AUSTRALIA IN THE WAR OF 1939-1945

SERIES ONE
ARMY

VOLUME IV
THE JAPANESE THRUST

AUSTRALIA IN THE WAR OF 1939-1945

SERIES 1 (ARMY)
    I. To Benghazi. *By Gavin Long.**
    II. Greece, Crete and Syria. *By Gavin Long.**
    III. Tobruk and El Alamein. *By Barton Maughan.*
    IV. The Japanese Thrust. *By Lionel Wigmore.**
    V. South-West Pacific Area—First Year. *By Dudley McCarthy.*
    VI. The New Guinea Offensives. *By David Dexter.*
    VII. The Final Campaigns. *By Gavin Long.*

SERIES 2 (NAVY)
    I. Royal Australian Navy, 1939-42. *By G. Hermon Gill.*
    II. Royal Australian Navy, 1942-45. *By G. Hermon Gill.*

SERIES 3 (AIR)
    I. Royal Australian Air Force, 1939-42. *By Douglas Gillison.*
    II. Air War Against Japan, 1943-45. *By George Odgers.**
    III. Air War Against Germany and Italy, 1939-43. *By John Herington.**
    IV. Air Power Over Europe, 1944-45. *By John Herington.*

SERIES 4 (CIVIL)
    I. The Government and the People, 1939-41. *By Paul Hasluck.**
    II. The Government and the People, 1942-45. *By Paul Hasluck.*
    III. War Economy, 1939-42. *By S. J. Butlin.**
    IV. War Economy, 1942-45. *By S. J. Butlin.*
    V. The Role of Science and Industry. *By D. P. Mellor.*

SERIES 5 (MEDICAL)
    I. Clinical Problems of War. *By Allan S. Walker.**
    II. Middle East and Far East. *By Allan S. Walker.**
    III. The Island Campaigns. *By Allan S. Walker.**
    IV. Medical Services of R.A.N. and R.A.A.F. *By Allan S. Walker.*

* Published.

The writers of these volumes have been given full access to official documents, but they and the general editor are alone responsible for the statements and opinions which the volumes contain.

THE JAPANESE THRUST

by

LIONEL WIGMORE

The Naval & Military Press Ltd

Published by
The Naval & Military Press Ltd
5 Riverside, Brambleside, Bellbrook
Industrial Estate, Uckfield, East Sussex,
TN22 1QQ England
Tel: +44 (0) 1825 749494
Fax: +44 (0) 1825 765701
www.naval-military-press.com
www.military-genealogy.com

In reprinting in facsimile from the original, any imperfections are inevitably reproduced and the quality may fall short of modern type and cartographic standards.

CONTENTS

	Page
Preface	xi
List of Events	xv

PART I: THE ROAD TO WAR

Chapter		Page
1	THE JAPANESE DILEMMA	1
2	AUSTRALIA'S PROBLEM	13
3	PLANS AND PREPARATIONS	28
4	TO MALAYA	46
5	THE MALAYAN SCENE	62
6	AWAITING THE FIRST BLOW	87

PART II: SOUTH-EAST ASIA CONQUERED

7	WIDESPREAD ONSLAUGHT	121
8	INVASION OF MALAYA	137
9	CRUMBLING RESISTANCE	153
10	MOUNTING DISASTERS	170
11	AUSTRALIANS INTO BATTLE: THE AMBUSH AT GEMAS	198
12	THE BATTLE OF MUAR	222
13	TO SINGAPORE ISLAND	250
14	NAKED ISLAND	284
15	DEFENCE OF WESTERN AREA	308
16	STRUGGLE FOR SINGAPORE	335
17	CEASE FIRE	368
18	RABAUL AND THE FORWARD OBSERVATION LINE	392
19	THE LOSS OF AMBON	418
20	THE DESTINATION OF I AUSTRALIAN CORPS	442
21	RESISTANCE IN TIMOR	466
22	THE END IN JAVA	495

PART III: PRISONERS OF THE JAPANESE

23	CHANGI, BICYCLE CAMP, AND OTHER MAIN CENTRES	511
24	THE BURMA-THAILAND RAILWAY	541
25	CAMPS IN BORNEO, JAPAN AND ELSEWHERE	593

APPENDIXES:

		Page
1	Australians in Mission 204	643
2	"ABDACOM" Directive to Supreme Commander, dated 3rd January 1942	646
3	General Bennett's Escape	650
4	Ordeal on New Britain	653
5	Future Employment of A.I.F.: General Sturdee's Paper of 15th February 1942	675
6	Central Army Records Office and the Prisoners of the Japanese	679
7	Books by Australian Prisoners of the Japanese	683
8	Abbreviations	684

INDEX 687

ILLUSTRATIONS

	Page
The Singapore waterfront	14
The *Queen Mary* in the Singapore graving dock	14
Lieut-General C. G. N. Miles and Brigadiers C. A. Callaghan and H. B. Taylor	15
Lieut-Colonel D. S. Maxwell and Major R. F. Oakes	15
The arrival of the 22nd Brigade at Singapore	46
Air Chief Marshal Sir Robert Brooke-Popham and General Sir Archibald Wavell	47
Lieut-General A. E. Percival and Major-General H. Gordon Bennett	47
Australians on a route march in Malaya	78
A cricket match between 27th Brigade teams	78
Australian troops moving through jungle	79
Mail delivery in Malaya	79
The camouflaged headquarters of the 8th Division in a rubber estate	110
A naval craft negotiating a river boom	110
Manhandling an anti-tank gun during training	111
A forward Australian patrol	111
Rice distribution in Malaya	174
Indian sappers preparing a bridge for demolition	174
Gemencheh bridge	175
The tank trap in the 2/30th Battalion area forward of Gemas	175
Laying an Australian 25-pounder field gun	206
Stretcher bearers attending a wounded Australian	206
The Muar ferry crossing	207
A 2-pounder of the 2/4th Anti-Tank Regiment in action near Bakri	207
Knocked-out Japanese tanks near Bakri	238
The crew of an anti-tank gun	238
The Parit Sulong bridge	239
The hut at Parit Sulong into which the Japanese forced wounded prisoners	239
Lieut-Colonel C. G. W. Anderson	270
The Simpang Rengam crossroads	270
The mouth of the Sungei Mersing	271
The Mersing bridge	271
Demolitions in Malaya	302
A.R.P. workers in Singapore	302
The Causeway, linking Johore Bahru and Singapore Island	303
The bombing of Singapore Island	303
Mandai road	334
Choa Chu Kang road	334
Air raid casualties in Singapore	335
Smoke from the naval base overshadows Singapore	398
Simpson Harbour, New Britain	399
Mount Nona, Ambon Island	430
Laha airfield, Ambon Island	430
Plains in the Usau district, Dutch Timor	431
Usau ridge	431

	Page
Lieut-General V. A. H. Sturdee and Major-General H. ter Poorten	494
Men of the 2/2nd Independent Company in Timor	494
Checking positions on a map in the Tjampea area, Java	495
H.M.T. *Orcades* at Batavia	495
The Changi area	526
The move to Selarang Barracks Square	526
Rice distribution, Changi	527
A 50-metre hut, Changi	527
News reception at Changi	574
Forms of rail and river transport	574
The Burma-Thailand railway and the main road	575
Australian officers' mess, Alepauk	575
The audience at a camp theatre on the Burma-Thailand railway	590
Mess parade at a camp on the Burma-Thailand railway	590
Pile-driving on the Burma-Thailand railway	591
Railway "workers"	622
A bridge, south of Thanbyuzayat, after attacks by R.A.F. Liberators	622
A better type of jungle camp	623
Cholera hospital, Hintok	623
A Japanese questionnaire circulated to prisoners of war in Korea	638
The camp hospital at Bakli Bay, Hainan Island	638
Leaflet dropped over Changi, 28th August 1945	639
The entrance to Changi Gaol	639
Released prisoners of war embark on a hospital ship	639
Survivors from Ambon on board a corvette	639

MAPS

	Page
The Far Eastern theatre	30
Area of deliberations Singapore conference, October 1940	42
Malaya	54
Location of forces, Malaya, 8th December 1941	105
The Japanese objectives	112
Japan's opening moves in Malaya	139
The withdrawal across the Perak	158
The attack on Hong Kong	171
Japanese landings in the Philippines	178
Western Johore, 25th January 1942	262
The Japanese conquest of Malaya	280
Dispositions Singapore Island, 7th February 1942	286
Western front, Singapore Island, 7 p.m. 10th February	344
The Japanese advance through the Indies and to Rabaul	393

SKETCH MAPS

The Philippines in danger zone	88
A.I.F. locations, Malaya, December 1941	99
Kota Bharu, 8th December	124
The fall of Jitra	148
The invasion of Borneo	179
The Japanese advance to Slim River	188
Kuantan	192
The ABDA and Anzac Areas	200
Perak to Johore	208
The Westforce front, 14th January 1942	211
The 2/30th Battalion dispositions, Gemas, 14th January	212
Bakri, 8 a.m. 19th January	228
The withdrawal from Bakri	237
Mersing-Endau area	251
Ayer Hitam, 24th-25th January	263
Nithsdale Estate, 26th-27th January	267
Namazie Estate, 7 a.m. 28th January	275
Ayer Bemban, 29th January	278
Dispositions, 22nd Brigade, 10 p.m. 8th February	310
Bulim line, 9th February	324
Causeway sector, 8 p.m. 9th February	328
"X" Battalion and Merrett Force	347
South-western front, Singapore Island, early morning 12th February	360
Dispositions round Singapore, daybreak 14th February	374
Central Sumatra	384
Bataan Peninsula	390
Rabaul	394
Dispositions, Rabaul, 2 a.m. 23rd January	401

	Page
New Ireland	413
The invasion of Ambon	421
Escape routes from Ambon	439
North-eastern Indian Ocean	448
South-east Sumatra	453
Burma	461
Timor	467
Dutch Timor	468
Portuguese Timor	478
The invasion of Java	498
West Java	500
Burma-Thailand	542
"A" Force camps, Burma-Thailand railway	550
"D", "F" and "H" Force camps, Thailand	563
North Borneo	595
Japan, Korea and Manchuria	617
Formosa	630
Mission 204, China	644
Gazelle Peninsula	654
New Britain and south-east New Guinea	658

PREFACE

THE heavy task of recording a series of reverses culminating in one of the greatest disasters suffered by British and Allied arms befell the writer of this volume. He has had to tell of shortages and shortcomings in men and materials—the more exposed to notice because in this period there was no victory to shed its mantle over them. The volume is thus a chronicle "Not of the princes and prelates with periwigged charioteers riding triumphantly laurelled to lap the fat of the years", but all too frequently of men whose moral and physical resources were tried to, and sometimes beyond, the bounds of human endurance.

The volume is mainly concerned with the operations of the Australian Army in the early months of the war against Japan. A very shallow understanding of Australia's contribution to the struggle would, however, be given if these were not shown in the light of the many and diverse circumstances which determined the nature of the conflict and to a large extent dominated the employment of the Allied forces. The writer therefore has endeavoured to place those operations in their setting and to relate them to the overall strategy determined in London and Washington, Berlin and Tokyo. In this endeavour he has necessarily overstepped the boundaries of an exclusively national viewpoint; but has indicated Australia's influence upon the decisions of her Allies and the reasons which underlay her own decisions. Although he has naturally described Australian participation in the military operations in greater detail than that of the other forces, this should not be taken as a measure of its relative importance or effect.

Again, the narrative is focused principally upon the ground forces. Accounts of the activities of the naval and air forces are left to the writers of volumes in the companion series, except for such references to those Services as seem necessary because of their bearing upon the course of events generally, and the experiences of the ground forces in particular. Furthermore, attention is necessarily directed principally to infantry action, for it would be impracticable to relate the activities of the ancillary forces on the same scale.

The choice of what the volume should or should not contain was largely a matter of discovering, selecting and fitting together what seemed most interesting and most significant in the stream of events; but the writer has sought also so to present the facts that the reader may have a sound and sufficient basis for judgment. With the object of re-creating the outlook and atmosphere of the time, the words of participants are freely quoted.

Most of the war diaries of the part of the 8th Division, A.I.F., which fought in Malaya were destroyed when Singapore fell. Soon after the Australians went into captivity, however, unit commanders were instructed to rewrite these diaries. The task was painstakingly performed during the period of several months before parts of the force were dispersed to various areas in Malaya, Thailand and elsewhere, and while the events of the campaign were still fresh in the minds of officers and men. Thus the diaries were compiled by reference to notes and other surviving records and by searching the recollections of those concerned; also a divisional narrative was compiled. The writer has drawn also on the despatches of Lord Wavell, Sir Robert Brooke-Popham, Lieut-General A. E. Percival and other commanders of the forces engaged in Malaya and in other areas; the Australian War Cabinet minutes; and the very large number of published memoirs of political and military leaders and of soldiers of all ranks. Those on which particular reliance has been placed are referred to in the footnotes.

The writer was greatly aided by interviews and correspondence with leading civil and military authorities; formation, unit and sub-unit commanders from generals to lieutenants; and men whose principal jobs were to use their weapons, drive a truck, maintain a telephone line, and so on. All these, by relating what they did, saw or experienced at particular times and places helped to confirm, correct, or amplify information contained in the records.

Indeed, one of the major difficulties has been the mass of material which had to be sifted, analysed, and taken into account. So extensive was the range of such sources and of the assistance given by individuals in response to requests that any fully detailed acknowledgment is impracticable. The sources mentioned in the volume are, however, the main ones from which information and quotations have been drawn. The writer has been helped in procuring documents or by comment on chapters when they were in draft form principally by: Lieut-Generals H. G. Bennett, Sir Vernon Sturdee; Brigadiers F. G. Galleghan, C. H. Kappe, D. S. Maxwell, H. B. Taylor, W. C. D. Veale; Colonels H. H. Carr, W. S. Kent Hughes, S. A. F. Pond, G. E. Ramsay, J. J. Scanlan, W. J. R. Scott, J. H. Thyer; Lieut-Colonels C. G. W. Anderson, B. J. Callinan, B. G. Dawson, W. E. Fraser, W. W. Leggatt, R. F. Oakes, L. N. Roach; Major A. E. Saggers; Captain W. B. Bowring. The comment, suggestions and information received from these soldiers were of great value in the process of revision, but it does not follow that any of them is in full agreement with the contents of the volume in its final form.

Major-General S. W. Kirby, the writer of the corresponding volume in the United Kingdom Official History of the Second World War, visited Australia in 1953 for discussions with Australians who took part in the events described in this book; collaboration with him, both then and since, has been invaluable in searching out and assessing facts and shaping this volume, especially as regards those circumstances and happenings outside the sphere of Australian records. The very thorough accounts of the composition and activities of the Japanese forces which he and his colleagues obtained and collated were generously made available to supplement those from other sources which the writer had to hand.

Voluminous reports of the prisoner-of-war period were studied. Information drawn from these was checked with and supplemented by the large number of diaries kept by the prisoners, and by the many interviews collected by officers of the Repatriation of Allied Prisoners of War and Internees organisation, which are now systematically catalogued in the library of the Australian War Memorial. The thoroughness with which the interrogations were carried out at the end of the war made it possible for answers to be found from the prisoners themselves to almost every question which arose. These reports, diaries, and interviews have been plundered, sometimes without acknowledgment, with the object of providing an authentic account of the life of the Australians in captivity. The medical aspects of the period of active service and of captivity have been described in more than 150 pages of the second volume of the medical series. In dealing with the period of captivity in the present volume the main endeavour has been to describe the changing organisation and problems of the various groups of prisoners, their movements from place to place, and the general character of their experiences. As an appendix shows, Australian men and women who with many others were prisoners of the Japanese, produced a remarkably large number of books in which their individual and group experiences are described in graphic detail. These books contain intimate accounts of the experiences of Australians in Changi, on the Burma-Thailand railway, in Sumatra, Java, Japan and elsewhere. It is hoped that this narrative will provide a frame into which those individual stories may be fitted.

In the preface of the first volume of this series the difficulty of obeying any one system of transliterating Greek and Arabic place names was mentioned. A similar problem is presented by Indonesian place names. In large-scale maps used by the Allies in the war Dutch spellings of places in the Netherlands Indies were generally followed, but as a rule these are unfamiliar to English-speaking readers, whose atlases have long preferred English phonetic spellings. The atlases, however, disagree with one another as to how the English forms should be arrived at. Thus the Dutch spellings of four places frequently mentioned in the following pages are: Soerabaja, Koepang, Tjilatjap, Makassar. The Naval Intelligence Division of the Admiralty, a main authority on this subject, considers that the best English forms are Surabaya, Kupang, Chilachap, Macassar. The *Oxford Atlas,* 1951, however, prints Koepang, the National American Geographical Association's map of the Pacific Ocean, 1952, Surabaja and Makassar. In this volume the English methods of transliteration have generally been employed, but exceptions are made where the Dutch form became so familiar to Australian soldiers that to abandon it might confuse them. Among these exceptions are Koepang, Tjilatjap and (in other volumes of this history) Noemfoor. In the case of Thai place-names, spellings familiar to the prisoners of war have been used.

The services of Mr A. J. Sweeting, a member of the staff of the Australian Official War History section, were in part available in compiling this volume. Mr Sweeting was responsible for procuring most of the documents, collating certain of the information used, preparing biographical footnotes, indexing the volume, and performing other such tasks. He also drafted, very largely in the form in which it now appears, the story of the fate of the force in Rabaul, and wrote the three chapters which describe the prisoner-of-war period. Thus to a large extent he is a co-author. Much painstaking work went into the maps drawn by Mr Hugh Groser.

The writer is grateful to his wife for unselfishness, forbearance and fortitude at times when heavy demands were made on her resources of those great qualities. He was stationed in Singapore (where it was his duty to keep in close touch with the course of events, but in a civilian capacity) from April 1941 to February 1942, and in Java almost until its last escape port was closed to Allied shipping. It seems certain that had he realised at first the magnitude of the task which writing this volume would present to him he would not have felt able to perform it. It is no less certain that but for his having drawn heavily and continuously upon the General Editor's knowledge of military affairs, and his experience, wisdom, and seemingly inexhaustible patience he would not have completed the work as it is now presented.

L.G.W.

Canberra,
 25th March 1956.

LIST OF EVENTS
FROM 1931 TO 20 MAY 1942
Events more particularly described in this volume are printed in italics

1931-32		Japan establishes puppet state of Manchukuo
1936	25 Nov	Japan signs Anti-Comintern Pact with Germany
1937	7 July	Beginning of general attack by Japanese forces on China
	13 Aug	Fighting begins between Japanese and Chinese troops at Shanghai
1938	29 Sept	Munich Agreement signed by United Kingdom, Germany, France and Italy
1939	1 Sept	German Army invades Poland
	3 Sept	Britain and France declare war on Germany; Australia declares war on Germany
1940	9 Jan	First A.I.F. contingent embarks for Middle East
	9 Apr	Germans invade Denmark and Norway
	10 May	German Army invades Holland and Belgium
	4 June	Embarkation from Dunkirk completed
	10 June	Italy declares war
	22 June	France signs armistice with Germany
	17 July	*Burma Road closed for three months*
	22 Sept	*Japan granted bases in Indo-China*
	27 Sept	*Tripartite Pact between Germany, Italy and Japan*
	27 Dec	German raider shells Nauru Island phosphate loading plant
1941	3-5 Jan	Battle of Bardia
	6 Feb	Australian troops enter Benghazi
	18 Feb	*Australian troops arrive at Singapore*
	6 Apr	German Army invades Greece and Yugoslavia
	20 May	German troops descend on Crete
	8 June	Allied invasion of Syria begins
	22 June	Germany invades Russia
	24 July	*Japanese troops land in south Indo-China*
	26 July	*United States Government freezes Japanese assets in the United States*
		General MacArthur appointed to command United States Army in Far East

xv

	25 Aug	British and Russian troops enter Iran
	7 Oct	Mr Curtin becomes Prime Minister of Australia
	17 Oct	*General Tojo becomes Prime Minister of Japan*
	7-8 Dec	*Japanese attack Malaya and Pearl Harbour*
	10 Dec	H.M.S. Prince of Wales and H.M.S. Repulse sunk
	11 Dec	Germany and Italy declare war on United States
	26 Dec	*Fall of Hong Kong*
1942	23 Jan	*Japanese force attacks Rabaul*
	30 Jan	*Japanese force attacks Ambon*
	31 Jan	*Defending forces in Malaya withdraw to Singapore Island*
	15 Feb	*Singapore Island surrenders*
	19 Feb	First Japanese air raids on Darwin
	19-20 Feb	*Japanese forces land on Timor*
	28 Feb-1 Mar	*Japanese forces land in Java*
	8 Mar	Japanese troops enter Rangoon
	9 Apr	United States forces on Bataan surrender
	6 May	United States forces on Corregidor surrender
	20 May	Allied forces withdraw from Burma

PART I

THE ROAD TO WAR

CHAPTER 1

THE JAPANESE DILEMMA

THE Japanese, an island people who had lived apart from the rest of the world until they were forced into contact with it in the eighteen-fifties, went to war with China in 1894 and defeated her. In 1905 they defeated Russia; in 1910 they annexed Korea. After the world war of 1914-18 Japan was given a mandate over the Mariana, Caroline and Marshall Islands, former German colonies.[1] In 1922 at the Washington Conference the United States prevailed upon the five principal naval Powers to agree to the following limits on naval strength in ships of the larger classes: U.S.A., 525,000 tons; Britain and her Dominions, 525,000; Japan, 315,000; France and Italy, each 175,000. Japan, stimulated by her successes and not spent, as were the European nations, by heavy efforts in the war, was at first unwilling to accept naval inferiority. She reluctantly agreed to the ratio when the corollary was added that, in effect, the United States would not further develop any naval base west of Hawaii, nor would Britain east of Singapore.

As an outcome of granting Japan a mandate over islands of the western Pacific (despite Australian reluctance[2]) and granting Australia a mandate over the former German colony of New Guinea, the limits of Australian and Japanese territory were now only 285 miles apart.[3] The dilemma in which Australia became increasingly involved had been clearly stated in the House of Representatives by the Australian Prime Minister, Mr Hughes, upon his return from the Imperial Conference of 1921.

For us (he said) the Pacific problem is for all practical purposes the problem of Japan. Here is a nation of nearly 70 millions of people, crowded together in narrow islands; its population is increasing rapidly, and is already pressing on the margin of subsistence. She wants both room for her increasing millions of population, and markets for her manufactured goods. And she wants these very badly indeed. America and Australia say to her millions "Ye cannot enter in". Japan, then, is faced with the great problem which has bred wars since time began. For when the tribes and nations of the past outgrew the resources of their own territory they moved on and on, hacking their way to the fertile pastures of their neighbours. But where are the overflowing millions of Japanese to find room? Not in Australia; not in America. Well, where, then? . . .

These 70,000,000 Japanese cannot possibly live, except as a manufacturing nation. Their position is analogous to that of Great Britain. To a manufacturing nation,

---

[1] Except that Guam, in the Marianas, remained an American possession.

[2] As one of the Allies during the 1914-18 war Japan had occupied the German island possessions in the Pacific north of the Equator, and Australia and New Zealand those south of it. At the Versailles Conference which followed the war, each of these countries pressed for annexation to it of the islands it had occupied. Agreement by the then Prime Minister of Australia, Mr W. M. Hughes, to their being allotted under mandate, making the holders responsible to the League of Nations for the administration of the islands, was secured only when a class of mandate was devised which gave practically permanent tenure, and left Australia free to apply her immigration laws to the territory under her mandate. When the mandates were issued, Japan deposited at the office of the League a declaration that her agreement to their issue in their existing form "should not be considered as an acquiescence . . . in the submission of Japanese subjects to a discriminatory and disadvantageous treatment in the mandated territories. . . ."

[3] Between Kapingamarangi Island, south of the Carolines, and the Malum Islands, north of Bougainville.

overseas markets are essential to its very existence. Japan sees across a narrow strip of water 400,000,000 Chinese gradually awakening to an appreciation of Western methods, and she sees in China the natural market for her goods. She feels that her geographical circumstances give her a special right to the exploitation of the Chinese markets. But other countries want the market too, and so comes the demand for the "Open Door". . . .

This is the problem of the Pacific—the modern riddle of the Sphinx, for which we must find an answer. . . . Talk about disarmament is idle unless the causes of naval armaments are removed.[4]

The Western Powers nevertheless continued their efforts to widen the naval disarmament agreements. At the same time ultra-nationalist groups in Japan increased in power and vehemence. In protest against the moderation of the Japanese Government, a fanatic shot and fatally injured the Prime Minister, Mr Hamaguchi, in 1930. In the following six years nine other Japanese leaders were assassinated.

In 1931 the Japanese War Minister, General Ugaki, who had been seriously ill for some months, resigned. His place was taken by General Jiro Minami, who until December 1930 had been Governor-General and Commander-in-Chief in Korea, and who regarded Japanese territorial expansion as a matter of urgency. Baron Wakatsuki, the new Prime Minister, was a believer in parliamentary influence; but Japan's political system was so constructed that the Cabinet's responsibility was to the Emperor rather than to Parliament. Further, the armed forces were able in effect not only to act independently of or even without the knowledge of the Cabinet, but to force the resignation of a Cabinet with which they were at odds.[5] Little critical public opinion existed in Japan; the army was practically exempt from democratic control, and popular support almost automatically attached to decisions which could be ascribed to the Emperor. Thus, when important policies were to be implemented, conferences were held in the presence of the Emperor so that he might be identified with them. His prestige was protected, however, by the convention that Ministers and not the Emperor were responsible for the results of these policies.

Such by-passing of Parliamentary control behind a facade of democracy was facilitated by Shintoism, the national religion, which fostered devotion to the Emperor. Further, the concept of national leaders being responsible to the people, and they for the actions of their leaders, was as yet strange to the mass of Japanese people, and their wishes had little real bearing upon these actions. Between the show of democracy in Japan and its reality lay, therefore, a great gulf. Indeed, it was not to be expected

---

[4] Imperial Conference, 1921. Statement by the Rt Hon W. M. Hughes, 30 Sep 1921. *Parliamentary Papers*, No. 146, pp. 10-11. Another British statesman at the conference made a prophecy. "Our temptation is still to look upon the European stage as of the first importance," said the South African Prime Minister, General Smuts. "It is no longer so . . . these are not really first-rate events any more. . . . Undoubtedly the scene has shifted away from Europe to the Far East and to the Pacific. The problems of the Pacific are to my mind the world problems of the next fifty years or more."

[5] A continuance of this state of affairs was to be reflected in the title of a sub-section of memoirs by Prince Konoye, thrice Prime Minister of Japan from 1938 onward—"The Independence of the Supreme Command and State Affairs from Each Other: The Anguish of Cabinets from Generation to Generation."

that its reality would have been assimilated in so brief a period of parliamentary institutions, by a nation with a background of centuries of subjection to feudal rule. This political childhood made the people readily susceptible to direction and deception from above, and to that most dangerous of all national delusions of grandeur—a sense of divine mission, inherent in the Japanese expansionist outlook.

In these circumstances, on the pretext that Chinese had torn up a section of the south Manchurian railway line which Japan controlled, the Japanese *Kwantung Army,* in September 1931, occupied strategic centres in the Mukden area, and fighting broke out with Chinese units.[6] This was a blow not only at China, but at the whole system of collective security represented by the League of Nations. It was a blow also at the liberal forces in Japan which had been holding in check those who sought in foreign adventure a solution of Japan's problems and satisfaction of personal ambitions. The effect was a resounding victory for militarism, which thenceforward committed Japan more and more deeply to aggression. In the same year, and in view of the worsening situation in the Far East,[7] a national coalition government in the United Kingdom, with Mr Ramsay MacDonald at its head, gave the "all clear" signal for hitherto delayed expenditure on a British naval base at Singapore. This project had been bitterly opposed in both the British press and Parliament, largely on the ground that it would imperil friendly relations with Japan. Prophetic comment, from a strategic point of view, came from General Sir Ian Hamilton, leader of the Allied land forces during the Gallipoli campaign of 1915. He did not doubt that Singapore could be held, he said, unless "we ourselves put a half-way house and then—half-garrisoning it, as is our wont—make a present of it to the wrong people".[8]

Defying the League of Nations, Japan gained control of the whole of Manchuria in 1931 and 1932, and there set up a puppet state known as Manchukuo. In January 1932, after anti-Japanese riots in Shanghai, Japan landed troops there and fighting occurred between this force and the Chinese army round Shanghai until May. From Manchuria her troops attacked the northern provinces of China inside the Great Wall, and forced China to cede control of the province of Jehol, adjoining Manchuria. In 1932 Japan gave notice of her intention to resign from the League and in December 1934 of her intention to abandon the Washington Treaty; by her military adventures she violated other obligations she had entered into for the preservation of peace. Although invited in January 1935 to join in a new treaty for limitation of naval armaments, she declined to do so when she was unsuccessful in demanding naval parity and a common upper limit of construction. Nevertheless, Japan found Germany willing

---

[6] Kwantung comprised territory in Manchuria, at the southern end of the Liaotung Peninsula, leased by China to Japan, and usually referred to by the Japanese at the time as Kwantung Province.

[7] The term Far East, whose general acceptance at the time makes its use necessary, derived from a European rather than an Australian point of view. To Australia the "Far East" is more realistically East Asia, or the Near North.

[8] *The Times,* London, 24 Mar 1924.

to accept her signature in 1936 to what was known as the Anti-Comintern Pact, ostensibly aimed against communism. Had this been its only aspect, the pact might have gained other signatories—America, for example, whose attitude to Japan was conditioned in part by Japan's value as a counter to the spread of communism in Asia, and especially in China. But in the circumstances of the time the pact suggested a *rapprochement* between the German and Japanese forms of aggressive nationalism, thus offering merely an alternative danger to the *status quo*.

Strength was given to Japan's expansionist influences not only by considerations of national prestige. With a population of 320 to the square mile, Japan was in difficult economic straits when she faced the world depression of 1929 onward. Her big industrial interests were naturally allied to such polices as would gain for them greater access to raw materials and markets. History—including America's—provided attractive examples of imperialist expansion.[9]

The endeavours of German socialists to readjust the economy of their country by peaceful action had been unimpressive, and a renewed trend towards the smash-grab course of foreign conquest was apparent in the rise of the Nazi party in Germany. Fear of Russia, this time as a Soviet state, had revived in Japan. Fear of the growth of communism in Japan itself strengthened the alliance between Japanese industrialists and militarists. In fact, extreme nationalism throve on opposition to communism, so that, in time (wrote a Japanese observer) "all liberal thought came to be classed as communistic—therefore criminal—and the nationalists soon tabbed Western culture and democracy as the same kind of enemy"; and "the entire school system became one more means of spreading the doctrine of reaction".[1]

In the face of such factors, Japan's principal moderating influences were a small group of liberal statesmen and parliamentary institutions which had been grafted on to an autocratic system of government but forty years before. It was "certainly arguable that, had outside influences not intervened, and had the Japanese nation been given one more decade in which to wax in political wisdom the cause of representative government in Japan might just have turned the corner. A focal point would thus have existed round which liberals and progressives could have rallied in order to resist the attack on free institutions which the army and the reactionaries were now about to launch";[2] but as things were, Japan was drifting to the most fateful turning-point in her history.

---

[9] "In the nineteenth century the major western countries . . . were acquiring vast additional territories. . . . The acquisition by the United States in 1898 of Hawaii, in which Japanese were the largest single element in the population, and of the Philippines, only a short distance south of the Japanese-held Formosa, could be interpreted by the fearful and the militarists as a further threat. When she set out to build an overseas empire Japan was but conforming to the pattern of the times."—K. S. Latourette, an American historian, in *A Short History of the Far East* (1947), p. 507.

[1] Masuo Kato, *The Lost War* (1946), pp. 182, 185.

[2] R. Craigie, *Behind the Japanese Mask* (1946), p. 25. (Craigie had become British Ambassador to Japan in 1937.)

Meanwhile Australia's increasing trade with Japan had drawn her closer to the centre of a stage on which Japan, Great Britain, the United States and China were the leading players. The course of events in this sphere illustrated the growing conflict between Australia's trade interests in the Pacific and her relations with Great Britain. During the world economic depression, Japan's increasing demands for Australian foodstuffs and raw materials when other markets were contracting were a factor in cushioning the effects of the depression upon Australian primary industry. By 1935-36, the balance in Australia's favour of her trade with Japan amounted to more than one-third of the sum Australia needed annually to pay interest upon the heavy indebtedness she had incurred to other countries. The influx of Japanese goods to Australia, and undependable Japanese commercial methods, caused misgivings among Australian manufacturers and importers; but the cheapness of Japanese goods helped Australians with small incomes to make ends meet while they were either struggling against the depression or recovering from it. Politically the Labour party appeared to be content with that fact, while a section of Australian commercial interests welcomed the growth of such trade relationships.

"The industrialisation of Japan," said a report published by the Bank of New South Wales in 1934, "promises to bring with it great possibilities for the development of markets for Australian foodstuffs and raw materials. . . . Australia needs markets for her primary products. The great potential markets for those products are the Far Eastern countries. Of these countries, China is at present the largest buyer of our wool, but if Japanese living standards are allowed to improve, there is a possibility of selling more foodstuffs to Japan in the future." After asking whether Australia had not reached "a point where her policy should be broadened to permit of the harmonisation of the changes which are occurring in the Far East with her own economic needs", the report questioned the wisdom of attempting to make the British Empire a self-sufficient economic unit. It added that "in the face of the rapid growth of Japanese industry, it is difficult to resist the conclusion that any survey of the rational ends of Australian trade policy in the circumstances of today must offer a more prominent place to interchange of goods with the East than it has occupied in the past".[3]

This trend of affairs was less palatable to English manufacturers, particularly when in 1935 Japan displaced Great Britain as the largest supplier of textiles to Australia; and in March 1936 a Manchester Trade Delegation visited Australia to seek means whereby the situation could be remedied. Nevertheless, the Australian public was taken by surprise when, on 22nd May 1936, the Government announced its decision to divert a portion of Australia's import trade "with the object of increasing our exports of primary produce, expanding secondary industry and bringing about a considerable increase of rural and industrial development".[4] This decision

---
[3] *Australia and Industrial Development in Japan* (Bank of New South Wales circular, Vol IV, March 1934).
[4] *Commonwealth Debates*, Vol 150, p. 2211.

would be implemented by a licensing system which would provide a tight control over importation of certain goods; and higher customs duties. Although this policy was aimed by no means exclusively at Japanese goods, it did in fact deal a severe blow at trade with Japan, more especially as duties on textiles other than those from the United Kingdom were raised, and British textiles were given a higher degree of preference than hitherto. The decision followed confidential and unsuccessful negotiations between representatives of the Australian and Japanese Governments for a trade agreement. The negotiations had come at a time when "credit difficulties had filled the public mind of Japan with an almost feverish sense of the urgency of making overseas sales . . . such that they could brook no curb in markets where the size of their purchases appeared to give the commanding word". Each government was "acutely conscious of its own country's difficulties, but dimly conscious of those of the other".[5]

Had economic factors only been involved, the outcome of the negotiations might have been different; but uneasiness was now being felt in political and military quarters in Australia about the international situation, and especially about Japan's actions in Manchuria. By the end of the year a compromise agreement was reached under which limits were placed upon the trade in wool and textiles between Australia and Japan. In the meantime, however, Australia had contributed to the fear on which Japan's expansionists were able to play that she was being excluded from the world's markets, and might be deprived of means of existence as an industrial nation.[6]

Australia and New Zealand had pressed for a British fleet to be stationed in the Far East in peacetime, but the British Government, at an Imperial Conference in 1937, re-affirmed its policy of stationing its fleet in European waters, with the proviso that units would be sent to threatened areas elsewhere as necessary. It was argued in favour of this policy that Japan would be unlikely to risk war with the British Commonwealth unless the latter became involved in war in Europe; and that the greater the concentration of British sea power in that sphere, the less would be the likelihood of such a war, and consequently of attack by Japan. The assurance was given, however, that in the event of war with Japan a fleet would be sent to the Far East to protect the sea routes to India, Australia and New Zealand; and that, even if war were concurrent in Europe and the Far East, a fleet would be sent to contain the Japanese. The Singapore base would have to withstand any attack before the fleet could arrive—a period estimated at from seventy to ninety days. British policy towards Japan was re-affirmed as the maintenance of friendly relations, short of sacrificing British interests either in China or Hong Kong.

---

[5] C. A. S. Hawker, in *Austral-Asiatic Bulletin*, Vol I, No. 1, April 1937, p. 7.

[6] Reference has been made, particularly in dealing with Australia's trade relations with Japan, to J. Shepherd, *Australia's Interests and Policies in the Far East* (1940).

The trend of Japanese policy and actions had been closely watched by the leaders of Britain's armed forces, and they did not fail to give warning of its danger. In a review by the Chiefs of Staff Committee presented to the Imperial Conference, the view was expressed that Japan was aiming at hegemony in the East just as was Germany in Europe. The committee underlined Mr Hughes' earlier reference to "the riddle of the Sphinx" by stating that Japan would have difficulty in supporting much longer her rapidly increasing population and was, moreover, singularly deficient in those raw materials necessary for industrial development along modern lines. Intense competition in foreign trade, enhanced by the cheapness of Japanese labour, had been countered in parts of the British Empire and other countries by various measures designed to limit an expansion of Japanese exports. This reduced Japan's power to purchase the raw materials on which her essential manufactures depended. The solution of this problem was the principal objective of Japanese policy, and the solution favoured was the creation of a more self-sufficient empire and the paramountcy of Japan in the Far East. There was very little doubt that Japan would seize the opportunity afforded by a European war, in which Britain was involved, to further her expansionist schemes.

After reviewing possible British and Japanese strategy in such an event, the committee concluded: "The Singapore defences are nearing completion, but they alone do not secure our strategic position in the East. The dispatch of a fleet to the Far East remains the operation upon which the security of the eastern half of the Empire depends." At the time, it was estimated that Britain, while keeping a force in home waters capable of meeting the requirements of a war with Germany, would be able to send to the Far East a fleet approximately equal to that of Japan; and that such a fleet should suffice to protect trade in the East and prevent Japan from undertaking any major operations against India, Australia, New Zealand, or Borneo.

This contention had long been challenged by leaders of thought in the Australian Army. In 1926 Lieut-Colonel Wynter[7] examined the theory in a lecture to the United Services Institute of Melbourne which was to influence greatly the doctrines and later the policies of Australian Army staffs.[8] He said that "Australia could not, as a matter of practical policy, avoid giving her first consideration to the problem of her own security". Australia would rely primarily on naval defence only if the Imperial Navy was strong enough to provide for the naval defence of Australia and at the same time provide for the defence of all other Imperial interests; and if the Imperial authorities would be willing, in any circumstances, to detach a sufficient naval force to ensure naval superiority in the western Pacific. He said that it was a reasonable assumption that if war broke out with "a Pacific Power" it would be at a time when

---

[7] Lt-Gen H. D. Wynter, CB, CMG, DSO, QX6150. (1st AIF: AAG, AIF 1917-19.) GOC Northern Comd 1939-40, 9 Aust Div 1940-41, Eastern Comd 1941-42; Lt-Gen i/c Admin LHQ 1942-45. Regular soldier; of Brisbane; b. "Winterton", Burnett River, Qld, 5 Jun 1886. Died 7 Feb 1945.
[8] The lecture was published later in the *Army Quarterly* (London) of April 1927.

Britain was involved in war in Europe. He questioned whether in such a situation Britain could or would detach a sufficient naval force to the Far East.

Henceforward the attitude of the leading thinkers in the Australian Army towards British assurances that an adequate fleet would be sent to Singapore at the critical time was (bluntly stated): "We do not doubt that you are sincere in your beliefs but, frankly, we do not think you will be able to do it."

Wynter's conclusions were that Australia should prepare to defend her own vital south-eastern area against invasion, and should develop a fleet base in Australia as an alternative to Singapore. Later writers developed this argument, pointing particularly to the vulnerability of Singapore to attack from the landward side.[9] Some of these conclusions were echoed in the Australian Parliament by the Labour party, which urged that Australia prepare to repel invasion of her own soil, chiefly by building her air strength and enlarging her capacity to manufacture munitions for her citizen army. If an Eastern first-class power sought an abrogation of a basic Australian policy, such as her immigration policy (declared the Labour leader, Mr Curtin, in the Australian House of Representatives in November 1936), "it would most likely do so when Great Britain was involved or threatened to be involved in a European war. Would the British Government dare to authorise the dispatch of any substantial part of the fleet to the East to help Australia? The dependence of Australia upon the competence, let alone the readiness, of British statesmen to send forces to our aid is too dangerous a hazard upon which to found Australian defence policy."

On the Government side of the House, Mr Hughes also argued against reliance upon the British Navy, and declared that the aeroplane came to Australia as "a gift from the gods" as a means of resisting invasion. The Government, however, continued to rely principally upon cooperation with the British Navy to safeguard Australia, and generally to concur in the overall plan of Imperial defence evolved by the British authorities.

In these circumstances it would have been wise of the Australian Services to have developed Far Eastern Intelligence branches and to have sought experience on which to base tactical doctrines that could be applied in a war against Japan. It was likely that the United Kingdom would be so preoccupied with preparations for European, African and

---

[9] See J. D. Lavarack, "The Defence of the British Empire, with Special Reference to the Far East and Australia", *Army Quarterly*, Jan 1933, and H. C. H. Robertson, "The Defence of Australia", *Army Quarterly*, Apr 1935.
In England an unorthodox naval writer, Commander Russell Grenfell, in *Sea Power in the Next War* (1938), reached conclusions similar to those of Wynter and others in Australia. In the middle and late 'thirties there appeared in Australia a large number of books, pamphlets and articles warning against the danger from Japan and advocating stronger defence measures. Among the books and pamphlets were: W. M. Hughes, *Australia and War Today* (1935), "Albatross" (E. L. Piesse), *Japan and the Defence of Australia* (1935), W. C. Wentworth, *Demand for Defence* (1939). W. S. Kent Hughes, then a member of the Victorian Parliament, campaigned energetically throughout 1935 for more adequate preparation for defence against Japan. He will reappear later in this volume. Newspaper articles by Maj-Gen H. Gordon Bennett, in 1937, will be mentioned later.

Indian operations that study of Far Eastern conditions would be given low priority by her leaders.

As early as 1917 military requirements had resulted in a systematic study of the Japanese language and history being initiated in Australia. In that year Mr James Murdoch,[1] who had spent many years in Japan and had written a comprehensive history of that country, was appointed lecturer in Japanese at the Royal Military College, Duntroon. It was arranged that eight suitable cadets should undertake a course in Japanese, and Murdoch held classes for a number of the staff including two officers, Captains Broadbent[2] and Capes,[3] who graduated in 1914 and had recently been invalided home from the A.I.F. In 1919 Murdoch was appointed first Professor of Japanese at the University of Sydney, and a Japanese citizen replaced him as lecturer at Duntroon.[4]

Meanwhile, in 1919 a "Pacific Branch" was established within the Prime Minister's Department under Major Piesse,[5] a lawyer who had acted as Director of Intelligence at Army Headquarters in the previous three years. In the following year the Government sent to Tokyo for a two-years language course, by attachment to the British Embassy, Captains Broadbent and Capes. In the same year, an officer who had also served in the A.I.F. and subsequently on the General Staff of the 2nd Military District, Captain Longfield Lloyd,[6] was appointed to the Pacific Branch. All three had already undertaken a course of Oriental studies and each had some knowledge of the Japanese language. Broadbent again visited Japan in 1923 with the Australian relief ship dispatched after the Japanese earthquake in that year, "his knowledge of the Japanese language and customs proving invaluable".[7] Later two Australian naval officers and a civil official of the Department of the Navy were also sent to Tokyo for language study.[8]

Oriental studies were not maintained with much energy in the army and the public service. Piesse left the Pacific Branch in 1923; Broadbent

---

[1] Professor James Murdoch. Professor of Oriental Languages, University of Sydney 1919-21. B. Kincardineshire, Scotland, 1856. Died 30 Oct 1921.

[2] Brig J. R. Broadbent, CBE, NX34728. (1st AIF: Capt 1st LH.) AA&QMG 8 Aust Div 1940-42; DA&QMG I Corps 1942-43 and 1944-45; II Corps 1943-44. Grazier; of Mt Fairey, NSW; b. Ballarat, Vic, 18 Feb 1893.

[3] Maj G. H. Capes. 1st AIF: Capt 5 Bn. Regular soldier and journalist; of Melbourne; b. Elsternwick, Vic, 6 Mar 1893. Died 6 Mar 1935.

[4] The Japanese lecturer, Rokuo Okada, resigned in 1921 and Professor J. F. M. Haydon, who had been teaching other modern languages at Duntroon and had studied Japanese with Murdoch and Okada, took over the teaching of Japanese also. In 1937 Mr A. R. Rix, a schoolteacher, and former student of Professor Murdoch, was appointed to Canberra High School and became part-time lecturer in Japanese at Duntroon. The teaching of this subject at Duntroon ceased, however, in 1938.

[5] Maj E. L. Piesse. Director of Intelligence, AMF 1916-19. Director Pacific Branch, Prime Minister's Dept 1919-23. Solicitor; of Hobart, Tas, and Kew, Vic; b. New Town, Tas, 26 Jul 1880. Died 16 May 1947.

[6] Lt-Col E. E. Longfield Lloyd, MC, VD. (1st AIF: Capt 1 Bn.) Aust Govt Commissioner, Japan 1935-40; Director Commonwealth Investigation Service 1944-52; Director-General Commonwealth Security Service 1945-49; British Commonwealth Counsellor, Allied Council, Japan 1946-47. Public servant; of Canberra; b. Sydney, 13 Sep 1890. Died 18 Jul 1957.

[7] F. S. G. Piggott, *Broken Thread* (1950), p. 182.

[8] They were, in 1925, Paymaster Lieutenant (later Paymaster Commander) T. E. Nave; in 1927, Paymaster Lieutenant (later Lieut-Commander) W. E. McLaughlin and Mr R. A. Ball. Ball had served as an infantry lieutenant in the 1st AIF.

instructed in Japanese at Duntroon for three years until, in 1926, he—
and also later Capes—resigned from the service. In the next eight years
no effort was made to maintain Australian officers in Japan. However,
after the dispatch to Japan in 1934 of a mission with Mr John Latham[9]
as leader and Longfield Lloyd as adviser, Longfield Lloyd in 1935 was
appointed Australian Trade Commissioner in Japan (the designation being
broadened later to Australian Government Commissioner). Piesse in that
year wrote a well-informed study of defence against Japan already mentioned.[1] Broadbent will reappear later in this history.

Thus, in the 'thirties, only meagre measures had been taken by the
Army to gain knowledge of the Japanese language and to acquire firsthand experience of Japan and the Far East generally. In the field of
tactics no effort appears to have been made to gain experience of and
develop doctrines about the kind of tropical bush warfare that was likely
to occur in a conflict with Japan. Valuable experience might have been
gained by attachment of officers to British garrisons in tropical Africa
or Burma, by sending observers to China, or by exercises in suitable
areas of Australia or New Guinea.

In July 1937 there occurred at the Marco Polo bridge, Peking, another
military "incident". Japan thereupon engaged in a major though undeclared war with China, biting deeply into Chinese territory, but meeting
with stubborn resistance. The signatories of a Nine-Power Treaty[2] except
Japan, who refused to attend, met in Brussels in November to determine
what course they should take in the face of this perilous situation, but
failed to reach agreement for firm collective action by which Japan might
have been restrained.

Affronts to British and American interests and feelings were frequent
in the course of the struggle. Among them were the shelling by a Japanese
battery of the British and American gunboats on the Yangtse Kiang in
December 1937, followed by the bombing and sinking by Japanese planes
of the American gunboat *Panay*. Alleging that Chinese terrorists and
currency smugglers were being harboured there, the Japanese, early in
1939, imposed a blockade of the British Concession area in Tientsin. Men
and women were subjected to search at the exits, some were stripped, and
it was clear that the Japanese sought to make life in the Concession, for
British people in particular, so intolerable that control would be surrendered to the Japanese or to the puppet Chinese authorities. Faced with
the threat of war in Europe, Britain finally agreed to a settlement of
the Tientsin issue.

Such incidents, and barbarous conduct by Japanese troops in China,
hardened British and American opinion against Japan. They also made

---

[9] Rt Hon Sir John Latham, GCMG. (1914-19: Lt-Cdr RANR.) Attorney-General 1925-29, 1931-34; Minister for External Affairs 1932-34; Leader Aust Mission to East 1934; Chief Justice High Court of Aust 1935-52; Aust Minister to Japan 1940-41. B. Ascot Vale, Vic, 25 Aug 1877.

[1] *Japan and the Defence of Australia*, by "Albatross" (Melbourne, 1935).

[2] Concurrent with the Washington Five-Power Treaty.

it apparent that because of her ambitions to establish a sphere of influence in which she could command the raw materials necessary to sustain and increase her strength, she was becoming increasingly reckless of war with Britain and the United States. By the end of October 1938, Japanese troops had landed at Bias Bay, 35 miles north-east of Hong Kong, and occupied Canton to the west, thus largely nullifying the value of Hong Kong as a base, and placing themselves in a position to subject it to swift and probably successful assault. In February 1939 Japanese troops occupied the island of Hainan, within easy striking distance of Indo-China.

Although she had studiously avoided a showdown with the Japanese in China, the United States gave notice in July 1939 that her commercial treaty with Japan would be abrogated; and increased her economic aid to China. Between 1931 and 1939, however, Japan had nearly doubled her industrial production, with a marked emphasis upon metals and engineering. Her military budget had risen from 29.4 to 71.7 per cent of total expenditure. With consequent heavy burdens upon her people, her economy was being dedicated to the gamble of war, on a scale affecting the whole future of the Far East and the Pacific. The weakness of her war potential lay chiefly in the fact that her home production of natural and synthetic oil amounted to only some 10 per cent of her annual requirements. Of her oil imports, about 80 per cent came from the United States and 10 per cent from the Netherlands East Indies.[3] She had built up a stock of 51 million barrels; but if she were to engage in war on the scale necessary to blast her way to the resources she coveted, she would have to ensure means of replenishing her storage tanks.

As Europe drifted to war, increasing attention was given by Australia to her relations with other countries in the Pacific Ocean area. The Prime Minister, Mr Menzies, explained in May 1939 that Australia's

primary responsibilities are around the fringes of the Pacific Ocean and because my colleagues and I realise that is so, we have decided to press on with all activity with a new Pacific policy, a policy which will not merely consist of making pious statements about our desires and friendships with Canada or the United States; but which will exhibit itself in a positive policy, the setting up of real machinery for the cultivation of friendship with those countries and putting that friendship on a permanent basis. . . . We make no contribution in Australia to the peace of the Pacific by sporadic, hostile action in relation to Japan. . . . I hope that we in Australia, small though we may be in point of numbers, will be able to make a real contribution to the world's peace by making a real contribution to the peace of the Pacific Ocean.[4]

Little time remained, however, for such a policy to take effect; and the trend of events yielded little ground for hope that it might succeed.

As both Germany and Japan became increasingly aggressive, United States strategists saw that the problem facing them was not merely the defence of American soil. From May 1939 onward, they began to formulate what became known as the "Rainbow" series of basic war plans

---

[3] To become, in 1950, the Republic of Indonesia.
[4] Address in the Town Hall, Sydney, 15 May 1939.

contemplating war against more than one enemy, in more than one theatre. These plans were in fact a logical outcome of the naval limitation agreements under which naval supremacy, formerly possessed by Great Britain, was now shared with the United States. Sharing of power meant sharing of responsibility. In the event of the British fleet becoming involved in war in Europe, the American fleet would have a weightier role in the Far East; and defeat of Britain by another power or powers might leave the United States outmatched in naval strength. Thus the plans contemplated hemisphere defence, including dispatch of American forces overseas, and cooperation with Great Britain and France. They paved the way for Anglo-American staff talks which occurred in 1940; for by then the system of collective security erected after the war of 1914-1918 had finally crumbled away, and given place to a new world conflict.

CHAPTER 2

AUSTRALIA'S PROBLEM

AUSTRALIA'S response to the outbreak of war in Europe in September 1939 was first to await indications of what Japan's policy would be; and when Japan soon declared that she would not join Germany, to prepare to send expeditionary forces to Britain's aid, as she had done in 1914.

At that time, however, the Anglo-Japanese Alliance had made it relatively safe for Australia to employ her forces in this way. Now Japan was a potential enemy. In this new situation it might not have been surprising had the Australian Government decided to build up forces as defensive reserves on her own soil and in her northern island territories, and to send any she felt she could spare to Malaya, where they would constitute a further safeguard to Australia and might relieve British forces for employment elsewhere. A tradition had been established in previous wars, however, of sending Australian forces to battlefields in which Britain's forces were in action, rather than of employing them in a garrison role. In the event it was upon building up formations for use in the Middle East and Western Europe that Australia's main military energies were concentrated on this occasion also. This left her own safety bound up with such protection as British forces in Asia might be able to give, and the fact that America, although she remained nominally neutral, might be considered to have replaced Japan as Britain's partner in the Pacific.

In the eight months after the declaration of war Australia raised a corps including the 6th and 7th Divisions; most of the 6th Division had sailed from Australia; a large part of the Australian Navy had gone to oversea stations, and an air contingent, the nucleus of a larger force to come, was established in England.

It was the policy of the United Kingdom and of Australia to avoid war with Japan. As a means to this end Britain, in October 1939, withdrew her gunboats—twenty in all—from the Yangtse Kiang and the West River and at length decided to withdraw three infantry battalions that had been stationed at Shanghai and Tientsin. On the other hand, in August, she had added some strength to the garrison of Singapore, which then contained only six battalions—three British, two Indian and one Malay— by sending there one of three brigade groups which were held ready by the Indian Army for oversea service. The air force at Singapore comprised five poorly-equipped squadrons, to which a sixth was added on 22nd September 1939.

The commanders of the military and air garrisons at Singapore asked London for reinforcements, but were told that none could be sent. The Overseas Defence Committee, on which sat representatives of the Colonial Office, the three Services, the Foreign Office, the Ministry of Home Defence, and the ubiquitous Treasury, recommended that the General

Officer Commanding in Malaya, Lieut-General Bond,[1] should increase his strength by improving the efficiency of the Volunteers, a local force whose British establishment was 2,370, including some 300 officers. This volunteer force included four battalions of the Federated Malay States Volunteers. About one-third of the personnel were Europeans and the remainder Malays and Chinese.

Malaya produced 38 per cent of the world's rubber and 58 per cent of the world's tin; 70 per cent of her exports were sold to the United States. The British Government, in need of dollars, intimated to the Malayan Government that first priority should be given to dollar-earning. The mobilisation and expansion of the Volunteers would take experienced managers and technicians from the rubber plantations and the tin mines; therefore the Volunteers were not mobilised.[2] At the end of September 1939 the Chiefs of Staff in London increased to 180 days their estimate of the time the garrison of Singapore would have to hold out before relief could come.

So matters stood in Malaya, when, in May and June 1940, Germany's defeat of France and Holland offered Japan the glittering chance her expansionists had sought to carry into effect in the Pacific, and through East Asia, the ambitions which underlay her actions in Manchuria and China.

Australian attention, however, still remained focused chiefly upon the struggle in Europe rather than upon defence against Japan. A contingent of Australian and New Zealand troops, diverted while on the way to Egypt, landed in the British Isles on 16th June; and it was expected that the 7th Division, then in training, would soon join the main body of the 6th Division in the Middle East. "As long as Great Britain is unconquered, the world can be saved," declared the Australian Prime Minister, Mr Menzies.

The crisis leading up to and succeeding the fall of France brought a rush of recruits to the A.I.F. This raised the number of enlistments for the 7th Division from 15,196 on 30th May to 54,897 on the 27th June. Thus ample manpower became available not only to complete the 7th, but also to form an 8th Division which the Australian War Cabinet had authorised on 22nd May. Many of those who now enlisted did so with the words of the British Prime Minister, Mr Winston Churchill, ringing in their ears: "Let us therefore brace ourselves to our duties, and so bear ourselves that, if the British Empire and its Commonwealth last for a thousand years, men will still say 'This was their finest hour'."

Nevertheless, the Australian War Cabinet had considered on 12th June an agendum which referred to the possibility of "recurrence of danger of aggression in the Pacific, which would certainly be accompanied by grave

---

[1] Lt-Gen Sir Lionel Bond, KBE, CB; GOC Malaya 1939-41. Regular soldier; b. Aldershot, England, 16 Jun 1884.

[2] It would not have strained Australian resources to have supplied the additional officers and instructors needed, but no suggestion that this be done seems to have arisen.

The Singapore waterfront, and mouth of Singapore River. A section of North Pier is on the left, Clifford Pier in the centre, and the Singapore Cricket Club on the right in the photograph.

The *Queen Mary* in the Singapore graving dock, August 1940.

(Australian War Memorial)

The 22nd Brigade embarked for Malaya in the *Queen Mary* at Sydney in February 1941. After farewelling the troops, Brigadier H. B. Taylor (right), who is seen with Lieut-General C. G. N. Miles, G.O.C. Eastern Command (centre) and Brigadier C. A. Callaghan, flew ahead of them to Malaya.

(Australian War Memorial)

Major R. F. Oakes (left) and Lieut-Colonel D. S. Maxwell, commander of the 2/19th Battalion, at the embarkation.

interference with our seaborne trade" and the "need for instant action in a number of ways to ensure that Australia will be able to continue the fight, or at least to exist". Underlying the question of what measures were to be taken was "whether or not we should continue to rely on the pre-war undertaking that a British squadron of capital ships would proceed to Singapore immediately on hostile action in the Pacific".[3]

A cable was dispatched to the British Government[4] asking as a matter "of the greatest possible urgency" for information covering the probable alternatives with which the Empire might be confronted, to enable Australia to review her policy on local defence and Empire cooperation, and to decide on the measures necessary to give effect to it. At the same time, further assistance which it might be possible for Australia to give was outlined. This included making available, in addition to a squadron of Hudson bombers (which it had been decided at the end of May to send to Singapore to replace a Royal Air Force Blenheim squadron) a further squadron of Hudsons, and one equipped with Australian-made Wirraways, an aircraft used mainly for training.

When the War Cabinet met on 18th June, France had asked Germany for peace terms, and a newspaper report had stated that these would include allotment to Japan of the New Hebrides and New Caledonia. The Cabinet considered the possibility of a Japanese invasion of Australia, and whether Darwin and Port Moresby should be reinforced. The Chief of the Naval Staff (Admiral Colvin[5]) advised the Ministers that defence of the northern part of Australia hinged on whether or not a battle fleet was based on Singapore; without it, the situation became radically changed. The Chief of the General Staff (General White[6]) pointed to the possibility that, by successful attack on British naval forces and bases, Japan could bring Australia to terms by the exercise of seapower alone, and would not need to invade her soil. By the end of the month certain passenger ships had been requisitioned, and were being fitted to carry 900 and 500 troops to reinforce the small garrisons at Darwin and Port Moresby respectively.

Japan had ardently pursued opportunity as the crisis heightened in Europe. On 15th April, within a few days of the invasion of Norway by German forces, the Japanese Foreign Minister, Mr Hachiro Arita, had spoken of an "intimate relationship" between Japan and the South Seas region, especially the East Indies. Early in June, he said "our concern

---

[3] War Cabinet Agendum 133, 1940.

[4] In this volume as in others in the series the word "British" is used in two senses: in one as pertaining to the United Kingdom; in another as pertaining to the British Empire as a whole. Where necessary the distinctive terms are used. There is a discussion of misunderstandings created by the lack of more precise and generally-understood adjectives in Volume I of this series.

[5] Admiral Sir Ragnar Colvin, KBE, CB; RN. (1914-18: Capt RN.) First Naval Member of Commonwealth Naval Board 1937-41; Naval adviser to High Commissioner for Aust 1942-44. Of Curdridge, Hants, Eng; b. London, 7 May 1882. Died 22 Feb 1954.

[6] Gen Sir Brudenell White, KCB, KCMG, KCVO, DSO. (1st AIF: GSO1 1 Div; BGGS Aust Corps; MGGS Fifth Army.) CGS Aust 1920-23 and 1940. Regular soldier; of Melbourne; b. St Arnaud, Vic, 23 Sep 1876. Killed in aircraft accident, 13 Aug 1940.

is not confined to the maintenance of the political *status quo*. Because of their resources . . . it is only natural that this country should be seriously concerned about the economic status of the Netherlands East Indies." By this time, Holland had been overrun by German forces. Into whose hands might the East Indies, with their enormous riches, fall? Japan was intent on staking her claim, for the prospect fitted admirably into the process of swinging away from economic dependence upon the sterling and United States dollar areas, and towards those in Eastern Asia where she hoped to build up an economic bloc under her leadership—or, as her expansionists termed it, a "Co-prosperity Sphere of Greater East Asia". This conception of becoming a "master race" was common to the utterances of German and Japanese leaders.

Japan turned her attention also to the routes of supply to China, some of which after three years of undeclared warfare Japan had been unable to block. If these could be sealed, Chinese resistance might be weakened, or might collapse, freeing Japanese forces for other tasks. The most important of the routes still open commenced at the Tonkinese port of Haiphong, passed through Hanoi, capital of Tonkin, north-eastern Indo-China, and then divided practically at a right-angle. One branch went to Lungchow, in the Chinese province of Kwangsi, where it connected with a road to Nanning; then forked north-east to Hunan and Kiangsi, and north-west to Kweichow and Szechwan. Another was from Haiphong over a metre-gauge, single-line railway track, traversing steeply mountainous country, to Kunming, terminus of the line; thence by road to Chungking, whither the Chinese Government had retreated.

Supply through Burma was from Rangoon via Lashio, and to a smaller extent, from Bhamo, a port on the Irrawaddy River. These Burmese routes joined some distance past the Chinese border, and the Burma Road then threaded through the great gorges of the Salween and Mekong Rivers, and clambered over towering mountain ranges, also reaching Chungking through Kunming.[7] The "North-West Road", which was the main route from Russia, was served by the Turkistan-Siberian railway at Sergiopol. Running south-east, it crossed the border of Sinkiang, China's westernmost province, and joined the ancient caravan route known as the Old Silk Road, to Lanchow. Thence supplies went to Chungking and other parts of China. Another route, of minor importance, left the Trans-Siberian railway near Lake Baikal, and crossed Outer Mongolia.

The French Government, in the face of impending disaster, agreed under Japanese pressure to prohibit transport of motor vehicles, petrol, and many other classes of supplies through Indo-China, and to admit Japanese military inspectors to see that the undertaking was observed. Then the Japanese Government sought from Britain action to prevent war material reaching Chungking via Burma, and through Hong Kong. The Japanese Minister for War, General Shunroka Hata, stated plainly that Japan should take advantage of the European situation to use

---

[7] Over this road some 22,000 tons of supplies had reached China in 1939.

drastic measures against any power trying to obstruct the execution of "Japan's national policy".

"Time pressed if they were to snatch for themselves in the South Pacific the spoils which might otherwise fall to a victorious Germany. Now, cried the expansionists, was the great moment in Japanese history. How were they to face their ancestors should this supreme opportunity be missed?"[8] Before the end of June, while the implications of Britain's plight were causing acute concern in the United States, Arita broadcast a statement that the destiny of the Far East and the South Seas, any development in them, and any disposal of them, was a matter of grave concern to Japan.

United States' vested interests in China were important, but in America opposition to involvement in war was strong. Thus while America as well as Britain had exercised a restraining influence upon Japanese actions in China, American policy was averse to full Anglo-American collaboration with the possibility of having eventually to back it up by force of arms. Neither nation was prepared psychologically or physically for such a show-down.

Herein lay a weakness which had served Japan's purpose as, step by step, she had put plans into operation for establishing her "New Order". Nevertheless, American influence and her enormous war potential were a powerful impediment to Japan's ambitions. Conversations were entered into by the United States Ambassador in Tokyo (Mr Joseph C. Grew) with Arita. Grew aimed to improve Japanese-American relations, particularly as by this time his Government was sending increasing quantities of military supplies from its small stocks to Britain, and was ill-prepared for war in the Pacific. He proposed an exchange of notes in which the United States and Japan would affirm "their wish to maintain the existing situation in the Pacific, except through peaceful change". Arita refused, declaring in a subsequent broadcast that the sword Japan had drawn in China was "intended to be nothing other than the life-giving sword that destroys evil and makes justice manifest". However, the Chinese did not see it that way; and neither did others.

The British Ambassador in Washington (Lord Lothian), accompanied by the recently-appointed first Australian Minister to Washington (Mr R. G. Casey), called on the American Secretary of State (Mr Cordell Hull) on 27th June and handed him an aide-memoire on the whole situation in East Asia, including the demands made by Japan on Britain. In this it was stated that having the whole responsibility for resisting the Axis powers in Europe, Britain found it impossible to oppose aggression in Eastern Asia also.

> Britain therefore believed there were only two courses open. One was for the United States to increase pressure on Japan either by imposing a full embargo on exports to Japan or by sending warships to Singapore, fully realising that these steps might result in war. The second was to negotiate a full settlement with Japan.[9]

---

[8] R. Craigie, *Behind the Japanese Mask*, p. 87.
[9] *The Memoirs of Cordell Hull* (1948), Vol I, p. 897.

After discussing Britain's proposals with President Roosevelt and his associates at the State Department, Hull told Lothian and Casey that sending the United States fleet to Singapore would leave the entire Atlantic seaboard, north and south, exposed to possible European threats. The main fleet was already well out in the Pacific, near Hawaii. As to the embargo proposal, the United States had been progressively bringing economic pressure on Japan for a year, and on several occasions the British Government had suggested caution lest this worsen rather than improve the situation.

When sounded as to America's likely reactions to an attempt by Britain and Australia to establish peace between Japan and China, Hull said that if Britain and Australia would make concessions, such as granting the right to mine iron ore in Australia (mentioned by Casey), and then ask Japan and China what concessions they would make, this would be in line with American desires.[1] However, the principles underlying Japan's application of her "New Order" would need negativing, or at least serious modifications; and no properties or interests of China should be offered to Japan. Hull suggested a third course, amounting to acquiescence in Japanese demands and moves where this was a matter of necessity, but avoiding assent and concessions which Japan could use as stepping-stones to further aggression; avoiding also military or economic action so drastic as to provoke immediate war with Japan.

Meanwhile the British Chiefs of Staff had considered the problems created in the Far East by the fall of France and Holland, and had decided that Japan's first move would probably be into Indo-China and perhaps Thailand (Siam); she might then advance against the Netherlands Indies, and at length against Singapore. It was now impossible to send an adequate fleet to Singapore, and Hong Kong was indefensible. They recommended that Britain should play for time, but should offer full support to the Netherlands Indies if they were attacked.

Since 1939 staffs in both Singapore and London had discussed whether the garrison of Singapore should be concentrated on the island or deployed partly in defence of the Malayan mainland. The air force commander urged that in the absence of a fleet, Malaya must rely mainly on air power, and, consequently, the army must defend airfields far and wide throughout Malaya. The United Kingdom Chiefs of Staff now decided that reliance must be placed chiefly on air power and that the whole of Malaya must be defended. They stated that Malaya required for its defence 22 air force squadrons with 336 first-line aircraft (only 8 squadrons were then available); and two additional infantry divisions plus a third until the air force had reached the required strength. None of these reinforcements

---

[1] Arrangements whereby Japan was to acquire iron ore to be mined at Yampi Sound, on the north-west coast of Western Australia, had fallen through when in 1938 export of iron ore was banned by the Australian Government.

was then available from Britain. The Chiefs of Staff recommended that Australia be asked to provide a division for Singapore.[2]

Whence, except Australia, could military reinforcements have been sought? Britain, facing possible invasion, could not spare a man or a weapon. The army in the Middle East was still small and ill-equipped and now faced almost certain attack by far more numerous Italian forces in North Africa and Abyssinia. India had already sent a brigade to Malaya and two brigades—later forming into the 4th Division—to Egypt.

In the first half of 1940 the 5th Division was formed in the Middle East from existing units. In the same period India recruited some 53,000 men, but her army, although it contained infantry units enough to form several more divisions, was short of technical troops and heavy equipment, and had a continuing responsibility for the defence of the North-West Frontier and for internal security. When France fell Britain accepted an Indian offer to form five more infantry divisions (6th, 7th, 8th, 9th, 10th); but to find officers, arms, and technical units, and particularly artillery, for these divisions would be a problem. Relatively little artillery had been needed by the Indian Army within India, and a policy had been adopted of manning very few artillery, engineer and signals units with Indians. Nevertheless India not only set about forming these five divisions for the general oversea pool, but planned to form five more to replace them when they went away.[3]

As an outcome of the appreciation by the British Chiefs of Staff, a recommendation that two squadrons of aircraft (already offered by Australia) and a division of troops be rapidly moved to Malaya came to Australia in a cable from the Secretary of State for Dominion Affairs (Lord Caldecote) on 28th June. He said that while it was not thought that war with Japan was necessarily imminent, the Chiefs of Staff, having reviewed Far Eastern strategy, considered that

> the security of our imperial interests in the Far East lies ultimately in our ability to control sea communications in the south-western Pacific, for which purpose adequate fleet must be based at Singapore. Since our previous assurances in this respect, however, the whole strategic situation has been radically altered by the French defeat. The result of this has been to alter the whole of the balance of naval strength in home waters. Formerly we were prepared to abandon the Eastern Mediterranean and dispatch a fleet to the Far East, relying on the French fleet in the Western Mediterranean to contain the Italian fleet. Now if we move the Mediterranean fleet to the Far East there is nothing to contain the Italian fleet, which will be free to operate in the Atlantic or reinforce the German fleet in home waters, using bases in north-west France. We must therefore retain in European waters sufficient naval forces to watch both the German and Italian fleets, and we cannot do this and send a fleet to the Far East.
>
> In the meantime the strategic importance to us of the Far East both for Empire security and to enable us to defeat the enemy by control of essential commodities at the source has been increased.
>
> The Japanese advance in China and Hainan has increased the threat to Malaya and any further advance, into French Indo-China, Dutch possessions or Thailand,

---
[2] They recommended also that the New Zealand Government be asked to send a brigade to Fiji, and that Government promptly did so.
[3] These were to be the 14th, 17th, 19th, 20th and 34th.

would endanger still more our position at Singapore, which is the key point in the Far East. Owing to the increased range of aircraft and the development of aerodromes, particularly in Thailand, we can no longer concentrate on the defence of Singapore Island entirely, but must consider the defence of Malaya as a whole, particularly the security of up-country landing grounds. For this reason, and because we cannot spare a fleet for the Far East at present, it is all the more important that we should do what we can to improve our land and air defences in Malaya.

The Dominions Secretary, after having stated that the Chiefs of Staff asked particularly whether the proposed division could be equipped as fully as possible from Australia's pool of military equipment, continued: "They realise that you could not equip these troops up to full western standards, nor would this be necessary in view of the unlikelihood of the Japanese being able to bring mechanised troops with the latest form of equipment to attack them. . . ." The Chiefs of Staff recommended movement by brigade groups as they became available if a whole division could not be sent immediately.

These significant views made clear to the Australian leaders the necessity for radically reviewing ideas about the Singapore base upon which Australia's defence plans had been largely founded; and they set off a train of intricate problems of home defence and use of the A.I.F. overseas for consideration by the Australian War Cabinet.

The Australian Chiefs of Staff reported to the War Cabinet that they were concerned with the necessity for ground protection of bases from which Australian air units would operate in Malaya. The 7th Division of the A.I.F., however, had just been organised. To send a division from Australia equipped on even a modest scale would not only seriously hamper training of the remainder of the A.I.F. in Australia, but also the equipment of necessary forces for home defence. Moreover, they felt that Australia's first obligation was to assist in the equipment of that portion of the 6th Division in the Middle East. They suggested three choices:

(1) Transfer of the 6th Division from the Middle East to Malaya, where Australia would assist in completing its equipment (the Chiefs of Staff said they recognised that there were serious general objections to this); (2) dispatch to Malaya of a brigade group, trained and equipped, from the 7th Division in Australia (this would not be ready to leave Australia for two or three months, depending on whether the 6th Division could be provided with equipment from other sources; the scale of equipment would be low; no anti-aircraft equipment and no anti-tank guns or armoured vehicles could be provided from Australia); (3) transfer of one brigade group at a time from Australia to India to relieve troops from India for use in Malaya. (These groups could complete their training in India, and Australia would complete their equipment as far and as quickly as possible; they could then be used for active operations.)

The War Cabinet decided to inform the British Government that it was unable on the information before it to send a division to Malaya; to draw attention to the related urgent need for completing equipment of the 6th Division and deciding its theatre of employment; but to leave the door open to further consideration when an appreciation then awaited from Britain arrived.

This later appreciation, by the British Chiefs of Staff, dealt with the situation in the Middle East. In it they reviewed factors on which the security of the Middle East hinged, and said that it was clearly necessary to strengthen the Imperial defence forces there at the earliest possible moment. The situation was, however, governed by the probability of a large-scale air offensive and even invasion of Great Britain in the near future, and shortages of equipment to meet these threats. Britain's policy therefore must be to concentrate immediate efforts on home defence, and to begin releasing equipment for the Middle East only when the situation could be more clearly judged following the impending trial of strength at home. Meanwhile, Britain would endeavour to send anything she could spare, including, if possible, modern fighters to re-equip squadrons in Egypt, and bombers to replace wastage.

The outlook in Australia and the United Kingdom, as presented by the Chiefs of Staff of both countries, was bleak. Both on political and strategical grounds, there were grave objections to dispatching a substantial force of men and equipment from Australia in such circumstances. It would be all too easy to make an unwise move. The Australian War Cabinet deferred decision, pending still further information which it was expecting; and on 10th July Mr Menzies told his colleagues that he thought it desirable that he should confer with the Prime Minister of the United Kingdom, and representatives of other Dominions, particularly New Zealand. This proposal was generally approved, although Mr Menzies did not in fact leave Australia until the following year.

While the destination of the A.I.F. was still under consideration, Britain was being pressed by Japan to withdraw the British garrison from Shanghai, as she had decided to do in 1939; and, as noted, to close Hong Kong and Burma to passage of war supplies to China. With the closing of the routes through Indo-China, the Burma Road became of prime importance, for the enormous length of the haul from supply centres in Russia made the "North-West Road" of relatively little value. Although the volume of supplies carried over the Burma Road was not large in relation to China's needs, it was regarded by China as a lifeline of her resistance.

In the course of Imperial consultation on the issue, Australia favoured compromise; and, in a statement to the House of Commons on 18th July, Mr Churchill said that the Government of Burma had agreed to suspend for three months the transit to China of arms and ammunition, petrol, lorries, and railway material. The categories of goods prohibited in Burma would be prohibited in Hong Kong. Asked whether the agreement would secure Japan's goodwill, Mr Churchill said succinctly: "I think that all that happens to us in the Far East is likely to be very much influenced by what happens over here." Clearly, he had no illusion that this humiliating step would do more than gain time. It cut across the feelings of all who admired China's prolonged resistance to the Japanese. China's leader, Generalissimo Chiang Kai-shek, declared that, if Great

Britain was trying to link the question of the Burma route with that of peace between China and Japan, it would practically amount to assisting Japan to bring China to submission. "So long as China has not attained the object for which she has been fighting," he said, "she will not lay down her arms"; to which the Chinese Foreign Office spokesman added, bitterly, "We are confident that we will win, whether we are betrayed or not."

Such hopes as were held for an improvement of relations with Japan were discouraged by the fall, on 16th July, of the relatively moderate Cabinet headed by Admiral Mitsumasa Yonai, and his succession by Prince Fuminaro Konoye, with General Tojo as War Minister and Mr Yosuke Matsuoka as Foreign Minister. Prince Konoye had been Premier at the time of the Japanese invasion of China in July 1937; Tojo was a leader of the powerful group within the army which was determined to conquer East Asia; Matsuoka, also an advocate of aggressive nationalism, had led the Japanese delegation out of the League of Nations in 1933, after defending Japan's seizure of Manchuria, and was regarded by the American Secretary of State as "crooked as a basket of fishhooks".[4]

Prince Konoye allowed himself only a week in office before announcing that there must be a "new national structure", since the enunciation of divergent views might mislead people, and the nation might miss an opportunity. He had reached agreement with the army, and on this he based confidence that he could solve the many problems which had accumulated. Nevertheless, he cautiously added that Japan would retain her autonomous position in foreign relations. She must not be blinded by the prospect of immediate gains, but must look ahead fifty or one hundred years towards the goal of national self-sufficiency, to be attained by developing Manchukuo, China, and the South Seas.

In July the United States initiated the first of a series of "economic sanctions" aimed at Japan, along the lines that Britain had urged earlier. Congress passed an Act authorising the President to prohibit or curtail export of munitions whenever he considered it necessary in the interests of defence. Soon afterwards the President prohibited the export, except to Britain and her allies, of aviation fuel and certain kinds of iron and steel scrap. Also in July Congress passed a bill authorising an immense expansion of the American Navy.

The Secretary of State for War, Mr Henry L. Stimson, concurrently told a committee of the House of Representatives, which was considering a "Selective Service" or Conscription Bill, that the executive and legislative branches of the Government were the trustees of the nation's security, and "a prudent trustee must take into consideration that in another thirty days Great Britain might be conquered and her fleet come under enemy

---

[4] Hull, Vol I, p. 902.

control". Although he had been speaking principally of Europe, he added that the Japanese fleet was the agent of a Power "working very closely with the Axis".

Those crowded and critical two months, June and July 1940, were followed by a comparative lull in the Pacific, but they had given a warning that none could ignore. They had also assured the passing, at length, of the United States Selective Service Bill, which President Roosevelt signed in September, rendering liable to service some 16,500,000 Americans, and had brought about an immense American naval construction program.

The British troops were withdrawn from Shanghai and Tientsin in August;[5] but at home Britain steadily gathered strength despite the hammering she now was suffering from the skies. A move to coordinate and develop the arming of British countries around the Indian Ocean basin was set afoot by calling a conference of their representatives, to be held in New Delhi in October. Announcing the appointment on 18th August of Sir John Latham, Chief Justice of Australia, and a former Deputy Prime Minister, as first Australian Minister to Japan, the Minister for External Affairs, Mr J. McEwen, said that this was "the culmination of the desire of Australia and Japan for a more direct and intimate relationship". Also in August informal Anglo-American staff talks began for the purpose of closer collaboration in both hemispheres.

Another fateful measure had been adopted by President Roosevelt. On 15th June, the day after the fall of Paris, he signed a letter establishing a National Defence Research Council and bringing under its direction a special committee he had recently appointed "to study into the possible relationship to national defense of recent discoveries in the field of atomistics, notably the fission of uranium".[6]

When on 28th August the Australian War Cabinet resumed consideration of the British proposal to send a division to Malaya, it had before it a series of cablegrams from the Dominions Office, a further and far from reassuring appreciation of the position in East Asia and the Pacific by the British Chiefs of Staff, and the views on this of the Australian Chiefs of Staff. Outstanding among the communications from Britain was one from Mr Churchill dated 11th August:

. . . We are about to reinforce with more first-class units the Eastern Mediterranean Fleet. This fleet would of course at any time be sent through the Canal into the Indian Ocean, or to relieve Singapore. We do not want to do this, even if Japan declares war, until it is found to be vital to your safety. Such a transference would entail the complete loss of the Middle East, and all prospect of beating Italy in the Mediterranean would be gone. We must expect heavy attacks on Egypt in the near future, and the Eastern Mediterranean Fleet is needed to help in repelling them. If these attacks succeed the Eastern Fleet would have to leave the

---

[5] A regiment of American marines remained in Shanghai until November, when it was withdrawn to the Philippines.

[6] From letter to Dr Vannevar Bush, quoted in *The White House Papers of Harry L. Hopkins* (1949) by R. E. Sherwood, p. 156-7.

Mediterranean either through the Canal or by Gibraltar. In either case a large part of it would be available for your protection. We hope however to maintain ourselves in Egypt and to keep the Eastern Fleet at Alexandria during the first phase of an Anglo-Japanese war, should that occur. No one can lay down beforehand what is going to happen. We must just weigh events from day to day, and use our available resources to the utmost.

A final question arises: whether Japan, having declared war, would attempt to invade Australia or New Zealand with a considerable army. We think this very unlikely, first because Japan is absorbed in China, secondly, would be gathering rich prizes in the Dutch East Indies, and, thirdly, would fear very much to send an important part of her Fleet far to the southward, leaving the American Fleet between it and home.

If, however, contrary to prudence and self-interest, Japan set about invading Australia or New Zealand on a large scale, I have the explicit authority of the Cabinet to assure you that we should then cut our losses in the Mediterranean and sacrifice every interest, except only the defence and feeding of this Island, on which all depends, and would proceed in good time to your aid with a fleet able to give battle to any Japanese force which could be placed in Australian waters, and able to parry any invading force, or certainly cut its communications with Japan. . . .

This very positive assurance, in marked contrast to what the United Kingdom Chiefs of Staff had said in June and had now repeated, about prospects from a strategical viewpoint of sparing naval forces from European waters, had a decisive effect. The Australian Chiefs of Staff declared that the defence of Singapore, and incidentally the holding of Malaya, remained of vital importance to Australia. Without Singapore the British fleet would have no suitable base for operations in the Far East. "We consider that this assurance . . . is of such importance," they said, "that we should strain all our efforts and resources to cooperate in the actual defence of the area as, strategically, it now becomes, as far as Australia is concerned, of greater ultimate importance than the Middle East." The security of Singapore, they said, would appear to depend largely on the defence of the whole of Malaya, and, to a less degree, the use by Japan of the air bases in Indo-China and Thailand; and denial of the use by Japan of air and naval bases in the Netherlands East Indies.

Accepting the premise that effective opposition to occupation of the East Indies was impracticable in the immediate future, the Australian Chiefs of Staff said that harassing and delaying action would be the best policy in Malaya and the East Indies. The strategic disabilities which would result from an unopposed Japanese occupation of the East Indies were so great that Australia should support the Dutch in the event of Japan attempting to seize the islands, unless the British Government considered that the delay of declaration of war against Japan would more than compensate for this loss. The Chiefs of Staff emphasised that they thought it desirable to undertake conversations with the Dutch as soon as sufficient forces were available to permit an offer of substantial help.

The British Chiefs of Staff had held that attack by Japan on Australia or New Zealand would be likely to be limited to cruiser raids, possibly combined with a light scale of seaborne air attack against ports. The Australian Chiefs of Staff, on the other hand, said that the Japanese leaders must be well aware that Britain's main fleet was contained in European waters, and might well accept as a reasonable risk the employment of naval forces including their capital ships and aircraft carriers. The possibility of attack on a medium scale, or even invasion, could not be ruled out, but a Japanese attempt to invade Australia when they could with far less risk obtain possession of the East Indies would be an unwise and improbable course of action. Once in possession of the Indies, they could, without serious risk, institute a blockade of Australia, and make raids on her coasts and shipping. They could also contemplate invasion of Australia if they were firmly in possession of the Indies, and the Singapore base was either in their hands or reduced to comparative impotence by the absence of a British (or American) main fleet.

In general assent to the Chiefs of Staff recommendations, the War Cabinet decided (at the meeting on 28th August) to assure Britain of its willingness to cooperate by the dispatch of the 7th Division to the theatre in which it could give the most effective support. In giving this assurance, the Government said it was realised that considerations of training and equipment precluded dispatch of the division to the Middle East then, although the intention ultimately to concentrate the Australian Corps in that region was noted. The War Cabinet would prefer that the 7th should go to India to complete its training and equipment, and to relieve for service in Malaya troops better equipped and more acclimatised; a less circumscribed role than that of garrison duties at Singapore would be more compatible with the psychology of the Australian soldier. However, should the British Government still desire the 7th Division to go to Malaya after carefully weighing the views to which the War Cabinet attached great importance, the latter would be quite agreeable to this course.

The War Cabinet also decided to inform the British Government that it felt that almost inevitably war would follow if Japan attacked the East Indies. Nevertheless, because of the military position in the United Kingdom and the Middle East, and the attitude of the United States, a binding one-way obligation to go to the assistance of the Dutch in this event should not be undertaken. The Empire's policy should be to take a realistic view of such an act of aggression in the light of its military position at the time. If the British Government concurred in the course, the views of the Empire should be put to the United States Government, with a suggestion that a similar attitude be adopted by it.

Reports of Japanese demands on French Indo-China became current in August, and talks between Hull, Lothian and Casey followed in Washington. Hull declared that a governing factor in the United States attitude was that it would be most undesirable, even from the British standpoint, for two wars to be raging at the same time, one in the East and the other in the West. If the United States should enter any war, it would immediately result in a great reduction of military supplies to Great Britain which she could ill afford to forego. The possibility of holding conferences on bases and unified defence in the Pacific was touched upon, but no positive advance in that direction was made at the time.

America and Britain continued to exert diplomatic pressure on Japan, but the French Government at Vichy, under German domination, yielded late in September to Japanese pressure. It declared that it recognised that the political and economic interest of Japan in East Asia was predominant, and conceded passage of Japanese troops into the Tonkin Protectorate in Northern Indo-China, with the use of bases therein. This move not only gave Japan advantages in her war with China; preceded by warnings by Britain and America, it showed that Japan was prepared to set them both at defiance to gain her ends. It also made bases available to the Japanese which in their hands encroached upon the security of Singapore, and constituted a menace to the whole area which the Singapore base had been designed to protect.

Thus the fall of France, with consequent weakening in her attitude to Japan, had produced circumstances greatly different from those contemplated when the Singapore base was planned. Then it had been assumed that Great Britain could count upon the support, or at least neutrality, of France in any conflict with Japan. Now French East Asian territory was to become enemy territory; and uncertainty about the future of what remained of the French fleet was a powerful factor in preventing British vessels being spared from the Atlantic and the Mediterranean to give reality to Singapore as a naval stronghold.

Once again, Japan was reflecting in her actions the tide of war in Europe; and not only what had happened on the Continent. Only a few days before Mr Churchill had said publicly that at any moment a major assault might be launched on Britain. He had stated at a secret session of the House of Commons that more than 1,700 self-propelled barges and more than 200 sea-going ships, including some very large ones, were gathered at the many invasion ports that were in German hands. The shipping available and assembled was sufficient, he said, to carry in one voyage nearly half a million men.

Between the end of August and the Japanese occupation of Tonkin late in September, however, the destination of the 7th Australian Division had been decided. It would go not to Malaya or India, but to the Middle East.

After its polite expression of reluctant agreement with the proposal to send the 7th Division to India or Malaya the Australian War Cabinet, on 7th September, had sent to London a fervent plea for ensuring the defence of the Middle East, and by inference had thus reinforced earlier arguments against diverting it to India or Malaya. Thereupon, on the 10th, Mr Churchill, with whose feelings this Australian opinion accorded, sent a memorandum to his Chief of Staff, General Ismay,[7] in which he said:

> The prime defence of Singapore is the Fleet. The protective effect of the Fleet is exercised to a large extent whether it is on the spot or not. For instance, the present Middle Eastern Fleet, which we have just powerfully reinforced, could in a very short time, if ordered, reach Singapore. It could, if necessary, fight an action before reaching Singapore, because it would find in that fortress fuel, ammunition, and repair facilities. The fact that the Japanese had made landings in Malaya and had even begun the siege of the fortress would not deprive a superior relieving fleet of its power. On the contrary, the plight of the besiegers, cut off from home while installing themselves in the swamps and jungle, would be all the more forlorn.
>
> The defence of Singapore must therefore be based upon a strong local garrison and the general potentialities of seapower. The idea of trying to defend the Malay Peninsula and of holding the whole of Malaya, a large country 400 by 200 miles at its widest part, cannot be entertained. A single division, however well supplied with signals, etc., could make no impression upon such a task. What could a single division do for the defence of a country nearly as large as England?
>
> The danger of a rupture with Japan is no worse than it was. The probabilities of the Japanese undertaking an attack upon Singapore, which would involve so large a proportion of their fleet far outside the Yellow Sea, are remote; in fact, nothing could be more foolish from their point of view. Far more attractive to them are the Dutch East Indies. The presence of the United States Fleet in the Pacific must always be a main preoccupation to Japan. They are not at all likely to gamble. They are usually most cautious, and now have real need to be, since they are involved in China so deeply. . . .
>
> I do not therefore consider that the political situation is such as to require the withholding of the 7th Australian Division from its best station strategically and administratively. A telegram should be drafted to the Commonwealth Government in this sense.[8]

This mandate by Mr Churchill, which overrode the advice of his military advisers but had Australia's backing, was embodied in a telegram which reached Australia on the 18th September, five days after the Italian Army crossed the frontier into Egypt. This event helped the argument that the I Australian Corps should be concentrated in the Middle East against an active enemy, rather than be divided between that theatre and Singapore.

---

[7] General Rt Hon Lord Ismay, GCB, CH, DSO. Chief of Staff to Minister of Defence 1940-46. Regular soldier; b. 21 Jun 1887.
[8] Quoted in W. S. Churchill, *The Second World War*, Vol II (1949), pp. 591-2.

CHAPTER 3

PLANS AND PREPARATIONS

WHILE the destination of the 7th Division was being decided, the 8th was being formed and trained. It was to include the 22nd, 23rd and 24th Infantry Brigades, and a proportionate number of corps troops was to be raised, bringing the total to approximately 20,000 all ranks. Major-General Sturdee[1] took command of the division on the 1st August 1940.

Although a corps and two divisional staffs had been formed for the A.I.F., it was still possible to find a highly-qualified staff for the 8th Division. Colonel Rourke,[2] who was transferred from the corps staff to the 8th Division as senior staff officer, had been a young artillery major in the old A.I.F. He later passed through the Staff College at Quetta, India, and instructed at the Royal Military College, Duntroon, and at the command staff school established in Sydney in 1938. The senior administrative officer, Colonel Broadbent, a Duntroon graduate and a Gallipoli veteran, as mentioned earlier had been attached to the British Embassy in Tokyo from 1919 to 1922, and was in charge of the Australian Food Relief Mission to Japan after the Japanese earthquake in 1923. He was one of very few Australian regular officers with experience of East Asia. In 1926 Broadbent had retired and become a grazier. Also on the staff were two citizen soldiers who had served as young officers in 1914-1918, and had won distinction then and in civil life—Major Kent Hughes,[3] then a Member of the Legislative Assembly in Victoria and a former Minister, and Major Whitfield,[4] a Sydney businessman.

The artillery commander was Brigadier Callaghan,[5] also of Sydney, who in the 1914-1918 war had won his way to command of a field artillery brigade. This was followed by continuous service in the militia, including command of the 8th Infantry Brigade from 1934 to 1938. The senior engineer, Lieut-Colonel Scriven,[6] who had designed the re-fortification

---

[1] Lt-Gen Sir Vernon Sturdee, KBE, CB, DSO, NX35000. (1st AIF: CRE 5 Aust Div 1917-18; GSO2 GHQ France 1918.) GOC Eastern Comd 1939-40; CGS AMF 1940-42 and 1946-50; GOC First Army 1944-45. Regular soldier; of Melbourne; b. Frankston, Vic, 16 Apr 1890.

[2] Brig H. G. Rourke, MC, VX14282. (1st AIF: Maj 7 Fd Arty Bde.) GSO1 8 Aust Div 1940-41; CRA 7 Div 1941-42; BGS I Corps 1942; LO (Joint Planning Cttee) War Office, London, 1942-45. Regular soldier; of Ashfield, NSW, 26 Jun 1896.

[3] Col Hon Sir Wilfrid Kent Hughes, KBE, MVO, MC, ED, MP; VX26600. (1st AIF: DAQMG Aust Mtd Div 1917-18.) DAQMG 8 Div 1940-41; AA&QMG Admin HQ 8 Div 1941-42. MLA in Vic 1927-49, Minister for Transport and Electrical Undertakings and Deputy Premier 1948-49; MHR since 1949; Minister for the Interior 1951-55. Company director; of Toorak, Vic; b. East Melbourne, 12 Jun 1895.

[4] Col N. H. Whitfield, MC, NX35030. (1st AIF: Capt 5 Pnr Bn.) DAAG 8 Div 1940-41; Director-General of Recruiting 1941-42; Admin LO Adv LHQ 1942-45. Managing director; of Randwick, NSW; b. Picton, NSW, 25 Oct 1896. Died 5 Nov 1950.

[5] Maj-Gen C. A. Callaghan, CB, CMG, DSO, VD, NX34723. (1st AIF: 1st Fd Arty Bde; CO 4 Fd Arty Bde 1918-19.) Comd Arty Eastern Comd 1939-40; CRA 8 Div 1940-42. Merchant; of Gordon, NSW; b. Sydney, 31 July 1890.

[6] Lt-Col E. G. B. Scriven, VX28449; CRE 8 Div 1940-41. Regular soldier; of Lower Sandy Bay, Tas; b. Brisbane, 5 Apr 1897. Accidentally killed 30 Jun 1941.

of Sydney in 1934, and the senior signals officer, Lieut-Colonel Thyer,[7] were regulars; Lieut-Colonel Byrne,[8] who commanded the Army Service Corps, Colonel Derham,[9] the medical services, and Lieut-Colonel Stahle,[1] the senior ordnance officer, were citizen soldiers, the two latter having held commissions in the old A.I.F.

The headquarters of the new division had been temporarily established on 4th July at Victoria Barracks, Sydney, and on 1st August were transferred to Rosebery Racecourse. The 22nd Brigade, raised in New South Wales, and the 23rd, raised in Victoria and Tasmania, were concentrated in the two bigger States; the 24th, drawn from Queensland, Western Australia and South Australia, assembled in Queensland.

Brigadier Taylor,[2] who had been training the 5th Brigade of the militia, was chosen to command the 22nd Brigade. He had gained a commission in the militia in 1913 and, during the war of 1914-1918, served with distinction in France as an infantry officer. After returning to Australia he resumed militia service and, in 1939, when he was given the 5th Militia Brigade, had successively commanded the Sydney University Regiment, the 18th Battalion, the New South Wales Scottish Regiment, and the 56th Battalion. In civil life the quality of his mind was evident in his having become a Doctor of Science in 1925. He had become Deputy Government Analyst of New South Wales in 1934.

As his brigade major, Taylor obtained Major Dawkins,[3] a regular who had become brigade major of the 5th Infantry Brigade in the 2nd Division. Taylor sought officers with last-war experience to lead his battalions, young militia officers as seconds-in-command, and a sprinkling of veterans among his N.C.O's and men, particularly for the steadying effect they were likely to have in the first action which the brigade or any part of it would have to face. Varley,[4] who was given command of the 2/18th Battalion, Maxwell[5] (2/19th) and Jeater[6] (2/20th) all reflected his requirements.

Varley, an Inverell grazier, with keen blue eyes and a sparsely-built frame which accentuated his military bearing, had returned as a captain,

---

[7] Colonel J. H. Thyer, CBE, DSO, VX12755. (1st AIF: Lt in Signal Coys 1918.) CO 8 Div Sigs 1940-41; GSO1 8 Div 1941-42. Regular soldier; of Melbourne; b. Natimuk, Vic, 30 Sep 1897.

[8] Lt-Col L. J. A. Byrne, ED, NX34829; CASC 8 Div. Works manager; of Lindfield, NSW; b. Sydney, 4 Jun 1896.

[9] Col A. P. Derham, CBE, MC, ED, VX13486. (1st AIF: S-Capt 2 Inf Bde 1915-16.) ADMS 8 Div. Medical practitioner; of Kew, Vic; b. Camberwell, Vic, 12 Sep 1891.

[1] Lt-Col L. R. D. Stahle, MBE, VX24581. (1st AIF: 10 Fd Amb; 34 Bn.) DADOS 8 Div. Managing director; of Toorak, Vic; b. Melbourne, 3 Nov 1892.

[2] Brig H. B. Taylor, MC, VD, NX34724. (1st AIF: Capt 19 Bn.) Comd 22 Bde 1940-42. NSW Deputy Govt Analyst; of Longueville, NSW; b. Sydney, 10 Aug 1890.

[3] Maj C. B. Dawkins, NX34726. BM 22 Bde 1940-41; GSO2 HQ 8 Aust Div 1941-42. Regular soldier; of Strathfield, NSW; b. Kerong Vale, Vic, 2 Jan 1901. Killed in action 11 Feb 1942.

[4] Brig A. L. Varley, MC, NX35005. (1st AIF: Capt 45 Bn.) CO 2/18 Bn 1940-42; Comd 22 Bde 1942. Stock and station agent; of Inverell, NSW; b. Lidcombe, NSW, 13 Oct 1893. Drowned at sea 14 Sep 1944.

[5] Brig D. S. Maxwell, MC, NX12610. (1st AIF: 3 LH Regt; Capt 52 Bn.) CO 2/19 Bn 1940-41; Comd 27 Bde 1941-42. Medical practitioner; of Cootamundra, NSW; b. Hobart, 8 Jan 1892.

[6] Lt-Col W. D. Jeater, NX34992. (1st AIF: 30 Bn; Lt 8 MG Coy.) CO 2/20 Bn 1940-41; Comd 8 Div General Base Depot 1941-42. Architectural draftsman; of Newcastle, NSW; b. Penrith, NSW, 2 Aug 1896.

aged 25, from the 1914-1918 war. He did not seek appointment in the militia until after the Munich crisis of 1938, but for the nine months before joining the A.I.F. he commanded the 35th Battalion. Maxwell, six feet three inches in height, was the shorter of two sons of a Tasmanian bank manager. Both had given distinguished service in 1914-1918 when they were affectionately known as "Big"[7] and "Little" Maxwell. They served as troopers in the light horse on Gallipoli, and later were commissioned in the infantry. In France, each was decorated for his exploits at Mouquet Farm. After his return to Australia Duncan Maxwell graduated in medicine at Sydney University, and went into private practice at Cootamundra. In August 1939, despite some misgivings arising from the contrast between the duties of a doctor and of a combatant, he returned to the infantry as second-in-command of the 56th Battalion, which had been newly raised in the Riverina. Three months later he became its commander. Although his infantry service between the wars had been so brief, his service in 1914-1918 and his personality underlay his selection to command of the 2/19th. Jeater, an architectural draftsman of Newcastle, had enlisted in the A.I.F. in August 1915, and gained a commission in the course of that war. In 1926 he obtained an appointment in the militia, and for three years from 1937 commanded a battalion.

Each commanding officer was allowed to enlist men from his own and adjoining militia districts, and naturally brought in a regional following. As an instance the 2/19th, although it included some men from as far afield as New Guinea, was

> to all intents and purposes a Riverina battalion. You could see it in the way they walked, the way they talked, and in the squint of their eyes. Pitt Street and Bondi Beach were foreign to them. Their hunting grounds were at Gundagai, Leeton, Griffith, Wagga, Narrandera and Lockhart. They told the yarns bushmen tell; about sheep and drovers and cocky farmers. . . . The Colonel's batman, "Young" Jimmy Larkin, had a milk round . . . [in Wagga] and had been a prisoner of the Bulgarians in the last war. The New Guinea men . . . clung together. Their stories were about Rabaul and Salamaua and Samarai. They talked about copra and gold and Burns Philp and Carpenters.[8]

In choosing their senior officers, the battalion commanders looked for those who had been in militia units, and consequently knew where to find good N.C.O.'s. The officers chosen were told, however, that they must select not more than three-quarters of the N.C.O's they needed; the remainder were to be selected after the main body of the brigade was in camp. "As you mould your men, so will your battalion be," Varley told his officers at the commencement of their classes. "Inculcate into them your finest ideals. Teach them the principles of team-work and good fellowship as opposed to individual effort and selfish disregard for the comrades with whom they are going to live, train and fight."

---
[7] Maj A. M. Maxwell, DSO, MC, VX74555. (1st AIF: 3 LH; Capt 52 Bn.) HQ 8 Div. Rubber planter; of Malaya; b. Hobart, 8 Jun 1888.
[8] Gilbert Mant, *You'll Be Sorry* (1944), pp. 36-7.

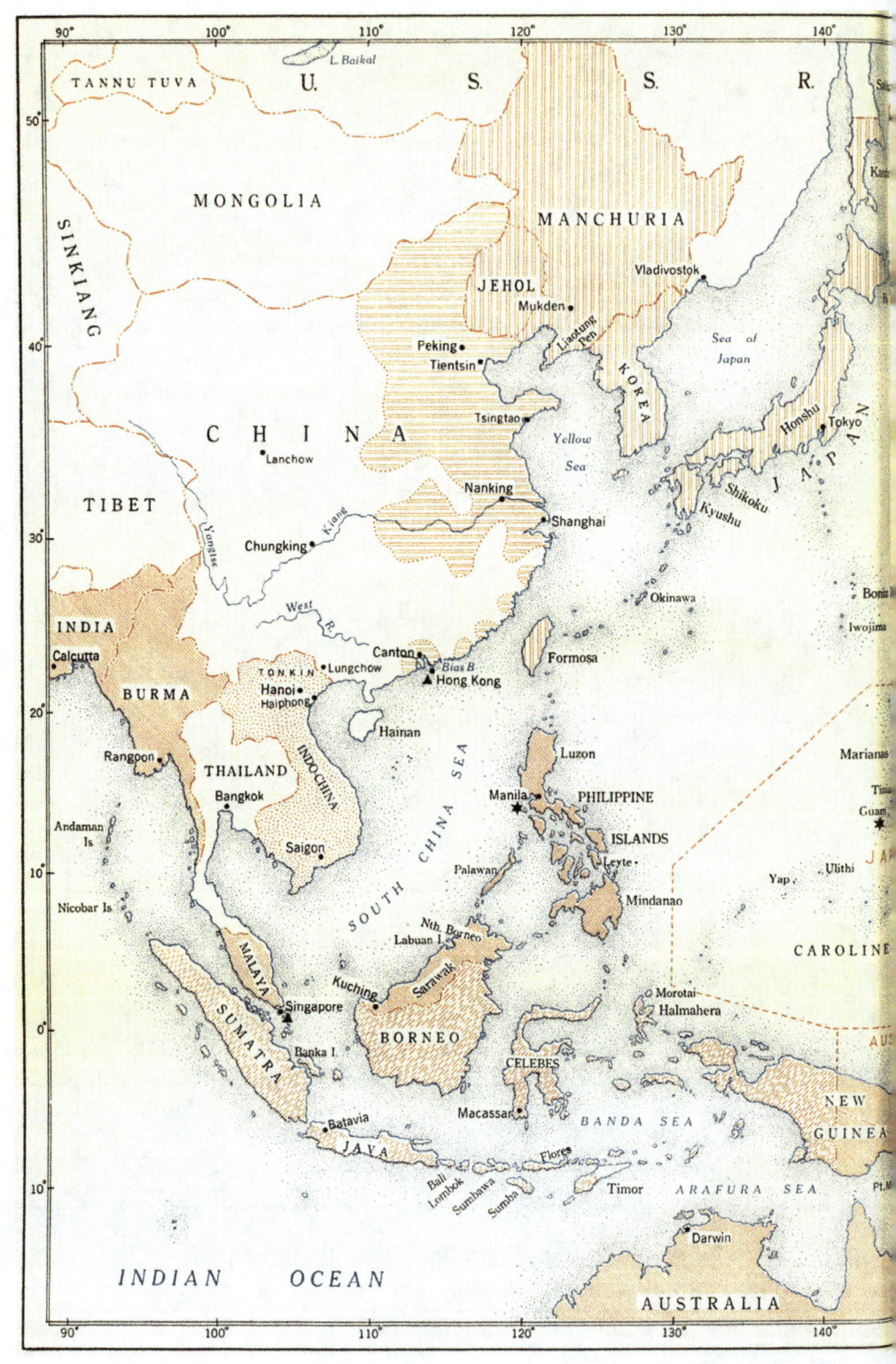

The Far Eastern Theatre

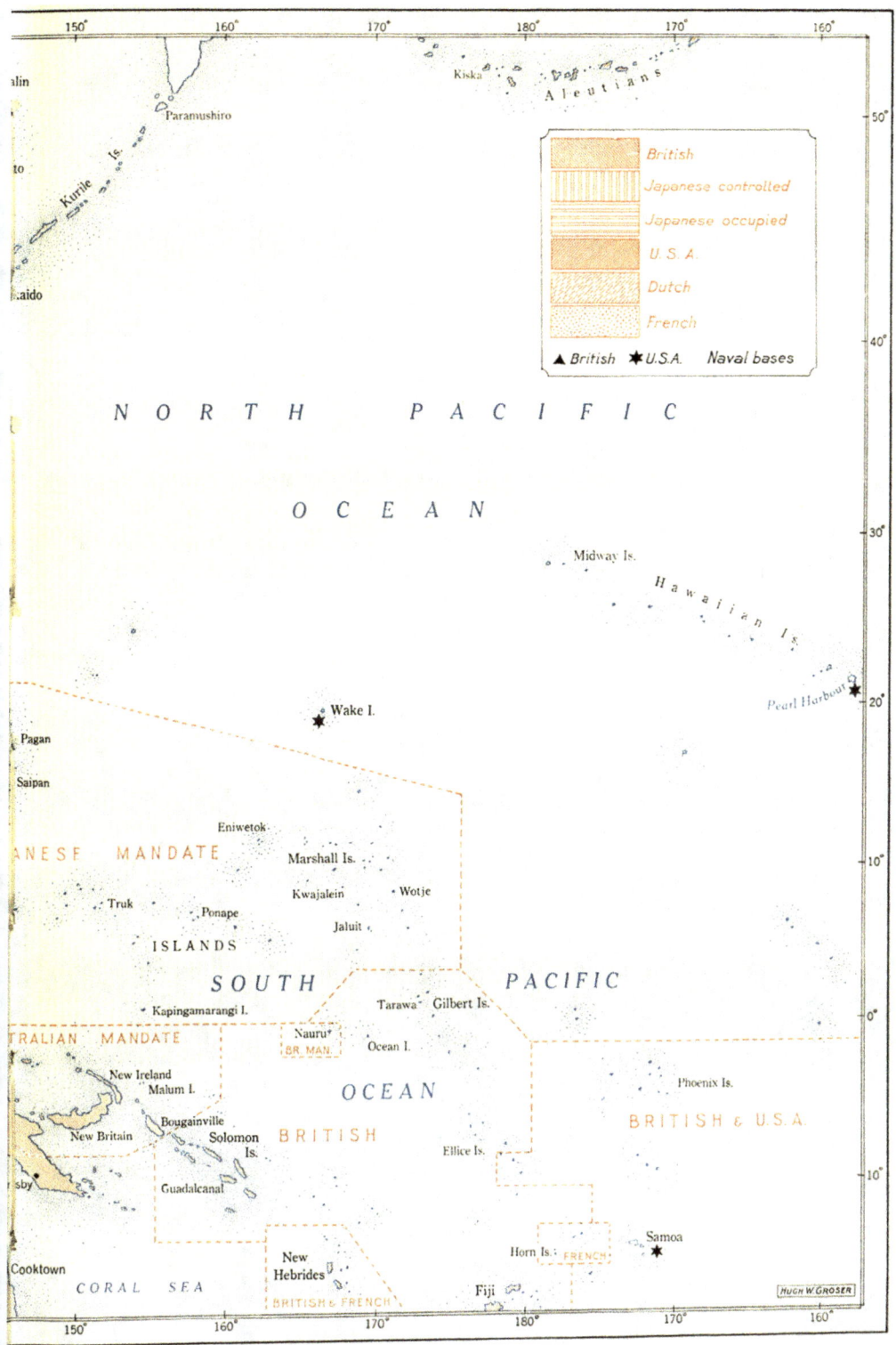

September 1938.

The officers and N.C.O's of 22nd Brigade first went into training on the 15th July, at Wallgrove camp, among undulating country some 25 miles from Sydney, and just south of the main road to the Blue Mountains. Drafts of recruits began to stream in from such centres as Tamworth, Newcastle, Wagga, Goulburn, and Liverpool and from "day-boy" centres in the metropolitan area where they had been receiving part-time training.

At Wallgrove and at Ingleburn, to which the brigade moved on the 20th August, the men rubbed shoulders, sizing each other up, settling into army routine. Those who needed the lesson soon learned to live simply and resourcefully. The "bull-ring" method familiar to the former A.I.F. was used for training; tactical exercises developed skill and initiative; band instruments were acquired; amenities were established; groups of individuals were welded into units. These in turn merged into the whole as the scope of training extended, and the life of the brigade got into full swing.

The training of the other brigades was of course similar in most respects; the 23rd at "Rokeby", near Seymour in Victoria and then Bonegilla, south of Albury on the Murray River; and the 24th (destined not to remain part of the 8th Division) at Grovelly, and later Enoggera in Queensland. The 23rd Brigade came into being on 1st July when its headquarters were temporarily established at Victoria Barracks, Melbourne; on 15th July Brigadier Lind,[9] who had been appointed its commander, arrived at "Rokeby" with Major Sheehan[1] as his brigade major. Brigade drafts came in the same day. Lind, like Maxwell, was a doctor. His first war service had been in the medical corps, ending with command of a field ambulance. In his student days at Melbourne University, however, he had been a subaltern in the citizen forces, and in 1919 he was appointed to command the Melbourne University Rifles. Since 1934 this enthusiastic doctor-soldier had led the 4th Infantry Brigade.

Lieut-Colonel Roach,[2] commander of Lind's 2/21st Battalion, was a Melbourne businessman and a devoted militia officer with varied military experience. After service on Gallipoli and in France, where he became a captain in the 5th Battalion in 1917, he joined the Indian Army, as did a good many other Australians. He saw active service in Persia and Afghanistan, retired in 1920 on medical grounds, and returned to Melbourne. There, since November 1939, he had commanded a militia battalion. Carr,[3] of the 2/22nd, had received his commission in the militia

---

[9] Brig E. F. Lind, CBE, DSO, VD, VX26781. (1st AIF: DADMS II Anzac Corps 1917-18; Comd 2 Fd Amb 1918-19.) Comd Aust Mil Contingent to Coronation 1937; Comd 23 Bde 1940-42. Medical practitioner; of Brighton, Vic; b. South Yarra, Vic, 23 Dec 1888. Died 2 May 1944.

[1] Maj-Gen E. L. Sheehan, CBE, TX2051. BM 23 Bde 1940-41; GSO1 11 Div 1942-43; BGS First Army 1943-46. Regular soldier; of Hobart; b. Melbourne, 23 Dec 1898.

[2] Lt-Col L. N. Roach, MC, ED, VX41587. (1st AIF: Capt 5 Bn; Indian Army.) CO 2/21 Bn 1940-42. Secretary; of Kew, Vic; b. Neutral Bay, NSW, 3 May 1894.

[3] Lt-Col H. H. Carr, ED, VX41567. CO 2/22 Bn 1940-42; AA&QMG No. 1 L of C Sub-Area 1943-45. Public servant; of Malvern, Vic; b. Ballarat, Vic, 4 Aug 1899.

in 1921, and gained command of a battalion in 1938. Lieut-Colonel Youl[4] (2/40th), a grazier, had become a major in the Royal Field Artillery[5] in the 1914-1918 war; he then joined the militia, and gained command of one of the two Tasmanian battalions.

On 13th August a heavy blow had fallen on Australia's leadership; the Chief of the General Staff (Sir Brudenell White), the Minister for the Army (Mr Street) and two other Ministers (Sir Henry Gullett and Mr Fairbairn) were all killed when the aircraft in which they were flying crashed near Canberra. In the consequent reorganisation, General Sturdee succeeded White. Sturdee had high qualifications for his new post. He had served as a captain and major of engineers on Gallipoli in 1915 and in France in 1916, commanded a pioneer battalion in 1917, and in 1918 served as a lieut-colonel on Haig's staff. Between the wars he had served for a total of nearly six years in England or India, and had been the third Australian soldier to attend the Imperial Defence College. He had been a director at Army Headquarters, first of Military Operations and then Staff Duties, during the seven years before the outbreak of war. His eventual appointment as Chief of the General Staff had long seemed inevitable, but the events of 1940 brought it rather sooner than might have been expected.

A challenging figure stepped into the history of the 8th Division on 24th September, when Major-General Gordon Bennett[6] was appointed its commander, in General Sturdee's stead. Bennett had been born at Balwyn, a suburb of Melbourne, in 1887, and at the beginning of his business career was a member of the staff of a leading Australian insurance company. At the age of 21 he was commissioned in the Australian Infantry Regiment, gained a captaincy in less than three years, and at 25, soon after the introduction of compulsory instead of voluntary military training in Australia, became a major with the 64th (City of Melbourne) Infantry. His overseas service commenced in 1914, as second-in-command of the 6th Battalion of the 2nd Brigade, A.I.F.

Bennett established a reputation for personal courage and forceful leadership under fire from the first day at Gallipoli. For example, in the famous though ill-fated advance to Pine Ridge, when his men realised that plans had miscarried, he characteristically rejected the suggestion that they should retire, and led an advance to a position where a party of enemy troops came into sight, in front of Turkish guns. Bennett stood to direct his men's fire, opened a map, and was shot in the wrist and shoulder. Although, when he went to the rear to have his wounds dressed, he was sent to a hospital ship, he was absent without leave from the ship next day, and back in the front-line. Ten days later Bennett led the

---

[4] Lt-Col G. A. D. Youl, MC, TX2111. (1914-18: Maj in RFA.) CO 2/40 Bn 1940-41. Grazier; of Leighlands Park, Tas; b. Perth, Tas, 6 Feb 1892.

[5] Not a few Australians obtained commissions in the British Army in 1914-18.

[6] Lt-Gen H. Gordon Bennett, CB, CMG, DSO, VD, NX70343. (1st AIF: CO 6 Bn; Comd 3 Bde 1916-19.) GOC 8 Div 1940-42, III Corps 1942-44. Public Accountant and company director; of Sydney; b. Balwyn, Vic, 16 Apr 1887.

6th Battalion in a final attempt by Anglo-French forces to capture the peak of Achi Baba.

> We advanced over open country in artillery formation, almost as though we were on a parade ground, and eventually deployed and advanced to what was known as the "Tommies Trench" (wrote a member of the 6th). . . . I remember that Major Bennett was continually exposed to Turkish machine-gun fire on the dangerous side of a creek whilst he directed and encouraged the advance of the battalion. Later, when we made our rush forward from the Tommies Trench, again with an utter disregard of danger, and with practically every officer in the battalion a casualty, he directed a further advance in the face of extremely heavy fire.[7]

When the brigade was relieved from the line, Bennett alone remained of the original officers with the battalion, and succeeded to its command. In 1916, at the age of 29, he was appointed to command the 3rd Brigade; and thus became probably the youngest brigadier-general in any British army at that time. Blamey,[8] to become commander of the A.I.F. in 1939, was then chief staff officer of a division; Lavarack,[9] to command the 7th Division, was an artillery major; Sturdee, to become Chief of the General Staff, was a major of engineers; Mackay,[1] to command the 6th Division, was a battalion commander.

Bennett's reputation continued to rise during his service with the A.I.F. in France, and on several occasions before the war ended he temporarily commanded the 1st Division. After the war he became chairman of the New South Wales Repatriation Board, and commanded the 9th Infantry Brigade from 1921 to 1926. Then, aged 39, he stepped up to command of a division (the 2nd), highest appointment available in peacetime to a citizen soldier, and held it for five years before being put on the unattached list. He became President of the New South Wales Chamber of Manufactures in 1931, and in 1933 President of the Federal body, the Associated Chambers of Manufactures.

Suddenly, in 1937, while fears of another world war were being fanned by aggression by Italy in Abyssinia and Japan in China, Bennett stepped before the public as the author of a boldly-displayed article in the *Sunday Sun* of Sydney. Declaring that the militia was "inefficient and insufficient", he asserted that nothing effective was being done to train senior citizen officers for high command. He alleged that attempts had been made to give command of all divisions to permanent officers to the exclusion of senior citizen officers, whom he considered more efficient. In succeeding articles he urged that all probable leaders be encouraged to fit themselves

---

[7] Quoted in "Celebrities of the A.I.F." by A. W. Bazley, *Reveille*, 1 Aug 1939.
[8] Field Marshal Sir Thomas Blamey, GBE, KCB, CMG, DSO, ED; VX1. (1st AIF: GSO1 1 Aust Div 1916-17; BGGS Aust Corps 1918.) GOC 6 Aust Div 1939-40, I Corps 1940-41; Deputy C-in-C ME 1941; GOC-in-C AMF 1942-46. Of Melbourne; b. Wagga Wagga, NSW, 24 Jan 1884. Died 27 May 1951.
[9] Lt-Gen Sir John Lavarack, KCMG, KCVO, KBE, CB, DSO; VX20310. (1st AIF: GSO1 4 Div 1917-19.) CGS Aust 1935-39; GOC Southern Comd 1939-40, 7 Aust Div 1940-41, I Aust Corps 1941-42, First Aust Army 1942-44. Governor of Queensland since 1946. Regular soldier; of Melbourne; b. Brisbane, 19 Dec 1885.
[1] Lt-Gen Sir Iven Mackay, KBE, CMG, DSO, VD; NX363. (1st AIF: CO 4 Bn 1916-17, 1 MG Bn 1918; Comd 1 Inf Bde 1918-19.) GOC 6 Div 1940-41, Home Forces 1941-42, NGF 1943-44. High Commissioner for Australia in India 1944-48. Schoolmaster; of Sydney; b. Grafton, NSW, 7 Apr 1882.

for command; that the training of the rank and file be more comprehensive; and that Australian industry be organised to produce war requirements at short notice.

In place of a further article by Bennett which the *Sunday Sun* had promised, there appeared a statement that the Military Board had instructed Bennett to discontinue the series; and that newspaper made a heated attack on the Board.[2] The controversy led to a lively discussion of Australia's lack of preparedness by the Federal Cabinet; no action was taken against Bennett for his criticism.

After war broke out, however, Bennett was not given an appointment until July 1940, when he was placed in charge of the Training Depot of Eastern Command and was officer commanding the Volunteer Defence Corps; but he eagerly sought a more active appointment. In 1939 only two officers of the Australian Army were senior to him—Sir Brudenell White, and Sir William Glasgow,[3] appointed High Commissioner to Canada at the end of 1939; yet Bennett, at 52, was not too old for any of the higher commands and had clearly demonstrated his capacity for leadership. He had been passed over for command of the Australian Corps and the 6th and 7th Divisions and, in the first instance, of the 8th. Behind this lay many factors, largely personal. Bennett's aggressive temperament had shown itself in criticism of his superiors and others at intervals throughout his military career. Relations between professional and militia officers depended of course upon their capacity to appreciate each other's virtues and the virtues of the two systems of training; but the references to the Staff Corps in his newspaper articles had caused resentment among professional officers. Bennett thus had become a controversial figure, and when leaders were sought who would command general support, strongpoints of resistance to his being chosen were encountered. Pressing Brudenell White, while he was Chief of the General Staff, Bennett was told that he had "certain qualities and certain disqualities" for an active command.[4] To a man of Bennett's ambitious temperament, being shelved was a particularly galling experience which made him all the more determined to vindicate himself and his opinions. This chance arose when Sturdee became Chief of the General Staff; for he regarded Bennett as suitable, on the basis of experience, to take his place in command of the 8th Division, and it seemed to him that Bennett's antipathy to professional officers had died down. The War Cabinet agreed to Sturdee's recommendation.

Bennett succeeded to the command of a formation the staff and brigadiers of which had already been chosen by his predecessor, a regular. Such a succession is not infrequent in war and peace, but, in the circumstances mentioned above, it was perhaps unfortunate that Bennett missed

---

[2] *Sunday Sun*, Sydney, 28 Nov, 5 and 12 Dec 1937.

[3] Maj-Gen Hon Sir William Glasgow, KCB, CMG, DSO, VD. (1st AIF: CO 2 LH Regt 1915-16; Comd 13 Bde 1916-18; GOC 1 Div 1918-19.) Min for Home and Territories 1926-27, for Defence 1927-29; Aust High Commissioner in Canada 1939-46. Grazier; of Gympie, Qld; b. Tiaro, Qld, 6 Jun 1876. Died 4 Jul 1955.

[4] From notes of an interview with General Bennett.

the opportunity of making the senior appointments in the division, and instead, took over a division in which they had already been made.

Events overseas resulted in some re-shaping of the 8th Division during the early stages of its existence. In September, General Blamey had urged that the 9th Division, which had been formed from troops diverted to England in June, be completed not from corps troops and reinforcements as had been planned, but from the brigades already formed in Australia. This request was agreed to, and in December the 24th Brigade was transferred to Egypt. A twelfth brigade was now needed to complete the infantry of the four divisions—6th, 7th, 8th and 9th—and in November the 27th Brigade was formed from recruits then training in Australia. This was the beginning of a transfer of brigades and even individual units from one division to another during the next few months, in response to emergencies which were to affect every division of the A.I.F. In this period the parts of the 8th Division were scattered throughout Australia. A difficult task was thus imposed on divisional headquarters at Rosebery Racecourse in New South Wales (which, in addition, had the task of administering all non-divisional A.I.F. units in that State).

Brigadier Norman Marshall,[5] chosen to command the new brigade, was a 54-years-old country man, son of a Presbyterian minister, who had risen from the ranks of the old A.I.F. to become one of the outstanding battalion commanders in France in 1917-18. At a critical moment at Villers Bretonneux in April 1918 "it was he (wrote C. E. W. Bean) who took hold and for the rest of the night controlled more than any other man the 15th Brigade's part in the operation". In 1940 he was commanding the 1st Cavalry Brigade of the militia; in July he stepped back a rank (an action typical of the man) to take command of an infantry battalion in the Second A.I.F., when other leaders of about equal seniority in the old A.I.F., such as Mackay and Allen,[6] were commanding divisions or brigades.

One regular and two citizen soldiers, all in their middle-forties, were chosen as his battalion commanders. Lieut-Colonel Boyes,[7] to command the 2/26th (Queensland) Battalion, had been commissioned in the regular forces in 1918 and until 1938 had occupied positions as adjutant and quartermaster of militia battalions. At the outbreak of war in 1939 he was brigade major of a militia brigade, and in April 1940 was chosen as a brigade major in the 7th Division. He was junior both to Lieut-Colonel Robertson[8] (2/29th Victorian Battalion) and Lieut-Colonel Galleghan[1]

---

[5] Brig N. Marshall, DSO, MC, QX16290. (1st AIF: CO 60, 54, 56 Bns.) CO 2/25 Bn 1940; Comd 27 Bde 1940-41. Grazier; of Stanthorpe, Qld; b. Callander, Scotland, 10 Feb 1886. Died 12 Sep 1942.

[6] Maj-Gen A. S. Allen, CB, CBE, DSO, VD, NX2. (1st AIF: 13 Bn and CO 45 Bn.) Comd 16 Bde 1939-41; GOC 7 Div 1941-42, 6 Div 1942-43, NT Force 1943-44. Chartered accountant; of Sydney; b. Hurstville, NSW, 10 Mar 1894.

[7] Lt-Col A. H. Boyes, VX13609; CO 2/26 Bn. Regular soldier; of Toorak, Vic; b. Melbourne, 23 Mar 1896. Killed in action 11 Feb 1942.

[8] Lt-Col J. C. Robertson, MC, VD, VX38973. (1st AIF: Lt 23 Bn.) CO 2/29 Bn. Fuel merchant and garage proprietor; of Geelong, Vic; b. Geelong, 28 Oct 1894. Died of wounds 18 Jan 1942.

[1] Brig F. G. Galleghan, DSO, OBE, ED, NX70416. (1st AIF: Sgt 34 Bn.) CO 2/30 Bn. Public servant; of Newcastle, NSW, and Sydney; b. Jesmond, NSW, 11 Jan 1897.

(2/30th N.S.W. Battalion), each of whom had the added qualification of having served in France with the old A.I.F. Robertson, pleasant and likeable and a capable man-manager, was a fuel merchant and garage proprietor of Geelong, Victoria, who had given long years of service between the wars to the militia, in which he was commanding a battalion in 1939. Galleghan, senior of the three (in fact senior to all the battalion commanders in the 8th Division, for he had commanded three militia battalions in succession since 1932) had been twice severely wounded as a young ranker in the old A.I.F., and had been commissioned on his return to Australia. As a public servant he had spent most of his life in the Newcastle area until 1936, when he transferred to the Commonwealth Investigation Service in Sydney. Tall, dark-visaged, possessed of drive and determination, he tended to ride roughshod over the opinions of others, and had won a reputation as a disciplinarian which preceded him to his new battalion.

Major Pond,[2] who became Marshall's brigade major, was also a citizen soldier—somewhat a departure from the principle established with earlier formations of having a regular in such appointments; on the other hand, since the end of 1939, he had occupied staff appointments in a militia division. Commanding officers were given freedom to select other officers for their units, subject only to age limitations laid down by General Bennett, who required that lieutenants should be 26 or younger (whereas in earlier formations 30 had been the upper age limit) and that captains should be correspondingly youthful. Inevitably there were exceptions to the general rules.

Brigadier Marshall, who established his headquarters at the Royal Agricultural Showground in Sydney in November, had the difficult task of controlling battalions raised and training in widely separated areas. The 2/26th Battalion went into camp at Grovelly in Queensland; the 2/29th at Bonegilla in Victoria; the 2/30th at Tamworth, N.S.W. It was not until February that it was possible to concentrate the brigade. Nevertheless the fact that most of the men had been drawn from infantry recruit training battalions was a partial compensation, and in those first few months, despite the handicap of limited equipment, a sound basis for more ambitious training was laid. This was tackled vigorously, and the battalions were soon welded into a fighting formation well prepared and eager for action.

Many men of the 8th Division, who in civil life had been avid newspaper readers, and listeners to radio news, gave comparatively little attention to what was happening overseas as they became absorbed in the reveille to "lights out" round of camp life, then began to look forward eagerly to home leave; but meanwhile events were shaping which would draw the 8th Division into their course. On 27th September 1940 a ten-

---
[2] Col S. A. F. Pond, OBE, ED, VX44770. BM 27 Bde 1940-42; CO 2/29 Bn 1942. Solicitor; of Caulfield, Vic; b. Surrey Hills, Vic, 8 Dec 1904.

year pact between Germany, Italy and Japan was signed in Berlin. The signatories undertook to "assist one another with all political, economic and military means if one of the high contracting parties should be attacked by a Power not at present involved in the European war, or in the Sino-Japanese conflict". The pact was the outcome of persistent German efforts to commit Japan fully to the Axis, but it was more significant of Japan's fear of missing opportunities for expansion which now seemed to lie open to her than of any affection she felt for Germany. The wording of the pact indicated clearly that extensive concession had been made by Germany to the Japanese viewpoint, especially in the passage which read:

The Governments of Germany, Italy, and Japan consider it as a condition precedent of a lasting peace that each nation of the world be given its own proper place. They have, therefore, decided to stand together and to cooperate with one another in their efforts in Greater East Asia, and in the regions of Europe, wherein it is their prime purpose to establish and maintain a new order of things, calculated to promote the prosperity and welfare of the peoples there.[3]

The flowery wording of this passage, and the reference to each nation of the world being given "its proper place" were further typical of Japan's official outlook at the time; and Japan's prospective share in the spoils was clearly stated in the article of the pact which declared that "Germany and Italy recognise and respect the leadership of Japan, in the establishment of a New Order in Greater East Asia".

Nevertheless, a lack of enthusiasm tinged with uneasiness haunted the conclusion of the pact. The British Ambassador to Japan recorded what he considered a well-substantiated story current at the time that while champagne corks popped at a party given by the Japanese Prime Minister to celebrate the occasion, Prince Konoye "was seen to melt into tears and the party, from all accounts, was a distinct frost". Ciano, Italy's Foreign Minister, despite his laudatory statement at the signing of the pact, wrote gloomily of the proceedings: "The ceremony was more or less like that of the Pact of Steel.[4] But the atmosphere is cooler. Even the Berlin street crowd, a comparatively small one, comprised mostly of school children, cheers with regularity, but without conviction. Japan is far away. Its help is doubtful. One thing alone is certain: That the war will be long."[5]

Plainly, however, Germany hoped that the pact would serve as a deterrent to United States aid to Britain, and would cause a diversion of British forces to East Asia, or at least tether those already there. To Japan it represented a counter to United States and British restraint upon Japanese expansionist moves. Matsuoka stated bluntly that Japan had concluded the pact because she recognised the principle of *hakko ichiu* (a Japanese term meaning the eight corners of the universe under one roof, or the whole world one family). "We three nations would be very

---

[3] British official transcript, *The Trial of German Major War Criminals*, Part 2, p. 261.
[4] Treaty of alliance between Germany and Italy, signed 22 May 1939.
[5] *Ciano's Diary, 1939-1943* (1947), p. 293.

glad to welcome any other Powers, whether it were the United States or another, if they should desire to join us in the spirit of *hakko ichiu*," he said. "However, we are firmly determined to eliminate any nation that may obstruct *hakko ichiu*."

Mr Bullitt, the United States Ambassador to France, was equally blunt in addressing the Council on Foreign Relations in Chicago. "The pact," he said, was "a contingent declaration of enmity", adding that "if ever a clear warning was given to a nation that the three aggressors contemplated a future assault upon it, that warning was given to the American people".

The Japanese Army and Navy quickly took advantage of a provision in the pact for the establishment in the three Axis capitals of mixed technical commissions. Japanese missions were promptly sent off to Berlin and Rome to pick up all the information they could that might help the Japanese forces. The head of the military mission to Berlin, Lieut-General Tomoyuki Yamashita, was to have plenty of opportunity to put it to practical use.

Far from acting as a deterrent to America, however, the pact was followed by a great acceleration of her aid to Britain, and of her own defence program. Already on 26th September a virtual ban had been placed upon export of any grade of iron or steel scrap to Japan. British and American policies in the Pacific and East Asia now drew closer together. Britain re-opened the Burma Road as from the 18th October, after her Ambassador in Washington had been assured by the American Secretary of State that "the special desire of this Government is to see Great Britain succeed in the war. Our acts and utterances with respect to the Pacific area will be more or less affected as to time and extent by the question of what course will most effectively and legitimately aid Great Britain in winning the war."[6] No doubt influenced by the growing cordiality of relations with the United States, Mr Churchill had informed President Roosevelt in advance of the intended re-opening of the Burma Road, adding:

> I know how difficult it is for you to say anything which would commit the United States to any hypothetical course of action in the Pacific. But I venture to ask whether at this time a simple action might not speak louder than words. Would it not be possible for you to send an American squadron, the bigger the better, to pay a friendly visit to Singapore? There they would be welcomed in a perfectly normal and rightful way. If desired, occasion might be taken of such a visit for a technical discussion of naval and military problems in those and Philippine waters, and the Dutch might be invited to join. Anything in this direction would have a marked deterrent effect upon a Japanese declaration of war upon us over the Burma Road opening.[7]

This proposal was discussed by the United States Standing Liaison Committee—a coordinating body for the military, naval, and diplomatic services which had been created in 1938. The committee agreed, how-

---

[6] *The Memoirs of Cordell Hull*, Vol I, p. 911.
[7] Quoted in Churchill, *The Second World War*, Vol II, p. 440.

ever, that sending a squadron to Singapore might precipitate action by Japan against the United States. Admiral Stark, the American Chief of Naval Operations, declared that "every day that we are able to maintain peace and still support the British is valuable time gained"; and General Marshall, the Chief of Staff of the Army, that the time was "as unfavourable a moment as you could choose" for provoking trouble.[8] Thus military considerations were added to political ones favouring a cautious policy by the United States in the Pacific; and Britain like the Netherlands East Indies (which, since February, had been stonewalling Japanese demands for trade concessions) had to continue to temporise. Nevertheless, several conversations took place about this time between the American Secretary of State, Mr Hull, the British Ambassador, Lord Lothian, and the Australian Minister in Washington, Mr Casey, about means whereby the United States, Britain, Australia, New Zealand and the Netherlands East Indies might exchange information as to the forces available to meet a Japanese attack. Lothian told Hull that Singapore was available to the United States Fleet at any time.

The entrance of the Japanese into Indo-China and the signing of the Tripartite Pact greatly discouraged the Chinese. On 18th October 1940 Chiang Kai-shek told the American Ambassador, Mr Nelson T. Johnson,[9] that he was anxious lest the Japanese seize. Singapore or cut the Burma Road.

> Before either of these disasters, China must have economic aid plus numbers of U.S. aircraft manned by American volunteers. Unless this aid came soon, China might collapse. If it came in time, the internal situation would be restored and the Japanese forestalled. The aircraft would also permit the Generalissimo to effect a "fundamental solution" of the Pacific problem by destroying the Japanese Navy in its bases. Proposed a month before British carrier aircraft attacked the Italian Navy at Taranto, the Generalissimo's plan might indeed have been the fundamental solution, but in the irony of history it was the Japanese who attempted the method at Pearl Harbour.[1]

The possibility of a joint defence agreement between the United States, Australia and New Zealand, had been mentioned by Casey in a cable to Canberra dated 3rd September. He said that the establishment of a permanent Joint Board of Defence (United States and Canada) and lease of sites for American bases in the British West Indies had inspired press references in America and elsewhere to the possibility of extension of arrangements on either or both of these lines to the Pacific and Australia. While he did not believe that for domestic political reasons the United States would consider any such extension before the presidential election in November, he thought it was not impossible after the elections. Casey asked for the views of the Australian Government defence advisers as

---

[8] Quoted in M. S. Watson, *Chief of Staff: Prewar Plans and Preparations* (1950), p. 117, a volume in the official series, *United States Army in World War II*.

[9] Nelson T. Johnson. American Ambassador to China 1935-41; American Minister to Australia 1941-46. B. Washington, DC, 3 Apr 1887.

[1] C. F. Romanus and R. Sutherland, *Stilwell's Mission to China* (1953), p. 9, a volume in the official series, *United States Army in World War II*.

to the most telling arguments that he could have up his sleeve for use as opportunity arose, respecting the value to the United States of joint use of existing bases or rights to lease and build their own bases in the south-west Pacific. On 24th September the War Cabinet sent him notes by the Australian Defence Committee[2] for the purpose.

On the same day, the Australian War Cabinet approved a proposal, suggested in August by the United Kingdom Chiefs of Staff, that a conference be held to consider the problems of defence of the East Asian area. Australia had proposed that it be held in Melbourne, but Singapore, where principally the British forces for the defence of the region were concentrated, was eventually chosen.

While preparations were being made for this conference, the War Cabinet was called upon to decide also the policy to be pursued by an Australian delegation to a conference to be held in New Delhi, convened by the Government of India with the consent of the United Kingdom to determine a joint war supply plan for the eastern group of Empire countries. The purpose of this Eastern supply conference was to ensure that maximum use would be made of the existing and potential capacity of each of the participating countries to supply the materials required in war. It was contemplated that the needs of each country, including essential needs of commerce and industry for maintenance of defence services and the civil population, should be met as far as possible within the group, and that any surplus production should be made available to Great Britain.

Before the departure of Sir Walter Massy-Greene, leader of the Australian delegation to this Eastern Group Conference, the Prime Minister instructed him, also in accordance with recommendations of the Defence Committee, that any policy of dependence on supplies from India was not acceptable to the Australian Government. This was particularly because of the risks associated with control of sea communications between the Eastern Group countries, political factors such as India's attitude to attainment of self-government, and the internal and external security of India. Mr Menzies emphasised that Australia was not prepared to import things she could produce, and there was no intention of entering into commitments which might cramp development and expansion of her secondary industries.[3]

Before the Singapore conference assembled the three commanders in Malaya—Admiral Layton,[4] General Bond and Air Vice-Marshal Babington[5]—prepared a joint appreciation which was sent to the Chiefs of Staff in London on 16th October. In it they affirmed that, in the circumstances,

---

[2] The Defence Committee consisted of the Chiefs of Staff of the three Services and the Secretary of the Defence Department.

[3] An Eastern Group Supply Council, on which the United Kingdom, India, Australia, South Africa, and New Zealand were represented, was established in India to implement the decisions of the conference. Sir Bertram Stevens became the Australian representative.

[4] Admiral Sir Geoffrey Layton, GBE, KCB, KCMG, DSO; RN. Vice-Adm Comdg 1st Battle Sqn and second-in-command Home Fleet 1939-40; C-in-C China 1940-41, Eastern Fleet 1941-42, Ceylon 1942-45. B. 20 Apr 1884.

[5] Air Marshal Sir John Babington, KCB, CBE, DSO. AOC RAF Far East 1938-41; AOC-in-C Tech Training Comd 1941-43. B. 20 Jul 1891. (Changed name to Tremayne in 1945.)

the air force was the principal weapon for the defence of Malaya. Its tasks should be to repulse any invading force while it was still at sea, shatter any attempted landings, and attack any troops who managed to get ashore. They urged that the British forces be authorised to advance into southern Thailand if the Japanese entered that country. They recommended that the air force be increased until its front-line strength was 566 aircraft, and the army until it contained 26 battalions and 14 field and 4 anti-tank batteries—the equivalent of about three divisions with artillery on a reduced scale.

The Singapore conference, held from 22nd to 31st October, was attended by staff officers from India, Australia, New Zealand and Burma, with an American naval officer as an observer.[6] Before the conference got under way the Australian and New Zealand delegates contended that its scope should not be limited to south-east Asia but that it should consider the whole problem of Pacific defence. This proposal was referred to and approved by the British and Australian Governments. The conference concerned itself also with points for later staff talks with representatives of the Netherlands East Indies and United States in the event of these being authorised. The assumptions on which the conference worked were that, on the outbreak of war with Japan, the disposition of the Allies' sea, land and air forces would be as at the time of the deliberations; that the United States would be neutral, but her intervention would be possible; that the Dutch might remain neutral, but their intervention was probable; that Australian and New Zealand naval forces would return to home waters, and a battle cruiser and an aircraft carrier would be sent to the Indian Ocean.

The delegates reviewed courses of action which appeared to be open to the Japanese if they entered the war on the side of the Axis powers; and concluded that, in such event, attack on the trade and communications of the Allies in the Pacific and Indian Oceans would be certain. They noted that the Chiefs of Staff in London considered an attack on Hong Kong probable, but that if American intervention were a strong possibility, attempts to invade Australia or New Zealand could be ruled out altogether. Other possibilities considered were: an attempt to seize islands in the Pacific Ocean to pave the way for invasion of Australia or New Zealand, and secure bases for attack on shipping in Australian and New Zealand waters; an attack on Malaya aimed at seizing Singapore; an attempt to seize bases in British Borneo preparatory to attack on Malaya; an attack on Burma by land and air from Indo-China and Thailand; an attack on the Netherlands East Indies or Timor to secure supplies and bases for further operations; an attack on Darwin; raids by warships and seaborne aircraft on points in Australia, New Zealand and elsewhere.

---

[6] The Australian delegates were Captain J. Burnett (Deputy Chief of the Aust Naval Staff), Major-General J. Northcott (Deputy Chief of the General Staff) and Air Commodore W. D. Bostock (Deputy Chief of the Air Staff). Staff officers who accompanied them were Lieut-Commander G. C. Oldham, Major C. H. Kappe, then on the staff of the 8 Div, and Squadron Leader W. L. Hely.

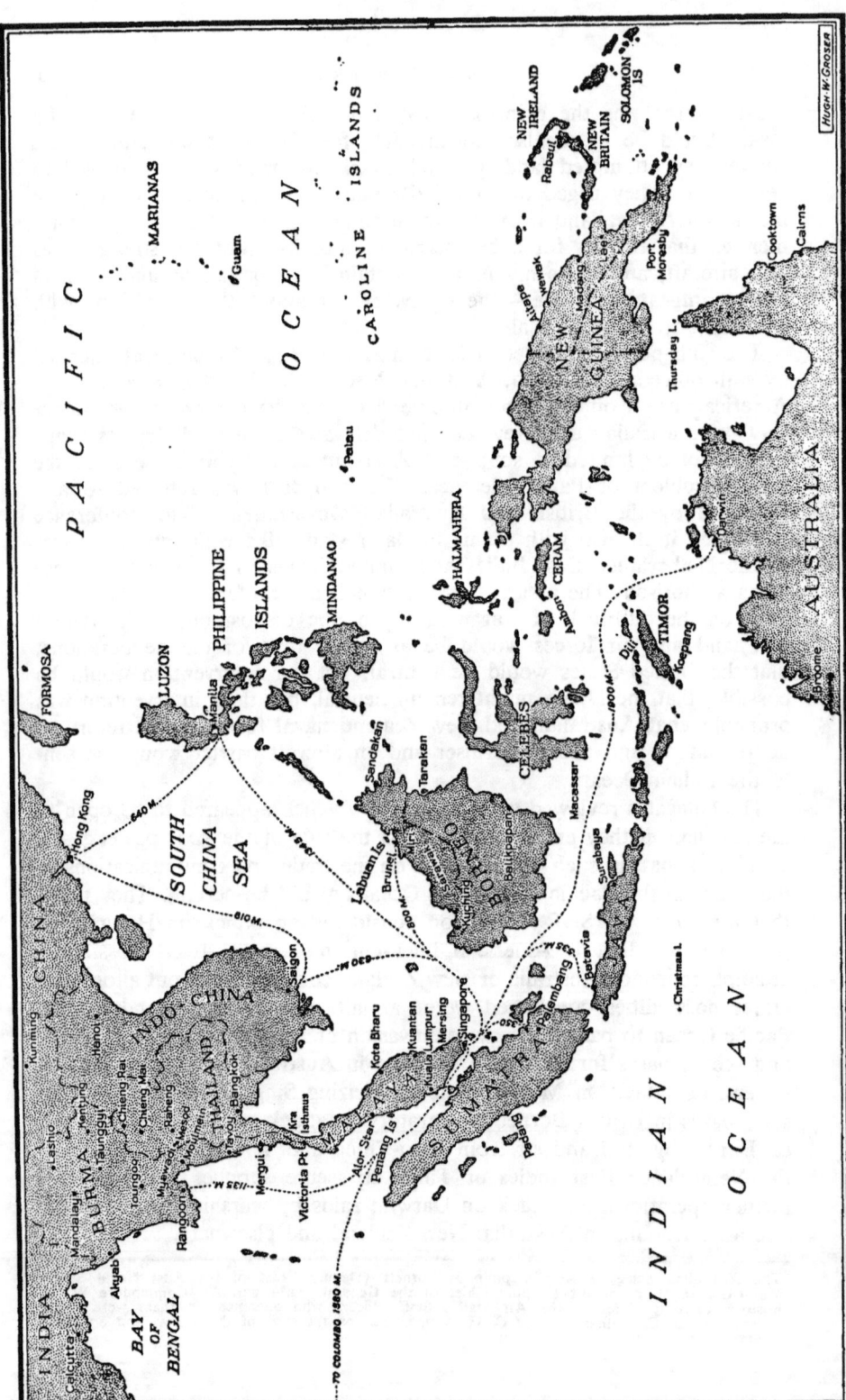

Area of deliberations, Singapore conference, October 1940

The conference decided that it was vital to defeat any attack on Malaya. A successful attack on the Netherlands East Indies or Timor (Portuguese and Dutch) would make it relatively easy to carry out naval and air attacks on Malaya, including Singapore, and on Darwin and the trade routes. An attempt to seize Darwin for use as a base was considered possible, although in view of the difficulties of maintaining a force there it was thought unlikely. Warning was given, however, that raids to destroy the facilities of the port must be guarded against.

The conference decided also that until sufficient naval forces were available for offensive action against the Japanese, it would be necessary to remain on the defensive, and to concentrate on the protection of vital points and vital trade and convoys. The first and immediate consideration must be to ensure the security of Malaya against direct attack. In view of the inadequacy of the naval forces then available, army and air forces in Malaya, including the reinforcements then being provided, were far below requirements in both numbers and equipment. This deficiency must be remedied immediately, and the further cooperation of India, Australia and New Zealand should be sought without delay. It was decided that Burma also was inadequately defended.

The conference considered that all available air forces should be used to prevent or at least deter the Japanese from establishing naval and air bases within striking distance of vital points in Malaya, Burma, the Netherlands East Indies, Australia and New Zealand. Advanced operational bases should be available throughout the area, so that aircraft could be concentrated at any point from its collective air resources. Preparation of the necessary facilities and ground organisation should therefore begin forthwith, irrespective of whether or not adequate aircraft were available.

While the possibility of a major expedition against Australia or New Zealand might be ruled out initially, such army and air forces must be maintained there as were necessary to deal with raids; and such naval and air forces as would ensure maintenance of vital trade, protect troop convoys, and carry out other local defence tasks. The conference noted the weakness inherent in the absence of fully-developed manufacturing industries in those countries, and that provision of adequate air forces in Australia and New Zealand in the near future was entirely dependent upon allotment by Britain of aircraft to meet rearmament and expansion programs.

Naval problems were reviewed, and it was noted that with the exception of capital ships, the minimum naval forces considered necessary to safeguard essential commitments in Australian and New Zealand waters could be provided by the return of Australian and New Zealand naval forces then serving overseas—provided that adequate air forces were maintained in the focal areas. Those available in the areas at the time were considered inadequate. The position in the Indian Ocean was dependent upon the arrival of naval reinforcements from elsewhere; among other things it would be necessary to replace the Australian and New Zealand ships on that station. Early provision of air forces in the Indian Ocean was essential. The strengthening of facilities at Suva, Port Moresby, Thursday Island and Darwin should be expedited, in preparation for possible operations by the United States and British naval forces.

As to the military requirements of Malaya and Burma, the conference pointed to the fact that the British Government had asked India, subject to her own security requirements, to have four divisions ready for service overseas in May, July, October and December 1941 respectively. Although it had been planned to send these to the Middle East, the Indian Government was unlikely to raise any difficulties about their ultimate destination, provided adequate warning was given. From the A.I.F. in Australia it should be possible to provide one strong brigade group and the necessary ancillary troops by the end of December 1940, if the British and Australian Governments agreed.

The most disturbing aspect of the report was its revelation in detail of the defence deficiencies in the danger zone extending from India to New Zealand. Although the Singapore naval base had been intended as a stronghold of sea power for the whole area, it was evident that its ability to serve this purpose to even a limited extent turned solely upon what the British Navy, desperately committed on the other side of the world, might be able eventually to spare. The Australian delegation recorded as its general conclusion that, in the absence of a main fleet in the area, the forces and equipment available for the defence of Malaya were totally inadequate to meet a major attack by Japan.

The conference estimated that Malaya needed an additional twelve battalions of infantry; six field or mountain regiments of artillery; eight anti-tank batteries; six infantry brigade anti-tank companies; three field companies of engineers; and three light tank companies, as well as 120 heavy and 98 light anti-aircraft guns and 138 searchlights. Additional requirements for Burma on a short-term basis included seven infantry battalions. The formations then in these areas were, with few exceptions, deficient in Bren guns and carriers, mortars, anti-tank guns and rifles, all forms of technical equipment, and mechanical transport. They were seriously short of rifles and ammunition, and equipment reserves were on a ninety-day reserve scale for normal garrison purposes only.

The aircraft deficiencies disclosed by the report were startling. The numbers of aircraft already available were stated to be 88 in Malaya and Burma, of which only 48 were classed as modern; 82 in Australia (42 modern).[7] New Zealand had only 24 and the Indian Ocean 4, all classed as obsolete. It was estimated that to equip the squadrons which the conference considered necessary (leaving replacements out of account) 534 modern aircraft were needed in Malaya and Burma; 270 in Australia; 60 in New Zealand; and 87 in the Indian Ocean. On the information

---

[7] The air force in Malaya now included the three Australian squadrons referred to previously. They were: No. 1 (Hudsons), No. 8 (Hudsons) and No. 21 (Wirraways).

before the conference, some 187 were needed in the Netherlands East Indies. A number of operational airfields, and advanced operational bases for land-planes and flying-boats, also were needed in Burma, Malaya, Australia, New Zealand and the Netherlands East Indies. The full extent of planned output of modern military aircraft in Australia in 1941 was 180 Beauforts, of which 90 were for the R.A.A.F. and 90 for Britain.[8] Prospects of being able to remedy deficiencies in arms, ammunition and equipment were shown to be bleak, although certain equipment and ammunition being produced in Australia might be supplied.

These disclosures left no room for complacency. When it considered the report, with the observations of the Australian delegation and the views of the Australian Chiefs of Staff, the Australian War Cabinet expressed grave concern at "the most serious position revealed in regard to the defence of Malaya and Singapore", which was "so vital to the security of Australia". Nevertheless, reluctance to send Australian troops to reinforce Malaya was still evident. The War Cabinet decided to tell the British Government that it considered it preferable to use Indian troops there for the reasons stated when the subject was previously under consideration. If, however, Imperial strategy should call for Australian troops in Malaya, dispatch of a brigade group at an early date, with the necessary maintenance troops and equipment on a modified scale, would be concurred in; but the War Cabinet added the proviso that the troops should be concentrated in the Middle East as soon as circumstances permitted.

The War Cabinet decided that work should begin immediately on the extension of air force stations in Australia and the New Guinea-Solomon Islands-New Hebrides area; and that the British Government be asked to expedite allotment of aircraft to Australia to enable her to meet her share of responsibility for the air defence of the mainland and the islands. The minimum number of aircraft required to provide initial equipment of the squadrons earmarked for this task was stated to be 320; the deficiency (in modern aircraft) 278.

As to the naval problem, the War Cabinet noted the assumption by the Singapore conference that, in a war with Japan, Australian and New Zealand naval forces would return to their home waters, and that a British battle cruiser and aircraft carrier would proceed to the Indian Ocean. It agreed to give whatever naval assistance it could by allotting anti-submarine and minesweeping vessels, mines, and depth-charges, for use beyond Australian waters. The Chiefs of Staff reported that they were already expediting the expansion of naval stations at Darwin and Port Moresby, and strengthening the defences of Thursday Island.

---

[8] The Beaufort was a twin-engined general purpose torpedo-bomber monoplane, used also for reconnaissance.

CHAPTER 4

TO MALAYA

IN the circumstances revealed by the Singapore conference report, and with the danger of war in the Pacific steadily growing, Air Chief Marshal Sir Robert Brooke-Popham[1] arrived in Singapore on 14th November 1940 as Commander-in-Chief in the Far East. He had been appointed, with Australia's concurrence, a few days before the conference began.

The new leader would command the land and air forces throughout the Far East. Such a charter was rare in British experience. The fact that the task was assigned to an air leader no doubt reflected the importance of air power in the command; but the British Cabinet had chosen an officer of great seniority who had served as both soldier and airman, and therefore might be more acceptable to both Services. Brooke-Popham, aged 62, was, however, relatively old for an active command of such extent.[2] Three years before the war he had retired from the post of Inspector-General of the Air Force to become Governor and Commander-in-Chief of Kenya.

From 1898 to 1912 Brooke-Popham had been an infantry officer. Then as a captain he had joined the Air Battalion, Royal Engineers—the beginning of a British military air force, later to become the Royal Flying Corps and later still the Royal Air Force. He gained distinction as an air officer in the war of 1914-18 and when it ended was one of its senior leaders. In the following nineteen years he held a series of high appointments, including command of the R.A.F. Staff College and the Imperial Defence College (school of future senior commanders of all three Services). A tall, spare man, of distinguished appearance, he had stepped from his vice-regal position to rejoin the Royal Air Force in 1939.

On the British Government's current list of priorities, defence of the United Kingdom came first, on the principle that on this all else depended; then the struggle in the Middle East. Provision for resistance to a Japanese assault was next.[3] There was thus little prospect that the deficiencies, especially of aircraft, to which the Singapore conference had drawn attention, would soon be remedied. Nevertheless, Brooke-Popham had been told by Mr Churchill that Britain would hold Singapore no matter what happened, and that there would be a continuous and steady flow of men and munitions to the areas of his command.

Brooke-Popham had been made responsible to the United Kingdom Chiefs of Staff for the higher direction and control, and general direction of training, of all British land and air forces in Malaya (which for the

---

[1] Air Ch Marshal Sir Robert Brooke-Popham, GCVO, KCB, CMG, DSO, AFC; C-in-C Far East 1940-41. B. Wetheringsett, Suffolk, 18 Sep 1878. Died 20 Oct 1953.

[2] For example, General Gort, who had commanded the British Expeditionary Force in France, was aged 54; General Wavell, then C-in-C Middle East, was 57; and General Auchinleck, soon to become C-in-C India, was 56.

[3] In June 1941, when Germany attacked the Soviet Union, the Far East was relegated to fourth place on the list.

(Australian War Memorial)

The *Queen Mary,* carrying some 5,750 Australians, including the 22nd Brigade, arrived at Singapore on 18th February 1941. A group of British officers, including the G.O.C. Malaya, Lieut-General L. V. Bond (carrying cane) and the Governor, Sir Shenton Thomas (on Bond's left), greeted the Australians.

(Australian War Memorial)

A group of Australians after disembarkation.

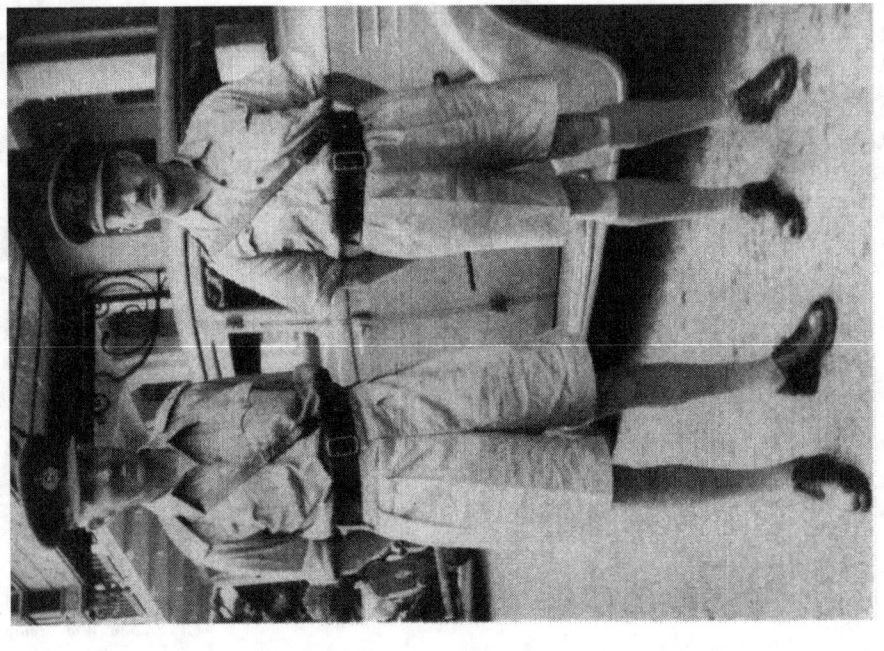

(*Lt-Gen H. Gordon Bennett*)

Lieut-General A. E. Percival, G.O.C. Malaya, and Major-General H. Gordon Bennett, G.O.C. A.I.F. Malaya.

Air Chief Marshal Sir Robert Brooke-Popham, Commander-in Chief Far East, and General Sir Archibald Wavell.

purpose would include Sarawak and North Borneo) and in Burma and Hong Kong. He was responsible also for the coordination of plans for the defence of these territories. He was similarly responsible for the British air forces in Ceylon, and squadrons which it was proposed to station in the Indian Ocean and the Bay of Bengal for ocean reconnaissance. The General Officers Commanding in Malaya, Burma, and Hong Kong, and the Air Officer Commanding in the Far East, were placed under his command. Despite these widespread responsibilities, his staff originally comprised only eight officers.[4] Civil administration, although obviously it must play an essential part in the defence of Malaya, lay outside his jurisdiction; so also did the naval forces, despite the fact that the approaches to his areas of responsibility were largely by sea.

The directive given to Brooke-Popham specified that he should deal chiefly with matters of major military policy and strategy, and should not assume administrative or financial responsibilities, or the normal day-to-day functions exercised by the army and air commanders. This, while perhaps intended to help him concentrate on the broader issues, tended to isolate him from those "normal day-to-day functions" which are underlying realities of planning at even the highest level. Indeed, as he was passing through Cairo on his way to Singapore, General Wavell,[5] the wise and learned Commander-in-Chief of the army in the Middle East, told him that he considered a general headquarters based on such a directive was impracticable.

Brooke-Popham opened his General Headquarters, Far East, at Singapore on 18th November. A primary task was to ensure the security of the costly naval base at Singapore, which occupied a large area of the northernmost part of Singapore Island, facing Johore Strait and the Malay state of Johore, on the mainland of Malaya. The two entrances from the sea to the strait, from the south-west and east of the island respectively, were covered by big coastal guns. Near the western end of the naval base area was a long, heavily-constructed causeway which formed the sole link with the mainland for surface traffic. After delays caused chiefly by political and financial difficulties, the base had been officially opened in February 1938. It was then hailed as, for example, "the Gibraltar of the East . . . the gateway to the Orient . . . the bastion of British might".[6] A correspondent gaily reported that there were "more guns on Singapore Island than plums in a Christmas pudding".[7] But in the fifteen years since the plan for this base had been introduced to the British Parliament, the range of aircraft had been increasing, to an extent which challenged the strategy on which the plan was founded.

---

[4] In August 1941, he was given authority for an establishment of 20 in all.
[5] Field Marshal Rt Hon Earl Wavell, GCB, GCSI, GCIE, CMG, MC. GOC-in-C Middle East 1939-41, India 1941-43; Supreme Comd SW Pacific (ABDA Area) Jan-Mar 1942; Viceroy of India 1943-47. B. 5 May 1883. Died 24 May 1950.
[6] *Sydney Morning Herald*, 14 Feb 1938.
[7] *Sydney Morning Herald*, 10 Mar 1938.

Brooke-Popham's problems were increased by inter-Service jealousies which, in his view, caused lack of cooperation and a tendency by one Service to go ahead with its plans, particularly for airfields, with scant regard for how they might fit in with defence requirements as a whole. Moreover, the working relationship between the civil and military authorities left a great deal to be desired in the event of swift and effective military action being necessary. The system of government of British Malaya was of a type which tended to develop in Asian and African areas where a European Power had established a trading post and thence extended its influence by a variety of encroachments and compromises. In 1941 Malaya comprised (*a*) the Straits Settlements, a Crown Colony including Singapore, Malacca, Penang and some other areas, (*b*) the Federated Malay States, whose sultans still sat on their thrones but which were largely governed by a central administration at Kuala Lumpur, and (*c*) six "unfederated" States ruled by sultans, beside each of whom was a British adviser with an administrative staff which was almost completely British at the higher levels.[8] The most important of these States was Johore, whose capital Johore Bahru lay at the northern end of the causeway connecting Singapore Island with the mainland. The sultan[9] of this State was a shrewd and urbane potentate and in 1941 had been on the throne since 1895, when he was 21. The Governor of the Straits Settlements was also High Commissioner for the federated and unfederated States and thus the coordinating authority for the whole area. This organisation with its complex of "influences" and pressures, political, administrative, commercial and personal, had for long served its purpose; but the closest possible collaboration was necessary to adapt it to the demands of war.

In practice it proved difficult, especially because of Malaya's importance as a source of strategic raw materials and of economic strength, to reconcile the aims of the military authorities, who placed defence requirements first, and of the civil authorities, whose concern continued to be primarily political and economic. Brooke-Popham considered the view of the Colonial Office to be that rubber and tin output was of greater importance than the training of the forces in Malaya; a belief which he based largely upon a telegram from London to the Governor, Sir Shenton Thomas,[1] asserting that "the ultimate criterion for exemption (from military service) should be not what the General Officer Commanding considers practicable, but what you consider essential to maintain the necessary production and efficient labour management".[2]

---

[8] Five of these States were in Malaya, the sixth was Brunei, 800 miles away in Borneo.

[9] H. H. Sir Ibrahim, GCMG, GBE.

[1] Sir Shenton Thomas, GCMG, OBE. Governor and C-in-C of Straits Settlements and High Commissioner for the Malay States 1934-42. B. London, 10 Oct 1879.

[2] The Governor subsequently described Malaya as a "dollar arsenal" and announced that during the eleven months ended July 1941 it had contributed 135,000,000 United States dollars to the Bank of England, compared with 98,000,000 in the first year of the war in Europe. "This," he said, ". . . represents a principal part of Malaya's contribution to the Empire's war offensive."

As failure to hold Malaya would involve not only loss of these resources, but other and far greater consequences, the need for some over-riding authority for defence purposes was strongly urged, but without avail. The circumstances tended therefore to a pull devil, pull baker relationship between the civil and military authorities.

Lack of a sense of urgency, arising from factors such as a long period of immunity from war in the area, the enervating climate, and a feeling of superiority towards Japan despite the shortcomings of Britain's Far Eastern defences also had a marked effect on the conduct of affairs. The wide gulf between the standard of living of the Europeans and that of the mass of the Asian population of Malaya separated them socially as well as economically, and in general prevented sympathetic reciprocal understanding of each other's viewpoints. This situation was accepted fatalistically by the Asians as a whole; but it produced extremes of hardships on one hand, and on the other an artificial existence which tended to restrict the Europeans' outlook and sense of reality. There were nevertheless many Asians and Europeans to whom this did not apply, and among whom mutual understanding was possible.

Malaya lacked a balanced economy, and a large proportion of the Asian population's staple diet of rice had to be imported. Rice was "a constant source of anxiety" in maintaining the six months' supply of food which had been laid down as a minimum military requirement.[3] Vast though Malaya's resources were as applied to the task of feeding distant factories, secondary industries that might have been turned to local production of munitions were almost wholly lacking. On the whole, however, Malaya rated as a prosperous and well-administered territory by standards of comparison at the time. British rule was generally accepted, and its corollary, military protection, was taken for granted.

Within a few weeks of Brooke-Popham's arrival two additional brigades (the 6th and 8th) arrived from India, and two British battalions (the 2/East Surrey and 1/Seaforth Highlanders) arrived from Shanghai. The military garrison then included 17 battalions of which six (one a machine-gun battalion) were British, ten were Indian, and one was Malay. In addition the headquarters of the 11th Indian Division (Major-General Murray-Lyon[4]) had reached Malaya. There was thus infantry enough to form two divisions; but the only mobile artillery was one mountain regiment, whereas two divisions should have possessed six artillery regiments between them, not counting anti-tank units.

The air force included two squadrons of Blenheim I bombers, two squadrons of obsolescent Vildebeeste torpedo-bombers, one squadron of flying-boats (four craft) and the three Australian squadrons (two with Hudsons, the third with Wirraways). Since September 1939, one R.A.F. squadron had departed and the three Australian squadrons had arrived.

---

[3] R. Brooke-Popham, *Despatch on Operations in the Far East, from 17 October 1940 to 27 December 1941*, p. 548.

[4] Maj-Gen D. M. Murray-Lyon, DSO, MC. GOC 11 Indian Div 1940-42. Regular soldier; b. 14 Aug 1890.

Only 48 of the 88 first-line aircraft—the Blenheims and Hudsons—could be counted as modern at the time, and the range of the Blenheims was inadequate.

Brooke-Popham's other territorial responsibilities were strung out along a 2,500-mile line from Colombo to Hong Kong. The doctrine of "Burma for the Burmese", demanding removal of British control, had taken a firm grip in Burma, and there was antipathy by Burmese to Indians, principally because of the hold which Indians had obtained on much of Burma's best agricultural land. Thus the internal situation, as well as the weakness of the forces stationed there (a few battalions mostly of Burman troops and virtually no air force), complicated the problem of Burma's defence. Brooke-Popham formed the opinion that Burma's safety depended largely upon holding Malaya, and that defence of Malaya must have priority, in view particularly of the weakness of the available air forces throughout his command.

Hong Kong, a British colony situated partly on the island of Hong Kong and partly on the mainland of China, with a population of some 1,500,000 people, "was regarded officially as an undesirable military commitment, or else as an outpost to be held as long as possible". Brooke-Popham held that it was very valuable to China as a port of access, and that had the Chinese "not been convinced of our determination to stand and fight for its defence, and been taken into our confidence and given opportunities to inspect the defences and discuss plans for defence, the effect on their war effort would in all probability have been serious. A withdrawal of the troops in Hong Kong coinciding with the closing of the Burma Road might have had a marked effect on Chinese determination to fight on. . . ." He held also that "had we demilitarised Hong Kong, or announced our intention of not defending it, the Americans might have adopted a similar policy with regard to the Philippines. In this case, they might have ceased to take direct interest in the Far East, and confined themselves to the eastern half of the Pacific."[5]

A rapid increase of population caused by a large and continuing influx of Chinese was one of the main local problems affecting the defence of Hong Kong. It placed an abnormal strain on the provisioning and other essential services of the crowded little colony, and made adequate security measures practically impossible. From his broad strategical viewpoint Mr Churchill considered at this time that there was not the slightest chance of holding or relieving the colony in the event of attack by Japan.

Brooke-Popham supported the proposal, already mentioned, that if the Japanese entered Thailand the British should occupy the southern part of the Kra Isthmus. He urged that efforts should be made to encourage the United States to show a firm front to Japan. One sequel to the arrival in London in December of his first appreciation was the appointment of Major-General Dennys[6] as military attaché at Chungking with the task

---

[5] Brooke-Popham, Despatch, p. 541.
[6] Maj-Gen L. E. Dennys, MC. Military attaché Chungking 1941. Regular soldier; b. 10 May 1890.

of organising a British military mission ("204 Mission") should war break out between Britain and Japan.[7]

Meanwhile the Chiefs of Staff in London had examined the report of the October conference at Singapore, and on 8th January replied that although they considered that the conference's estimate that 582 first-line aircraft were required was the ideal, nevertheless experience indicated that their own estimate of 336 would give a fair degree of security; and in any event no more could be provided before the end of 1941. They would try to form five fighter squadrons for the Far East during the year. (There were then no modern fighters there.) They accepted the conference's estimate of 26 battalions (including three for Borneo) and indicated that this total would be reached by June. Mr Churchill, however, was unwilling to agree to any diversion of forces to the Far East and on 13th January the Chiefs of Staff received from him a minute in which he said that

the political situation in the Far East does not seem to require, and the strength of our Air Force by no means warrants, the maintenance of such large forces in the Far East at this time.

Five days earlier Mr Churchill and the Chiefs of Staff had decided that "in view of the probability of an early German advance into Greece through Bulgaria it was of the first importance, from the political point of view, that we should do everything possible, by hook or by crook, to send at once to Greece the fullest support within our power".[8] There was little to offer the Greeks; and Churchill evidently considered that there was nothing at all for Singapore.

Meanwhile some reinforcement of the garrison of Singapore was due soon to arrive from another quarter. At the beginning of December, the Australian Government's offer to send a brigade group to Malaya if necessary was gratefully accepted by Mr Churchill, who added that the Australian force would be relieved in May 1941 by the equivalent of a division from India. Churchill said to the Australian Government that he believed the danger of Japan going to war with the British Empire was definitely less than it was in June after the collapse of France.

The naval and military successes in the Mediterranean and our growing advantage there by land, sea, and air will not be lost upon Japan (he continued). It is quite impossible for our Fleet to leave the Mediterranean at the present juncture without throwing away irretrievably all that has been gained there and all the prospects of the future. On the other hand, with every weakening of the Italian naval power the mobility of our Mediterranean Fleet becomes potentially greater, and should the Italian Fleet be knocked out as a factor, and Italy herself broken as a combatant, as she may be, we could send strong naval forces to Singapore without suffering any serious disadvantage. We must try to bear our Eastern anxieties patiently and doggedly until this result is achieved, it always being understood that if Australia is seriously threatened by invasion we should not hesitate to com-

---

[7] About 40 Australians, then serving in Malaya, were later enlisted in this mission. See Appendix 1 for a brief account of their activities.
[8] Churchill, *The Second World War*, Vol III (1950), p. 14.

promise or sacrifice the Mediterranean position for the sake of our kith and kin. . . .
I am also persuaded that if Japan should enter the war the United States will come
in on our side, which will put the naval boot very much on the other leg, and
be a deliverance from many perils.

. . . With the ever-changing situation it is difficult to commit ourselves to the
precise number of aircraft which we can make available for Singapore, and we
certainly could not spare the flying-boats to lie about idle there on the remote
chance of a Japanese attack when they ought to be playing their part in the deadly
struggle on the North-western Approaches. Broadly speaking, our policy is to build
up as large as possible a Fleet, Army, and Air Force in the Middle East, and
keep this in a fluid condition, either to prosecute war in Libya, Greece, or
presently Thrace, or reinforce Singapore should the Japanese attitude change for
the worse. In this way dispersion of forces will be avoided and victory will give
its own far-reaching protections in many directions. . . .[9]

Arrangements were made in Australia for the 22nd Infantry Brigade and attached troops, 5,850 all ranks, to embark for Malaya early in February preceded by a small advanced party. The Chief of the General Staff (General Sturdee) visited Malaya in December on his way back from a visit to the Middle East, and inspected the areas and accommodation that the A.I.F. was to occupy.

On 27th December a vessel with a Japanese name, and showing a Japanese flag, shelled and wrecked the phosphate loading plant on Nauru Island, north-east of the Solomon Islands and just south of the Equator. The island, a prolific source of phosphates of particular importance to Australia, was among the German possessions in the Pacific occupied by Australian forces in 1914. Placed by the Versailles Treaty under mandate to Great Britain, Australia, and New Zealand, it had then been continuously administered by Australia. The raider, after she had signalled that she was about to fire, hoisted a German flag. It later transpired that she was the *Komet,* which with the *Orion,* another German raider, had sunk near Nauru early in the month five ships engaged in the phosphate trade.

As 1941 dawned, America intensified her diplomatic and material assistance to the Allies. "We were convinced," wrote the American Secretary of State subsequently, "that an Allied victory was possible, and we were determined to do everything we could to bring it about, short of actually sending an expeditionary force to Europe or the Orient. We were especially convinced that an Axis victory would present a mortal danger to the United States. . . . We were acting no longer under the precepts of neutrality, but under those of self-defense."[10]

American policy crystallised in a directive from President Roosevelt in mid-January 1941. At informal talks in London in August 1940 between British and American officers, the United Kingdom Chiefs of Staff had made it clear that despite the importance of Malaya they were not prepared to support its defence at the cost of security in the Atlantic and

---
[9] Quoted in Churchill, Vol II, pp. 628-9.
[10] *The Memoirs of Cordell Hull,* Vol II, p. 919.

the Mediterranean. Roosevelt agreed at the end of November to further Anglo-American staff talks being held at Washington; and in preparation for these, steps were taken to plot a clear course for the United States to follow. In the resultant directive, which followed a White House conference between the President and his Secretaries of State (Mr Cordell Hull), War (Mr Henry L. Stimson), Navy (Mr Franklin Knox), Chief of Naval Operations (Admiral Stark), and Chief of Staff (General Marshall) Roosevelt laid it down that

> The United States would stand on the defensive in the Pacific with the fleet based on Hawaii; the Commander of the Asiatic Fleet would have discretionary authority as to how long he could remain based in the Philippines and as to his direction of withdrawal—to the East or to Singapore; there would be no naval reinforcement of the Philippines; the Navy should have under consideration the possibility of bombing attacks against Japanese cities; it should be prepared to convoy shipping in the Atlantic to England, and to maintain a patrol offshore from Maine to the Virginia Capes.
>
> The Army should not be committed to any aggressive action until it was fully prepared to undertake it; the United States military course must be very conservative until her strength had developed; it was assumed that she could provide forces sufficiently trained to assist to a moderate degree in backing up friendly Latin-American governments against Nazi-inspired "fifth column" movements.
>
> The United States should make every effort to go on supplying material to Great Britain, primarily to disappoint what Roosevelt thought would be Herr Hitler's principal objective in involving the United States in war at this time; "and also to buck up England".[1]

For the purpose of the Washington staff talks, which it was emphasised must be held in the utmost secrecy, the British delegation wore civilian clothes and were known as "technical advisers to the British Purchasing Commission". The talks, which commenced at the end of January and lasted until late in March, resulted in a plan for the grand strategy of Anglo-American cooperation, and embodied the "Beat Hitler first" principle (the principle that, in a war against both Germany and Japan, the aim should be to concentrate first against Germany and go on the defensive in the Pacific and Far East). Provision was made for continuing exchange of information and coordination of plans. In sanctioning such measures, Roosevelt took a big political risk, for

> It is an ironic fact that in all probability no great damage would have been done had the details of these plans fallen into the hands of the Germans and the Japanese; whereas, had they fallen into the hands of the Congress and the press, American preparation for war might have been well nigh wrecked and ruined. . . .[2]

Canada, Australia[3] and New Zealand were represented at meetings of the British delegates but not at the joint meetings.[4] Despite the growing

---

[1] The directive is quoted in M. S. Watson, *Chief of Staff: Prewar Plans and Preparations*, pp. 124-5.
[2] R. E. Sherwood, *The White House Papers of Harry L. Hopkins*, pp. 273-4.
[3] The Australian representatives were Rear-Admiral M. W. S. Boucher, Maj-Gen Northcott, and Air Vice-Marshal S. J. Goble.
[4] The Australian Government received telegrams from both the Australian Legation at Washington and the Dominions Office in February 1941 reporting that President Roosevelt had told Lord Halifax that even if the United States were involved in a war with Japan the Atlantic and Britain would be the main theatre and the United States would have to fight a "holding war" in the Pacific.

partnership between the United States and Britain, the United States Joint Planning Committee gave warning in a memorandum preparatory to the talks that "it is to be expected that proposals of the British representatives will have been drawn up with chief regard for the support of the British Commonwealth. Never absent from British minds are their post-war interests, commercial and military. We should likewise safeguard our eventual interests. . . ."[5]

Britain's critical plight in American eyes at the time was indicated by an accompanying statement that the conversations should include "the probable situations that might arise from the loss of the British Isles"; and the "Beat Hitler first" policy was maintained in the outcome of the talks as basic to the common aim. It was agreed that America's paramount territorial interest was in the western hemisphere, though dispositions must provide for the ultimate security of the British Commonwealth of Nations, a cardinal policy in this respect being retention of the Far East position "such as will assure the cohesion and security of the British Commonwealth".[6]

Should Japan enter the war, military strategy in the Far East would be defensive, it was agreed; but the American Pacific Fleet would be used offensively in the manner best calculated to weaken Japanese economic power, by diverting Japanese strength away from the Malay Archipelago. It was held that augmentation by the United States of forces in the Atlantic and Mediterranean would enable Britain to release the necessary forces for the Far East. The British delegation proposed that the United States send four cruisers from its Pacific fleet to Singapore, but this proposal was rejected on the grounds that they would not be enough to save Singapore; that the United States might later be compelled either to abandon these vessels to their fate and face Japan with a weakened Pacific fleet, or reinforce them to the extent of applying the navy's principal strength in the Far East, with resultant risk to the security of the British Isles.

The agreements reached at the talks were not formally accepted by either the British or the United States Governments, but planning proceeded along the lines agreed on by the staffs. Whether or not Japan became aware of this policy, it certainly suited her designs. European and American possessions in the area which Japan sought to dominate, whose peoples were insufficiently armed and trained by their rulers to enable them to defend themselves, were an inducement to aggression, especially if, by diversion of America's main effort towards Europe, the extent of possible intervention in the Pacific by the United States Fleet would be lessened.

At this stage Germany retained her mastery of Europe, but Italian failures were proving an embarrassment to her in Greece and North Africa, and Britain was gaining strength. Russia, neutral but wary, was still a

---
[5] Quoted in M. S. Watson, *Chief of Staff: Prewar Plans and Preparations*, p. 371.
[6] Watson, p. 376.

Malaya

danger to Japan, who therefore maintained large forces along the borders of Manchuria and Mongolia. Despite the pro-British attitude of American leaders, isolationist sentiment in the United States was still strong. Perhaps the greatest single deterrent to further Japanese aggression was the presence of the American fleet in the Pacific. Was there any way by which Japan might remove this obstacle? "If war eventuates with Japan, it is believed easily possible that hostilities would be initiated by a surprise attack upon the fleet or the naval base at Pearl Harbour," wrote Knox to Stimson on 24th January 1941. Knox added: "The inherent possibilities of a major disaster to the fleet or naval base warrant taking every step, as rapidly as can be done, that will increase the joint readiness of the Army and Navy to withstand a raid." In this Stimson completely concurred. The United States Ambassador in Tokyo, Mr Grew, cabled to Hull on 27th January that there was talk in Tokyo that a surprise mass attack on Pearl Harbour was planned by the Japanese military forces in case of "trouble" between Japan and the United States. This report was passed on to the War and Navy Departments. The new Japanese Ambassador to Washington, Admiral Kichisaburo Nomura, who called on Hull on 12th February, gave an impression of sincerity in seeking to avoid war between the two countries. He said, however, in the course of interviews during which President Roosevelt and Hull at least did some frank talking, that his chief obstacle would be the military group in control in Tokyo.

The Lend-Lease Act, which provided means whereby Britain could obtain the supplies she needed from the United States without paying cash for them, was to become law on 11th March, providing a further answer by America to Japan's signature of the Tripartite Pact. Evidence given by Hull in support of Lend-Lease before the House Committee on Foreign Affairs in January, in which he hit hard at Japan's proposed "New Order" in Eastern Asia, stung the fiery Japanese Minister for Foreign Affairs to belligerent reply.

"Japan must demand America's reconsideration of her attitude," declared Matsuoka, "and if she does not listen there is slim hope for friendly relations between Japan and the U.S.A. I will try my hardest to make the United States understand, but I declare that this cannot be accomplished by courting—the only way is to proceed with unshakeable resolve."[7]

Undaunted by an accompanying assertion by Matsuoka that Japan must dominate the Western Pacific, the Dutch rejected any suggestion of having the East Indies incorporated in a "New Order", under the leadership of any Power whatsoever. Japan found opportunity further to assert her claim to such leadership, however, by acting as mediator between Thailand and Indo-China, the latter under Vichy (French) government

---

[7] During this sultry period in Pacific affairs there appeared in Australia a Major Sei Hashida, of the Japanese Army. The Japanese Consul-General said Hashida had come to investigate wool, metal and other industries in relation to Japan's military requirements. Hashida said he was travelling for health reasons. A request to the Minister for the Army by the Consul-General that Hashida be permitted to inspect Army establishments in Australia was declined.

but now subject to Japanese domination. Fighting between Thai and French forces had flared up at the end of December, in a territorial dispute which it was suspected had been promoted by Japan. Terms for an armistice, presented by a Japanese general, were signed aboard a Japanese warship at the end of January, and a peace treaty was subsequently concluded in Tokyo.[8]

Matsuoka said early in February that the situation between Japan and the United States had "never been marked by greater misunderstanding". The United States, however, gained means of knowing a great deal more about what was in the minds of Japanese leaders than the latter intended that they should. Although it was a top secret at the time, means of deciphering the secret code used in communications from Japan to her representatives in America were discovered by American experts. By this means, known as "Magic", many of Japan's secrets were bared. As an instance, Roosevelt was able to know not only what Nomura was saying to Hull, but Matsuoka's instruction to Nomura of 14th February —to the effect that United States recognition of Japanese overlordship of the Western Pacific was the price sought for avoidance of war. At the same time it was learned that Japan contemplated the acquisition of military bases in Indo-China and Thailand, and ultimately an attack on Singapore; that her aims included incorporation of south-east Asia and the south-west Pacific in the Greater East Asia Co-prosperity Scheme.[9]

In London, in the second week of February, Mr Churchill

> became conscious of a stir and flutter in the Japanese Embassy and colony. . . . They were evidently in a high state of excitement, and they chattered to one another with much indiscretion. In these days we kept our eyes and ears open. Various reports were laid before me which certainly gave the impression that they had received news from home which required them to pack up without a moment's delay. This agitation among people usually so reserved made me feel that a sudden act of war upon us by Japan[1] might be imminent. . . .[2]

Thereupon Churchill sent Roosevelt a message, dated 15th February, in the course of which he said:

> Any threat of a major invasion of Australia or New Zealand would of course force us to withdraw our Fleet from the eastern Mediterranean, with disastrous military possibilities there. . . . You will therefore see, Mr President, the awful enfeeblement of our war effort that would result merely from the sending out by Japan of her battle-cruisers and her twelve 8-inch gun cruisers into the Eastern oceans, and still more from any serious invasion threat against the two Australian [sic] democracies in the South Pacific.[3]

---

[8] When he was informed of the decision to enforce mediation on Thailand and Indo-China, on terms which would suit Japan's purpose, the Emperor of Japan remarked "I do not approve of anything in the nature of a thief at a fire. However, in dealing with the fast-changing world of to-day, it would not be gratifying to err on the side of benevolence." (Entry for 3 Feb 1941 in the diary of Marquis Koichi Kido, Lord Keeper of the Privy Seal, and one of the most influential of the Emperor's advisers.)

[9] *The Roosevelt Letters* (edit. Elliott Roosevelt), Vol III (1952), p. 355.

[1] It is now known that in January 1941 Admiral Yamamoto, Commander of the Japanese Fleet, ordered his staff and Rear-Admiral Inishi, Chief of Staff of the *Eleventh Air Fleet*, to study and work out details of an attack on Pearl Harbour such as Yamamoto had conceived.

[2] Churchill, Vol III, p. 157.

[3] Quoted in Churchill, Vol III, p. 158.

In Australia, cable messages from Japan were intercepted which instructed Japanese firms to reduce staffs and send home all who were not required, particularly women, by 1st March. In assessing the action likely to be taken by Japan in the near future pursuant of her southward expansion policy, the Senior Intelligence Officer at Army Headquarters, Colonel Chapman,[4] reported that as at 8th February there were indications that the most suitable time for any such action would be in the three or four weeks ending in mid-March. An endeavour to convey a sense of urgency to the Australian public was apparent in newspaper reports of meetings of the Advisory War Council[5] on 5th and 12th February. Records show that keen concern about the safety of Australia had been expressed by Mr Curtin, to the extent that at the later meeting he suggested a test mobilisation of Australia's forces. Although this proposal was not adopted, he also drafted a suggested press statement. This was modified in response to objections that it might create a panic, but the statement issued contained a declaration that "it is the considered opinion of the War Council that the war has moved to a new stage involving the utmost gravity . . . there should be neither delay nor doubt about the clamant need for the greatest effort of preparedness this country has ever made".

The alarm soon died down; but it had served to draw more attention than hitherto to the danger from Japan, as compared with the needs of the Middle Eastern theatre of war. Mr Curtin, who would become Australia's Prime Minister later in 1941, had declared publicly on 11th February that it was imperative that both the front and back doors of Singapore should be safeguarded, and Darwin and Port Moresby should be made as strong as possible. Islands of the Pacific must not become the spring-boards for an attack on Australia, and increased naval strength should be afforded to the Australia Station. Mr Menzies, who was in Cairo on his way to discuss the war situation with Mr Churchill and others in England, was asked to press for a frank appreciation by the United Kingdom authorities as to probable actions by Japan in the immediate future which would make war unavoidable, and possible moves she might make which would be countered by other means. Mr Menzies had passed through the Netherlands East Indies, Malaya, and India on his way from Australia.

At this stage Mr David Ross,[6] a former air force officer, then Superintendent of Flying Operations of the Australian Department of Civil Aviation, was instructed to go to Dili, capital of the Portuguese section of the island of Timor, ostensibly as the Department's representative there, but also to send Intelligence reports, especially about what the Japanese

---

[4] Col James A. Chapman, OBE, VX59424. (1st AIF: Maj 30 Bn.) DMI AHQ 1941-42; Col i/c Admin HQ 7 MD 1942; Comd 12 Inf Bde 1942, Tas Force 1943-44; AMLO Middle East 1944-46. Regular soldier; of Toorak, Vic; b. Braidwood, NSW, 7 Aug 1895.

[5] The Advisory War Council, formed in 1940, included senior Ministers and senior members of the Opposition parties.

[6] Gp Capt D. Ross. Superintendent of Flying Operations, Dept of Civil Aviation; Aust Consul in Portuguese Timor 1941-42; Director of Transportation and Movements RAAF 1943-46. Public servant; of Ivanhoe, Vic; b. Melbourne, 15 Mar 1902.

were doing there, and to tell the Government how Australia's interests in the area might be promoted.

Brooke-Popham flew to Australia and attended a meeting of the Australian War Cabinet on 14th February which discussed an appreciation of the position in the Far East by the Australian Chiefs of Staff. This followed receipt of the views of the United Kingdom advisers on the report of the October Singapore conference, and the tactical appreciation at that time by the commanders of the forces at Singapore. The British advisers held that the views of the Singapore commanders on the general defence position were unduly pessimistic, and that both the threat of attack on Burma and the need for additional land forces for defence of Burma and eastern India had been over-estimated. Nevertheless, the weaknesses in British land and air forces in the Far East, particularly the air forces, were "fully recognised", and "everything possible was being done to remedy this situation, having regard to the demands of theatres which are the scene of war". Brooke-Popham urged the War Cabinet to press on in every possible way with local manufacture of munitions. Reviewing prospects in his command, he said that although the defences on the mainland part of Hong Kong might be overcome shortly after war began, the island could defend itself for at least four months. In Malaya, even if Johore were captured by Japan, and use of facilities at the naval base lost, this would not prevent Singapore Island from holding out.

The supreme need at the moment was more munitions and more aircraft, Brooke-Popham declared; but he added that Japanese planes were not highly efficient, and he thought that the air forces in Malaya would cause such loss to the Japanese Air Force as to prevent it from putting the British forces out of action. Japanese fighter aircraft were not as good as Brewster Buffaloes, of which sixty-seven were on the water from the United States to Singapore. The training of the British and Australian Air Forces was more thorough and sounder than that of the Japanese. He said he did not look upon the Japanese as being air-minded, particularly against determined fighter opposition, and that the Japanese were not getting air domination in China despite overwhelming numerical superiority. He spoke, however, of the necessity for a clear definition of actions by Japan which would be regarded as justifying retaliation, and said that he hoped the line would be drawn at Japanese penetration of southern Thailand. He estimated the minimum naval strength necessary at Singapore at a battle squadron of four or five battleships and three or four cruiser squadrons totalling between ten and twelve cruisers, but said that with the British commitments elsewhere it would not be possible to provide this unless America joined in.

Neither the Australian Chiefs of Staff nor the War Cabinet were as confident regarding the situation as the United Kingdom authorities or Brooke-Popham. The Australian Chiefs of Staff gave warning that the current trend of events pointed to Japan having made up her mind to secure freedom of action in Indo-China and Thailand for her forces, preparatory to securing control of those two countries. If the penetration included southern Thailand, they said, it might be regarded as a disclosure of intention to attack Malaya, and Japanese movement in strength into southern Thailand should be considered a cause of war. Numerous reports recently received had given evidence of great activity by the Japanese in increasing the defences and facilities of her mandated islands east of the Philippines, such as would facilitate seizure of further bases from which she could harry American lines of communication with the West Indies, and attack sea communications vital to Australia. Japan could make available forces greatly superior to the British and Dutch naval forces in the Far East and, in the absence of American intervention, was free to take any major course of action she might determine. She could provide a preponderance of military forces in any two of the three principal areas—Malaya, the Netherlands East Indies and Australia—and air forces greatly superior in numbers to the combined total of British and Dutch air forces in the Far East. If Australia deferred reinforcement of her "outer zone" of defence until hostilities began, she might find that Japan had forestalled her; but arrival of Australian troops at other than British territories, while she was at peace with Japan, might serve as a pretext for war.

The Australian Chiefs of Staff were anxious to establish air forces in the islands as far north as possible. The Chief of the Air Staff, however, was not willing to station air forces in the islands unless there were army garrisons to protect the airfields. With reluctance, General Sturdee agreed to send a battalion group to Rabaul for this purpose, and to hold two other such groups ready to go to Timor and Ambon when war became an immediate threat. The Chiefs of Staff recommended that these moves and preparations be made, but advised that the concurrence of the Dutch authorities be sought for the stationing of Australian forces in the Netherlands East Indies, particularly Timor; and that the 8th Division, instead of joining the Australian Corps in the Middle East as had been intended, be retained for use in the Australian area and East Asia.

The War Cabinet approved these recommendations; and decided to raise two reserve motor transport companies and one motor ambulance unit for service in Malaya, to overcome a shortage of drivers there which Brooke-Popham had mentioned. Soon after, the Cabinet decided, "in principle", to move one A.I.F. Pioneer battalion and one A.I.F. infantry brigade group less one battalion, to the Darwin-Alice Springs area. These, with units already at Darwin, could provide one battalion for Timor and one brigade group for the Darwin area, as well as coast and anti-aircraft units. It authorised the distribution of one militia battalion between Port Moresby and Thursday Island; and the sending of one A.I.F. battalion to Rabaul. Thus there would be three A.I.F. divisions in the Middle East, a brigade at Singapore, another at Darwin, and another in training in Australia, where also a proportion of the militia was always in training.

The original plan to send a brigade group to Malaya, where it would be directly under Malaya Command, had given way to a decision to send also part of the divisional headquarters, on the ground that the staff of a brigade was insufficient to handle an Australian force in an overseas country. Major Kappe[7] left Australia on 31st January with a small advanced party, and General Bennett on 4th February, by air, to set up the headquarters in Malaya. On 2nd February the 22nd Brigade and attached units boarded the 81,000-ton *Queen Mary,* formerly famous as Britain's largest liner. The vessel (whose designation was then "H.T.Q.X.") rode in Sydney Harbour, off Bradley's Head, site of Taronga Park Zoo. Although efforts had been made to keep the destination of the troops, known as "Elbow Force", as secret as possible, the embarkation became a great public occasion. Crates marked "Elbow Force, Singapore", which had been waiting to be loaded on the ship, were among the factors which robbed security precautions of much of their effect. Relatives and friends of the men, and sightseers from city and country, crowded rowing boats, yachts, launches, and ferries, and massed at vantage points around the harbour when, on 4th February, the *Queen Mary,* accompanied by the 45,000-ton *Aquitania* and the Dutch liner *Nieuw Amsterdam* (36,000 tons) carrying troops to the Middle East, put out to sea escorted by the Australian cruiser *Hobart.*[8]

The convoy as a whole lifted approximately 12,000 members of the A.I.F. Their cheers mingled with those of many thousands of spectators ashore and afloat, the toots of ferries and tugboats, the screams of sirens, and the big bass of the *Queen Mary's* foghorn as the convoy steamed down the harbour and through the Heads. Despite the brave showing of the farewell, it impressed on many more deeply than before the extent to which Australia was committed to a war on the other side of the world while it showed signs of spreading to the Pacific, and possibly to her own soil.

Colonel Jeater was addressing his men at sea next day on subjects which included the necessity for security measures, when the *Queen Mary* picked up a radio message that when the convoy had been at sea only twelve hours an enemy raider was within 39 miles of the ships.[9] The voyage was otherwise uneventful until the *Mauretania,* carrying reinforcements to the Middle East, joined the convoy early on 8th February. At Fremantle, which the convoy reached on the 10th, small vessels circled the ships and collected parcels and letters from the men. These local craft

---

[7] Brig C. H. Kappe, OBE, VX48789. GSO2 (Ops) 8 Div; CO 8 Div Sigs. Regular soldier; of Ballarat, Vic; b. Ballarat, 2 Dec 1900.

[8] With the 22 Bde HQ and the 2/18, 2/19 and 2/20 Bns, the *Queen Mary* carried the 2/10 Fd Regt; a battery of the 2/4 A-Tk Regt; 2/10 Fd Coy; 8 Div Sigs; 10 AGH, 2/4 CCS, 2/9 Fd Amb; 2/2 MAC, 2/5 Fd Hyg Sec; 2 Mobile Bacteriological Laboratory; 17 Dental Unit; 4 Supply Pers Sec; Res Motor Tpt Coy; a field bakery; 2/4 Fd Workshop; 2/2 Ord Store; 8 Div Cash Office, 8 Div Provost Coy, 8 Div Postal Unit, and other headquarters details. The total was some 5,750 troops. Brigadier Taylor left Sydney the same day by flying-boat for Malaya.

[9] 2/18th Battalion war diary. In fact there was no enemy raider within thousands of miles of the *Queen Mary* at that time. The message probably originated as security propaganda.

were searched when they returned to shore, and 6,000 pieces intended for mailing, which might have spread details of the force far and wide, were confiscated.[10]

The convoy weighed anchor again on 12th February, and next day Major Whitfield, Deputy Assistant Adjutant-General of the 8th Division, cleared air thick with rumours about the destination of the force when he told the men that they were going to Malaya, and described their probable role. On the 16th the British cruiser *Durban* came into sight, and swung into line abreast of the Australian cruiser *Canberra,* which had taken over escort duty from the *Hobart* at Fremantle. The scene which followed stirred the emotions of the entire convoy, as the *Queen Mary* swung to port, circled behind the other ships, and then when they were again in formation, charged past them at twenty-six knots. Wholehearted cheers burst from the men thronging the decks of the vessels, and from the nurses who accompanied them. New Zealanders cheered Australians; Australians cheered New Zealanders, with equal vim. Bands rolled great chords of music across the waters; then the convoy headed by the *Canberra* set course towards the sinking sun, and the *Queen Mary* and the *Durban* headed for the tropics and a land where never yet an Australian contingent of soldiers had set foot. The splitting of the convoy was eloquent of Australia's now divided responsibilities—for assistance to the Imperial cause in the European war, and for helping to man barriers against onslaught by Japan.

A broadcast by Moscow Radio on 11th February to the effect that the *Queen Mary* had arrived in Singapore laden with Australian troops was recorded in Australia. The time of the broadcast was approximately nineteen hours after the vessel could reasonably have got there had she not, as happened, altered course shortly after leaving Sydney, and travelled via Fremantle instead of around the north of Australia. Whether or not this change of course misled enemy raiders, the *Queen Mary,* after several nights of stifling heat for the troops pent up under blackout conditions, arrived safely at Singapore on 18th February, and poured them into their new and strange environment.

---

[10] Security officers soaked in water the letters confiscated at Fremantle, and dropped them overboard when the *Queen Mary* was a day and half from Singapore; yet some of the letters were recovered and came soon after into possession of Malaya Command.

CHAPTER 5

THE MALAYAN SCENE

FROM the waterfront the Australians gazed eagerly at Singapore with its profusion of sights, sounds, and smells, and at the medley of uniforms on the wharf which "might well have come from the wardrobe of a theatrical company".[1] Before nightfall on 18th February 1941, the infantry were packed into railway carriages and on their way to barracks at Port Dickson, on the west coast of the Malayan Peninsula, and at Seremban, some 20 miles inland and 206 miles from Singapore. Headquarters of the A.I.F. in Malaya was established at Sentul, a suburb of Kuala Lumpur, capital of the Federated Malay States, 42 miles north-west of Seremban. The signals were at Kampong Bahru, a near-by suburb; the artillery and supply units and the general hospital at Malacca, on the west coast south of Port Dickson; and the motor ambulance convoy at Kajang, between Seremban and Kuala Lumpur.

There was a puzzling absence of women and children in the villages and towns through which the Australians passed in the early days of their travels in Malaya.

> As we got to know the people (wrote the author of a chronicle of the 2/18th Battalion[2]) we learned that we had been given the reputation of being unholy terrors where women and children were concerned. . . . However, the cheerful Digger soon proved the fallacy of this scare, and it was not long before all fear on the part of their yellow and black neighbours was dispelled. In fact, as soon as a convoy of troops was sighted approaching a town or village, the streets became lined with shouting youngsters holding up their thumbs and crying out "Hello, Jo". That was their nickname for the Aussies, and it has stuck. Any Australian is always "Jo" wherever he is in Malaya.

There is reason to believe that this early fear of the Australians was the outcome partly of Japanese radio propaganda and partly of indirect official British propaganda, the latter misguidedly designed to heighten their reputation as warriors. But the warriors soon showed themselves to be in the main the sort of individuals to whom children take an instinctive liking, and whose relationships with others were on a man-to-man basis in which human values were of far more concern than rank, riches, race, creed or colour. The Asians were quick to show their liking for them. Soon the Australians "learnt a smattering of the Malay tongue, which is the easiest of all to pick up, and gradually became familiar enough with (Malayan) dollar currency to promote successful two-up schools. They grossly overpaid the Chinese rickshaw men, to the chagrin of the local inhabitants. The 2/19th lines were swarming with cocoa-brown Malaya youngsters delighted that we had commandeered their school. They were jolly children, with merry eyes and flashing teeth, and

---
[1] W. Noonan, *The Surprising Battalion* (1945), p. 3.
[2] *Men May Smoke*, June 1941.

they spoke English excellently and gravely. Real friendships were made between some of the men and these boys, and they cried when we left.[3] They taught us Malay and collected Australian postage stamps avidly."[4]

Soon men who had manoeuvred on windswept, sunburned plains in Australia were training amid lush tropical growth in steamy, unremitting heat, their clothes sodden with perspiration. There was apparently no time to be lost; a training instruction issued by Malaya Command warned that "the first three months of 1941 are likely to prove the critical period of the war, not only at home (Great Britain) and in the Middle East, but also in Malaya. . . . We must . . . use every effort to make ourselves fully efficient as early as possible." Among the troops, rumours of imminent battle had been rife when the *Queen Mary* reached Singapore, and the expectation had gained ground that the men would see action within a fortnight. They soon found, however, that the possible imminence of war had not disturbed the social life of Singapore.

> I still have very vivid memories of my first mental reactions on our arrival in Singapore (wrote an officer afterwards). We were being sent to a war station. We were equipped—even if only 50 per cent equipped—for war. Yet the first sight that met our eyes on the first evening was officers in mess dress and fashionable women in evening dress. It was not only incongruous, it was wrong. Either we were crazy or they were crazy. Either there was danger or there was no danger. If the latter why had we been sent there, and why were more troops on the way from India?

It was argued against this point of view that nothing was to be gained, least of all in morale, by foregoing social activities and leaving people to spend their leisure in boredom, or perhaps less innocuous and no more useful pursuits than those in which they now engaged. The real issue appears to have been how much leisure the community, and especially the forces stationed in Malaya, could afford at this stage. In retrospect it is obvious that the danger of Japanese aggression was taken far too lightly; and that an all-out effort, stripped down to the stark demands of war, was urgently necessary. As it was, the garrison maintained an easy-going, leisurely routine. Officers' wives and children were allowed to remain, and their presence tended to be a distraction from an alert and active approach to a struggle for existence. This was to become still more serious when the struggle was in progress, and urgent problems of how to get wives and children to safety would face officers upon whom rested responsibility for the lives of their men and the defence of Malaya. On the other hand the Australians were new to the contemporary scene, and free of such domestic diversion. It was to be expected therefore that some at least of them would view the situation more critically than those upon whom it had crept by passage of time and the embrace of custom.

A jungle-clad range of mountains, generally some 4,000 feet high and rising to 7,186 feet, forms the backbone of the Malayan Peninsula, with mostly low-lying land on either side. The plain on the west side of the

---
[3] Upon transfer of 2/19th Battalion from Seremban to Port Dickson.
[4] G. Mant, *You'll Be Sorry* (1944), p. 81.

range is relatively narrow, but was more highly developed and more closely populated. Here were Malaya's main traffic arteries—a trunk road from Singapore to Singora, on the east coast of Thailand, with an extensive road system between it and the Malayan west coast; and the main line of a single-track metre-gauge railway to Bangkok, capital of Thailand, with laterals to the west coast and a branch to Singora. Another track started from this line at Gemas, 150 miles from Singapore, and ran on the east side of the range to the port of Tumpat, between Kota Bharu and the Thai frontier. From Pasir Mas, inland from Kota Bharu, a branch led back to the main track at Haad Yai junction, near Singora. A motor road which left the west coast road system in the Malayan State of Kedah crossed the frontier near Kroh and led to Patani, another east coast port. It linked with a route, shown on a current official map as in part cart track and in part footpath, southward from Kroh to Grik. A road then ran adjacent to the Sungei[5] Perak back to Kuala Kangsar, on the trunk road. Thus there were on the west ready means of access to and from Thailand.

The large eastern portion of Malaya was poorly served by roads. They were principally one from Johore Bahru through Mersing to Endau, and two linking the east and west coasts. Of these two, one ran to Mersing from the trunk road at Ayer Hitam, crossing the railway line at Kluang; and the other from Kuala Kubu through a gap in the range at Fraser's Hill to Kuantan. Most of the State of Kelantan, in the north-east, was roadless, and its only substantial transport link with the rest of Malaya was the eastern branch of the railway. Sandy beaches line Malaya's east coast, and there are many, largely interspersed by mangrove swamps, on the west. Most of the rivers are not broad, but the Perak, in the northern half of the west coast, is half a mile wide well inland, at Kuala Kangsar. Apart from cultivated areas, devoted principally to rubber, rice and coconut growing, Malaya was mostly covered by jungle. There visibility throughout the day often extended for only a few yards, in a green dusk under the thick vegetation.

Malaya is some 400 miles long in a direct line. The main road and west-coast railway from Singapore to the border of Thailand were about the length of the railway between Sydney and Melbourne. The width of the peninsula varies from 60 to 200 miles, and its area is 52,500 square miles, or about a sixth of the area of New South Wales. The island of Penang, near the north-west coast, is 350 miles distant in a direct line from Singapore. Singapore Island, at the foot of the peninsula, is 217 square miles in extent—about 1-120th the area of Tasmania.

The population of the whole of Malaya in 1940 was nearly 5,500,000 people, of whom only about .5 per cent were Europeans.[6] Chinese, far more astute and adapted to industry and commerce than the easy-going Malays, represented some 43 per cent of the population, the Malays 41

---

[5] River.

[6] In 1940 there were 2,379,000 Chinese, 2,278,000 Malays, 744,000 Indians, 18,000 Europeans, 48,000 Eurasians and 58,400 others in Malaya. During 1941 the European population decreased to about 9,000. In the past twenty years the percentage of Chinese had rapidly increased.

per cent. The rest were principally Indians, a large proportion of them coolies on plantations. Though few in number, the Japanese had extensive interests in the photographic industry, owned iron mines near Endau in Johore, at Kuala Dungun in Trengganu, and in Kelantan, and rubber estates of which many were at strategically important points. They also operated freighters from the east coast to Japan. Thus they were in a position to keep a close watch on defence activities, and to acquire an intimate knowledge of Malaya.

Lying only 73 miles north of the Equator, and bounded on both sides by the sea, Malaya has a heavily humid climate. This keeps the heat down to a mean of about 81 degrees Fahrenheit in the shade, but its constancy, day and night, summer and winter, is exhausting, particularly to newcomers. In the jungle the atmosphere is especially oppressive, and made jungle exercises by troops uncomfortable and exhausting. Singapore itself, covered by jungle and mangrove swamp when it was acquired by Sir Stamford Raffles in 1819, had grown rapidly in importance and affluence as a junction of the vast streams of wealth flowing between East and West. It had in 1941 a population of about 720,000, and the port received some 31,000,000 tons of shipping a year (compared with about 12,000,000 then entering Sydney in a year).

Although the men did not know it, the directive given to General Bennett had contemplated that the force sent to Malaya would be used to strengthen its defence merely until it could join the Australian Corps in the Middle East in mid-1941. Meanwhile it was to come under the operational control of the General Officer Commanding, Malaya, with the reservations, as Bennett's directive stated, that:

(a) The Force will retain its identity as an Australian force;
(b) No part of the Force is to be employed apart from the whole without your consent;
(c) Should the G.O.C. Malaya in certain circumstances of emergency insist on an extensive operational dispersal of your Force you will, after registering such protest as you deem essential, comply with the order of the G.O.C. Malaya and immediately report the full circumstances to Army Headquarters, Melbourne.

Thus the directive embodied well-established principles for the employment of Australian forces overseas, giving Bennett a large degree of freedom of action subject to such overriding requirements as an emergency might impose.

Malaya presented to Bennett and those under his command many problems, of which the most important was training. In the expectation that the division would go to the Middle East, it had been organised and conditioned largely for rapid mechanised movement over good roads and in open country. Now it must be prepared to fight not only where such movement was possible, and approaching enemy forces could be easily seen and fired upon, but also in densely-vegetated country, where malaria was rife, roads were few or non-existent, and enemy troops might be completely concealed only a few yards away. The country was inhabited mainly by people whose colour, features, clothes and language made Europeans among them especially conspicuous. On the other hand, Japanese were not easily distinguished from them by newcomers such as the Australians. To the Asian people of Malaya, subjects of a European race and lacking democratic self-government, war with Japan would mean something quite different from what it meant to the Australians, and their goodwill or trustworthiness could not be taken for granted. The heat, frequent sudden downpours of rain, swamps, rivers, and other obstacles would make troop movement exhausting and difficult. Tactics would have to be adapted to meet the new requirements.

Most of Malaya was conveniently but often misleadingly referred to as "the jungle", in much the same way that Australians refer to "the bush" when they mean anything from areas covered by bushy vegetation to rural or remote parts of Australia, whether timbered or open country, inhabited or not. The Malayan "jungle" might include or be interspersed with rubber, coconut palm, pineapple and other plantations; villages, open grassy areas, and both primary and secondary jungle in the real sense of the term. At its outer edges, the primary jungle is dense and difficult to penetrate except by paths made by human beings or animals, and gives a misleading impression of impenetrability. Inside, it comprises a labyrinth of trees, standing in what, except to those fully conditioned to it, is apt to seem a stifling, eerie silence. It is possible to move here with a certain amount of freedom, but only those skilled in finding their way in these surroundings are likely to avoid becoming lost in the course of extensive movement. Secondary jungle—that which has been cleared and then allowed to grow again—is usually a mass of dense, tangled undergrowth.

The only antidote to jungle fear—in itself a terrifying enemy—is jungle lore sufficient to enable men to regard the jungle as a friend rather than an enemy, or at least as neutral. To this had to be added, for the purposes of warfare, skill and resolution in outwitting and overcoming enemy troops who also might seek to turn the jungle to their advantage.

Learning to live in moist tropical heat at almost sea level on the Equator was a very different and easy matter compared to learning to know the jungle (wrote an Australian officer). Strenuous efforts were made by small and large parties to obtain jungle training. A few individuals even went bush with the Sakai.[7] Nevertheless, the true jungle is not the fearsome place most writers describe in great detail. As one of the Australian planters said to us on our arrival: "There are only two things in the jungle that will chase you. All the rest will run away from you much faster than you can run away from them, if you give them the chance." The two jungle terrors were the seladang and the hornets. The former was a heavy and cumbersome water buffalo type of beast. The latter were fast black dive bombers with yellow bands around their middles. Twelve stings could kill a bullock. The red ants were annoying and irritable, but the hornets were really dangerous. Poisonous snakes abound in Malaya, the worst being the Hamadryad or King Cobra and the banded krait. I never heard of anyone being killed by snake bite among the troops in Malaya. Fifteen foot pythons were kept as pets to keep down the rats and mice. There were tigers and elephants in certain parts of Malaya. The latter

---

[7] Aboriginal people of Malaya.

were not dangerous unless annoyed. The former caused plenty of scares but no real trouble. The sentry in the jungle at night was more scared by his own imagination than by any denizens of the jungle itself.

Use of long-range weapons would be difficult and sometimes impossible where masses of vegetation would tower before the mouths of guns, and hamper observation of the objective and effect of fire. Opportunity for ambush, by either attacker or defender, lay almost everywhere. Movement was of course almost completely concealed from air observation, but vehicles quickly became bogged in the damp, soft soil off the roads. Thus the supplies necessary to operations in the jungle would often have to be manhandled. Strict precautions would have to be taken against malaria. Movement in rubber was far less restricted, but here too it was difficult to keep direction and use supporting weapons to full advantage. Little imagination and initiative had been exercised in the training of the forces generally in Malaya at the time the Australians arrived. A notable exception was the 2/Argyll and Sutherland Highlanders, part of the 12th Indian Brigade which had arrived in Malaya late in 1939, whose leaders had made a relatively enterprising and vigorous approach to the problem.[8]

What steps were taken by the Australians to master these conditions? A booklet issued by Army Headquarters, Melbourne, in 1940 contained pithy advice on operations in Malaya in sharp contrast with some of the ideas prevailing there at the time. Evidently based on studies of the Japanese in action, it gave warning that the most likely enemy possessed a high standard of armament and technical training, great physical endurance and few bodily requirements compared with British troops; was ruthless, had a talent for misleading his opponent, a large potential "fifth column" in Malaya, and a very high standard and ample experience of landing operations. After landing he was capable of moving inland at great speed, self-contained for several days. As thick country did not favour static defence, offensive action should be taken against the enemy, whenever and wherever he was met. The booklet emphasised the need for training all ranks in moving through jungle, since "the difference between trained and untrained troops is immense".[9]

The first training instruction issued by A.I.F. Headquarters in Malaya echoed the necessity of making the troops "jungle-minded". It asserted, however, that "our enemy will not be so trained . . . is unaccustomed to any surprise and reacts badly to it. Generally speaking, he is weak in small unit training, and the initiative of his small units is of a low standard." A Malaya Command training instruction previously mentioned said experience had shown that the Japanese soldier was "peculiarly helpless against unforeseen action by his enemy".

---

[8] The battalion trained in the Mersing area to which the 12th Indian Brigade had been allotted, and where later the 22nd Australian Brigade would be stationed. Angus Rose, one of the battalion's officers, records (*Who Dies Fighting*, 1944, pp. 9-12) that its early preparations for jungle training received little encouragement from Malaya Command, "and they assured us that if we were not drowned in the seasonal rains, we would be decimated by malaria". Training manuals were "pompous, heavy, often platitudinous and otherwise equivocal", and accordingly, "everyone had completely different tactical conceptions or else none at all".

[9] *Tactical Notes for Malaya*, issued by General Staff, A.H.Q., Melbourne, 1940.

Brigadier Taylor had flown ahead of his brigade to Malaya to arrange a tour of British and Indian units on the mainland in order to discover what methods of training had already been evolved. Although he found the units helpful and cooperative, he formed the opinion that none of them was very advanced in jungle training. He concluded that although the 22nd Brigade had made large strides in orthodox training in Australia, the principles on which they had trained there would now have to be adapted to the new conditions; in the jungle there were no fields of fire, tactical features lost their significance, roads and tracks were vital; static defence spelled defeat, and all round protection would be essential. As Taylor saw it, the section and platoon commanders would become all-important. "If they lost, you had lost," he wrote afterwards. Major Anderson,[1] one of Taylor's officers, who had campaigned in East Africa in the previous world war against the German-led Askari, and thus possessed experience particularly valuable in Malayan conditions, wrote later also that "in jungle fighting, owing to the closeness of the country, the tempo of fighting is much faster than in ordinary warfare, and errors of tactics and judgment, and indecision on the part of junior commanders, have a far greater influence on the general scheme of operations than is generally realised".

As often occurred when Australian and British troops were together in the tropics, the British considered that the Australians had too little respect for the heat of the midday sun, and the Australians considered that the British had too much respect for it.

The local planters thought the Australians were crazy to attempt so much hard physical training in the tropical heat, that is, during the daytime (an officer wrote). Plenty of sweat was lost, but the physical effects were good rather than bad. On the other hand, the complete contempt in which Australians held the siesta hour on arrival abated very rapidly and they ultimately adopted the custom. Neither mad dogs nor Englishmen—except a few "flanneled fools"—seemed to go out in the noon-day sun in Malaya.[2]

In the early stages of section training the Australians suffered much from fatigue and cramp, and skin diseases were common. Salt reduced cramp and fatigue, and medical officers with the keen cooperation of Colonel Maxwell of the 2/19th Battalion, himself a doctor by profession, were able to reduce the prevalence of skin diseases.[3] As equipment was streamlined, speed of movement both by day and night improved, and gradually the men developed a sense of direction when moving in dense vegetation where the range of vision was severely limited. Training sylla-

---

[1] Lt-Col C. G. W. Anderson, VC, MC, NX12595. (1914-18: King's African Rifles in British East Africa.) CO 2/19 Bn 1941-42. MHR 1950-51 and since 1955. Grazier; of Crowther, Young, NSW; b. Capetown, Sth Africa, 12 Feb 1897.

[2] On one occasion a ship arrived at Port Swettenham with 800 tons of frozen meat and many motor vehicles for the AIF. The Australian officers in charge, keen to get the unloading done swiftly, worked the native wharf labourers hard for six hours until they were wilting, whereupon Australian troops who had been sent for took over, despite the fact that it was not considered desirable politically or medically to employ white men as labourers in Malaya. These moved cargo at three times the rate achieved by the poorly-nourished coolies, and emptied the ship in record time.

[3] For medical aspects of the war with Japan, see the medical series in this history by Allan S. Walker.

buses included village fighting, wide enveloping movements, moving as advance-guards with carriers through a defile (in effect any jungle-lined road in Malaya), and night attack. Much was learned by trial and error, and by frequent consultation between Taylor and his battalion commanders.

On 28th February the Deputy Chief of the Australian General Staff, Major-General Northcott,[4] had arrived in Singapore to attend a staff conference, which will be mentioned later. He informed General Bennett that (in accordance with an agreement with the Dutch) the 23rd Brigade was being moved to the Northern Territory; that two of its battalions would be sent to Timor and one to Ambon; and that the 27th Brigade would probably go to Alice Springs.[5] Thus it seemed that in the near future about one-third of Bennett's division would be in central Australia, one-third either in Darwin or the Dutch Indies and one-third in Malaya —an extremely unsatisfactory arrangement from the point of view of the commander.[6]

After Northcott had described this plan he told Bennett that he must either arrange with Malaya Command to take over an area command in Malaya, or return to Australia to take command of the larger part of the division.

> Chose former (wrote Bennett in his diary). I must expect to stay here unless Japanese situation cleared up. I asked that a complete Div HQ be formed here or alternatively my Div HQ be sent from Australia and that I be authorised to form a complete Base HQ. He said he would recommend it to Military Board.

At the same meeting Bennett asked among other things for a casualty clearing station, more equipment, interpreters of Japanese, and certain staff officers including Colonel Derham, his senior medical officer. On the 3rd March Bennett sent a telegram to Melbourne asking that a second infantry brigade, a machine-gun battalion and a pioneer battalion and other smaller units be sent to Malaya. Next day, in a further effort, he sent letters to General Sturdee urging that the division be kept intact; to his artillery commander, Brigadier Callaghan; and to a close friend who was on the staff of the Minister for the Army. On 11th March Bennett learnt from Sturdee that his force would not be increased. Bennett's staff was strengthened, however, by sending to Malaya later in March Major Kent Hughes, his D.A.Q.M.G., in whom he had great confidence.[7] At

---

[4] Lt-Gen Sir John Northcott, KCMG, KCVO, CB. (1st AIF: Capt 12 Bn.) Deputy CGS 1939-41, GOC 1 Armd Div 1941-42, CGS 1942-45. Governor of NSW 1946-57. Regular soldier; of Melbourne; b. Creswick, Vic, 24 Mar 1890.

[5] General Bennett understood at the time that the battalions of the 23rd Brigade would go to Timor and Ambon in the near future. Actually the arrangement was that they should go there if war with Japan broke out.

[6] As an outcome of this plan Lt-Col E. G. B. Scriven, the Chief Engineer of the division, was sent from Darwin to the Netherlands Indies on a reconnaissance. He was killed in a motor-car accident at Koepang in Timor on 30th June.

[7] Bennett wrote in his diary: "Kent Hughes arrived—like a breath from Heaven. As AQ he will be really good—he knows his job." Kent Hughes, a citizen soldier, had had long experience in administrative appointments in the war of 1914-18. He was staff captain of the 3rd Light Horse Brigade in 1915-17, and DAQMG of the Australian Mounted Division in 1917-18. He had become a major in 1917 at the age of 21, and had joined the Second AIF, still as a major, 23 years later.

length, on 20th March, Bennett was informed by Army Headquarters that his whole divisional headquarters was to join him, and also a field park company, stores depot, reserve motor transport company and convalescent depot. These were welcome additions, but far short of what Bennett had asked for, which was, in effect, the division less the brigade group committed to the Netherland Indies. The senior officers of the divisional staff arrived at Bennett's headquarters on 6th April. Colonel Rourke took over as senior general staff officer and Colonel Broadbent as senior administrative officer.

The 22nd Brigade took part in March in a "Far Eastern Defence Exercise", staged by Malaya Command, and aimed at testing all stages of transition from peace to war by the civil authorities and Services. On the theoretical assumption that an enemy had landed at Mersing, where the 12th Indian Brigade was stationed, the Australian brigade was to move from the Seremban-Port Dickson area via Kluang to help repel the invaders. This necessitated movement by road and rail over a distance of about 150 miles.

In the course of the movement, a sharp disagreement occurred between General Bennett and Brigadier Taylor about its timing. Although with the aid of intermediaries the difference was patched up, its causes lay deeper than the incident, in the temperaments of the two, and in there being only one brigade, but both a divisional commander and a brigadier. The task of a divisional headquarters normally was to control three infantry brigades, a group of artillery regiments under a brigadier, divisional engineers, signallers and others, with, perhaps, units of armour, machine-gunners, pioneers and more. When a divisional commander and his staff controlled virtually only a single brigade group a difficult situation was created. Bennett's division in Malaya was, at the time, Taylor's brigade and little more. Friction resulted from the exercise of both divisional and brigade authority within these narrow confines.

In April the infantry practised bayonet assault and snap shooting in the jungle, aimed at increasing their speed of movement and reaction. The more experienced infantry officers—especially Major Anderson as a veteran of jungle warfare—attached great importance to training junior commanders and their men in the use of weapons for personal defence. They did so on the ground that the likelihood of meeting the enemy suddenly at close quarters in the jungle called for a high degree of self-reliance, and speedy mental reaction such as would gain for them the advantages of surprise and the initiative. This training was to stand them in good stead, and to cost the enemy dearly, especially when he came within the reach of their bayonets in events which were to follow.[8] As a result of an exercise during April General Bennett reached conclusions of particular interest in view of what was to happen in battle. Among these were that communications and information presented a major prob-

---

[8] A Japanese company commander told Major Anderson in the prisoner-of-war period that the number of Japanese casualties from bayonets had caused them great concern.

lem, as information had taken too long to come through; and that "A" and "B" Echelon mechanical transport must not be used as troop-carrying vehicles except in very special circumstances.

In May groups from each battalion took part in an elephant hunt in mountainous and enclosed country. Under the supervision of Malays they lived and travelled in the jungle for four days, and made shelters, beds and rafts from bamboo. By July each battalion was sending out self-contained companies on a 30-mile circuit on four-day exercises, which took them through rubber and jungle, with the company commander solely responsible for maintenance and protection. At night, companies went into perimeter defence, where they were "attacked" by roving platoons and learnt their weaknesses in defence and counter-attack. After company training came battalion training, which took the form of rapid movement by transport, the organisation and training of flying columns to seize important localities ahead of the main body, movement through jungle roads, protection against ambush, cooperation with artillery and aircraft, and battalion attack and defence. In attack a focal point was used in lieu of a "start-line" when units moved on predetermined compass bearings, the objective being some easily recognised line such as a road, track or village, well behind the supposed location of the enemy. In defence the battalions were allotted areas of responsibility which they constantly patrolled.

The 8th Division from its commander downwards was now undergoing a test to which Australian troops had not hitherto been put. In the South African War (to go no farther back) and in 1914-1918, Australians had volunteered in formidable numbers to go to "the front" and had been sent there briskly. In both those wars they had manned fighting formations, and had done little base or garrison service. In 1940 and 1941 first one then another and another Australian division had been sent to the Middle East and, in 1914-1918 style, had gone into action there with little or no delay. By July 1941 they had fought in Africa, Europe and Asia and few formations on the Allied side equalled them in experience. The 8th Division, on the other hand, although enlisted like the others in the wave of anxiety and enthusiasm that followed the fall of France, had been dispersed far and wide on garrison duty of a kind not contemplated by the officers and men when their units were being formed. In tropical conditions, which themselves imposed nervous strain, this resulted in a sense of frustration and the sort of grumbling by which men relieve their feelings. Strained relations existed at divisional headquarters from time to time.

The feelings of the Australian troops in Malaya were aggravated by remarks in letters from wives, girls and friends showing that they had gained from newspaper articles published in Australia the impression that the men were leading exotic lives in the tropics. Sometimes a wife or girl would add that she too knew how to have a gay time. Such remarks, made in ignorance of the toil, sweat and tedium of the men's lot, bit into the feelings of many. They referred to themselves satirically as "Menzies' Glamour Boys", and they named a row of huts "Pansy Alley". When a newsreel showing Mr Menzies inspecting Australians in the Middle East came on the screen at Seremban there was a chorus of hoots because it was he who, as Prime Minister, embodied the decision to send them to Malaya. This was merely a means of relieving their pent-up feelings, but other members of the audience were astonished, and might understandably have attached to it more significance than it possessed.

Week-end leave, organised sport, and the efforts of organisations and individuals in providing amenities did much to counter the men's feeling of frustration. As soon as General Bennett established his headquarters at Kuala Lumpur in March 1941 the Surveyor-General of the Federated Malay States, Major W. F. N. Bridges, a son of General Bridges who had commanded the First A.I.F. in 1914-15, called upon him and asked whether he could help. Bennett asked him whether he could establish a leave club in Kuala Lumpur, staffed preferably by European women. In three days the people of Kuala Lumpur had opened one, with British women cooking for and waiting on the troops. In July a building erected on a recreation ground in the heart of Singapore for use as an Anzac Club was opened. The building was a personal gift from a Singapore resident, Mr H. W. T. Fogden, "as a mark of an Englishman's appreciation of the Dominion troops". The club was organised and financed by the Australian Comforts Fund, and staffed largely by Australian and New Zealand women in Singapore as voluntary workers. The Chinese community at Seremban organised a "garden" where Australian troops could obtain Chinese or English food at cost price. British women in the district voluntarily helped to staff it.

Friendships between the Australians and others extended through the community, and included many English people;[9] although those who considered that that rather vaguely conceived factor, "the prestige of the white man" was best maintained by being aloof from "the natives" were apt to look askance at the Australians because of their easy-going ways with Asians.

An issue regarding the employment of the 8th Division which caused General Bennett keen concern first arose in mid-April, when he received from Malaya Command a message forecasting that the principal role of his force would be in support of the 11th Indian Division in north-west Malaya. He saw in this the possibility that part of his division might come under command of General Murray-Lyon and noted in his diary: "I may

---

[9] "The British community gave the Australians a grand welcome at all times and in all places—far better than any of us could have deserved," wrote Major Kent Hughes. "Both in Singapore and up country they took us into their homes as guests. They made us honorary members of their clubs (a very special and prized privilege in those parts). Women, who had never cooked an egg or done a hand's turn for themselves, in a land where domestic labour is cheap and plentiful, turned to and organised Anzac hostels and rest-rooms. . . . Everyone was out to help the new chums from 'down under' in every way possible. In fact their activities, plus the Australian propaganda in the newsreels, at one time made the British Tommy feel a bit annoyed, and quite frankly I do not blame him if he did feel a bit neglected. He was part of the Malayan scene. The Australians were novelties."—From an unpublished manuscript "Singapore, Before and After".

be left in the cold if operations come locally." Apart from its personal aspect, such an arrangement would of course have been contrary to the directive which had been given him, except with Bennett's consent or in an emergency. Although it did not eventuate, he remained on guard against any such move.

There were two incidents in May either of which might have caused serious trouble. General Bennett was asked by the Governor to supply troops to quell a strike of plantation workers for an increase in pay.[1] Such an action would have cut right across Australian principles, and Bennett explained that Australian policy made it necessary for him to decline. He received next day a letter from Malaya Command stating that the A.I.F. was legally bound to undertake the task, and this he reported to Australia. There followed a clash between other troops and strikers, in which some of the latter were killed. The upshot of Bennett's report was that a cable was sent from Australia to Malaya Command confirming that the A.I.F. was not to be used to break strikes. Bennett learned subsequently that India also objected.

On 26th May a report reached Bennett that two junior Australian officers had crossed the frontier into Thailand, and been arrested. Their action, of minor consequence in an individual sense, had grave possibilities in that it might be seized upon by the Japanese to make a case for entering Thailand on the ground that Thai neutrality had been violated. Although the incident blew over, news of it leaked out, and was used by enemy propagandists.

The arrival and activities of Australian troops in Malaya, with their unusual characteristics, naturally had made a newsy subject, useful for emphasising Imperial solidarity and the accumulating strength of British defences in the area. Thus the force was given extensive publicity, and Australian news was increasingly featured in Malayan newspapers with the aid of a service established by the Australian Department of Information. At one stage, however, steps were taken by the Services authorities to soft-pedal news about the A.I.F. on the ground that the prominence given to the Australians tended to create ill-feeling on the part of other troops who had gained less recognition. While this might have been justifiable as a local measure, it affected overseas publicity also, and was resented not only by Bennett but by newspaper correspondents who gathered in increasing numbers in Malaya as the Far Eastern crisis approached a climax.

Skilful handling of publicity at this Far Eastern nerve-centre was obviously necessary not only for such effect as it might have upon the potential enemy. Favourable influence upon the American public, hesitant of commitment to war with Japan, was vitally important. It was necessary also to create an alert and responsive public opinion in Malaya and elsewhere in the Far Eastern area. The Services Press Bureau, set up in

---
[1] The workers were seeking a daily increase of pay of 10 cents for males and 5 cents for females over the then current daily rates of 50 and 45 cents respectively. In terms of Australian currency 10 cents equalled about 3d.

May 1941, in charge of the Commander-in-Chief, China Station, with a naval commander at its head who had been brought from retirement and conspicuously lacked practical knowledge of the press, was frequently in conflict with newspapermen. It became all too apparent, then and later, that the Services "were undoubtedly hampered in the Far East through lack of officers experienced in dealing with the press".[2] The Far Eastern Bureau of the British Ministry of Information (headed by an expert in Far Eastern Affairs, who was keenly cooperative towards Australia[3]) and the Malayan Department of Information were also engaged in publicity work, but the Services Press Bureau was of course a vital source of news on which they as well as the newspapermen were dependent. While shortcomings in Malaya were all too real, Brooke-Popham's policy was to emphasise the growing strength of Malay's defences. Muzzled though he was, by the policy of avoiding action which might be considered provocative to Japan, he could at least growl. To make the best of this required a thorough understanding of pressmen and the conditions of their work, with ability to assess the influence of their dispatches upon the mind of the public not only in Malaya but throughout the world. Individuals concerned possessed these qualifications in varying degree. On the whole, the administration of publicity policy through the Services Bureau was a source of dissatisfaction, and resulted in absurdities such as the following extract from a dispatch to a London newspaper in October 1941:

> I bring you good news—there is no need to worry about the strength of the Air Force that will oppose the Japanese should they send their army and navy southward. . . . The Air Force is on the spot, and is waiting for the enemy—clouds of bombers and fighters are hidden in the jungle, and are ready to move out on to camouflaged tarmacs of our secret landing fields and roar into action at the first move of the Japanese towards this part of the world. . . . The planes . . . consist of the most modern planes Britain, Australia and America are producing.[4]

In view of the presence of many Japanese in Malaya and the discrepancy between such statements and the facts, it seemed highly improbable that the Japanese Intelligence services would be misled;[5] but over-optimistic publicity did contribute to a false sense of security in Malaya, and to undue complacency as a result. An American radio reporter quoted an American girl who returned from a visit to the United States as saying:

> There is so much flag-waving and war spirit and talk about the war at home that it's a relief to get back to the peace and quiet and indifference of Singapore.[6]

While the A.I.F. in Malaya was preparing to fight, if need be, at this approach to Australia, the course of affairs in East Asia was largely an

---
[2] Brooke-Popham, *Despatch on Operations in the Far East*, p. 547.
[3] Mr R. H. Scott (later Sir Robert Scott, KCMG, CBE). Scott had held a succession of consular posts in the Far East between 1927 and 1939 when he was seconded to the British Ministry of Information.
[4] Quoted in *Straits Times*, 27 Oct 1941.
[5] There was even a Japanese-owned newspaper, which at one stage advocated administration of Malaya being handed over to Australia.
[6] C. Brown, *Suez to Singapore* (1942), p. 182.

intensification, with German encouragement, of already existing trends towards war in the area. Possibly the advantage gained by Japan in dictating the settlement of the struggle between Indo-China and Thailand prompted the Japanese Foreign Minister to declare in February 1941 that Japan was fully prepared to act as mediator, or take whatever action was calculated to restore normal conditions, not only in "Greater East Asia", but anywhere in the world. He was told, however, by the British Prime Minister that "in a cause of the kind for which we are fighting, a cause which is in no way concerned with territory, trade, or material gains, but affecting the whole future of humanity, there can be no question of compromise or parley". Matsuoka subsequently declared that his words were not to be regarded as an offer of mediation in the European war. This retraction was stated in the House of Commons to have followed consultation with Germany; and in fact the German Foreign Minister, von Ribbentrop, was at the time seeking to persuade Japan, through General Oshima, Japanese Ambassador to Berlin, that a surprise intervention by Japan was bound to keep America out of the war. America, he argued, was not armed and would hesitate to expose her navy to any risks west of Hawaii, if Japan had first made a surprise attack. It was unlikely that America would declare war if she then would have to stand by helplessly while Japan took the Philippines without America being able to do anything about it. In view of the coming "New World Order", it seemed to be in the interest of Japan to secure for herself, during the war, the position she wanted to hold in the Far East at the time of a peace treaty.[7]

In an order dated 5th March about collaboration with Japan, Herr Hitler decreed that it must be the aim of the collaboration based on the Tripartite Pact to induce Japan, as soon as possible, to take active measures in the Far East. The High Commands of the branches of the armed forces must comply in a comprehensive and generous manner with Japanese desires for information about German war and combat experience, and for assistance in military economics and in technical matters. Among the guiding principles he laid down were (1) the common aim was to be to force England to the ground quickly, thereby keeping the United States out of the war (Hitler added that beyond this Germany had no political, military or economic interests in the Far East which would give occasion for any reservations with regard to Japanese intentions); (2) the seizure of Singapore, as the key British position in the Far East, would mean a decisive success for the three Powers; (3) attacks on other bases of British naval power—extending to those of American naval power only if the entry of the United States into the war could not be prevented—would result in weakening the enemy's power in that region, and also, like the attack on sea communications, in tying down substantial forces of all kinds.[8]

---
[7] *The Trial of German Major War Criminals*, Part 2, pp. 264-5.
[8] *War Trials*, Part 2, pp. 266-7.

Growing concern with the situation in the Far East from another viewpoint was reflected in a series of talks, which were an outcome of the Singapore conference of October 1940 and were designed to establish full cooperation between the participants. At a conference held in Singapore in February 1941 between United Kingdom, Dutch and Australian representatives,[9] with United States observers in attendance, plans for mutual reinforcements, principally of air forces and submarines, were made. As already mentioned, the Australian Chiefs of Staff had advised earlier in February that Australia should arrange with the Dutch to station Australian forces in the Indies and particularly in Timor, if war broke out with Japan. As a result of the February conference at Singapore the Australian Government agreed to hold units in readiness to reinforce the garrisons both of Dutch Timor and of Ambon Island, also administered by the Dutch. Both of these, lying between New Guinea and Java, could be regarded as near stepping-stones to Australia from the north. Australia agreed also to provide an air striking force, based on Darwin, to operate from advanced bases to be established in collaboration with the Dutch at these two places. It was decided that immediate steps should be taken secretly to dispatch to them equipment and other requirements for Australian Army and Air Force units. The Australian Government was greatly concerned at the failure of the conference to draw up a coordinated naval plan for eastern waters and considered that early completion of such a plan was of paramount importance. Although the conference did not propose allocation of naval forces to operate from Darwin, the War Cabinet subsequently decided that the development of Darwin as a defended base for operations of the three Services must continue.

As to Mr Churchill's pledge that if Japan set about invading Australia or New Zealand on a large scale, Britain would cut her losses in the Mediterranean and proceed to their aid, the War Cabinet noted a cable sent from London on 12th March by Mr Menzies, which made it evident that he had been talking to others than Mr Churchill on the subject. In the course of the cable he said:

> It was stressed to me that such a step would not be practicable until after the lapse of a considerable period, and might not be possible even then. It was urged that it was imperative to resolve a general declaration of this nature into a plan of specific measures that really would be possible in event of such a contingency arising. There are large forces in the Middle East, including three Australian divisions, and they could not be just left to their fate. To withdraw them, however, would take time, shipping would have to be provided, convoys organised, and naval protection afforded in the meantime. Much could happen in the Far East during that period, and it was unwise to delude ourselves regarding the immediate dispatch of a fleet of capital ships to Singapore if such reinforcement was impossible. It was far better to face the facts by preparing a definite plan of naval reinforcement east of Suez on a progressive basis according to the probable outcome of events in the Mediterranean.

Mr Menzies added that he had asked that this be done.

---

[9] Maj-Gen J. Northcott, Deputy Chief of the General Staff, and Col W. M. Anderson, Director of Staff Duties, were the Australian Army representatives.

The Singapore conference in February had agreed upon a list of possible actions by Japan which from a strategic viewpoint would demand counter-action. The action which the conference thought most likely was the development of Japan's hold on Indo-China and Thailand and an attack on Malaya with the object of capturing Singapore. The Australian War Cabinet decided to ask the United Kingdom Government whether a satisfactory procedure could be evolved to ensure that counter-measures against Japan when necessary could be taken without delay. In London, after considering the conclusions reached at the February conference, the Chiefs of Staff declared that any decision whether or not to help the Dutch would have to be made by the British Government at the time the issue arose.

In Washington at this time, as mentioned earlier, discussions were taking place between British and American staff officers. In consequence the British Chiefs of Staff appointed permanent representatives in the American national capital to maintain contact with the American Chiefs of Staff —a move that was to have important consequences in the development of cooperation between the forces of the two great powers.

The arrival of the 6,000 Australians at Singapore had greatly encouraged Air Chief Marshal Brooke-Popham, who urged that Hong Kong should be reinforced with two additional battalions, making a total of six, and that the policy be adopted of holding that port against the Japanese until it could be relieved and used as a base for offensive operations against them. The Chiefs of Staff in London disagreed; Mr Churchill declared that there was "not the slightest chance of holding Hong Kong or relieving it"; but Brooke-Popham did not then change his opinion.

In March and April a second Indian division arrived in Singapore. It was the 9th, under Major-General Barstow,[2] but consisted of only two brigades (the third having been sent at the last moment to Iraq) and had no artillery. There were now five Indian brigades and one Australian brigade in Malaya, and three British regular battalions (not including three that formed parts of Indian brigades); but only enough field artillery to provide the normal quota of one division; and no tanks. However, the garrison had been more than trebled since the fall of France and Holland, and had acquired more than the additional 12 battalions of infantry recommended by the October conference; but, as has been mentioned, that conference considered that an additional 12 battalions would suffice only if the first-line air strength had been increased to 566 aircraft. Not one-fifth as many aircraft were yet in sight.

Air Vice-Marshal Pulford[3] succeeded Air Vice-Marshal Babington as Air Officer Commanding Far East Command on 24th April 1941. In May

---

[2] Maj-Gen A. E. Barstow, CIE, MC. GOC 9 Indian Div 1941-42. Regular soldier; b. 17 Mar 1888. Killed in action 28 Jan 1942.

[3] Air Vice-Marshal C. W. H. Pulford, CB, OBE, AFC. AOC No. 20 Group 1940-41; AOC RAF Far East 1941-42. Regular airman; b. Agra, India, 26 Jan 1892. Believed died about 10 Mar 1942.

two more new senior commanders arrived in Malaya. Lieut-General Percival[4] took over as G.O.C. Malaya in place of General Bond on 16th May, and about the same time Lieut-General Sir Lewis Heath[5] and the headquarters of III Indian Corps arrived. The fact that there were now three divisions in the field plus the equivalent of a fourth had made the addition of a corps headquarters essential.

General Percival had been commissioned at the age of 26 upon the outbreak of the 1914-1918 War, in which he rose to command a battalion, then to temporary command of the 54th Brigade, and won three decorations. His service between the wars included four years (1925-29) with the West African Frontier Force, and two (1936-38) as a senior staff officer in Malaya. He had then become a brigadier, on the General Staff of Aldershot Command. He had the unusual distinction of having graduated not only at the Army Staff College at Camberley but at the Naval Staff College, and of having attended a course at the Imperial Defence College. This had made him a member of a relatively small group from which senior commanders and chiefs of the general staff were customarily drawn. He had gone to France with the British Expeditionary Force soon after the outbreak of war in Europe; but in April 1940 had returned to London to become one of the three Assistant Chiefs of the Imperial General Staff. After the fall of France he asked to be transferred to a field formation and was given command of the 44th Division, recently evacuated from France and needing extensive reorganisation. Percival was unassuming, considerate and conciliatory, but whether he possessed the imagination, drive and ruthlessness required of a commander in circumstances such as were to arise in Malaya remained to be seen.

He had, however, challenged the then current strategical assumptions about Malaya when in 1937, as a staff officer there, he prepared an appreciation and plan of attack on Singapore from the point of view of the Japanese. The fundamental assumptions were that the British fleet would arrive at Singapore within a maximum of seventy days of outbreak of war with Japan; that its arrival would automatically avert danger of Singapore being captured; and that the role of the garrison was merely to hold out for that period. Percival held that as a result of the political situation in Europe it was unlikely that the British fleet would be able to reach Singapore in the time. He outlined a form of attack on Malaya which could be undertaken in such circumstances. This consisted of operations to seize airfields in southern Thailand and northern Malaya, and naval and air facilities in Borneo, preliminary to capture of Singapore itself. Percival consequently deduced that defence of northern Malaya and of Johore were of increased importance and that stronger forces were urgently needed. This prophetic viewpoint was subsequently adopted in prin-

---
[4] Lt-Gen A. E. Percival, CB, DSO, OBE, MC. GOC 43 Div 1940, 44 Div 1940-41, Malaya 1941-42. Regular soldier; b. Aspenden, Herts, Eng, 26 Dec 1887.

[5] Lt-Gen Sir Lewis Heath, KBE, CB, CIE, DSO, MC. Comd 5 Indian Div 1939-41; GOC III Indian Corps 1941-42. Regular soldier; b. Poona, India, 23 Nov 1885. Died 10 Jan 1954.

(Australian War Memorial)

The Australians were soon hard at work. Long route marches helped to harden them and make them familiar with the Malayan countryside.

(Australian War Memorial)

A cricket match between two 27th Brigade teams, played in September 1941, soon after the brigade's arrival in Malaya.

A delivery of mail to the 2/15th Field Regiment, after the outbreak of war.

(*Australian War Memorial*)

Australian troops moving through thick jungle including pandanus palms.

(*Australian War Memorial*)

ciple by the Chiefs of Staff in London, and it was not surprising therefore that Percival was chosen to help implement the resultant new defence plan.

General Heath was two years older than Percival and until recently had been senior to him. Before the 1914-1918 War he had served for three years with the King's African Rifles; in that war he fought in Mesopotamia and suffered permanent injury to one arm. In 1940 he commanded the 5th Indian Division in the operations against the Italians in Abyssinia, and thus he had more recent experience of large-scale warfare than any other senior commander in Malaya. Heath's corps, with headquarters at Kuala Lumpur, included the 9th Indian Division, now deployed on the east coast of Malaya, and the 11th Indian Division, in northern Malaya. On Singapore Island and in eastern Johore Major-General Simmons[6] (who had served in Palestine during the disturbances of the late 'thirties) commanded the equivalent of another division—1st Malaya, 2nd Malaya and 12th Indian Brigades—and the coastal and anti-aircraft artillery. General Percival's reserve was the 8th Australian Division. The two Indian divisions each possessed only two brigades, and were short of artillery; the Australian division possessed only one brigade.

Burma also gained some reinforcements. At the October conference it had been held that five brigades and ancillary troops were required in Burma, which at that time had the equivalent of two brigades, mostly of Burman infantry units. The establishment of a Burma Army had begun only in 1937, when Burma was separated from India. When war broke out four battalions of the Burma Rifles were in existence, and these were now being increased to eight. The Burma Rifles, however, were considered to be of only limited value. Consequently when, in the course of 1941, two Indian brigade groups, the 13th and 16th, arrived in Burma, they represented a far stronger relative reinforcement than their mere numbers suggested. India had been the main source of military reinforcements for the Far East and her army was now being fairly rapidly expanded; but successive crises in the Middle East and Iraq and Persia (Iran) had drawn away one new Indian formation after another. By June these theatres had claimed all but three of the eight Indian divisions formed in 1939 and 1940.

It must have become increasingly clear to Japan that she could not count upon America standing aside in a Pacific war; but what of Russia? Matsuoka had visited Moscow, Berlin and Rome during March and April, and returned with a pact of neutrality between Japan and the Soviet Union (the Soviet having been warned by the Allies, in the meantime, that Germany was preparing to attack her). This eased the commitments of both countries on the Far Eastern borders where Japanese and Russian forces faced each other. It paved the way for westward movement if need

---

[6] Maj-Gen F. Keith Simmons, CBE, MVO, MC. Comd Shanghai Area, British Troops in China 1939-40, Singapore Fortress Troops 1941-42. Regular soldier; b. 21 Feb 1888. Died 22 Sep 1952.

be of Russia's eastern forces, and facilitated southward deployment of Japan's.[7]

In Berlin Matsuoka told Ribbentrop, the German Foreign Minister, that he was doing everything to reassure the English about Singapore. It might be possible that his attitude toward the English would appear to be friendly in words and in acts. However, Germany should not be deceived by that. He assumed this attitude not only to reassure the British, but also to fool the pro-British and pro-American elements until, one day, he would suddenly open the attack on Singapore. Having thus bared his character, Matsuoka continued that the Japanese Navy had a low estimate of the threat from the British Navy. It also held the view that it could smash the American Navy without trouble. However, it was afraid that the Americans would not take up the battle with their fleet, and that thus the conflict with the United States might be dragged out to five years. This possibility, he said, caused considerable worry in Japan.

Evidently Matsuoka was not "through with toadying" as he had stated on a previous occasion; but his cagey lack of precision about a Japanese attack on Singapore was not appreciated by those with whom he now dallied. A decision to attack Russia in the spring of 1941 had been made by Hitler on 31st July 1940, but on his orders Japan was not told of it.

In Singapore in April there were staff talks between American, Dutch and British officers, including representatives of Australia and New Zealand.[8] The British and Dutch delegates learnt that the United States considered Singapore very important but not absolutely vital; that its loss, while undesirable, could be accepted. While maintaining at Hawaii a naval force superior to the Japanese, the United States would if necessary reinforce her Atlantic Fleet from her Pacific Fleet. She intended to use the Pacific Fleet offensively against Japanese mandated islands and sea communications, and to support British naval forces in the South Pacific, but did not intend to reinforce her Asiatic Fleet; she did not expect that the Philippines would hold out very long against determined Japanese attack, and anticipated being forced to withdraw from those islands.

In the main, the conference decided that a defensive policy would have to be maintained in the eastern theatre against superior Japanese forces until Allied naval and air strength was substantially increased. Surface craft would be used primarily for the protection of vital sea communications, and submarines and aircraft to attack Japanese southbound expeditions. The likelihood of attacks upon Australia and New Zealand as initial Japanese operations was ruled out, whether or not the United States remained neutral. The British Commander-in-Chief, China Station, would exercise unified strategical direction over all the naval forces of the

---

[7] *The Trial of the German Major War Criminals*, Part 2, p. 269. Field Marshal Keitel, Hitler's Chief of Staff, later stated that the Soviet was enabled in the next few months to transfer 18 to 20 divisions from the east to help stem Germany's advance.

[8] The Australian delegation comprised: Admiral Sir Ragnar Colvin; Paymaster Capt J. B. Foley; Col H. G. Rourke and Gp Capt F. M. Bladin.

associated powers in the eastern theatre, except those employed in local defence or operating under the Commander-in-Chief, United States Asiatic Fleet. Part of this would come under orders of the Commander-in-Chief, China, immediately, and the rest under his strategic direction when Manila became untenable. Similar strategic direction of air forces would be exercised by Brooke-Popham.

The plan, known as ADB-1, adopted by the conference was rejected by the United States authorities, largely because Admiral Stark and General Marshall did not like its strategic features or what they considered to be its political implications; and particularly the possibility that its acceptance might lead to the American Asiatic Fleet being deployed in an area that was not strategically valuable to America. The British staffs, however, drew up a plan designated PLENAPS, based on ADB-1, for emergency use. As events were to show, it was as well they did.

Differences of opinion persisted between Mr Churchill and his military advisers on the relative importance of the Middle East and Malaya in Britain's grand strategy. In April Mr Churchill repeated in a directive his view that the likelihood of Japan entering the war was remote, and if she did the United States would almost certainly enter it on Britain's side. Meanwhile there was no need to make further dispositions for the defence of Malaya and Singapore beyond "the modest arrangements already in progress". The Chief of the General Staff disagreed; and the Future Operational Planning Section presented to the Defence Committee in June a paper in which, referring to the Far East, they said:

> The threat in this area is only potential; consequently it tends to become obscured by other threats which are more grimly real. But, should it develop, this threat may bring even greater dangers than those we now face. Singapore is of course the key. . . . It is vital to take, as soon as possible, the necessary measures to secure the defence of Singapore.

Early in May the Australian War Cabinet, to which the significance of the decision to concentrate against Hitler first if war broke out with Japan was becoming more specific, had held an emergency meeting to consider the proposed transfer of units of the United States Pacific Fleet to the Atlantic. In general terms it concurred in the plan; but in a cable to the British Government, it urged that America's Pacific Fleet be not reduced below a certain limit; also that consideration be given to the immediate release of adequate British capital units to reinforce Singapore if war against Japan broke out. The War Cabinet approved, subject to certain conditions, plans for coordinated strategic command of forces in the Far East, including American forces. It noted the view of the Commander-in-Chief, Far East, that reinforcement of Malaya by land and air forces since October had so materially strengthened his position that he was most optimistic of the ability of Singapore to continue to operate as a fleet base.

The realities of the situation in the Far East, particularly as they affected Australia, were more sharply defined when Mr Menzies returned to Australia from his visit to England, bringing with him comprehensive

British reports on the military situation. Even though the review he had obtained of the defence position in the Pacific from the United Kingdom Chiefs of Staff might not be very encouraging in certain respects (he said to the War Cabinet on 10th June) Australia now certainly knew where she stood, the degree to which she must rely on her own efforts, and the necessity for expanding them to the utmost extent. He continued that Mr Churchill had no conception of the British Dominions as separate entities, and the more distant the problem from the heart of the Empire the less he thought of it. (Menzies added, however, that if Churchill were driven from office it would be a calamity.) Certain remarks in the course of the United Kingdom review about the land and air forces in Malaya and their equipment indicated a degree of complacency about the defence of the Pacific region, he said, and "it is now evident that, for too long, we readily accepted the general assurances about the defence of this area".

As to Britain's ability to send a fleet to the Far East, the Chiefs of Staff in London had replied: "All we can say is that we should send a battle cruiser and a carrier to the Indian Ocean. Our ability to do more must be judged entirely on the situation at the time." In view of this, said Menzies, Australia must re-insure herself against the most unfavourable likelihood by the maximum local defence effort. On the question of what would constitute an act of war by Japan, Mr Menzies quoted a cable from the British Government agreeing that any attack on the line from Malaya to New Zealand through the Netherlands East Indies equally concerned all affected parties, and must be dealt with as an attack on the whole line.

The passages in the London Chiefs of Staffs' review to which Menzies referred as indicating "a degree of complacency" were to the effect that the land forces in Malaya should reach their full strength (the 26-battalion total) by the end of April 1941, "with the exception of certain artillery units"; it was not practicable to give firm dates regarding arrival of the various items of army equipment needed in Malaya, but the deficiencies were not serious "with the exception of anti-aircraft and anti-tank guns, small arms ammunition and artillery ammunition"; most of the 450 shore-based aircraft which the Japanese could marshal for an attack in the Far East were of obsolete types, and the Chiefs of Staff had no reason to believe that Japanese standards were even comparable with those of the Italians;[9] though British air strength in the Far East was below that neces-

---

[9] Colonel Thyer, of General Bennett's staff, had a long discussion later with three of Brooke-Popham's senior officers, representing the navy, army and air force. "I shall never forget," he related, "the overall opinion they gave me of the Japanese Army and Air Force. It can be summed up in the expression used by the army man who had been in Shanghai and Hong Kong—'The Japanese Army is a bubble waiting to be pricked.'"

Compton Mackenzie (*Eastern Epic*, 1951, p. 227) wrote: "General Percival . . . was depending for his judgment about Japanese intentions and Japanese fighting efficiency on the Far East Combined Bureau, and that efficiency was always under-estimated. Yet Lieut-Colonel Wards, an expert about the Japanese Army who came to advise the military authorities in Malaya, was insistent that a Japanese battalion was, in training, discipline and intrepid efficiency, as good as a crack battalion of the unmilked Indian Army of 1939 and that meant as good as any battalion anywhere in the world. People shook their heads over what they considered the 'defeatism' of Wards' opinions, and his expert knowledge was not invited again." (The term "unmilked" meant that trained officers and men had not been drawn off, as was to happen, for new formations.)

sary for reasonable security in the absence of a fleet, they did not consider that in the present situation Britain was running more serious risks there than elsewhere, but every effort was being made to restore the balance at the earliest possible moment. (The Chiefs of Staff also said that the Brewster Buffalo appeared to be eminently satisfactory and would probably prove "more than a match for any Japanese aircraft".) Menzies' cable from London about the practicability of fulfilling Churchill's pledge that Britain would cut her losses in the Mediterranean if it were necessary for her to proceed to Australia's aid, was supported in effect by a declaration of the Chiefs of Staff in London. They said that the security of Britain's position in the Middle East remained essential to her strategy for the defeat of Germany, and "any withdrawal, however small, would involve the movement of forces by sea, and the necessity for retaining a strong fleet in the Mediterranean would be increased rather than lessened during the period of such withdrawal. Even if it were decided to abandon our Mediterranean interests, the fleet would have to remain until the end in order to cover the withdrawal of the armies."

Thus, in a matter of fundamental importance to Australia, because of its bearing upon what forces she could send overseas consistent with her own safety, a choice had to be made between Mr Churchill's rather rhetorical pledge and what his experts considered practicable.

The War Cabinet decided that a United Kingdom suggestion that two additional infantry brigades be sent to Malaya could not be considered apart from a complete review of the manpower situation; but next day (11th June) in response to a request from Brooke-Popham a compromise was reached. It was decided that of the two A.I.F. infantry brigades in Australia, the 23rd, which had been sent to Darwin in April, in conformity with the agreement to reinforce Ambon and Timor in an emergency, should remain there; but the 27th, then at Bathurst in New South Wales, should go to Malaya.

After the departure of the 27th Brigade Group the A.I.F. troops remaining in Australia would include in addition to the 23rd Brigade Group, the 2/4th Machine Gun and the 2/4th Pioneer Battalions, and four recently-formed Independent Companies. These companies were partly officered from the 8th Division, and two of them were to take part in the operations described in this volume.

In mid-1940 the British Army formed a number of commando units or independent companies, one of whose tasks would be to make raids on German-occupied territory. Later in the year the War Office offered to send a group of instructors to Australia to train Australian and New Zealand independent companies on lines developed in Britain by the enterprising regular officers, explorers, ski-runners and others who had built up the British companies.[1] The mission to Australia, which had arrived in November 1940, comprised Lieut-Colonel J. C. Mawhood, Captains

---

[1] See D. W. Clarke, *Seven Assignments* (1948); F. Spencer Chapman, *The Jungle is Neutral* (1949); B. J. Callinan, *Independent Company* (1953).

Calvert[2] and Spencer Chapman,[3] and two sergeants. Both Calvert and Chapman had been members of a ski battalion formed early in 1940 for service in Finland. These chose as a suitable area for a guerilla warfare school the rugged national park of Wilson's Promontory in southern Victoria and there, in February 1941, "No. 7 Infantry Training Centre" was established at Foster.[4] Volunteers were called for and inevitably some came from units of the 23rd and 27th Brigades and other parts of the 8th Division which seemed likely to remain on garrison duty in Australia for some time. There, every six weeks, enough officers and N.C.O's were trained to staff one Australian and one New Zealand independent company, and in the second half of 1941 four Australian companies were formed. The training, wrote Chapman later, was

as practical as we could make it. Calvert, with his infectious enthusiasm, taught them how to blow up everything from battleships to brigadiers. . . . I taught them how to get a party from A to B and back by day or night in any sort of country and arrive in a fit state to carry out their task. This included all kinds of sidelines —a new conception of fitness, knowledge of the night sky, what to wear, what to take and how to carry it, what to eat and how to cook it, how to live off the country, tracking, memorizing routes, and how to escape if caught by the enemy.[5]

Each company had 17 officers and 256 men and possessed its own signals and its own medical officer and detachment. It was thus more in the nature of a streamlined battalion than a reinforced company. In August 1941 Calvert and Chapman were sent to Burma and Singapore respectively to instruct in bush warfare, and the Wilson's Promontory School was carried on by Australians they had trained.

On 15th August the 27th Brigade, with some eight months' training behind it, arrived in Singapore. It travelled in three Dutch liners—*Johan Van Oldenbarneveldt*, *Marnix Van St Aldegonde* and *Sibajak*—having embarked at Sydney and Melbourne in late July. The principal army units in the convoy were:

> Headquarters 27th Brigade
> 2/26th Battalion
> 2/29th Battalion
> 2/30th Battalion
> 2/15th Field Regiment (armed with mortars only)
> 2/12th Field Company
> 2/6th Field Park Company
> 2/10th Field Ambulance

Despite Brooke-Popham's policy of emphasising the growing strength of Malaya's defences, the arrival was given bare mention in an official "handout".

---

[2] Brig J. M. Calvert, DSO; RE. Comd 77 Chindit Bde, Burma. Regular soldier; b. 6 Mar 1913.
[3] Lt-Col F. Spencer Chapman, DSO. 5/Seaforth Highlanders; i/c left behind parties, Malaya, 1942-45. Schoolmaster; b. London, 10 May 1907.
[4] It was commanded until May by Major W. J. R. Scott, DSO, and afterwards by Major F. S. Love, DSO, MC.
[5] Spencer Chapman, *The Jungle is Neutral*, pp. 8-9.

Meanwhile important changes had occurred in the staff of the 8th Division. In July Brigadier Marshall, who had been ill for some time, relinquished command of the 27th Brigade, Lieut-Colonel O'Donnell[6] replaced Lieut-Colonel Scriven in command of the divisional engineers, and Colonel Rourke, Bennett's chief staff officer, left Malaya to become the artillery commander of the 7th Division, then in Syria. His departure left the 8th Division with only two regular staff officers—Kappe and Dawkins—who, before 1939, had graduated from the Staff Colleges at Camberley or Quetta. In other A.I.F. formations the quota had generally been much higher.[7]

Were the new appointments to be made from within the 8th Division or should the considerable talent now existing in the A.I.F. as a whole be utilised? Among the most senior battalion commanders in the Middle East in July 1941 there were, after five campaigns, several with outstanding claims for higher rank: for example, Eather, who had commanded the 2/1st Battalion throughout the Libyan campaign, and was then administering command of the 16th Brigade in Palestine; King, who had been a Grade II staff officer on the 6th Division in Libya and had commanded the 2/5th Battalion in Greece and Syria; Moten, who had led the 2/27th Battalion throughout the Syrian campaign; Martin, who had commanded the 2/9th Battalion at Giarabub and was then leading it at Tobruk. (Soon each of these was to be promoted, and would lead a brigade with distinction throughout the war.) Regular soldiers with qualifications similar to Rourke's and more recent experience of operations were also available for important general staff appointments. The more senior of these included Irving, who had trained in England after the first war, had spent two years at Quetta in the middle 'thirties and was then Blamey's liaison officer at Middle East Headquarters; Wells, who had been at Quetta in 1934-36, had been the senior liaison officer of the Anzac Corps in Greece and would soon become G.S.O.1 of the 9th Division; Elliott, who had trained abroad at Singapore in the early 'twenties, had been to Quetta and was then a Grade II staff officer on the I Australian Corps and would in November become the G.S.O.1 of the 7th Division. Obviously each of these was well qualified to fill the vacant post, and would bring with him experience of recent operations in the Middle East.

On the other hand, Bennett, although commanding only two brigades, had long sought powers of promotion delegated to General Blamey as commander of the Australian Corps. When it was learned that he favoured the appointment as G.S.O.1 of his Chief Signals Officer, Lieut-Colonel Thyer, who as brigade major of the 8th Brigade for three years before the war had gained a reputation as an exponent of infantry tactics, Army Headquarters hastened to propose him. Major Kappe was promoted to fill the now vacant post of Chief Signals Officer. To fill the appointment

---
[6] Col I. J. O'Donnell, OBE, ED, VX43938. OC 2/10 Fd Coy; CRE 8 Aust Div. Civil engineer; of Camberwell, Vic; b. Myrtleford, Vic, 6 May 1905.

[7] For example, in January 1941, there were on the headquarters of I Corps 12 such officers, in the 6th Division, six, in 7th Division eight, and in the 9th Division (then forming) three.

of commander of the 27th Brigade Bennett sought the promotion of Maxwell, then commanding the 2/19th Battalion, who though junior to some of the battalion commanders in the 8th Division, was of equable temperament, had become familiar with Malaya, and was highly regarded by Bennett as a leader. Eventually this was agreed to, and Major Anderson was promoted to command the 2/19th.[8]

The 27th Brigade having arrived, the A.I.F. in Malaya thus consisted of the headquarters of the 8th Division and two of its three "brigade groups"—the term used to describe an infantry brigade plus its share of artillery, engineers and other supporting troops. There were two field regiments (one armed with old 18-pounders and the other with 3-inch mortars) but the third remained in Australia; the anti-tank regiment (armed partly with the new 2-pounder but partly with 75-mm guns and captured Italians guns) lacked one battery, which had been sent to Rabaul. The division was without its "divisional cavalry", a unit then armed with light tanks and tracked machine-gun carriers, useful for reconnaissance or pursuit. The 8th Divisional Cavalry had been sent to the Middle East, and its name changed to 9th Divisional Cavalry, the intention being to attach it to that division. Already, in June and July, it had fought as part of the 7th Australian Division and later the 6th British Division in Syria.

Furthermore, in battle a divisional commander would normally have under his command certain fighting units from the "corps troops" held at the disposal of the senior commander. These might include a machine-gun battalion (equipped with the heavier belt-fed Vickers gun as distinct from the light machine-gun which the infantry normally carried[9]), a pioneer battalion trained to fight as infantry or to carry out relatively simple engineering work, heavy tanks, anti-aircraft artillery and additional field artillery and signals. Possession of all three brigades and a pool of corps troops enabled a divisional commander to plan to send two brigades into battle and yet hold in reserve a third brigade and groups of corps and divisional units—cavalry, machine-gunners, pioneers—equal in fire power to a fourth. The Australian division lacked such a reserve. If both brigades were committed there would be little left.

---

[8] In August, when Maj-Gen Rowell visited Malaya on his way from the Middle East to become Deputy Chief of the General Staff, he discussed with Bennett the question of future appointments to the rank of brigadier and Grade 1 staff officers, and said that it would ultimately cripple the efficiency of the 8th Division if such appointments came only from within the division. "The proper answer," he wrote to General Sturdee soon afterwards, "is to consider AIF (ME) and AIF (Malaya) as one pool." After the war Bennett said that he thought this would have been a good arrangement, provided that the exchange worked both ways.

The principal appointments on the staff of the 8th Division in August were: *GOC*: Maj-Gen H. G. Bennett; *GSO1*: Col J. H. Thyer; *GSO2*: Maj C. B. Dawkins; *LO*: Maj C. J. A. Moses; *AA&QMG*: Col J. R. Broadbent; *DAAG*: Capt M. Ashkanasy; *DAQMG*: Maj W. S. Kent Hughes; *ADMS*: Col A. P. Derham; *LSO*: Maj P. L. Head; *DADOS*: Lt-Col L. R. D. Stahle; *DAPM*: Capt W. A. Miller; *CRA*: Brig C. A. Callaghan; *CRE*: Lt-Col I. J. O'Donnell; *CO Sigs*: Lt-Col C. H. Kappe; *CASC*: Lt-Col L. J. A. Byrne.

[9] Some Vickers guns were issued to Australian infantry battalions in Malaya. For instance, they were issued to the 2/30th Battalion in place of Bren guns, at first unavailable, for use in carriers. When they were replaced by Brens, four Vickers guns were retained by the battalion for other use.

CHAPTER 6

AWAITING THE FIRST BLOW

THE thunder of Germany's attack on the Soviet Union had rolled round the world on 22nd June 1941. That Japan had not been told it was pending was a blow to her pride; and the violation of the German-Soviet Non-aggression Pact of 1939 did nothing to inspire confidence in German pledges. Despite his having urged so recently upon Matsuoka that Japan should attack Singapore, Ribbentrop cabled on 10th July to General Ott, German Ambassador in Tokyo, asking him to "employ all available means in further insisting upon Japan's entry into the war against Russia at the soonest possible date". Ribbentrop added "the natural objective still remains that we and Japan join hands on the Trans-Siberian railroad before winter starts".[1]

Earlier, Japan might have been glad of opportunity to gain control of Vladivostok and Russia's maritime provinces; but now she had no intention of abandoning her southward advance. Matsuoka was replaced as Foreign Minister by Admiral Toyoda. On 2nd July an Imperial Conference in Tokyo decided to continue efforts to settle the "China Incident" (the euphemism by which the Japanese referred to their military failure in China), secure all Indo-China, and proceed with preparations for war with Britain and the United States. On 14th July, Japan demanded the right to occupy bases in southern Indo-China, which would become a joint protectorate of Japan and France; and on the 21st the Vichy French Government yielded. Three days later Japanese troops began moving into southern Indo-China. In this momentous advance they secured the use of a naval base at Camranh Bay, 750 miles from Singapore, and airfields within 300 miles of Kota Bharu, nearest point in Malaya. Having reached Indo-China's western frontier, they directly menaced Thailand, whose Prime Minister had unsuccessfully sought a declaration by the United States and Britain that in attacking Thailand Japan would automatically be at war with them. That the Thais lacked such assurance, and means of successfully resisting Japanese pressure unaided, heightened the danger to Malaya.

In Washington, where talks between the Japanese Ambassador, Admiral Nomura, and the American Secretary of State, Mr Cordell Hull, were now in their fifth month, with no formula for peace in sight, the reaction to the Japanese march into Indo-China was drastic. On 26th July President Roosevelt froze Japanese assets in the United States, thus virtually ending all trade between the two countries; similar action was taken by Britain, and, within a few days, by the Netherlands Indies. On the same day Roosevelt appointed General Douglas MacArthur, hitherto military adviser to the Philippine Commonwealth under American tutelage, to be com-

---

[1] *The Trial of German Major War Criminals*, Part 2, p. 273.

mander of the United States Army Forces in the Far East; and ordered that the Philippine Army be embodied in the American Army.

In 1934 the United States had made an agreement with the "Commonwealth of the Philippines" whereby the Commonwealth would become an autonomous republic in July 1946. In 1935 General MacArthur was appointed military adviser to President Quezon (who in 1936 made him a field marshal[2]). He borrowed two American officers, Majors Dwight D. Eisenhower (subsequently President of the United States of America)

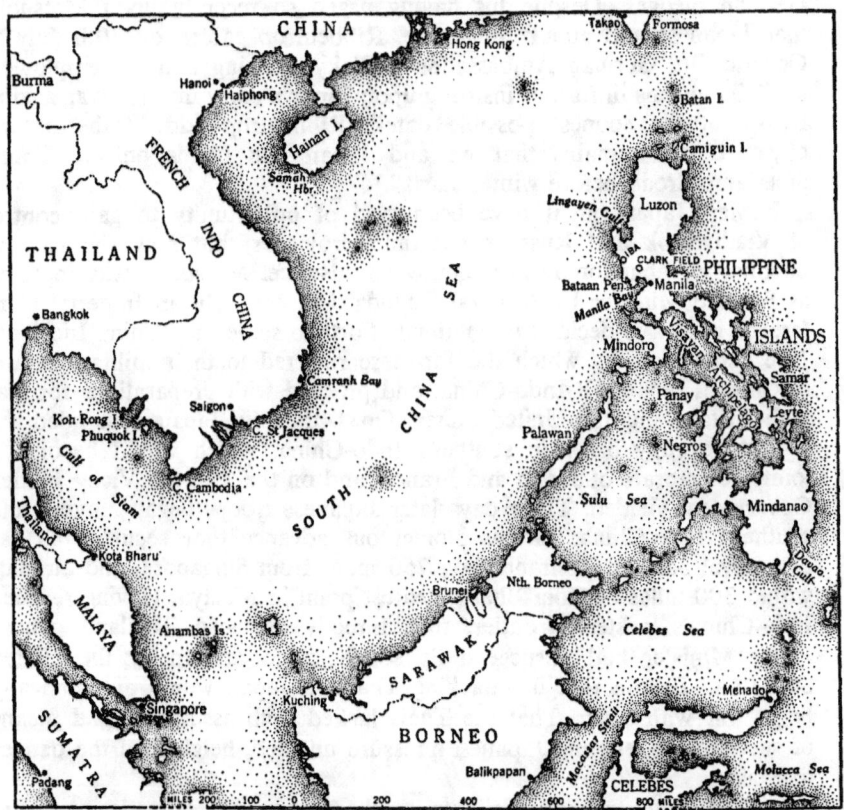

and James B. Ord (accidentally killed in 1938) for his general staff. Eisenhower and Ord drafted a plan whereby a Filipino army of 200,000, including trained reserves, was to be formed by 1946. Service was to be compulsory; six months' continuous training for privates, one year for N.C.O's and eighteen months for reserve officers. Professional officers were to be trained at a military academy modelled on America's West Point. The annual quota was to rise from 20,000 in 1937 to 35,000 in 1941. The force was to be organised in small divisions 7,500 strong.

---

[2] The braided cap which MacArthur wore thereafter was that of a field marshal in the Philippine Army.

A nucleus for the new army was drawn from the Philippine Constabulary, and some twenty Filipino officers were lent from the Philippine Scouts, a locally-enlisted corps which was and would remain a part of the United States Army. From 1938 onwards potential officers were selected from the ranks also, given six months' training, and commissioned pending the arrival of subalterns from the military academy.[3]

General MacArthur was an eminent soldier who had been Chief of Staff of the United States Army from 1930 to 1935. He had served briefly in France in 1918, first as senior staff officer of a division and, from August to November, as a brigade commander; and in the Far East as a young officer from 1903 to 1906, again from 1922 to 1925, and in 1928.

For many years the American staffs had accepted a plan whereby, in a war with Japan, only the Manila Bay area in the Philippines would be strongly defended, it being considered impossible to hold the whole archipelago. In February 1941, however, General MacArthur, as a retired American Army officer employed by the Philippine Government, wrote to the United States Chief of Staff in Washington, explaining that late in 1941 there would be a Philippine Army of some 125,000 men and he was contemplating full-scale defence of all Luzon and the Visayan Archipelago, blocking the straits leading to its inland sea. He asked for 32 artillery guns to assist this project. General George Grunert, then commanding the American garrison in the Philippines, supported the project, but underlined the lack of equipment and the poor condition of the Philippine Army, and the facts that the Philippine Navy consisted of two torpedo boats and the air force had only 45 machines. After his appointment in July 1941 to command all American army forces in the Far East, MacArthur again pressed his proposal, and from August onwards the American forces in the Philippines were gradually reinforced.

As part of this plan for reinforcing the Philippines, the Australian Government, in September 1941, agreed to an American proposal whereby bases suitable for the new American heavy bombers would be constructed at Rabaul, Port Moresby, Townsville and Darwin, thus establishing a friendly air route from Hawaii to the Philippines; and in November B-17s (Flying Fortresses) were flown over this route. Between September and December two tank battalions, some artillery and 35 Flying Fortresses reached the Philippines. By December MacArthur's troops included about 100,000 men of the partially-trained Philippine Army.[4]

The American troops and the Philippine Scouts were well-trained regulars but short of equipment; for example the tanks had armour-piercing but no explosive shells for their 37-mm guns. The artillery pieces were

---

[3] From General Eisenhower's memorandum to President Quezon, 22 June 1942, published in *Military Affairs*, Summer 1948. Eisenhower left the Philippines in 1939.

[4] The US Army troops in the Philippines numbered 19,000 Americans, of whom 8,500 had arrived since July 1941, and 12,000 Filipinos. They included 5,000 of the army air force with some 250 aircraft of which 35 were Flying Fortresses and about 130 were fighters; the 31st Infantry Regt, 4th Marine Regt, artillery and technical troops, two recently-arrived tank battalions of the National Guard, the Philippine Scouts, including three infantry regiments, and the 26th Cavalry. The Philippine Army was eventually organised into ten weak divisions, most of them commanded by American brigadier-generals.

75's and 155's of 1918 vintage; the Philippine Army lacked equipment and had received little training. (The 31st Division had begun to mobilise on the 1st September; all three of its infantry regiments were not assembled until 25th November, and the mobilisation of the two artillery battalions was not completed until 8th December. On an average the infantrymen had then had between three and four weeks' training; the gunners had not fired a practise shot; no division possessed an anti-tank battalion.)

The American Asiatic Fleet, based on Manila Bay, included a strong flotilla of submarines, a flotilla of destroyers, but only two cruisers, *Houston* and *Marblehead*.

On 25th November MacArthur appointed Major-General Jonathan Wainwright, hitherto commanding the Philippine Division, to North Luzon, where he was to deploy a force of four Filipino divisions (11th, 21st, 31st, 71st) and prepare to meet a Japanese attack in that quarter. MacArthur considered that Wainwright would have until April to make those preparations, as the Japanese would not attack before then.

Thus there were parallels between American problems and policy in the Philippines and British problems and policy in Malaya, the American decisions following the comparable British ones, but a year or so later. In both areas an initial policy of holding only the naval base area had been replaced by a policy of holding a wider area. At length a Commander-in-Chief had been appointed in both areas. The naval forces in both areas were inadequate, and the policy was to rely largely on air defence; but too few aircraft were available. Both commanders possessed a relatively small force of well-trained troops and a larger body of less well-trained ones. Both commanders were excessively optimistic; and both were gravely short of equipment.

The danger that the economic restraints imposed by Britain and the United States upon Japan might precipitate war was evident in an intercepted message from the Japanese Foreign Minister, Admiral Toyoda, on 31st July 1941 to the Ambassador in Berlin, General Oshima, telling him to explain why Japan was moving south instead of against Russia.[5] Commercial and economic relations between Japan and other countries, led by England and the United States, were becoming, he said, "so horribly strained that we cannot endure it much longer". Japan "must take immediate steps to break asunder this ever-strengthening chain of encirclement which is being woven under the guidance of and with the participation of England and the United States, acting like a cunning dragon seemingly asleep". Thus the United States had gained by its interception

---

[5] Japanese diplomatic communications were in various codes. Messages in these "were intercepted and read at the Philippines primarily for the purpose of local information. They were sent, as intercepted, to the Navy Department in one of the Navy's own codes. All intercepted diplomatic traffic was sent to Washington. . . . Intercepted Japanese diplomatic traffic received by the Washington unit was pooled with similar traffic intercepted by the Army and was decrypted and translated by the Navy and the Army. . . . The resulting information was distributed daily . . . to the Chief of Navy Operations, and to others in the Navy Department. The President and the State Department similarly were furnished this information daily." From *Appendix to Narrative Statement of Evidence at Navy Pearl Harbour Investigations*, containing former top secret portions of reports of Pearl Harbour Investigations, made public in 1946.

and decoding system the valuable warning that from now on, at any moment, the storm might break.

The fact that Germany's strength was now being used largely against the Soviet Union gave relief to Britain in some important respects; but to help the Soviet to withstand the German assault, large quantities of weapons and supplies needed elsewhere were diverted to her. "In order to make this immense diversion and to forego the growing flood of American aid without crippling our campaign in the Western Desert," Mr Churchill wrote later, "we had to cramp all preparations which prudence urged for the defence of the Malay Peninsula and our Eastern Empire and possessions against the ever-growing menace of Japan."[6]

In these critical circumstances, and in response to an invitation from President Roosevelt, Mr Churchill set off on 4th August aboard Britain's newest battleship, *Prince of Wales*, to see the American President. They met in Placentia Bay, Newfoundland, on 10th August. The principal news released after the meeting was that they had agreed on an Anglo-American declaration of principles, to become known as the Atlantic Charter, based on a draft by Churchill. In private conference, however, Roosevelt indicated to Churchill that because he was uncertain that he could carry Congress with him in a declaration of war, and because more time was needed to strengthen America's forces, he must seek to delay a break with Japan. He nevertheless agreed to issue a warning, also on the lines of a Churchill draft, that any further Japanese encroachment in the south-west Pacific would produce a situation in which the United States would be compelled to take counter-measures, even though these might lead to war.[7] Though Churchill had hoped for more, he was well pleased, for the Japanese menace lay in his mind in "a sinister twilight" compared with other demands; and he believed that eventual entry of the United States into the war would "overwhelm all evils put together".[8]

Mr Duff Cooper,[9] who had been Minister for Information in the United Kingdom, arrived in Singapore in September. He was commissioned as a Minister of State to investigate the situation in the Far East, and to inquire into the feasibility of setting up an authority to deal on the spot with political questions which were then being referred to the British Cabinet for decision.[1] Australia's desire for a voice in the conduct of affairs at Far Eastern key points was evident in the appointment of Mr Bowden,[2] Australian Government Commissioner in China, as Australian

---

[6] Churchill, *The Second World War*, Vol III, pp. 351-2.
[7] On Cordell Hull's insistence the terms of this warning were greatly toned down.
[8] Churchill, Vol III, pp. 522-3.
[9] Rt Hon Sir Alfred Duff Cooper, GCMG, DSO (later Viscount Norwich). First Lord of Admiralty 1937-38; Minister of Information 1940-41; Ambassador to France 1944-47. B. 1890. Died 1 Jan 1954.
[1] This move recalls that, at General Wavell's request, Mr Oliver Lyttelton had been made Minister of State in the Middle East as a means of overcoming delays hitherto caused by having to refer political problems to London.
[2] V. G. Bowden, CBE. (1915-18: Major RE.) Aust Govt Commissioner in China 1935-41; Aust Govt Representative in Singapore 1941-42. B. Sydney, 28 May 1884. Executed by Japanese 17 Feb 1942.

Government Representative in Singapore, and of Sir Frederic Eggleston[3] as Australia's first Minister to China. Sir Frederic combined eminence as a scholar and a legal authority with political sagacity. Bowden brought to his new task the experience he had gained not only in more than 25 years in China and Japan, but in service with the British Army in France from 1915 to 1919. Divergence in the viewpoint of the Australian and the British Governments and military authorities about the extent and urgency of the need for reinforcements in the Far East had resulted in Sir Earle Page, Australian Minister for Commerce, being given a mission to emphasise Australia's viewpoint in London.

In London in August and September the sending of a battle fleet to Singapore had been under sharp discussion. The Admiralty had recommended that four battleships of the "R" class (completed in 1916-17) should be sent to the Indian Ocean and should be reinforced early in 1942 with two more slow battleships, a battle cruiser and, in an emergency, an aircraft carrier. When he returned from the Atlantic Conference Mr Churchill opposed this plan. Instead of the old, relatively slow battleships, he wished to send to the Indian Ocean the recently-completed battleship, *Duke of York,* an old but fast battle cruiser, and an aircraft carrier. These, he said, would have "a paralyzing effect upon Japanese naval action". The Admiralty held that none of the three new battleships could be spared while there was a possibility of the new German battleship *Tirpitz* making a foray into the Atlantic; that a British fleet smaller than that which Japan was likely to employ (and Japan possessed 10 battleships) would not deter the Japanese from advancing into the Indian Ocean. This difference of opinion continued, but Churchill had his way. At length, late in October, the Admiralty agreed to send the *Prince of Wales,* the battle cruiser *Repulse* and the aircraft carrier *Indomitable* to Singapore.[4] On 3rd November, however, the *Indomitable* ran aground in Jamaica during a training cruise, and no other carrier could be spared.

Meanwhile discussion of future land and air policy in Malaya was being continued. Air Chief Marshal Brooke-Popham and his subordinate commanders decided that they should anticipate a Japanese seizure of Singora, the only port of any size on the east coast of the Kra Isthmus. The proposed operation was given the code-name MATADOR. They estimated that British forces established round Singora would be liable to attack by one division advancing overland from Bangkok and a maximum of two landed from the sea; and decided that a force of three brigade groups supported by six air force squadrons would be needed to take and hold the Singora area. British officers in plain clothes reconnoitred the area; they met Japanese officers, also in plain clothes, doing the same thing.

---

[3] Sir Frederic Eggleston. (Lt 1st AIF.) Aust Minister to China 1941-44, to USA 1944-46. Barrister and solicitor; of Melbourne; b. Brunswick, Vic, 17 Oct 1875. Died 12 Nov 1954.

[4] This episode recalls the remark of Stafford Northcote in 1882: "Argue as you please, you are nowhere, that grand old man, the Prime Minister [Gladstone], insists on the other thing."

On 2nd August General Percival had asked the War Office for reinforcements, insisting that he needed as a minimum a total of 48 battalions. One division was wanted to defend the Perlis-Kedah area; one for Kelantan-Trengganu-Pahang; one, with a tank regiment, for a reserve to III Indian Corps in northern Malaya; one for the defence of Johore; one and a tank regiment for Singapore Island. The Chiefs of Staff accepted this appreciation, but said that they could not provide the reinforcements required. In the event, the only substantial reinforcement to reach Singapore between August and December was the 28th Indian Brigade. which arrived in September, poorly trained and incompletely equipped. The Chiefs of Staff later informed Brooke-Popham that they also could not afford the reinforcements he sought for MATADOR, and pointed out that there must be no advance into Thailand before the Japanese invaded it. In reply to an inquiry by the Chiefs of Staff, Brooke-Popham said that he would need 36 hours' notice before undertaking MATADOR.

In such circumstances, there obviously was little chance that the operation would be successful. Further unreality was given to the situation by a conference at Singapore on 29th September over which Mr Duff Cooper presided. The conference was attended by Air Chief Marshal Brooke-Popham; the naval Commander-in-Chief, China, Vice-Admiral Layton; the Governor of the Straits Settlements, Sir Shenton Thomas; Sir Earle Page (on his way to London via America), the British Ambassador to China, Sir Archibald Clark Kerr; and the British Minister to Thailand, Sir Josiah Crosby. It decided that the Japanese were concentrating against Russia; must be aware of the danger of going to war against the United States, the British Commonwealth and the Netherlands Indies; and, in any event, were unlikely to attempt a landing in Malaya during the northeast monsoon, due to begin in October.[5] The conference emphasised, however, the propaganda value of even one or two battleships at Singapore, the need for an announcement by the British, American and Dutch Governments that a coordinated plan of action existed, and the need for closer liaison with the Russians in the Far East.

Page discussed with Duff Cooper a proposal to establish a central governmental authority coordinating all British Far Eastern and Pacific interests, with either a United Kingdom or Australian Minister presiding.[6] Page reported to Australia that he thought an officer of the necessary calibre working in liaison with the Foreign Office would do the job better. Page was in Malaya for ten days, and saw a good deal of General Bennett and the A.I.F.

It was not only at Singapore that Page heard optimistic estimates. On his way through Manila he was assured by General MacArthur that after five years of intermittent war in China, Japan had become over-

---

[5] In Washington also at the time, despite the many indications of Japan's ambitions in the south, there was "a persistent conviction . . . that Japan was merely biding its time for an attack upon the Siberian maritime provinces". M. S. Watson, *Chief of Staff: Prewar Plans and Preparations*, p. 494.

[6] Duff Cooper also visited Australia and discussed the subject with the Australian War Cabinet.

extended, and needed a long period of recuperation before she could undertake another major struggle. She had gone to the limit of her southward expansion if she wished to avoid it, and under present conditions further expansion could be successfully resisted. Page learned in Washington that despite the American attitude at the Washington staff talks and the April Singapore conference, the Philippines were being strengthened. He was assured by General Marshall that by early 1942 the American forces would "constitute such a serious menace to Japan that she would be forced out of the Axis".

Twenty-three days before this conference at Singapore, the Japanese leaders had made the crucial decision. At an Imperial Conference on 6th September it was decided that preparations for war must be complete by the end of October; that the diplomatic efforts to reach a settlement must continue, but that if they had not succeeded by the early part of October the decision to get ready for war would then be made. On 2nd October the Nomura-Hull negotiations at Washington reached a deadlock. On the 16th Konoye, who had continued to strive against the group in his Cabinet which was intent on war, resigned. On the 17th General Tojo became Prime Minister. He was also Minister for War and Minister for Home Affairs (and thus in charge of the police). On the 5th November another Japanese Imperial Conference was held. It decided that unless America agreed by 25th November to the Japanese terms—no more aid to China, no increase in British and American forces in the Far East, no interference in Indo-China, and American cooperation with Japan in obtaining raw materials—Japan would go to war.[7]

Mr Kurusu was sent to Washington to join Admiral Nomura in the now hopeless negotiations. Tojo said later that Kurusu knew of the

---

[7] The last offer, known as Proposal B, was a concession in appearance rather than in reality. Its terms were:
    Japan and the United States to make no armed advance into any region in south-east Asia and the south-west Pacific area;
    Japan to withdraw her troops from Indo-China when peace was restored between Japan and China or an equitable peace was established in the Pacific area;
    Japan meantime to remove her troops from southern to northern Indo-China upon conclusion of the present agreement, which would later be embodied in the final agreement;
    Japan and the United States to cooperate toward acquiring goods and commodities that the two countries needed in the Netherlands East Indies;
    Japan and the United States to restore their commercial relations to those prevailing prior to the freezing of assets, and the United States to supply Japan a required quantity of oil;
    The United States to refrain from such measures and actions as would prejudice endeavours for the restoration of peace between Japan and China.
To Hull, the commitments the United States would have to make in accepting the proposal, were "virtually a surrender. We . . . should have to supply Japan as much oil as she might require, suspend our freezing measures, and resume full commercial relations with Tokyo. We should have to discontinue aid to China and withdraw our moral and material support from the recognised Chinese Government of Chiang Kai-shek. We should have to help Japan to obtain products of the Netherlands East Indies. We should have to cease augmenting our forces in the western Pacific. Japan, on her part, would still be free to continue her military operations in China, to attack the Soviet Union, and to keep her troops in northern Indo-China until peace was effected with China. . . . Her willingness to withdraw her troops from southern Indo-China to northern Indo-China was meaningless because those troops could return within a day or two. . . . The President and I could only conclude that agreeing to these proposals would mean condonement by the United States of Japan's past aggressions, assent to future courses of conquest by Japan, abandonment of the most essential principles of our foreign policy, betrayal of China and Russia, and acceptance of the role of silent partner, aiding and abetting Japan in her effort to create a Japanese hegemony over the western Pacific and eastern Asia. . . ."—*The Memoirs of Cordell Hull*. Vol II, pp. 1069-70.

Japanese military leaders' program. The American leaders knew through intercepted signals that 25th November was the deadline.

In November and early December 1941 trickles of reinforcements continued to arrive at British and American bases in the Far East. The decision not to reinforce Hong Kong had been reversed, and in October the Canadian Government agreed to send a brigade headquarters and two battalions there. These disembarked on 16th November, bringing the number of battalions in the garrison to six. The newcomers were the Winnipeg Grenadiers and the Royal Rifles of Canada. The Grenadiers had been mobilised since 1st September 1939 and the Rifles since 8th July 1940; but 448 new volunteers had recently been drafted to the battalions, including 120 who had received less than the sixteen weeks' training normally given to Canadian troops before they were sent overseas.

In September, as has been mentioned, the 28th Indian Brigade reached Singapore; in November and December the lamentable shortage of artillery in Malaya was partly remedied by the arrival of two field regiments and one anti-tank regiment from the United Kingdom, and one field regiment from India. In common with other Indian units, the 28th Brigade, comprising three Gurkha battalions, had lost a proportion of its officers and trained men to form cadres for new units being trained in India as part of the expansion of the Indian forces.

The share Malaya had been given of the available forces is broadly indicated by the disposition of British divisions among the major theatres at the beginning of December 1941:

	United Kingdom	Middle East	Persia-Iraq	Far East (Malaya)
Armoured divisions (U.K.)	6	3	—	—
Infantry divisions (U.K.)	21[8]	2	—	—
Dominion infantry divisions	2	6	—	1
Indian infantry divisions	—	2	3	2
Totals	29	13	3	3

The deficiencies in Malaya extended to the provision of military training schools. In the Middle East there was a wide range of well-staffed army schools. To these schools the Australian and other contingents which trained in that theatre owed much of their swiftly-acquired efficiency; and the A.I.F. there had now established a full range of schools of its own. When Brigadier Rowell,[9] formerly General Blamey's chief of staff in the Middle East, passed through Malaya late in August 1941 on his way home to Australia he found Malaya "badly served for schools". The relatively small Australian force there was unable to provide them out of

---

[8] Excluding 9 "county" divisions for home defence. At this time the 18th British Division was on the way to the Middle East.
[9] Lt-Gen Sir Sydney Rowell, KBE, CB, VX3. (1st AIF: 3 LH Regt 1914-15.) BGS I Aust Corps 1940-41; Deputy CGS AMF 1941-42; GOC I Aust Corps 1942; Dir Tac Investigation War Office 1943-46; CGS 1950-54. Regular soldier; of Adelaide; b. Lockleys, SA, 15 Dec 1894.

its own resources, and he proposed that candidates from the 8th Division be sent to Australian schools in the Middle East. Events were to show that it was then too late for such a policy to produce effective results. Malaya Command had, however, established an officer training school at Changi, and had given a fair proportion of the vacancies to the A.I.F. In the course of 1941 the candidates from British and Indian units had dwindled and those from the A.I.F. increased; in August, 30 Australian and 9 British cadets graduated.

The poorly-trained reinforcements sent to Malaya, as to the Middle East, by inefficient training depots in Australia presented a more difficult problem to the small force in Malaya than to the large force in the Middle East, which had long before set up its own big and first-class reinforcement depot to re-train men arriving there. When a large batch of reinforcements reached Malaya in October, the best any unit could say about them was that their training had been bad, and the men were not well disciplined.[1]

Incidents had occurred in Singapore and Kuala Lumpur in August between Australians on leave and British military police. Bennett, having received a report that his men were being provoked, thereupon arranged with Percival and Heath that A.I.F. discipline be maintained only by Australian military police. Nevertheless, trouble between some Australian and British troops on leave occurred from time to time. When dissimilarities in dress, discipline and rations were suggested as principal causes of ill-feeling, Bennett proposed an exchange system whereby selected British officers and other ranks might serve with A.I.F. units, and selected Australians with British units. This system, which was readily agreed to by Percival, began in November. Although the cost of living in the British messes severely limited the extent to which the Australians were able to avail themselves of the system, it was a thoughtful and practical step towards dissipating animosities—often the outcome of misunderstanding—which flourish in static garrison conditions. On the other hand, when General Percival, seeking to remove one bone of contention, wrote to Bennett asking that a War Office edict be applied to the A.I.F. restricting the use of motor vehicles for recreational purposes to a once-monthly basis for which troops should pay a nominal mileage rate, Bennett rightly refused to agree. He explained that it was the "policy of the A.I.F. to maintain health and morale at Government expense".[2] With General Bennett's concurrence General Percival arranged that British units should wear Australian felt hats. This, however, led to unfortunate results, for misconduct among felt-hatted soldiers in Singapore was apt to be attributed to Australians, whether or not this was so.

From the point of view of the British regular officer, Malaya in 1940 and 1941 was a backwater. There was a tendency for the most enterprising

---

[1] The besetting sin of the Australian depots seems to have been to skip elementary training and hurry on to more interesting technical work before men were ready for it.

[2] When AIF Headquarters was at Sentul, about four miles from the centre of Kuala Lumpur, army transport was the only satisfactory means of reaching the centre.

officers to seek appointments in more active theatres; in addition the expansion of both British and Indian armies caused the ratio of fully-experienced leaders to become smaller and smaller. In these circumstances, and having regard for the need for the closest possible liaison, it now seems to have been unfortunate that a substantial number of Australians was not absorbed into Malaya Command, where they might not only have had an invigorating effect, but have enabled the point of view of their large contingent to be seen more clearly. It was equally unfortunate that differences in rates of pay and allowances as between the United Kingdom and Indian forces also prevented adequate Indian Army representation on Malaya Command headquarters. "In 1941 there were scores of highly trained Indian Army staff officers in Malaya," wrote one of them,[3] "but none, with a few junior exceptions, on the staff of Malaya Command, for the simple reason that a regimental Indian Army officer, from a monetary point of view, lost considerably, even if it meant one or even two steps up in rank, in taking a staff appointment on Malaya Command headquarters." This situation restricted the range of choice in appointments to that command; and the already-mentioned obstacle to participation by Australians in the system of exchanges with British units hampered movement between each of the forces such as might have led to better mutual understanding and cohesion, and greater drive and enthusiasm.

In matters of Australian policy, as when in May General Bennett had refused to permit Australian troops to be used to suppress strikes of plantation workers for higher pay, he exercised his powers as the commander of an independent force responsible to his own Government—just as General Blamey was doing in the Middle East. Nevertheless, in discussions with General Percival on the status of the A.I.F., he emphasised his willingness to cooperate with British units and to accept orders, especially in an emergency, without hesitation; except where departures from Australian policy were involved. This was of course a strictly correct attitude, not necessarily implying a cordial relationship between the two commanders. Indeed, General Sturdee, Chief of the General Staff, cabled to Blamey early in August asking him to consider Bennett as a possible substitute for General Sir Iven Mackay in command of the Australian Home Forces. Sturdee gave as his reason that Bennett was "very senior", and an "energetic junior commander" would fit in better with Malaya Command requirements. He added that he could if necessary find a successor to Bennett from the 8th Division. Although the move was not made, the suggestion indicated Sturdee's concern about the situation as he assessed it at that stage.

By the end of August, after the arrival of the 27th Brigade, the 8th Australian Division in Malaya had been released from Command Reserve and given a definite area of responsibility such as Bennett sought for it. The task of the III Indian Corps being the defence of northern Malaya,

---
[3] Brigadier C. C. Deakin, DSO, OBE. He was at the time commanding officer of the 5/2 Punjab (12th Indian Brigade) and had served on exchange in Australia from 1937 to 1940.

General Percival ordered that the division take over the defence of Malacca and Johore. The east coast of Johore, the southernmost state on the Malayan Peninsula, offered obviously tempting means, from an enemy point of view, of landing within easy striking distance of Singapore Island rather than perhaps encountering resistance in Thailand and fighting all the way down the peninsula from the border to gain similar advantage. If success could be gained swiftly enough, the lines of communication upon which the III Indian Corps depended might be cut, and it might be isolated in the north. The responsibility entrusted to the two-brigade Australian division was thus a vital one, and particularly onerous in view of the weight of attack which could be expected in these circumstances.

General Bennett established his headquarters at Johore Bahru on 29th August, and on that day also the 22nd Brigade replaced the 12th Indian Brigade in the Mersing-Endau area, where it was anticipated that any such attack would be made. The 27th Brigade, which had remained on Singapore Island since its arrival, was to deployed mainly in north-western Johore, but with battle stations which would make it available for support of 22nd Brigade and counter-attack.

Among General Percival's reasons for agreeing to move the Australians was that he was anxious to give them a more responsible role; and that, under the new arrangement, there was a greater probability that the division would be able to operate as a formation under its own commander instead of being split up. Bennett had left Percival in no doubt of his feelings about the prospect, if the force remained in reserve and war began, of its being sooner or later sent forward piecemeal to relieve Indian units; and he had not failed to emphasise that it would be contrary to A.I.F. policy for the division to be dispersed in this way. The 12th Indian Brigade now became Percival's reserve.

In anticipation of the move, General Bennett had called on the Sultan of Johore and quickly established such friendly relations that the Sultan thenceforward granted all Bennett's requests for the use of buildings, camp sites and the like; and volunteered other help, such as the use of a polo ground for sports. The new role allotted to the Australians strengthened Bennett's case for obtaining other units of his division still in Australia; but, in the course of discussions during his visit to Malaya, Brigadier Rowell had told Bennett that recruits were coming forward so slowly in Australia that Bennett was unlikely to get even the machine-gun battalion and pioneer battalion for which he had been asking since March.

Defence of Singapore Island against attack through the Mersing area was considered to hinge upon possession of the junction, at Jemaluang, of the road from Endau and Mersing westward to Kluang with one in the east from Singapore through Kota Tinggi to Jemaluang. Capture of Jemaluang by the enemy would give him the choice of thrusting toward the trunk road and railway which served the whole of the defending forces in the northern part of Malaya, or of advancing south toward Johore Bahru, separated from the Naval Base and Singapore Island generally only by a narrow strait. The Sungei Endau, reaching the sea at Endau, some 20 miles north of Mersing, was regarded as offering waterway approach to Kahang, on the east-west road and near the Kahang airfield. By capturing Kahang an enemy might cut this road and also gain access through Kluang, on the main railway line, to the western road system.

Thus the first line of defence was to be the 22nd Brigade. Bennett planned that it should hold the beaches at Mersing with the 2/18th and 2/20th Battalions,[4] and have the 2/19th in reserve at Jemaluang. A company of the 2/20th under Captain Carter[5] was posted at Endau, and one of the 2/18th and subsequently of the 2/19th at a boom across the

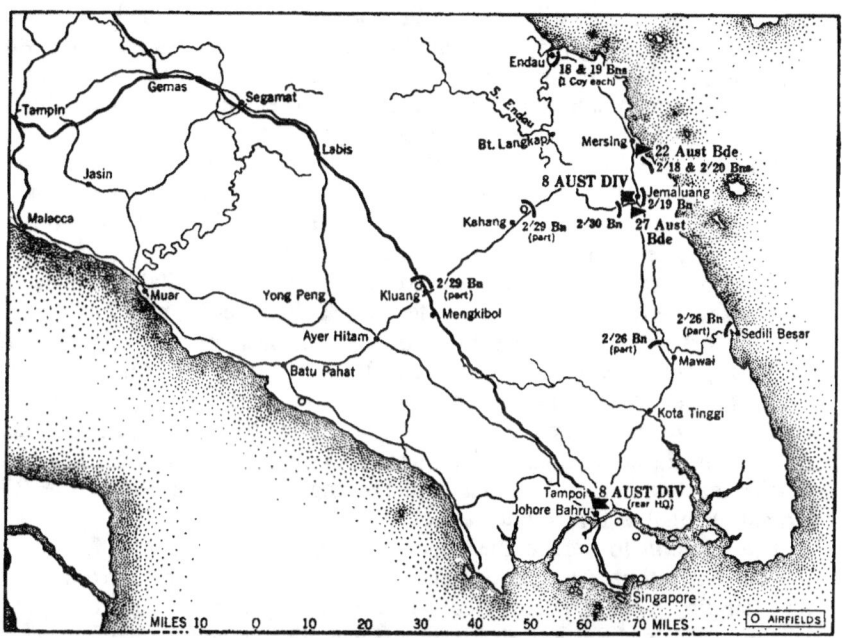

A.I.F. locations, Malaya, December 1941

Sedili Besar. In the event of war, the 27th Brigade would share responsibility for the area. Its 2/26th Battalion would take over the boom and protect the road from Sedili Besar north to the 2/19th Battalion. The 2/30th was to be a mobile unit, stationed a mile and a half west of the Jemaluang road junction, under the direct orders of General Bennett; and the 2/29th would be responsible for the Bukit Langkap iron mine area and the airfields at Kahang and Kluang.

The 22nd Brigade went to work promptly and energetically to strengthen and extend the rather sketchy defences which existed in its area. In the course of the next three months it built what was practically a new defensive system, and although this took much of its time and effort, it

---

[4] Early in August Major Assheton, second-in-command of the 2/18th Battalion, was promoted to command the 2/20th in place of Colonel Jeater, who had been ill. Jeater took command of the Australian General Base Depot.

[5] Maj W. A. Carter, NX34852; 2/20 Bn. Bank officer; of Hurstville, NSW; b. Stawell, Vic, 1 Oct 1910.

underwent extensive and persistent local training.⁶ The 2/30th Battalion set about cutting tracks through dense vegetation to assist it in fulfilling its role in the event of the main road becoming impassable. The most important of these was one from the east-west road west of Jemaluang, skirting a height known as Gibraltar Hill in the Nithsdale Estate (a defensive position for the battalion's forward company), bypassing Jemaluang junction, and joining the road to Mersing north of Jemaluang.

"We can expect them to be bold," wrote Brigadier Taylor of the Japanese, in assessing the 22nd Brigade's role. "They greatly admire German methods and will develop the maximum strength in the minimum of time. Japanese infantry can maintain themselves for several days without transport in difficult terrain." He saw the brigade's task as being to destroy any enemy landing on the beaches between Jemaluang and Mersing and to harass them elsewhere as much as possible.

A major issue generally in Malaya, while defensive preparations were being made in 1941, had been whether or not to attempt to hold the beaches in the event of enemy assault, or to place forces back from the beaches in defence of roads leading into the interior. It was argued against holding the beaches that this would string out the available forces and leave insufficient available for counter-attack. Brooke-Popham had ordered that the first line of defence must be the beaches, on the principle that the enemy would be most vulnerable to land, air and (if naval vessels were available) sea attack when disembarking. He regarded the system adopted by the Australian command as a satisfactory way of meeting the problem, in that the 22nd Brigade had perimeter defence for units mutually supporting each other and primarily defending the beaches, with the 27th Brigade available for counter-attack.⁷

The decision to defend the beaches seems to have been influenced by the current estimate of the damage which could be inflicted from the air on a landing force. General Heath recorded later that, before the opening of the campaign, the Royal Air Force was always confident of its power to stop any invasion of Malaya, and estimated that it would be able to inflict upon any enemy convoy as high a loss as 40 per cent. Assessment of the striking capacity of the air force, to which the leading role was assigned, was of course fundamental to the strategy for the defence of Malaya.

By late September, the 27th Brigade had settled down to somewhat dispersed locations in its new area—the headquarters of the 27th Brigade and the 2/29th Battalion in the Segamat area, through which the trunk road and railway from Singapore passed over the north-western border of Johore; the 2/26th Battalion at Jasin; the 2/30th at Batu Pahat, a

---

⁶ The work included construction of a 400-bed casualty clearing station, largely recessed into a hillside.

⁷ At a conference on 30th August with his unit commanders in the Mersing area, Brigadier Taylor laid it down that defence was to be on a system of platoons, self-contained in all respects and able to fire in all directions. The platoons were to be distributed in depth, and mutually supporting; areas between them were to constitute mortar and artillery tasks. The men had been told that they might be surrounded by the enemy and be called upon to counter-attack with movement and fire.

port on the west coast of Johore; and the 2/15th Field Regiment at Tampin, on the northern border of Malacca. These localities offered good training areas, and the troops had soon become acclimatised and settled down to solid training. Having been a battalion commander in the 22nd Brigade, Brigadier Maxwell was able to pass on the local experience he had gained in that role. His commanders sought to improve wherever possible upon what the 22nd Brigade had achieved in preparing itself for action under Malayan conditions.

Bennett naturally continued to take a keen interest in the units of his division which were still in Australia. When 10 per cent of the men of those units were taken away and sent as reinforcements to the Middle East he protested strongly. Late in October he decided to visit the brigade in Darwin. He was informed, however, that the Australian War Cabinet had decided that he might visit the Middle East but that a visit to Darwin was unnecessary in view of a new decision to remove the units of the 8th Division in Australia from his control. Thenceforward the 8th Division comprised two brigades, and such divisional units as were allotted to it. The 23rd Brigade and the remaining divisional troops, including at this stage the machine-gun and the pioneer battalions, became detached forces with roles in the Northern Territory, New Britain and the Indies.

Brigadier Rowell, however, had been a sympathetic advocate of the 8th Division's needs when he arrived in Melbourne. At Bennett's request he recommended to General Sturdee that the 2/4th Machine Gun Battalion be sent to Malaya, particularly because of its value in beach defence; that efforts be made to rearm the Australian artillery regiments in Malaya (one of which had old 18-pounders and 4.5-inch howitzers and the other 3-inch mortars) with 25-pounders; that an additional anti-tank battery, and corps signals be sent; and that an A.I.F. administrative headquarters separate from the divisional headquarters be formed in Malaya (both under Bennett's command) thus freeing the divisional staff for its proper role.

The establishment of the administrative headquarters was agreed to, and it began to operate in October, from the same building in Johore Bahru as that occupied by divisional headquarters. Kent Hughes was promoted to lieut-colonel and placed in charge of the administrative staff, which moved in November to a camp at Tampoi Hill near the A.I.F. General Base Depot. There were now 15,000 Australian troops in Malaya, including an increasing number of base units. Thus the establishment of such a headquarters was overdue.

The new arrangements gave General Bennett roles similar to those played by General Blamey in the Middle East. Blamey had the right to report directly to the Minister for the Army and Bennett, assuming a similar right, had sent on 31st March to the Minister, Mr Spender, a report on the events to that date. On 18th April he had received a cable from the Military Board instructing him not to communicate directly with the Minister. Later he was informed that, although Blamey was not responsible to the Military Board, he (Bennett) was. There the matter rested until September, when Sturdee cabled that Spender had suggested that Bennett should have the right to communicate directly with the Minister. A few days later Bennett received a letter from Spender stating that he had the right. Next, on 30th October 1941, Bennett was formally appointed "G.O.C., A.I.F., Malaya".

On 6th November General Blamey arrived at Singapore on his way to Australia to confer with the Ministers. In particular (as he informed Bennett), he sought firstly to try to persuade them to reverse a decision that would necessitate breaking up one of the divisions in the Middle East; secondly to press that the 8th Division be sent to the Middle East.[8] Blamey was still in Australia when, on 18th November, Bennett left Malaya by air to visit the A.I.F. in the Middle East. Bennett's subsequent comments suggest that he was not impressed by what he saw there. He wrote that the offensive in the Western Desert at the time, "lacked drive, punch and coordination", that the "elephantine" headquarters of the army in Egypt "had grown usually at the expense of the number of men available to fight"; and that "too many officers were so far removed from the battles that were being fought that they lost touch with reality. Departments became watertight and out of touch with other departments. Perfect cooperation was extremely difficult."[9]

On 3rd December Bennett noted in his diary "Indo-China has been well prepared as a springboard from which to make the dive into Thailand, Malaya and Netherlands East Indies. I fear that the move may start before my return, so I have decided to push off at once." On 8th December, at Mergui (Burma), on his return flight, he learned how well-founded his fears had been.

The numbers of fighting units in Malaya on 7th December 1941, exclusive of engineers, mechanical transport, signals and ancillary units, the local volunteers and Indian and Malayan State forces, were:

    31 infantry battalions (the infantry strength of about 3½ divisions)
    7 field regiments (5 of 24 guns; 2 of 16 guns)
    1 mountain regiment (24 guns)
    2 anti-tank regiments (1 of 48 guns; 1 of 36 guns)
    2 anti-tank batteries (1 of 8 Breda guns; 1 of six 2-pounders).

A large proportion of these units was poorly trained and equipped. There were also ten battalions of volunteers, only sketchily trained and equipped; five battalions from Indian States for airfield defence; a battalion maintained by the Sultan of Johore, with some light artillery; and small forces, ranging up to a weak battalion, maintained by other of the Unfederated States. The total strength of regular and volunteer forces was nearly 88,600, of whom 19,600 were British, 15,200 Australian, and the greater number Asian (Indian 37,000, locally enlisted 16,800).

---

[8] In view of the Far Eastern situation, however, the War Cabinet decided on 18th November that no action be taken on this request.

[9] H. G. Bennett, *Why Singapore Fell* (1944), pp. 55-6.

The army's strength was thus far short—to the extent principally of 17 infantry battalions, 4 light anti-aircraft regiments and 2 tank regiments —of what it had been agreed was required. There were no tanks, though these had been asked for as early as 1937; few armoured cars; insufficient anti-tank rifles in the infantry units; and a serious shortage of mobile anti-aircraft weapons.

The arrival at Singapore on 2nd December of the battleship *Prince of Wales* and the battle cruiser *Repulse* caused a wave of relief and even of elation to sweep over Malaya in particular. Though they were without the intended aircraft carrier, their presence seemed to many onlookers to have ended the critical period. Britain had shown that she "meant business", it was said among the crowds who watched these great vessels. Japan had stuck her neck out too far, and now she would have to pull it in again. The toast was to the British Navy. But, based at Singapore on 8th December, in addition to these vessels, were only three small and out-dated cruisers, seven destroyers (four of them small and obsolete), three gunboats, and a cluster of minor craft ranging from auxiliary anti-submarine vessels to motor-launches.[1]

Thus in Malaya, hub of Far Eastern defence, the ragged edge of want still ran throughout the Services. Broadly speaking, they had got what was left over after demands with higher priority—especially those of the Middle East—had been met. The drain on British resources included dispatch to Russia during 1941 of 676 aircraft and 446 tanks—enough to satisfy fully Malaya's needs for these weapons; but Russia, actually engaged in war, was given priority. In Malaya there were not only shortages of equipment, but defects in quality and efficiency. A severe shortage existed of experienced officers to administer the forces, train them, and provide dependable leadership in battle; and of experienced men to leaven the rank and file.[2] This was especially serious in the III Indian Corps, Percival's largest fighting formation.

The size of the Indian Army generally at this time was misleading without consideration of its quality. It had been so stinted of funds that a committee under the chairmanship of Major-General Auchinleck[3] found in 1938 that it was "showing a tendency to fall behind the forces of such minor states as Egypt, Iraq and Afghanistan. Judged by modern standards the army in India is relatively immobile and under-armed and unfit to take the field against land or air forces equipped with up-to-date weapons". At the outbreak of war in Europe the shortage of modern weapons and vehicles was acute, and a huge expansion scheme was commenced. India's Congress Party had called for assurances that India, who had not been consulted about participation in the war, would be treated as a free

---

[1] Thirteen auxiliary anti-submarine vessels, 4 mine-sweepers, 12 auxiliary mine-sweepers (and 5 at Penang), 5 auxiliary patrol vessels, 11 motor-launches, 6 boom defence tugs and depot ships. A cruiser and three destroyers (including HMAS *Vampire* and HMAS *Vendetta*) which belonged to other stations were refitting at Singapore.

[2] A senior Australian officer commented that the quality "went quickly from cream to skimmed milk".

[3] Field Marshal Sir Claude Auchinleck, GCB, GCIE, CSI, DSO, OBE. C-in-C India 1941, 1943-46; C-in-C Middle East 1941-42. Regular soldier; b. 21 Jun 1884.

nation. In the absence of satisfying response, it had adopted a policy of passive resistance to British rule; but, despite this, the main difficulties lay not in recruiting men, but in training large numbers in little time, and in providing them with suitable officers.

Of the Indian Army's officers in July 1939, 2,978 were British and 528 Indian. To meet the needs of the expansion, "Indianisation" (officering of Indian units by Indians) which had been proceeding at a snail's pace since 1918, had suddenly to be accelerated. Meanwhile officers of existing units had to be distributed widely over new ones, and many additional British officers found. The whole tempo of thought and action needed to be adjusted to the urgent demands of the times. Yet, drawn from a largely illiterate population in which existed a multiplicity of races, castes, creeds and languages, the Indian recruit needed a much greater period of training than recruits from more advanced and less diversified communities; and as the Indian Army tended to curb rather than to stimulate the national aspirations of Indians, his loyalty was apt to attach to leaders who by experience and force of character could win his respect rather than to the cause in which he was enlisted. To transferred officers, and especially to the many new officers required, some of them even unable to speak more than a few halting words of Urdu, the language in which they had to make themselves understood by their men, this was a lengthy and sometimes impossible task. Under expansion many Indian officers had far less experience and other qualifications than those previously held necessary; and this applied to non-commissioned officers also. In turn, the training and leadership of the men suffered.

Expansion, therefore, had been accompanied by a substantial lowering of the traditional standards of the Indian Army. It affected those Indian units sent to Malaya after the 12th Brigade went there in 1939 to a progressive extent as the expansion took its course.[4] Thus, in Malaya, where 18 out of the 31 battalions (excluding the Volunteers) were Indian, it was likely that those Indian battalions would fall far below 1939 standards of efficiency.

It had been a general practice to include two Indian battalions and one British regular battalion in an Indian infantry brigade but, as a result of the expansion of the Indian Army, this was no longer always possible. Of the six Indian brigades in Malaya in December only three—6th, 12th and 15th—contained a British battalion. It seems strange, therefore, that three British regular battalions—2/Loyals, 2/Gordons and 1/Manchester (a machine-gun battalion)—were all relegated to the Singapore Fortress, a direct attack on the island being the least probable course of action.

---

[4] From Sep 1939 to Sep 1941 seven Indian divisions went overseas or were organised there:

Date	Division	Destination	Location 7 Dec 1941
Sep 1939	4th	Middle East	North Africa
Aug 1940	5th	Middle East	Cyprus
Jan 1941	11th	Malaya	Malaya
Mar 1941	9th	Malaya	Malaya
May 1941	10th	Iraq	Persia
Jul 1941	8th	Iraq	Iraq
Sep 1941	6th	Iraq	Persia

Location of forces, Malaya, 8th December 1941

In Malaya Command, on 7th December, General Heath's III Indian Corps was responsible for defence of Malaya north of Johore and Malacca, including the island of Penang. Of the corps' two divisions, each of two brigades, the 11th, as noted earlier, was in the north-west and the 9th in the north-east (with its 8th Brigade in the Kota Bharu area, near the border with Thailand, and its 22nd at Kuantan, about half-way down the eastern coast). The 28th Brigade was Heath's reserve. The 8th Australian Division (two brigades) had the task of defending the States of Johore and Malacca, with the Johore State forces under its command. Defence of Singapore and the adjoining islands was the responsibility of the Singapore Fortress troops, under Major-General Simmons. The 12th Indian Infantry Brigade Group (Brigadier Paris[5]), General Percival's reserve, was in the Port Dickson area. Anti-aircraft regiments (Brigadier Wildey[6]) were allotted the defence, in cooperation with other arms, of selected targets in the Singapore area against air attack. An independent company with a strength of 300 British and Indians was formed early in 1941 for amphibious and special operations in enemy territory, but had not completed its training in December 1941. Detachments of troops in Borneo, a small volunteer force in British North Borneo, and a Coast Artillery detachment at Christmas Island (in the Indian Ocean, south of Sumatra) for protection of phosphate deposits, were also under Malaya Command. Percival had endeavoured to ensure that in view of the wide area covered by the command, and because operations might develop simultaneously in various parts of the area, responsibility for control of operations should be decentralised as much as possible.[7]

---

[5] Brig A. C. M. Paris, MC. Comd 12 Indian Inf Bde 1940-41; GOC 11 Ind Div 1941-42. Regular soldier; b. 28 May 1890. Drowned at sea March 1942.

[6] Brig A. W. G. Wildey, MC. Comd AA Def Malaya 1940-42. Regular soldier; b. 24 Jul 1890.

[7] In further detail, the principal formations in Percival's army were:
   Northern Malaya
      III Indian Corps (Lt-Gen Heath)
         9th Indian Division (Maj-Gen Barstow)
            8th Bde (Brig Key: 2/10 Baluch, 2/12 FF Regt, 3/17 Dogra, 1/13 FF Rifles)
            22nd Bde (Brig Painter: 5/11 Sikh, 2/18 Garhwal)
         11th Indian Division (Maj-Gen Murray-Lyon)
            6th Bde (Brig Lay: 2/Surrey, 1/8 Punjab, 2/16 Punjab)
            15th Bde (Brig Garrett: 1/Leicesters, 2/9 Jat, 1/14 Punjab, 3/16 Punjab)
         Two additional battalions (3/16 Punjab attached to 15th Bde, and 5/14th Punjab at Penang)
         III Corps reserve—28th Bde (Brig Carpendale: 2/1, 2/2, 2/9 Gurkha)
         One volunteer infantry battalion and fixed coastal defences (Penang Garrison)
         Airfield defence troops (three Indian State Forces battalions)
         Line of communication troops (volunteers)
   Johore and Malacca
      8th Australian Division (Maj-Gen Bennett)
         22 Bde (Brig Taylor: 2/18, 2/19, 2/20 Bns)
         27 Bde (Brig Maxwell: 2/26, 2/29, 2/30 Bns)
         (The forces of the State of Johore were also under Bennett's command)
   Singapore Fortress
      Maj-Gen Simmons controlled, in addition to fortress troops, the following mobile formations:
         1 Malaya Bde (2/Loyals, 1/Malaya Regt)
         2 Malaya Bde (1/Manchester, 2/Gordons, 2/17 Dogra)
         Straits Settlements Volunteer Force
         Two Indian State Force battalions (airfield defence)
      The anti-aircraft defences (Brig Wildey) included two heavy and two light anti-aircraft regiments and a searchlight regiment.
   Command Reserve
      12th Indian Bde (Brig Paris: 2/A & SH, 5/2 Punjab, 4/19 Hyderabad)
   Borneo
      2/15 Punjab.

A large well-led labour corps would have been of great value to the defending force in Malaya, but all efforts to form such a force had failed. General Bond had foreseen this need in 1940 and succeeded in obtaining two Indian labour companies. In April 1941 Malaya Command obtained permission from the War Office to raise six companies locally, but the Malayan Government advised against this on the grounds that it would interfere with rubber production and in any event local labourers might be difficult to recruit. Since the rate of pay fixed by the War Office was only a fraction of the ruling rate, recruiting proved not merely difficult but impossible. General Percival then asked for more Indian companies, but without success. He next tried, also without success, to obtain labourers from Hong Kong. On the 18th November, the Treasury having fixed a higher rate of pay than the original War Office figure, Percival informed the War Office that he proposed to begin recruiting labourers in Malaya on the 24th. The rate proved to be still too low to attract labourers; and the only labour companies available in December were the two Indian companies obtained in 1940.

The dispositions for the defence of Malaya were fundamentally unsound in December 1941. Although they were based on the assumption that Malaya would contain an air force strong enough to inflict crippling losses on an invading convoy, such an air force was not present; yet the army was deployed over a wide area largely to protect outlying airfields. It was realised that the enemy might land on the Kra Isthmus and advance down the west coast, or at Kota Bharu and capture the three airfields there, or at Kuantan where there was another airfield, or in the Mersing area with the object of taking Singapore from the north, or on the island itself. The army was dispersed so as to meet every one of these possible attacks. In a force including ten brigades only one was retained in Force reserve. Thus it was practically inevitable that wherever the enemy made his initial attack he would be in superior strength as soon as he had put his main force ashore; and that, if he gained a success in the early stages, the defender's reserves would be drawn into the battle, but only gradually, because of poor communications, and the enemy would be given an opportunity of defeating the defending army piecemeal.

Elsewhere in Brooke-Popham's command the two principal responsibilities were Burma and Hong Kong. Of these Hong Kong was of course in the more exposed position and the less likely to survive determined assault. Despite Mr Churchill's earlier reluctance, for this reason, to reinforce the outpost, two Canadian battalions had arrived there in mid-November, as mentioned earlier, bringing the infantry strength to five battalions (two Canadian, two Indian, one Scottish), with a machine-gun battalion (English), two regiments of coastal artillery, a medium artillery regiment, a local Volunteer Defence Corps about 2,000 strong, and a Chinese machine-gun battalion in course of formation. The total strength of mobilised personnel, including auxiliary units, was about 14,500. Hong Kong could put into the air four craft—two Walrus amphibians and two Vildebeestes. The naval forces comprised one destroyer (two others left under orders for Singapore on 8th December), eight torpedo motorboats, four gunboats, and some armed patrol vessels.

Burma presented more vital considerations. Lying across the eastern land approach to India, it was also a back-door to China, Malaya and Thailand; and it afforded landing grounds—principally at Tavoy, Mergui and Victoria Point on the Tenasserim coast—for overland movement of planes to and from Malaya. The forces in Burma comprised sixteen battalions of regular infantry, mostly Burmese and Indian; three Indian mountain batteries; a Burma Auxiliary Force field battery; and two air squadrons with a total of four Blenheim I bombers,[8] sixteen Buffaloes, and a reserve of sixteen Buffaloes.[9] An American Volunteer Group, comprising three fighter squadrons equipped with Tomahawk planes, had commenced training in Burma in August 1941 and it was understood that if Burma were attacked part or the whole of the group would remain for its defence. The Governor of Burma, Sir Reginald Dorman-Smith,[1] presided over a war committee inclusive of Burmese ministers, two British counsellors and the General Officer Commanding.[2]

In Washington on 25th November 1941, President Roosevelt had conferred with his advisers. Mr Stimson, Secretary for War, noted in his diary that at the conference the President, speculating on the possibility of United States forces being attacked without warning, perhaps as early as 1st December, said the question was "how we should manoeuvre them into the position of firing the first shot without allowing too much danger to ourselves".[3] Hull handed to Nomura next day "with the forlorn hope that even at this ultimate minute a little common sense might filter into the military minds in Tokyo",[4] comprehensive proposals which in effect upheld the principles of the United States' stand.[5] On the 27th Stark and Marshall presented a memorandum to Roosevelt in which, while still seeking time, they recommended action substantially on the lines which had emerged from the Singapore conferences. Warnings were sent to the commanders of United States forces, including General MacArthur and Admiral Kimmel, Commander-in-Chief of the U.S. Fleet at Pearl Harbour, to be on the alert for any attack. A message from Togo, Japan's Foreign Minister, to Nomura was intercepted which stated that the negotia-

---

[8] The bomber squadron's other Blenheims were in Malaya for bombing practice.

[9] Twenty-four of the Buffaloes were temporarily out of action with engine valve gear trouble.

[1] Col Rt Hon Sir Reginald Dorman-Smith, GBE. Minister of Agriculture and Fisheries 1939-40; Governor of Burma 1941-46. B. 10 Mar 1899.

[2] Lieut-General D. K. McLeod. Responsibility for the defence of Burma was transferred from Brooke-Popham to the Commander-in-Chief, India, on 15 Dec; and Lieut-General Hutton took over from McLeod on the 29th.

[3] Quoted in H. Feis, *The Road to Pearl Harbour* (1950), p. 314.

[4] *The Memoirs of Cordell Hull*, Vol II, p. 1083.

[5] These proposals included a non-aggression pact among the governments principally concerned in the Pacific; an agreement by them to respect the territorial integrity of Indo-China; relinquishment of extra-territorial rights in China; a trade agreement between the United States and Japan on liberal lines; removal of the freezing measures; and withdrawal of Japanese armed forces from China and Indo-China.

tions would be ruptured. "I do not wish you to give the impression that the negotiations are broken off," said Togo. "Merely say to them that you are awaiting instructions and that, although the opinions of your government are not yet clear to you, to your own way of thinking the Imperial Government has always made just claims and has borne great sacrifices for the sake of peace in the Pacific."[6]

Clearly, common sense had not "filtered into the military minds in Tokyo"; and on 5th December the Dominions received from the United Kingdom Government information that it had received assurance of armed support from the United States (*a*) if Britain found it necessary either to forestall a Japanese landing in the Kra Isthmus or to occupy part of the isthmus as a counter to Japanese violation of any other part of Thailand; (*b*) if Japan attacked the Netherlands East Indies and Britain at once went to their support; (*c*) if Japan attacked British territory. The message continued that Brooke-Popham had been instructed to move into the Kra Isthmus if it were established that escorted Japanese ships were approaching it, or if the Japanese violated any other part of Thailand; and to act on plans agreed to by the Dutch for implementation if the Japanese attacked the Netherlands East Indies.

Roosevelt made a final conciliatory gesture by sending the Japanese Emperor on 6th December (7th December in Australia) a message in which he declared that both he and the Emperor had "a sacred duty to restore traditional amity and prevent further death and destruction in the world". China, still unsubdued, and therefore limiting the extent of the forces which Japan might use elsewhere, saw hope that at last powerful allies might help to shorten her ordeal. The leader of a Chinese mission which visited Malaya in November had declared that "China makes a pledge to conclude no separate peace and to continue fighting to the limit of her strength until all the aggressor nations are defeated and humbled".

Behind a barrier of secrecy Japan had been preparing a daring and far-flung offensive. Though, as has been shown, the barrier had been perforated by the American success in intercepting and deciphering Japanese code messages, it was only by post-war investigation that the full extent of the Japanese preparations, and their background, became known to those against whom they were aimed.

By the end of July 1941 the Japanese Planning Board[7] had prepared a study called "Requirements for the Mobilisation of Commodities for the Prosecution of War". Such a war, the board said, must be regarded as fundamentally a war of resources. The board asserted that if Japan were to continue her course of relying for her requirements on Britain and America, she "would undoubtedly collapse and be unable to rise again".

---
[6] Complaining that circumstances had so changed since he left Japan that "I cannot tell you how much in the dark I am", Nomura had unsuccessfully sought when Tojo became Prime Minister to be relieved of his ambassadorship to the United States. "I do not want," he said, "to continue this hypocritical existence, deceiving myself and other people."
[7] Established in May 1937, as national control of Japan's economy was being increased.

She must therefore make a final decision promptly. If she decided upon war, she must capture the rich natural resources of the southern area at the outset. Unless command of the air and sea was immediately secured, the minimum requirements of the mobilisation of supplies could not be fulfilled.

On this basis, the supreme commands of the Japanese Army and Navy studied four alternative proposals:

1. To capture the Netherlands East Indies first and then attack Malaya and the Philippines.
2. To carry out operations against the Philippines, Borneo, Java, Sumatra and Malaya in that order.
3. To carry out operations in the order Malaya, Sumatra, Borneo, Java and the Philippines to delay for as long as possible the entry into the war of the United States.
4. To start operations against the Philippines and Malaya simultaneously and proceed southward promptly and at length assault Java from both east and west.

The Army favoured the third course, which insofar as it might delay America's entry into the war fitted in with German wishes. It would, however, involve serious risk to the Japanese lines of communication, over which the Americans might in time exert a stranglehold if they could muster sufficient strength in the Philippines. The second course appealed to the Navy, as offering an easy concentration of military strength and a secure line of communications; but to this the objection was raised that it might allow sufficient time for Sumatra and Malaya to be so strengthened as to be impregnable. By the middle of August the fourth plan had been adopted, provisionally upon sufficient military strength being available; and the preparation of detailed operational plans was commenced. Under the supervision of Admiral Isoroku Yamamoto, Commander-in-Chief of the Combined Fleet, a "table-top" exercise was carried out in September which provided for (*a*) a naval operation to gain command of the sea in the western Pacific, leading to capture of American, British and Dutch areas in the southern region, (*b*) a surprise assault against Hawaii. The utmost secrecy surrounded study and exercise for the latter, which had been under consideration since the previous January, and was intended primarily to hamstring American retaliation for attack on the Philippines. Although some officers favoured landing a force to seize the island of Oahu, in which Pearl Harbour is situated, it was decided that there would not be enough transports for this purpose as well as for the southward move. Further discussions with the army followed, and drafting of the Combined Fleet's operation orders was then commenced.

An order for mobilisation of a "Southern Army" was issued on 6th November. This army, commanded by Count Terauchi, would include the *XIV, XV, XVI* and *XXV* "Armies"—each the equivalent of a British corps.[8]

---

[8] For this reason the titles of Japanese armies and British corps are both printed in Roman numerals in this series.

(Lt-Gen H. Gordon Bennett)

The headquarters of the 8th Division in a rubber estate. The dense vegetation of Malaya lent itself to concealment and camouflage.

(Australian War Memorial)

A naval craft negotiating a river boom in eastern Malaya.

(Australian War Memorial)
Members of the 2/4th Anti-Tank Regiment manhandling a gun into position during training.

(Australian War Memorial)
A forward Australian infantry patrol, after the outbreak of war.

Divisions and independent brigades included in the four armies and their areas of operation, were:

XIV (Philippines), *16th, 48th Divisions, 65th Brigade, 56th Regiment*;
XV (Thailand and Burma), *33rd, 55th Divisions*;
XXV (Malaya, Northern Sumatra), *Guards, 5th, 18th, 56th Divisions*;
XVI (Borneo, Celebes, Ambon, Timor, Java), *2nd, 38th, 48th Divisions, 56th Regiment,* naval landing detachments;
The *21st Division* (from January onwards) and the *21st Brigade* were in reserve.

Thus the Japanese rated the army in Malaya more highly than any of the four main forces they had to overcome, allotting four divisions including the *Guards* to the task. The *48th Division* and *56th Regiment* were to join the *XVI Army* after completing their task in the Philippines, and the *38th Division* after the capture of Hong Kong.

The main force of the *Southern Army*, with the cooperation of the navy, was to assemble in southern China, Indo-China and various islands and if attacked by American, British or Dutch troops was to act in self-defence. Then, if negotiations with the United States fell through, it would carry out its offensive in three principal phases: in the first the main objectives would be Malaya and northern Sumatra, the Philippines, British Borneo, Hong Kong, Guam and Wake Islands; in the second it would advance to Rabaul, Ambon, Timor, and southern Sumatra; in the third capture Java and invade central Burma. Finally a defensive perimeter would be established running from the Kuriles to Wake Island, the Marshall and Gilbert Islands, New Guinea, Timor, Java, Malaya and the Burma-India border. It was hoped that the capture of Java, the culmination of the southward drive, would be completed within 150 days.

In the Philippines the *XIV Army* was to be supported by the *Third Fleet* and air forces. In Malaya the *XXV Army* was to be supported by the *Second Fleet* and air forces. Guam and Wake Islands and later New Britain and New Ireland were to be taken by the *Fourth Fleet,* using forces of marines, plus the *144th Infantry Regiment,* the whole force being about 5,000 strong in combat troops and supported by the *24th Air Flotilla* and, for New Britain, by the Carrier Fleet.

This fleet, commanded by Admiral Nagumo, and comprising six aircraft carriers and a supporting force including two battleships and two heavy cruisers, was allotted to an attack on Pearl Harbour. By 22nd November it had concentrated in a bay in the Kurile Islands, and on 3rd December was at a stand-by point about half-way to Hawaii. After the attack on Pearl Harbour the Carrier Fleet was to refit and refuel, then to support the landing at Rabaul; and landings on Ambon and Timor islands (principally, in respect of Timor, by striking at Darwin). Admiral Yamamoto kept his main battleship force, the *First Fleet,* in reserve.

A total of 500 ships, amounting in all to 1,450,000 tons, was allotted to transport the military forces. Southern air operations were to commence from bases in Formosa and French Indo-China, and new bases being established on islands off the coast of French Indo-China. Con-

The Japanese objectives

centration and deployment of the land forces was hampered by bad weather, the long distances to be covered, difficulty in assembling materials and fuel shortage at some points. By 5th December, however, Count Terauchi had reached Saigon from Tokyo via Formosa and was making preparations for the moment when his forces would be unleashed. What was the quality of these forces, and what were their characteristics?

Before 1941 the Japanese Army had twice overcome a European adversary—the Russians in Manchuria and Korea in 1905, and, in 1914, the little German garrison of Tsingtao in China. European military observers had closely and admiringly observed that army in the Russo-Japanese War, and, in the period between the two world wars, European officers who studied the Japanese Army had defined most of the characteristics which were to be displayed in December 1941 and January and February 1942. Their observations, however, had not sunk very deeply into the consciousness of European officer corps accustomed to regard Asian military leaders generally as deficient in first-rate organising and technical ability, and the rank and file as lacking the fibre and initiative of their own men.

Japanese social conventions conferred upon the Japanese Army certain qualities of substantial military value. In the Japanese citizen was implanted an ever-present conviction of obligation to the divine Emperor, to the Japanese community, and to its individual members. Distinctions of rank were so rigidly drawn that these obligations and the code of behaviour by which they were expressed could be precisely defined, and were fully understood by the Japanese people, but by few others. The greatest honour a soldier could attain was to die for the Emperor. A soldier who was taken prisoner was regarded as an outcast. A commander whose force suffered defeat should and often did commit suicide. In the ranks the subordination of one grade to another was extreme. Officers and N.C.O's sometimes slapped the faces of their juniors if they misbehaved. Senior privates slapped new recruits.

As in most large European conscript armies, the officers belonged to three main groups. All senior appointments and, in peace, most of the junior ones were occupied by regular officers who had been trained at the military academy. Secondly, there were the reserve officers selected from among the better-educated conscripts and, after service in the ranks, trained at reserve officer schools; after commissioning they usually were transferred into the reserve ready to be employed in the expansion of the army in war. Thirdly, there were officers who had been promoted from the ranks after long service as senior non-commissioned officers.

In peace the conscripts, about 80 per cent of whom were peasants and labourers, were trained for two years and then passed into the reserve, but in 1941 Japan had been fighting China for four years, and many veteran reservists had been recalled for a second tour of duty. The peacetime training of the Japanese soldier was probably more exacting than in any other army, particularly in hardening him to endure extremes of heat and cold, fatigue and hunger. In the 'thirties, for example, a skilled English observer recorded operations in Manchuria in which the troops went entirely without food for three days in weather so cold that the water froze in their flasks. By 1941 most of the formations had been further seasoned by arduous and recent active service.

Components of the *XXV Army* provided instances of this. The *18th Division* had fought round Canton in 1938; in 1939 it advanced into Kwangsi Province and took Nanning. In 1940 and 1941 it was on duty in the Canton area, with units active at Hainan and Foochow. Thus when this division embarked for operations against Malaya it had been more or less continuously on active service for four years. The *5th Division* also had been continuously on active service in China from 1937 until late 1941, when it went to Hainan. The *Guards Division* had served in south China in 1940; in 1941 it had been either in Hainan training for the Malayan campaign, or taking part in the occupation of Indo-China.

In December 1941 the Japanese Army included 51 divisions. Ten (not including the division in Indo-China) were allotted to the new *Southern Army* which was to carry out the drive to the south.[9] Of the remainder 21 were in China, 14 in Manchuria and Korea, and 5 in Japan. In addition to these divisions Japan possessed 10 depot divisions, used to train reinforcements for units overseas; 22 independent brigades of infantry; and 37 other formations of approximately brigade size; also she was reorganising her divisions on a nine-battalion instead of a twelve-battalion basis. Thus she possessed the means of forming a number of additional divisions without raising new units.

The Japanese Navy, like the British and American, possessed its own infantry. In Japan these were the "Special Naval Landing Forces", flexible organisations but usually consisting basically of the equivalent of a British "battalion group" of about 1,200 to 1,500 men, including a rifle battalion, a heavy weapons company, and a few light tanks or armoured cars. Two or three such units might be combined to form a force equivalent to a British brigade group. The S.N.L.F's were named after the naval bases where they were recruited, thus the "*6th Kure S.N.L.F.*" was the 6th force, or battalion, from Kure.

Since Japan had broken away from naval limitation plans she had made her navy more powerful than the combined strength of other naval forces in the Pacific. Its main components were 11 battleships, 10 aircraft carriers, 18 heavy cruisers, 21 light cruisers, 100 destroyers and 63 submarines; these were divided administratively into six fleets, from which task forces were drawn. The two principal task forces were the fast carrier

---

[9] In 1941 the Australian Director of Military Intelligence, Colonel James Chapman, in a review of the situation at the time, wrote that Japan's economic and political situation was likely to result in her adopting a break-through course. He estimated that Japan had a mobile striking force of some ten divisions for operations in new theatres, such as Malaya or towards Australia. In the event of Japan attacking Malaya, it was possible that her forces would seek first to destroy Malaya's northern air bases, and establish themselves within easy bombing range of Singapore Island.

force assigned to attack Pearl Harbour, and a "Southern Force" to be used against the Philippines, Malaya and the Netherlands East Indies.

As with their American opponents, the Japanese Army and Navy each possessed its own air force, and, in the army air force, there was emphasis on giving close support to ground troops. The combined strength of the air forces was about 5,000 first-line aircraft, with adequate reserves for immediate requirements.

As mentioned, the Japanese Army of 1941 was re-forming its standard infantry division so that it would contain three instead of four infantry regiments. In the operations to be described, some divisions contained four regiments grouped in twos to form two brigades, and some three regiments. Other reorganisation and re-equipment was in progress. The following summary, therefore, aims at providing only a generally accurate account of the Japanese Army as it was in December 1941.

The Japanese triangular infantry division fairly closely resembled a British division in organisation and basic equipment, a main difference being that the Japanese division possessed relatively few field and anti-tank guns; probably a reflection of its long war in China against a lightly-armed enemy.

The word "regiment" is used in a variety of meanings in a British army. In this account of the structure of the Japanese Army it is used in its European sense, to indicate a group of (usually) three units. (Thus the Japanese "artillery regiment" was the equivalent of the British "divisional artillery".) In 1941 a Japanese artillery regiment was armed with 36 75-mm field guns, or field guns and 150-mm howitzers. This weakness —36 weapons compared with 72 in a fully-equipped British divisional artillery—was offset somewhat by the fact that the infantry regiments had an infantry gun company likely to be equipped with six 70-mm howitzers firing an 8-pound shell, or light guns of other models. Each infantry regiment was equipped also with 12 mortars and more than 80 grenade dischargers.

The Japanese infantry division did not include a machine-gun battalion, but each regiment possessed 24 medium ("Juki") machine-guns in addition to 84 light machine-guns. The reconnaissance regiment of the division had 12 light tanks, a 9-ton vehicle armed with a 37-mm gun and two machine-guns. The Japanese medium tank was of 15 tons with a 57-mm gun and two machine-guns.

The organisations described as Japanese "armies" consisted basically of two to four divisions and perhaps some smaller formations. A Japanese "Area Army" (e.g. the *Southern Army*) included two or more such "armies" and thus was the equivalent of a British army.

The mystical Japanese approach to warfare, and their eagerness to fling themselves furiously into battle, seems to have led to a neglect of important branches of staff work such as Supply and, particularly, Intelligence. They collected information assiduously but failed adequately to carry out the more important part of Intelligence work—collation, interpretation, and circulation—or to pay sufficient heed to it. The geographical information with which their armies were provided was inadequate; for example, the post-war report of the operations of the *XXV Japanese Army* in Malaya states that the best maps of Malaya distributed to that army were on a scale of 1:300,000 until just before Japan struck, when some on a scale of 1:100,000 were provided. The United States official historian of the operations in the Philippines concludes that, until they captured American maps in Manila, the Japanese "probably used a road map of the Philippines and hydrographic charts of their own".[1] The strength of the Australian force in Malaya was greatly over-estimated despite the ease with which information from Singapore was available.

"Japanese training manuals state that the chief aim in battle is to develop an enveloping attack on the enemy and destroy him on the field of battle," set out a booklet on the Japanese Army issued by Army Headquarters, Melbourne, in January 1942 (too late to reach Malaya before the fighting began). "Envelopment therefore is normally used in operations. In this connection it should be noted that the Japanese troops are very hardy. . . . Owing to their ability to exist on a small ration and without material comforts, their radius of action is not limited by transport requirements to the extent to which British troops are limited." Elsewhere the same booklet said:

> General tactics appear to consist of a vigorous advance using the roads until contact is gained; a direct frontal attack is avoided. Small parties carry out attacks on flanks and rear by an outflanking movement through the jungle, river and sea. These tactics show considerable initiative and usually cause a general withdrawal. Japanese infiltration methods exert considerable moral effect on troops who may be attacked in the rear.

In China the Japanese engineers had demonstrated notable speed and efficiency in construction or reconstruction of roads and river crossings —skills likely to be developed in operations against an enemy fighting guerilla-fashion and relying largely on demolition to fend off their attackers. Japanese signal equipment was of fair quality but, in general, somewhat out of date by European standards of 1941. Japanese signallers placed most emphasis on wire communication, but employed wireless where wire could not be used.

By December 1941 the Japanese Army possessed an experience of landing operations far greater than that of any other force. It had developed several types of partly-armoured, flap-fronted, shallow-draught landing craft, each able to carry up to 100 men and to travel at from 8 to 12 knots. In addition it had employed in operations the sampans commonly used in large numbers by the Japanese for fishing, ferrying and cargo-carrying. The Japanese forces were adept at a variety of ruses such as employing pyrotechnics to simulate weapon fire, calling out to the enemy in his own language, setting booby traps, and shaking bushes

---

[1] L. Morton, *The Fall of the Philippines* (1953), a volume in the official series *United States Army in World War II*, p. 599.

by means of ropes in order to draw fire. Japan was not a large-scale producer of motor vehicles, but was one of the largest manufacturers of bicycles. The availability of bicycles, either on issue or where they could be commandeered, and their usefulness on low-grade Asian roads and jungle tracks caused the Japanese to employ them on an increasing scale in military operations.

Except for their siege operations against the German garrison at Tsingtao in 1914, and a 24-days' conflict with the Russians in Manchuria in 1939, the Japanese Army had not fought a fully-equipped enemy since 1905. The tactics and equipment, the strengths and weaknesses of the Japanese Army of 1941 were products largely of the long war in China against stubborn soldiers lightly-armed and generally ill-led, but cunning guerillas fighting in terrain which presented immense difficulties to the movement of mechanised forces. Hence, largely, came the Japanese skill in landing operations and road-making and bridging; their changing organisation and tendency towards forming *ad hoc* forces; their relatively light equipment and reliance on mortars and small guns rather than on the standard field gun, and on light tanks; their emphasis on envelopment tactics; partly also their development of a large and grimly-efficient corps of military police (*Kempei Tai*) possessing wide powers and trained to employ those powers ruthlessly.

PART II

SOUTH-EAST ASIA CONQUERED

CHAPTER 7

WIDESPREAD ONSLAUGHT

NEWS of an increasingly strong concentration of Japanese sea, land and air forces in southern Indo-China and the South China Sea was received by Air Chief Marshal Brooke-Popham during November. A telegram from the British War Office gave warning that the Washington negotiations might collapse at any moment, and that Japan might be expected then to attack Thailand, the Netherlands East Indies, or the Philippines. Aircraft, believed to be Japanese, flew over Malaya so fast and so high that they escaped identification.

Because of a report from Saigon that the Japanese intended landing troops in southern Thailand on 1st December, Air Headquarters was warned on 29th November to be ready to support Operation MATADOR at twelve hours' notice. Additional air forces were moved into north Malaya,[1] and daily air reconnaissances were carried out, though with the stipulation that there must be no attack on any convoy thus located.[2] Degrees of readiness of the forces generally were stepped up, and relief which had been proposed of the 22nd Australian Brigade in the Mersing area by the 27th Brigade was indefinitely postponed.

Late in November General Percival visited Sarawak. He was impressed by the fact that this part of Borneo was nearly as large as England, and there were large Japanese-owned rubber plantations near the airfield seven miles south of its capital, Kuching; yet the forces comprised only one Indian battalion (the 2/15th Punjab) to supplement partially-trained and poorly-equipped local forces. Obviously there was little hope of holding Sarawak against serious attack; but resistance might make the enemy use a greater force than otherwise would be necessary. Listening to radio news on 29th November, Percival heard that all troops away from barracks

---

[1] On 8th December, after certain moves by detachments had taken place in the early morning, the Air Force in Malaya was located as follows:

Base	Unit	Type	No.
Singapore Island			
Seletar	No. 36 (TB) Sqn RAF	Vildebeeste	6
	No. 100 (TB) Sqn RAF	Vildebeeste	12
	No. 205 (FB) Sqn RAF	Catalina	3
Tengah	No. 34 (B) Sqn RAF	Blenheim IV	16
Sembawang	No. 453 (F) Sqn RAAF	Buffalo	16
Kallang	No. 243 (F) Sqn RAF } No. 488 (F) Sqn RNZAF }	Buffalo	30
Northern Malaya			
Sungei Patani	No. 21 (F) Sqn RAAF	Buffalo	12
	No. 27 (NF) Sqn RAF	Blenheim I	12
Kota Bharu	No. 1 (GR) Sqn RAAF	Hudson	12
	Det No. 243 (F) Sqn RAF	Buffalo	2
Gong Kedah	Det No. 36 (TB) Sqn RAF	Vildebeeste	6
Kuantan	No. 8 (GR) Sqn RAAF	Hudsons	12
	No. 60 (B) Sqn RAF	Blenheim	8
Alor Star	No. 62 (B) Sqn RAF	Blenheim I	11
			158

There were also 3 Catalinas manned by Dutch crews on Singapore Island, making a total of 161 first-line aircraft in Malaya on the outbreak of war.

[2] Rumours to the effect that Thailand was the objective had been spread by the Japanese to conceal their real intentions.

in Singapore had been ordered back to them at once. Returning with all speed aboard a destroyer, he found on arrival on 1st December that Brooke-Popham had ordered the second degree of readiness, and the Volunteers were being mobilised. Soon troops were recalled from leave and other precautions were taken, including the rounding up of Japanese civilians.

Admiral Phillips,[3] who had flown from Colombo to Singapore in advance of *Prince of Wales* and *Repulse* and taken up duty as Commander-in-Chief Eastern Fleet (leaving local naval defence to Vice-Admiral Layton[4]) flew on 4th December to confer at Manila with the Commander-in-Chief of the United States Asiatic Fleet, Admiral Thomas C. Hart. The conference was ended abruptly by news that a large Japanese convoy was on its way from Camranh Bay towards the Gulf of Siam. As Phillips was leaving for Singapore because of this situation, Hart told him that he had just ordered four of his destroyers, then at Balikpapan (Borneo), to join Phillips' force.

Authority to order MATADOR in certain contingencies without reference to the War Office reached Brooke-Popham on 5th December, in consequence of the previously mentioned assurance of American armed support if Britain found it necessary either to forestall a Japanese landing in the Kra Isthmus, or in certain other circumstances. The contingencies specified to Brooke-Popham for instituting operation MATADOR were:

(a) If he had information that a Japanese expedition was advancing with the apparent intention of landing on the Kra Isthmus; or
(b) If the Japanese violated any other part of Thailand.

It had, however, been impressed on him only a few days before by the British Chiefs of Staff that such an operation, if the Japanese intended to land in southern Thailand, would almost certainly mean war with Japan. He therefore considered it his duty to be scrupulously careful in acting on the telegram.

Also on 5th December, *Repulse* had left Singapore at slow speed, preceded by three Vildebeeste planes as an anti-submarine patrol, and screened by the destroyers *Tenedos* and *Vampire* (the latter a vessel of the Royal Australian Navy which had been refitting at Singapore) for Darwin.[5] In Australia that day, Cabinet decided at a special meeting to cancel army leave, and authorised Australian participation in the provisional plans for cooperation with the United States and the Netherlands Indies.

Soon after midday on 6th December[6] a Hudson of No. 1 Squadron R.A.A.F., operating from Kota Bharu reported three transports with a

---

[3] Admiral Sir Tom Phillips, KCB; RN. Lord Commissioner of the Admiralty and Vice-Chief of Naval Staff 1939-41; C-in-C Eastern Fleet 1941. B. 19 Feb 1888. Killed in action 10 Dec 1941.
[4] The appointment of Commander-in-Chief, China Station, held by Layton, lapsed at the outbreak of war with Japan, the Admiralty having decided to merge the command of the China Station with that of the Eastern Fleet.
[5] Concerned about the exposed position of *Repulse* and *Prince of Wales*, the British Admiralty had cabled on 1st December to Phillips suggesting that they be sent away from Singapore. *Prince of Wales*, however, required a few days at Singapore to repair defects before putting to sea again.
[6] Malayan time (2 hours 40 minutes behind Australian Eastern time). Local times are used in this and succeeding chapters.

cruiser as escort about 80 miles south of Cape Cambodia, steering northwest. This report was followed by two other sightings, the first considerably farther east, of twenty-two transports with a heavy escort of cruisers and destroyers steering west; and the second, similarly constituted, but slightly south, which might either have been the same convoy or another steering a parallel course. As one of the Hudsons on reconnaissance was chased by an enemy plane, it was apparent that the Japanese knew they had been seen. However, the air force was under orders not to attack owing to Brooke-Popham's anxiety lest, by holding out a bait, the Japanese might provoke the first blow, and make the British appear the aggressors. Had the main group of Japanese vessels continued its observed course, it would have reached the Kra Isthmus, a narrow neck of land joining Thailand to Malaya. Did this clearly indicate an attack on Thailand—so clearly that Brooke-Popham could set MATADOR in motion—or would the expedition attack Malaya?

In this grave situation, Brooke-Popham consulted Layton and Phillips' Chief of Staff, Rear-Admiral Palliser.[7] They concluded that probably the expedition would follow the course of the vessels first observed, and anchor at Koh Rong on the west coast of Indo-China. No word had been received of an actual breakdown of the Washington talks, and this Japanese move might be but another step towards, yet not into, Thailand, in the war of nerves in which Japan was engaged. Brooke-Popham decided that he would not be justified in ordering MATADOR but he gave instructions that all forces bring themselves to the highest degree of readiness, and that air contact with the expedition be maintained. Battle stations were accordingly taken up.

Though time to move forces into Thailand before an enemy could forestall them was the essence of Operation MATADOR, attempts to maintain contact with the Japanese ships had meanwhile failed. One Catalina flying-boat sent to take over the search in the early part of the night returned to Singapore at 8 a.m. on the 7th without having seen anything of the enemy convoys because of bad weather; another, dispatched at 2 a.m. on 7th December, failed either to report contact or return to base.

The reconnaissance plan for 7th December provided for a cover by British, Australian, and Dutch aircraft of the more direct approaches to Singapore and the Mersing-Endau area, and a sweep into the Gulf of Siam. Vildebeestes were dispatched to maintain the anti-submarine patrol ahead of *Repulse*, which had been recalled from its intended voyage to Australia. Because of bad weather the aircraft which were to make the sweep into the Gulf of Siam did not take off until 6.45 a.m. Two of them, which had encountered rain, low clouds and bad visibility, returned shortly afterwards, and the third sighted nothing. A plane dispatched at 12.20 p.m. to make a reconnaissance of the anchorage at Koh Rong also returned, owing to the bad weather. Admiral Phillips returned that morning from Manila.

---

[7] Admiral Sir Arthur Palliser, KCB, DSC; RN. Chief of Staff Eastern Fleet 1941-42; Comd 1 Cruiser Sqn 1943-44; a Lord Commissioner of the Admiralty and Chief of Supplies and Transport 1944-45. Died 22 Feb 1956.

Reports to Air Headquarters during the afternoon included the sighting at 3.45 by a Hudson of No. 8 Australian Squadron of a Japanese vessel stated to have a large number of men on deck in khaki. A merchant vessel and a cruiser were sighted by another Hudson at 5.50, about 112 miles north of Kota Bharu, and the cruiser fired at it. At 6.48 p.m., through dense cloud, four Japanese vessels were seen off the coast of Thailand about 150 miles from Kota Bharu, steaming south—some thirty hours after

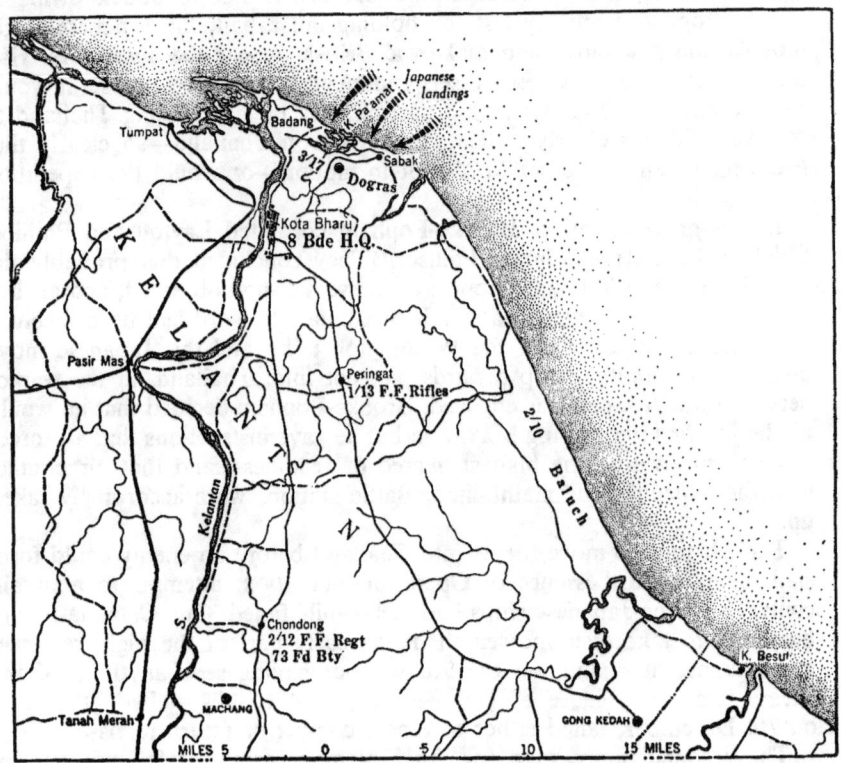

Kota Bharu, 8th December 1941

the Japanese had first been sighted. Although official accounts vary, Brooke-Popham recorded that this latter report did not reach him until about 9 p.m. Percival held that if the Japanese were headed for Singora, it was unlikely that they could be forestalled by Operation MATADOR. He therefore told Brooke-Popham that he considered the operation would be unsound. At a conference held at the naval base, at which Brooke-Popham, Phillips, and Percival were present, it was decided not to order MATADOR that night, but General Heath, of the III Indian Corps, who was to be responsible for its execution, was ordered to be ready to put it into effect at dawn. Brooke-Popham considered that in view of the bad conditions for reconnaissance, and on the information available, there was no certainty that the Japanese were about to open hostilities. He recalled warnings that MATADOR would almost certainly mean war with Japan, and that he had no authority to order attack on a Japanese expedition at sea until the Japanese had committed some definite hostile act. Apparently he either did not regard the firing on the Hudson, preceded by the disappearance without signal of the Catalina, in this sense; was not fully informed on these points; or did not think the facts sufficiently established to warrant their acceptance.

Before midnight, Japanese ships anchored off the coast near Kota Bharu. The 8th Indian Brigade's front in this locality comprised six beaches each about five miles long, and a 10-mile river front. Three airfields—Kota Bharu, Gong Kedah, and Machang, so located that they were roughly at the three points of a triangle, with Kota Bharu at its apex—were guarded by the 1st Hyderabad and the 1st Mysore State Infantry. Beaches north and east of the town were heavily wired, and concrete machine-gun pill-boxes were spaced along them at distances of about 1,000 yards. To the south, however, were dummy pill-boxes and stretches of sparsely-wired beach. The principal units in the 8th Brigade were:

3/17th Dogras (beaches north and east of Kota Bharu).
2/10th Baluch (20 miles of beaches south of Dogras).
1/13th Frontier Force Rifles (in reserve).
2/12th Frontier Force Regiment (on loan from 22nd Indian Brigade and in reserve, with one company patrolling towards the frontier with Thailand).
73rd Field Battery; 21st Mountain Battery.

Soon after the ships were sighted, the Japanese began shelling two pill-boxes guarding a small river-mouth between the Sabak and Badang beaches held by the Dogras. Japanese troops landed at this point about 12.30 a.m. on 8th December, and fierce fighting followed.

When the ships were reported to Air Headquarters, a Hudson was ordered to the scene with flares to reconnoitre; but before it took off definite information was received that transports were offshore apparently about to land troops. The Officer Commanding the Kota Bharu airfield thereupon received authority to take offensive action with all No. 1 Squadron's available Hudsons (ten). Vildebeestes at Gong Kedah and five air squadrons at Kuantan, Sungei Patani, Tengah and Alor Star were ordered to attack shipping in the Kota Bharu area at first light. In a series of sorties from Kota Bharu, the Australian airmen bombed and machine-gunned enemy ships and crowded landing barges, inflicting damage and casualties. Dutch submarines also operated against the enemy.[8]

The monsoon, which might have been expected to hinder Japanese landings during this season, had in fact facilitated the enemy approach by pro-

---

[8] The Dutch submarines, based on Singapore, operated under the strategic control of Admiral Layton. One of them (*K12*) sank the transport *Toro Maru* (1,939 tons) off Kota Bharu on 12th December. The *O16* severely damaged the transports *Tosan Maru* (8,666 tons), *Sakina Maru* (7,170 tons), *Ayato Maru* (9,788 tons) and *Asosan Maru* (8,812 tons) at Patani the same day. The *K12* was credited with sinking a naval tanker, *Taisan Maru* (3,525 tons) near Kota Bharu on 13th December, but this may have been the burnt-out *Awagisan Maru*. By 21st December three of them—including *O16*—had been sunk. A more detailed account of the naval operations in this period appears in G. Hermon Gill, *Royal Australian Navy, 1939-42*, in the Navy series of this history.

viding cloud cover. On the other hand it had badly affected the surfaces of such roads as could be used in moving British ground forces to the point of attack. Arrangements were made for counter-attacks on the beaches after dawn, with the understanding that air support would be given.

Landing of Japanese troops was continuing when soon after 4 a.m. some seventeen Japanese aircraft, from southern Indo-China, came over Singapore Island. Most of the bombs fell at the Seletar and Tengah airfields, causing little damage, but in Raffles Square, close to the harbour, and predominantly Singapore's European shopping and commercial centre, about 200 casualties resulted among the Asian population. Radar had detected the approaching raiders more than half an hour before their arrival, but the Operations Room of Fighter Control was unable to obtain any response from civil A.R.P. headquarters, Singapore's street lights remained ablaze throughout the raid, and no effective warning was received by the populace. Many, in fact, thought it was a realistic practice by British planes, and watched from windows, streets, and gardens. The rumble of exploding bombs broke the news to the citizens of Singapore that war had come to Malaya.

While Malaya was being attacked, 7th December[9] was dawning at Hawaii, 3,440 miles east of Japan, and 2,010 miles from San Francisco. The periscope of a submarine had been sighted off the entrance buoys to Pearl Harbour, America's great Pacific naval and air base on Oahu Island, by a mine-sweeper at 3.42 a.m. Hawaiian time. As American submarines had been forbidden to operate submerged in this area, the sighting was reported to the destroyer *Ward,* on patrol duty, which made a search. It was not, however, until 6.45 a.m. that the *Ward* located and sank a midget submarine. A report of this action filtered through to the duty officer of the Commander-in-Chief, Pacific Fleet, by 7.12 a.m. However, a number of unconfirmed reports of submarines had been received in the past few days, and despite the critical state of affairs between America and Japan, and the warnings which had accompanied it, immediate precautions were limited to ordering a ready-duty destroyer out to assist *Ward,* and a stand-by destroyer to get up steam.

Suddenly, at 7.55 a.m. (1.45 a.m. on 8th December in Malaya) a cloud of planes appeared over Oahu. In a series of attacks lasting until 10 a.m. Japanese bombs blasted warships and naval and army aircraft at this vital point of America's Pacific defence system. So complete was the surprise that the planes were not recognised as hostile until the bombs fell. One of a number of midget submarines succeeded in entering the harbour through the gate in the submarine net. It fired its complement of two torpedoes ineffectively, and was sunk. Another was beached on the coast of Oahu, and captured with its commander next day. All the

---
[9] Because Hawaii was on the other side of the International Date Line, the date was a day earlier than in Malaya.

midget submarines were lost, but despite attempts to locate the main Japanese force, it escaped without being seen.

When the results of the raid were assessed, it was apparent that America's naval strength in the Pacific had been struck a crippling blow. Of the eight battleships in Pearl Harbour, four were sunk, one was run aground to prevent sinking, and three were damaged but remained afloat. Two destroyers were so badly damaged as to need complete rebuilding, one had its bow blown off. Three light cruisers were damaged, but left Pearl Harbour late in January 1942. Altogether 19 vessels were hit; about 120 planes destroyed; and service casualties amounted to 2,403 killed and 1,178 wounded.[1]

Great as was the destruction thus wrought, there remained of the United States Fleet in the Pacific the surviving vessels, damaged and undamaged, in the harbour;[2] and elsewhere a powerful force in the aggregate of one battleship (being overhauled) and three carriers, with heavy and light cruisers, destroyers, submarines, and other craft. Though the fleet's battleships—its main strength in orthodox terms—were for the time being out of action, the components still serviceable were capable of giving in their turn demonstrations of sea-air power such as had been demonstrated by the Japanese in the raid. The vessels transferred to the Atlantic earlier in the year were of course exempt from the disaster. The heavy cruiser *Pensacola,* an escorting tender, four transports, and three freighters, were on their way at the time to Manila. Carrying 4,600 soldiers, airmen and naval replacements, and a number of aircraft, the convoy was diverted to Suva, and sailed thence to Brisbane.

As the news of Japan's offensive on the opening day was put together, it was found that her forces had attacked not only Thailand, Malaya, and Pearl Harbour, but a series of points along a quarter of the world's circumference which lay between them. These points included Midway, Wake, and Guam Islands—outposts of United States power in the Pacific and knots in a tenuous lifeline between America and the Philippines; the Philippines themselves; Ocean Island; and the British colony of Hong Kong.

Midway Island, 1,140 miles north-west of Oahu, had been officially described in 1938 as second in importance only to Pearl Harbour from a strategical viewpoint. As a landing-point between America and East Asia, it had been visited by Mr Kurusu in November on his way from Japan to the United States to join Admiral Nomura in the critical diplomatic negotiations then in progress.[3] Its garrison on 7th December[4]

---

[1] From S. E. Morison, *The Rising Sun in the Pacific* (1948), p. 126, in the series *History of United States Naval Operations in World War II.*

[2] Excluding vessels heavily damaged though not sunk, auxiliaries, and smaller craft, these comprised two heavy cruisers, four light cruisers, 29 destroyers, eight destroyer mine-sweepers, and five submarines.

[3] A lively account of the pains taken to give Kurusu an impression that the defences of Midway were considerably stronger than in fact they were appears in *Marines at Midway,* by Lt-Col Robert D. Heinl Jr, U.S.M.C., published in 1948 by the Historical Section of the Marine Corps.

[4] Midway is on the same side of the International Date Line as Pearl Harbour.

was the 6th Defence Battalion of the American Marine Corps. The carrier *Lexington* was on her way with a marine fighter squadron which it was intended should be flown in to Midway that day. The raid on Pearl Harbour resulted in the *Lexington* being diverted from this task in an endeavour to locate the attacking force. News of the raid on Pearl Harbour reached Midway while it was in progress, but it was not until 9.30 that night that a radar set indicated the presence of "what seemed to be surface targets".[5] Five minutes later salvos of fire from seaward were pounding its defences. Casualties on Midway in what proved to be another hit-run raid were light, but the enemy surprise tactics had once more been effective in causing extensive damage.

Wake Island, 2,600 miles west of Oahu, and within relatively short range of Guam and clusters of islands held at the time by the Japanese, was towards the end of 1941 being converted into a modern naval air base, primarily for reconnaissance purposes, but also as a stage in trans-Pacific flights. It was in fact used in staging Flying Fortresses to reinforce air strength in the Philippines. Although preparations were being rushed, Wake's defences were highly vulnerable when, shortly after sunrise on 8th December,[6] a message arrived that Pearl Harbour was being attacked. Wake was garrisoned by a detachment of United States Marines, supplemented on 4th December by a Marine fighter squadron with aircraft new to them, and deficient in several important respects. The total combat force amounted to 449 all ranks. Posts were hurriedly manned when the news of Pearl Harbour was received, and air patrols were sent up; but Wake lacked radar equipment. It was not until the officer commanding a battery near the southern tip of the island saw strange aircraft overhead at 11.58 a.m. (local time) that warning of attack was received. The aircraft had been masked by a rain squall and, as the officer jumped to a field telephone, Japanese bombs were falling. When the raid was over, at 12.10, Wake was littered with wreckage.

In the Marianas one lonely island, Guam, was a United States outpost; but its development had been neglected, and, as at Wake, the garrison was small. It consisted of 365 marines and 308 locally-recruited men, equipped with small arms only. News of the attack on Pearl Harbour reached the Governor, Captain George J. McMillan of the United States Navy, at 5.45 a.m. and at 8.27 Japanese aircraft commenced successive bombing raids on the Marine headquarters, and native villages.

All Hong Kong's troops were at their battle stations by the evening of 7th December. Definite reports were received during the evening of concentrations of Japanese forces in villages bordering the frontier of

---

[5] *Marines at Midway*, p. 11.
[6] 7 Dec at Pearl Harbour.

the colony, on the mainland. A broadcast warning in code from Tokyo to Japanese nationals that war was imminent was picked up at 4.45 a.m., Hong Kong time, on 8th December, and passed to the authorities concerned. News of the Japanese attack on Malaya arrived at 5 a.m.

Thus when at 8 a.m. Japanese planes dive-bombed Kai Tak airfield on the mainland, Hong Kong's garrison was standing to arms. It had been recognised that the five air force planes stationed there were hopelessly inadequate to cope with any substantial attack. All of them were soon either destroyed or damaged. Japanese troops simultaneously crossed the frontier, and during the day and succeeding night forced forward units to withdraw to positions near what was known as the Gin Drinkers' Line,[7] where the main body of the brigade assigned to defence of the mainland was stationed.

Before dawn on 8th December in the Philippines General Lewis H. Brereton, MacArthur's air commander, had been told of the raid on Pearl Harbour and had given instructions that all his air units should be prepared for action; but he received orders not to take the offensive until authorised by MacArthur's headquarters to do so. His plan was to attack targets in Takao Harbour, Formosa, especially enemy transports and warships, and to reconnoitre airfields on Formosa. At dawn Japanese aircraft attacked a seaplane tender in Davao Gulf, south-east of Mindanao Island, and commenced raids on north Luzon Island. For reasons which remain obscure it was not until about 11 a.m. that Brereton received instructions that "bombing missions" could be executed. Preparations were then made for an air offensive against Formosa at daybreak next day.

In these circumstances, many aircraft were on the ground when fifty-four Japanese bombers made a surprise high-level bombing attack on Clark Field, about 40 miles north-west of Manila. This commenced about 12.15 p.m., and was followed by low-level strafing by thirty-four Zeros. When the attacks ceased at 1.37 p.m., Clark Field was ablaze, there had been heavy loss of life, and almost the entire force of aircraft at the base had been destroyed or put out of commission. Iba Field, on the coast north-west of Clark Field, was also attacked, by 104 aircraft, just as a squadron of fighters was returning from a search over the South China Sea. At the end of the day, half the heavy bomber strength of the United States Far East Air Force had been lost, with fifty-six fighters and 25 or 30 other aircraft.

On this first day of the Japanese onslaught a minor attack was made on a Pacific outpost manned by a small Australian garrison. At 11.30 a.m. on the 8th a flying-boat appeared over Ocean Island, circled it and dropped five bombs, which caused no damage. Soon after 1 p.m.

---

[7] A line constructed on strong ground five or six miles north of the harbour strait separating mainland and island, and covering the isthmus between Tide Cove and Gin Drinkers' Bay.

that day a flying-boat (believed to be the same) appeared over Nauru, also garrisoned by Australians,[8] circled the island at about 6,000 feet, and disappeared in a north-easterly direction about half an hour later.

Because of the difference between Malayan and Greenwich Mean Time (7 hours 30 minutes as from 1st September 1941), it was during the evening of 7th December in England that the British Government received a report that the Japanese were attempting to land at Kota Bharu. When the Australian War Cabinet met on 8th December, a British Admiralty message had been received indicating that hostilities against Japan should be commenced. It agreed that the situation should be accepted as involving a state of war against Japan. As mentioned, the Australian Government had agreed to hold forces ready at Darwin to reinforce Timor and Ambon. In Cabinet Mr Curtin stated that in response to a request by the Netherlands East Indies authorities he had approved of arrangements being made immediately for dispatch of A.I.F. troops to Koepang in Timor. These arrangements were confirmed. The situation generally was surveyed and various consequent decisions were made. Approval by the Minister for the Army for the dispatch of A.I.F. troops to Ambon was given the same day. Australia and New Zealand formally declared themselves at war with Japan.

The Japanese Ambassador to Washington and Mr Kurusu were in the waiting room of the American Secretary of State's office, about to present a long reply to America's note of 26th November, when Mr Cordell Hull received a telephone call from President Roosevelt. The President said he had received an unconfirmed report that the Japanese had attacked Pearl Harbour. Hull already had received a series of decoded intercepts of the Japanese reply. This contained no declaration of war or even notice that diplomatic relations had ended, but said that owing to the attitude of the American Government Japan considered it impossible to reach an agreement through further negotiations. As the Pearl Harbour report had not been confirmed, Hull decided to see the Japanese envoys. When they faced him, he was aware that Pearl Harbour had been attacked more than an hour before. After making a pretence of reading the note they presented, Hull eased his feelings.

"I must say," he declared, "that in all my conversations with you during the last nine months I have never uttered one word of untruth. This is borne out absolutely by the record. In all my fifty years of public service I have never seen a document that was more crowded with infamous falsehoods and distortions . . . on a scale so huge that I never imagined until today that any government on this planet was capable of uttering them."

---

[8] In 1941, as an outcome of raids by German armed merchant cruisers, small garrisons, each with two field guns, had been established on the remote phosphate-producing islands of Nauru and Ocean. On Ocean Island there were in December about 50 men under Captain A. L. Bruce (of Manly, NSW); on Nauru a similar force under Captain J. C. King (Mosman, NSW).

At this, Nomura "seemed about to say something. His face was impassive, but I felt he was under great emotional strain. I stopped him with a motion of my hand. I nodded towards the door. The Ambassadors turned without a word and walked out, their heads down."[9]

A declaration of war by Japan on America followed; and next day Congress reciprocated.

Japan's plan of attack was imposing in its breadth and daring. To sustain the huge task she had undertaken would make big demands on Japan's forces and economy; but it might be expected to place a still heavier strain upon the deficient defensive strength within the threatened area. Like a burglar seeking to rob a householder made complacent by prosperity, Japan could hope to find her victims asleep, or as nearly so as might be in a military sense. In this, largely, she was not disappointed. Indeed, the most ambitious of her leaders could hardly have hoped for such success as the first day's raids yielded. Not only was surprise achieved in the actual appearance of her forces at several widely-spaced points of attack, but also in the skill of Japanese airmen and the performance of their craft. Mentally as well as materially, the defenders were staggered by the onslaught.

Perhaps the most surprising thing about the attack on Pearl Harbour was that it was a surprise. This great naval and air base, like the Singapore Base, represented an enormous investment of public funds. Unlike the Singapore Base, it was occupied by a powerful fleet and air force, and though installation of a radar system had been delayed, mobile sets were in operation for a few hours a day.[1] The likelihood of a Japanese surprise attack on the base had been accepted; vital code messages from Tokyo were being intercepted, decoded, and perused; and a series of other indications of the rapid approach of zero hour in relations between Japan and the United States had been noted.[2] On the other hand there had been during late 1941 a persistent conviction in Washington, as in Malaya, that Japan would attack the Soviet Union's Maritime Provinces rather than committing herself elsewhere.

However, in concentrating their attacks upon warships and aircraft, the Japanese had neglected Pearl Harbour's permanent installations, such as workshops, power plant, and the main fuel storage depot. Thus ships could be, and were, raised; damage repaired; and ships and aircraft reinforced. Japan had disposed of for some while, but not permanently,

---

[9] *The Memoirs of Cordell Hull*, Vol II, pp. 1096-97. Hull gained the impression that neither Nomura nor Kurusu had heard at this stage of the Japanese attack.

[1] The approach of aircraft was detected on one set, but the possibility of their being enemy planes was ignored.

[2] Whether adequate information was conveyed to the responsible authorities, and the allocation of responsibility for failure to take the necessary precautionary measures, are matters outside the scope of this volume. They and other aspects of the attack on Pearl Harbour were the subject of a series of official investigations.

the danger of serious interference by the United States Pacific Fleet. As against this temporary advantage, she had united in opposition to her the people of a power with resources far greater than her own.

Japan's formal decision to go to war against Great Britain, the United States, and the Netherlands on the ground that negotiations with the United States had failed, had been made at an Imperial Conference on 1st December. It was decided that notification to the United States should precede the raid on Pearl Harbour by such a brief period that it would not interfere with the advantage to be gained by surprise.[3]

An operation order issued by Admiral Yamamoto to the Japanese Combined Fleet on 1st November had announced that Japan intended "to drive Britain and America from Greater East Asia, and to hasten the settlement of the China Incident. . . . The vast and far-reaching fundamental principle, the goal of our nation—*Hakko Ichiu*—will be demonstrated to the world."

Twenty submarines, comprising an Advance Striking Force, had approached Pearl Harbour independently of the Carrier Force. Clamped to each of five of them was a midget submarine, 41 to 45 feet long, fitted with two small torpedoes, and with two-man crews whose task meant almost certain death to them. The Carrier Force, after a long and hazardous voyage in stormy seas, reached a point 275 miles north of Pearl Harbour about 6 a.m. on the day of the attack, and launched 360 of its aircraft in the series of attacks. Sunday had been deliberately chosen because it was customary for the fleet to be at base over the week-ends. Church bells were ringing as the bombs began to fall. Total Japanese losses in the operation, additional to the five midgets, were 29 aircraft.

Midway was shelled by another force, known as the *Midway Neutralisation Unit*; Wake Island was bombed by planes from Kwajalein Atoll, in the Marshall Islands; and Guam by planes from Saipan in the Mariana Islands. Missions against Nauru and Ocean Islands were flown by four-engined flying-boats based, until 13th December, at Majuro (Marshall Islands). Later reference will be made to the forces engaged against Hong Kong. In the Philippines the first-day attacks were mainly by large groups of army and navy aircraft from Formosa, though the attack on the seaplane tender at Davao in Mindanao was by dive bombers from a carrier based on Palau, about 400 miles north of New Guinea. In the main attacks the Japanese, intent on neutralising MacArthur's air power, succeeded far beyond their hopes. They had feared that delay, caused by bad weather, in taking off from Formosa would result in stiff opposition.

---

[3] Nomura had been instructed by Tokyo to deliver the reply to the United States at 1 p.m., Washington time (which was dawn in Hawaii and around midnight in East Asia). But delay occurred in Nomura's office in getting the long message decoded and typed, and he and Kurusu did not reach Hull's office until 2.5 p.m. As has been shown, the landing at Kota Bharu occurred before the raid on Pearl Harbour. Thus it was not until after both these attacks had occurred that the Japanese emissaries delivered the message. Referring to the fact that it was not given to Great Britain, Togo said at the eventual trials of Japanese accused of war crimes that he thought Washington would pass it to London.

The *XXV Japanese Army* employed against Malaya[4] was commanded by Lieut-General Tomoyuki Yamashita,[5] who had headed the Japanese military mission sent to Germany and Italy to study their methods of waging war. Exclusive of its *56th Division,* which would stand by in Japan, it comprised 125,400 men (of whom nearly 37,000 were line of communication troops), 7,320 vehicles and 11,516 horses.[6] Considerable difficulty had been experienced in getting the widely-dispersed units together in time for the task ahead. The plan for Malaya was that, with sea and air cooperation, the main strength would land near the frontier of Thailand and Malaya and advance to the Sungei Perak, on Malaya's west coast, in fifteen days. Meanwhile strength would be built up for advance to the southern end of the Malay Peninsula, opposite Singapore Island. Assault on the island, and on Singapore, was to follow. Landings on the south-east coast of the peninsula, in the Kuantan-Mersing area, to assist the main drive were contemplated.

The *5th Japanese Division* was to make the main landings at Singora and Patani in Thailand near Malaya. The main body of the *9th Infantry Brigade (11th* and *41st Regiments)* would then make for west Malaya along the Singora-Alor Star road, and the *42nd Regiment* (of the *21st Brigade)* along the Patani-Kroh road. The *56th Regiment* detached from the *18th Division* would make a subsidiary landing at Kota Bharu, and push southward along the Malayan east coast. Additional flights of the

---

[4] The order of battle of the *XXV Army* for the Malayan campaign was:
Imperial Guards (motor transport) including a divisional infantry group headquarters, *3rd, 4th* and *5th Konoye Regts,* each regiment 2,600 strong. Total strength 12,600.
5th Division (motor transport) including *9th Infantry Brigade (11th* and *41st Regts)* and *21st Infantry Brigade (21st* and *42nd Regts)* each regiment 2,600 strong. Total strength 15,300.
18th Division (horse transport), including *23rd Infantry Brigade (55th* and *56th Regts)* and *35th Infantry Brigade (114th* and *124th Regts),* each regiment 3,500 strong. Total strength 22,200.
1st Independent Anti-Tank Battalion.
Eight independent anti-tank companies.
3rd Tank Group, consisting of four tank regiments—*1st, 2nd* and *6th (Medium)* and *14th (Light)*—and ancillary units.
3rd Independent Mountain Artillery Regt, 3rd and *18th Heavy Field Artillery Regts.*
21st Heavy Field Artillery Battalion.
Two trench mortar battalions (*3rd* and *5th*) horsed.
14th Independent Mortar Battalion.
17th Field Air Defence Unit (consisting of four field anti-aircraft battalions).
Three independent field anti-aircraft companies.
1st Balloon Company.
Three independent engineer regiments (*4th, 15th* and *23rd*).
5th Independent Heavy Bridging Company (two horsed, one mechanised).
Three bridging material companies (*21st, 22nd* and *27th*).
Two river crossing material companies (*10th* and *15th*), one horsed, one mechanised.
21st River Crossing Company (horsed).
2nd Field Military Police Unit.
2nd Railway Unit (consisting of two railway regiments, one railway material depot, two railway station offices and two special railway operating units).
25th Army Signal Unit, consisting of one telegraph regiment (horsed), one independent wire company (mechanised), three independent wireless platoons (two mechanised, one horsed) and five stationary wireless units.
Line of communication headquarters and units. (These included four L. of C. sector units, eight independent motor transport battalions, twelve independent motor transport companies, two horse transport units, ten land service companies, five construction service companies, also survey, water, road, construction, ordnance and medical units.)

[5] Yamashita's divisional commanders were: *Guards,* Lt-Gen Takumo Nishimura; *5th,* Lt-Gen Takuro Matsui; *18th,* Lt-Gen Renya Mutaguchi.

[6] At the beginning of operations the *3rd Tank Group* comprised four tank regiments (three medium, one light) and ancillary units. The *2nd (Medium) Tank Regiment* was transferred to *XVI Army* on 29th January 1942. The group then had 79 medium tanks, 100 light tanks, and 238 other vehicles. The medium tanks, weighing 16 tons, each carried one 57-mm gun and two 7.7-mm machine-guns; the light tanks (8 tons) one 32-mm gun and one 7.7-mm machine-gun.

5th Division, including its fourth infantry regiment, would reach Singora during December. The *56th Division* would be used for the Kuantan-Mersing landings if they became necessary.[7]

The *143rd Regiment* of the *55th Division* (*XV Japanese Army*) would land, concurrently with the first landings in Malaya, north of Singora, to protect the rear of the *5th Division*, secure the railway between Bangkok and the frontier with Malaya, and then capture Victoria Point, on the air reinforcement route to Malaya. The *Guards Division*, lent to *XV Army* for the early stages of its invasion of Thailand generally and its advance into Burma, would send a small detachment by sea to Bangkok, capital of Thailand, on the morning of 8th December. There it would await arrival of the rest of the division by land from Indo-China. The *Guards* would then revert to *XXV Army*, and, moving overland, follow up the advance of *5th Division*. The *18th Division*, less the *56th Regiment* which would have landed at Kota Bharu and the *124th Regiment* which would have invaded British Borneo, would land at Singora and Patani early in January, move into northern Malaya and Penang, and prepare to invade Sumatra.

It was assumed that Singapore could not be captured before early in March. In convoying the attacking land forces, a feint would be made towards Bangkok to disguise the intention of the move. Japanese naval authorities had opposed landing troops without first mastering the sea approaches, but Yamashita, who was prepared to rely largely on air protection, got his way. To overcome the problem presented by British airfields being close to or within range of the landing points, and the fact that Japanese planes operating from the mainland of Indo-China would be able to operate over these points for only a short while, an airfield was hurriedly constructed on Phuquok Island, off the French Indo-China coast, and within 300 miles of Kota Bharu. Even so, single-seater fighters would find it difficult to make the long hop, perhaps engage enemy aircraft, and get back before their tanks ran dry. It was therefore decided that as soon as possible the planes must be enabled to land and refuel in Thailand near Malaya. In the execution of the plan, the *3rd Air Group* (612 planes) would protect the convoy and cooperate with naval air units (187 planes) at the landings; then seek to destroy air opposition, and cooperate with the ground forces in their advance into Malaya.

Two slow transports left Samah Harbour, Hainan Island, on 3rd December, and others early on the 4th, under protection of the *Southern Force*, and carrying the first flight of the *5th Division*. The *143rd Regiment* sailed from Saigon during the afternoon of 5th December. It had been arranged that the two convoys should hug the coast to avoid detection or conceal as long as possible their real destination; then meet at a point (9°25′ north, 102°20′ east) in the Gulf of Siam on the morning of the 7th. They would then speed direct to their objectives.

---

[7] The division was not in fact called upon for assistance in the Malayan campaign, but was used in the invasion of Burma.

After the convoy carrying the *5th Division* had rounded Cape Cambodia, an aircraft identified by the Japanese as a Catalina dived at the fighter escort, was attacked, and disintegrated. "If this enemy seaplane had observed our convoy and reported it by wireless, our Malaya landing operation might have been a dismal failure," related Yamashita's Chief of Staff, General Susuki, although as has been shown Japanese ships in convoy had in fact been sighted earlier. Fears that the expedition would be frustrated, or at least encounter serious opposition by British sea and air forces, persisted as the Japanese reached their rendezvous. A force of some 5,500 men, commanded by Major-General Takumi, made for Kota Bharu in three ships with a naval escort, and cast anchor at 10.20 p.m. High seas then running caused difficulty in launching the landing craft and maintaining their direction. Confusion occurred about the prearranged landing places, and this was heightened by the British gunfire once the invading force was sighted. Under air attack, one transport, the *Awagisan Maru*, caught fire and was abandoned; a fire started on another but was put out; and the third was damaged. The units which first landed lost heavily under fierce fire as they sought to penetrate the wire on the beaches. Successive waves of troops "all swarmed together in the one place" according to a Japanese account, and units became mixed with each other. By dawn, however, the survivors were on their way inland.

Rough seas also hampered landing operations at Singora and Patani, and many landing craft overturned, sank, or ran aground, but by 3.30 a.m. the first landings had been made. Although some resistance was offered by Thai military and police forces at Singora, it had been overcome by about midday.[8] The troops in the first flights landed numbered approximately 13,500 at Singora, and at Patani 7,550. The total number of troops landed at these places and at Kota Bharu was about 26,640, of whom 17,230 were combat troops. Yamashita, who had travelled on one of the transports, was among the first to land at Singora.

The United States was aghast at the news of the raid on Pearl Harbour in particular; but there was now no doubt about her being in the war against Japan, and that meant that she would be at war with Germany and Italy also. The raid, sneak attack though it was, had been, technically, a brilliant achievement; but there had been shoddy thinking behind Japan's grand strategy. The United States, with the enormous resources she could mobilise, could quickly recover from the set-back she had received. She was in the war not in consequence of British pleading or intrigue, not of some abstract principle, not merely of a long-range view of her own

---

[8] General Susuki related that officers with the Japanese Consul in Singora were fired upon as they approached the back gate of the police station. They left their cars and crawled to the gate, shouting "The Japanese Army has come to save you". Susuki does not mention that this assurance was received with any enthusiasm, but he says that the party saw the Chief of Police and made "necessary arrangements".

interests; she was in the war in response to a smack on the nose.[9] Britain's Prime Minister, after the long strain of not knowing what the outcome of the Battle for Britain would be, and what might result if Japan were to join actively with Britain's enemies, went to bed that night and "slept the sleep of the saved and thankful". He was to write:

> All the rest was merely the proper application of overwhelming force. The British Empire, the Soviet Union, and now the United States, bound together with every scrap of their life and strength, were, according to my lights, twice or even thrice the force of their antagonists. . . . I expected terrible forfeits in the East; but all this would be merely a passing phase . . . there was no more doubt about the end.[1]

In his first waking moments next day, Mr Churchill decided that he would again visit the President of the United States, as quickly as possible. He thereupon sought and obtained from King and Cabinet their assent to his proposal.[2]

Swallowing the fact that Japan had ignored German urgings to attack the Soviet Union, and instead had enlisted the United States for active service against the Axis, Hitler presented Japan's Ambassador to Berlin with the Grand Cross of the Order of Merit of the German Eagle in gold. They discussed Pearl Harbour. "You gave the right declaration of war," he said.[3]

---

[9] The attack disposed of President Roosevelt's concern about the possibility of delay in getting a vote from Congress for war, and about unity among the American people in the effort which must be demanded of them. "There was just one thing that they [the Japanese] could do to get Roosevelt completely off the horns of the dilemma, and that is precisely what they did, at one stroke, in a manner so challenging, so insulting and enraging, that the divided and confused American people were instantly rendered unanimous and certain."—R. E. Sherwood, *The White House Papers of Harry L. Hopkins*, p. 430.

[1] Churchill, *The Second World War*, Vol III, pp. 539-40.

[2] Churchill set out on 12th December. Addressing a joint session of Congress during the visit, later in the month, he declared: "We have, indeed, to be thankful that so much time has been granted to us. If Germany had tried to invade the British Isles after the French collapse in June, 1940, and if Japan had declared war on the British Empire and the United States about the same date, no one can say what disaster and agonies might not have been our lot. But now . . . our transformation from easy-going peace to total war efficiency has made very great progress."

[3] *The Trial of German Major War Criminals*, Part 2, p. 285.

CHAPTER 8

INVASION OF MALAYA

BY dawn on 8th December, seventeen sorties had been carried out by Hudsons of No. 1 Squadron R.A.A.F. against Japanese ships and troops engaged in the landing at Kota Bharu. Continuous heavy rains had created conditions in which the Kota Bharu airfield would normally have been regarded as unserviceable, and a thick blanket of cloud hung low over the sea. However, ground staff and crews sprang to their tasks, and low-level attacks were made on enemy vessels, amid intense anti-aircraft fire from the Japanese. It appeared, when results were reviewed, that one transport had been blown up, one containing tanks and artillery had been set ablaze, and one had disappeared after receiving direct hits.[1] Of the squadron's ten serviceable Hudsons, two, with their crews, had been lost. The captain of one of the latter was Flight Lieutenant Ramshaw,[2] who had first located the Japanese convoys. Most of the other Hudsons were damaged, but were made again serviceable after daylight. They, and other aircraft mustered for early daylight operations, then attacked landing craft and Japanese troops ashore.

Air Force headquarters planned an all-out effort against Japanese transports at Kota Bharu at dawn on the 8th, but when the squadrons arrived over the area the ships had withdrawn. At 7.30 a.m. Japanese bombers and fighters began delivering heavy attacks on Malaya's northern airfields, using light bombs against planes and personnel, and avoiding serious damage to airfield surfaces. They were notably successful in arriving over the airfields while defending craft were descending or taking off. The performance of the enemy aircraft, and the accuracy of the bombing, came "as an unpleasant surprise"[3] to Malaya Command, despite Intelligence reports of the performance of the Zero fighters which had been sent to the Far Eastern Air Command headquarters.[4] It appeared that the fighters had been given increased range by auxiliary fuel tanks, torpedo-shaped and made of aluminium, which could be jettisoned when their contents had been used. Eight attacks were made in ten hours on Kota Bharu airfield, which was frequently strafed by low-flying aircraft.

On the beaches where the Japanese had landed, the ground forces received little air support, and it soon became apparent that the Japanese had complete mastery of the air in the vicinity. Although the Dogras stuck gamely to their task, a gap made by the enemy remained open.

---

[1] The *Awagisan Maru* was sunk, and *Ayato Maru* and *Sakewa Maru* were damaged.
[2] F-Lt J. C. Ramshaw; No. 1 Sqn RAAF. Draftsman; of Malvern, Vic; b. Bangalore, India, 18 Oct 1914. Killed in action 8 Dec 1941.
[3] A. E. Percival, *Despatch on Operations of Malaya Command, from 8th December 1941 to 15th February 1942*.
[4] It transpired that the information had lain unnoticed among the accumulation of Intelligence material at the headquarters. Its establishment did not include an Intelligence staff at the time the report was received, and the Combined Intelligence Bureau was inadequate for the needs of the three Services.

Brigadier Key,[5] commanding the 8th Indian Brigade, decided that if the airfield were to be held this gap must be closed before dusk; but the 1/13th Frontier Force Rifles and the 2/12th Frontier Force Regiment, ordered forward for the purpose, were delayed by numerous rivers and creeks, and by the nature of the country generally. In the confused situation which resulted, Key received during the afternoon a report that the airfield was already being attacked from the ground.

This report was a repeat of one already dispatched to Air Headquarters at Singapore during the temporary absence from his headquarters of the station commander, Wing Commander Noble.[6] On his return, Noble was dismayed to find the station headquarters ablaze and the staff preparing to leave, as Singapore had acted on the report and ordered a withdrawal. Having ordered his staff to remain, Noble joined Key in a reconnaissance of the airfield and discovered from the Indians that the Japanese were not yet about the perimeter defences.

In the meantime the Australians of No. 1 Squadron were working on their Hudsons under periodic air attack. During the afternoon, they detected what they thought to be aimed small-arms fire in their vicinity; a supposition which their commanding officer verified. Faced with the headquarters order to withdraw, Noble began an orderly retreat after Key had agreed to it. When the last of the few serviceable Hudsons had flown off at dusk, the Australian ground staff joined the station headquarters staff and left by truck for Krai, where they were to entrain for Singapore.

In view of this occurrence, the reappearance of Japanese transports off the beach soon after dark, and the prospect of his forward troops becoming isolated and overwhelmed, Key, with higher approval, ordered withdrawal during the night to a position north of Kota Bharu township—a course which he found had been decided upon also by Malaya Command. By midnight, the troops and guns on the airfield had been evacuated, and it was in enemy hands. The purpose for which troops had been stationed in Kelantan had thus disappeared in twenty-four hours.

The fact that the main Japanese landings were at Singora and Patani had been revealed in the course of dawn air reconnaissance on 8th December; and later in the morning many Japanese planes, mostly fighters, were found to be using the Singora airfield. The Japanese had forestalled Operation MATADOR, for which the troops of the 11th Indian Division had been standing by at half an hour's notice in drenching rain since the afternoon of 6th December. As the division was disposed, with three battalions beside trains, two in camp with their trucks loaded, and one forward near the frontier, they were ill prepared for any other move. There they remained, despite what was happening, and endeavours to obtain authority from Malaya Command for action, until about 1.30 p.m. Then, when vital hours had been lost, orders which had been issued at

---

[5] Maj-Gen B. W. Key, DSO, MC. Comd 8 Ind Bde 1940-42; GOC 11 Ind Div 1942. Regular soldier; b. 19 Dec 1895.

[6] Gp Capt C. H. Noble, OBE. Station Comd Kota Bharu 1941, Lahat 1942, Ender 1942-43; Assist Comdt RAF Base Batavia 1942. Of Melbourne; b. Bristol, Gloucester, England, 18 Apr 1905.

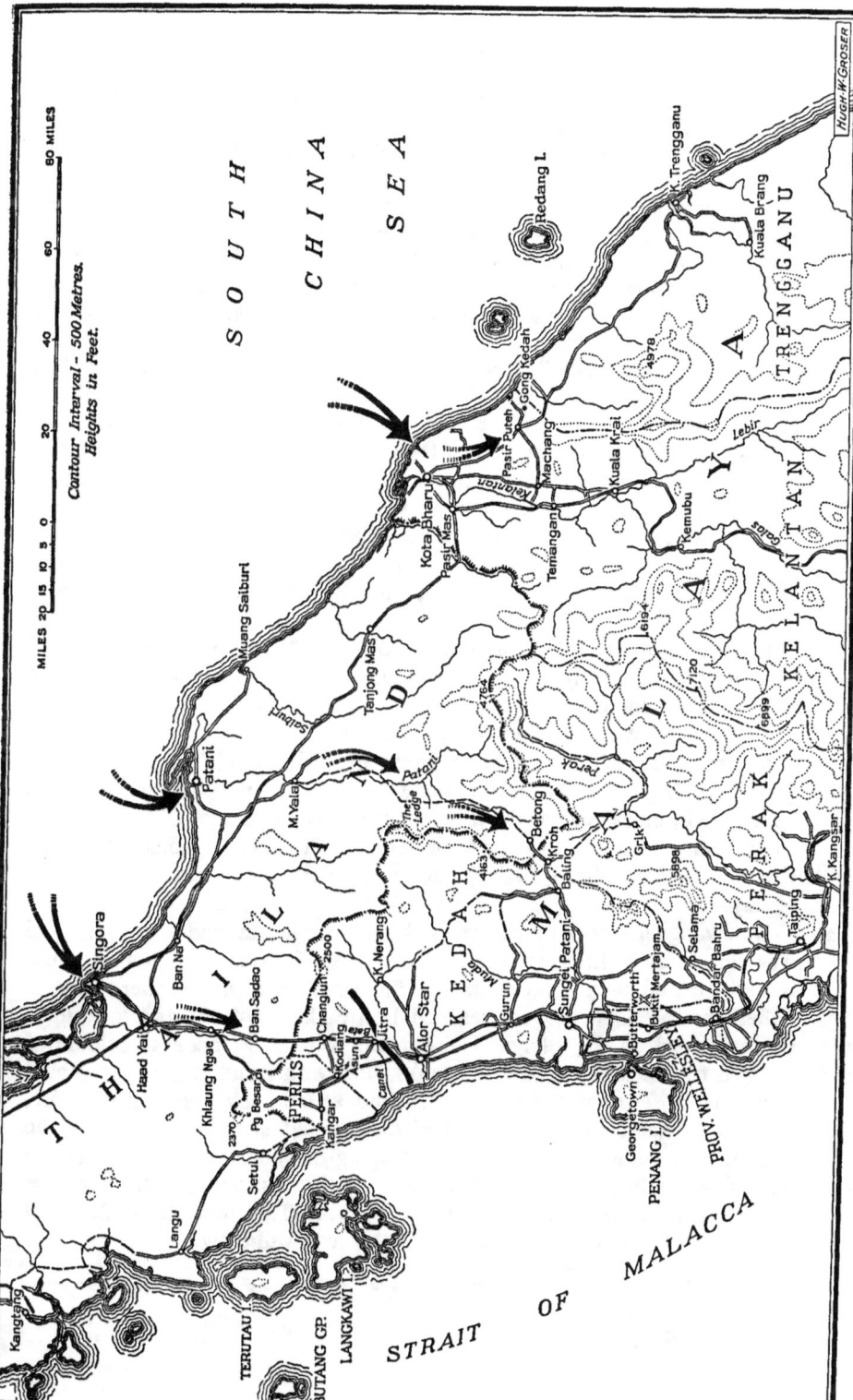

Japan's opening moves in Malaya

11.30 a.m. reached III Indian Corps headquarters requiring it to adopt the alternative plan and occupy selected defensive positions on the Singora and Kroh-Patani roads, and to dispatch a mobile column towards Singora, in an endeavour to obstruct the Japanese advance. The 28th Indian Brigade was allotted to the 11th Division as a reserve force, and entrained at Ipoh at 5 p.m. That such a restricted manoeuvre was all that remained of the dynamic plan to move into Thailand was naturally dispiriting to the troops and their commanders. Even this might be forestalled by the enemy; and the men would be tired and confused before they could give battle.

The main defensive line now to be held, running from east of Jitra to the west coast, was in the State of Kedah, astride the main road and railway from Malaya into Thailand. Its right flank rested on jungle-clad hills which had been considered by the planners of Malaya's defence system to be militarily impenetrable. Selected for the protection of the airfield at Alor Star and others south of it, the line was the only so-called prepared position of such extent on the Malayan mainland. Its system of communication trenches and line signal communications was, however, incomplete; it had not been wired, and anti-tank mines had not been laid.

In fulfilment of orders, a force known as "Krohcol" (Lieut-Colonel Moorhead[7]) based on Kroh, and comprising in the first instance 3/16th Punjab, was sent to seize a position known as "The Ledge", thirty miles beyond the frontier. Another force, "Laycol" (Brigadier Lay[8]) comprising two companies and the carrier platoon of 1/8th Punjab, with anti-tank guns and engineers, advanced along the Changlun road towards Ban Sadao, eight miles beyond the frontier on the way to Singora. An armoured train, manned by a platoon of the 2/16th Punjab and some engineers, entered Thailand from Padang Besar, in Perlis, northernmost state of Malaya.

The vanguard of Krohcol crossed the frontier in mid-afternoon, and was immediately fired upon by Thai armed constabulary. As a result, it had cleared only three miles of the road past the frontier when it halted for the night. Laycol reached Ban Sadao at dusk, and took up a position north of the village. There, about 9 p.m., a Japanese column of thirty-five vehicles, preceded by tanks, and with headlights blazing, bore down on it. Two of the tanks were knocked out by gun and rifle fire, but the Japanese infantry, who had dismounted at the beginning of the action, were soon engaged in an enveloping movement. Laycol thereupon withdrew, destroying two bridges and partly destroying a third on its way. The train party reached Khlaung Ngae, in Thailand, blew a 200-foot railway bridge on the line to Singora, and also withdrew.

---

[7] Lt-Col H. D. Moorhead. CO 3/16 Punjab. Regular soldier; b. 6 Jul 1898. Killed in action 20 Jan 1942.

[8] Brig W. O. Lay, DSO. Comd 6 Indian Bde 1939-42, 8 Indian Bde in Feb 1942. Regular soldier; b. 26 Nov 1892.

By the end of the day, the initiative was clearly in the hands of the Japanese. Having established themselves in Thailand,[9] near the border, they had aircraft within easy striking distance of the whole of northern Malaya; others, making a total of about 530, were operating from southern Indo-China.

Putting this advantage to immediate use, the Japanese were already hammering at their opponents' offensive and defensive air power. This caused heavy losses, dislocation, and confusion, and from the outset established ascendancy in the air. On land, they had been able to marshal their forces practically without hindrance, and to commence penetration of Malaya. The air forces in Malaya had been unable to inflict upon the enemy the crippling initial blow which it was their role to deliver, and the whole purpose underlying the disposition of ground and air forces in northern Malaya was endangered if not defeated. Of 110 operational aircraft based in the area at the beginning of the day, only 50 remained fit for use.[1] Although he was at the time unaware of the full extent of either the enemy air strength or the British losses, Air Chief Marshal Brooke-Popham telegraphed to the British Chiefs of Staff urging that reinforcements, especially of long-range bombers and night fighters, be sent with all speed.[2]

An Order of the Day by Brooke-Popham, prepared long before to facilitate its distribution and translation into several languages, showed how ludicrously wide of the mark had been the official thinking or publicity policy from which it had sprung. "We are ready," it was asserted. "We have had plenty of warning and our preparations are made and tested. . . . Our defences are strong and our weapons efficient. . . . We see before us a Japan drained for years by the exhausting claims of her wanton onslaught on China. . . ."

Could the real situation be retrieved or modified by naval action? To Admiral Sir Tom Phillips, when it appeared likely that Malaya's land and air forces would be hard pressed as a result of the Japanese landings, it seemed "inacceptable to retain a powerful naval force at Singapore in a state of inaction".[3] He therefore decided that, with fighter protection

---

[9] Indo-China's compliance with Japan's demands had brought powerful Japanese forces close to Thailand's eastern border, and exposed her coastline also to Japanese attack. Although the British Minister at Bangkok, Sir Josiah Crosby, had been optimistic of the Thai attitude to the Japanese, it was obvious that the prospect of successful resistance, without powerful British aid, to the forces Japan could throw against Thailand were slight. The Thai Minister for Foreign Affairs informed the British Minister on 9th December that his government had signed, under duress, an agreement with Japan allowing passage of Japanese troops across Thailand to attack Malaya or Burma.

[1] Further disappointment followed the arrival next day of twenty-two Glenn Martin Dutch bombers, and nine Buffalo fighters. Although the Dutch aircraft had come in fulfilment of the mutual reinforcement plan worked out while the Japanese threat was growing, it was found that the crews had not been trained in night fighting. As effective fighter cover could not be provided for day bombing, arrangements had to be made for their return to the Netherlands East Indies until the necessary training had been given.

[2] Mr Churchill had contemplated on 5 December offering a component of the RAF, about 10 squadrons strong, to operate on the southern flank of the Russian armies and help protect Russian naval bases on the Black Sea. However, on 10 December, while the British Foreign Secretary, Mr Anthony Eden, was on a mission to Moscow, Churchill told him of the "urgent necessity to reinforce Malaya with aircraft from the Middle East", and asked him to withhold the offer. Churchill, *The Second World War*, Vol III, pp. 475, 553-4.

[3] Vice-Admiral Sir Geoffrey Layton, *Despatch on Loss of H.M. Ships Prince of Wales and Repulse.*

if possible, or by avoiding detection during approach, he would endeavour to attack at dawn on the 10th the vessels of the Japanese invasion force. Known as "Z" Force, *Prince of Wales, Repulse,* and an escort of four destroyers which included the Australian vessel *Vampire,* sailed from Singapore Base at 5.35 p.m. on 8th December. Their course was eastward of the Anambas Islands, to avoid possible enemy mines near the coast; and then northward.

On the Kota Bharu front, in darkness and heavy rain, Brigadier Key's troops were with difficulty withdrawn from the forward positions. Contact with some units was lost. Others had to cross a flooded river over which the bridge they hoped to use had collapsed. Some of the men were swept away in the attempt; others were left behind. The brigade was in its new position, however, by dawn on 9th December, with the 4/19th Hyderabad, brought from command reserve, in a supporting position. A dawn attack by the enemy on the right flank of the position was accompanied by heavy fire, and further infiltration followed. European women and children, the Sultan of Kelantan and his household, and others had been evacuated from the town. Having decided that the position was unsuitable for defence, Key ordered a general withdrawal southward. The brigade accordingly pulled back at night through the Hyderabads to Chondong, on the way to the road and rail junction at Kuala Krai, and by the 11th December was occupying positions at Machang. The withdrawal had been accompanied by demolitions along the road and railway, and at the Gong Kedah and Machang airfields, whence airmen and aircraft had been withdrawn.

Meanwhile General Barstow (commanding the 9th Indian Division, of which the 8th Brigade was a part) had submitted to General Heath (commanding the III Corps) a proposal that the brigade be withdrawn to Kuala Lipis, midway between east and west Malaya, where the railway joined a road running westward across the central range of mountains. In doing so he pointed to the danger of continued reliance upon a single track of railway from Kuala Krai southward as the brigade's line of communication. The purpose of maintaining troops in Kelantan having now disappeared, they might be lost if they remained there, he declared. On the other hand they might be more useful in the west, where the main threat seemed likely to develop. Heath agreed, but, as General Percival demurred, Heath decided to go to Singapore on the night of 11th-12th December to impress upon him this point of view. Such was the scarcity of aircraft for army communication purposes that he had to travel from his headquarters by train.

The Japanese air offensive had been so successful that within forty-eight hours of the landing at Kota Bharu the equivalent of three bomber squadrons and one fighter squadron had been lost in the air or on the ground. So that the remaining craft should be exposed as little as possible to attack on the ground, squadrons had been withdrawn from Alor Star and Sungei Patani airfields in the north-west, and Kuantan on the east coast, as well as from those in Kelantan. Despite the obvious desirability of retaliating against Japanese aircraft concentrations across the border, it was decided to abandon bomber attacks by day, on the ground that the necessary fighter escort craft could not be spared from the primary task of protecting the Singapore Base and reinforcement convoys. Such was the effect on the troops forward of Alor Star of the smoke and the sound of explosions resulting from demolitions at that airfield on 10th December —emphasising as they did the reverses suffered at this early stage of the struggle—that orders were given that petrol and oil were to be allowed to run to waste rather than be fired when airfields had to be evacuated. Demolitions by explosives were to be undertaken only by the army. It was thus evident that morale among the troops, a high proportion of whom were entering upon their first experience of war in circumstances suggesting collapse rather than dynamic defence, was already a matter of concern.

Air Headquarters had been asked by Admiral Phillips to make reconnaissances to the northward on behalf of his force, and to give fighter protection off Singora. However, for reasons ascribed principally to the airfield situation and the short range of Buffalo fighters, only a reconnaissance for 100 miles to the north-westward of the force from 8 a.m. on 9th December was definitely promised before the force sailed. In a signal to Phillips at sea late during the night of 8th-9th December, the hope was expressed that a dawn reconnaissance of the coast near Singora could be carried out on the 10th,[4] but it was stated that provision of fighter protection was impossible. The Admiral nevertheless decided to persist in his mission, provided his ships were not sighted by enemy aircraft during 9th December.

Frequent rainstorms and low cloud favoured concealment of the force, but on the afternoon of the 9th Japanese naval aircraft were sighted from *Prince of Wales*. Phillips thereupon decided that as the prospect of catching the Japanese off their guard had been lost, the risk of continuing towards Singora was no longer justified. At 8.40 p.m., therefore, the force turned south-south-east.

Yet when a signal was received, near midnight, that the Japanese were reported to be landing at Kuantan, not far off the return track of "Z" Force, the Admiral again decided to seek the enemy; but Kuantan was found to be all quiet. Then, before resuming the homeward course, it was decided to investigate vessels, seen in the distance before reaching Kuantan, which it was thought might be landing-craft. The destroyer *Tenedos,* which at 6.35 p.m. on 9th December had been ordered to return to Singapore as her fuel was running low, reported soon after 10 a.m. from a position 140 miles to the south-east that she was being bombed by enemy planes. Phillips thereupon ordered his force to assume first-degree readiness.

Meanwhile, as was revealed in post-war interrogations, a submarine, and apparently not aircraft, had reported the whereabouts of "Z" Force

---

[4] Both reconnaissances were made.

on the afternoon of 9th December. When the report reached Saigon, long-range planes were about to take off for a further attack on Singapore. Torpedoes were quickly included in their loads, and they were assigned to attack the warships, but failed to find them. Another submarine reported "Z" Force early on 10th December as it was steaming south. While it was still dark reconnaissance planes were dispatched from Saigon to search the area where "Z" Force had been reported, followed just before dawn by a striking force of 27 bombers and 61 torpedo planes, from *21st* and *22nd Air Flotillas*. The aircraft searched without success until they were near Singapore, then turned north. It seemed as though they would have to report a third failure. Then, about 11 a.m., as they flew despondently back, one of the reconnaissance aircraft sighted the *Prince of Wales* and *Repulse* and directed the striking force to its quarry.

Soon after this opportunity presented itself to the enemy, high-level bombers attacked, scoring a direct hit on *Repulse*. Later, torpedo bombers attacked. The *Prince of Wales* was hit by two torpedoes and her speed reduced to 15 knots; her steering gear failed, and she became an easy target. Using bombs and torpedoes, the airmen continued their onslaught until nearly 1 p.m. *Repulse* sank at 12.33 p.m. and *Prince of Wales* at 1.15 p.m. Although for some unexplained reason *Prince of Wales,* as the flagship, did not break wireless silence or order *Repulse* to do so as soon as the attack occurred, *Repulse* sent a signal about an hour later. When this reached the Operations Room at Air Headquarters, eleven Buffaloes of No. 453 Squadron R.A.A.F. were sent from Sembawang. As they arrived over the scene of the battle they saw *Prince of Wales* go down, and hundreds of men struggling in water heavily covered with oil. The men were being picked up by the destroyers, unmolested by the enemy. They had fought with superb coolness and courage, and of their conduct in the water the officer commanding the Buffaloes[5] recorded:

> I have seen a show of spirit in this war over Dunkirk during the "Battle of Britain", and in the London night raids, but never before have I seen anything comparable with what I saw yesterday. . . . After an hour, lack of petrol forced me to leave, but during that hour I had seen many men in dire danger waving, cheering, and joking as if they were holiday-makers at Brighton waving at a low-flying craft. It shook me, for here was something above human nature.[6]

Once again, the Japanese had demonstrated unexpected efficiency in their air arm. It was noticed that the torpedoes, dropped from a height of between three and four hundred feet, appeared to run perfectly straight from the point where they were dropped. Admiral Phillips and Captain Leach[7] went down with the flagship, 845 highly trained naval personnel were lost, and the British Navy was shorn of two capital ships dispatched, with great misgivings on the part of the Admiralty, to Far Eastern waters.

---

[5] F-Lt T. A. Vigors, DFC (of Fethard, Co. Tipperary).

[6] Published with Vice-Admiral Layton's Despatch.

[7] Capt J. C. Leach, DSO, MVO; RN. Comd HMS *Prince of Wales* 1941 (Flag Capt and CSO to Vice-Adm Comd 2 Battle Sqn; Flag Capt to C-in-C Eastern Fleet). B. 1 Sep 1894. Lost in *Prince of Wales* 10 Dec 1941.

With them disappeared all prospect that the Japanese landings in Malaya might be seriously impeded by British naval action. The value of Singapore naval base at this stage, and all that it meant to Australian security and British interests generally in East Asia, had virtually vanished. The general effect of the disaster, with other reverses suffered on land and in the air, was grave in the extreme.

The news reached Mr Churchill in what was the morning of 10th December in England, while he was opening his dispatch boxes before rising for the day. "In all the war," he was to write, "I never received a more direct shock. . . . As I turned over and twisted in bed the full horror of the news sank in upon me. There were no British or American capital ships in the Indian Ocean or the Pacific except the American survivors of Pearl Harbour. . . . Over all this vast expanse of waters Japan was supreme, and we everywhere were weak and naked."[8]

In a broadcast during the evening, Mr Duff Cooper, who that day had been appointed Resident Minister for Far Eastern Affairs, sought to mitigate the effect upon public confidence of the loss of the ships, implying as it did that with the war less than three days old, Japan had gained command of the seas around East Asia. His terms of reference required that he should relieve the Commanders-in-Chief as far as possible of responsibilities outside their normal sphere; give them broad political guidance; and settle on the spot political questions which might otherwise have to be referred to London. He was to be assisted by a War Council, comprising himself as chairman, the Governor of the Straits Settlements and High Commissioner for Malaya (Sir Shenton Thomas), the Commander-in-Chief Far East (Air Chief Marshal Brooke-Popham), the Commander-in-Chief Eastern Fleet (Vice-Admiral Layton[9]), the General Officer Commanding Malaya (Lieut-General Percival), the Air Officer Commanding Far East (Air Vice-Marshal Pulford), and Mr Bowden representing Australia. General Bennett, as commander of the Australian force in Malaya, was at liberty to attend the meetings when he was able to do so.[1] The Council held its first meeting also during the evening.

Reviewing the Far Eastern situation on 11th December, the British Chiefs of Staff saw better prospects of sending land and air reinforcements eastward than might have been expected. Contrary to gloomy forecasts of what might happen to the Soviet Union when she was attacked by Germany, Russian victories had countered the danger of a German thrust through the Caucasus to Iraq and Persia, and the situation in the Middle East had been improved by General Auchinleck's success in Libya. The Chiefs of Staff decided that the 18th British Division and some anti-tank and anti-aircraft regiments, on their way to the Middle East, should be placed at the disposal of General Wavell, then Commander-in-Chief,

---

[8] Churchill, Vol III, p. 551.

[9] Vice-Admiral Layton, who as mentioned above had relinquished command of the China Station to Admiral Phillips early on 8th December, took over command of the Eastern Fleet on 10th December, after Phillips had gone down with his flagship.

[1] Bennett recorded: "I agreed to assist in every way I could, but reserved the thought that we were going to be too busy fighting the enemy to attend many War Council meetings."

India. All aircraft which could be spared from Europe would be sent to India, which would become the base for all reinforcements of the Far East. It was decided also that command of Burma would be transferred from Brooke-Popham, now overloaded with responsibility, to Wavell.

Little consolation could, however, be offered to Admiral Layton in response to a request by him for additional naval vessels and aircraft. He was informed on 17th December that one of four old "R" class battleships was being sent to the Far East, and the Chiefs of Staff hoped eventually—perhaps by April 1942—to reconstitute the Eastern Fleet at a strength of five modern capital ships, with the four "R" class battleships (mentioned above) and three or four aircraft carriers.

The threat to the west of Malaya had speedily developed after the Japanese landings in Thailand. Thai opposition to Krohcol ceased suddenly on the afternoon of 9th December, and the column spent the night at Betong. Next day it became apparent that by means of a forced march the Japanese had forestalled the column in its objective, and were seeking to get behind the 11th Division by thrusting along the road through Kroh. Transported by two sections of the 2/3rd Australian Reserve Motor Transport Company,[2] the 3/16th Punjab had got to within about five miles of The Ledge when the leading company, advancing afoot, came under fire. As in the case of Laycol, Japanese tanks then appeared, followed by truck-loads of troops, and then more tanks. One of the Punjab companies was trapped, and another temporarily cut off; but despite the advantage which the tanks gave the enemy, the Indians fought on. The 5/14th Punjab, less a company, and the 10th Mountain Battery, arrived meanwhile at Kroh and took up a supporting position north of Betong.

In north-western Malaya, on rain-sodden soil, forces were hurriedly disposed along and in advance of the Jitra line. The 15th Indian Brigade (Brigadier Garrett[3]) was assigned to the right sector, extending for 6,000 yards to and including a road branching through Kodiang to the railway line at Kangar, in Perlis; and the 6th Indian Brigade (Brigadier Lay) to the left, an 18,000-yards stretch from this road to the coast. The 28th Brigade (Brigadier Carpendale[4]) was in reserve. Support was to be given by two batteries of the 155th Field Regiment, a battery of the 22nd

---

[2] This unit and the 2/3 Motor Ambulance Convoy had been specially recruited in Australia and attached to III Indian Corps. In asking for the transport company the British War Office specified that it should be formed on a British war establishment; that its men should be between 35 and 45 years of age; and that apart from uniforms and small arms it would be equipped by Britain. The age of many of the men was in fact above 45 years, and it contained a high percentage of veterans of the 1914-18 war, who gave it a solid backing of experience. Its actions showed that men of more than 45 could be usefully employed in forward areas, and in fact they stood up to fatigue better than many of the younger men. The unit, commanded by Major C. M. Black, consisted of a headquarters, four operating sections, and a workshop section. It was recruited in New South Wales and Queensland, and reached Malaya in April 1941. In the pre-war period it was stationed at Ipoh, and gained high praise for the assistance it gave in the preparation of defences.

[3] Brig K. A. Garrett, MC. Comd 15 Indian Bde 1940-41, 6/15 Indian Composite Bde 1941. Regular soldier; b. 12 Nov 1894.

[4] Brig W. St J. Carpendale. Comd 28 Indian Bde. Regular soldier; b. 26 Jul 1892.

Mountain Regiment, three batteries of the 80th Anti-Tank Regiment, the 137th Field Regiment and an anti-aircraft battery due to arrive later.

The right of the 15th Brigade's sector was allotted to the 2/9th Jat, in boggy soil covered by padi (rice crop), bisected by a creek with a jungle growth extending up to 50 yards from each bank. Company and platoon posts were so widely dispersed that they gave the young and untried troops a feeling of isolation. On the left of the Jats, and separated from them by 2,000 yards of swamp and trees, were the 1/Leicester, whose position was the stronger of the two.

In the 6th Brigade sector the 2/East Surrey occupied a position from the Kodiang road to the railway, and the 2/16th Punjab the remaining distance to the coast. Between one Punjab company astride the railway and one adjoining the coast were several miles of canal, patrolled by parties from the remainder of the battalion, which was to come into battalion reserve on completion of its covering role. Outposts were placed on both roads running through Jitra to the north and north-west. A detachment of the 1/14th Punjab (the 15th Brigade reserve battalion) was at Asun, on the main (Singora) road, three miles north of the main position. On the Kodiang road, at Kanjong Iman, were two companies of the 1/8th Punjab (the 6th Brigade reserve) and a mountain battery detachment. Between the two outposts were four miles of thick jungle. In front of them were two delaying and demolition detachments.

Confronted by a Japanese advance-guard south of the frontier early on 10th December, one of the detachments, from 1/14th Punjab, gradually withdrew, seeking to delay the enemy as it did so. The divisional commander, General Murray-Lyon, thereupon told Garrett that to gain time for preparation of the main positions he must hold the approach to Jitra till 12th December, and assigned the 2/1st Gurkha Rifles (less a company) from the 28th Brigade to assist him. Garrett sent the Gurkhas to Asun, and concentrated the 1/14th Punjab forward round Changlun. The foremost troops on the Kodiang road were withdrawn to Kodiang, carrying out demolitions along the railway as they went. This move amounted to evacuation of the British forces from Perlis, and was the occasion of a protest by its Sultan that it constituted a violation of Britain's treaty with the State. Other moves were made that day to strengthen and consolidate the defensive forces.

During the morning of 11th December, the Japanese pressed the 1/14th Punjabs where they had concentrated at Changlun. Two anti-tank guns were lost, and a further withdrawal was ordered to a position about two miles north of Asun. This operation was in progress when, about 4.30 p.m., in heavy rain, Japanese medium tanks, followed by motorised infantry, attacked the rear of the column. Most of the Indians had never before seen a tank, and they presented to them a strange and terrifying apparition in the absence of such a weapon on the British side. Taking advantage of the surprise and confusion, the Japanese broke through, overran two anti-tank and two mountain guns, and approached the bridge in front of the Asun outpost position held by the 2/1st Gurkha. The bridge demolition charge failed to go off, but the leading tank was stopped by fire from anti-tank rifles, and blocked the road, thus halting the tank advance. Japanese infantry, however, attacked the Gurkhas in front and from the flanks, cleared the road and allowed the tanks to resume their advance. They broke through the outpost position, overwhelmed most of the forward troops and isolated the battalion headquarters. Only small

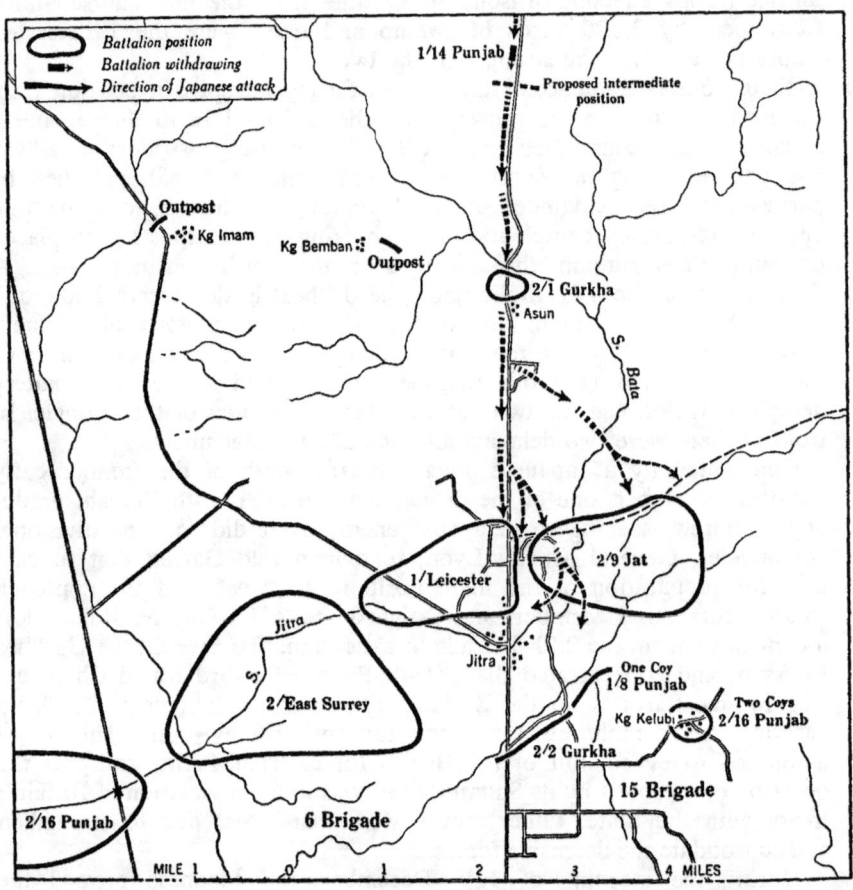

The fall of Jitra

parties succeeded in fighting their way out. Others found their way back to the brigade next day.

By 8.30 p.m. the tanks had overrun a forward patrol of the 1/Leicesters, but once more the leading tanks were disabled, forming a temporary roadblock. However, they continued firing while the Leicesters hastily constructed a further obstacle of tree trunks, wire, and mines. On the Kodiang road, withdrawal was continued on 11th December. A premature bridge demolition resulted in the trucks and carriers of the covering and outpost troops, four mountain guns, and seven anti-tank guns being left behind although there had been no fighting.

In the absence of Garrett, who was missing, the 15th Brigade was placed at this stage under the command of Carpendale; the 2/2nd Gurkhas from the 28th Brigade were ordered to join the 15th Brigade, replacing the 1/14th Punjab as brigade reserve. The remaining battalion (the 2/9th Gurkhas) having been disposed for the protection of the Alor Star-Sungei Patani area, Murray-Lyon was left without a divisional reserve. On the main road before dawn on 12th December the Japanese succeeded in reaching the right forward company of the Leicesters. Exaggerated reports were received of enemy action against the Jats during the night. During three hours of sharp fighting, the Leicesters held the Japanese at bay in this area, but the enemy managed to penetrate some distance between the two battalions. Meanwhile Carpendale had asked for and obtained from Lay, without reference to Murray-Lyon, successive reinforcements. Thus when the divisional commander visited the 15th Brigade headquarters at 9 a.m. he found that four companies of the 6th Brigade had arrived in Carpendale's sector.

As this situation developed on the Jitra front, the Japanese increased their pressure towards Kroh. Successive attacks in strength during the afternoon of 11th December were repulsed by the 3/16th Punjab in their position near The Ledge, but at the cost of heavy casualties, and outflanking movements were threatening the position. Colonel Moorhead, who correctly estimated that his force was opposed by three battalions (the Japanese *42nd Infantry Regiment*) was given permission to retire if necessary. Consequently he arranged for the 3/16th to withdraw through the 5/14th Punjab early on 12th December. Murray-Lyon, concerned at the speed at which the threat to his line of communication from this quarter was developing, at what seemed to him to be a serious threat to his right flank at Jitra, and the fact that his reserve had been committed and his men were tired, now decided to ask for permission to withdraw his division from Jitra to Gurun, 30 miles southward.

Whatever General Heath might have done about this request, the fact is that as he was at the time on his way by train to Singapore to confer with Percival about the Kelantan front, Percival received it in his stead. As he saw the situation such a withdrawal would have a most demoralising effect upon both the troops and the civil population, and would also immediately prejudice chances of denying west coast airfields to the enemy. Accordingly, with the endorsement of the War Council, he ordered that pending further instructions the battle for north-west Malaya should be fought out in the Jitra position.

As it later transpired, the commander of the Japanese *9th Infantry Brigade* (Major-General Kawamura), who had gone forward at noon on 12th December, ordered the *41st Infantry Regiment* to take over the task of advance-guard, and at night to attack the eastern side of the main road near Jitra while *11th Infantry Regiment* attacked the western side.

The advance-guard,[5] however, had again attacked in battalion strength east of the road, before the orders could be put into effect. Under the impetus of the attack, the left forward company of the Jats was overwhelmed, and a wedge was driven between the Jat and the Leicester battalions. Soon the Japanese battalion was in contact with 2/2nd Gurkhas holding the south bank of the Sungei Bata east of the main road bridge, and was attacking the Leicesters' right flank. At this stage the Japanese were repulsed by the carrier platoon (sixteen Bren guns in tracked vehicles) of the 2/East Surrey who had been sent from 6th Brigade, and the Gurkhas and Leicesters stood their ground. Parties which had been cut off in earlier fighting (among them Brigadier Garrett) were now coming in, and being used as reinforcements.

However, with the enemy now pressing on this flank, a gap of about one mile and a half which separated the Leicesters and the Gurkhas had become a serious danger. Deciding to concentrate upon defence of the vital bridge over the Bata, Murray-Lyon gave orders that the Leicesters should be moved to close the gap, and that the Jats should be withdrawn. In the event, these orders were misconstrued, and did not reach the right forward company of the Jats. Attacked while they were at a disadvantage in taking up new positions, the Leicesters lost heavily, and movement became badly confused. The situation in the Jat sector rapidly deteriorated, and soon troops and transport were streaming in disorder southward over the bridge. Exaggerated reports made the outlook seem even worse than it really was. Murray-Lyon ordered withdrawals from the 6th Brigade sector, sought to restore order, and at 7.30 p.m. again asked for permission to withdraw to Gurun.

Having now arrived at Singapore, Heath, after consultation with Percival, replied that the task of the 11th Division was to fight for the security of north Kedah; that he estimated it was opposed by one Japanese division at most; and that the best solution seemed to be to halt the advance of the enemy tanks on a good obstacle and dispose the forces of the 11th Division so as to obtain considerable depth, and scope for its artillery. Murray-Lyon was accordingly given discretionary power to withdraw. He was informed that Krohcol—far distant, and a distraction which had complicated his task—would cease to be under his control from midnight.

A difficult, disorganised, and costly withdrawal from Jitra followed. Murray-Lyon's plan was that the division should move to Gurun in two stages, the first of which would be a position on the south bank of the Sungei Kedah, at Alor Star. No transport was available for the troops, so they had to march fifteen miles. The Bata bridge was destroyed at 2 a.m. on the 13th after a Japanese attempt to rush it had been frustrated by 2/2nd Gurkhas, and they withdrew through a rearguard of the 2/9th Gurkhas. However, owing to darkness, breakdowns of communications, and the generally tangled situation, withdrawal orders failed to reach several units, who were thus left stranded in their positions. Parties from

---

[5] The advance-guard of the *5th Division* comprised the *5th Reconnaissance Regiment*; a mountain artillery company; a tank company; an engineer platoon; and the *II/41st Battalion*.

these units eventually made their way back as best they could by land, river, and sea. Some were ambushed and dispersed; some reached the coast and boarded native craft—sampans, tongkans, and junks—in which they paddled, sailed, and drifted to various points. Some Leicesters were shipwrecked, and others reached Penang, before rejoining their battalion at Ipoh. Two British officers, with a few Gurkhas and a Jat, landed in Sumatra, eleven days after the withdrawal had been ordered.

The 15th Brigade emerged from the battle barely 600 strong, and the 1/Leicester alone of its units had any carriers or mortars left. The 6th fared less badly, but had suffered serious losses in men and equipment. The 2/1st Gurkha had been reduced to one company, and other units of the 28th Brigade had suffered substantial casualties. Two commanding officers and twenty-five other officers had been killed or lost. Losses of guns, vehicles, and signalling equipment were heavy, and particularly serious in some instances owing to lack of sufficient reserves in Malaya from which to replace them. Many of the men who remained with or later rejoined the division were badly affected by their experiences and unfit for further action in the near future.

The fact, established in post-war investigation, that merely an advance-guard of the Japanese *5th Division* had dislodged the 11th Division from Jitra, emphasises the advantage gained by the hitherto underrated enemy from his swift, dynamic development of the offensive in contrast to a hesitant deployment of the defending forces. Adequate air reconnaissance could have corrected the misleading impression which Murray-Lyon obtained of the immediate danger to the position. Even a few tanks, and adequate employment of anti-tank guns, might have countered the disastrous physical and psychological effect which the enemy tanks achieved. The long Jitra line had been manned at the expense of defence in depth on the road, which obviously, as they were advancing with tanks and mechanical transport, the Japanese would use. Their troops were thus able to exploit this weakness, and the inexperience in battle of most of those who opposed them. Having been poised for Operation MATADOR, cancelled only after fatal delay, the 11th Division was caught on the wrong foot in its hastily assumed static defence role while the Japanese imposed a war of movement. Being in Singapore when the unforeseen crisis occurred, Heath had not been able to exercise on the spot at Jitra his authority and perspective as corps commander in the direction of the battle. Premature use of reserve units robbed Murray-Lyon of means of influencing it at the critical stage.

The Japanese losses at Jitra, according to their records, were 27 killed and 83 wounded. Hastening from Patani towards Kroh was a Japanese column later revealed to be the Japanese *42nd Infantry Regiment* with two companies of light tanks and a battery of field artillery. Both the Japanese mechanised columns, confined to the roads, would have been vulnerable to air attack had British aircraft been employed for the purpose; but almost in a matter of hours the Japanese had gained command of the air. Now, too, they had command of the seas, enabling them to land troops at will in front, on the flanks, or to the rear of the British land forces; and of the three divisions deployed for the defence of the mainland, one had already been dislodged and largely disintegrated.

Although the facts were muffled in official communiqués, sufficient became known of the outcome of the first five days' fighting to shock seriously the confidence of troops and civilians alike in the defences of Malaya. No prospect existed of substantial reinforcement from overseas until at least the following month. Consequently the policy adopted was to resist the enemy as fully as circumstances permitted, but as far as possible to avoid forces being cut off and destroyed in detail.

Fears which had been entertained that the Asian population of Singapore would panic under bombing attacks proved, however, to have little justification. "One of the most pleasing features of the past three days," declared the *Straits Times* on 10th December, "has been the behaviour of Asiatic members of the passive defence services, particularly those engaged in A.R.P. work. . . . They have proved to be full of courage, completely amenable to discipline, and have shown pride in the uniforms they wear."

As well as sending aircraft and naval vessels to Malaya, the Netherlands East Indies quickly mobilised forces to defend their own soil. Their Commander-in-Chief, General ter Poorten, had broadcast an exhortation in which he declared that it was better "to die standing rather than live on our knees".

CHAPTER 9

CRUMBLING RESISTANCE

JAPAN'S three-pronged thrust into Malaya was succeeding on all fronts by 13th December. British hopes of halting the enemy near the frontier were rapidly diminishing. Concern increased lest part or the whole of the British forces in northern Malaya be cut off, and thus divorced from their primary task of protecting the Naval Base.[1]

Close relationship became necessary between these forces, both east and west of the main range, to avoid isolation from each other and from the forces in the south. Thus they became increasingly committed to a continuous process of retreat, accompanied by delaying actions to gain time during which, it was hoped, sufficient reinforcements would arrive to turn the tide of battle. General Heath's recommendation—reinforced by what was happening at Jitra—that the 8th Brigade be withdrawn from Kelantan, was accepted by General Percival at their conference on 12th December. It was approved by Air Chief Marshal Brooke-Popham with the proviso that the enemy must be prevented from using the railway. On the night of the 12th-13th Percival placed his reserve, the 12th Indian Brigade, at the disposal of the III Indian Corps and sent it forward by rail to Ipoh, where the leading battalion, 2/Argyll and Sutherland Highlanders, arrived on the afternoon of the 13th. Heavy fighting occurred on the 12th and 13th at Machang, 25 miles south of Kota Bharu, and the junction of a road to the east coast. The Japanese were sufficiently checked to enable the withdrawal to the railhead at Kuala Krai to be continued without serious interference.

A.I.F. Headquarters in Malaya had followed the course of operations with growing concern. As senior staff officer, Colonel Thyer had come to the conclusion that the Japanese would move towards Endau from Kuantan, and that any landings from the sea in eastern Johore would be at Endau rather than Mersing. Assuming, as was extremely likely, that the Japanese were aware of the strong defence system established by the Australians in the Mersing area, it certainly was not improbable that the enemy would seek an alternative to head-on encounter where it was strongest. At any rate, Thyer recommended that the detachment at Endau be strengthened, and that a company be placed at Bukit Langkap to prevent a thrust down the Sungei Endau which might cut the road from Jemaluang westward to Kluang. In this Brigadier Callaghan, in charge of the Australian division during General Bennett's absence in the Middle East, concurred, and he redisposed his troops accordingly.

---

[1] Brooke-Popham received from the Chiefs of Staff in the latter part of December a cable stating: "His Majesty's Government agree your conception that vital issue is to ensure security of Singapore Naval Base. They emphasise that no other consideration must compete with this."

General Bennett, who had returned to Malaya on 10th December, toured his units on the 12th. When he found that his dispositions had been altered he was emphatic in his disapproval, on the ground that the effect was to commit units to definite roles and areas before the enemy intentions were known. In particular he was adamant that the 2/30th Battalion should be retained intact for counter-attack in the event of the Japanese reaching Jemaluang, or (a hint perhaps of the direction in which his thoughts were turning) for action elsewhere with the 27th Brigade, instead of being committed in part to forward positions. Thus he ordered the former positions to be resumed.

On 13th December Bennett wrote to the Australian Minister for the Army: "The third brigade of my division would have been a godsend to us now. As you know, it has been repeatedly asked for, and my requests have been repeatedly refused. However, we will have to do the best with what we have. . . ."[2] In a letter to Australian Army Headquarters he wrote that "the morale of our men has never been higher", but, referring to there being insufficient air cover for the defending troops, he said "I fear a repetition of Crete". Anticipation of a Japanese landing in the south was sharpened when on the same day a message was received from Malaya Command that a large convoy was moving from the southern tip of Indo-China towards the south-east coast of Malaya. Percival called next day on Bennett, who recorded:

> He is anticipating a possible attack on Singapore Island direct from the sea, and asks what would be the position of the A.I.F. if such an attack developed and help from the A.I.F. were required. I replied that the A.I.F. were here to defend Singapore and that if the troops on the island needed help, the A.I.F. would certainly go to their assistance. He realises that there are insufficient troops on the island to defend it effectively and is very perturbed at the danger. I told him that I needed more troops to defend Johore effectively, implying that the Mersing front should not be weakened unless the emergency were grave.[3]

Although the anticipated landing did not occur, it further emphasised the insecurity of the forces on the mainland of Malaya, and reinforced the policy of withdrawal. At this time also, with the prospect of congestion of airfields on Singapore Island resulting from progressive evacuation of those in the north, Air Headquarters ordered that stocks of bombs with refuelling and rearming parties be withdrawn to Sumatra, so that facilities might be developed there for the transit of reinforcing aircraft and the operation of bombers.

On the 16th, referring to the situation in northern Malaya, Bennett wrote to Army Headquarters in Melbourne:

> I have seen a total absence of the offensive spirit, which after all is the one great remedy for the methods adopted by the Japanese. Counter-attacks would put a stop to this penetration. . . . The position has arrived when something must be done —urgently. I strongly urge that, should the request be made, at least one division of the A.I.F. from the Middle East be transferred to Malaya.

---
[2] H. G. Bennett, *Why Singapore Fell*, p. 69.
[3] Bennett, p. 70.

Bennett also sent a letter to be read to all ranks of his command, in which he said:

> The recent operations in northern Malaya have revealed the tactics adopted by the Japanese in their offensive movements. It is simply that they endeavour to infiltrate between posts, or if that is difficult, to move small parties via the flank to threaten the flank or the rear of our position. . . . This is not a new system; it is as old as war itself. . . . Our training during the past twelve months has been to outflank any enemy position which is being held; similarly in any attack, the main attack should come from the flanking party. All units in defence will hold a small reserve in hand which will have the duty of moving around the enemy flanks and creating despondency and alarm by firing into their rear elements. Should it be possible for a small party of the enemy to penetrate between two posts and open fire on the rear of posts, arrangements must be made for alternate sections in a post to face the rear and deal with this enemy party by fire. At the same time a patrol must be sent forward to capture or destroy the enemy which has been successful in penetrating the position. It is imperative that the offensive spirit be maintained. . . . There will be no withdrawal; counter-attack methods, even by small parties, will be adopted.

A few days later, in an instruction on tactics to be employed, Percival also emphasised that enemy outflanking and infiltration tactics must not lead to withdrawals, which, he said, should take place only on order of higher authority. The enemy could not be defeated by sitting in prepared positions and letting the Japanese walk round them. "We must play the enemy at his own game and attack on every occasion," he declared, adding that the efficiency, cunning and alertness of the individual were of primary importance.[4]

An example of the kind of jungle warfare in which the Japanese had been schooled was provided on 18th December, when four carriers of the 2/12th Frontier Force Regiment were ambushed by troops who dropped grenades into them from the branches of trees they had climbed. This simple ruse might have been suggested by falling coconuts, but it was far removed from the training which most of the British forces had been given. Nevertheless, the 8th Brigade's withdrawal was well controlled, and losses of men and materials were relatively light. Evacuation by rail from Krai of stores and equipment was carried out so successfully under the direction of Lieut-Colonel Trott,[5] the senior administrative officer of the 9th Division (an Australian who had transferred from the A.I.F. to the Indian Army in January 1918) that of the 600 motor vehicles with the force only sixty were lost in Kelantan. Forty casualties occurred when the railway station was bombed during the morning of 19th December, but the railhead had been evacuated by the end of the day. The brigade's strength had been reduced by 553 all ranks who had been either killed or wounded, or were missing. Its losses of machine-guns, mortars, and anti-tank rifles had been heavy. In the area Kuala Lipis-Jerantut in which the brigade was next concentrated, it was centrally situated, with access by road to either the east or west of the peninsula.

---

[4] Percival, *Despatch on Operations of Malaya Command*, Appendix "D".

[5] Brig W. A. Trott, MC. (1st AIF: Pte to Capt 2 Bn 1914-17; and Indian Army.) AA&QMG 9 Indian Div 1941-42; Comd 8 Indian Bde 1942. Regular soldier; b. Newtown, NSW, 17 May 1894.

Meanwhile, the 3/16th Punjab on the Kroh front to the west had been attacked at dawn on 12th December, and the Japanese had begun to by-pass its position. Then, as the 3/16th was about to be withdrawn, it was again attacked, and shelled by heavy artillery. Spare drivers of the 2/3rd Australian Reserve Motor Transport Company fought as infantry in the endeavour to extricate the force. Although the withdrawal was accomplished, the battalion's determined resistance since its first encounter with the enemy had cost it half its strength by the time it passed through the 5/14th Punjab north-east of Betong, and reached a position three miles west of Kroh on the road to Baling. The 5/14th, now the covering troops, withstood a further attack early on the 13th until its flanks were endangered.[6] It then fell back to Betong, where it destroyed the road bridge, and by dusk had joined the 3/16th. The road southward from Kroh to Grik, and thence to the main west coast road at Kuala Kangsar, was thus uncovered. Although north of Grik it was little better than a mountain track, there was a danger that the Japanese would use it as a means of striking at the lines of communications of the Indian Corps, farther to the south. Heath therefore decided on 13th December to send a company of the 2/Argyll and Sutherland Highlanders and some armoured cars[7] from Ipoh to Grik, and the rest of the battalion to Baling in support of Krohcol. On 14th December he handed over command of the column to Brigadier Paris of the 12th Brigade, and instructed him to hold the Kroh-Baling road. Paris ordered Krohcol to withdraw during the night of 14th-15th December, leaving the Argylls to defend Baling.

The first mass slaughter of civilians in Malaya had occurred on 11th December, when after daily air raids on Penang airfield from 8th December, Georgetown was raided. Thronging the streets to watch the aircraft, thousands of the inhabitants of this principal town on Penang Island, off the coast of north-west Malaya, were bombed and machine-gunned by the raiders. In the absence of anti-aircraft defences and British fighter aircraft, about 2,000 casualties were inflicted. Smaller raids occurred on the two following days. In the panic which these raids caused, so many civilians fled from the town that essential services broke down. Corpses were left in the streets, and ferry transport between the island and the mainland had to be taken over progressively by the military (including some members of the 2/3rd Australian Reserve M.T. Company).

The military importance of Penang Island[8] lay principally in its port facilities, its stocks of ammunition and stores, and the fact that it was a terminal of two overseas cables. The intention had been to hold the island,

---

[6] A section of 2/3 Aust Reserve MT Coy was used on 13 Dec to guard a golf course area at Kroh, as it was thought that the enemy might land paratroops there.

[7] Some members of the 2/3 Aust Reserve MT Coy manned the cars. Finding the machine-guns useless they fired from open turrets with Lewis guns.

[8] The garrison of Penang comprised Fortress Headquarters and Signals; 11th Coast Regiment, Hong Kong and Singapore Royal Artillery (two 6-inch batteries); 36th Fortress Company Royal Engineers; a company of 5/14th Punjab; an Independent Company; a detachment of 3rd Indian Cavalry; the 3rd Battalion, Straits Settlements Volunteer Force; a mixed reinforcement camp; and administrative detachments.

but on 12th December the Fortress Commander (Brigadier Lyon[9]) and the British Resident Counsellor decided to evacuate all European service families, all civilian European women and children, and inmates of the military hospital. Departure of most of the Europeans on the night of the 13th, and the haste with which it was done, shocked the Asian inhabitants of Malaya generally, and indeed many Europeans also. Few civilians had means of knowing the overall military situation, and how the Japanese were compelling withdrawals. What they did know was that the protection on which, as a subject people, the Asians of Penang Island had learned to rely, was abruptly withdrawn, ties of loyalty and economic bonds were severed, and the Asians were left to whatever fate might befall them. Rather than thus abandon them, a few European civilians stayed behind.

The Europeans on the island at the time of the attack were few in number compared with the Asian population, whose evacuation was not considered feasible even had they elected to leave their homes. It was not easy, however, for the simple people of Malaya to distinguish between the practical limits of what could be done, and racial discrimination. On the other hand Japanese propagandists had been urging the Asians in pamphlets and radio broadcasts to "burn up the whites in a blaze of victory", thus indicating that they intended violent discrimination against the Europeans, but suggesting that the non-European inhabitants of Malaya might expect friendly treatment. Had they been withdrawn they would have been divorced from their homes, and their safety still could not have been assured. However, the effect at the time, when the enemy was delivering so many other successful blows, was particularly damaging to British prestige. At a meeting on 14th December the War Council decided that unless the Japanese on the mainland could be halted, the island must be abandoned militarily also. Apart from military necessity, withdrawal of the garrison would remove the likelihood of the civilian population being exposed to further air raids.

The withdrawal from Jitra to an area south of the Sungei Kedah by the 11th Indian Division on 12th-13th December gained little respite for its weary troops, or for reorganisation of its depleted units. Intermittent firing, and penetration by Japanese troops to the south bank of the river, from which they were expelled in a counter-attack by the 2/9th Gurkha, indicated that further pressure was accumulating. Eight carriers of the 2/East Surrey were cut off when a bridge was prematurely demolished. Murray-Lyon decided that the withdrawal must be continued. In heavy rain, and with many mishaps, a badly congested stream of traffic moved on during the night of the 13th-14th to Gurun.

The Gurun position, 19 miles south of Alor Star—the junction of a large, flat, rice-growing area with undulating country thickly covered by rubber plantations—was regarded by Percival as perhaps the best natural defensive position in Malaya. The plantations, on either side of the main road and the railway, were served by a network of roads. Kedah Peak,

---

[9] Brig C. A. Lyon, DSO. Comd Penang Fortress Troops 1941. Regular soldier; b. 11 Aug 1880.

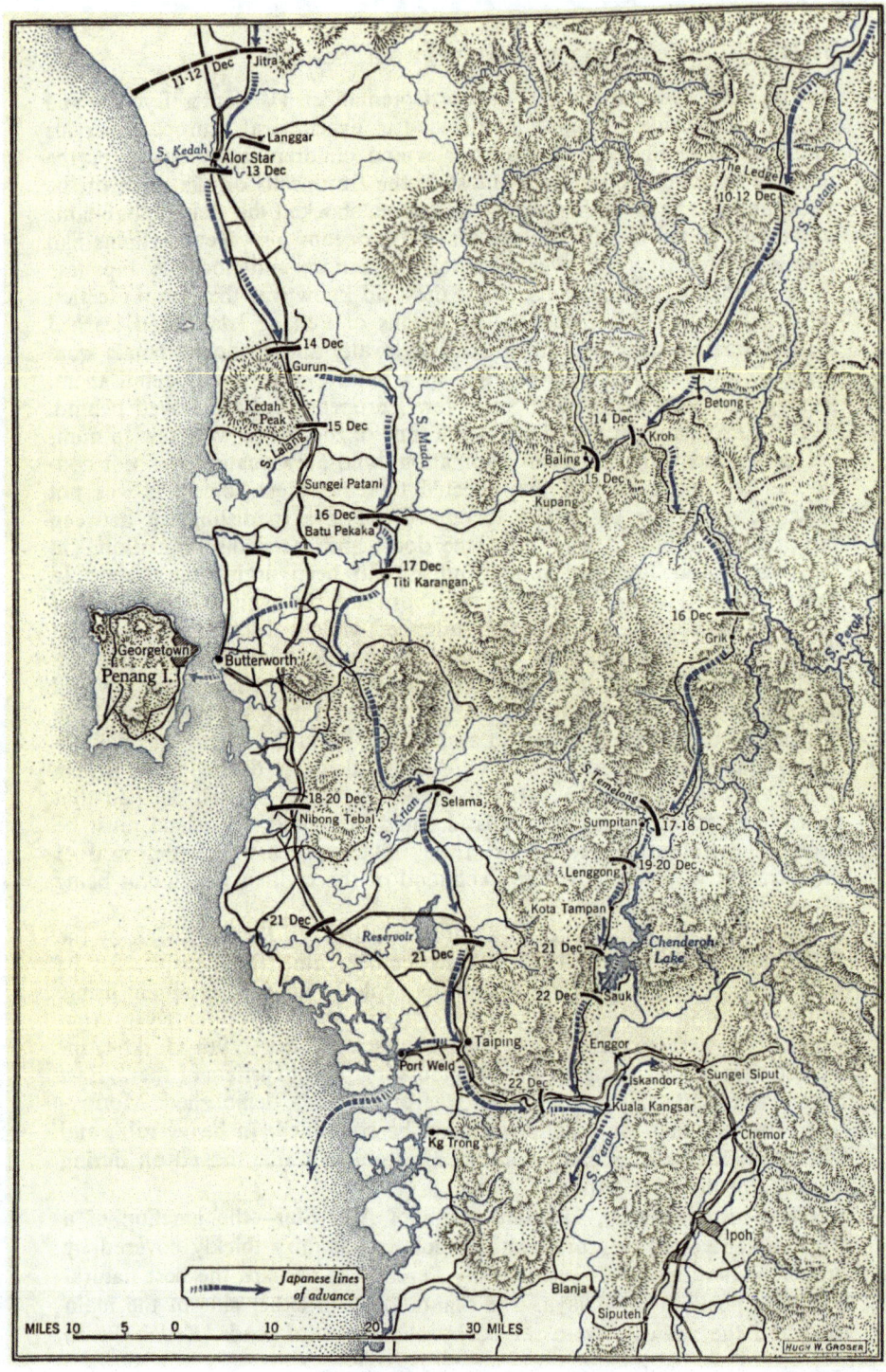

The withdrawal across the Perak

a 3,978-foot jungle-clad mountain, stood between the road and the coast. The position had not, however, been prepared before the war for defence. This task therefore faced the fatigued and disconcerted troops. Dispositions taken up on 14th December were: right sector, 28th Brigade, reconstituted under Brigadier Carpendale (Brigadier Garrett having resumed command of 15th Brigade); left, 6th Brigade, astride road and railway and to Kedah Peak; in reserve, 15th Brigade, now only about 600 strong, astride the road a mile south of Gurun. The 6th Brigade's position was about four miles north of the village of Gurun, and three-quarters of a mile south of where a road from the west coast joined the main road. The 2/16th Punjab were on the railway, with the 2/East Surrey on their left and the 1/8th Punjab astride the main road. The brigade reserve comprised the carrier platoon of 2/16th Punjab.

A Japanese patrol quickly approached the crossroads, and at 2 p.m. three tanks, followed by troops in lorries, came into action. Although one tank was hit and the others withdrew, the enemy infantry forced back the defending patrol and gained control of the road junction. A counter-attack led by Brigadier Lay checked further penetration, but when Heath visited the 11th Division's headquarters during the afternoon, Murray-Lyon said he considered his troops unfit for quick successive encounters, and emphasised the danger that the enemy would cut in on his rear by using the Grik road. He recommended that any further withdrawals should be such as to provide sufficient time for rest and concentration. Although Heath replied that the division must hold the Japanese for the time being at Gurun, he told Percival by telephone during the evening that he considered it should be withdrawn to the Sungei Perak, with an intermediate stand at the Sungei Muda to allow Penang to be evacuated.

From 10 p.m. until 1 a.m. on 15th December, the 1/8th Punjab was under heavy mortar fire. Then, as Lay was organising a further counter-attack to regain the crossroads, the Japanese thrust through the battalion and infiltrated the 6th Brigade area. Having seen Japanese passing his right flank, the battalion commander concluded that it had been isolated. He withdrew what remained of it, and a company of 2/East Surrey under his command, towards the coast. The enemy thereupon overwhelmed the headquarters of the East Surreys, killing the commanding officer and five others, and broke into brigade headquarters. There they killed all its occupants, including seven officers but not Lay.

Carpendale redisposed 28th Brigade in an endeavour to stem the enemy advance, but in the hazardous situation which had developed Murray-Lyon decided early on 15th December to make a further immediate withdrawal. He ordered his division to a position on the Sungei Lalang, seven miles south of Gurun. Later in the day, as reports indicated how badly the division had been disrupted, he decided that it should continue during the night to behind the Sungei Muda. Helped largely by supporting fire from the 88th Field Regiment, contact with the enemy was soon broken, and next morning the division was south of the Muda; but losses of vehicles and equipment were again heavy.

Any prospect of more than a brief stand at the Muda was slight, and an outbreak of cholera and typhoid on Penang Island, off the coast a little to the south, appeared likely in the rapidly worsening conditions then existing there. Heath therefore ordered that the small garrison now left on the island be evacuated by daylight on 17th December. Hurried steps were taken to destroy and demolish everything likely to be of value to the enemy, but the result showed serious shortcomings. Although little effort was required to wreck the broadcasting station, it was left virtually intact. Many small craft such as would be valuable to the enemy in coastal operations remained in the harbour after the garrison had gone—a fact for which the circumstances offered insufficient excuse. About 500 Asians of the Straits Settlements Volunteer Force who eventually were offered evacuation elected to remain to protect their families.

A complex situation now faced Heath and his commanders while 11th Division paused at the Muda. Day and night alternation of fighting and retreat, accompanied by the frequent isolation of units; deficiencies and losses in leadership, upon which the Indians were especially dependent; and rapid decrease in the means of resistance, had severely strained the stamina and resources of the 11th Division. Lack of suitable and adequate training and equipment had been a severe handicap. The road from Kroh through Baling linked with the road system in the Muda area; and the route from Kroh southward through Grik reached the trunk road and the railway west of Kuala Kangsar. How long could the enemy force which had captured Kroh be kept from the division's present right flank and rear? How long was it safe to keep the division west of the Perak in all the circumstances?

Heath decided on the morning of 16th December to place it behind the Sungei Krian, which was flanked by swamps and presented the principal natural obstacle between the Muda and the Perak. He ordered the 6th and 15th Brigades to Taiping, between the Krian and Kuala Kangsar, to rest and refit; and the 28th Brigade, in relatively good condition, to occupy a position covering the Krian, from the road and rail bridge at Nibong Tebal westward to the sea. Krohcol having been disbanded, the 5/14th Punjab was withdrawn to Taiping and the 3/16th Punjab, with the 10th Mountain Battery, was ordered to hold a crossing of the Krian at Selama, 15 miles east of Nibong Tebal. The 12th Brigade Group (Brigadier Paris) was ordered to cover the withdrawal by fighting a rearguard action through Titi Karangan, where the Baling road linked with the road system south of the Muda, to Selama. There it was to pass through the 3/16th Punjab to Taiping.

In an endeavour to make good the losses on the west coast, Brooke-Popham asked, also on 16th December, that a brigade group and reinforcements from India for III Corps be dispatched immediately. In the upshot, it was arranged that the 45th Brigade Group of the 17th Indian Division, due to sail from Bombay on 22nd December for Burma, would be diverted to Singapore, and that reinforcements for the 9th and 11th Divisions would be sent from India as quickly as possible.

Meanwhile Paris, realising that continued withdrawal of 11th Division might expose his troops to attack from the west, had ordered the 5/2nd Punjab to hold a bridge over the Muda at Batu Pekaka, north of Titi Karangan, and moved the Argylls from Baling to Kupang, six miles westward. His concern was soon justified, and it became apparent that the Japanese had not been deterred by the nature of the route from Kroh to Grik. The company of Argylls, with armoured cars, was attacked on the 16th a little north of Grik, and fell back under the impact to a point where they were joined by two Volunteer Force platoons. On the same day a Japanese force which had swung inland from the main road confronted the 5/2nd Punjab. Led by infantry in Malay clothes, the enemy attempted to rush the Batu Pekaka bridge. They were driven off, however, and the bridge was destroyed. Early next day the 5/2nd Punjab was withdrawn. Despite destruction of the bridge the Japanese quickly advanced, and by 10 a.m. were in contact with the main body of the Argylls, who had been moved meanwhile to Titi Karangan as ordered by Heath. The ensuing action was of special interest, for the enemy force was now opposed by a battalion which had received realistic training in jungle warfare.

The Argylls' layout was in keeping with their normal tactics of fighting in self-contained, dispersed company groups of varying composition, controlled by directives rather than by detailed orders, each company group ready to form a firm base if attacked, or if not engaged to strike at any enemy attacking another group. The position, however, was an unfavourable one for a delaying action, and the battalion was handicapped by having been engaged in a succession of sudden moves since 10th December. Both an attack and a withdrawal plan were prepared, with an ambush to fix the Japanese frontally astride the road half a mile north of Titi Karangan.

Apparently the fact that the leading Japanese were in native dress had not been conveyed to the Argylls, for this caused surprise. The enemy opened fire first, and the ambush failed. They quickly developed the "fix-encircle" tactics in which the Argylls also had been trained. Although the latter brought withering machine-gun fire to bear upon an enemy group which moved off the road into rubber trees, the enemy light mortar fire was highly effective. As the engagement progressed it became apparent that there was no choice other than a costly counter-attack or withdrawal. The battalion commander, Lieut-Colonel Stewart,[1] under orders to hold Titi Karangan until noon, chose to attack, and was about to give the order when he received permission to withdraw at his discretion. Deciding that the hazards of attack would now be unwarranted, he reversed his decision.

---

[1] Brig I. MacA. Stewart, DSO, OBE, MC. CO 2/A&SH 1940-42; Comd 12 Indian Bde 1942. Regular soldier; b. 17 Oct 1895.

As it happened, the Argylls almost succeeded in causing the prescribed delay, for the rear parties during the withdrawal did not pass through Titi Karangan until 11.55 a.m. So swift was the Japanese pursuit that five minutes later a rearguard armoured car near the village ambushed a leading group of fifteen Japanese and killed them. Another enemy party which emerged from a forest road nearly a mile to the rear, after a wide encircling movement, was met by Argyll armoured cars and carriers, and held until the battalion was clear.

> The Jap tactics were constant [wrote Stewart afterwards]—frontal fixing and local encirclement, perhaps to a depth of 1,000 yards, by the leading battalion commander, while the regimental commander, without waiting for the situation to develop, launched a wide and deep (perhaps to four miles) encircling attack with a reserve battalion to cut the road in rear. If that attack ever got established the British situation was bound to become an intensely critical one. Fortunately, it never succeeded against the Argylls, but the very careful and close timings and the great speed of action necessary for jungle fighting will be noted. Had the battalion been asked to delay another quarter of an hour, its counter-attack would have had to go in. . . . By that time too the wide Jap encircling move would have got established across the road behind, and what had been a most successful action would within a few moments have turned into a disastrous defeat.[2]

Reaching Selama, south-east of the Sungei Krian, on 17th December, the 12th Brigade (less the Argyll company on the Grik road) came under command of the 11th Division, which by dawn on 18th December was south of the river.

The road from Kroh through Baling was now no longer a potential danger to the British communications; but events on the Grik road showed that another was swiftly developing. In fact, as it later transpired, the Japanese *42nd Infantry Regiment* had taken the more ambitious course offered by this route. Although they had left their light tank battalion behind because of the state of the surface between Kroh and Grik they quickly forged ahead, and under their pressure the small force which stood in their way withdrew to Sumpitan, south-east of Selama. Meanwhile Heath had decided to send the 1st Independent Company[3] to its aid; and he now resolved again to use the 12th Brigade as a means of halting this further enemy advance towards the 11th Division's rear. He had in mind that unless these moves were successful, the division would have to be pulled back to the Sungei Perak or even farther.

Impressed by the aggression of the enemy, and lacking adequate Intelligence, Percival concluded that the Japanese were employing one division along the trunk road, one on the Patani-Kroh-Grik road, and one in Kelantan, with reserves at call in Indo-China, as against his two Indian brigades on the east of the Malayan Peninsula and the equivalent of a division on the west. He considered relieving the 11th Indian Division with the 8th Australian, but decided against it on the ground that piecemeal employment of the Australian force would be undesirable, and its removal

---

[2] I. M. Stewart, *History of the Argyll and Sutherland Highlanders, 2nd Battalion* (1947), pp. 25-26.
[3] This unit, comprised of a headquarters and one British and three Indian platoons, had been formed in April 1941 for action behind the enemy lines.

as a whole from Johore would leave the State weakly held by troops unfamiliar with the ground. With their command of the seas, the Japanese would be free to launch landings at Mersing or elsewhere on its eastern coast. On the other hand, the necessity of holding the airfields of central Malaya, from which otherwise the enemy could the more readily attack the naval base and reinforcement convoys approaching Singapore, dictated that the Japanese must be kept as far north as possible. The upshot of Percival's deliberations was that he decided against any major redisposition of his forces for the time being, but authorised a withdrawal by the weakened 11th Division to the line of the Perak if necessary.

By this time only about a hundred aircraft were available in Malaya for the defence of the base, protection of convoys, and any other duties for which they could be spared. The latter included little action to check the enemy advance. The main weakness of the Perak as an obstacle was that it ran not across the north-south communications, but more or less parallel with them, during the greater part of its course from Kuala Kangsar. On 18th December, after conferring with Heath, Percival issued a series of further orders, which required principally that a flotilla comprising a sloop and some light craft be formed to oppose enemy movement by sea between the mouths of the Krian and the Perak; that delaying positions be prepared east and south-east of the Perak, at Ipoh and Tanjong Malim; that the 9th Indian Division be retained on the east coast to prevent enemy use of the airfield at Kuantan and penetration from that quarter; that what became known as "Roseforce" be formed to raid Japanese communications west of the Perak; that the 6th and 15th Indian Brigades be amalgamated as the 6th/15th Brigade; and that the 12th Brigade be incorporated with them in the 11th Division.

Percival's resolve to limit losses of strength in northern Malaya was in line with a direction which had been given by Mr Churchill on 15th December. In a cable to General Ismay for the Chiefs of Staff Committee, Churchill, then on his way to the United States to confer with Roosevelt, urged them to beware lest troops required for the defence of Singapore Island were used up or cut off on the Malayan Peninsula. "Nothing," he said, "compares in importance with the fortress."[4] Indeed, this had now so impressed itself upon him that he required, after consultation with General Auchinleck, the Commander-in-Chief Middle East, and the Australian Government, that consideration be given to moving the I Australian Corps from Palestine to Singapore. On the same day Mr Duff Cooper had disclosed to Mr Bowden, Australia's representative in Singapore, misgivings about the military situation, and said he saw the probability of a gradual withdrawal to a line approximately covering the southern half of Johore, to be held pending arrival of reinforcements about a month hence. On 18th December a conference was held in Singapore, attended by representatives of Great Britain, the United States, Holland, Australia[5]

---

[4] Churchill, Vol III, p. 565.
[5] The Australian representatives were General Bennett, Captain J. A. Collins (navy) and Group Captain J. P. J. McCauley (air).

and New Zealand, as a result of which a report was sent to the British Chiefs of Staff. In this it was held that the additional forces needed to meet Malaya's needs must include four fighter and four bomber squadrons with reserves, and aircraft to complete squadrons already in Malaya and their reserves; an infantry division and a brigade group, three light and two heavy anti-aircraft regiments, an anti-tank regiment and fifty light tanks, and reinforcements for the III Indian Corps. The conference endorsed Percival's policy of holding the enemy as far north as possible. On 19th December, however, Churchill said in a further cable to Ismay that Duff Cooper had conveyed to him anxieties similar to his own. He added: "The Commander-in-Chief (Far East) should now be told to confine himself to defence of Johore and Singapore, and that nothing must compete with maximum defence of Singapore. This should not preclude his employing delaying tactics and demolitions on the way south and making an orderly retreat."[6]

To the pleas for reinforcements were added those of General Northcott, the commander of the recently-formed Armoured Division, then visiting Malaya, and General Bennett, cabling on 18th December to the Chief of the Australian General Staff, General Sturdee. Northcott strongly recommended that all possible reinforcements be sent, including a machine-gun battalion to be dispatched immediately. Bennett said: "In my opinion retreat through Kedah into Perak (State) is grave. Situation will grow worse unless troops of quality are available to intervene. My force not yet engaged but cannot leave present location without grave risk and cannot be split as it is already dangerously thin. I consider Australian division from Middle East by fastest means essential to save situation. . . ." On 19th December, in a cable to the Department of External Affairs, Bowden raised an issue particularly significant in the light of later events.

"I feel strongly," he declared, "that before further Australian troops are committed every possible guarantee should be taken that they will not be abandoned with those already here." Bowden added that in his view the real defensive strength of Malaya fell far short of previous publicity; and that assurances should be sought immediately from Great Britain that Malaya would not continue to be regarded as a secondary theatre of war, but that reinforcements and supplies of modern arms and equipment would be rushed to Malaya even at the cost of slowing down the African offensive. On the same day he received an assurance from his department that the Australian Government was far from satisfied with the results of the policy of subordinating the requirements of the Malayan theatre of war; that despite the assurances given by Brooke-Popham during his visit to Australia that all was well with the Malayan defences, there was anxiety in Australia about the position. On 23rd December the department received through the British High Commissioner in Australia a message from Duff Cooper referring to the appointment of Bowden to

---
[6] Churchill, Vol III, pp. 565-66.

the Far Eastern War Council and saying "We are glad to have him with us, and share your confidence in the soundness of his views."

Saddled with the task of defending the Grik road, Paris sent Stewart with the Argylls who had fought at Titi Karangan, and a troop of field guns, to Lenggong, about midway between Kuala Kangsar and Grik. Behind them, at Kota Tampan where the Sungei Perak ran close to the road, he stationed a company of the 5/2nd Punjab. Seeking room for manoeuvre, Stewart sought on 19th December to gain control of the road north of Sumpitan, where it entered a jungle defile. As however the Independent Company, now under his command, lost heavily in the endeavour, it was withdrawn, and the Argylls, after a brisk engagement, took up positions at dusk along the road between Sumpitan and Lenggong. There ensued a lull until, at 4.15 p.m. next day, a Chinese from Temelong on the Perak (described by Stewart as "one of that gallant race for whom all Argylls have affection") reported that four hours previously he had seen a Japanese force moving down the river in boats and on foot. They were forcing local Asians to carry what were evidently mortars, and were demanding direction to Kota Tampan. If this force gained the causeway across a swamp south of Kota Tampan, Stewart recorded, "it was the end, not only of the Argylls but of Kuala Kangsar and much of the 11th Division as well. . . . The testing time of the Argylls' speed had indeed come." With the aid of the 2/3rd Australian Motor Transport Company, a detachment raced back down the road and repulsed a Japanese thrust along a track from the river.[7] It was found that the Japanese were calling "Punjabi, Punjabi", in an attempt to pass for members of a platoon of the 5/2nd Punjab which had been stationed at the river and which they had dispersed at the outset of their attack.

Although the thrust had been checked, the possibility of further encircling moves was obvious. The withdrawal of the rest of the battalion to Kota Tampan was therefore commenced. It was quickly followed up by the Japanese, who ran into a series of ambushes and lost heavily. By 10 p.m., having covered Kota Tampan until dark as required, the battalion was behind the causeway, which was then demolished. Next morning (the 21st December) when the withdrawal had been completed, the Argylls were again attacked, but the enemy withdrew after close fighting. Instructions were later received for the battalion to retire at night through the rest of 5/2nd Punjab, who were moving up to cover the western and southern shores of Chenderoh Lake. Stewart decided, however, to dispose of a further attack then developing. This occurred during the afternoon, was again resolutely met, and the enemy was dispersed.

---

[7] In his unit's history Stewart recalled that the 2/3 MT Coy had been closely associated with the 2/Argylls during all the fighting on the mainland. He added: "It is difficult to find words to express the excellence of their quality. They would take on any job, at any time, and under any conditions with a coolness and a quick practical efficiency that was indeed an inspiration to a weary unit coming out of battle. In the foolish and usually unjust recriminations that have in places followed the Malayan campaign, we Argylls hope that our Australian cousins, many of them Scots, will read and accept this genuine and heartfelt tribute."—*History of the Argyll & Sutherland Highlanders, 2nd Battalion*, pp. 42-3.

The Argylls then moved back through the 5/2nd Punjab, who were concentrated at Sauk, south-west of Chenderoh Lake and 11 miles from the junction of the Grik road with the trunk road west of Kuala Kangsar. The 4/19th Hyderabad, withdrawn from Kelantan, was posted to protect the main road at Sungei Siput, east of the Iskandor and Enggor bridges by which the main road and the railway respectively crossed the Perak. Japanese who tried to cross the Krian at Selama on 20th December were repulsed by the 3/16th Punjab; but because of the growing threat to the vital crossings of the Perak, the 11th Division, including the 12th Brigade, had been withdrawn behind that river by the early morning of 23rd December. The Iskandor and Enggor bridges were destroyed, and during the following night a pontoon bridge at Blanja, south of Kuala Kangsar, was sunk. The 12th Brigade was now at Sungei Siput, and 28th Brigade at Siputeh, at a junction of the road from Blanja.

Extensive changes of commanders were made on the same day. With the commanders of all three original brigades of 11th Division in hospital, Stewart of the Argylls was appointed commander of the 12th Brigade, Lieut-Colonel Moorhead (3/16th Punjab) of the 15th Brigade, and Lieut-Colonel Selby[8] (2/9th Gurkha Rifles) of 28th Brigade. On the ground that an officer with the widest possible experience of bush warfare was needed to command the division in the situation which had developed, Murray-Lyon was replaced by Brigadier Paris of the 12th Brigade. On this day too Lieut-General Sir Henry Pownall[9] reached Singapore. The United Kingdom Chiefs of Staff had decided some weeks before war with Japan broke out, but when the importance of the role which would have to be fulfilled by the army in Malaya was increasingly apparent, that an army officer with up-to-date experience should replace Air Chief Marshal Brooke-Popham as Commander-in-Chief Far East; and on 27th December Pownall took over this command.[1] Pownall, a cool, clear-headed soldier, had been a student at the Imperial Defence College under Brooke-Popham, and Chief of Staff to General Gort,[2] commander of the British Expeditionary Force in France in 1939-40. The fact that this decision became generally known in Malaya soon after it was made could hardly have strengthened Brooke-Popham's authority thenceforward.

Reviewing the situation as it existed on 23rd December, Percival was to record:

> It was now clear that we were faced by an enemy who had made a special study of bush warfare on a grand scale and whose troops had been specially trained in

---

[8] Brig W. R. Selby, DSO. CO 2/9 Gurkha Rifles; Comd 28 Ind Inf Bde. Regular soldier; b. Doncaster, Yorkshire, England, 31 Aug 1897.

[9] Lt-Gen Sir Henry Pownall, KCB, KBE, DSO, MC. CGS Brit Exped Force 1939-40; Vice CIGS 1941; C-in-C Far East Dec 1941 to Jan 1942; Ch of Staff ABDA Comd Jan-Feb 1942; GOC Ceylon 1942-43; C-in-C Persia-Iraq 1943; Ch of Staff to Supreme Allied Comd SEAC 1943. Regular soldier; b. 19 Nov 1887.

[1] Brooke-Popham pointed out in a report to the Chiefs of Staff that at this stage the land forces which they had agreed were the minimum required had not been supplied; and that the aircraft in the Far East were 370 short of the accepted estimate, and largely obsolescent.

[2] Field Marshal Viscount Gort, VC, GCB, CBE, DSO, MVO, MC. CIGS War Office 1937-39; GOC-in-C BEF 1939-40; Governor and C-in-C Gibraltar 1941-42; C-in-C Malta 1942-44. B. 10 Jul 1886. Died 31 Mar 1946.

those tactics. He relied in the main on outflanking movements and on infiltration by small parties into and behind our lines. For support of his forward troops he relied on the mortar and the infantry gun rather than on longer range weapons. His snipers operated from trees. He exploited the use of fireworks. For mobility he made a wide use of civilian bicycles seized in the country. His tanks he had up to date operated mainly on the roads. His infantry had displayed an ability to cross obstacles—rivers, swamps, jungles, etc.—more rapidly than had previously been thought possible. Finally, speed was obviously of vital importance to him and he was prepared to press his attacks without elaborate preparations.[3]

As has been mentioned much of the information now emerging from Japanese operations in Malaya had been available from various sources before the war; but a gap had existed between this and the realisation which, as Percival's review showed, was now being forced upon leaders in Malaya.

Bennett had sent one of his staff officers, Major Dawkins, to III Indian Corps headquarters on 19th December to make personal inquiries into the cause of the retreat. In the course of his report Dawkins said that outflanking moves by the Japanese had taken place through all types of country. Either the enemy was well supplied with guides—voluntary or enforced—or he had a trained corps of scouts capable of using the compass and leading companies with accuracy and speed.

There is no terrain which is impassable to infantry suitably equipped and trained (he said). Jungle, forest and rubber areas are *par excellence* infantry country—every move is screened from air and ground observation, the value of fire of weapons of all natures is very limited, and troops on the offensive can close to within assaulting distance unmolested. The force which has the initiative will have so great an advantage over the enemy that securing and retaining the initiative must be the prime aim of every commander irrespective of grade.

Operations so far, Dawkins continued, had confirmed the suitability of the tactical training carried out by the A.I.F. in Malaya. The enemy had clearly demonstrated reluctance to stand when offensive action was taken against him. He did not press his attacks where they did not attain initial success. The statement that the Japanese were fighting with "fanatical courage" was a gross exaggeration. Well-trained troops of high morale and suitably equipped should easily wrest the initiative from him. Referring to the desirability of "travelling light" in the jungle, Dawkins recommended that the scales of clothing, equipment, ammunition and transport should be reviewed and drastic reductions made to ensure mobility.

Deciding that the time might be near when the A.I.F. would be called upon to defend Johore, Bennett also on 19th December sent some of his staff and Brigadier Maxwell (27th Brigade) to Gemas, on the trunk road just before it entered the State from the north-west, to reconnoitre in detail a suitable defensive position. To the Australian Minister for the Army he wrote a letter giving his views on what he considered to be "the incompetence of higher commanders" in Malaya.[4] He decided on the 21st to withdraw the 2/10th Australian General Hospital from Malacca

---

[3] Percival, Despatch, p. 1280.
[4] Entry in General Bennett's diary.

and the Convalescent Depot from Batu Pahat before 3rd January. On the 23rd, at Jemaluang, he held a conference of commanders of brigades, battalions and ancillary units at which he reviewed the campaign to date, described the methods used by the Japanese, and indicated those to be employed in operations by the Australians. They were not to withdraw, he said, merely because their flanks were threatened, but to send out strong counter-attacking parties. Units must concentrate on practising the attack and adopt ruses to defeat fifth column activity.

The British commanders in Singapore were now concerned by the threat offered by the road across Malaya from Kuantan on the east through Jerantut and Kuala Lipis to Kuala Kubu, on the trunk road in the west. If the Japanese drive down the west coast passed Kuala Kubu while the 9th Division was still in its position on the east of Malaya, the division would be cut off. After consultation, Brooke-Popham, Percival and Air Vice-Marshal Pulford decided to withdraw the division if and when this danger made it expedient. On the 23rd December Percival took the first precautionary steps for the defence of north Johore and Singapore Island, when he ordered Bennett to make preliminary arrangements to deal with an enemy advance down the main road from Kuala Lumpur, capital of the Federated Malay States, towards Singapore and also with landings by "small enemy forces" on the west coast.[5] He ordered the Commander of Singapore Fortress to arrange for reconnaissance of the north shore of Singapore Island to select defensive positions in the event of enemy landings—an order which, issued at this stage, indicated how little that possibility had entered into previous planning and preparation.

Reconnaissances and attacks on enemy transport had been carried out from 13th December by Norgroup, a small operational air formation associated with the III Corps headquarters, and based on Ipoh. By 19th December, however, this airfield had been so heavily bombed that it was abandoned, and the supporting craft were back at Kuala Lumpur. The Japanese quickly used the airfields they captured, especially as in the circumstances of their evacuation efforts to wreck them had been inadequate. Even stocks of aviation spirit had been left intact, and piles of road metal were readily available to repair what damage had been done to the runways. On 21st and 22nd December increasingly heavy Japanese air raids were made on the Kuala Lumpur airfield, where the Buffaloes of No. 453 Squadron R.A.A.F. were stationed. Despite valiant efforts by the pilots, the superiority in numbers and performance of the enemy craft told heavily against them. By nightfall on the 22nd, only four of the squadron's sixteen Buffaloes remained in operational condition. To conserve strength for protection of the naval base and reinforcement convoys, Air Vice-Marshal Pulford ordered the remnants of the squadron back to Singapore, and evacuation of the field to begin early next day.

---

[5] Percival, Despatch, Appendix "C".

Thus the air force had been swept out of northern Malaya, except that a composite fighter squadron (Nos. 21 and 453) was formed to cooperate with III Corps, using Kuala Lumpur as an advanced landing ground.

There had meanwhile been little activity by Malaya's bomber aircraft, for the report on 13th December that a large convoy was steaming towards south-eastern Malaya had caused most of them to be held in readiness to help oppose a landing. Daily seaward reconnaissances were made to determine the convoy's destination, and it was not until 24th December that it was concluded that this had been British Borneo. Other reconnaissances were flown to obtain warning of any movements by Japanese forces in coastal craft along Malaya's east and west coasts. The first air reinforcements, comprising eight Hudson light bombers, were manned at Darwin by Australian crews from Singapore, and delivered on 23rd December. Hopes which had been pinned on route-ing planes through Burma to Malaya vanished, however, when after Japanese air raids on the airfield at Victoria Point in southern Burma, the field was evacuated on 13th December, and occupied by Japanese troops two days later. Thereafter such planes as had sufficient range were to be flown from Rangoon to Sabang, off northern Sumatra, and thence to Singapore. Fighter planes had to be sent by sea, with consequent delay in their arrival. It was arranged by the British Air Ministry on 17th December that 51 Hurricane fighters, in crates due to reach Durban in convoy next day, should then be trans-shipped and sent to Singapore with pilots and ground staff for one squadron. Arrangements also were made for 52 Hudsons to be sent, but as these would take several weeks to reach Malaya endeavours were made to have flown there or to the Netherlands East Indies a number of American four-engined bombers then in Australia.

At the political level in the conduct of the war, a rapidly mounting sense of urgency was shown in cables to the Australian Prime Minister (Mr Curtin) by the Australian Minister in London (Sir Earle Page) and the High Commissioner (Mr Bruce). They were disturbed by a feeling that the United Kingdom Chiefs of Staff, though greatly concerned and endeavouring to provide substantial reinforcements for the Far East, were not sufficiently seized with the necessity of meeting swiftly the immediate needs of the situation. "We might only have three or four weeks to save the position, and immediate action might save us five or six years of war," said Page. He noted in his diary on 19th December, after attending a meeting of the Imperial Defence Committee, that "there was a great tendency to emphasise the importance of the Libyan campaign to the detriment of reinforcements to the Far East".

Mr Churchill had been pondering the issue during his voyage to America for discussions with President Roosevelt. He landed at Washington airport after dark on 22nd December, and "clasped his strong hand with comfort and pleasure".[6]

---

[6] Churchill, Vol III, p. 587.

CHAPTER 10

MOUNTING DISASTERS

THE Japanese forces as a whole were now riding a wave of victories. In the colony of Hong Kong, which had become a perilously-situated extremity of British power, the enemy troops continued on 9th December their advance on the Gin Drinkers' Line. This line, ten and a half miles long, occupied a commanding position on the mainland, but had little depth. Major-General Maltby,[1] commander of the British troops in China and of the Hong Kong Fortress, estimated that the line might be held for seven days or more, but only if there was no strong and capable offensive against it. It was hoped that sufficient delay would be imposed to enable final measures, possible only when war was certain, to be taken for defence of the main stronghold, the island of Hong Kong itself.

The island, with an area of thirty-two square miles, is traversed by an east-west range of steep, conical hills, rising to 1,800 feet at Victoria Peak. The densely-populated city of Victoria occupied principally a flat, narrow strip of land along the north-western shore. Some shelters against bombing and shelling had been provided, but for the majority of its 1,750,000 inhabitants, mostly Chinese, no such protection was available. Its water supply came partly from the mainland, and partly from reservoirs on the island itself. In both respects it was vulnerable to enemy action. Since it was first occupied by the British in 1841, the island had graduated, like Singapore, from earlier use by pirates and fishermen, through increasingly lucrative stages, to affluence as a great port and commercial centre on the main Far Eastern trade route.[2] The colony had been extended in 1860 to include part of the peninsula of Kowloon, and 359 square miles of adjacent territory was acquired in 1898 on a ninety-nine years' lease; but development of the island as a naval base had given way, as a result of the Washington Agreement of 1922, to construction of the Singapore Base.

The total force for defence of the colony, including naval and air force personnel and non-combatant services, was about 14,500 men. Its principal components, as mentioned earlier, were two United Kingdom, two Indian, and two Canadian battalions. Both the United Kingdom and the Indian battalions had lost some of their most experienced officers and men by transfer to service elsewhere. The Canadians had not received the concentrated and rigorous training necessary to fit them for battle. The outbreak of war had prevented their carriers and lorries, dispatched later than the troops, from reaching Hong Kong. The artillery on the island was manned largely by Indians and volunteers; some of the guns dated

---

[1] Maj-Gen C. M. Maltby, CB, MC. GOC British Tps in China and Commander Hong Kong Fortress 1941. Regular soldier; b. 13 Jan 1891.

[2] In the mid-nineteenth century one of Hong Kong's uses was as a transit depot for Chinese going to Australian and Californian goldfields.

The attack on Hong Kong

from the 1914-18 war, and were drawn by hired vehicles driven by Chinese civilians. Protracted naval defence of Hong Kong was out of the question, for only three destroyers, a flotilla of eight motor torpedo boats, four gunboats, and some armed patrol vessels were stationed there at the outbreak of war with Japan, and two of the destroyers sailed for Singapore on 8th December. Prospects of naval reinforcement were negligible. On the other hand, denial of the port to the enemy was considered highly important.

As in Malaya and elsewhere, a poor opinion had been widely held of the quality of the Japanese forces despite much available information to the contrary. They were considered, for instance, to be poorly qualified for night operations; to prefer stereotyped methods; and to be below first-class European standards in the air.

Until the arrival of the Canadian troops it had been considered practicable to employ only one infantry battalion on the mainland, but three were then allotted to it, with a proportion of mobile artillery. At the time of attack the 5/7th Rajput occupied the right sector of the Gin Drinkers' Line, the 2/14th Punjab the centre, and the 2/Royal Scots the left, the whole force being commanded by Brigadier Wallis.[3] On the island, under the Canadian commander, Brigadier Lawson,[4] were a machine-gun battalion (1/Middlesex) for beach defence, the Winnipeg Grenadiers in the south-west sector and the Royal Rifles of Canada in the south-east. The defences included some thirty fixed guns of up to 9.2-inch calibre, but lacking radar equipment. Anti-aircraft armament was on a small scale, and such aircraft as the colony possessed had been put out of action in the first day of war.

Pre-conceived ideas about the Japanese had rapidly to be revised as their attack developed. Their patrols and small columns, led by guides familiar with the terrain, moved swiftly over cross-country tracks by day and night, and the Japanese forces as a whole acted with such speed and efficiency that it was apparent they had been intensively trained for their task. Although on 9th December they engaged chiefly in patrol action, they surprised the defenders of Shing Mun Redoubt, a key position largely dominating the left sector of the Gin Drinkers' Line, and captured it, including a Scots company headquarters, near midnight. This gravely affected the situation generally, and a company of the Grenadiers was brought from the island to strengthen the mainland forces. A Japanese attack from the Redoubt next morning was halted by artillery and a Rajput company which had been moved into a gap on the right of the Scots; but the centre and left companies of the Scots had become dangerously exposed, and they were withdrawn late in the afternoon to an inner line. Shelling and air attacks were carried out by the enemy during the day. At dawn on the 11th Japanese troops turned the left flank of the Scots,

---

[3] Brig C. Wallis. CO 5/7 Rajput; Comd Mainland Bde Hong Kong 1941. Regular soldier; b. 7 Mar 1896.

[4] Brig J. K. Lawson. Comd Canadian Expeditionary Force to Hong Kong 1941. Killed in action 19 Dec 1941.

and though the Grenadier company and a detachment of the Hong Kong Volunteer Defence Corps were brought into action,[5] the position became so critical that withdrawal of the mainland forces, except 5/7th Rajput, was ordered. The Rajputs were to occupy Devil's Peak Peninsula, covering the narrow Lye Mun Passage between the peninsula and the island.

The Japanese extended their activities during the day to attempted landings on Lamma and Aberdeen Islands, and stepped up artillery and air attack. Withdrawal of the British forces from the mainland, as ordered, was carried out during the night. Because of the weight of the attack and other factors, including rapidly increasing water transport difficulties, Devil's Peak Peninsula too was evacuated, with naval aid, early in the morning of 12th December. The withdrawal imposed an exhausting task on the Indian battalions who, short of transport, had to manhandle mortars and other equipment over difficult country and to fend off the enemy, while under dive-bombing attacks and mortar fire. The whole of the northern portion of the island now came under mortar and artillery fire. This, and the fact that the resistance on the mainland had lasted only four days, was of course disconcerting to the civilian population as well as to the British forces.

The Japanese forces on the mainland comprised principally the three regiments of the *38th Division*—the *228th* and *230th Regiments* with three mountain artillery battalions on the right, and the *229th Regiment* on the left. Expecting a longer resistance, they had rapidly to readjust their plans to what had happened. At 9 a.m.[6] on the 13th a launch flying a white flag reached the island from Kowloon, with a letter to the Governor of Hong Kong and Commander-in-Chief, Sir Mark Young, from Lieut-General T. Sakai, commander of the Japanese *XXIII Army,* demanding the surrender of the colony. The offer was sharply rejected, an increasingly heavy bombardment of the island followed, and Japanese were seen to be collecting launches in Kowloon Bay. The British forces were reorganised into the East and West Brigades. The East Brigade, commanded by Wallis, comprised the Royal Rifles of Canada and the 5/7th Rajput; companies of the 1/Middlesex were also under command, and two companies of Volunteers in reserve. The West Brigade—the Royal Scots (in reserve), the Winnipeg Grenadiers and the 2/14th Punjab, with the rest of 1/Middlesex and four Volunteer companies, also in reserve—was placed under Lawson. The Middlesex companies were manning pill-boxes on the perimeter of the island.

Serious fires, civil disorder, sniping by "fifth columnists" and desertion of locally-enlisted army transport drivers soon contributed to the island's difficulties. Accurate and intensive Japanese shelling began putting guns out of action on the 14th, and on the 15th was mainly directed at pill-boxes along the north shore. A night landing on the north-east part of the island was attempted by Japanese troops using small rubber boats and

---

[5] The Winnipeg Grenadiers thus was the first Canadian infantry unit to be in action in the 1939-45 war.
[6] Hong Kong winter time, then in force.

rafts, but was repulsed. Resistance was encouraged by reports that Chinese forces were moving towards Hong Kong, though Maltby considered that they could not give effective assistance until early in January. Continuous pounding from land and air, mainly of military objectives, had caused extensive damage and put a heavy strain on the defenders when, on 17th December, the Japanese renewed proposals for surrender. These were again rejected, and next day Japanese shelling and air raids became less discriminate, as had been hinted by the envoys. Petrol and oil tanks were set ablaze, and burned for several days. Further concentration of water transport craft by the enemy was observed. Shelling of the north-east sector was particularly heavy, and frequently cut communications with the pill-boxes. By now, the destroyer (*Thracian*) had been disabled, and the only British naval vessels in action were two gunboats and a depleted motor torpedo boat flotilla.

Japanese forces swarmed over the strait and landed on a two-mile front in the north-east of the island on the night of 18th-19th December. Despite concentrated fire from the Rajputs to whom the sector had been allotted, and shelling by British artillery, the Japanese *229th Regiment* occupied Lye Mun Gap and Mount Parker, the *228th Regiment* won its way to Mount Butler, and the *230th Regiment* to Jardine's Lookout. There they dominated the approaches from the area to the Wong Nei Chong Gap, behind which the West Brigade was disposed from north to south across the island. Although the enemy gained access to the North Point power station area, resistance was maintained at the station throughout the night by a force known as the "Hughesiliers",[7] with power company employees, nine Free French personnel, and some wounded of the 1/Middlesex. Most of the force fought in near-by streets next day until killed or captured. Resistance was continued in the main office of the building until 2 p.m.

Trying to check or repulse the invaders, Lawson sent forward three platoons and then a company of Grenadiers, while Fortress Headquarters organised other reinforcements. The Grenadiers at first made good progress. Led by Company Sergeant-Major J. R. Osborn, some of them captured Mount Butler and held it for three hours. They were then dislodged, and rejoined remnants of their company trying to get back to brigade headquarters.

> Enemy grenades began to fall in the company position. Osborn caught several and threw them back. At last one fell where he could not retrieve it in time; and the Sergeant-Major, shouting a warning, threw himself upon it as it exploded, giving his life for his comrades.[8]

Few of the company, however, escaped being killed, wounded, or taken prisoner; and, at 10 a.m. on the 19th, Lawson reported to Fortress Headquarters that, as the Japanese were firing at point-blank range into his headquarters at Wong Nei Chong Gap, he was about to fight it out in

---
[7] Formed by a Colonel Hughes of men of 55 and over, many of them prominent in the colony's affairs.

[8] C. P. Stacey, *The Canadian Army 1939-45* (1948), p. 285. (Osborn was posthumously awarded the Victoria Cross.)

(Australian War Memorial)
Rice stocks were distributed to the civilian population to avoid them falling into Japanese hands.

(Australian War Memorial)
Indian sappers prepare a bridge for demolition, as the rice distribution, by various forms of transport, continues.

(*Australian War Memorial*)

Gemencheh bridge taken from the direction of the advancing Japanese. Captain D. J. Duffy's company of the 2/30th Battalion was disposed in ambush positions to the right and left of the cutting beyond the bridge. Post-war photograph.

(*Australian War Memorial*)

Scene of the tank trap in the 2/30th Battalion area forward of Gemas. Five Japanese tanks were destroyed in this area on the morning of 15th January 1942.

the open. He and nearly all the staffs at the headquarters—West Brigade, West Group artillery, and a counter-battery group—were killed. Maltby himself took over command of the brigade until next day, when he passed it to Colonel Rose,[9] of the Hong Kong Volunteer Defence Corps. The Governor, Sir Mark Young, emphasised to Maltby the importance of fighting to the end, however bad might be the military outlook, on the ground that every day gained was a direct help to the British war effort.

A motor torpedo boat attack on Japanese being ferried to the island met with some success, but fire from both sides of the harbour, and from fighter aircraft, prevented it from being developed as planned. As the Japanese became established in the north-east, and brought in support and supplies under cover of their positions, efforts by the West Brigade to dislodge them gradually gave way to defence on its north-south line. The Rajputs having been practically destroyed in opposing the landings, the East Brigade was withdrawn from a line slanting south-westward on the right of the former Rajput line to one running east-westward to Repulse Bay, covering Stanley Peninsula and Fort Stanley. Misunderstanding of an order lost the brigade its mobile artillery in the process. The brigade was organised in its new position for a counter-attack on 20th December along two lines of advance—one via the Repulse Bay road to the Wong Nei Chong Gap, and the other along the western slopes of Violet Hill south-east of the Gap. The advance was commenced at 8 a.m., but two hours later a company of Royal Rifles encountered Japanese troops surrounding the Repulse Bay Hotel, at the head of Repulse Bay. The Canadians drove them off, and found a number of European women and children in the hotel being defended by a mixed party led by a Middlesex lieutenant. The advance generally was soon halted by superior numbers (two battalions of *229th Regiment*) and as night closed in the brigade fell back on its former positions.

It became increasingly evident as the fighting on the island continued that Japanese command of the air and sea, and the weight of their attack, made defeat inevitable in the absence of speedy aid from outside. All available forces, including navy, air, and army service corps personnel joined in heroic efforts to retrieve the situation. In the course of the desperate fighting the Scots took revenge for their reverse on the mainland, but suffered further severe casualties. The 1/Middlesex distinguished itself particularly in defence of Leighton Hill. Maltby recorded that the Hong Kong Volunteer Defence Corps proved themselves stubborn and gallant soldiers. Progressively weakened, the defenders were however driven southward and westward, and a wedge was driven between the East and West Brigades. On the night of 24th December a bombardment commenced of the centre of Victoria, capital of the colony; of the naval dock-

---

[9] Col H. B. Rose, MC. Comd Hong Kong Volunteer Defence Force 1938-42. Regular soldier; b. 17 Jul 1891.
   Col P. Hennessy, DSO, MC, the Canadian next in seniority to Lawson, had been killed earlier in the day.

yard; and of Fortress Headquarters. Japanese patrols were penetrating the outskirts of the city.

Christmas morning presented a desperate situation, especially as failure of the water supply was imminent. Again the Japanese sent envoys—this time a British officer and a civilian whom they had captured—to testify to the formidable array of men and guns they had seen massed for final assault. It was nevertheless decided to fight on, but the military situation so deteriorated that soon after 3 p.m. Maltby told the Governor that no further effective resistance was possible. Responsible also for the civilian population, Sir Mark Young thereupon authorised negotiations for a ceasefire. He formally surrendered the colony later in the afternoon. Holding out at Fort Stanley, Brigadier Wallis demanded confirmation in writing of verbal orders brought to him through the Japanese lines to surrender. It was not until 2.30 a.m. on 26th December that he ordered that a white flag be hoisted.

Many factors additional to Japanese command of air and sea, and the extent and efficiency of their land forces, entered into the defeat. Commenting on the enemy tactics, Maltby said later that patrols

> . . . advanced by paths which could have been known only to locals or from detailed reconnaissance. Armed agents in Kowloon and Hong Kong systematically fired during the hours of darkness on troops, sentries, cars and dispatch riders. . . . After the landing on the island had been effected, penetration to cut the island in half was assisted by local guides who led the columns by most difficult routes . . . marked maps found on dead officers gave a surprising amount of exact detail, which included our defences and much of our wire. Every officer seemed to be in possession of such a map. . . . They seemed to be in possession of a very full Order of Battle, and knew the names of most of the senior and commanding officers.[1]

The British battle casualties in the defence of Hong Kong were estimated at nearly 4,500; and 11,848 combatants were lost in the fighting and as a result of the surrender. The official total of Japanese battle casualties was 2,754. Capture of the colony by the Japanese was not only a blow at British power and prestige in the Far East: it also provided the enemy with an additional stronghold in the regions they had determined to dominate, and cancelled Hong Kong as a means of bolstering Chinese resistance.

Japanese forces were sweeping over United States possessions also. Pearl Harbour, stricken as it was and presenting a tempting chance to acquire a stronghold menacing even American home waters, was not further molested. Midway Island suffered only submarine bombardments in the period with which this volume deals. But after air attacks lasting two days, invading and supporting forces overwhelmed on 10th December the small garrison on Guam Island. The Japanese were able to develop the island as a naval and air base about equidistant from New Guinea and the Philippines. An attempt to land at Wake Island on the 11th was defeated; but on the 23rd a second and more formidable invasion force

---

[1] C. M. Maltby, *Despatch on Operations in Hong Kong*, p. 701.

bore down on the isolated garrison. Heavily outnumbered, and amid the wreckage of sixteen bombing raids, the Americans nevertheless fought until they too had no choice but to surrender. By the evening the enemy was in possession of that base also.

Although what happened at Pearl Harbour, Wake, and Guam belongs to naval rather than to army history, the blow to American seapower thus inflicted was fundamental to the course of the war, and thus to the nature of the struggle in which land forces became engaged. It affected, for instance, defence of the Philippine Islands, where resistance to continued assault became a struggle isolated from the aid which otherwise America might have been able to give.

In the Philippines as in Malaya, the overwhelming initial successes of the enemy airmen left little to be feared from the defending air forces. The Japanese were nervous of submarine action, but no decisive opposition was to be expected from such surface units of the United States Asiatic Fleet as remained in Philippine waters. The Japanese plan was to seize bases at the northern and southern ends of the Philippine archipelago, and then, in the third week of the war, to land their main force—including the *16th* and *48th Divisions*—on Luzon. Thus by 20th December, enemy marines had seized Batan and Camiguin Islands, north of Luzon. Landings had then been made at Aparri, on the north coast of Luzon; near Vigan (north-western Luzon); at Legaspi, near the south-eastern tip of the island; and at Davao, in the south-eastern portion of Mindanao Island. Aircraft had again bombed airfields in the vicinity of Manila, and destroyed the near-by naval dockyard at Cavite on Manila Bay. Fourteen Flying Fortresses, the only survivors of their kind in the Philippines, had left for the Batchelor Field in the Northern Territory of Australia.[2]

By 9th December the army and navy planning staffs in Washington had decided that the Philippines could not be held, but, at President Roosevelt's insistence, the navy was instructed to do what it could to help MacArthur. On 14th December Colonel Eisenhower, by then on General Marshall's staff, prepared a paper emphasising the need "to convert Australia into a military base from which supplies might be ferried northward to the Philippines"; a principal which was thenceforward accepted.[3]

In the Philippines the defending army was organised into four commands: North Luzon (four divisions), South Luzon (two divisions), the harbour defences of Manila Bay, and the Southern Islands (three divisions). One Philippine Army division and the "Philippine Division" of the United States Army were in reserve.

The *48th Japanese Division* was landed in Lingayen Gulf on 22nd December, and part of the *16th Division* in Lamon Bay, south-east of Manila on 23rd and 24th December. On the 23rd General MacArthur decided to withdraw the forces on Luzon into the Bataan Peninsula, and next day he moved his headquarters to the island fortress of Corregidor

---

[2] These aircraft continued to operate over the Philippines, using the Del Monte field in Mindanao as an advanced base.

[3] L. Morton, *The Fall of the Philippines*, p. 153.

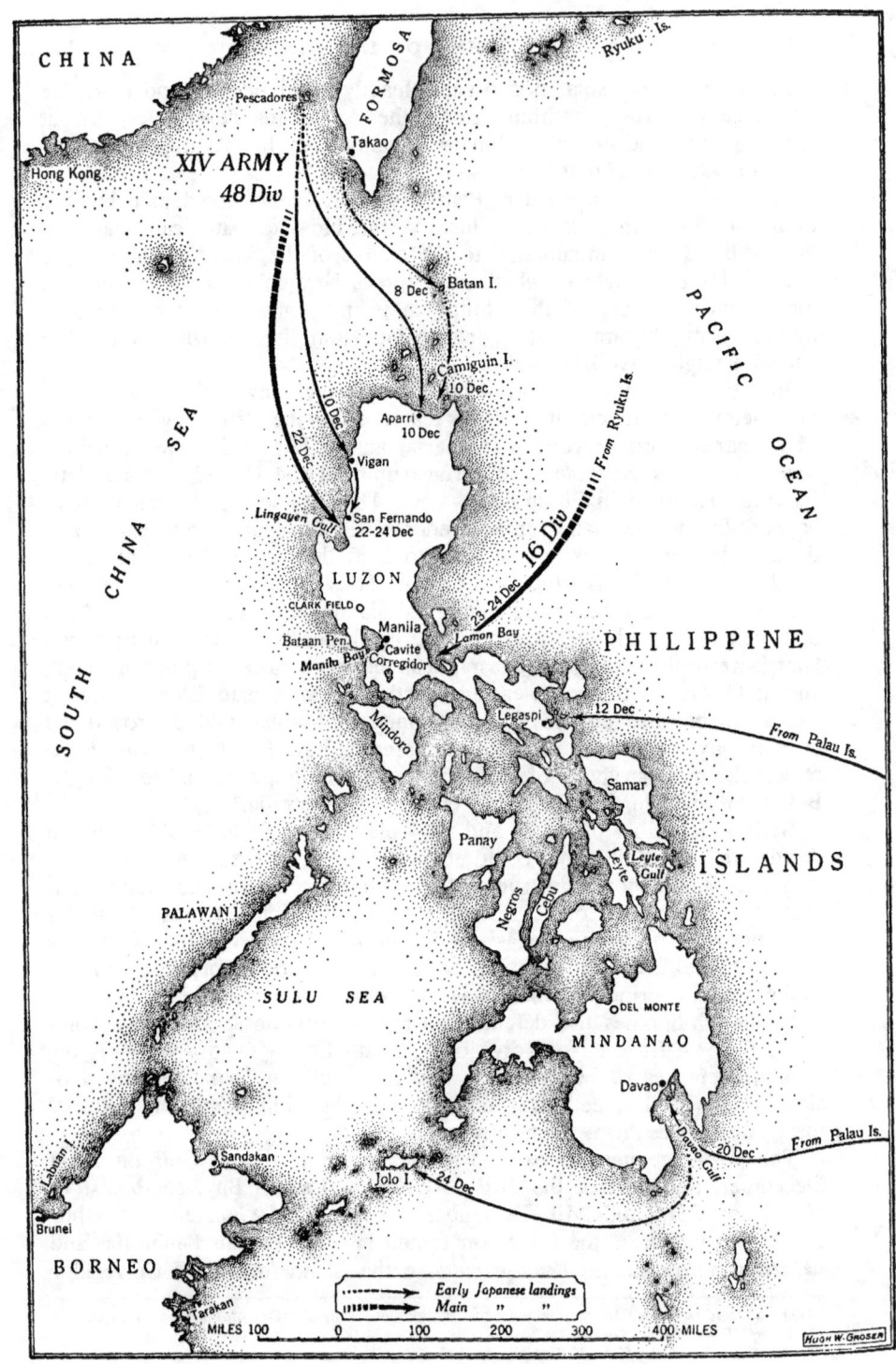

Japanese landings in the Philippines

in Manila Bay. By 2nd January both North and South Luzon Forces, with a combined strength of about 50,000, had succeeded in withdrawing into Bataan, which is about 30 miles long and 20 wide. They formed a line across the neck of the peninsula. Also on the 2nd the Japanese entered Manila.

Prospects of relief for MacArthur's forces were now about as remote as Hong Kong's had been. Not only had the Philippines been practically eliminated as a danger to Japan's southward moves; the islands could now be used as an aid to other operations. Having played its part in the landings, the Japanese *Third Fleet* proceeded as planned against Dutch Borneo, Celebes, Ambon and Timor.

An invasion of British Borneo had been planned by the Japanese high command as part of the opening phase of their overall plan. Tactically, possession of this territory would safeguard their communications with Malaya, and facilitate subsequent movement on Java. It would also secure for Japan supplies of oil which she urgently needed.

Occupying an area along the northern and north-western seaboards of the island of Borneo, the greater part of which was owned by the Dutch, British Borneo comprised the two principal states of British North Borneo and Sarawak; between these two areas, Brunei, a small native state under British protection; and Labuan, an island Crown colony at the northern entrance to Brunei Bay. Generally clad in dense jungle, the island of Borneo as a whole was largely undeveloped and unexplored, but both the British and the Dutch portions were rich in oil and other resources.

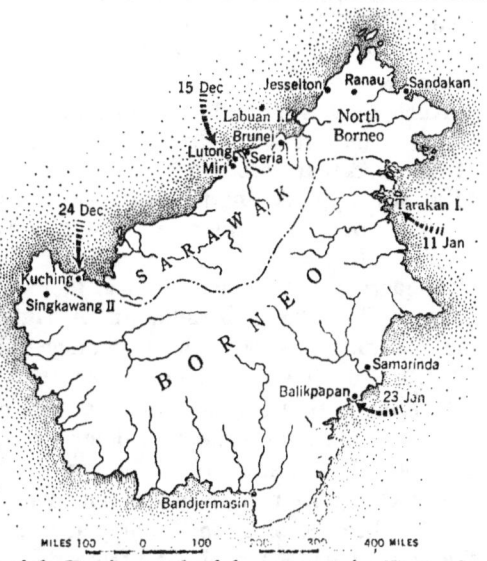

Although, like the near-by Philippine Islands, it lay at the approaches from Japan to Malaya and the Netherlands East Indies, neither the Dutch nor the British had found it practicable to spare more than small detachments for its defence.

Defence of British Borneo's oilfields at Miri, in Sarawak near its boundary with Brunei, and at Seria in the latter state, had therefore been ruled out in favour of destruction of the installations on the fields and at Lutong, near by, where the oil was refined.

A company of the 2/15th Punjab Regiment had been sent in December 1940 to Miri to cover the demolitions when they became necessary, and in August 1941 partial application of a denial scheme had reduced the output of oil by 70 per cent. The rest of the 2/15th Punjab, sent in May 1941 to Kuching, capital of Sarawak, was to defend this centre near the south-western extremity of the state because of its airfield, seven miles south of the town, and because a Dutch airfield known as Singkawang II lay only 60 miles to the south-west. The other forces in Sarawak, comprising a local Volunteer Corps, a Coastal Marine Service, the armed police, and the Sarawak Rangers (native troops) were bracketed with the Punjabs in a command known as "Sarfor" (Lieut-Colonel Lane).[4] It was realised, however, that such a force could not be expected to cope with any large-scale attack upon the town, and when in September 1941 it appeared that this must be expected, a conference of British and Dutch authorities decided that the airfield only would be defended. Demolitions of the oilfield installations and of the refinery were carried out on 8th December. On the 13th the detachment at Miri, with the oil staffs, left by sea for Kuching.

This was the day on which a Japanese convoy left Camranh Bay (Indo-China) and caused concern in Malaya lest it be headed for Mersing or thereabouts. With an escort of cruisers and destroyers, and two seaplane tenders for reconnaissance, it carried the Japanese *35th Infantry Brigade Headquarters* and the *124th Regiment* from the *18th Division,* and the *2nd Yokosuka Naval Landing Force.* The convoy anchored off Miri a little before midnight on the 15th December, and swiftly occupied the oilfields without opposition other than by rough seas during landings. In raids on the 17th, 18th, and 19th Dutch bombers sank a destroyer (*Shinonome*) and some landing craft. By 22nd December, however, fifteen Japanese medium attack planes and fighter aircraft were using an airstrip at Miri despite the damage which had been done to it before the Punjab company withdrew.

Kuching was raided by Japanese bombers on 19th December, and Dutch planes reported to Air Headquarters, Far East, on the morning of the 23rd that a convoy (carrying part of the force which had reached Miri) was approaching the town. Bombers at Singkawang II were ordered to attack, but the enemy forestalled the operation by a raid on that airfield. As a result, the field was so damaged that with the concurrence of Air Headquarters the planes stationed there were withdrawn during the afternoon to Palembang, in Sumatra. A Dutch submarine torpedoed four of the six transports near the anchorage off Kuching on the night of the 23rd, but a landing had been made by dawn next day. Another Dutch submarine sank a second Japanese destroyer (*Sagiri*) the following night before being herself sunk by a depth-charge. Five Blenheim bombers from Singapore Island also raided the convoy, causing minor loss.

A message from Malaya Command reporting the approach of the convoy had been received in Kuching at 9 p.m. on the 23rd—two hours after the convoy had been sighted from the near-by coast. Although in pursuance of his orders Lane had disposed troops for the defence of the

---

[4] Lt-Col C. M. Lane, MC. Regular soldier; b. 19 Jul 1899.

airfield, the message contained an order for its destruction. Reporting that it was too late to alter his plans, he received a reply next day reiterating the order. He was to resist the Japanese as long as he could, and then to act as he thought best in the interests of Dutch West Borneo. On 24th December, despite resistance which cost the enemy seven landing craft and a number of casualties, they had forced their way up the Santubong River to Kuching, and captured the city by 4.30 p.m. At nightfall they were advancing on the airfield; and next day, concerned lest Japanese encircling moves might cut off his force, Lane ordered its withdrawal into Dutch West Borneo. The force was attacked as this was in progress, and all but one platoon of the rearguard of two Punjabi companies were killed or captured. A further 180 men became separated from the force during the night at a river crossing and most of the transport was abandoned. This party, however, rejoined the column when, having parted near the border from its Sarawak State Forces component, it reached Singkawang II airfield on 29th December. Women, children, and Volunteers who had accompanied the column were sent to a point on the coast from which they were evacuated on 25th January. The Punjabis meanwhile came under Dutch command, as part of a garrison of 750 Dutch Bornean troops for defence of the airfield and its surrounding area.[5]

In Malaya, intensive air attacks on ground troops which began on 23rd December added to the pressure of the Japanese thrust down the western part of the peninsula. In keeping with the orders issued by General Percival on 18th December, successive positions along the trunk road south-east of where it crossed the Perak were chosen as means of delaying the enemy. The next major stand was to be made at Kampar, north of a junction of the road and the railway, and 23 miles south of Ipoh. General Heath ordered the reconstituted 15th Brigade Group to occupy this position while the 12th Brigade was disposed north of Ipoh and the 28th Brigade south of it and on the road to Blanja.

The problems presented to the Japanese in crossing the Perak caused a lull on this front, and Christmas Day was observed by the British forces in varying ways and circumstances. The scene which met General Bennett as he visited some of his men at their Christmas dinner was typical of something which orthodox disciplinarians were apt to deplore. "I found the officers waiting on the men at table," he recorded, "the light-hearted men addressing them in the local fashion as 'boy' and demanding better service. While the men enjoyed their Christmas fare, the sergeants relieved them by taking over their guard duties."[6]

"I wondered," Bennett commented, "if they realised that they would soon be fighting for dear life." He had reported on 23rd December to the Chief of the General Staff (General Sturdee) that positions were

---

[5] Japanese forces attacked Singkawang from 26th January. After a gallant resistance the Punjabis made a long and arduous march to the south coast, hoping to escape to Java, but were compelled to surrender on 9th March.

[6] Bennett, *Why Singapore Fell*, p. 83.

being prepared in the vicinity of Gemas, on the main road into Johore, and at Muar, on the coastal road west of it, adding:

> When enemy advance is checked lost ground must be regained. This will require at least three divisions in my opinion. Again strongly urge that at least one of our divisions from Middle East be sent here as early as possible. Percival concurs.[7]

Sturdee replied next day that the Australian Government had decided to send to Malaya a machine-gun battalion and 1,800 reinforcements.

Further and very insistent warning came from the Australian Representative in Singapore (Mr Bowden). In the course of a cable received in Australia on Christmas Day, he declared:

> ... deterioration of our position in Malaya defence is assuming landslide proportions and in my firm belief is likely to cause a collapse in whole defence system.... Present measures for reinforcing Malayan defences can from a practical viewpoint be regarded as little more than gestures. In my belief only thing that might save Singapore would be immediate dispatch from Middle East by air of powerful reinforcements, large numbers of latest fighter aircraft with ample operational personnel. Reinforcements of troops should be not in brigades but in divisions and to be of use they must arrive urgently. Anything that is not powerful modern and immediate is futile. As things stand at present fall of Singapore is to my mind only a matter of weeks. If Singapore and A.I.F. in Malaya are to be saved, there must be very radical and effective action immediately ... plain fact is that without immediate air reinforcements Singapore must fall. Need for decision and action is a matter of hours not days.

The Australian Prime Minister, Mr Curtin, responded dynamically to this compelling situation. He addressed to both President Roosevelt and Mr Churchill, as they were conferring in Washington, a cable dated 25th December in which, after referring to reports he had received, he said:

> Fall of Singapore would mean isolation of Philippines, fall of Netherlands East Indies and attempt to smother all other bases. This would also sever our communications between Indian and Pacific Oceans in this region. The setback would be as serious to United States interests as to our own.
>
> Reinforcements earmarked by United Kingdom Government for Singapore seem to us to be utterly inadequate in relation to aircraft particularly fighters....
>
> It is in your power to meet situation. Should United States desire we would gladly accept United States command in Pacific Ocean area. President has said Australia will be base of utmost importance but in order that it shall remain a base Singapore must be reinforced. In spite of our great difficulties we are sending further reinforcements to Malaya. Please consider this matter of greatest urgency.

To the Australian Minister in Washington, Mr Casey, was sent an even more emphatic statement of the situation. "Please understand that stage of suggestion has passed," he was told. "... This is the gravest type of emergency and everything will depend upon Churchill-Roosevelt decision to meet it in broadest way."

Churchill cabled, also on the 25th, that Roosevelt had agreed that the leading brigade of the 18th British Division (which when Japan came into the war was rounding the Cape in American transports on its way to the Middle East, and was then diverted to Bombay and Ceylon) should go

---

[7] Bennett, p. 82.

direct to Singapore in the transport *Mount Vernon*.[8] He reminded Curtin of his (Churchill's) suggestion that an Australian division be recalled from Palestine to replace other troops going to Malaya, or sent direct to Singapore if that could be arranged. While indicating that he did not favour using up forces in an attempt to defend the northern part of Malaya, he spoke of Singapore as a fortress "which we are determined to defend with the utmost tenacity".[9] Referring to current consultations between himself and Roosevelt, and between their respective staffs, he said that not only were the Americans impressed with the importance of maintaining Singapore, but they were anxious to move a continuous flow of troops and aircraft through Australia for the relief of the Philippine Islands. The President was agreeable to troops and aircraft being diverted to Singapore should the Philippines fall, and was also quite willing to send substantial United States forces to Australia, where the Americans were anxious to establish important bases for the war against Japan.

The people of Australia were warned of the critical situation in a newspaper article by Mr Curtin published on 27th December. In this he declared:

> . . . the war with Japan is not a phase of the struggle with the Axis Powers, but is a new war . . . we take the view that, while the determination of military policy is the Soviet's business, we should be able to look forward with reason to aid from Russia against Japan. We look for a solid and impregnable barrier of democracies against the three Axis Powers and we refuse to accept the dictum that the Pacific struggle must be treated as a subordinate segment of the general conflict. . . . The Australian Government, therefore, regards the Pacific struggle as primarily one in which the United States and Australia must have the fullest say in the direction of the democracies' fighting plan. Without any inhibitions of any kind, I make it quite clear that Australia looks to America, free of any pangs as to our traditional links or kinship with the United Kingdom. We know the problems that the United Kingdom faces. . . . But we know, too, that Australia can go and Britain can still hold on. We are, therefore, determined that Australia shall not go, and shall exert all our energies towards the shaping of a plan, with the United States as its keystone, which will give to our country some confidence of being able to hold out until the tide of battle swings against the enemy.[1]

This stung Mr Churchill, who later declared that it "produced the worst impression both in high American circles and in Canada".[2] Nevertheless, a concerted plan of the kind Curtin sought speedily emerged from the crisis; for on the night of 27th December in America (28th in Australia) Roosevelt proposed to Churchill the appointment of an officer to command the British, American, and Dutch forces in the war against Japan. He had suggested to his Chiefs of Staff that the officer should be General MacArthur,[3] but after discussion agreed to propose General

---

[8] The division had been trans-shipped at Halifax into the largest transports then in the services of the United States. They included the converted liners *Manhattan*, *Washington*, and *America* (re-named the *Wakefield*), the *Mount Vernon* and *West Point*.

[9] Churchill, *The Second World War*, Vol III, p. 593.

[1] Melbourne *Herald*, 27 Dec 1941.

[2] Mr Churchill (*The Second World War*, Vol IV, 1951, p. 8) "weighed painfully . . . the idea of making a broadcast direct to the Australian people".

[3] Mr Casey reported: "I understand that, although not devoid of human frailties, he is a good man."

Wavell. Churchill at first demurred, and his Chiefs of Staff opposed the nomination on the ground that responsibility for the all-too-likely disasters in the area would be placed on the shoulders of a British general rather than an American. It was, however, urged on him next day by Marshall, and the British Prime Minister thereupon sought and obtained his Cabinet's approval of the plan. Trying to meet the immediate needs of Malaya, he had cabled on 25th December to General Auchinleck, Commander-in-Chief in the Middle East, suggesting that he should be able to spare at once, despite the needs of the Libyan offensive, four Hurricane fighter squadrons and an armoured brigade. Auchinleck immediately set afoot arrangements to comply. At this date the reinforcements under orders for Malaya comprised the 45th Indian Brigade Group; the 53rd Brigade Group (18th Division) with one anti-tank and two anti-aircraft regiments and the crated Hurricanes previously mentioned; reinforcements for the two Indian divisions; the 2/4th Australian Machine Gun Battalion; and reinforcements for the 8th Australian Division.

Quickly assenting to the establishment of a united command of forces resisting Japan, Curtin asked that Australia be represented on a joint body which it was proposed to set up, responsible to Churchill and Roosevelt, from whom Wavell would receive his orders. "I wish to express our great appreciation of the cohesion now established," he cabled to Churchill, "and would like to say to you personally how appreciative we are of the great service you have rendered in your mission to the United States of America." The clash between the two Prime Ministers had emphasised how differently the war appeared at this stage from the viewpoints of the United Kingdom and of Australia, and pointed clearly to the need for a better mutual understanding. It thus was an argument in favour of Curtin's request for representation in the new controlling body, if one were needed additional to the facts that Australia had land forces in Malaya, Ambon, and Timor, in the A.B.D.A. (American, British, Dutch, Australian) area as it was about to be defined, and in Darwin to which it was later extended; that the I Australian Corps would soon be assigned to A.B.D.A., and Australia was to become increasingly the main base of operations against Japan. Notwithstanding all this, Australia was given no direct representation on the controlling body, which comprised the United States Chiefs of Staff, and the Imperial Chiefs of Staff represented by senior officers in Washington, thousands of miles distant from the A.B.D.A. theatre of war at Australia's northern portals.

While these high-level decisions were helping to shape the future, the 12th Indian Brigade again came to grips with the enemy in the fight for time in Malaya. The Japanese attacked at Chemor, north of Ipoh, in the afternoon of 26th December, and although by the end of next day the brigade had given little ground, its casualties were heavy and its men exhausted after twelve days of continuous action. Seeking to conserve his forces for the defence of Kampar, General Paris decided to move his two forward brigades to positions south of Ipoh. During the night of 27th-28th December the 28th Brigade was moved to the right flank of Kampar, and the 12th Brigade was disposed in depth along the main road from Gopeng to Dipang, while the 15th Brigade prepared the Kampar position.

Meanwhile "Roseforce", which Percival had ordered to be formed to raid Japanese communications west of the Perak, had come into existence, commanded by Captain Lloyd.[4] Two naval motor launches, part of the Perak flotilla which also Percival had brought into existence, were used to transport the two-platoon force from Port Swettenham, south of Kuala Selangor, on 26th December for a landing up the Trong River, west and a little north of Ipoh. It was accompanied by Major Rose[5] of the Argylls, whose pleas to be allowed to organise commando activities had given rise to the plan (though it was on a much smaller scale than he had urged).

The blight which had fallen on British endeavours in Malaya seemed to have fallen on this expedition also when the engine of the launch allotted to Lieutenant Perring's[6] platoon could not be started. After half an hour's delay Lloyd ordered Lieutenant Sanderson's[7] platoon to go on alone. Thus delayed, and necessarily restricted in their objective, Sanderson and his men landed about 9 a.m. on 27th December near a road to the village of Trong. They eventually succeeded in ambushing a Japanese car carrying officers, followed by three lorries and a utility, on the main south coast road. The car was hit by a grenade and ran off the road. Sanderson emptied a drum of Tommy gun ammunition into it, killing the passengers. The two leading lorries capsized over an embankment, and their occupants also were shot. The remaining lorry halted, and the utility turned over. Their occupants hid behind a culvert, but were killed by grenades.

Having thus demonstrated what might have been done on a much larger scale to hamper and disconcert the enemy, the platoon rejoined the rest of the force. Five British soldiers who had become separated from their units in earlier fighting attached themselves to it, and it returned to Port Swettenham on the 29th. Sanderson's platoon had the distinction of being the first body of Australian infantry to go into action against the Japanese in the Malayan campaign. Soon after, the depot ship for the

---

[4] Maj D. T. Lloyd, NX70438; 2/30 Bn. Clerk; of Hunter's Hill, NSW; b. Hunter's Hill, 10 Oct 1912. Lloyd's force comprised two platoons, one commanded by Lt R. E. Sanderson, with three guides attached from the 1 Perak Bn FMSVF, and volunteers from the 2/19, 2/20 and 2/30 Bns; the other by Lt M. Perring with the same number of guides and men from the 2/18, 2/26 and 2/29 Bns. Each platoon totalled twenty-five men in all; each was allotted 13 Thompson guns, 2 Brens, 12 rifles, 8 Gurkha kukris and four .38 pistols. In addition each man carried two bakelite grenades and a quantity of SAA. Rose travelled as an observer for Malaya Comd with Sanderson's platoon, and Lloyd moved with Perring's.

[5] Lt-Col A. J. C. Rose; 2/A&SH. Regular soldier; b. 16 Aug 1909.

[6] Lt M. Perring, NX45187; 2/18 Bn. Farmer and grazier; of Manilla, NSW; b. Manilla, 30 Aug 1916.

[7] Lt R. E. Sanderson, NX52523; 2/19 Bn. Clerk; of Forbes, NSW; b. Forbes, 10 Jun 1919.

Perak flotilla was bombed and sunk, five vessels on their way to reinforce the flotilla were sunk or driven ashore, and both the flotilla and Roseforce were disbanded.

The little that had been done to form units for irregular warfare was represented principally by the Independent Company, previously mentioned, which became committed to the battlefront before it could be used in its special role; and by Lieut-Colonel Spencer Chapman's Special Training School.[8] Chapman, who after suffering many frustrations had at last obtained permission to organise parties to operate behind the Japanese lines, crossed the Perak on Christmas Day intending to meet Roseforce at a rendezvous and guide it to suitable targets. "Except for the occasional exercise we had had in the Forest Reserve at Bukit Timah, on Singapore Island, it was the first time I had been in real jungle," he recorded in describing his adventure. The rendezvous failed, but he returned convinced that the Japanese lines of land communication, now becoming as extensive as those of the British forces, were very vulnerable to attack by men with the necessary training. His account of what he saw as he lay by a roadside and watched the enemy was illuminating. As he later described it, there were:

hundreds and hundreds of them, pouring eastwards towards the Perak River. The majority of them were on bicycles in parties of forty or fifty, riding three or four abreast and talking and laughing just as if they were going to a football match. Indeed, some of them were actually wearing football jerseys; they seemed to have no standard uniform or equipment and were travelling as light as they possibly could. Some wore green, others grey, khaki or even dirty white. The majority had trousers hanging loose and enclosed in high boots or puttees; some had tight breeches and others shorts and rubber boots or gym shoes. Their hats showed the greatest variety: a few tin hats, topees of all shapes, wide-brimmed *terai* or ordinary felt hats; high-peaked jockey hats, little caps with eye-shades or even a piece of cloth tied round the head and hanging down behind. Their equipment and armament were equally varied and were slung over themselves and their bicycles with no apparent method. . . .

The general impression was one of extraordinary determination: they had been ordered to go to the bridgehead, and in their thousands they were going, though their equipment was second-rate and motley and much of it had obviously been commandeered in Malaya. This was certainly true of their means of transport, for we saw several parties of soldiers on foot who were systematically searching the roadside *kampongs*, estate buildings and factories for bicycles and most of the cars and lorries bore local number plates. . . .

All this was in very marked contrast to our own front-line soldiers, who were at this time equipped like Christmas trees with heavy boots, web equipment, packs, haversacks, water-bottles, blankets, ground-sheets, and even great-coats and respirators, so that they could hardly walk, much less fight.[9]

Not only was the Japanese *5th Division* now concentrated in the vicinity of the Perak, but the *Guards Division,* allotted initially to the *XV Army*

---

[8] General Percival later wrote (*Daily Telegraph,* London, 14 Feb 1949) of the planning of "stay-behind" parties: "Of course, it should all have been part of the military plan, but at that time these activities were not under any of the Service Ministries."

[9] F. Spencer Chapman, *The Jungle is Neutral,* pp. 27-8.

for the occupation of Thailand, was arriving in the Taiping area to take part in the drive on the western front in Malaya. The Japanese were thus in a position to force the pace with fresh troops while the British forces engaged on this front became progressively more battle-worn and depleted of men and material. As the struggle developed, the enemy tactics generally continued to impose on the British a wide dispersal of forces and to necessitate frequent hasty movement of units to and from threatened areas, thus adding to the disruption and fatigue of actual combat. In the relatively open country of the Kampar position both sides would be able to use artillery to a greater extent than hitherto, but the Japanese still had the exclusive and powerful aid of tanks. In the air they could strike freely behind the British lines, and keep a close watch on the movement of opposing forces—formidable advantages at a time when air forces had become to a large extent the eyes and long-range artillery of land forces; and apt to be severely damaging to the morale of all but thoroughly trained and disciplined troops. The Japanese advance in the west now increasingly threatened the junction at Kuala Kubu, on the trunk road, of communications with the 9th Indian Division in the east.

The dominant feature of the Kampar position was Bujang Melaka—a 4,070-foot limestone mountain with steep sides thickly covered by jungle, whose western slopes descended to near the right of the main road where it reached Kampar. The mountain afforded good observation posts for artillery, commanding a wide and open tin-mining area to the north, west and south, although a large area of rubber plantations lay to the south-west. It was thus a local offset to enemy air observation while the position remained in British hands. The main sector of the Kampar position, adjacent to the township of Kampar, rested against the mountain and was occupied by the 15th Brigade (the combined 6th and 15th) with the 88th Field Regiment and 273rd Anti-Tank Battery under command. On the right, at Sahum, astride a road which looped the mountain and rejoined the main road below Kampar, was the 28th Brigade, to check any attempt to bypass Kampar by this route. To guard against attack from the direction of Telok Anson, in the south-west, the 12th Brigade was to be withdrawn to Bidor after completing its covering task, and the 1st Independent Company was to be stationed at Telok Anson.

The 12th Brigade was attacked at Gopeng on the afternoon of 28th December, and by midday on the 29th had been forced back to within three miles of Dipang. Brigadier Stewart was given permission to withdraw through Dipang after dark, and the 2nd Anti-Tank Battery had already gone back when a further enemy thrust, supported by tanks, nearly succeeded in disrupting the defence. The situation was saved only by resourceful action by Lieut-Colonel Deakin[1] (5/2nd Punjab), whose men checked the enemy less than a mile north of Dipang. The brigade was thus enabled to withdraw to Bidor. Three attempts to demolish the Dipang bridge over the Sungei Kampar failed, but the fourth was successful.

---

[1] Brig C. C. Deakin, DSO, OBE. GSO1 1 Aust Div 1937-40; CO 5/2 Punjab 1941. Regular soldier; b. Cruck Meole, Shropshire, England, 16 Jul 1896.

Further enemy advance along this road was discouraged by artillery fire, but enemy parties now appeared right of the Sahum position, and patrols were encountered south-west of Kampar. On New Year's Day a heavy assault, preceded by a bombardment, was made on the main position where it was held by the Combined Surreys and Leicesters, now known as "the British Battalion". The fighting lasted throughout the day,

The Japanese advance to Slim River

and, although the position was held, the Japanese gained a foothold on its extreme right, at Thompson's Ridge. As pressure failed to develop at Sahum, Paris withdrew from that position all but a battalion and supporting artillery, and ordered the 28th Brigade's 2/2nd Gurkha Rifles to the Slim River area—another prospective strongpoint in the British line of withdrawal—as a further precaution against attack from Telok Anson and thereabouts.

Also on 1st January, a tug towing barges was seen at the mouth of the Sungei Perak, and a large group of sea craft appeared at the mouth of the Sungei Bernam, the next large river to the south, bordering the States of Perak and Selangor. The two rivers, navigable for several miles, were only nine miles apart at the coast, and linked by a road which led to Telok Anson. A landing occurred during the night at the Bernam. Instead, therefore, of enjoying a respite at Bidor the 12th Brigade was sent to the area between Telok Anson and Changkat Jong, where the road forked north towards Kampar and north-east towards Bidor. The 2/1st Gurkha and 5/14th Punjab, in divisional reserve, had been placed on the road from the junction to Kampar in anticipation of the new threat. As was later established, the seaborne troops were the *11th Infantry Regiment,* embarked at Port Weld, with a battalion of the *4th Guards Regiment* which came down the Perak in small commandeered boats and landed at Telok Anson early on 2nd January. They were to thrust from there towards the trunk road.

The Japanese again attacked the Kampar position on 2nd January and pressed heavily upon the defenders. Although the position was still being held at the end of the day, street fighting had occurred in Telok Anson; the 1st Independent Company was withdrawn from the township through the Argylls; and by nightfall the 12th Brigade had been forced back to a position two miles west of Changkat Jong. As this thrust now endangered the rear of the troops at Kampar, Paris decided that Kampar must be abandoned. In the ensuing moves the 28th and 12th Brigades withdrew to the Slim River area, where on 4th January they were covered by the battered 15th Brigade at Sungkai. The British Battalion at Kampar, led by Lieut-Colonel Morrison,[2] had borne for two days the weight of the Japanese *41st Infantry Regiment* (of the *5th Division*) supported by tanks and artillery.

The best news at this stage was that the 45th Indian Brigade—first of the reinforcements being hurried to Malaya—had reached Singapore. Semi-trained though it was, and with no experience of jungle warfare, it sustained hopes that if only the enemy could be delayed long enough, sufficient forces could be deployed on the mainland to save Singapore and its naval base. The promised brigade group of the 18th British Division was due in mid-January and the rest of the division, the 44th Indian Infantry Brigade, the 2/4th Australian Machine Gun Battalion, and Australian and Indian reinforcement drafts, later in the month or early in February.

The fact that the whole of the 18th British Division was to be committed to Malaya reflected critical decisions made by the United Kingdom Chiefs of Staff at a meeting on 1st January. They had decided that although defeat of Germany must continue to be the primary aim, the security of Singapore and maintenance of Indian Ocean communications were second in importance only to the security of the United Kingdom and its sea

---

[2] Brig C. E. Morrison, DSO, MC. CO Leicester/Surrey Bn. Regular soldier; b. 17 Jun 1893.

communications. Despite the prize which appeared within grasp in Libya, where a successful offensive was in progress, development of the campaign in that theatre was made subject to the proviso that it must not prevent reinforcement of the Far East on a scale considered sufficient to hold the Japanese. The reinforcements for this purpose were to comprise (it was hoped) two divisions and an armoured brigade for Malaya, two divisions for the Netherlands East Indies, and two divisions and a light tank squadron for Burma. Endeavours were to be made to send to Malaya also eight light bomber squadrons, eight fighter squadrons, and two torpedo bomber squadrons; and to Burma six light bomber squadrons and six fighter squadrons. The United States was to be asked to do its utmost to strengthen the Netherlands East Indies air force with supplies via Australia. In fulfilment of this policy, the main body of the 18th Division, then at Bombay, was ordered at once to Malaya—despite misgivings which had been expressed by Wavell, when Commander-in-Chief in India, at the extent to which the resources to have been available in India were being diminished. Consent was obtained from the Australian Government on 6th January to the dispatch of the I Australian Corps (including the 6th and 7th Divisions) from the Middle East to the Far East; but this movement, which would make big demands on shipping, could not begin until the first week in February.

These decisions were in sharp contrast to the relative importance originally assigned to the Far East by Mr Churchill; the question now was whether or not sufficient time could be gained for them to become effective.

On the civil front in Malaya, realisation of the rapidly increasing peril which faced the established order was dawning bleakly:

> We enter into a New Year in local conditions that are simply fantastic (declared the *Straits Times*, an influential morning daily paper in Malaya). . . . Even a month ago we were preparing for the usual New Year land and sea sports in Singapore. All accommodation at the hill stations was booked, prospects for the Penang race meeting were being discussed and hotels were announcing that very few tables were still available for the New Year's festivities. . . . Terrible changes have taken place with a rapidity that still leaves us a little bewildered, but as we recover from the initial shock, so do we become better able to see things in their proper perspective. . . .[3]

This "proper perspective" was not, however, reflected in some official communiqués and statements, which seemed to be devoted to propping up prestige rather than to bringing home to the people of Malaya the real facts of the situation.[4] The task of those concerned in wording them was admittedly not easy. Not only had care to be taken to avoid disclosure of information which might aid the enemy; thought had to be given also to the effect of news of British reverses upon the Asian population, whose outlook and interests were substantially different from those of the British

---
[3] *Straits Times*, 1 Jan 1942.
[4] "Everybody in this country seems to have been lulled into a false sense of security by confident statements regarding continuous additions to our armed might. The only people who have not been bluffed by them are the Japanese."—*Straits Times*, 9 Jan 1942.

community. In the upshot the effect on neither community was satisfactory; nor did some sections of the civil administration engender confidence.

> . . . the administration is displaying so little vigour (wrote a British observer in a day-by-day account of events) that the Asiatics are entirely uninspired and there's an atmosphere of apathy—almost of resignation—about the whole place. One can't resist the conclusion that the average citizen has little confidence that Singapore will hold—or even that the British intend to put up much of a fight for it. Why else should the trades people have stopped all credit facilities?[5]

Mr Duff Cooper expressed in a letter he sent by airmail to Mr Churchill his dissatisfaction with civil defence preparations. To the War Council on 31st December he pointed out that a breakdown in the civil defence organisation might be fatal to the defence of Singapore, and spoke of the need for some bold step which would revive public confidence. He then proposed that the Chief Engineer of Malaya Command, Brigadier Simson,[6] be appointed Director-General of Civil Defence with plenary powers in Singapore Island and the State of Johore. In the terms in which he received the appointment from the Governor, however, Brigadier Simson was given such restricted powers that the position did not carry with it the freedom of action intended by Mr Duff Cooper, and even these powers did not extend beyond Singapore Island. Furthermore, the course of events was to give him little time to use them for what they were worth.[7]

General Heath had hoped that his 9th Division east of Malaya's central range might become available for transfer along the east-west road to Kuala Kubu for assault on the Japanese left flank. It was decided, however, that to safeguard arrival at Singapore of the prospective reinforcement convoys, the division must hold Kuantan airfield and also deny the enemy access to central Malaya by the railway north of Kuala Lipis.

The importance of these considerations did not escape the Japanese. Equipped with horse transport, and using coastal seacraft, the *56th Infantry Regiment* so surmounted the formidable difficulties presented by the undeveloped state of Kelantan and Trengganu that leading elements of the regiment were in contact with patrols from the 22nd Indian Brigade on 23rd December. Supported by the 5th Field Artillery Regiment, this brigade was on both sides of the Sungei Kuantan so that it might resist

---

[5] G. Playfair, *Singapore Goes Off The Air* (1944), p. 50.

[6] Brig I. Simson. CE Scottish Comd 1941; CE Malaya 1941-42. Regular soldier; b. 14 Aug 1890.

[7] Mr Duff Cooper subsequently related that in a report to the British Government before Japan struck, he wrote: "Great Britain was more closely and vitally concerned with the world of the Pacific than any other European power, but we were continuing to handle its problems with the machinery that existed in the reign of Queen Victoria. Four government departments were concerned: the Foreign Office, the Colonial Office, the Dominions Office, and, so far as Burma was concerned, the India Office. To these had been added since the outbreak of war [in Europe] the Ministries of Information and Economic Warfare. The need for some form of coordination was obvious and, should war break out in the Far East, would become imperative."
In his report he recommended the appointment of a "Commissioner General for the Far East", who, if war came, would be the head of a Far Eastern War Council. "The man I had in mind was Mr Robert Menzies, whom I knew and admired. He was out of office at that time and I felt that good use could be made of his services in the post that I was suggesting. As a former Prime Minister of Australia and one who had travelled in Europe and America, he would carry the necessary guns, and I believed he would know how to use them. I discussed the matter later with him in Melbourne and I think he liked the idea of the appointment. Events, however, intervened."—Duff Cooper, *Old Men Forget* (1954).

attack from the sea, or on land from the north. The airfield was six miles from the coast, west of the river and near the main road. Under orders from Heath, who was anxious lest part of the force and its equipment be cut off east of the river, the commander, Brigadier Painter,[8] on 30th December set afoot a withdrawal which would leave only the 2/18th Royal Garhwal covering the river east of the ferry crossing near the coast. By this time, however, a substantial Japanese force was near by, and in a forestalling attack with air support seriously hampered the movement; but guns and transport were successfully withdrawn during the night. The Japanese quickly entered Kuantan, attacked the covering troops, and bombarded the ferry head.

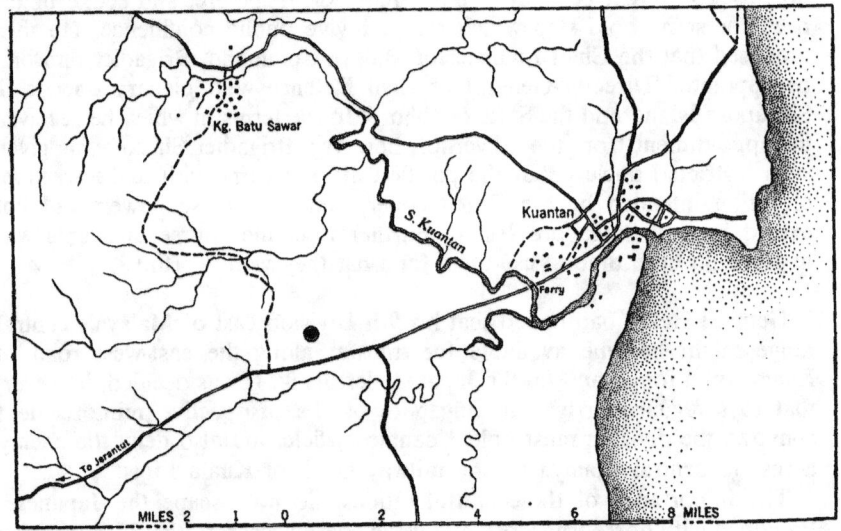

On 31st December Painter received instructions to resist as long as possible, but not to jeopardise his brigade. After discussion with General Barstow, Painter disposed the 2/12th Frontier Force Regiment to hold the airfield and ordered that the 2/18th Royal Garhwal should cross the river that night. Two companies were cut off, but the rest made the crossing, and the ferry was sunk. The Japanese succeeded in infiltrating towards the airfield, and at the same time the decision to withdraw the 11th Division from Kampar on the 2nd-3rd made it essential to withdraw the 9th from the Kuantan area. Therefore on the 3rd orders were received from Heath to withdraw the brigade to Jerantut, where part of the 8th Indian Brigade was stationed. A further Japanese attack succeeded in isolating the rearguard of the 2/12th Frontier Force Regiment as it was leaving the airfield. Despite courageous action by Lieut-Colonel Cumming[9] (for which subsequently he was awarded the Victoria Cross) the greater

---

[8] Brig G. W. A. Painter, DSO. Comd 22 Indian Bde 1941-42. Regular soldier; b. 24 Feb 1893.

[9] Brig A. E. Cumming, VC, OBE, MC. CO 2/12 FFR 1940-42, 9 Jats 1942; Comd 63 Gurkha Bde 1943-44. Regular soldier; b. 18 Jun 1896.

part of two companies was lost. The rest of the brigade reached Jerantut without being further engaged, and by 7th January was disposed in the vicinity of Fraser's Hill.

Concurrently with these developments on the eastern front, General Percival had urged upon General Heath that the airfields at Kuala Lumpur and Port Swettenham be denied to the enemy at least until 14th January. Realising that unless provision were made to cope with further Japanese landings southward along the west coast he might be unable to fulfil this requirement, he sent units to Brigadier Moir,[1] commanding the Lines of Communications, with orders to prevent landings at Kuala Selangor. To delay the enemy on the trunk road he ordered dispositions in depth, headed by the 12th and 28th Brigades in the Trolak-Slim River area to cover crossings of the river, and with the main defensive position some ten miles south of it, near Tanjong Malim.

At this stage the *42nd Infantry Regiment of the Japanese 5th Division,* with a tank battalion, was under orders to press on along the trunk road towards Kuala Lumpur. The *III/11th Battalion,* followed by the *4th Guards Regiment,* was to advance by land and sea to Kuala Selangor and Port Swettenham, thence also towards Kuala Lumpur. Other troops were to be ready to exploit these moves.

Attempts to land in the Kuala Selangor area on 2nd and 3rd January were repelled by artillery fire from Brigadier Moir's force, which General Heath then reinforced. On 4th January, Japanese troops using a track north of Kuala Selangor drove back forward patrols, and reached the north bank of the Sungei Selangor. Next morning they were in contact with the 1st Independent Company covering bridges over the river in the Batang Berjuntai area, only eleven miles from Rawang on the trunk road. Brigadier Moorhead, commanding the 15th Indian Brigade, was now made responsible for the coastal sector. On 6th January he withdrew across the river his forces at Batang Berjuntai, and destroyed the bridges.

The 12th Brigade had moved into the Trolak position early on 4th January, and set to work preparing defences. That night the 15th Brigade was withdrawn from its covering position at Sungkai to occupy the main Tanjong Malim position. Constant attack by Japanese aircraft necessitated much of the 12th Brigade's work being done at night. Coming on top of the men's previous exertions and shortage of sleep, this resulted in extreme fatigue. Describing the condition of the 5/2nd Punjab at the time, its commander, Lieut-Colonel Deakin, was to write:

> The battalion was dead tired; most of all, the commanders whose responsibilities prevented them from snatching even a little fitful sleep. The battalion had withdrawn 176 miles in three weeks and had only three days' rest. It had suffered 250 casualties of which a high proportion had been killed. The spirit of the men was low and the battalion had lost 50 per cent of its fighting efficiency.

The foremost part of the position comprised dense jungle through which the trunk road and railway ran roughly parallel, a few hundred

---
[1] Brig R. G. Moir, DSO, MC Comd HQ L of C Area Malaya. Regular soldier; b. 6 Jun 1894.

yards apart. The 4/19th Hyderabad (three companies) was forward; the 5/2nd Punjab was in the centre; and the Argylls were at the exits from the jungle at Trolak village and on an estate road branching from the trunk road. The 5/14th Punjab, from corps reserve, was at Kampong Slim under short notice to come forward to a check position about a mile south of Trolak.

The density of the vegetation was relied upon to keep enemy tanks and transport to the road; but although the 11th Division had enough anti-tank mines to pave large sections of the road with them, Stewart had only twenty-four, with some dannert wire and movable concrete blocks, to help impede an enemy advance. On the ground that his area gave little scope for artillery, only one battery of the 137th Field Regiment was deployed in support, while the rest waited between Kampong Slim and the Slim River bridge. Positions allocated by Brigadier Selby to the 28th Brigade were the 2/2nd Gurkha in the Slim River station area; the 2/9th Gurkha astride the road at Kampong Slim; and the 2/1st Gurkha in reserve at Cluny Estate—two miles and a half eastward. For the time being, however, the brigade was being rested in the Kampong Slim area. Instead of occupying the position at Tanjong Malim, the 15th Brigade was sent on 5th January to reinforce Moorhead's coastal force.

Bombers pounded the 12th Brigade positions on the morning of the 5th, and Japanese infantry then advanced along the railway. Waiting until they came within close range, the Hyderabads posted at this point directed on them such concentrated fire that the attack wilted. Next day the Japanese began an outflanking movement. A further infantry attack occurred soon after midnight on the 6th-7th along both the road and the railway; then, after a heavy barrage of mortar and artillery fire, and in clear moonlight, tanks suddenly appeared on the road.

These, it quickly became apparent, were part of a mechanised column with infantry interspersed between the armour. Under covering fire, the infantry soon disposed of the first road-block in its path; the forward company of Hyderabads was overrun; and with guns blazing the column charged on. Other Japanese troops renewed the pressure along the railway, and some of the tanks used an abandoned and overgrown section of old road in a flanking manoeuvre, with the result that rapid progress was made in this thrust also. The column was checked only when the leading tank entered a mined section of the road in front of the forward company of the 5/2nd Punjab near Milestone 61. Fierce fighting ensued, but here the first of two more disused deviations, which it had been intended to use for transport when the time came for the battalion to withdraw, enabled the enemy to move to the flank and rear. Again overrunning the position, the Japanese column advanced until it came upon more mines, in front of the reserve company of the 5/2nd Punjab. Furious fighting at this point lasted for an hour, but by exploiting the third loop section the Japanese achieved the same result as before. The suddenness of the penetration so disorganised communications that it was not until 6.30 a.m., when the position had been lost, that a dispatch rider delivered to General Paris' headquarters at Tanjong Malim his first message from the 12th Brigade. Even this contained only a vague reference to "some sort of break-through", for the information received by Stewart had lagged behind the night's swiftly-moving events.

In was in fact about this time that four enemy medium tanks reached the first of two road-blocks hurriedly erected by the Argylls. The blocks, and such resistance as the battalion, lacking anti-tank guns, was able to offer to the tanks, were also overcome, and an attempt to destroy the bridge at Trolak failed. Although the Argyll companies on the railway and the estate road held out until they were surrounded, and then tried to fight their way out, all but about a hundred of them were lost. Thus the tactics in which the Argylls had been trained had been used with disastrous effect against them and the other units of Stewart's brigade. At 7.30 a.m. the tanks reached the 5/14th Punjab moving up in column of companies to occupy their check position. Caught by surprise, the Punjabis were dispersed and a troop of anti-tank guns sent from the 28th Brigade to assist them in the position they were to occupy was overrun before it could fire a shot.

Unaware as he was that by daylight the Japanese had reached the Argylls, Paris had ordered Selby to deploy the 28th Brigade in the positions assigned to it, and Selby had issued his orders at 7 a.m. The 2/9th Gurkha were occupying positions near Kampong Slim when, about 8 a.m., the leading Japanese tanks roared past, and caught the 2/1st Gurkha Rifles moving in column of route to Cluny Estate. Thrown into confusion, the battalion dispersed. The tanks next paused briefly to fire on two batteries of the 137th Field Regiment parked beside the road, and reached the Slim River bridge about 8.30 a.m. An anti-aircraft battery brought two Bofors guns to bear on them at 100 yards' range, but the shells bounced off the tanks, while they poured fire into the gun crews. Before the bridge could be destroyed, the tanks crossed it and continued their triumphant course. Two miles south of the bridge they met the 155th Field Regiment moving up to support the 28th Brigade. There, after the regiment's headquarters had been overrun, and six hours after the column had commenced its thrust, they were stopped. Although under heavy fire, a howitzer detachment got a 4.5-inch howitzer into action. With their leading tank disabled, the Japanese thereafter confined themselves to tank patrols, and during the afternoon withdrew to the bridge.

Selby meanwhile had established the 28th Brigade headquarters, with headquarters of the 12th Brigade which had withdrawn down the estate road, on a hill east of Kampong Slim. On the incomplete information available to him, he decided to hold out until dusk and then withdraw his men down the railway, and across the river to Tanjong Malim. Pressed by increasing numbers of Japanese, the 2/9th Gurkha had difficulty in breaking contact for this move. The one bridge which had been successfully blown was that which had carried the railway line across the Slim

River. A hurriedly constructed plank walk served as a perilous substitute. Because of the congestion at its approaches, a number of men entered the water downstream. Some were swept away by the current, and others lost their way.

Next day—8th January—the strength of the 12th Brigade was fourteen officers and 409 men. The 2/1st Gurkha had been lost, and of the other two battalions of the 28th Brigade there remained a total of only 750 men. The guns and equipment of two field batteries and two troops of antitank guns, and all the transport of the two brigades, had been forfeited. Although it had absorbed the 12th Brigade to make good its losses from Jitra to the Perak, the 11th Indian Division had suffered another disastrous debacle.

After the campaign opened there was no reason to under-estimate the enemy; indeed the tendency was now to over-estimate him. Yet as events proved, the precautions taken to meet attack along the main route of the Japanese advance were surprisingly inadequate. Once again, the impetus of the enemy had thrown the machinery of control out of gear, and the defenders off balance. The Japanese had repeated their success at Jitra, and by similar means. It was discovered later that the battle was won by the Japanese *42nd Infantry Regiment,* aided by a tank battalion and part of an artillery regiment. The spearhead of the attack comprised one tank company, an infantry battalion in carriers and lorries, and some engineers.

The tactics employed by the Japanese from the commencement of their invasion of Malaya—in particular their enveloping type of attack and the flexibility and momentum of their movements—had been consistent. They could hardly have been cause for surprise had the substance of Intelligence reports on the subject been adequately circulated and sufficiently digested by commanders; yet the enemy had employed them with unfailing success. The overall tactical weakness of the dispositions which had been forced on the army for the defence of airfields was of course a fundamental disadvantage, and tended in itself to dictate withdrawal to what it was hoped would be some firm rallying point; but as the need at least to delay the enemy's progress was imperative, it might have been expected that all means to this end would have been used. The road from Jitra southward had presented many opportunities for ambushes, and outflanking tactics to counter those employed by the Japanese. By such means they might have been made to pay heavily for their impetuous actions, and to proceed with caution and thus at a reduced speed. Effective counter-initiative might indeed have thrown their advance seriously out of gear. It is now known that the commander of the *5th Japanese Division,* pursuant of the fundamental principle of the Japanese Army in the campaign that the British forces must be given no respite, had ordered his frontline units to attack without losing time in arranging liaison and cooperation with each other, and to disjoint the British chain of orders as much as possible. To counter such tactics required, however, well-trained and well-led troops, fighting with dash and determination; and as has been shown General Heath had all too few of them under his command. General Bennett's emphasis in cables to Australia on the need for additional "quality" troops was underlined by this situation.

In the losses of men and materials which it involved, the disaster at Slim River far more than offset the value of the reinforcements which had reached Singapore on the 3rd January, and seriously prejudiced prospects of later resistance. To the Australians preparing to defend Johore, it gave urgent warning. The 11th Division had ceased to exist as an effective formation. Time, such as had existed in the easy-going, pre-war days in Malaya, was necessary to concentrate and deploy forces for the next stand. The outcome of the Battle of Slim River, and enemy moves in other directions, showed that time was running very short indeed.

CHAPTER 11

AUSTRALIANS INTO BATTLE: THE AMBUSH AT GEMAS

GENERAL Percival had decided before the debacle at Slim River that the most he could hope to do pending the arrival of further reinforcements at Singapore was to hold Johore. This would involve giving up three rich and well-developed areas—the State of Selangor (including Kuala Lumpur, capital of the Federated Malay States), the State of Negri Sembilan, and the colony of Malacca—but he thought that Kuala Lumpur could be held until at least the middle of January. He intended that the III Indian Corps should withdraw slowly to a line in Johore stretching from Batu Anam, north-west of Segamat, on the trunk road and railway, to Muar on the west coast, south of Malacca. It should then be responsible for the defence of western Johore, leaving the Australians in their role as defenders of eastern Johore.

General Bennett, however, believing that he might soon be called upon for assistance on the western front, had instituted on 19th December a series of reconnaissances along the line from Gemas to Muar. By 1st January a plan had formed in his mind to obtain the release of his 22nd Brigade from the Mersing-Jemaluang area and to use it to hold the enemy near Gemas while counter-attacks were made by his 27th Brigade on the Japanese flank and rear in the vicinity of Tampin, on the main road near the border of Malacca and Negri Sembilan. Although he realised that further coastal landings were possible, he thought of these in terms of small parties, and considered that the enemy would prefer to press forward as he was doing by the trunk road rather than attempt a major movement by coastal roads, despite the fact that the coastal route Malacca-Muar-Batu Pahat offered a short cut to Ayer Hitam, far to his rear. It was therefore on the possibilities of action along the trunk road that his mind was fixed.

It is not in the nature of retreat to inspire confidence; and certainly what had happened to the 11th Division between Jitra and Kuala Lumpur, with its series of failures, heavy losses, and progressive demoralisation, had not done so. While General Yamashita basked in the sunshine of success, Generals Percival and Heath might have reflected, as Hitler was to do a year later, that "it is a thousand times easier to storm forward with an army and gain victories, than to bring an army back in an orderly condition after a reverse or a defeat".[1] (Later, perhaps, they might console themselves with the thought that, because of the priority given to the war against Germany, retreat in Malaya was in some part the price of the Allied

---
[1] *Fuehrer Conferences on Naval Affairs*, 12 Dec 1942.

successes which evoked that strangely chastened remark from the strutting Fuehrer.)

To Bennett, concerned with the part which the A.I.F. was now to play in the dangerously deteriorating situation, it seemed that the withdrawals in Malaya had been the outcome of faulty leadership. On 4th January he proposed to Percival that upon withdrawal of the III Indian Corps into Johore, all forces in that State should come under Bennett's command; alternatively, that the A.I.F. be responsible for the west of the State, and the Corps for the east. Percival rejected both proposals, on the grounds that fusion of the Corps and the A.I.F. must lead to command and administrative difficulties, and replacement of the 22nd Australian Brigade on the east coast by troops unfamiliar with the area would weaken the defences of that area. He said that the only practical solution seemed to be to make the A.I.F. responsible, after the withdrawal, for the east of the State and the Corps for the west; and at a conference next day he issued orders embodying this principle, with the proviso that there must be no withdrawal without his permission south of the line Endau[2]-Batu Anam-Muar.

Bennett reported to Australia on 6th January that Heath's men were tired and in most units lacking determination; that "unless great changes in outlook take place withdrawal will continue, exposing my left flank and ultimately creating impossible position for A.I.F." He continued that he had therefore urged that his fresh and fit 22nd Brigade should be replaced in its existing position by an Indian brigade, and placed in the forefront of the fight in western Johore; that the retiring units should occupy a supporting position, and the former "purely defensive attitude" should be replaced by "strong counter-attack methods". General Sturdee, who had received Bennett's report, replied that while he felt it would be most unwise to attempt from Australia to influence dispositions in Johore, it was difficult to believe that when the enemy reached northern Johore he would not attempt concurrently landings in eastern Johore. These, he said, seemed likely to be pressed with even more determination, and would be actually closer to Singapore.

In global perspective, the misfortunes being suffered at the time by the defenders of Malaya were far more than counter-balanced by the significance of a document signed by the representatives of 26 nations on New Year's Day, 1942, as the outcome of the meetings between Mr Churchill and President Roosevelt in August and December 1941. It was a document which gave birth to the United Nations, pledged to the principles embodied in the Atlantic Charter created at the August meeting, with the addition of religious freedom, and to united action against the Axis Powers. This great marriage of aims and action, precipitated by

---

[2] Later amended to Mersing.

Japan's attack on Pearl Harbour, was to have a tremendous effect not only upon the course of the war, but also upon world affairs thereafter.[3]

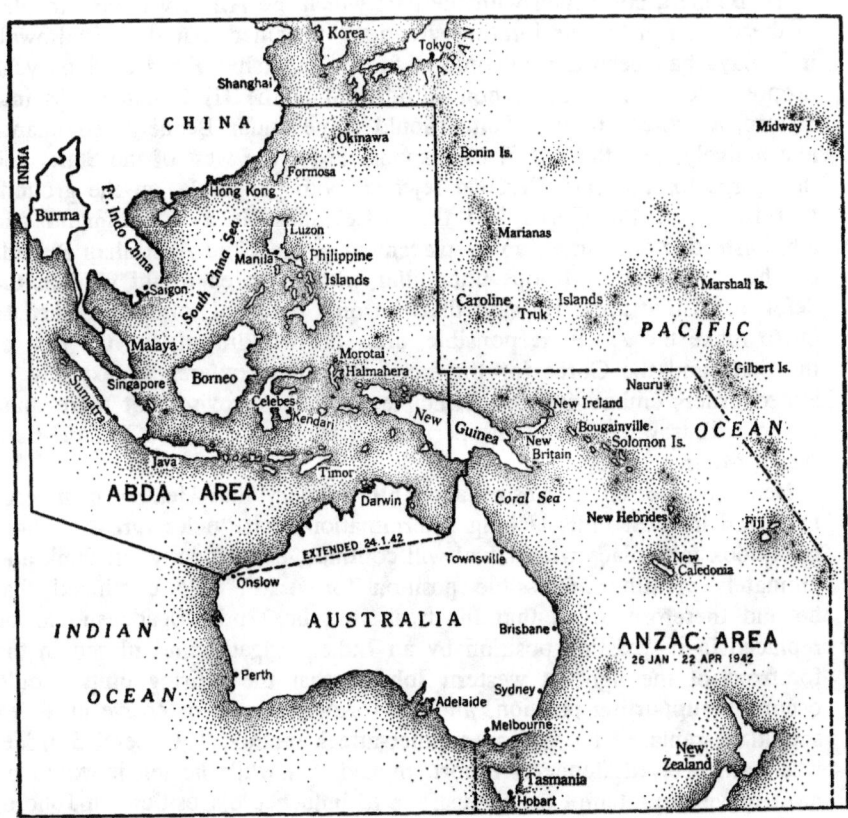

It was of course in keeping with the more immediate purposes of the document that the setting up of a united command against Japan should proceed. The main architect of the A.B.D.A. Command organisation was

---

[3] The text of the document was:
A Joint Declaration by the United States of America, the United Kingdom of Great Britain and Northern Ireland, the Union of Soviet Socialist Republics, China, Australia, Belgium, Canada, Costa Rica, Cuba, Czechoslovakia, the Dominican Republic, El Salvador, Greece, Guatemala, Haiti, Honduras, India, Luxemburg, the Netherlands, New Zealand, Nicaragua, Norway, Panama, Poland, South Africa, and Yugoslavia.
The Governments signatory hereto,
Having subscribed to a common program of purposes and principles embodied in the Joint Declaration of the President of the United States of America and the Prime Minister of the United Kingdom of Great Britain and Northern Ireland, dated August 14, 1941, known as the Atlantic Charter,
Being convinced that complete victory over their enemies is essential to defend life, liberty, independence, and religious freedom, and to preserve human rights and justice in their own lands as well as in other lands, and that they are now engaged in a common struggle against savage and brutal forces seeking to subjugate the world, DECLARE:
(1) Each Government pledges itself to employ its full resources, military or economic, against those members of the Tripartite Pact and its adherents with which such Government is at war.
(2) Each Government pledges itself to cooperate with the Governments signatory hereto, and not to make a separate armistice or peace with the enemies.
The foregoing declaration may be adhered to by other nations which are, or which may be, rendering material assistance and contributions in the struggle for victory over Hitlerism.

the Chief of Staff of the United States Army, General Marshall. The principal problem had been how to reconcile the varying national interests of those countries concerned—Britain, the United States, the Netherlands East Indies and Australia—in such a command, and to allow of employment of their forces in such ways as would be acceptable to them. As, however, the United States was anxious to build up American forces in Australia for recovery of its power in East Asia, there existed a ready basis of agreement between these two countries. Britain's interests were involved primarily in the retention of Singapore and of control of the Indian Ocean, as well of course as in the defence of Australia; while the Dutch sought to safeguard their East Indian possessions. Because of the importance she attached to maintaining resistance by China, and the fact that the only practical supply line to that country was by the Burma Road, the United States sought the inclusion of Burma in the command.[4] The British representatives demurred on the ground that Burma had so recently been transferred from the Far Eastern to Indian Command, and was dependent upon India for administration, reinforcements, and supplies. Finally it was agreed that it should be included in the A.B.D.A. area for operational purposes, though it would continue to be administered from India. Australia and New Zealand were excluded from the A.B.D.A. area in the first directive, but, in response to a protest by Australia, it was agreed that a naval force under the strategical direction of the Commander-in-Chief of the United States Navy should operate in what would be known as the "Anzac Area", to include the eastern coast of Australia and the whole of New Zealand. Eventually (on 24th January) after representations by General Wavell and with Australia's concurrence, the A.B.D.A. area was extended to include the portion of Australia north of a line from the south-eastern corner of the Gulf of Carpentaria to Onslow on the west coast, thus including Darwin and as much elbow-room as was deemed necessary for its defence.

When formally assigning the command to Wavell on 29th December, Churchill cabled: "You are the only man who has the experience of handling so many different theatres at once, and you know we shall back you up and see you have fair play. Everyone knows how dark and difficult the situation is."[5] The first directive, dated 3rd January, reached Wavell on the 4th.[6] It set out that the A.B.D.A. area had been constituted to comprise initially all land and sea areas, including the general regions of Burma, Malaya, the Netherlands East Indies and the Philippine Islands,

---

[4] "At Washington I had found the extraordinary significance of China in American minds, even at the top, strangely out of proportion. I was conscious of a standard of values which accorded China almost an equal fighting power with the British Empire, and rated the Chinese armies as a factor to be mentioned in the same breath as the armies of Russia. I told the President how much I felt American opinion over-estimated the contribution which China could make to the general war. He differed strongly. There were five hundred million people in China. What would happen if this enormous population developed in the same way as Japan had done in the last century and got hold of modern weapons? I replied that I was speaking of the present war, which was quite enough to go on with for the time being." (Churchill, *The Second World War*, Vol IV, p. 119.)

[5] "It was almost certain that he would have to bear a load of defeat in a scene of confusion."—Churchill, Vol III, p. 600.

[6] The directive appears as Appendix 2 to this volume.

as were defined in an annexure; and that Wavell had been designated Supreme Commander of this area and of all armed forces therein of the A.B.D.A. governments, and of such forces in Australia as had been allotted by their governments for service in or support of the area.

The basic strategic concept of the ABDA Governments for conduct of war in your area (continued the cabled directive) is not only in immediate future to maintain as many key positions as possible, but to take offensive at the earliest opportunity and ultimately to conduct an all-out offensive against Japan. The first essential is to gain general air superiority at the earliest moment through employment of concentrated air power. The piecemeal employment of air forces should be minimised. Your operations should be so conducted as to further preparations for the offensive.

General strategic policy will be therefore:
   (a) to hold Malaya barrier defined as line Malay Peninsula, Sumatra, Java, North Australia as basic defensive position of ABDA area and to operate sea, land and air forces in as great depth as possible forward of barrier in order to oppose Japanese southward advance;
   (b) to hold Burma and Australia as essential support positions for the area and Burma as essential to support of China and to defence of India;
   (c) to re-establish communications through Dutch East Indies with Luzon to support Philippines garrison;
   (d) to maintain essential communications within the area.

Conditions common to the employment of Australian forces in oversea theatres of war were embodied in the directive, to the extent that interference was to be avoided in the administrative processes of the forces of the governments concerned, and there might be free communication between the commanders of those forces and their respective governments; and each national component of a task force would normally operate under its own commander and would not be subdivided into small units for attachment to other components except in cases of urgent necessity.

It was decided that Wavell should report to a new British-American military committee consisting of the American Chiefs of Staff and the senior representatives in Washington of the three British Services. This body was named the Combined Chiefs of Staff.[7]

Onerous though the task would be, and risky to his reputation as a general, Wavell was not the kind of man to shirk it. Realising that it involved a race against time, and anxious to gain a practical grasp of the situation which would face him, he left Delhi by air on 5th January, and reached Singapore early on the 7th. He hoped that the enemy could be delayed north of Johore till the end of January, allowing the 18th Division to reinforce the defence, and the I Australian Corps to be landed and to prepare a counter-offensive. He had in mind that the Indian troops in Malaya might then be withdrawn to reinforce the Netherlands East Indies.

When, however, Wavell visited the III Corps on 8th January, and assessed its condition after the Battle of Slim River, he promptly decided that it must be withdrawn to Johore for rest and reorganisation before

---

[7] The alternative proposals for the higher direction of ABDA Command are set out in M. Matloff and E. M. Snell, *Strategic Planning for Coalition Warfare 1941-1942* (1953), a volume in the official series *United States Army in World War II*.

again facing any major encounter with the enemy. He told Heath, whom he thought tired, of this decision, and said that, though he should cover Kuala Lumpur as long as possible, he should not await a full-scale enemy attack. After he had discussed the situation with Bennett, he decided to give the Australian commander the responsibility he sought, and laid down next day the following plan for the defence of what remained of Malaya in British hands:

(a) III Indian Corps, after delaying the enemy north of Kuala Lumpur for as long as possible [Wavell did not expect it to be longer than 11th January] to be withdrawn by rail and road into Johore, leaving sufficient mobile rearguards to cover the demolition scheme.

(b) The 8th Australian Division, leaving its 22nd Brigade Group in the Mersing area on the east coast, to move forthwith to the north-western frontier of Johore and to prepare to fight a decisive battle on the general line Segamat-Mount Ophir-mouth of Muar River. The 22nd Brigade Group to join the remainder of the Australian division as soon as it could be relieved by troops from Singapore Island. [Wavell considered that this could not be completed before the arrival of the 53rd Brigade.]

(c) The 9th Indian Division, to be made up from the freshest troops of the III Indian Corps and the 45th Indian Brigade, to be placed under General Bennett for use in the southern portion of the position allotted to the Australian division.

(d) The Australian division as soon as possible to send forward mobile detachments to relieve the rearguards of III Indian Corps and to harass the enemy and delay him by demolitions.

(e) III Indian Corps on withdrawal to take over responsibility for the east and west coasts of Johore south of the road Mersing-Kluang-Batu Pahat, leaving Bennett free to fight the battle in north-west Johore. The Indian Corps to rest and to refit the 11th Indian Division and to organise a general reserve from reinforcements as they arrived.

The plan conceded the enemy a further southward advance of nearly 150 miles. Although it involved weakening the east coast defences, Wavell held that in view of the state of III Indian Corps, and since the well-developed road systems in Selangor and Malacca made delaying tactics difficult, a risk must be taken temporarily on the east coast, which was not immediately threatened, for the sake of the west which was so threatened. He was confident that Bennett—although initially the forces available to him for operations in north-western Johore would include only one of the Australian brigades—would conduct "a very active defence", and he still hoped that a counter-stroke could be delivered once the Australian Corps had arrived. He hoped also that expected air reinforcements would enable close support to be given to forward troops, and that small naval craft would be able to cope with enemy attempts to land on the coast. Wavell ordered that work be begun on defences on the north side of Singapore Island, where, he was concerned to find, "no defences had been made or even planned in detail"; and he received from Duff Cooper "a gloomy account of the efficiency of the Civil Administration and the lack of cooperation between the civil and military".

As a result of the creation of Wavell's new command, Duff Cooper's position as Resident Minister now lapsed, and meetings of the Far Eastern War Council were suspended pending decision whether it was to continue to function. It was decided on the 10th January that it should resume as "War Council, Singapore", with its scope limited to the area under Malaya Command and the administration of the Governor. As in fact it had never operated in the wider sphere implied by its former title, and had acted as a consultative rather than a directing body, this made little difference to its activities.

On the initiative of the Chinese of Malaya, who thereby displayed a refreshingly lively approach to the subject of civilian cooperation in the struggle, there had been formed a Chinese Mobilisation Council. Seeking to avoid in Singapore a collapse of essential services such as had occurred in Penang, it was to be primarily concerned with maintaining a supply of labour. Delegates to the council included representatives of such widely diverse bodies as the Malayan Kuomintang (allied to the then ruling party in China) and the Malayan Communist Party. Its president was a leading Malayan business man, Mr Tan Kah-kee.

The activities of the small British naval force remaining at Singapore had become confined almost wholly to protection of convoys, and Admiral Layton had transferred with his staff to Batavia, leaving Rear-Admiral Spooner[8] in local command.

At this time Mr Bowden sent to the Secretary of the Department of External Affairs, Colonel Hodgson[9]—who referred it to the Minister, Dr Evatt—a letter containing penetrating comment on some of the men principally concerned in the conduct of affairs in Malaya. Of Mr Duff Cooper he wrote that he was an able man but not a dominant one, and did not provide the War Council with the strong leadership that a body of that sort should have. Brooke-Popham had shown "an extraordinary diffidence of manner for a man in his position" and was "definitely too old for such a post in wartime". Pownall had become the outstanding man in the Council; Percival appeared to be able but not a particularly strong personality; Air Vice-Marshal Pulford was "very worried and greatly overworked". The Governor, Sir Shenton Thomas, appeared to Mr Bowden as more ready at producing reasons for not doing things than for doing them, and in the Malayan civil service there seemed to be too much of the old bureaucratic doctrine that action means to risk making blunders, and inaction means safety.[1]

---

[8] Vice-Adm E. J. Spooner, DSO; RN. Comd HMS *Repulse* 1938-41; i/c Naval Establishments at Singapore, 1941-42. B. 22 Aug 1887. Died 15 Apr 1942.

[9] Lt-Col W. R. Hodgson, CMG, OBE. (1st AIF: Lt 2 Fd Arty Bde.) Secretary Dept of External Affrs 1935-45; Aust Minister to France 1945-48, Ambassador 1948-49. B. Kingston, Vic, 22 May 1892.

[1] Commenting on 12th January on the pending departure of Duff Cooper from Malaya, the *Straits Times* said that rightly or wrongly the public had regarded him as the last bulwark against "that minute-paper mentality to which many of our present anxieties must be attributed". Appealing for his retention, the paper said that alternatively a military governor of Singapore Island should be appointed "to cut through that cumbrous procedure which is so hopelessly unsuited to the days in which we live. . . ."

These opinions, hewn in the stress of the times, could hardly have done full justice to those concerned. They were none the less the opinions of an able man, concerned for the welfare of his country, and anxious that the gravity of the situation in Malaya should not be obscured in responsible quarters in Australia by the veneer of Malayan official optimism.

On the 10th Wavell flew to Batavia, where he met the principal officers who were to be on his staff. It was a strange turn of fortune that placed this learned, high-principled old soldier again in chief command in the main eastern theatre (which the Far East had now become in succession to the Middle East). Despite the importance of the task assigned to him, it is doubtful whether Churchill ever had full confidence in him. Indeed, he had not even met him until August 1940; and in July 1941 he had sent him upstairs from Cairo to Delhi. Now Wavell faced even more baffling problems than those the Middle East had presented in mid-1941 with revolution in Iraq, Crete lost, a German force on the Egyptian frontier, and the likelihood that he would be asked to attack in Syria.

On Wavell's right, MacArthur's main Filipino-American army had fallen back, as shown in Chapter 10, to a line across the neck of the Bataan Peninsula. The Japanese had recently occupied not only British North Borneo, but also Tarakan in Dutch Borneo, and Menado in the Celebes. Such British and Dutch naval forces as were available were engaged chiefly in escorting supplies and reinforcements to Singapore. There were only small American surface naval forces in the A.B.D.A. Command, and Japanese planes had mastery in the air. Thus not only was the enemy at the throat of communications with the Philippines, but there was little to prevent him from occupying more island bases whence his aircraft could attack Java and dominate the supply route to it from Australia. In Malaya the British forces might be driven back to Singapore Island. On Wavell's left, in Burma, the Japanese had not yet made a major attack.

As Wavell's directive required, his staff included officers of the various Services of four nations. The position of Commander-in-Chief, Far East, was to lapse, and Pownall, who had held it hardly long enough to gather the reins, had flown from Singapore with him to become his Chief of Staff. The Deputy Commander-in-Chief was Lieut-General George H. Brett of the American Army Air Force, until recently in command of the nucleus American forces in Australia. Admiral Hart (United States Navy) was Chief of the Naval Staff, with Rear-Admiral Palliser (British Navy) as his deputy. Major-General Brereton (United States Army Air Force) was in command of the Allied air forces, pending the arrival of Air Marshal Sir Richard Peirse[2] (R.A.F.). It seemed likely that Australia would soon be providing the largest military contingent in the combined force, and

---

[2] Air Ch Marshal Sir Richard Peirse, KCB, DSO, AFC. Dep Chief of Air Staff 1937-40; AOC-in-C Bomber Comd 1940-42, India 1942-43; Allied Air C-in-C SE Asia Comd 1943-44. Regular airman; b. 1892.

Wavell sought some Australian officers for inclusion in his staff.³ The Allied land forces under his direction were commanded by the following officers:

> Java, Lieut-General H. ter Poorten
> Burma, Lieut-General T. J. Hutton⁴
> Malaya, Lieut-General A. E. Percival
> Philippines, General D. MacArthur
> Darwin, Major-General D. V. J. Blake⁵

Headquarters were to be in a hotel at Lembang, near Bandung, the site of the Netherlands East Indies Army headquarters. At the first conferences of the Combined Staff, the Dutch and American officers urged the necessity of holding and reinforcing such forward air bases as survived in Allied hands: Ambon, Kendari (Celebes), Samarinda (Dutch Borneo), Sabang (Sumatra). However, each had only a small garrison, and Wavell was unable to see how with his very limited resources he could afford to reinforce them. He therefore clung to his plan to concentrate on the line Darwin-Timor-Java-southern Sumatra-Singapore.

Wavell had not yet formally assumed command because his headquarters had not been fully established, and he was not, in the words of his directive, "in position effectively [to] carry essential functions of supreme command".⁶ In the meantime, on 13th January, he flew to Singapore again to visit his main sector in Malaya. There, on the morning of the 9th, Percival had issued orders to Bennett consequent upon those given by Wavell to him.

As supplemented on the 10th, Percival's orders provided that troops in Johore be divided into two forces. The force under Bennett, to be known as Westforce, would comprise:

> 9th Indian Division;
> A.I.F. less 22nd Brigade;
> 45th Indian Brigade Group;
> 2/Loyal Regiment (from Singapore Fortress) less one company;
> Artillery, engineer, and administrative units not included in formations;
> An Indian pioneer battalion.

Westforce was to hold north-west Johore, principally along the line Batu Anam-Muar. The composition of the other main force—III Indian Corps—would be:

---

³ On 21st January Colonel Lloyd, until recently General Morshead's senior staff officer in Tobruk, was promoted major-general and appointed senior administrative officer. (Maj-Gen C. E. M. Lloyd, CBE, VX4. DAAG 6 Div 1939-40; AQMG I Corps 1940; GSO1 9 Div 1941, HQ AIF ME 1941-42; DSD LHQ 1942-43; AG LHQ 1943-45. Regular soldier; of Melbourne; b. Fremantle, WA, 2 Feb 1899. Died 31 May 1956.) Wavell recorded in his dispatch that Lloyd did the job most efficiently, and was "a staff officer of great quality".

⁴ Lt-Gen Sir Thomas Hutton, KCIE, CB, MC. CGS India 1941; GOC Burma 1942; Secretary War Resources and Reconstruction Committees of Council (India) 1942-44; Secretary Planning and Development Dept 1944-46. Regular soldier; b. 27 Mar 1890.

⁵ Maj-Gen D. V. J. Blake, VP7416. (1914-18: Maj AFC.) In charge Administration Southern Comd 1939-41; Comdt 7 MD 1941-42. Regular soldier; of Melbourne; b. Harris Park, NSW, 10 Nov 1887.

⁶ The official time and date of the opening of the ABDA Command were midday GMT on 15 January 1942.

(*Australian War Memorial*)
Laying an Australian 25-pounder field gun, Malaya, January 1942.

(*Australian War Memorial*)
Stretcher bearers attending a wounded Australian.

The Muar ferry crossing, looking south-east. The 45th Indian Brigade, on the left flank of Westforce, was disposed along 24 miles of river front, with detachments forward of the river.

(*Australian War Memorial*)

The rear 2-pounder gun of the 13th Battery, 2/4th Anti-Tank Regiment, in action ahead of Bakri on 18th January. From this position the forward and rear guns accounted for nine Japanese tanks.

11th Indian Division;
22nd Australian Brigade Group and attached troops, including 2/17th Dogra Battalion from Singapore Fortress, under Brigadier Taylor (to be known as Eastforce);
Corps troops, inclusive of artillery, engineer and administrative units.

The III Indian Corps was to defend the remainder of Johore up to and including the line Endau (on the east coast) through Kluang to Batu Pahat on the west coast. Although the 11th Indian Division was included in this force, it was to be placed in areas where it could be rested and reorganised, and the 12th Indian Infantry Brigade was to be withdrawn direct to Singapore. The plan split the Australian division—something which Percival hitherto had sought to avoid, and which Bennett accepted with reluctance, thinking perhaps that events might soon restore his 22nd Brigade to him.

On the ground that an Indian Army officer was now required to pull together and establish confidence in what remained of the 11th Division, Brigadier Key was appointed to command it in place of Major-General Paris. Brigadier Lay, having returned to duty, was given command of the 8th Indian Infantry Brigade (9th Division) and Colonel Challen[7] replaced Brigadier Moorhead in command of the 15th Brigade (11th Division).

Percival impressed on Bennett that the new position must be held and declared that "if this position is lost, the battle of Singapore is lost". Percival's ground forces on the peninsula amounted to three under-strength divisions, including the weak 11th Division. He expected to have the equivalent of one more division by the end of the month, and a number of reinforcements. It was almost impossible for the time being to give any effective air support to the infantry. On the other hand the Japanese were now bombing targets, including Singapore Island, with increasing freedom, as well as supporting their forward troops. The seas around Malaya lay open to the enemy.

While these plans were being made, the Japanese were building their strength in Malaya. The *21st Regiment* of the *5th Division* landed at Singora on 8th January and the *Guards Division*, having been relieved of its duties in Thailand, had its *5th Regiment* in Ipoh. Preparations were being made to land at Endau towards the end of January the portion of the *18th Division* which as yet had not been employed in Malaya, and at the same time the Anambas Islands, off the east coast of Malaya, were to be occupied so that they might be used as an advanced naval base.

The principal immediate danger to the safe withdrawal of III Indian Corps to Johore, however, was presented by the Japanese *4th Guards Regiment*. The main body of this regiment crossed the Sungei Selangor unopposed on the night of 9th-10th January, and forced its way to Klang. There it captured the bridge over the Sungei Klang held by the Jat-Punjab Battalion of the 15th Brigade, and forced its withdrawal to Batu Tiga by 1 a.m. on 11th January. The battalion, reduced to about 200 all ranks, was then embussed and moved southward through Kajang, on the trunk

---
[7] Brig B. S. Challen. 2 Punjab Regt; AQMG III Indian Corps 1941; Comd 15 Indian Bde 1942. Regular soldier; b. 17 Jan 1897.

road. Concurrently, the *II/4th Battalion* of the *Guards Division* had been moved by sea to near Port Swettenham, at the mouth of the Sungei Klang, and landed unopposed on the afternoon of the 10th. It then set out for Kajang, hoping to come on to the flank of the 11th Indian Division. In

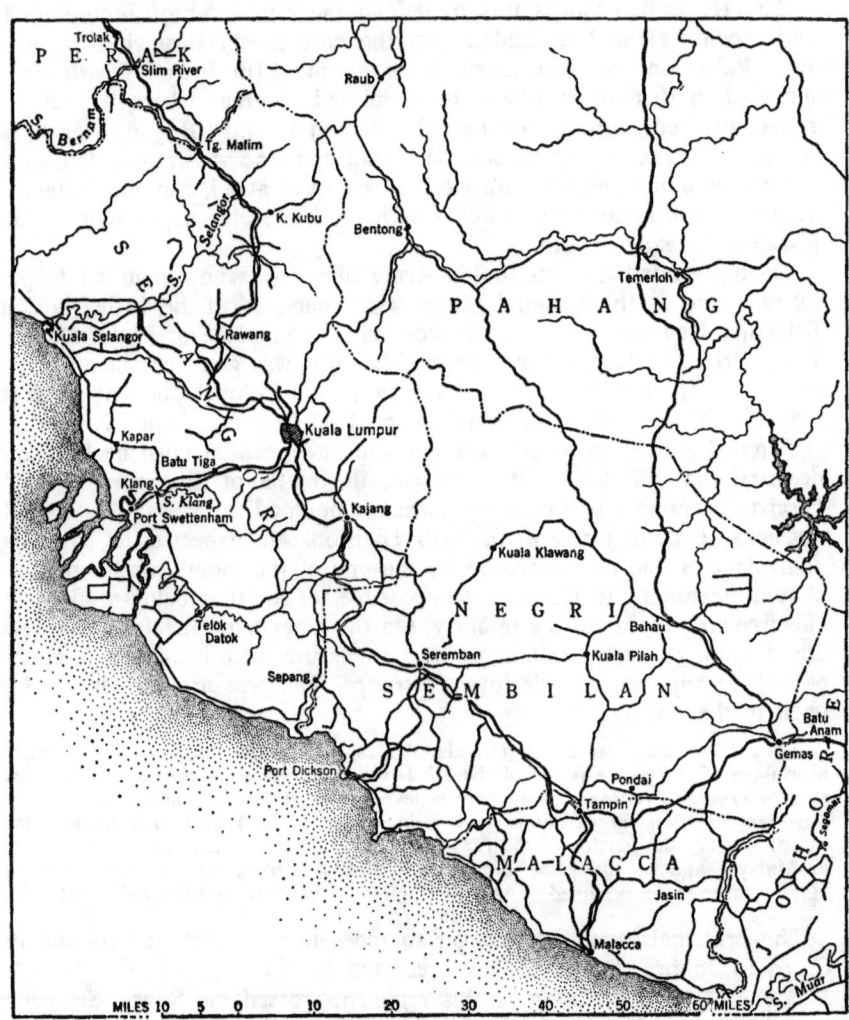

this endeavour it was too late, for the British Battalion, acting as the rearguard of the 11th Division, had withdrawn from Kuala Lumpur at 4.30 a.m. on the 11th, and the division was clear of Kajang when the *Guards* battalion arrived there that evening.

For days past, smoke had billowed up at Kuala Lumpur from great quantities of stores which could not be moved because of the swift collapse at Slim River. Even so, much was left to the enemy. The southward move from the city had begun on the morning of Saturday, 10th January.

> All Saturday and Sunday, all day and all night, the great withdrawal continued (wrote a war correspondent who witnessed it). An interminable convoy, composed of all manner of vehicles, began to roll south: large lorries filled with British troops so dog-tired that they slept in spite of bumps and jolts; civilian motor-cars commandeered by the military and hastily camouflaged by being spattered with mud; lorries bearing the names of half the rubber estates in Malaya; dispatch-riders darting in and out of the traffic on their motor-bicycles; eleven steam rollers . . . which had steamed all the way down from Kedah and Perak; two fire-engines also making their way south; enormous tin-dredges towed by Diesel tractors . . . so broad that they took up most of the road, and so heavy that their treads curled up the tarred surface; low trollies towing sticks of heavy aerial bombs saved from the northern airfields for further use; private motor-cars, from Austins to Rolls Royces, carrying Local Defence Volunteers, A.R.P. wardens, police officials; camouflaged staff cars through whose windows one caught a glimpse of red tabs and hatbands; Red Cross ambulances, ordnance vans, trucks fitted with cranes and lathes and all equipment needed for field repairs. . . .
>
> In the villages and towns along the route Malays and Chinese and Indians stood in silent little groups. . . . Neither pleasure nor malice nor sympathy were to be seen in their impassive countenances. . . . War was a phenomenon completely strange to these pacific, indolent, happy people. And now they saw the white tuans [masters], who had always been in Malaya since they could first remember, heading south. . . .[8]

The white tuans had indeed been humbled. Not only were they giving up great military, commercial, and personal possessions; they were being forced to leave behind them millions of Asians whom they were pledged to protect. It was a bitter moment, relieved only by hope of ultimate victory.

Enemy troops entered Kuala Lumpur at 8 p.m. on 11th January, thus completing the first phase of the Japanese plan for the conquest of Malaya. Preparing for the next, and establishing control in the capital, the invaders paused, and the 11th Division moved without further fighting to successive positions in its withdrawal to Johore. No longer able to enter the trunk road at Kuala Kubu, the 9th Indian Division withdrew southward through Bentong and Bahau, and on the 13th reached the Segamat area, where it came under Bennett's command.

> It is naturally disturbing to learn that the Japanese have been able to overrun the whole of Malaya except Johore (cabled the Australian Prime Minister to Mr Churchill on the 11th), and that the Commander-in-Chief considers that certain risks have to be accepted even now in carrying on his plan for the defence of this limited area.
>
> It is observed that the 8th Australian Division is to be given the task of fighting the decisive battle. . . . I urge on you that nothing be left undone to reinforce Malaya to the greatest degree possible in accordance with my earlier representations and your intentions. I am particularly concerned in regard to air strength. . . .

To this Churchill replied on the 14th—

> I do not see how any one could expect Malaya to be defended once the Japanese obtained the command of the sea and while we are fighting for our lives against

---

[8] Ian Morrison, *Malayan Postscript*, pp. 104-5. Morrison, whose Australian-born father was the famous "Chinese" Morrison, had become correspondent in Malaya for *The Times* of London.

Germany and Italy. The only vital point is Singapore Fortress and its essential hinterland. Personally, my anxiety has been lest in fighting rearguard actions down the peninsula to gain time we should dissipate the force required for the prolonged defence of Singapore. . . . Some may think it would have been better to have come back quicker with less loss. . . . Everything is being done to reinforce Singapore and the hinterland. . . .

Faced with the great challenge to the A.I.F. and to himself in the Westforce plan, Bennett briskly set about his task. As approved in principle by Percival, the crossings over the Sungei Muar and Sungei Segamat in the vicinity of Segamat were to be secured strongly against all forms of attack. Bennett directed that, westward of these, localities were to be held at focal points, with striking forces available to prevent the enemy from moving around the flanks. An ambush force and road-block were to be placed along the main road west of Gemas, on which it was expected that the principal enemy force would converge. Believing that the Japanese would not stand up to resolute blows, Bennett wanted to ensure that they were hit hard when they first encountered the A.I.F. In the coastal area to the west the 45th Indian Brigade Group[9] would cover the main coast road at Muar, south of the river, with detachments and patrols along the river to Lenga, about 25 miles inland. Discussing the plan with General Barstow, commander of the 9th Indian Division, Bennett "told him definitely that there would be no withdrawal. He said that was all right, but if the troops could not stand, a withdrawal would be forced on us." Bennett "reiterated that there would be no withdrawal". Barstow "accepted the decision and immediately set to work to pass on the determination to his brigadiers".[1]

Bennett impressed on Brigadier Maxwell (27th Brigade) and his battalion commanders that "fixed defensive positions were dangerous, and that a fluid defence with as many men as possible for counter-attack was sounder".[2] He expounded these tactics also to Brigadier Duncan,[3] commander of the 45th Indian Brigade. As the 27th Brigade was disposed on 13th January in the Segamat sector, the foremost position, on the trunk road three miles west of Gemas, was occupied by the 2/30th Australian Battalion (Lieut-Colonel Galleghan) with Major Ball's[4] battery of the 2/15th Field Regiment, and the 16th Anti-Tank Battery (less a troop) under command. The role of the battalion was to act as a shock-absorber at the first contact with the enemy, inflict as many casualties as possible, and hold its ground for at least 24 hours before falling back on the main positions. The 2/26th Battalion (Lieut-Colonel Boyes), with the 29th Field Battery under command, was on the Paya Lang Estate, north of the trunk road, and between Gemas and Batu Anam. Behind the 2/26th

---

[9] This brigade, mobilised in Aug 1941, was one of the three brigades of the 17th Indian Division. It had embarked from India in December for Burma and been diverted to Malaya.
[1] H. G. Bennett, *Why Singapore Fell*, p. 102.
[2] Bennett, p. 106.
[3] Brig H. C. Duncan. Comd 45 Indian Inf Bde 1941-42. Regular soldier; b. 19 Aug 1895. Killed in action 20 Jan 1942.
[4] Maj A. F. Ball, ED, NX 12309; 2/15 Fd Regt. Bank officer; of Strathfield, NSW; b. Woollahra, NSW, 16 Oct 1906.

was the 2/29th Battalion (Lieut-Colonel Robertson), at Buloh Kasap, between Batu Anam and Segamat. Headquarters of the 27th Australian Brigade and of the 2/15th Field Regiment were near Segamat, and advanced headquarters of Westforce at Labis, south-east of Segamat. Units of the 9th Indian Division were allotted various responsibilities from Segamat to Batu Anam, and westward of the main road to guard approaches through Jementah, on a road from Malacca and the west coast. Their dispositions were: 8th Indian Brigade: 1/13th Frontier Force Rifles

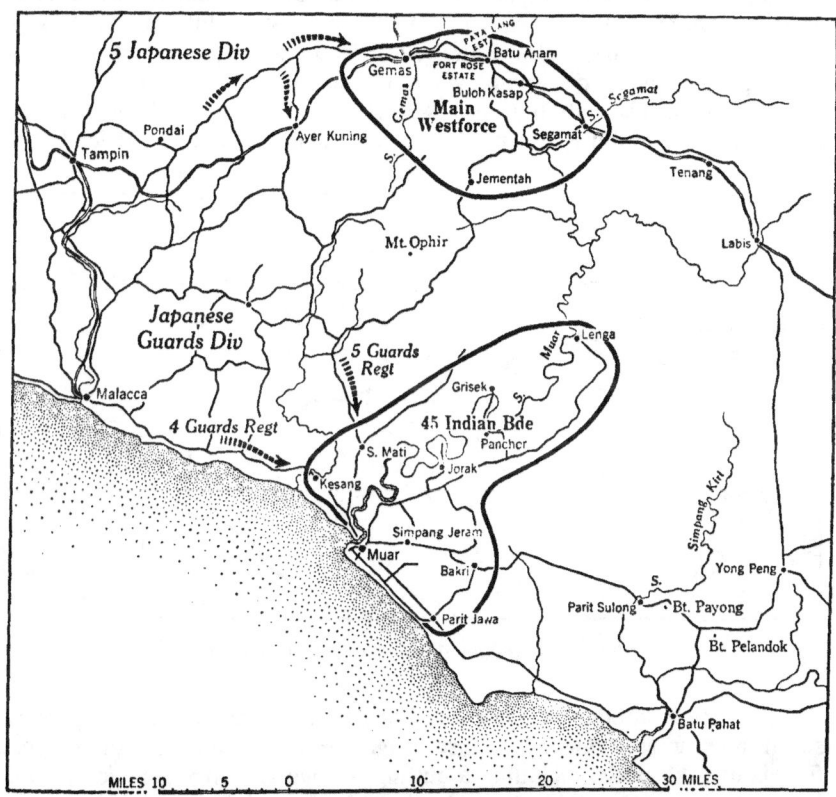

The Westforce front, 14th January 1942

astride the road west of Batu Anam; 2/10th Baluch between Batu Anam and Buloh Kasap; 3/17th Dogras, Segamat. 22nd Indian Brigade: 5/11th Sikhs near bridge over Sungei Muar four miles west of Segamat on the road to Jementah; 2/18th Garhwals about the junction of the roads Batu Anam to Jementah and Segamat to Jementah; 2/12th Frontier Force Regiment, between the Garhwals and the Sikhs. The 2/Loyals, in reserve, were responsible for the local defence of Segamat. The 29th Australian Field Battery was placed in the area occupied by the 1/13th Frontier Force Rifles. Other Indian units were supported by Royal Artillery units.

The ambush was a device which Bennett had for long discussed with his commanders pursuant to his belief that resolute aggressive action might check the Japanese advance, and perhaps disrupt their plans. He saw in the situation now facing him means of putting it into practice, though on a smaller scale than originally had been contemplated. It was expected that the III Indian Corps would make a clean break away from the enemy, who would be unopposed for thirty miles. Bridges along the road would be left intact to heighten the impression of helter-skelter retreat, and tempt the Japanese to become over-confident and careless as they continued their advance.[5] High hopes were entertained of what could be done by the 2/30th Battalion, forged and toughened by strenuous training and severe discipline, when it encountered the enemy in such circumstances. The battalion area was closely reconnoitred,[6] and the spot chosen for the ambush consisted of a length of the main road leading at

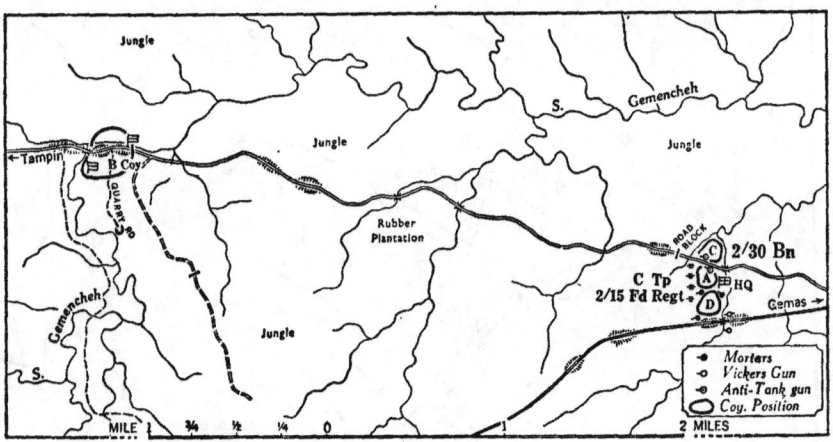

2/30th Battalion dispositions, 14th January

this point to a wooden bridge over a small river—the Gemencheh—about seven miles west of Gemas. Dense jungle grew on both sides of the road for about 500 yards, including a cutting, twelve feet high and forty yards long, which ended within 60 yards of the bridge, giving way to low scrub offering little or no concealment. On the far side of the bridge the road ran in a straight line for about 250 yards with open ground on either side. Percival, who visited the spot with Bennett, considered that it was too far in advance of where the main stand was to be made, near the Paya Lang Estate, but Bennett upheld the choice.

As Galleghan disposed his forces, positions forward of battalion headquarters, extending from north of the road to the railway line, were

---

[5] In the event only one bridge—a steel and concrete structure at Pondai—was demolished.
[6] Maxwell had lived for two or three months at Segamat; and his brother Arthur, now a liaison officer with the A.I.F., had a plantation near by at Ayer Kuning.

occupied by "C" Company (Captain Lamacraft[7]), on the right, with responsibility for establishing a road-block ahead of its positions, "A" Company (Major Anderson[8]) in the centre, and "D" Company (Captain Melville[9]) on the left. "B" Company (Captain Duffy[1]), entrusted with the task of manning the Gemencheh ambush, three miles ahead, took up its position amid teeming rain on 13th January while Japanese planes droned overhead to bomb and machine-gun rearward targets. Lieutenant Head's[2] platoon lined the cutting with company headquarters near by. Platoons commanded by Lieutenants Geikie[3] and Jones[4] were in echelon along the road. Rear headquarters were established close to a track known as Quarry road, along which the company was to withdraw after taking maximum toll of the enemy. Galleghan was insistent in putting into practice his belief that the use of transport in the battle area should be kept to a minimum.

To prevent Japanese troops not caught in the ambush from attempting a flanking movement, two sections of Head's platoon were posted on opposite sides of the road where they could cover both the road and the flats beside it. A small holding force was given the task of securing the junction of the road with Quarry road. This force comprised headquarters details under Warrant-Officer Gordon,[5] the company sergeant-major, on the right and a detachment of Jones' platoon on the left, under Sergeant Garner.[6] Two signal lines were laid, one to battalion headquarters and one to the supporting battery, which was to fire on enemy troops following those who had been caught in the ambush.[7] On his way to the ambush position Duffy had noticed the artillery signal wire lying conspicuously beside the road. The N.C.O. in charge of the truck from which the line was being laid undertook to send a party on foot to camouflage it after it had been laid. Galleghan, inspecting the position soon after first light on the 14th, also noticed the wire and gave instructions for its concealment. Wireless telegraph equipment was not provided. Engineers of the 2/12th Field Company prepared the bridge for demolition. All transport and carriers were sent to B Echelon except one truck for each

---

[7] Capt A. M. Lamacraft, ED, NX34738; 2/30 Bn. Company secretary; of West Chatswood, NSW; b. Glebe, NSW, 13 Jul 1908.

[8] Maj R. H. Anderson, ED, NX70435; 2/30 Bn. Salesman; of Greenwich, NSW; b. Stanmore, NSW, 19 Mar 1908.

[9] Lt-Col W. S. Melville, NX34711. 2/30 Bn 1940-42; CO 11 Bn 1943-45. Solicitor; of Inverell, NSW; b. Kogarah, NSW, 10 Jul 1911.

[1] Lt-Col D. J. Duffy, MC, ED, NX34792; 2/30 Bn. Staff supervisor; of Rockdale, NSW; b. Sydney, 30 Apr 1910.

[2] Lt H. Head, NX70439; 2/30 Bn. Clerk; of Mudgee, NSW; b. Scone, NSW, 30 Jun 1915.

[3] Lt N. B. C. Geikie, NX32594; 2/30 Bn. Wool valuer; of Darling Point, NSW; b. Sandgate, Qld, 20 Jan 1919.

[4] Maj F. A. Jones, EM, NX70513; 2/30 Bn. Journalist; of Casino, NSW; b. Maclean, NSW, 24 Mar 1917.

[5] WO2 V. M. I. Gordon, NGX33; 2/30 Bn. Barman; of Bowen Hills, Qld; b. Melbourne, 18 Oct 1906.

[6] Sgt D. F. Garner, NX36285; 2/30 Bn. Ironmonger; of Narrandera, NSW; b. Fairfield, Vic, 6 Sep 1911.

[7] The signallers with 2/30 Bn ran short of wire as they were linking the battalion's various positions, so they stopped an Indian signals truck as it was withdrawing into Johore and took the length they needed. "Who shall I say took the wire?" asked the Indian sergeant. "Colonel Ned Kelly, of Australia," said Galleghan, who was near by.

company, two ammunition trucks with Intelligence, two carriers and signals trucks, and Galleghan's car.

The 27th Brigade was now ready for its first experience under fire. Withdrawal of the III Indian Corps was completed on the night of 13th-14th January. As all wheeled transport had to pass through Segamat this became a dangerous bottleneck, but, surprisingly and fortunately, enemy planes failed to take advantage of it.

Galleghan told his commanders and staff on the eve of battle: "The reputation not only of the A.I.F. in Malaya, but of Australia, is in the hands of this unit." Soon after 10 a.m. on the 14th he passed on to his companies the code word "Switch", indicating that control of the front had passed from Heath to Bennett. Thus the men were braced for battle when, shortly before 4 p.m., a few Japanese on bicycles rounded the bend near the Gemencheh bridge. Soon a column of blithely chattering Japanese push cyclists, riding five or six abreast, was streaming over the bridge. They resembled a picnic party rather than part of an advancing army, except that they carried arms. Reporting by telephone to battalion headquarters that the cyclists were moving through, Duffy found that the voice at the other end of the line reached him only faintly. Sounds along the road forward of his position suggested that motor transport, with perhaps the main body of the enemy convoy, was following. He therefore let from 200 to 300 of the cyclists pass, to be dealt with by troops in the rear. As it happened, only three motor cyclists appeared, followed by several hundred more push cyclists. When these were tightly packed into the ambush, and on the bridge, and it seemed to Duffy that the head of the column would have reached the Quarry road position, he gave the order for the bridge to be blown.

The charge hurled timber, bicycles and bodies skyward in a deadly blast. Almost simultaneously, Duffy's three platoons hurled grenades among the enemy and swept them with fire from Bren guns, Tommy guns and rifles. The din was so great that when Duffy ordered artillery fire the artillery forward observation officer thought his battery's guns were firing. Both he and Duffy soon found, however, that their signal lines back from the ambush position had gone dead—cut, it was believed, by Japanese who had discovered them at the crucial moment in the artillery fire plan. In the absence of wireless telegraph equipment[8] there remained no means whereby the artillery could be given the signal to fire as had been planned on to the enemy troops and transport which it was assumed would bank up on the far side of the bridge.

Battalion headquarters, straining their ears for the sound of the bridge being blown, heard nothing they could rely upon as a signal that the action had commenced, and that would indicate when and where artillery fire was required. On the other hand, they knew that premature or wrongly

---

[8] Wireless telegraph had been found to be unreliable in the Malayan jungle, and it was suspected in some quarters that it gave the enemy means of pin-pointing positions. It might nevertheless have served to convey a message to the artillery after the bridge had been blown, had there been a set with the company.

directed fire might be disastrous. Thus the Australians were now threatened by the "fog of battle" that had hampered the III Corps throughout its long withdrawal from the north.

But there was no frustration of Duffy's men in their immediate task. The ambush had caught the Japanese completely by surprise. Their rifles and automatic guns were strapped to their cycles, and there was little opportunity to use either their bayonets or their grenades. The best hope of those who had survived the onslaught lay in pretending to be dead. In twenty minutes it was all over. Of the sight across the river, Duffy related: ". . . the entire 300 yards of road was thickly covered with dead and dying men—the result of blast when the bridge was blown up and the deadly fire of our Bren guns, specially told off to attend to the section on the far side of the bridge."[9] Undoubtedly the first encounter with the Australians had been costly to the enemy.

Duffy now ordered withdrawal, especially as so many Japanese had been let through the ambush before the action commenced. In the withdrawal Head and some of his platoon became engaged with these Japanese, who had turned back. He shot an enemy officer, but was himself wounded and had to be supported by Sergeant Doolan[1] to the rendezvous at Quarry road. Geikie, who with his platoon also encountered the enemy, led several successful bayonet attacks and he too was wounded, but not badly. Gordon's and Garner's parties, after fighting fiercely, joined company headquarters in the jungle near Quarry road. Jones' platoon also withdrew, fighting a rearguard action.

As it appeared that the Japanese were in strength on the trunk road, Duffy led his company in single file through the jungle in an attempt to move round the enemy's flank. He did not discover until 5.15 that contact had been lost between the party immediately following him and the rest of the company. With Duffy were Captain Kearney,[2] his second-in-command; Sergeant Garner and his party from Jones' platoon; approximately one section from each of Geikie's and Head's platoons; the Forward Artillery Observation Officer and his party; and the engineers group—a total of thirty-eight. All three platoon commanders were with the others, who therefore would not be short of leaders in finding their way.

Hearing Japanese near by, but deciding against attack in the circumstances, Duffy headed south, towards the railway line. Soon after the party moved off wild firing broke out and continued for about fifteen minutes. The party formed a circle and went to ground, but although they were not seen by the Japanese, Lance-Sergeant Nagle,[3] the company orderly room sergeant, was killed by the fire and one man was wounded. In the course of their further endeavours to rejoin their battalion the party came

---

[9] A. W. Penfold, W. C. Bayliss, and K. E. Crispin, *Galleghan's Greyhounds, The Story of the 2/30th Australian Infantry Battalion* (1949), p. 89.

[1] Sgt A. A. Doolan, NX36597; 2/30 Bn. Shop assistant; of Stawell, Vic; b. Baan Baa, NSW, 23 Dec 1907. Died while prisoner 9 Nov 1943.

[2] Capt P. D. Kearney, NX70437; 2/30 Bn. Traveller; of Cremorne, NSW; b. Cremorne, 25 Jul 1917.

[3] L-Sgt A. G. Nagle, NX7951; 2/30 Bn. School teacher; of Bellingen, NSW; b. Cowra, NSW, 22 Aug 1909. Killed in action 14 Jan 1942.

under fire of artillery where it was shelling the enemy; but with the exception of a patrol led by Garner, they reported to battalion headquarters at noon on 16th January.

Jones, with the rearguard, followed Geikie's platoon from the ambush position; and both thought they were following Duffy. They were in fact following Head, who had continued the original eastward movement through the jungle with a group including part of 12 Platoon, and was unaware of the presence of the others. When the pain he was suffering compelled Head to give up the lead, Doolan took over and brought the column out of the jungle next morning. It was then discovered that Jones and Geikie were part of the column, and Jones took charge. Two attacks by parties of Japanese were beaten off, the latter one by the rearguard comprising two sections of Jones' platoon under Corporal Huntley.[4] Of these men, six were missing when the column reached the battalion perimeter during the morning.[5] "We'll pin them down—you get back," they had said.

Garner's patrol, which had been sent by Duffy to warn battalion headquarters of his party's approach, comprised Garner, Lance-Corporal Hann[6] and Private Noble.[7] In an encounter with a Japanese patrol Noble killed three of its members with his machine-gun. He and Garner reached brigade headquarters on 16th January but Hann, who became separated from them by jumping into a river when he was fired upon, was captured and imprisoned in a hut. Released by a Tamil—of whom many were employed at the time in Malaya—he donned a turban and other Indian clothing and made his way to the house of a second Tamil, who gave him food and cigarettes. With two other Tamils as guides, Hann set off again and eventually met an Australian patrol, hurriedly pulled off his turban, and was recognised.

Tension at battalion headquarters naturally had increased as it was realised that the signal lines to Duffy's company had been cut, and that action of some kind probably was in progress. Patrols were sent out to endeavour to restore communications. The patrols became involved in several clashes with enemy troops and one, led by Lance-Corporal Heckendorf,[8] was cut off but rejoined the battalion later with valuable information obtained behind the enemy lines. It was discovered that the Japanese were in control of the Gemencheh ambush area (where they restored the

---

[4] Cpl N. L. S. Huntley, NX27854; 2/30 Bn. Station manager; of Hay and Booligal, NSW; b. Summer Hill, NSW, 14 Aug 1908.

[5] The missing men were: L-Cpl C. F. Mulligan (of Paddington, NSW), Ptes F. G. Collett (of South Hurstville, NSW), J. R. Bland (of Rose Bay, NSW), T. C. Trevor (of Seaforth, NSW), E. W. Sams (of Forbes, NSW), and J. R. Cochrane (of Brookvale, NSW).

[6] L-Cpl I. G. Hann, NX25741; 2/30 Bn. Barman; of Moree, NSW; b. Moree, 9 May 1917. Died while prisoner of war, 18 Feb 1945.

[7] Pte J. A. Noble, NX37430; 2/30 Bn. Labourer; of Geurie, NSW; b. Dubbo, NSW, 27 Apr 1914.

[8] Sgt E. E. Heckendorf, NX36791; 2/30 Bn. Station hand; of Lockhart, NSW; b. Lockhart, 11 Apr 1910.

bridge for traffic within six hours of its having been blown up[9]) and were advancing in force, with tanks, towards the battalion's main position.

Preceded by a storm of machine-gun fire, two Japanese tanks appeared soon after 9 a.m. on 15th January near the road-block in front of Lamacraft's company, but turned tail under assault by anti-tank guns. Next came three tanks—two medium and one light—which fired along the road. Armour-piercing shells either passed through or ricochetted off them, but when high-explosive shells also were used the first tank was set ablaze, the second one was disabled, and the third towed it away. The blazing tank served as a screen for three more tanks which then appeared, soon followed by another. The tanks, and machine-guns dismounted from two of them, were quickly sending a stream of fire along the road. This was supplemented by fire from mortars and machine-guns brought up by Japanese infantry, but the Australian mortar and anti-tank fire was so effective that the first of the four tanks was hit, the second disabled, the third set on fire, and the fourth wrecked by a mortar bomb which exploded after entering its turret. Artillery now opened fire on the troops in the Japanese rear. The Japanese still pressed forward along the road and commenced flanking movements, but the combined effect of the Australian artillery and infantry fire was too much for them. The assault was over within an hour, at heavy cost to the enemy. It was during the ensuing lull that Jones' party rejoined the battalion, with its stimulating news of the success of the Gemencheh ambush.

To Galleghan, with the information now available to him, this seemed to be the time for an attack which he had planned. Melville's company was chosen to advance on a hill occupied by the Japanese about 1,000 yards from the company's position, hold it if possible till dusk, and then return. As reports flowed in to battalion headquarters it was realised that the Japanese were massing much more quickly than had been thought likely. Their use of tanks, so soon after the Gemencheh bridge had been blown, added to the danger that the battalion would be overpowered or cut off if it attempted to hold on to its advanced position. It was accordingly decided that a plan for the battalion's withdrawal behind the Sungei Gemas should be put into effect that evening.

The struggle was not only between ground forces, with the Australians outnumbered: taking advantage of their command of the air, Japanese planes were bombing Gemas, and suddenly dive bombers pounded battalion headquarters. Except at the command post, no trenches had been dug, and the men could only lie on the ground as the bombs exploded around them. A divisional signals wireless truck attached to the battalion was destroyed, but from it emerged an unscathed signaller holding a broken buzzer key.[1]

---

[9] The speed with which the Japanese repaired the bridge was attributed to there being a sawmill near by, from which ready-cut timber was available. The work could, of course, have been hampered and perhaps made impossible by artillery fire but for the failure of the signals from the ambush area and consequent uncertainty at battalion headquarters as to what had happened and the whereabouts of Duffy's company.

[1] Suspecting that the Japanese had been able to locate battalion headquarters by the wireless signals from it, Galleghan abandoned use of radio telegraphy for short-distance communications.

The dive bombers next attacked in the area held by Anderson's company, apparently seeking to destroy anti-tank guns and 25-pounders, but without success:

> At fifteen minutes to one o'clock a great cry went up from the platoon on my left, and there on the flank was "Don" Company advancing in open formation across the clearing. It was magnificent to see them, each man in place, with his rifle held high across his body, walking forward as if on a training exercise. . . . We had prepared for this for two years, and as we others watched we yelled and roared with excitement to see "Don" Company doing its job so well.[2]

While Melville was leading his men forward a report was received that the Japanese were only 300 yards ahead of the start-line. It was by then too late to change the plan, and the company was soon under heavy fire from ground and air. Although the supporting artillery fire was landing too far behind the Japanese, the company pushed them back and inflicted heavy casualties on them. Melville was soon wounded, but directed his men until they were out of range of his voice, when Captain Morrison[3] took command.

Thick undergrowth hampered the advance of Lieutenants Parry's[4] and Donohue's[5] platoons on the left flank and gave the Japanese ideal cover. Privates Dever,[6] Hilton[7] and Williams[8] of Parry's platoon, using bakelite grenades and then their bayonets, captured two Japanese guns and destroyed their crews. Private Beattie,[9] racing towards a Japanese machine-gun which was holding up Lieutenant Hendy's[1] platoon on the right flank, was killed within twenty yards of the gun. The platoon was temporarily surprised by fire from Japanese perched in rubber trees around them, but it was not until the men came under cross-fire and were confronted by several tanks that their attack was halted and they withdrew. When they met Parry's platoon it was making headway, but as the tanks now were a serious threat Morrison ordered the company to return to its former position.

In carrying out a supporting attack by Anderson's company Lieutenant Clarke's[2] platoon had been forced to ground. Lieutenant Booth,[3] com-

---

[2] Sgt S. F. Arneil, of Anderson's company, in *Stand To*, Jan-Feb 1954.

[3] Capt R. H. K. Morrison, NX12519; 2/30 Bn. Bank officer; of Mosman, NSW; b. Summer Hill, NSW, 1 Mar 1916.

[4] Lt K. W. Parry, NX12541; 2/30 Bn. Bank officer; of Cremorne, NSW; b. Orange, NSW, 5 Jan 1922.

[5] Capt K. G. C. Donohue, NX70451; 2/30 Bn. Circulation manager; of Randwick, NSW; b. Sydney, 26 May 1919. Died 20 Oct 1950.

[6] Pte L. C. Dever, NX46711; 2/30 Bn. Station hand; of Greta, NSW; b. Rix's Creek, NSW, 1 Mar 1912.

[7] Pte E. P. Hilton, NX37604; 2/30 Bn. Labourer; of Glen Innes, NSW; b. Tenterfield, NSW, 27 Mar 1922.

[8] Pte D. H. Williams, NX36593; 2/30 Bn. Labourer; of Leeton, NSW; b. Cootamundra, NSW, 11 Apr 1902. Missing presumed died 11 Feb 1942.

[9] Pte R. G. Beattie, NX47652; 2/30 Bn. Labourer; of Greta, NSW; b. Noonan Flat, NSW, 6 Jul 1913. Killed in action 15 Jan 1942.

[1] Lt L. F. G. Hendy, NX70443; 2/30 Bn. Steel salesman; of Edgecliff, NSW; b. Strathfield, NSW, 21 Apr 1918.

[2] Lt G. R. Clarke, NX70442; 2/30 Bn. Bank officer; of Concord, NSW; b. Waverley, NSW, 14 Nov 1917.

[3] Lt L. H. Booth, NX70440; 2/30 Bn. Pay clerk; of Coogee, NSW; b. Coogee, 16 Apr 1919.

manding a platoon which gave covering fire, had been wounded and two sections of Booth's platoon led by the company's second-in-command, Lieutenant Boss,[4] had also encountered tanks. Both these sections had therefore returned to their original positions, but not before there had been some very spirited action.

> Two-thirds of the way to our goal (wrote a section leader) the machine-gun fire, though still badly aimed, suddenly increased. "Don" Company having now withdrawn to the left, all the Japanese fire-power available was concentrated on our front. Behind us the second-in-command of our company brought up another platoon which traversed the Japanese front from the right of the road and stopped some of the barrage. At the same time the sounds of tanks moving up to confront us could be clearly heard. . . . Not hearing the order to withdraw being shouted by the platoon commander at the rear, we kept moving forward, and forty yards from the fence across the front, came upon four men of "Don" Company, three of them wounded, with a little red-haired fellow lying guard over them. They had all been caught on the fence, which was high and thick at this point. It was obvious to us then that we would have to return.[5]

Directed by Major Ball, a troop of guns of the 30th Battery, which had been placed forward of Anderson's company, was firing over open sights while these withdrawals were occurring, and probably was responsible for keeping the Japanese tanks in check.

The counter-attack appeared to have surprised the Japanese and to have forestalled an attack by them. One of the most notable of many individual acts arising from the engagement was performed by Corporal Abbotts.[6] Although himself badly wounded in the chest during an attack on a machine-gun post, he carried a wounded man back to the aid post.

Other air attacks were made during the morning, on battalion headquarters and company areas. Early in the afternoon, to the accompaniment of heavy mortar fire and a final air attack, tanks moved against Lamacraft's company. As another signal line had been cut, the company could not ask battalion headquarters for mortar fire, and the tanks were protected by trees from the anti-tank guns; but they were spiritedly attacked with hand grenades and bullets from the cover of trees and logs in the course of a running fight. Lieutenant Clemens,[7] shot through the heart, was the first of the battalion's officers to be killed in the campaign. The fire from the tanks was wild and largely ineffective, and they withdrew.

Valuable aid to the infantrymen had been given throughout the day by the mortars under Captain Howells,[8] whose three sections, acting on information from the forward companies and from Private Reid[9] of the mortar platoon from his observation post in a tree, had been remarkably

---
[4] Capt J. A. Boss, NX12540; 2/30 Bn. Clerk; of Sydney; b. Sydney, 16 Jun 1918.
[5] Sgt S. F. Arneil in *Stand To*, Jan-Feb 1954.
[6] Sgt F. Abbotts, NX46176; 2/30 Bn. Timber carrier; of Taree, NSW; b. Birmingham, England, 23 Aug 1901.
[7] Lt P. W. Clemens, NX32588; 2/30 Bn. Public servant; of Canberra; b. Melbourne, 9 Jun 1919. Killed in action 15 Jan 1942.
[8] Capt E. R. Howells, NX12535; 2/30 Bn. Bank officer; of Sydney; b. Narrogin, WA, 17 Jan 1914.
[9] Pte K. S. Reid, NX50207; 2/30 Bn. Salesman; of Croydon, NSW; b. Stanmore, NSW, 7 Jan 1920. Died while prisoner of war 30 Sep 1943.

accurate. The medical officer, Captain Taylor,[1] and his men had worked bravely in rescuing the wounded under fire. The Red Cross symbol on the ambulances brought forward for the purpose was respected by the Japanese.

Owing to the rapidly mounting strength of the Japanese on the immediate front, the battalion began to withdraw in mid-afternoon. Although they were being fired at by a Japanese tank over open sights, and were also under heavy mortar fire, Bren carriers under Captain Tompson[2] persisted, until they were ordered to withdraw, in attempts to pull out anti-tank guns. They then picked up other weapons, walking wounded, and a section of Lamacraft's company, on their way back to Gemas. Heavy mud had bogged anti-tank and field guns, and only one—a 25-pounder—was saved. Most of the trucks in the area were got out, several (carrying ammunition) under fire. Driver Pearce[3] was killed when a cannon shell hit his truck, but Warrant-Officer Schofield[4] kept the vehicle under control. Galleghan ordered Melville, Booth and three others, all wounded, into his car and himself moved on foot, accompanied by his Intelligence officer, Lieutenant Eaton,[5] with Lamacraft's company, which was the last out. The car was fired on from the air and one of its occupants was again hit. Melville maintained pressure on the man's severed artery while Booth, wounded in one leg, stood on the running board to maintain a lookout for planes.

In the two days' action the battalion's casualties were one officer and sixteen other ranks killed, nine men missing and four officers and fifty-one others wounded. The battalion had taken heavy toll of the enemy, and although the withdrawal took place in daylight, a clean break was made. The behaviour of the Australians under intense fire did great credit to them and to their training.

Japanese losses in the 35-day advance to Kuala Lumpur had been light. They had captured big quantities of material and a large number of prisoners. The *5th Division* was tired, however, and was therefore given a few days' rest. What was known as the *Mukaide Force* was thereupon organised to come forward as the spearhead of the advance along the trunk road. It consisted of the *1st Tank Regiment* with an infantry battalion and machine-gun and artillery support. Unable to overcome the resistance of the Australians and having suffered heavy casualties, it was brought on 15th January under command of the *9th Brigade* which threw additional strength—evidently the *11th Infantry Regiment*—into the battle. Further to force the issue the *21st Brigade* (*21st* and *42nd Regiments*)

---

[1] Capt J. L. Taylor, MC, NX70453; RMO 2/30 Bn. Medical practitioner; of Roseville, NSW; b. Sydney, 28 Mar 1914.

[2] Capt R. C. Tompson, NX12542; 2/30 Bn. Bank officer; of Manly, NSW; b. Manly, 8 Dec 1913.

[3] Dvr T. F. Pearce, NX47566; 2/30 Bn. Labourer; of Rappville, NSW; b. Lismore, NSW, 29 Jul 1917. Killed in action 15 Jan 1942.

[4] WO2 P. A. Schofield, NX27012; 2/30 Bn. Bank clerk; of Manly, NSW; b. Werris Creek, NSW, 1 May 1907.

[5] Lt R. W. Eaton, MBE, NX70758; 2/30 Bn. Shipping clerk; of Mosman, NSW; b. Lismore, NSW, 26 May 1918.

were detoured by a southern road leading to the left flank and rear of the 27th Australian Brigade. These moves were testimony to the blows struck by the Australian 2/30th Battalion in the role to which it had been assigned of checking the enemy at the trunk road approach to the Westforce positions in Johore.

Enemy aircraft had continued throughout the first fortnight of January to support Japanese ground forces both directly and indirectly. Though the effect on the morale of insufficiently trained troops in the defending forces was severe, they had caused few casualties and little material damage, and had missed big opportunities, such as the withdrawal through Segamat, of delivering what might have been shattering blows. Raids on Singapore Island, particularly on Tengah airfield west of the trunk road into the city, had been intensified. The defending aircraft, inferior in both numbers and performance, had been employed mainly in protection of the island, patrols of the sea approaches to eastern Malaya and northern Sumatra, a raid on railway yards and shipping at Singora on 7th January, and attacks on the airfields at Ipoh, Sungei Patani, and Kuantan in Japanese possession. British hopes that sufficient time would be gained to deploy reinforcements in Johore had been stimulated by the safe arrival on 13th January of a convoy of large American vessels bringing the 53rd British Infantry Brigade Group of the 18th British Division, the British 6th Heavy and 35th Light Anti-aircraft Regiments, the 85th British Anti-tank Regiment, and fifty-one Hurricane fighter aircraft. A swarm of Japanese aircraft appeared as the convoy neared Singapore, but stormy weather had closed in, giving the ships far more protection than the aircraft at the disposal of Malaya Command could supply. The British brigade group which included three battalions—2/Cambridgeshire, 5/Norfolk, and 6/Norfolk—135th Field Regiment and 287th Field Company, was without its transport or its guns, which were following in another convoy. These needs had therefore to be met from local resources. Percival hoped to use the 53rd Brigade, if time permitted, to release the 22nd Australian Brigade for Bennett's command; but having been at sea for eleven weeks, the 53rd Brigade was not considered to be fit for immediate employment. Arrival of the Hurricanes was hailed in some quarters as the beginning of the end of Japanese air supremacy. The machines were, however, in crates, and accompanied by only twenty-four pilots, and these lacked experience of Malayan conditions. Time was needed for assembling and conditioning the aircraft and giving experience to the pilots.

CHAPTER 12

THE BATTLE OF MUAR

THE blow dealt to the enemy by the Australians at Gemas, following so closely upon the arrival of the reinforcement convoy on 13th January, was seized upon as a means of reviving confidence in the outcome of the struggle for Malaya. A speaker over Singapore radio declared flamboyantly that the news gave good reason to believe that the tide of battle was on the turn, "with the A.I.F. as our seawall against the vicious flood". General Bennett was quoted in the *Singapore Times* of 16th January as saying that his troops were confident that they would not only stop the Japanese advance, but put them on the defensive. This elation was natural but short-lived, for disturbing reports soon began to come in from the left flank of Westforce in the Muar area (allotted, as has been shown, to the 45th Indian Brigade).

Two battalions of the 45th had been placed, at Bennett's instructions, on this flank, along the Sungei Muar's winding course, which on a map resembles an uncompleted edge of a jigsaw puzzle. The battalions were the 4/9th Jats, with one company in each of three areas—Grisek, Panchor, and Jorak—and fighting patrols north of the river; and the 7/6th Rajputana Rifles, from Jorak to the mouth of the river, with two companies north of it. The sectors were of fifteen and nine miles respectively. The 5/18th Royal Garhwal was in reserve based on Bakri, with a company forward at Simpang Jeram on the inland road from Muar, and a detachment south of Parit Jawa, where another road came in from the coast to Bakri. The brigade was allotted the 65th Australian Battery (Major Julius[1]) of the 2/15th Field Regiment as support.

The main crossing of the Muar, from the network of roads in Malacca, was near the river mouth, by ferry across a wide expanse of water to the township of Muar. The river flowed through thick jungle and inevitably only sections of it were manned. The possibility of enemy coastal landings between Muar and Batu Pahat to the south was another hazardous element in the situation. Both the road along the coast and the one inland through Bakri offered access from Muar to the trunk road at Yong Peng, far to the rear of the main body of Westforce. The disposition of two companies of the Rajputana Rifles on the far side of the river no doubt reflected Bennett's policy of "aggressive defence" and his enthusiasm for ambushing the enemy, but it was at the expense of the forward line south of the river. However, the fact that he assigned to this inexperienced brigade the task of protecting his left flank seems clearly to indicate that he did not expect any strong enemy thrust in this direction; and as General Wavell had ordered that the 22nd Australian Brigade should join the remainder of its

---
[1] Maj W. W. Julius, DX141; 2/15 Fd Regt. Regular soldier; of Darwin; b. Grafton, NSW, 17 Jan 1909. Killed in action 19 Jan 1942.

division as soon as it could be relieved by troops from Singapore Island, he could regard the brigade as a prospective reserve.

On 15th January, the day on which the battle of Gemas ended, General Barstow, keenly cooperative but still uneasy about the prospect, strongly urged General Bennett to prepare lines of retreat. Bennett, who had been caustic in his comments about the rapid movements down the peninsula since the Japanese first struck, again told him there would be no retreat. Bennett felt confident that the performance at Gemas could be repeated at Batu Anam, which he expected would be the next point of contact with the enemy force advancing along the trunk road. Aircraft had reported congested Japanese traffic north of Tampin, where the road struck inland to Gemas (but also near a road and rail junction which gave access to Malacca, and the coastal road to Muar). At Bennett's request, Australian airmen attacked the area that day and the next, aided on the second day by six Glenn Martin bombers operated by Dutch airmen stationed with the Australians at Sembawang, on Singapore Island.

Successive Japanese air attacks on Muar from 11th January were followed by the appearance on the 15th of Japanese troops at the northern approach to the ferry. They were fired upon by the 65th Battery, but the telephone line to the battery's observation post on the far side of the river was severed, thus handicapping the battery in its task.[2] One of its guns, in charge of Sergeant Buckman,[3] was thereupon brought to the southern end of the ferry crossing and fired over open sights. A Rajput company, also on the far side, reported just before its telephone line failed that Japanese were coming down the road from Malacca. The battalion's advanced headquarters in the township found itself out of telephone contact with two other companies also, and with rear headquarters near Bakri.

As there were no bridges in the vicinity of Muar and as all boats thought likely to be useful to the enemy had been removed from the northern bank, the river presented a difficult obstacle, and some 800 rounds of harassing fire during the night by a troop of the Australian gunners commanded by Captain Steele[4] were a further deterrent. The Japanese nevertheless made rapid progress on the 16th January. Two guns under Lieutenant Withycombe[5] were at one stage during the afternoon blazing over open sights from a position taken up on the southern bank at landing craft which appeared at the mouth of the river. Although these withdrew, enemy troops meanwhile had made a crossing upstream. The Rajput

---

[2] Lt J. N. Shearer (of Lindfield, NSW), subsequently posted missing, was in charge of the post. His driver, Gnr H. M. M. Fisher (Dural, NSW), was at the ferry crossing with a prisoner suspected of aiding the enemy when he was fired upon. He dived into the river, and hid all day under the ferry ramp. At nightfall he swam to the southern bank, and supplied valuable information to his unit.

[3] Sgt G. I. Buckman, NX24072; 2/15 Fd Regt. Clerk; of Haberfield, NSW; b. Bowraville, NSW, 4 Jul 1912. Killed in action 18 Jan 1942.

[4] Maj R. E. Steele, EM, NX34686; 2/15 Fd Regt 1940-42; with guerillas in Philippines 1943-44; Aust Army representative Allied Air Forces, Brisbane 1944-45. Commercial traveller; of Burwood, NSW; b. Eastwood, NSW, 25 Mar 1915.

[5] Lt P. S. Withycombe, EM, NX70315; 2/15 Fd Regt. Solicitor; of Mayfield, NSW; b. Melbourne, 27 Jul 1916.

company east of Muar was attacked, and though the flanking company whose positions extended to the river mouth was sent to its aid, a company of Japanese reached the township from the east and overwhelmed battalion headquarters. Both the Rajput companies north of the river had been lost, and few men of the other two companies got back. During the night the remnant of the battalion withdrew down the coast to Parit Jawa, and thence to Bakri. The Rajput commander, his second-in-command, and all his company commanders had been killed or were missing.

Meanwhile, gunners under Lieutenant McLeod[6] on their way with guns for attachment to the advanced headquarters of the 5/18th Royal Garhwal at Simpang Jeram had been ambushed near the headquarters early on the 16th, and one gun and three men were lost. The Garhwalis were attacked the same day, soon after 11 a.m., and moved off the road into the shelter of rubber trees. Close fighting followed, in which hand grenades and bayonets were used; but after a costly and unsuccessful counter-attack at 1 p.m. a withdrawal was ordered. By this time the officer commanding the force was among the killed. Communications to the rear had failed soon after the attack opened, and before the situation became serious. The 4/9th Jats on the right were not attacked, but having discovered that the enemy had crossed the river their commander withdrew the forward companies and concentrated on the road from Panchor to Muar. The Australian battery stuck to its task at Muar until 8.30 p.m., then made for Bakri by the coast road through Parit Jawa. The Japanese were then free to continue their advance by both this road and the one through Simpang Jeram.

The enemy force used to achieve this result was, as is now known, the *Guards Division*, which had occupied the town of Malacca on 14th January. Although he had intended to rest his troops at this stage, General Nishimura concluded that if he could quickly overcome resistance in the Muar-Batu Pahat area it would greatly assist the Japanese forces on the trunk road, and be a triumph for his division. Thus spurred, he decided to press on, with the *4th Guards Regiment* less one battalion on the right and the *5th Guards Regiment* on the left. The former was to occupy the attention of the forces holding the town of Muar while the latter made an upstream crossing of the river during the night and attacked from the east. The *4th* was then to make for Batu Pahat along the coast road while the *5th* thrust along the inland road to Yong Peng. The other battalion of the *4th Regiment* was to go by sea down the coast, land between Batu Pahat and Rengit and conceal itself until the time came to cut the British line of withdrawal from Batu Pahat down the coast road.

The Rajputs forward of the Muar were quickly trapped and overcome, but Nishimura was badly worried by the problem of how to cross the river. It was readily solved by the *5th Regiment* using a number of small boats, taken from ricefields, to cross to larger craft on the opposite side. These craft were then brought back and used to transport larger parties of men. By dawn a sufficient number had been ferried over to continue the advance. Once the crossing had been made the untried Indians whom they encountered were no match for the *élite* troops of the Japanese Army, especially as the secrecy and suddenness of the manoeuvre took

---

[6] Lt R. McLeod, NX70902; 2/15 Fd Regt. Clerk; of Bondi, NSW; b. Bondi, 24 Feb 1920.

the defenders by surprise. The boats which had been collected were used again for the main crossing at the mouth of the Muar, made without opposition on 17th January.

Bakri, headquarters of the 45th Indian Brigade, and only 30 miles from the trunk road at Yong Peng, was now threatened. Still worse, Japanese were reported late on 16th January to have landed south-west of the town of Batu Pahat (in keeping with the enemy plan just outlined) and to have moved inland. They were thus a threat to the 45th Brigade from its rear, and to Westforce communications, as well as to the immediate locality. On the east coast, strong Japanese patrols were being encountered north of Endau[7]—clear warning of attack upon the Australian 22nd Brigade in the Mersing area. Because of the collapse of resistance on the Muar, Bennett decided on the evening of 16th January to send his reserve battalion, the 2/29th (Lieut-Colonel Robertson), less one company and a platoon, to reinforce the Muar front instead of using it as he had planned to relieve the 2/30th after its action at Gemas. Unaware of the extent of the enemy forces in the Muar area, he directed that it should be used to counter-attack towards Muar, and gave it a troop of 2/4th Australian Anti-Tank Regiment and one of armoured cars from the Loyals for what he considered good measure. In briefing the officers concerned, he said that his information was that Muar had been taken with a force of about 200 men. He emphasised that the Muar-Yong Peng road was vital, and that should the enemy be encountered in strength it must be held for seven days to enable the forces north of Yong Peng to be withdrawn.

Dealing with the chessboard problems confronting him, General Percival decided that he would allot to the III Corps the task of protecting Westforce communications. He extended the corps' responsibilities to the trunk road from Ayer Hitam to Yong Peng and thence to Batu Pahat, and ordered the newly-arrived 53rd Brigade Group to the Ayer Hitam area. There, on 17th January, it came under corps command and was allotted to General Key, then commanding the 11th Indian Division.[8] The 6/Norfolk was sent to hold the defile between Bukit Pelandok on the south and Bukit Belah on the north, near where the road from Yong Peng branched south-westward to Batu Pahat and north-westward to Muar. The 2/Cambridgeshire went to relieve the garrison at Batu Pahat. From Bukit Pelandok to Batu Pahat and to Muar were long stretches of road which would need constant and effective patrolling as a precaution against enemy penetration between the forces disposed at those places.

At a conference between Percival, Bennett, and Key at noon on 17th January, the question of withdrawal from Segamat, consequent upon the situation at Muar, was discussed. Largely on the ground that this would be damaging to morale it was decided to try to hold both the Muar and

---
[7] Contact by a 2/19th Battalion patrol (22nd Australian Brigade) had been made at 11 a.m. on 14th January, and thus constituted the first encounter with the enemy by the Australians in Johore.
[8] General Paris had reverted to command of the 12th Brigade, then in Singapore for reorganisation.

the Segamat areas. Percival ordered that the 2/19th Australian Battalion at Jemaluang be relieved immediately by the 5/Norfolk and go to Muar, where it would operate as part of Westforce. Bennett was disappointed that the 53rd Brigade was not used to relieve the whole of the 22nd Australian Brigade of its tasks on the east coast, but Percival held that, apart from any other reason, there was not time in the existing situation to carry out the relief. Because of the inexperience of the 5/Norfolk, Lieut-Colonel Anderson, commanding the 2/19th Battalion, left his second-in-command, Major Oakes,[9] with three other officers and several N.C.O's to help the newcomers to take over their positions.[1] It soon became evident in the conduct of the advanced party of the Norfolks that they were ill-fitted by their training for warfare in Malaya.[2]

Brigadier Duncan (45th Brigade) meanwhile had been ordered by Bennett to clear the Muar area of the enemy as soon as possible. Bennett's assessment of the situation on the information available to him at this stage was evident in an order which required that the 2/29th Battalion should revert to the main body of Westforce "on completion of immediate task".[3] Duncan had allocated defensive positions about a mile from Bakri on both the Muar and Parit Jawa roads, and planned to launch counter-attacks once the isolated 4/9th Jats had come in and the Australians had arrived. When the 2/29th got to Bakri during the afternoon of the 17th the position on the Muar road was held by the 5/18th Garhwal, but it was to move by night to Parit Jawa.

After interviewing Duncan and discussing the situation with Major Julius of the 65th Battery, which was now available to support the 2/29th Battalion, Robertson decided to rest his men during the early part of the night about a mile and a half forward of Bakri, and then to attempt to capture Simpang Jeram at daylight on the 18th. He quickly gained evidence of the presence of the enemy, for an armoured car sent forward to reconnoitre the road returned with the information that it had been fired upon at a Japanese road-block about two miles forward of the battalion's position. A patrol clash followed this incident, and by 7 p.m. the forward troops were under heavy mortar fire. A small force of Japanese then arrived, and in the darkness hand grenades and bayonets were used in disposing of them. The Garhwalis were nearing Parit Jawa village when they were ambushed and dispersed. Only some 400 men straggled back to a position on the Parit Jawa road a mile from Bakri held by remnants of the 7/6th Rajputana Rifles. About midnight Julius reported to Robert-

---

[9] Lt-Col R. F. Oakes, NX12525. (1st AIF: 3rd MG Bn and AFC.) 2/19 Bn 1940-42; CO 2/26 Bn 1942. Grazier; of Maryvale, NSW; b. Manly, NSW, 19 Feb 1896.

[1] The move by 5/Norfolk commenced, but was later cancelled.

[2] "They were a fine body of men," wrote an Australian officer later, "but almost dazed by the position in which they found themselves. Their training had been for open warfare, and not the very close warfare of the Malayan countryside. They demonstrated the unreality of their approach to the situation by lighting up all the buildings in the area, stringing their transport along highly vulnerable and prominent crossroads, and by the CO telling the second-in-command, in my presence, that his first job was to get the mess going." The 2/19th Battalion's diarist recorded: "Their personal gear was new to us; trunks, valises, baths, etc., all in the mud, much to the amusement of our lads."

[3] Westforce Operation Instruction No. 1.

son the withdrawal of the Garhwalis from the Parit Jawa area, and asked for protection for his guns. Robertson consequently sent Captain Sumner's[4] company of the 2/29th (minus a platoon which had been left in the Gemas area) to a position covering the junction at Bakri of the Parit Jawa and Muar roads. A troop of the gunners, however, came under counter-battery fire about 1 a.m. on 18th January. The fire was so intense and accurate that one of the guns was disabled, an ammunition trailer was set on fire by direct hits, and the troop had to withdraw.

With the rear of the 2/29th Battalion's main position threatened by penetration from the coast via Parit Jawa, five Japanese light tanks approached the position frontally at 6.45 a.m. unaware that an anti-tank gun awaited them at each end of a cutting through which the Muar road ran. Solid armour-piercing shells were first used against the tanks, but it was found that these went straight through them and out the far side. The tanks continued to advance, firing with all guns as they came. The leading tank was level with the foremost anti-tank gun when the gun sergeant (Thornton[5]) gave a notable exhibition of courage and coolness. Turning his back on the other tanks, he fired high-explosive shells into the first three as they went down the road. When the other tanks entered the battalion perimeter they came under fire of the rear gun also. All were disabled. Although he was wounded in the engagement, Thornton prepared his gun for further action, and soon three more tanks approached the position.

> A couple attempted to turn and make a get-away (wrote Lieutenant Ben Hackney[6]) but still those boys with the anti-tank guns were sending a stream of shells into them. At last they could not move forward any further and became as pill-boxes surrounded, sending fire in all directions; until one by one they were smashed, set on fire, and rendered useless and uninhabitable. There came then from the tanks sounds which resembled an Empire Day celebration as the ammunition within them burnt, and cracked with sharp bursts, and hissed, with every now and again a louder explosion as larger ammunition ignited.

Those of their crews who had survived the shell fire were finished off by bullets and grenades. The loss of eight tanks by the enemy produced a lull, but the company in the left forward position then came under heavy automatic fire and sniping from the branches of trees by Japanese who apparently had infiltrated during the night. First one, then two more carriers came forward, and though their armour failed to resist Japanese bullets and nearly every man in them was wounded, they silenced the enemy machine-guns. Behind these were Japanese infantry, but they were held in check by the Australians.

---

[4] Capt A. B. Sumner, VX39013; 2/29 Bn. Butcher; of Geelong West, Vic; b. Geelong, 5 Jan 1915. Missing presumed died 13 Sep 1944.

[5] L-Sgt C. W. Thornton, VX42501; 2/4 A-Tk Regt. Farmer; of Berrigan, NSW; b. Berrigan, 10 Apr 1918.
The guns were part of a troop of four, commanded by Lieutenant R. M. McCure (North Brighton, Vic) of the 2/4th Australian Anti-Tank Regt.

[6] Lt B. C. Hackney, NX71148; 2/29 Bn. Grazier; of Bathurst, NSW; b. Sydney, 2 Mar 1916.

Meanwhile Anderson and his 2/19th Battalion, 700 strong,[7] preceded by its carriers (Lieutenant Pickup[8]) were met at Yong Peng by Colonel Thyer, General Bennett's senior staff officer, and joined by a troop of British anti-tank guns. Anderson, Thyer, and others comprising a reconnaissance party went ahead with Major Arthur Maxwell, sent to guide them to 45th Brigade headquarters.

During a conference with Thyer, Anderson, and Robertson at Bakri, Brigadier Duncan received the first report to reach the British forces that the Japanese *Guards Division* had joined in the struggle for Malaya, and was being employed in the Muar area. He explained that he had sent patrols to order the Jats into Bakri as soon as possible by an estate road which joined the road to Bakri near the 2/29th Battalion's position. It

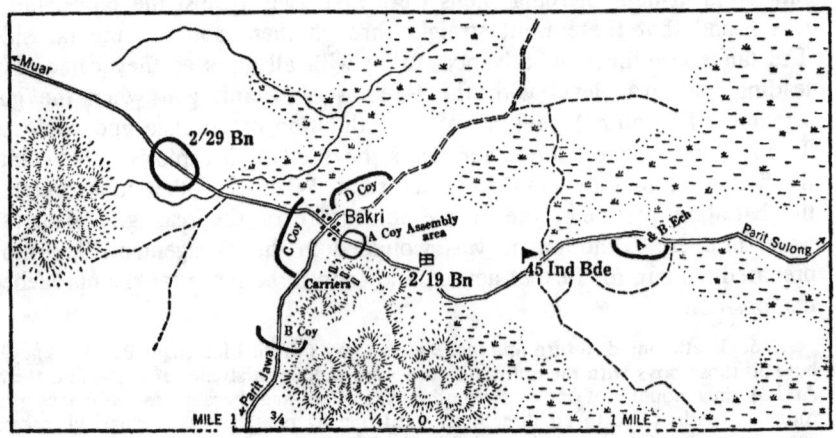

Bakri, 8 a.m. 19th January

was decided to deploy the 2/19th to add depth to the position and, when the Jats came in, to take the offensive. On his way back to Westforce headquarters Thyer came upon disconcerting evidence of unpreparedness by the Norfolks at Bukit Payong defile—transport head to tail along the road and as Thyer later described it "a sitting bird for air action".

Having left a platoon under Lieutenant Varley[9] to guard the concrete bridge over the Sungei Simpang Kiri at Parit Sulong, the 2/19th Battalion, under the battalion second-in-command, Major Vincent,[1] reached Bakri during the morning of 18th January and deployed at Bakri village and in positions near by on the roads to Parit Jawa and Muar, covered by guns of the 65th Battery. At midday an armoured car patrol sent from Bakri towards the 2/29th Battalion position reported having encountered

---

[7] "D" Company of the 2/19th comprised only one platoon and company headquarters, detachments having had to be left on the east coast.
[8] Capt A. C. Pickup, NX34741; 2/19 Bn. Signwriter; of Bathurst, NSW; b. Bathurst, 17 Feb 1910.
[9] Lt J. A. Varley, MC, NX60090; 2/19 Bn. Clerk; of Inverell, NSW; b. Inverell, 23 Sep 1920.
[1] Maj T. G. Vincent, MC, NX34967; 2/19 Bn. Barrister-at-Law; of Edgecliff, NSW; b. Sydney, 19 Nov 1905. Killed in action 9 Feb 1942.

a road-block, and having been fired upon from both sides of the road. As Robertson had been promised that Sumner's company would be returned to his positions, it was sent with carrier, armoured car, and mortar support, to dispose of the block and rejoin the battalion. Its initial attack failed but eventually, with the aid of platoons led by Lieutenant Glasson[2] and Sergeant Lloyd Davies[3] of the 2/19th Battalion, Sumner's company got through, leaving the road free of obstruction. The company found Major Olliff[4] now in command, for Robertson and a dispatch rider on whose machine the commander was riding pillion also had encountered a road-block. Although both were wounded they had managed to get to within a hundred yards of battalion headquarters before Robertson fell off. He was picked up by a carrier in charge of Lieutenant Gahan[5] which rushed to his rescue, but died half an hour later. Trucks which came through with Sumner's company were sent back to Bakri carrying wounded men.

A Jats officer reached Bakri at 4 p.m., and reported to Duncan that his battalion was six miles north-west of the village. By 5 p.m. Bakri and the 2/19th Battalion's positions were under shell fire, but nothing had been done to bring the Jats in. Anderson, chafing under the delay, which was playing into the hands of the Japanese, realised that the Jats now could not arrive in time for his battalion to take the offensive that day. He offered a jungle-trained Australian patrol to escort the Jats officer, but finally, as enemy patrols had been reported on the route he was to take, the officer's departure was delayed until early next morning. Duncan recalled to the brigade perimeter for the night those of the Rajputs and Garhwalis who were able to return. They had with them only two British officers, many had lost their equipment, and they were in poor condition for further fighting. A British field battery allotted to the 2/19th reported to Anderson during the night, but, on the ground that further artillery would be a drain on manpower for escort duties, it was ordered to rejoin the main body of Westforce. This left artillery tasks to the 65th Australian Battery which had resisted the initial attack on Muar, and was still in action.[6]

Bayonets and grenades were again successfully used in dealing with two attacks on the 2/29th Battalion's left forward troops as they were about to withdraw into night perimeter. The Japanese were dressed in an olive-green uniform and equipped with respirators, grenade dischargers, grenades and entrenching tools, and the officers carried Samurai swords. Captured Bren-type guns of Japanese calibre were found to be fitted with a bayonet

---
[2] Lt D. J. R. Glasson, NX12538; 2/19 Bn. Law student; of Double Bay, NSW; b. Blayney, NSW, 7 Aug 1920. Missing presumed died 22 Jan 1942.

[3] Sgt J. L. Davies, NX56212; 2/19 Bn. Farmer; of Brobenah, via Leeton, NSW; b. Leeton, 19 Aug 1919. Missing presumed died 22 Jan 1942.

[4] Maj S. F. Olliff, VX44193; 2/29 Bn. Manager; of Armadale, Vic; b. London, 17 Jun 1905. Killed in action 19 Jan 1942.

[5] Capt N. J. Gahan, VX39021; 2/29 Bn. Bank officer; of Eltham, Vic; b. Ivanhoe, Vic, 20 Sep 1916.

[6] The battery had fired 4,795 rounds by midnight of 18th-19th January

attachment. After the failure of these attacks, the night and the following morning were relatively quiet.

After the initial crossing of the Muar, General Nishimura had ordered his *5th Regiment*, with artillery and tank support, to attack the positions on the inland road to Bakri and cut the road immediately behind them, as quickly as possible. Perhaps under the heady influence of the success gained by Japanese troops in overcoming the defenders of Muar, a tank company advanced without infantry against the 2/29th Battalion and was wiped out. Bereft of its aid, the infantry (*III/5th Guards Battalion*) were unable to break the resistance and, as later described by Nishimura, the engagement became "severe and sanguinary".

It was not until General Percival received the news that the *Guards* were being employed in the Muar area that he fully realised the danger of the situation.[7] He learned also that a Japanese force had been seen crossing a ford some miles north of Batu Pahat; that the 6/Norfolk had been attacked from the air near Bukit Pelandok; and that the 2/Cambridgeshire had encountered enemy patrols south-west of Batu Pahat. In the Segamat sector artillery had ceaselessly pounded the enemy line of approach during the night of 15th-16th January, after the withdrawal of the 2/30th Australian Battalion to the Fort Rose Estate. Ground action on the 16th and 17th consisted chiefly of exchanges of shell fire. The Japanese were busily repairing or providing substitutes for demolished bridges along the two railway lines and the trunk road which converged at Gemas, and were also engaged in flanking movements. During the afternoon of the 17th they pressed the southern flank of the 2/30th, which was withdrawn during the night to an eastward position, nearer Batu Anam. Next day the invaders increased their artillery fire on Batu Anam and concentrated their infantry activities against the 1/13th Frontier Force Rifles astride the main road and railway thereabouts. Late in the afternoon they overran the battalion's forward positions and two guns of the 16th Australian Anti-Tank Battery were lost. Repeated air attacks were made upon townships from Batu Anam to Yong Peng, and upon the road between Gemas and Labis. By thus engaging the forces in the central sector the Japanese were gaining time for their major outflanking movements along the west coast from Muar.

General Bennett, his concern growing at the possibility of his force being cut off, obtained General Percival's assent on the afternoon of 18th January to a withdrawal behind the Sungei Segamat preparatory to consolidation farther back. Deciding that Bennett was likely to have his hands full in dealing with the situation on the trunk road and the railway, Percival placed the whole of the forces on the Muar front under command of General Heath as from 9.45 p.m. This, however, had little reality, for Heath's only means of communicating with 45th Brigade,

---

[7] Percival later explained (*The War in Malaya*, p. 228) that "throughout the campaign we were so blind from lack of ground visibility and lack of air reconnaissance that we frequently underestimated the strength of the enemy".

other than by dispatch rider,[8] was by wireless through Westforce headquarters; and the course of events was again being dictated by the enemy.

As ordered by Bennett, the withdrawal from Segamat consisted of leap-frogging moves by his 27th Brigade and the 9th Indian Division to a new line covering the trunk road and the railway at Labis, about 25 miles north of Yong Peng.

Because of the danger to Batu Pahat, General Key early on 19th January ordered the 15th Brigade (Brigadier Challen) to defend the township, and reinforced the garrison with the British Battalion. He obtained permission to move the 5/Norfolk of the 53rd Brigade, previously allocated to Jemaluang, to Ayer Hitam. With the 2/Cambridgeshire at Batu Pahat and the 5/Norfolk so dispersed, the brigade had only the 6/Norfolk at this stage with which to hold the Bukit Pelandok defile, now threatened by the Japanese move inland from near Batu Pahat. Key therefore ordered the 3/16th Punjab (about half strength) to its aid. At a conference with Heath, Bennett and Key during the afternoon of the 19th, Percival decided that the 53rd Brigade should be further reinforced by the 2/Loyals (a battalion which had not left Singapore Island throughout its training in Malaya, but had been recently allotted to the 22nd Indian Brigade from the Singapore garrison); that the 45th Brigade should be withdrawn through the 53rd Brigade to west of Yong Peng; and that the withdrawal from Segamat should continue. A company of the Loyals which had been retained to garrison Blakang Mati Island, off the southern coast of Singapore Island, was sent up to the 6/Norfolk during the day, but rejoined its battalion on the evening of 20th January.

Meanwhile the situation in the west was rapidly worsening. Brigadier Duncan intended that an attack should be made along the road to Muar during the morning of the 19th by Lieutenant-Beverley's[9] "A" Company of the 2/19th Battalion, to allow the Jats to come in and to test the strength of the enemy. The company, which occupied a rubber-planted ridge to the left and a little forward of battalion headquarters, was relieved by a section of carriers, and assembled for its task, but was kept waiting for the British anti-tank gun support allotted to it. Captain Keegan's[1] "B" Company was held in reserve at its night position on the Parit Jawa road, and Captain Snelling's[2] "C" Company was on the Muar road. Both positions were near Bakri village.

Heavy firing from the carriers was heard at 8 a.m., and they were driven from the ridge under strong attack by a force which apparently had been deployed from the Parit Jawa road east of Keegan's company. Anderson quickly gave the Japanese a taste of the tactics they themselves had been employing, first by sending two of Beverley's platoons into the

---

[8] Patrolling between the 53rd and 45th Brigades appears to have been neglected, and use of dispatch riders as a communications link with Bakri not to have been attempted at this stage.
[9] Capt F. G. Beverley, NX34902; 2/19 Bn. Orchardist; of Griffith, NSW; b. Mildura, Vic, 4 Apr 1909.
[1] Maj R. W. Keegan, NX35027; 2/19 Bn. Barrister-at-Law; of Willoughby, NSW; b. North Sydney, 31 Aug 1907. Missing presumed died 11 Feb 1942.
[2] Capt R. R. L. Snelling, NX70191; 2/19 Bn. Master printer; of Clifton Gardens, NSW; b. Wellington, NZ, 26 Dec 1900. Missing presumed died 22 Jan 1942.

fight—one, led by Lieutenant Weily,[3] to make a frontal attack, while Lieutenant Crawford[4] led another along the ridge against the enemy's right flank. When the attack had been launched, Keegan's company was moved back, parallel with the road, towards the ridge, to come in on the enemy's rear. These tactics caught the assailants on the wrong foot. Lieutenant Reynolds,[5] one of Keegan's commanders, recorded that the Japanese "literally ran round in circles". He was standing among a litter of dead around a gun position when one of the prostrate figures partly raised himself, with a grenade in one hand. Reynolds shot him, but was hit under the right arm and on the head when the grenade exploded. He urged his men on as he fell close to another badly-wounded Japanese.

> I saw him pushing his rifle laboriously towards me (wrote Reynolds afterwards), so I picked up my pistol from under me and with my left hand took careful aim and pulled the trigger for all my worth, but it would not fire. I can tell you I was extremely annoyed. Luckily my batman saw the Jap up to his tricks, so he shot him. At the same time Captain Harris,[6] 2 i/c., dashed up and kicked the rifle out of the Jap's hands.

After binding Reynolds' wounds, his batman was attacked by two Japanese wearing only short trousers. He disposed of them with two shots fired from his hip, and Reynolds was able to make his way to an aid post. The third platoon (Lieutenant Ritchie[7]) of Beverley's company was thrown in against the Japanese right flank, to complete their confusion. It joined Keegan's company in a bayonet charge and hand-to-hand fighting. The Japanese were routed, leaving some 140 dead, as against ten Australians killed and fifteen wounded, most of them in Beverley's company. While two men were searching the battlefield to see if all the Japanese were dead, and count them, a supposed corpse suddenly sprang to his feet and made a dash, unarmed, at one of them—Private "Bluey" Watkins.[8] The company diarist recorded that "Bluey", "who had done quite a lot of fighting in Sydney, threw aside his rifle and bayonet and came to grips. A good fight was witnessed for a short time until [Private] Farrel[9] came to the rescue with his .303. The explosion almost deafened Bluey, and for some time afterwards he was shouting loudly his story to his mates."

During the action, the battalion's transport sergeant (Sergeant Meal[1]) brought news that the transport, in charge of the headquarters company commander, Captain Newton,[2] and behind Bakri on the road to Parit

---

[3] Capt J. G. Weily, NX58094; 2/19 Bn. Bank clerk; of Orange, NSW; b. Orange, 10 May 1920.
[4] Lt B. D. G. Crawford, NX12601; 2/19 Bn. School teacher; of Summer Hill, NSW; b. Casino, NSW, 17 Apr 1909. Missing presumed died 22 Jan 1942.
[5] Lt P. R. Reynolds, NX12527; 2/19 Bn. Grazier; of Cumnock, NSW; b. Cumnock, 20 Aug 1917.
[6] Capt F. L. Harris, NX34662; 2/19 Bn. Grazier; of Tumut. NSW; b. Tumut, 29 Oct 1912.
[7] Lt J. M. Ritchie, NX59618; 2/19 Bn. School teacher; of Yeoval, NSW; b. Rylstone, NSW, 19 Jun 1915. Missing presumed died 9 Feb 1942.
[8] Pte J. Watkins, NX26753; 2/19 Bn. Carpenter; of Panania, NSW; b. Swansea, Wales, 28 Jan 1916. Missing presumed died 8 Feb 1942.
[9] Pte A. B. Farrel, NX35902; 2/19 Bn. Butcher; of Griffith, NSW; b. Austinmer, NSW, 17 Sep 1916.
[1] Sgt F. C. Meal, NX56207; 2/19 Bn. Motor mechanic; of Temora, NSW; b. Junee, NSW, 4 Sep 1904.
[2] Maj R. W. J. Newton, MBE, ED, NX34734; 2/19 Bn. Electrical engineer; of Petersham, NSW; b. Sydney, 22 Dec 1906.

Sulong, had been suddenly attacked by 400 to 500 Japanese, who apparently had come from the direction of Parit Jawa. They were establishing a road-block, and Meal had been seriously wounded in getting through. This wedge between the battalion and its transport threatened the line of communication of the forces in the Muar area. A section of carriers was sent to force a way through to Newton, but was unable to get past the block.

Japanese airmen scored a direct hit on brigade headquarters[3] at 10 a.m. Duncan was stunned and Major Julius, commander of the 65th Battery, was mortally wounded. All Duncan's staff, except Major R. Anderson, formerly liaison officer between III Indian Corps and Bennett, but now acting as brigade major, were killed or wounded.[4] All copies of the brigade to Westforce signals cipher were destroyed, causing delay in re-establishing signals communication. At the brigade major's request, Lieut-Colonel Anderson took command of the brigade. Responsibility was thus thrust upon this Australian battalion commander for a brigade which but for the missing Jats had practically ceased to exist except as a liability. He quickly decided that in view of the threat to the line of communication, the 2/29th must be speedily withdrawn to a position behind Bakri road junction, and the front confined to the one road leading from there back to Yong Peng. He contemplated another stand at Parit Sulong if further withdrawal became necessary. Parit Sulong lay behind eight miles of straight causeway through swampy soil devoid of cover, and three miles of road nearest the village lined with rubber trees. If the force could gain the shelter of the rubber, it might concentrate fire on enemy troops coming along the causeway.

However, although the Jats were now due, they had not arrived at Bakri, and, rather than abandon them, Anderson decided to delay withdrawal of the 2/29th Battalion for the time being. The further delay resulted in his companies becoming fully committed as the morning of the 19th wore on to meeting threats from the south and north-west. Keegan's company was again heavily attacked, but with the assistance of Bren carriers and Indian mortars manned by gunners of the 65th Battery under Lieutenant Quinlan[5] of the 2/19th, it drove the Japanese off and inflicted further substantial losses.

Meanwhile the enemy had further infiltrated between the two battalions. The long-awaited Jats, who had made a two-company attack on a small village on the 18th to drive off Japanese blocking their way, reached the

---

[3] A truck loaded with wounded from the 2/29th Battalion, including Lieutenant Hackney, was parked near brigade headquarters at the time. "Outside the brigade headquarters was an ugly sight," he wrote, "—men's bodies lying about everywhere . . .—portions of soldiers' stomachs hanging on limbs amongst the leaves of the trees—torn bloodstained limbs scattered about with only a lump of bloody meat hanging to them to indicate the body from which they were torn—just beside the road a naked waist with two twisted legs lay about two yards from a scarred bleeding head with a neck, half a chest and one arm. . . . There were some still alive but bent over, and others crawling, with every manner of injury."

[4] Anderson had volunteered to replace Duncan's former brigade major when news reached Westforce headquarters that the latter had become a casualty. He was "a tower of strength" during the subsequent withdrawal from Bakri, until killed by a bomb while firing a Bren gun at a Japanese plane.

[5] Lt J. E. Quinlan, NX35443; 2/19 Bn. Clerk and stock classer; of Cootamundra, NSW; b. Coolamon, NSW, 30 Aug 1915. Missing presumed died 22 Jan 1942.

2/29th's position early in the afternoon. They had lost contact with their transport in moving off from where they had been waiting.[6] About 200 of them came under heavy machine-gun and shell fire in the 2/29th Battalion area. Largely because of their inexperience, many were killed or wounded. Part of the Jats battalion detoured by a track through swamp past the position, but others were cut off and decided next morning to make for Yong Peng by the shortest route. Those of the Jats who mustered at Bakri numbered six officers and about 200 men. Their commander, Lieut-Colonel Williams,[7] had been killed. Anderson ordered them to form up in the brigade area so that, when others who were expected came in, assistance might be sent to Newton. Olliff was ordered to disengage from the enemy at 6 (later 6.30) p.m., and an artillery barrage to assist his battalion's withdrawal was arranged. Such reserves as Anderson possessed were sent to help resist attacks, which had reached serious proportions, on his companies. Later, after he had sized up the condition of the Jats, and when the rest of them failed to arrive, Anderson reluctantly decided that endeavours to assist Newton would have to wait until next morning.

Japanese machine-gunners were beaten off the right flank of the 2/29th Battalion after the Jats had appeared. An attack in force on the left flank followed, but the Australians chased the enemy some hundreds of yards in a counter-attack. In the course of the battalion's withdrawal Olliff and others were killed, and contact was lost with the leading company, which came under heavy machine-gun fire while crossing open ground. The main body of the battalion swung east, and reached Bakri with relatively few casualties. After an attempt to clear the road had failed, others followed them. These, however, came under artillery and mortar fire and lost direction. Comprising seven officers and 150 others in several groups, including Jats, they were eventually gathered together by the battalion's adjutant, Captain Morgan.[8] Finding themselves isolated, they set off across country towards Yong Peng. Most of them eventually fell into Japanese hands.

At Bakri that night a company commander of the 2/29th Battalion, Captain Maher,[9] took command of the battalion, comprising seven officers and 190 others, and Lieutenant Ross[1] took command of the 65th Battery. The battalion moved into the 2/19th Battalion's perimeter, on the Parit Sulong side of Bakri. After waiting for others to come in, Captain Snelling's company evacuated the village by midnight. The Japanese attempt to get through Bakri to the rear of Bennett's force on the trunk

---

[6] On finding that the Jat infantry had moved off, the officer in charge of their transport found the route they had taken had been blocked by the Japanese. After disabling the vehicles he set off with his men, guided by a Volunteer major who was familiar with the area, to try to reach the road between Bakri and Parit Sulong. With some Indians and Australians they met on the way, they succeeded in joining Anderson's column.

[7] Lt-Col J. W. Williams; CO 4/9 Jat. Regular soldier; b. 28 Nov 1899. Killed in action 18 Jan 1942.

[8] Lt-Col M. C. Morgan, VX38985; 2/29 Bn. Regular soldier; of Seymour, Vic; b. Hobart, 28 Apr 1916.

[9] Capt M. B. Maher, VX39116; 2/29 Bn. Clerk; of Essendon, Vic; b. Tungamah, Vic, 13 Nov 1910. Killed in action 21 Jan 1942.

[1] Capt J. F. Ross, MC, NX70474; 2/15 Fd Regt. Engineer; of Newcastle, NSW; b. Melbourne, 13 Dec 1912.

road had so far been thwarted, but the cost had been heavy, and both Australian battalions, with the remnants of the 45th Brigade, had an enemy road-block immediately at their rear. To make matters worse, the two forward companies of the 6/Norfolk at the Bukit Pelandok defile had been surprised and forced back during the day by Japanese who had come in from the coast, and who thereupon gained control of the road to Bakri at that point. Unless they could be dislodged, Anderson's force would be sealed off in the Bakri area. Brigadier Duke[2] of the 53rd Brigade ordered a counter-attack at dawn next day.

The now-familiar Japanese tactics, by which the defending forces on the trunk road were being moved southward by threats to their line of communication, were again succeeding despite resistance by Australian troops in the Bakri area similar to that at Gemas, and were imperilling the whole of Westforce. Having regarded the Segamat-Muar line as the last real defensive position on the peninsula, General Yamashita was agreeably surprised.

In a complicated process of withdrawal as ordered from the Segamat sector on 19th January, the 8th Indian Brigade, in covering positions behind the Sungei Muar at Buloh Kasap in the central sector, was confronted by tanks and cyclist troops on the opposite bank. Despite bridge demolitions, a party of Japanese made a crossing; but serious infiltration was prevented. At night the 9th Indian Division was withdrawn through positions behind the Sungei Segamat, to which the 27th Australian Brigade and the 5/11th Sikhs had been withdrawn. The movement was hampered and endangered by the township of Segamat having caught fire as a result of an Australian officer's attempt to prevent foodstuffs falling into Japanese hands; but the men plunged through the heat and showering sparks, and at dawn on 20th January had reached the Tenang area, midway between Segamat and Labis.

In an attempt to recapture the Bukit Pelandok defile, two companies of the 3/16th Punjab led by the battalion commander, Lieut-Colonel Moorhead, set out at 4 a.m. on 20th January to reach a company of the 6/Norfolk which had retained its position on the northern slopes of Bukit Belah, overlooking from the north the road to Parit Sulong. Another company of the Punjabis moved to occupy a height about 500 yards farther north, and did so unopposed. It was intended that upon completion of these moves the Norfolks, assisted by covering fire from the Punjabis, should capture Bukit Pelandok. The two companies were mistaken for Japanese, however, and fired on by the Norfolks. As soon as this had been stopped, Japanese blazed at the troops from near-by concealment, with the result that Moorhead was killed and his men and the Norfolks were driven off the feature. So serious were the losses that despite the urgent need to clear the road to Bakri, Brigadier Duke decided that he would have to await the arrival of the Loyals before making a

---

[2] Brig C. L. B. Duke, CB, MC. Comd 53 Brit Bde. Regular soldier; b. 27 Nov 1896.

further endeavour. It later transpired that a Norfolk detachment which had relieved Lieutenant Varley's platoon at the Parit Sulong bridge, having been without rations since the 18th, and thinking that it had been cut off, had left its vital post during the morning of the 20th and set off across country to Batu Pahat. The Japanese were free therefore to establish themselves at the bridge also, thus blocking Anderson's line of withdrawal.

When Key visited Bennett's headquarters the same morning Bennett naturally urged upon him the need to clear the defile and send a relief force to Anderson. As his Australian reserve troops had been committed, he asked that the 53rd Brigade be employed for this operation. Key feared, however, that the brigade, or a substantial part of it, might find itself also cut off in attempting such an operation, thus adding to the already heavy losses and further endangering Yong Peng. The issue was therefore referred to Percival, who instructed Bennett to withdraw the 27th Brigade to Yong Peng instead of halting it near Labis as had been intended. An order to the 45th Brigade to withdraw had been sent by the III Corps during the night. Key instructed Duke during the afternoon to make a further attempt to clear the road to Parit Sulong. On Duke representing that the troops hitherto employed were not in condition to attack, Key agreed that the 2/Loyals, who had been continuously on the move for three days and nights and had not yet fully assembled in the brigade area, be used with artillery support as early as possible next day.

With his force hemmed in at Bakri, Anderson had given orders before daylight on the 20th for a five-mile withdrawal towards Parit Sulong by nightfall, to the edge of the open swampland where further passage in daylight would expose it to air attack. The force was now organised as a battalion of five rifle companies, with two companies of Jats (Major H. White) and a composite force of Rajputs and Garhwalis (Captain Woods) attached. The advance-guard was Captain Keegan's company, followed on the right of the road by Captain Beverley's and on the left by Captain Westbrook's[4] (comprising two platoons of the 2/29th and one of the 2/19th). The body of the column included transport, guns, Indian troops, and Captain Snelling's company of the 2/19th (in reserve). The rearguard, commanded by the adjutant of the 2/19th (Captain Hughes[5]), comprised the 2/29th's "B" Company and two companies of Jats. One anti-tank gun was detailed for work at each end of the column, and all gunners not required as such served as infantry. The 2/19th's Intelligence officer (Lieutenant Burt[6]) acted as adjutant of the force.

Keegan's company moved off at 7 a.m., but was held up at a swamp defile by Japanese dug in on a slight rise south of the road, and by a

---

[4] Capt K. L. Westbrook, NX34771; 2/19 Bn. Estate agent-auctioneer; of Bowral, NSW; b. Mayfield, NSW, 9 Apr 1916.

[5] Maj L. Hughes, NX35079; 2/19 Bn. Branch manager retail store; of Wollongong, NSW; b. Chilton, Durham, Eng, 10 Apr 1910. Killed in action 9 Feb 1942.

[6] Capt S. F. Burt. NX34960; 2/19 Bn; Aust Intelligence Corps. Farmer and grazier; of Wallendbeen, NSW; b. Dunedin, NZ, 18 Feb 1908.

road-block. The company fought vigorously, and Lieutenant Ibbott[7] led a gallant flank attack in which he and three of his men reached the Japanese trenches before they were killed. The delay imposed by the Japanese was serious, however, for the force had not gained sufficient room, and being so bunched together was very vulnerable to air or artillery attack. The fact that Keegan's company was so close to the enemy prevented it being given supporting fire. Anderson therefore decided that

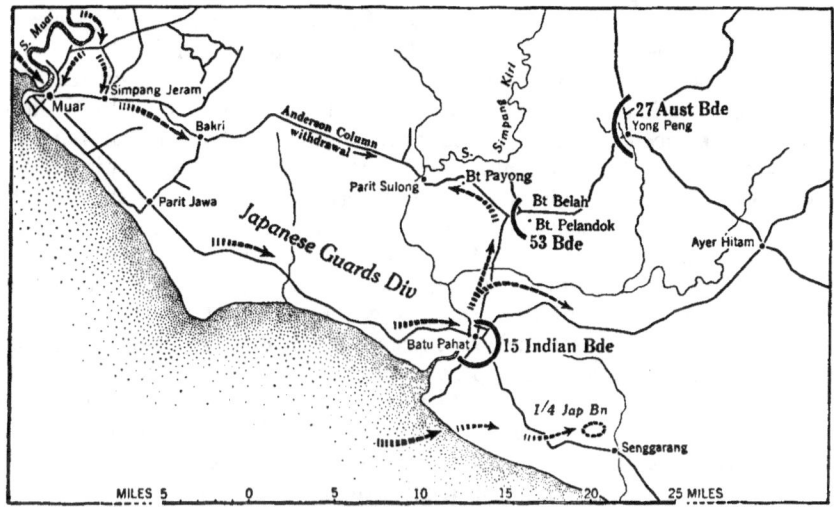

The withdrawal from Bakri

a rapid and spirited assault was necessary to gain space, and ordered Beverley to lead his men singing into the the struggle. This he did, and these were the words they sang:

> Once a jolly swagman camped by a billabong
> Under the shade of a coolibah tree. . . .

"Waltzing Matilda", never sung by Australians with more enthusiasm than when they meet in surroundings strange to them, had become a battle song.

Although the attack went wide, the company drove the Japanese from its course, reached the area, now abandoned, where Newton and the 2/19th's transport had been, and then attacked the enemy from the rear. The halted column now came under shell fire, and the situation again called for swift and decisive action. Keegan's company again attacked, and in a final assault, led by Anderson, the Japanese were routed and their road-block was destroyed. Anderson himself put two machine-gun posts out of action with grenades (which, as a result of his 1914-18 war experience, he always carried), and shot two Japanese with his pistol.

---

[7] Lt A. G. C. Ibbott, NX12600; 2/19 Bn. Farmer; of Cootamundra, NSW; b. Benalla, Vic, 20 Jan 1906. Killed in action 20 Jan 1942.

Beverley's company now became the advance-guard as the force forged slowly ahead through Newton's former transport harbour, where bodies and disabled vehicles gave evidence of a prolonged struggle.

The body of Captain Macdonald[8] was found there. A man who had escaped related that Macdonald was leading a party withdrawing from the area when he was badly wounded. He handed over his men to a sergeant, gave covering fire as they departed, and remarked that it was "like shooting grouse on the moors". The diarist who recorded this incident added that "before he died he did a wonderful job, as was evident by the number of dead Japanese around him".

The attack on the transport group had opened at 7 a.m. on the 19th, soon after it had been joined by the platoon under Lieutenant Varley which had been relieved at the Parit Sulong bridge by the Norfolks. Newton's and Varley's men, numbering about 150, were disposed in perimeter formation, but a gap was forced in it and the quartermaster, Captain Duncan,[9] was killed. When the firing started, the transport officer, Captain Bracher,[1] had ordered drivers to take their vehicles back towards Parit Sulong, and about twenty vehicles, including a carrier, reached the road. It was in one of these that Sergeant Meal got to battalion headquarters at Bakri. Three, despite constant air strafing, reached Yong Peng; one had to be abandoned at Parit Sulong. The driver of the carrier was shot, and it ran off the road into a ditch. A water truck overturned and caught fire. With the road to Yong Peng thus blocked, the others tried to reach the battalion, only to be barred by the road-block Meal had passed as it was being constructed. Another carrier, trying to force a passage, was wrecked by a land-mine.

The attack on the transport group continued until late afternoon. With the enemy almost surrounding his position, Newton thought that the battalion must have been overcome, or have withdrawn in another direction. He therefore ordered his men to withdraw across the road and through the jungle. Varley's platoon became separated from the others in this movement. Next day, after hearing that the Parit Sulong bridge was held by the Japanese, Newton decided to strike south through Batu Pahat, and grouped his men in small parties for the purpose.[2]

Anderson's column encountered another and stronger block soon after midday on the 20th, comprised of some of Newton's vehicles reinforced by tree-trunks, and with troops entrenched on a slight ridge beside it. The strength of the Japanese at this point was estimated at two companies or more, with six heavy machine-guns covering the road where it ran between swampy, tree-covered country, and Beverley's company as the advance-guard became closely engaged. The rear of the column was now

---

[8] Capt H. C. H. Macdonald, NX12599; 2/19 Bn. Grazier; of Wagga Wagga, NSW; b. Melbourne, 28 Mar 1904. Killed in action 19 Jan 1942.

[9] Capt D. I. McI. Duncan, NX70233; 2/19 Bn. Clerk; of Cremorne, NSW; b. Inverell, NSW, 11 Jun 1906. Killed in action 19 Jan 1942.

[1] Capt W. P. Bracher, NX12594; 2/19 Bn. Telephone linesman; of Wagga Wagga, NSW; b. Hastings, England, 3 Jan 1897.

[2] Some of Newton's men rejoined Westforce later; some reached the coast and got to Sumatra; others, including Newton, were captured where they fought.

(*Australian War Memorial*)

Two of the nine Japanese tanks knocked out by anti-tank guns forward of Bakri on 18th January.

(*Australian War Memorial*)

The crew of the rear anti-tank gun, which accounted for six of the nine tanks destroyed.

(Australian War Memorial)

The Parit Sulong bridge towards which the survivors of the 2/19th and 2/29th Battalions and of the 45th Indian Brigade fought their way. The wreckage of some of the column's vehicles may be seen to the right of the bridge. Post-war photograph.

(Australian War Memorial)

The hut at Parit Sulong into which the Japanese forced wounded Indian and Australian prisoners. Most of the wounded were afterwards massacred.

being pressed by the main body of the enemy. Westbrook's composite "D" Company was brought in on Beverley's left flank, and a platoon led by Lieutenant Cootes[3] was sent round this flank to test the enemy's strength but was cut off.[4] Shells again burst among the closely-packed transport, by now increasingly occupied by wounded men. The Jats at the rear became difficult to control, and the rearguard gave ground. Four trucks were lost before Brigadier Duncan rallied his men and led a counterattack by Jats and Australians. The trucks were recaptured, but Duncan lost his life.[5]

Anderson had gone to the rear when news of the trouble reached him, and had left his second-in-command, Major Vincent, to direct the forward attack.[6] Lieutenant Carr[7] (2/29th Battalion) was killed while leading a left forward attack during this period. Anderson found when he returned that Vincent had done excellent work, especially in directing mortar fire on to the enemy. As it was now necessary to press on if the day's objective was to be reached, and the morale of the Japanese appeared to have been shaken, Anderson decided to use his reserve company (Captain Snelling) to add momentum to the assault. Under cover of a small rise, Anderson addressed the company, directing them through Beverley's company, on the right, as he considered their best chance of success lay in this direction. As rapid fire commenced preparatory to the endeavour

> Every man was fighting mad (wrote the 2/19th Battalion's diarist). Mortar shells were directed on to targets by infantrymen a few yards from the target; gunners were fighting with rifles, bayonets and axes (range too short for 25-pounders except to Jap rear areas west). A gun crew pushed its 25-pounder round a cutting and blew out the first road-blocks (vehicles) at 75 yards' range. Carriers pushed within 5 yards of Japanese M.G's and blew them out. . . . Men went forward under heavy M.G. fire and chopped road-blocks to pieces. . . .

Leading the assault, Snelling had his thigh shattered, but the Japanese were routed, many at the point of the bayonet. His company pursued the enemy along the road while the block was being removed under fire from snipers.

The number of wounded with the convoy now became a serious problem. As Hackney saw the situation from the truck in which he lay:

> During each halt more wounded fellows would be brought in and placed on the vehicles; sometimes lifeless-looking bundles being carried by their mates, others being helped along. Each time a few words as to how it happened, and always it was while they were doing a job, somewhere, perhaps in front or along the sides, or in the rear, as all the time the enemy surrounded this ferocious little force. . . . Overhead always circling around and around were enemy aircraft which often added

---

[3] Lt R. J. G. Cootes, VX39165; 2/29 Bn. Cartage contractor; of Kyabram, Vic; b. Malvern, Vic, 30 Jan 1917. Killed in action 12 Mar 1942 (after capture).

[4] Survivors eventually reached Yong Peng.

[5] In a narrative of the withdrawal, Anderson referred to Duncan as "a very able and gallant officer, whom the Indian troops held in highest regard".

[6] Anderson wrote subsequently: "Vincent was a first-class officer. He had an imaginative brain in training, so that his conduct in battle was that of a veteran, with personal courage and great stamina."

[7] Lt W. P. Carr, VX39014; 2/29 Bn. Estate agent; of Geelong, Vic; b. Geelong, 1 Oct 1916. Killed in action 20 Jan 1942.

their lot, by either bombs or machine-guns, to the efforts of their ground forces. . . . Very often a bullet or a shell splinter would find its way to our truck. . . . On one occasion a burst of machine-gun bullets tore a line of holes along the off side of the vehicle. I heard a peculiar grunt beside me, and looking round saw that the poor fellow sitting there, already badly wounded, had been killed. His body slumped forward, revealing a fresh blood patch where a bullet had entered his back.[8]

Darkness fell upon the battered and weary but still dogged column, and it moved on, through the open country it had had to avoid in daylight. At its next halt, three miles ahead, it was joined by Varley and his platoon. By midnight, Anderson had learned that an Indian soldier had reached the column with a report that Parit Sulong was now held by Japanese. Two dispatch riders sent to investigate found the village looted, were challenged in an unknown tongue at the bridge, and quickly raced back. Thus, when it had seemed that the column had fought its way to freedom, another and perhaps more desperate struggle had to be faced.

Meanwhile the withdrawal from Segamat had continued, with little pressure by the enemy. Soon after dawn on 21st January the 27th Brigade took up positions covering the junction at Yong Peng of the road from Muar. The 22nd Indian Brigade was a little north of Labis, and the 8th Indian Brigade twelve miles to its rear. The consequent shortening of communications made it easier for General Bennett to control both the force under his command on the trunk road and those on the Muar road. Movement of these forces obviously required close coordination and, as mentioned, the only communication with Anderson was by wireless telegraph through Bennett's headquarters. General Percival therefore ordered at 8.33 a.m. that Bennett should command all troops on the Muar road, at a time to be arranged with Key.[9] The latter went to the headquarters of the 53rd Brigade to see what was being done about the attack he had ordered, only to find that for some reason, stated to have been faulty transmission of the order by a liaison officer, no arrangements for it had been made. In the absence of Brigadier Duke on a reconnaissance, the brigade major informed him in response to his inquiries that an attack could be organised by 2 p.m. Leaving tentative instructions for this to be done, Key visited Bennett, offering his assistance in preparing the necessary orders. The upshot was that the brigade was ordered to attack accordingly, with the Loyals as the attacking battalion. The order was conveyed by Major Parker,[1] a West Australian in the Indian Army, serving on Key's staff, who reached the 53rd Brigade headquarters about noon. Colonel Thyer, sent forward to Brigadier Duke by General Bennett, reached the headquarters of the 53rd Brigade soon afterwards. Finding Duke absent

---

[8] From a narrative by Lieutenant Hackney.

[9] Percival later commented: "There are very obvious disadvantages in such rapid changes of command, but in very mobile operations they are not easy to avoid. The problem is further complicated when the army is made up of contingents from different parts of the Empire which, quite naturally, prefer to serve under their own commanders. But the avoidance of too much insularity should in the future be one of the corner stones of our military doctrine." (*The War in Malaya*, p. 231.)

[1] Col P. W. Parker. GSO2 11 Indian Div. Regular soldier; b. 15 Apr 1900.

on reconnaissance, Thyer went forward to the Loyals where he was informed that the battalion was ready for its forward move; but in fact considerable delay appears to have occurred in organising its transport. At 2.30 p.m. at the far end of the causeway through swamp to the Bukit Pelandok defile Thyer and the commander of the Loyals, Lieut-Colonel Elrington,[2] met Brigadier Duke. As Thyer later recorded, he found

> the reconnaissance for the attack and the issue of the plan being made completely in the open, in full view of the defile only a thousand yards away. When it was suggested that this was an unsound and risky manner in which to conduct the preparations for an attack . . . [I] was informed by the brigade commander that he was convinced that there were no troops on the hill feature. It was then suggested that if this were the case, the forward battalion, the Punjabs, should be sent forward to occupy the hill immediately instead of waiting for a set-piece attack by the Loyals. Failing this, at least fighting patrols should be sent forward to probe the position and locate enemy localities.

Because of what he had seen at the causeway, and when, an hour after the scheduled time for the attack by the Loyals, it had not begun, Thyer decided to report the situation to his commander. Signals communications had been destroyed by an air raid on Yong Peng, so he made the report in person. He got back to the Loyals soon after 4 p.m. with orders from Bennett that the attack begin immediately. He found, however, that the battalion still was not in position. Duke told him that the artillery was not yet ready to give adequate support, and reconnaissance had been hindered by transport difficulties. The time for the attack was moved to 6 p.m., and later to 6 a.m. next day. The commander of the Australian divisional artillery, Brigadier Callaghan, was informed by Bennett that the brigade had asked for additional artillery support for the attack, but Bennett considered such a measure neither practicable nor necessary. At the 53rd Brigade headquarters, Callaghan was informed at 9 p.m. by the brigade major, in the absence of Duke, that a field battery had completed its preparations, and "the Brigadier was quite happy that the support it would provide would be adequate".

Meanwhile (at 12.30 p.m. on 21st January) Percival had held another conference at which it was decided that a further reorganisation of forces should occur upon withdrawal from Yong Peng.[3] They were to comprise:

Eastforce: All troops in the Mersing and Kahang area, to hold Jemaluang with detachments forward in the Mersing area.

Westforce: 9th Indian Division and the A.I.F. (less its 22nd Brigade) under General Bennett's command, covering Kluang on the railway and Ayer Hitam on the trunk road.

11th Indian Division: 53rd Brigade when released from Westforce, 15th Brigade, and 28th Brigade, commanded by General Key, to hold the Batu Pahat area and operate on the west coast road.

This day of continued and exasperating delays by the 53rd Brigade—arising it seemed at the time to Australian officers from failure to realise

---
[2] Lt-Col M. Elrington, MC. CO 2/Loyals. Regular soldier; b. 28 Dec 1897.
[3] A decision to withdraw from the Mersing-Yong Peng-Batu Pahat line had arisen from circumstances related in the next chapter.

the urgency of the situation, and no doubt largely from the brigade's lack of training and experience for the task it was set—was a day of disaster to Anderson's column. Making the most of the cover of darkness, the force came to the end of the open country, and was halted in the shelter of rubber trees at 2 a.m. on 21st January. A detachment led by Sergeant Lloyd Davies, sent to reconnoitre the bridge at Parit Sulong, was attacked there, and returned at 7.15. Although two Malays who had been encountered insisted that the bridge was held by the Sultan of Johore's men, Anderson disbelieved their report, and deployed his forward companies through the trees. Soon, after its night-long trek, the column had to fight again. The leading men met rapid fire, and were charged by 120 Japanese, whom they halted and held in the open by means of a flank attack. While Japanese heavy tanks came up to the rear of the column, where they were stopped by a section of 25-pounders of the 65th Battery under Sergeant Barton,[4] carriers came forward and disposed of the frontal assault. Thus the head of the column, now comprising Keegan's and Beverley's companies, reached the outskirts of Parit Sulong about 9.30 a.m., only to find that houses and other vantage points had been turned into Japanese machine-gun nests. The rear of the column (Maher's and Westbrook's companies) was being increasingly assailed by tanks and mechanised infantry. Between the head and rear of the column there was now a distance of only 1,200 to 1,500 yards. Aircraft were swooping down and spattering it with bullets. Wireless communication with Westforce had failed during the night, but was re-established by the signallers despite the inferno in which they were working. A message was received during the morning that assistance (by means of the attack sought by Bennett) was coming. So, with this hope, and cheered also by the sound of guns between Parit Sulong and Yong Peng—which they took as evidence of the approach of a relieving force though in fact they were registering shots —the column fought on.

Such mortar ammunition as remained had to be used in maintaining the column's position, and hampering the enemy at the rear, rather than in supporting an attack on the village. A bend in the road, high rubber trees and short range prevented artillery being trained on the bridge. All gunners and drivers who could be spared, and the less seriously wounded men, were sent to fight on the flanks while the main strength of the column was exerted at its head and tail. Reynolds, though wounded at Bakri, did notable work on the left flank. At 11 a.m. Indian troops, led by Major R. Anderson, were ordered to attack the village from the west. Coming under heavy fire they swung wide, but got round to the north bank of the Simpang Kiri west of the bridge, and exchanged fire with Japanese across the water. Keegan's and Beverley's companies were held up until, with the aid of Pickup's carriers, which soon after midday engaged the enemy machine-guns at point-blank range, the companies managed to thrust through the village and also reach the north bank. Beverley was now sent

---

[4] Sgt S. J. Barton, NX30078; 2/15 Fd Regt. Station hand; of Walcha, NSW; b. Rookwood, NSW, 16 May 1909.

to investigate the possibility of attacking the bridge, but as the afternoon wore on, and pressure from the rear increased, Anderson decided that the column's remaining resources, especially of mortar bombs, were insufficient for attack with any real chance of success. Air strafing increased, and soon after 4 p.m. bombs added many more casualties. The lot of the wounded had become pitiable in the extreme, and at 5 p.m. the medical officers of the two Australian battalions, Captain Cahill[5] (2/19th) and Captain Brand[6] (2/29th) suggested to Anderson that the Japanese be asked to let through two ambulances carrying men who were dying for lack of treatment.[7] Anderson considered the chance remote, but agreed to the suggestion with the proviso that the men sent forward should be only those whose condition the doctors considered hopeless.

During the late afternoon and until after dark, the rearward part of the column was under intense fire. In a lull which followed, the rumble of approaching tanks was heard, and Lieutenant Ross and Sergeant Tate[8] ran to a gun already set up in an anti-tank position on the road. In the darkness they were unable to locate the ammunition, but found some grenades. Armed with these, they jumped into the ditches lining the road and made towards the tanks. Forty yards from the gun they used the grenades to such effect that they stopped the leading tank. Racing back to the gun, they found its crew in position, and though the tank could not be seen at this distance the gun was aimed at where Ross and Tate had encountered it. The first shot hit the target, and after others had been fired it burst into flames, forming a temporary road-block behind which the gunners continued to fire on the enemy armour. This gallant incident, in which Tate was wounded, gave the column's oddly assorted fighting parties, made up of such men as became available from time to time, the opportunity to get at the other tanks during the night. Using grenades and anti-tank rifles, they went to work on them with grim resolve.

Distant gun fire had again been heard, but it seemed (rightly) that it had drawn no nearer the bridge. The column had had little food for two days, and its mortar and 25-pounder gun ammunition was almost exhausted. Anderson therefore sent a message to Bennett asking that if possible aircraft be used at dawn to bomb the approaches to the far end of the bridge, and to drop food and morphia. As the cipher books used by the signallers in the Muar area had been destroyed, he received a reply "Look up at sparrowfart". It had been framed by Thyer to convey (as it did) to him but not to the enemy that planes would be over at first light next day.

---

[5] Capt R. L. Cahill, MBE, NX35149; AAMC. Medical practitioner; of Bondi Junction, NSW; b Sydney, 20 Jan 1914.

[6] Capt V. Brand, MC, VX39085; RMO 2/29 Bn. Medical practitioner; of St Kilda, Vic; b. Melbourne, 16 Jul 1914.

[7] "These RMOs with the limited facilities at their disposal had done magnificent work under the grimmest conditions," wrote Anderson afterwards. ". . . The fortitude and cheerfulness of the wounded was amazing. . . . Captain Snelling, who was wounded twice again by air strafing, was outstanding for his example of courage and cheerfulness."

[8] Sgt B. Tate, NX28467; 2/15 Fd Regt. Barman; of Bondi, NSW; b. Daylesford, Vic, 17 Dec 1905. Missing presumed died 15 Sep 1944.

Captain Maher was wounded by shrapnel, and then killed when a shell blew up the car in which he had been placed. At 10 p.m. a volunteer driver of one of the ambulances returned with news that the commander of the Japanese at the bridge had demanded the surrender of the column, offering to take care of the wounded in that event. He had ordered the ambulances to remain on the bridge approach to act as a road-block, covered by machine-guns which would be fired if they attempted to move. Anderson's decision was hard to make, but still with hope of relief he refused to consider the Japanese demand.

After dark Lieutenant Austin,[9] gravely wounded in the neck and shoulder, and a driver, also wounded, released the brakes of each vehicle, rolled them down the slope away from the bridge, and then amid the din of battle drove them back to the perimeter. There, throughout the night, they and the rest of the column were assailed by the fire of tanks, artillery, and machine-guns.

The Loyals were in position before dawn on 22nd January for their delayed attack on Bukit Payong, but Brigadier Duke insisted on further testing of the range of his artillery preparatory to opening up a barrage to cover the operation. As the ranging shots fell short,[1] he ordered further postponement of the attack until 9 a.m. All prospect of taking the Japanese by surprise now had been lost, and the troops on the start-line were heavily attacked from the air.

> With no artillery support forthcoming (Thyer wrote later), Brigadier Duke felt that he would have little chance of getting through to Parit Sulong. . . . It was further contended by 53rd Infantry Brigade that the chances of holding the defile, after it had been captured, were remote. Also the failure to capture and hold it successfully would have jeopardised "their main task of preventing the enemy penetrating to Yong Peng". The fact that they had been relieved of this responsibility does not seem to have been completely understood. Brigadier Duke decided to cancel the operation and reorganise into a defensive position. This decision was made after reference to H.Q. Westforce.

The brigade was accordingly grouped to prevent enemy advance along the causeway.

No such frustration afflicted the Japanese in renewing shell fire on Anderson's column at dawn the same day; but then—during a brief period while Japanese aircraft were absent from the scene—two cumbersome planes came over, dropped the food and morphia for which Anderson had asked, and went off after releasing bombs upon the Japanese at the far end of the bridge.[2] Anderson decided, however, that the effect of the bombing had been insufficient to make it practicable to cross the river;

---

[9] Lt R. W. L. Austin, NX70159; 2/19 Bn. Law student; of Woollahra, NSW; b. Sydney, 16 Mar 1919.

[1] Thyer reported a 100-yards margin of error. The failure was attributed by Heath to faulty fuses, and climatic conditions.

[2] Anderson was under the impression that there was only one aircraft, "an old fashioned Vildebeeste", but the rubber trees amid which he was engaged gave only a limited view overhead. Australian Air Force records state that the task was performed by two Albacores escorted by three Buffalo fighters, from the RAAF station at Sembawang.

and though the distant gun fire of the promised relieving force still seemed no nearer, it was reasonable for him to hope that further assistance would follow. Enemy tanks were again active, and made a flank attack supported by infantry. The number of casualties became so great that the column would be unable to fight much longer.[3] As a last bid, when relief failed and hope was fading, Anderson ordered Beverley's company to test the resistance at the bridge. The response by the Japanese convinced Anderson that no chance of success lay in this direction. At 9 a.m., when the column faced annihilation if it remained where it was, he ordered destruction of carriers, guns, and transport, and withdrawal eastward through swamps and jungle by all capable of attempting it.[4]

Our fellows, although so far fewer than the enemy in numbers, had seemed for ages to be sending back nearly as much fire as came into our area (the wounded Hackney subsequently wrote), but now there was noticeable a definite slackening off of the fire from our position. It was not very long before we knew why—it became known to most that orders had been given for all men to get out as best they could. An odd burst from a machine-gun, and some rifle fire kept going out from our troops, but as time went on there were less and less of our men about. In small parties and sometimes singly, we could see our fellows going up the northern bank of the river east of the bridge.

The gallant 65th Battery had fired 6,519 rounds in the action from the Muar to Parit Sulong. Wireless-telegraph communications had been maintained by Corporal Bingham[5] and Signalman Benoit,[6] of the 8th Divisional Signals, under constant shell fire in an open truck in Anderson's column. By 10 a.m. an orderly withdrawal from Parit Sulong had been made, except by Anderson, Major Vincent, Captain Hughes, and Padre Greenwood[7] of the 2/19th, Lieutenant Bonney[8] of the 2/29th, and twenty men whom it was still possible to assist from the shambles; by a platoon of the 2/19th led by Sergeant Hunt[9] who failed to receive the withdrawal order;[1] by a small party under Sergeant Davies; and by Private Quigley,[2]

---

[3] The vehicle carrying Hackney and other wounded was at last without a driver, so Hackney drove it whenever movement was necessary, manipulating the clutch, hand throttle and hand-brake with his hands and the leg he was still able to use. "Even the sight of a fiddling little aeroplane from our fellows outside bucked everyone up considerably," he wrote later. But a shell burst near him as he stood during a pause propped against the vehicle, sending splinters into his back and the leg he had been still able to use. When a move again became necessary and his truck was impeding others, he dragged himself back to the driving seat and somehow got the truck along. "I had ceased to care how the damn thing went forward," he added, "as long as I got it out of the way and along the road."

[4] The withdrawal order anticipated a message sent soon after by Bennett to Anderson stating that there was little prospect of relief reaching the column, and leaving it to his discretion to withdraw. "Sorry unable help after your heroic effort," ran the message. "Good luck."

[5] Cpl G. J. Bingham, DCM, NX51770; 8 Div Sigs. Telegraphist; of Petersham, NSW; b. Merriwa, NSW, 2 Nov 1913.

[6] Sig M. A. W. Benoit, MM, VX32772; 8 Div Sigs. Electrical testman; of Bayswater, Vic; b. Ballarat, Vic, 26 Sep 1919. Missing presumed died 24 May 1943.

[7] Chap Rev H. Wardale-Greenwood, VX38675. Presbyterian minister; of Rainbow, Vic; b. Durham, England, 20 May 1909. Died Borneo 18 Jul 1945.

[8] Lt L. G. Bonney, VX39068; 2/29 Bn. Farmer; of Alvie, via Colac, Vic; b. Colac, 26 Dec 1917.

[9] Capt W. G. Hunt, MM, NX52483. 2/19 Bn; 44 Bn; 19 Garrison Bn. Labourer; of Epping, NSW; b. Sydney, 4 Jun 1918.

[1] Hunt and his platoon fought their way out by way of the west coast.

[2] Pte J. B. Quigley, NX32671; 2/19 Bn. Transport driver and mechanic; of Emu Plains, NSW; b. Paddington, NSW, 7 Mar 1901. Missing presumed died 22 Jan 1942.

Lieutenant Crawford's batman, slightly wounded in the forearm, who chose to remain with Crawford and other badly wounded men.

Anderson's force had done all that could reasonably have been expected of it, and more. That did not alter the fact that another heavy loss, amounting to a brigade and a large part of two Australian battalions, had been inflicted on the defenders of Malaya. Looking to the battles of the future, however, it was significant that, as Anderson later commented:

> The well-trained Australian units showed a complete moral ascendancy of the enemy. They outmatched the Japs in bushcraft and fire control, where the enemy's faults of bunching together and noisy shouting disclosed their dispositions and enabled the Australians to inflict heavy casualties at small cost to themselves. When the enemy was trapped they fought most gamely. In hand-to-hand fighting they made a very poor showing against the superior spirit and training of the A.I.F.

Further, by their stand at Bakri and by their dogged struggle along the road to Parit Sulong, the force imposed delay on the Japanese advance which was of vital importance at the time, particularly in the area of Bennett's command. Percival was to record:

> The Battle of Muar was one of the epics of the Malayan campaign. Our little force by dogged resistance had held up a division of the Japanese *Imperial Guards* attacking with all the advantages of air and tank support for nearly a week, and in doing so had saved the Segamat force from encirclement and probable annihilation. The award of the Victoria Cross to Lieut-Colonel Anderson of the A.I.F. was a fitting tribute both to his own prowess and to the valour of his men.[3]

Those left behind at Parit Sulong soon met a fate largely typical of what many already had experienced, and many more were to experience, at the hands of the Japanese. Among the wounded who could not be taken away was Hackney, who has been quoted freely not only because of his courage and stamina during the struggle, but also because later he wrote a vivid and compelling account of what happened to him and to those around him.[4] The aftermath at Parit Sulong cannot be better described than by drawing further upon his narrative, and by quoting it in part.

Hackney and Lieutenant Tibbitts[5] were together when the withdrawal occurred. Tibbitts obtained a Bren gun, and while he was away looking for more ammunition, Hackney blazed away from beneath the truck, hoping thereby to give those who had left a better chance to get clear of the enemy. When Tibbitts returned, and in the period of suspense till the Japanese would reach them, they spoke of "a wash; being in other than bloodstained, torn, filthy clothes; a bed and a sleep", and of other things they "had not known before were so good". The Japanese were slow in moving in, but at last, when firing from the column had ceased, "from all directions, but particularly north and west, chattering creatures began to come into sight, often screaming something to somebody not far away". They herded the wounded together with kicks, curses, blows from rifle

---
[3] Percival, *The War In Malaya*, p. 233.
[4] "Dark Evening" (in typescript of 116 pages) by Ben Hackney.
[5] Lt A. H. Tibbitts, VX57746; 2/29 Bn. Clerk; of East Kew, Vic; b. Melbourne, 15 May 1916. Missing believed killed, 22 Jan 1942.

butts, and jabs from bayonets. Unable to walk, Hackney was aided by Tibbitts, both of them under a series of blows. Across the bridge, they and the other prisoners were made to strip and sit in a circle. Hackney estimated that this maimed and bloodstained remnant of the force numbered 110 Australians and 40 Indians.

Many Japanese seemed to delight in kicking where a wound lay open, and so great was their satisfaction at any visible sign of pain that often the dose was repeated.

No part of the prisoners' bodies was spared from the brutality of their captors. Their clothes were searched by an English-speaking white man dressed as a British soldier, and then returned to them in a heap. As many as possible were forced into a shed, which became so overcrowded that many were piled on top of others, thus adding to their excruciating pain. Appeals for water and medical attention were ignored, and a move to another building was made under compulsion of more brutality. Japanese guns, tanks and troops streamed by throughout the rest of the afternoon. Whenever they stopped, troops ran to see the prisoners and add to their sufferings. One of the dead was placed in an upright position on a table top propped against a truck. There the body "seemed to create enormous amusement to the Japanese concerned, and was an object of ridicule to many Japanese afterwards". An Indian lying in front of the building regained consciousness. The Japanese in charge at the spot gave him a series of kicks, bashed him with a rifle, thrust into him again and again with his bayonet, then heaved the corpse into the water near by.

Then, it seemed, the outburst of savagery was to be checked. An officer shouted orders; helmets and mugs filled with water were produced, and packets of cigarettes. While these were held just out of reach of thirst-crazed men, newly-arrived Japanese photographed the scene. The water was then thrown away, and the cigarettes were withdrawn.

At sunset the prisoners were roped or wired together in groups. Jerking the fetters, kicking and bashing the victims, their captors led them away, except a few, including Hackney, left for dead or about to die. Petrol was collected from the column's stranded vehicles. Feigning death, Hackney later heard a stutter of machine-guns, and saw a flicker of fire. Crawling inch by inch later in the night, but steeling himself to suffer inertly more kicks, blows, and bayonet thrusts, even letting his boots be tugged off his feet despite agonising pain, Hackney dragged himself to a coolie building. There, by a protracted process of rubbing against a corner of a foundation block, he severed the rope binding his wrists together. After more agonised crawling, he found water and came upon two members of his battalion—one of them Sergeant Ron Croft.[6] Both smelt strongly of petrol. Croft told Hackney that he and his comrade had been among a few who were not tied when the prisoners were fired upon. They fell, though not

---

[6] Sgt R. F. T. Croft, VX39208; 2/29 Bn. Salesman; of Richmond, Vic; b. Richmond, 14 Jul 1914. Missing presumed died 15 Apr 1942.

hit, and feigned death. Petrol was then thrown on the group, and ignited, but Croft managed to free himself and the other man, who was badly wounded, from the rest.

Croft now helped this man to thick jungle near the river. Weak and nerve-racked, and smaller than Hackney, who weighed fourteen stone, he yet managed to return and stagger off with Hackney across his shoulder.

> Sheer strength alone did not enable him to carry his burden. It was something more than that—his wish and willingness to help; courage, guts, and manliness.[7]

On a hillside track north of Parit Sulong, where it had been agreed that the parties withdrawing from the village should meet, Keegan received a report that Anderson had been killed. Obviously even the men who had remained unwounded were in no condition for further fighting until they had been rested and re-equipped. Keegan therefore gave them orders that, grouped as nearly as possible in their original companies, they should make their way to Yong Peng, about fifteen miles away. Ahead lay more swamp, rubber plantations, and jungle with its tangle of vines and roots. The unwounded men hacked a way where necessary. Night fell on the main body of the survivors—Captain Harris, Lieutenant Reynolds, and 310 others—before they reached an island amid swamp as shown in their maps, so all lay where they could. Mud and water oozed around their bodies, but to most exhaustion brought sleep. The group pushed on next day, aided by Chinese, and with frequent pauses for the sake of the wounded. The sounds of fighting grew louder as they neared Yong Peng. Thanks to arrangements made by Harris, who led an advanced party, they were given drinks of tea or water at each Chinese shop or house on the way. Major Vincent, coming up with a party of fifty men of the 2/29th Battalion and some Indians, gave them news that Anderson, far from having been killed, was close behind. Then ambulances for which Harris had arranged picked up the wounded, and one of the drivers dryly remarked "My word, we are glad to see you fellows! You don't realise what we have had to put up with, waiting here for you during the last few days." The rest of the group and others, including Anderson and his party, reached Yong Peng during the evening.[8] Keegan and ten others

---

[7] The man whom Croft had first rescued died next day, after the three had been joined by an English soldier. The survivors reached a Malay house, where they were given food and allowed to wash and sleep for a while. Hackney, still unable to stand, persuaded the others that it would be best for him to stay at the house while they pushed on next day.
The rest of Hackney's story concerns chiefly his personal survival after he had been carried off by the Malays and left some distance from the house. Though his body was riddled by wounds, sapping his physical strength, he managed to crawl from place to place until 27th February. He was mostly refused help by Malays, who appeared to fear reprisals if they harboured him, but generally aided by Chinese, at the risk of their own and their families' lives. Then, thirty-six days after he had begun his attempt to escape, he was caught by a party of Malays, one of them dressed as a policeman, taken back to Parit Sulong, and handed over to the Japanese. There he received more of the brutal treatment he had previously endured, but this lessened in the course of a series of moves. When he entered Pudu gaol, at Kuala Lumpur, on 20th March, he had lost more than five stone in weight, but his wounds had almost healed, and he found himself again in the company of Englishmen and Australians—including Captain Morgan, adjutant of his battalion. Later, Hackney and others were transferred to the main prisoner-of-war camp at Changi, on Singapore Island.

[8] One party of 137 had been led on a compass bearing to Yong Peng by Pte M. Curnow of the 2/19th, who had been outstanding as a runner between Colonel Anderson and "A" Coy during the action at Bakri.

had arrived in the morning. An armoured car—one of two in charge of Sergeant Christoff[9] of the 2/30th Battalion, which had made a series of spirited sorties westward from Yong Peng while the fate of Anderson's column was at issue—helped to bring in survivors.

Before he washed or had a meal, Anderson reported to Bennett, who wrote: "He was cool and calm and talked as if the whole battle was merely a training exercise. From this I understood why he was able to keep his men in hand. With such coolness, self-control, strength of character, and with such kindly affection and consideration for his men, he could overcome all difficulties."[1]

The 45th Brigade now had no commander or headquarters, no battalion commanders or officers second-in-command, and only one of its adjutants. Only two or three of its remaining British officers had had more than a few months' experience. Anderson had 271 left of his battalion, including fifty-two wounded who made their way back. Of the 2/29th Battalion, which had first taken the weight of the main Japanese advance near Bakri, only 130 men mustered at Yong Peng. Its commander and most of its officers had been killed or were missing. The 65th Battery numbered 98 at this stage, including 24 wounded who had made their way from Parit Sulong. Both battalions were ordered to be ready for battle again within a few days.

From Nishimura's viewpoint, the resistance between Bakri and Parit Sulong had been again a cause of anxiety. The British troops in the Bukit Pelandok positions had been dispersed by two battalions of the *4th Guards Regiment* sent to the area between Bukit Pelandok and Parit Sulong from near Batu Pahat to prevent reinforcements reaching Bakri; but the delay imposed on the force engaged against Anderson's column had been overcome only after Nishimura had "strenuously encouraged" attack. In his hour of triumph when the struggle ended, he contemplated leaving the battalion he had disposed in concealment south of Batu Pahat to fend for itself while the rest of his division stole a march on the *5th Division* by continuing the pursuit to Yong Peng and taking the lead along the trunk road. However, when he learned of the stage reached in the Westforce withdrawal, he decided that after his men had completed their task on the Muar-Yong Peng road he would swing his main force to the area of Batu Pahat.[2]

The enemy losses in the Muar area were a company of tanks and the equivalent of a battalion of men. Japanese accounts pay tribute to the valour of the troops who fought them there and at Gemas.

---

[9] Sgt G. J. Christoff, DCM, NX54034; 2/30 Bn. Motor driver; of Collarenebri, NSW; b. Walgett, NSW, 25 Aug 1911. Killed in action 30 Jan 1942.

[1] Bennett, *Why Singapore Fell*, p. 146.

[2] In a subsequent account of events at this stage Nishimura said he considered that it would not be *Bushido*—the Japanese soldier's equivalent of good form—to intervene in such circumstances. He congratulated himself, however, upon having forced the Westforce withdrawal.

CHAPTER 13

TO SINGAPORE ISLAND

THE Japanese had bitten deeply into the left flank of Westforce in the battle of Muar. With two divisions deployed from the trunk road and railway to the coast, General Yamashita was able to apply to a greater extent the strategy and tactics characteristic of his campaign. Displaying extreme mobility, his forces continued to make swift and unremitting use of the initiative they had gained. General Percival's forces were now being forced from the northern half of Johore, though that State was their last foothold on the Malayan mainland. The Japanese were stimulated by victory; their opponents were suffering the physical and psychological effects of withdrawal. Already Australian troops—the 27th Brigade—were sharing the loss and exhaustion imposed upon the III Indian Corps since the beginning of the struggle by constant fighting by day and movement by night.

To the east, Mersing, extensively prepared for defence on the ground that it offered a tempting back-door approach to Singapore Fortress, had been comparatively little affected at this stage; but, as shown, the likelihood that it would be attacked had resulted in the 22nd Brigade Group being kept there, and had prevented the Australians from being employed as a division in resisting the enemy's main thrust. Because of the Japanese possession of Kuantan and their progress in that and other sectors, the brigade had begun early in January to prepare to meet attack from the north and north-west rather than to resist a landing. Particular attention was paid to the Sungei Endau area and north of it. The river, with its tributaries, offered means of enemy approach in shallow draught vessels to the road running across the peninsula from Mersing, through Jemaluang, Kluang and Ayer Hitam to Batu Pahat. An Endau force was formed on 7th January, with Major Robertson,[1] of the 2/20th Battalion, in command. It comprised one company of the 2/19th Battalion and one of the 2/20th Battalion, the anti-aircraft platoon of the 2/18th, and a number of small vessels under command.

Enemy infiltration of the area was soon evident, for during the morning of the 14th a reconnaissance patrol saw thirty Japanese soldiers crossing the Sungei Pontian, about 15 miles north of Endau, oddly clad in steel helmets, black coats and khaki shorts. Next day Endau was bombed and machine-gunned, and a party of Japanese riding bicycles was engaged eight miles north of the Sungei Endau by a platoon led by Lieutenant Varley, son of the commander of the 2/18th Battalion, which had been sent forward for the purpose.[2] Both Endau and Mersing were attacked

---

[1] Lt-Col A. E. Robertson, NX34912; 2/20, 2/19 Bns (CO 2/19 Bn Feb 1942). Accountant; of Willoughby, NSW; b. NE Ham, Essex, 24 Jun 1906. Died while prisoner 31 Mar 1943.

[2] The platoon was in contact with the enemy for two days and inflicted a high proportion of casualties. In extricating his men Varley swam a flooded river and got a boat for them.

from the air on the 16th. When, on the 17th, it became apparent that the Japanese were gathering in the Endau area in strength, Brigadier Taylor decided that the Endau force had fulfilled its role, and ordered its withdrawal. Before this had been completed the area was again attacked by Japanese aircraft.[3] Because these attacks suggested some major move in the area, bridges on the way from Endau to Mersing were demolished and the road was cratered.

General Heath visited Brigadier Taylor's headquarters at Mersing on 18th January, and it was decided at a conference that the road leading south from Jemaluang through Kota Tinggi to Singapore Island, rather than defence of Mersing, must be considered vital—another indication of the concern being felt about attack from the flank and rear. It was also decided that the garrison being maintained at Bukit Langkap, west of Mersing on the Sungei Endau, must be reduced to strengthen Jemaluang. The new formation to be known as Eastforce was to be commanded by Taylor under Heath's control as from 6 a.m. on 19th January. It would comprise the 22nd Australian Brigade Group and all troops and craft in the Mersing-Kahang-Kota Tinggi areas.

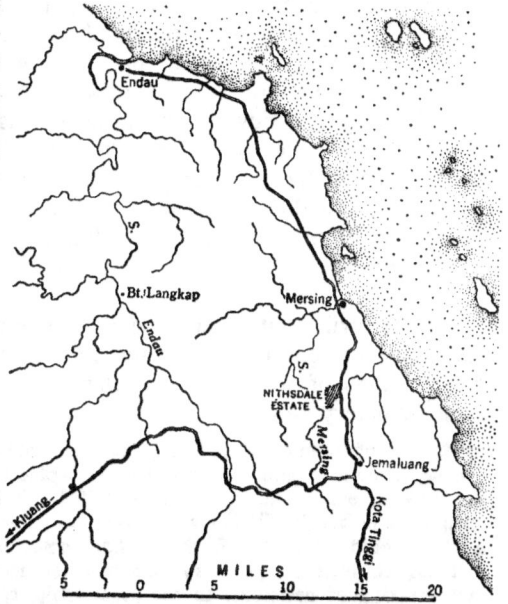

Its Australian components were the 2/18th and 2/20th Battalions, the 2/10th Field Regiment, the 2/10th Field Company, and the 2/9th Field Ambulance. Also included at this stage were the 2/17th Dogras, the Jat Battalion (amalgamated 2nd Jats-1/8th Punjabs), two companies of the Johore Military Forces, and the Johore Volunteer Engineers.

Patrols reported a gradual enemy approach to Mersing in the next two days, and the 2/20th Battalion area was under frequent air attack. During the morning of the 21st a patrol led by Lieutenant Ramsbotham[4] ambushed a party of Japanese near the north bank of the Sungei Mersing, and killed a number of them. The others attempted a flanking move, and entered a minefield. Though the mines had become immersed in water from

---

[3] During the 16th and 17th January HMS *Shun an* (Lt O. R. T. Henman) and HMS *Kelena* (Lt Connor Craig) went up and down the Endau under heavy bombing and rifle fire, firing broadsides from brass 3-pounders at the enemy on the north bank. The *Kelena* was sunk, but the *Shun an* was used to evacuate the garrison at Bukit Langkap, farther south on the Endau.

[4] Capt F. Ramsbotham, NX59561; 2/20 Bn. Clerk; of Bondi Junction, NSW; b. Murwillumbah, NSW, 22 Nov 1916.

heavy rains, and failed to explode, the Japanese were disposed of by machine-gun, mortar and artillery fire. In the afternoon a concentration of Japanese in the same locality was successfully dealt with by the 2/10th Field Regiment's guns.

An attempt was made early on 22nd January by a company of Japanese to capture the Mersing bridge. This, however, had been well wired, and the attackers wilted under concentrated mortar and machine-gun fire. A section of the 2/20th Battalion crossed the river and machine-gunned enemy posts, and houses in which the Japanese had hidden. Artillery which ranged along the road completed the task, and the rest of the enemy force moved westward. Enemy posts and concentrations elsewhere in the Mersing area were pounded by the Australians' guns, for which good fields of fire had been provided as a result of the evacuation of civilians on the outbreak of war with Japan. In keeping with the withdrawal policy laid down, Taylor moved his headquarters and the 2/18th Battalion less a company back to the Nithsdale Estate, 10 miles north of Jemaluang. The 2/10th Field Regiment maintained effective fire throughout the day, and the move was completed without interference during the night. The 2/20th Battalion was left covering the approach to Mersing.

On the civil front meanwhile the Governor, Sir Shenton Thomas, had responded to complaints that the civil administration was failing to meet the demands of war. In a circular issued to the Malayan civil service in mid-January he declared:

The day of minute papers has gone. There must be no more passing of files from one department to another, and from one officer in a department to another. It is the duty of every officer to act, and if he feels the decision is beyond him he must go and get it. Similarly, the day of letters and reports is over. All written matter should be in the form of short notes in which only the most important matters are mentioned. Every officer must accept his responsibility to the full in the taking of decisions. In the great majority of cases a decision can be taken or obtained after a brief conversation, by telephone or direct. The essential thing is speed in action. . . . Officers who show that they cannot take responsibility should be replaced by those who can. Seniority is of no account. . . .

On this the *Straits Times* commented: "The announcement is about two and half years too late," adding "but no matter. We have got it at last." It would, however, have required a staunch faith in miracles to entertain the idea that habits engendered by Malaya's venerable system of government could thus be changed overnight.

A further exchange of cables between the British and the Australian Prime Ministers had again indicated their differences in outlook. Replying on 18th January to Mr Churchill's cable of the 14th about the withdrawal in Malaya, Mr Curtin pointed out that Australia had not expected the whole of Malaya to be defended without superiority of seapower. On the contrary, the Australian Government had conveyed to the United Kingdom Government on 1st December 1941 the conclusion reached by the Australian delegation to the first Singapore conference that in the absence of a main fleet in the Far East the forces and equipment available in the area for the defence of Malaya were totally inadequate to meet a major attack by Japan. There had been suggestions of complacency with the present position which had not been justified by the speedy progress of the Japanese. Curtin reminded Churchill that the "various parts of the Empire . . . are differently situated, possess various resources, and have their own peculiar problems. . . ."

To this Churchill replied first with a review of his war strategy in which he said he was sure that it would have been wrong to send forces needed to beat General Rommel in the Middle East to reinforce the Malayan Peninsula while Japan was still at peace. He added that none could foresee the series of major naval disasters which befell Britain and the United States in December 1941. In the new situation he would have approved sending the three fast Mediterranean battleships to form, with the four "R's" and the *Warspite,* just repaired, a new fleet in the Indian Ocean to move to Australia's protection, but

> I have already told you of the *Barham*[5] being sunk (Churchill added). I must now inform you that the *Queen Elizabeth* and *Valiant*[6] have both sustained underwater damage from a "human torpedo" which put them out of action, one for three and the other for six months. . . . However, these evil conditions will pass. By May the United States will have a superior fleet at Hawaii. We have encouraged them to take their two new battleships out of the Atlantic if they need them, thus taking more burden upon ourselves. We are sending two, and possibly three, out of our four modern aircraft carriers to the Indian Ocean. *Warspite* will soon be there, and thereafter *Valiant*. Thus the balance of seapower in the Indian and Pacific Oceans will, in the absence of further misfortunes, turn decisively in our favour, and all Japanese overseas operations will be deprived of their present assurance. . . .

But Curtin, while appreciative, still was not reassured. "The long-distance program you outline is encouraging, but the great need is in the immediate future," he replied on the 22nd. "The Japanese are going to take a lot of repelling, and in the meantime may do very vital damage to our capacity to eject them from the areas they are capturing."

The immediate future as General Wavell saw it was reflected in a cable which he had sent to General Percival on 19th January:

> You must think out the problem of how to withdraw from the mainland should withdrawal become necessary (he said) and how to prolong resistance on the Island. . . . Will it be any use holding troops on the southern beaches if attack is coming from the north? Let me have your plans as soon as possible. Your preparations must, of course, be kept *entirely secret*. The battle is to be fought out in Johore till reinforcements arrive and troops must not be allowed to look over their shoulders. Under cover of selecting positions for the garrison of the Island to prevent infiltration of small parties you can work out schemes for larger forces and undertake

---

[5] *Barham* was torpedoed on 25 Nov.

[6] *Queen Elizabeth* and *Valiant* were put out of action in Alexandria harbour on 19th December, a month before Churchill's cable.

some preparation such as obstacles or clearances but make it clear to everyone that the battle is to be fought out in Johore without thought of retreat. . . .

Reporting the situation to Churchill, Wavell said that the number of troops required to hold the island effectively probably was as great as or greater than the number required to defend Johore. "I must warn you," he added . . . "that I doubt whether island can be held for long once Johore is lost."

Next day General Percival sent to Generals Heath, Bennett, and Simmons (the Singapore Fortress Commander) a "secret and personal" letter, with instructions that it should be shown only to such senior staff officers and column commanders as they might think should see it. In this Percival said that his present intention was to fight for the line Mersing-Kluang-Batu Pahat, on which was situated three important airfields, and on which the air observation system was based. He outlined a plan, however, to come into operation if withdrawal south of this line and to Singapore Island became necessary. It provided that there would be three columns—Eastforce, Westforce, and 11th Indian Division—falling back respectively on the Mersing road, the trunk road, and the west coast road to Johore Bahru. The movements of the columns would be coordinated by the III Corps, which would establish a bridgehead covering Johore Bahru through which they would pass on to the island. Selected positions would be occupied on each road, and ambushes laid between them. The positions and sites were to be reconnoitred and selected immediately. With this letter therefore Percival set afoot provisional measures for the abandonment of the Malayan mainland.

Also on 20th January General Wavell again visited Singapore. There he came to the conclusion that General Percival's forces would have to fall back to the Mersing-Kluang-Batu Pahat line, and that there was every prospect of their being driven off the mainland. He found that despite the instructions he had given for preparation of defences in the northern part of Singapore Island, very little had been done to this end. He told Percival to endeavour to hold the enemy on the mainland until further reinforcements arrived; but to make every preparation for defence of the island. After discussing dispositions for the latter purpose, he ordered that the 18th British Division, as the freshest and strongest formation, be assigned to the part of the island most likely to be attacked; that the 8th Australian Division be given the next most dangerous sector; and that the two Indian divisions, when they had been re-formed, be used as a reserve. Percival contended that the main attack would be on the north-east of the island, from the Sungei Johore, and favoured placing the 18th Division there, and the Australians in the north-west. Although Wavell thought this attack would be on the north-west—in the path of the enemy's main advance down the peninsula—he accepted Percival's judgment on the ground that he was the commander responsible for results, and had long studied the problem.

At this time also the question of Australian representation on the staff of A.B.D.A. was under discussion. In Wavell's plan for the organisation of his A.B.D.A. headquarters the only provision for a senior Australian officer was as deputy intendant general in the administrative branch. In a statement to the Australian Advisory War Council on 19th January on this subject, Mr Curtin said that this was another sidelight on the attitude of the United Kingdom towards Australian participation in the higher direction of the war in an area in which Australia was vitally concerned. Attached to the statement was a comparison of the military careers of Generals Wavell and Blamey, Commander-in-Chief of the Australian forces in the Middle East.[7] Curtin continued:

> When General Wavell was Commander-in-Chief in the M.E. his successes were mainly against Italians or black troops in Abyssinia, East Africa and Libya. He suffered defeats by the Germans in Libya in April 1941 and again in June 1941, when he launched a counter-offensive. He also was defeated by the Germans in the Greek campaign, though General Blamey conducted the actual operations of extricating the British forces.

Despite the implications of this passage, Curtin added:

> There can be no question of criticising this appointment, but apparently no Australian can expect consideration for a high command even though Australia may supply the largest share of the fighting forces as in the case of Greece and Malaya.

Curtin went on to say that exclusion of Australian officers from senior posts in A.B.D.A. was unjustifiable if Australia was to have three divisions and possibly a fourth in the area. A vital principle was at stake as much as the question of a share in the political higher direction.

> It is my view (concluded Mr Curtin) that the G.O.C., A.I.F., should either be given a high place on the staff of the Supreme Commander or a Field Command in an area where the A.I.F. is wholly concentrated under his operational control, subject only to the Supreme Commander. Alternatively, he should be brought back to Australia and be given a suitable post.

The Council concluded that the position allotted on Wavell's staff was "quite unacceptable", and that "the G.O.C., A.I.F., should be given a status that will ensure he is fully consulted in regard to all operational, administrative, and other plans insofar as they affect the A.I.F.". It recommended that representations be made to the British Government on these lines.

---

[7] This was in the form of a chronological summary in parallel columns of Wavell's and Blamey's military careers. It showed, for example, that Blamey (who was seven months younger than Wavell) had become a GSO1 in July 1916, Wavell in October 1916; Blamey had become a brigadier on the general staff (in France) in June 1918, Wavell (in Palestine) in March 1918; Blamey had become Second Chief of the General Staff in Australia in 1923 when Wavell was a GSO1 at the War Office. Blamey, having retired from the regular army, had been appointed to command a division in 1931; Wavell had become a divisional commander in England in 1935; from April 1941 Blamey had been first Wavell's and later Auchinleck's deputy commander-in-chief in the Middle East.

Indeed there was not much to choose between them so far as experience in staff and command appointments in war were concerned; but whether both London and Washington would not vigorously dispute a proposal that a Dominion commander be appointed was another matter.

The War Cabinet endorsed this conclusion.[8] On 21st January it had before it a proposal which carried the question of Australian representation into a higher sphere. This had come from the Dominions Office, and had been rejected by the Advisory War Council. It was to the effect that a Far Eastern Council be established in London on a Ministerial plane, presided over by Mr Churchill, and including a representative of Australia. Its function would be to "focus and formulate views of the represented Powers to the President", whose views would also be brought before the Council. Again endorsing the Advisory War Council's attitude, the War Cabinet decided to reply that both these bodies unanimously disagreed with the proposal. The Far Eastern Council would be purely advisory, and quite out of keeping with Australia's vital and primary interest in the Pacific sphere. It was desired that an accredited representative of the Australian Government should have the right to be heard in the British War Council in the formulation and direction of policy, and that a Pacific War Council be established at Washington, comprising representatives of the Governments of the United Kingdom, the United States, Australia, China, the Netherlands and New Zealand; this body to be a council of action for the higher direction of the war in the Pacific.

On the morning of 22nd January, after hope had been lost of rescuing Colonel Anderson's column at Parit Sulong, General Bennett ordered the 53rd Brigade to hold its positions behind the Bukit Pelandok defile, on his left flank, at least until midday on the 23rd, to help the remnants of the column to escape and enable other positions to be organised. The causeway between the defile and Yong Peng was to be held till 7 p.m. on the 23rd. Yong Peng was to be evacuated by midnight. Anti-aircraft guns were concentrated along the main road and railway and air cover for the withdrawal from Yong Peng was arranged. During the 22nd, however, Bennett received a report that the brigade was falling back, and sent orders that it must stand fast. He was informed also that resistance at Batu Pahat showed signs of cracking. His diary for the day concluded:

> Held usual Press conference today. Same correspondents present, representing British, American and Australian press. They were waiting for me just as I sent the Bakri men my last message. I told them the story but am afraid my chagrin and disappointment made me somewhat bitter and critical.[9]

---

[8] Wavell cabled to Army HQ Melbourne on 29th January that a senior Australian officer was on his general staff; the HQ of I Aust Corps would be within easy reach and General Lavarack, its commander, could be taken into consultation when necessary. He added: "There will thus be no lack of representation of Australian point of view." Wavell suggested that if further representation were required an Australian might become deputy to his chief of staff, General Pownall, or might, if suitably qualified, relieve his Chief of General Staff, General Playfair. He pointed out that the position as his own deputy, equivalent to that held by General Blamey in the Middle East, was held by an American, General Brett. He proposed to recommend creation of an area command under ABDA which would include the portion of Australia placed under his command, with Ambon and Timor, and that the commander be an Australian. In the upshot, however, ABDA was short-lived, and such adjustments were not made.
Concurrently, the Australian War Cabinet was informed in a cable from Churchill that the United States would be willing, he believed, to reinforce Australia's home defence troops by 40,000 to 50,000 Americans, subject to sufficient shipping being available. On the recommendation of the Australian Chiefs of Staff, it was decided to welcome the suggestion. As this relates principally to a later stage in the war with Japan, it is dealt with in Volume V of this series.

[9] Bennett, *Why Singapore Fell*, p. 144.

After a conference on the morning of 23rd January General Percival gave orders implementing the first stage of the plan for withdrawal to Singapore Island which he had outlined in his secret letter on the 20th. These provided that Westforce would come under General Heath's command as soon as the last troops had been withdrawn south of the Yong Peng road junction, and that the 53rd British Brigade, to move back through the 27th Australian Brigade, should revert at Ayer Hitam to General Key's (11th Indian Division) command. The general line Jemaluang-Kluang-Ayer Hitam-Batu Pahat was to be held, and there was to be no retraction from it without his permission. He had in mind that positions farther south were not good, and also the pending arrival of the rest of the 18th British Division. For this it was highly desirable that the enemy should be kept from the mainland airfields which lay behind the new defence line. A further concern was the growing strength of the Japanese near Mersing, and the possibility of another east coast landing.

General Bennett had assigned to the 2/30th Battalion the task of holding Yong Peng until first light on the 23rd, and of then covering Ayer Hitam from the north. Two of its companies were to remain at Yong Peng until the 53rd Brigade had completed its withdrawal. As the first stage of this movement was in progress the appearance of some of the newly-arrived Hurricanes in the sky seemed to the Australians to promise the air power so conspicuously lacking hitherto in Malaya, as it had been in Greece and Crete where their comrades had fought. "You bloody beauts!" they fervently exclaimed. Perhaps it was fortunate that they did not know that of the two airfields on the mainland which had remained in use by defending aircraft after the Japanese reached Muar, the Kahang airfield had been evacuated on the 22nd.

On the railway on 23rd January the 22nd Indian Brigade had taken up positions to guard the Kluang airfield, with the 2/18th Garhwal to their north at Paloh, where a road ran south-west to the main road near Yong Peng. Under attack the Garhwalis withdrew, and their headquarters became separated from their rifle companies. Lacking this contact, the companies continued their withdrawal and reached Kluang that night—by which time the Kluang airfield also had been abandoned by the air force. The 8th Indian Brigade, on the main road covering the approach from the north, held off the enemy during the day and at night passed through Yong Peng. It was then transported to the Rengam area, on the railway line south of Kluang.

In the course of its withdrawal from the road between Yong Peng and Bukit Pelandok the 53rd Brigade was repeatedly attacked by enemy tanks and infantry. Bridges on the causeway were blown before the movement had been completed. Two companies of the Loyals were forced into swamp through which the causeway ran, and became isolated, for the time being, with the result that the battalion was badly depleted when, as had been arranged, it came under command of the 27th Brigade, and was posted to the rear of the 2/30th Battalion. The 53rd Brigade reached Ayer

Hitam on 24th January, and was thereupon sent to Skudai. The task undertaken by the Japanese *Guards Division* in the Muar area now had been completed.

Early on the 24th, when the last of the southward-bound units had passed through the 2/30th Battalion and the Loyals, the Yong Peng bridge was blown up and, Percival related, "we breathed again".[1] The dangerous isolation of Westforce resulting from the collapse of resistance in the Muar area had been overcome, and the front was relatively straight from coast to coast. But as will be shown, its western end was fraying dangerously; and the Japanese were active also at the eastern end.

The 44th Indian Brigade, commanded by Brigadier Ballentine,[2] with attached troops and 7,000 Indian reinforcements, had reached Singapore on 22nd January, but as Percival considered it as little fitted for battle as the 45rd Indian Brigade he kept it on the island. The reinforcements, still less trained and with very few N.C.O's among them, were drafted sparingly to units. On 24th January there arrived the 2/4th Australian Machine Gun Battalion,[3] comprising 942 all ranks, and 1,907 largely untrained reinforcements for other units.[4] Some of these had defective rifles. The machine-gunners were allotted accommodation in the Naval Base area and ordered to prepare machine-gun positions on the north coast of the island. Thus the influx contributed little to the defence of the mainland, and the value of the newly-arrived Indian infantry for the defence of the island was considered uncertain.

Batu Pahat, where another threat to the defending forces was now developing, was, like Muar, a small coastal port, on the south bank of an estuary crossed by a ferry. One road connected it to Yong Peng, and one to Ayer Hitam, also on the trunk road. Another ran down the coast, turned inland at Pontian Kechil, and joined the trunk road at Kulai near

---

[1] Percival, *The War in Malaya*, p. 235.

[2] Brig G. C. Ballentine. Comd 44 Indian Bde. Regular soldier; b. 13 May 1893.

[3] The battalion had been formed in Western Australia in November 1940 and trained there and in South Australia before being sent to Darwin in October 1941. Thus, in January 1942, it had had 14 months' training—as much, for example, as most units of the 6th, 7th and 9th Divisions when they went into their first battles in North Africa or Syria. It was commanded by Lt-Col M. J. Anketell, a militia officer who had served as a subaltern in the 44th Battalion in France in 1917-18. The battalion had sailed from Darwin on 31st December to Port Moresby where part of the unit was trans-shipped to the *Aquitania* and the remainder stayed in the *Marella*. These ships reached Sydney on 8th January and Fremantle on the 15th. Fremantle was the machine-gunners' home port. No leave was granted but most of the unit became absent without leave, and 94 had not returned when the ships sailed for Singapore. In the Sunda Strait the battalion was trans-shipped into small Dutch vessels which landed it at Singapore. The only other machine-gun battalion in Malaya was the 1/Manchester.

[4] The arrival of such reinforcements in Malaya may be explained partly by the fact that the practice had developed of sending raw recruits to the Middle East where they received their basic training under expert instructors in the excellent training organisation established there. This does not, however, excuse the blunder of sending untrained men forward (early in January) to a division then going into battle. Even if there was a shortage of adequately trained reinforcements in Australia early in December, the needs of the 8th Division could have been foreseen. If necessary a shipload of reinforcements could have been sent from the Middle East where, in mid-December, after all units had been filled, there were 16,600 in the reinforcement pool (including 10,000 recently arrived), and whither, in 1941, a percentage of the men in some 8th Division units in Australia had been sent as reinforcements. In Australia on 8th December there were also 87,000 militiamen on full-time duty, many thousands of whom had already received months of training. Soon after war with Japan broke out these were debarred from enlisting in the AIF lest their units be unduly depleted by a large number of such transfers. Even so, these militiamen constituted a pool from which fairly well-trained volunteers might have been sought.

Johore Bahru, capital of Johore. Thus the area offered scope to the *Guards Division* for further influencing the course of the campaign. Nishimura's hitherto concealed *I/4th Battalion* had engaged in minor encounters with the British forces at Batu Pahat from 18th January onward. A sweep by the British Battalion and the Cambridgeshires on the 21st to clear the Bukit Banang area south of the town was unsuccessful, and Japanese troops were encountered north-east of the town also. Generals Heath and Key visited Brigadier Challen during the day, and told him that he must not only hold the area, but keep open the road to Ayer Hitam. Soon after they had gone, it was found that the Japanese had placed a block across it. The road was temporarily cleared next day by the 5/Norfolks from Ayer Hitam and the British Battalion from Batu Pahat; but a British field battery was attacked at a point on the coastal road about five miles south of Batu Pahat, its commander was killed, and a gun was abandoned. On the 23rd the Ayer Hitam road was again blocked, and the 5/Norfolks, who were to have moved along it from Ayer Hitam into Batu Pahat to reinforce the garrison, were sent via Skudai and Pontian Kechil instead.

Challen now feared that his 15th Brigade would find itself in a situation similar to that which had developed at Bakri. Unable to get instructions because his wireless had failed, he decided to withdraw from the town to a position in depth on the coastal road between Batu Pahat and Senggarang. Communication was restored while this movement was in progress, and it was reported to the 11th Division. Concerned that such a withdrawal would give the enemy access to the left flank and communications of Westforce and endanger the new defence line, Key ordered it to be cancelled, and Batu Pahat to be reoccupied. This order was confirmed by Heath after consultation with Percival. Although the Japanese had penetrated the town to some extent, and concealed themselves in houses, Challen's men re-entered it and took up defensive positions for the night.

At this ominous stage of events in Malaya, Japanese forces had overcome (on 23rd January) the Australian garrison at Rabaul, administrative centre of the Mandated Territory of New Guinea.[5] The enemy had thus extended his far-flung battle line east of the A.B.D.A. area, and made his first assault on territory under Australian control. Within the A.B.D.A. area Japan had used the middle prong of a trident thrust to the south to occupy Balikpapan (Dutch Borneo), also on the 23rd, and Kendari (Celebes) on the 24th. Disturbing reports had reached General Wavell of Japanese progress in Burma. The day after the fall of Rabaul he received notification that his responsibilities had been extended to the defence of Darwin and a strip of the adjoining coastal area considered necessary for this purpose.[6] Taking this adjustment into account, the total number of men in the Australian land forces in the A.B.D.A. area,

---

[5] See Chapter 18.
[6] Wavell's directive provided that none of the forces of 7th Military District in the area, numbering 14,050, was to be transferred from Australia without the consent of the Australian Government.

including "Sparrow Force" on Timor Island and "Gull Force" on Ambon Island, was 34,370. Six squadrons of the Royal Australian Air Force were also in the area—three in Malaya, one on Ambon, and two based on Darwin and Timor—and a small advanced party of I Australian Corps reached Java on 26th January. These considerations gave further weight to the complaint that Australia was inadequately represented in the higher direction of A.B.D.A. and on Wavell's staff.

Reporting on 24th January to the Combined Chiefs of Staff on the outlook in his command, Wavell said that the only possible course was to use such limited resources as were available to check the enemy's intense offensive effort as far forward as possible by hard fighting, taking offensive action whenever possible. This policy would involve heavy losses by land, sea and air, and ability to make further efforts would depend on these losses being rapidly made good.

In Malaya, 24th January was another fateful day. Heath now commanded a front on which Eastforce was in contact with the enemy in the Mersing area; Westforce, with the 9th Division (8th and 22nd Indian Brigades) on the railway covering Kluang and the 27th Australian Brigade covering Ayer Hitam, was temporarily disengaged; and the 11th Indian Division had the 15th Brigade precariously situated at Batu Pahat, the 28th Brigade at Pontian Kechil, and the 53rd Brigade on its way from Skudai to Benut, on the west coast road between Pontian Kechil and Batu Pahat. During the day Percival issued an outline plan indicating the method to be adopted in the event of withdrawal to Singapore Island, but without a time-table. The withdrawal by the 2/18th Garhwal Regiment from Paloh on 23rd January had created a dangerous situation, and the 8th Indian Brigade gained little respite at Rengam before it was ordered forward to enable the 22nd Brigade to counter-attack on the 24th. It was planned that the 5/11th Sikhs, commanded by Lieut-Colonel Parkin,[7] should swing to the west and come in on the line at Niyor, the junction of a branch road from the railway to the road linking Kluang and Ayer Hitam. However, as progress of the rest of the brigade up the railway was slow, the Sikhs were ordered to reach it at an intermediate point. Lacking a map of the area, Parkin kept to the route originally ordered, but his battalion encountered a road-block and formed a perimeter for the night of the 24th-25th.

On the west coast the attempt to reinforce the 15th Brigade was resumed at dawn on the 24th, and the 5/Norfolk, having moved up the coast road, reached it soon after 7 a.m. Street fighting was in progress at Batu Pahat, with a Cambridgeshire company holding a position in the centre of the township. The Norfolks were ordered to occupy a rise overlooking the exit to the coast road, but the supporting artillery was able to give little aid because ammunition lorries had been omitted by error from the reinforcing convoy. By nightfall the battalion was still short of its objec-

---

[7] Lt-Col J. H. D. Parkin, DSO; CO 5/11 Sikh. Regular soldier; b. 22 Apr 1898.

tive. Pressure from north-east of the township increased next morning, and a reconnaissance report indicated that an enemy force (presumably Nishimura's *1/4th Battalion*) was concealed near Senggarang. It was therefore in a position to cut Challen's line of communication, as Nishimura had planned to do. With his fears of becoming isolated thus confirmed, Challen again sought permission to withdraw, but was told that a decision could not be given until after a conference which General Percival was to hold during the afternoon. Meanwhile the 53rd Brigade, consisting at this stage of the 6/Norfolk and the 3/16th Punjab, each of only two companies, had reached Benut. It took two squadrons of the 3rd Cavalry and a field battery under command, and Brigadier Duke sent the Norfolks forward with armoured car and artillery support, to leave a garrison of one company at Rengit and then press on to Senggarang. The head of the column, less the company left at Rengit, reached Senggarang at 8 a.m. but the Japanese in the area successfully attacked its tail half a mile south of the village, and established a series of road-blocks.

In the central sector heavy air attacks on the crossroads at Ayer Hitam, where the 2/30th Australian Battalion and the 2/Loyals were stationed, had made it obvious that the Japanese would press home their advantage. The roar of demolitions along the road had indicated that the 2/12th Australian Field Company was doing its best to make this as difficult for them as possible. The company had been hard at work during the whole of the struggle from the time of the Gemencheh ambush, and as occasion arose its members shared in the fighting.

Viewing this now familiar pattern of threat and compulsion, Percival decided, after his conference in the afternoon of 25th January with Heath, Bennett, and Key, that the 15th Brigade should immediately link with the 53rd Brigade in the Senggarang area; Westforce to withdraw at night to the general line Sungei Sayong Halt-Sungei Benut on the railway and trunk road respectively. This line was to be held at least until the night of 27th-28th January, and subsequent withdrawals were to be made to positions specified in advance. Eastforce and the 11th Division were to move in conformity with Westforce, under orders from Heath. Bennett was to hold a good battalion in reserve, whenever possible, to deal with the danger of penetration from the Pontian Kechil area. The 2/Gordon Highlanders, from Singapore Island, were to relieve the Loyals.

There remained a slender hope that the Japanese advance might be stemmed in southern Johore, but withdrawal to Singapore Island was an insistent probability. With this in mind Heath had selected areas for delaying action on a series of lines to the rear. He gave maps to Key and Bennett on which these lines had been marked, with tentative times for withdrawals; and he subsequently ordered Eastforce to withdraw to Jemaluang. Key ordered the weak 53rd Brigade to clear the road from Rengit to Senggarang by dawn on the 26th, and 15th Brigade to reach Benut by the 27th; Challen to take command of the troops at Senggarang and Rengit as he reached them. Bennett issued orders for the movement required of Westforce. On the basis of Heath's maps he issued that day or the next—records differ on this point—an outline withdrawal plan. This required that the 9th Division should withdraw down the axis of the railway and the 27th Brigade down the trunk road, denying successive positions to the enemy. As there was no road from a few miles south of Layang Layang to Sedenak down which the 9th Division might withdraw its artillery and transport, it was necessary for this to be sent from Rengam by estate roads to the 40½-mile post on the trunk road while it was still covered. Between Rengam and Sedenak the division would be restricted to such equipment as could be manhandled, and would have to make its way on foot.

During the afternoon of the 25th, Brigadier Taylor held a conference of his commanding officers. The day before, when Kluang airfield was endangered and he was ordered to destroy Kahang airfield, he had moved his headquarters to a point east of Jemaluang. He now issued orders for his headquarters to be established on the Kota Tinggi road south of Jemaluang, and for the 2/20th Battalion to withdraw from its strongly prepared positions to Jemaluang crossroads that night. The enemy, however, was to be made to pay for the concession. Lieut-Colonel Varley, of the 2/18th Battalion, gained approval of a plan for a large-scale ambush in the Nithsdale and adjacent Joo Lye Estates. This would operate on the withdrawal of the 2/20th, and after carrying it out the 2/18th would pass back to a position on the Kota Tinggi road. Bombing of Mersing during the day was heavy, but the 2/20th made its withdrawal with precision, and the 2/18th meanwhile took up its ambush positions.

In the railway sector on the 25th the Sikhs were preparing to advance on Niyor when they received orders to withdraw to Kluang. Parkin decided that the attack should be made to secure freedom for this movement. In the ensuing engagement the Japanese were routed with bayonets, and the withdrawal was then made with relative ease. The rest of the 22nd Brigade was engaged during the day, but with the headquarters and headquarters company of the Garhwal, who rejoined it during the afternoon, withdrew at night (25th-26th) to Rengam, where the Sikhs rejoined next morning. The same night the 8th Brigade was withdrawn to Sungei Sayong Halt.

Fighting had occurred meanwhile on the trunk road sector (where as is now known the main body of the Japanese *5th Division* was being employed). The 2/30th Battalion (Colonel Galleghan) and the 2/Loyals (Colonel Elrington) were covering the northern approach to the vital road junction at Ayer Hitam. "A" Company (Major Anderson) of the 2/30th, a "B" Company platoon (Lieutenant Cooper[8]), a few newly-arrived reinforcements, and a detachment of mortars (Sergeant McAlister[9]) occupied a hill position on the right, 4,000 yards north of the junction,

---

[8] Lt J. H. Cooper, NX12530; 2/30 Bn. Sharebroker's clerk; of Wollstonecraft, NSW; b. Wollstonecraft, 11 Apr 1914.

[9] Sgt A. J. McAlister, NX15405; 2/30 Bn. Farm labourer; of Hurstville, NSW; b. Gundagai, NSW, 9 Dec 1915.

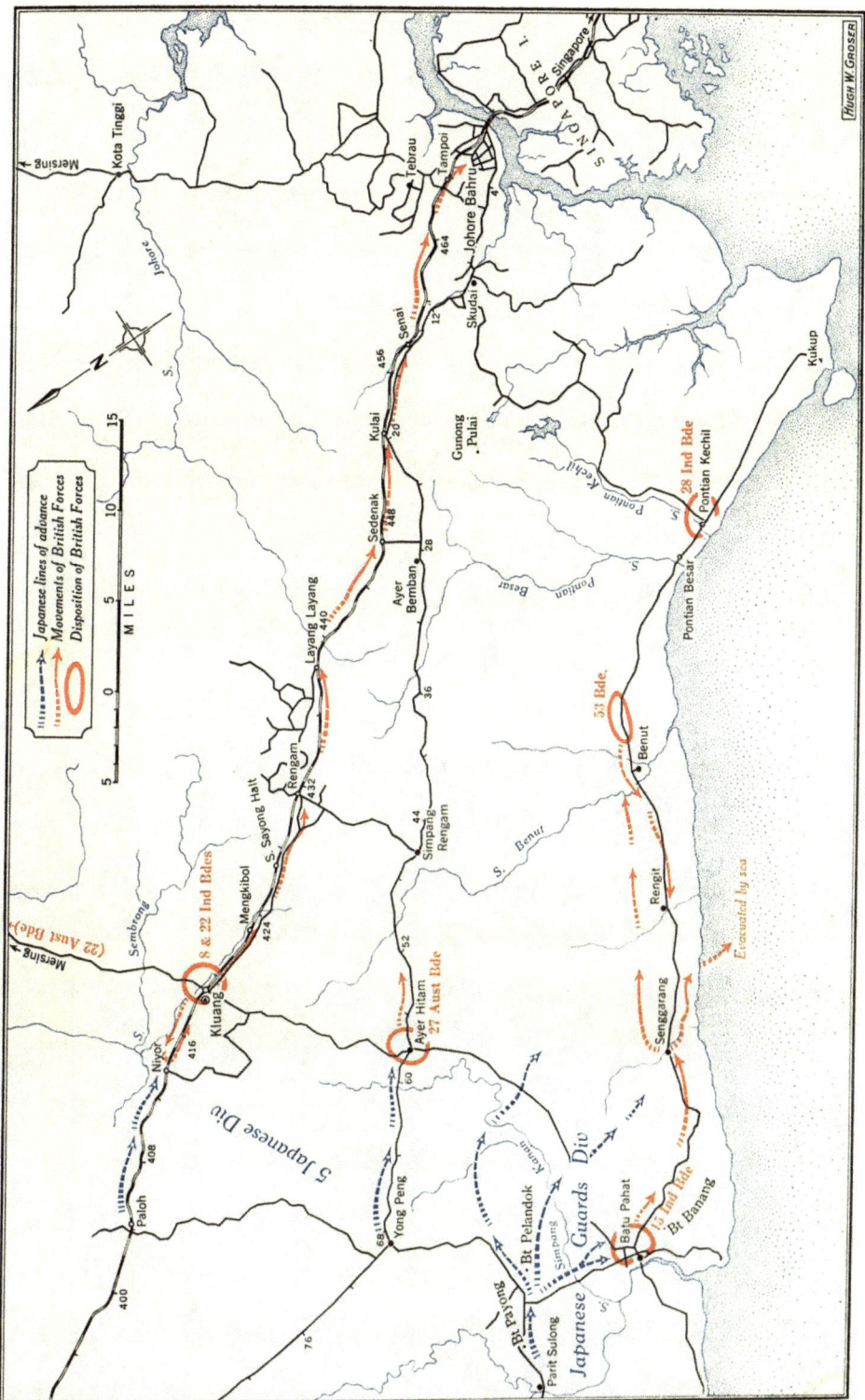

Western Johore, 25th January

with the Loyals forward astride the road. Between these positions and the rest of the battalion was the Sungei Sembrong and an area of swamp, scrub, and jungle. The area offered good fields of fire. Anderson's men took full advantage of grass and bracken on their hill for concealment from air observation, and dry rations were passed from hand to hand among them with a minimum of movement.[1] The battalion maintained these precautions for two days, despite a growing feeling that it might be better to be bombed than to be driven mad by mosquitoes. On 24th January the Loyals came down the road under enemy pressure, and on Brigadier Maxwell's instructions were redisposed by Galleghan with "A" Company under Anderson's command. Despite his senior rank, Elrington elected to remain with his men and accept direction, on the ground that Anderson was more familiar than he with the local situation.

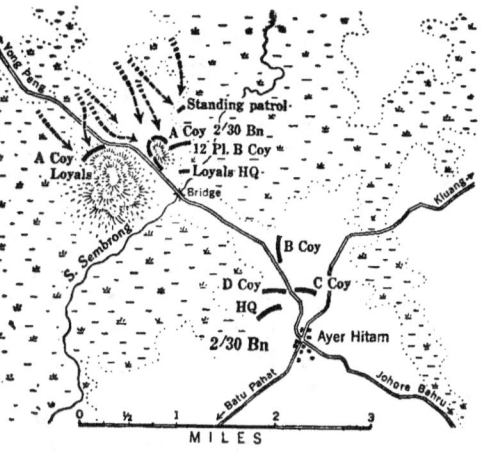

Ayer Hitam, 24th-25th January

Heavy tropical rain added to the discomfort of the troops on the 25th. Japanese aircraft were overhead trying to locate them and destroy the bridge over the river. Patrol actions, in which Sergeant Russell[2] of the 2/30th was outstanding, commenced at dawn and gradually developed into general fighting in the forward area, with heavy fire against the defenders and the bridge. Near mid-afternoon attacking troops were led by an officer bearing a large Japanese flag. He was shot down, and so were a second and a third who attempted to carry it forward. Beaten back by Australian small arms and mortar fire, the Japanese abandoned their emblem. In the latter part of the afternoon the Japanese made a two-company attack on the right flank of Anderson's company but were similarly repulsed by the Australians and the Loyals, and left many casualties lying on the ground. A second attack in greater strength became bogged down in swamp and under mortar fire. Then, as light was failing, the enemy heavily attacked a company of Loyals west of the road. The Loyals held on until some of them were in hand-to-hand conflict, but were outnumbered, and after suffering heavily were forced from their positions.

---

[1] "After Gemas the Japanese air observers never again located the battalion positions on the ground, and there is no known case of a further casualty from bombing, by direct attack on the battalion positions, although two or three casualties were caused by air attacks on near-by objectives. This successful evasion of air attack was considered to be due to the elimination of transport from the battle area and to strict battle discipline throughout the unit."—*Galleghan's Greyhounds*, p. 159.

[2] Sgt E. S. Russell, NX28821; 2/30 Bn. Forestry worker; of Bondi, NSW; b. St. Kilda, Vic, 9 Feb 1913. Killed in action 11 Feb 1942.

The forward left flank was thus exposed, but as Japanese came on to the road and could be dimly seen by a platoon under Lieutenant Brown,[3] which occupied the top of a cutting, the platoon's fire forced them to ground. In retaliating the Japanese used "a queer weapon which emitted red balls of flame and much smoke to little effect".[4] Though they tried later to rush the position and mounted machine-guns, the platoon held them off with mortars, Bren guns and grenades. The rest of the battalion, however, and the artillery positions behind Ayer Hitam, were now under intensive shelling and bombing. As the brigade was due to withdraw that night, the battalion was pulled back. The Japanese having gained the road, the withdrawal from the forward positions was made partly through swamp and abandoned rice-fields, in darkness and under persistent enemy machine-gun fire. Although they had to struggle through mud at times waist-deep, the stretcher-bearers succeeded without exception in their tasks. Captain Peach,[5] the adjutant, who had brought forward the withdrawal order, succeeded under similar conditions in conveying it to the Loyals and returning to the bridge over the Sungei Sembrong. At 9 p.m., when he was assured that only the enemy were forward of it, he ordered its demolition. Captain Duffy successfully commanded a rearguard partly consisting of his ("B") company and some Loyals, and covering 25-pounder fire was given by the 30th Battery of the 2/15th Field Regiment. Although the Japanese had been made to pay heavily, the casualties of the 2/30th Battalion were only four killed and twelve wounded or missing. The battalion took up during the night a position it had been assigned at the 41-mile post, five miles south of Simpang Rengam. The Loyals were withdrawn to Singapore Island and replaced as had been arranged by the Gordons, who occupied a position at Sungei Benut (milestone 48½) with the 2/26th Battalion at milestone 44½.

In the west, Brigadier Challen succeeded, with the aid of a bombardment by the river gunboat *Dragonfly*, in withdrawing his forces during the night of 25th-26th January from Batu Pahat. Although he had been ordered by General Key to reach Benut by the 27th, he discovered at Senggarang on the morning of the 26th that the enemy had occupied the bridge and near-by buildings at the southern end of the village. The Cambridgeshires cleared the buildings, but were held up by enemy fire along the swamp-lined road leading to the Japanese blocks. Under attack also from the air on artillery positions and transport, successive attempts to force a way south were unavailing.

Thus Brigadier Duke (53rd Brigade) found himself called upon as at Bukit Pelandok, though with a depleted brigade, to conduct a relieving operation. On orders from Key, who visited his headquarters at 10.30

---

[3] Lt G. V. Brown, NX30914; 2/30 Bn. Hardware salesman; of Mosman, NSW; b. Sydney, 24 Oct 1917.

[4] *Galleghan's Greyhounds*, p. 157. The Japanese sometimes used fireworks in endeavours to create confusion and panic.

[5] Lt-Col F. S. B. Peach, NX76207; 2/30 Bn. Regular soldier; of Bexley, NSW; b. Arncliffe, NSW, 4 Oct 1915.

a.m. on the 26th, he mustered and sent from Benut at 12.30 p.m. a column under a British territorial officer, Major C. F. W. Banham, of artillery, armoured cars, carriers and a detachment of infantry, with orders to deploy at Rengit. The column nevertheless was in close formation when it ran into a road-block a little north of the village, and was almost wiped out. Only Banham's carrier broke through and continued on its way. After negotiating the succession of blocks established by the enemy, it dramatically toppled over the last one and reached Senggarang at 2 p.m. just as Brigadier Challen was about to launch a full-scale attempt to break through to the south.

On Banham's report of the obstructions he had encountered, Challen decided that it would be useless to attempt to get his guns and vehicles to Benut. He therefore ordered them to be destroyed, the wounded to be left under the protection of the Red Cross, and the remaining troops to make their way across country past the enemy.[6] That night, after having blocked the road south of Rengit, the Japanese captured that village. About 1,200 of Challen's men, guided by an officer of the Malayan police force, moved east of the road from Senggarang and reached Benut next afternoon. Others, led by Challen, moved west of the road, and halted at a river during the night of the 26th-27th. Challen was taken prisoner while he searched for a crossing. Lieut-Colonel Morrison, of the British Battalion, thereupon took command, led the men to the coast west of Rengit, and sent an officer to Pontian Kechil to seek aid. General Percival decided when he learned of their plight to evacuate them by sea. By using two gunboats (*Dragonfly* and *Scorpion*) and a number of small craft from Singapore, this daring and difficult task was carried out during successive nights, and completed on 1st February.

In dislodging and dispersing the 15th Brigade, the Japanese *Guards Division* had carried out a series of adventurous enveloping movements. Despite the obstacles presented by rivers, jungle, and swamp, and the fact that units went astray from time to time, the movements were generally well coordinated. The *5th Infantry Regiment* lost the equivalent of a battalion in the fighting between Muar and Batu Pahat, but the division's total losses were small in comparison with the results which it achieved in overcoming resistance in the Batu Pahat area and influencing the course of the struggle on the mainland generally.

Concurrently with the withdrawal of the 15th Brigade from Batu Pahat, enemy forces were increasingly active at the eastern end of the Johore defence line. A convoy which comprised four cruisers, one aircraft carrier, six destroyers, two transports, and thirteen smaller craft was sighted 20 miles north-east of Endau by Australian airmen at 7.45 a.m. on 26th January, but their warning signal was not received. Thus it was only when they returned to base on Singapore Island at 9.20 a.m. that the news reached Air Headquarters.[7] Only thirty-six aircraft were available

---

[6] The infantry comprised at this stage the British Battalion, 5/ and 6/Norfolk and 2/Cambridgeshire.

[7] The report gave the strength of the convoy as two cruisers, 12 destroyers, and two transports.

as a striking force. As it was thought that the Japanese vessels would be in shallow water by the time they could be attacked, the Vildebeestes in the force were rearmed with bombs instead of torpedoes which they normally carried. The bomber group in Java was ordered to send all available bombers to Endau, and A.B.D.A. Command was asked for American bombers to supplement the endeavour. It was not until early in the afternoon that the first wave of the local force (9 Hudsons and 12 Vildebeestes) took off, escorted by 23 fighters. Heavy opposition was encountered in the target area, which was reached about 3 p.m., but the attackers were able to avail themselves of cloud cover. Direct hits were made on two transports and a cruiser, and bombs were dropped among troops in barges and on the beaches, for a loss of 5 Vildebeestes.

About 5 p.m., when the second attack was made, by 9 Vildebeestes and 3 Albacores, with 12 fighters, the clouds had disappeared, and the damage inflicted upon the enemy was slight, but 5 more Vildebeestes, 2 Albacores and a fighter were lost. Five Hudsons from Sumatra returned to Singapore after bombing troops and landing-craft in the Sungei Endau during the evening. Early next morning two obsolescent destroyers—*Vampire* (Australian) and *Thanet*—sent from Singapore, encountered three modern Japanese destroyers. Under concentrated attack, *Thanet* quickly sank. *Vampire,* trying to cover *Thanet* with a smoke-screen, was next engaged, and another destroyer and a light cruiser joined in the action against her. She nevertheless succeeded in eluding the enemy, and escaped to Singapore. Thus the enemy was able to complete the landing operation. On the other hand the number of defending aircraft in service in Malaya had been reduced to near vanishing point. Not only had a high proportion of them been lost, but others had been badly damaged; two squadron leaders had been killed, and a number of the airmen had been wounded.

The Japanese force which landed was the *96th Airfield Battalion* and its signal unit, to operate the Kahang and Kluang airfields as soon as they had been captured. This was not known when the convoy was sighted on the 26th, and, in the light also of the evidence of concentration of enemy troops from the north, it then appeared that the 22nd Brigade could expect to be attacked on a large scale. Arrangements were completed for Varley's ambush, but with the stipulation, in keeping with the general withdrawal orders, that the troops employed in it must withdraw through the 2/20th Battalion at Jemaluang immediately the ambush had been sprung, to the section of the road to Kota Tinggi allotted to them. Captain Edgley's[8] company of the 2/18th was west of the road from Mersing, near a height known as Gibraltar Hill and where jungle growth formed a defile; Major O'Brien's[9] east of the road to the south of the defile; Cap-

---

[8] Capt J. L. Edgley, NX34780; 2/18 Bn. Solicitor; of Fairfield, NSW; b. Dorrigo, NSW, 2 Jul 1912. Killed in action 27 Jan 1942.

[9] Maj C. B. O'Brien, EM, NX34793; 2/18 Bn. School teacher; of Maroubra, NSW; b. Eaglehawk, Vic, 29 Dec 1906.

tain Johnstone's[1] company astride the road to the rear of these positions; and Captain Okey's[2] company in reserve. It was proposed to let about a battalion of Japanese pass the two forward companies and to come upon a block established by Johnstone's company. Guns of the 20th and 60th Batteries of the 2/10th Field Regiment, supplementing the battalion mortars and machine-guns, would pound the trapped enemy troops at this stage, and an artillery barrage would creep forward, spreading to both sides of the road into the Nithsdale Estate, as Edgley's men moved in behind it on to the road. After mopping up, they would then move south towards O'Brien's company, whose task was to dispose of any Japanese who survived on its front. The success of the plan depended upon all concerned withholding fire until a sufficient number of Japanese had entered the trap. This required a degree of self-control which would severely test the training of the 2/18th Battalion.

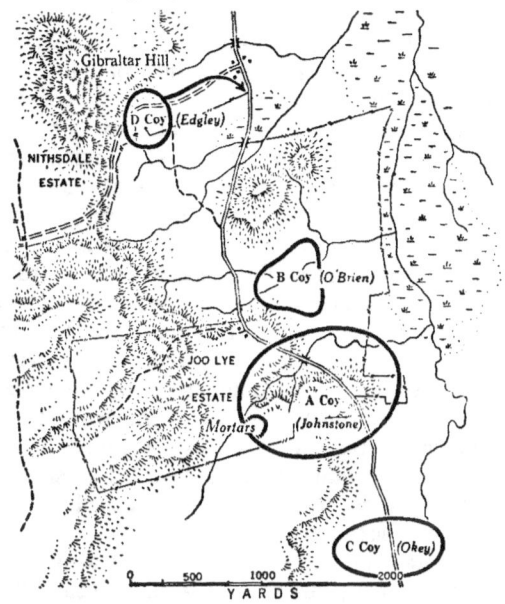

Nithsdale Estate, 26th-27th January

A force estimated at 1,000 Japanese, reported to be moving from Endau to Mersing, was not expected to reach the positions until after daylight on the 27th. However, patrols had exchanged shots with a Japanese patrol in the ambush area late in the afternoon of the 26th. After dark increasing numbers of Japanese, finally estimated at battalion strength, were observed but allowed to pass into the area as arranged, despite the ideal target presented by enemy troops marching along the road in column of route. Indiscriminate enemy fire, accompanied by the noise of crackers, broke out soon after midnight, apparently intended to make the Australians disclose their positions; but their orders to hold fire were strictly observed. Lieutenant Warden's[3] platoon of Johnstone's company was attacked at 2 a.m., and retaliated with bayonets. Although the encounter was expensive for the Japanese, it resulted also in the death of the platoon commander, and two others. An hour later, when the

---

[1] Maj F. T. Johnstone, ED, NX12511; 2/18 Bn. Law clerk; of Armidale, NSW; b. Armidale, 15 Jun 1906.

[2] Maj D. T. Okey, NX35116; 2/18 Bn. Schoolmaster; of Chatswood, NSW; b. Greymouth, NZ, 10 Jun 1903.

[3] Lt W. G. Warden, NX34942; 2/18 Bn. Apprentice plumber; of Pennant Hills, NSW; b. Inverell, NSW, 2 Jul 1920. Killed in action 27 Jan 1942.

pressure indicated that a large body of Japanese was engaged, the mortar and artillery fire was ordered. Varley, who for some while had been vainly trying to get through to the forward companies by telephone, succeeded at this critical stage and ordered them to carry out the agreed plan. Johnstone's company heard a stream of shells rushing over them into the defile,[4] which became a shambles. After about 20 minutes the barrage had moved far enough up the road to allow the forward companies to go into action. Soon after, Varley received a telephone message from Edgley that his company had not come into contact with the enemy, and was about to withdraw as arranged. That was the last report Varley received from him. It transpired that the company's leading section attacked Japanese who were repairing a bridge; thereupon the Japanese fled to positions which had been hastily taken up by their force on high ground astride the road at the southern end of the defile. A two-platoon attack failed to dislodge them, and a platoon sent to their left flank was repulsed. In savage encounters, the Australians discovered that the position was strongly held, and came under an increasing volume of mortar and machine-gun fire, accompanied by grenades. Because of this, and communication difficulties, the fight was still raging when daylight came. O'Brien's company was also engaged, though with smaller numbers of the enemy, with whom it dealt successfully. It therefore moved towards the Japanese stronghold encountered by Edgley and itself encountered severe resistance.

Meanwhile Varley found himself again cut off from line communication with his men; but at 7.45 a.m. Sergeant Wagner,[5] the battalion's Intelligence sergeant, who had gone forward through the enemy to the forward positions, provided information which enabled the artillery again to concentrate on its target with notable results. Varley then ordered Johnstone to assemble men for a counter-attack. They were about to move off, and the move by O'Brien's company to assist Edgley's was afoot, when a message was received from Brigadier Taylor in consequence of detailed orders he had received from Heath under the general withdrawal plan. It was to the effect that as the brigade (less its 2/19th Battalion) was responsible for holding the whole of the road back to Johore Bahru, no further troops must be committed to the action, and the companies engaged must be withdrawn to Jemaluang.

The order was reluctantly obeyed, especially as it meant leaving Edgley's company—and to an extent O'Brien's also—to fight their way out. The withdrawal of the battalion, including such of the forward troops as could be extricated, was covered by Okey's company. In the final count its losses in the ambush action were found to be six officers and 92 others killed or missing; but the Japanese losses appeared to have been far heavier. Edgley's company was subsequently reconstituted of survivors—about a platoon strong—who had made their way back to the battalion,

---

[4] The two artillery batteries fired 900 rounds in the first hour of the operation.
[5] Lt C. A. Wagner, DCM, NX29683; 2/18 Bn; and guerilla forces in Philippines, 1943. Pump hand (boot trade); of Woollahra, NSW; b. Bondi, 12 Aug 1916. Killed in action 21 Dec 1943.

and others, under Captain Toose.[6] A series of further movements in keeping with the withdrawal plan were made unmolested by Eastforce, commanded by Varley[7] while Taylor carried out a bridgehead task to which, as will be seen, he had been allotted. Reports from men who came in after being cut off indicated that the setback imposed on the Japanese was such that they did not occupy Jemaluang until 29th January.

A Japanese account of the experiences of the Kuantan landing force (two battalions of the *55th Infantry Regiment* with artillery and engineers) which made its way to the Mersing area indicates that it encountered severe difficulties in making its way from Kuantan through jungle and swamp. Men handling artillery pieces sank deep in the mire; troops ate tree roots, coconuts, and wild potatoes, and at times could find dry resting places only by climbing trees. The fighting near Jemaluang was "an appalling hand-to-hand battle". Seriously weakened, the force withdrew towards Mersing, and strong reinforcements were sent from Kluang to Jemaluang. The *55th Infantry Regiment* was then diverted to Kluang to join the main body of the Japanese *18th Division*. The progress of the *5th* and *Guards Divisions* having made unnecessary the earlier plan to land the *18th Division* in the Mersing area, this formation had landed at Singora on 22nd and 23rd January and had been brought south, bringing the Japanese strength on the west of the peninsula to three divisions. Because of the terrain of Malaya and insufficient means of transporting the *18th Division's* horses by sea, these had been left behind in Canton; nor had it mechanical transport of its own; but lorries had been made available by the other formations to transport its main force from Singora to the scene of action.

In the central sector the withdrawal plan was being carried out meanwhile under varying pressure. Low-flying Japanese planes were constantly overhead, and the Gordons and the 2/26th Battalion were intensively strafed. A sheet of paper blown from the cockpit of a Japanese fighter and picked up in the 2/26th Battalion area bore an accurate sketch of the dispositions. Early in the afternoon of the 26th January snipers and machine-gunners attacked the Gordons' forward companies. Japanese troops who then approached along the edges of the road were checked by mortar and 25-pounder gun fire. Near the close of the day, however, it was reported that the Gordons had run out of food and water and their ammunition was running short.[8] Under further enemy pressure they were withdrawn, but fortunately the Japanese did not immediately seize their advantage.

In the afternoon General Heath had held a conference at which he issued a definite program for movements culminating in a withdrawal to

---
[6] Capt A. V. C. Toose, NX12347; 2/18 Bn. Bank officer; of Kempsey, NSW; b. Comara, NSW, 31 Oct 1910.

[7] Major W. E. Fraser replaced Varley in command of the 2/18th Battalion during this period.

[8] Colonel Thyer wrote later: "On enquiries being made it was discovered that the battalion carried no reserve of rations, and that the water supply had not been replenished since the day before. The location of the ammunition point at the 35-mile post had been notified."

Singapore Island on the night of 31st January-1st February. General Bennett accordingly issued at 12.20 a.m. on the 27th an operation instruction to Westforce. This embodied the following schedule, which it was emphasised must be adhered to:

Night 26th-27th January—hold present positions.
Night 27th-28th January—withdraw to line rail mile 440, road mile 44.
Night 29th-30th January—withdraw to line Sedenak road mile 32.
Night 30th-31st January—withdraw to line rail mile 450, road mile 25.
Night 31st January-1st February—On to island.

The order contained a discrepancy in that an appendix showing these stages coordinated with the movements of Eastforce and the 11th Indian Division specified the Westforce positions for the night of 27th-28th January as rail mile 437 and road mile 42.

General Barstow gave orders to the 9th Indian Division based on his interpretation of this instruction. These required the 22nd Indian Brigade to hold the foremost position on the railway till the night of the 28th-29th; the 8th Indian Brigade to hold Sedenak till the night of the 30th-31st; and the 22nd Indian Brigade to hold the next position till the night of 31st January-1st February. Barstow specified block positions to be occupied in front of each of the points the brigades were to deny, and instructed his brigadiers to coordinate the movements of their brigades by agreement. The 22nd Indian Brigade block for the 27th-28th was from the railway milestones 432 to 437. Brigadier Painter pointed out that a network of estate roads between Rengam and Layang Layang would enable this to be easily outflanked, and perhaps allow the enemy to get between the two brigades. (The roads ran through some six miles of rubber plantation separating the brigades.) He was told, however, that it was necessary to hold the area to cover the right flank of the 27th Australian Brigade's position on the trunk road until 4 p.m. on the 28th. Barstow selected and ordered the 8th Brigade to occupy during the evening of 27th January a ridge astride the railway at milestone 439½ to the rear of Layang Layang, covering the railway and a road bridge at that point in the brigade block. The brigade accordingly moved back, and the 22nd Brigade took up its position, with the 5/11th Sikh a mile and a half south of Rengam, among the estate roads mentioned, and the rest of the brigade at rail mile 435. The Sikhs, however, were driven back during the afternoon to rail mile 434.

On the trunk road, the 27th Brigade's positions were strafed from low altitudes[9] during the 27th—especially when the 9th Division's guns and transport came through—and concentrated shelling of the 2/26th Battalion's area broke out in mid-afternoon. Front and flank attacks on the Australians followed, and they became heavily engaged. The Japanese

---

[9] It was noticed that the Japanese airmen were now operating to a regular schedule, from 8 a.m. to 11.30 a.m. and from 1 p.m. to approximately 4.30 p.m., thus observing what the Australians described as "trade union hours". The regularity of their artillery salvos reminded veterans of the German artillery in the 1914-18 war. Such habits might well have been an outcome of the visit to Germany of a Japanese military mission, headed by General Yamashita, while Japan was preparing for her onslaught. Reports of fair-complexioned officers with the Japanese at various stages in the campaign heightened the suspicion of German influence.

Lieut-Colonel C. G. W. Anderson, commander of the 2/19th Battalion.

The Simpang Rengam crossroads, at the 46-mile post, looking south. The 2/26th Battalion held this area on 26th and 27th January. Postwar photograph.

(Australian War Memorial)

(British Ministry of Information)

The mouth of the Sungei Mersing.

(Australian War Memorial)

The Mersing bridge. The central span was blown by sappers of the 2/10th Field Company on the morning of 25th January 1942. The makeshift bridge was built by the Japanese.
Post-war photograph.

again supplemented their fire with crackers of a type known to Australians as Jumping Jacks. These, as recorded in the battalion's narrative, "burst with a flash of coloured fire and then changed direction suddenly and would again explode". It was noticed that one cracker would perhaps explode ten times. Apparently they were intended to affect morale, but although the absence of air support such as had been given in the withdrawal from Yong Peng was a bitter disappointment, the crackers were regarded by the Australians as a form of comic relief amid the strain of constant bombardment and fighting. Again, the fact that apparently the Australians were inflicting a far greater number of casualties on the Japanese than they themselves suffered, despite the enemy's command of the air, was reassuring. The battalion had difficulty in breaking off the engagement for the scheduled withdrawal after dark, but eventually, with the staunch support of the 30th Battery, got back by midnight to its milestone 42 position, covering a road into the Namazie Estate, with the Gordons a little ahead of them on the trunk road to their left.

The full significance of the dispersal of the 15th Brigade after the fall of Batu Pahat had become apparent to General Percival during 27th January. He considered the remaining troops on the west coast road were not strong enough to stop the advance in that sector for long, and that the whole of his forces on the mainland were now endangered. In the evening he sent a message to General Wavell in which he said:

> A very critical situation has developed. The enemy has cut off and overrun the majority of the forces on the west coast. . . . Unless we can stop him it will be difficult to get our own columns on other roads back in time, especially as they are both being pressed. In any case it looks as if we should not be able to hold Johore for more than another three or four days. We are going to be a bit thin on the island unless we can get the remaining troops back. Our total fighter strength now reduced to nine and difficulty in keeping airfields in action.

Wavell replied the same day giving Percival discretion to withdraw to the island if he considered it advisable.

At a conference early on 28th January between Percival, Heath and Bennett, a plan was adopted by which the mainland would be evacuated on the night of 30th-31st January—a day earlier than was contemplated in the schedule on which Heath and Bennett had been working. Wavell was notified of this and when cabling approval told Percival that he must fight for every foot of Singapore Island. Wavell also conveyed the decision to Australia in a cable dated 29th January which General Sturdee read to the Advisory War Council next day. In this he said the Japanese were making three main thrusts, in one of which warships with large convoys were proceeding by the Moluccas probably against Ambon, but Koepang might be threatened.

The Australians in Malaya had greatly distinguished themselves, he continued. Percival should have the equivalent of approximately three divisions to hold Singapore Island, about half of whom would be fresh. Of the very limited naval forces available in Java a considerable proportion was in harbour for repair or refit, and practically all the rest except submarines were engaged on escort duties. Endeavours were being made to collect a striking force, but it would be small. No more formations of land troops would be available for about three weeks, when the Australian Corps would begin to arrive. It had been intended to use this Corps to relieve Indian troops in Malaya and carry out a counter-offensive, but in view of the changed situation the Corps must be used in the first instance to secure vital areas in Sumatra and Java. The air striking force amounted to little more than eight to ten American heavy bombers, which had been doing most effective work, but were insufficient to meet all threats. Considerable reinforcements of British and American air forces were on their way.

All I can do in the immediate future (said Wavell) is to check enemy by such offensive action by sea and air as limited resources allow and to secure most important objectives which I conceive to be Singapore, air bases in central and southern Sumatra, naval base at Surabaya, aerodrome at Koepang.

Picture looks gloomy but enemy is at full strength, is suffering severe losses, and cannot replace his losses in aircraft as we can. Things will improve eventually as we keep on fighting but may be worse first.

The Advisory War Council discussed Wavell's omission of Ambon from the key points to be held. The Chiefs of Staff held that withdrawal from Ambon would be a very difficult operation and in any event it was important to deny it to the Japanese as long as possible.

For the crossing from the Malayan mainland to Singapore Island it had been planned to form an outer and an inner bridgehead, to safeguard the movement as fully as possible. Anti-aircraft guns were to be grouped to counter Japanese air attacks upon the long stream of men and material which would pass along the Causeway across Johore Strait, and provision was made to ferry troops across the water if the Causeway became unusable. The outer bridgehead would be held by the 22nd Australian Brigade and the 2/Gordons; the inner one by the Argylls, now reorganised but only 250 strong. The Australian brigade would include its 2/19th Battalion, hurriedly reorganised by Colonel Anderson after the losses it had sustained between Bakri and Parit Sulong. General Heath at first allotted command of both bridgeheads to the Argylls' commander, Colonel Stewart, but General Bennett asserted that as the outer bridgehead troops were to be mainly Australians and Taylor was the senior in rank, they should be under Taylor's command. Eventually the outer bridgehead was placed under Taylor and the inner one under Stewart. Bennett also pressed for a detailed plan for the withdrawal, pointing out that no times for the various units to cross the Causeway, and no order of march, had been specified. Finally, he protested to Percival against the Australian machine-gun battalion being used to prepare the III Corps positions on the island instead of those to be occupied by Australian troops; but on this point Percival replied that the work must be carried out according to a program laid down by the Fortress Commander, Major-General Simmons. Detailed routes and timings were worked out by Heath with Bennett.

The prospect of holding a bridgehead area in southern Johore for any lengthy period had been discussed but rejected. Some defences had been prepared in the Kota Tinggi area before the war, but they were inadequate; the forces in the bridgehead area would be dependent upon the Causeway and such temporary provision as might be made for traffic to and from the island; and by landing on the island from another direction the Japanese might at last fulfil their threat to the rear of the mainland forces which had hovered over the defenders for so long. Water supply on the mainland would also present an awkward problem, for in view of the situation on the west coast the prospect of holding a sufficiently large area to include the Gunong Pulai catchment area, between Pontian Kechil and the trunk road, and main source of supply to the Johore Bahru area, was not entertained.

The 11th Indian Division was made responsible for holding Skudai on the trunk road against enemy approach from the west coast. Key therefore ordered the remnant of the 53rd Brigade at Benut to withdraw on the night of 29th-30th January to the island, and the 28th Brigade to hold the Pontian Kechil area till dusk on the 29th; then to take up positions in depth on the road to Skudai. Bennett visited the Sultan of Johore after the conference and was entertained by him at length and presented with gifts. Bennett, determined not to be engulfed in defeat, told him that it was quite possible that he might have to attempt escape to avoid becoming a prisoner of war, and might be seeking his aid, especially to obtain a boat for the purpose. That night Bennett instructed his staff to issue orders accelerating the withdrawal of Westforce by one day as had been decided. These were issued next morning (29th January). They provided that the final position on the mainland, to have been held for two days, now would be held for one day only.

In the railway sector another disaster was brewing. Brigadier Lay informed the 22nd Indian Brigade during the night of 27th-28th January that he was moving the 8th Brigade south of Layang Layang and would telephone again later. Before he could do so, however, the railway bridge over a creek near the $439\frac{1}{2}$-mile position on the railway line was prematurely blown, thus disrupting the railway telegraph line—the only means of communication between the two brigades since their wireless sets had been sent back with their transport—and preventing rations and ammunition being sent forward by rail. The position was made worse by the fact that the 22nd Brigade moved farther towards Sedenak than Barstow had ordered, and left unmanned the ridge near Layang Layang that he had decided it should occupy. In the early hours of the 28th the 22nd Brigade heard transport moving on the estate roads on its right flank, and at dawn Brigadier Painter found that enemy troops were between him and the 8th Brigade. He thereupon decided that immediate withdrawal was essential to regain contact. By 10.15 a.m. the brigade had been concentrated and had begun to move down the western side of the railway.

Meanwhile General Barstow had somewhat varied his previous orders to the brigades, to make sure that the positions specified for them in General Bennett's withdrawal program at that time—before the accelerated program had been adopted—were securely held. Early on the 28th he went forward to see for himself how the brigades were faring. With him went his senior administrative officer, Colonel Trott, and the Australian liaison officer with the Indian division, Major Moses.[1] At Lay's headquarters he learned of the bridge having been blown, and that the ridge from which it was to have been covered was unoccupied. He immediately ordered Lay to send his leading battalion—the 2/10th Baluch—to the ridge, and with Trott and Moses continued on up the line on a trolley, intending to visit the 22nd Brigade. Finding the Baluchis resting beside the line about a mile short of the creek, he personally ordered them forward, and continued his journey. At the creek the three officers discovered that although the bridge had sagged it was still passable on foot. They therefore crossed it, and walked along the railway embankment towards Layang Layang station, spaced out with Barstow in the lead. Soon they were challenged and fired upon. In their spontaneous move for cover, the general went to the right of the embankment and the others to the left. Attempting to rejoin Barstow, they again came under fire in such volume that they decided the only course left to them was to make their way back.

Bullets again whizzed past them as, having waded the creek, they reached the ridge where the Baluchis were to have been, only to find it occupied by the enemy. After making a detour they again reached the railway, and met the vanguard of the Baluchis moving forward; but more fire from the ridge sent them to cover. Trott thereupon went back to report the situation to the 8th Brigade and 9th Division, while Moses remained with the Baluchis thinking that Barstow might be rescued after the ridge had been gained. However, the Baluchis failed in the attempt and were driven back under heavy fire. No further endeavour was made during the day to reach the 22nd Brigade, and the battalion was withdrawn during the night. The 22nd Brigade thus was left to find its way out of the trap set for it by the Japanese as best it could.

It later transpired that Barstow's body was found at the foot of the embankment by the enemy. His courage and initiative, at a time when morale was being severely tested, had won for him the high regard of the Australians and others with whom he had been associated.[2] Moving back along the railway, the 22nd Brigade advance-guard at midday on 28th January found Japanese troops in possession of Layang Layang station and suffered about fifty casualties in an unsuccessful endeavour

---

[1] Lt-Col C. J. A. Moses, CBE, NX12404. HQ 8 Aust Div; T/CO 7 Cav Regt 1942-43. General manager, Australian Broadcasting Commission; of Sydney, NSW; b. Atherton, Lancs, England, 21 Jan 1900.

[2] "Not only was General Barstow a popular officer, especially among the Australians who knew him, but he was one of the most efficient British leaders with whom the Australians were associated. He was fearless and was a good front-line soldier. He was inspiring to his troops and though hampered by some very weak officers within his command, managed to keep his men fighting well." Bennett, *Why Singapore Fell*, p. 157.

to eject them. Lacking fire support, means of evacuating his wounded other than on hand-borne stretchers, and communication with the 8th Brigade, Painter decided to move his brigade across country west of the railway, hoping to reach the 8th Brigade's left flank. A track shown on his only map of the area came to an end in dense jungle, through which his men hacked a way on a compass bearing until the moon went down and they were halted.

On the trunk road the Japanese had begun 28th January with probing patrol movements. The Gordons, in the foremost position at mile-post 41½, were engaged in skirmishes, and fire was soon concentrated on the 2/26th Battalion on the Gordons' right, amid rubber trees. The supporting position was held by the 2/30th Battalion, at the junction of the estate road with the trunk road, which for two miles to the rear was bordered by jungle. Both Brigadier Maxwell and Colonel Galleghan were uneasy about the position because of the opportunities, remarked upon by Brigadier Painter, that the estate roads offered to the enemy, who if he reached

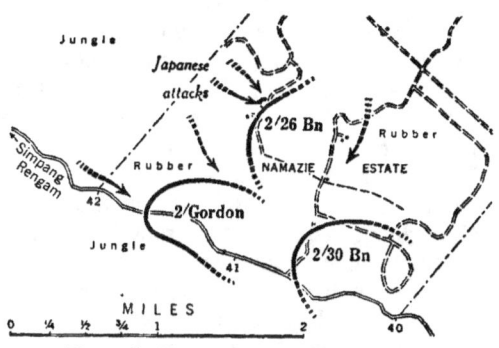

Namazie Estate, 7 a.m. 28th January

the jungle to the rear might isolate the two battalions. A plan discussed by Maxwell and Galleghan to organise a battalion ambush at the entrance to the jungle defile was set aside after weighing its possibilities.

A series of fire attacks on the Gordons and on the flanks of the 2/26th Battalion, with constant air support, lasted throughout the morning. The return fire was so effective that the attackers were held in check, but other enemy troops meanwhile worked round through the rubber to the right of the 2/30th Battalion. Near midday, a patrol came upon about six of them, near where "D" Company was stationed in a rearward position on this flank, and reported their presence to company headquarters. A fighting patrol of two sections, led by Corporal Moynihan,[3] was thereupon sent to dispose of what seemed to be a small infiltration. In an encounter they found themselves outweighed in fire power, and had difficulty in withdrawing. Galleghan concluded that, as he had anticipated, the Japanese were trying to get to the jungle defile at the rear of the brigade's positions, and sent Captain Duffy with two platoons to the area to meet the threat as best he could. Leading one of the platoons, Lieutenant Jones saw two men sitting on a rise covered by a type of vine familiar in rubber plantations, about where a "D" Company standing patrol was expected to be.

---

[3] Cpl W. J. Moynihan, NX32703; 2/30 Pn. Hairdresser; of Mascot, NSW; b. Botany, NSW, 9 Nov 1918. Missing presumed died 12 Sep 1944.

"Yes, we are 'Don' Company," was the reply to a challenge from a distance.

<blockquote>
"Like hell they are! They're Japs!" came immediately from one of the platoon, who confidently opened fire on the two Japanese, as indeed they were, and wearing British steel helmets. Immediately the whole hillside seemed to spring into life with Japanese troops, who were lying there, having been very effectively concealed by the cover plant. . . . The platoon was heavily outnumbered, but unhesitatingly engaged the enemy and quickly inflicted forty to fifty casualties with steady fire. Corporal Swindail[4] accounted for a Jap only twenty yards away, who had Lieutenant Jones pinned down. Swindail had to expose himself to pick off his man and was himself wounded before succeeding. As Lieutenant Jones was armed only with a revolver, Swindail flung his rifle to his officer, who then completed the job.[5]
</blockquote>

The other platoon, led by Lieutenant Cooper, arrived at this critical stage and the Japanese were repulsed. The two platoons took up a position covering the approach to the battalion's rear at a point where the rubber and the jungle met. However, "D" Company's headquarters and the battalion headquarters area between this point and the trunk road came under fire, and it was evident that the threat was increasingly serious. Three more platoons, two armoured cars and a section of mortars were moved to the area, and the forward units were told of the situation. At Galleghan's request Boyes sent him a company of the 2/26th Battalion to come under command and reinforce his right flank. Three platoons, covered by two others, were ordered to attack under Captain Duffy's direction the high ground occupied by the Japanese, and a strong outflanking attack was to be made.

The frontal attack was launched at 4.40 p.m., under a storm of covering small arms fire. Although the Japanese made expert use of cover, the Australians got in among the foremost of them with bayonets, the armoured cars blasted machine-gun posts and other targets, and under this fierce assault the enemy fell back. There were no tanks at hand to tip the scales against the Australians, whose bayonets again caused screaming confusion; but the Japanese now produced containers which exploded into clouds of yellow fumes. At first it seemed that they had resorted to the use of poison gas. With no respirators available to them the Australians were robbed of their advantage by fits of coughing and by their eyes watering so profusely that they could scarcely see. One container, which appeared to have been fired from a rifle or mortar, burst close to company headquarters and emitted more fumes. To cope with the effect which the fumes produced as they spread, the forward troops in the vicinity were withdrawn, and the intended outflanking attack was withheld.

At the regimental aid post it was soon discovered that the fumes were merely an irritant and that those who had encountered them soon recovered. However, the enemy had gained further freedom of movement and might reach the defile as night was falling. It seemed obvious that the aim was to force another brigade into the jungle. Meanwhile Captain

---

[4] Cpl D. T. Swindail, NX29840; 2/30 Bn. Labourer; of Rozelle, NSW; b. Sydney, 20 Jun 1917.
[5] *Galleghan's Greyhounds*, pp. 167-68.

Wyett[6] had come forward from 27th Brigade headquarters with authority to issue orders on Brigadier Maxwell's behalf. Orders were issued for withdrawal at nightfall, with special precautions against attack in passing through the defile.[7] Westforce in due course ordered the 9th Indian Division to conform by withdrawing during the night to Sedenak. This order was passed on to the 8th Indian Brigade; but, as has been shown, communication with the 22nd Indian Brigade had now failed.

The 2/26th Battalion, last in the order of withdrawal, had difficulty in breaking contact, but the move was successfully made. Owing to lack of troop-carrying transport at the forward positions, however, a twelve-mile march was now superimposed upon the day's fighting and all that had gone before it. Boyes set aside standing orders and used portion of his "A" Echelon vehicles in successive runs carrying men over portions of the route. Even a water cart managed to make several trips with up to twenty-five men and many weapons, filling the bottles of the marching troops as it returned. Such aid as this, and the spirit in which it was given, did much to help the men overcome their fatigue.

Early on the morning of 29th January, before it had received the Westforce order for the generally accelerated withdrawal, the 9th Indian Division's headquarters ordered the 8th Indian Brigade forward in an endeavour to rescue the 22nd Indian Brigade. On receipt of the Westforce order this move was cancelled, and the 8th Brigade was instructed to withdraw during the night to rail mile 450½, about two miles and a half north of Kulai. The 22nd Indian Brigade, which at the time was struggling on through increasingly difficult country, was thus finally cut off.[8]

The 27th Australian Brigade, now in more rubber and jungle country at milestone 31, near Ayer Bemban forward of a branch road to Sedenak, had another heavy day's fighting on the 29th. The 2/26th Battalion was astride and mostly west of the trunk road. Behind them were the Gordons, and the 2/30th was in reserve at the road junction. After a sharp early clash had brought Australian artillery fire on to the Japanese, a party of thirty of them dressed in European, Indian and native clothing was allowed to reach a position between the two forward companies of the 2/26th, and there was wiped out. Others were found to be massing behind a rise, and were attacked with grenades and bayonets. By mid-morning all four Australian companies were being fiercely and persistently attacked. The Japanese tried to set up mortars and machine-guns in full view of the Australians, and were mown down in most instances before the weapons could be fired. Their casualties mounted rapidly, but so did their reinforcements, and in mid-afternoon, when it was estimated that

---

[6] Maj J. W. C. Wyett, TX2155; HQ 8 Div and HQ 27 Bde. Chemist; of Hobart; b. Beaconsfield, Tas, 22 Jul 1908.

[7] Accounts differ as to whether the order was issued by Wyett or Galleghan. The latter has recorded that because brigade headquarters were out of communication with him, he assumed command of the forces engaged with the Japanese at this point, and ordered the withdrawal.

[8] Hungry and exhausted. and harried by enemy patrols, the 22nd Brigade became incapable of attack, and largely disintegrated. Lieut-Colonel Parkin (5/11th Sikhs), with some of his officers and about thirty men, eventually reached Singapore Island with others whom they picked up on the way. The remainder of the brigade was captured.

three Japanese battalions had been brought forward, one battalion with infantry guns was seen forming up on the road.

The Australian artillery quickly took advantage of the new target and the battalion's mortars thickened the fire. A sharp counter-attack by the 2/26th Battalion's "D" company (Captain Tracey[9]), which again found use for its bayonets, finally disposed of this threat, but was badly weakened by an accurate bombing attack. Bombing and shelling of the battalion generally was added to the weight of the infantry attacks, and more fumes of the kind experienced the day before were released in the area occupied by "B" Company (Captain Swartz[1]). The battalion nevertheless stood its ground, and, as night set in, the Japanese gave up their costly and unusually protracted assault.[2]

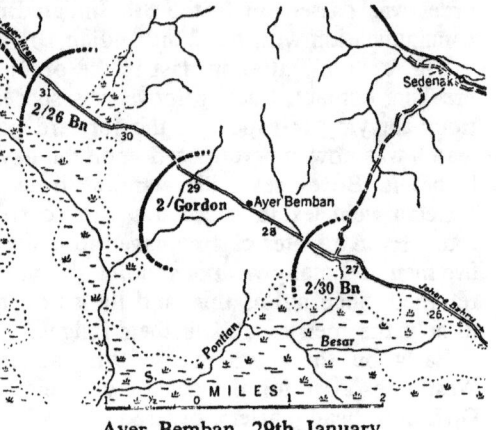

Ayer Bemban, 29th January

Despite fatigue the battalion's morale was high, for the splendid performance of the 29th and 30th Field Batteries had done much to offset the lack of air support or protection; and the battalion's casualties were only six killed and twenty-five wounded, as against the evident slaughter of a large number of Japanese. Orders to withdraw to the 21¼-mile post, forward of Kulai, were carried out afoot for the first six miles, but were

---

[9] Maj C. P. Tracey, ED, NX70508; 2/26 Bn. Bank clerk; of Lismore, NSW; b. Hurstville, NSW, 4 Oct 1908.

[1] Maj R. W. C. Swartz, MBE, ED, MP; 2/26 Bn. MHR since 1949. Commercial executive; of Toowoomba, Qld; b. Brisbane, 14 Apr 1911.

[2] In the 2/26 Bn's war diary, Capt H. L. Sabin, the adjutant, later wrote of its experiences on the mainland: "Only on two occasions during 13 days of active operations were British or Allied planes sighted, and on both occasions they did not provide air support but merely flew over Bn area. . . . Jap planes would skim the tree tops and drop bombs in sticks of three. Casualties from dive-bombing were more numerous than casualties from other causes. . . . Not on any occasion were the enemy successful in *forcing* a withdrawal on our front. All withdrawals were carried out according to plan and the enemy showed no aggressive spirit or initiative to follow up withdrawals. On two occasions the enemy shelled the route of withdrawal for a few minutes only. The enemy usually attacked on the front and on meeting resistance immediately withdrew and moved to a flank. If unable to get around flank he did not press home any attack. He seemed reluctant to stand up to fire and when once put to the ground remained there. His forming up areas for attacks often were within view of our troops and on two occasions on a main road. Counter preparation artillery fire disorganised these attempts with heavy casualties. His aircraft worked in close cooperation with forward troops but did not closely support them during actual contact. If an attack failed, aircraft would bomb and machine-gun our position and then a further attack would develop. During an attack his aircraft would dive low near our areas, as if they were going to drop bombs, in an attempt to keep our heads down. On two occasions, after vainly trying to dislodge us from our defensive position, a concentration of choking gas was put over our forward troops as a final measure. This was dropped from low flying aircraft in bakelite bombs. It was non-persistent and of a very local effect. As we were not carrying respirators at the time it is not known if the service respirator would be effective protection. . . . He (the Japanese) is a poor shot with rifle and L.M.G., and on one occasion just prior to a withdrawal by our troops he concentrated several L.M.G's on our position. All bullets were at least 10 feet above the ground and there were no casualties."

completed before midnight. Japanese shelling hampered the movement, but caused only two more casualties.

A Japanese account of the engagement (in "Malaya Campaign 1941-1942", a report captured at Lae, New Guinea, in 1943) stated that the frontal resistance was so powerful that a pincer movement was attempted, but "the warriors continued their suicidal resistance like wounded boars". Near the end of the battle "the enemy, defying death, strangely and impudently counter-attacked with bayonets along the whole line". The force which had detoured to the right flank made a fierce attack, but was repelled, and "finally, one severely wounded soldier was the sole survivor of the rosy-cheeked commander's unit". Artillery came forward through jungle and swamp to by-pass demolished bridges, and when the battle was over "the infantry force commander grasped the artillery force commander's hands tightly and shed tears of gratitude".

The 2/30th Battalion took up a covering position, and the Gordons were withdrawn to Singapore Island. No further serious attack occurred on the west coast, though a successful ambush by a 2/2nd Gurkha fighting patrol of a party of Japanese stopped what appeared to be an attempt to establish a road-block behind the 28th Brigade.

General Wavell flew to Singapore again on 30th January with Air Marshal Sir Richard Peirse, newly arrived from England as Wavell's Chief of Air Staff and Commander of the Allied Air Forces in the A.B.D.A. Command. At a conference with Generals Percival, Heath and Bennett, General Wavell reviewed the situation in his command generally. Despite his stout-hearted demeanour, the facts offered a menacing prospect. After the conference final orders were issued by III Indian Corps for the withdrawal to the island. The routes as specified in the outline plan of 28th January were confirmed. This provided that the 11th Indian Division would move by the trunk road from Kulai through Skudai, and along the waterfront of Johore Bahru to the Causeway. Westforce would withdraw to Senai, south of Kulai, where the 9th Indian Division would take a route through the centre of Johore Bahru. The 27th Brigade and other Australian units would use an unmetalled loop road through rubber estates to Tebrau, and enter the town from the north-east along the main east coast road, following units of Eastforce not required for bridgehead duty. Colonel Kent Hughes, now in charge of the lines of communication,[3] foreseeing the possibility of the Tebrau loop route being needed, had ordered the engineers to strengthen the culverts and improve the road generally. Block timings for use of the Causeway were not given, but formations were given the times at which their rear elements must be clear of their current positions. In the case of Westforce this was 1 a.m. on 31st January, by which time it was hoped what remained of the 22nd Indian Brigade would have come in. Bennett ordered the 2/30th

---

[3] A hastily improvised organisation commanded by Major P. L. Head manned the trains on the line to Singapore with drivers and firemen after the withdrawal from Kuala Lumpur. A motor car fitted with flanged wheels was used on the rails to evacuate wounded from Kluang. Men from the Tampoi Hill base depot transported forces from the Mersing area, and a large labour corps, principally of Chinese, was employed. At one stage three trains a day were being unloaded at Johore Bahru. Large supplies of foodstuffs and other stores were placed in godowns (storage sheds) near the Causeway—where before long they were taken over by the Japanese.

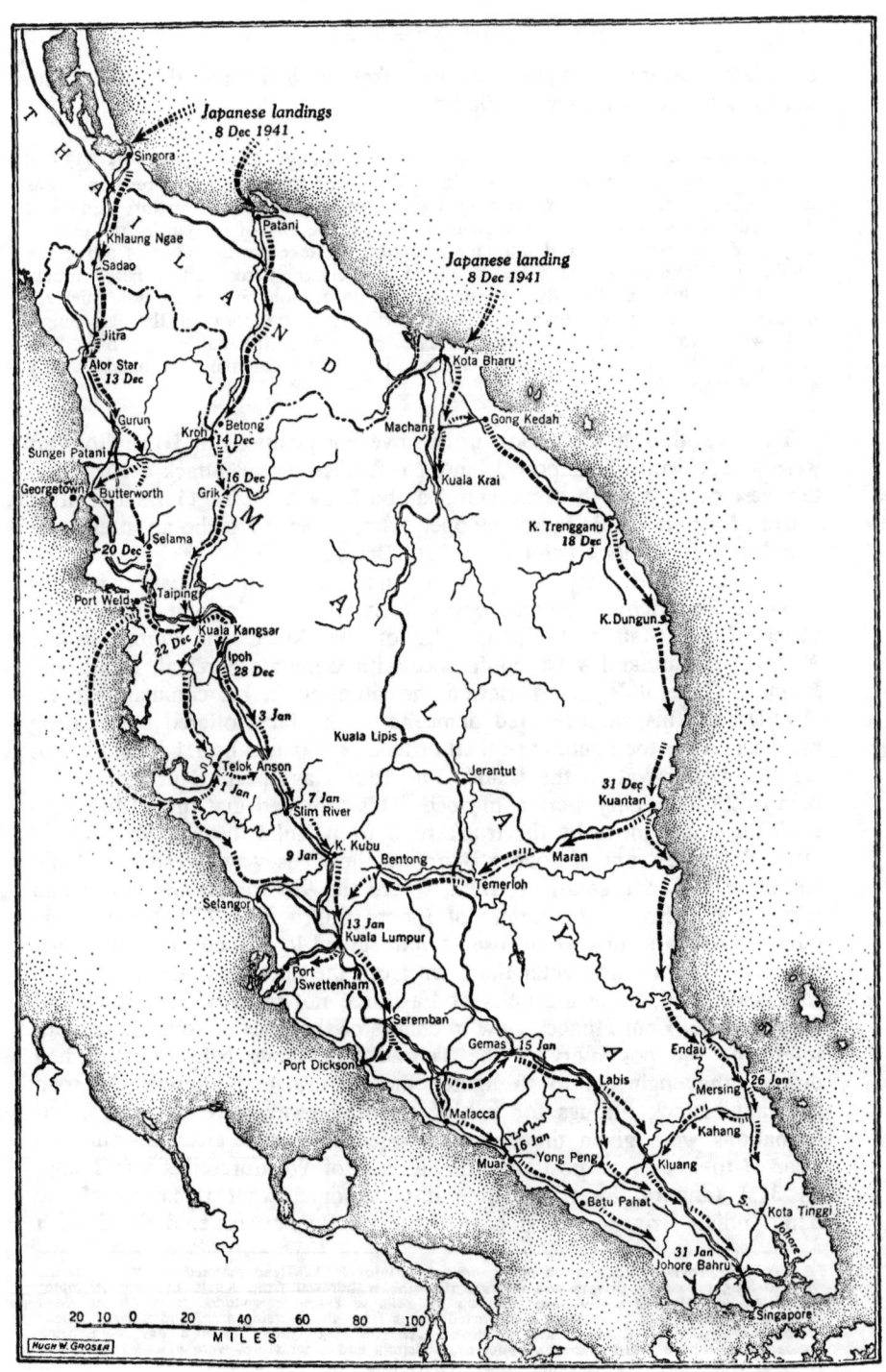

The conquest of Malaya

Battalion to be withdrawn to the left flank of the 2/26th Battalion by 3.30 p.m. There was to be no further withdrawal before 10 p.m. Embussing at the 14-mile post was to be completed by 3 a.m. on 31st January.

In Singapore General Wavell discussed the defence of the island with the Governor, with General Percival, Air Vice-Marshal Pulford, General Simmons, and Rear-Admiral Spooner, the senior naval officer. On the ground that to leave fighter aircraft on its now-exposed airfields would invite their destruction, he ordered all but the equivalent of one squadron to be withdrawn to Sumatra, with the proviso that it would be reinforced as occasion served. "This decision," he later recorded, "was open to criticism as depriving the land forces at a dangerous time of protection against air attack, but it was inevitable. Crete had shown, and events in Java and Burma were to show later, that it is impossible to maintain a weak air force within close range of a stronger enemy one, and that the sacrifice of aircraft entailed by the attempt brings no real relief to the land forces in the end."[4]

After he had given his orders, Bennett left for new divisional headquarters on the island. "I toured slowly through Johore Bahru," he noted, "past derelict cars and destroyed houses and the bomb holes that were everywhere. There was a deathly silence. There was not the usual crowd of chattering Malays and busy Chinese. The streets were deserted. It was a funeral march. I have never felt so sad and upset. Words fail me. This defeat should not have been. The whole thing is fantastic. There seems no justification for it. I always thought we would hold Johore. Its loss was never contemplated."[5]

This last day before the defenders abandoned the mainland produced curiously little interference by the enemy. The final stages of the withdrawal from the east and west coasts were completed, and the 9th Indian Division, less its still-missing 22nd Brigade, duly converged upon the 27th Brigade near Kulai, where the railway swung in to the road, and ran side by side with it for some miles.[6] Demolitions and artillery fire delayed the enemy following up the withdrawal of the 28th Brigade, which reached Skudai.

The day was nevertheless a time of high nervous tension, particularly for those responsible for the critical move across the Causeway of the great mass of men and material comprising Eastforce, Westforce, and the 11th Indian Division. The bulk of the artillery, ammunition, supplies and ancillary forces naturally had to be sent across ahead. If, with his strength in the air and on land, the enemy could seriously disrupt the movement of the infantry, disaster might swiftly follow. Once daylight came the anti-aircraft guns concentrated for defence of the crossing would be unlikely to prevent punishing blows from the air, seeing that the

---

[4] Wavell, *Despatch on Operations in the South-West Pacific, 15th January 1942 to 25th February 1942*, p. 11.

[5] Bennett, *Why Singapore Fell*, p. 161.

[6] Arrangements were made at this stage for Volunteers officers familiar with the country to stay behind in Johore and endeavour to locate the 22nd Indian Brigade and guide it to Johore Strait. Air and sea cooperation in the endeavour to rescue the brigade was organised.

Japanese had been bombing the island with clockwork regularity despite the anti-aircraft batteries clustered there.

Still hoping that the 22nd Indian Brigade would turn up, General Heath directed that Westforce should hold its final position at Kulai as long as possible, provided its withdrawal over the Causeway was completed by dawn. The 11th Division would make an earlier withdrawal from Skudai, down the main road, and the 9th Division would complete its withdrawal from Kulai by 11 p.m. to conform to this movement. Colonel Thyer told General Heath of General Bennett's order that Westforce was to be clear of Kulai by 1 a.m. If this time were set back, the rear of the force would be exposed to attack by Japanese following up the 11th Division. Heath undertook to see Bennett and vary the original orders, but apparently did not meet him again that day. At 5 p.m., when Thyer visited the joint 9th Division and 27th Australian Brigade headquarters at Kulai, he found that Heath nevertheless had postponed the 27th Brigade's final withdrawal by two hours, to 3 a.m.

Thyer was thus in the dilemma that, in the temporary absence of his commander at this crucial stage, he was responsible for carrying out the last order Bennett had given; yet another order, which he believed endangered the prospect of successful withdrawal unless the timing for the 11th Division were altered, had been given by the commander of III Corps, whose command included Westforce. Thyer took the stand that, as the situation had not altered since Bennett gave his order, there should be no change of the timings of any part of Westforce without Bennett's authority. The 9th Division orders to the 8th Brigade were altered accordingly, and a message notifying the action was sent to III Corps and Westforce headquarters. A liaison officer was sent to Key to inform him of the message and ask him if he could delay his division's retirement in anticipation of an order to do so. Key came forward and discussed the problem with Thyer, but said that his orders had been issued and his troops were already moving. Thyer thereupon arranged for the 27th Brigade to post a detachment at the Skudai road junction, and some armoured cars to patrol the road from Skudai northward.

At 7 p.m., with Kulai in flames, and Japanese attacking Indian troops on the railway near by, a fighting patrol from the 2/26th Battalion was rushed to the flank of Kulai. To avoid the village, the 2/30th Battalion moved across country in darkness from the 21-mile post to a pre-selected position where the trunk road and the railway ran side by side, and where they would thus cover the withdrawal of both the Indians and the Australians. The position was occupied at 9 p.m. Having in mind the threat to Kulai and the movement of the 11th Division, Thyer took the responsibility of advancing the time for the withdrawal of Westforce, so that the rear elements would leave the embussing point at 1 a.m.

Most of the force had embussed by midnight. There were anxious moments, for of necessity the vehicles were close together, and had the enemy attacked from land or air the result might have been disastrous.

As it happened only light shelling was experienced. Thirty vehicles had passed into the loop road when it was reported that the leading vehicle had come to a broken bridge. Should the rest follow the 11th Division down the trunk road, with the right flank unprotected? A dispatch rider sent to the rear of the division to ask it not to demolish the Skudai bridge returned with the report that the bridge had been blown. To Thyer this report suggested the grisly prospect of a Westforce withdrawal across country on foot. However, it was then discovered that the bridges on the loop road were intact. Thus the movement continued, and Westforce, with the aid of the 2/3rd Reserve Motor Transport Company which had distinguished itself from the beginning of the campaign, completed its crossing of the Causeway just before daylight. Bennett watched the last of the force coming in.

The Australians and the Gordons manning Taylor's outer bridgehead crossed next, and the inner bridgehead followed. The Argylls marched not as a defeated regiment—though it had been so battered in battle that a mere ninety had remained when it was withdrawn from the fighting —but resolutely to the skirl of bagpipes playing "A Hundred Pipers" and "Hielan' Laddie". Brigadier Stewart was the last to make the crossing.

The navy, which had made preparations to ferry the forces across Johore Strait as best it could if the Causeway had become impassable, was thus relieved of what might have been a desperate task with assorted craft ranging in size up to two pleasure steamers from the Yangtse Kiang in China. The massive Causeway, 70 feet wide at the water line and wider at its base, now had to be demolished as fully as possible. While civilian refugees were still streaming across it, squads had been laying depth-charges in such a way as to leave at least one pair of lock gates available for boats until the last moment. Soon after 8 a.m. the charges were touched off. The roar of the explosion seemed to express the frustration and fury of the forces which had been thrust back and penned up in "the island fortress", as it was still regarded. When the deluge of spray and debris had fallen, water was seen racing through a seventy-foot gap.

"So now the army was back on the island," said Lieut-Commander J. O. C. Hayes, the navy's liaison officer with the army during the withdrawal, in a subsequent broadcast. "It was the same sensation as after Dunkirk. We knew where we were. There could be no more retreat without calamity. But driving along the north shore that morning, back to the naval base, now an empty settlement, I doubted for the first time that Singapore *was* impregnable. Somehow it did not look its part. . . ."

CHAPTER 14

NAKED ISLAND

THE situation facing General Wavell, as he saw it at the beginning of February, was that Ambon Island had fallen to the enemy on 31st January; there was still a convoy at Balikpapan which might at any time move south on Macassar or Bandjermasin; and a third force, reported to be in the South China Sea, might be heading for Singapore or Sumatra. Rangoon was endangered by the enemy advance in Burma, and the British forces had been driven from the mainland of Malaya. In Wavell's view much depended on the ability of the forces on Singapore Island to make a prolonged resistance. He considered that an active defence should enable the island to be held for some time—perhaps for some months—while the forces at his command were being strengthened.

Mr Churchill's thoughts had turned, while he was concluding his talks in Washington, to the possibility of a withdrawal to Singapore Island such as had now occurred. "How many troops would be needed to defend this area?" he had asked in a message to General Wavell on 15th January. "What means are there of stopping landings [such] as were made in Hong Kong? What are defences and obstructions on landward side? Are you sure you can dominate with fortress cannon any attempt to plant siege batteries? Is everything being prepared, and what has been done about the useless mouths?"[1]

These questions, which but for his preoccupation with more immediate issues he might well have asked much earlier, brought a disconcerting reply. On what Wavell told him, Churchill reflected: "So there were no permanent fortifications covering the landward side of the naval base and the city! Moreover, even more astounding, no measures worth speaking of had been taken by any of the commanders since the war began, and more especially since the Japanese had established themselves in Indo-China, to construct field defences. They had not even mentioned the fact that they did not exist." He added that he had put his faith in the Japanese "being compelled to use artillery on a very large scale in order to pulverise our strong points at Singapore, and in the almost prohibitive difficulties and long delays which would impede such an artillery concentration and the gathering of ammunition along Malayan communications. Now, suddenly, all this vanished away, and I saw before me the hideous spectacle of the almost naked island and of the wearied, if not exhausted, troops retreating upon it."[2]

In a message to the Chiefs of Staff Committee in London on 19th January Churchill ordered that a plan be made at once to do the best

---

[1] Churchill, *The Second World War*, Vol IV, p. 42. The term "useless mouths" denoted in military parlance those who in circumstances such as those faced at the time on Singapore Island could not usefully be employed for military purposes.

[2] Churchill, Vol IV, p. 43.

possible while the battle of Johore was going forward, and went into extensive detail of what he considered the plan should comprise. Among his stipulations were that:

> The entire male population should be employed upon constructing defence works. The most rigorous compulsion is to be used, up to the limit where picks and shovels are available.
> Not only must the defence of Singapore Island be maintained by every means, but the whole island must be fought for until every single unit and every single strong point has been separately destroyed.
> Finally, the city[3] of Singapore must be converted into a citadel and defended to the death. No surrender can be contemplated.

Having thus outlined what an unfettered military governor might have done, but not a Percival fettered by all the complications of civil and military administration in Malaya and of relations with the London authorities, Churchill cabled to Wavell on the 20th:

> I want to make it absolutely clear that I expect every inch of ground to be defended, every scrap of material or defences to be blown to pieces to prevent capture by the enemy, and no question of surrender to be entertained until after protracted fighting among the ruins of Singapore City.[4]

Obviously Mr Churchill was in fine mental fighting trim; but he did not explain what the hundreds of thousands of unarmed and untrained civilian men, women, and children, few with protection from bombs and shells or with prospect of escape from Singapore Island, were to do while all this was going on. Meanwhile Wavell had dispatched to him a message, previously mentioned, which in effect emphasised how far the author of these ringing demands was from the realities at the scene of action. Schemes were being prepared for defence of the northern part of the island, said Wavell, but "I doubt whether island can be held for long once Johore is lost. . . ."

On this, Mr Churchill swiftly readjusted his perspective, turning his thoughts to Burma and of the reinforcements then on the way to Singapore which might be diverted to Rangoon.

> What (he asked in a message to his Chiefs of Staff on 21st January) is the value of Singapore [to the enemy] above the many harbours in the south-west Pacific if all naval and military demolitions are thoroughly carried out? On the other hand, the loss of Burma would be very grievous. It would cut us off from the Chinese, whose troops have been the most successful of those yet engaged against the Japanese. We may, by muddling things and hesitating to take an ugly decision, lose *both* Singapore and the Burma Road. Obviously the decision depends upon how long the defence of Singapore Island can be maintained. If it is only for a few weeks, it is certainly not worth losing all our reinforcements and aircraft. [Moreover] one must consider that the fall of Singapore, accompanied as it will be by the fall of Corregidor, will be a tremendous shock to India, which only the arrival of powerful forces and successful action on the Burma front can sustain.[5]

---
[3] Singapore was not officially raised to the status of a city until 1952.
[4] Churchill, pp. 45, 47.
[5] Churchill, p. 50.

But both Mr Churchill and his Chiefs of Staff did hesitate to take the "ugly decision"; and while they did so the Australian War Cabinet received from Sir Earle Page warning that the issue was being weighed. On this, and reports of the situation at the time in Malaya, the War Cabinet decided at an emergency meeting on 23rd January that strong representations be made to Mr Churchill. Mr Curtin thereupon sent a cable in language hardly less forthright than Britain's Prime Minister had been using about Singapore. In this he referred to the substance of the reports, and continued:

> After all the assurances we have been given the evacuation of Singapore would be regarded here and elsewhere as an inexcusable betrayal. Singapore is a central fortress in the system of the Empire and local defence ... we understood that it was to be made impregnable, and in any event it was to be capable of holding out for a prolonged period until the arrival of the main fleet.
> Even in an emergency diversion of reinforcements should be to the Netherlands East Indies and not to Burma. Anything else would be deeply resented, and might force the Netherlands East Indies to make a separate peace.
> On the faith of the proposed flow of reinforcements, we have acted and carried out our part of the bargain. We expect you not to frustrate the whole purpose by evacuation.

As against the concern which Mr Churchill had expressed about Burma and India, Mr Curtin went on to say that the heavy scale of the Japanese attack on Rabaul, and the probability of its occupation, if this had not already occurred (it was on the 23rd that Rabaul fell), presaged an early attack on Port Moresby.[6] After making a wide sweep of problems and proposals for defence in the Pacific arising from the dangers with which Australia was faced, and an urgent plea for additional aircraft, he added:

> The trend of the situation in Malaya and the attack on Rabaul are giving rise to a public feeling of grave uneasiness at Allied impotence to do anything to stem the Japanese advance. The Government, in realising its responsibility to prepare the public for the intense resisting of an aggressor, also has a duty and obligation to explain why it may not have been possible to prevent the enemy reaching our shores. It is therefore in duty bound to exhaust all the possibilities of the situation, the more so since the Australian people, having volunteered for service overseas in large numbers, find it difficult to understand why they must wait so long for an improvement in the situation when irreparable damage may have been done to their power to resist, the prestige of the Empire, and the solidarity of the Allied cause.

Evidently the Australian War Cabinet—and the Advisory War Council, which subsequently endorsed the cable—still hoped that Singapore could be held, at least for a period which would repay the cost in men and material of doing so; but to leave Australia's 8th Division on the island, and to agree to the diversion to a front so distant from Australia as Burma of forces then going to its aid, might well have exposed the Australian Government to a tidal wave of protest.

Australia's attitude offered Mr Churchill an opportunity to throw responsibility on Australia for the consequences of the subsequent landing on

---

[6] See Chapter 18.

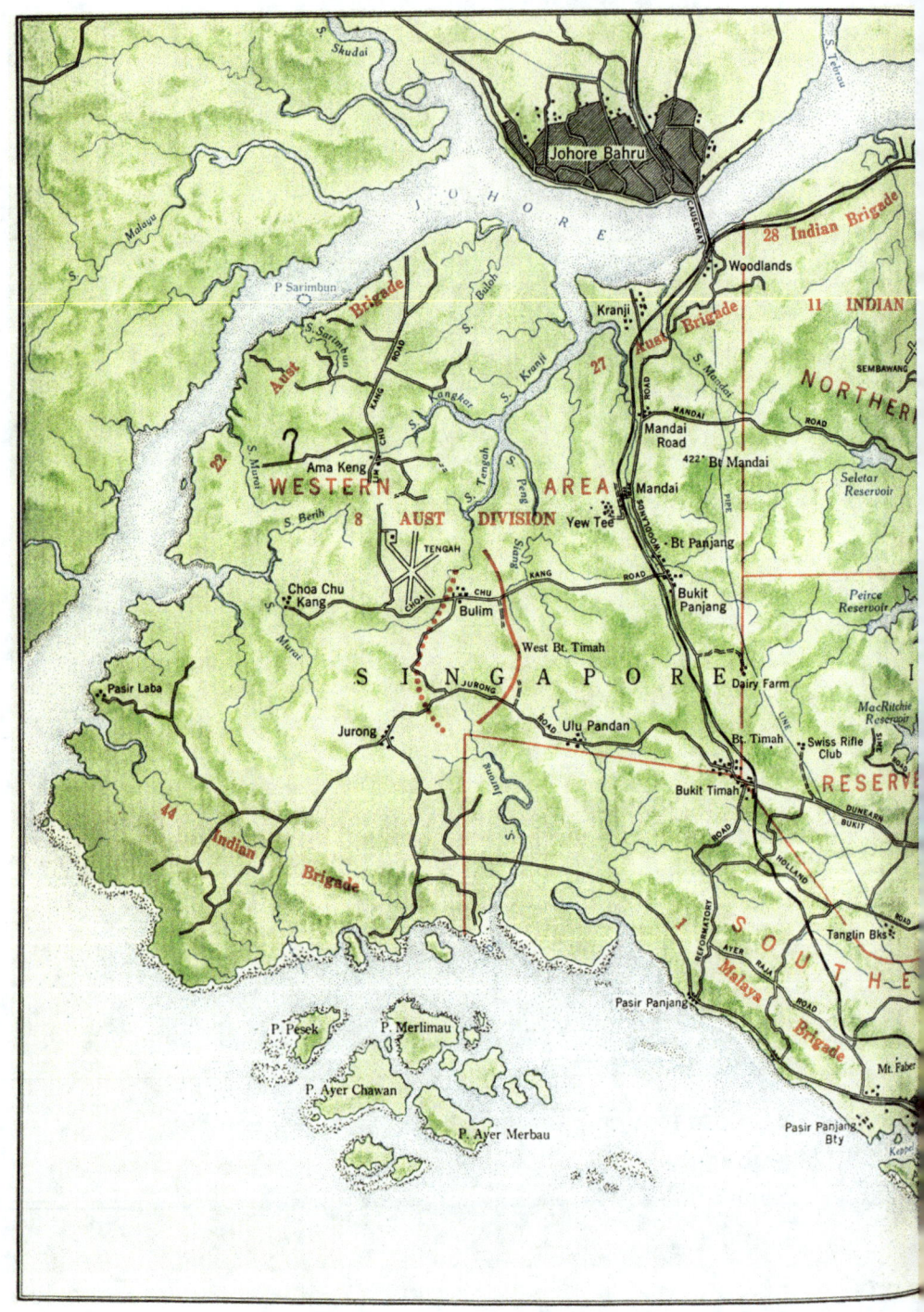

Dispositions, Singapore

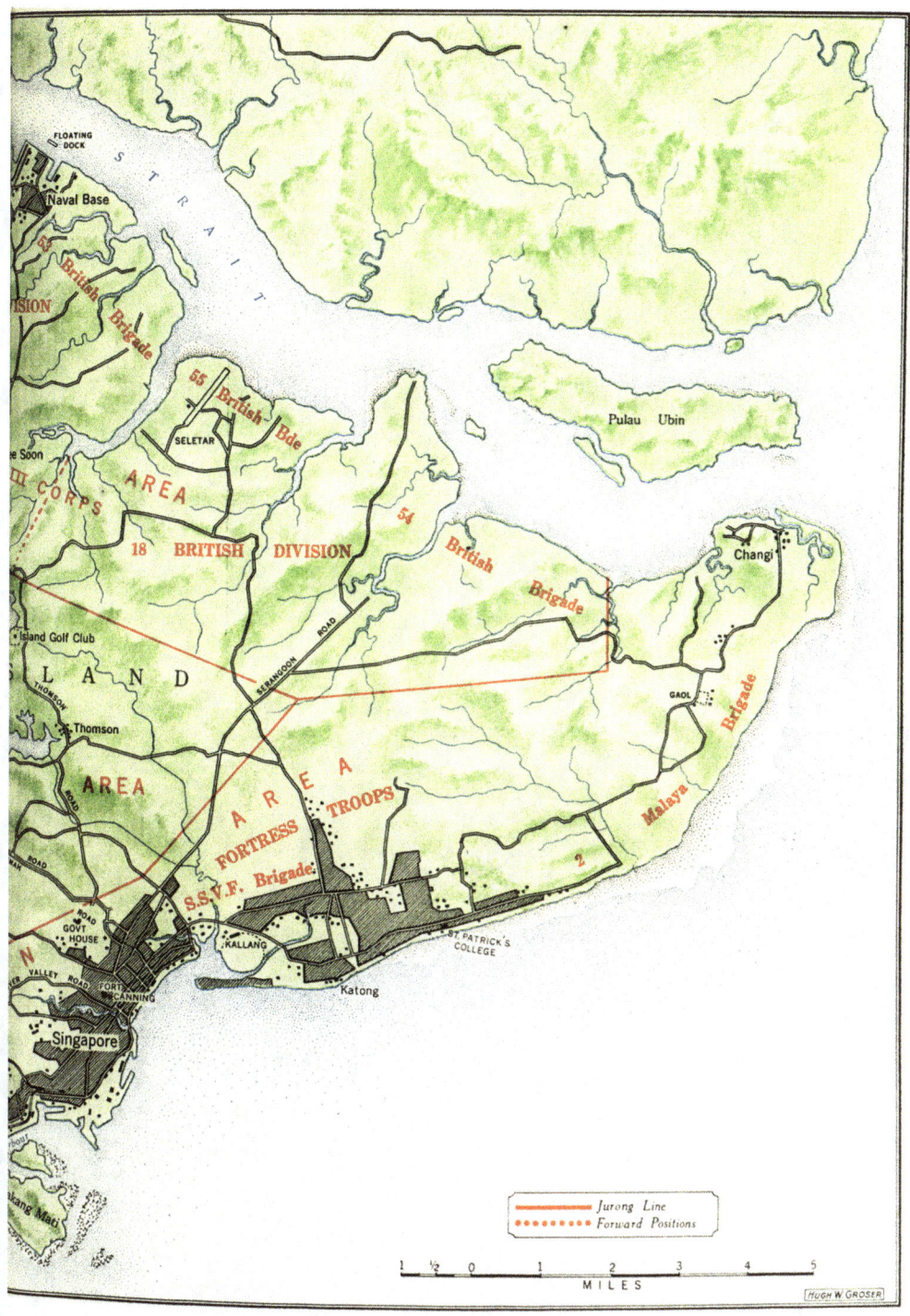

Island, 7th February 1942

the island of the remainder of the 18th British Division; but to do so would have been to abdicate the responsibility for conduct of Britain's part in the war in both the east and the west to which he firmly held. "It is not true," he wrote in retrospect, "to say that Mr Curtin's message decided the issue. . . . I was conscious . . . of a hardening of opinion against the abandonment of this renowned key point in the Far East. The effect that would be produced all over the world, especially in the United States, of a British 'scuttle' while the Americans fought on so stubbornly at Corregidor was terrible to imagine." Reflecting that there was no doubt what a purely military decision should have been, he related that "by general agreement or acquiescence, however, all efforts were made to reinforce Singapore and to sustain its defence. The 18th Division, part of which had already landed, went forward on its way."[7] In other words, the decision was made despite the irreconcilability of the political with the military factors; but Percival's success or failure in defending the island would depend on the latter. The 18th Division would provide him with more men and weapons; but not with means of overcoming the Japanese supremacy at sea and in the air. Defending an island in these circumstances, divided from the enemy by only a strip of water narrower than that between England and the Isle of Wight, was an unenviable task. How unenviable it was may be gauged by imagining what might have happened had the German forces established themselves as close to the English shoreline in the Battle for Britain, and had there been no effective resistance by the Royal Air Force or the Royal Navy.

While the fate of Singapore Island was being thus debated, increasingly powerful and numerous Japanese air attacks on the town and other parts of the island were contradicting the comforting assurances about its future to which its inhabitants had become accustomed. Six hundred civilians were killed during January, and 1,512 injured. Facing the realities of death and destruction, the civilians speedily responded in such ways as were open to them. An Australian war correspondent, Douglas Wilkie, wrote in a dispatch late in January:

> Europeans here have given up talking about "white" and "coloured" races—those Europeans are proud to be trying to help Asiatics show the world that Singapore can take it. . . . Singapore Island's three-quarter million Asiatics can take it. They have taken it with a smile when the Japanese dropped bombs indiscriminately on the outlying native suburbs and villages, killing innocent civilians whom Tokyo threatens nightly to "liberate", blasting nothing but precious gimcrack furniture and savings of a coolie's life-time. . . .
> The European A.R.P. workers, who braved death alongside Singapore's splendid body of Asiatic wardens, roof-spotters and fire-fighters, have learnt things not easily forgotten. European women shielding children in the same shelter with Chinese mothers, who have exchanged smiles of relief as a stick of bombs passed a few hundreds of yards away, have discovered many things which will not vanish when Singapore's ordeal has passed.[8]

---

[7] Churchill, pp. 51-2.
[8] *The Herald* (Melbourne), 19 Jan 1942, p. 4.

Perhaps the forecast overshot the mark, for feelings made incandescent by danger are apt to cool rapidly after it has passed; but the dispatch breathed the spirit of the time. Much more could have been asked of these people, and would have been given, had the opportunity and the leadership which the occasion demanded been provided. As it was, the cumbrous administrative machinery never reached the necessary momentum; and dynamic leadership was among the many deficiencies which the defence of Malaya continued to suffer.

To the conflict of interests and personalities which resulted in muddle and procrastination in the use of manpower was added the fact that Asian workmen, broadly designated coolies, were apt to disappear from their jobs when air raids were imminent, or were threatened in Japanese broadcasts and leaflets.[9] This was not surprising, however, in view of the fact that so little had been done, while there was yet time, to provide civilian shelter.[1] A European broadcasting official closely concerned with the day-to-day happenings in Malaya, commented: "It's easy to criticise the Asiatic workmen who have deserted their posts and cannot be persuaded to return, but what better can be expected from them when their families are in such obvious jeopardy and have no more solid protection than the street-side drains or their own flimsy dwellings?"[2]

The Australian Government was given, as January drew to a close, less reason to feel hopeful of the outcome of an attempt to hold Singapore. Reporting on the 26th to the Minister for External Affairs, Mr Bowden said he had begun to doubt whether it really was the firm intention to hold the island. After a War Council meeting that day, when a rapid collapse of British defence seemed to him probable, he had asked Rear-Admiral Spooner at what stage he would demolish the naval base. The Admiral replied that he would have to begin as soon as the Japanese reached the Strait of Johore.

> I replied (continued Bowden): "My deduction from that is that Singapore will not be held, for with the naval base and all natural resources of Malaya gone, Singapore will have nothing more than sentimental value."

Bowden recorded that the Rear-Admiral, Malaya, concurred; the General Officer Commanding, Malaya, said nothing; only the Governor naturally maintained that Singapore would be held and said he would cable the Imperial Government for its confirmation of this intention.

---

[9] "The real trouble appears to be lack of cooperation, red tape—on the services side just as much on the civilian side—and confusion as to where lies the final power for organising labour forces." Extract from leading article in the *Straits Times*, Singapore, 26 Jan 1942.

[1] Brigadier I. Simson, who on the recommendation of Mr Duff Cooper was appointed on 31st December 1941 as Director-General of Civil Defence, recorded that he accepted the position under pressure as he considered it too late at that stage to organise effectively the civil defence of a cosmopolitan population under bombardment, and that his terms of reference as amended on 1st January were too limited. Much was done in constructing shelters, but "owing to all this work not having been begun or even seriously considered until half-way through the campaign, only a small percentage of the real requirements for such a large population were met". He added: "In the bombed and burnt-out kampongs and town areas, the Chinese behaved magnificently."

[2] G. Playfair, *Singapore Goes Off the Air*, pp. 66-7.

From Percival's remarks at the War Council meeting, said Bowden, it appeared likely that Singapore Island would be in a state of siege within a week. "What I then anticipate," he continued, "is that the Japanese air force will concentrate on putting our fighter defence out of action by rendering our airfields useless, following which they would concentrate on our land defences, port facilities and essential services and ultimately make a combined attack from land and air and possibly from the sea." Bowden added that he did not see how the fall of Singapore could be prevented unless provision could be made for substantial and effective reinforcement of fighter aircraft with all necessary ground crews for servicing; concentrated bombing of Japanese airfields on the peninsula; and some powerful form of diversion such as landing in force somewhere up the peninsula to cut the now extended Japanese line of communication. He seriously doubted whether such measures could be put into effect in the time that might be available. It appeared to him that no answer had been found to Japanese infiltration tactics but retreat. Various incidents had suggested lack of decision.

Two and sometimes three raids were made daily during the latter half of January by formations of twenty-seven to fifty-four bombers escorted by fighters, with the island's four airfields as their main targets. Despite the way anti-aircraft guns spattered the sky with metal, the planes maintained perfect formation, and bombed from heights of more than 20,000 feet with considerable accuracy. As the Japanese troops advanced into Johore, the defending aircraft were forced to operate solely from the island. There the raiders took such heavy toll of them that by the end of the month the whole of the surviving bomber force was withdrawn to bases in southern Sumatra, whence it was intended that they should fly sorties to the aid of Singapore. When General Wavell visited Malaya on 30th January, three of the airfields were about to come within range of the Japanese artillery. His orders for further withdrawals of aircraft left only eight Hurricanes and six Buffaloes on the island.

The main body of the 18th British Division reached Singapore on 29th January, and, with its 53rd Brigade, was taken into command reserve. Its machine-gun and reconnaissance battalions arrived on 5th February. On the island were then concentrated all the troops who had been withdrawn from the Malayan mainland, those who recently had arrived from overseas, and the then garrison of the "fortress"—a total approximating 85,000 men, of whom about 15,000 were engaged in base, administrative, and non-combatant duties. The remaining 70,000 included many in second-line combat units. Operational command was assumed by Percival, but despite the urgency of the situation no overall control of both civil and military affairs was established. The infantry comprised 21 Indian battalions, including four Indian States Forces battalions for airfield defence; 13 of United Kingdom troops; 6 Australian; 2 Malay; and 3 of the Straits Settlements Volunteer Force—45 battalions in all. There were also 3 machine-gun battalions—one Australian and two United Kingdom—and a reconnaissance battalion.

These figures do not, in themselves, give a fair indication of fighting strength, for the battalions varied widely in quality, condition, and equipment. Only one of the Indian battalions was up to numerical strength, three (in the 44th Brigade[5]) had recently arrived in a semi-trained condition, nine had been hastily reorganised with a large intake of raw recruits, and four were being re-formed but were far from being fit for action. Six of the United Kingdom battalions (in the 54th and 55th Brigades of the 18th Division) had only just landed in Malaya, and the other seven battalions were under-manned. Of the Australian battalions, three had drawn heavily upon recently-arrived, practically-untrained recruits. The Malay battalions had not been in action, and the Straits Settlements Volunteers were only sketchily trained. Further, losses on the mainland had resulted in a general shortage of equipment. The experiences of the troops had affected their morale in varying degree. The general effect was bad.

The civilian population of Singapore was now so swollen by refugees from the mainland and Penang Island that the total was about a million.

Percival expected that the Japanese would take at least a week to prepare their attack, but that it would be made as soon as possible to free forces for use elsewhere and to open up the Indian Ocean. He estimated that they could deploy against the island about 60,000 men of the three divisions they had on the mainland (the actual number of infantry battalions was twenty-seven) but thought that with their reserves in Malaya and Indo-China or elsewhere they could bring to bear a total of seven or eight divisions. While it seemed to him likely that the main assault would be on the north-west or north-east of the island, he could not ignore the possibility of seaborne ventures against the south-west or south-east, or that troops would be dropped from the air.

Singapore Island, with a total area of 220 square miles, extends for about 26 miles from east to west, 14 miles from north to south, and has 70 miles of coastline. The main arm of the Johore Strait east of the Causeway is from 1,100 to 5,000 yards wide, but its western arm is only 2,000 yards across at its widest point, and narrows to 600 yards. The naval base was in the northernmost part of the island, east of the Causeway. The most closely populated area of the island was in the south and east. A large part of the remainder, especially the centre and west, was thickly covered by rubber and other plantations, and by secondary jungle,

---

[5] The 44th Brigade had been formed in Poona (India) in July 1941 of three under-strength battalions comprising about equal proportions of trained regular soldiers, reservists, and recruits from training battalions. The ancillary units were raised from scratch during August, September, and October, except the signal section, which came into existence just before the brigade sailed for Malaya. In the first six months of its existence the brigade was "milked" of some 250 men required in the formation of new units, and it took in 250 replacements during its last month in India, many of them with only 4 to 5 months' service and under 18 years of age. Few experienced Indian Viceroy-commissioned officers and non-commissioned officers remained in the brigade. The number of Indian Army British officers averaged fewer than three regulars to a battalion, the others having been drawn from outside India, with at most 12 months' experience of Indian troops and their language. These circumstances applied almost identically to the 45th Indian Brigade which had been employed in the Muar area as part of Westforce.

Feb 1942   THE FIXED DEFENCES   291

with relatively few roads. The centre held the heavily-timbered, hilly municipal catchment area and MacRitchie, Peirce, and Seletar reservoirs. The trunk road, in its first nine miles from the Causeway towards the town, ran at the foot of the western slope of the island's main watershed, which includes the highest points on the island—Bukit Mandai (422 feet) and Bukit Timah (481 feet). East of the road and the main heights was the Pipe-line, augmenting from the mainland the island's supply of water.[6] The Pasir Panjang ridge, about four miles long and rising to 270 feet, lay between the south-western outskirts of the town and the village of Pasir Panjang on the south coast.

The western portion of Singapore Island rises to coastward hills. In the north-west these reach the edge of coastal swamps. The island is almost bisected from north to south by two tidal river systems. Of these, the Sungei Peng Siang and Sungei Tengah, flowing north, join the Sungei Kangkar from the west to form the Sungei Kranji. The Sungei Jurong, rising south of the source of the Peng Siang, flows to the south coast. Between the headwaters of these two rivers lies a neck of land, about 4,000 yards wide, most of it between the Choa Chu Kang and the Jurong roads. These roads, branching from the trunk road at Bukit Panjang and Bukit Timah villages respectively, were the principal ways to and from the island's western area. At Tengah airfield, about half-way between Bukit Panjang and the west coast, the Lim Chu Kang road ran due north, through Ama Keng village, with branches to north-western coastal areas. The other airfields—Sembawang, Seletar, and the Kallang civil airport—were in the eastern part of the island.

Formidable heavy artillery defences had been installed on the island in the years from 1934 to 1941 to protect the naval base from sea attack —a fact which had been used extensively in building up the legend of Singapore's impregnability. The fixed defences comprised two fire commands, covering the eastern approach to the base, the approaches to Keppel Harbour, in which lay the commercial port, and the western arm of Johore Strait. Each command had one 15-inch and one 9.2-inch battery, and a number of 6-inch batteries. Some of the guns, however, were incapable because of location, lack of range, or limited traverse of being used against targets in Johore. The heavy guns useable for the purpose had very little high-explosive ammunition, and their armour-piercing shells were relatively ineffective against land targets because the shells were apt to bury themselves deep in the soft ground, which muffled the force of their explosion. Nevertheless, measures were now taken to bring the batteries into use as fully as possible against any Japanese approach from the mainland, while keeping in mind the possibility of assault, perhaps at the same time, from the sea. The 152 anti-aircraft guns available at the beginning of February were sited to cover vital points, such as Keppel

---

[6] In peace the population of Singapore Island consumed about 27,000,000 gallons of water a day of which 17,000,000 came from the three reservoirs on the island and 10,000,000 were piped from Johore. The problem of maintaining the supply in the event of the island becoming isolated had been considered and in January consumption was reduced to 15,000,000 gallons a day (less than that which the reservoirs on the island could supply).

Harbour, and the airfields. Lack of a warning system since the evacuation of the mainland reduced the effectiveness of their fire.

The permanent beach defences, commenced in 1936 when Percival was principal staff officer to General Dobbie,[7] did not extend to the coastline of the Western Area despite the appreciation prepared by Percival of the danger of attack down the mainland, for it had been hoped to keep any enemy sufficiently far north to make this unnecessary. The development of air power, and the Japanese occupation of Indo-China in 1940 and 1941, had robbed Singapore Island of much of the security hitherto provided by its seaward defences. On the other hand it emphasised the need to defend the mainland as a means of preventing enemy bases being established within striking distance of the island from the north. Thus little provision had been made against the possibility of a struggle on the island itself. Even when this possibility had become acutely obvious as the Japanese forces swept into Johore, nothing was undertaken which reflected the British Prime Minister's demand for heroic measures such as employing the entire male population with picks and shovels upon constructing defence works; and endeavours to provide an adequate amount of Asian labour became to a large extent bogged down in administrative and other difficulties. Perhaps the most vital feature in the situation as it developed was the neck of land on Singapore Island which, as previously mentioned, lies between the sources of the Sungei Kranji and the Sungei Jurong. This offered means of switching forces between east and west and of shortening the front and reducing the area to be defended if this became necessary. Yet a partially dug anti-tank ditch west of the headwaters of the rivers was almost the only token of endeavour to provide defensive works in this area. Thus "the wearied, if not exhausted, troops" who had been withdrawn from the mainland to what they expected to be an island stronghold now shared Mr Churchill's dismay at "the hideous spectacle of the almost naked island".

In a secret letter to formation commanders on 23rd January giving an outline plan for the defence of the island Percival had said that the northern and western shores were too intersected by creeks and mangroves for any recognised form of beach defence, and that the general plan in each area would include small defended localities to cover known approaches, such as rivers, creeks and roads to the coast or tracks along which vehicles could travel. He added that these localities would be supported by mobile reserves in assembly areas from which they could operate against enemy parties seeking to infiltrate near these communications or in the intervening country.

General Simmons was made responsible for developing the plan, with a special staff on which the Australians were represented by Major Daw-

---

[7] Lt-Gen Sir William Dobbie, GCMG, KCB, DSO. GOC Malaya 1935-39; Gov of Malta 1940-42. Regular soldier; b. Madras, 12 Jul 1879.

kins, one of General Bennett's staff officers. As Percival saw the situation, there were two alternatives open to him. These were to endeavour (1) to prevent the enemy from landing or, if the enemy succeeded in doing so, to stop him near the beaches and destroy him or drive him out by counter-attack; (2) to hold the coastline thinly and retain large reserves for a battle on the island. Though he considered that the extent of the coastline relative to the forces at his disposal made it impossible to build up a really strong coastal defence, he chose the former alternative, despite the weakness which had resulted from dispersion of forces on the mainland.[8]

As it finally emerged, the defence plan provided that the defences, other than anti-aircraft, should be organised in three areas. The boundaries of these areas, and the forces allotted to them, were:

Northern Area: From Changi (exclusive) on the eastern tip of Singapore Island to the Pipe-line (exclusive)—III Indian Corps, comprising 11th Indian and 18th British Divisions. Commander, General Heath.

Western Area: From the Pipe-line (inclusive) to the Sungei Jurong (exclusive)— 8th Australian Division and 44th Indian Brigade. Commander, General Bennett.

Southern Area: From the Sungei Jurong (inclusive) to Changi (inclusive)— Fixed Defences, 1st and 2nd Malaya Infantry Brigades, Straits Settlement Volunteer Force and Fortress Troops. Commander, General Simmons.

The Southern Area corresponded approximately to the south coast defences already held by the Singapore Fortress troops. It excluded the Pasir Laba Battery, inside the western entrance to Johore Strait, and therefore in the Western Area. Percival would hold a small central reserve—the 12th Indian Brigade (Brigadier Paris) which now comprised only two battalions. Of these the Argylls numbered 400, including 150 marines, and the 4/19th Hyderabad 400, most of the latter semi-trained. Commanders of the Northern and Western Areas were each to hold an infantry battalion at an hour's notice at night to move to the support of other areas as might be required. Percival arranged to expand rapidly the force of Chinese irregulars (Dalforce[9]) which had been operating in an auxiliary role on the mainland under Lieut-Colonel J. D. Dalley, of the Federated Malay States Police Force.

The loss of the 22nd Indian Brigade shortly before the withdrawal across the Causeway had left the 9th Indian Division with only one under-manned brigade (the 8th), which was now taken into the 11th Indian

---

[8] In his subsequent Despatch (p. 1312), Percival gave as his reasons for the choice that "there was a lack of depth in which to fight a defensive battle on Singapore Island in front of the vital town area. The Naval and Air Bases, depots, dumps and other installations were dispersed all over the Island and some of them would certainly be lost if the enemy was allowed to get a footing on the Island. Further, the close nature of the country and the short visibility would favour the enemy who would be sure to adopt aggressive tactics. Finally, the moral effect of a successful enemy landing would be bad both on the troops and on the civil population."

[9] "This force was recruited from all classes of Chinese—college boys and rickshaw pullers, loyalists and communists, old and young. Later it became the centre of the resistance movement in Malaya and did much to help British troops marooned in that country. The members of Dalforce . . . were exceedingly tough, and in spite of their lack of training would, I have no doubt, have made excellent fighters had we been able to arm and equip them properly. As it was, the effort, though most praiseworthy, came too late to have any real effect on the course of events." (Percival, *The War in Malaya*, p. 263.)

An Australian officer described them as "a motley crew, equipped with shot-guns and service rifles".

Division; as shown above, Major-General Beckwith-Smith's[1] 18th British Division was included in III Indian Corps. Detachments from Dalforce were allotted to area commanders to patrol swamp areas where landings might occur, and act as a nucleus of such fighting patrols as might operate on the mainland. Such craft as the navy could muster, now based on Keppel Harbour, were to patrol the sea approaches and to operate inshore as required by area commanders. The sole remaining air squadron based on the Kallang civil airport, close to the town area, was to cooperate with the ground defences against attacks, and to spot Japanese concentrations. Operational headquarters of Malaya Command and Navy and Air Force headquarters were at Sime road, on the northern outskirts of the city, and Malaya Command administrative headquarters near its centre, at Fort Canning.

Morale, both military and civilian, was now a matter of increasingly serious concern. The feeling of security engendered by the former peace and prosperity of Malaya under British control, and fostered by the publicity policy hitherto pursued, had hardly yet given place to a real sense of urgency on the part of all concerned; but confidence in being able to surmount the enemy's superior might, and in the control of operations, had been badly shaken by the course of events. Greater credence naturally tended to be given in these circumstances, especially by Singapore's Asian people, to the assertions pumped out by the Japanese-controlled Penang radio. These were in fact often more revealing than the official communiqués. The long withdrawal and the heavy losses on the mainland could hardly have been otherwise than dispiriting to the troops. The far-famed and fabulously costly naval base had become useless; the air force had practically disappeared. British prestige was rapidly ebbing, Australia as well as the Netherlands East Indies now appeared to lie in the path of the Japanese advance, and as Percival has put it, "it was understandable that some among the troops should begin to think of their own homes overseas which were now being directly threatened".[2]

The naval base having come under observed artillery fire and small arms fire, and being within closer range of enemy aircraft to which only limited opposition could be offered, had become unusable for naval purposes; but so strong was the popular legend of the impregnability of the base that one of the greatest shocks suffered by the forces upon their withdrawal to the island was the discovery that it had been abandoned by the navy, and was being demolished. To many, including some senior officers, it seemed that the primary purpose of being in Malaya had disappeared, and further fighting would result in wholesale slaughter and destruction with no corresponding gain. This humanitarian outlook gained strength from the fact that what had been termed an impregnable fortress was under existing conditions not a fortress at all, but a very vulnerable

---

[1] Maj-Gen M. B. Beckwith-Smith, DSO, MC. GOC 18 Brit Div 1941-42. Regular soldier; b. 11 Jul 1890. Died while prisoner 11 Nov 1942. Beckwith-Smith had temporarily commanded the 1st Division at Dunkirk.

[2] Percival, Despatch, p. 1312.

island with the heavy military liability of a large civilian population. Not only were the civilians exposed to shells and bombs; they faced the all-too-evident likelihood that eventually they would be at the mercy of Japanese soldiery drunk with victory and looted intoxicants. The broader picture from the military viewpoint of the importance of keeping the Japanese forces engaged, and thus gaining time to build up resistance elsewhere, was apt to be clouded by these considerations.

Seeking to counter rumours that Singapore itself was not to be defended—a possibility which as has been shown had been weighed by Mr Churchill—General Percival said in the course of a press statement:

> The battle of Malaya has come to an end and the battle of Singapore has started. . . . Our task is to hold this fortress until help can come—as assuredly it will come. This we are determined to do. In carrying out this task we want the help of every man and woman in the fortress. There is work for all to do. Any enemy who sets foot in our fortress must be dealt with immediately. The enemy within our gates must be ruthlessly weeded out. There must be no more loose talk and rumour-mongering. Our duty is clear. With firm resolve and fixed determination we shall win through.

The sentiment was heroic, but circumstances such as those outlined challenged the realism of the statement.

Once again, there appears to have been a discrepancy between orders issued by General Wavell and General Percival's action. As has been related, Wavell had instructed Percival to place the 18th Division on the front most likely to be attacked, and the 8th Australian Division in the next most dangerous sector. Despite his having then expressed the belief that the Japanese were most likely to attack the north-east, Percival himself recorded that when the dispositions were made he regarded the western sector of the island as the danger area, adding "I had specially selected for it the Australian Imperial Force . . . because I thought that, of the troops which had had experience of fighting on the mainland, it was the freshest and most likely to give a good account of itself".[3] This was a notable tribute to the fighting qualities of the Australians by a man who had so recently employed them in action; but as he realised, the western area was a particularly difficult one. It was in fact very questionable whether any troops, no matter how fresh and able they might be, could do more than act as a buffer force in the circumstances in which the Australians were placed. Extended over a front vastly disproportionate to their numbers, how could the two brigades hope to hold such forces as the Japanese could throw in?

In contrast to this assessment of where the main danger lay, by far the greater strength of artillery was allotted to the Northern Area—five field artillery regiments, two anti-tank regiments, and one mountain regiment in addition to its three fixed batteries—whereas the Western Area received eventually only three field artillery regiments and three anti-tank batteries, additional to one fixed battery. The Southern Area had one field regiment

---

[3] Percival, *The War in Malaya*, p. 262.

and one anti-tank battery. The allocation to the Western Area meant that less than 5 per cent of its three-brigade frontage could be engaged by the guns at any one time, and only about one-seventh of the front could receive support at one time or another. In retrospect it seems strange that the two Australian brigades should have been divided by the Kranji. Had the Causeway sector been included in the Northern Area, making the Kranji the north-eastern boundary of the Western Area, the 27th Brigade could have been used as the sort of reserve which the area required; and the Australians would have been able to fight as they preferred, in a compact, self-reliant force.

Extensive reorganisation was undertaken to repair as far as possible the effects of the misfortunes suffered on the mainland. Lieut-Colonel Coates,[4] principal staff officer of the 9th Indian Division, became commander of the 6th/15th Indian Brigade in place of Brigadier Challen, missing since the brigade was dispersed on the west coast. The brigade now comprised the British Battalion, the Jat Battalion (amalgamated 2/ and 4/Jat) and 3/16th Punjab. Colonel Trott was given command of the 8th Indian Brigade, comprising the 1/13th Frontier Force Rifles, 2/10th Baluch, two companies of Bahawalpur Infantry, and the Garhwal Battalion, being formed from survivors and reinforcements of the 2nd and 5th Royal Garhwal Rifles. The two Australian battalions which had fought at Muar had been so depleted that the 2/29th took in 500 reinforcements, and 370 went into the 2/19th. The 2/18th received ninety men to replace its losses on the east coast. Of the 2/29th Battalion's company commanders at this stage, only one (Captain Bowring[5]) had survived the Muar action, and nineteen new officers, mostly from reinforcements, had been appointed to the battalion. Commenting on the quality of the reinforcements, Thyer wrote later:

> Of those allotted to the 2/29th Battalion, the great majority had arrived from Australia as late as the 24th of January. . . . Some had sailed within a fortnight of enlistment. A large proportion had not qualified at a small arms course, nor been taught bayonet fighting. Naturally they were ignorant of the conditions in Malaya or elsewhere . . . some reinforcements to all battalions had never seen a Bren gun and none of them had handled a sub-machine-gun or an anti-tank rifle. Worse still was the fact that there were some who had never handled a rifle. . . . There was a serious lack of trained specialists, such as signallers, mortar men and carrier drivers.

The training they needed might have been given in Malaya had there been time for it; but it was too late now. Major Pond, formerly Maxwell's brigade major, took command on 25th January of the 2/29th, and set about giving it what basic training was possible; but it needed at least a three months' course before it could be considered fit for battle. Though Anderson had worked hard to prepare the 2/19th for further action after the disaster at Parit Sulong, it also was far from this goal.

[4] Col J. B. Coates, OBE, MC. GSO1 9 Ind Div 1941-42; Comd 6/15 Ind Inf Bde Feb 1942. Regular soldier; b. 24 Sep 1897.
[5] Capt W. B. Bowring, MC, VX44362; 2/29 Bn. Accountant; of Mildura, Vic; b. Mildura, 6 Sep 1916.

The Sungei Kranji, 1,200 yards wide where it reached Johore Strait west of the Causeway, offered a natural boundary in the northern part of the Western Area. The 27th Brigade was placed east of it, in what became known as the Causeway sector, and the 22nd Brigade west of it, on a front extending to the Sungei Berih, about half way down the west coast.[6] This gave the 22nd a frontage to the Strait of about 16,000 yards, compared with the 27th's 4,000 yards, despite the fact that the 22nd Brigade's frontage was closer to the mainland. However, the 2/29th Battalion, to be retained in the Causeway sector, was to be regarded as a divisional reserve. Its handicap in a role requiring well-controlled mobility was the large proportion of raw reinforcements it contained. The 44th Indian Brigade (Brigadier Ballentine) was allotted to the south-west sector, with an even longer frontage—21,000 yards of coastline from the Berih to the Jurong—but it appeared to be less immediately exposed to attack. Thus the divisional defence plan provided that the brigade might be used as a reserve in the event of attack on the 22nd Australian Brigade.

In detail, the dispositions of infantry and ancillary forces in the Western Area were:

Causeway sector: 27th Australian Brigade, Brigadier Maxwell (2/26th, 2/29th, 2/30th Battalions) with 13th Anti-tank Battery, 2/12th Field Company, "B" Company 2/4th Machine Gun Battalion, and 2/9th Field Ambulance under command; 2/10th Field Regiment, less one battery, in support.[7]

North-west sector: 22nd Australian Brigade, Brigadier Taylor (2/18th, 2/19th, 2/20th Battalions) with 15th Anti-tank Battery, 2/10th Field Company, "D" Company 2/4th Machine Gun Battalion, 2/10th Field Ambulance under command; 2/15th Field Regiment, less one battery, in support.

South-west sector: 44th Indian Brigade, Brigadier Ballentine (6/1st, 7/8th, 6/14th Punjab Regiments) with 16th Anti-tank Battery, a field company of Indian Sappers and Miners, "C" Company 2/4th Machine Gun Battalion under command; 19th Battery 2/10th Field Regiment and 65th Battery 2/15th Field Regiment in support.[8]

Bennett's headquarters were at Hillview Estate, on Jurong road, about 1,400 yards north-west of Bukit Timah village. Jurong road, branching at the village from the main road between Singapore and the Causeway, led into Ballentine's sector. Northward, the main road to the Causeway gave access to Maxwell's sector and to the Choa Chu Kang road into Taylor's sector. The troops under Bennett's command quickly set to work wiring, digging, and otherwise preparing to give battle as best they could in the absence of previously prepared defences. In many instances the swampy nature of the ground made it impossible to dig trenches, and breastworks had to be thrown up.

---

[6] Frontages on the island, down to brigades, were allocated by General Keith Simmons and his staff, including Major Dawkins of the 8 Aust Div.

[7] Afterwards some senior officers criticised the decision to switch the artillery regiments from the brigades with which they had trained and fought. The artillery commander, Brig Callaghan, allotted the 2/10th Field Regiment to the 27th Brigade because it so happened that it was the last field regiment over the Causeway, and allotting it to that area would avoid unnecessary movement on busy roads at night.

[8] During 6th-7th February a 5th Field Regt group (Royal Artillery) under Lt-Col E. W. F. Jephson replaced the two Australian batteries, which then reverted to their regiments.

Maxwell was anxious particularly about the southern portion of the five miles from north to south of his sector, fearing enemy penetration towards the rear of his forward troops. He placed the 2/30th Battalion (Lieut-Colonel Galleghan) at and near the entrance to the Causeway; the 2/26th (Lieut-Colonel Boyes) to the left of this position, covering the coast and the area near the mouth of the Kranji. Although the 2/29th was in reserve it was given extensive responsibility for rear protection. The 2/26th Battalion's sector consisted largely of swamp, and its main positions were established on the higher ground, with standing patrols and listening-posts forward. Of the two foremost companies, "B" (Captain Swartz) was north of the Kranji road, which bisected the area between the trunk road (linked by the Causeway with the trunk road on the mainland) and the mouth of the Kranji, and "A" (Captain Beirne[9]) on "B" Company's left. The area of the junction of the Kranji road and the railway which ran more or less parallel with the trunk road and a little west of it, was held by "C" Company (Captain Walker[10]). "D" Company (Captain Tracey[1]) was in reserve near where the Kranji road met the trunk road (of which the part running through the brigade sector was known as the Woodlands road). Even the relatively high ground was found unsuitable for trenches and weapon pits. Although breastworks were erected, they gave relatively poor protection. A carefully devised plan had been drawn up for coordinated machine-gun, mortar and artillery fire covering the battalion fronts. The 60th Battery was posted about a mile and a half east of Mandai Road village to support the 2/30th Battalion, and the 20th Battery was west of Yew Tee village, to support the 2/26th Battalion. Brigade headquarters were at the Singapore Dairy Farm, east of the trunk road and seven miles back from the Causeway—a long way for effective contact with the battalions, but close to Bennett's headquarters, and placed there presumably with his concurrence. Positions immediately to the right (east) of the Causeway sector were occupied by the 28th Indian Brigade (Brigadier Selby).

Brigadier Taylor, having discharged his responsibilities as commander of the outer bridgehead during the withdrawal to the island, found himself faced with an even more difficult problem. In keeping with General Percival's plan of defending the beaches, each of the 22nd Brigade's battalions had to be given a frontage of about three miles. Taylor placed his 2/20th (Lieut-Colonel Assheton[2]) with a platoon of the 2/4th Machine Gun Battalion and a company of Dalforce under command, on the right, with a frontage of 8,000 yards from the Kranji to near the Sungei Sarimbun on the west coast; the 2/18th (Lieut-Colonel Varley) with a machine-gun platoon under command from this point to the Sungei Murai; and the 2/19th Battalion (Lieut-Colonel Anderson) with a machine-gun

---

[9] Capt B. R. Beirne, QX6463; 2/26 Bn. Solicitor; of Toowoomba, Qld; b. Toowoomba, 7 Oct 1912.
[10] Capt R. R. Walker, NX70509; 2/26 Bn. Auctioneer; of Lismore, NSW; b. Lismore, 21 Nov 1913.
[1] Captain Tracey was shortly to become coordinating officer under a new commander of the battalion, and to be succeeded in command of "D" Company by Captain G. B. Ferguson (of Brisbane).
[2] Lt-Col C. F. Assheton, NX3797; CO 2/20 Bn. Civil engineer; of Tamworth, NSW; b. Kalgoorlie, WA, 21 Sep 1901. Killed in action 9 Feb 1942.

platoon under command, from the Murai to the Sungei Berih and the Choa Chu Kang road. The brigade was thus left without a reserve battalion, but each battalion was required to hold one company in reserve in its headquarters area. Brigade headquarters were centrally situated a little south of Ama Keng village. The Jind Infantry Regiment, one of the better units of the Indian State Forces, was guarding the near-by Tengah airfield, in the south-eastern portion of the brigade area, and came under Taylor's command.

Brigadier Ballentine, commander of the 44th Indian Brigade, also placed his three battalions—all Punjabis—in forward positions to guard his front, less two companies held in reserve. The 6/14th Punjab was on the right, the 6/1st in the centre, and the 7/8th on the left, the latter facing south. Thus, as at Muar, an Indian brigade occupied Bennett's left flank; and the 44th was about as raw as the 45th Brigade had been. The frontage comprised a continuous fringe of mangrove swamps.

During the early days of February the island's airfields were being constantly attacked by Japanese bombers, making it difficult to operate even the few remaining aircraft from them. From the air, and from observation posts at Johore Bahru, the enemy had an almost unimpeded view of activity on the island during the day, unless it was under cover. It became necessary to work by night in constructing defensive positions in cleared areas, and to camouflage them before dawn. Such recruited labour as was made available was of little value under bombardment from air and land. The Japanese appeared to use a variety of weapons, including 4-inch mortars, light and medium field guns, and light anti-aircraft guns firing on a flat trajectory, but these caused surprisingly few casualties among the Australian infantry. The Australians, however, were at a loss to understand why their own guns first refrained from fire against Johore Bahru, and especially against its public administration building, in view of the obvious use being made of it by Japanese spotters. Restriction of artillery fire generally against the Japanese was the result of a stock-taking of ammunition carried out by Malaya Command. This, in relation to the policy (which persisted despite current circumstances) to plan for a three months' siege, was described as serious, and a plan to ration ammunition accordingly had been drawn up. The plan provided that, except during attack or defence, 25-pounder guns should be restricted to twelve rounds a day, 18-pounders to 25 rounds, and 4.5-inch howitzers to 29 rounds. On 4th February Malaya Command ruled that allocations of ammunition were not transferable from gun to gun, and not accumulative from day to day.

Because of the superior facilities for observation possessed by the enemy —whose reconnaissance aircraft were flying as low as 400 to 500 feet— artillery action was further restricted by orders that guns at battle positions were to be silent, and that most of the shooting should be by roving sections or troops of guns continually changing their positions. Malaya

Command even issued an instruction that notification must be sent to Command Headquarters before making "warlike noises", such as those resulting from range practice, on the ground that the civil population must be informed in advance, to avoid panic. Apart from hampering warlike preparations, which at this stage needed to be made with all speed, this instruction was significant of the unrealistic state of mind existing at the time. Endeavours were made, without success, to get the Command to agree to a more liberal use of ammunition.

In such restrictive circumstances Bennett, dealing with a report that the artillery wished to open fire on the Johore administration building as the presence of an enemy observation post in its tower was suspected, ordered that the town was not to be fired on unless there was definite proof of the enemy's presence. This the Japanese quickly supplied. A further order, that there should be no firing on a defined area along the Sungei Tebrau, was intended to allow men who it was still hoped would come in from the lost 22nd Indian Brigade to move along the edge of the river east of Johore Bahru to the Strait. As they or other survivors from the mainland might seek to cross the Strait in small craft, orders were given also that the forward artillery observation posts and the Pasir Laba fort should not challenge or engage craft less than 100 feet long unless they were in large numbers or engaged in obviously hostile actions. The Australian artillery policy generally, laid down by its commander, Brigadier Callaghan, with Bennett's approval and within the framework of Malaya Command orders, was that targets should not be engaged except to register zones of fire; for observed shooting on identified enemy targets; for counter-battery fire when enemy guns were actually firing; for defensive fire on request by company or senior commanders, or by pre-arranged signal; or as ordered by Callaghan's headquarters. The signal for defensive fire was to be a succession of red Very lights.

The Pasir Laba fort, placed under Western Area Headquarters command, was equipped with two 6-inch coastal defence guns, and had two 3.7-inch howitzers, two 18-pounders, and a company of the Malay Regiment, for its local defence. The arcs of fire of the coastal defence guns had been arranged so that they could fire to the south-west, but the commander of the fort was arranging for the arc of the northernmost of these to be increased to enable it to fire to a point opposite the front of the 2/18th Battalion—the centre battalion of Taylor's brigade. The howitzers and 18-pounders were old, shod with iron tyres, and not equipped for indirect fire.

Taylor sought to have the 2/10th and 2/15th Field Regiments placed under command of his and Maxwell's brigades respectively, but Bennett concurred in a recommendation by Callaghan that the regiments remain in support, i.e. controlled directly by Callaghan but cooperating with the brigades. Among Callaghan's reasons were that it might be necessary for the artillery in the Causeway and north-west sectors to fire in support of either or both the sectors, or to act similarly as regards the north-west and south-west sectors; and that by virtue of the broader perspective of his command, he would be in a better position than a brigade commander to avoid guns being surrounded as a result of enemy outflanking movements. However, the two regiments were ordered on 2nd February to form one extra troop each, equipped with six surplus 4.5-inch howitzers, to be known as "G" Troop, and to comprise such drivers and others as could be spared for the purpose.

Despite the limitations placed on the artillery in the preparatory period, Bennett propounded again, at a conference with his three brigade commanders on 2nd February, his policy of aggressive defence. Anti-aircraft searchlights and beach-lights were to be switched on each night, and their positions altered daily. A request that sufficient transport be held in Taylor's brigade area for two companies, as the only immediately available reserve of troops, was not granted, on the ground that it would be unwise to hold such transport in unit areas.

With difficulty, beach-lights, supplemented by headlights removed from cars, were obtained to illuminate areas where the Japanese might attempt landings. Barbed wire and telephone cable also were difficult to obtain in sufficient quantity to serve the widely dispersed units. In abandoning the naval base the navy had left large quantities of stores, clothing and foodstuffs behind them. As a result of action by Galleghan and men of the 2/30th Battalion, the 27th Brigade received from it clothing, tinned food, biscuits, tobacco, soft drinks, kitchen utensils, mapping requisites, telephone hand-sets, signal cable, and truckloads of beer. As a large shipment of parcels from Australia arrived at this time, the men were able for the time being to take a light-hearted view of their circumstances. Occasional artillery fire on observed targets in Johore Bahru was now cheering the Australians generally.

Despite the obvious desirability, no arrangements had been made to leave concealed patrols on the mainland equipped with wireless sets with which they could send back information about the enemy. The Strait was patrolled, however, by light naval craft. Bennett ordered that boats be manned by Australians who could act as listening posts, and that Australian patrols should cross the Strait at night and reconnoitre on the mainland for a day or more. Patrols were sent across also from the III Corps area. Two Punjabis who appeared in the 27th Brigade's sector on 3rd February reported that they had been able to cross the Causeway. They had found that the gap caused by the demolition charges was fordable at low tide, and the above-water obstructions had not stopped the two men. In these circumstances companies and mortar units in the sector were ordered to prepare second and third positions.

Consideration was given at the Australian divisional staff level to the Kranji-Jurong neck of land as offering a means whereby, if a contraction of the widely dispersed forces in the Western Area became necessary, units west of the Sungei Kranji and the Sungei Jurong could be disposed along 4,000 yards of relatively good country instead of the 40,000 yards of difficult coastline they occupied. Colonel Thyer, who believed that the thin defences along the coast were unlikely to stand against a strong attack, ordered a reconnaissance of the neck, and preparation of a plan for its use if necessary.

Concern at being under-manned was expressed by brigade commanders and senior staff at a conference held by Bennett on 3rd February. "As they left," Bennett noted, "I realised the unfairness of asking them and their men to fight with such meagre resources." He thereupon ordered Major Robertson, of the 2/20th Battalion, to form a Special Reserve Battalion from surplus Army Service Corps and ordnance men and 2/4th Machine Gun Battalion reinforcements. Visiting the 2/18th and 2/19th Battalions on 4th February, Bennett found the area thickly covered by trees, with mangroves growing to the water's edge. The battalion posts were hundreds of yards apart, with small fields of fire, and he became still more concerned about the prospect the Australians faced. The terrain and the circumstances were indeed ideal for the infiltration tactics which the Japanese had consistently employed on the mainland. As an officer of the 2/19th Battalion was to write,[3] the unit had found itself after arrival on Singapore Island—

dumped in a scraggy waste of stunted rubber and tangled undergrowth, apparently miles from anywhere, our vision limited to the next rise in the undulating ground and our means of movement confined to a few native foot-tracks winding through the wilderness. . . . Maps showed us that we were a mile and a half from the west coast, with . . . the 2/18th away to the north in a similar desolation of waste and confusion. . . . A mile of single-file track led through the belukar [secondary jungle] eight feet high, where the visibility was no more than a stone's throw, to Tom Vincent's headquarters, where "D" Company looked out on the beauties of a mangrove swamp which was under water at high tide. A wooden foot-bridge crossed the swamp to a small hill on the coast occupied by a platoon. On its southern flank lay the broad reaches and monotonous mangrove swamps of the Sungei Berih. . . . A long trek through more swamps and belukar brought us to another platoon position, covering a hill on the coast large enough to be held by at least a company, and behind these two coastal positions the remainder of "D" Company was shrouded by the lank undergrowth of the hinterland.

With a rather confused idea of "D" Company's position, we set off on a long trail to "B" Company, further north across another mangrove swamp and into a sloping wilderness where Dick Keegan nestled among the shrubs and vines which concealed his headquarters. Away to the west a grove of coconut palms lay at the foot of an extensive cleared hill which had the appearance of a pineapple farm.

This in turn was bounded to the north by a small river, the Sungei Murai, the opposite bank of which formed the left boundary of the 2/18th. The coconut grove was a pleasant, low-lying piece of ground on the water's edge with lush grass in which to rest and enjoy the meat and drink of the coconut. It was also an excellent place for a Jap landing. The rest of "B" Company was swallowed up in the ridiculous immensity of its area.

---

[3] Lt-Col R. F. Oakes, in "Singapore Story", made available in typescript to the writer of this volume.

(*Australian War Memorial*)

A.R.P. volunteers fighting fires in the Singapore docks area. The bearded citizen on the right claimed to have been fighting such fires from Ipoh in Northern Malaya, southwards along the peninsula until Singapore was reached.

(*Australian War Memorial*)

Stocks of rubber were burned to prevent them from falling into the hands of the advancing Japanese.

(Australian War Memorial)

On 31st January the rearguard of the defending British forces in Malaya withdrew to Singapore Island, and the Causeway was blown. The 70-foot gap in the Causeway can be seen below the Johore Administration building.

(Australian War Memorial)

The withdrawal to Singapore Island exposed the island's airfields to shelling as well as air bombardments, and most of the defending air forces were withdrawn to Sumatra. Thenceforward Singapore Island was subjected to increasingly heavy air attacks. Bombs are seen falling in the background of this picture, taken in February 1942.

To Australia, Bennett reported on 4th February that he considered the best policy would be a strong counter-offensive as soon as reinforcements of aircraft and quality troops could be arranged.[4]

At a "depressing" conference with Percival, Heath and Simmons on the same day, civil control, especially of labour, was severely criticised. Under constant bombing, the unloading of ships was slow. Bennett recorded having suggested that a military adviser to the Government be appointed, "who should be the strong man behind the throne, one who would force the civil administration out of its peacetime groove". Percival "seemed impressed with the idea", and asked Bennett after the conference if he would undertake the task. Bennett asked for time to consider the proposal. Next day he told Percival that he would prefer to become Military Governor of Singapore (a position which Mr Duff Cooper had contemplated creating if Singapore were invested), but would accept the other position provided the civil governor agreed to act under his instructions in all things. In the upshot no such appointment was made.

Meanwhile the Japanese increased the intensity of their shelling and bombing, and Tengah airfield became so damaged that it was abandoned by the air force. Major Fraser, with Major Shaw[5] (8th Division Engineers) and Captain Wyett commenced on 4th February reconnoitring the Kranji-Jurong area, formulating plans, and pegging out positions to take advantage of its features for defensive purposes. Captain McEwin[6] and four platoon commanders of the 2/4th Machine Gun Battalion were subsequently sent to assist in the work. The anti-tank line, which existed mostly as a mark on a map, was a westward curve bisecting the Choa Chu Kang and Jurong roads a little west of Bulim and east of Jurong villages respectively. The roads were not cut, but they were sited for anti-tank mines. Except for swampy ground running into its northern and southern boundaries, the Kranji-Jurong area was undulating and sparsely timbered. In some parts, particularly in the vicinity of West Bukit Timah, which was regarded as a reserve locality, there were open fields of fire running some 200 to 250 yards forward of partially prepared defence works. On a spur in the Bulim village area there were some section posts comprising breastworks of timber and stone. Fraser had instructions to carry his reconnaissance down to section posts, to peg out anti-tank defences and weapon pits, and to await news of Chinese labour being made available for the digging. Machine-gun and artillery cooperation in defending the area was to be arranged. It was proposed to allot initially two battalions, and possibly a third, to the positions, but Fraser soon

---

[4] After the war Bennett explained that his scheme was "to land a brigade group at Malacca or Port Dickson, or both, or even at Port Swettenham, move to the main road and then attack the enemy at the southern end of Johore from the rear".

[5] Maj J. A. L. Shaw, DSO, NX34966; OC 2/12 Fd Coy. Civil engineer; of Manly, NSW; b. Marrickville, NSW, 26 Aug 1902.

[6] Capt O. S. McEwin, WX3442; 2/4 MG Bn. Sales manager; of Cottesloe, WA; b. Sydney, 15 Jul 1910. Killed in action 12 Feb 1942.

concluded that much larger forces were needed for the task of holding them.

On 5th February the Japanese heavily bombarded the 18th Division's part of the Northern Area allotted to the III Corps, and carried out movements on the mainland opposite it, apparently seeking to give the impression that an attack was impending from this direction. They caused surprise by using a gun with such range that it shelled Government House close to the hub of the city; and their aircraft so damaged the liner *Empress of Asia* off the south-west coast of the island that she caught fire, and was abandoned in a sinking condition.[7] The vessel was one of four ships bringing the remainder of the 18th British Division, some other troops, and transport vehicles. Most of the troops were rescued by the navy, but nearly all their weapons and equipment were lost. Percival and Bennett, from a hill in the 44th Brigade sector, saw the *Empress of Asia* burning. On their left they saw the position held by a Punjab company, and two miles or more to the right the next company's position, with mangrove swamp between the two. Percival "again expressed his concern at the thinness of the defence and asked how we could defend the place", wrote Bennett in his diary. "He agreed with my reply which was, 'only with more soldiers'."[8]

Guns were at last ranged on the Johore administration building, and severely damaged it, to the Australians' keen satisfaction, but an observation balloon above Johore Bahru withstood all attempts to shoot it down. Callaghan had to go to his rear headquarters, and later to hospital, with an attack of malaria, and Lieut-Colonel McEachern,[9] of the 2/4th Anti-Tank Regiment, acted as commander of the Australian artillery.

From 5th February onward sounds from the mainland of sawing, hammering, and other activities were heard by the Australians. A series of changes in command took place at this critical stage. Lieut-Colonel Anderson, commanding the 2/19th on Varley's left, was admitted to hospital, and his place was taken by Major Robertson of the 2/20th Battalion. Command of the Special Reserve Battalion was given to Major Saggers,[1] of the 2/4th Machine Gun Battalion. An "X" Battalion, also formed of spare men and reinforcements, was placed under command of Lieut-Colonel Boyes. Major Oakes of the 2/19th Battalion, who had admired and been closely associated with Brigadier Maxwell when Maxwell was the battalion's commander, was promoted to lieut-colonel to command the 2/26th Battalion in Boyes' stead. Arrangements had been made whereby an extra platoon comprised of men culled from various ancillary

---

[7] Strangely, the vessel was the only one lost under air attack on any convoy bringing reinforcements to Malaya; a fact no doubt attributable in part to air strength having been conserved for convoy escort duties.

[8] Bennett, p. 170.

[9] Brig C. A. McEachern, DSO, ED, QX6176. CO 2/4 A-Tk Regt 1940-42. Solicitor; of Brisbane; b. Dongara, WA, 9 Sep 1905.

[1] Maj A. E. Saggers, ED, WX3454; 2/4 MG Bn; CO Special Reserve Bn Feb 1942. Merchant; of Dalkeith, WA; b. Parramatta, NSW, 29 Nov 1899.

units and reinforcements was added to each rifle company, and to battalion headquarters for defensive purposes.²

Time was needed for the officers and men concerned to become adjusted to the new circumstances. Time was indeed the greatest all-round need in seeking to put Singapore Island into a fit state for defence; but it quickly became all too evident that the Japanese plan of operations did not provide for it.

A stir was caused at Malaya Command Headquarters on 6th February by a report, after an air reconnaissance from Palembang, in Sumatra, that a cruiser, four destroyers, and four merchant ships were anchored off the Anambas Islands north-east of Singapore. To Percival and his staff it seemed that their fears of a seaborne attack on Singapore might be about to materialise, though A.B.D.A. Command told Percival on the 7th (correctly as it turned out) that the convoy was aimed at southern Sumatra.

On 7th February the Japanese artillery increased its fire on the 18th Division's area and extended its range to the outer suburbs of the city. Bombing of targets in the city was on a larger scale than hitherto, and Japanese troops were found to have landed during the night on Ubin Island. On their face value these activities suggested that landings might be expected in the north-east, possibly in conjunction with a sea attack. Concurrently, however, patrols led by Lieutenant Homer,³ of the 2/20th Battalion, and Lieutenant Ottley,⁴ of the 2/19th, had explored the mainland opposite their battalion sectors. Their reports, received during the night of 7th-8th February, indicated large concentrations of Japanese troops in the area.

As the Japanese were later to disclose, they had taken into account in pre-war planning of their attack on Singapore Island that the mainland opposite its north-west coast offered rivers, roads and concealment well suited to assembling guns, troops and landing craft, and that it faced the narrowest portion of the Strait of Johore. Further, it seemed likely

---

² Lt-Col Anderson, with Maj M. Ashkanasy (Bennett's DAAG) and the 2/19 Bn Intelligence Officer, Lt S. F. Burt, had been authorised after Muar to prepare a revised establishment for an infantry battalion based on experience on the mainland. Anderson held that under Malayan conditions more fire-power was necessary, and four-platoon companies were desirable because three platoons were needed to form a mutually assisting perimeter. With enemy infiltration tactics it was always likely that one platoon would be cut off. The other platoons then became exposed, and without a reserve platoon all power of manoeuvre was lost. He held also that the allocation of transport to battalions was excessive, and that carriers were of little or no use owing to their noise and vulnerability to grenades. The plans drawn up provided for battalions of about 900 men, by bringing many formerly employed as drivers, in clerical work, and so on, into the companies. Bren and Lewis guns were given to the additional platoons, but there was a shortage of Tommy guns.

In post-war comment, Anderson criticised the "totally unsuitable establishments of our infantry units" saying that the initiative of commanders was "drastically curtailed by the three-section platoon, and the three platoon company, and for that matter a three-battalion brigade; but particularly in the lower formations. With greater manpower a battalion commander has some prospect of resting men, but more than that, he has a good margin for employing sub-units without damaging the tactical value of his companies and platoons. To be able to employ fighting patrols of platoon strength behind the enemy lines would have been invaluable, and would very seriously have cramped the style of Japanese leaders, but freedom from such tactics encouraged them to exploit outflanking movements, without the necessity of having to retain sufficient reserves for their own L of C's."

³ Lt R. Homer, NX45803; 2/20 Bn. Clerk; of North Bondi, NSW; b. Sydney, 12 Mar 1916. Died of wounds 10 Feb 1942.

⁴ Lt D. Ottley, NX34250; 2/19 Bn. Sawmiller; of Bombo, NSW; b. Wyalong, NSW, 23 Jul 1915. Killed in action 9 Feb 1942.

to them that the foremost westward defence line on the island would be along the line of the Sungei Kranji and Sungei Jurong, with only outposts west of it; in which case they could expect to land in the area almost unopposed in the first instance.

Detailed planning for the capture of Singapore had been commenced by General Yamashita and his staff as soon as Japanese troops occupied Kuala Lumpur. Opinion among the Japanese command was divided as to how strong resistance would be. Some interpreted the rapid withdrawal down the peninsula as a sign of panic having set in and held that once the British forces reached the island they would do little but surrender or try to escape. Others quoted broadcasts to the effect that the troops had been exhorted by Mr Churchill to fight to the end, and referred to the strength of the island's fortifications, which in the Japanese reports had been ludicrously exaggerated. Eventually it was decided to employ the entire available fighting strength for the conquest of Singapore, and to assemble 1,000 rounds a gun for the supporting field artillery and 500 a gun for the heavy batteries. Yamashita issued his consequent orders from his command post at Kluang on 31st January. His airmen were to cooperate in the attack with a heavy concentration of planes, and provision was made for intense artillery fire against installations and artillery on the island. The main strength of the army artillery as distinct from the divisional artillery would be on the upper reaches of the Sungei Malayu for counter-battery and support purposes during the period of preparation for landings and the early stages of the invasion, when the divisional artillery would directly cooperate with the front-line troops. A total of 168 guns would be employed.

The *5th* and *18th Divisions* were concentrated in the area of the Sungei Skudai, north-west of the 22nd Australian Brigade's front, for the main attack. The *Guards Division* (with the *14th Tank Regiment* attached) assembled in the Tebrau area, opposite what remained of the Naval Base, to execute a feint and then a subsidiary attack. On 4th February commanders received at Skudai orders for these actions, and the artillery bombardment of the island was commenced. Despite the damage which might have been caused by the large array of guns on Singapore Island during this preparatory period, the rationed artillery fire caused little hindrance to the Japanese.

For the main attack, sixteen battalions, with five more in reserve, were allotted for use on the 22nd Australian Brigade's front, principally in the area between the Sungei Buloh and the Sungei Murai held by only two battalions—the 2/20th and 2/18th Australian. The first objective would be the Tengah airfield, to be reached by the morning of 9th February, and the second a line from Bukit Panjang to Ulu Pandan, on the Jurong road east of the Sungei Jurong. The *18th Division* would attack with seven battalions on the Japanese right, and the *5th Division* (to which was attached the *1st Tank Regiment*) with nine battalions, on the left. The feint by the *Guards* was to heighten the belief (attributed in Japanese

Intelligence reports to Malaya Command) that the main attack would be against the Naval Base and thereabouts, and so to keep the British forces dispersed as widely as possible. For this purpose also dummy camps were erected east of the Sungei Tebrau, convoys of vehicles were employed to give the impression of eastward movement, and artillery fire was concentrated on the north-east of the island. The slightness of the patrol opposition encountered by the *Guards* battalion on Ubin Island disturbed the Japanese commanders, for it seemed to them that the feint had failed in its purpose of distracting attention from the north-west area.

CHAPTER 15

DEFENCE OF WESTERN AREA

DAWN on 8th February brought with it still greater enemy air activity. Aided by observation from a balloon moored over Johore Bahru, from aircraft, and from vantage points on the ground, guns pounded the island with increasing ferocity during the day. The weight of these attacks fell principally in the 22nd Brigade's sector. General Bennett's headquarters were bombed during the morning, and although only one man was killed, documents at this operational nerve-centre were sent flying.[1]

The shelling and bombing played havoc with communications generally, and especially with those of the 22nd Brigade. Although the bombardment seemed wasteful in relation to the number of casualties it caused, it was to pay the Japanese handsomely as a means of hampering control of the defenders' operations. As it continued, line communications were cut, in some instances every ten yards or so. The 22nd Brigade's wireless sets had been called in for overhaul when the brigade got back to the island, and were returned only on the morning of 8th February. They were sent up to the battalions in the afternoon, but effective use was not made of them. The artillery response to the bombardment included fire to the mainland opposite the 44th and 22nd Brigades; but the scale and intensity of the enemy fire were far more evident than any retaliatory measures.[2]

Taylor's headquarters and those of his battalions were among the targets attacked by guns and aircraft. In the 2/19th Battalion area the bombardment prevented Major Robertson from completing his reconnaissance on taking over command. The Causeway sector also was under fire. The shelling increased during the evening until it reached drumfire intensity. Australian signallers were unable, despite constant and valiant efforts,[3] to cope with the damage to lines, and most of Taylor's companies lost touch with their battalion headquarters.

---

[1] General Bennett's diary entry that "anyhow, a little less paper in this war will improve matters" (*Why Singapore Fell*, p. 173) reflected his attitude to what he considered excessive staffing behind the fighting men.

[2] Referring to the continuous artillery and mortar fire during a period of 15 hours on 8th February, Lieut-Colonel Varley, commanding the 2/18th Battalion, wrote in his personal diary: "During my four years' service 1914-18 I never experienced such concentrated shell fire over such a period. Pozieres was the heaviest shelling I experienced in that war. In 2½ days I lost 50 out of 56 men. The German shells seemed more effective in causing casualties. On this occasion 80 shells were counted falling in D Coy area (Captain Chisholm) in one minute; Lt Jack Vernon's platoon area had 67 in 10 minutes and this was typical of the whole area. Battalion HQ had 45 shells in 7 minutes; half an hour's spell then another similar dose and so on throughout the whole area all day. Our signal communications were cut and repaired and cut again."

The fact that the battalion's casualties were light, despite the intensity of the barrage, was attributed by Varley to the necessity for the construction of slit trenches holding one or two men having been impressed upon all ranks, and their having provided themselves with this cover. Varley warned his companies to expect attack by enemy troops during the night.

[3] Lieut-Colonel Oakes was to write that the devotion to duty of the signallers, both divisional and regimental, was outstanding, adding: "I myself, from the shelter of a slit trench in which I was crouching saw a regimental signaller lying in the open near by, in the middle of a severe shelling bout, transmitting messages on a line phone he had connected up. And this was typical of the whole tribe throughout the campaign."

As a guide to his company commanders in the absence of other orders, Taylor had instructed them that, if strong enemy attack overwhelmed portion of a force, the remaining elements should fight their way back to company headquarters. As a last resort, battalions should form perimeters around their headquarters. The battalions had been trained in such manoeuvres. At 8 p.m. Taylor sent a direction to Lieut-Colonel Assheton, commander of the 2/20th Battalion, that if he were forced to form a perimeter the battalion should then fall back on the 2/18th at Ama Keng, north of the Tengah airfield. His intention was that there, with the 2/19th farther to the left, the three battalions should hold a line from Ama Keng to the Sungei Berih in the hope that reserves would be sent up and would operate after first light. The instructions were realistic in the circumstances as they developed, but no prepared defences existed along the Ama Keng-Sungei Berih line. Further, because of the extent of the 22nd Brigade's front, adequate means of mutual support in such operations were absent.

Bennett, perturbed by the pitch of the gunfire, rose from his bed in a bungalow near Bukit Timah village and rang his duty officer, Major Dawkins, telling him to ask the 22nd Brigade headquarters if it had any reports from forward posts, and to instruct them to switch on their beach-lights.

They replied that all lines to forward posts had been cut by shell fire and that linesmen were out effecting repairs (wrote Bennett afterwards). Dawkins mentioned that he thought the brigadier had ordered that no beach-lights were to go on in order that the patrol which was going over to the mainland might get across the straits safely.[4]

As Dawkins did not appear to be worried even after contact with the brigade, Bennett returned to bed; but being uneasy he got up again and motored with two of his staff officers to his operations room, which he reached at 11 p.m. There at 11.30 p.m. he received from Taylor a telephone call telling him of extensive landings on his sector, and of penetration having occurred. Taylor estimated the enemy strength as six battalions, spoke of his lack of reserves with which to meet the situation, and asked for a fresh force to be made available for counter-attack at dawn. Bennett thereupon undertook to send the 2/29th Battalion (Lieut-Colonel Pond) to his aid.

Although the damage to communications had made it difficult for Taylor to piece together a clear picture of what had happened, the landings, aided by heavy concentrations of mortar as well as artillery fire, had in fact begun soon after 10.30 p.m. in all his battalion sectors. It had been arranged that calls for defensive artillery fire should be given in the first instance by means of Very lights fired from the area being attacked; and that the calls should be relayed by observation posts. However, it was uncertain because of the nature of the terrain whether such signals from even the observation posts would be seen at the gun positions, and not enough Very pistols were available to supply all the posts requiring them.

---

[4] Bennett, *Why Singapore Fell*, p. 174.

The artillery liaison officers at battalion headquarters were therefore to convey requests from battalion to battery or regimental headquarters. Because of the extent of the front, four primary tasks, covering river mouths, road ends, and beaches, had been indicated in each battalion sector. It followed from these circumstances that with signal lines being constantly cut, and forward wireless sets unused, delays would occur in bringing down defensive fire; also that in the event of many demands

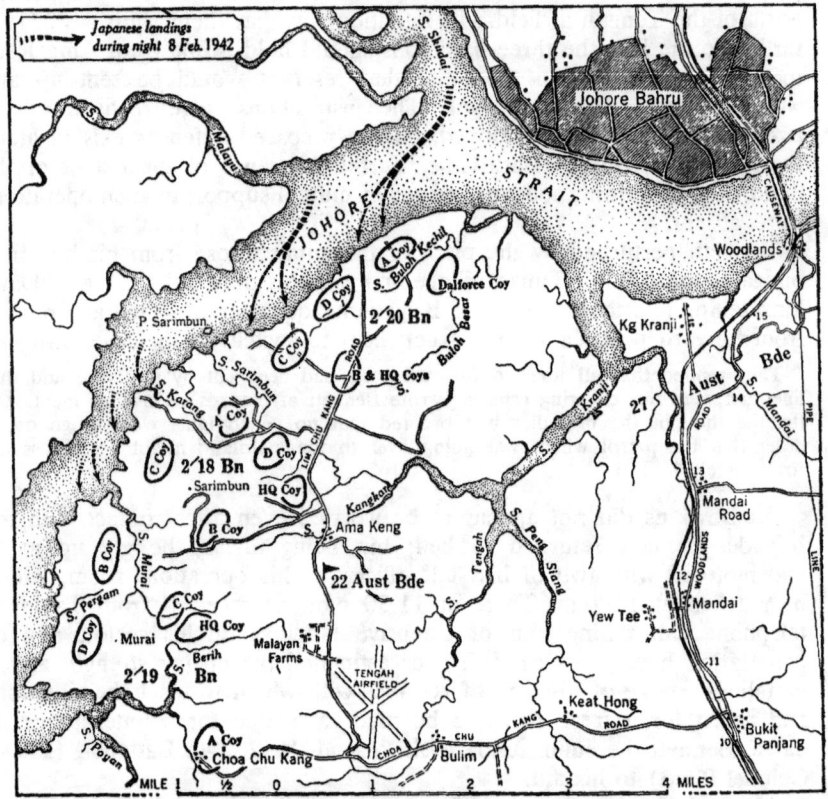

Dispositions, 22nd Brigade, 10 p.m. 8th February

being received, the artillery could respond to only some of them. So it happened, and as Very lights shot up but did not bring the desired result, the Japanese reaped the benefit of their bombardment, while the Australians were at a loss to understand why their artillery had, it seemed, left them in the lurch.

Even the calls which eventually reached the guns were so rapid that the guns were unable to keep up with the tasks. As an instance, one request through a liaison officer was to "bring down fire everywhere". Again, lack of visibility because of the beach-lights not being used seriously limited observation. Nevertheless, the artillery records indicate that the guns were constantly firing to meet such needs as became known and could be met under the fire plan, for what it was worth in the circumstances. Had communications been in order, and had the beach-lights been operated,[5] the invaders' casualties might have been greater. As it was, having carried out their characteristic policy of disrupting communications, and in the absence of artillery fire directed on to them as they neared their landing-points, they were able to leap ashore for the most part in darkness, opposed only by infantry weapons.

Men of the 2/4th Machine Gun Battalion attached to Captain Richardson's[6] "D" Company of the 2/20th blazed at boats and barges as they came inshore near the end of the Lim Chu Kang road. A barge carrying explosives caught fire and fortuitously lighted the scene at one point for several minutes. Other barges were set alight, and few of the Japanese managed to scramble ashore. Soon afterwards more landing craft reached a swamp area near by and were hotly engaged. Many were beaten off or sunk, but, as happened at other points on the front, the men and weapons immediately available to meet the invaders were insufficient to cope with their numbers and the tactics they employed.

As the Japanese poured in, they pressed on Richardson's right flank. A machine-gun on this flank had been knocked out in the afternoon's bombardment, but the other machine-gunners were firing at ranges down to ten yards. Such barbed wire obstacles as had been erected were valuable in temporarily halting enemy parties where they were exposed to withering fire. The water in the cooling system of the guns was boiling as the fight continued. As a counter to this fire, the Japanese tethered a barge to a fish trap about 100 yards offshore and poured mortar and machine-gun fire from it into the area. The machine-gunners nevertheless stuck to their task until about 1.30 a.m., and those who could be spared from the guns used bayonets on the enemy. The machine-gunners had fired about 10,000 rounds from each gun when, almost without ammunition, and with reports of Japanese on both flanks, Lieutenant Wankey[7] ordered his platoon's machine-guns to be destroyed, and organised the platoon into a fighting patrol, taking the platoon's wounded with it. He had counted some twenty landing craft, carrying an average of twenty-five men each.

Richardson's infantry meanwhile had been engaged in hand-to-hand fighting with the Japanese as they came inland. Although signals for close

---

[5] The lights were manned by men of the British 5th Searchlight Regiment. A record attached to the Australian artillery headquarters' diary indicates that they were placed under command of Brigadier Taylor, who delegated his power to the unit commanders in charge of the sectors in which the lights were situated. N.C.O's in charge of them were instructed that they were not to be used without specific instructions. The cable of one light was destroyed and the light put out of action before the landings, but although the other lights were in working order, authority was not received to switch them on. Brigadier Taylor's subsequent explanation was that insufficient time had been available for the preparatory work necessary to protect the lights; he felt sure that once they were exposed they would be shot out by the enemy; and he therefore considered it better to reserve their use for actual emergency, when they should operate, as would artillery, on the signal for defensive fire being given. However, perhaps because of misunderstanding or confusion, they failed to do so.

[6] Capt R. J. D. Richardson, NX35012; 2/20 Bn. Grazier; of Raymond Terrace, NSW; b. Orange, NSW, 21 May 1915.

[7] Lt M. E. Wankey, MC, WX9392; 2/4 MG Bn. Letterpress machinist; of North Perth, WA; b. Narrogin, WA, 4 May 1918.

defensive fire were sent up they brought no apparent response. Ammunition ran short, and the company was withdrawn to a position along a fighter strip about 800 yards from the shore. With a Bren gun and a haversack of grenades, Sergeant Dumas[8] distinguished himself in covering the withdrawal of his platoon. The company, reinforced at its position by a reserve platoon and three carriers, held until 5.30 a.m., when, on orders from Lieut-Colonel Assheton, the platoon and carriers were withdrawn to help form a battalion perimeter. Richardson's company failed to receive a message conveying a similar order, but when at first light what were thought to be tanks were heard approaching, a further withdrawal of 200 yards was made to a knoll which, it was hoped, would provide a satisfactory obstacle to them, at least on its northern and eastern sides.

Because of the landing on the right of Richardson's company, orders had been brought about midnight to Major Merrett's[9] which in its position farther to the right had been practically undisturbed, to fall back to the right of the battalion perimeter. A composite platoon of pioneers and bandsmen at the end of the Lim Chu Kang road which had been heavily engaged with the enemy was also withdrawn to the battalion perimeter soon after.

On the left, Captain Carter's[10] company had suffered severely from the preliminary bombardment, and from mortar fire from the near-by island of Sarimbun which had been occupied by the enemy before the main landings commenced. Japanese then landed in strength in the company area, supported by machine-gun fire from the opposite shore. Despite fierce fighting, the invaders forced a passage along the Sungei Sarimbun between Assheton's battalion and the right flank of the 2/18th (Lieut-Colonel Varley). The company was accordingly ordered, in the early hours of the morning, back to the battalion perimeter.

By 2 a.m. on 9th February, Headquarters Company (Major Cohen[1]), "B" Company (Captain Ewart[2]) which had been in reserve, what remained of Carter's company, and the battalion's forward transport, were in the perimeter. There they were joined by two Dalforce platoons. Merrett's company arrived at about 7 a.m. As Richardson's men had not reached the position they were to have occupied in the northern part of the perimeter, two of Merrett's platoons were placed astride the Lim Chu Kang road and one was placed in their left rear. Richardson's company, still on the knoll it had occupied earlier, was thus exposed to the full force of attack by the Japanese who had advanced into the surrounding area. During the night the battalion perimeter had become a target for thousands

---

[8] Sgt H. S. Dumas, NX31208; 2/20 Bn. Clerk; of Point Piper, NSW; b. Adelaide, SA, 27 Mar 1914. Missing presumed died 10 Feb 1942.

[9] Maj R. O. Merrett, ED, NX35002; 2/20 Bn. Millinery manufacturer; of Manly, NSW; b. Mosman, NSW, 7 Jul 1905.

[10] Carter was in hospital at the time of the Japanese landings on Singapore Island, and the company was commanded by Lieutenant J. V. Mudie.

[1] Maj R. H. Cohen, NX499; 2/20 Bn. Company director; of Manly, NSW; b. Waverley, NSW, 14 Apr 1911. Killed in action 9 Feb 1942.

[2] Maj A. C. M. Ewart, NX498; 2/20 Bn. Mechanical engineer and company manager; of Parramatta, NSW; b. Parramatta, 9 Nov 1909.

of rounds of light machine-gun fire, and Japanese infantry were pressing hard on the right flank. The Australians used their 3-inch mortars to marked effect, and from time to time threw the enemy back by bayonet attack. As dawn broke the struggle continued.

Two main landings had occurred on the 2/18th Battalion's front, one on the right against "A" Company (Captain Johnstone) and one on the left against "C" Company (Captain Okey). Johnstone's company had two platoons (7 and 8) forward on small hills which as the tide rose became islands. The tide had reached this stage at the time, and two motor craft landed about eighty Japanese on the island occupied by 8 Platoon (Lieutenant Vernon[3]). Many of the Japanese in this wave were killed, and the survivors dispersed; but under heavy mortar fire another landing followed, in greater strength. Again, the Japanese lost heavily, but the platoon was badly weakened, and Vernon decided that the time had come to withdraw to company headquarters. The water presented a serious obstacle, particularly as some of his men were wounded and some of the fit men could not swim. With keen resourcefulness, he tied together a number of rifle slings, fastened one end of the line at each side of the water, and thus contrived an aid by which the non-swimmers and the wounded were assisted to cross. He himself made repeated crossings to help the wounded. At a near-by island position, 15 Platoon (Lieutenant Gibson[4]) was attacked. Although it fought desperately, the odds proved too great, and its few survivors also withdrew. No. 7 Platoon (Lieutenant Richardson[5]) was by-passed on both flanks. It stayed in position throughout the night, and next day, then tried to reach its battalion. Only a few of the men succeeded.

Meanwhile company headquarters had lost contact with its forward troops, and, with Japanese estimated at two or more companies approaching, the plan to assemble the company in a defensive perimeter was abandoned, and, about 3.30 a.m., the headquarters and the newly-formed reserve platoon moved off towards battalion headquarters north of Ama Keng.

A still more dangerous situation resulted from the landing in the sector held by Okey's company, amid a wild complex of hills and inlets between the mouth of the Sungei Murai and the terminus of a road to the coast north of it. The area adjacent to the river mouth had been recognised as a likely landing place, and as it could not be adequately defended by small arms fire, had been included in the defensive fire plan as a task for artillery and mortars. A machine-gun platoon was sited in two sections close to the water's edge at the end of a narrow peninsula dividing the river mouth from an inlet north of it. When the Japanese were seen

---

[3] Capt J. M. Vernon, MC, NX34879; 2/18 Bn. Station hand; of Inverell, NSW; b. Beecroft, NSW, 7 Dec 1907.

[4] Capt J. E. M. Gibson, NX31612; 2/18 Bn. Clerk; of Tamworth, NSW; b. Cairns, Qld, 8 May 1916.

[5] Lt G. D. Richardson, NX35127; 2/18 Bn. Civil servant; of Raymond Terrace, NSW; b. Raymond Terrace, 23 Nov 1917.

approaching, Very lights were fired by Okey's forward troops, but answering fire was not evident to them. In scattered positions on the hills, the infantry saw the enemy swarm ashore. One of the machine-gun sections, with Lieutenant Meiklejohn,[6] the machine-gun platoon commander, opened fire against six approaching barges, and kept on firing for two hours, despite retaliation by hand grenades, as the Japanese landed and crossed the neck of the peninsula. Then, with ammunition running short, Meiklejohn led his section along a jungle path where they came upon a party of Japanese resting. He shot some with his revolver, and another was knocked out with a swing from a tripod, but Meiklejohn lost his life in attempting to cover his section's withdrawal. The other section made a similar stand on the beach until it was informed that a near-by infantry platoon was almost surrounded, and about to withdraw. While coming out, this section also encountered Japanese troops. Private Spackman,[7] attacked by a Japanese officer with a sword, bayoneted him and used the sword against another Japanese. Although most of the section were wounded, it reached battalion headquarters.

It appeared that, true to form, the Japanese were avoiding head-on encounters as far as possible, and taking advantage of the gaps which existed among the widely-spaced points of resistance to penetrate the Australian rear. The invaders made their way on to roads through the battalion sector towards the Lim Chu Kang road. They were thus approaching battalion headquarters, and when Varley was able to assess the situation he sought, at 1.30 a.m., with Taylor's approval, to concentrate his men in the battalion perimeter about Ama Keng and the road junction 500 yards to the north, where he would have greater command and they would be available for mobile action when daylight came. Taylor placed the 2/10th Field Company (Major Lawrence[8]) consisting of 200 men who had been employed throughout the preceding week in the battalion perimeter, under Varley's command. Varley ordered Major O'Brien's company, stationed at the branch of the road from the Murai which is shaped like a question mark, to dispose of a party of Japanese reported to be in the vicinity, and clear a way for Okey's withdrawal. The Japanese, however, were encountered in greater strength than had been expected, and others had infiltrated to the Australian rear, with the result that the company was cut off and divided. Efforts to rejoin the battalion failed, and only remnants of the company eventually reached rear positions where they were collected and redrafted.

Okey's company had been heavily engaged meanwhile. The characteristic Japanese tendency to bunch together under fire was again evident where No. 15 Platoon was occupying a hill position, and many of the invaders fell before the fire of automatic weapons and hand grenades with

---

[6] Lt J. T. Meiklejohn, WX9393; 2/4 MG Bn. Warehouseman; of Victoria Park, WA; b. Katanning, WA, 7 May 1920. Killed in action 8 Feb 1942.

[7] Cpl C. J. Spackman, WX7715; 2/4 MG Bn. Dairy hand; of Karridale, WA; b. Pingelly, WA, 27 Feb 1917.

[8] Maj K. P. H. Lawrence, ED, VX45686; OC 2/10 Fd Coy. Civil engineer; of Hartwell, Vic; b. Toora, Vic, 14 Feb 1901.

which the platoon sought to repel them. Then, as the weight of the attack increased, the platoon withdrew and found its way back to "D" Company (Captain Chisholm[9]), in reserve near battalion headquarters. The rest of Okey's company became split up in the darkness, amid hills, swamp and jungle, and under attack. Those who got to O'Brien's former headquarters found that the patrol left there to meet them had been driven away from the position. Of the whole of Okey's company, only four officers and 41 others reached battalion headquarters early on the morning of 9th February. There, with three officers and forty others of Captain Johnstone's company, they went into position on a rise west of the Lim Chu Kang road. Chisholm's company, comprising five officers and 136 others east of the road was covering the road approach to Ama Keng from the north at 3.30 a.m., but in the darkness had also lost contact with some of its men. The 2/10th Field Company went into a sector extending from the Sungei Murai road to the Lim Chu Kang road, 250 yards south of the junction.

In the 2/19th Battalion area, under cover of darkness, Lieut-Colonel Robertson had moved his headquarters, bombed during the day, to a position just north of the upper reaches of the Sungei Berih. His "B" Company (Major Keegan) and a headquarters company platoon were forward near the shoreline, with the Sungei Murai between them and Varley's battalion. The left forward position was occupied by "D" Company (Major Vincent). Captain Thomas'[1] "C" Company was a little west of battalion headquarters, and "A" Company (Captain Cousens[2]) was at Choa Chu Kang village, south-east of the Berih at the end of the Choa Chu Kang road. This road ran eastward to the southern boundary of the Tengah airfield, and through Bulim and Keat Hong villages to Bukit Panjang village, on the road from the Causeway to Singapore.

This battalion which as has been shown was largely comprised of reinforcements, was responsible for the left flank of the 22nd Brigade, adjacent to the right flank of Ballentine's 44th Indian Brigade. The boundary between the two brigades was the Choa Chu Kang road and the wide tidal basin formed by the Sungei Berih and the Sungei Poyan which separated the forward elements of the brigades. With its broad expanse, the estuary could be expected to attract Japanese landing craft. It was accordingly included in defensive fire plans for the 2/15th Field Regiment and the batteries of the 44th Indian Brigade sector. More machine-guns were posted in the area than elsewhere on the Australian front. These were concentrated chiefly on the estuary and on high ground north of the village. But because of the opportunities they had had for observation, the Japanese were perhaps as well aware of these dispositions as were Taylor and

---

[9] Capt J. W. S. Chisholm, NX34713; 2/18 Bn. Grazier; of Graman, NSW; b. Goulburn, NSW, 5 Jun 1906.

[1] Maj R. E. Thomas, NX70189; 2/19 Bn. Private secretary; of Cammeray, NSW; b. Sydney, 13 Mar 1916.

[2] Maj C. H. Cousens, NX34932; 2/19 Bn. Radio announcer; of Sydney; b. Poona, India, 26 Aug 1903.

Robertson. At any rate, only five or six craft entered the estuary, where they were driven off or sunk by artillery fire, and the few Japanese who landed were disposed of by a detachment of Punjabis of the 44th Brigade.

The main assault on Robertson's front was made at a small promontory, covered by coconut trees, in the northern corner of Keegan's sector. There a platoon saw craft approaching estimated at up to fifty in number, and promptly shot off signals for defensive fire, but again without apparent result. An attempt to transmit the request through battalion to brigade headquarters failed because the line had been cut. Fierce fighting broke out, and quickly spread to the whole of the sector. Though Keegan's company held its main ground, and inflicted heavy losses, the Japanese advanced past its right along the Murai. To counter this movement, the greater part of Thomas' company was moved up to the headwaters of the river. Its patrols soon reported what appeared to them to be enemy troops moving on Ama Keng at the battalion's rear.

By 3 a.m., as the struggle in his sector continued, Keegan decided that to save his company with its large proportion of wounded, it must be withdrawn. Keegan and remnants of his platoons succeeded in reaching the perimeter which had been organised around battalion headquarters. Thomas' company also was withdrawn, and ordered to send a fighting patrol to investigate a report of Japanese movement east of this position and astride the battalion's line of withdrawal; but before it left the perimeter it was attacked. The Japanese were held off, and Vincent's company, unmolested at its position near the Sungei Berih, had been withdrawn to the perimeter by 6.30 a.m., but lost two platoons which were cut off by the enemy on the way. Meanwhile a patrol had been sent to contact Cousens' company, but apparently failed to do so.

In the 44th Indian Brigade's sector, apart from the artillery fire on landing craft in the Berih basin, and the encounter by the Punjabis already mentioned, the night was uneventful. Next morning the two 6-inch guns of Pasir Laba Battery were put out of action by air bombardment and artillery fire.

Japanese post-war accounts showed that the full volume of artillery fire available to their *5th* and *18th Divisions* had been concentrated on important points on the opposite shore, preparatory to the landings, for which thirteen infantry battalions were available, with five in reserve. Expected obstacles in the Strait, and opposition by water craft, were not met during the crossings, but the accounts refer to intense fire having been encountered at the landing points, and to stubborn resistance on land. In the ecstatic language employed by a Japanese army information service narrator, as translated,

> the courageous warriors of our landing forces . . . gradually closed in on the enemy position through the concentrated fire of machine-guns and mortars. Words cannot describe the glorious hand grenade and hand-to-hand fighting encountered in various

places by these courageous warriors after destroying layer after layer of barbed wire entanglements. . . .[3]

As successive waves of Japanese got ashore, wearing compasses on their wrists to help them to find their way, the Australians became hopelessly outnumbered.[4] Particularly to raw reinforcements among the Australians, this first experience of battle was like some wildly disordered nightmare, the more stark because of the contrast between the beauty of the tropical night and the savagery of action. Despite the stand at first made against the invaders, the long and sparsely-manned front lost cohesion and drive as contact failed and isolation increased. Some were overrun or outflanked. Others saw that to stay in their exposed positions, out of reach of orders, invited death or captivity, and would serve no useful purpose. As in a bushfire in their own country, with the flames rapidly encircling the men who sought to keep it in check, withdrawal offered the only prospect of being able to continue the fight. Runners and liaison officers did their best to make up for the earlier and concurrent damage to communications, and signallers were constantly and heroically at work repairing them, but the transmission delays gave the Japanese further advantage.

At 3 a.m. (9th February), as General Bennett became increasingly aware of the seriousness of the situation, he ordered the Special Reserve Battalion (Major Saggers) and the reserve company of the 2/4th Machine Gun Battalion to stand to, and at 4.45 a.m. ordered them to the 22nd Brigade area, with instructions as to the position the Reserve Battalion was to occupy. Delay occurred in moving the 2/29th Battalion, which he had ordered to the area soon after midnight, for in its defensive role it was widely dispersed and had first to be concentrated. Because of this, and a hitch in supplying it with transport, it did not reach the Tengah airfield area until 6 a.m. There, at 7.45 a.m., it was joined by Saggers' battalion, with the exception of one company which lost its way and did not arrive until 11 a.m. At 8.30 a.m., General Percival ordered his only reserve, the 12th Indian Brigade (Brigadier Paris) to Keat Hong to come under Bennett's command. Meanwhile, in response to a request by Bennett, ten Hurricanes had engaged in a dawn battle with eighty-four Japanese aircraft coming from Johore; then, with one of their number lost, they hastily landed, refuelled, and made a second attack. Despite the desperate odds against them, they fought to considerable effect.

---

[3] *Malaya Campaign* (ATIS translation). In another document the commander of the *18th Division* (General Mutaguchi) described how, with the left wing of his landing forces, he took part in the battle, using hand grenades, and received minor injuries. This part of the force, he related, took the wrong road in the darkness and entered the operational area of the *5th Division* near Ama Keng.

[4] An Australian officer related that: "The Japanese barges carried mortars and much ammunition. The mortars were set at a fixed elevation and were fired rapidly as the barges moved across, so that when they first began to move, the bombs were falling short of the shore, yet the elevation was not changed. The bombs falling in the water gave a moderate screen of spray and smoke, then as the barges moved on, the mortar barrage advanced across our positions. This barrage looked worse than it was and casualties were few. In many cases, however, men withdrew before this creeping barrage or else were destroyed by it. Thus when the Japanese beached they met stern opposition in some places and were repulsed, but in other cases there were substantial gaps in our line, into which they penetrated very rapidly."

As yet no attempt had been made to land in the 27th Brigade sector, but it had been severely shelled during the 8th and the night of the 8th-9th. Several more Indians had made their way from the mainland across the Causeway during daylight on 8th February, thus further demonstrating how little reliance could be placed on the gap blown in the structure as an obstacle to enemy troops. At night (8th-9th February) Lieutenant Smyth,[5] of the 2/30th Battalion, who had just gained his commission, and Privates Calvert[6] and Barnes,[7] crossed the Strait in a boat to act as a listening and observation post near the mainland. Like the Japanese on many of their patrols, they were clad only in shorts and sandshoes. On their way back, after they had located some enemy machine-gun positions, another boat appeared through the darkness. Smyth at first thought it might be another Australian patrol boat, and challenged it from a distance of only a few feet. The response was an attempt to ram Smyth's boat. With instant decision he leapt into the enemy craft, threw a hand grenade among its occupants, and leapt back again. Then, on a pre-arranged plan, the Australians capsized their craft and swam off towards separate points on their own shore.

Soon Calvert and Barnes heard calls for help, but were unable to find their officer. Whether he had been wounded by his own grenade, had been hit by subsequent fire from the enemy boat, or had suffered some other mishap was not discovered; but his action had saved his men's lives.

Heavy machine-gun fire broke out from the enemy shore after this incident, and a call for defensive artillery fire was sent up from the position to the right of the Causeway, occupied by Major Anderson's company of the 2/30th Battalion. Forward Vickers gunners blazed at the Japanese, and 25-pounders and 4.5-inch howitzers joined in the fire, which lasted for about half an hour. The Australian gunners in this area were aided by a beach-light which illuminated barges about 700 yards to the left of the Causeway. This exchange, to the accompaniment of much yelling from the Japanese, was followed a little later by another burst of fire from their side, but no other engagement occurred during the night. Very lights seen shooting skyward from the 22nd Brigade's sector gave a hint, however, of enemy assault in that direction.

By 6 a.m. on 9th February Brigadier Taylor had concluded that the situation on his front was becoming desperate. He had reports of his battalions being hard pressed, and of Japanese penetration to his rear. Firing was being heard in Ama Keng, 200 yards forward of his brigade headquarters. Thereupon he ordered the headquarters to a position just behind Bulim, placing the brigade protection platoon and some brigade personnel west of the Tengah airfield, to link with Pond's battalion. His

---

[5] Lt F. M. Smyth, NX68127; 2/30 Bn. Regular soldier; of Neutral Bay, NSW; b. Sydney, 23 Aug 1914. Killed in action 8 Feb 1942.

[6] Pte C. L. Calvert, NX72474; 2/30 Bn. Casual shearer and farm worker; of Dubbo, NSW; b. Dubbo, 20 Nov 1920. Died while prisoner 25 Jun 1943.

[7] Pte J. H. Barnes, NX37531; 2/30 Bn. Labourer; of Weetaliba, NSW; b. Marrickville, NSW, 21 Jan 1922.

plan was to form a line, with the aid of the Jind battalion stationed at the airfield, from the north of the field to west of the junction of the Lim Chu Kang and Choa Chu Kang roads, to link with Cousens' company of the 2/19th at Choa Chu Kang village. Going to the airfield area he met Pond. To Taylor's surprise, as he did not know that the Reserve Battalion was to be made available to him, he met Saggers also, soon after 8 a.m. Taylor ordered him to dispose two companies in depth behind Pond's battalion, and the missing company to extend the left flank when it arrived. He also disposed the reserve company of the 2/4th Machine Gun Battalion which he found had been sent to his aid. Meanwhile small parties coming in from forward battalions had reported that they had been overrun or by-passed by large Japanese forces, and that companies were fighting their way back to the airfield.

From their perimeter on the 22nd Brigade's right flank the men of the 2/20th Battalion saw large numbers of Japanese crossing the Lim Chu Kang road forward of their position towards the east. The Japanese were scattered by mortar fire, and a platoon cleared the road for some way northward, hoping that this would help Richardson's company to rejoin the battalion. It was found, however, that the Japanese were crossing the road southward of the perimeter also. After further attempts to deal with the situation, Assheton concluded that the stream of invaders made the odds too great, and at 9.15 a.m. ordered a withdrawal to Ama Keng, where he hoped to join forces with Varley's 2/18th Battalion.

Moving to a protective position on the left flank, Ewart's "B" Company was ambushed, the battalion Intelligence officer, Lieutenant Lennon,[8] was killed, and Ewart was wounded. The ambushing party was in turn destroyed by Lieutenant Cornforth's[9] platoon of "A" Company and the survivors of Ewart's company pressed on. They, however, found the Japanese in the position they were to occupy, and lost more men in a further clash. Covering the withdrawal from its position in the former perimeter, Major Merrett's company less Cornforth's platoon held out under attack until 10 a.m. Then, when withdrawal was attempted, it came under heavy machine-gun fire from high ground at its rear, and split into small parties in attempts to avoid it. Cornforth's platoon, separately engaged after disposing of the ambush, was joined by Lieut-Colonel Assheton, and ordered also to withdraw.

Richardson's company clung to its position until it received at 10.30 a.m. Assheton's earlier order to withdraw into the 2/20th Battalion perimeter. Although, with Wankey's machine-gun platoon, it reached the former headquarters of the battalion, only dead men were found there. Pushing on through country now overrun by the enemy, it was split into two parties by an ambush at Ama Keng. Forced into the swamps, men

---

[8] Lt J. J. Lennon, NX65413; 2/20 Bn. School teacher; of Wee Waa, NSW; b. Inverell, NSW, 9 Sep 1914. Killed in action 9 Feb 1942.
[9] Lt R. G. W. Cornforth, NX59134; 2/20 Bn. Salesman; of Mosman, NSW; b. Mosman, 19 Jan 1919.

were lost in making river crossings, but remnants of both parties reached Bulim, exhausted and without arms. At this stage seven of the battalion's officers had been killed, three wounded, and one captured, and many other ranks had been lost.

Having established the nucleus of a battalion perimeter north of Ama Keng as previously stated, and while waiting for more of his men to come in, Varley had given orders that his headquarters be moved back to the southern edge of Ama Keng, and had gone to report to brigade headquarters. When he returned he found that his headquarters had been moved farther back than he had intended, to the north-western corner of Tengah airfield.[1] Although this affected his plan to form the perimeter he stayed in the forward area to direct his forces as they came in, and about a third of his battalion was in position just before dawn. Soon the Japanese attacked the rise occupied by remnants of Johnstone's and Okey's companies, and drove them east of the road. The enemy began to press the flanks of the engineers at Chisholm's rear, and moved behind a long ridge west of the road towards the Tengah airfield.

Major Lawrence, commanding the engineers, had received no orders for some hours, so, at 8 a.m., he went to see Varley and was given orders for Chisholm to move his company westward and attack the Japanese in the rear. His return was delayed by having to avoid parties of Japanese, in the Ama Keng village area, and when he got back he found that the situation had gone from bad to worse. Not only had the number of Japanese increased, but six of their aircraft were swooping over the area, raking it with machine-gun bullets. Johnstone initiated an attack by eighty of his and Okey's men and about fifty engineers with bayonets, hand grenades, and a Bren gun, covered by rapid rifle fire from other engineers. Despite the barrage of mortar and machine-gun fire with which the Japanese defended themselves from a rise they now occupied, the Australians got to within twenty yards of them. Lawrence, however, was unable to find Chisholm, and Johnstone's men and the engineers had insufficient force to cope with the situation unaided. At this critical stage, orders were passed by word of mouth to withdraw to a hill about half a mile to the south. Most of the infantry moved accordingly, but as no order reached the engineers, under Captain Dolamore[2] in Lawrence's absence, they held on, knowing that in doing so they were giving other men a chance to come in. Seriously wounded men were loaded on to a truck, but had to be abandoned when it was stopped by a road-block. Walking wounded were helped to the airfield by their mates. Corporal Johnson,[3] a field company cook, made seven trips across swamp for this purpose. At last, near 9.30 a.m., when some Australians were

---

[1] The move was subsequently attributed to a misunderstanding by the second-in-command of the battalion.

[2] Capt W. H. Dolamore, VX27638; 2/10 Fd Coy. Civil engineer; of Bairnsdale, Vic; b. Malvern, Vic, 27 Apr 1909.

[3] Sgt C. H. Johnson, VX28836; 2/10 Fd Coy. Baker and chef; of Sth Melbourne; b. Launceston, Tas, 1 May 1902.

seen passing behind the position, Dolamore decided that his company's task was completed, and ordered its withdrawal. Not only had these technical troops made a valiant stand, but Lieutenant Heathcote,[4] commanding the last section of the engineers to leave, provided another example of courage. Under heavy fire, he halted two trucks and he and 14 men loaded them with about twenty wounded infantry. He and another were killed and two sappers were wounded. Near brigade headquarters, Lieutenant Dobbie,[5] commanding a section of engineers, came upon a party of Assheton's and Varley's men, and led them and the rest of the engineers back to the north-eastern end of the airfield, where they linked with a company of the Johore Volunteer Engineers.

In Major Robertson's sector, the machine-gunners, stationed on the estuary of the Sungei Berih and the Sungei Poyan, ordered to meet Vincent's company at its headquarters, were delayed in getting their guns from the water's edge, and by the time they reached the company headquarters' site it had been abandoned. Encountering Japanese troops now in possession of the area, the party destroyed their machine-guns and split into small groups. One platoon disappeared, but the other reached Cousens' company. Meanwhile the battalion position had been surrounded, and Robertson ordered an attack, with carriers in close support, hoping to break through towards Tengah. The attack began about 7 a.m., but a ridge across the line of withdrawal was held in strength by the Japanese, and only 200 yards were gained, at the cost of heavy losses and disablement of four carriers. The battalion's transport was captured, contact with Thomas' company was lost, and under increasing enemy pressure dispersal through the swamps was ordered as the only practicable alternative to capture or extinction. Some detachments failed to receive the order, and many men were killed, captured, or died of exhaustion. Robertson, Keegan, Chaplain Greenwood, and about forty others managed to reach the Jurong road and rejoin the brigade. Other groups found their way to rear areas and were reassembled for further action.

Cousens' company had remained unmolested at Choa Chu Kang, but contact with the rest of the battalion was lost. When some of the Australians cut off in the earlier fighting emerged from the swamps and reached the company's position, Cousens, about 8 a.m., sent Lieutenant Shaw, a British Intelligence officer attached to him, to try to reach battalion headquarters. On his way, Shaw met Taylor on the Choa Chu Kang road, was told that battalion headquarters had been isolated, and was given an order to Cousens to withdraw his company and the machine-gun platoon with it to the south-eastern corner of Tengah airfield. The move began at 9 a.m.

Lieut-Colonel Assheton with a group of his and Varley's men meanwhile had sought to attack from a small defensive locality north of the

---
[4] Lt C. T. Heathcote, VX39027; 2/10 Fd Coy. Mining engineer; of Melbourne; b. St Kilda, Vic, 1 Feb 1917. Killed in action 9 Feb 1942.
[5] Lt F. A. Dobbie, VX45595; 2/10 Fd Coy. Clerk; of Camberwell, Vic; b. Bendigo, Vic, 12 Mar 1908. Died while prisoner 15 Aug 1943.

airfield, but found the enemy pouring in too strongly to leave him any hope of success. Endeavouring to protect withdrawal of the wounded, he went forward with three Bren gunners to a small knoll. There the party was met by a blast of machine-gun fire at short range. Assheton, encouraging the machine-gunners by moving from one to the other in the positions he allotted to them, was hit and one of the machine-gunners killed. Another was wounded, but the third continued to fire upon the Japanese as they advanced in close order. Two men who attempted to rescue Assheton found that he too was dead. Nevertheless, his and the machine-gunners' valiant action achieved its purpose, for the force was enabled thereby to disengage, and withdrew across country to Bukit Panjang village.

Varley also tried to make a stand, after the Japanese broke through the positions he had established near his former headquarters. Having been forced to withdraw to near Malayan Farms with a party of his men, he sent his wounded to the rear in trucks found in the area, and told one of them, Sergeant Wagner, to ask brigade headquarters for instructions. Then, joined by Captain Griffin[6] with about thirty more members of the battalion, and Major Merrett with about twenty-five men of the 2/20th, he disposed the group for defence of the near-by portion of the airfield. However, Wagner soon returned with orders from Taylor as a result of which Varley led his force to the south of the airfield for reorganisation in the Bulim village area, behind Pond's battalion.

From early morning on 9th February, while resistance was still being maintained by the Australians north of the Tengah airfield, Brigadier Taylor, as shown, had sought to establish a stop-line from the northern end of the airfield to the Choa Chu Kang village behind which he might build strength and from which a counter-attack might be launched. In his initial dispositions, the Jind Battalion was on the right and the 2/29th Battalion on the left, with Saggers' battalion in reserve. Communication between brigade and Western Area headquarters was intermittent and inadequate, but at 9.30 a.m. a liaison officer reached Taylor with orders from Bennett to counter-attack and recapture Ama Keng village, using Pond's 2/29th Battalion for the purpose.[7] Taylor went forward with Lieut-Colonel Wright,[8] commander of the 2/15th Field Regiment, and discussed a plan for the counter-attack with Pond, who prepared to carry it out; but as the Japanese worked round to the east of the airfield, the brigadier subsequently decided that to do so would involve unjustifiable risk.

---

[6] Capt R. S. Griffin, NX34712; 2/18 Bn. Sales representative; of Sydney; b. Brisbane, 8 Jun 1910. Killed in air raid while prisoner 15 Jun 1943.

[7] The question arises whether in these circumstances it would have been advantageous if Bennett had visited the 22nd Brigade and seen for himself the situation on that front. On the one hand was the desirability of being on hand at his headquarters ready immediately to receive and act upon information from his three brigades or instructions from Malaya Command. On the other the main attack had fallen on the 22nd Brigade and it was being driven back in some confusion; communications were seriously disorganised and by going forward to it the divisional commander could not only gain his own impressions of the state of affairs but could exert an immediate influence upon them.

It is a problem that faces every commander, senior and junior, in a force that is hard pressed or actually withdrawing, and is frequently a subject of debate.

[8] Lt-Col J. W. Wright, DFC, NX12233. (1st AIF: 12 LH Regt; 2 and 4 Sqns AFC.) CO 2/15 Fd Regt. Company secretary; of Wahroonga, NSW; b. Quirindi, NSW, 4 Jan 1892.

As Taylor saw the situation, his two main problems were now to prevent the Japanese from getting around the airfield towards the Kranji-Jurong area, as yet unmanned; and to protect the right flank of the 44th Indian Brigade. He estimated that by midday the Japanese could have landed twelve battalions. To meet such a situation he had at his disposal some 500 men of his own brigade; Pond's and Saggers' battalions; the Jind Battalion and the reserve company of the 2/4th Machine Gun Battalion—a force small in comparison, and one comprising units either hastily organised, in process of reorganisation, or, in the case of the Jind, trained solely for airfield defence. Were he to hazard one of the only intact battalions upon a counter-attack possibly or probably foredoomed to failure, he might jeopardise all prospect of a successful stand in his sector. He was doubtful also of being able to hold the stop position for long, especially as once night came it would be particularly vulnerable to attack and outflanking movements. In these circumstances he cancelled the counter-attack order about 11 a.m., decided to readjust his line so that it would face west on a line from east of the Tengah airfield through Bulim towards the Jurong road, and sent Beale,[9] his brigade major, to inform Brigadier Ballentine and General Bennett of his intention.

On the airfield during the morning the carrier platoon attached to the 2/18th Battalion opened fire with six machine-guns on an enemy company in close formation, with such effect that a Japanese movement to the east of the 2/29th Battalion was checked for the time being. The Jind Battalion on the airfield had stood its ground despite bombing and machine-gun fire until, by 11.30 a.m., because of Japanese movements which threatened to outflank them to the north-east, the field was made unserviceable and the battalion withdrawn. The men of the 2/29th, although so many of them were newly-arrived reinforcements, in action for the first time, stuck to their job, and a party of Saggers' men with Thompson machine-guns held out against an attempt to get round Pond's right flank. By midday, however, enemy pressure necessitated sending a company of the 2/29th (Captain Lloyd) to the airfield to strengthen this flank.

Major Merrett, with fifty men of the 2/20th who had collected at Bulim, was sent to the left flank of the 2/29th. Brigadier Paris reported to General Bennett during the morning, and was directed to join forces with Taylor's brigade. Ballentine telephoned Bennett's headquarters about midday, pointing out that unless the Japanese were held the 44th Indian Brigade would soon be outflanked and in danger of being cut off. Thyer told him that there was every possibility that Taylor would have to withdraw to the Kranji-Jurong area, and that he should make plans for this. As a result, Ballentine ordered withdrawal of his beach defence guns, and forward posts of the Australian machine-gunners attached to him.

The 12th Indian Brigade reported to the 22nd Australian Brigade at midday that it had begun to arrive at Keat Hong, a mile and a half east of Bulim. About 1 p.m. Taylor gave orders for occupation of the line

---

[9] Maj R. F. S. Beale, VX12397; BM 22 Bde. Regular soldier; of Sydney; b. Mosman, NSW, 4 Nov 1900. Executed by Japanese 15 Feb 1942.

through Bulim towards the Jurong road. The positions to be occupied were in fact forward positions of the Kranji-Jurong area already surveyed,[1] and Captain Wyett, who had been engaged in that task, assisted the movement. A detachment of the Johore Volunteer Engineers which had arrived during the morning went into position on the right, north of Bulim and the Choa Chu Kang road; the 2/18th Battalion, about 330 strong, astride the road forward of Bulim village and to the south of it; and the 2/29th between the 2/18th and the Jurong road, with a company which had

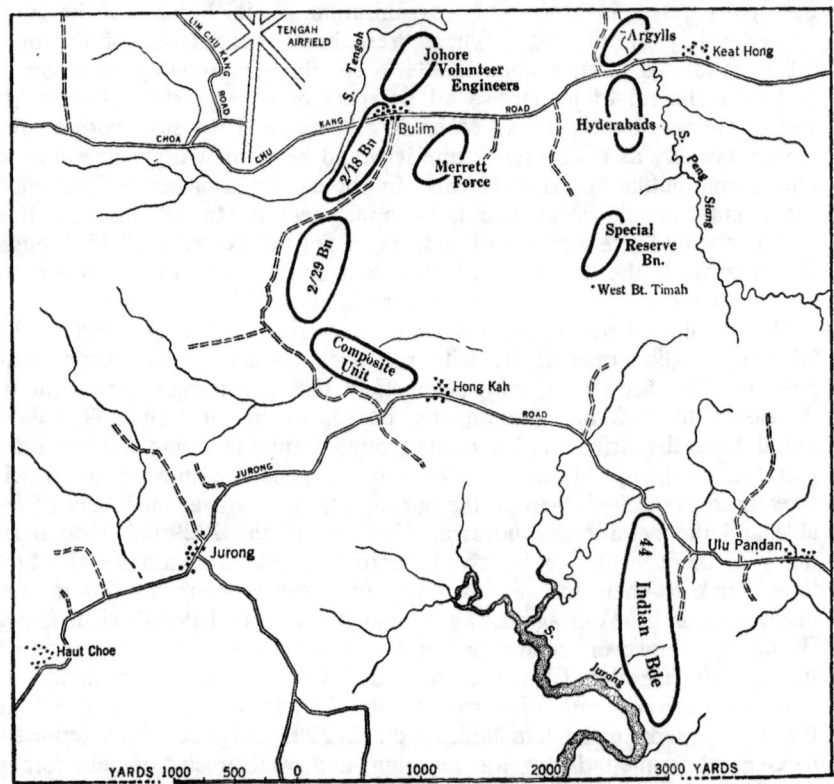

Bulim line, 9th February

become detached from the Special Reserve Battalion, about 150 survivors of the 2/10th Field Company, and a small party of the 2/20th Battalion on its left. The company of the 2/19th Battalion which had been at Choa Chu Kang village, and about sixty men of the 2/20th Battalion, came under command of Major Merrett as "Merrett Force", which was placed in a reserve position near the 2/18th Battalion.

Paris reached Taylor at 1.30 p.m. He discussed with him the disposition of the 12th Brigade, which at this stage comprised the Argylls, 400

---

[1] Planning and pegging of a defence system had been almost completed on 8th February, and a good deal of digging had been done, though the Chinese labourers had dispersed under bombing attacks. Australian engineers had extended the anti-tank ditch.

strong including 150 marines, and the 4/19th Hyderabads, numbering 440 including many newly-arrived reinforcements. The Argylls were placed north of the Choa Chu Kang road, and the Hyderabads, guided into position by Major Fraser (who like Wyett had been engaged in surveying the Kranji-Jurong area, and was now Bennett's liaison officer with the brigade) continued the line 600 yards south of the road towards the West Bukit Timah reserve position, extending northward of that feature. To this latter position Taylor ordered Saggers' Reserve Battalion, less its company in the Bulim line.

Beale and Major Moses, the Australian liaison officer with the 44th Indian Brigade, met early in the afternoon at Ballentine's headquarters, where a plan for Ballentine's and Taylor's brigades to occupy jointly the Kranji-Jurong area was formulated. Bennett, however, hoping perhaps that Paris' brigade would enable Taylor to stand his ground, refused when Moses returned to Western Area headquarters at 2.30 p.m. to sanction the plan.[2]

Percival, who, as well as sending Paris to the western sector had drawn Heath's 6th/15th Brigade (Colonel Coates) into command reserve, at an hour's notice to move, called on Bennett soon after. Bennett thought he "seemed very worried",[3] as well he might have been in view of the events of the night and morning, and the menacing situation with which he was now confronted. Decisions were reached as a result of discussion between the two generals based on a further report of the situation on Taylor's front. They were that Maxwell's brigade should continue to hold the Causeway sector, and that with the other forces available to him Bennett should try to stabilise the position in the Kranji-Jurong area. For this latter purpose the 44th Indian Brigade was to withdraw at once to the southern part of the line. Particularly because of the food and petrol dumps east of Bukit Timah village, the 6th/15th Brigade would be ordered up to the Singapore racecourse, near the village, where it would come under Bennett's orders.

Obviously Percival had concluded that the situation was very grave. He had now committed his two reserve brigades to deal with the threat from the west; and when he got back to his headquarters he and his staff began drawing up a plan for withdrawal, if the Japanese succeeded in breaking through the Sungei Kranji-Bulim-Sungei Jurong line, of the whole of his forces to a defensive perimeter. This would include Kallang airfield, the MacRitchie and Peirce reservoirs, the depots in the Bukit Timah area and hills immediately west of Bukit Timah village, and would reach the south coast at Pasir Panjang village. On this line, if necessary, "the final battle for Singapore" as the subsequent order put it, would be fought.

With the loss of Tengah airfield, and only Kallang serviceable to the few remaining aircraft—which despite overwhelming odds had been in the

---
[2] War Diary of AIF Headquarters.
[3] Bennett, *Why Singapore Fell*, p. 176.

air almost continuously throughout the week—it was decided to withdraw them to Sumatra. Hopes were entertained that they would be able to use Kallang as an advanced landing ground. Orders were received by Bennett's headquarters from Malaya Command to blow an ammunition magazine near the junction of the Peng Siang and the Kranji, in the 27th Brigade's sector, and the task was passed to the engineers. In the early belief that attack on the island would come from the sea, most of the ammunition on the island was stacked there and at Nee Soon, and it was estimated that the Kranji magazine held 60,000 tons.

In implementing the decisions reached with Percival, Bennett instructed his artillery commander about 4 p.m. to support the 27th and 22nd Australian Brigades and the 44th Indian Brigade along the Kranji and thence to the Jurong. Extensive reconnaissances and plans had been made during the past week for such an eventuality, and orders were issued immediately whereby the artillery would deploy accordingly, with the 2/10th Regiment on the right, 2/15th in the centre, and the 5th on the left (south). As the despatch of the 2/29th Battalion to the 22nd Brigade sector had left the 20th Battery (2/10th Regiment) without infantry protection, it was being moved at this time from a position near the junction of the Kranji and the Peng Siang to east of the main road to the Causeway. The new order necessitated the battery occupying positions which the 60th Battery had been shelled out of, and required extensive realignment of communications being carried out under fire.

While Taylor's men were re-forming at Bulim, Taylor accompanied Paris on a reconnaissance of the Kranji-Jurong rear line, saw Saggers' men going into position there, and inspected the Bulim line. Pond's battalion, covering the readjustment, was not pressed by the enemy when it broke contact and cleared the airfield road junction.

Near the end of the afternoon Bennett decided to withdraw his headquarters from Jurong road to Holland road, and left for the new location. Ballentine withdrew his headquarters to Jurong, though not before the headquarters had been heavily bombed. Though serious congestion occurred while the rest of his brigade was pulling out of the south-west sector, its withdrawal to the Kranji-Jurong line was completed by 10 p.m. Meanwhile only minor patrol activity occurred in front of Bulim. It seemed that the Japanese, having swiftly carried through the first phase of their offensive in Taylor's sector, needed time to develop the second.

In retrospect, Taylor's front, with its excessive dispersal of units, had been about as capable of withstanding a concentrated assault as a sieve is of holding water. Thus it could not reasonably be expected that the enemy could be prevented from landing.[4] If, however, the 22nd Brigade could then make a stand between the Kranji and the Berih or thereabouts, further toll might be taken of the invaders; a forward base for counter-attack

---

[4] Even when their legions were ensconced behind the heavily fortified Atlantic Wall, Hitler's generals were to take such a possibility into account (in planning to repel the Normandy invasion). In 1944 and 1945 when the Japanese were on the defensive they seldom tried to hold the beaches.

might be established; and time might be gained for a build-up of forces between the Kranji and the Jurong. However, such tactics would depend upon sufficient contact and control being maintained to ensure an orderly withdrawal. In the darkness, and when communications failed, this ceased to be a practical possibility by forces so widely dispersed as the forward policy required, and the line through Bulim presented the next best chance of checking the enemy.

To what extent did artillery play its part in opposition to the Japanese landings? As against the 168 artillery guns massed by the Japanese for the assault, 266 were available for the island's defence generally. These were, however, scattered all over the island, and as has been shown a much smaller allocation of artillery had been made to the Western Area than to the Northern Area, which so far had not been attacked. However much this dispersion might have been considered necessary for defence of the island from almost any quarter, it meant that as the situation had developed the defenders of the Western Area particularly were at a great disadvantage compared with the Japanese. The enemy had superior means of observation; their area of attack was limited and clearly defined; and they therefore could concentrate therein the whole or part of their fire where and when it would best serve their purposes.

To these advantages possessed by the enemy was added the fact that disruption by bombardment of line signals in the Western Area, and the circumstances relating to wireless transmission, undoubtedly caused serious delays and lack of precise direction during the initial landings when maximum artillery support was needed. However, during the night of 8th-9th February, the 2/15th Regiment fired 4,800 rounds, more than 90 per cent of them after the first reply to defensive fire signals; and the 2/10th Field Regiment, in Maxwell's sector, fired 400 rounds to the area from the mouth of the Sungei Skudai to the mouth of the Malayu in which the Japanese had been reported to be massing. Added to this was support from Jephson's[5] group. During the morning of 9th February this group, and the 2/10th Field Regiment, fired on Japanese in the Malayan Farms area, and the 2/15th Regiment fired on the Tengah airfield as the Japanese gained possession of it during the day. Ironically, the Australian artillery received on the evening of the 9th an order from Malaya Command cancelling its previous limitation of non-operational ammunition expenditure which had so heavily handicapped defensive artillery action while the Japanese were building strength for their assault.

By the end of 9th February the invaders had gained their first objective —Tengah airfield—and were transporting additional men and material, including tanks, across Johore Strait as quickly as they were able. Seeking to hold the Choa Chu Kang and Jurong roads to the centre of the island were the forces on the Bulim line and those which had occupied the Kranji-Jurong line proper—the 12th Indian Brigade on the right, the

---

[5] Lt-Col E. W. F. Jephson, MC. CO 5 Fd Regt RA. Regular soldier; b. 5 Nov 1897.

Special Reserve Battalion near the centre, and the 44th Indian Brigade on the left, with the 15th Indian Brigade in reserve.

From the Causeway sector groups of men of the 22nd Brigade had been seen early on 9th February crossing the Sungei Kranji and its south-eastern tributary the Peng Siang. This and the news of the fighting in the 22nd Brigade sector which filtered through to Brigadier Maxwell deepened

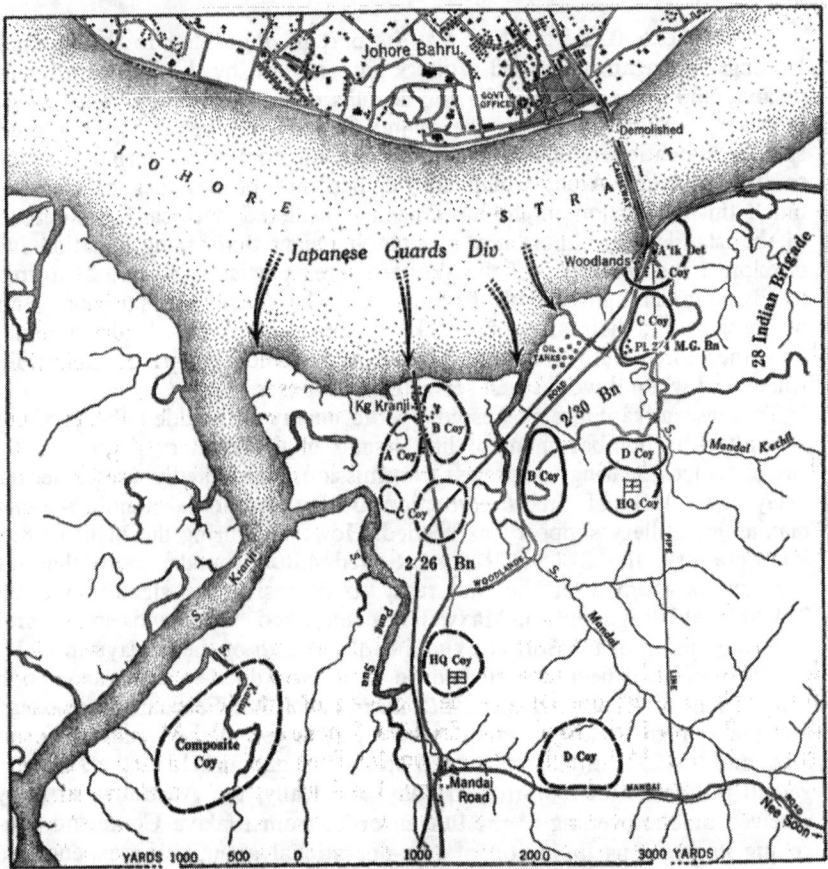

Causeway sector, 8 p.m. 9th February

the concern he felt about the gap to the south of his two battalions, left by the transfer of his 2/29th Battalion to the 22nd Brigade. It appeared to him that the enemy had committed himself to making his main attack in that sector. Opposed by only one brigade on a long and therefore thinly-held front, the invaders appeared to be pushing rapidly towards the headwaters of the Sungei Kranji and the Choa Chu Kang road, leading to the southern extremity of the 27th Brigade sector at Bukit Panjang. From there to the rear of the battalion positions was a distance of three miles. Maxwell felt convinced that the enemy would exploit this gap rather than assault the relatively concentrated forces north of it—the 2/26th Battalion in the swampy area near the mouth of the Kranji, the 2/30th Battalion adjoining the Causeway and the III Indian Corps east of them. It had been estimated during the night of 8th-9th February that the Japanese had landed eight battalions in the west, and others might now have followed them. If Maxwell's troops remained in the positions they occupied they might be cut off by enemy troops from that direction streaming through the gap and so gaining access both to Singapore and to the rear of the 28th Indian Brigade.

Consequently he sought, at 11 a.m., permission to withdraw his 2/26th Battalion to a line from the junction of the main (Woodlands) road from the Causeway and the Kranji road, to a point on the Peng Siang due west of the 12-mile post (nearly two miles north of Bukit Panjang). This would align his troops on a north-south axis, facing west, and do something to close the gap. The request was refused, but Maxwell was authorised to use the fourth platoon of each rifle company in the battalion to form a composite company. With "D" Company of the 2/26th, the composite company would be responsible for 600 yards to the battalion's rear along the east bank of the Kranji and the Peng Siang, thus serving the purpose Maxwell had in mind.

Artillery and air attack on the 27th Brigade's sector were intensified during the morning, and threatened to cut its line communications as the 22nd Brigade's had been cut the day before. As on that occasion, signallers distinguished themselves by constant endeavours to keep the lines in order despite the extent and hazards of the task. The communications problem was accentuated by the distance from the battalion positions of brigade headquarters. A further request was made by Maxwell to Western Area headquarters about midday that he be permitted to occupy a north-south line from the junction of the Kranji-Woodlands road to the 12-mile post on the Woodlands road. The brigade would thus be withdrawn from the area west of the road, and its right flank would be two miles south of the Causeway. This appears to have been granted, conditionally upon the withdrawal of the brigade not being commenced before the oil tanks near the Causeway, in the 2/30th Battalion's sector, had been demolished.[6] The move would in fact bring the brigade into the north-south alignment of the forces in the Western Area which as has been shown was ordered by General Bennett during the afternoon.

At 1.30 p.m. Brigadier Maxwell held a conference with Lieut-Colonel Galleghan, commander of the 2/30th Battalion, and then ordered him to obtain hospital treatment for ear trouble which was causing him partial deafness; Major Ramsay[7] was to take command of the battalion during his absence. Lieut-Colonel Oakes who, because of a delay in his transfer,

---

[6] General Bennett said after the war that he himself did not give permission for any withdrawal from the Causeway.

[7] Col G. E. Ramsay, ED, NX34999; 2/30 Bn (CO Feb 1942). Public relations officer; of Cremorne, NSW; b. East Maitland, NSW, 8 Jan 1899.

had only that day taken over the 2/26th Battalion from Lieut-Colonel Boyes, was also called in. During the course of the afternoon he was ordered to extend his left flank along the Kranji and Peng Siang for the time being, as had been authorised during the morning. The 2/30th Battalion was to be responsible for enabling the engineer detachment to wreck the oil tanks before first light on 10th January; the withdrawal of both battalions was to follow immediately upon completion of this task.

Instead of then stringing the battalions out along more than 3,000 yards from the 12-mile post to the Kranji-Woodlands road, however, Maxwell decided to concentrate them along what evidently he considered the vital portion of the line. Thus the 2/30th was to be immediately forward of Bukit Mandai, inclusive of the road to Nee Soon, where it would be in a position to resist passage to the rear of the 28th Indian Brigade. The 2/26th Battalion would be to the south of this position, extending the line towards the next vital road junction—that of the Choa Chu Kang and the Woodlands roads. In the event of being forced to give ground, the brigade would have freedom of manoeuvre, by withdrawal either to the east towards Nee Soon, or to the south along the Woodlands road or the Pipe-line east of it.[8] Oakes was to give the order for the withdrawal from the Causeway-Kranji positions, and to coordinate the movements of the two battalions.[9] He returned to the 2/26th late in the afternoon with a heavy responsibility on his shoulders, especially as he was new to his command and unfamiliar with the sector in which it was situated; but he was an officer in whom Maxwell had great confidence. The withdrawal would expose the left flank of the 11th Indian Division for a distance of about two miles. It was necessary therefore that it should be informed of the plan, so that its commander could make any necessary readjustment of his forces also—a task that would be possible provided he received adequate notice. This would normally be transmitted by Western Area headquarters, and by liaison between the 2/30th Battalion and the Indian unit adjacent to it. Ramsay received the orders through his Intelligence officer, Lieutenant Eaton, who returned from brigade headquarters with Oakes. Eaton told him that the situation on the 22nd Brigade's front was considered to be extremely serious. Ramsay, concerned at leaving a position which he considered his battalion capable of holding, subsequently discussed the plan by telephone with Oakes. The two agreed that having regard to the tactical position generally, and their lack of adequate knowledge of what was happening on the 22nd Brigade front, they would not be justified in asking their brigade headquarters to reconsider the order.

---

[8] Brigadier Maxwell pointed out (post-war) that at this stage his brigade positions were not being attacked other than by aircraft and artillery; that his decision therefore was made on tactical grounds and not in response to enemy pressure on the front the brigade occupied at the time.

[9] Oakes' recollection after the war was that he had not been given such definite orders about withdrawal, and himself took a larger responsibility for the subsequent movements of the two battalions.

Meanwhile, having staged the diversionary landing on Ubin Island, the Japanese *Guards Division* had been assembling for an attack on the Causeway sector. The width of suitable landing points between the Causeway and the Kranji was considered too narrow to allow more than one battalion to cross the Strait at a time, and the Japanese Command feared that after the warning given by the crossings to the 22nd Brigade's sector, the operation would involve heavy casualties. As against this, the command took the view that the attack would contain British forces in and about the area which otherwise might be employed elsewhere, and if the *Guards* could gain access to the main road from the Causeway into Singapore, the Japanese would virtually command the island. With these considerations in mind the command decided to accept the risks involved. In barges assembled at the mouth of the Sungei Skudai, a battalion of the *4th Guards Regiment* was launched upon the initial assault on the night of 9th February.

Movements to extend the left flank of the 2/26th Battalion were in progress when about 8.30 p.m. the Japanese lifted their bombardment of the Causeway sector, and barges were seen by the Australians approaching its shore. Soon after 9 p.m. enemy troops began landing against the battalion's two forward companies. The main assault was about a pier between the mouths of the Sungei Mandai and the Sungei Kranji, where wire and other defensive works had been demolished by the bombardment. Other landings were made in swamps along the frontage, and some Japanese went up the Sungei Mandai (between the 2/30th and the 2/26th Battalions) and the Sungei Mandai Kechil (in the 2/30th Battalion area).

Lights in the 2/26th Battalion area did not function, and although all serviceable flares[1] were used in calling for defensive artillery fire, they brought no immediate response. The battery which had been sited west of the Woodlands road in support of the 2/26th Battalion had been ordered to move after dark to the Mandai road area because of the concern felt, presumably at Western Area headquarters, about the brigade's left flank, and it was not in action when the attack started. It was not until the attack had been observed from Ramsay's sector that the battery supporting his battalion, and his mortars, fired to Oakes' sector. The other battery opened up later. Australian machine-gunners on the front of the 2/26th did not come into action until twenty minutes after the first landing because they had not seen the flares, which were to be their fire signal also. The battalion's mortars fired on the Kranji pier area, scoring heavily, but the Japanese persisted in their endeavours, with the result that they were soon engaged in hand-to-hand fighting with Oakes' forward platoons.

Soon after 9 p.m. a standing patrol forward of the 2/30th Battalion's "B" Company (Captain Duffy) reported enemy movement on the mouth of the Sungei Mandai, but only a small force of Japanese landed at this stage, and these came under mortar and machine-gun fire. News then

---
[1] Some of the cartridges, swollen by humidity, would not fit the flare pistols.

arrived of the landing against the 2/26th Battalion generally, and Japanese were seen gathering on the mainland shore about 300 feet west of the Causeway. A beach-light

outlined the figure of a Japanese officer at the head of the Causeway, shouting and gesticulating to imaginary troops apparently to divert attention from the activities farther up the bank (wrote the diarist of the 2/30th Battalion). Several well-placed shells deprived him of any further interest in activities whilst the main weight of shell fire fell on the troops he had been striving to cover. Subsequent flashes revealed them to be in the act of entering barges, but the accuracy of the shell fire at least discouraged them in that endeavour.[2]

Meanwhile, the battery supporting the 2/30th was running short of ammunition because additional supplies had not arrived. Fire to the mainland foreshores had to be restricted, and despite streams of bullets from two machine-guns manned by the battalion's carrier crews at vantage points near the Causeway, a line of Japanese barges managed to reach the Sungei Mandai Kechil. There, apparently, they awaited reinforcements. Ramsay regarded the spot as a bottleneck, into which fire could be poured from machine-guns and mortars when the right time arrived. Pending that, standing patrols were used to keep touch with the Japanese and prevent infiltration.

By midnight the forward troops of the 2/26th Battalion had concentrated in the vicinity of Kampong Kranji, where although they had suffered heavy casualties they held firmly. Some Japanese who managed to enter a house in the centre of the position were dislodged with automatic fire and grenades. Corporal Rogers[3] and four others with guns, grenades and finally bayonets drove back an enemy party which attempted to charge along the road into the area. The corporal felled a Japanese with the muzzle of his gun when its magazine was empty. As he fell the Japanese grasped Rogers' legs and brought him down too, but Lance-Corporal Lee[4] finished the struggle with his bayonet. Confused fighting followed, with both the Australians and the Japanese uncertain of the movements of their opponents. A report came from the 2/30th Battalion of the penetration of the Sungei Mandai, and a patrol led by Sergeant Brennan[5] was sent to deal with it. The patrol came upon some Japanese attempting to draw a barge to the bank of the river, and wiped them out with grenades.

Demolition of the oil tanks, situated forward of Duffy's company of the 2/30th, was delayed because the truck with the explosives and gear for the task was hit by a shell. Lieutenant Watchorn,[6] in charge of the demolition party, had to walk four miles to make good the loss, while the Japanese were building up their strength. Eventually, with the assist-

---

[2] Narrative with the 2/30th Battalion war diary.

[3] Cpl J. Rogers, QX1690; 2/26 Bn. Station hand; of West Maitland, NSW; b. West Maitland, 5 Dec 1901. Died while prisoner 16 Dec 1943.

[4] Sgt G. F. Lee, QX12611; 2/26 Bn. Labourer; of Lanefield, Qld; b. Brisbane, 4 Sep 1917.

[5] Sgt R. N. Brennan, QX10622; 2/26 Bn. Station hand; of Maryborough, Qld; b. Wondai, Qld, 15 Jul 1915.

[6] Capt A. B. Watchorn, MC, VX9737; 2/12 Fd Coy. Student; of Sandy Bay, Tas; b. Hobart, 27 Sep 1916.

ance of Sergeant Wilstencroft[7] and the other members of his party he coolly set the charges within earshot of the enemy.

Colonel Oakes, who had been under the impression that the 12th Indian Brigade was responsible for the area immediately left of his battalion, received about 3 a.m. from one of his officers a report that that brigade's position extended no farther north than Bukit Panjang. This appears to have influenced the extent of the move by the two battalions which he was soon to set afoot. About 4.30 a.m., as 2,000,000 gallons of petrol went up in flames and smoke from the tanks, the surrounding area was vividly illuminated. Blazing spirit flowed down creeks into the Mandai Kechil and on to the waters of the Strait. It was assumed that this inflicted serious loss on the Japanese.[8] Concurrent fires at the naval base added to the lurid impact of the scene. The task upon which the predetermined withdrawal of the 2/26th and 2/30th depended having been performed, the battalions withdrew. The mortars and machine-guns of the 2/30th swept the Japanese in its sector with two final barrages. Shouts and screams from the enemy made it evident that the fire was finding its mark. The signal line to the 2/2nd Gurkhas on the 2/30th Battalion's right had been disrupted, but a written message was sent to inform them of the 2/30th's new position. It was assumed that information about the withdrawal plan would have reached the 28th Indian Brigade, of which the Gurkhas were a part, through the usual higher command channels.

Although the withdrawal conceded the Japanese the forward area of the Causeway sector, the resistance had caused them heavy casualties, and they had been able to make little headway. Then, as the stream of fire from the tanks flowed on to the water in the vicinity, further impeding their progress, reports which reached General Nishimura made the situation appear so serious that he asked *XXV Army Headquarters* for permission to cancel the attack in the Causeway sector and to land on Singapore Island behind the *5th Division*. Headquarters staff officers were hurriedly sent to investigate the situation. It was then found that opposition had subsided, and the operation continued as originally planned. These circumstances were of course unknown to Brigadier Maxwell, whose information about the situation on his front was insufficient to enable him to assess the actual strength of the enemy landing, or the fact that a division was available to exploit it. In any case, cancellation of the withdrawal order while the fighting was in progress would of course have been a hazardous proceeding, particularly as Maxwell had no reserve with which to influence the outcome and no troops guarding the stretch south of the Kranji road.

The Japanese had used collapsible boats, small landing craft and pontoons for their crossings of the Strait. The small landing craft were

---

[7] Sgt R. Wilstencroft, MM, NX50642; 2/12 Fd Coy. Roadmaking ganger; of Annandale, NSW; b. Fairy Meadow, NSW, 19 Sep 1903.

[8] The Japanese had been apprehensive that the vast amount of petrol and oil stored on Singapore Island would be used to lay a sheet of flame over the waters of the Johore Strait wherever invasion was attempted. That it was not done fitted in with the pattern of unpreparedness of Singapore's landward defences.

brought by rail and sea along the west coast, and hand-carried in the final stages to the embarkation points to avoid detection; the collapsible boats and pontoons were mainly carried on trucks. The collapsible boats, constructed of plywood with rubber joints and built in two sections, were capable of being assembled by one man in two minutes. Propelled by a 30 horsepower 2-cylinder outboard motor, each could carry twelve fully-equipped troops with a four-man crew; linked together in threes they were capable of carrying field artillery pieces. Two types of pontoons were used. One, similar to but heavier in construction than the collapsible boats, was linked together in threes to carry heavy vehicles and tanks up to 16 tons. The other type, of steel construction, was commonly used for bridge building, but could also be used as a landing craft. Altogether 297 craft of all types (including 200 collapsible boats) were allotted for the operation, but the number used was about 10 per cent less.

Little time had been available for training the infantry in the crossings to be made. The assault troops of the *Guards Division* practised boarding on 8th February in an area near the embarkation point; the *5th* and *18th Divisions* on 4th February in an area to the rear. However, both these divisions had had previous experience in amphibious operations: the *5th* had received specialised training before the outbreak of war, and the *18th* had carried out river crossings in south China.

Mandai road, about two miles from Mandai Road village, showing the dense vegetation encountered by the troops even on Singapore Island.

(*Australian War Memorial*)

Choa Chu Kang road, near Bulim village. In this area a Japanese attack was repulsed by the 2/29th Battalion on the morning of 10th February. Post-war photograph.

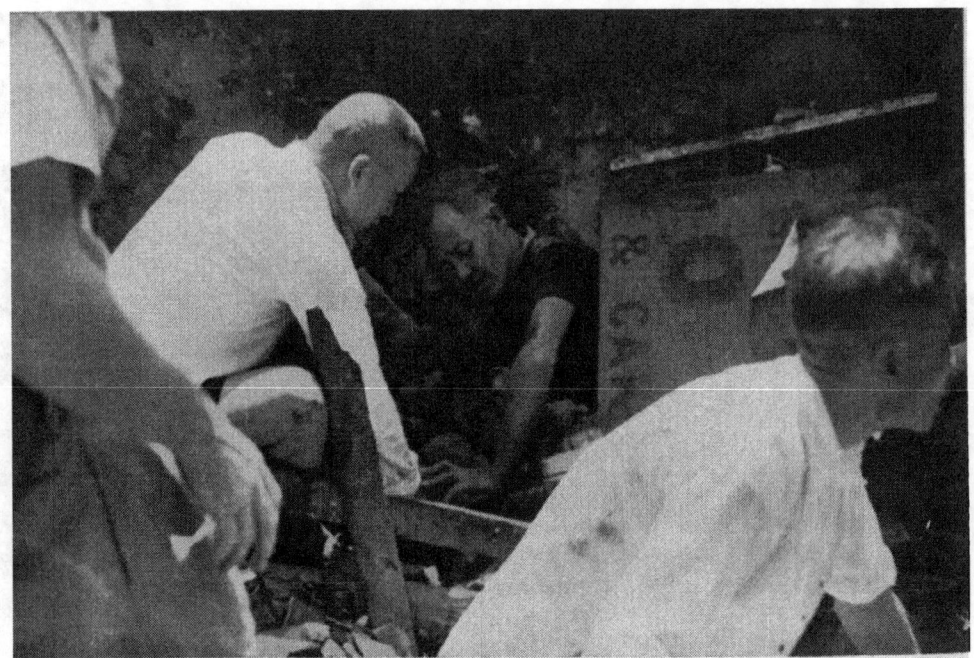

(*Australian War Memorial*)

The plight of the civilians of Singapore, swollen to over a million by refugees from the north, worsened as the area held by the defenders was reduced and air attacks and shelling increased in intensity. In the above photograph a Chinese doctor attends an air raid casualty.

(*Australian War Memorial*)

Two grief-stricken Chinese women lament the death of a child.

CHAPTER 16

STRUGGLE FOR SINGAPORE

IN the situation which faced General Bennett on the morning of 10th February, much depended on the Kranji-Jurong line. If the Japanese could not be held there, and prevented from exploiting their gains in the Causeway sector, presumably General Percival's plan to form a defensive arc on the outskirts of Singapore would have to be put into effect. This would involve abandoning most of the island and, unless they could be destroyed, the outlying masses of ammunition and stores which General Percival had taken into consideration in his original plan to meet the enemy on the beaches.

To the forces assigned to the Kranji-Jurong area was added the 6th/15th Indian Brigade (Colonel Coates) which, as has been shown, was placed under General Bennett's command on the afternoon of 9th February. Bennett had ordered it during the evening of the 9th to take up a position in the line on the right of the 44th Indian Brigade. This action appears to have been taken largely because of an erroneous report by a liaison officer that the 44th had been cut off on the Jurong road, was fighting its way through, and had suffered heavy casualties. A consequence of the order was that the 44th Brigade was required to sidestep from the positions which it was in process of occupying north of the Jurong road to others south and inclusive of it, with the brigade's left in touch with the 2nd Malay Battalion at Kampong Jawa on the eastern bank of the Sungei Jurong. The move was difficult in the darkness and the rough country to which the brigade was allotted, especially as it was only partially trained and had no opportunity of reconnoitring the new positions.

Only patrol encounters occurred during the night of the 9th-10th February near the Bulim line. Soon after midnight Major Beale returned from a visit to Western Area headquarters with orders for withdrawal of Brigadier Taylor's forces, after denying Bulim till 6 a.m., to the line being formed between the Kranji and the Jurong. Taylor, at 4.15 a.m., directed his commanders accordingly. He then visited 12th Brigade headquarters, and told Paris of the dispositions; saw some of his men taking up their new positions; and went to the rear to remove the grime from burning oil dumps with which he like many others had become covered. The 2/29th Battalion was to extend the 12th Brigade's line astride the Choa Chu Kang road and link with the Special Reserve Battalion in its position north of West Bukit Timah. Major Merrett, whose force comprised remnants of the 2/19th and 2/20th Battalions, received orders to withdraw to about Keat Hong village, and the 2/18th Battalion was to go into reserve in the same locality. The 2/10th Field Company and the company of the 2/4th Machine Gun Battalion were to revert to divisional command.

In the course of the withdrawal, the 2/18th Battalion's carriers remained in position, with shells falling among them, until its infantry had gone. The carriers were about to leave when two large groups of Japanese were seen, one marching along the road and the other south of it. Waiting in concealment until these came within close range, the crews blazed into them with their machine-guns, temporarily halted the enemy, and withdrew with their vehicles.

Three of the 2/29th Battalion's companies, under Lieut-Colonel Pond's second-in-command, Major Hore,[1] reached the Argylls.[2] The dispositions of the 12th Indian Brigade had been changed meanwhile to the extent that the 4/19th Hyderabad, formerly on the left flank of the Argylls near the junction of the Kranji-Jurong line with the Choa Chu Kang road, had been withdrawn at 2 a.m., apparently without Western Area headquarters or the 22nd Brigade having been informed, to the rear of the Argylls. Hore therefore decided in consultation with Colonel Stewart, the Argylls' commander, to go into position on the Argylls' left. This of course meant that the 12th Brigade forward line did not reach as far south as it would have done had the Hyderabads remained in it, and had the Australians been placed on their left to link with the Special Reserve Battalion as intended. The other company of the 2/29th Battalion had become detached, for seeing the other companies coming under fire as they reached the Choa Chu Kang road, Pond led it across country to the southern slopes of West Bukit Timah. There he put it into position in contact with 6th/15th Indian Brigade on its left, and went northward looking for the rest of his battalion. In doing so he located the Special Reserve Battalion headquarters, but as has been shown, the other companies of the 2/29th Battalion were farther north than had been intended, and Pond failed to find them. After returning to his remaining company, he unsuccessfully sought means of telephoning his brigade headquarters. Finally, he went to the headquarters for orders.

Meanwhile, at 12.50 a.m. on 10th February, Percival's provisional plan for a defence arc round Singapore had been issued as a secret and personal instruction to senior commanders and staff officers. It specified that the northern sector of the arc would be occupied by the III Indian Corps (11th Indian and 18th British Divisions) commanded by General Heath. General Bennett's responsibility would be the western sector, and General Simmons' the southern sector. At the time the instruction was drawn up, the allocation of the 12th and 44th Indian Brigades had not been decided, but it was intended that at least one of these would be in command reserve. Bennett's front was to extend from north-east to west of Bukit Timah village, and to about 750 yards west of the junction of

---

[1] Maj F. Hore, VX44803; 2/29 Bn. Buyer; of Ormond, Vic; b. Mincha, Vic, 13 Jan 1907.

[2] "The 93rd [Argylls] had met this fine unit before, and in the undignified 'pot calling the kettle black' recriminations that have at times occurred over Singapore, it is well to say that if the 93rd had to choose a unit with whom they would like to go into battle, they would not look beyond the 2/29th Australians."—I. MacA. Stewart, *History of the Argyll and Sutherland Highlanders 2nd Battalion*, p. 104.

Reformatory and Ayer Raja roads (some 1,500 yards from Pasir Panjang village). The instruction set out that—

> Reconnaissances of areas will be carried out at once and the plans for the movement of formations into the areas allotted to them will be prepared. Formations will arrange to move back and locate in their new areas units located in their present areas which are under command of H.Q. Malaya Command.

Percival had imparted the plan verbally to Heath and Simmons during the previous evening. He issued it so that responsible senior officers might know his intentions in case the situation developed too rapidly for further orders to be issued. Despite Bennett's antipathy to warnings which might cause his commanders to "look over their shoulders", the substance of the instruction was embodied in an order issued from his headquarters at 7.30 a.m. on the 10th. Although it indicated that the commanders might have to evacuate their sectors, it stated that no action except reconnaissance was to be taken pursuant of the order. In the event of the new positions being occupied, the A.I.F. sector would be manned by the 27th Brigade on the right of Bukit Timah road (the name of the trunk road in the vicinity of Bukit Timah village) and the 22nd Brigade on the left, with the 44th Indian Brigade in reserve.

Typed copies of the order were dispatched. It naturally made commanders think in terms of how to withdraw should circumstances require it, and subsequent events suggest that in the confused situation in which they found themselves and with signal lines badly disrupted, it acted to some extent as a magnet to their thoughts. When Brigadier Taylor read the order its limited nature escaped him, and he interpreted it as requiring the new positions to be manned forthwith. He accordingly ordered the units under his command—other than the 2/29th Battalion and the Special Reserve Battalion, which were committed to the Kranji-Jurong line—to positions along the line of Reformatory road, in the sector provisionally allotted to his brigade. He had learned at this stage that an additional Australian unit, to be known as "X" Battalion, was being formed in Singapore by Lieut-Colonel Boyes, and would come under command of the 22nd Brigade. This, and remnants of the 2/18th Battalion under Lieut-Colonel Varley, he allotted to positions immediately west of the section of Reformatory road between Ulu Pandan road and Bukit Timah road, with Merrett Force in their rear a little east of Reformatory road. Each of these units was given a machine-gun platoon in support, leaving one in reserve at brigade headquarters. The 15th Anti-Tank Battery was to cover roads in the area, and an armoured car detachment would also be in reserve.

On his way to reconnoitre the new positions Taylor reported to Bennett, who tersely reproved him for his actions, but did not countermand the orders given by the brigadier. Taylor thereupon continued his reconnaissance. The total strength of the 2/18th and Merrett Force at this stage was about 500.

Early the same day (10th February) Brigadier Maxwell visited Western Area headquarters and was ordered to open his headquarters in a position where he would be at call of Area headquarters if required. This he did, in the Holland road locality, although in that position he was out of signal communication with his 2/30th and 2/26th Battalions in the Causeway sector. Meanwhile, the 2/30th under Major Ramsay had taken up its new positions in the Bukit Mandai area, east of the junction of Mandai road with the trunk road from the Causeway. The move by the 2/26th Battalion had been more extensive. With delegated responsibility on his shoulders for dispositions, its commander, Lieut-Colonel Oakes, ordered it to take up a line, east of the railway and the trunk road, from Bukit Mandai back to Bukit Panjang. This gave it a frontage of 4,000 yards, with each company occupying a hill position, and roadless gaps of up to 1,000 yards of dense vegetation between them.

Also early on the 10th General Wavell visited the island once more, and quickly went with Percival to see Bennett at his headquarters. The ensuing conference coincided with a Japanese bombing attack. Debris showered down and some casualties resulted, but the generals were unharmed. By this time, as has been shown, both Australian brigades had retracted from the fronts allotted to them, and were facing west. To Percival, Bennett seemed "not quite so confident as he had been up-country. He had always been very certain that his Australians would never let the Japanese through and the penetration of his defences had upset him. As always, we were fighting this battle in the dark, and I do not think any of us realised at that time the strength of the enemy's attack."[3]

As Percival and Wavell left Bennett they passed

an undisciplined-looking mob of Indians moving along the road. They were carrying rifles and moving in no sort of formation. Their clothing was almost black. I must confess (wrote Percival) I felt more than a bit ashamed of them and it was quite obvious what the Supreme Commander thought. Only recently have I learnt the truth. This was the administrative staff of a reinforcement camp on the move. The quartermaster had some rifles in store and, good quartermaster as he was, had determined that they must be taken. So, having no transport, he had given one to each man to carry. . . . Many of our troops looked more like miners emerging from a shift in the pits than fighting soldiers. It is difficult to keep one's self-respect in these conditions, especially when things are not going too well.[4]

The two generals next visited General Heath, and went on to see General Key, whose headquarters were north of Nee Soon near the Seletar Reservoir. There they found that as the trunk road from the Causeway had been exposed to the enemy, Maxwell's line of communication now ran back through Key's area rather than Western Area. Percival decided to put the Australian brigade under Key's command as soon as he had seen Bennett again. Meanwhile, regarding the junction of the Mandai road with the road from the Causeway as being vital to Key's left flank, he sent a

---
[3] Percival, *The War in Malaya*, p. 275.
[4] Percival, pp. 275-6.

personal instruction by dispatch rider to Maxwell to place his troops in more advanced positions in the area.

Percival also ordered General Heath to withdraw three battalions from the Northern Area and send them to the Bukit Timah area, which he now considered vital, and where they were to be a reserve under Bennett's command. These, from different brigades of the 18th British Division, comprised the division's Reconnaissance Battalion, the 4/Norfolks (54th Brigade), the 1/5th Sherwood Foresters (55th Brigade) and a battery of the 85th Anti-Tank Regiment. They were commanded by Lieut-Colonel Thomas,[5] and designated "Tomforce".

Back with Bennett early in the afternoon of the 10th, Wavell and Percival were informed that although the positions of the troops west of Bukit Timah village were not definitely known, the Kranji-Jurong line had been lost. As it transpired, the Japanese had quickly followed up the withdrawal from Bulim, and made contact with the main body of the 2/29th Battalion and the Argylls astride the Choa Chu Kang road. Out of touch with his brigade headquarters, lacking artillery support, and in danger of encirclement, the Argylls' commander, Stewart, on his own initiative, decided to place them and the Australians in depth along the road, behind the Sungei Peng Siang, and some way back from the position they had been holding. Hore therefore moved his men to high ground near Keat Hong village, where they became the forward battalion; then, suffering from a mortar shell wound, he handed over command to Captain Bowring and left by motor cycle to seek orders from his brigade or divisional headquarters. Bowring told Stewart that he would remain in the position until by-passed by the Japanese, when he would fall back in stages.

While the Japanese were thus moving towards Bukit Panjang, as Brigadier Maxwell had feared they might, from the west, Brigadier Paris (12th Indian Brigade) received reports that his patrols had been unable to make contact with the unit of the 27th Brigade on his right (just as the 2/26th Battalion had been unable during the night to locate the 12th Brigade). Out of touch with Western Area headquarters, but concluding that an enemy thrust from the north along the trunk road towards Bukit Timah might be expected, he decided on his own responsibility to leave the 4/19th Hyderabad in its position on the Choa Chu Kang road between Bukit Panjang village and Keat Hong; and to place the three companies of the 2/29th Battalion in the village immediately covering the junction of the two roads, with the Argylls to the south.

Bowring and Paris met while the Australian companies were going into their covering position, and Bowring asked for an anti-tank battery to assist them in their task. Believing, however, that the enemy could not yet have landed tanks, Paris refused to meet the request. He similarly declined a later request by Bowring for a battery of the 2/10th Australian Field Regiment.

---

[5] Maj-Gen L. C. Thomas, CB, CBE, DSO, MC. Comd "Tomforce" 1942, 88 and 36 Indian Inf Bdes. Regular soldier; b. 20 Oct 1897.

The moves ordered by Paris were completed early in the afternoon of the 10th. Thus the northern portion of the line between the headwaters of the Kranji and the Jurong was abandoned, and the right flank of the forces in the southern portion of the line—the Australian Special Reserve Battalion (Major Saggers) and the 6th/15th and 44th Indian Brigades—was left in the air. The 6th/15th Brigade had the British Battalion north of the Jurong road, the 3/16th Punjab echeloned back from its right flank, and the Jat Battalion in reserve. On the 44th Brigade front the 6/1st Punjab was on the Jurong road, the 6/14th Punjab was farther south, in touch with the 2nd Malay Battalion, and the 7/8th Punjab was in reserve to the rear of the 6/1st.

General Percival's secret instruction indicating that a defensive line might be formed around Singapore had reached Brigadier Ballentine about 10.30 a.m. He thereupon notified Colonel Coates (6th/15th Indian Brigade) of its requirements, and told his battalion commanders that in the event of a retirement they were to move along tracks to Pasir Panjang village. Both brigades, and Saggers and his men at West Bukit Timah, were heavily bombed during the morning. Wild firing broke out in the 6/1st Punjab position about 1 p.m. This was followed by hasty withdrawal down the Jurong road of a number of vehicles, one of the battalion's companies, and some men of the British Battalion. The Punjabis reported—incorrectly as it transpired—that the British Battalion had withdrawn, and permission was given to the battalion to readjust its line. However, the rearward movement quickly got out of control, and soon most of the brigade was streaming towards the village. There it was halted and reformed by Brigadier Ballentine, who received orders to move it to the junction of Ulu Pandan and Reformatory roads.

In the situation created by the withdrawal of the 44th Brigade, Coates moved his brigade back along the Jurong road, to within about two miles of Bukit Timah. Finding itself isolated and without orders, the company which Pond had placed in the Kranji-Jurong line withdrew in search of some Australian headquarters. Saggers used his men to extend the new 6th/15th Brigade position south of the road. Brigadier Williams[6] (1st Malaya Brigade), with his right flank uncovered, withdrew the 2nd Malay Battalion to Pasir Panjang, but left outposts on the bridge over the Sungei Pandan.

At his early afternoon conference with Generals Percival and Bennett, while these events were in train, General Wavell said he considered it vital that the Kranji-Jurong line be used as a bulwark against the Japanese thrust from the west towards Bukit Timah, and urged that it be regained. Percival thereupon ordered Bennett to launch a counter-attack, and told him that in view of the situation which had developed in the Causeway sector the 27th Brigade would be placed under command of the 11th Division (General Key) as from 5 p.m. Percival also ordered that a large

---

[6] Brig G. G. R. Williams; Comd 1 Malaya Bde 1941-42. Regular soldier; b. 30 Mar 1894.

reserve of petrol stored a few hundred yards east of Bukit Timah be destroyed.

Japanese troops had reached the Kranji ammunition magazine before engineers arrived to destroy it, and much of the ammunition which had been reserved for a prolonged resistance fell into their hands. On Wavell's orders, the last of the serviceable aircraft and the remaining airmen on Singapore Island were withdrawn to the Netherlands East Indies. Air Vice-Marshal Maltby,[7] who had been acting as Assistant Air Officer Commanding at Air Headquarters, went with them to become the commander of the R.A.F. and R.A.A.F. units under the A.B.D.A. Command. In an order of the day Wavell declared:

> It is certain that our troops on Singapore Island greatly outnumber any Japanese that have crossed the Straits. We must defeat them. Our whole fighting reputation is at stake and the honour of the British Empire. The Americans have held out in the Bataan Peninsula against far greater odds, the Russians are turning back the picked strength of the Germans, the Chinese with almost complete lack of modern equipment have held the Japanese for 4½ years. It will be disgraceful if we yield our boasted fortress of Singapore to inferior enemy forces.
>
> There must be no thought of sparing the troops or the civil population and no mercy must be shown to weakness in any shape or form. Commanders and senior officers must lead their troops and if necessary die with them.
>
> There must be no question or thought of surrender. Every unit must fight it out to the end and in close contact with the enemy. . . . I look to you and your men to fight to the end to prove that the fighting spirit that won our Empire still exists to enable us to defend it.

In a covering note, General Percival said ". . . In some units the troops have not shown the fighting spirit expected of men of the British Empire.

"It will be a lasting disgrace if we are defeated by an army of clever gangsters many times inferior in numbers to our men. The spirit of aggression and determination to stick it out must be inculcated in all ranks. There must be no further withdrawals without orders. There are too many fighting men in the back areas.

"Every available man who is not doing essential work must be used to stop the invader."

There was a Churchillian ring in Wavell's exhortation; and indeed Mr Churchill sent him on this same day a cable on which obviously Wavell had drawn with characteristic loyalty but perhaps, under pressure of events, without mature consideration.

> I think you ought to realise the way we view the situation in Singapore (said Churchill). It was reported to Cabinet by the C.I.G.S. [Chief of Imperial General Staff] that Percival has over 100,000 men, of whom 33,000 are British and 17,000 Australian. It is doubtful whether the Japanese have as many in the whole Malay Peninsula. . . . In these circumstances the defenders must greatly outnumber Japanese forces who have crossed the straits, and in a well-contested battle they should destroy them. There must at this stage be no thought of saving the troops or sparing the population. The battle must be fought to the bitter end at all costs. The 18th

---

[7] Air Vice-Marshal Sir Paul Maltby, KBE, CB, DSO, AFC. AOC 71 (AC) Group 1940-41, Brit Air Forces in Java 1942. Regular airman; b. 5 Aug 1892. Maltby had reached Singapore on 4th January as Chief of Staff designate to the Commander-in-Chief Far East, but the appointment lapsed on the formation of ABDA Command.

Division has a chance to make its name in history. Commanders and senior officers should die with their troops. The honour of the British Empire and of the British Army is at stake. I rely on you to show no mercy to weakness in any form. With the Russians fighting as they are and the Americans so stubborn at Luzon, the whole reputation of our country and our race is involved. It is expected that every unit will be brought into close contact with the enemy and fight it out. . . .[8]

Mr Churchill said nothing about the Malayan campaign having been virtually lost at sea and in the air within a few days of its commencement; nothing about the disastrous dispersal of the army on the mainland to protect airfields now valuable only to the enemy; nothing about the Japanese monopoly of tanks; though indeed his figures did indicate that about half the force at Percival's disposal comprised Asian soldiers. These, in the main poorly trained and inexperienced, and with many officers who were more or less strangers to their units, were pitted against other Asians who had become veterans of campaigns in China and were fighting ardently for their country instead of as subject people. The United Kingdom troops included the newly-arrived 18th Division; more than half the total number of Australians, with a divisional organisation but only two brigades, consisted of other than front-line troops. It will be seen later that Wavell was greatly mistaken in his estimate that the American-Filipino forces at Bataan were facing "far greater odds than the troops on Singapore Island"; nor was the island a Russia or a China, with their vast spaces for manoeuvre and enormous reserves of manpower. Singapore had been indeed a boasted fortress, but it was not the enemy who had been deceived by the boast. To Mr Churchill himself, as has been shown, it had become with a shock of discovery "the naked island".

Wavell himself left Singapore at midnight, after injuring his back in a fall down some steps during an air raid blackout. Some of the events hitherto described in these pages were not known to him, but despite his order that Singapore must be held to the last, he went "without much confidence in any prolonged resistance".[9] He cabled to Mr Churchill stating that the battle for Singapore was not going well.

Indeed, time was running swiftly against the defenders. Even the effect of a last stand in an endeavour to buy time for resistance elsewhere would depend upon how quickly the essential parts of Percival's disrupted and battered military machine could be reassembled and made to function.

Seeking meanwhile to retrieve the situation caused by timely notification not having reached him of the 27th Australian Brigade's withdrawal from his left flank near the Causeway, General Key employed his reserve (8th Brigade) throughout the day (10th February) to occupy high ground overlooking the road and the Causeway. The troops made substantial gains, though at the cost of heavy fighting and many casualties. One of Key's staff officers took to Lieut-Colonel Ramsay (2/30th Battalion) during

---

[8] Churchill, *The Second World War*, Vol IV, pp. 87-8.
[9] Wavell, *Despatch on the Operations in the South-West Pacific 15th January 1942 to 25th February 1942*, para 27.

the morning a request that he send a platoon up to the junction of the Mandai road with the trunk road from the Causeway. Ramsay went forward with a small detachment, and decided to send up a company; but, on returning to his headquarters, received an order from his brigade headquarters to keep his troops in position. Thus when General Key himself visited the battalion about 1 p.m. and again asked for troops to be sent to the junction, Ramsay referred to this order and asked that the issue be taken up with his brigadier.

At 2 p.m., after receipt of Percival's plan for a defensive line round Singapore, Brigadier Maxwell issued an order to his 2/26th and 2/30th Battalions to withdraw down the Pipe-line east of the trunk road to a rendezvous near the racecourse if they were unable to hold the enemy near Bukit Mandai. The order reached the 2/26th at 4 p.m., but was delayed in transmission to the 2/30th. The 27th Brigade came meanwhile under command of the 11th Division, and the 2/30th received the information at 5 p.m., with an order to move to the trunk (Woodlands) road on a line south from Mandai road. Maxwell reported to General Key about 6.30 p.m. Three companies of the 2/30th Battalion moved at 9 p.m. to high features immediately behind the junction of the two roads, with the fourth guarding the approaches along the Pipe-line north of Mandai road. It was understood by Ramsay that the 2/10th Baluchis would come up on the battalion's right.

General Bennett had issued at 4.5 p.m. on the 10th, through his G.S.O.2, Major Dawkins, instructions for the counter-attack ordered by Percival. Despite the rapid deterioration of the front, the weakness of the forces now available, and difficulties of organisation and control—factors more clearly apparent in retrospect than they would have been to Bennett with the limited information available to him at the time—these instructions required that the Kranji-Jurong line should be regained in three phases. The first objective was to be gained by 6 p.m. on the 10th; the second by 9 a.m. on the 11th; and the third—the reoccupation of the Kranji-Jurong line—by 6 p.m. that day. The 12th Brigade, with the 2/29th Battalion under command, was to be on the right in the attack; 6th/15th Indian Brigade in the centre; and the 22nd Australian Brigade on the left. The 44th Indian Brigade and Tomforce were in reserve positions. The 2/15th Australian Field Regiment was to be under 12th Brigade command and the 5th Field Regiment was to support the 6th/15th Indian and 22nd Australian Brigades.

Obviously this plan required very speedy action, with little or no time for reconnaissance of the ground over which the attack was to be made, and for correlating action by artillery and other arms; the more so because communication was largely by liaison officers, and the infantry units concerned were scattered and largely disorganised. The 6th/15th Brigade was the most intact, with about 1,500 men. The Argylls, of the 12th Brigade, were less than 400 strong, including the administrative personnel, and the Hyderabads were melting away so rapidly that Brigadier

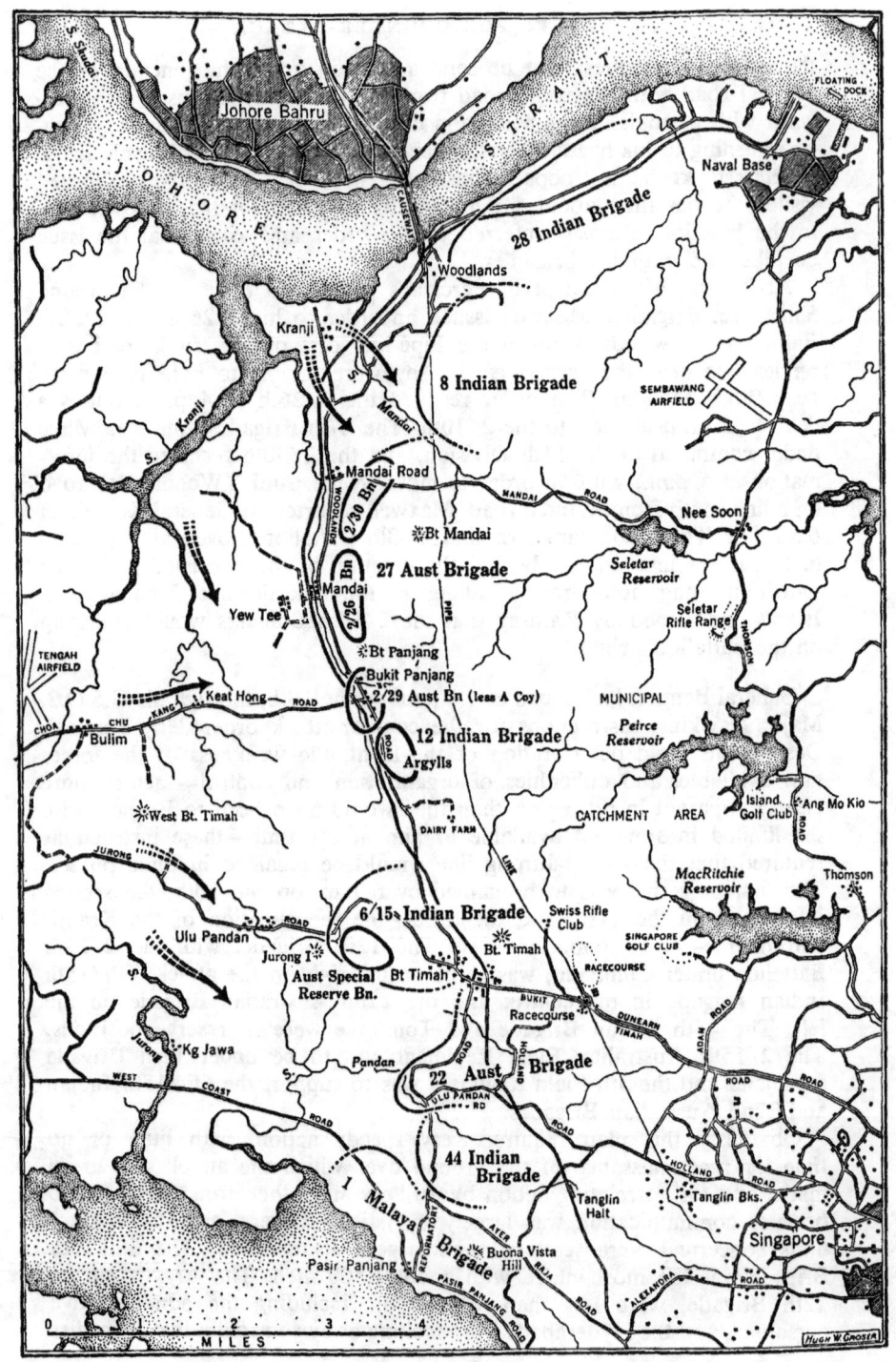

Western front, Singapore Island, 7 p.m. 10th February

Paris could place little reliance upon them. The 22nd Brigade now included "X" Battalion, of about 200 Australians mustered by Lieut-Colonel Boyes, but the total number of troops available to Taylor was still small.[10]

After making his reconnaissance for occupation of Reformatory road, Brigadier Taylor received the counter-attack orders from Western Area headquarters, and issued corresponding brigade orders. In the latter part of the afternoon he again visited General Bennett, who gave him a somewhat more advanced objective. Taylor referred to the weakness of the forces at his disposal, and the difficulty of occupying positions in darkness, but Bennett stood firm as to his requirements. The brigadier therefore directed "X" Battalion to occupy a height known as Jurong I on the right, and Merrett Force (Major Merrett) to occupy the left at Point 85, west of Sleepy Valley Estate. The depleted 2/18th Battalion, and two platoons of the 2/4th Machine Gun Battalion, he retained in reserve at Reformatory road. Colonel Coates advanced the 6th/15th Indian Brigade to the small extent necessary to occupy its first-stage position, with the Jats (who it was intended should link with the 12th Brigade) on the right and the Punjabis on the left, both north of the Jurong road; and the British Battalion astride the road. The Special Reserve Battalion (Major Saggers) remained to the left of the British Battalion.

Any similar moves by the 12th Brigade (Brigadier Paris) were forestalled by the enemy. Soon after nightfall on 10th February Captain Bowring (2/29th Battalion) was informed that all the brigade's forward troops had been withdrawn behind the 2/29th. He therefore moved his "C" and "D" Companies nearer the crossroads, leaving his "B" Company on high ground south-west of the junction, with orders to rejoin the others if it were too heavily attacked. Some of the 4/19th Hyderabads, however, were filtering through the Australians when, between 7 and 8 p.m., Japanese troops appeared, and heavy fighting ensued. Japanese tanks then joined in the attack, and although two or three were incapacitated the pressure, in the absence of anti-tank guns, became too great. Heading enemy troops estimated as at least two battalions strong, the tanks made their way along the trunk road towards Bukit Timah, and one of Bowring's companies, west of this road, became detached. The others moved south-east along the Pipe-line, and were subsequently allotted to other positions. Some linked with the battalion's "A" Company, and were reconstituted under Lieut-Colonel Pond. They included Captain Bowring with four of his officers and forty-five others who though out of contact with brigade headquarters had waited near Bukit Panjang until nearly midnight before withdrawing, and as will be seen were further occupied on the way back.

---

[10] The casualties in the 22nd Brigade over the period 8-10 February were 362 killed, presumed dead or died of wounds, and 175 wounded. The 2/29th Battalion, attached to the 22nd Brigade from the 9th, lost 14 killed and 26 wounded. As in Greece and Crete, where also large numbers of Australians were taken prisoner, the ratio of killed to wounded in 22nd Brigade seems disproportionately high. In Malaya the figures for killed are likely to be fairly precise, but the system of recording wounded has probably broken down. If the figure for killed is accepted and the number of wounded calculated at the normal ratio of 2½ to 1 the total losses in the 22nd Brigade seem likely to have been about 1,200 over the three-day period.

While the Australians were being attacked, the Argylls hurriedly improvised road-blocks of motor vehicles, and laid some anti-tank mines. About 10.30 p.m., when the leading Japanese tanks reached this point, a lone Argyll armoured car went into action against them, and was quickly knocked out. A large force of Japanese tanks and infantry followed, and although delayed at the road-blocks, the tanks pushed them aside and reached the outskirts of Bukit Timah village before they halted. The road in the Argylls' area "was solid with tanks and infantry for the rest of the night",[1] and from positions in rubber east of the road the battalion heard someone shouting in English and Hindustani "Stop fighting. The war is over. All British and Indians are to rally on the road." Stewart planned that his men should lie low until daylight, and then harry the enemy flank; but in the small hours of 11th February a force of Japanese moved up a track to within a few yards of battalion headquarters. Rather than engage in a confused struggle in the darkness, Stewart thereupon decided, with Paris' agreement, to withdraw his men to the near-by Singapore Dairy Farm, which might serve as a base for further endeavour. His forward companies, however, were attacked and dispersed. Some of the battalion became engaged in near-by areas; others withdrew to the Tyersall Palace area.

Major Fraser, making a liaison trip from Western Area headquarters to the 12th Brigade after 2 a.m. on 11th February, came upon two of the brigade's staff officers who were seeking to discover the whereabouts of its battalions. With their concurrence Fraser decided to establish a road-block about 300 yards south of Bukit Timah village, and employed three Australian tractors and men of the 2/4th Australian Anti-Tank Regiment for the purpose. The block had no sooner been constructed than Japanese mortar fire began to fall just to the south of it. The staff officers having meanwhile withdrawn Fraser became senior officer on the spot. He organised gunners of the regiment to cover the block and form a local perimeter, then moved back about 300 yards towards two troops of British howitzers. Coming under fire from Japanese patrols at the side of the road he and his batman disposed of a machine-gun post with grenades. When he got to the howitzers he found that their crews had no orders and did not know what was happening, so he ordered them to fire over open sights at any tank which approached, then move back and be prepared to support a counter-attack on the village which he knew General Bennett intended. Fraser then went to the junction of Bukit Timah and Holland roads, which he reached about 6.20 a.m., to organise defence around that point.

Having displaced 12th Brigade and gained entrance by midnight on 10th-11th February to Bukit Timah, the enemy was able to seal off the eastern end of Jurong road, and thus sever the line of communication with 6th/15th Indian Brigade and the Australian units also in forward positions for the counter-attack towards the Kranji-Jurong line ordered by Percival.

---

[1] Stewart, *History of the Argyll and Sutherland Highlanders 2nd Battalion*, p. 110.

Japanese fighting patrols pushed southward into the Sleepy Valley area at the rear of Merrett Force.

Unaware of these happenings, the men of "X" Battalion had nevertheless received with concern the unexpected order to advance into an area which none of them knew, and which soon would be cloaked in darkness. They were tired from their many and varied individual experiences since the Japanese landings. Now, as a scratch force, they were equipped with rifles, fifteen sub-machine-guns, eight light machine-guns, five 2-inch mortars, and two 3-inch mortars. Some of the men were armed with only hand grenades, and others carried only ammunition. Machine-gun carrier vehicles were to join the battalion next day. Lieut-Colonel Boyes' second-in-command was Major Bradley,[2] of the 2/19th Battalion, and his company commanders were Majors O'Brien (of the 2/18th) and Keegan (2/19th) and Captain Richardson (2/20th).

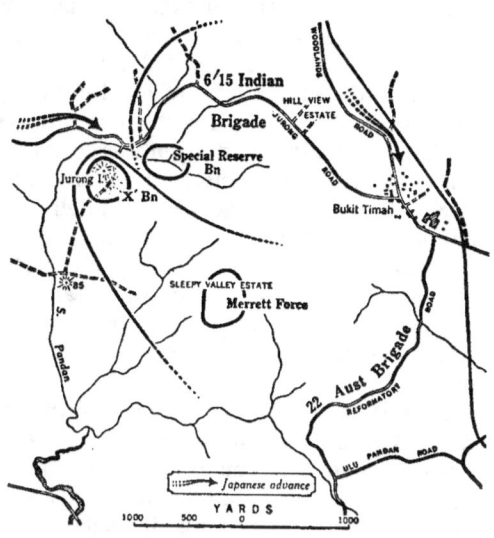

English troops through whom they passed in the Bukit Timah area, lurid with flames, reported that the enemy was just ahead. Snipers fired at them, and there were sounds of heavy fighting on the right. Boyes and Saggers, of the Special Reserve Battalion, met as "X" Battalion moved up. Taking a road bearing left from Jurong road, "X" Battalion found Jurong I trig. station, but not the Punjabis of the 6th/15th Indian Brigade who were to be on their right. Merrett Force, about 200 strong, which was to have been on their left, had followed a track from Reformatory road, but after forging a mile westward through bog and tangled growth, hanging on to each other's bayonet scabbards to maintain contact, had formed a small defensive perimeter in Sleepy Valley to await daylight before pushing on.

Of the three companies of "X" Battalion O'Brien's took up the right forward position and Richardson's the left, with Keegan's looking after the rear, close to battalion headquarters. Although the men were suspicious and uneasy in their surroundings, most of them had fallen asleep by 1 a.m. At 3 a.m. (11th February) the *18th Japanese Division,* advancing along the Jurong road, launched a sudden and well-concerted attack on the

---

[2] Maj B. H. J. Bradley, NX34993; 2/19 Bn. Electrical engineer; of Leichhardt, NSW; b. Grahamstown, NSW, 17 May 1903. Killed in action 11 Feb 1942.

battalion front and flanks. This was soon aided by flames from a petrol dump near battalion headquarters, which the Japanese ignited with hand grenades.

Overborne in the rush, sentries were unable to give adequate warning. Some of the Australians were bayoneted in their sleep; others, half awake, sought to defend themselves, but many succumbed. In the full glare of the fire, the headquarters were an especially easy target, and Boyes and Bradley were killed. Assailed by small arms fire, grenades and mortar bombs, and then involved in hand-to-hand fighting, the battalion was soon overwhelmed. Groups dispersed in various directions, some to be again attacked on their way. Keegan was severely wounded in one such encounter and it became impossible to remove him. A party led by Lieutenant Richardson[3] was challenged in English, and he went forward with his batman to investigate. Soon he shouted, "I'm O.K. but you clear out". Although, thanks to his warning, the party succeeded in doing so, neither Richardson nor his batman was seen again. O'Brien's company missed the main assault, and got away relatively intact, but the battalion's losses were so great that it ceased to exist, and its remnants were drafted to other units.

Sounds of this struggle, and of firing to the rear, indicated to Merrett that his force was threatened with isolation, and he ordered his men to move back to Reformatory road at dawn. As the move commenced, at 5.45 a.m., the force came under fire, and a series of encounters followed, in which the force became divided into groups fighting different actions. Only remnants of this unit also got back to the Australian lines, and were re-drafted.

Of the forces in forward positions for the counter-attack ordered by General Percival, there remained on 11th February after the dispersal of "X" Battalion and Merrett Force, only the 6th/15th Indian Brigade and the Australian Special Reserve Battalion, astride Jurong road forward of Bukit Timah village. The strength of the battalion, on the left of the brigade's British Battalion, was about 220. Its commander, Major Saggers, had reported to General Bennett at Western Area headquarters at 8 p.m. on the 10th, and been ordered to remain in position. From 1 a.m. on the 11th the battalion had heard firing at its rear and on both flanks. At 3 a.m. the men could see the blaze which occurred when "X" Battalion was attacked, but did not realise its significance. Finding all communication to his rear severed, Colonel Coates decided at 5.30 a.m. to cancel the counter-attack his brigade was to have made at dawn.

His orders failed to reach the Jats, who went forward on their original instructions and became isolated.[4] The British Battalion and Saggers' men withdrew before dawn to a better defensive position about 400 yards to

---

[3] Lt W. J. Richardson, NX35011; 2/20 Bn. Student; of Gordon, NSW; b. Meadowbank, NSW, 27 Jun 1919. Missing presumed died 11 Feb 1942.

[4] The battalion remained in the locality, unable to make its way back, until the fall of Singapore, then it broke up. Its commander, Lieut-Colonel Cumming, and some of his British and Indian officers eventually made their way to Sumatra, and were transported to India.

their rear. As dawn broke the Australians could see Japanese troops silhouetted against the sky on a hill they had just left, and sharp exchanges of fire soon began.

The Japs pushed up to our line firing around and dodging behind trees, crawling along drains and using every fold in the ground (Saggers wrote later). Many had cut a bush and used this to push in front of themselves as they crawled forward, while others smeared mud and clay over their faces and clothing.

Brigade headquarters was attacked from Bukit Timah village, and Coates moved forward to the British Battalion's headquarters, where in the midst of increasingly hot fighting he ordered a withdrawal across country to Reformatory road, in view of the obvious prospect that the brigade would become isolated if it tried to remain where it was, and annihilated if it attempted to pass through the village. By the time the move was under way the forward troops had held the enemy for nearly three hours, despite increasingly fierce small arms and mortar fire, and the danger that they might find themselves stranded by the tide of invasion. To assist other units to get away, one company of the British Battalion and one company ("E") led by Lieutenant Warhurst[5] of the Special Reserve Battalion joined just before 9 a.m. in a bayonet attack which quickly lessened the enemy pressure. The brigade then withdrew in three columns, British, Australian, and Indian. They had gone about a mile through the heavy scrub in the area when they came into an open saucer-shaped depression and were caught in a storm of rifle, light automatic and mortar fire from huts in front of them, and on both flanks. "Almost instantly the columns became intermingled," wrote Saggers later, "and all control appeared lost. The more numerous Indians . . . rushed across from their flank and intermingled with our troops . . . many held up their rifles, butts uppermost, as a sign of surrender, and one produced a white flag which he held up." Tommy-gun fire was pumped into the huts, but many men fell before the remnants of the columns escaped from the ambush.[6] Even when they reached Reformatory road they were machine-gunned as they crossed it. East of the railway line, where the force was temporarily halted during a search for a headquarters from which instructions could

---

[5] Lt V. I. Warhurst, NX70433. 2/4 MG Bn; Special Reserve Bn. Regular soldier; of Glenunga, SA; b. Hyde Park, SA, 22 Jan 1918. Killed in action 11 Feb 1942.

[6] Recounting further incidents of the ambush, Saggers wrote: "One Indian officer, singlehanded, charged the spot in the hedge from which the fire of the Jap light automatic appeared to be coming, but the Japs got him when he was 40 yards away. . . . Lieutenant Jimmy [J. J.] Till's last known action was to rush a Jap L.A. section and shoot its entire crew of six with his Bren gun. He had been wounded in the arm just prior to this." In the confusion, many men went off the course of the withdrawal movement, and found themselves among the advancing enemy. Lieutenant D. V. Mentiplay "was hiding in scrub with the Japs all around him and he saw a murderous Jap bayoneting our wounded. This so enraged Vic that he charged this Jap with his bayonet. The Jap, who was on slightly higher ground, met the attack, and Vic's rush carried him on to the point of the Jap's bayonet, which entered his throat under the chin and came out the back of his neck. The bayonet missed the jugular vein by a fraction of an inch . . . he threw himself backwards off the bayonet and fell on the flat of his back. Pulling his revolver from his waistbelt he shot the Jap and then seeing red he rushed at the other Japs in the vicinity and shot another five, then threw his empty revolver at a machine-gun crew. Fortunately for Vic they thought he threw a grenade and ran for their lives . . . he threw himself into a native duck pond and hid himself partially under an overhanging shrub. . . . By shamming dead and waiting until the tide of battle had passed over the area he moved to a native hut, where he found a badly wounded British officer who asked Vic to shoot him. This of course he refused to do, and donning native clothes he cautiously made his way back to our lines which he reached at dusk and promptly collapsed. The British officer had a slightly wounded companion with him and they would not hear of Vic remaining with them."

be obtained, Saggers could muster only eighty of his men, and there remained only about 400 of the Punjabis and the British Battalion. Neither the 12th nor the 6th/15th Indian Brigades, brought from reserve to help Bennett check the enemy, now remained effective, and Brigadier Taylor's slender force on the line of Reformatory road stood directly in the path of the enemy advance on Singapore.

As survivors and stragglers drifted in during the small hours of 11th February to the Reformatory road area, and sounds of battle to the north and north-west were heard, Taylor realised that the situation in his sector was rapidly becoming critical. Moving south from Bukit Timah, Japanese attacked his headquarters in Wai Soon Gardens at 5 a.m., but were held off while dawn approached. To the right, on a rise overlooking Reformatory road, was Varley's 2/18th Battalion, which had been transferred to this position from the Bukit Panjang area. It was about to move to ground offering a better field of fire, and to connect with brigade headquarters, when it also was attacked, but the move went on. As the Japanese increased their pressure on brigade headquarters, staff and attached officers, signallers, machine-gunners and infantry counter-attacked across Reformatory road, driving the enemy back from a near-by ridge. Beale, the brigade major, and Lieutenant Barnes,[7] commander of the brigade's defence platoon, were wounded leading bayonet charges. The Intelligence officer, Lieutenant Hutton,[8] was killed as he assailed a Japanese machine-gun crew with hand grenades. Lance-Corporal Hook[9] and Corporal Bingham were both severely wounded while leading a group of signallers against another machine-gun post. The Japanese were checked also when Lieutenant Iven Mackay,[1] Varley's carrier officer, with three carriers, charged up Reformatory road to Bukit Timah road, thence south to Holland road, and back to battalion headquarters. Using machine-guns and hand grenades, he and his men dealt out death and confusion. Enemy accounts indicate that having reached the objectives they had been given, and as delay had occurred in transporting artillery and ammunition to the island, the two Japanese divisions (*5th* and *18th*) paused at this stage. The vigour of their attacks had suggested, however, that they would have pressed on had the resistance been less determined.

In the early hours of 11th February General Bennett received news of the Japanese having reached Bukit Timah village. He thereupon ordered Tomforce to come up at once to re-possess this village and then Bukit Panjang village. Lieut-Colonel Thomas ordered the force to carry out a sweeping movement to 2,000 yards on each side of the road for these purposes—a difficult task particularly because of the steep terrain on the right. The Reconnaissance Battalion was to advance astride the trunk

---

[7] Lt W. G. Barnes, NX52625; 2/18 Bn. Wool student; of Strathfield, NSW; b. Strathfield, 24 Jul 1919.

[8] Lt K. W. Hutton, NX35003; 2/20 Bn. Audit clerk; of Roseville, NSW; b. Roseville, 4 Dec 1919. Killed in action 11 Feb 1942.

[9] L-Cpl R. L. Hook, VX27656; 8 Div Sigs. Accountant; of Donald, Vic; b. Donald, Vic, 2 Sep 1916. Died of wounds 18 Feb 1942.

[1] Lt I. J. Mackay, NX34743; 2/18 Bn. Clerk; of Sydney; b. Sydney, 2 Sep 1920. (Son of Lt-Gen Sir Iven Mackay.)

road, with the 4/Norfolks on the right of the road, and the Sherwood Foresters on the left. Still at the junction of Bukit Timah and Holland roads, where he had been organising resistance by such men as were available, Major Fraser met the commander of the Reconnaissance Battalion at 6.30 a.m., outlined the local situation to him, and discussed plans for the attack. In response to urgent requests from the anti-tank gunners in the perimeter position covering the road-block near Bukit Timah village, he arranged for a detachment to go to their assistance. He was still engaged in furthering the movement of the battalion when he met Lieut-Colonel Pond with part of the 2/29th Battalion, and informed him that he was under Tomforce command. When Thomas arrived Fraser informed him of the action he had taken; then he returned to Bennett's headquarters and reported on the situation in the area from which he had come. It was decided to move Western Area headquarters back to Tanglin Barracks.

Meanwhile Captain Bowring and the portion of the 2/29th Battalion which had withdrawn with him from Bukit Panjang had taken up a position on the right of the trunk road behind Bukit Timah village, guarding guns of the 2/15th Australian Field Regiment. The guns were withdrawn about 6 a.m., but as the infantrymen were experiencing only occasional sniping from the enemy they remained in position. They came under fire from the Reconnaissance Battalion about 8 a.m., however, and when contact was established Bowring was taken to Thomas. Although the Australians had had practically no sleep for four nights, Thomas declined to relieve them, on the ground that their experience and knowledge of what was happening made them too valuable to be dispensed with at that stage.

Dissatisfied with the progress being made by Tomforce Bennett later instructed Fraser to return to the force with a message urging that it should press on with more vigour. As he was about to leave Fraser was informed that Major Dawkins would be sent in his stead, allowing him to gain some rest after his activities during the night. Dawkins was killed on his way forward, but the message was delivered by Bennett's aide, Lieutenant Gordon Walker.[2] The Reconnaissance Battalion encountered strong resistance near Bukit Timah railway station, adjacent to the junction of the Reformatory and Bukit Timah roads.[3] The Foresters, to whom Pond with his part of the 2/29th Battalion gave left flank and rear protection, also came under fire near by, but got to within 400 yards of the village. At 10.30 a.m., however, they were forced back some distance and Pond and his men found themselves pinned down a little east of the station. The Norfolks swung over to the Pipe-line and gained heights overlooking the village from the north-east, in the vicinity of the Bukit Timah Rifle Range, but were held there by Japanese who had penetrated the area.

---

[2] Maj G. H. Walker, NX12593. HQ 8 Div; HQ III Corps. Pastoralist; of Cootamundra, NSW; b. Grove Park, Kent, England, 16 Sep 1911.

[3] Tomforce records state that when Colonel Thomas learned that the enemy had captured Bukit Timah village he disposed the Reconnaissance Battalion astride the road in support of the road-block.

As it transpired, the Japanese *18th Division* was holding the Bukit Timah area, and the *5th Division* was on commanding heights east of the trunk road in this locality, each division with two regiments forward. Thus, although heavy fighting occurred, Thomas found it necessary to withdraw his force during the afternoon to positions covering the Racecourse and Racecourse village. Pond received no orders and he and his men remained in position for some hours. They had been joined about midday by Bowring's force which had been eventually relieved by the Reconnaissance Battalion to enable it to do so. As enemy troops had been seen by-passing them, Pond withdrew his force after dark, and in the course of skirmishes it became split into groups. With remnants of his headquarters company, Pond withdrew last, and reached General Bennett's headquarters at dawn next day.

General Percival had woken at 6 a.m. on 11th February at his headquarters in Sime road to the sound of machine-gun fire which seemed to be about a mile away. He decided therefore to move to Fort Canning, and did so just before the main reserve petrol depot east of the Racecourse caught fire and added its smoke to the depressing pall from other such conflagrations. He then went up Bukit Timah road to see for himself how Tomforce was getting on.

It was a strange sensation (he wrote later). This great road, usually so full of traffic, was almost deserted. Japanese aircraft were floating about, unopposed except for our anti-aircraft fire, looking for targets. One felt terribly naked driving up that wide road in a lone motor car. Why, I asked myself, does Britain, our improvident Britain, with all her great resources, allow her sons to fight without any air support?[4]

This was a cry which had been in the hearts of his men for the past two months, as they suffered the miseries of their long withdrawal with little or no answer to the onslaughts of Japanese airmen, and under constant threat of seaborne attack to the flanks and rear. It had deeply concerned the Australian Government, seeking to gain the air reinforcements which, but for the demands of another war on the other side of the world, might have provided the answer.

Concerned at a gap west of MacRitchie Reservoir in the forces defending the near approaches to Singapore, Percival sent a unit composed of men from reinforcement camps to the eastern end of the Golf Course. He placed the 2/Gordons from Changi under Bennett's orders, and made General Heath responsible for the whole of the area east of the Racecourse. With this responsibility on his shoulders, Heath considered the possibility that the enemy might thrust towards the reservoirs from the north, where the *Guards Division* had gained a footing, and between them from the Bukit Timah area, now held by the enemy. He therefore ordered another formation of brigade strength, commanded by Brigadier Massy-Beresford,[5] to deny the enemy approach to Thomson village, east of MacRitchie Reser-

---
[4] Percival, *The War in Malaya*, p. 279.
[5] Brig T. H. Massy-Beresford, DSO, MC. Comd 55 Bde. Regular soldier; b. 10 Apr 1896.

voir, and the Woodleigh pumping station, farther east. This formation, known as Massy Force, which was also to form a link between Tomforce and the reservoirs, took up positions during the afternoon at the eastern end of MacRitchie Reservoir. It comprised the 1/Cambridgeshire, from the 55th Brigade, the 4/Suffolk (54th Brigade), the 5/11th Sikh (from Southern Area), a detachment of the 3rd Cavalry, one field battery, and eighteen obsolescent light tanks recently landed, and manned by a detachment of the 100th Light Tank Squadron.

Mr Bowden, Australian Government representative in Singapore, had cabled to Australia on 9th February: "It appears significant that February 11th is greatest Japanese patriotic festival of the year, namely, anniversary of accession of their first Emperor, and it can be taken as certain that they will make a supreme effort to achieve capture of Singapore on this date."[6] General Yamashita, commander of the Japanese forces in Malaya, chose the morning of the 11th to send aircraft with twenty-nine wooden boxes, each about eighteen inches long, to be dropped among the forces now seeking desperately to retain their last foothold on the illusory stronghold of British interests in the Far East. They contained a note addressed "To the High Command of the British Army, Singapore". It read:

Your Excellency,
I, the High Command of the Nippon Army based on the spirit of Japanese chivalry, have the honour of presenting this note to Your Excellency advising you to surrender the whole force in Malaya.

My sincere respect is due to your army which true to the traditional spirit of Great Britain, is bravely defending Singapore which now stands isolated and unaided. Many fierce and gallant fights have been fought by your gallant men and officers, to the honour of British warriorship. But the developments of the general war situation has already sealed the fate of Singapore, and the continuation of futile resistance would only serve to inflict direct harm and injuries to thousands of non-combatants living in the city, throwing them into further miseries and horrors of war, but also would not add anything to the honour of your army.

I expect that Your Excellency accepting my advice will give up this meaningless and desperate resistance and promptly order the entire front to cease hostilities and will despatch at the same time your parliamentaire according to the procedure shown at the end of this note. If on the contrary, Your Excellency should neglect my advice and the present resistance be continued, I shall be obliged, though reluctantly from humanitarian considerations to order my army to make annihilating attacks on Singapore.

In closing this note of advice, I pay again my sincere respects to Your Excellency.
(signed) Tomoyuki Yamashita.
1. The Parliamentaire should proceed to the Bukit Timah Road.
2. The Parliamentaire should bear a large white flag and the Union Jack.

Captain Adrian Curlewis,[7] one of Bennett's staff officers, was given the note from a box which fell in the Australian lines. Covered in grime

---

[6] On 11th February the Japanese celebrated the anniversary of the founding of the Japanese Empire. Stretching the point for the occasion Yamashita issued a communiqué which began: "The Imperial Army Forces, who had been smashing the stubborn resistance of the enemy since early in the morning of the 11th, entered the city of Singapore at 0800 hours and routed the British forces everywhere." The communiqué went on to specify, however, that the forces had entered "one corner of the north-west sector" of the city.—"Malaya Campaign" (ATIS translation of captured Japanese publication).

[7] Capt A. H. Curlewis, NX70316; HQ 8 Aust Div. Barrister; of Mosman, NSW; b. Mosman, 13 Jan 1901. (District Court Judge NSW since 1948.)

from the smoke-laden air, he took it to Fort Canning, and handed it to Colonel Thyer, who was there.

Yamashita's statement of the plight of Singapore was all too true. On the face of it, the note was a courteous and considerate offer to cease hostilities. Perhaps certain terms might even be obtained to modify the bitterness and humiliation of surrender. This, in any event, could hardly be long postponed, as the events of the day were making increasingly evident. With the loss of all the food and petrol dumps in the Bukit Timah area, only about fourteen days' military food supplies remained under Percival's control; the remaining petrol stocks were running perilously low; Singapore's water supply was endangered as the enemy approached the reservoirs and the pumping station, and water gushed from mains broken by the Japanese bombardment. Incendiary bombs dropped on the crowded and flimsy shops and tenements which occupied much of the city area might start a holocaust which nothing could arrest. What civilians and troops might suffer in this event, or if the Japanese forces in the heat of battle were to break into Singapore, was a horrifying speculation.

But General Percival was under orders from General Wavell, who, in keeping with Mr Churchill's instructions, had decreed that "there must be no thought of sparing the troops or the civil population". Whatever Percival's intellect or feelings might have dictated, his orders were clear. Percival cabled to Wavell, telling him of the Japanese demand for surrender. "Have no means of dropping message," Percival added, perhaps unconscious of the irony of these words, "so do NOT propose to make reply, which would of course in any case be negative."

As yet, the Japanese *Guards Division* on the 11th Indian Division's left flank was playing a minor role, but General Heath's anxieties grew when he learned early on 11th February that the 27th Australian Brigade had been ordered to recapture Bukit Panjang.[8] As this would remove the brigade from use against the *Guards*, a proposed attack by the Baluchis to regain ground on the 2/30th Battalion's right flank was cancelled, and the battalion was ordered to a defensive position astride the Mandai road about two miles back from Mandai Road village. Maxwell had moved his headquarters to a point near Nee Soon, some 8,000 yards east of Mandai Road village. Orders for Colonels Ramsay and Oakes, timed 8.44 a.m., were conveyed by Captain Anderssen[9] of the 2/26th Battalion, who had reported at brigade headquarters on his way from hospital to rejoin the battalion. The move on Bukit Panjang was to commence at 11 a.m., which was the earliest Maxwell thought it possible. Travelling at first on a motor cycle, and then on foot, Anderssen did not reach Ramsay's headquarters

---

[8] No conclusive evidence has come to light as to who issued the order, although an attack on the enemy rear supplementary to a frontal attack by Tomforce would have been a logical move to retrieve the situation in this most critical area. According to General Key (11th Division) and his senior staff officers Brigadier Maxwell told them at the time that it came from General Bennett, but General Bennett has denied having given it. Brigadier Maxwell has recorded emphatically that it came from General Percival. It would have been contrary to military practice for either Percival or Bennett to issue it direct to the 27th Brigade while the brigade was under Key's command. However, in the confusion of the time the chain of command might have become somewhat dislocated.

[9] Capt L. N. Anderssen, QX6456; 2/26 Bn. Sales manager; of Ingham, Qld; b. Ingham, 25 Jul 1913.

until about 10.30 a.m. When he got to the headquarters Oakes had been occupying, he found that all but "C" Company of the 2/26th Battalion had moved, and as Oakes was not there he was unable to give him the order. As it happened, a message had reached Ramsay meanwhile by runner from Oakes, indicating that he was moving his men down the Pipe-line towards the Racecourse, but Ramsay could of course assume that this movement would be cancelled by the counter-attack order.

Clashes by the forward troops of the 2/30th Battalion with Japanese troops during the morning had made it evident that they were present in strength, but the Australians were in the disconcerting circumstance of having contact neither with the Baluchis nor with the 2/26th Battalion to the left. By the time Colonel Ramsay received the order to move on Bukit Panjang, extensive fighting was in progress between his men and the enemy, but most of the battalion broke contact without serious difficulty. Captain Booth's[1] company in its rear position guarding approaches to the Pipe-line at Mandai road had found early in the morning that the Japanese had penetrated between it and the main battalion positions. The company was ordered to hold on as long as possible to allow the other companies to get clear, and fought hard to do so. Eventually, because of enemy infiltration on its right flank and at its rear its commander ordered withdrawal. This was in progress when a two-pronged attack was made on the right and left of its position.

Men, machine-guns and mortars were rushed back, and two of the forward machine-guns were fired at almost point-blank range as Japanese swarmed over a ridge in front of them. Mortars, too, were used to marked effect, but after suffering considerable losses the enemy deployed along the company's flanks under cover of high ground. The Australian company therefore continued to withdraw, with its forward troops fighting from tree to tree to give cover to the rear. Having used its last round, the mortar section loaded its weapons on a truck, but the Japanese put it out of action before it could be driven away. The machine-gunners also lost their vehicle, in similar circumstances. Following the route of the Pipe-line, the Australians were pressed with more persistence than the enemy had shown on the mainland. Particularly as wounded men had to be carried by hand, a section commanded by Lieutenant Hendy was detailed to act as a rearguard. It fought gamely, though the number of Japanese swarming over the recently contested ground and along the line of withdrawal showed that a substantial force was being employed to force the pace. It was only when the company reached the battalion rendezvous a mile short of Bukit Panjang that contact was broken, and it rejoined the main body.

Colonel Ramsay, unable to locate or obtain further news of the 2/26th Battalion, out of touch with his brigade headquarters, unaware of the strength of the enemy in the Bukit Panjang area, and with Japanese forces to his rear, concluded that he would be unable to justify throwing his battalion alone into a counter-attack in such circumstances. He therefore

---
[1] Capt E. H. Booth, NX70486; 2/30 Bn. Master printer; of Sydney; b. Burwood, NSW, 3 Oct 1911.

decided to lead his men eastward through the municipal catchment area to Upper Thomson road, by a track parallel to Peirce Reservoir where he hoped to regain touch with brigade headquarters. With a heavy overlacing of jungle growth, the track was, in the words of the Headquarters Company commander, Captain Howells, "as cool and cloistered as a cathedral aisle". During mid-afternoon the leading troops came upon Captain Matthews,[2] the brigade signals officer, who with a party of his men was laying a cable to the now-abandoned attack rendezvous. Ramsay was thus able to speak to Maxwell, telling him of the move, and arranging transport for his wounded. He received orders to continue his move to Thomson road. Near nightfall about seventy men of the 2/26th Battalion led by Captain Beirne emerged on the track. They related that the battalion had been ambushed while moving along the Pipe-line, south-eastward from the Bukit Panjang area. With this addition the column eventually reached its objective and was placed between the Peirce Reservoir and the Seletar Rifle Range to block a possible Japanese attempt to cut the road south of Nee Soon, perhaps by way of the track the column had used.

Oakes had become aware of the break-through towards Bukit Timah when about 10 p.m. on 10th February the 2/26th Battalion regimental aid post truck, well to the rear of his headquarters and near a company of the 2/29th Battalion, was captured. His Intelligence officer, Lieutenant Moore,[3] whom, in the absence of contact, he had sent during the morning to brigade headquarters, returned in the afternoon with Maxwell's order for the battalion to rendezvous at the Racecourse in the event of further withdrawal. Early next day a report reached Oakes that large bodies of Japanese, supported by tanks, were moving along the Choa Chu Kang road within a few hundred yards of his headquarters, making for Singapore. Japanese planes appeared to be concentrating on the main road south of the battalion area. The battalion had almost run out of rations at the time. Deciding that it was too widely dispersed to mount an attack, Oakes ordered his men to withdraw south-east to the rendezvous, each company to move as a separate fighting force if the column was broken. The move began at 10.15 a.m. on 11th February—a quarter of an hour before the time specified in Brigadier Maxwell's order (of which Oakes was unaware) for the counter-attack on Bukit Panjang.

After a two-hour march "D" Company (Captain Tracey) which was in the lead, reached ground overlooking the Singapore Dairy Farm, a former site of the brigade headquarters, and the men were astonished to see what were estimated at 2,000 troops sitting in the open. Opinion was divided as to whether they were Japanese or Indians, but it was decided, especially as the battalion could not be assembled for attack without being observed, to continue the withdrawal. The company thereupon swung

---

[2] Capt L. C. Matthews, GC, MC, VX24597; 8 Div Sigs. Salesman; of Kensington and Norwood, SA; b. Stepney, SA, 15 Aug 1912. Executed by Japanese 2 Mar 1944.

[3] Lt C. H. Moore, QX6466; 2/26 Bn. Shop assistant; of Gladstone, Qld; b. Mt Morgan, Qld, 30 Jan 1917.

east into jungle growth, and followed a compass course until it came to a dirt road north of the Swiss Rifle Club, where a sharp clash occurred with Japanese troops. In this, Private Hayman[4] distinguished himself by getting wounded men away on two occasions and returning to the fight. After fending off the enemy attack, the company acted as a rearguard and with the rest of the battalion, less "A" and "C" Companies, reached the Singapore Golf Course.

Meanwhile "A" Company (Captain Beirne) to the rear, with a "B" Company platoon replacing one of its own, had encountered other Japanese. Calling out that the company was surrounded, a Japanese spokesman promised that if it surrendered the troops would be back in Australia in a fortnight. Private Lloyd[5] was captured and sent back with a similar message. Someone else, who claimed to be an Argyll, shouted that he was a prisoner and that the enemy was a thousand strong. Machine-guns were seen behind buttresses of the Pipe-line. However, Beirne decided that the company should fight its way out, and after a short but furious encounter it succeeded in joining the 2/30th Battalion on the track to Nee Soon. A platoon which was cut off during this move rejoined the 2/26th Battalion, at the Golf Course.

Last in the column, "C" Company was met by Captain Anderssen at 11.45 a.m. and given a copy of the order for recapture of Bukit Panjang. However, as it was obvious that the order could not now be put into effect, and as it indicated that the Japanese had got through to the Racecourse and Sime road, the company set out to follow the Pipe-line to the Dairy Farm and then to move east on a compass bearing. It eventually found its way to the General Base Depot at the Island Golf Club which was in charge of Lieut-Colonel Jeater.

Oakes decided that his group should move from the Singapore Golf Course to Bukit Brown, south-east of it, for the night and Captains Tracey and Roberts[6] were sent in search of brigade or other headquarters where orders could be obtained. Tracey eventually got through by telephone from Fort Canning to General Bennett's headquarters and received orders for the battalion to move at first light from Bukit Brown to Tyersall Park, which surrounded the Singapore residence of the Sultan of Johore. There it met remnants of the 12th Indian Brigade.

Taking into consideration the circumstances on his left flank, General Heath had decided meanwhile to abandon the Naval Base area. The 53rd Brigade readjusted its line to face north-west, covering the Sembawang airfield, and the 8th Brigade continued the line southward, across the east-west road to Nee Soon. The 28th Brigade went into reserve beside Thomson road, south of Nee Soon. What remained of the 18th Division

---

[4] Pte V. J. Hayman, QX13178; 2/26 Bn. Station hand; of Wowan, Qld; b. Mt Morgan, Qld, 26 Oct 1902.

[5] Pte S. K. Lloyd, QX10800; 2/26 Bn. Timber salesman; of Pillar Valley, NSW; b. Lucabia, NSW, 3 Sep 1916.

[6] Capt S. S. Roberts, QX19066; 2/26 Bn. Garage owner; of Toowoomba, Qld; b. Toowoomba, 15 Jul 1907.

after supplying troops to Tomforce and Massy Force remained where it was. During the afternoon of the 11th General Percival, with Heath's concurrence, ordered Massy Force to occupy Bukit Tinggi, west of the MacRitchie Reservoir, and establish contact with Tomforce; but enemy troops got there first. Massy Force thereupon went into a position from the reservoir to the northern end of the Racecourse, where the contact with Tomforce on its left was made.

Steps had been taken before 9 a.m. on 11th February to consolidate the 22nd Brigade position. Brigadier Taylor decided to move his headquarters back along Ulu Pandan road to its junction with Holland road, where line communications had been laid on. Part of the 2/18th Battalion lost contact during its move under heavy fire to new positions, but with such other fragmentary forces as became available, the front was held. The latter included about ninety men under Major Robertson of the 2/20th Battalion, who had been got together as a nucleus of a "Y" Battalion which it was intended to form largely of reinforcement troops. Heavy fighting and casualties followed, with Captain Chisholm from time to time leading parties of men, including British and Indian troops, to wherever they were most needed, and Mackay's men again giving valiant aid. Heavy artillery fire became available early in the day, and was effectively used among Japanese troops massing for attack. Bennett's headquarters at Holland road closed after mortar bombs had fallen in its grounds, and was reopened at Tanglin Barracks, south of Tyersall Park and Holland road.

Early in the afternoon Brigadier Taylor, with General Bennett's concurrence, shortened his front, and swung it so that it would be in line on its right flank with Tomforce. Its main position would face west in an arc from the southern junction of the railway and Holland road to near the junction of Ulu Pandan and Reformatory roads, with its apex at Ulu Pandan IV. Bennett ordered as many men as could be made available from the 2/4th Machine Gun Battalion to be sent to fight as infantry on this front, and arranged with Percival that the 2/Gordon Highlanders should be ordered up to fill a gap between the brigade and Tomforce on its right. On the left, the 44th Indian Brigade continued the 22nd Brigade line southward to Ayer Raja road. From there to the coast at Pasir Panjang was occupied by the 1st Malaya Brigade, reinforced by the 5/Bedfordshire and Hertfordshire (less two companies) from the 18th Division, and a battalion formed from Royal Engineer and Indian Sapper and Miner units.

Taylor directed that a composite company of forty men of the 2/20th Battalion led by Captain Gaven,[7] which had reached him at noon, should be on his right flank (where they were joined by "D" Company of the 2/29th). The bulk of the 2/4th Machine Gun Battalion was to be in the centre, with Robertson's force and some of the machine-gunners on the

---

[7] Capt F. Gaven, NX34885; 2/20 Bn. Public servant; of Seaforth, NSW; b. Sydney, 26 Oct 1908.

left. The British Battalion and some other United Kingdom troops who had come under Taylor's command were to support the line, and the 2/18th Battalion was to go into reserve. The new line was manned, though with difficulty, under constant attack from land and air. Pressure had been particularly heavy in the northern part of the bulge in Reformatory road, and of 71 men led by Captain Griffin (2/18th Battalion) who had occupied a foremost feature in the area, only 22 came out of action. Private Beresford[8] acted as No. 1 of a light machine-gun crew while five successive No. 2's were wounded, and until the gun was destroyed by Japanese fire. Small groups of men arrived during the day to rejoin their units, whose strength therefore was constantly changing. In response to a request by Brigadier Ballentine, the British Battalion and some other troops who had become attached to it were placed under his command. Artillery support by both Australian regiments and the 5th Regiment, Royal Artillery, continued throughout the night of 11th-12th February, and appeared to be hampering further development of the enemy attack.[9] General Percival recognised that Brigadier Taylor's men had held their ground "most gallantly".[1] They had in fact been attacked by the *56th* and *114th Regiments* of the *18th Japanese Division* at heavy cost to the Japanese in casualties.

The Indian Base Hospital at Tyersall caught fire during the day. The huts of which it was comprised blazed fiercely, and despite gallant rescue work by Argylls and Gordons, most of the inmates perished. As another grim day ended, Percival was faced with the need for further revision of his plans. At midnight on 11th-12th February he gave Heath command of all troops to and including the trunk road[2] near Racecourse village, on his left. These included Tomforce, formerly under Bennett's command, which was now combined with Massy Force. The new boundary for Bennett's forces was from this point to Ulu Pandan road, and General Simmons was responsible for the rest of the front to the coast.

The tempo of battle increased sharply on 12th February. With half the island in their possession, the Japanese sought to enforce their demand for surrender. While Heath continued to realign his forces, the 2/10th Baluch held off Japanese tanks and troops attempting to reach Nee Soon. Massy Force was attacked and gave ground. At 8.30 a.m. enemy tanks dashed down Bukit Timah road as far as the Chinese High School before they were turned back by United Kingdom troops, and a patrol of the Australian 73rd Light Aid Detachment firing at the tanks with rifles—their only weapons. The patrol was from a modified infantry battalion formed

---

[8] Pte E. S. Beresford, MM, NX40461; 2/18 Bn. Station hand; of Werris Creek, NSW; b. Currabubula, NSW, 23 Aug 1920.

[9] Brigadier Taylor related that an officer of the 5th Field Regiment (Lieutenant Thompson) had arrived during the afternoon with two 4.5-inch howitzers, and continued: "I asked him who sent him up and he replied 'I thought somebody up here might be in need of help so I came'. This young officer was of great help and did excellent work."

[1] Percival, *The War in Malaya*, p. 279.

[2] Known as Bukit Timah road between Bukit Timah village and Singapore.

by Lieut-Colonel Kappe, commander of the Australian divisional signallers, of about 400 men who could be spared from signals and other duties. (Kappe named it "the Snake Gully Rifles".) The patrol was led by Captain Couch,[3] of the 2/20th Battalion. The thrust by the tanks caused confusion in Massy Force, and resistance had to be hastily reorganised. The force was withdrawn during the morning from the Racecourse area to the general line of Adam and Farrer roads, which meet

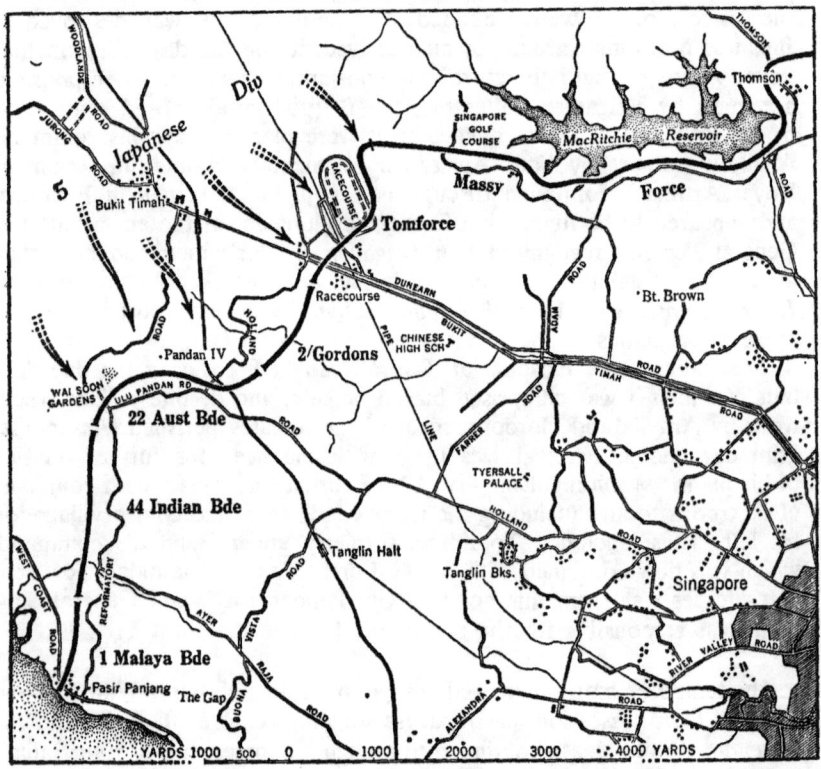

South-western front, early morning 12th February

Bukit Timah road about 3,000 yards south-east of Racecourse village. Couch's force of Australian signallers and others, stationed between Massy Force and the 22nd Brigade, resolutely checked Japanese attempting to penetrate its area.

Percival again drove forward to see for himself what was happening. This convinced him that there was a real danger that the Japanese would break through in the area. Reflecting that, as things were, there would then be little to stop the enemy from entering the city, he went to see Heath. They agreed that it would be foolish to keep troops guarding the

---

[3] Capt N. W. Couch, NX46360; 2/20 Bn. Storekeeper; of Kempsey, NSW; b. Kempsey, 10 Jul 1916.

northern and eastern shores of Heath's area while the city was thus endangered. Percival therefore decided to put into effect his plan to form a defensive line round Singapore, though now it would have to be smaller than the one he had previously planned. He therefore ordered Heath to withdraw the 11th Indian Division and the remainder of the 18th British Division to positions covering the Peirce and MacRitchie Reservoirs, and General Simmons to prepare to withdraw his troops from the Changi area and the beaches east of Kallang. These were major decisions, bearing also on the civil administration, so he then went to see the Governor. Sir Shenton Thomas, with characteristic phlegm, had remained at Government House despite repeated shellings. He reluctantly agreed to order destruction of Singapore's radio broadcasting station, and of portion of the stock of currency notes held by the Treasury.

The line to be occupied included the Kallang airfield and ran thence via the Woodleigh pumping station, a mile south-west of Paya Lebar village, to the east end of the MacRitchie reservoir; to Adam road, Farrer road, Tanglin Halt, The Gap (on Pasir Panjang ridge west of Buona Vista road), thence to the sea west of Buona Vista village. Sectors allotted were: Kallang airfield-Paya Lebar airstrip, 2nd Malaya Brigade; airstrip to Braddell road one mile west of Woodleigh, 11th Division; thence to astride Bukit Timah road, 18th Division; to Tanglin Halt, the forces under General Bennett's command (including 2/Gordons); Tanglin Halt to the sea, 44th Indian Brigade and 1st Malaya Brigade.

General Bennett, too, had been taking stock of the perilous situation. Lieut-Colonel Kent Hughes had urged that all Australian transport and troops, except the men in hospitals, be brought out of the city proper, and a plan had developed to create an A.I.F. perimeter in the area around Tanglin Barracks up to Buona Vista road, where the Australians would make their last stand together. Colonel Broadbent, Bennett's senior administrative officer, had set about the task of preparing for the move.

Meanwhile Brigadier Taylor, dazed with fatigue but unable to sleep, sent for Lieut-Colonel Varley, who had been with his 2/18th Battalion in reserve during the night, and asked him to take over, temporarily, command of the brigade. "I realised," Taylor recorded, "that I would have to get a few hours' rest in a quiet spot; my brain refused to work and I was afraid that if I carried on without rest the brigade would suffer." Having given the order, he collapsed and, with Captain Pickford,[4] his Army Service Corps officer, was taken to divisional headquarters. Pickford hurried in with the news, and Taylor, reviving, entered after him. After reporting to Bennett, Taylor returned to his brigade headquarters with some maps which were required. As he got back into his car, his acting brigade major, Captain Fairley,[5] took the responsibility of ordering the driver to take the brigadier to hospital, irrespective of what he said.

---

[4] Capt C. Pickford, ED, NX34653; 8 Div AASC. Accountant; of Earlwood, NSW; b. Sydney, 27 Jul 1909.

[5] Maj J. G. Fairley, NX34719; HQ 22 Bde. Assurance representative; of Sydney; b. Glasgow, Scotland, 5 Jul 1902.

Taylor, however, insisted on being driven back to Western Area headquarters again on the way.

The 22nd Brigade had spent a relatively quiet night, attributed largely to close and effective cooperation between British and Australian field artillery, and fire by fixed defences guns to the area of Bukit Timah village and of the main road north of it. Before noon on the 12th an armoured car detachment commanded by Corporal Brisby[6] encountered an enemy convoy a little south of the Ulu Pandan-Reformatory roads junction, which indicated a move past the brigade front to the southern flank. The detachment disabled thirteen trucks and one car, creating a temporary roadblock at this spot. Varley was informed during the morning that he had been promoted by Bennett to brigadier, and remained in command of the brigade. The number of Australian troops at his disposal was approximately 800, including 400 in the 2/4th Machine Gun Battalion. Valuable aid was being given by about 100 Sherwood Foresters.

The 27th Brigade was now out of action as such. In the withdrawal from the Northern Area ordered by General Percival, the 2/30th Battalion came temporarily under command of the 53rd Brigade (Brigadier Duke). Men of the 2/29th Battalion not posted on the 22nd Brigade front were being rested, refitted and reassembled by Lieut-Colonel Pond in the Tanglin area. The 2/26th, among spacious and beautiful homes in the Tyersall Park area, experienced a strange reaction to their struggles in plantations and jungle. Their respite was brief, for at midday they were sent under shelling and air attack to occupy a position left of Bukit Timah road and forward of Farrer road, on the right flank of Bennett's final perimeter. The move was made more difficult and hazardous by the activities of snipers, who seemed to be in every house and tree, while "hundreds of enemy planes were carrying out every kind of attack on Singapore city and troops. Five enemy raids were counted in twenty minutes."[7]

Bennett received news during the day that the last of the Australian nursing sisters and the matrons of the two Australian general hospitals had embarked for Australia. The 2/10th A.G.H., at Manor House and Oldham Hall, though under shell and mortar fire, was still behind the front line, but the 2/13th, at St Patrick's College beyond the Kallang airport, would be exposed by the withdrawal to the defensive line planned by Percival. Bennett decided that as the city was under such heavy assault from land and air it would be better to leave the inmates where they were. "I consider that the end is very near," he noted, "and that it is only a matter of days before the enemy will break through into the city."[8] That day Brigadier Callaghan, commander of the Australian artillery, returned to his headquarters from hospital, but Colonel McEachern remained in command of the artillery.

---

[6] Cpl H. H. Brisby, NX45700; 2/20 Bn. Farm labourer; of Waverley, NSW; b. Sydney, 15 May 1919.
[7] 2/26th Battalion war diary.
[8] Bennett, *Why Singapore Fell*, p. 184.

The Japanese *18th Division* persisted in attempts to thrust between Varley's and Ballentine's brigades near the Ulu Pandan-Reformatory roads junction. On Varley's right, penetration was occurring in the area between the Ulu Pandan-Holland roads junction and Racecourse village to the north, across the northern flank of the machine-gunners on Ulu Pandan IV. Evidently therefore an attempt was being made to envelop or by-pass the Australian forward positions. Machine-gun detachments sent to the railway bridge across Holland road halted a force approaching the 2/Gordons on the right flank. An armoured car detachment led by Stanwell,[9] of the 2/4th Machine Gun Battalion, engaged in a sharp fight, until the car was disabled, with enemy troops on Holland road just south of Racecourse village. The results obtained in these engagements by armoured cars led naturally to thought of what might have been achieved had the Australians been equipped with tanks.

Varley ordered up the 2/18th Battalion, now commanded by Major O'Brien, with Captain Okey as his second-in-command, to deal with the Japanese turning movement on his left. Late in the afternoon he ordered it to drive Japanese from a rise which they had captured from the Punjabis, south of Ulu Pandan road and east of Reformatory road. The brigade area, however, was constantly under bombardment and Japanese planes were circling like hawks, swooping from time to time to strike. The Japanese, in good cover, were covering their approaches with fire, and the positions occupied by the machine-gun battalion and Robertson's "Y" Battalion were swept by bullets and mortar bombs. Lieutenant Mackay brought forward a water truck, machine-guns, and three armoured cars manned by British troops. Captain Chisholm, in charge of a force allotted to the task, himself acted as forward observation officer for counter-artillery fire. O'Brien's men, numbering about sixty in the vicinity of the ridge, reached its forward slopes but as night fell they had not dislodged the enemy.

Japanese, thickly clustered on hills west of Reformatory road, also thrust strongly against the brigade's northern positions, with the result that they gained a height between the road and Ulu Pandan IV. Under pressure from both flanks, the Australians were gradually forced back. The commander of the 2/4th Machine Gun Battalion, Lieut-Colonel Anketell,[1] was mortally wounded, and his battalion, after mowing down successive waves of Japanese, became almost surrounded. Fifty of the 400 Australians were killed or wounded.

Thus when Varley reported to Bennett's headquarters the situation on his front, he was given permission to redispose his forces for the protection of the Holland and Buona Vista roads junction to his rear. The 2/18th Battalion had been reduced to 250 all ranks. The machine-gun battalion was able to disengage only after it had repulsed the enemy on

---

[9] Cpl O. M. Stanwell, WX7789; 2/4 MG Bn. Shop assistant; of Bayswater, WA; b. Moora, WA, 24 Jul 1905. Died while prisoner 12 Mar 1945.

[1] Lt-Col M. J. Anketell, WX3376. (1st AIF: Lt 44 Bn.) CO 2/4 MG Bn. Trustees officer; of Claremont, WA; b. Briagolong, Vic, 13 Oct 1890. Died of wounds 14 Feb 1942.

its front with bayonets. The 44th Indian Brigade withdrew to the area of the railway bridge over Buona Vista road, linking with the 5/Bedfordshire and Hertfordshire on its left. A partial withdrawal was made by the forces farther south. Although a hitch occurred in maintaining contact with the Gordons, they eventually moved back also. On their right in the new line were the 2/26th Battalion and Captain Couch's signals detachment.

In the northern area during the afternoon of 12th February the 2/10th Baluch, with artillery support, had frustrated a Japanese attempt to capture the road junction at Nee Soon. The 53rd Brigade, aided by the 2/30th Australian Battalion, gave cover to the withdrawal of the 8th and 28th Brigades to their sectors in the perimeter, and remained on the road immediately south of Nee Soon. The Australian battalion exploded an ammunition dump on the Seletar Rifle Range and then moved to the vicinity of the Island Golf Club and Ang Mo Kio village on upper Thomson road, east of the Peirce Reservoir. Ramsay's men slept briefly before dawn, in buildings formerly used as the Australian General Base Depot, and then went into new positions near by as reserve. Both the 18th Division and the troops in the Changi area and on the beaches east of Kallang were withdrawn without contact with the enemy.

Acute difficulties had been experienced by the ancillary arms of the Australian forces in playing their part while movement of the infantry was so rapid, and units became so fragmentary and dispersed. The signallers, who in the face of many difficulties had established a very thorough system of communication between commanders and their forces in the period before the Japanese landings, worked unceasingly to repair land lines damaged by incessant Japanese bombardment. They sought to reorganise their network as headquarters, from battalions to division, moved from place to place. The artillery were required constantly to seek out new gun positions, only to move again as the tide of battle ebbed. Curiously optimistic reports reached their headquarters after the counter-attack had been ordered on 10th February. These were to the effect that the 11th Indian Division had successfully attacked and was holding the line from the Causeway to Bukit Timah; that 600 Japanese aircraft had been destroyed on the ground; and that no further withdrawals were to be made. The artillery diarist recorded that these "induced intense optimism amongst most personnel, and the general feeling was that the British forces had 'turned the corner' and could now expect continued attacks rather than continued withdrawals". However, once artillery unit commanders reported the situation in their areas, this elation was short-lived. In the small hours of 11th February vehicles in the advanced artillery headquarters area adjacent to Holland road came under small arms fire, and in consequence the headquarters was withdrawn to Tanglin Barracks. At midday the 2/10th Field Regiment, which because of the movements of 27th Brigade was no longer required with the 11th Indian Division, was ordered to support the 22nd Australian and 44th Indian Brigade fronts. The fact that towards the close of the day strong artillery support was being given in the Reformatory road area was to the credit of artillery and signals alike.

The few fighters remaining on Singapore Island, replaced from Sumatra as this became necessary to maintain their number, had been almost continuously airborne during daylight from the beginning of the month until they were withdrawn. Against overwhelming numbers, they had mostly sought to ward off Japanese attacks, but with little warning to enable them to get into the air before the enemy planes appeared, and handicapped also by having to dodge craters on Kallang airfield as they took off and landed. The pilots became more adept in overcoming these difficulties as time went on, and on the final day of their operations (9th February) their records claimed six Japanese aircraft shot down and fourteen seriously damaged, for the loss of two Hurricanes and one pilot. "It was significant," commented Air Vice-Marshal Maltby, "that by 5th February the surviving pilots were mostly experienced men who had had previous battle experience before coming to the Far East."[2] Although the forces on the island were not generally aware of it, a series of air operations was carried out from 30th January to 13th February by bombers from Sumatra against the Japanese air forces on Alor Star, Penang, and Kluang airfields, and the Singora docks in Thailand.

In the cable in which he referred to the likelihood that the Japanese would attempt to capture Singapore on 11th February, Bowden had asked for direction as to whether he and his political and commercial secretaries, Messrs J. P. Quinn and A. N. Wootton respectively, should stay there or take an opportunity which might occur of leaving on a cargo steamer next day. With their aid, he had supplied particularly valuable reports on the course of events in Malaya and had been the means whereby an Australian viewpoint was presented to the War Council. The reply to his enquiry, confirmed subsequently by the Australian War Cabinet, was that he should stay, as "we shall otherwise be deprived of independent information and effect on morale would be bad. . . . We deeply value what you have done for Australia and her soldiers and we know you will continue to safeguard Australia's interests whatever may befall. Very best wishes." Next day he received a further cable telling him that "if worst comes, you and your staff are to insist on receiving full diplomatic immunities, privileges and courtesies. . . . Through protecting Power we shall insist on you and your staff being included in any evacuation scheme agreed on with Japanese Government. . . . If necessary, show paraphrase of this to Japanese administration." Bowden replied: "We shall continue to do utmost to serve Australia in whatever ways remain open to us."

As has been shown, the rapid Japanese advance on Singapore had caused a number of units to split into parties making their way across country

---
[2] *Report on the Air Operations during the campaigns in Malaya and Netherlands East Indies from 8th December 1941 to 12th March 1942,* p. 1382.

out of touch with their units. Some were without officers. Inadequate provision was made for straggler collecting posts, and in the confusion of the time, with unit headquarters moving from place to place, and communications having frequently to be reorganised, many men found it difficult to link up again. Some sought food and rest among the civilian population; some looked for means of escape. On his way to the Australian base depot—which was not in direct contact with the rest of the A.I.F.—to investigate a report that most of the Australian stragglers had come from that establishment, Lieut-Colonel Kent Hughes found on 10th February that the men at the depot apparently had been ordered through some misunderstanding to move into the town. With the help of the provosts and base depot N.C.O's he reversed the movement. Men who had made their way back from forward areas were collected and fought again once their contact with an organised fighting force had been restored. There was, however, a residue of Australian and other troops who had become desperate and defiant of authority—a circumstance hardly surprising in view of the intensity of the Japanese bombardment from land and air and the many other factors already mentioned which tended to undermine confidence in the outcome of the struggle. On 12th February Bowden cabled that a group of Australians and others had boarded a vessel without authority and in it had sailed for the Netherlands East Indies.

The contraction of the front had reduced the military food supplies under control to enough for only seven days' consumption in addition to what was held by units, and to the civil food reserves. Except for reserves on Pulau Bukum, only a small dump of petrol remained on which the defenders could draw. Breaks in water mains were gaining over repairs, and pressure was falling so ominously that water-carrying parties were organised. The disaster which Bowden had foreseen when he sought direction as to whether he should stay was rapidly approaching. He sent a further message to Australia that all merchant shipping under British naval control had left Singapore, and that "except as a fortress and battlefield Singapore has ceased to function".

The Japanese had realised that the Kranji-Jurong line offered strong defensive positions. Having used the Sultan's palace at Johore as a command post for the crossings to the island, General Yamashita transferred on 10th February to the Tengah airfield, to direct the progress of his forces against this line and on to the city. As yet, owing to delays in the crossings of the Strait, the full strength of the Japanese forces had not been deployed on the island; but the *5th Division* reached Bukit Timah village on the night of the 10th, and the *18th* was about a mile to the west. The *Guards Division* was driving eastward towards Nee Soon in the northern sector. Yamashita had expected that the defenders would make their final resistance north and west of Bukit Timah and north of Mandai. When by 11th February these positions had been penetrated, it was presumably with swelling pride that he invited their surrender. In the absence of response, the *Guards* continued their eastward movement, with the intention of then turning south beyond the municipal catchment area towards Paya Lebar, a north-eastern suburb of Singapore. The *5th Division* advanced on the evening of the 11th north-east of Bukit Timah village to the Bukit Timah Rifle Range and the Racecourse. The *18th Division*, advancing on the line of Jurong road, overcame the forces seeking to check their advance west of Bukit Timah village, and reached the Reformatory road area. There they assembled for a drive to the south, once the main strength of the Japanese artillery had completed its crossing of Johore Strait. The Japanese army artillery units, advancing towards Bukit Timah, encountered intense artillery fire from dusk on 11th February, and were checked in their move. As air opposition diminished and then disappeared, anti-aircraft units cooperated in the ground fighting, while aircraft gave maximum support to the Japanese troops.

CHAPTER 17

CEASE FIRE

ON Friday, 13th February, whatever hope remained that Singapore might be saved was on its deathbed. Troops were disposed along an arc between the enemy and the town, but it was by no means firmly held, nor was it fortified. Behind it, instead of an area cleared for battle and organised for a maximum defensive effort, were thickly-clustered shops, offices, schools, churches, houses, gardens, and about a million civilians, many of them refugees from the mainland. Most of the civilians, especially the Asians, were pitifully exposed to the effects of bombardment, and without prospect of evacuation. In this densely congested area, where there was now little room for discrimination by the enemy between what was or was not a legitimate military target, bombs and shells were blasting away the last essentials of resistance.

The 2/30th Australian Battalion remained north of the defensive arc, in positions near Ang Mo Kio village, until 12.30 p.m., when the 53rd Brigade (Brigadier Duke), last of the forces to leave the Northern Area, had passed through. Then, in the course of its own withdrawal,

> the old optimism, that always arose at the sight or news of supporting units, returned as the battalion passed through the long columns of British and Indian troops. But only one thing could have inspired any real sense of security: the appearance of British planes. The inevitable red-spotted variety soon dispelled futile dreams of this nature. . . . Disappointment at not seeing more planes in the air in the last few weeks had been great. . . . Though the campaign was nearly at its weary end, many of the troops had not seen a plane of either side brought down.[1]

Thomson road was choked with transport converging on this artery into Singapore, and Japanese planes were doing ghastly work. At Tanglin Barracks, on their way to Australian perimeter positions, the troops discovered that the barracks stores

> contained practically everything that they could desire; there was clothing of all descriptions, military of course, and food in abundance . . . without delay the troops began to help themselves to much needed stocks of clothing and, ignoring plain army rations, selected some choice lines of luxury foods which they had not seen for many a long day. There was also a fine collection of wines and spirits, together with a good supply of beer, which under the circumstances was not enjoyed to the full. . . . It is unusual for Australian soldiers to deliberately pass up the opportunity of enjoying a glass of beer, particularly Australian beer. But there it was, in a very large barrel, by one of the barrack roads, and a stray soldier was imploring passers-by to come and drink with him. They passed him by, preoccupied and only vaguely interested. . . .[2]

Brigadier Taylor, who had been given a sleeping draught at the 2/13th A.G.H. the previous day, had left it in the morning with Lieut-Colonel Anderson and other officers who had been patients there, to resume duty.

---
[1] *Galleghan's Greyhounds*, p. 216.
[2] *Galleghan's Greyhounds*, p. 218.

He was given the task of forming the Australian perimeter, oval shaped and 7 miles in circumference. Holland road was the main axis, and the divisional headquarters, in Tanglin Barracks, was at the centre. Colonel Anderson rejoined his 2/19th Battalion.

The segments of the arc which General Percival had ordered to be occupied by his forces generally were: Kallang airfield to Paya Lebar airstrip, the 2nd Malaya Brigade; airstrip to a mile west of Woodleigh on Braddell road, the 11th Division; Chinese cemetery area north of Braddell road, the 53rd Brigade; Thomson road to Adam Park, the 55th Brigade (inclusive of Massy Force); astride Bukit Timah road, the 54th Brigade and remnants of Tomforce; Farrer road sector, 2/Gordons; junction of Farrer road and Holland road to the railway north of Tanglin Halt, the 8th Australian Division; astride Buona Vista road west of Tanglin Halt, the 44th Brigade; Pasir Panjang ridge and Pasir Panjang village, the 1st Malaya Brigade.[3]

General Bennett, having reviewed the situation on either flank of the A.I.F., had decided as previously related to collect all the A.I.F., except a few units, inside the Australian perimeter. The north-western portion of the perimeter was the segment allocated to the A.I.F. in the general line which General Percival had ordered to be occupied. The Australian perimeter was fully manned on all fronts in case the Japanese should penetrate the general line and endeavour to attack the Australians on either flank or even from the rear. Most units of the A.I.F. were concentrated in the perimeter, and many of the base units were used to man sectors of the Australian line. The swimming pool at Tanglin was filled with fresh water and this, together with the reserve supplies of food, ensured that the A.I.F. troops would not go short of sustenance for some days at least.

The withdrawals were followed by a lull in the fighting, except on the Pasir Panjang ridge, which formed a salient running north-westward from the general defensive line. There, after a two-hour bombardment, the *18th Japanese Division* thrust towards the Alexandra area where the island's largest ammunition magazine, the ordnance depot, and the principal military hospital were situated.

The 1st Malay Battalion, a regular unit, officered principally by Englishmen familiar with the language and customs of their men, showed during the struggle for the ridge how well more such forces could have been employed in the defence of their homeland.[4] Despite their determined resistance, however, they were gradually overpowered. The Japanese won their way to heights known as Pasir Panjang III and Buona Vista hill, and along the Pasir Panjang road by the southern shore. As those on the ridge reached The Gap, near the Buona Vista road, where under peaceful

---

[3] The 1st Malaya Brigade comprised at this stage the 2/Loyals (less one company), 1st Malay Battalion, 5/Bedfordshires and Hertfordshires (less two companies), and a composite battalion of Royal Engineers.

[4] "On this and the following day the regiment fully justified the confidence which had been placed in it and showed what *esprit de corps* and discipline can achieve. Garrisons of posts held their ground and many of them were wiped out almost to a man. It was only when it was weakened by heavy losses that a regiment was forced to give ground." Percival, *The War in Malaya*, p. 284.

conditions there had been a popular lookout over part of Singapore and neighbouring islands, a desperate fight ensued around the Malay battalion's headquarters. On the right, the 2/Loyals became exposed to enfilade fire from the ridge, and by 5 p.m. the Japanese had wrested from the 5/Bedfordshire and Hertfordshire a hill a little west of the Buona Vista road. As no troops were immediately available to attempt to regain the ridge forward of The Gap, the 1st Malaya Brigade and the Bedfordshire and Hertfordshire were withdrawn at nightfall to what was known as the Alexandra switchline. This was where Alexandra road runs northward between the ridge and other high ground east of it, of which Mount Faber is the principal feature.

As its left flank became exposed by the Japanese advance, the 44th Indian Brigade was withdrawn down the railway to Alexandra road and thence to the Mount Echo area at the south-east corner of the A.I.F. perimeter. The withdrawal accelerated movements whereby this perimeter was manned during the day by the Australians, including the 27th Brigade now reassembled under Brigadier Maxwell. The only Australian units not accommodated in the perimeter were the 2/13th A.G.H., at Katong on the east coast outside the general perimeter, and the 2/10th A.G.H., the Convalescent Depot, and the 2/10th and 2/12th Field Ambulances. The 2/Gordons—the only non-Australian unit in the perimeter—were still under General Bennett's command. Although the Japanese were making their way eastward through areas north and south of the perimeter, it was not attacked in force from this stage onward.

The sufferings of Singapore's civilians meanwhile were reaching an intolerable pitch. Despite inadequate provision for their protection, they had borne stoically and resourcefully ever since the beginning of the campaign an increasing scale of air raids. Now with artillery also pounding streets, shops and dwellings, and a water supply failure imminent, many more were being killed, many maimed, and many were losing all they possessed.

A scene, typical of many since the bombing of Singapore began, met the eyes of an officer as he drove along Orchard road. A stick of bombs had just fallen.

A petrol station on our left blazed up—two cars ahead of us were punted into the air, they bounced a few times before bursting into flames. Buildings on both sides of the road went up in smoke. . . . Soldiers and civilians suddenly appeared staggering through clouds of debris; some got on the road, others stumbled and dropped in their tracks, others shrieked as they ran for safety. . . . We pulled up near a building which had collapsed onto the road—it looked like a caved-in slaughter house. Blood splashed what was left of the lower rooms; chunks of human beings—men, women and children—littered the place. Everywhere bits of steaming flesh, smouldering rags, clouds of dust—and the shriek and groan of those who still survived.

Farther on the officer slowed down in obedience to a signal from a frail Chinese woman who offered him her small child.

She was spattered in blood and the youngster was bleeding profusely from a head wound. I cheered her up in her own language and she smiled through her tears as we helped her into the ambulance while the chaps attended to the child's wounds.[5]

In terms of power politics, such sufferings were negligible. Although no warm regard existed between Germany and Japan, the effect of Japan's onslaught in drawing off substantial forces from the war in Europe had been perceived with gratification by Herr Hitler and his followers. A report by Admiral Raeder, head of the German Navy, to the Fuehrer on 13th February showed how much more was now expected of Germany's Far Eastern ally.

Rangoon, Singapore and, most likely, also Port Darwin will be in Japanese hands within a few weeks. Only weak resistance is expected on Sumatra, while Java will be able to hold out longer. Japan plans to protect this front in the Indian Ocean by capturing the key position of Ceylon, and she also plans to gain control of the sea in that area by means of superior naval forces. Fifteen Japanese submarines are at the moment operating in the Bay of Bengal, in the waters off Ceylon, and in the straits on both sides of Sumatra and Java. With Rangoon, Sumatra, and Java gone, the last oil wells between Bahrein and the American continent will be lost. Oil supplies for Australia and New Zealand will have to come from either the Persian Gulf or from America. Once Japanese battleships, aircraft carriers, submarines, and the Japanese naval air force are based on Ceylon, Britain will be forced to resort to heavily-escorted convoys if she desires to maintain communications with India and the Near East. Only Alexandria, Durban, and Simonstown will be available as repair bases for large British naval vessels in that part of the world.[6]

Possibilities such as these, as they related to the area of his command, had to be weighed by General Wavell. He cabled to Mr Churchill on the same day: ". . . The unexpectedly rapid advance of enemy on Singapore and approach of an escorted enemy convoy towards southern Sumatra necessitate review of our plans for the defence of the Netherlands East Indies, in which southern Sumatra plays a most important part. With more time and the arrival of 7th Australian Division,[7] earmarked for southern Sumatra, strong defence could be built up. But ground not yet fully prepared. . . ."

How much of the more time that was needed could Singapore's forces wrest from the enemy? The Japanese were within 5,000 yards of the main seafront, bringing the whole city within artillery range, when Percival summoned a conference at Fort Canning at 2 p.m. Mainly because there was no reserve available for the purpose, General Bennett now agreed with his fellow commanders that there remained no prospect of successful counter-attack. They emphasised the effect on their troops of continuous day and night operations, with no hope of relief,[8] and recog-

---
[5] D. H. James, *The Rise and Fall of the Japanese Empire* (1951), pp. 229-30.
[6] *Fuehrer Conferences on Naval Affairs*, 13 Feb 1942.
[7] Part of I Aust Corps being transferred from the Middle East. As will be seen in Chapter 20, the 7th Division could not reach Sumatra before 15 March.
[8] Light was thrown on this factor, as it applied to the Australians, by Lieut-Colonel Pond in the diary of the 2/29th Battalion: "The factor of tiredness of unseasoned troops was a very pressing one and it was found that most of the reinforcements were, after 48 hours without sleep, completely exhausted, though a number of the officers and more experienced men were still comparatively fresh after 4 or 5 days with only 3 or 4 hours' rest in the whole period. In other words, untrained troops must be nursed until they are used to the demands being made on them, and to the noise and uncertainty of warfare . . . 2/29 Bn, as re-formed, had not had sufficient time to implant any thorough discipline and the unit's fighting ability was consequently much reduced."

nised that the plight of the civilians, in the event especially of domination by the Japanese of all food and water supplies, could not be ignored. Percival considered that in these circumstances it was unlikely that resistance could last more than a day or two, and that there "must come a stage when in the interests of the troops and the civil population further bloodshed will serve no useful purpose". He therefore asked Wavell for wider discretionary powers. The reply next day, reflecting a situation more readily seen from Wavell's point of view than from under the ominous smoke-pall of Singapore, was:

> You must continue to inflict maximum damage on enemy for as long as possible by house-to-house fighting if necessary. Your action in tying down enemy and inflicting casualties may have vital influence in other theatres. Fully appreciate your situation, but continued action essential.[9]

As Bennett returned from the conference to his headquarters

> there was devastation everywhere. There were holes in the road, churned-up rubble lying in great clods all round, tangled masses of telephone, telegraph and electric cables strewn across the street, here and there smashed cars, trucks, electric trams and buses that once carried loads of passengers to and from their peaceful daily toil. The shops were shuttered and deserted. There were hundreds of Chinese civilians who refused to leave their homes. Bombs were falling in a near-by street. On reaching the spot one saw that the side of a building had fallen on an air raid shelter, the bomb penetrating deep into the ground, the explosion forcing in the sides of the shelter. A group of Chinese, Malays, Europeans and Australian soldiers were already at work shovelling and dragging the debris away. Soon there emerged from the shelter a Chinese boy, scratched and bleeding, who immediately turned to help in the rescue work. He said, "My sister is under there." The rescuers dug furiously among the fallen masonry, one little wiry old Chinese man doing twice as much as the others, the sweat streaming from his body. At last the top of the shelter was uncovered. Beneath was a crushed mass of old men, women, young and old, and young children, some still living—the rest dead. The little Oriental never stopped with his work, his sallow face showing the strain of anguish. His wife and four children were there. Gradually he unearthed them—dead. He was later seen holding his only surviving daughter, aged ten, by the hand, watching them move away his family and the other unfortunates. This was going on hour after hour, day after day, the same stolidity and steadfastness among the civilians was evident in every quarter of the city.[1]

Rear-Admiral Spooner had decided that rather than allow them to fall into the hands of the enemy as at Penang, the small ships and other sea-going craft still in Singapore Harbour, including some naval patrol vessels, should be sailed to Java. These craft, with which he himself would leave, would carry about 3,000 persons, as well as their crews, thus providing a last chance of organised evacuation. It was decided to send in them principally service people and civilians who could be spared, and also some chosen because their experience and knowledge would be useful elsewhere.

Of the vacancies, 1,800 were allotted to the army. Especially because of reports of what had happened to nurses who had fallen into the hands

---
[9] Quoted in Churchill, *The Second World War*, Vol IV, p. 91.
[1] Bennett, *Why Singapore Fell*, pp. 186-7.

of the Japanese at Hong Kong, all women in the nursing services were to be included. Staff officers and technicians no longer required were to be sent at the discretion of formation commanders. Air Vice-Marshal Pulford, who had declined to leave until air personnel capable of evacuation had gone, was also to go.

The 1,800 were to include 100 from the A.I.F. Bennett decided that this Australian group would be led by Colonel Broadbent, his principal administrative officer, and appointed Lieut-Colonel Kent Hughes to succeed him in this position. Lieut-Colonel Kappe, Chief Signals Officer, was nominated by Malaya Command to leave. With him were to be twenty-seven of his best signals technicians. Captains Fisk[2] and Pople,[3] on Bennett's list, with seven other ranks, boarded a vessel. The remainder were too late in leaving Tanglin and were unable to get away.

Percival again visited the Governor, who, because a shell had entered a shelter under Government House, killing several people, had moved to the Singapore Cricket Club; and he said goodbye to Pulford. Referring to the course of the campaign, Pulford remarked, "I suppose you and I will be held responsible for this, but God knows we did our best with what little we had been given."[4] By this time Singapore's public services had come almost to a standstill for lack of labour. Corpses lay unburied; and water had ceased to reach many taps, because it was gushing unchecked from broken mains at lower levels. Hospitals were trying to cope with ever-increasing numbers of wounded soldiers and civilians.

The next day, 14th February, brought no relief to the defenders and civilians of Singapore. In their principal thrusts north of the town, where both the *5th Japanese Division* and the *Guards Division* were now employed, the enemy got to within a few hundred yards of the Woodleigh Pumping Station, vital to the maintenance of the city's water supply, before they were held by the 11th Indian Division; forced a gap between the 53rd and 55th Brigades which had to be plugged with a battalion from the 11th Indian Division; and sent tanks down Sime road, some of which were stopped only after they had reached the edge of the Mount Pleasant residential area. In the south-western area of the city, a series of attacks which commenced at 8.30 a.m. was stoutly resisted by the 1st Malaya Brigade. Heavy losses occurred on both sides, but the Japanese poured in fresh troops and, about 4 p.m., with the aid of tanks, penetrated the brigade's left flank, forcing it to withdraw to the vicinity of Alexandra road. Japanese naval units which entered the Naval Base during the day were surprised to find it deserted and undefended. However, because of delay in getting supplies across Johore Strait on to the island, the enemy artillery was running short of ammunition, and "deep consideration was

---

[2] Lt-Col E. K. Fisk, NX95. Aust Signals Corps; Civil Affairs 1945. Clerk; of Lindfield, NSW; b. Sydney, 19 Oct 1917.
[3] Maj F. H. Pople, NX12293. Aust Signals Corps. PMG engineer; of Beecroft, NSW; b. Granville, NSW, 20 Nov 1909.
[4] Percival, *The War in Malaya*, p. 287.

given to preserving progress and battle strength in the army's fighting henceforth".[5]

Though the 2/13th Australian General Hospital north-east of the city fell into enemy hands without harm to its occupants, a ghastly episode occurred when Japanese troops advancing along the Ayer Raja road reached the Alexandra military hospital in pursuit of some detached Indian troops who fell back into the hospital still firing. The Japanese bayoneted a number of the staff and patients, including a patient lying

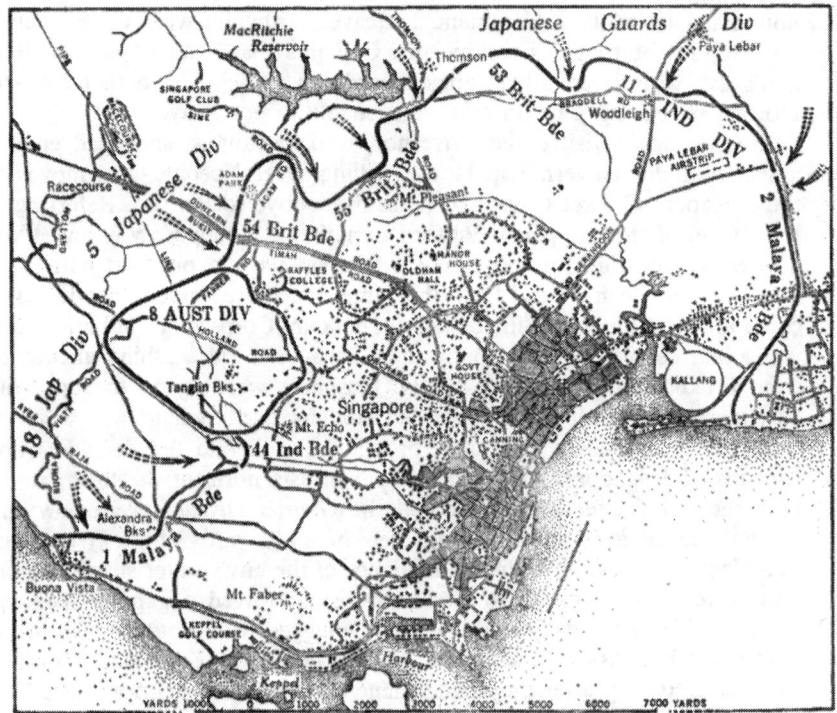

Daybreak, 14th February

on an operating table. They herded 150 into a bungalow, and the next morning executed them. Among those who lost their lives was Major Beale, who had been taken to hospital after being wounded on the 11th.

It seemed likely after the withdrawal of the 1st Malaya Brigade that the Australian perimeter would soon be completely by-passed. General Bennett concluded that his troops might become isolated from the rest of the defending forces, and sent a cable to Army Headquarters in Melbourne:

A.I.F. now concentrated in Tanglin area two miles from city proper. Non-fighting units less hospital including my headquarters in position. Can rely on troops to

---

[5] Malay Operations Record, *XXV Japanese Army*.

hold to last as usual. All other fronts weak. Wavell has ordered all troops to fight to last. If enemy enter city behind us will take suitable action to avoid unnecessary sacrifices.[6]

Bennett as well as the Japanese was concerned with the availability of artillery ammunition. Information had been received from Malaya Command the day before that there was a serious shortage of field gun ammunition, particularly for 25-pounders, as so many dumps had been captured by the invaders. The Australian ammunition column had shown courage and resource in salvaging shells; but now it was found that no further supplies of 25-pounder ammunition could be obtained from dumps or the base ordnance depot, which was under fire and ablaze. Bennett therefore ordered that the A.I.F. guns should fire only in defence of the Australian perimeter, "and then only on observed targets, on counter-battery targets, and H.F. targets where enemy troop and battery movements were definitely known to be taking place".[7]

General Percival had received early on 14th February from the Director-General of Civil Defence (Brigadier Simson) a report that the town's water-supply was on the verge of a complete failure. At a conference held by Percival at 10 a.m. at the municipal offices, attended also by the Chairman of the Municipality, by Brigadier Simson and the Municipal Engineer, the latter reported that more than half the water being drawn from the reservoirs was being lost through breaks in the water mains caused by shells and bombs. He said that the supply might last for 48 hours at most, and perhaps not more than 24 hours. Percival arranged to withdraw about 100 men of the Royal Engineers from the 1st Malaya Brigade's sector to assist in repairing the mains. He then visited the Governor, telling him that despite the critical water situation he intended to continue the fighting as long as possible.

Staunch though he had been in refusing to admit even the possibility of defeat, the Governor cabled to the Colonial Office:

> ... There are now one million people within radius of three miles. Water supplies very badly damaged and unlikely to last more than twenty-four hours. Many dead lying in the streets and burial impossible. We are faced with total deprivation of water, which must result in pestilence. I have felt that it is my duty to bring this to notice of General Officer Commanding.[8]

Percival reported the situation to General Wavell, adding that though the fight was being continued, he might find it necessary to make an immediate decision. Wavell replied that fighting must go on wherever

---

[6] Percival, who was unaware of the message at the time, later commented that it seemed to him "a most extraordinary procedure". He added that no doubt Bennett was entitled to communicate to his own Prime Minister, "but surely not to inform him of an intention to surrender in certain circumstances when he had not even communicated that intention to his own superior officer". (Percival, *The War in Malaya*, p. 284.)
In evidence at the Ligertwood inquiry in 1945 Bennett said: "I decided to let Australia know we had no hope; it was no good going on sacrificing more lives, and it would be better to surrender at that stage than go on fighting." He explained later that "If enemy enter city behind us" implied that Malaya Command HQ in the city behind the AIF might be overrun. In that event, he would be in a position to make his own decision.

[7] War diary of HQ RAA, AIF Malaya.

[8] Quoted in Churchill, Vol IV, p. 90.

there was sufficient water for the troops, and later dispatched a further message:

> Your gallant stand is serving a purpose and must be continued to the limit of endurance.

He nevertheless reported to Mr Churchill that he feared Singapore's resistance was not likely to be very prolonged. The British Prime Minister wrote later that at this stage he decided that

> now when it was certain that all was lost at Singapore . . . it would be wrong to enforce needless slaughter, and without hope of victory to inflict the horrors of street fighting on the vast city, with its teeming, helpless, and now panic-stricken population.[9]

He therefore cabled to Wavell:

> You are of course sole judge of the moment when no further result can be gained at Singapore, and should instruct Percival accordingly. C.I.G.S. concurs.

At a second conference at the municipal offices, about 5 p.m. on the 14th, the Water Engineer reported that the water-supply position was a little better. Percival asked Brigadier Simson for an accurate report at 7 a.m. next day of the prospect at that time. Curiously, though the Japanese had gained control of the reservoirs, water continued to flow to the pumps at Woodleigh.

As mentioned, the Australian Government Representative, Mr Bowden, largely because of his membership of the War Council in Singapore, had supplied information which, with General Bennett's reports, had helped to mould Australian policy.[1] Now the Council had ceased to function, and Singapore's civilian administration was rapidly coming to a standstill. Bowden had received from the Australian Minister for External Affairs an assurance that his Government would try to arrange an exchange of Bowden and his staff against the Japanese diplomatic staff in Australia. However, he received information on 14th February suggesting that capitulation was very close; and a member of Percival's staff offered him an opportunity of leaving with some senior officers and certain persons selected by the Governor. Bowden, Wootton and Quinn thereupon decided that, as their remaining in Singapore would serve no useful purpose, they would accept the offer. The vessel upon which they would embark would be the *Osprey*, a launch designed to seat ten persons. Bowden drafted his last message to Australia: "Our work completed. We will telegraph from another place at present unknown." Although by the time it was lodged the means of transmission had been reduced to a small handset operated at the point where the cable entered the water, the message reached its destination. The three men went to the launch at 6.30 p.m. By this time groups of soldiers including Australians were at large seeking escape,

---

[9] Churchill, Vol IV, p. 92. It seems doubtful whether his reference to a "panic-stricken population" was more than rhetorical.

[1] On the other hand, although Maj W. A. Tebbutt, as liaison officer between Army Headquarters, Melbourne and the Far East Combined Bureau, had sought permission of that headquarters to advise Bowden on service matters, it had been refused.

and a few, armed with Tommy guns and hand grenades, threatened to open fire on the launch unless they themselves were taken aboard. When, at 11.30 p.m., the *Osprey* moved out, with thirty-eight aboard, rifle shots were fired at it, but no one was hit. The launch party, which included Colonel Dalley, of Dalforce, and some of his men, transferred in the harbour to a forty-foot diesel-engined vessel, the *Mary Rose*.

Meanwhile, General Bennett had been giving close consideration to the question of escape if capitulation were enforced. Colonel Broadbent was the only senior officer who had been sent away with the special party, and there was doubt whether he would be able to reach Australia. Bennett considered it advisable that other officers from his headquarters should, if possible, return to Australia and give first-hand information of Japanese methods and strategy. Major Moses, who had been acting as liaison officer with the 44th Indian Brigade, had told Bennett's aide de camp, Lieutenant Walker, on 12th February that he intended to "have a crack at getting away". Walker thereupon broached the subject of getting Bennett away; but as Moses was then to be appointed brigade major of the 22nd Brigade in place of Beale, he dropped out of the project for the time being. As it happened the appointment was filled by Captain Fairley. When Moses returned, Walker had invited Captains Curlewis and Jessup,[2] two of Bennett's staff officers, to join the escape party. Curlewis, who had been President of the Surf Life Saving Association of Australia, was known to be a strong swimmer, and Jessup spoke Malay and Dutch. From 12th February onward, steps had been taken to put an escape plan into operation.

Some further gains were made by the enemy during the night, but the general defence line was held. Brigadier Simson reported next morning (15th February) that the water-supply had deteriorated to the extent that most of the water was running to waste because repairs could not keep pace with breakages; and supply to the higher parts of the town had failed. After a Communion service at Fort Canning, a conference was held at 9.30 a.m. of the area commanders and others. The commanders reported on the tactical situations on their fronts; Brigadier Simson said that such water-supply as existed could not be guaranteed for more than 24 hours, and that if a total failure occurred it would result in the town being without piped water for several days.

Percival said that only a few days' reserve of military rations remained, but there were still fairly large civilian food stocks. Hardly any petrol remained other than that in the tanks of motor vehicles, there was a serious shortage of field gun ammunition, and reserves of shells for Bofors anti-aircraft guns were almost exhausted. The only choices available, he continued, were to counter-attack immediately to regain control of the reservoirs and the military food depots and drive back the Japanese artillery to an extent which would reduce the damage to the water-supply; or to surrender.

---

[2] Capt H. E. Jessup, VX51823; HQ 8 Aust Div. Pearler and planter; of Aru Is., and Brisbane; b. Brisbane, 17 Jun 1912.

The area commanders again agreed that a counter-attack was out of the question. Consideration was given to what might happen if the Japanese smashed their way into the town, amid its civilians. Bearing the tremendous responsibility of determining what to do in the circumstances, Percival decided with the unanimous concurrence of the others at the conference to seek a cessation of hostilities as from 4 p.m.,[3] and to invite a Japanese deputation to visit the city to discuss terms of capitulation.

It was further decided that a deputation representing the military and civil authorities should go to the enemy lines as soon as possible, to propose the cease-fire and to invite the Japanese to send a deputation to discuss terms. Orders were to be issued for the destruction of all secret and technical equipment, ciphers, codes, secret documents, and guns. Personal weapons were excepted, in case the Japanese would not agree to the proposal to be made to them, or the weapons were needed before agreement was reached.

Percival was strengthened in his resolve by a message received from Wavell that morning:

> So long as you are in position to inflict losses to enemy and your troops are physically capable of doing so you must fight on. Time gained and damage to enemy of vital importance at this crisis. When you are fully satisfied that this is no longer possible I give you discretion to cease resistance. Before doing so all arms, equipment, and transport of value to enemy must of course be rendered useless. Also just before final cessation of fighting opportunity should be given to any determined bodies of men or individuals to try and effect escape by any means possible. They must be armed. Inform me of intentions. Whatever happens I thank you and all troops for your gallant efforts of last few days.

Percival thereupon notified Wavell of his decision, and again reported to the Governor, but Bennett was not informed, as obviously he should have been, of Wavell's view that opportunities should be given for escape.[4] However, Bennett in turn called his senior commanders together, told them of the decision to negotiate with the enemy, and the question of escape was discussed. It was agreed that to allow any large-scale unorganised attempts to escape would result in confusion and slaughter. Officers recalled how Japanese troops had run wild after capturing cities in China, and it was agreed that the Australians should be kept together and sentries posted. Bennett thereupon issued an order that units were to remain at their posts, and concentrate by 8.30 a.m. next day[5] (but said after the war that this did not mean that no-one was to attempt to

---

[3] General Bennett's recollection later was that the time agreed upon at the conference was 3.30 p.m.

[4] Neither did Percival include the message in the extract from Wavell's cable which appeared in his (Percival's) book, *The War in Malaya*, p. 292.

[5] A copy of the order, preserved during captivity, and subsequently made available by General Bennett, read as follows: "Confirming verbal orders transmitted by LO's. Units will take reasonable precautions for security during night. All ranks stand fast within unit areas and will concentrate at first light to be completed by 0830 hours. All precautions must be taken to ensure that the spirit of the cease-fire is not destroyed by foolish action. All arms will be unloaded under strict supervision immediately. Amn will be left in present positions. Unit assembly areas will be notified in accompanying administrative instruction. Unit representatives will report divisional headquarters on completion of assembly. Two days rations will be issued to units for issue to personnel on completion of assembly. All water bottles to be filled tonight. Q will arrange delivery to units. Essential personnel to guard food ammunition dumps and water points may remain armed. All secret documents to be destroyed. No lighting restrictions. All informed. Ack."

escape after the surrender). The order was of course important not only to the Australians, but to the other troops and to the inhabitants of Singapore generally because of the effect which either a disciplined surrender or disorder and disintegration in the Australian perimeter might have upon their fate. Similarly, it was important to all concerned that order should be maintained in the other formations also.

Meanwhile fighting continued north and south of the city, yielding further gains to the enemy against troops exhausted by day and night pressure against them. In the north-east, the defenders fell back towards the Kallang airfield, and the northern line generally was retracted despite local counter-attacks. The 2/Loyals were under attack throughout the day in the south-west of the city, and during the afternoon withdrew, with the Malay Battalion and the 5/Bedfordshire and Hertfordshire, to a line from Keppel Golf Links northward, near the southernmost portion of the A.I.F. perimeter. This perimeter now became a salient sandwiched between enemy forces, and appeared likely soon to be completely enveloped.

The joint deputation, sent along Bukit Timah road to the Japanese *5th Division's* lines, returned about 1 p.m. with instructions that Percival was to proceed with his staff to a meeting with Lieut-General Yamashita, the Japanese commander. This took place about 5.15 p.m. in the Ford motor factory north of Bukit Timah village. Although Percival received no copy of the galling terms, he recorded them from memory in his subsequent dispatch:

(a) There must be an unconditional surrender of all military forces (Army, Navy and Air Force) in the Singapore area.
(b) Hostilities to cease at 2030 hours, British time[6]—i.e. 2200 hrs Japanese time.
(c) All troops to remain in positions occupied at the time of cessation of hostilities pending further orders.
(d) All weapons, military equipment, ships, aeroplanes and secret documents to be handed over to the Japanese Army intact.
(e) In order to prevent looting and other disorders in Singapore town during the temporary withdrawal of all armed forces, a force of 100 British armed men to be left temporarily in the Town area until relieved by the Japanese.[7]

Yamashita insisted that these terms be accepted immediately; and Percival felt that he was in no position to bargain. In complying he told Yamashita that there were no ships or aircraft in the Singapore area, and that the heavier types of weapons, some of the military equipment and all secret documents had already been destroyed pursuant of orders he had issued after his commanders' conference.[8]

---

[6] The reference is to 8.30 p.m. according to the time which had been observed in Malaya under British administration.

[7] As recorded in a gazette (*Negri Sembilan Shu Koho*, Vol I, No. 36) the terms were:
  1. The British Army shall effect complete cessation of hostilities not later than February 15 at 10 p.m. (Nippon time).
  2. The British troops shall disarm themselves in their present positions not later than 11 p.m.
  3. The Imperial Army will permit the British troops to station not more than 1,000 armed constables [not 100 as recorded by Percival] in order to maintain peace and order in Singapore until further notice. The Imperial Army shall fire on the British troops immediately in the event of the slightest infringement upon any of the terms on the part of the British troops.

[8] Although Percival did not know it at the time, the Australian artillery had not been destroyed, as Bennett was uncertain of the outcome of the approach to the Japanese.

This news, unlikely to be palatable to Yamashita, was received more placidly than Percival had expected. Japanese accounts of their circumstances during the assault on Singapore suggest that it was a relatively minor consideration. A report attributed to Yamashita's chief of staff, Lieut-General Suzuki, related that of the 1,000 rounds of shells allotted to each Japanese cannon, 400 had been fired against Singapore Island from Johore Bahru, and another 400 before the morning of 13th February.[9] At that stage the Japanese had been experiencing an "unimaginably vehement" bombardment, and a bayonet charge to have been made in the *18th Division's* area in the south of the city was held up by heavy fire.

Describing in a radio talk the scene as he and Yamashita watched the battle on 15th February from a height near Bukit Timah, Suzuki said:

> My eye was caught by a Union Jack fluttering in the breeze on the top of Fort Canning. . . . I figured that it would be a good week's work to take the heights that still intervened between us and our object. . . . Behind Singapore was an island with a fort. To the left was the Fort Changi. It was no simple matter to take these forts. I figured that a fairly large number of days would be required to capture this last line of defence of the city. . . . Presently, it was intimated to me . . . that the bearer of a flag of truce had come.

This account is of course consistent with Singapore having been surrendered for reasons not obvious at the time to the Japanese, such as the threatened failure of food, ammunition and water supplies. It is also a tribute to the defenders' artillery and to the men who stood in the path of the Japanese thrusts to the heart of the city.

The magnitude of the disaster which had befallen them was not easily grasped by the battle-weary forces now at the mercy of an enemy alien to them in language, custom and thought. What lay ahead? When, if ever, would they see their homes again? From the point of view of the Australian troops, what would happen in their absence, with Singapore no longer an obstacle between the Japanese and Australia, and they themselves powerless to defend their own soil? Perhaps this was their bitterest thought.

On the other hand, the prospect of a cease-fire offered at least a chance of temporary oblivion in long-delayed sleep. Some were past caring for the time being what happened after that. Some, though they were required to stay in their positions, considered prospects of escape. Some who had failed to rejoin their units searched the waterfront for a way out of the shambles, and its atmosphere of futility and defeat. There remained to General Bennett the choice between becoming a prisoner of war or acting on his escape plan.

> I personally (he wrote subsequently) had made this decision some time previously, having decided that I would not fall into Japanese hands. My decision was fortified by the resolve that I must at all costs return to Australia to tell our people the

---

[9] *Japan Times and Advertiser*, 8 Apr 1942.

story of our conflict with the Japanese,[10] to warn them of the danger to Australia, and to advise them of the best means of defeating Japanese tactics.[1]

After directing that his men should be supplied with new clothing and two days' rations, Bennett set out early in the afternoon with Moses and Walker to tour the Australian lines and look for a way through the Japanese forces. The attempt would be hazardous—the risks involved without doubt greater than those involved in remaining—but Bennett's personal courage was beyond question. He took leave of a number of his officers and, during the evening, orders for a "cease-fire" as from 8.30 p.m. came through. When this time arrived he handed over his command to his artillery commander, Brigadier Callaghan (who had administered the 8th Division during his visit to the Middle East) and moved off. With him went Moses and Walker.[2] The three got away from Singapore Island about 1 a.m.

In the Australian lines Japanese troops were heard cheering as they received news that the campaign was about to end; but sniping, shelling and bombing continued until the "cease-fire". Then the rattle and roar of battle sank to a strange and solemn hush. In the comparative silence, the small sounds of everyday life, and the groans and cries of the wounded, seemed to be magnified and given a keener significance. The dense smoke still hovering over the city, principally from burning fuel and oil depots but also from homes, shops and offices, became a stifling shroud. Beyond it the fall of Singapore reverberated throughout the world as one of the greatest disasters in British history.

During the invasion of the island the *No. 3 Japanese Flying Corps* had engaged chiefly in cooperation with the ground troops, and in attacking ships seeking to escape from Singapore; the *12th Air Corps* in gaining air superiority over Singapore; and the *57th Air Corps* in attacking key positions, particularly those occupied by the opposing artillery. The aircraft made 4,700 sorties and dropped 773 tons of bombs. The Japanese anti-aircraft units, with few and then no British planes to engage their attention, used their weapons for cooperation in ground fighting. Thus

---

[10] Bennett said subsequently that he feared the 8th Division would be blamed for the defeat in Malaya.

[1] Bennett, *Why Singapore Fell*, p. 198. After the campaign the lessons to be drawn from the fighting in Malaya were rapidly set down and circulated. For instance, in response to a request by Wavell to Percival for an experienced commanding officer who would convey his experience of Japanese tactics, Colonel Stewart of the Argylls, had been sent from Singapore. His information, and notes on the same subject compiled by Colonel Francis G. Brink, an American observer who had been in Malaya, were closely examined by the officers of I Australian Corps, whose role at this stage was to be the defence of Java. Two manuals were compiled by Bennett and issued by III Australian Corps, stationed in Western Australia, after Bennett became its commander in April 1942. One of these, entitled *Notes on Japanese Tactics in Malaya and Elsewhere and Tactics to Counter-Attack and Destroy the Enemy*, dealt in close detail with the subject; in May 1942 the notes were embodied in a 20-page *Army Training Memorandum* and circulated to the Australian Army at large with a foreword by General Blamey requesting their close study by all officers responsible for training troops to meet the Japanese. The other, *Tactics in Modern Warfare*, largely embodied these tactics for use by the III Corps, with emphasis on the need for offensive action.

[2] As has been shown, Captains Curlewis and Jessup had been invited to join the escape party. Curlewis, however, expressed doubts to Moses about the propriety of leaving the men. Moses said the party had grown to six, including Lieutenant V. Baynes (Longueville, NSW) of the 2/30th Battalion who possessed a knowledge of navigation. It would therefore be split into two. Eventually Bennett, Moses and Walker left, but not the others.

the defending troops became exposed to the full and unopposed weight of the Japanese air attack, and were targets for their anti-aircraft guns as well as of their field artillery. Nevertheless, the Japanese casualties in the capture of the island were 1,714 killed and 3,378 wounded. As against this, British forces numbering about 85,000, and masses of stores, weapons, and other material which could ill be spared from the resources necessary elsewhere to stem the Japanese onslaught generally, fell into their hands. It was to Yamashita's credit that he kept his troops, other than those engaged in police duties, from any mass entry to the city, and that order was maintained.

After a seventy-day campaign, the whole of Malaya was at the feet of the enemy. The Japanese forces in this period had advanced a distance of 650 miles—in which the Australians had been engaged over a distance of 150 miles—at an average rate of nine miles a day, from Singora (Thailand) to Singapore's southern coast. The casualties among the defenders were: United Kingdom, 38,496; Australian, 18,490;[3] Indian, 67,340; local Volunteer troops, 14,382; a total of 138,708, of whom more than 130,000 became prisoners. The Japanese suffered 9,824 battle casualties during this period. They had evolved no new principles of warfare, but their tactics had been far more flexible than those employed by the defenders.

On the morning of 16th February a Japanese officer arrived at the Australian headquarters with instructions that the general officer commanding should present himself to the Japanese military authorities with his senior commanders. Brigadier Callaghan[4] responded to this summons, accompanied by Brigadiers Maxwell, Taylor and Varley, Colonels Thyer and Kent Hughes, and Captain Geldard.[5] Objections by the Australian officers to their troops being herded into the Raffles College area, and being deprived of their steel helmets, as was happening at the time, were accepted, and these actions ceased. As an outcome of the meeting the Australian troops were issued with instructions about the surrender of arms and ammunition and were told to remain in their area. Most of the arms, even small arms, had already been put out of action at the time of the surrender. Later in the day a conference of G.O.C's was held at Malaya Command with the Japanese. General Percival raised strong objections to the order that all troops would move to Changi on the following afternoon without their arms and equipment, but carrying ten days' rations. The Japanese insisted that the order must be obeyed but allowed a certain number of trucks to carry the rations. The move took place the following day. To some of the troops the long and humiliating march to Changi was almost more than they were able to bear in their weakened state. They were cheered, however, by the kindness of the Asian people who

---

[3] The Australian figure includes 1,789 killed and 1,306 wounded.

[4] On 17th February General Percival promoted Callaghan to the temporary rank of major-general, with command of the Australians, thus giving him the necessary status in dealing with the Japanese.

[5] Capt H. S. Geldard, MC, NX70339. (1st AIF: Lt 53 Bn.) HQ 8 Aust Div. Company director; of Greenwich Point, NSW; b. Armidale, NSW, 29 Aug 1891.

pressed gifts on them as they marched. Many units did not reach the area until the early hours of the following morning.⁶

The fall of Singapore, coming at a time of political as well as military crisis, was a heavy blow to Mr Churchill personally as well as to the prestige of British arms. As against this, Britain had gained, by the Japanese attack on Pearl Harbour, an ally whose resources, if sufficient time could be won in which to develop and apply them, would bring overwhelming strength to the struggle against the Axis powers. In President Roosevelt, Churchill had gained a warm-hearted and understanding friend.

> I realise how the fall of Singapore has affected you and the British people (cabled the President on 19th February). It gives the well-known back-seat driver a field day, but no matter how serious our setbacks have been—and I do not for a moment underrate them—we must constantly look forward to the next moves that need to be made to hit the enemy. I hope you will be of good heart in these trying weeks, because I am very sure that you have the great confidence of the masses of the British people. I want you to know that I think of you often, and I know you will not hesitate to ask me if there is anything you think I can do. . . . Do let me hear from you.⁷

The seas between Singapore and Sumatra and Java were dotted for several days with small craft as those who had got away in the official groups, and some making individual endeavours, sought to run the gauntlet of Japanese air and sea forces in the area. The official evacuation had been carried out in a confused way as men sought to find the craft to which they were allotted, but which had become dispersed under the Japanese bombardment of Singapore and its seafront. The 2/3rd Reserve Motor Transport Company, having no role once the army had concentrated on Singapore Island, was ordered to embark in the steamer *Kinta* (1,220 tons). The *Kinta's* crew dispersed in an air raid, but the Transport Company supplied competent deck and engine-room hands and the *Kinta* sailed on the 9th and reached Batavia. Desperate men no longer with their units, and civilians not listed for evacuation but determined to escape, also sought to take what opportunity offered. Of the hundred men to have been sent officially from the A.I.F. only thirty-nine, including Broadbent, eventually got away. A patrol boat carrying Admiral Spooner, Air Vice-Marshal Pulford and others was forced ashore on a deserted and malarial island in the Tuju group, 30 miles north of Banka Island. There, with few stores and no doctor, eighteen of them died, including Spooner and Pulford, before the survivors were found and taken into captivity by the Japanese.⁸

General Bennett, Major Moses and Lieutenant Walker, with some planters who had been serving in the Volunteer forces in Malaya, took charge of a native craft and made an adventurous trip to the east coast

---

⁶ Part III of this volume deals with the prisoner-of-war period.

⁷ Quoted in Churchill, Vol IV, p. 94.

⁸ Included in the literature of escapes from Singapore are *Let's Get Cracking* (Sydney, 1943), the story of the evacuation of a press party written by Athole Stewart, Press Conducting officer to the AIF in Malaya; and graphic accounts in *Through* (Sydney, 1949), published by the 8th Division Signals Association.

of Sumatra. There the three Australians transferred to a Singapore Harbour Board launch, the *Tern,* and by this and other means crossed Sumatra to Padang, on its west coast.[9] There Bennett met other escapers, including Brigadier Paris (12th Indian Brigade) and Colonel Coates (6th/15th Indian Brigade) who had fought in his area on Singapore Island; and

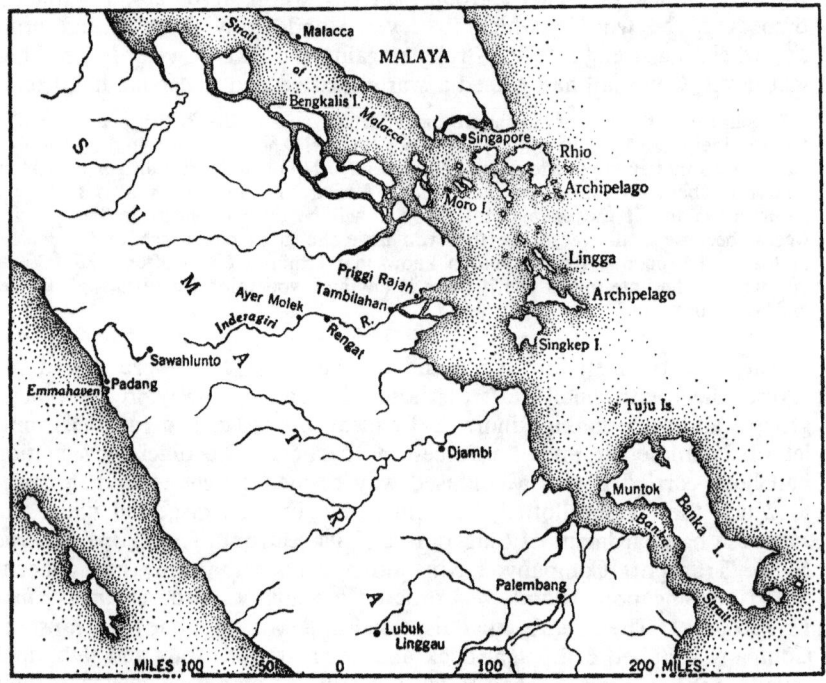

he received a telephone call from General Wavell. Bennett and his officers were flown thence to Java, and he then went ahead of them on a Qantas plane to Australia. He reached Melbourne on 2nd March and called on General Sturdee, then Chief of the General Staff.

To my dismay, my reception was cold and hostile (wrote Bennett afterwards). No other member of the Military Board called in to see me. After a few minutes' formal conversation, Sturdee told me that my escape was ill-advised, or words to

---

[9] Bennett, Moses and Walker left the launch at Djambi, some 80 miles up the Djambi River in southern Sumatra. They were about to set off on the next stage of their journey when they heard that help was needed by badly wounded women and children, stranded on Singkep Island from a ship which had been sunk by bombs. A Dutch doctor had procured a launch (the *Heather*) in which to go to their aid, but had no one who could manage its diesel engine. Knowing that some of the crew of the diesel-driven *Tern* were experienced in handling such engines Bennett "told the story to these young men from Britain and asked if they would like to volunteer for the task. . . . These men had struggled for many days in their attempt to escape from the Japanese and had just reached safety. Yet they volunteered without hesitation to go back again into the jaws of death. . . ." (Bennett, *Why Singapore Fell,* pp. 210-11.) Thus the *Heather* made the trip, and many people were rescued in consequence. The crew who undertook the task, comprising Capt L. A. Carty, RASC, Sgt Chismon and Corporal Billings, eventually reached India. Carty related their experiences in a letter to Bennett dated 31 Sep 1942.

that effect. I was too shocked to say much. He then went on with his work, leaving me to stand aside in his room. This same Military Board had issued a circular not many months before instructing all ranks that, if captured, their first duty was to escape. . . .[10]

A meeting of the War Cabinet was held and was attended by Sturdee and Bennett, who gave an account of the Malayan campaign. As soon as it was over, without consulting Sturdee, the Prime Minister made a press statement in which he said:

> I desire to inform the nation that we are proud to pay tribute to the efficiency, gallantry and devotion of our forces throughout the struggle. We have expressed to Major-General Bennett our confidence in him. His leadership and conduct were in complete conformity with his duty to the men under his command and to his country. He remained with his men until the end, completed all formalities in connection with the surrender, and then took the opportunity and risk of escaping.[1]

The *Mary Rose,* carrying Bowden and others, passed unmolested from Singapore Harbour on 15th February through many small and apparently new sampans, manned it was thought by Japanese in Malay clothes. The original plan was that the launch should proceed to the Inderagiri River in Sumatra, whence its occupants presumably could have reached Padang and Java as Bennett had done. It was decided, however, to make for Palembang, in the south-east of the island. At the entrance to Banka Strait before dawn on 17th February a searchlight suddenly shone on the *Mary Rose,* and two Japanese patrol vessels trained their guns on her. With no white flag to show, the party used a pair of underpants to indicate surrender, and was taken to Muntok Harbour, Banka Island. There, as its members' baggage was being examined, Bowden remonstrated with a Japanese guard about some article being taken from him. The party was then marched to a hall where hundreds of other civilian and service captives were held. Bowden asked that he be allowed to interview a Japanese officer in order to make known his diplomatic status. Another altercation with a guard resulted. Though Bowden was an elderly, white-haired man, he was punched and threatened with a bayonet, and the guard sought to remove his gold wristlet watch. Then, when a second guard had been brought, he was told by signs that he was to accompany the two. Squaring

---

[10] Bennett, *Why Singapore Fell,* p. 217. An order issued by Australian Army Headquarters, Melbourne, in October 1941, contained the following passages:
"In the very undesirable event of capture by the enemy a prisoner of war has still certain very definite duties to perform:
 (*a*) Not to give away information.
 (*b*) To obtain and endeavour to transmit information home.
 (*c*) TO ESCAPE. This is the most important duty of all, for the following reasons:
  (1) In order to rejoin your unit and again be of use to your country.
  (2) In order to bring back information, e.g. the location and lay-out of the camp, your experiences inside and whilst being taken there."
Under a sub-heading "Early escape" the order continued: ". . . Remember that the information you can collect and give if you escape early is the latest and therefore 'red hot'. So keep on the alert and take in everything you see. In the event of your being unable to make good your escape before arriving in camp take the earliest opportunity to report yourself to the Senior Officer or NCO P/W."

[1] In 1945, at the end of the war, the Commonwealth Government appointed Mr Justice Ligertwood to be a Commissioner to inquire into and report upon the circumstances connected with the action of General Bennett in relinquishing his command and leaving Singapore. The findings of the Commissioner, and an examination of those findings by an eminent military lawyer are given in Appendix 3 to this volume.

his shoulders, he was led from the hall by the guards who carried rifles with bayonets fixed. About half an hour later two shots were heard, and the guards returned cleaning their rifles. It subsequently appeared that the guards kicked Bowden as he was being marched along, made him dig his own grave, and shot him at its edge.

Many others were discovering at this time what it meant to be at the mercy of the Japanese. An outrage had occurred the day before to the survivors from the *Vyner Brooke*. Those aboard this vessel, which left Singapore on 12th February, included the sixty-four Australian nurses in charge of Matron Drummond[2] of the 2/13th Australian General Hospital, who had been ordered out as the enemy pressed on that city. The vessel was bombed and sunk off Banka Island on the afternoon of the 14th. Two of the nurses were killed during the bombing, nine were last seen drifting on a raft, and the others reached land. Of the latter, twenty-two landed from a lifeboat on the north coast of the island, a few miles from Muntok. Although two of them had been badly wounded, they were supported by the others in a long walk along the beach to a fire lit by earlier arrivals from the same vessel, some of them also wounded. On the 16th, when it was found that Japanese were in possession of the island, an officer was sent to Muntok to negotiate their surrender. Some of the women and children in the group, led by a man, set off soon after for Muntok. The Australian nurses stayed to care for the wounded.

About ten Japanese soldiers in charge of an officer then appeared. The men in the party capable of walking were marched round a small headland. To their horror the women saw the Japanese who had accompanied the group wiping their bayonets and cleaning their rifles as they returned. The nurses were next ordered to walk into the sea. When they were knee-deep, supporting the two wounded among them, the Japanese machine-gunned them, and killed all but one. The survivor, Sister Vivian Bullwinkel,[3] regained consciousness and found herself washed ashore and lying on her back, while Japanese were running up the beach, laughing over the massacre. After a further period of unconsciousness she found herself on the beach surrounded by the bodies of those who had fallen with her.

> I was so cold that my only thought was to find some warm spot to die (she related). I dragged myself up to the edge of the jungle and lay in the sun where I must have slept for hours. When I woke the sun was almost setting. I spent the night huddled under some bamboos only a few yards from my dead colleagues, too dazed and shocked for anything to register. Next morning I examined my wound and realised I had been shot through the diaphragm and that it would not prove fatal. For several days I remained in the jungle. I found fresh water where I could get a drink and have a bath. . . . On the third day, driven by hunger, I went down to the lifeboat to see if there were any iron rations in it. . . . A voice called

---

[2] Maj Irene M. Drummond, SFX10594. Sister i/c 2/4 CCS 1940-41; Matron 2/13 AGH 1941-42. Nursing sister; of Millswood, SA; b. Ashfield, NSW, 26 Jul 1905. Killed while prisoner 16 Feb 1942.

[3] Lt Vivian Bullwinkel, ARRC, Florence Nightingale Medal, VFX61330; 2/13 AGH. Nurse; of Broken Hill, NSW; b. Kapunda, SA, 18 Dec 1915.

"Sister", and I found an Englishman there.... After machine-gunning the sisters the Japanese had bayoneted the men on stretchers. He too had been bayoneted through the diaphragm, and left for dead.[4]

Sister Bullwinkel and the Englishman were again taken captive, about ten days later. He died during internment, but Sister Bullwinkel, despite her wound and the sufferings of the prisoner-of-war period, survived and at length returned to Australia. Among those who died in the massacre was Matron Drummond of the 2/13th A.G.H. Matron Paschke[5] of the 2/10th A.G.H. was among the nine who drifted from the *Vyner Brooke* and were not seen again.

The escapers generally from Singapore were broadly in three categories —those who had deserted or had become detached from their units during hostilities; those officially evacuated; and those who escaped after Singapore fell. As has been related, the official evacuation was a confused undertaking. For many of those chosen to leave—mostly women and children, nurses, specialists, and representatives of various units to form experienced cadres elsewhere—the transport which was to be available could not be found when the parties had been organised. The servicemen among these were given the choice of rejoining their units (as Kappe and most of his signals party had done) or of escaping on their own initiative. Two naval gunboats and four small converted river steamers in which evacuees eventually left Singapore were bombed and sunk, but many of these, and others, survived the misfortunes which befell them.

The dividing line between desertions and escapes was in some instances indefinite, particularly as a report that the "cease-fire" on Singapore Island was to take effect as from 4.30 p.m. on 15th February had gained wide circulation and many acted on it in good faith.[6] Some, as the plight of the city worsened, consciously deserted. Once the fighting had ceased, others felt free to get away if they could. Thus before and after capitulation Singapore's shores were combed for craft of any kind which gave hope of escape. The extent of the movement from the island is indicated by the fact that although many who took part in it died and others were captured, about 3,000 reached Java, Ceylon and India through Sumatra.

South and west of Singapore Island the seas are strewn with islands. It was chiefly by way of these that hundreds of craft—sampans, tongkangs, junks and European craft from launches to gunboats—were navigated with varying degrees of skill, or drifted under the influence of wind and currents, towards Sumatra. Many of their occupants owed their lives to Indonesian villagers and others who gave generously of their frugal resources, and in some instances risked their lives to aid them;[7] to the help

---

[4] From an account by Sister Bullwinkel in a narrative by Sister Veronica Clancy who was also on the *Vyner Brooke* and was interned with her.

[5] Maj Olive D. Paschke, RRC, VX38812. Matron 2/10 AGH. Trained nurse; of Dimboola, Vic; b. Dimboola, 19 Jul 1905. Presumed died 14 Feb 1942.

[6] The deputation sent to the Japanese lines had been instructed to propose that hostilities should cease at 4 p.m.

[7] An escaper noted: "Saved as usual by some Malays carrying burning torches . . . taken to village . . . given food, clothes, and a hut. . . . The Malays behaved as if they acted as hosts to shipwrecked evacuees every night."

and hospitality of the Dutch;[8] and to selfless efforts by servicemen and civilians who voluntarily or officially acted as part of the escape organisation. Many escapers were drowned; others were killed by bombs and bullets; some as has been shown died at the hands of the Japanese, or of disease and starvation. Most of those who reached Sumatra were evacuated through the west coast port of Emmahaven, a few miles from Padang.

Two officers became principally active in organising aid for the participants in the strange migration. Captain Lyon[9] of the Gordons, assisted by a Royal Army Medical Corps private, established a dump of food and a shelter hut on an uninhabited part of an island near Moro, in the southwestern part of the Rhio Archipelago. Here, until the evening of 17th February, first aid and sailing directions were given, and rations were provided for the next stage of the journey. Even after Captain Lyon and his assistant left, others got food and instructions left behind in the hut.

Meanwhile Major H. A. Campbell, of the King's Own Scottish Borderers, had arranged with the Dutch authorities in Sumatra means whereby transport, food and clothing were provided. The three main routes used were from the south through Djambi (the first to be closed by the Japanese); through Bengkalis Island to the north-west; and, in the main up the Inderagiri River to Rengat, thence by road to a railhead at Sawahlunto. All three routes led to Padang.

It was the Rengat route that by constant travel and personal contact Campbell organised. Instructions about the route and navigation of the Inderagiri were supplied at Priggi Rajah, at the mouth of the river. At Tambilahan a surgical hospital was set up and further aid was given. Escapers were rested and re-grouped into suitable parties at Rengat, and Ayer Molek near by. Though the Dutch themselves were endangered by the Japanese, now invading Sumatra, a generous number of buses was made available to carry the escapers to the railhead. A British military headquarters was set up at Padang to handle evacuations, and help the Dutch defend the town if necessary. Naval vessels and a number of small craft took parties thence to Java. Two ships left for Colombo and one, with Colonel Coates, formerly of the 6th/15th Indian Brigade, as officer-in-charge of 220 troops aboard, got there. The other, whose passengers included Brigadier Paris and his staff, was sunk on the way.[1]

The behaviour of the escapers varied greatly. Some, generally regarded as being among the deserters, and including Australians, blackened the reputation of their fellow countrymen and prejudiced the chances of those

---

[8] An official report says: "No praise can be too high for the Dutch population in Sumatra. The way they combined hospitality with efficiency in spite of many cases of barbaric ingratitude evoked the admiration of nearly every one of the many hundreds whom they helped to escape to freedom and to the chance to fight another day."

[9] Lt-Col I. Lyon, MBE; 2/Gordons. Regular soldier; b. 17 Aug 1915.

[1] A stark account of the sufferings and eventual death of most of this party is given in *Lifeboat* (1952), by Walter Gibson, who had served as a corporal with the 2/A & SH during the Malayan campaign.

who followed.[2] Among those whose courage and resource gained them distinction were Lieut-Colonel Coates,[3] of the Australian Army Medical Corps, and Captain W. R. Reynolds, an Australian who had been mining in Malaya. Coates was among those of a medical party evacuated from Singapore whose vessel was bombed and disabled, but who reached Tambilahan in a launch. There, aided by other doctors, he carried out a series of operations on wounded people at what became one of a chain of hospitals established by the Royal Army Medical Corps across Sumatra to Padang. Eventually he remained in Padang, with a Major Kilgour of the British medical corps, looking after troops not evacuated.

Reynolds had left Malaya aboard a 90-ton former Japanese fishing boat. On his way he picked up and towed to Sumatra a motor vessel whose engines had failed. Aboard her were 262 Dutch women and children. When Reynolds heard that a large party of evacuees was stranded at Pulau Pompong, in the northern part of the Lingga Archipelago, he made two trips back into the danger zone to evacuate them. Then he placed his vessel at the disposal of the Dutch authorities, and is credited with having helped 2,000 people to Sumatra. On 15th March, when Japanese troops were expected to arrive next day at Rengat, he was officially advised to leave. After a hazardous trip up the east coast of Sumatra he reached India.

Travelling in a launch owned by the Sultan of Johore which had been manned by two Royal Navy officers and a crew, Colonel Broadbent made an adventurous trip to Sumatra, and landed at Tambilahan. It was this launch which picked up Lieut-Colonel Coates and his party whose vessel, as mentioned, had been bombed and disabled on its way from Singapore. Broadbent attended to the housing of about 60 Australian soldiers at Tambilahan. He then went to Rengat, took part in establishing a collecting station, and became responsible for staging a growing number of people to Padang. There he handed over to Brigadier Paris (who at this stage had not left) responsibility for all but about 125 Australians who had reached this point. Other Australians had already been sent forward and had left Sumatra by ship. At length Broadbent and the substantial group of Australians under his command reached Tjilatjap on the south coast of Java, where they and others boarded a fast cargo ship, the *Van Dam,* one of the last vessels to leave for Australia. After picking up on the way five survivors (two of them Australians) of those aboard a vessel which had left a few hours ahead of her, the *Van Dam* reached Fremantle on 6th March.

During and after the collapse of resistance in Singapore largely because of the imminent failure of its water supply, the American-Filipino army of 80,000 troops pent up in the Bataan Peninsula with 26,000 refugees

---

[2] It is on record that a Dutch Javanese police inspector, who acted as host to a party of 12 Australians, found upon returning from absence on duty that his house had been ransacked, and food, bedding and parts of his dress uniform taken.

[3] Lt-Col Sir Albert Coates, OBE, VX39198. (1st AIF: Pte, 7 Bn.) 2/10 AGH. Surgeon; of Melbourne; b. Ballarat, Vic, 28 Jan 1895.

was being starved into submission. Pre-war plans had provided that six months' supplies for 43,000 men should be stored in the peninsula at the outbreak of war but

> MacArthur's order to fight it out on the beaches had invalidated this plan, and when war came supplies and equipment were moved forward to advance depots to support the troops on the front lines.[4]

On 3rd January there were only 30 days' field rations for 100,000, and soon the daily allowance of food was reduced to a dangerously low level.

The Japanese plan provided for the capture of Luzon by the end of January. This would release the *48th Division* which, as mentioned, was to take part in the invasion of Java. Late in December, however, the invasion of Java was brought forward one month on the time-table and early in January preparations were being made to transfer the *48th Division,* in replacement of which General Homma, commanding the *XIV Japanese Army,* received the *65th Brigade,* of six battalions. Soon Homma had only a division and a half to oppose 80,000 troops in Bataan, 12,000 on Corregidor, and the three Philippine divisions in the central and southern islands.

However, on 9th January, Homma, whose staff greatly under-estimated the strength of MacArthur's force, launched an attack by three regiments against the Bataan line. After thirteen days of fierce fighting the weary defenders withdrew to a line 12 miles from the tip of the peninsula. The Japanese attacked again but, after three weeks, had made no real progress against a line manned by far stronger forces than their own and well supported by tanks and artillery. On 8th February Homma ordered his force in Bataan to fall back and reorganise and appealed to Tokyo for reinforcements. Battle casualties and tropical disease had reduced the *XIV Japanese Army* to a skeleton. After the war Homma told an Allied Military Tribunal that if the American and Filipino troops had launched an offensive in late February or in March they could have taken Manila

---

[4] L. Morton, *The Fall of the Philippines,* p. 254.

"without encountering much resistance on our part". From the end of February until 3rd April there was little contact between the opposing armies.

Meanwhile, on 8th February, seven days before the surrender at Singapore, President Quezon had proposed that an agreement be sought with Japan whereby the American troops be withdrawn from the Philippines and the Philippine Army disbanded. This proposal was contained in a message from the American High Commissioner, Mr Francis B. Sayre, supporting the proposal, if American help could not arrive in time, and by one from MacArthur in the course of which he said:

> Since I have no air or sea protection you must be prepared at any time to figure on the complete destruction of this command. You must determine whether the mission of delay would be better furthered by the temporizing plan of Quezon or by my continued battle effort. The temper of the Filipinos is one of almost violent resentment against the United States. Every one of them expected help and when it has not been forthcoming they believe they have been betrayed in favor of others. . . . So far as the military angle is concerned, the problem presents itself as to whether the plan of President Quezon might offer the best possible solution of what is about to be a disastrous debacle. It would not affect the ultimate situation in the Philippines for that would be determined by the results in other theatres. If the Japanese Government rejects President Quezon's proposition it would psychologically strengthen our hold because of their Prime Minister's public statement offering independence. If it accepts it we lose no military advantage because we would still secure at least equal delay. Please instruct me.[5]

Roosevelt promptly sent a long telegram to MacArthur in the course of which he ordered that American forces must keep the flag flying in the Philippines as long as any possibility of resistance remained. MacArthur was authorised, however, to arrange for the capitulation of the Filipino elements "when and if in your opinion that course appears necessary and always having in mind that the Filipino troops are in the service of the United States". Roosevelt added:

> The service that you and the American members of your command can render to your country in the titanic struggle now developing is beyond all possibility of appraisement. I particularly request that you proceed rapidly to the organization of your forces and your defenses so as to make your resistance as effective as circumstances will permit and as prolonged as humanly possible.
> If the evacuation of President Quezon and his Cabinet appears reasonably safe they would be honored and greatly welcomed in the United States. They should come here via Australia. This applies also to the High Commissioner. Mrs Sayre and your family should be given this opportunity if you consider it advisable. You yourself, however, must determine action to be taken in view of circumstances.

By the beginning of March the troops on Bataan were receiving only enough food to keep them alive. The cavalrymen shot their horses and they were eaten; there was much malaria and a shortage of quinine; dysentery was widespread. Resistance could not last much longer.

---

[5] Quoted in Stimson and Bundy, *On Active Service in Peace and War* (1948), p. 398. Stimson was the U.S. Secretary of War.

CHAPTER 18

RABAUL AND THE FORWARD OBSERVATION LINE

EASTWARD of the Malay Peninsula the Japanese, having captured Tarakan and Menado on 11th January, were ready in the last week of January to thrust their trident farther south. One prong was aimed at Kavieng and Rabaul, one at Kendari on the south-eastern coast of Celebes, and, later, Ambon on the opposite side of the Molucca Sea, and one at Balikpapan in Dutch Borneo, the site of big oil refineries. These advances into Dutch and Australian territory would carry the Japanese forces across the equator, and establish them in bases whence they would advance to the final objectives on the eastern flank—the New Guinea mainland, and Timor and Bali, thus completing the isolation of Java.

The capture of Rabaul, Kavieng, Kendari and Balikpapan were to take place on the 23rd and 24th January; the advance to the final objectives was to begin about four weeks later. In this phase, as always throughout their offensive, the length of each stride forward was about the range of their land-based aircraft. Thus aircraft from one captured base would support the attack on the next. If no such base was available, carrier-borne aircraft were employed.

As an outcome of the Singapore Conference of February 1941 and discussions between the Australian Chiefs of Staff and Air Chief Marshal Brooke-Popham, the Australian War Cabinet had agreed to send an A.I.F. battalion to Rabaul, capital of the Mandated Territory of New Guinea. It decided also to encourage "unobtrusively" the evacuation to the mainland of women and children not engaged in essential work in New Guinea.

Rabaul, situated on the Gazelle Peninsula, lies on Blanche Bay, inside the hooked north-eastern tip of New Britain, largest and most important island of the Bismarck Archipelago. Formerly part of German New Guinea, the island had been seized in September 1914 by an Australian Expeditionary Force under Colonel Holmes,[1] and remained under military government until May 1921.[2] In fulfilment of a mandate from the League of Nations, Australia then established a civil administration throughout the Territory. This included a district service which offered unusual opportunities for adventure and advancement.

New Britain is crescent-shaped, 370 miles long with a mean breadth of 50 miles, with a rugged range of mountains along its whole length. Most of the coconut and other plantations near Rabaul were served by roads, but others, scattered along the coastal areas in the western part of the island, were reached principally by sea. New Britain's climate is

---

[1] Maj-Gen W. Holmes, CMG, DSO. Comd AN & MEF 1914-15, 5 Inf Bde 1915-16, 4 Div 1916-17. B. Sydney, 12 Sep 1862. Killed in action 2 Jul 1917.
[2] See S. S. Mackenzie, *The Australians at Rabaul*, 1927 (*Official History of Australia in the War of 1914-18*, Vol X).

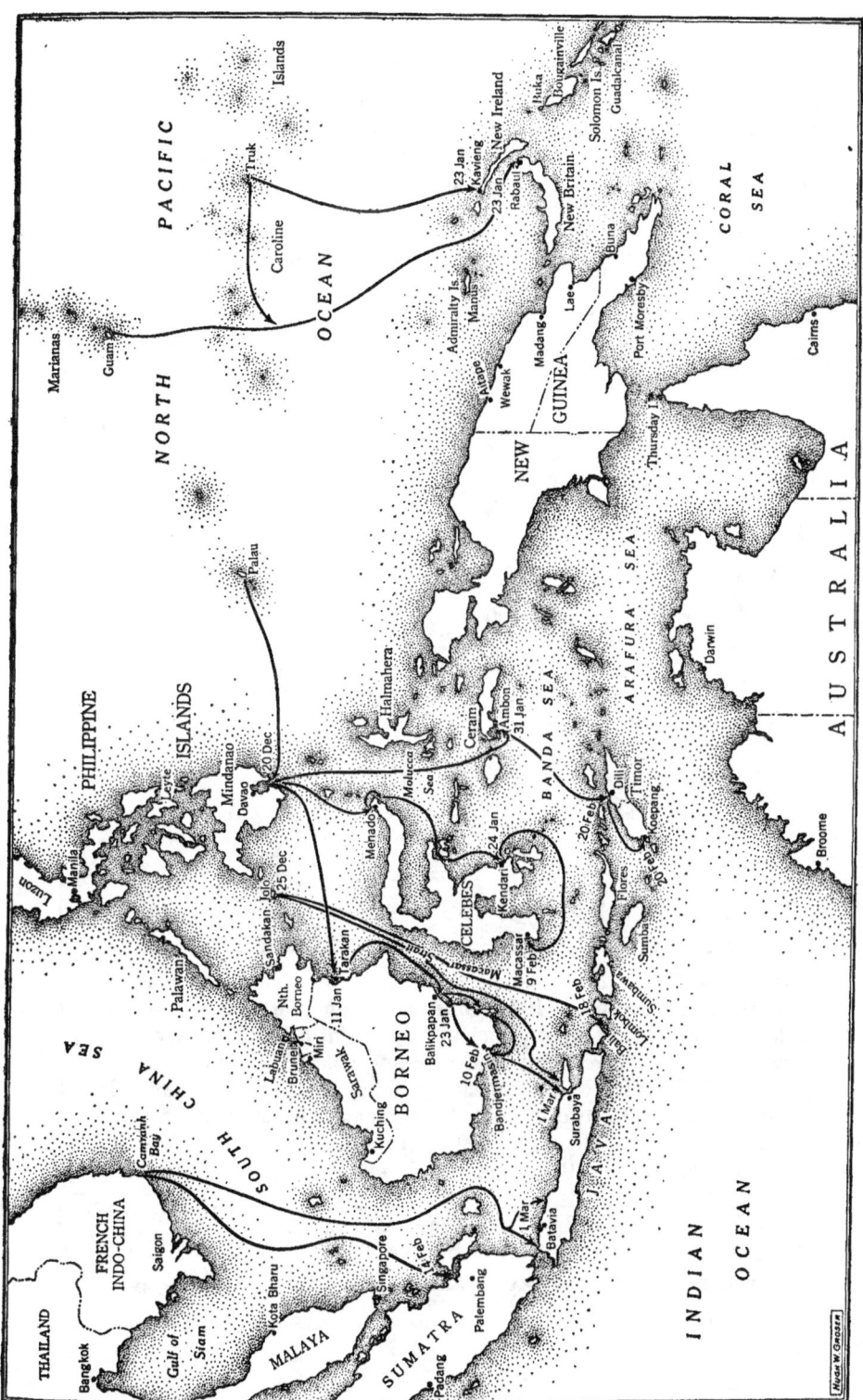

The Japanese advance through the Netherlands Indies and to Rabaul

no worse nor better than that of thousands of other tropical islands, with a moderately heavy rainfall, constant heat, and humidity.

Lieut-Colonel Carr's 2/22nd Battalion of the 23rd Brigade arrived during March and April 1941 to garrison this outpost, protect its airfields and seaplane anchorage, and act as a link in a slender chain of forward observation posts which Australia was stringing across her northern frontiers. The one other military unit in the territory, apart from a native constabulary, was a detachment of the New Guinea Volunteer Rifles, comprising some eighty men, raised by Lieut-Colonel Walstab,[3] the Super-

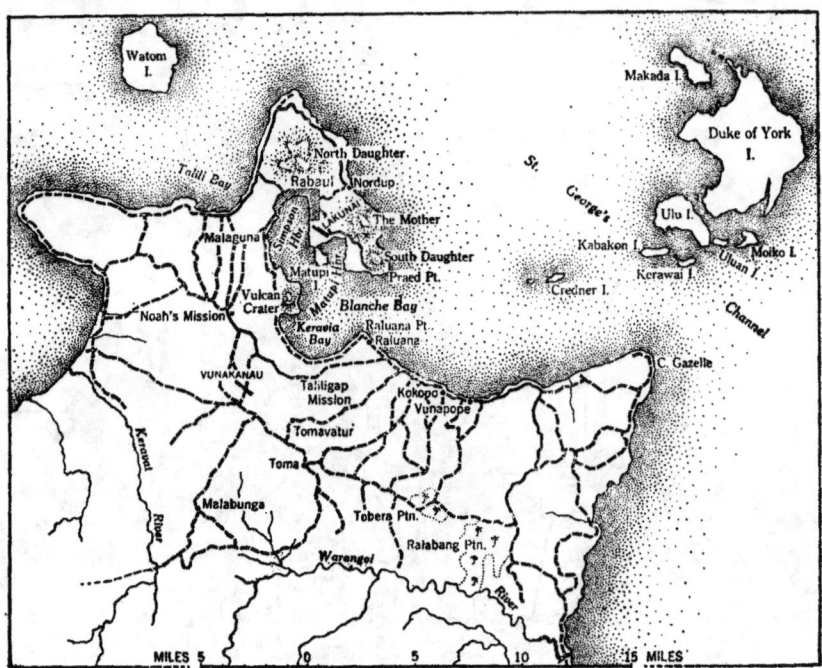

intendent of Police, for part-time training soon after the outbreak of war in 1939. Until December 1941, other small units arrived to swell Carr's battalion group. They were principally a coastal defence battery with two 6-inch guns and searchlights under Major Clark,[4] in March and April (sent partly because of the attack by German raiders on Nauru Island in December 1940); two out-dated 3-inch anti-aircraft guns under Lieutenant Selby[5] (two officers and fifty-one others) on 16th August; and the 17th Anti-Tank Battery (six and 104) under Captain Matheson[6] on

---

[3] Col J. Walstab, DSO, VD, VX17626. (1st AIF: CO 5 Bn 1916-17.) HQ I Aust Corps. Police superintendent; of Caulfield, Vic; b. Victoria Barracks, Melbourne, 8 Oct 1885.

[4] Maj J. R. P. Clark, TX6041. OC Praed Point Bty 1941-42. Clerk; of New Town, Tas; b. Hobart, 26 Jun 1903.

[5] Maj D. M. Selby, NX142851. OC AA Bty Rabaul 1941-42; Legal Offr Angau 1943-45. Barrister; of Vaucluse, NSW; b. Melbourne, 13 Mar 1906.

[6] Maj G. Matheson, ED, VX45210; OC 17 A-Tk Bty 1941-42. Insurance inspector; of Bendigo, Vic; b. Carlton, Vic, 4 Feb 1909.

29th September. Other detachments included one from the 2/10th Field Ambulance under Major Palmer⁷ and six nurses.

The harbour which the little force was to defend lies in a zone containing several active volcanoes, some of which had erupted in 1937. Blanche Bay contains two inner harbours, Simpson and Matupi, and forms one of the best natural shelters in the South Pacific, capable of holding up to 300,000 tons of shipping. The inner part of the bay is almost surrounded by a rugged ridge which rises at Raluana Point, reaches a height of about 1,500 feet north of Vunakanau airfield, then decreases, as it swings north, to about 600 feet west of Malaguna. Farther north the ridge rises sharply to three heights which dominate the north-eastern part of the bay—North Daughter, The Mother and South Daughter. On the southern slopes of South Daughter lies Praed Point, overlooking the harbour's entrance, where the coastal battery had been established. On the northern shores of Simpson Harbour, between the slopes of North Daughter and The Mother, was a flat stretch of ground up to three-quarters of a mile wide on which lay Rabaul and Lakunai airfield. Overlooking the town was the volcano Matupi, barren and weather-beaten, from whose crater from mid-1941 to October that year poured a mighty column of black volcanic ash. Cheek by jowl with Matupi was the gaping but idle crater of Rabalanakaia, from which Rabaul derives its name.

The European population of Rabaul, amounting to about 1,000,

was well served by two clubs, three hotels and three European stores (wrote Lieutenant Selby) but the main shopping centre consisted of four streets of Chinese stores where the troops could spend their pay on a multitudinous variety of knick-knacks to tempt the eyes of the home-sick soldiery. In the centre of the two was the Bung, the native market, where the [native people] displayed and noisily proclaimed the excellence of their wares, luscious paw-paws, bananas, pineapples, tomatoes and vegetables. Among the magnificent tree-lined avenues strolled a polyglot population, the local officers looking cool in their not-so-spotless whites, troops in khaki shirts and shorts, the tired-looking wives of planters on a day's shopping, Chinese maidens glancing up demurely from beneath their huge sunshades, their modest-looking neck to ankle frocks slit on each side to their thighs, bearded German missionaries, hurrying Japanese traders and ubiquitous [natives], black, brown, coffee coloured or albino, the men with lips stained scarlet by betel nut juice, the women carrying the burdens and almost invariably puffing a pipe.⁸

Rabaul was approached by three main roads—Battery road, which ran from Praed Point Battery past Lakunai airfield to the town; Namanula road, from Nordup on the coast over the Namanula ridge to Rabaul; and Malaguna road. On the outskirts of the township the Malaguna road joined the Tunnel Hill road (a short linking road to the north coast road system), and the Vulcan road which followed the coast past Kokopo until it reached Put Put on the east coast below the Warangoi River. A steeply-graded road named Big Dipper ascended between Vulcan and

---

⁷ Lt-Col E. C. Palmer, OBE, NX35096. 2/10 Fd Amb and Comd 10 Fd Amb 1942-45. Medical practitioner; of Bulli, NSW; b. Coolgardie, WA, 22 Jan 1909.

⁸ The writer is indebted to Major Selby for allowing him to use an account of these events written in July 1942, after Selby's return to Australia. While this volume was in the press, Selby's narrative was published with the title *Hell and High Fever* (Sydney, 1956).

Rabaul to Four Ways where a number of secondary roads met, and continued on through Three Ways into the Kokopo Ridge road running north of Vunakanau through Taliligap until eventually it linked with the Vulcan road east of Raluana. Above the ridge the country was flat and covered in thick jungle, but around Vunakanau airfield was a large undulating area of high kunai grass. Narrow native pads or tracks on the Gazelle Peninsula linked village to village, but they were usually steep and tiring to follow. Rivers and streams were plentiful. The smaller streams could usually be crossed by wading, but the larger, of which the Keravat, flowing north, the Toriu, flowing west, and the Warangoi, flowing east, are the principal ones, could be crossed easily only by boat.

In July the 1st Independent Company, commanded by Major Wilson,[9] passed through Rabaul on its way to Kavieng, New Ireland, an island slanting across the top of New Britain. Sections were to be disposed for the protection of air bases there and at Vila (New Hebrides), Tulagi (Guadalcanal), Buka Passage (Bougainville), Namatanai (Central New Ireland) and Lorengau (Manus Island), thus farther extending the forward observation line chosen by the Chiefs of Staff until it spread in an arc from east of Australia's Cape York to the Admiralty Islands, north of New Guinea, a distance of about 1,600 miles.

From July to October Rabaul township was covered by dust and fumes from Matupi, which blackened brass, rotted tents and mosquito nets, irritated the throats of soldiers and civilians and killed vegetation. On 9th September, mainly because of the dust nuisance, the headquarters of the Administrator (Brigadier-General Sir Walter McNicoll[1]), with some of his staff, was moved from Rabaul to Lae, on the mainland of New Guinea.

That month the Australian Chiefs of Staff recommended to the War Cabinet acceptance of an American proposal to provide equipment, including minefields, anti-submarine nets, anti-aircraft equipment and radar, for the protection and expansion of the anchorage at Rabaul to make it suitable as a base for British and American fleets. The War Cabinet approved the proposals the next month and an inter-service planning team visited Rabaul in November. However, the Australian Chiefs of Staff reported in December, after the outbreak of war, that the project was unlikely to be implemented. They said it was important to retain the garrison at Rabaul as "an advanced observation line", but its reinforcement was not possible because of the hazard of transporting a force from the mainland and of maintaining it; account should be taken of the psychological effect which a voluntary withdrawal would have on the minds of the Dutch in the Netherlands. The Chiefs of Staff concluded that though the scale of attack which could be brought against Rabaul from bases

---
[9] Maj J. Edmonds-Wilson, SX9068. OC 1st Indep Coy. Farmer and grazier; of Georgetown, SA; b. Red Hill, SA, 16 May 1907. Died 4 Jan 1951.

[1] Brig-Gen Sir Walter McNicoll, KBE, CB, CMG, DSO. (1st AIF: 7 Bn and CO 6 Bn; Comd 10 Inf Bde 1916-18.) MHR 1931-34; Administrator of New Guinea 1934-43. Of Melbourne and Geelong, Vic; b. South Melbourne, 27 May 1877. Died 26 Dec 1947.

in the Japanese mandated islands was beyond the capacity of the small garrison to repel, the enemy should be made to fight for the island, rather than that it should be abandoned at the first threat.

About the same time the War Cabinet, as an outcome of the Singapore Conference of February 1941, agreed to spend £666,500 on behalf of the United States for further development of New Caledonia, south of the New Hebrides, as an operational base. After the Chiefs of Staff had repeated earlier warnings that a division, supported by strong air forces, would be needed to defend the island, the War Cabinet approved the dispatch of the 3rd Independent Company (21 officers and 312 other ranks) to Noumea as a gesture to the Free French and to carry out demolitions if necessary.

Meanwhile, as an outcome of the proposals to expand the Rabaul base, a new commander had arrived at Rabaul. He was Colonel Scanlan,[2] an experienced soldier of the 1914-18 war, who took over the already established headquarters of "New Guinea Area" on 8th October.

During December a force of four Hudson aircraft and ten Wirraways commanded by Wing Commander Lerew[3] was established at Rabaul. Japanese planes, travelling singly and at great height, began to appear over the area. In mid-December compulsory evacuation to Australia of all European women and children not engaged in essential services began.[4]

Scanlan, mainly occupied since his arrival in preparing a plan for the defence of Rabaul by a force equivalent to a brigade group and with a greatly expanded scale of equipment, made no radical redeployment of his existing force of 1,400 men. These had been disposed by Carr covering the harbour area, with an improvised company at Praed Point, a company in beach positions at Talili Bay, westward across the narrow neck of the peninsula; one at Lakunai; and others along the ridge around the bay, at Four Ways and defending Vunakanau airfield. On New Year's Day the Area commander ordered his men to fight to the last and concluded with the words, underlined and in capitals: "There shall be no withdrawal." The troops lacked regular news of the outside world and the camps were alive with wild rumours, some of them inspired by propaganda broadcasts from Tokyo. Lieutenant Selby felt that a regular official news service would do much to dispel misgivings which Scanlan's order helped to increase. Scanlan's headquarters considered such a service impracticable, but a few days later issued an order forbidding troops to listen to Tokyo.[5]

Other officers who saw as clearly as did the Chiefs of Staff the isolated and vulnerable condition of the force, were sufficiently disturbed by the

---

[2] Col J. J. Scanlan, DSO, TX16307. (1st AIF: 7 Bn 1914-16, CO 59 Bn 1918.) Comd HQ NG Area 1941-42. Deputy Governor Hobart Gaol; of Hobart; b. Albert Park, Vic, 19 Oct 1890.

[3] Gp Capt J. M. Lerew, DFC, 73. Comd 24 Sqn 1941-42, 7 Sqn 1942; Overseas HQ London 1944-45. Regular airman; of Melbourne; b. Hamilton, Vic, 20 Aug 1912.

[4] The Director of Health, Doctor E. T. Brennan, decided that the nurses employed by the New Guinea Administration were in an essential service, but at the direction of the Government Secretary, Major H. H. Page, made it clear to them that if they wished they also could leave the territory. Only one elected to do so.

[5] As an outcome Selby himself produced an "AA News Bulletin" which proved so popular that he issued it daily. He sent a copy to HQ NG Area and was asked to put that headquarters on his circulation list.

lack of a comprehensive scheme for withdrawal to ask Colonel Scanlan to define their functions in the event of the garrison being overwhelmed. The Army Service Corps officer to the force placed before New Guinea Area Headquarters in January a plan to hide portion of the battalion's two years' food supply in the mountains, but this precaution, fundamental to continued resistance in that area, or even to survival, seems to have gone almost neglected.[6]

The first heavy raid on Rabaul came about 10.30 a.m. on 4th January. Twenty-two Japanese bombers, flying in formation at 18,000 feet, made a pattern-bombing attack with fragmentation bombs on Lakunai airfield. More than fifty were dropped. Three hit the runway, seventeen landed on the native compound, killing about fifteen people and wounding as many more, and the rest fell harmlessly in the sea. Two Wirraways which took off from Lakunai failed to intercept the raiders, and Selby's anti-aircraft battery fired at them, but without effect, their shells bursting far below.[7] Late in the day about eleven flying-boats made two runs over the Vunakanau airfield; one pattern of bombs straddled the end of the strip, but the others fell wide of it, killing only one native.

On the 9th a Hudson piloted by Flight Lieutenant Yeowart[8] made a courageous flight from Kavieng over Truk, 695 miles north of Rabaul, where he saw a large concentration of shipping and aircraft presumably being assembled for a southward thrust. By the 18th it had been established that the bulk of the Japanese *Fourth Fleet* was concentrated at Truk and its reconnaissance aircraft were ranging over the area held by the 2/22nd Battalion and the 1st Independent Company. Further bombing raids on the Rabaul area were made during January. The battery on the slopes of North Daughter, although equipped with obsolescent guns and lacking modern predictors, kept the aircraft at a high level.

Soon after midday on the 20th the garrison received warning from Sub-Lieutenant Page,[9] a coastwatcher[1] at Tabar Island, east of New Ireland, that twenty enemy aircraft were headed towards the town. A further formation of thirty-three approaching from the west was not

---

[6] The exception was that Major Mollard, second-in-command of the 2/22nd Battalion, in conjunction with Captain Appel, in charge of troops situated for the defence of Vunakanau airfield, moved three truck-loads of tinned food from an A.S.C. dump at Vunakanau to Malabunga Mission. This was later distributed to troops passing through Malabunga.

[7] This appears to have been the first militia unit to go into action in Australian territory.

[8] F-Lt R. A. Yeowart, 270647. Nos. 6, 12, 32 Sqns 1940-42; OC Test and Ferry flights Nos. 1 and 7 Aircraft Depots 1943-45. Accountant; of Brisbane; b. Brisbane, 22 Aug 1915. (Yeowart was attached to No. 24 Squadron during this period.)

[9] Sub-Lt C. L. Page; RANVR. Planter; of Tabar Is; b. 1911. Believed executed by Japanese 21 Jul 1942.

[1] A member of a naval coastwatching organisation in the Territories and the Solomon Islands. This had its beginnings in 1919 and was greatly extended after the appointment in 1939 of Lt-Cdr Eric Feldt, a graduate of the Australian Naval College who left the Navy after the 1914-18 war to enter the Govt Service in New Guinea. The scheme "provided for the appointment of selected personnel adjacent to or on the coast with means of instant communication with the Navy Office, who should, in time of war, report instantly any unusual or suspicious happenings in their area, sightings of strange ships or aircraft, floating mines and other matters of defence interest. Appointees included reliable persons such as postmasters, police and other Government servants; missionaries at mission stations on little-frequented parts of the coast, pilots of civil airlines on or near coastal routes, and, in the Territories of Papua, New Guinea, and the British Solomon Islands, Patrol Officers and District Officers and other officials, besides planters." (Eric Feldt, *The Coastwatchers*, 1946.) The Coastwatching Organisation is described in the naval volumes of this history.

Smoke from the naval base overshadows Singapore. February 1942.

(*Australian War Memorial*)

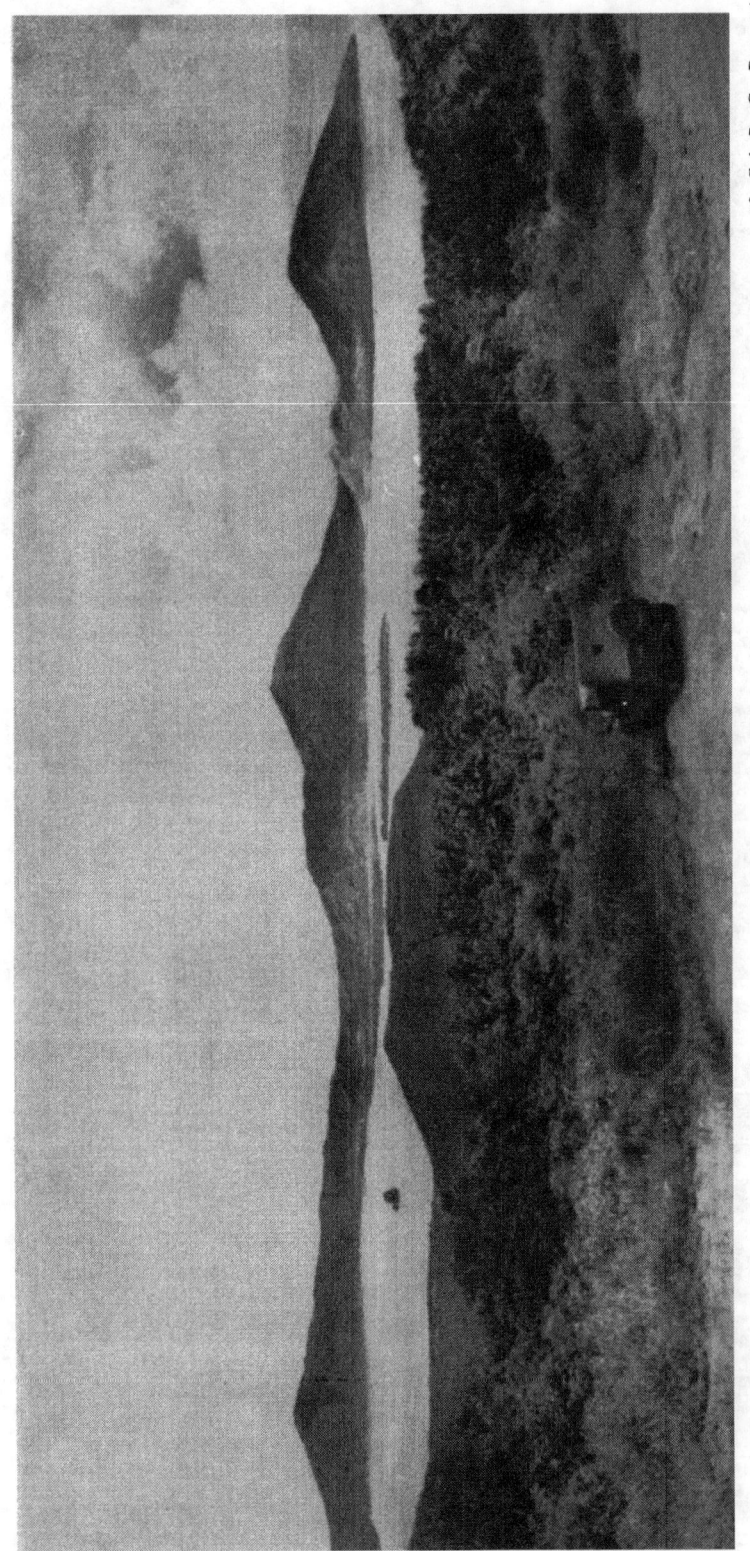

Simpson Harbour, fronting Rabaul, capital of the Mandated Territory of New Guinea in 1942, viewed from Taliligap on the Kokopo Ridge road. Post-war photograph.

(*Lt-Col B. G. Dawson*)

detected until it was over Rabaul at 12.40 p.m. A few minutes later a report was received that another fifty aircraft were over Duke of York Island, between Cape Gazelle and New Ireland. When the first formation was sighted two Wirraways were patrolling at 15,000 feet. Six others took off, though the odds seemed insuperable and to the pilots it must have seemed that they were going to certain death. One crashed in the kunai grass near Vunakanau and the others were still attempting to gain height as bombs were falling. Within a few minutes the remaining Wirraways, outnumbered, outpaced and outmanoeuvred, were forced out of action. Three were shot down, two crash-landed, one landed with part of its tailplane shot away, and only one remained undamaged. Six members of the squadron were killed and five wounded or injured in their brave but foredoomed action.

The Japanese now delivered leisurely high-level bombing attacks against shipping, wharves, airfields and other objectives. Heavy bombers, flying-boats and seaplanes patrolled in pageant formation while Zero fighters attacked shipping in the harbour, wharves and military encampments, and performed impudent aerobatics. The Japanese used about 120 aircraft, and the raid lasted three-quarters of an hour. At its end the Norwegian merchantman *Herstein* lay burning in the harbour, the hulk *Westralia* had been sunk, and a Japanese heavy bomber, brought down by anti-aircraft fire, was smouldering against the side of The Mother. Only three of Lerew's aircraft—one Hudson and two Wirraways—remained undamaged. That afternoon he concentrated these at Vunakanau and handed over Lakunai for demolition.

There was a lull in the air attacks on the 21st, but early that morning Scanlan's headquarters intercepted a message from a Catalina flying-boat that four enemy cruisers were 65 miles south-west of Kavieng, heading towards Rabaul. Scanlan learnt also that Kavieng had been heavily attacked that morning. In the afternoon Carr and his adjutant, Captain Smith,[2] were called to Area Headquarters, where Colonel Scanlan informed them that he expected the cruisers to be near Rabaul about 10 o'clock that night, and that he did not intend to allow the troops "to be massacred by naval gunfire". He ordered Carr to move all troops from Malaguna camp, which lay in an exposed position along the foreshore of Simpson Harbour and an improvised company, under Captain Shier,[3] to be sent to Raluana. All other companies were to be prepared for immediate movement. Scanlan added that the troops were to be told that it was "an exercise only" —a decision which resulted in some men going to battle stations lacking hard rations, quinine and other essentials.

That day Lerew began arrangements to evacuate his force. Two Wirraways left in the afternoon for Lae by way of Gasmata, and before daylight on the 22nd the remaining aircraft—a Hudson—had taken off from Vuna-

---

[2] Maj I. L. Smith, VX44388. 2/22 Bn and 1 Para Bn. Articled law clerk; of Balwyn, Vic; b. Canterbury, Vic, 2 May 1915. Killed in aircraft accident 14 Oct 1943.

[3] Capt F. E. Shier, VX44908; 2/22 Bn. Manager; of South Yarra, Vic; b. Hampton, Vic, 7 Aug 1909.

kanau carrying the wounded. The airfield was then demolished, over 100 aircraft bombs being buried in the strip and then exploded.

Just before 8 a.m. on the 22nd a further attack was launched by forty-five fighters and dive bombers. Under severe machine-gunning and dive-bombing, Captain Appel's[4] company at Vunakanau, inspired and encouraged by their leader, replied with small arms and machine-gun fire. The dive bombers then turned to the Praed Point battery, easily located from the air because during its construction all the palm trees and tropical undergrowth in the area had been removed, and a wide metalled road ran like a pointer to the emplacements.

The intense bombing and machine-gunning that followed had the effect of silencing the coast defence guns. A heavy pall of smoke and dust, so thick that it resembled a semi-blackout, hung over Praed Point. Some of the dazed survivors said that the upper gun had been blasted out of the ground, crashing on the lower gun and injuring the commander. Eleven men were killed, including some sheltering in a dugout who were buried alive when it collapsed.[5]

With the silencing of the Praed Point battery, the evacuation of the air force,[6] and the cratering of the airfields, Scanlan decided that the justification for the original role of the force no longer existed. He ordered that demolitions be carried out and the township evacuated. At 3.30 p.m. he received news from the anti-aircraft battery position that an enemy convoy was approaching and sent his brigade major, McLeod,[7] to confirm it. Through the battery telescope McLeod saw eleven ships "just visible on the horizon, and steaming south-east". The convoy appeared to him to consist of destroyers, cruisers, transports and one aircraft carrier. About twenty vessels had been counted in the convoy before it disappeared to the south-east half an hour later.

At 4 p.m. the engineers blew a bomb dump within the town. The blast of the great explosion shattered valves of wireless sets in Rabaul and put the radio transmitter at headquarters out of action. The only means then existing of passing messages was by a teleradio, which had been established at Toma. Thus, as Rabaul received confirmation of the arrival of the enemy convoy, its main link with the outside world snapped.

Scanlan, who had now established his headquarters between Three Ways and Taliligap, decided that the enemy's probable landing places would be within the harbour. To prevent the possibility of part of his force being cut off should the Japanese establish themselves astride the

---

[4] Lt-Col E. S. Appel, MC, VX8370; 2/22 Bn. Pharmaceutical chemist; of Ripponlea, Vic; b. Castlemaine, Vic, 16 Oct 1904.

[5] Afterwards the siting of the guns was criticised. Normally they are sited more or less on the same level, but where a wide arc has to be covered the fire of one gun will mask the other towards the extremities of the arc, and blast effects are a serious problem. To meet the requirements of as wide an arc of fire as possible and to avoid masking and blast, the Praed Point guns had been sited one above the other. It was a departure from Australian precedent, but quite logical, and had in fact been adopted at the Pasir Laba battery in Singapore before the war.

[6] Some members of Scanlan's force, influenced by the withdrawal in trucks of the remaining RAAF ground staff towards Sum Sum, on the south coast in accordance with a pre-arranged plan, joined in the movement, without orders, and were taken off in flying-boats on the 23rd and 24th.

[7] Lt-Col N. R. McLeod, NX102558. BM HQ NG Area 1941-42, 8 Bde 1945. Regular soldier; of Point Piper, NSW; b. Thursday Island, 10 Jan 1918.

connecting isthmus, he decided to move his troops from the Matupi area and concentrate the companies south of Blanche Bay. Major Owen's[8] company at Lakunai, having demolished the airfield there, was moved to prepared positions at Vulcan; "R" Company from Praed Point to a reserve position at Four Ways; and a company under Captain McInnes[9] from Talili Bay to a covering position at Three Ways, about a mile south of Four Ways, to prevent enemy penetration from the beach at Vulcan or from Kokopo, along the Kokopo Ridge road. Appel's company was to retain its position at Vunakanau for airfield defence. Captain Travers'[1] company, supplemented by "R" Company, would remain at Four Ways as battalion reserve, with possible roles of defence against penetration from the Talili or Kokopo areas, or as reinforcement to Appel's company at Vunakanau. Major Palmer's detachment of the 2/10th Field Ambulance and the six nurses, who had been running a military hospital on Namanula ridge, he moved with the patients to the comparative safety of Vunapope Mission at Kokopo. Finally he ordered Lieutenant Selby of the anti-aircraft battery to destroy his guns and join Captain Shier's company at Raluana. The force was now west and south of Rabaul.

Dispositions, 2 a.m. 23rd January

It was a sad moment for the gunners to whom the guns had long been a source of pride and inspiration. A round was placed in the chamber and one in the muzzle of each gun. The oil buffers were disconnected and lengths of telephone wire attached to the firing handles. The ringsight telescope was draped over the muzzle of No. 2 gun and the gun telescopes were removed from their brackets. Everybody took cover. The wires were pulled, there was a roar, then another, and pieces of metal

---

[8] Lt-Col W. T. Owen, VX45223. 2/22 Bn and CO 39 Bn. Bank teller; of Leongatha, Vic; b. Nagambie, Vic, 27 May 1905. Killed in action 29 Jul 1942.

[9] Maj C. L. McInnes, ED, VX46497. 2/22, 2/14 Bns. Bank officer; of Shepparton, Vic; b. Brunswick, Vic, 28 Sep 1906.

[1] Maj R. E. Travers, VX44162; 2/22 Bn. Grazier; of Metung, Vic; b. Warragul, Vic, 19 Feb 1901. Executed by Japanese 27 Jan 1942.

whistled overhead. When the artillerymen emerged from their shelter both barrels had split and for a couple of feet from the gun mouths they "opened out like a sliced radish". It was found impracticable to destroy the ammunition, amounting to about 2,500 rounds.

At 5 p.m. Scanlan ordered road-blocks to be dropped on three secondary roads which led to the new positions from Talili Bay, and anti-tank mines to be laid. McInnes supervised this, posting a section on each road-block and sending patrols along Tavilo and Kokopo Ridge roads and down Big Dipper road.

Meanwhile Owen had disposed his company in prepared positions on the Rabaul side of Vulcan crater. He placed the N.G.V.R. and the anti-tank guns under Lieutenant Clark[2] of the 17th Anti-Tank Battery near the Big Dipper-Vulcan road junction; Lieutenant Grant's[3] platoon of the 2/22nd forward on the left, north of the lower slopes of Vulcan; 9 Platoon on the right on two spurs approximately 1,200 yards south-west of Grant's platoon and 8 Platoon in reserve, about 1,000 yards to the rear of the forward platoons near company headquarters.[4] To the fire power of each of the forward platoons Owen added a medium machine-gun, retaining the three mortars near his company headquarters. The men who had been attached from the coastal defence battery and the engineers were disposed between the Vulcan position and the Big Dipper road. By 5 p.m. all were settled in their positions and watching civilians making their way in trucks, cars and on foot along the road to Kokopo under a cloud of black smoke from the burning wharves and the demolitions in Rabaul township.

At Raluana Shier's improvised company received some slender reinforcement during the day. The men were short of tools and it was not until 11 p.m. that digging of the platoon positions was completed. Soon afterwards Shier ordered a redeployment, placing Lieutenant Henry's[5] platoon right of the Mission with a patrol to the junction of the Vulcan-Kokopo roads, Lieutenant Tolmer's[6] pioneers at the Mission, and Lieutenant Milne's[7] platoon on the left at the Catchment (a small water reservoir), supported by a medium machine-gun manned by five New Guinea riflemen.

Meanwhile the anti-aircraft gunners had arrived at Three Ways. Thence they were ordered by Scanlan to join Shier at Raluana.

My men (wrote Selby afterwards) had had no infantry training—neither had I. . . . We climbed back into the two trucks and moved on through Taliligap. A misty rain

---

[2] Lt A. Clark, VX43797; 17 A-Tk Bty. Grazier; of Yea, Vic; b. Melbourne, 14 Mar 1911.

[3] Lt W. G. Grant, VX44911; 2/22 Bn. Accountant; of Brighton, Vic; b. Brighton, 30 Jan 1916.

[4] Owen's company included three 3-inch mortars, two medium machine-guns, two anti-tank guns, a platoon of NGVR manning two medium machine-guns and one mortar, a detachment of artillerymen commanded by Captain S. G. Nottage (of Woodville, SA) and two Bren carriers.
Although the battalion was not fully equipped with light machine-guns it possessed 16 Vickers medium machine-guns which were used to form an MG company. In addition there were 4 Bren gun carriers and the anti-tank battery, the latter armed with 16 2-pounder anti-tank guns, but possessing only solid steel ammunition, and only enough for each gun to enable rapid rate of fire to be maintained for about a minute.

[5] Lt L. D. Henry, VX38976; 2/22 Bn. Regular soldier; of Seymour, Vic; b. Croydon, Vic, 11 Jun 1914. Killed in action 26 Jan 1942.

[6] Maj A. R. Tolmer, MC, VX35754. 2/22, 49, 2/4 Bns; 1 NG Inf Bn. Sales manager; of Brighton, Vic; b. Broome, WA, 17 Aug 1914.

[7] Lt G. A. C. Milne, VX44781; 2/22 Bn. Salesman; of Hampton, Vic; b. Melbourne, 8 Apr 1916.

was falling, the road was a slippery ribbon of mud and . . . lights were forbidden. . . . We went at a walking pace down the narrow twisting road, a gunner walking in front with his hand on the mudguard to guide me through the darkness. It was nearly midnight when we reached Raluana and we were given a most welcome cup of soup, our first refreshment since lunchtime. Captain Shier and I walked around the defences. There was no wire on the beach and only one short length of trench had been dug. On Shier's orders I placed the Vickers gun and its crew on the beach and posted five gunners with rifles to cover it. The rest of us were ordered to proceed to the old German battery position a few hundred yards up the hill where we were to support the troops on the beach.

Soon after midnight Owen's company, waiting beside Vulcan, heard the hum of an approaching aeroplane and a parachute flare was dropped towards the crater, illuminating the whole harbour. Other flares had been dropped continuously over Vunakanau airfield throughout the night. About 1 a.m. landing craft could be seen making in the direction of the causeway, and red Very lights in Matupi Harbour signalled the success of Japanese landings. At 2.25 the men heard movement and voices within Simpson Harbour and landing craft were seen making towards the left platoon. Corporal Jones,[8] patrolling forward of the company positions, fired a Very light at 2.30—a signal to his comrades that the Japanese had arrived at the near-by beach.

The Australians could see the landing craft and their occupants silhouetted against a boat and dumps ablaze in Rabaul harbour and township. Lieutenant Grant immediately telephoned Major Owen, who passed the news to battalion headquarters.

We could see dimly the shapes of boats, and men getting out (said one soldier later). As they landed the Japanese were laughing, talking and striking matches . . . one of them even shone a torch. . . . We allowed most of them to get out of the boats and then fired everything we had. In my section we had one Lewis gun, one Tommy gun, eight rifles. The Vickers guns also opened up with us. We gave the mortars the position . . . and in a matter of minutes they were sending their bombs over.[9]

The beach was wired forty yards ahead of the platoon's position and the mortars, accurately directed by Sergeant Kirkland,[1] were landing their bombs just in front of the wire. Two attempts to rush the positions were frustrated by the intense fire of the Australians. Thwarted in their flank assaults on Owen's positions, the Japanese now began moving toward Vulcan, away from the wire which stretched across the company front. Soon after 2.30 the right platoon reported that Japanese were moving up the ravines from Keravia Bay. A few minutes later the telephone line between company and battalion headquarters went dead. Some of the Japanese were carrying flags towards which others rallied. They were engaged by rifle and machine-gun fire and immediately halted in the cover of the ravines.

---

[8] Cpl J. N. Jones, VX29630. 2/22, 49 Bns. Drainer; of Corowa, NSW; b. Finley, NSW, 2 Jun 1917.

[9] Sgt K. G. Hale, VX25895; 2/22 Bn. Printer; of Buninyong, Vic; b. Buninyong, 18 Jan 1919.

[1] Sgt A. J. Kirkland, VX22014. 2/22, 2/4 Bns. Clerk; of Surrey Hills, Vic; b. Melbourne, 1 Jan 1918.

Meanwhile Captain Shier's company in its hastily and ill-prepared positions at Raluana was faring less well. At 2.45 a.m. Japanese had landed on the beach between Tolmer's platoon at the Mission and Milne's at the Catchment. The enemy overran the forward sections of company headquarters and Captain Shier gave the order to withdraw. The company fell back in stages, platoon by platoon, to transport waiting on the Vulcan Ridge road, and began embussing. At 3.30 the Japanese began infiltrating through the position and were fired on by a rearguard section which remained. At 3.50 the last of the company, including the artillerymen, withdrew from Raluana, joining a procession of trucks moving slowly in the darkness up the steep winding track towards Taliligap.

At 4 a.m. a green flare, which appeared to the defenders along Vulcan beach to be the signal for concerted action, was sent up to about 1,000 feet over Rabaul. Soon afterwards a Japanese launch was seen moving along the eastern side of the harbour, clearly indicating that the Japanese were established in Rabaul itself. A string of transports, each about 2,000 tons, entered the harbour from the east and disgorged landing parties. The first transport made towards Malaguna, others for Matupi Island. Some landed troops at Vulcan, Raluana and other places on the Kokopo coast. One party, consisting of a ship's launch towing two landing barges each containing about twenty men, attempted a landing in front of the Catholic Church between Vulcan and Malaguna. The N.G.V.R's mortars under Lieutenant Archer[2] accurately ranged on the position, one bomb landing in the second barge.

The sun was rising when Grant reported to Owen at 6 o'clock that his supply of ammunition had been exhausted. Two fast trips were made by Captain Field[3] and Private Olney[4] to replenish it. The barges which had made the original landing on "A" Company's immediate front had been withdrawn, leaving the casualties behind, but the Japanese could now be seen taking cover in the ravines, and it was clear that further landings, beyond the range of effective mortar fire, had been made on the lower slopes of Mount Vulcan. There the invaders were engaged by Grant's platoon with small arms and machine-gun fire, and dispersed round the side of Vulcan, losing a machine-gun and crew which Private Saligari[5] put out of action with light machine-gun fire.

Soon afterwards Owen's right platoon reported that enemy patrols were working wide round their right flank, attempting to encircle them. Japanese were moving on the rearward slopes of Vulcan towards Four Ways. Owen decided that his position was no longer tenable: a pre-arranged attack by Travers' company from Four Ways had failed to

---

[2] Lt J. C. Archer, OBE, NGX458; NGVR. Administrator of Northern Territory from 1956. Civil servant; of Rabaul; b. Castlemaine, Vic, 28 Jul 1900.

[3] Maj D. F. Field, ED, VX38844; 2/22 Bn. Salesman; of Kew, Vic; b. Moonee Ponds, Vic, 21 Jun 1907.

[4] Pte J. N. Olney, VX35583. 2/22 Bn; "M" Special Unit. Caretaker; of Warburton, Vic; b. Whittlesea, Vic, 13 Sep 1911.

[5] Pte E. P. Saligari, VX24181; 2/22 Bn. Farm labourer; of Cavendish, Vic; b. Cavendish, 13 Mar 1914.

eventuate, the troops were being attacked by low-flying Japanese planes, transports in the harbour were shelling his positions, and his line of withdrawal along Big Dipper road was endangered. At 7 a.m. he ordered Grant to withdraw his platoon, with the carriers, by road to Four Ways, while the remaining platoons provided covering fire.

Landing craft were now disembarking troops near Big Dipper road, and were being engaged by anti-tank guns. Small merchant ships could be seen berthing at Main Wharf. As Grant's men clambered aboard the waiting truck, a further four or five landing craft moved towards the beach between Big Dipper road and Owen's headquarters. The two platoons remaining held their positions until 7.30, when Owen ordered them too to withdraw to Four Ways. Except that it was clear that fighting had ceased at Raluana, Owen had no knowledge of events in other sectors. Consequently he directed the withdrawing troops to move to Tobera, south of Kokopo, if they discovered that Four Ways had been captured. Soon after the order had been given the men began to withdraw through the bush towards Four Ways, under fire from the ships in the harbour, and followed by Owen and Captain Silverman,[6] medical officer to the coastal battery, who had established an R.A.P. in the area.

These companies at Vulcan and Raluana had been out of touch with the battalion commander, Carr, and with Scanlan, since soon after 2.30, when the line which ran from Owen's company at Vulcan through Raluana and thence to Carr's headquarters at Noah's Mission, between Three Ways and Four Ways, went dead. At 3 a.m., from his command post now established at Taliligap, Scanlan had ordered Travers' company to move from Four Ways to prepared positions at Taliligap covering the Kokopo Ridge road. An observation post at Taliligap commanded a view of both Lakunai and Vunakanau airfields and of the whole harbour. At dawn an assembly of thirty-one vessels could be seen at the entrance to the harbour. Steaming along the harbour in line abreast were three destroyers, and landing craft or barges dotted the deep waters and foreshores of the harbour. A merchant ship was berthed at the Government Wharf. As it was evident that Owen's company must be hard pressed, Lieutenant Dawson,[7] the young and enterprising Intelligence officer of the 2/22nd Battalion, was sent to lead it out from its beach positions along a track which passed through Tawliua Mission and led down to the beach.

> I set off in a car with a driver and an Intelligence orderly (said Dawson later). On turning the last curve before the mission we saw there in the middle of the road a full platoon of Japs and several natives. With them was one of the local German missionaries shaking hands with an officer who appeared to be the platoon command. I had seen the German earlier in the morning and he had then impressed me as being very pleased about something. . . . The impression I got was that the natives had led the Japs up the . . . track because it was utterly impossible to find it from the lower end. That was the reason I was going down to lead "A" Company out. The Japs opened fire at a range of about 50 yards. The car stopped.

---
[6] Capt H. N. Silverman, VX129333. RMO Heavy Bty Rabaul. Medical practitioner; of Julia Creek, Vic; b. Fitzroy, Vic, 4 Dec 1910. Missing believed died 30 Jan 1942.
[7] Lt-Col B. G. Dawson, VX47614. 2/22 Bn; 2/5 Indep Coy; CO 1 NG Inf Bn 1945. Student; of Portland, Vic; b. Ballarat, Vic, 16 Feb 1920.

The Australians dismounted. Private "Curly" Smith[8] was killed as he rounded the front of the car, but the driver, Private Kennedy,[9] and Dawson escaped into the bush. Carr, unaware of Dawson's encounter with the Japanese and his failure to reach Owen, had rung Scanlan at 6.30 and informed him that Owen's company was withdrawing. Scanlan thereupon ordered McInnes' company, astride the main Kokopo road at Three Ways, to cover the withdrawal of Owen's company. At 6.45 Scanlan decided to withdraw his own headquarters to Tomavatur.

By 3.10 Travers' company, which had been ordered to the pre-arranged Taliligap position astride the Kokopo Ridge road, had arrived in its position and was digging in. Travers disposed his men on a front of about 2,000 yards astride the Kokopo Ridge road. He placed a platoon under Sergeant Morris[1] on the left covering the road and approximately 300 yards of front to the forward slopes of a knoll; Lieutenant Lomas'[2] from the Kokopo Ridge road to the left of a large re-entrant on the reverse slope of the knoll; and Lieutenant Donaldson's[3] from the re-entrant to Vunakanau. Company headquarters were sited in rear of Morris' platoon, with the anti-tank guns, machine-guns and mortars near by. At 5 a.m. Travers sent a patrol from Morris' platoon to Taliligap Mission.

Half an hour later the survivors of Shier's company from Raluana began to arrive after a difficult trip without lights in the darkness. Some trucks had overturned on the slippery road. The survivors' arrival was reported to Carr who ordered that Tolmer's platoon join Travers and the remainder continue to Four Ways and join the battalion reserve.

Thereupon Travers ordered Tolmer to a position forward on his left flank near Gaskin's House. The area was under low-flying machine-gun attacks and light bombs were being dropped. At 8.15 telephone communication with battalion headquarters failed. It was never restored.

During the morning a detachment of Fortress Signals at Toma managed to dispatch a message by teleradio (drafted by Lieutenant Figgis,[4] the Area Intelligence Officer) to Port Moresby to the effect that a "landing craft carrier" was off New Britain and that a landing was taking place. The message was corrupted during transmission and as received at Port Moresby merely reported: "Motor landing craft carrier off Crebuen [Credner] Island." It was Rabaul's last message.

Meanwhile McInnes and Appel at Three Ways and Vunakanau respectively, and the Reserve Company at Four Ways, had seen no enemy

---

[8] Pte L. W. Smith, VX37810; 2/22 Bn. Fisherman; of Sorrento, Vic; b. Fitzroy, Vic, 21 Nov 1911. Killed in action 23 Jan 1942.

[9] Pte N. Kennedy, VX23834; 2/22 Bn. Hosiery operator; of North Balwyn, Vic; b. Abbotsford, Vic, 6 Mar 1920. (Later Kennedy reached the nurses' quarters at Kokopo; they disguised him as a native by covering him with boot-black. Eventually he was captured by the Japanese. He was lost at sea in the *Montevideo Maru* on 1 Jul 1942.)

[1] Sgt O. Morris, VX30759; 2/22 Bn. Bookkeeper; of Horsham, Vic; b. Middlesex, England, 1 Jul 1900. Lost in sinking of *Montevideo Maru* 1 Jul 1942.

[2] Maj F. J. Lomas, MC, VX38184. 2/22 Bn; 2/7 Cav Cdo Sqn. Clerk; of Red Cliffs, Vic; b. Warracknabeal, Vic, 6 Jan 1914.

[3] Capt J. G. Donaldson, VX44779; 2/22 Bn. Trustee officer; of Heidelberg, Vic; b. Heidelberg, 16 Sep 1913.

[4] Maj P. E. Figgis, MC, VX44411. 2/22 Bn; "M" Special Unit. Clerk; of St Kilda, Vic; b. St Mawes, England, 16 Nov 1915.

troops since the action began, although all areas had been attacked from the air. The company under Appel in prepared positions round Vunakanau airfield was constantly dive-bombed and machine-gunned throughout the morning. At 7.20 a.m. Captain Smith, the adjutant, phoned to Appel that battalion headquarters was closing at Noah's Mission and moving southward to Malabunga junction. Appel passed the message to Scanlan.

Soon after 8.30 Grant's platoon from the Vulcan position arrived at Three Ways. The crews of two machine-guns which McInnes had posted along the Kokopo Ridge road to hold the line between his own and Travers' companies now reported that they had been surrounded, and were forced to withdraw under covering fire from McInnes' mortars. Soon afterwards Three Ways came under rifle and automatic fire from a ridge about 800 yards distant.

McInnes' position was rapidly becoming untenable. At 8.45 Appel telephoned McInnes, who informed him that Grant's platoon had passed through Three Ways and was moving along Bamboo road in the rear of Vunakanau. He then said that his own company would have to withdraw. Appel asked him to hold his position if possible, and asked that Major Mollard,[5] who had been sent forward by Carr to coordinate the defence of the Kokopo Ridge road by the two companies there, be brought to the telephone. When Mollard arrived Appel suggested that if McInnes could hold his present position and close the gap between his own and Travers' company on the Kokopo Ridge road, the front would possess good length and depth, and force the enemy to come out into the kunai grass country. On the other hand, he added, if McInnes withdrew the whole front would have broken down.

Mollard, after reiterating the necessity to withdraw, ordered Appel to cover McInnes' withdrawal and that of the remnant of Owen's company under Grant, and then to move his own company to an area at the junction of Bamboo and Tavilo roads, south of Vunakanau.

Appel now sent a dispatch rider to battalion headquarters at Malabunga junction. The rider found the headquarters at Glade road, 500 yards from the junction, and returned with a message that the battalion would move to the Keravat River and take up new positions; meanwhile Appel's company should continue to hold the junction of Bamboo and Tavilo roads until all transport of the withdrawing companies had passed through. It was the last communication Appel had with his battalion headquarters.

Mollard, now concerned lest the line of withdrawal of "R" Company through Three Ways be cut, hastened by car to Four Ways to order its evacuation. It was then about 9 a.m. All transport available, no matter to which company it belonged, was requisitioned and troops were bundled into the vehicles in whatever order they arrived. Sergeant Walls[6] recalled

---

[5] Maj J. C. Mollard, VX43446; 2/22 Bn. Mantle manufacturer; of Melbourne; b. Perth, WA, 28 May 1908.
[6] Lt R. K. Walls, MC, VX24197. 2/22 Bn; "M" Special Unit. Barrister and solicitor; of Hamilton, Vic; b. Coleraine, Vic, 30 May 1914.

afterwards that he himself was clinging to the side of a taxi containing a corporal and six members of his section. It had gone about 400 yards from Four Ways when the convoy halted and he was ordered by Major Mollard to move towards Malabunga, making a wide circuit of the road which the enemy were wrongly believed to have crossed.

About 10 o'clock Mollard ordered the withdrawal of McInnes' company from Three Ways. Soon the troops were speeding along the road in trucks continually harassed from the air.

The sense of urgency in the forward area was soon transmitted to the rear. Carr had moved his headquarters from Noah's Mission to Glade road about 8 o'clock. Thenceforward he was out of touch with his forward companies except by dispatch riders, although telephone communication was maintained between the battalion commander and Scanlan throughout. Soon after 9 o'clock rumours reached battalion headquarters that the Japanese were coming through "in thousands" and could not be held. Enemy aircraft, flying low, were machine-gunning and shelling all roads, Vunakanau airfield and battalion headquarters area. As if to confirm the rumours, trucks now began to come through the fire and were seen speedily withdrawing along Glade road towards Toma. The adjutant, Captain Smith, and the regimental sergeant-major, Murray,[7] attempted to halt some of the trucks and establish a defensive position near Glade road, but the men said the enemy was advancing quickly, and some trucks refused to stop. Other trucks followed the early arrivals and, since serious congestion appeared likely on the narrow road, offering a target for further air attacks, Carr ordered the withdrawal to continue to Area Headquarters at Tomavatur.

After a telephone discussion with Carr, Scanlan—as much out of touch with the progress of fighting as his battalion commander because of the breakdown in communications, but who had observed the trucks streaming down the road past Tomavatur towards Toma—decided that it was useless to prolong the action. He ordered Carr to withdraw his battalion towards the Keravat River. Carr pointed out that this was now impracticable, since his battalion was already spread out in other directions. He suggested that the northern companies withdraw to the Keravat, the southern to the Warangoi, both to hold those positions as long as they could; and the centre companies to move back along the Malabunga road. Scanlan agreed, adding that it would now be "every man for himself", which Carr took to mean withdrawal in small parties. Carr gave these orders to his battalion signallers for transmission to all companies. To avoid congestion at the road junction he posted a picquet at the Malabunga road junction with orders to direct, in accordance with the agreed plan, any trucks arriving there.

It remains to record the experiences of Travers' company on the Kokopo Ridge road, out of touch with its headquarters since soon after 8 a.m.,

---
[7] WO1 E. A. A. Murray, EM, VX42537; 2/22 Bn. Labourer; of Murrumbeena, Vic; b. Horsham, Vic, 10 Aug 1914.

with its line to Three Ways severed, and faced with the possibility of attack from the rear by troops advancing from Vulcan. At 9 o'clock Travers ordered a redeployment to meet the new threat, placing Lomas' and Morris' platoons on a knoll 500 yards to the rear of his previous position facing the original left flank. Lieutenant Garrard,[8] with company headquarters, took up a position between these two platoons and Tolmer's pioneers; Donaldson's remained in its previous position facing Kokopo, with the task of flank protection.

At 11 o'clock the pioneers moved forward of Gaskin's house to a knoll astride the Kokopo Ridge road, 400 yards farther forward along the road to Kokopo. At 11.30 Tolmer's batman, Private Holmes,[9] called out that two natives of the island were approaching. Tolmer, who immediately joined him, saw the two wearing white mission lap-laps, closely followed by Japanese. He fired on the natives, killing one, whereupon his men joined in and killed the other and, Tolmer estimated, ten Japanese. Simultaneously Japanese began to move in on Donaldson's platoon and company headquarters. Those encountered by Tolmer's platoon succeeded in occupying Gaskin's house, where they were held; others worked round the left flank, cutting off the company from its trucks.

At midday Travers withdrew Tolmer's platoon to Taliligap, where, half an hour later, it came under machine-gun fire from a knoll to the right of Taliligap. At 12.45 p.m. Travers ordered Lomas and Tolmer to withdraw their platoons through Donaldson's positions towards Vunakanau, and attempt to contact Appel's company, believed still to be occupying the airfield, on which aircraft could be seen dropping bombs. Heavy fire could be heard near Morris' and Garrard's positions.

Lomas withdrew his platoon in good order, passing behind Donaldson's perimeter defence and heading in the direction of Vunakanau as directed. He was not again seen by Travers. Tolmer reached Donaldson at 1.15, with orders from Travers to hold on until the rest of the company had passed through, and took up a position on the right flank facing Taliligap. There was a lull, while both sides regrouped; then at 2 o'clock Travers, who had throughout proved himself a fearless and capable leader, ordered the two covering platoons to join him at Taliligap heights. There Donaldson received orders to advance along the Kokopo Ridge road and recapture two M.M.G. trucks which had been cut off with the company's transport 300 yards west of Taliligap.

Just before 3 p.m. Donaldson set off along the road, covered by fire from Tolmer's pioneers. The men came under light small arms and mortar fire before reaching a platoon on the left of the road, where Donaldson asked Sergeant Morris to support his advance with fire from the left flank.

---
[8] Lt H. G. Garrard, VX24726; 2/22 Bn. Furniture designer; of Prahran, Vic; b. Perth, WA, 4 Jan 1918. Executed by Japanese 4 Feb 1942.
[9] Pte W. Holmes, VX22843; 2/22 Bn. Hotel employee; of Manangatang, Vic; b. Londonderry, Ireland, 6 Mar 1902.

In the subsequent advance Lance-Corporal Simson[1] was outstanding. He made his way forward, skilfully using all available cover, and came upon ten Japanese into whom he fired with his Tommy gun, accounting for all of them. Advancing farther, he killed a similar group. Both trucks were brought back, one of them driven by Private Clinton[2] under very heavy small arms and mortar fire. Enemy troops encountered were checked by sub-machine-gun fire from Donaldson's platoon, in which Corporal Sloan,[3] another Tommy-gunner, was a dominating figure. When the counter-attack had ended, Donaldson estimated the enemy casualties at fifty. His own platoon had suffered none.

At 3.10 Travers ordered the company to withdraw through the kunai to Glade road, and his men did so, closely pursued by Japanese who at times reached within 100 yards of the rear of the column, only to be checked by sub-machine-gun fire. Under fire from mortars and machine-guns, and constantly harried from the air, the company reached Toma road at 5 p.m. There a bridgehead was formed and in a deep valley a mile to the west the men bivouacked for the night.

Organised resistance to the Japanese on New Britain had now ended. The force split up into small parties and withdrew south-west to the north coast and south-east to the south coast. The strength of the force at Rabaul on 23rd January was estimated at 76 officers, 6 nurses and 1,314 others. Of this number 2 officers and 26 men were killed during the fighting that day. Some 400 subsequently escaped to Australia; about 160 were massacred by the Japanese at Tol in early February. The remainder became prisoners. The special circumstances in which the force was placed, and the ordeal and fate of many of its members are narrated separately in Appendix 4 of this volume.

The Japanese force which undertook the capture of Rabaul was the *Nankai* or *South Seas Force,* commanded by the slight, balding Major-General Tomitaro Horii, who had originally commanded the *55th Division,* whence the principal units of the *South Seas Force* had been drawn. The main units of the force, formed in November 1941 to carry out landing operations in cooperation with the *Fourth Fleet,* were the *I, II,* and *III Battalions* of the *144th Infantry Regiment* commanded by Colonel Kusunose; a mountain artillery battalion; the *15th Independent Engineer Regiment;* anti-aircraft artillery; and transport and medical detachments, probably about 5,300 strong. Evidently these were supported at the outset by three special naval landing forces, each of about battalion strength. The force had left Japan towards the end of November, rendezvoused in the Bonin Islands area, and on 10th December carried out the landing operations at Guam. Evidently the Japanese expected strong resistance in the

---

[1] S-Sgt A. B. Simson, VX43045. 2/22 Bn and FELO. Accountant; of Geelong, Vic; b. Naracoorte, SA, 26 May 1917.

[2] Pte F. R. Clinton, VX29738. 2/22, 2/4 Bns. Truck driver; of Heidelberg, Vic; b. Prahran, Vic, 11 Feb 1914.

[3] Cpl J. K. Sloan, VX24455; 2/22 Bn. Salesman; of Brighton, Vic; b. Melbourne, 17 Jan 1913.

next phase of the operations—or were taking no risks—and allotted a naval force including two aircraft carriers and two battleships to the task.[4]

The convoy carrying the *South Seas Force* left Guam on 14th January with a naval escort, being "patrolled continuously" by naval planes until the 17th, when it was joined by the *Fourth Fleet* from Truk; it then totalled "more than 30 ships" (Dawson from his observation post at Tawliua counted 31 on the morning of the 23rd). While the convoy was at sea aircraft of the *24th Air Flotilla* "strafed the enemy's air bases" at Rabaul, Vunakanau, Kavieng and Salamaua and "shot down about 10 enemy planes over the New Britain Island area on the 21st and 22nd".

On the afternoon of the 22nd the convoy passed between New Ireland and New Britain, sailing between both islands in clear sight during the daytime in a zigzag movement at reduced speed to kill time. "Undoubtedly," says the report of the *South Seas Force,* "the enemy was aware that the convoy entered deep between both islands in the daytime . . . but it seemed that they judged this movement of ours meant we would land in the Kokopo vicinity, because the units stationed directly at Rabaul were withdrawn and positions were taken up facing the Kokopo area to the south. Thus, our successful landings were made by taking advantage of the enemy's unpreparedness at that point."

Horii landed the *I Battalion* (Lieut-Colonel Tsukamoto) at Praed Point, the *II Battalion* and regimental headquarters of the *144th* in the vicinity of Nordup. These two battalions advanced rapidly to occupy Lakunai airfield and the Rabaul township. The first wave of the *III Battalion* (Lieut-Colonel Kuwada) left the stern of the *Mito Maru* at 0200 and succeeded in making a landing on the beach in the neighbourhood of Kazanto (Vulcan—where Owen's company was stationed) at 0230, and at Minami Point (Raluana) where they seized "the gun emplacement".[5] The *III Battalion* started its drive towards Vunakanau but "being blocked by sheer cliffs and unable to find the road shown in the aerial photo[6] . . . was forced to advance through jungles. Bitter fighting broke out at the landing point of the *9th Infantry Company* . . . which happened to be just in front of the position which the enemy newly occupied after their change of dispositions." Another diarist records that during the advance to Vunakanau "there were places on the road where the enemy had abandoned vehicles, where ammunition was scattered about and where due to the pursuit attacks of our high speed *Butai* [detachment] were pitiful traces of the

---

[4] A captured diary records that "at our next landing point, New Britain, there is based a strong air and naval force . . . we will suffer losses until the time we make an opposed landing . . . do not think that things will go as smoothly as . . . at Guam". By way of contrast to the forebodings expressed by this diarist, the post-war report of the *South Seas Force* states that the Japanese believed that Rabaul was garrisoned by "an Australian Army force about 500 strong . . . likely to be reinforced by an additional 1,500, and by a volunteer defence corps of some strength and a patrol police force". The same report states that the area had "batteries stationed at two points on the seashore and part of the Australian Air Force" (about 11 planes).

[5] The old 1914 German gun emplacement was being prepared by the Australians for further use when the invasion occurred.

[6] Horii had been dissatisfied with the Intelligence provided for the landing at Guam, and gained permission to attach an officer of his staff to the *Fourth Fleet* at Truk. Thence the officer made two flights over Rabaul taking aerial photographs which were used as a basis for planning the attack.

confused flight and defeat of the enemy. Leapfrogging all *Butai* we advanced on foot to the aerodrome and at 1400 hours captured it." Evidently the resistance in the *III Battalion* area, where "furious reports of big guns and rifle fire" could be heard from Rabaul, caused some concern, however, and in the afternoon the *I Battalion* was transferred by water craft from Rabaul to Keravia Bay and strengthened the *III Battalion* in its thrust towards Vunakanau. Horii ordered the pursuit of the Australians to be continued on foot on the 24th January, and later a destroyer and three transports were allotted to facilitate these operations, which were impeded by the difficult terrain.

During the fighting on 23rd January the Japanese lost 16 killed and 49 "injured" (presumably wounded in action). Eight aircraft (presumably wrecked), two fortress cannons, 2 anti-aircraft guns, 15 anti-tank guns, 11 mortars, 27 machine-guns, 7 light machine-guns, 548 rifles, 12 armoured cars (Bren carriers), 180 automobiles and 17 motor cycles, were reported to have been captured by the invaders.

Meanwhile, on 21st January, two days before the Japanese landing at Rabaul, Kavieng, 125 miles to the north-west, had been attacked soon after 7 a.m. by about sixty Japanese aircraft, including bombers, dive bombers and fighters.[7] The Japanese concentrated their dive-bombing on the town, gun positions on the airfield and along the ridge running laterally to the western beaches, where the 1st Independent Company had established concealed machine-gun positions. The aircraft were met by brisk fire and one crashed into the sea beyond Nusa Island. Soon after the raid began the *Induna Star*[8] cast her moorings at the main wharf and was attempting to reach the comparative safety of Albatross Channel when she was attacked by six aircraft. Although the ship's Bren gun team under Corporal Reed[9] put up a stout defence, during which six of the team were wounded including two mortally,[1] control of the vessel was lost and she ran on a reef about two miles south of Kavieng.

By 9 o'clock the aircraft had gone. The defenders of Kavieng accounted for four planes and damaged others during the almost incessant air attacks. Soon afterwards the captain of the *Induna Star* arrived at Kavieng in a canoe to report the beaching of his ship. He was ordered to return and attempt to bring it back to the wharf. A message was then sent to Rabaul, reporting details of the action, including the supposed loss of the *Induna Star*.

After visiting the areas occupied by his men that day, Major Wilson concluded that his positions at Kavieng would be untenable should landings be made simultaneously at Panapai and the western beaches. He

---

[7] There was a lull in the air attacks on Rabaul on this day.

[8] A vessel of 81 tons gross register, purchased for the use of the Independent Company soon after its arrival at Kavieng.

[9] Cpl G. B. Reed, VX20657; 1st Indep Coy. Grazier; of Albury, NSW; b. Ballarat, Vic, 1 Apr 1911. Lost in sinking of *Montevideo Maru*, 1 Jul 1942.

[1] Trooper G. Anderson and Signalman R. H. Munro. Anderson though twice wounded and in great pain continued to fire the Bren until the ship ran onto the reef.

decided to move his men from the area except for a portion of Captain Goode's[2] platoon at the airfield and a few other troops required for demolitions in the town. At the civil hospital the wounded had begun to arrive and Captain Bristow,[3] ably assisted by Sister D. M. Maye of the Administration's nursing service, was operating. After consulting them Wilson decided that the seriously wounded should be sent to the near-by Lamacott Mission under the sister's care.

At 11 a.m. the *Induna Star* returned, leaking badly and considered unseaworthy by her skipper. However, since she represented the Independent Company's only means of escape a month's rations were taken aboard

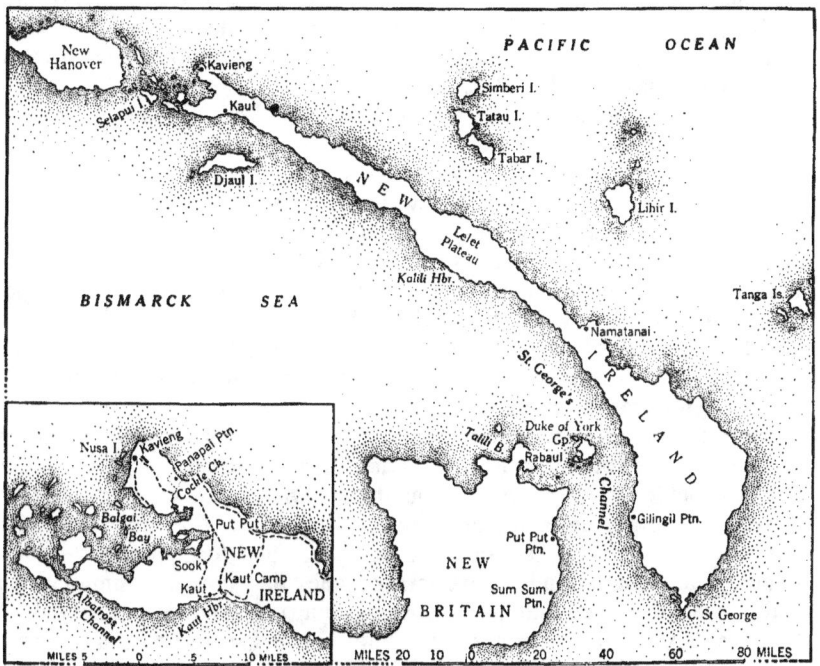

and the crew was ordered to take the ship to Kaut Harbour, patch the hull, and await orders. During the afternoon the men were moved on foot to camps on the Sook River (adjacent to one set up by the civil administration) and at Kaut overlooking the harbour. Wilson moved his main wireless set to a position of relative safety about half a mile south-west of the airfield, where he established his headquarters. Soon after these moves had been completed a message was received from Rabaul that an enemy force of "one aircraft carrier and six cruisers" was approaching from the north-west.

---

[2] Capt A. E. Goode, VX44549; 1st Indep Coy. Jackeroo; of Deniliquin, NSW; b. Olton, Birmingham, Eng, 20 Dec 1910.

[3] Capt V. G. Bristow, VX39436; RMO 1st Indep Coy. Medical practitioner; of Heidelberg, Vic; b. Parkville, Vic, 10 May 1914.

At 8 o'clock on the 22nd Wilson learnt from Rabaul that no further information had been received, but Rabaul promised to keep in touch with him. It was the last message passed between the two forces. The rest of the day was spent by the Independent Company preparing for an attack, and moving supplies to Sook and Kaut. At 10.30 p.m. the plantation manager at Selapui Island, Mr Doyle, arrived in a motor-boat bringing a report from the company's outpost that there had been no sign of the enemy. It was dark and raining, but Wilson asked him to return to Selapui, since the outpost was now out of touch by wireless, and warn the men to make for Kaut if they saw Kavieng being attacked. Only Wilson, Lieutenant Dixon,[4] three soldiers and five civilians (some of them Catholic priests) remained in Kavieng during the night. The men stayed in two houses close to the water front, so that demolition of the wharves could begin early on the 23rd.

At 3.5 a.m. sounds were heard at Saunders Wharf. Visibility was poor and it was raining lightly. Five minutes later enemy landing barges were reaching the western beaches, Very lights were being fired and there was much shouting and shooting. A few minutes later the house Wilson and its owner were occupying was surrounded but the two men left by car unmolested, except for a few stray and ineffective shots. At the airfield Wilson met Lieutenant Burns[5] and ordered him to blow it and the supply dumps. He then drove to the end of the runway and at 3.18 saw and heard the sounds of the demolitions. Captain Goode received severe concussion, but withdrew with all members of his platoon in good order towards a pre-arranged rendezvous at Cockle Creek.

Soon afterwards Wilson arrived at his headquarters south-west of the airfield and after ordering the destruction of the wireless equipment retired also to Cockle Creek. There he found that Dixon and his party had not arrived from Kavieng, and learnt from other reports that the landing had been made by a force estimated between three and four thousand strong.[6] Landings at Panapai and the western beaches had not been simultaneous, and it was this fact that had allowed their unimpeded withdrawal. At 6.45, as Dixon still had not arrived, the men began to withdraw towards Sook. As it was impossible to carry the wounded through the thick jungle, they made their way on foot. Corporal Noonan[7] gallantly refused assistance though wounded in both legs.

Next morning they met a party sent out by Captain Fraser[8] from Sook, and moved there on foot and in canoes. Some of the men arrived during the afternoon, others not until next day, and then almost exhausted.

---

[4] Lt G. W. P. Dixon, VX50082; 1st Indep Coy. Engineer; of Brighton Beach, Vic; b. Melbourne, 25 Dec 1919.

[5] Lt J. L. Burns, VX39159; 1st Indep Coy. Accountant; of East Malvern, Vic; b. Bruthen, Vic, 14 Apr 1918.

[6] The Kavieng invasion force consisted of 2 cruisers and 3 destroyers plus converted merchant ships carrying the major part of the *Maizuru Special Naval Landing Force*, a company of the *Kashima*, and an anti-aircraft unit.

[7] Cpl A. P. Noonan, SX6384; 1st Indep Coy. Hotel manager; of Georgetown, SA; b. Georgetown, 11 Jul 1913. Lost in sinking of *Montevideo Maru*, 1 Jul 1942.

[8] Capt A. Fraser, QX6470; 1st Indep Coy. Clerk; of Ingham, Qld; b. Ingham, 9 Mar 1919.

On the 27th the men learnt that Dixon and his party had been captured at Kavieng. Lieutenant Dennis[9] and a civilian arrived from Kaut during the day with news that an enemy aircraft carrier was anchored at Djaul Island and an enemy submarine was patrolling the mouth of the Albatross Channel. Wilson learnt also that the *Induna Star* was lying on a mudbank in Kaut Harbour. However the new arrivals believed that she could be made seaworthy. The men were now suffering from malaria and diarrhoea, and some of the civilians were complaining that the soldiers' presence was endangering them. Wilson decided that two courses were open to him: to concentrate his force at Kaut and attempt to refloat the *Induna Star* in the hope of reaching New Britain, or to move to Lelet plateau, where healthier conditions existed.

An offer by Captain Fraser and Warrant-Officer Harvey[10] to take a rescue party to Kavieng and attempt to bring back Lieutenant Dixon was refused, since the reports received were contradictory and the time needed would have endangered the remainder of the company.[1] On the 28th, after destroying all equipment too heavy to carry, and leaving the wireless set with the civilians with instructions not to take any action to destroy it until three days had passed, Wilson moved his men to Kaut, and set them to work repairing the *Induna Star*. It was not until the evening of the 30th that the craft was pumped free of water, her hull patched and the main engine functioning satisfactorily. That morning Wilson had sent Lieutenant Sleeman[2] to Sook with dispatches for Moresby about his proposed move to New Britain; in the afternoon Sleeman returned with the news that the wireless had been destroyed, but bringing a message from Army Headquarters, Melbourne, ordering Wilson to "remain and report, also to do as much damage as possible to the enemy". After conferring with his medical officer, Captain Bristow, Wilson decided that the condition of his men precluded any such role.

> They had mostly been struggling through jungle and swamp for nine days (he wrote afterwards); prior to that they had been constantly on duty for many months and were now suffering from fatigue, malaria and dysentery, and skin diseases. Furthermore there was only two months' supply of food left, including that on the "Induna Star" [and] our only main and effective role, that of observation reports was now impossible. Added to this, our only chance of leaving the island was to go at once before the enemy discovered the whereabouts of the "Induna Star".

That night Wilson embarked his men, intending to sail down the coast in the darkness and lie up during the day in the hope of reaching the east coast of New Britain. By daylight on the 31st Kalili Harbour had been reached without incident. There Wilson learnt that fighting on New Britain had ceased, that the natives on New Ireland were becoming increas-

---

[9] Lt D. J. A. Dennis, VX48779; 1st Indep Coy. Jackeroo; of Warncoort, Vic; b. Colac, Vic, 8 Jan 1920.

[10] WO2 C. R. Harvey, SX2676; 1st Indep Coy. Farmer; of Salisbury, SA; b. Salisbury, 12 Feb 1909. Lost in sinking of *Montevideo Maru*, 1 Jul 1942.

[1] Lt Dixon and his party, it was learnt later, were captured before noon on the 23rd. Dixon was threatened with death for refusing to divulge the whereabouts of his company and on the 26th faced a firing squad. However he was reprieved and on the 27th was sent to Rabaul.

[2] Lt F. N. Sleeman, QX6468; 1st Indep Coy. Clerk; of Townsville, Qld; b. Sydney, 4 Mar 1915.

ingly hostile; and that the Namatanai detachment of the Independent Company was believed to be in the mountainous country south-east of Namatanai, with representatives of the civilian administration equipped with a teleradio set "and therefore in a reasonable position".[3] Thereupon Wilson decided to attempt to reach Port Moresby. That night the journey down the coast continued. Early next morning an enemy destroyer was sighted lying inshore about three-quarters of a mile astern. Soon afterwards the destroyer swung out from the shore and set off westwards.

All that day the schooner lay hidden in a harbour near Gilingil Plantation. The night was overcast and Wilson decided to run straight for Woodlark Islands with a favourable wind and a heavy following sea. At 9.30 a.m. on the 2nd, when the ship was some 90 miles south-east of Rabaul, she was sighted by an enemy plane. It circled and machine-gunned the ship without doing serious damage, and then dive-bombed. One bomb struck the *Induna Star* amidships, destroying the lifeboat and causing a number of casualties. Since the ship was now taking a dangerous amount of water, Wilson considered further resistance useless, and ordered the ship to heave to.

We then received instructions from the enemy to proceed towards Rabaul, which we did slowly, accompanied by enemy planes, all available hands taking shifts on the pumps (wrote Major Wilson). At 1813 hours an enemy destroyer came up to within 500 yards, then sent a boat which took the wounded and officers aboard the destroyer. A line was passed to the "Induna Star" which was towed. The next morning we were lying off the eastern end of New Ireland when all but six of the personnel were transferred to the destroyer from the "Induna Star" and we proceeded to Rabaul and captivity. Three men had been killed during the action and these had been buried at sea from the "Induna Star"; one of the wounded died on the enemy destroyer during the night and was buried immediately, honours being paid by the enemy, myself giving what I remembered of the burial service.[4]

Meanwhile on the 23rd and 24th January Japanese forces had landed at Kendari and Balikpapan. The force that was to take Balikpapan—the *56th Regiment* plus the *2nd Kure Naval Landing Force*—set out from Tarakan in 16 transports on 21st January. An American submarine, American flying-boats and Dutch aircraft reported the convoy, and on the evening of the 23rd Dutch aircraft destroyed the transport *Nana Maru*. That night the convoy began disembarking its troops at Balikpapan, under the protection of the cruiser *Naka* and seven destroyers. There was no opposition ashore, the Dutch garrison having withdrawn inland after damaging the oil installations.

Since early in January Admiral Glassford's American naval force, based at Surabaya, had been allotted a general responsibility for the eastern flank from Bali to eastern New Guinea, while the Dutch squadron operated

---
[3] The fate of the remaining detachments of the Independent Coy is related in the next volume in this series.

[4] The foregoing account is based mainly on Major Wilson's report, written at Manila on 20 Sept 1945, from notes compiled during the period 21st January 1942 to 2nd February 1942.
The casualties in the Independent Company in this period were: 8 wounded on 21st January (two of whom subsequently died); one killed in action on the 23rd (the day of the Japanese landing); 3 killed (or died of wounds) and 24 wounded on 2nd February, during the bombing of the *Induna Star*.

in the centre and the British-Australian squadron on the west. Admiral Glassford's squadron—two cruisers and four destroyers—had learnt of the advance of the Japanese convoy on the 20th, when it was anchored off Koepang. The destroyers set out towards Balikpapan but a mishap delayed the cruisers. After midnight on the 23rd-24th, as the Japanese were disembarking, the destroyers were nearing Balikpapan. Since the Dutch had set fire to the oil tanks the American destroyers as they approached could see the enemy's transports silhouetted. They attacked in the early hours of the 24th. The Japanese were taken completely by surprise. The escorting destroyers raced off searching for imagined submarines while the American destroyers fired torpedo after torpedo at the convoy, sinking three transports—*Sumanoura Maru, Tatsukami Maru* and *Kuretake Maru*—and a torpedo boat. A Dutch submarine sank the *Tsuruga Maru*; and, as mentioned, Dutch aircraft had sunk the *Nana Maru* and probably also the *Jukka Maru*. It was the heaviest loss suffered by a Japanese convoy during their whole offensive.

At Kendari the American seaplane tender *Childs* was getting under way in the early morning of the 24th January when to the astonishment of her crew they saw a flotilla of enemy vessels approaching. The *Childs* made off, concealed in a sudden rain storm. The Japanese ships contained the *Sasebo Combined Naval Landing Force*—the equivalent of a brigade group of marines, and the same force as had taken Menado on 11th January. The resistance of the troops ashore was soon overcome.

CHAPTER 19

THE LOSS OF AMBON

AFTER Rabaul, Kendari and Balikpapan the next important enemy objective on the eastern flank was Ambon. Initially the Japanese had planned to take it by 6th February, but they had now advanced its place on the time-table.

As mentioned earlier, Australia had agreed as an outcome of talks with Netherlands East Indies staffs early in 1941 to hold troops and air force squadrons ready at Darwin to reinforce Ambon and Timor if the Japanese entered the war; and in consequence, on 17th December, the 2/21st Battalion landed at Ambon. Part of No. 13 Squadron R.A.A.F., with Hudson bombers, had been established there since 7th December.

The 2/21st Battalion, like other units of the 23rd Brigade group, had had a frustrating period of service. With other units of the 8th Division, it had been formed soon after the fall of France, and filled with men eager to go overseas and fight. By March 1941 they had been training for nine months; yet they were still in Australia. It had been a hard blow to the men of the 2/21st that three junior battalions, trained with them at Bonegilla, had already sailed abroad. It was a disappointment when, in March, they were ordered to Darwin to spend perhaps the remainder of the war garrisoning an outpost in Australia. Good young leaders sought and obtained transfers to the Armoured Division, and the Independent Companies then being formed in great secrecy at Foster in Victoria.

In Darwin a proportion of the men became restive and resentful. As had happened during the corresponding period in Malaya, the period of waiting proved a severe test for soldiers who were reading daily of the exploits of their comrades in North Africa, Greece, Crete and Syria. The number of breaches of discipline in some units increased disturbingly as the months went on. The spirits of the 2/21st Battalion were depressed when on two occasions 10 per cent of its men were sent to the Middle East as reinforcements.

The decision to reinforce Ambon and Timor had presented a difficult problem to Brigadier Lind, the commander of the 23rd Brigade. His task at Darwin, where he was under the command of Major-General Blake of the 7th Military District, was to provide the main defence of the Northern Territory against possible attack by Japan. This in itself was a tall order, considering the Territory's size and situation; yet in May 1941 he was instructed that if Japan attacked southward, two of his battalions would be dispersed, one to Ambon 580 miles away, one to Timor 500 miles away. Lind and his infantry battalion commanders, Lieut-Colonel Roach (2/21st) and Lieut-Colonel Youl (2/40th) immediately reconnoitred both islands. After this Lind reported to General Blake that the forces were inadequately armed for their tasks, and that a military liaison should be established with the Dutch staff at their main headquarters at Bandung.[2] In Melbourne in July, Lind repeated his contentions directly to the Chief of the General Staff, Lieut-General Sturdee, and in October, after a more detailed tactical reconnaissance of the islands, in which the company commanders also took part, he presented a similar viewpoint. He suggested that all requirements for "Sparrow Force" (Timor) and "Gull Force" (Ambon), as they were named, be made the responsibility of an officer appointed to Army Headquarters for that purpose; that this officer should visit or have visited the islands so as to have some idea of the problems involved; and that he should visit them at regular intervals to keep touch.

On 5th December, three days before the Japanese onslaught from Pearl Harbour to Malaya, the Netherlands Indies Government asked Australia to send aircraft to Ambon and Timor in accordance with the long-standing agreement. The Australian War Cabinet approved, and, at dawn on 7th December, two flights of Hudsons (of No. 13 Squadron) flew to Laha field on Ambon and one flight (of No. 2 Squadron) to Koepang.[3] That day Brigadier Lind, at Darwin, received orders to move the 2/21st Battalion to Ambon and the 2/40th to Timor. They became detached forces operating under the direct command of Army Headquarters in Melbourne. The brigade headquarters, the 2/4th Pioneer Battalion,[4] the 2/14th Field Regiment, and parts of the ancillary units of the brigade group were all that remained of the brigade in the Northern Territory, although it was soon reinforced with militia units from the south.[5]

---

[2] In this chapter, and elsewhere, in accordance with the principles set out in the preface, the place names, with certain exceptions, have been transliterated in the English not the Dutch style, despite the fact that the participants were familiar with the Dutch forms. The "oo" sound is written "u" and not "oe"; thus the puzzling Oesaoe becomes Usau, Penfoei becomes Penfui. As mentioned in the preface, Koepang is among the exceptions made to this general rule.

[3] No. 13 Squadron was commanded by Wing Commander J. R. G. McDonald and, after McDonald's death on 10th December in an aircraft accident, by Squadron Leader J. P. Ryland. Some days later the third flight of No. 13 Squadron occupied Namlea airfield on Buru Island, near Ambon Island. At the end of December this flight went to Babo in Dutch New Guinea and its place at Namlea was taken by a flight from No. 2 Squadron which moved up from Timor.

[4] The 2/4 Pioneer Bn had replaced the 2/3rd in the Northern Territory in October.

[5] In 1942 Brigadier Lind, then about to retire, was again to express his opinion of the deployment of the Australian forces on Ambon and Timor Islands in an outspoken memorandum which he asked should be "forwarded without delay through the normal channels to Minister for the Army, GOC Australian Army in the Field, to Records for filing with War Diaries of 23 Aust Inf Bde and of 2/21 Bn and 2/40 Bn". It "placed on record that in the case of the detachment of 2/21 Bn to Amboina [Ambon] and of 2/40 Bn to Timor the following conclusions are accurate:
  (1) Eight months were available for provision of necessary adequate personnel and armament and for provision of the necessary cooperation with N.E.I., with the Navy and with the Air Force.
  (2) No satisfactory army liaison with N.E.I. Comd Bandoeng [Bandung] was established with result that preparations for reception of forces concerned were inadequate and the capacity for effective cooperation with N.E.I. Forces at Amboina and Timor was not developed.
  (3) No effective L. of C. was established in the case of either Force.
  (4) Forces involved were not informed of arrangements for Naval cooperation—if such existed—under conditions in which such was essential. Such cooperation did not materialise.
  (5) Effective air support was non-existent—no covering aircraft were available at time of Japanese attacks at Amboina and Timor.
  (6) Forces involved were NOT provided with adequate Fire Power—although eight months intervened from inception of project to its execution.
    (a) No Fd Arty was made available.
    (b) No A.A. Arty was made available at Ambon.
    (c) Provision of Light Automatic weapons was limited to 26 per Bn and spare parts were not available.
  (7) These forces were embarked and dispatched on tasks of first magnitude without orders from executive authority at A.H.Q.
  (8) Competent authority on the spot was deprived of opportunity to make essential representations relevant to projected operations."

"Gull Force", commanded by Colonel Roach, consisted of the 2/21st Battalion and 213 men in detachments of anti-tank artillery, engineers and other arms and services. Roach felt no less keenly than Lind about the need for adequate planning, coordination and equipment. On 13th December he wrote to Major Scott,[6] who was staff officer for his force at Army Headquarters, to say that there had been insufficient reconnaissance, and that he had not enough anti-tank guns and no field guns. He asked for a troop of 25-pounders, two more anti-tank troops, six more mortars, anti-aircraft guns "if available", two additional infantry companies and more automatic weapons "if you can spare them". The letter ended with the postscript: "As a test of communications could you acknowledge this please."

On 17th December—the day Gull Force disembarked at Ambon—Roach again wrote to Scott listing deficiencies in the arms and equipment of the force, and concluding "Health and morale good". On the 23rd he sent the following signal to Army Headquarters, Melbourne:

Imperative to have at once all those items mentioned para. K [guns and machine-guns] plus a further Field Troop. When will they arrive? No items mentioned other paras yet arrived. Surgical equipment inadequate refer Col. Barton.[7]

What was the task which seemed to Colonel Roach to demand so urgently the additional equipment and reinforcements for which he asked? The island on which Gull Force was established is 386 square miles in area, and 32 miles long. It is just below the western end of the much larger island of Ceram, and is in a central position between New Guinea, Timor, Celebes, and Halmahera Islands. Slanting from south-west to north-east, the larger portion of the island is joined by the Paso Isthmus to the smaller portion, Laitimor Peninsula, which resembles an undershot lower jaw. Between the upper (Hitu Peninsula) and lower jaws is the deep Bay of Ambon, about 10 miles long, and capable of sheltering a large fleet. At the head of this is Binnen Bay, which was used as a seaplane alighting area, with a base on its southern shore, at Halong, about three miles north of the town of Ambon.

Laha airfield was on the Hitu Peninsula, about half-way along the northern shore of the Bay of Ambon, and there was a newly-constructed landing ground near the northern extremity of the island, at Liang. Thus the island had much to offer as a base either for the Allies or the Japanese.

The island was one of the outer possessions of the Netherlands East Indies. The Portuguese founded a settlement on it in 1521, it was taken over by the Dutch in 1605; and British and Dutch administration alternated until in 1814 it was restored to the Dutch. In the early days of its

---

[6] Col W. J. R. Scott, DSO, VX71997. (1st AIF: Maj 20 Bn.) GSO1 G Branch (Special Operations) AHQ 1941-42; CO 2/21 Bn 1942. Insurance inspector; of Killara, NSW; b. Bingara, NSW, 21 Jun 1888.

[7] Col N. D. Barton, CBE, NX70413. (1st AIF: Maj 7 LH Regt.) CO 2/12 Fd Amb 1940-42; DDMS NT Force 1942-43; ADMS 11 Div 1943-44; CO 2/9 AGH 1945. Medical practitioner; of Parkes, NSW; b. Wellington, NSW, 5 Jun 1894.

European administration it was important chiefly as a centre of the spice trade. Extremely rugged and jungle-covered, it was traversed only by paths and tracks, with the exception of a primary road from Latuhalat across the toe of the Laitimor Peninsula to its bay shore, thence to the town

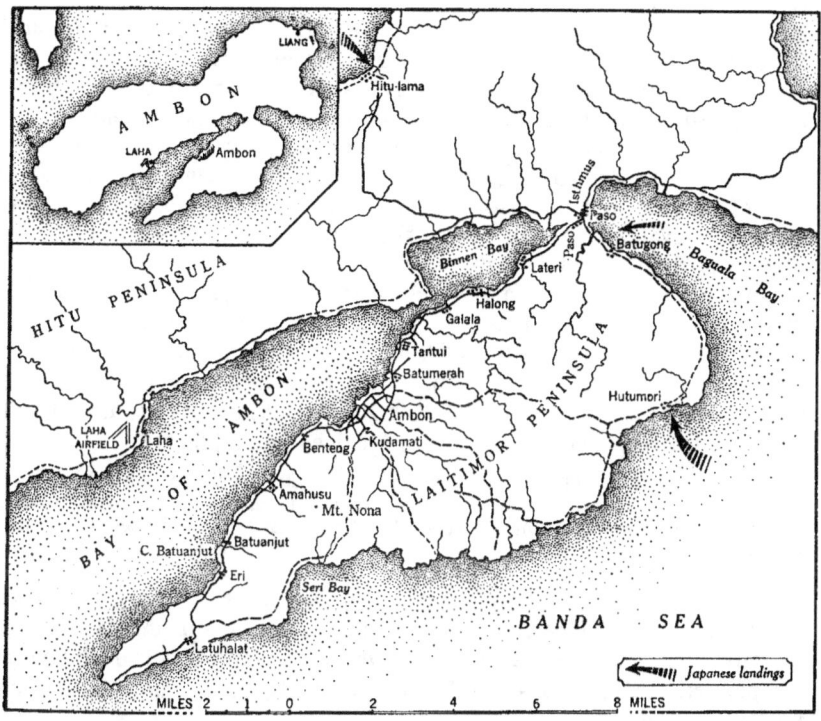

The invasion of Ambon

and the head of Binnen Bay. There it bifurcated, one part running across the northern portion of the island to a flat area of the north coast at Hitu-lama, and the other towards Liang.

The Dutch garrison of the Molucca Archipelago was mainly concentrated on Ambon, and the island's garrison had been reinforced also from Java. By the end of December the Netherlands Indies forces on the island, commanded by Lieut-Colonel J. R. L. Kapitz, numbered about 2,600 men. They comprised several small companies of Indonesian troops, mainly officered by Dutchmen, and some Dutch coast artillery. The companies were below strength, and lacked their full complement of commissioned and non-commissioned officers. Gull Force had a total strength of about 1,100.[8] Kapitz became commander of all forces on Ambon, Dutch and Australian.

---

[8] The troops attached to the 2/21st Battalion were: C Troop 18th Anti-Tank Battery; one section 2/11th Field Company; a detachment of the 23rd Brigade Signal Section; an AASC section; a detachment of the 2/12th Field Ambulance; the 23rd Dental Unit; 104 LAD; and other small detachments. A small reinforcement of one officer and 16 other ranks arrived on 20th January.

The principal fortifications were at Paso, on the Paso Isthmus, to deny entry from the north and east to the Laitimor Peninsula, inclusive of the town of Ambon. At Benteng, adjacent to the town, was a battery manned by Dutch permanent artillerymen. It was emplaced in concrete, with its accommodation and telephone system underground, and commanded the Bay of Ambon and the Laha airfield. The aircraft based on the island in December included some American and Netherlands Navy flying-boats, some Dutch bombers, and two fighters, as well as the Hudson bombers of No. 13 Squadron R.A.A.F. The flying-boats were at Halong and the others at Laha and (by mid-December) at Namlea on Buru Island. Mines had been laid to hamper enemy access to important positions in the Bay of Ambon and to Paso and the Laitimor Peninsula from the east. The only naval vessels stationed at the island were two motor-boats taken over from the harbourmaster.

Gull Force, at first accommodated mainly at Tantui camp, a little north of the town of Ambon, had been allotted positions in both the east and the west of the island, interposed with those of the Dutch force. This was the situation when Colonel Roach, on 23rd December, sent a third appeal for more arms and men. On the 24th Roach sent a signal stating that his previous messages had not been acknowledged and adding:

> Present combined army forces inadequate hold vital localities more than day or two against determined attack from more than one direction simultaneously. To be of any appreciable value we consider imperative have following additional forthwith.

The reinforcements he sought included two troops of field and two of anti-tank artillery (there was no mobile artillery on the island), six mortars, four medium machine-guns, bush nets and medical equipment. He pointed out that anti-aircraft guns would be useful, and carriers had not arrived, adding:

> Owing enemy strategy now employed indications are this position will be precarious even with above additional if adequate support other services NOT provided. Would appreciate indication proposed policy.

This signal and a report of the same day in which Roach had mentioned deficiencies in rations and of certain types of ammunition, drew a reply from the Deputy Chief of the General Staff, Major-General Rowell, on 26th December:

> Concerned at your remarks regarding ammunition and food reserves since adequate supplies were dispatched Ambon before your arrival. Carriers left direct for Ambon 19/12 anticipate arrive first week January. Additional units you ask for not repeat not available. Your task in cooperation with local Dutch forces is to put up the best defence possible with resources you have at your disposal.

This clearly meant that what Gull Force had or was about to receive was all that could be spared to enable it to "put up the best defence possible". On the 27th (ten days after the arrival of Gull Force) Army Headquarters signalled "send dispositions combined forces". Roach complied, and on the 29th sent a further signal saying that they would do their utmost, and adding:

> Additional requested would make immeasurable difference this strategically important centre as feel confident enemy will waver before Australian fire and bayonets. All most eager administer salutary punishment.

However, in a letter to Scott on 1st January, Roach wrote more pointedly:

> I find it difficult to overcome a feeling of disgust, and more than a little concern at the way in which we have seemingly been 'dumped' at this outpost position ... without any instructions whatever[9] ... and ... with (so far) a flat refusal to consider any increase in fire-power and the number of troops, whilst the cooperation and assistance from the other two arms of the Service must be of very limited value indeed.

On the 3rd January Army Headquarters signalled to Roach that large supplies of ammunition and rations had been on the way for some weeks (evidently Rowell's signal of the 26th December referred to these supplies, about which Roach had not been informed).

On the night of 6th-7th January seven Japanese flying-boats dropped thirty-three bombs at three points on Ambon. Two Hudsons, a Buffalo fighter and a workshop were damaged at Laha airfield; three native civilians but no soldiers were killed.

Four days later Roach sent a signal indicating that a Japanese attack on the island was expected soon, saying that "prospects are gloomy" and suggesting that Colonel Leggatt[1] (of the 2/40th in Timor) and he should fly to Darwin, furnish information and discuss a plan. Also on the 11th January Area Combined Headquarters at Halong[2] sent a signal to Melbourne pointing out that Japanese air bases were now established about 360 miles distant, and urgently requesting "immediate reinforcements by fighters and dive bombers". It suggested Tomahawks and Wirraways in

---

[9] Roach later recorded that an operational instruction from AHQ, dated 6th December and relating to the forces in Timor and Ambon, did not reach Ambon until 13th January. It stated that: "The Australian Military Forces allotted to Ambon and Dutch Timor will be under the direct operational control of AHQ. The normal L of C will be through 7 MD, the headquarters of which will act as HQ L of C, for maintenance arrangements. It may be necessary to use other L of C to meet the sea transport situation at the time." As regards Ambon itself, the order was that "The Force Comd (CO 2/21 Bn) will retain command of all Australian troops at Ambon. Dutch authorities will retain civil control of Ambon and the military and administrative command of all Dutch troops. Gull Force Comd will cooperate with the Dutch Comd in all operational plans. The AIF troops will remain under the administrative command in respect of personnel of Comd 23 Inf Bde AIF who will also have the right to inspect troops at Ambon and examine operational plans of the area in collaboration with the Dutch Commander when directed by AHQ to do so. A CDH capable of controlling local defence and air operations will be formed. This CDH is to consist of Dutch Navy and Army Comds and Australian Army and Air Force Comds acting in cooperation."

Roach stated in June 1942 that, apart from the signal on 26th December from General Rowell, he had before he received this order "no other clue as to the probable policy—whether ours was to be a sort of delaying show, whether we were to hold on indefinitely ... whether naval or air support subsequently could be anticipated, or whether we should include withdrawal from Ambon in our plans". He commented that "every commander of a detached force can reasonably expect to receive all available information, and instructions as to his role and task. Such advices, plus the local situation, are factors determining his plan."

[1] Lt-Col Sir William Leggatt, DSO, MC, ED, VX44907. (1st AIF: Lt 60 Bn.) 2/22 Bn; CO 2/40 Bn 1941-42. MLA, Vic, 1947-55. Barrister; of Mornington, Vic; b. Malekula Is, New Hebrides, 23 Dec 1894. (Leggatt had replaced Youl as commander of the 2/40 in Nov.)

[2] Area Combined Headquarters was an overall control device developed in the United Kingdom when more than one Service was operating on the same task; for example the passage of convoys across the North Atlantic. At Halong, Australian, Dutch and American Services were represented.

the largest numbers possible and added "only token resistance possible with present unsuitable aircraft all of which will certainly be destroyed in one day's action against carrier-borne forces".[3]

On the 13th January Roach sent a signal to headquarters in Melbourne that "in view of overwhelming enemy combined forces successfully operating Menado area and indications early attack on similar scale here we could NOT hold out for more than ONE day"; that he understood that no such support as he had asked for could be expected; and that to avoid purposeless sacrifice of valuable manpower and arms he recommended immediate evacuation of the combined force.

Army Headquarters replied that Roach's messages "should cease at once", and added "your staunch defence will have important effect . . . in regard future Australian Dutch cooperation". Next day Roach received a signal that Major Scott was flying to Darwin and would take over command of Gull Force; Roach to return to Southern Command.

General Sturdee told General Wavell about this situation. Wavell replied, on the 15th:

> So far as I can judge position at Ambon not critical and in any case I am opposed to handing out important objectives to enemy without making them fight for it. Quite appreciate feelings of lonely garrison but am sure Australians will put up stout fight whatever happens. No doubt it is wise to change commander. If circumstances allow hope fly there for short visit soon.

Scott, 53 years of age and thus some years older than the oldest battalion commander in the A.I.F., had served on Gallipoli, had been an outstanding company commander in fighting in France in 1916, 1917 and 1918, and for a period, as a captain, had commanded a battalion in action. Between the wars he served for a year in the militia infantry and later as a staff officer. In June 1940 he was appointed to the general staff at Melbourne.

Meanwhile, on Ambon the local defence plan had been rearranged. On 10th January Colonel Roach sent his second-in-command, Major Macrae,[4] to a conference with Kapitz, who said his company commanders had told him they could not work successfully with Australian companies. This was attributed to language difficulties, presumably as between Australians and Indonesians. Roach, with his Indian Army experience in mind, wanted to put his troops among the Indonesians. His dispositions provided for one Australian company at Laha, one at Paso, and one in reserve. Kapitz, however, offered the Australians a choice of two sectors, either to be taken over entirely by them. One was a line across the upper

---

[3] On 14th January the Chief of Air Staff RAAF (Air Chief Marshal Sir Charles Burnett) sent a personal message to Wing Commander Scott, the senior RAAF officer at ACH Halong, which said (in part): "The position of Ambon is within the control of the Commander-in-Chief in N.E.I. and must form part of the whole strategical plan and cannot be considered alone. It must therefore be held until orders are received from the Supreme Commander, General Wavell. I feel sure you would be the first to protest if Australians were withdrawn leaving the Dutch alone to meet the attack. Congratulate those concerned on good work accomplished."

[4] Maj I. F. Macrae, OBE, VX44787; 2/21 Bn. Manager; of Upper Hawthorn, Vic; b. Melbourne, 16 Jul 1905.

part of the island, from Paso to Hitu-lama; the other south of the town, in the vicinity of Mount Nona in the south-western portion of the Laitimor Peninsula, and also the Laha airfield, where "C" Company (Captain Sandy[5]) had been stationed since arrival. The latter sector was accepted.

An Australian rifle section, with engineers and two Bren carriers, was accordingly allotted to an outpost position at Latuhalat, on the southern shore of the Laitimor Peninsula near its south-western tip. It was hoped that it would be able to hamper any attempted landing there, and if necessary fight a delaying action in any Japanese thrust across the peninsula towards Eri. Eri, on the bay shore, was to be defended along a steep and lengthy line by "A" Company (Major Westley[6]). A platoon of "B" Company under Lieutenant Chaplin,[7] was to be stationed at Cape Batuanjut, between Eri and Amahusu. Battalion headquarters and "D" Company (Captain Newnham[8]) were to occupy a 2,800-yard line dipping sharply from the Nona plateau to the beach at Amahusu, between Eri and the town of Ambon. Newnham's company was ready with vehicles loaded either to move forward to Eri or north to Benteng hill, south of Ambon. Seeing danger of his position being commanded by enemy troops who might seize the Nona plateau, 1,600 feet above it, Newnham obtained agreement that the pioneer platoon (Lieutenant Jinkins[9]) be posted there. The transport and other details, and the 104th Light Aid Detachment, were to be at Kudamati, on a slope near the southern outskirts of the town. "C" Company (now under Captain Watchorn[1]), with "B" Company (Captain Perry[2]) less one platoon were to defend Laha airfield, which was the Australians' main responsibility. Also at Laha were about 300 troops of the Dutch force, with two Bofors anti-aircraft guns.

On the ground that the main attack was likely to be from the deep indentation made by the Bay of Baguala on the east, the principal Dutch forces were to occupy positions at and near Paso, which was to be held stubbornly. In the view of the Dutch command, a Japanese landing on the steep, jungle-covered south coast of the Laitimor Peninsula was impracticable, and Laha was militarily inaccessible by overland routes. A company and a mortar unit were assigned to oppose any landing at Hitulama, and to delay with the support of other troops any thrust across country towards Paso from that direction. Another company was allotted to the Australian left flank at Eri as a result of subsequent developments.

---

[5] Maj D. A. Sandy, ED, VX44354. 2/21 Bn, and various appointments connected with PW & I. Production and sales executive; of St Kilda, Vic; b. Melbourne, 11 Mar 1915.
[6] Maj G. de V. Westley, ED, VX44808; 2/21 Bn. Estate agent; of Balwyn, Vic; b. Hawthorn, Vic, 14 Apr 1910.
[7] Lt W. J. Chaplin, GM, VX46446; 2/21 Bn. Clerk; of Ormond, Vic; b. Glenhuntly, Vic, 10 Apr 1921.
[8] Capt C. F. Newnham, ED, VX44777; 2/21 Bn. Warehouse superintendent; of Hawthorn, Vic; b. Hawthorn, 22 Mar 1909.
[9] Maj W. T. Jinkins, MBE, VX44818. 2/21 Bn and "Z" Special Unit. Builder and contractor; of Hawthorn, Vic; b. Moreland, Vic, 29 Nov 1912.
[1] Capt N. E. Watchorn, VX45224; 2/21 Bn. Grazier; of Larpent, Vic; b. Christchurch, NZ, 2 Apr 1903. Executed by Japanese 15 Feb 1942.
[2] Capt D. G. Perry, VX44346; 2/21 Bn. Customs agent; of Caulfield, Vic; b. Caulfield, 4 May 1917. Executed by Japanese 15 Feb 1942.

The Dutch positions, and the Australian positions on the Laitimor Peninsula, were designed to cover the main approaches to the town. Resort to guerilla warfare if the positions could not be held was "contemplated" by Kapitz, but no plans for guerilla resistance were made.

Owing in part to neglect of precautions, there was considerable wastage among the Australians at Laha from malaria and dysentery. Among the victims was Captain Sandy, who late in January was evacuated to Australia. He was replaced on 20th January in command of the companies at Laha by Major Newbury.[3]

The change in the dispositions of the defending forces had entailed digging new defence works and reorganising communications and supply. It placed the Australian and Dutch companies in unfamiliar positions. But perhaps the most disturbing factor for Gull Force was the sudden change of command. Having recommended to the Director of Military Operations that Roach be recalled, Scott had offered to command Gull Force himself and had been appointed. He reached Ambon on the night of the 16th, and Roach accepted an opportunity to fly to Darwin early next morning. Thus Scott took over, at a critical period in the Japanese southward thrust, a force which had just been re-disposed, and whose officers and men were strangers to him. There was naturally considerable resentment among the members of Gull Force at Roach having been recalled. Fortunately the second-in-command, Major Macrae, was a capable and tactful officer, for whom the force had a high regard.

The Japanese air raid on Ambon Island on 6th-7th January was probably part of the prelude to their landings at Menado and Tarakan on the 11th. Thereafter enemy air raids on Ambon had increased in number and strength. Both the Dutch fighters were shot down on 15th January. In a daylight raid by 36 aircraft on the 16th some of the Hudsons were destroyed on the ground and two riflemen and two signallers of the 2/21st Battalion were killed. Because of the Japanese preponderance in the air, and on the grounds that the flying-boat base had been made useless by bombing, the Dutch naval aircraft were withdrawn that day; the American airmen left soon after.

In these raids the two Bofors guns manned by the Dutch—the only anti-aircraft guns on the island—achieved disappointing results. The Australians tried to defend Laha with Lewis guns supplemented, after the seaplane base at Halong had been abandoned, with heavy machine-guns from Catalina flying-boats, on improvised mountings.

The Japanese had made extensive air reconnaissances, and Scott regarded attack by the convoy at Menado as imminent. Among the difficulties of the situation, as Scott saw them, were that Gull Force was widely distributed and the country was very steep and tangled; the only means of transport between Gull Force headquarters at Tantui and the Laha

---

[3] Maj M. W. H. Newbury, VX43876; 2/21 Bn. Softgoods manager; of Brighton, Vic; b. Kew, Vic, 6 Apr 1908. Executed by Japanese 6 Feb 1942.

airfield was the Dutch harbourmaster's launch. Scott complained later that there was no plan for storage of food, water, or ammunition in the hills where guerilla resistance could if necessary be maintained in the final stages of the defence.

On the 24th January—the day of the Japanese landing at Kendari— 35 aircraft from the carriers *Soryu* and *Hiryu* attacked Ambon. It was the first task these carriers had undertaken since the attack on Pearl Harbour and Wake Island. Two other carriers (*Shokaku and Zuikaka*) of the Carrier Fleet were then supporting the attack on Rabaul. The use of carriers at Rabaul had been desirable because of its distance from land-based aircraft. Their use at Ambon and later Timor and Darwin was evidently a result of caution—hardly justified by the facts—about those bases where Australian air and land forces were deployed. In this phase it was only against such bases that the Carrier Fleet was employed.

The evacuation of the few remaining serviceable Hudsons of No. 13 Australian Squadron began on 28th January. Soon no air or naval support would remain.[4]

The approach to Ambon Island of a Japanese convoy, estimated at five warships and seventeen transports, with five unidentified vessels some hours astern, was reported by Australian airmen on 29th January. On Dutch orders, the Australian engineers destroyed naval oil reserves, and oil and bomb dumps, hangars, and equipment at Laha. They sought to make the surface of the airfield unserviceable. Shortly before dusk on the 30th, Jinkins and his men on Nona sighted ships off the coast of the Laitimor Peninsula.

There followed, during the night, two Japanese landings, by marines at Hitu-lama and by an army regiment on the southern coast of the Laitimor Peninsula. By choice of these points the enemy avoided any major opposition on the beaches, and grasped the initiative, though the southern landing would necessitate traversing extremely rugged country served only by rough tracks. The defenders were at the disadvantage that, having an insufficient number of troops to man the coastline generally, their forces were committed to certain points which had seemed most vulnerable to attack, and to a largely static defence, unless they could be redistributed with sufficient speed once the Japanese plan became apparent.

To reinforce Paso against thrusts from the north-west and from the south, Kapitz withdrew to Paso the Dutch company at Hitu-lama, and one on the road to Liang, leaving only platoons for delaying actions. Only small detachments of the Dutch forces were in the vicinity of the south coast landings.

At Hitu-lama, the defending infantry and machine-gunners were quickly overwhelmed as Japanese troops swarmed ashore, and mortars were cap-

---

[4] Most of the RAAF men were flown out in Hudsons, but one party, including the base commander, Wing Commander Dallas Scott, had to stay behind when the last Hudson became unserviceable. At Namlea Squadron Leader A. B. McFarlane and eight others who remained to undertake demolitions, were later picked up by a flying-boat and taken to Darwin.

tured while an attempt was being made to get them back to Paso. Bridges on the road which were to have been destroyed were left intact, allowing the landing force to thrust quickly across the Hitu Peninsula.

Successive landings occurred on the Laitimor Peninsula, principally at Hutumori due east of the town of Ambon, and south of Paso. Once ashore, the Japanese split forces for thrusts westward to the town, and northward to Paso. Captured Ambonese were forced to act as guides.

The Paso defences had been designed principally against attack from the north and the west; they were now being attacked from the south. The roadless jungle-covered terrain to the south had been thought to be a defence in itself against assault from that direction. For this reason, and because of the concealment it had been thought desirable to retain against air attack, there had been insufficient clearing for fields of fire. It soon became apparent, however, that the Japanese were capable of astonishingly quick progress over such country, and that concealment was far more important to them as an aid to infiltration than it was as cover to the defenders.

As an instance, Japanese troops arrived within 100 yards of the Paso southern flank without having been detected, and entered a gap caused by dispatch of a platoon to aid in resisting an attack on Batugong, a fortified position on the line of approach from the south. The gap had been left owing to failure of the telephone line to staff headquarters. Batugong fell early in the morning of the 31st and the Japanese were thus able to encircle troops on the eastern flank of the Paso position. The Dutch forces were not equipped with means of radio communication, and their telephone system was quickly affected by the efficiency of the Japanese in cutting the lines. Colonel Kapitz, and the commander of the Paso position, Major H. H. L. Tieland, soon lost a general view of how the situation was developing.

At noon Kapitz transferred his headquarters from near Halong to Paso. While the thrusts from the south were developing, an attack from the east on the Paso defences by portion of the force which had landed at Hitulama set in. Confusion caused by failure of communications, and by surprisingly swift attack from unexpected quarters, had a demoralising effect. Resistance at some points was slight or not sustained, and such counter-attack as was attempted failed to stave off encirclement of the Paso defences.

A perimeter defence by units which remained in action was finally ordered, but towards the end of the afternoon the commanders of the units found that communication with the Paso headquarters had failed. It later transpired that both Kapitz and Tieland with their staffs had left the headquarters. At 6 p.m. a motor-cycle with sidecar was seen on the road to the west of the Paso position showing white flags and travelling towards the Japanese. Firing on the Paso perimeter was suspended on the orders of the Dutch company commanders, and the troops were allowed to rest and eat. Tieland visited them, however, with an order to recommence fighting, on the ground that the white flag had not been accepted by the enemy.

After a conference between Tieland and the company commanders, it was agreed that execution of the order be postponed while two of the commanders went with him to see Kapitz, at the Lateri Battery, on Binnen Bay near Halong. Giving an account later to Scott of what had happened, one of Kapitz's company commanders said Kapitz complained that reports to him by his officers had made the situation appear worse than it really was when he decided to show the white flag. He considered that they had been intimidated by the bold action of small numbers of Japanese who had penetrated the lines, and was ashamed that fighting had been given up so soon. The officers with the white flags had not succeeded in reaching the enemy, who apparently were not inclined to open up negotiations. However, after one of the commanders had testified to the seriousness of the fighting of which he had knowledge, it was agreed that a waiting-and-prepared-for-action attitude be assumed in the last occupied positions in the Paso area.

When Tieland and the company commanders returned to the position, they found that the resting troops had been taken prisoner by a Japanese unit. These officers were told that they must consider themselves prisoners also.

The Australians had received from Dutch headquarters before 3 a.m. on the 31st a report that the enemy had landed on the south coast of the Laitimor Peninsula. Jinkins reported from Mount Nona at daylight that ships were apparently anchored off the coast, and warships were patrolling the coast and across the mouth of the Bay of Ambon. Thus the threat was from the east, whereas the southern dispositions on the peninsula had been designed to meet one from the bay. Kapitz therefore ordered an Ambonese company under Captain E. P. Bouman from Eri, where it had just been sent to the left flank of Westley's company, to Kudamati, which now seemed likely to become the front-line instead of the rear. Lieutenant Russell,[5] liaison officer at Dutch headquarters, reached the Australians during the morning of the 31st with a report that the headquarters staff had left the town of Ambon. He said they had left intact maps and telephones, which he then destroyed.[6]

---

[5] Lt G. T. Russell, VX46435; 2/21 Bn. Marketing assistant; of Toorak, Vic; b. Melbourne, 10 Jan 1916.

[6] Scott subsequently quoted Russell as having reported to him: "About 0900 hours I was out of the H.Q. for a few minutes and got a report that some Jap soldiers were just above our H.Q. I went back and as I did so I saw Kapitz and all his Dutch staff disappearing down the road. I ran after them and asked where they were going and Kapitz . . . said they were leaving at once for a new H.Q. I asked for orders and he gave none. . . . I only had my batman with me and we were now quite alone. I reported to you by 'phone and got your instructions to report at once to you at B.H.Q. I then returned to Dutch HQ and destroyed maps and papers which had been left intact as well as the four or five telephones which were also left connected and intact. These and the switchboard I destroyed and then with my batman got into my truck and drove to Amahoesoe and reported to you."
Scott subsequently sent a dispatch rider to Paso to try to locate Kapitz, with a message to the effect "I don't know your H.Q. location. I have no information as to the position. I have no instructions." The reply, according to Scott, gave no location of H.Q., and no instructions. This was the last communication between Scott and Kapitz during the action.

Scott ordered Captain Turner,[7] second-in-command of Westley's company, to take charge at Kudamati, and that engineer, army service, ambulance, pay and postal personnel quartered in and north of the town of Ambon should move into the position. On the ground that, as events were shaping, effective control would be difficult to maintain from Amahusu, he decided to move his headquarters to Eri. Turner disposed Bouman's company to defend the approach to Mount Nona.

Japanese troops were seen occupying the hospital, less than half a mile north of the Kudamati position, about 4 p.m. on the 31st. They were fired upon, but with poor results as they were too far away. Next day (Sunday) Japanese army vehicles were seen moving up the road to the hospital. With them were two Australian ambulance trucks. Captured troops were seen alighting from the vehicles. It thus appeared that the town, and the Australian casualty clearing station in it, had fallen into Japanese hands. The Kudamati position came under shell fire.

Japanese advancing from the town towards Kudamati were hotly engaged by transport men under Lieutenant Smith[8] early on Sunday morning (1st February), and withdrew. The Japanese then commenced an outflanking movement in the same direction which threatened to drive a wedge between the Kudamati position and the Benteng Battery to the west, with which there was no liaison. A runner was sent to a warrant-officer in charge of a party of Australians so placed that they might be able to counter this threat. The officer and most of his command, including the only two signallers there, could not be found. The situation was made worse by the fact that the telephone lines to Australian headquarters had been cut, it was assumed by artillery fire.

When a request was made to Bouman for aid in dealing with the threat, it was found that his company had lost heavily in machine-guns as a result of Japanese shelling, and that most of his troops had disappeared. Bouman nevertheless undertook to give the necessary cover.

Benteng Battery, which since daylight had been under fire from mountain guns on near-by heights, itself ceased fire about 9 a.m., and it became apparent that the guns were being disabled. With this vital defensive position out of action, the enemy concentrated the full power of their artillery upon the Kudamati position, instead of exposing their troops in further attempts to storm it. Japanese vessels entered the bay. A mine-sweeper struck a mine, broke in half and sank swiftly.

Owing to their hurried transfer to Eri, and then to Kudamati, many of Bouman's Ambonese had gone without several meals, and were very fatigued. After going to Scott for information early on Sunday, Bouman came under fire when attempting to rejoin his men. Late in the day, he found the company's machine-gun position deserted. Shell craters and bullet holes indicated that it had been under heavy fire. After dark,

---

[7] Capt J. M. Turner, MBE, VX45196; 2/21 Bn. Bank officer; of North Balwyn, Vic; b. St Kilda, Vic, 26 Aug 1910.

[8] Lt D. W. Smith, VX34426; 2/21 Bn. Pastoral manager; of Booligal, NSW; b. London, 25 Nov 1906.

Looking south-east from Laha across the Bay of Ambon to Mount Nona.
Post-war photograph.

Laha airfield, looking towards the northern end of the strip where much of the fighting took place.
Post-war photograph.

(*Australian War Memorial*)

(*Australian War Memorial*)

Dutch Timor. Plains in the Usau district (looking north-west towards the head of Koepang Bay) where Japanese paratroops landed on 19th-20th February 1942. Post-war photograph.

(*Australian War Memorial*)

Usau Ridge, where resistance by the 2/40th Battalion ended on 23rd February 1942. Post-war photograph.

Bouman reached the company's main position, where there remained only the officer in command, some N.C.O's, and a few soldiers. He was informed that the position had been attacked by parties of Japanese, and shelled by mortars and mountain artillery. The greater part of the troops had disappeared during the night 31st January-1st February. Bouman ordered that the remaining troops should endeavour to safeguard the Australian right wing, and next morning set out again to see Scott.

The Kudamati position, inclusive of "B" Echelon with much of the battalion's ammunition, stores, and transport, was in fact being by-passed by the night of 31st January. The Amahusu line had been readjusted when it became apparent that its rear was to become its front. A patrol was dispatched on Sunday morning along the road towards Kudamati when a report was received that that position had been cut off. The patrol became engaged with the enemy, and fell back to a position where it could make a stand. An attempt was made to get the wounded men of the patrol by ambulance to Ambon hospital, but the driver was halted by the Japanese, and returned with a letter from a Japanese commander stating that no wounded would be allowed through until after the Australians had surrendered; also that Colonel Kapitz had surrendered with his force, and the Australians were hopelessly outnumbered.

Attacks on the left flank of the Amahusu position continued throughout the day. A party comprising cooks and headquarters mess details, placed under Sergeant Martin[9] in a position covering the road approach from Ambon, held up the enemy advance for a while. Martin and others relayed mortar fire control orders to a mortar position under Sergeant Smith[1] up the line. This fire, and rifle grenades from his party, dispersed the Japanese.

In the early afternoon Captain Newnham's headquarters and Sergeant Smith's mortars were under small arms fire. Soon after 4 p.m. the platoon (Lieutenant Chaplin) from Batuanjut was sent forward to the Amahusu position and relieved Sergeant Martin's hard-pressed detachment.

> From this time onwards (wrote Newnham soon afterwards) many Dutch and Ambonese troops were drifting back from Kudamati and Batumerah; some even stated they were from Paso direction. It was estimated that by 1800 hrs over 100 troops had been fed and watered, the majority saying they had not been fed for two days. Confusion was caused by these troops coming through fire positions, many being in a panicky state; some were directed out of the line, but many were placed in fire positions, and others were sent to the Intelligence officer (Lieutenant Chapman[2]) for employment around Position H.Q.[3]

Meanwhile Mount Nona reported that Japanese were appearing on the Nona plateau, and a platoon less a section, under Lieutenant Anderson,[4]

---

[9] Sgt L. E. Martin, VX28878; 2/21 Bn. Carpenter; of Box Hill, Vic; b. Windsor, Vic, 16 Oct 1916. Died while prisoner 5 Aug 1945.
[1] L-Sgt H. L. Smith, VX26133; 2/21 Bn. Truck driver; of Malvern, Vic; b. Bridgetown, WA, 8 Jul 1907. Died while prisoner 21 Jul 1945.
[2] Capt W. A. M. Chapman, VX45199. 2/21 Bn; and Staff appointments. Student; of Kew, Vic; b. Melbourne, 29 Jan 1921.
[3] Report by Capt C. F. Newnham re Amahusu and Erl.
[4] Lt S. F. Anderson, VX24574; 2/21 Bn. Jackeroo; of Malvern, Vic; b. Melbourne, 2 Oct 1918.

was sent to aid Jinkins' platoon, a platoon being sent forward from Eri to replace Anderson's. On the plateau, Anderson and a corporal were moving ahead of the others when they were attacked by Japanese with hand grenades, and Anderson fell, hit in the legs. He told the senior N.C.O., a corporal, that he was done for and that the corporal should do the best he could for the platoon. The corporal returned to the men and led them back to the line.

Jinkins' platoon had been attacked by Japanese who got to within 30 yards before being challenged. They tried to deceive the Australians by replying that they were Ambonese but without success; a Japanese bullet killed Sergeant Kay.[5] The rush of enemy troops was stopped with grenades and fire from sub-machine-guns, and they were driven back yelling loudly. Thrusts at the platoon's flanks were defeated, despite heavy mortar fire directed at the Australian position.

Jinkins shouted to Anderson during the attack in an effort to discover if he was near. When Anderson replied, Jinkins and a few of his men were facing a charge by forty or fifty Japanese in close formation. Bowling grenades, and then discharging them from rifles as the Japanese receded, they drove them off. Disregarding Anderson's call to them not to bother about him, Jinkins and two others found him gravely wounded, and weak from loss of blood. Although they came under heavy machine-gun fire, and Anderson fainted during the rescue, they got him to their position.

During the night, Jinkins moved his platoon 100 yards westward. At daylight on 2nd February from his point of vantage he saw that the Kudamati position had been vacated, and that the Japanese who had attacked his platoon had occupied the position it had left.[6] Runners whom he had dispatched to battalion headquarters had not returned. Later in the morning Japanese warships were seen shelling positions to which the battalion had withdrawn, and Jinkins decided to endeavour to lead his platoon to them.

At 10.30 p.m. on the 1st Colonel Scott telephoned Captain Newnham and asked him to think over a suggestion that in view of the enemy's possession of Nona, Newnham's company should fall back to Eri "where the unit could make a stand for two or three days". Newnham consulted his officers, and then told Scott that he agreed. An hour later, at midnight 1st-2nd February, the movement began. Scott hoped that air or naval support from Australia might arrive next day, in consequence of the message which he understood had been sent from Laha to Army Headquarters.

The withdrawal was complicated by the presence of the troops who had entered the Amahusu line from Dutch positions. While it was in progress, a barrage of mortar fire was maintained against the enemy, until the weapons became too hot for use. The last platoon to withdraw countered

---

[5] Sgt B. G. Kay, VX27174; 2/21 Bn. Concrete hand; of Box Hill, Vic; b. Rosebery, Vic, 25 Oct 1913. Killed in action 1 Feb 1942.

[6] It was afterwards discovered that they numbered 500.

a Japanese attack with hand grenades, and close-range fighting occurred in one of the trenches. Captain Major,[7] second-in-command of Newnham's company, which now had attached to it some Indonesians to whom owing to difference in language it was difficult to convey orders, was the last to leave the line. Despite the nearness of the Japanese, he marched his men to Eri, which he reached at daylight on the 2nd.

Enemy seaplanes had strafed the Eri positions, and the Japanese warships shelled them constantly. These attacks, and a grass fire started by the shelling, caused some withdrawals. Unrest became evident among the Australians on the 2nd. Some asserted that there had been too much "sitting down and taking it", and that they wanted to "get stuck into them". Seaplanes were machine-gunning the road. In the circumstances, Scott decided to evacuate the road positions, and get everybody up the near-by hill, thus consolidating his force.

The position was reviewed at a lengthy conference between Scott, Macrae, Westley, and Newnham after nightfall. Among the factors considered were exhaustion of the troops, especially those from Amahusu; food and water scarcity, now that the position was so crowded with Australian and other troops; the difficulty, owing to the nature of the terrain, of making any effective counter-attack at night; and the likelihood of heavy losses under bombardment if the troops remained where they were.

> It was apparent that all commanders and officers present were nearing exhaustion (wrote Newnham later) and on two occasions a senior officer dropped off to sleep through sheer fatigue. The conference lacked a definite spirit and I can recall saying to the C.O. that in my present condition, having only had four hours' (approx.) sleep since Thursday, 29 January (it was then 8 p.m. on Monday) it was difficult to think along offensive lines.

Capitulation was discussed, but Major Macrae strongly opposed it on the grounds that negligible casualties had as yet been inflicted on the battalion, and the troops round Eri had not even joined battle.

Scott withheld a decision that night, except to authorise Macrae to lead a fighting patrol of twenty-three to Latuhalat, from which the patrol stationed there had returned stating that the Japanese had landed in the vicinity of their position. Macrae's party, some of them so exhausted that they fell asleep as soon as they stopped moving, reached at dawn a gorge intersecting the road above Latuhalat. The bridge over the gorge had been destroyed by the patrol, so Macrae halted his men there, in a banana plantation, to attack any Japanese attempting to cross the gorge at this point. After he and others had slept for a few hours, Macrae sampled some nuts he found while looking for bananas to feed his party, and became violently ill. Lieutenant Chapman, who was with him, sent to Eri for a stretcher, and was told by the bearers when they arrived that the battalion was going to surrender. He was given permission by Macrae to escape with twenty members of the party. Macrae, accompanied by a warrant-officer and a sergeant, was carried back to Eri.

---

[7] Capt J. F. Major, VX44506; 2/21 Bn. Bank officer; of East Malvern, Vic; b. St Kilda, Vic, 10 Oct 1915. Died while prisoner 11 May 1944.

Some Australians had left the Eri line during the night and the early morning of 3rd February. Scott concluded that if the troops generally remained in the position they would be bombed and shelled with no prospect of retaliation. The supply position was critical. The Japanese flag was seen flying over the Laha position. Scott therefore dispatched the battalion's medical officer, Captain Aitken,[8] to the enemy lines to obtain the terms of surrender.[9]

With supplies of food and ammunition exhausted, and their position cut off, Turner and his men at Kudamati surrendered at noon.

On Mount Nona, as it appeared impossible to get Anderson in his wounded condition down the steep cliff which the platoon must descend in withdrawing, two men—Privates Buchanan[1] and Wakeling[2]—volunteered to carry him by a more practicable route leading to the Japanese lines. Of 500 Japanese whom they encountered, 400 marched back by compass-bearing to the Benteng barracks with the stretcher in front. Two Japanese carried it towards the end of the trip.

The remainder of Jinkins' platoon found Amahusu village empty, with the exception of an Indonesian who said that the Japanese had captured Eri, and driven the Australians to the toe of the peninsula. One of the Australians (Private Lewis[3]) walking to Eri for medical aid, came upon a Dutch officer bearing a note from Kapitz to Scott to tell him that the Dutch had surrendered on the 1st February. With this was a message from the Japanese to the effect that they had decided to cease hostilities until noon next day; and urging Scott to give in.

Hearing no sound of fighting at Eri, the Dutchman returned to Amahusu with Lewis, where they parted. Lewis reported to Jinkins at a spot where the platoon was hiding, and he thereupon decided that he should get the note and make sure Scott saw it. Securing a bicycle, Jinkins rode into a Japanese road-block, and asked for a "shogun",[4] meaning someone in authority. An officer arrived who could speak English, and sent Jinkins under escort to the Benteng barracks, where he was taken to a Major Harikawa. The major took Jinkins to see Anderson, who had been fed and given medical treatment; then to the Residency, where General Ito of the *38th Japanese Division* had established himself. Later Jinkins was taken to see Kapitz, who wrote a second note to Scott. An attempt was made by a Japanese to get information from Jinkins, who counted ten before he answered questions, and then gave non-committal answers.

---

[8] Capt W. Aitken, VX31470; RMO 2/21 Bn. Medical practitioner; of Coburg, Vic; b. Coburg, 3 Feb 1915.

[9] Newnham subsequently recalled Scott as having said: "This is a very humiliating business. I hope these fellows realise what surrender means, but I don't think I could have rallied the unit and made a further stand."

[1] Pte A. D. Buchanan, VX41748; 2/21 Bn. Labourer; of Carrum, Vic; b. Natimuk, Vic, 1 Dec 1912. Died while prisoner 4 Aug 1945.

[2] Pte S. W. Wakeling, VX39764; 2/21 Bn. Labourer; of Albert Park, Vic; b. Ballarat, Vic, 16 Oct 1904. Died while prisoner 27 Jun 1945.

[3] Pte J. B. Lewis, VX26874; 2/21 Bn. Motor driver; of Pearsedale, Vic; b. Mornington, Vic, 20 Oct 1918. Died while prisoner 11 May 1944.

[4] Shogun ("Barbarian-Subduing-General") was the title of the virtual ruler of Japan under her feudal system abolished in 1868.

Drawing his sword, the Japanese said "Why do you answer so slowly?", and received the reply "Because you don't speak good English". The Japanese looked insulted, but replaced his sword and walked away. Then Harikawa drove Jinkins to the Amahusu line, told him there were no Japanese past this point, and gave him a captured A.I.F. motor-cycle to use. Shaking hands with him, he said: "If you do not come back, I hope we shall meet in the field."

Jinkins found that Scott had already been in touch with the Japanese, and was about to march the battalion to an area forward of the Amahusu line. Although Scott gave Captain Bouman an opportunity to surrender with his remaining men before the Australians did so, Bouman declined it, and took part in the Gull Force surrender negotiations. All weapons were destroyed, ammunition was buried, and grenades were made useless. Defeat was made more bitter by the battalion being photographed by Japanese cinematographers as it reached the enemy.

Kapitz and his staff at Lateri Battery had been taken prisoner in the early hours of 1st February by the Japanese unit which had captured the resting troops in the Paso position late on 31st January. There are indications that upon the surrender of the forces in the Dutch sector, there came into possession of the Japanese details of the positions occupied by the Australians and Bouman's company; of the strength of the island's forces; the situation of land and sea minefields; and other facts important to the enemy in completing their occupation of the island. Such information could for instance have facilitated the shelling of the Benteng Battery, the entry of Japanese warships into the Bay of Ambon, and the assault on the Australian positions from land, sea, and air.

Telephonic communication with Laha had ceased once the Australians on the Laitimor Peninsula lost touch with Dutch headquarters, connected to Laha by cable. Scott, however, sent a wireless message to Newbury, who informed him that news of the strength of the Japanese, and of their landings, had been transmitted to Australia. The R.A.A.F. wireless personnel had then left. The mortar and machine-gun positions particularly at Laha had been intensively bombed from the air. The Australians replied with small arms fire. They also manned the anti-aircraft guns when the local crews went to cover during air attacks.

The first land attack on the Laha position came late in the afternoon of 31st January, apparently by an advanced party of the force which had landed at Hitu-lama. The Japanese encountered a platoon of Captain Perry's company north-east of the airfield, but though the platoon was heavily outnumbered, the party was repulsed. Mortar and machine-gun fire was exchanged next day, and it was evident that the Japanese were being heavily reinforced (probably as a result of the fall of Paso). A concentrated attack on the position, by troops, dive bombers, fighter planes, and artillery, commenced on 2nd February.

Lieutenant McBride,[5] in charge of a platoon at a beach position, received a message from Major Newbury during the night of 1st-2nd February that some Japanese appeared to have filtered through a platoon on the north side of the airfield and that he was to take his platoon to the spot.

About 0100 hours (Monday, 2nd February) heavy machine-gun and mortar fire was directed at our positions (wrote McBride soon afterwards) and small parties of the enemy infiltrated between the platoons holding that area. My platoon proceeded to deal with this enemy detachment and there was hand-to-hand fighting. The enemy were located because of their habit of talking and calling out in a high tone to each other. . . . The fighting took place in an area covered by tall grass and the numbers of the enemy force could not be correctly arrived at. The enemy failed to make use of the natural cover afforded them and seemed to be poorly trained in night fighting. In individual combat the enemy troops were no match for our men and did not display any fortitude when wounded.

McBride almost trod on a Japanese, and was shot through both arms. He was assisted by his batman, Private Hawkins,[6] to the field dressing station in the village of Laha.

Support was moved up also from Captain Watchorn's company, stationed south of the airfield. At dawn on the 2nd a concentrated attack was made by the Japanese, and about 10 a.m. resistance ceased.

Next day, at the advanced dressing station in the jungle behind the airfield, McBride found that the Japanese had occupied the airfield. Despite his weak condition, he began to organise an escape party. Captain White,[7] of the 2/12th Field Ambulance, and all his men, decided to stay with the wounded. Full details, from an Australian point of view, of the fighting at Laha, have not become available, for reasons given below. Tribute was paid by Private Wegner,[8] brought from Laha by the Japanese, to the inspiration and gallantry of Newbury's leadership.

In the defence of Ambon, the main part of Gull Force lost 15 killed. In addition 309 officers and men who were at Laha were either killed in action or killed by the Japanese in mass executions which evidently took place on 6th February, and between the 15th and 20th. Japanese witnesses said after the war that the executions took place as a reprisal for the loss of life caused to the Japanese when a mine-sweeper (as mentioned above) struck a Dutch mine in Ambon Bay on 1st February.[9]

It is now known from Japanese sources that their force consisted in the main of the *38th Infantry Division Headquarters* under Major-General Takeo Ito, and the

---

[5] Maj I. H. McBride, MBE, VX44612. 2/21 Bn; Staff and Int appts. Schoolmaster; of Camberwell, Vic; b. Melbourne, 16 Jan 1917.

[6] Pte G. A. Hawkins, VX53582; 2/21 Bn; and HQ 17 Inf Bde. Transport driver; of Shepparton, Vic; b. Bristol, England, 1 Dec 1906.

[7] Capt S. B. McK. White, NX70920; 2/12 Fd Amb. Medical practitioner; of Neutral Bay, NSW; b. Melbourne, 5 Nov 1915. Missing presumed died 20 Feb 1942.

[8] Pte A. C. Wegner, VX27317; 2/21 Bn. Labourer; of Colac, Vic; b. Rosebery, Vic, 14 Jul 1905. Died while prisoner 23 Jun 1945.

[9] The heavy losses suffered by the survivors of Gull Force while in captivity will be recorded in a later chapter.

228th Infantry Regiment.¹ (It was the *38th Division* which had taken Hong Kong.) The force had spent nine days in training at Davao, in the Philippines, where the troops were informed of their destination. Ito decided that the main Allied force was round Ambon and that he would land on the south-eastern part of the peninsula where the defences would probably be weak.

The main part of the convoy appeared south of Ambon Island as a ruse; went northward; and again turned, to land at Hutumori. Other vessels carried the *1st Kure Naval Landing Force,* about 820 strong, which had been added to Ito's force, and an army unit of about company strength, to the north coast for the landing at Hitu-lama. There the approach was aided by heavy clouds which Genichi Yamamoto, of the Navy Press Corps, enthusiastically acclaimed as "aid from Heaven".²

From Hitu-lama, the Japanese reached Binnen Bay by midday on 31st January, and by nightfall an advanced party was at Laha. Next day a party reconnoitred the hills at the back of the position, and on 2nd February an attack was made in which the Japanese suffered heavy losses.

Japanese readers were given by Yamamoto a highly dramatic account of the struggle. Although apparently he did not himself witness the fighting, he reported that, from accounts given by the commander and his men, the Naval Landing Force's "human bullet battle" was "a record of blasting through forbidding mountains, thickly woven jungles, and impassable roads, or literally going over the bodies of dead comrades, and hacking with blood and death in the midst of the enemy . . . a battle during which took place such heroism as to make the Gods weep".

The attack on Laha was "like fighting against the blast of a furnace", but on the second day of the attack in coordination with the terrific attack by land, the Japanese air force was bombing the enemy fortifications, while warships were pounding the battery and bombarding the trench mortar positions of the enemy behind the Laha aerodrome from the sea. For all their numerical superiority, the defending forces began to betray signs of weakened resistance towards sundown, under the relentless pressures of the Japanese from land, sea and air. Yamamoto admitted, however, that "the desperate resistance of the Australians after the break-through of the Japanese death band was not to be despised".³

A Japanese prisoner of war later testified that when the surrender came, there remained of the defending force at Laha about 150 Australians, two or three Dutchmen, and a few natives.

The main enemy force, with horses and bicycles, landed unopposed at Hutumori, according to Japanese accounts. Thrusting along narrow tracks, one part of it went northward to Paso, and the other across the Laitimor Peninsula to the town. Resistance to the latter force was quickly overcome until the Australian positions south and south-west of the town were encountered. There frontal attacks became necessary, and it was not until artillery had been moved up, and all weapons trained on the positions, that the Japanese won the island.

The battle of Ambon Island disclosed in miniature many of the deficiencies of Allied defence against the Japanese onslaught generally. Without support at sea or in the air, the forces on the island had been overcome by an enemy whose strength and ability had been grossly under-estimated by many concerned. The speedy defeat of the Dutch forces was due in part it seems, here as elsewhere, to failure of communications.

---

¹ The force was 5,300 strong and included, in addition to the infantry regiment, a light tank unit, a mountain artillery battalion and part of a howitzer battery, two anti-aircraft batteries, two engineer companies, and other detachments.

² Reprint from *Nippon Times,* 31 Jan 1943.

³ In a citation announced by the Japanese Navy Ministry, Admiral Yamamoto, Commander-in-Chief of the Combined Fleet, stated that the landing party "conducted a series of dangerous fights against better equipped enemy troops, entrenched in a solid fortress", Radio Tokyo, 31 Jan 1943.

The resistance by the Australians, while it hinged largely upon the Paso position being held, or at any rate on continuation of the fight by the Dutch forces, fell short of what might have been done had there been a greater sense of urgency in the preparation of Gull Force for its task, and had it not experienced the handicaps mentioned in this chapter. Nevertheless, in the absence of aid from elsewhere, it was inevitable that a force such as the Japanese brought to bear against Ambon Island should succeed in its task, with little more delay than actually occurred. There remains the possibility that, had the necessary provision been made, the Japanese might have been hampered, after their occupation of the island, by guerilla warfare. It is doubtful, however, if this could have been maintained for long, and on any significant scale, on an island so small, and so far removed from Allied aid as Ambon was destined to be.

Because of the change of commanders in mid-January, and Scott's scant knowledge of the ground and the personnel of Gull Force, he had to rely upon Macrae to a far greater extent than would have been necessary under normal circumstances. Despite sharp divergencies of outlook and opinion which existed between the two men, Scott recorded of Macrae: "His loyalty to me from start to finish has been one of the finest things which I have met with in a long life. . . . He is an officer of undoubted courage. He is imbued with many traits of personal character which might be regarded as ideal in any officer."

Of Gull Force, despite his having been severely critical of it, Scott reported that it "did in fact hold up a complete Japanese division with its transports and adequate naval and air support for at least two weeks, and inflicted heavy loss upon the enemy. . . . It can be stated that had Gull Force been withdrawn from Ambon before the Japanese attack, the Japanese division . . . could have proceeded straight to Darwin. . . . I am unable to say whether this force would have been destroyed on arrival at Darwin during January-February 1942, but there can be said to be at least considerable doubt on this point."

Certainly, had the island not been garrisoned, or had the Japanese known how small the force was which held it, they could have attacked on a smaller scale and used the surplus for other operations. Ambon and Timor, however, were convenient stepping-stones in the Japanese southward movement, and it would have been risky to leave either as a possible base for attack on their sea communications. Thus when resistance on Ambon had been overcome, the invaders prepared for a further advance, not to Darwin but to Timor.

As has been mentioned, Lieutenant McBride on 3rd February began to organise the escape of the men who like himself were lying wounded or sick at the advanced dressing station at Laha. He collected about 20 patients who were able to walk and led them northward. In an Ambonese village on the northern side of the island he learnt that Wing Commander

Scott[4] and 10 men of the R.A.A.F. had attempted to escape by boat, but had been captured by a Japanese naval launch. After nine days McBride, with eight others, rowed a prahu to Ceram, where with the assistance of the Dutch District Officer and the natives he and four others reached Amahai. There he joined Lieutenant Snell of the Dutch Army, a Dutch medical officer and four Dutch soldiers. The combined party went on to Dobo in the Aru Islands, where they picked up 72 Dutch native troops and, now in two motor-boats, went on to Merauke in Dutch New Guinea, joining on the way a prahu containing a Dutchman, with his wife and child and 16 men of the A.I.F. From Merauke the combined party went on to Karumba in the Gulf of Carpentaria, a four-day voyage.

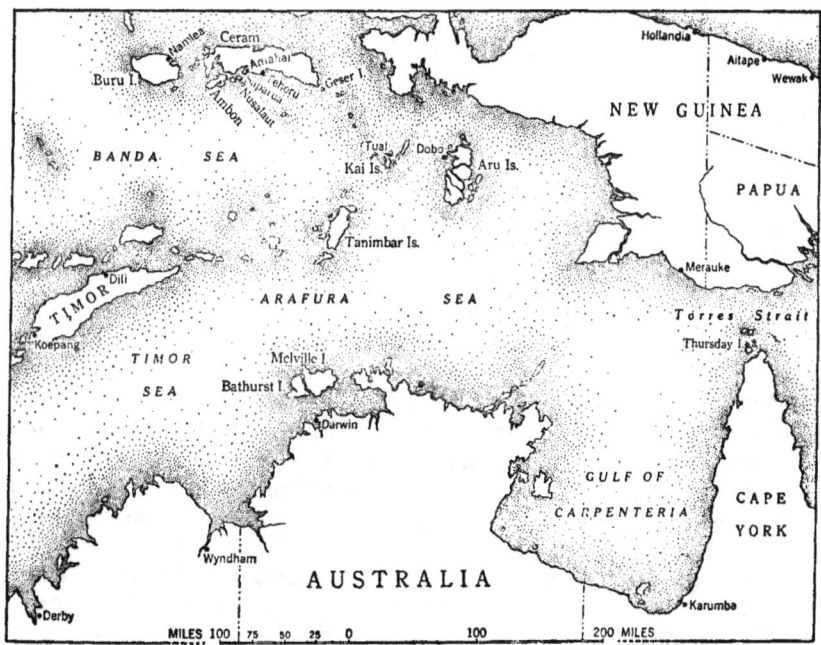

Another party of escapers was led by Lieutenant Chapman. With the 20 men of Macrae's patrol he had gone from Latuhalat to Seri Bay, obtained a prahu and set sail. They went to Nusalaut Island, then Saparua Island and Amahai, being helped by natives on the way. Thence they made their way towards Geser Island, off the south-east tip of Ceram. At the village of Tehoru natives told them that 50 Japanese were ahead of them in a motor launch. Thereupon ten of the men decided "to take their chance in the bush" rather than continue the voyage. The remainder continued to Geser and thence reached Tual in the Kai Islands on 26th February, where

[4] W Cdr E. D. Scott, AFC. No. 1 Sqn 1939-40; Comd No. 6 Sqn 1940-41; Comd RAAF component ACH Halong 1941-42. Regular airman; of Heidelberg, Vic; b. Heidelberg, 5 Oct 1913. Died while prisoner 6 Feb 1942.

the ten who had set out to walk along Ceram rejoined them. From Tual Chapman sent a signal through normal channels to Bandung:

> 1 officer 20 O.Rs escaped Ambon. Request instructions and transport.

On the 28th February Bandung replied that he should proceed to Dobo in the Aru Islands, where after eight days a ship would arrive. At Dobo Chapman's party found a Dutch infantry company. No ship arrived, but the Australians went on to Merauke in luggers, and were taken thence in a naval vessel which landed them at Thursday Island on 12th April. This party finally included Chapman, 10 Australians, 16 Dutch troops and 2 Dutch women and 4 children.

A third group was led by Lieutenant Jinkins, who escaped after six weeks in prison camp, accompanied by Lieutenants Jack[5] and Rudder[6] and four other ranks. Both the Gull Force commander, Scott, and his second-in-command, Macrae, might have joined this escape party had they wished. However, when the independent opinions were sought of two of Scott's officers both declared Scott and Macrae should remain: Scott because as Commanding Officer he "was responsible to the Australian Government for the prisoners of war and it was therefore his duty to remain" and Macrae because "the Commanding Officer was a stranger to the battalion . . . did not know any of the officers or men, their qualities or their weaknesses", and Macrae's departure would deprive him "of his only counsellor".[7] Scott and Macrae abided by this decision. The party of escapers sailed from island to island, reaching Australia after a voyage of six weeks.

Private Johnson[8] organised the escape to Australia of another party of six which eventually reached Dobo and there joined a group of three who had originally been with McBride, and another group including Private Digney,[9] another Australian, and two American airmen who had been shot down some time before. They eventually reached Thursday Island.

While the Ambon operation was in progress the American aircraft carrier force made its first foray into the western Pacific. This force— initially *Saratoga, Lexington, Yorktown, Hornet* and *Enterprise*—had not been at Pearl Harbour when it was attacked, but the shock of that calamity had been so severe that from 8th December until mid-January the carriers had not ventured westward. On the last day of 1941 new American naval commanders took charge both at Washington and Pearl Harbour—Admiral Ernest J. King as Chief of Naval Operations at Washington and Admiral Chester W. Nimitz as Commander-in-Chief of the Pacific Fleet. "Morale

---

[5] Lt-Col A. G. Jack, VX44705. 2/21 Bn and AAOC. School teacher; of Bendigo, Vic; b. Bendigo, 6 Jun 1917.

[6] Capt R. O. D. Rudder, NX76229. 2/21 Bn and AASC. Shipping clerk; of Haberfield, NSW; b. Haberfield, 10 Jul 1916.

[7] Lt-Col W. J. R. Scott, "Report on Ambon and Hainan", Part II, p. 5.

[8] WO1 D. Johnson, VX39936. 2/21 Bn and Water Transport. Transport driver; of Newmarket, Vic; b. Melbourne, 24 Dec 1912.

[9] Cpl H. Digney, VX60812. 2/21 Bn and Water Transport. Driller; of West Footscray, Vic; b. Footscray, 30 Jul 1922.

at Pearl Harbour, which had reached an all-time low with the recall of the Wake relief expedition, now rose several hundred per cent," wrote the historian of the United States Navy.[1] "He [Nimitz] restored confidence to the defeated Fleet." King instructed Nimitz that he must hold the line of communications through Samoa and Fiji to Australia and New Zealand. As mentioned, this policy had been accepted by President Roosevelt since late December, the necessity for it having been urged upon General Marshall as early as 14th December by Brigadier-General Eisenhower, then newly appointed to his planning staff. Eisenhower said to Marshall: "Our base must be Australia, and we must start at once to expand it and to secure our communications to it. In this last we dare not fail."[2] Marshall had promptly adopted the idea. (None of this was known to Australians at the time and the legend developed that American forces were sent to Australia solely to help Australia and in response to Australian appeals.) The arrival at Brisbane of the "*Pensacola* Convoy", diverted after the attack on Pearl Harbour from its original destination in the Philippines, had led to the establishment of an American base in Australia.

On 6th January an important reinforcement for the America-Australia route sailed from San Diego in California. It was a force of marines for American Samoa, and was escorted by two carriers, *Yorktown* and *Enterprise,* and attendant naval vessels. The marines were disembarked at Samoa on the 23rd January, the day on which Japanese troops supported by the Japanese Carrier Fleet landed at Rabaul, 2,500 miles to the west.

The American leaders feared that the enemy, having taken Rabaul, might next thrust farther east, from the Marshall Islands against Samoa, capture of which would place them firmly astride the American reinforcement route. To counter this *Yorktown* and *Enterprise* were ordered on 25th January with 5 cruisers and 10 destroyers to make a foray north from Samoa and bomb Japanese bases in the Marshalls. Between them these ships on 1st February bombed or bombarded Kwajalein, Wotje, Jaluit and other atolls. Little damage was done, but the carrier crews gained experience and confidence. Thus the week of the Japanese success at Ambon was the week also of the tentative beginnings of an American naval offensive in the Pacific.

---

[1] S. E. Morison, *The Rising Sun in the Pacific,* p. 256.
[2] D. D. Eisenhower, *Crusade in Europe* (1948), p. 25.

CHAPTER 20

THE DESTINATION OF I AUSTRALIAN CORPS

IN the period between the fall of Ambon and the fall of Singapore the Japanese had been steadily advancing their western flank. When the army cooped up in Singapore had been overcome, only flimsy Allied land and air forces remained to defend the rich western islands of the Indies.

The naval forces in General Wavell's command still included eight cruisers, eleven destroyers and a Dutch and an American submarine flotilla. In his air forces, however, there were only some ten depleted Dutch squadrons, and the remnants of the air force from Malaya, which on 14th February consisted of 22 Hurricanes and 35 Blenheims, many of them unserviceable. This force, commanded by Group Captain McCauley,[2] was operating from P.2 airfield near Palembang in Sumatra; Air Vice-Marshal Maltby was then reorganising his headquarters in Java. The Dutch-controlled army in Java consisted of about 25,000 men organised in four regiments, each of three battalions, and a very little artillery. There were also in Java five regiments of British anti-aircraft artillery, which had been sent there to defend the airfields, but had lost much of their equipment as a result of enemy action and other factors.

For several years the little army of the Netherlands Indies had been in process of expansion. The conquest of Holland by the Germans in 1940 made the continuance of this expansion, never an easy task for so small a nation, exceedingly difficult. The Indies Army depended chiefly on the homeland for its officers, for cadres of European soldiers, and for equipment. In 1940 and 1941 the proportion of Europeans to Indonesians in the army was reduced until it was about one in forty; additional weapons were obtained from America and Australia but there were not enough. In any event they were of different calibre from the Dutch weapons, and at length the Indies forces had rifles of 6.5-mm (Dutch), 7.62-mm (American), 7.7-mm (Australian) and 8-mm. Reorganisation was still in progress in December 1941, and in the words of a Dutch general staff officer "things were more or less chaotic".

Destined for the Indies, however, was the I Australian Corps, a more formidable formation than the Japanese had yet encountered, but most of it was still far away. An advanced party of the Corps had arrived at Batavia by air on the 26th January. It included the commander, General Lavarack; his Brigadier, General Staff, Brigadier Berryman;[3] his senior

---

[2] Air Marshal Sir John McCauley, KBE, CB. RAAF Malaya 1941-42; Deputy Chief of the Air Staff RAAF 1942-44; Air Cmdre (Ops) 2 Tactical Air Force, Europe, 1944-45. Chief of Air Staff RAAF since 1954. Regular airman; b. Sydney, 18 Mar 1899.

[3] Lt-Gen Sir Frank Berryman, KCVO, CB, CBE, DSO, VX20308. (1st AIF: 4 AFA Bde and BM 7 Inf Bde.) GSO1 6 Div 1940-41; CRA 7 Div 1941; Deputy CGS LHQ 1942-44; Comd II and I Corps during 1944; Chief of Staff Adv LHQ 1944-45. Regular soldier; of Melbourne; b. Geelong, Vic, 11 Apr 1894.

administrative officer, Brigadier Bridgeford;[4] Chief Engineer, Brigadier Steele;[5] and six other officers. Eight more officers, including Brigadier C. E. M. Lloyd, arrived on the 28th January. From that day Lloyd, as has been mentioned, became Intendant-General on Wavell's staff.

On the 27th January Lavarack met Wavell, who told him of his general plans: to hold Burma, south Sumatra, Java, Timor and Darwin, with an advanced position in Malaya. Wavell said that Lavarack's role would be to hold south Sumatra with one division and central Java with another, Dutch troops being deployed in between in western Java. Lavarack, obedient to his standing instructions from his Government, objected to the division of the Corps, but Wavell insisted that it was necessary, and at length the proposal was submitted to and approved by the Australian Government. From 1st to 9th February Lavarack and Berryman reconnoitred south Sumatra and central Java and prepared appreciations of the situation the Corps faced in both areas.[6]

The day these tasks were completed Lavarack received a cablegram from the Australian Prime Minister, Mr Curtin, seeking his views on a policy of launching a counter-offensive as soon as reinforcing troops and aircraft arrived. Lavarack replied to this somewhat vague proposal that he agreed with the fundamental policy, but urged the need for reinforcements, perhaps from Australia.

Lavarack's senior Intelligence officer, Lieut-Colonel Wills,[7] had prepared on 2nd February a paper in which he predicted that the next Japanese objectives would be (a) Timor (thus to cut air communications between Java and Australia) and (b) the Sumatra airfields and refineries; and that the enemy could attain these objectives by 2nd March. Java would then be isolated, Wills continued, and the small Dutch garrison, "split up into penny packets throughout the island" and of problematical fighting value, would not hold out for long. On the information available, the leading Australian division could not be ready for action in the Indies before 15th March at the earliest.[8] Wills concluded that adequate Australian troops

---

[4] Lt-Gen Sir William Bridgeford, KBE, CB, MC, VX38969. (1st AIF: 29 Bn and 8 MG Coy.) Comd 25 Bde 1940; DAQMG I Corps 1940-42, First Army 1942-43, NG Force 1943-44; GOC 3 Div 1944-46. Regular soldier; of Melbourne; b. Smeaton, Vic, 28 Jul 1894.

[5] Maj-Gen Sir Clive Steele, KBE, DSO, MC, VD, VX19. (1st AIF: Lt 5 and 6 Fd Coys.) CRE 6 Div 1939-40; CE I Corps 1940-42; E-in-C LHQ 1942-45. Consulting engineer; of Melbourne; b. Canterbury, Vic, 30 Sep 1892. Died 5 Aug 1955.

[6] An important outcome of the presence of the advanced parties in Java was the compilation of a paper on Japanese tactics in Malaya which was to form the basis of instructions issued to the Australian Army at home in 1942. This paper was the result of a long interview between General Allen and Brigadier Berryman on the one hand and Colonel Stewart of the Argylls on the other. It was swiftly circulated not only throughout the army in Australia but to the Australian brigades which subsequently were sent to Ceylon. There a copy was distributed to each company and was compulsory reading for all officers, sergeants and corporals.

[7] Brig K. A. Wills, CBE, MC, ED, SX3199. (1914-18: Capt 2/15 Bn, the London Regt and the Northumberland Fusiliers.) GSO3 (Air) I Corps 1940-41; GSO2 (Int) I Corps 1941-42; GSO1 (Int) First Army 1942-43; DDMI HQ NG Force 1943-44; Controller Allied Int Bureau GHQ SWPA 1944-45. Merchant; of Adelaide; b. Adelaide, 3 Mar 1896.

[8] The information then available at Wavell's and Lavarack's headquarters about the movements of I Australian Corps was that the first convoy, carrying one brigade group and some other units, would sail from the Middle East on 2 February and arrive in the Indies on 1 March; the remainder of the 7 Division would sail about 19 February and arrive on 15 March; the 6 Division would sail between the 19 and 29 March.

could not arrive in time; that if part of the Corps arrived before the Japanese attacked it would be lost; and that

> by attempting to bring 6 Aust Div, 7 Aust Div and Corps troops to southern Sumatra and Java, under the circumstances and bearing in mind the time factor, the defence and safety of Australia itself is being jeopardised.

Early on the 13th, when it seemed that Singapore would soon fall, Lavarack prepared an appreciation to send to the Australian Chief of the General Staff, General Sturdee, for the information of the Prime Minister. It contained echoes of Wills' paper, but took into account further information about the projected arrival of the I Australian Corps. Lavarack said that the fall of Singapore would release large Japanese forces; that one Australian division plus the few Netherlands East Indies troops in Sumatra would delay the enemy for only a short period, and he was "unable to judge whether such delay would justify the probable loss of 7 Aust Div equipment and possibly the loss of a large proportion of its personnel". Hs considered that, even with the addition of the 6th Australian Division, the prolonged land defence of Java was impossible. The I Australian Corps was now the only striking force within reasonable distance of the Far East, and he stressed the value of its two highly-trained, equipped and experienced divisions. The main body of the 7th Division would begin to arrive on the 25th February and would probably not be ready for full-scale operations until the third week of March; the 6th Division would probably not be ready for full-scale operations in central Java until "the middle of April at the earliest".[1]

Lavarack showed this message to Wavell, who expressed agreement but asked him to delay sending it until Wavell himself had sent a somewhat similar appreciation to the Combined Chiefs of Staff and the War Office. Wavell did this, adding to his appreciation the suggestion that there would be strategic advantages in diverting one or both the Australian divisions either to Burma or Australia. "This message," he added, "gives warning of serious change in situation which may shortly arise necessitating complete reorientation of plans."

While Wavell's appreciation and Lavarack's were on their way, General Sturdee was writing a comprehensive paper on the future employment of the A.I.F. He pointed out that the first flight of 17,800 troops of the Australian force was then in Bombay being re-stowed into smaller ships for transport to the Netherlands Indies. So far, he said, the Allies had violated the principle of concentration of force. The object should now

---

[1] The complications of trying to switch a large force so quickly from west to east were underlined when, on the 7th February, a three-days-old signal reached General Lavarack from General Allen, commanding the 7th Division, stating that Allen and the advanced part of his staff were held up at Calcutta, and that his destination was Indo-China (probably a mutilation for "Indonesia"); could Lavarack arrange onward move! The following reply was sent:
"For General Allen. Your destination stated in your unnumbered signal 4 Feb probably mutilated but is NOT repeat NOT Indo-China but Java repeat Java. Can NOT repeat NOT assist your onward move. If BOAC or Qantas passage not yet available suggest you inquire Karachi or Bangalore whether any B-17 aircraft flying Java. If so you may have to join in Ceylon."

At length, on 13th February, when Allen and five members of his staff arrived at Batavia, their air journey had taken 17 days, two days longer than it took the first units of their division to arrive by sea.

be to hold some continental area from which an offensive could be launched when American aid could be fully developed. Thus the sea and if possible the air routes from America should be kept open. The area to be held must be large enough to provide room for manoeuvre. The Dutch forces in Java "should be regarded more as well-equipped Home Guards than an Army capable of undertaking active operations in the field". It seemed doubtful whether the 7th Australian Division could reach south Sumatra in time, and if they were unable to do so probably the whole Corps would be concentrated in central Java. Assuming the Australian Corps could reach Java in time, the defence of Java would depend on the Australian Corps of two divisions, one British armoured brigade (Sturdee did not know that Wavell had already ordered it to Burma) and two inadequately organised and immobile Dutch divisions (in fact an overstatement of the Dutch strength). He considered the prospects of holding Java "far from encouraging". If Timor were lost it would be impossible to ferry fighter and medium bomber aircraft to Java from Australia.

Sturdee concluded that the only suitable strategic base was Australia, with its indigenous white population, considerable fighting forces, and sufficient industrial development. The alternatives were Burma and India. Burma was already in the front line; India had a long sea route from America, and the attitude of its people was likely to be uncertain if the East Indies fell into Japanese hands.

The Australian Military Forces, he added, were being built up to some 300,000 but lacked much essential fighting equipment and were inadequately trained. He recommended that the Government should give immediate consideration to

(a) The diversion to Australia of:
    (i) that portion of the A.I.F. now at Bombay and *en route* to Java;
    (ii) the British armoured brigade in the same convoy.
(b) The diversion of the remaining two flights to Australia.
(c) The recall of the 9th Australian Division and the remaining A.I.F. in the Middle East at an early date.

After this had been written but before it had been delivered, Lavarack's cable and then Wavell's arrived, confirming, in Sturdee's opinion, the views he had expressed.[2]

There was likely to be opposition to the policy recommended by Sturdee and Lavarack. Indeed, in Wavell's cablegram there was an indication of one form which the opposition might take: a proposal to send one Australian division, or both, to Burma.

Sturdee and Lavarack had the advantage, when preparing these and later appreciations, that they were reproducing proposals and arguments which they had been expressing during the last decade, whereas the British and American Ministers and their advisers were viewing calamities which they

---

[2] The full text of General Sturdee's appreciation, which expressed a policy adopted and thereafter maintained by the Government (and later in some regards by General MacArthur) appears as Appendix 5.

had not foreseen and which were occurring in areas about which they knew little. The Australian leaders belonged to a school of thought which had long contended that the situation of February 1942 would come about: Singapore fallen; the British and American fleets temporarily impotent against Japan; and Australia, the only effective base, being required to hold out until British or American reinforcements could arrive in strength.

Acting on the advice of Sturdee and influenced by Lavarack's message, Mr Curtin, also on 15th February, sent a cable to Mr Churchill, repeated to the Prime Minister of New Zealand and General Wavell, to the effect that Australia was now the main base and its security must be maintained; "penny-packet" distribution of forces should be avoided; the Indies could not be held; the A.I.F. should return to Australia to defend it.

> When we are ready for the counter-offensive (he added) sea power and the accumulation of American forces in this country will enable the A.I.F. again to join in clearing the enemy from the adjacent territories he has occupied.

It was not until the 17th, however, that Curtin sent a cable to Churchill repeating the precise requests suggested in Sturdee's paper: that the three Australian divisions and, if possible, the 7th British Armoured Brigade be sent to Australia.

On the 16th Wavell had sent a cable to Churchill which to some extent reinforced Curtin's. He said that he considered the risk of landing the Australian Corps on Java unjustifiable, and summed up:

> Burma and Australia are absolutely vital for war against Japan. Loss of Java, though severe blow from every point of view, would not be fatal. Efforts should not therefore be made to reinforce Java which might compromise defence of Burma or Australia.
>
> Immediate problem is destination of Australian Corps. If there seemed good chance of establishing Corps in island and fighting Japanese on favourable terms I should unhesitatingly recommend risk should be taken as I did in matter of aid to Greece year ago. I thought then that we had good fighting chance of checking German invasion and in spite results still consider risk was justifiable. In present instance I must recommend that I consider risk unjustifiable from tactical and strategical point of view. I fully recognize political considerations involved.
>
> If Australian Corps is diverted I recommend that at least one division should go Burma and both if they can be administratively received and maintained. Presence of this force in Burma threatening invasion of Thailand and Indo-China must have very great effect on Japanese strategy and heartening effect on China and India. It is only theatre in which offensive operations against Japan possible in near future. It should be possible for American troops to provide reinforcement of Australia if required.[3]

Meanwhile, on the 17th, Lavarack had cabled that the *Orcades* with 3,400 troops, mostly Australian, had been ordered to Batavia, that he had represented to Wavell that they should not be disembarked, but that Wavell did not agree, being "anxious to avoid appearance precipitately

---

[3] On 14th February, the day after Wavell's warning message quoted on an earlier page, the U.S. War Department had decided to do what Wavell now suggested. It had decided to send the 41st Division and 8,000 service troops to Australia, where hitherto the only American ground forces had been some artillery units diverted while on their way to the Philippines. The events leading up to the decisions to send American ground forces to Australia in 1942 will be dealt with in more detail in the next volume of this series.

changed plan which might compromise relations Dutch and prestige generally; also wishes them to protect aerodromes in Java". Lavarack added that he considered there was no possibility of employing the A.I.F. to advantage in Java. Sturdee, when handing on this cable, commented that if the troops landed and were distributed in Java it would be difficult if not impossible to withdraw them.

The Australian War Cabinet considered Lavarack's *Orcades* cable on the 18th and decided to tell Wavell that Lavarack considered the Australian troops now at Batavia could not be employed to advantage in the Indies.

Next day—the 19th—when the Australian Advisory War Council considered the problem, it had before it also a cable sent from London on the 18th by the Australian representative to the United Kingdom War Cabinet, Sir Earle Page. He reported that the Pacific War Council (Churchill and the United Kingdom Chiefs of Staff plus representatives of Holland, Australia and New Zealand) had considered, on the 17th, the recommendation sent by Wavell on the 16th (and repeated to Australia by Page) that at least one Australian division should be sent to Burma. The Pacific War Council had thereupon recommended to the Combined Chiefs of Staff at Washington that resistance should be maintained by all forces already in Java, but no attempt should be made to land the Australian Corps in the Indies. It had also recommended that the Australian Government be asked to agree that the 7th Division "already on the water" should go to Burma, these being, in Page's words, "the only troops that can reach Rangoon in time to make certain that the Burma Road will be kept open and thereby China kept in the fight. The position of this convoy makes it imperative that permission should be given to this course within 24 hours." The Council had added that the 70th British Division, less one brigade, would be sent from the Middle East to Rangoon, and the remaining brigade used to garrison Ceylon; the remaining Australian divisions (6th and 9th) should go "as fast as possible back into the Australian area".[4]

Also on the 18th Page sent to Australia a copy of a telegram to the Combined Chiefs of Staff in Washington recording the deliberations of this meeting of the Pacific War Council. In it the proposal about the 7th Division was phrased thus:

> In view of the imminent threat to Rangoon and the vital importance of keeping open the supply route to China, the Australian Government should be asked to permit the 7th Australian Division, the leading elements of which are now off Colombo and are the nearest fighting troops to Rangoon, to proceed to Burma and assist in the defence of that country until they can be relieved.

The 7th Division was not in a single convoy ready to set out at short notice for Rangoon. It had embarked at Suez in five flights, three of them each containing a brigade group and a proportion of other troops; one

---

[4] It appears that in practice the Council did not originate such plans as these, but had before it definite proposals formulated by Mr Churchill and the Chiefs of Staff.

(in *Orcades*) containing principally two battalions; and one containing divisional headquarters and administrative units, and the cavalry and signals units. On the 17th February, when the Pacific War Council made its recommendation, the *Orcades* had reached Batavia, the second convoy (21st Brigade Group) was between Bombay and Colombo, the third (25th Brigade Group) was due at Colombo on the 18th, the fourth (18th Brigade Group) was two days' sail west of Bombay, where it was to trans-ship into smaller transports (a task that would take five days), and the fifth, three days' sail west of Colombo.

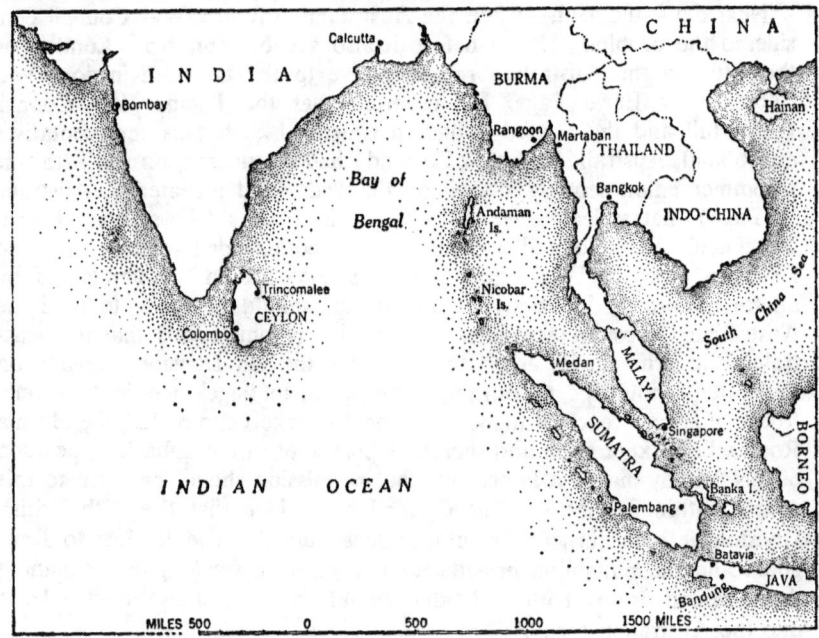

In addition, the transports had been hurriedly assembled from far and wide, and the staffs in Egypt, wisely as it seemed at the time, had loaded each group of ships as they became available, putting men on troop transports and heavy equipment on cargo ships, and had sent them off. Consequently the men were not necessarily in the same convoy as their heavy equipment. In January it had seemed that there would be time in Sumatra and Java to sort things out. To have insisted on each part of the force being "tactically loaded" would have delayed the movement of the Corps as a whole. Because he knew this Lavarack had pointed out on the 13th that the 7th Division could not be ready for operations in Sumatra until about 21st March. It was unlikely therefore that it could be ready for action in Burma even as early as that.

At the Australian Advisory Council meeting which considered these proposals the non-Government members recommended that the 7th Division should go to Burma, but the War Cabinet decided to reject this advice and not to vary its request for the return of all three Australian divisions to Australia.

Thus the Pacific War Council in London was convinced, it seemed, that the 7th Division could save Rangoon, keep the Burma Road open, and thus keep China in the war.[5] The non-Government members of the Advisory War Council considered that the 7th Division should go to Burma. The Australian War Cabinet, however, accepted the advice of General Sturdee that the whole A.I.F. should return to Australia. It was natural that in this crisis the thoughts of British Ministers and generals (including those of Wavell, until recently Commander-in-Chief in India) should turn towards Rangoon and Calcutta. As has been shown, however, it was entirely consistent of General Sturdee to advise concentration on the defence of Australia at that stage, and the development of Australia as a base for a later offensive. Inevitably Curtin's refusal to yield to the proposals formulated in London was opposed not only by Churchill but Roosevelt, for the stand the Australian leader had taken touched American policy on the raw.

The American leaders and people in general felt a strong affection for the Chinese. From the President downwards they regarded European imperialism in general and British imperialism in particular as an active force for evil in the world, and their own American colonial policy as an active force for good. Partly as an outcome of their sentimental regard for China they saw in the Chinese a potential military power which might greatly help them against the Japanese. To the British leaders Burma was a gateway to India; to the American leaders it was a gateway to China. Australian senior soldiers, on the other hand, were sharply aware of the internal insecurity of the Asian colonies, compared with Australia with its united and patriotic people, and of the Asian colonies' lack of industrial equipment and skilled operators, in both of which Australia was relatively rich.

Sturdee's paper was dated the 15th February; Curtin's cable to Churchill requesting the return of all three divisions was sent on the 17th (the day on which, as it happened, Sumatra was evacuated). In the following six days there developed a cabled controversy of a volume and intensity unprecedented in Australian experience. On the one hand were the Australian Ministers and their Chief of the General Staff; on the other were Mr Churchill, President Roosevelt, their Chiefs of Staff, General Wavell, Mr Bruce (the Australian High Commissioner in London), and Sir Earle Page. The messages sent between the 19th and the 22nd which passed through Page's hands alone cover twenty foolscap pages, many of them closely typewritten. They include discussion of problems other than the destination of I Australian Corps, but most of them deal chiefly with that subject.

---

[5] This was said in the account of the Pacific War Council's deliberations which Page sent to Curtin. The actual resolution was less emphatically phrased.

On the 18th Wavell recommended through the War Office that the whole Australian Corps be diverted to Burma, or, if Burma were unable to receive it all, that part be landed at Calcutta. This cable was repeated to Australia. The same day Bruce cabled to Curtin declaring that it was "essential" to agree to the 7th Division going to Burma, and giving such reasons as keeping the Burma Road open, Chinese morale, strengthening Australia's position in demanding help, and the feelings of the Dutch.

On the 19th (the day Darwin was bombed) Lavarack cabled to Curtin that the 7th Division should be sent to Burma "if Australia's defence position reasonably satisfactory". Sturdee still advised that the home defence position was not satisfactory; and Curtin sent a cablegram to Page confirming his previous decision. That day the Dominions Office sent a cable to the Australian Government stating that General Marshall had said that an American division would leave for Australia in March and asking whether, in consequence, the destination of the 6th and 9th Australian Divisions might not be left open; "more troops might be badly needed in Burma". The same day Page sent a cablegram to Curtin asking him to change his mind and quoting arguments by Churchill.

On the 20th (the day on which, as described in the following chapter, Timor was invaded) Curtin sent a long telegram to Page and repeated it to Casey (the Australian Minister to Washington), Lavarack and Wavell, justifying the Australian decision and confirming it. That day Page informed Curtin that the original destination of the A.I.F. "convoy" (not "convoys") had not hitherto been altered during the negotiations, but that instructions had now been issued to divert it to Australia.

Still on the 20th Churchill cabled Roosevelt that "the only troops who can reach Rangoon in time to stop the enemy and enable other reinforcements to arrive are the leading Australian division", but the Australian Government had "refused point blank" to let it go. He appealed to Roosevelt to send him a message to pass on to Curtin. Roosevelt did so, emphasising that he was speeding troops and planes to Australia and concluding "Harry [Harry L. Hopkins] is seeing Casey at once". That evening Churchill sent to Curtin a telegram in which appeal, reproach, warning, and exhortation were mingled.[6]

---

[6] This telegram of 20 February and Curtin's reply of 22nd February were:
Prime Minister to Mr Curtin   20 Feb 42
I suppose you realise that your leading division, the head of which is sailing south of Colombo to the Netherlands East Indies at this moment in our scanty British and American shipping (*Mount Vernon*), is the only force that can reach Rangoon in time to prevent its loss and the severance of communication with China. It can begin to disembark at Rangoon about the 26th or 27th. There is nothing else in the world that can fill the gap.
2. We are entirely in favour of all Australian troops returning home to defend their native soil, and we shall help their transportation in every way. But a vital war emergency cannot be ignored, and troops *en route* to other destinations must be ready to turn aside and take part in a battle. Every effort would be made to relieve this division at the earliest moment and send them on to Australia. I do not endorse the United States' request that you should send your other two divisions to Burma. They will return home as fast as possible. But this one is needed now, and is the only one that can possibly save the situation.
3. Pray read again your message of January 23, in which you said that the evacuation of Singapore would be "an inexcusable betrayal". Agreeably with your point of view, we therefore put the 18th Division and other important reinforcements into Singapore instead of diverting them to Burma, and ordered them to fight it out to the end. They were lost at Singapore and did not save it, whereas they could almost certainly have saved Rangoon. I take full responsibility

21-22 Feb   EXCHANGE OF CABLES   451

On the 21st February Curtin was informed through Casey (Hopkins having seen him) that the American Government had decided to send the 41st United States Division to Australia; it would sail early in March. On the 22nd, Curtin having replied to Churchill's telegram of the 20th with equal asperity, Churchill sent Curtin the following cable:

We could not contemplate that you would refuse our request, and that of the President of the United States, for the diversion of the leading Australian division to save the situation in Burma. We knew that if our ships proceeded on their course with my colleagues on the Defence Committee for this decision; but you also bear a heavy share on account of your telegram.

4. Your greatest support in this hour of peril must be drawn from the United States. They alone can bring into Australia the necessary troops and air forces, and they appear ready to do so. As you know, the President attaches supreme importance to keeping open the connection with China, without which his bombing offensive against Japan cannot be started, and also most grievous results may follow in Asia if China is cut off from all Allied help.

5. I am quite sure that if you refuse to allow your troops which are actually passing to stop this gap, and if, in consequence, the above evils, affecting the whole course of the war, follow, a very grave effect will be produced upon the President and the Washington circle, on whom you are so largely dependent. See especially the inclination of the United States to move major naval forces from Hawaii into the Anzac area.

6. We must have an answer immediately, as the leading ships of the convoy will soon be steaming in the opposite direction from Rangoon and every day is a day lost. I trust therefore that for the sake of all interests, and above all your own interests, you will give most careful consideration to the case I have set before you.

Prime Minister of Australia to Prime Minister   22 Feb 42

1 I have received your rather strongly worded request at this late stage, though our wishes in regard to the disposition of the A.I.F. in the Pacific theatre have long been known to you, and carried even further by your statement in the House of Commons. Furthermore, Page was furnished with lengthy statements on our viewpoint on February 15.

2. The proposal for additional military assistance for Burma comes from the Supreme Commander of the A.B.D.A. area. Malaya, Singapore, and Timor have been lost, and the whole of the Netherlands East Indies will apparently be occupied shortly by the Japanese. The enemy, with superior sea- and air-power, has commenced raiding our territory in the north-west, and also in the north-east from Rabaul. The Government made the maximum contribution of which it was capable in reinforcement of the A.B.D.A. area. It originally sent a division less a brigade to Malaya, with certain ancillary troops. A machine-gun battalion and substantial reinforcements were later dispatched. It also dispatched forces to Ambon, Java, and Dutch and Portuguese Timor. Six squadrons of the Air Force were also sent to this area, together with two cruisers from the Royal Australian Navy.

3. It was suggested by you that two Australian divisions be transferred to the Pacific theatre, and this suggestion was later publicly expanded by you with the statement that no obstacle would be placed in the way of the A.I.F. returning to defend their homeland. We agreed to the two divisions being located in Sumatra and Java, and it was pointed out to Page in the cablegram of February 15 that should fortune still favour the Japanese this disposition would give a line of withdrawal to Australia for our forces.

4. With the situation having deteriorated to such an extent in the theatre of the A.B.D.A. area, with which we are closely associated, and the Japanese also making a southward advance in the Anzac area, the Government, in the light of the advice of its Chiefs of Staff as to the forces necessary to repel an attack on Australia, finds it most difficult to understand that it should be called upon to make a further contribution of forces to be located in the most distant part of the A.B.D.A. area. Notwithstanding your statement that you do not agree with the request to send the other two divisions of the A.I.F. Corps to Burma, our advisers are concerned with Wavell's request for the Corps and Dill's statement that the destination of the 6th and 9th Australian Divisions should be left open, as more troops might be badly needed in Burma. Once one division became engaged it could not be left unsupported, and the indications are that the whole of the Corps might become committed to this region, or there might be a recurrence of the experiences of the Greek and Malayan campaigns. Finally, in view of superior Japanese sea-power and air-power, it would appear to be a matter of some doubt as to whether this division can be landed in Burma, and a matter for greater doubt whether it can be brought out as promised. With the fall of Singapore, Penang, and Martaban, the Bay of Bengal is now vulnerable to what must be considered the superior sea- and air-power of Japan in that area. The movement of our forces to this theatre therefore is not considered a reasonable hazard of war, having regard to what has gone before, and its adverse results would have the gravest consequences on the morale of the Australian people. The Government therefore must adhere to its decision.

5. In regard to your statement that the 18th Division was diverted from Burma to Singapore because of our message, it is pointed out that the date of the latter was January 23, whereas in your telegram of January 14 you informed me that one brigade of this division was due on January 13 and the remainder on January 27.

6. We feel therefore, in view of the foregoing and the services the A.I.F. have rendered in the Middle East, that we have every right to expect them to be returned as soon as possible, with adequate escorts to ensure their safe arrival.

7. We assure you, and desire you to so inform the President, who knows fully what we have done to help the common cause, that if it were possible to divert our troops to Burma and India without imperilling our security in the judgment of our advisers we should be pleased to agree to the diversion.

to Australia while we were waiting for your formal approval they would either arrive too late at Rangoon or even be without enough fuel to go there at all. We therefore decided that the convoy should be temporarily diverted to the northward. The convoy is now too far north for some of the ships in it to reach Australia without refuelling. These physical considerations give a few days for the situation to develop, and for you to review the position should you wish to do so. Otherwise the leading Australian division will be returned to Australia as quickly as possible in accordance with your wishes.

This information astonished not only Curtin in Australia but Page in London. Page promptly followed it up with a telegram to Curtin pointing out that it conflicted with the information he had received and also with a statement in Churchill's cable of the 20th that the leading ship of the convoy would soon be steaming in the opposite direction from Rangoon.

Page learnt next day that the leading convoy had pursued its course towards Java up to 9 p.m. on the 20th, when the Admiralty, on Churchill's orders, had directed that it should turn north towards Rangoon. The final appeal was sent to Curtin ten minutes later in the belief that a reply would arrive in time for the convoy's route to be changed again without complications, if necessary. In the event, the reply from Australia was not received until the morning of the 22nd, by which time the Admiralty had learnt that some ships had not enough fuel to reach Australia.[7]

On the 23rd Curtin sent a cable to Churchill complaining that Churchill had treated his Government's approval of the diversion of the convoy towards Rangoon as merely a matter of form, and that by doing so he had added to the dangers of the convoy. He added:

Wavell's message considered by Pacific War Council on Saturday reveals that Java faces imminent invasion. Australia's outer defences are now quickly vanishing and our vulnerability is completely exposed.

With A.I.F. troops we sought to save Malaya and Singapore, falling back on Netherlands East Indies. All these northern defences are gone or going. Now you contemplate using the A.I.F. to save Burma. All this has been done, as in Greece, without adequate air support.

We feel a primary obligation to save Australia not only for itself, but to preserve it as a base for the development of the war against Japan. In the circumstances it is quite impossible to reverse a decision which we made with the utmost care, and which we have affirmed and reaffirmed.

Our Chief of the General Staff advises that although your telegram of February 20 refers to the leading division only, the fact is that owing to the loading of the flights it is impossible at the present time to separate the two divisions, and the destination of all the flights will be governed by that of the first flight. This fact reinforces us in our decision.

That day Churchill, not a little disgruntled, as his later telegrams show, informed Curtin that the convoy had been turned about, would refuel at Colombo, and proceed to Australia.

Meanwhile Sumatra had been lost and ABDA Command dissolved. Even before the end of January it had seemed likely that the first blows

---

[7] Memorandum from General Ismay to Mr Churchill, 24 Feb 1942, passed on to Sir Earle Page, to whom Churchill expressed regret that Page had not been kept better informed.

against the western islands of the Indies would be felt by Sumatra. Japanese bombers operating from captured fields in Malaya had bombed the Palembang airfield (P.1) in south-eastern Sumatra from early February onwards. During the first fortnight of that month, however, they had not found the second and more distant Palembang airfield (P.2), 40 miles to the south-west of P.1, where, as previously mentioned, Group Captain McCauley's depleted squadrons were then established.

Except round the oilfields in the south and the refineries near Palembang, the island of Sumatra (in common with most of the Indies outside Java itself) was little developed in 1942. Only one through road—on the western side—ran from north to south. The southern tip of the island, however, was better served with roads than the rest, and a railway ran from Palembang to the port of Oosthaven, facing the Sunda Strait separating Sumatra from Java. In mid-February Palembang and the airfields were garrisoned by a number of Dutch platoon or company groups, plus some British anti-aircraft detachments, and some small groups of R.A.F. men armed as infantry.

The Japanese land assault on the Palembang area was made by two main Japanese forces: the *229th Regiment* (of the *38th Division*) which sailed from Hong Kong to Camranh Bay and thence, on the 9th and 11th February, towards southern Sumatra; and a force of some 360 paratroops flown from airfields in Malaya. About 260 paratroops were dropped round P.1 airfield on 14th February, and next day about 100 were dropped near the refineries. There was close fighting against the paratroops throughout the 14th.

Meanwhile, on Wavell's orders, given on the 13th, Admiral Doorman had sailed westward to intercept the Japanese convoy. Doorman himself was then south of Bali, and it was the 14th before he had collected his forces. At dusk that day he sailed from a point north of Sunda Strait with the Dutch cruisers *De Ruyter*, *Java*, and *Tromp*, the British *Exeter*, the Australian *Hobart*, and ten destroyers. About midday on the 15th aircraft from the Japanese carrier *Ryujo* and land-based aircraft from Borneo attacked the Allied squadron. No Allied ships were hit but Doorman decided to withdraw southward.

It was not until the night of the 15th-16th that the leading Japanese infantry, having moved up the river Musi in landing craft, reached Palembang and joined the paratroops. Already Wavell had ordered the withdrawal of the garrison to Java by way of Oosthaven, where a number of small ships were waiting.

On the 14th Brigadier Steele, the Chief Engineer of I Australian Corps, had been sent to Sumatra to examine the proposed demolitions of the P.1 airfield. He was on his way from the airfield to the refineries at 9.30 a.m. when the Japanese paratroops landed. At Dutch headquarters he learnt that a few N.E.I. companies were on their way to reinforce Palembang; and he was joined by Lieut-Colonel MacCallum,[8] a medical officer on Lavarack's staff who was also reconnoitring in Sumatra. That afternoon, after having helped to organise the troops in the area, Steele, who was the senior Australian officer on Sumatra, went to Oosthaven to see what was being done about the reception of the *Orcades*, which was due to land her Australian troops there next day. The *Orcades*, a fast liner which had steamed far ahead of the other ships containing the 7th Division, carried 3,400 men, including two battalions—the 2/3rd Machine Gun (Lieut-Colonel Blackburn[9]) and the 2/2nd Pioneers (Lieut-Colonel Williams[1]).

On the 11th February Lavarack had prepared an instruction for Blackburn placing him, on arrival at Oosthaven, in command of all Australian troops in Sumatra until the arrival of the divisional commander or a brigade commander. At length he was to move his force into the Palembang area, but at the same time guard his communications to Oosthaven. Steele, who had seen this order, held a conference of the senior Australian and British officers at Oosthaven on the morning of the 15th. It was discovered that there were no Dutch troops south of Prabumulih near the P.2 airfield. Steele then formed a headquarters to control the defence of Oosthaven with himself in command, and as "G.S.O. 1" Lieut-Colonel MacCallum (who although now a medical officer had been a brigade major in France in the war of 1914-18). The forces in the area comprised a light tank squadron of the 3rd Hussars (which had been disembarked on the 14th), a British light anti-aircraft battery, and five improvised companies of men of the R.A.F. each of about 100 riflemen. Steele gave

---

[8] Brig W. P. MacCallum, CBE, DSO, MC, ED, NX439. (1st AIF: BM 5 Bde 1917-18.) ADMS HQ AIF (ME) 1941-42; Dep Dir-Gen Medical Services, GHQ Aust 1942-44, Adv LHQ 1944-45. Physician; of Edgecliff, NSW; b. Darlinghurst, NSW, 3 Apr 1895.

[9] Brig A. S. Blackburn, VC, CMG, CBE, ED, SX6962. (1st AIF: Capt 10 Bn.) CO 2/3 MG Bn 1940-42; Comd Blackforce in Java, 1942. Solicitor; of Adelaide; b. Woodville, SA, 25 Nov 1892.

[1] Lt-Col J. M. Williams, OBE, ED, NX12296. 2/17 Bn and CO 2/2 Pnr Bn. Production engineer; of Sefton, NSW; b. Helensburgh, NSW, 23 May 1904.

the force the task of defending the Oosthaven area and covering the evacuation of the air force troops from P.2 and of unarmed men and civilians from Oosthaven.

At midday the *Orcades* arrived off the harbour. Steele went aboard and arranged for Blackburn to bring his men ashore, form them into a brigade and advance on P.2 and thence Palembang. The troops were disembarking when the captain of the destroyer *Encounter* which was in the harbour received a signal from Wavell's headquarters ordering that no troops be disembarked and that the 3rd Hussars be put aboard the *Orcades,* which was to sail immediately. In the course of the day MacCallum was informed by a Dutch liaison officer that Japanese seaborne troops had landed at Palembang and had taken it, but that the oil refineries had been demolished except for two small plants.

On the morning of the 16th, after a conference of his own and Dutch officers, Steele, who had not yet learnt of Wavell's order for the evacuation of Sumatra, issued orders for the withdrawal from Sumatra of all British troops by 11 p.m. on the 17th, in cooperation with the N.E.I. forces. Late on the 16th ABDA Command received a message from Steele asking for naval and air support during the embarkation of 6,000 men by 6 p.m. on the 18th. It had also received a comprehensive report about events on Sumatra when a liaison officer returned with an account of what Steele was doing. The same day P.2 was evacuated.

Reports now reached Steele that Japanese vessels, laden with troops, had moved upstream to Menggala. A rearguard of British anti-aircraft gunners and R.A.F. riflemen under Major Webster[2] of the Corps staff had been placed in position at Mandah, where the road and railway from the north crossed a river. Steele now advanced the time for evacuating Oosthaven to 2 a.m. on the 17th. The embarkation of troops was carried out accordingly, all equipment that could be lifted having been taken on board the ships. On the 15th, 16th and 17th about 2,500 R.A.F. men, 1,890 British troops, 700 Dutch troops and about 1,000 civilians were embarked in twelve vessels. Lieut-Colonel Stevens[3] of the staff of ABDA Command, who had organised the embarkation, went aboard the steamer *Rosenbaum* with the rearguard at 7.30 a.m. on the 17th. There remained at the quay a K.P.M. steamer to pick up any late arrivals, and two more small ships were in the roads. A small group of officers remained ashore.

After the main evacuation an urgent appeal was sent out by ABDA Command on the 17th to embark all aircraft spares and technical stores. This signal was picked up by the Australian corvette *Burnie,* covering the embarkation, and she reported that the vessels had sailed. She intended to demolish oil tanks and quays. *Burnie* was promptly instructed not to destroy anything in Oosthaven without the concurrence of the local military authority. Nevertheless the proposed demolitions took place. On the 18th, ABDA Command learnt that late-arriving troops were still being

---

[2] Lt-Col I. G. Webster, VX6. DAQMG Base and L of C Units 1940-41, I Corps 1942; AQMG I Corps 1944-45. Wholesale merchant; of East St Kilda, Vic; b. St Kilda, 25 Sep 1908.
[3] Brig F. H. Stevens, OBE; ABDA Comd. Regular soldier; b. 16 Dec 1903.

embarked at Oosthaven in one remaining vessel. The enemy did not press on to Oosthaven, and on the 20th the Australian corvette *Ballarat*, whose captain knew Oosthaven well, went in with an air force salvage party of some 50 men and recovered valuable equipment.

No sooner had Sumatra been overcome than a Japanese force descended upon Bali at the opposite end of Java. When he learnt of the Japanese convoy advancing on Bali Admiral Doorman was at Tjilatjap with the cruisers *De Ruyter* and *Java* and four destroyers; the small cruiser *Tromp* was at Surabaya; and four American destroyers were in the Sunda Straits. Doorman decided to attack the enemy convoy on the night of the 19th-20th. The ships from Tjilatjap were to move in from the south at 11 p.m., and the *Tromp* and the four American destroyers would arrive from the north-west three hours later. One of the Dutch destroyers, the *Kortenaer*, ran aground leaving Tjilatjap. When Doorman's squadron reached Bali about 10 p.m. on the night of the 19th-20th one Japanese transport, escorted by two destroyers, remained. In a confused action the Dutch destroyer *Piet Hein* was sunk and the Japanese transport damaged; the Allied squadron withdrew. About three hours later the *Tromp* and the four American destroyers came in. In the succeeding action hits were scored by both sides but no serious damage was done.

When he received news of the action the Japanese admiral, who was north of Bali with the cruiser *Nagara* and three destroyers, sent two destroyers to help the other ships. These encountered the *Tromp's* force in Lombok Strait, east of Bali, at 2.20 a.m. and there both *Tromp* and a Japanese destroyer were severely damaged. Thus, although the Japanese were out-gunned at all times, they inflicted heavier loss than they received.

By the 20th, the airfields of Timor, Bali and Sumatra having been lost, the Allied air force in Java was now virtually cut off from reinforcement by air. That day the Combined Chiefs of Staff informed General Wavell that all land forces hitherto approaching him from the west were being diverted elsewhere, but that the troops on Java must fight on. Wavell was told also that Burma would be transferred to the control of the Commander-in-Chief, India—a course which Wavell had always advocated —and he was instructed on the 21st to transfer his headquarters "at such time and to such place within or without the ABDA area as he might decide". In reply Wavell recommended that his headquarters be not transferred but dissolved since he now had practically nothing to command, and the control of the forces in Java could be better exercised by the Dutch commanders.

Also on the 20th Mr Curtin informed General Lavarack of the Australian Government's opposition to the diversion to Burma and that the Government had been influenced in this policy by Lavarack's advice. Curtin asked Lavarack to explain the unsatisfactory situation of Australia's home defences to Wavell and ask for his sympathetic cooperation. He asked whether, if the worst came to the worst, there would be some chance of withdrawing the men from *Orcades,* which had arrived at Batavia on the 17th and disembarked its troops there on the 19th.

Curtin and his advisers apparently did not realise that Lavarack had been in the Middle East since 1940 and could not speak with authority on the present situation of Australia's home defences. That day Lavarack saw Wavell, however, and discussed with him the plans for the 7th Division and the troops in *Orcades.* After the meeting Lavarack wrote in his diary that General Wavell was

> sympathetic but feels cannot give way on subject of 7 Div. Also did not do so on subject of landed troops for reasons air requirements . . . and moral effect, particularly on Dutch. Promised, however, to make arrangements for evacuation if necessary and possible, and said had spoken to Admiral Palliser re this. Saw Palliser and found no positive arrangement, but promised to do all possible.

It was now decided to use *Orcades* to take away the advanced parties of the Australian Corps and the 7th Division. Consequently, on the 21st, Lavarack cabled to Curtin informing him that these advanced parties were embarking in *Orcades* for Colombo pending a decision as to their destination, and that he himself was flying to Australia to report. The Australian troops who had been landed in Java were being retained for defence of airfields, but arrangements were in train for their embarkation when the final decision was taken about Java.

Lavarack still did not know whether or not the Corps might go to Burma and, before he set out by air for Australia, instructed Allen that if the Corps went into action during his absence Allen was to command it, with Brigadier Bridgeford as his senior general staff officer, while Berryman commanded the 7th Division. Before the embarkation of the advanced parties Berryman issued an instruction to Blackburn, now promoted to brigadier, placing the following A.I.F. units under his administrative command:

	Approximate strength
2/3rd Machine Gun Battalion	710
2/2nd Pioneer Battalion	937
2/6th Field Company	222
Company headquarters and one platoon of Guard Battalion	43
105th General Transport Company	206
2/3rd Reserve Motor Transport Company	471
2/2nd Casualty Clearing Station	93
Stragglers	165
Details	73

For operations "Blackforce", as it became known, would be directly under the command of the Dutch Commander-in-Chief, General ter Poorten.

General Wavell and his staff were still in Java, and a message from Wavell to the War Office indicated that they would remain there until ordered to go. On the 21st the Dominions Office cabled to Curtin that the Chiefs of Staff in London had suggested to the Combined Chiefs in Washington that ABDA Command headquarters should move to Fremantle pending further instructions. That day Wavell cabled to Washington describing the situation in Java and seeking instructions. Fewer than 40 fighter aircraft and 40 bombers remained, he said, and little could be done to prevent a Japanese invasion. He was endeavouring to evacuate about 6,000 surplus R.A.F. and R.A.A.F. men and 1,400 American air force men. There would remain 3,000 to 4,000 R.A.F. men, 5,500 British troops, 3,000 Australians, 700 Americans, and 650 officers and men of his own headquarters.

The Combined Chiefs on the 22nd sent Wavell a telegram stating that:

> All men of fighting units for whom there are arms must continue to fight without thought of evacuation, but air forces which can more usefully operate in battle from bases outside Java and all air personnel for whom there are no aircraft and such troops particularly technicians as cannot contribute to defence of Java should be withdrawn. With respect to personnel who cannot contribute to defence, general policy should be to withdraw U.S. and Australian personnel to Australia.

On the 23rd the Combined Chiefs accepted Wavell's proposals and Wavell decided to dissolve his command from 9 a.m. on the 25th.[4] It had been in existence just six weeks.

On the 21st February Wavell had sent to Churchill (who had suggested that he should again become Commander-in-Chief, India) a characteristic signal which concluded:

> Last about myself. I am, as ever, entirely willing to do my best where you think best to send me. I have failed you and President here, where a better man might perhaps have succeeded. . . . If you fancy I can best serve by returning to India I will of course do so, but you should first consult Viceroy both whether my prestige and influence, which count for much in East, will survive this failure, and also as to hardship to Hartley [the Commander-in-Chief, India] and his successor in Northern Command.
>
> I hate the idea of leaving these stout-hearted Dutchmen, and will remain here and fight it out with them as long as possible if you consider this would help at all.
>
> Good wishes. I am afraid you are having very difficult period, but I know your courage will shine through it.[5]

Here this great commander, perhaps the noblest whom the war discovered in the British armies, passes out of the Australian story. It was under his command-in-chief that Australians, including some who had until recently been round him in Java, had taken part in the first successful British campaign, and later in other operations in the Middle East, some of which succeeded and some of which failed. The failures of the second quarter of 1941 had led to his removal to India, a removal which he accepted in written and spoken word as he accepted every decision of his seniors as being right and proper. The Japanese onslaught brought him a second time to the command of the main theatre of war. There he deported himself with immense energy for a man whose first taste of active

---

[4] General Brereton, commanding the American Army Air Force in Java, flew to India with his heavy bombers on the 24th. General Brett, Wavell's American deputy, had already returned to Australia.

[5] Quoted in Churchill, *The Second World War*, Vol IV, pp. 127-8.

service had been gained 42 years before; with a fastidious regard for the proprieties, and with characteristic wisdom and self-effacement.

General Lavarack first learnt that the 7th Division was destined not for Burma but Australia when he arrived at Laverton airfield near Melbourne on the evening of 23rd February. He asked General Sturdee, who met him there, when he should be leaving again.

> Sturdee then astonished me with the information that the whole set-up was now changed (he wrote in his diary) and that the whole of I Aust Corps was now ordered to Australia, by arrangement though not agreement between the British and Australian Governments.

Mr Curtin now set about trying to extricate the 3,000 Australian troops from Java. On the 24th he cabled to Page and Casey that his Government insisted that Wavell be given authority to ensure that the Australian troops in Java be evacuated ultimately to Australia. Page, however, could only reply that, although Wavell had been given authority to evacuate certain personnel, the Pacific War Council had recommended to the Combined Chiefs at Washington six days before that resistance should be maintained in Java by the troops already available there. Curtin, probably impressed by the undesirable moral effects of withdrawing troops already deployed on the soil of an ally, did not persist, and the 3,000 Australians remained in Java.

In London Sir Earle Page was disappointed about the decision not to send Australians to Rangoon, and he now adopted the suggestion of Colonel Wardell,[6] the Australian Army liaison officer at Australia House, that the 7th Division should reinforce, at least temporarily, the garrison of Ceylon. (Retention of Ceylon was essential to continued control of the Indian Ocean.) Page discovered that the garrison of Ceylon consisted of the 34th Indian Division (two Indian infantry brigades and one Ceylon brigade with only one battery of field artillery). There were 116 anti-aircraft guns. One brigade group of the 70th British Division would arrive in mid-March.[7]

On the 24th Page sent this information to Curtin with a recommendation that the 7th Australian Division should be landed in Ceylon at least until the brigade of the 70th Division arrived.

Thereupon Curtin cabled to Page (on the 26th) complaining that Page was not advocating the Australian point of view; on the contrary he had subscribed to the diversion of the 7th Division to Burma and was now seeking its diversion to Ceylon. Curtin said that a further reply would be sent about Ceylon, and meanwhile he instructed Page to "press most

---

[6] Brig A. W. Wardell, MC, NX371. (1st AIF: Capt 10 MG Coy.) Comd 25 Bde 1940, AIF UK 1940-41; Service adviser to Aust Representative, Imperial War Cabinet, 1942-43. Regular soldier; of Melbourne; b. St Kilda, Vic, 10 May 1895.

[7] All or parts of the 70th British Division, a regular formation formerly named the 6th, had served beside Australians of the 6th, 7th and 9th Divisions in the Western Desert, Crete and Syria. Several Australian units had fought as part of the 6th British Division in Syria, and the 70th Division had relieved the 9th Australian Division in Tobruk.

strenuously" the importance of Australia's security as a base for a counter-offensive against Japan. In a cable containing more than 2,000 words, Page defended his policy and insisted that the security of Australia had always been his first consideration; but he doggedly continued to press for an answer to his proposal about Ceylon and on 2nd March Curtin sent Churchill a cablegram in which he said:

1. We are most anxious to assist you in your anxieties over the strengthening of the garrison at Ceylon.
2. The President while fully appreciating our difficult home defence position in relation to the proposed return of the A.I.F. was good enough to suggest that he would be glad if we would see our way clear to make available some reinforcements from later detachments of the three divisions of the A.I.F. which have all been allocated from the Middle East to Australia.
3. For the purpose of temporarily adding to the garrison of Ceylon, we make available to you two brigade groups of the 6th Division. These are comprised in the 3rd Flight of the A.I.F. and are embarking from Suez. We ask that adequate air support will be available in Ceylon and that if you divert the two brigade groups they will be escorted to Australia as soon as possible after their relief. We are also relying on the understanding that the 9th Division will return to Australia under proper escort as soon as possible.
4. As you know we are gravely concerned at the weakness of our defences, but we realise the significance of Ceylon in this problem and make this offer believing that in the plans you are at present making you realise the importance of the return of the A.I.F. in defending both Australia and New Zealand.[8]

Two questions need to be answered: Was the I Australian Corps necessary to the defence of Australia; and could the available Australian troops have saved Rangoon and kept the Burma Road open in 1942?

It is not part of the task of the writer of this volume to answer the first question in detail. It is enough to say here that the next volume of this series will show that within a few months of its arrival in Australia the Corps and the divisions it included were needed to halt the Japanese advance in New Guinea.

To examine the question whether the available Australians could have saved Rangoon (as Mr Churchill and his Chiefs of Staff believed at the time and as Mr Churchill evidently still believed in 1951 when he published the fourth volume of *The Second World War*) it is necessary to turn back to the second week of February, just after a visit by General Wavell to the Burma front. Indian and British troops were then holding a front west of the Salween River. Wavell wrote later that:

all commanders expressed themselves to me as confident of their ability to deal with the Japanese advance.[9]

It was then that Wavell decided to divert the 7th Armoured Brigade, intended for Java, to Burma, and it arrived on 21st February.

---

[8] The 16th and 17th Brigades landed in Ceylon in late March and remained there not for the few weeks predicted but for sixteen. Their experiences are described in the following volume of this series.

[9] A. P. Wavell, *Despatch on Operations in Burma from 15th December 1941 to 20th May 1942*, para 17.

The force defending southern Burma was the 17th Indian Division, which included the 16th and 46th Indian and 2nd Burma Brigades. Farther north, in the southern Shan States, was the 1st Burma Division, including one Indian and two Burma brigades, but for the present the Japanese invading force—mainly the *33rd and 55th Divisions*, each less one regiment—was concentrated against southern Burma. The conclusion had been reached that "the battalions of Burma Rifles, which formed so large a proportion of the army in Burma, were undependable".[1]

From 22nd February control of operations in Burma was taken away from ABDA Command and returned to the Commander-in-Chief in India. About the same time General Alexander,[2] then commanding Southern Command in England, was appointed to the army in Burma; but he would not be able to arrive there until the first week of March. On 25th February, as mentioned, Wavell closed his ABDA Command headquarters and was appointed Commander-in-Chief in India again; on the 27th he reached Delhi.

Meanwhile the front west of the Salween River had been crumbling. On 11th February Martaban was lost. On the 14th the 17th Division (Major-General Smyth[3]) began to withdraw to the Bilin River. By 17th February the whole division was heavily engaged, and that night the Japanese crossed the Bilin. Counter-attacks failed to restore the position and, on the 19th, General Hutton decided to withdraw behind the

---

[1] Wavell, Despatch, para 16.

[2] Field Marshal Rt Hon Earl Alexander, KG, GCB, GCMG, CSI, DSO, MC. GOC 1 Div 1938-40; GOC-in-C Southern Comd 1940-42; GOC Burma 1942; C-in-C ME 1942-43, Allied Armies in Italy 1944; Supreme Comd Mediterranean Theatre 1944-45. Gov-Gen of Canada 1945-52. Regular soldier; b. Co. Tyrone, Ireland, 10 Dec 1891.

[3] Maj-Gen Sir John Smyth, Bt, VC, MC. Comd 127 Inf Bde 1940; Comd 17 Indian Div 1942. Regular soldier; b. 24 Oct 1893.

Sittang River. On this line the enemy would be close to the main road and railway to Mandalay and thence the road to China; and incidentally the road and railway to Mandalay was one of two main land routes for evacuation from Rangoon.

On the 18th February, General Hutton had cabled ABDA Command and the War Office that in the event of a fresh enemy offensive in the near future he could not be certain of holding the position on the Bilin River. If this line were lost the enemy might penetrate the line of the Sittang River without much difficulty and the evacuation of Rangoon would become an imminent possibility. The best he could hope for was that the line of the Sittang River could be held, possibly with bridgeheads on the eastern bank. A withdrawal to that river would, however, seriously interfere with the use of the railway to the north and thus with the passage of supplies to China. To hold the line of the river permanently and to undertake the offensive, he would want the extra division which had already been promised him from India but was not scheduled to arrive until April. Meanwhile he could only hope that the V Chinese Army would fill the gap. To defend Rangoon against a seaborne attack on the scale which had now become possible, he would require a second additional division, and to provide for a reserve and for internal security a third division was desirable. He required therefore, over and above the two divisions which he already had, an additional three. His major problem, however, was whether the prospects of holding Rangoon and denying the oilfields justified the efforts to provide these reinforcements, which could only be at the expense of India. He himself thought that, provided reinforcements could be sent earlier than at that time visualised the effort would be justified but, failing an acceleration of the reinforcement program, the risk of losing Rangoon was considerable.

This was two days before Mr Churchill cabled to Mr Curtin that the leading Australian division was "the only force that can reach Rangoon in time to prevent its loss and the severance of communication to China", and added "it can begin to disembark at Rangoon about the 26th or 27th". On the 20th the 17th Indian Division began to withdraw to the positions west of the Sittang. The Japanese followed up fast. In two days of heavy fighting—in the course of which, at 5.30 a.m. on the 23rd, the bridge over the river was blown while two brigades and part of a third were on the far side—the division lost practically all its heavy equipment. Its infantry strength was reduced to 80 officers and 3,404 other ranks, of whom only 1,420 still had their rifles. The effective units east of Rangoon were now only the 7th Armoured Brigade (two armoured regiments and one British infantry battalion) which had just disembarked, and a second British battalion watching the coast south of Pegu. Farther north was the Burma Division, which had only three Indian battalions and two battalions of the Burma Rifles, some of whose men had deserted.

On 21st February the Chiefs of Staff in London, having reviewed the position described in telegrams from General Hutton, had asked General

Wavell whether he still wished the 7th Australian Division to be diverted to Burma. Next day Wavell cabled both to the Chiefs of Staff and Hutton that he saw no reason why air attack should close Rangoon port, and that the only prospect of success lay in a counter-offensive, for which the 7th Armoured Brigade and an Australian division would be needed. On 23rd February Hutton agreed to accept the 7th Australian Division provided it arrived in time, but added that a final decision whether "the convoy" should enter the port would have to be made 24 hours before its arrival.

If the 21st Australian Brigade had continued its voyage to Rangoon it could have begun disembarking about the 26th, three days after the disaster on the Sittang. The convoy containing the second brigade of the division was then still at Colombo, having sailed there direct from Aden and arrived on the 18th; the third brigade was at Bombay about seven days' voyage from Rangoon; the commander and part of the headquarters of the division and part of the headquarters of the corps were in the *Orcades* steaming west from Java and due at Ceylon on the 27th. None of these convoys was "tactically loaded". Lavarack had estimated that the division could not be ready for operations in Java (where some preliminary organisation had been done by the advanced parties) before 21st March, and it seems improbable that the division could have been reasonably equipped and ready for action in Burma sooner than that.

On the 24th and 25th February the Japanese again attacked Rangoon from the air in full force, but again, as had happened in late December, the defending fighters shot down so many of the attackers that the raids were not repeated after the 25th. Already, however, there was chaos in the city.

Rangoon burned. Once more a multitude of refugees poured down the roads from the city, crammed the outgoing trains, and fled into the jungle. . . . The "E" evacuation warning signal was hoisted on February 20th, 1942, and an exodus gave the capital of Burma over to fire and the looters. The Governor, Sir Reginald Dorman-Smith, remained with his senior officials, preparing a demolition of the port and powerhouse. At this midnight of disaster, troopships and transports of the 7th Armoured Brigade drew alongside the quays, and the 7th Hussars, 2nd Royal Tank Regiment and a battalion of the Cameronians began disembarking their Stuart tanks and carriers. They rendered incalculable service during the rest of the campaign. Indeed, these 150 tanks probably saved the army, for they convoyed or carried thousands of troops out of encirclement, broke the Japanese road-blocks, held at bay the Japanese armour, and acted as the artillery of the rearguard all the way northward to the frontier of India.

The last days of Rangoon were at hand. Singapore had fallen, releasing Japanese troops and air forces from Malaya. But it was the loss of sea power which decided the issue. With Singapore there passed also the command of the Indian Ocean; Rangoon became indefensible, and without Rangoon the British Army in South Burma could not be supplied at that period since there were no land links with India.[4]

When Wavell reached Delhi on the 27th (the day after the 21st Australian Brigade might have begun to disembark) he learnt that it was proposed in Burma to evacuate Rangoon. He immediately cabled that

---

[4] *The Campaign in Burma* (1946), prepared for South-East Asia Command by the United Kingdom Office of Information.

nothing of the sort should be done until he arrived, and he ordered that convoys carrying a fresh Indian brigade—the 63rd—to Burma, which had been turned back from Rangoon, should sail into that port. He himself arrived by air at Magwe, on the Irrawaddy, on the 1st March and there confirmed his order that Rangoon be not abandoned. That day he flew on to Rangoon, and thence up to the front, where he replaced the commander of the 17th Division "who was obviously a sick man".[5] Next day Wavell flew to Lashio and interviewed Chiang Kai-shek, and on the 3rd flew back to India. At Calcutta he met General Alexander, who had just arrived by air, and instructed him to hold Rangoon as long as possible.[6] Alexander alighted at Magwe airfield on the 4th March and reached Rangoon on the 5th. The 63rd Indian Brigade, newly disembarked, was about 16 miles north of Rangoon, but its vehicles were still on board the transports. There was a gap of 40 miles between the 17th and the Burma Division (each with an effective strength of about a brigade) and Japanese were across the road between them. Alexander ordered attacks north and south so that the two divisions could link, and these gained some success, but meanwhile the Japanese cut the Rangoon-Pegu road, south of Pegu, and by 6th March one regiment of the armoured brigade and a brigade of the 17th Division were isolated in Pegu. At midnight of the 6th-7th Alexander ordered that plans for demolition in Rangoon be put into operation, the city evacuated, and the forces regrouped north of Rangoon in the Irrawaddy Valley. In the next few days the force in Pegu succeeded in extricating itself and it and the other forces round Rangoon were withdrawn to the Irrawaddy Valley ready to retreat northward. The Japanese entered Rangoon before dawn on the 8th March.

In the conditions outlined above it would have been astonishing if the 7th Australian Division—landed at Rangoon a brigade at a time between about the 26th February and the 6th March, with the transport and heavy weapons arriving on different vessels from those carrying the men, with no previous reconnaissance or base organisation, no tropical equipment and no tropical experience—could have been landed, organised, and launched into a successful counter-offensive against two hitherto victorious Japanese divisions in time to save Rangoon.[7] It is even more doubtful whether, had the 7th Division done this, the success could have been maintained in the face of increasing Japanese air power and Japanese naval control of the eastern part of the Bay of Bengal and beyond. A force defending Rangoon could have been adequately supplied only by sea,

---

[5] Wavell, Despatch, para 21.

[6] In his Despatch Wavell wrote with characteristic candour and calm: "While my intervention on this occasion postponed the evacuation of Rangoon for a week and enabled reinforcements of an infantry brigade and a field regiment to be landed, it eventually placed General Alexander in a difficult position and led to his forces being nearly cut off, as described in his report. On balance I am satisfied that we gained by the delay."

[7] On 24th February Lavarack, on his return to Australia, informed the Advisory War Council that the ships conveying the first and second flights of the AIF from the Middle East had not been tactically loaded, and, if the first flight had been diverted to Burma, the troops could not have been landed as an effective fighting force, as it was probable that many of the units would have had incomplete fighting equipment. It would have taken approximately 21 days after their arrival to re-sort the equipment available and have the troops ready for the field.—Advisory War Council Minute No. 786, 24 Feb 1942.

and the Japanese had the means of cutting the sea route to Rangoon, as they were soon to demonstrate.

It is now evident that the 7th Division would have arrived in time only to help in the extrication from Pegu and to take part in the long retreat to India. In that event it could not have been returned to Australia, rested, and been sent to New Guinea in time to perform the crucial role it was to carry out in the defeat of the Japanese offensive which would open there in July. The Allied cause, therefore, was well served by the sound judgment and solid persistence of General Sturdee, who maintained his advice against that of the Chiefs of Staff in London and Washington; and by the tenacity of Mr Curtin and his Ministers, who withstood the well-meaning pressure of Mr Churchill and President Roosevelt.

CHAPTER 21

RESISTANCE IN TIMOR

LIKE Ambon and Sumatra, the island of Timor was a stepping-stone towards Java, heart of the Dutch empire in the East Indies. The Australian garrison sent to Timor in December 1941 to reinforce the local force was likely to be attacked once Ambon had fallen.

The area of Dutch Timor, comprising the south-western portion of Timor, was 5,500 square miles. Koepang, the capital and principal port, 517 miles from Darwin and 670 from Java, looked out on Koepang Bay. The principal airfield of Dutch Timor, at Penfui, was six miles south-east of the town. Four near-by seaplane anchorages, the principal one at Tenau, five miles south-west of Koepang, formed one seaplane base. Koepang Bay and the adjacent Semau Strait provided good shelter for shipping. There was in Dutch Timor a population of at least 400,000 Timorese and 4,000 to 5,000 other people, including Dutch, Chinese, and Arabs.

The eastern part of the island, and a small enclave at Ocussi on the north-west coast, were under Portuguese control. This colony had an area of 7,700 square miles and a population of about 300 Portuguese, 500,000 Timorese, 2,000 Chinese and a few Japanese and Arabs. Early in 1941 the interest shown by Japan in the establishment of an air service with Portuguese Timor had aroused the suspicion of the Dutch and Australian authorities. The Australian Cabinet had decided in October that, because of the threat to Australia that would arise from a Japanese occupation of Portuguese Timor, she must be prepared to cooperate to the fullest possible extent in measures for the defence of the Portuguese as well as the Dutch part of the island. To imagine that the Japanese would respect it as the territory of a neutral power, or that its small force was capable of defending it, would have been to take an extravagantly optimistic view.

Dili, situated on the north coast of the island, 450 miles from Darwin, had an airfield a mile west of the town, and ship and seaplane anchorages. It stood amid a flat, swampy area bounded by a semicircle of hills, at its greatest distance some three miles behind the shore. The hills merge into a series of mountainous corrugations extending over by far the greater part of the colony. Dili contained the residence of the Governor,[1] and the principal European community. The colony was divided into provinces each with its administrator, and each province into "postos" under a junior official.

The island of Timor as a whole is 290 miles long, and up to 62 miles wide. Mountains, highly dissected and extremely rugged, occupy most of the island, and rise to 9,000 feet. The north-eastern portion of Timor particularly is dominated by them—in fact it was feelingly described by an Australian officer as "one lunatic, contorted, tangled mass of moun-

---
[1] Manuel de Abreu Ferriera de Carvalho.

tains", in which "the mountains run in all directions, and fold upon one another in crazy fashion". Much of the south-west is open country, which in 1941 could be easily traversed afoot or on ponies. Timorese ponies—small sturdy animals of which it was estimated that there were at least 100,000—were the basic form of transport on the island generally. A main trunk road ran from Tenau to Atapupu on the north coast, thence into Portuguese Timor, where it more or less followed the coast. Offshoots ran inland, and there were innumerable tracks, mostly suitable for horses. Only three roads crossed the island from north to south; two of these were at the Dutch end. Ships and seaplanes could use many points round the coast other than those mentioned, and there were many potential airfields. An existing airfield at Atambua, 180 miles from Koepang, was swampy and of little value.

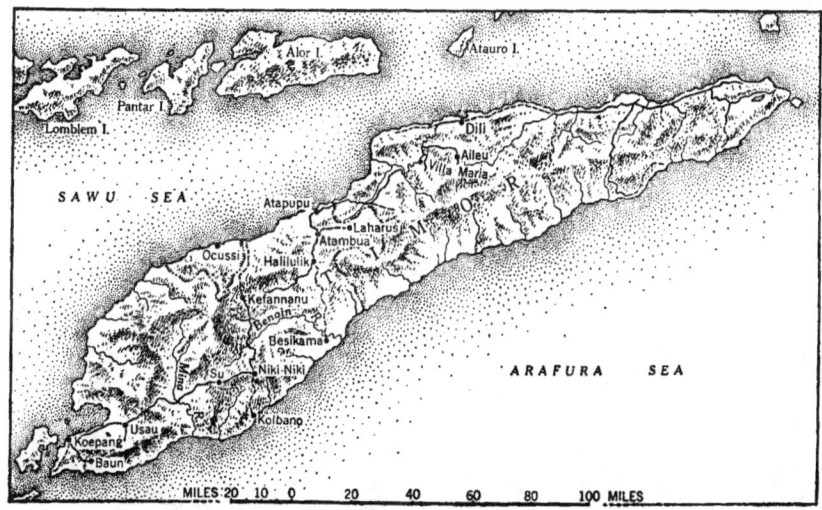

A force of about 500 troops was under command of Lieut-Colonel Detiger, the Dutch Territorial Commander of Timor and Dependencies in December 1941, and there was a similar force under Portuguese command. The number at Dili (about 150) was considered insufficient to turn even a small-scale Japanese attack.

This was the situation when, on 12th December, the 2/40th Australian Battalion, detached like the 2/21st from the 23rd Brigade at Darwin, arrived, with the 2/2nd Australian Independent Company,[2] at Koepang. The commander of the force, Lieut-Colonel Leggatt, aged 47, was a Melbourne lawyer who had served as an infantry subaltern in France in the previous war, and in the militia between the wars. He had been appointed to command the 2/40th, replacing Lieut-Colonel Youl, just a month before

---

[2] Specially trained on Wilson's Promontory, Victoria, and stationed for several weeks at Katherine in the Northern Territory before embarking for Koepang.

the war with Japan broke out. A battery of coast artillery was included in the force, which contained approximately 70 officers and 1,330 men and was transported in the ships *Westralia* and *Zealandia*. The only air force on the island was No. 2 Australian Squadron (under strength) flying Hudson bombers. The main task of the small Allied force was to defend the Bay of Koepang and the airfield. Positions south of Koepang were to be held by the Dutch, and those to the north by the Australians, who were also made mainly responsible for the defence of the Penfui airfield. When the agreement was made to reinforce Timor with Australian troops and aircraft, the possibility of the island being subjected to large-scale attack seems not to have been envisaged. It was seen rather as part of an outpost line whence aircraft might operate northward.

Known as "Sparrow Force",[3] the Australian contingent was at first administered by Colonel Leggatt from a force headquarters, but on the

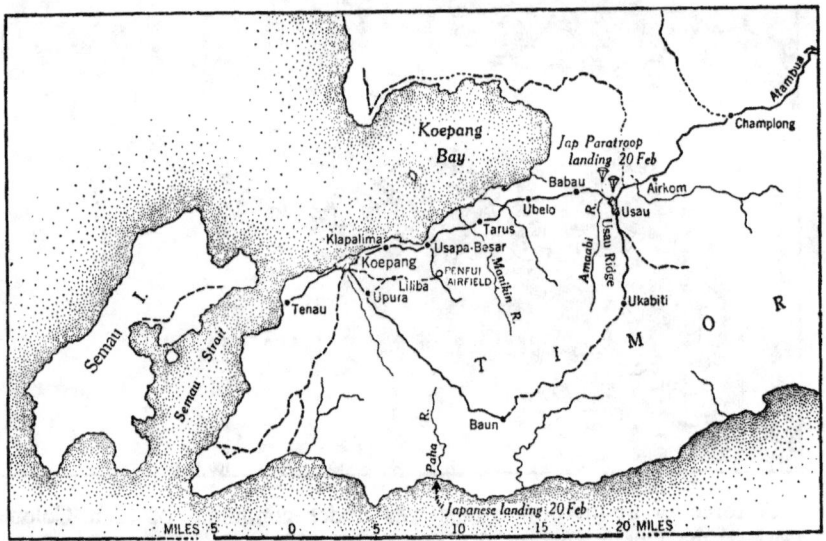

ground that the arrangement led to unnecessary duplication this headquarters was soon disbanded and the force was controlled from battalion headquarters at Penfui. A rear headquarters was established at Tarus and a base at Champlong. Fixed defences were concentrated at Klapalima, a battery position on the coast three miles and a half north-east of Koepang. It was found after disembarkation that many valuable stores, including wireless sets, had been lost, or damaged in handling at Darwin, and by local labour at the landing. Sanitary preparations for the force

---

[3] The units in Sparrow Force were: 2/40 Bn; 2/2 Independent Coy; 2/1 Heavy Bty; 79 Light AA Bty; 2/1 Fortress Engrs; 2/1 Fortress Sigs; B Troop 18 A-Tk Bty; Section 2/11 Fd Coy; detachments of 23 Bde Sigs, 2/12 Fd Amb, AASC; 75 LAD, 22 Dental Unit. The heavy battery had two 6-inch guns, the light anti-aircraft battery (whose arrival is mentioned later) had six Bofors guns and six Brens, the anti-tank troop four 2-pounders. Infantry and other units had six 3-inch mortars, 12 medium machine-guns, 55 Lewis guns, and 44 sub-machine-guns. There were ten machine-gun carriers, and four armoured cars, the latter having been borrowed from the Dutch.

had not been completed, and most of the Australians were attacked by dysentery and malaria. These circumstances, and the need to labour on beach and airfield defences and other work, severely hampered training. Reporting on the force soon after its arrival, Leggatt mentioned that only a token defence of the island could be provided, owing particularly to its 400 miles of coastline and the degree of dispersion necessary even in the area near Koepang. He twice asked for an officer to be sent to Timor to carry out an inspection, but none came.

Preceded by about 100 additional troops from Java, Colonel van Straaten arrived at Koepang by air on 15th December to command the Dutch forces on the island. He was to be under Leggatt's command. A conference held that evening was attended by the Dutch Resident at Koepang (Mr Niebouer); the Australian Consul at Dili, Mr Ross;[4] van Straaten; Leggatt; Detiger; the Commander of the old 16-knot Dutch training cruiser *Soerabaja* (5,644 tons); the Officer Commanding the Australian air force squadron, Wing Commander Headlam;[5] the Commander of 2/2nd Independent Company, Major Spence;[6] and staff officers. Van Straaten said he had been informed by the Governor-General of the Netherlands East Indies, Jonkheer Tjarda van Starkenborgh Stachouwer, that as a result of negotiations between the United Kingdom, Dutch, Australian and Portuguese Governments it had been agreed that in case of aggression against Portuguese Timor by Japan, the Governor of Portuguese Timor would ask for help, and Australian and Netherlands East Indies troops would be sent there; further, that if the Government of the Netherlands Indies considered the matter urgent, and an attack on Dili was imminent, the Portuguese Governor would be informed and would ask for these troops to be sent. The colonel added that he was instructed by the Governor-General to say that Japanese ships were now in the vicinity of Portuguese Timor, and it was urgent that troops be sent to Dili. It was agreed that Leggatt and Detiger leave for Dili next day by the *Canopus*,[7] and convey this information to the Governor at 8 a.m. on 17th December. Ross flew back to Dili to arrange the interview.

Netherlands Indies troops numbering 260, and 155 of the Independent Company embarked on the *Soerabaja* at 8 a.m. on 16th December, leaving the remainder of the Independent Company to follow aboard the *Canopus* on its return to Koepang. Wearing civilian clothes, Leggatt and Detiger were introduced by Ross to the Governor on the 17th, and Leggatt conveyed to him the message he had received through van Straaten. The Governor said that his instructions were definitely to ask for help only

---

[4] Gp Capt D. Ross. Aust Consul in Timor 1941-42; Director of Transportation and Movements 1943-46. Superintendent of Flying Operations, Dept of Civil Aviation; of Ivanhoe, Vic; b. Melbourne, 15 Mar 1902.

[5] Air Cdre F. Headlam, OBE. Comd No. 2 Sqn 1941-42; Comd various training schools 1942-44; Staff Officer Administrative HQ North-West Area 1945. Regular airman; of Hobart; b. Launceston, Tas, 15 Jul 1914.

[6] Lt-Col A. Spence, DSO, QX6455. OC 2/2 Indep Coy 1941-42; Comd Sparrow Force 1942; CO 2/9 Cav Cdo Regt 1944-45. Journalist; of Longreach, Qld; b. Bundaberg, Qld, 5 Feb 1906.

[7] A steam yacht of 773 tons displacement, normally part of a civil force used in peacetime by the NEI government for customs and police duties, but in time of war attached to the navy.

after Portuguese Timor was attacked. He was told that this would be too late; the troops were on their way, and must land. He then asked that the matter be put in writing, and when this had been done, asked for half an hour to discuss the matter with his Ministers. At 9.45 a.m. he said a message had been received from Lisbon, and he wanted an hour to decode it. This was agreed to, but meanwhile the *Soerabaja* had arrived off Dili, escorted by Australian aircraft. At 10.50 a.m. the Governor announced that the message was to the effect that he definitely must not allow troops to land unless Portuguese Timor was attacked, and that therefore his forces must resist such a landing.

Obviously the Governor was seeking to follow a diplomatically "correct" procedure which would avoid prejudice to Portugal's neutrality. The delegation, however, expressed the hope that there would be no fighting, pointing out that the Portuguese force was too small to succeed. The Governor said that when the landing occurred he would see the commander of his troops, and "ascertain what arrangements could be made".[8] Leggatt and Detiger then boarded the *Soerabaja,* and reported the interview to van Straaten.

That afternoon the troops landed. Spence told his men that they might have to fight as soon as they stepped ashore; but they and fifty Dutch troops landed unopposed, on a sandy beach about two miles and a quarter west of Dili, in the early afternoon. A small party of signallers went into the town under Lieutenant Rose,[9] to take over the radio station and signal Sparrow Force at Koepang. They were agreeably surprised to find the inhabitants apparently friendly towards them, and to experience no difficulty in taking over the radio station.

The Dutch were to occupy the town, and the Australians the airfield about a mile and a half west of it on the coast. As a precaution, the Australians took up positions near their objective, while Spence advanced with his No. 1 Section to the airfield and met the Governor, the Dutch Consul at Dili, and Ross. Australian occupation was agreed to by the Governor, though apparently with reluctance. Spence was unable to discover the whereabouts of the Portuguese troops, or their strength. The Australians then moved in, and at dusk were digging in around the two runways, and the hangars.

The attitude of the Portuguese authorities continued to cause concern. Leggatt and Detiger returned to Koepang on 17th December, but Leggatt was back in Dili for a few hours on the 19th. He found that at van Straaten's request the Governor had sent most of the Portuguese force out of Dili, but that the Portuguese Council was meeting that day to discuss the situation brought about by the landing. Subsequent indications were interpreted as meaning that the Governor was definitely against the occupation, was obstructing by all means in his power, and probably would assist any Japanese attack. Leggatt reported to Australian headquarters that the pro-British Portuguese in Dili could form a government,

---
[8] Report by Lieut-Colonel Leggatt.
[9] Capt J. A. Rose, NX65630. 2/2 Indep Coy; "Z" Special Unit. Salesman; of Manly, NSW; b. Wagga Wagga, NSW, 8 Jul 1920.

with the support of the Allied force, and that Ross recommended that that support be given if the Governor persisted in his attitude. On 31st December a message was received by Sparrow Force to be passed to Ross that, owing to a severe Portuguese reaction and threats to break off diplomatic relations, British proposals had been submitted to Portugal with Australia's approval. These were that the Dutch force withdraw to Dutch Timor and be replaced by more Australians from Koepang. The message added that this might relieve the situation, as the Portuguese were highly antagonistic to the Dutch, and had presented a note amounting to an ultimatum.[1] Sparrow Force replied to the message from Australia that the arrangement whereby forces had to be maintained at Koepang and Dili meant that they were weak at both points. If the proposals were carried into effect Koepang would be further weakened.

By 22nd December the remainder of the Independent Company, comprising a third platoon (Captain Laidlaw[2]) with signallers and engineers had reached Dili, and the company had received its only transport vehicles —two one-ton utilities and three motor-cycles. The Australians quickly set about obtaining a thorough knowledge of the country in which they might have to fight.[3] They formed friendships with the people of Dili so quickly that a picquet with transport had to be sent to the town to bring men back to their lines after the hospitality they enjoyed on Christmas Day.

Platoons were on the move to various tactical positions when the men were attacked by malaria, with the result that early in January the company had practically no fighting strength. Captain Dunkley,[4] the medical officer, established a hospital at Dili and within a few days it was crowded with seventy severe cases. Shortage of transport seriously hampered the moves, especially as so many of the men were ill, and it limited the extent of dispersal of men, supplies and equipment. By early February company headquarters and the hospital were at Railaco, in the hills behind Dili on the road to the town of Ermera.

Two sections of Captain Baldwin's[5] platoon were dispersed near by over a series of heavily wooded spurs. A detached section (Lieutenant McKenzie[6]) was stationed at the airfield, and Laidlaw's platoon was in the Bazar-Tete area, where it was in a position to control the coast road running west from Dili, and had an observation post overlooking the airfield. Fifty-five reinforcements who arrived on 22nd January had gone

---

[1] Throughout the colonial history of Timor the Portuguese had mistrusted the Dutch, fearing that they would seek to annex their part of the island. Now they suspected that the Dutch would use the war as an excuse for doing so.

[2] Maj G. G. Laidlaw, DSO, NX70537. 2/2 Indep Coy; 2/2 Cdo Sqn. Salesman; of Maryville, NSW; b. Gosford, NSW, 12 Dec 1910.

[3] The company's mapping work was so extensive that it enabled the Allied Geographical Section of South-West Pacific Area Headquarters, established later, to produce early in 1943 the most detailed map of Portuguese Timor that had been made.

[4] Maj C. R. Dunkley, WX11064. (1st AIF: Pte 28 Bn 1918.) RMO 2/2 Indep Coy 1941-42; CO 109 Convalescent Depot 1944-45. Medical practitioner; of Fremantle, WA; b. Ascot Vale, Vic, 5 Oct 1899.

[5] Maj R. R. Baldwin, VX50054. 2/2 Indep Coy 1941-43; and Staff appointments. School teacher; of South Yarra, Vic; b. South Yarra, Vic, 16 Dec 1909.

[6] Maj C. F. G. McKenzie, MC, WX5369. 2/2 Indep Coy; 2/2, 2/12 Cdo Sqns. Butcher; of Busselton, WA; b. Geraldton, WA, 17 May 1915.

into training with Captain Boyland's[7] platoon at a position known as "Three Spurs" between Railaco and Dili. The Dutch force was stationed in the town. Its officers showed little of the activity of the Australians in acquainting themselves with their surroundings, and disapproved of their friendly, easy-going attitude towards the other races on the island.

Back in Koepang Leggatt kept touch with Dili and forged ahead with defensive preparations. In its first operation order, on 25th December, Sparrow Force was told "Japan is moving southward. . . . Landings may be expected around Koepang Bay and on the west coast in Semau Strait, and at any point or points on the south coast, by a force up to the strength of a division." The order added that there was no naval support, nor could reliance be placed upon it becoming available. Of the 371 Dutch troops under command of Sparrow Force in Dutch Timor, 188 were in the Koepang area. Captain Johnston's[8] (A) and Roff's[9] (B) companies of the 2/40th were assigned to beach defence between Koepang and Usapa-Besar, six miles north-east of the capital; Captain Burr's[1] (C) to Penfui; and Captain Trevena's[2] (D) was to be kept on wheels as a mobile reserve. One platoon (Sergeant Miller[3]) of Headquarters Company (Major Chisholm[4]) would act as a covering force to the fixed defences at Kapalima, and a "reinforcement company" (Lieutenant Tippett[5]) would provide protection for headquarters. Combined Defence Headquarters were at the R.A.A.F. control room at Penfui; advanced headquarters also at Penfui; and base at Champlong, 29 miles from Koepang, in foothills overlooking the bay, and on the road through the centre of Dutch Timor to the north coast and Portuguese Timor. The responsibility of the Dutch troops in the Koepang area was to defend the stretch of beach from Koepang to Tenau.

Christmas Day was the occasion also of a message from Army Headquarters about Japanese tactics in Malaya, thus giving warning of what to expect should Timor be attacked. It was an interesting epitome of what had been learned to that date, setting out that the Japanese were full of low cunning, and used noise to lower morale and cause premature withdrawal; that it was customary for them to send a screen of troops, often dressed in ordinary shorts, shirts, and running shoes, to locate positions; and that, when this had been done, strong forces, often a battalion, deployed to the rear and worked round the flanks of their enemy. All

---

[7] Capt G. Boyland, WX6490; 2/2 Indep Coy. Clerk; of Northcote, Vic; b. Leederville, WA, 4 Jan 1911.

[8] Capt N. H. Johnston, TX2118; 2/40 Bn. Salesman; of Launceston, Tas; b. Zeehan, Tas, 1 Sep 1908. Killed in action 22 Feb 1942.

[9] Capt N. H. Roff, TX2124; 2/40 Bn. Schoolmaster; of Launceston, Tas; b. Midhurst, Sussex, 1 Jul 1903. Killed in action 22 Feb 1942.

[1] Capt D. F. Burr, VX44782; 2/40 Bn. Laboratory technician; of Carnegie, Vic; b. Sth Melbourne, 22 Jul 1914.

[2] Maj A. G. Trevena, VX44425; 2/40 Bn. Wool buyer; of Clifton Hill, Vic; b. Abbotsford, Vic, 28 Aug 1900.

[3] Lt H. D. Miller, TX2717; 2/40 Bn. Accountant; of Moonah, Tas; b. Burnie, Tas, 14 Aug 1914.

[4] Maj J. Chisholm, TX2159; 2/40 Bn. Agricultural officer; of Sprent via Ulverstone, Tas; b. Ulverstone, 13 Apr 1902.

[5] Lt M. D. Tippett, TX3999; 2/40 Bn. Salesman; of Devonport, Tas; b. Waratah, Tas, 28 Jun 1916.

this was done very rapidly, continued the message, and every endeavour was made to maintain the momentum of attack. The Japanese were prepared to live on the country to a greater extent than British troops, and were therefore less dependent upon lines of communication. Theirs was essentially a war of movement and attack, and experience had proved that the best way to defeat them was by counter-attack. ("Cannot defeat enemy by sitting in prepared positions and letting enemy walk round us," ran the message. "Must play him at his own game, and attack him every possible occasion."[6])

Leggatt was perturbed by the circumstances in which his force was placed in Dutch Timor. In a letter to Brigadier Lind on 4th January he wrote:

We are looking after 4½ miles of beach and there is still about 6 miles of beach on our right flank which we should cover, but all I can do is to put a mobile reserve well out on that flank to deal with anything that tries to come through there. The Dutch have about 7 miles of beach to cover from the eastern end of the town to Tenau and about 180 men at present with which to do it. The camp is situated alongside the aerodrome along a road ending abruptly and most decidedly about three miles further south. No movement is possible off the roads now or for the next three months, and even in the dry season no movement is possible by MT or even by carriers across country for any distance because of the rough coral country. . . . No ship has called here yet from Australia and we have no news about our carriers and extra MT, our leave personnel or our reinforcements—all of course badly needed and awaited eagerly. There is still a great deal to be done regarding naval and air force cooperation. We get on quite well with the RAAF here but they are just as much in the dark about things as we are. Ships and planes come and go with very little, if any, warning.

Lieut-Colonel Roach, returning to Australia from command of Gull Force on Ambon Island, called at Koepang on 17th January. He and Leggatt fully agreed that the forces for the defence of both Ambon and Timor were inadequate.

The steamer *Koolama* and the sloop *Swan* arrived on the 19th January bringing about 100 reinforcements (with little training) and some men returning from leave. On the 23rd the first batch of what was intended to be a steady stream of American aircraft assembled in Australia for use in Java landed en route at Penfui.

Seven Japanese aircraft arrived overhead on the 26th, machine-gunned the camp and airfield, damaged two aircraft on the ground, and shot down an unarmed machine. On the 30th (the day of the first Japanese landings on Ambon Island) Penfui was again raided, this time by forty-two aircraft. They destroyed a Hudson on the ground, attacked a dispersal airfield on the Mina River, destroying another Hudson, and shot down a Qantas flying-boat over the sea. These, and succeeding raids directed principally against shipping at and near Koepang, sharpened expectations of an invasion of Timor in the near future.

---

[6] The message was sent also to Gull Force on Ambon Island, and Robin Force on New Caledonia.

General Wavell, in Java, had decided on 27th January that Timor was threatened. Its airfield was essential, since short-range aircraft could not reach Java from Australia without refuelling after the flight over the Timor Sea.

> I somewhat reluctantly departed from the principle I had laid down that we could not afford to reinforce these small garrisons (he wrote later) and asked the Australian Government for permission to move a battalion from Port Darwin to Koepang, while the Americans agreed to send an artillery regiment from Port Darwin. I sent a battery of light AA artillery from Java.[7]

The Australian War Cabinet at first would not agree to this request on the ground that Australia had only two trained battalions at Darwin, but on 5th February, on the advice of the Chiefs of Staff, decided that the 2/4th Pioneer Battalion should go to Timor. Ships would not be available until 15th February.

Meanwhile on 9th February the Japanese had come nearer. That day a force which had embarked at Kendari, now an effective enemy air base, landed at Macassar.

In anticipation of the Australian Government's decision, Brigadier Veale,[8] hitherto Chief Engineer of the 7th Military District, had been instructed to take command of Sparrow Force with its additional battalion. Captain Arnold,[9] Veale's staff captain, and a small advanced party reached Timor on 9th February. Veale, with his brigade major, Cape,[10] arrived on the 12th.

The 49th American Artillery Battalion which was allotted to Sparrow Force was one of two which had been landed at Darwin on 5th January from the transport *Holbrook*. The *Holbrook* had been part of the "*Pensacola* Convoy" carrying reinforcements to the Philippines but diverted to Australia when the war broke out. The 79th Light Anti-Aircraft Battery (a British unit sent by Wavell), less one troop arrived at Koepang from Surabaya on the 16th.[1] On the same day, Japanese bombers passed over Koepang and bombed the convoy, escorted by the American cruiser *Houston*, the American destroyer *Peary* and the Australian sloops *Swan* and *Warrego*, which was bringing the other units from Darwin. About the same time, Wavell, having decided that an attack on Timor was imminent, ordered that the convoy turn back, and it did so, arriving at Darwin on the 18th. No ships were hit.

The Australian airmen, and some American pilots whose craft had been wrecked in Dutch Timor, were flown out of Penfui on the 19th.

---

[7] Wavell, *Despatch on the Operations in the South-West Pacific, 15th January 1942 to 25th February 1942*, p. 10.

[8] Brig W. C. D. Veale, MC, DCM, ED, VX43445. (1st AIF: Lt 5 Fd Coy Engrs.) CO 2/3 Pnr Bn 1940-41; CE 7 MD 1941-42; Comd Sparrow Force 1942; CE Second Army 1944-45, First Army 1945. Civil engineer; of Glen Osmond, SA; b. Bendigo, Vic, 16 May 1895.

[9] Maj G. J. Arnold, MBE, ED, VX40601. 23 Bde; Sparrow Force; DAAG Adv LHQ 1944-45 and various staff appointments. Motor car salesman; of Camberwell, Vic; b. Parkville, Vic, 18 Feb 1901. Died 4 Jun 1954.

[10] Col T. F. Cape, DSO, MBE, VX74788. BM Sparrow Force 1942; GSO1 HQ NG Force 1942-43, Directorate of Military Ops 1943-44, Adv LHQ 1944-45. Regular soldier; of Edgecliffe, NSW; b. Vaucluse, NSW, 5 Aug 1915.

[1] It was commanded by Major J. Dempsey.

Sparrow Force was informed that Penfui would cease to be an operating station, and become a refuelling point only. Its use even for this purpose became questionable when news was received that the Den Pasar airfield at Bali, used as a further stage in flying fighter aircraft to Java, had been so heavily bombed as to be unserviceable, and was under frequent attack. Darwin was asked by Leggatt to state the future role of Sparrow Force in these circumstances, but no reply was received.

On the ground that a strong Portuguese garrison force was on its way to take over the defence of Portuguese Timor, plans to withdraw the Dutch troops from Dili were afoot early in February.[2] Leggatt sought to withdraw the Independent Company also, partly because of its serious malarial casualties and partly so that it might replace Trevena's company as a mobile reserve to safeguard the Koepang-Champlong line of communication, and enable the 2/40th Battalion to operate as a more compact unit. Veale thereupon decided to withdraw the company to Penfui and sent a message to Major Spence instructing him to move his troops overland to Atambua, where transport would be provided; but the message arrived too late to be acted upon. However, Captain Callinan,[3] second-in-command of the company, left Railaco for Dili on 19th February to confer with van Straaten about movement of the Allied forces from Portuguese to Dutch Timor. That day news arrived of a devastating Japanese air raid on Darwin. The report stated that a Japanese aircraft carrier, a cruiser and five destroyers were 80 miles east of Kolbano, on the south coast of Dutch Timor.

The Portuguese force to replace the force at Dili was about due when, near midnight of 19th-20th February, Private Hasson,[4] one of the sentries on the Dili airfield, reported noises which he thought might indicate that the Portuguese had arrived. Lieutenant McKenzie, at the section's headquarters on the airfield, passed the report on to Callinan by ringing him at the Dutch headquarters at Dili. After advising him to send a patrol to investigate, Callinan switched him through to van Straaten, who ridiculed McKenzie's suggestion that an enemy landing might be in progress. Next came a report from another sentry that he could hear foreign voices. Reluctantly, because the voices might have been of Dutch troops who, van Straaten had told him, were due to reinforce the Australians on the strip, McKenzie again lifted the receiver to ring Callinan.

The sound of shell fire reached Callinan at this moment. The first of eight rounds hit the Dutch headquarters, but left the Japanese consulate building next door unscathed. Callinan was unhurt, but he heard moans from Dutch troops farther down the corridor. Sections of the building

---

[2] The Portuguese Government had protested vehemently to the Dutch and United Kingdom Governments against the Allied troops being sent to Dili. The upshot was an agreement that these troops would be withdrawn from Portuguese Timor when Portuguese troops from East Africa arrived to replace them. The Portuguese left Lorenco Marques on 28th January, and were still on their way to Timor when the Japanese captured it.

[3] Lt-Col B. J. Callinan, DSO, MC, VX50081. 2/2 Indep Coy (OC May-Nov 1942); Comd Sparrow Force 1942-43; CO 26 Bn 1945. Civil engineer; of Moonee Ponds, Vic; b. Moonee Ponds, 2 Feb 1913.

[4] Pte J. Hasson, WX13535. 2/2 Indep Coy; 2/2 Cav Cdo Sqn. Truck driver; of Ballidu, WA; b. Toodyay, WA, 17 Dec 1916.

caved in from another hit as he left it. He found van Straaten still sceptical about a landing, and convinced that the shells were coming from a submarine; then Dutch artillery returned the fire, and McKenzie saw a warship and a transport. He again rang van Straaten. The Dutch commander persisted that the attack was coming from a submarine, adding that it might land a few troops who would attempt to blow the airstrip and withdraw; but McKenzie preferred to believe the evidence of his own eyes. He sent another patrol, and a Bren gun team to cover the entrance to the airfield from Dili. An attempt was made to signal with a Lucas lamp to a post above company headquarters, but it failed owing to fog. The patrol returned with a negative report. Had he been too hasty? Once again, McKenzie rang Callinan.

The conversation was interrupted by a burst of fire from the Bren team. They were in action against the enemy, mowing down the foremost of a party of Japanese soldiers who a moment before had been loudly laughing and chattering as they marched along the road. Private Ryan[5] at the Bren first thought they were the expected Dutch reinforcements, and held fire until the Japanese were so close that those not put out of action by his first burst were able to throw grenades into the gunpit. These seriously wounded Ryan, and killed Private Smith.[6] Now, however, the Japanese evidently thought they were being trapped, and withdrew. Corporal Delbridge[7] and Private Doyle[8] crawled into the pit and bandaged Ryan, who refused to budge from his gun and urged them to leave him alone. During a lull in a second Japanese attack, Delbridge and Doyle moved into undergrowth. Ryan attempted to fire as soon as the Japanese came within good range, but his gun jammed. One of the Japanese called in English "Surrender! You are no longer an enemy. Take off your coat and give it to us."

"If you want my coat, come and take it off yourself," was Ryan's reply.

Another party of Japanese ran into heavy machine-gun fire at the back of the hangar at this stage. Trying to ring Dili again, McKenzie found that the line was dead. Doyle, the section runner, quickly claimed the task of taking a message to the Dutch headquarters, though he knew that in doing so, he would have to pass through the Japanese.

> Then commenced a dangerous journey. Doyle mounted an old Dutch push bicycle . . . called farewell to his friends, then crouching low over the handle-bars, pushed off for the strip entrance, where the Japanese troops were preparing to attack, speeding along as fast as his legs would take him.
>
> Through the strip entrance he rode, Japanese troops on either side of him, fast through the darkness until he arrived on the main Dili road. The sight of a dashing

---

[5] Pte M. P. Ryan, WX13624; 2/2 Indep Coy. Labourer; of Wembley, WA; b. Goomalling, WA, 8 Jun 1919.

[6] Pte F. C. Smith, WX12840; 2/2 Indep Coy. Shop assistant; of Mt Lawley, WA; b. Perth, WA, 26 May 1921. Killed in action 20 Feb 1942.

[7] Cpl A. Delbridge, WX10538; 2/2 Indep Coy. Labourer; of Gosnells, WA; b. Melbourne, 18 Sep 1917.

[8] L-Cpl C. E. Doyle, WX13042; 2/2 Indep Coy. Shop assistant; of Bayswater, WA; b. Bray, Ireland, 16 May 1921. Killed in action 29 Sep 1943.

Australian riding a push bicycle hell for leather through their lines must have amazed the Japanese to such an extent that they did not open up. Whatever it was, not a shot was fired at him by the enemy.

He rode into the township, found Captain Callinan, and delivered the message. He told him that the Bren gun team had been knocked out, and how precarious the situation was at the strip; then not being satisfied with the one-way trip he mounted his bicycle again and with a reply message from Captain Callinan headed back for the section.

This time he was not so fortunate. He rode the cycle along the main road until he approached the strip entrance where the fighting was taking place, contacting a group of Japanese. Turning sharply he gathered speed, and crouching low over the handlebars, riding the old Dutch cycle like an Olympic games star, he headed back towards the town.

The Japanese opened fire with rifles and L.M.G's, hitting the push-bike and forcing Doyle to leave his vehicle at top speed, to land on his feet, and crouching low disappear along the side of the road.[9]

Excepting what Doyle accomplished by his bravery, the now-familiar story of failure of communications in the face of the Japanese onslaught was repeated at this stage. Trying to transmit a message from Dili to company headquarters, Callinan found that the radio was disabled. When it had been repaired, no response could be obtained. The road between Dili and the headquarters was the one along which the Japanese had advanced from their landing point between Dili and the airfield. At the airfield, Corporal Curran[1] was sent by McKenzie to check up at all the positions under his command. Curran found that the men were in good fettle, and well placed to carry out the role for which they had been trained, of a small force containing a large one. McKenzie himself occupied a fighting position, and with rifle and machine-gun fire the Australians made their enemies pay for each attempt to infiltrate their positions. Curran, who had been given responsibility for blowing the airstrip, bayoneted several Japanese on a bridge over a ditch on the western edge of the airfield; Privates Poynton[2] and Thomas[3] distinguished themselves as Tommy gunners.

As dawn approached, with the danger that it would reveal that the airfield was being held by only a section against overwhelming odds, McKenzie reviewed the situation. The reinforcements promised by van Straaten had not arrived, and McKenzie was unable to obtain orders from higher authority. The Japanese attack strengthened. He arranged for a dawn counter-attack to cover withdrawal. This attack, carried out with determination and vigour by Poynton and Thomas, and Private Hudson[4] with a rifle, enabled the airstrip to be cratered by the sappers and the withdrawal to proceed. Ryan remained beside the body of Smith in the

---

[9] From a detailed record compiled in 1945 by Cpl S. A. Robinson, Mil Hist Section.

[1] Lt K. S. Curran, VX47342; 2/2 Indep Coy. Labourer; of Traralgon, Vic; b. Traralgon, 19 Dec 1920.

[2] L-Sgt J. W. Poynton, DCM, WX12552. 2/2 Indep Coy; 2/2 Cdo Sqn. Carpenter; of Claremont, WA; b. Ballarat, Vic, 4 Apr 1922.

[3] Pte H. E. Thomas, WX12679; 2/2 Indep Coy. Labourer; of Subiaco, WA; b. Midlands Junction, WA, 28 Nov 1911.

[4] Pte W. D. Hudson, WX13305; 2/2 Indep Coy. Labourer; of Kalgoorlie, WA; b. Tambellup, WA, 3 Nov 1919.

gunpit, and with Signalman Gannon,[5] who also had been wounded and refused to let others hold back to help him.

The section set off in independent groups. McKenzie and Private Hooper[6] left the main party at a Dutch artillery position and went to Dili. There McKenzie found that Callinan had left with the Dutch forces, under the impression that they were retiring to a secondary position at Taco-Lulic to direct the battle from there. Callinan had taken with him Doyle, who had got back to Dili after his dash on a bicycle. An Australian signaller at the radio station was still trying to transmit a message to company headquarters. McKenzie sent Hooper to bring the main party into Dili, intending to lead them by an indirect route to Railaco.

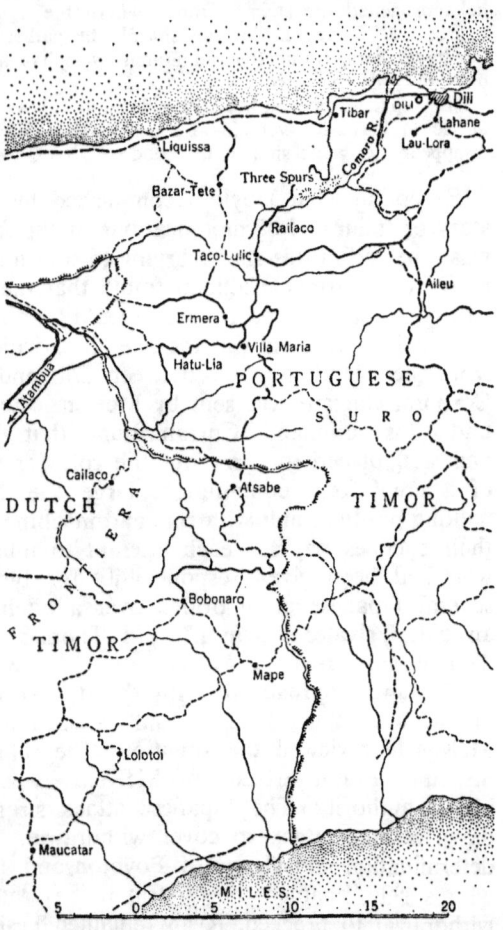

Private Holly[7] reached Tibar without encountering any Japanese, and met a platoon patrol which had come down from Three Spurs to investigate the cause of explosions they had heard when the strip was blown. Within four hours of having left the strip, he was at company headquarters with the patrol, breaking the news of what had happened to McKenzie's section. Meanwhile Callinan, having accompanied the Dutch some distance before discovering that they intended leaving Portuguese Timor, had informed van Straaten that he must leave him and return to Australian headquarters. Van Straaten agreed, and Callinan and Doyle set off for Railaco in a direct line. On the way they almost walked into an ambush, only avoiding it by scrambling

---

[5] Sig B. I. Gannon, WX10548; 2/2 Indep Coy. Counter hand; of Hollywood, WA; b. Mundaring, WA, 15 Jul 1942. Missing believed killed in action 20 Feb 1942.

[6] Pte N. S. W. Hooper, WX11349; 2/2 Indep Coy. Farm hand; of Ardath, WA; b. Cottesloe, WA, 5 Jun 1919.

[7] Pte C. J. Holly, WX12409; 2/2 Indep Coy. Butcher; of Perth, WA; b. Birmingham, England, 1 Jun 1919.

up a hillside chased by shots from the Japanese, and hiding among some bushes. From this position they saw McKenzie's main party and some Dutch troops approaching a junction of roads to Lahane and Lau-Lora in a van and an old truck they had acquired. The party, anticipating an ambush, took up positions to attack the Japanese. Lance-Corporal Fowler,[8] Privates Poynton, Thomas, Growns,[9] and Signalman Hancock,[1] firing from a ditch beside the road, were highly successful. Poynton knocked out a Japanese machine-gun and its crew, then advanced with hand grenades and repeated the feat.

Callinan and Doyle meanwhile had pushed on towards Aileu. That night—the second of the assault on the Dili area—McKenzie and his main party, except for Fowler, Poynton, Thomas and Hancock, set off for Railaco, and on the 25th rejoined their platoon. The four continued their fire until dusk, then withdrew along the road towards Atambua taken by van Straaten and 150 Dutch troops, whom they overtook early next morning. Curran, with two sappers (Lance-Corporal Richards[2] and Williamson[3]) had set out for Three Spurs to convey the news of the landing, rightly judging that as the night had been foggy the fighting would not have been seen from there. Williamson had a bad attack of malaria, and the three were without food for nearly three days. When after a hazardous trip they reached Three Spurs on 27th February they found that the camp was being prepared for demolition.

Company headquarters received from Captain Laidlaw in the Bazar-Tete area on the morning of 20th February an account of what was then happening at Dili. His platoon's observation posts commanded a view of a warship shelling the town, and Japanese troops landing. Laidlaw sent a running description of the scene by radio to Railaco, and then led a patrol towards Tibar. This met the patrol from Three Spurs which had been encountered by Holly.

Lieutenant Campbell[4] of No. 7 Section, patrolling at Tibar, had also seen the warship, and sent a runner to Three Spurs with the news. A party of fifteen accompanied by the Company Quartermaster Sergeant, Walker,[5] had left for Dili on leave before the runner arrived. Unaware that the Japanese were in Tibar, they drove through the village and reached the Comoro River before they were halted and taken prisoner by Japanese sentries. All but four were then sent on in the truck towards Dili. The fate

---

[8] Cpl J. F. Fowler, WX11366. 2/2 Indep Coy; 2/2 Cdo Sqn. Farmer; of Wongan Hills, WA; b. Doodenanning, WA, 24 Apr 1912.

[9] Cpl F. W. Growns, WX13530. 2/2 Indep Coy; 2/2 Cdo Sqn. Truck and tractor driver; of Ballidu, WA; b. Claremont, WA, 30 Dec 1920.

[1] Sig P. Hancock, WX203. 2/2 Indep Coy; LAC 14 Sqn RAAF. Salesman; of Mt Lawley, WA; b. Perth, WA, 26 Oct 1914.

[2] Cpl R. C. Richards, TX4709; 2/2 Indep Coy. Turner and fitter; of Hobart; b. Latrobe, Tas, 6 Jun 1920.

[3] Pte R. McK. Williamson, SX12657. 2/2 Indep Coy; RAE; FELO. Electrical fitter; of Port Pirie, SA; b. Port Pirie, 13 Sep 1918.

[4] Capt A. Campbell, WX6446. 2/2 Indep Coy; 2/2 Cdo Sqn. Traveller; of Perth, WA; b. Perth, 26 Mar 1916.

[5] S-Sgt J. W. E. Walker, VX41872; 2/2 Indep Coy. Grocery assistant; of Jeparit, Vic; b. Spotswood, Vic, 10 Sep 1919. Executed by Japanese 20 Feb 1942.

of the four—Lance-Sergeant Chiswell[6] and Privates Alford,[7] Hayes[8] and Marriott[9]—illustrated how the Japanese military code of honour so often worked out in practice. They were forced to march for some distance; then their hands were tied behind their backs; and they were pushed into a drain beside the road. As they lay helplessly there the Japanese fired on them, killing three. Hayes lay unconscious with a bullet through his neck. When he regained consciousness and moved the Japanese bayoneted the four, wounding him again in the neck. Reviving, he found that his wristlet watch had gone, but that in the act of taking it his wrists had been freed. Despite his pain and weakness, Hayes crawled away into a ricefield, where he was found by native people. They took him to their village, where a woman tended his wounds. They then dressed him in their clothes, and took him on a pony to Laidlaw's positions at Bazar-Tete.

With the departure of the Dutch,[1] the Independent Company was left to fend for itself. As the situation became apparent to the Australians, they continued to move farther back into the hills. As the Three Spurs site was being vacated Percy the magpie, an Adelaide bird, which had been brought to Timor as a mascot, was last seen perched nonchalantly on a demolition charge.

By the end of February, company headquarters had been established at the Villa Maria, a house twenty miles from Dili, and a little inland of Ermera. Boyland's platoon was farther inland, at Hatu-Lia. Laidlaw's platoon continued to patrol the Bazar-Tete—Tibar area. There, on the last day of the month, they had their first encounter with the enemy. Seeing a convoy of Japanese trucks travelling along the coastal road between Dili and Liquissa, they went down to the road and attempted to mine it. However, the convoy came into view on its way back to Dili before this dangerous task—delayed while the section casually brewed itself some tea —had been completed. When the first truck passed them without hitting a mine, Lieutenant Nisbet,[2] one of twelve lining the road, stepped from cover and aimed a machine-gun at the driver. The gun jammed, and the convoy dashed through rifle fire and bursting grenades. One of the trucks was wrecked, but the rest got away.

---

[6] L-Sgt G. A. Chiswell, VX38419; 2/2 Indep Coy. Milkman; of Irymple, Vic; b. Irymple, 20 Sep 1919. Executed by Japanese 20 Feb 1942.

[7] Pte F. J. Alford, WX10460; 2/2 Indep Coy. Labourer; of Victoria Park, WA; b. Fremantle, WA, 17 May 1922. Executed by Japanese 20 Feb 1942.

[8] Pte K. M. Hayes, WX12317; 2/2 Indep Coy. Typewriter salesman; of South Perth, WA; b. Maylands, WA, 15 Jan 1921.

[9] Pte H. W. Marriott, WX13254; 2/2 Indep Coy. Saw bench hand; of Kalgoorlie, WA; b. Yarloop, WA, 5 Feb 1907. Executed by Japanese 20 Feb 1942.

[1] A Dutch account states that at 6 a.m. on 20th February (following the Japanese landing during the night) the Dutch Commander decided to occupy the ridge of a hill south of Dili "with the reserve troops still at his command (about 40 men) in order to assemble the remnants of the troops". But "on occupying the ridge it appeared that the enemy had already extended their encircling movement a good deal farther than the Netherlands Commandant could have guessed. . . . The detachment consequently ran the danger of being cut off entirely, and so it was decided to retire, keeping to the east as much as possible, and avoiding the bigger roads. . . . The plan originally drawn up by the Netherlands Commandant to make his retreat via the base of the Australian Independent Company had to be cancelled, as little progress was made by the retreating detachment owing to the heavy terrain that had to be crossed."

[2] Lt-Col T. G. Nisbet, WX11073; 2/2 Indep Coy; OC 2/9 Cdo Sqn 1945. Process engraver; of Dalglish, WA; b. Glasgow, Scotland, 12 Nov 1919.

The incident showed the Japanese that the Australians were prepared to give fight without waiting for the enemy to seek them out; and on 2nd March Laidlaw learned that Japanese troops were on their way to Bazar-Tete to deal with this danger. From a near-by spur, Laidlaw and his men watched them enter the village and approach their position. Under Australian fire, the Japanese went to ground and commenced their characteristic encircling movement. Realising the threat, the Australians withdrew along a spur, with Japanese moving up spurs on either side of it. Privates Knight[3] and Mitchell[4] were killed, and three were wounded.[5] It then appeared that one party of Japanese was moving west of Bazar-Tete, and the other between Bazar-Tete and Railaco. The withdrawal would have to be made between these two forces.

The firing had been heard by Baldwin's platoon, now situated at Lonely Cross Spur, farther into the hills south-west of Railaco; and next morning 150 Japanese approached this position. Their forward party, of about fifty soldiers, marching gaily along, with rifles slung over their shoulders, entered an ambush of twenty-two men of McKenzie's section and of platoon headquarters, directed by Lieutenant Baldwin. In a moment, a Japanese officer was shot, and Japanese were falling before they could unsling their rifles. The action continued until the main body of the Japanese brought up mortars. Having accomplished their purpose, Baldwin and his men withdrew without casualties, but leaving the ground littered with enemy bodies. The withdrawal was part of a plan agreed upon earlier whereby Baldwin's platoon should withdraw to Mape, and Laidlaw's to Hatu-Lia. It was made difficult by the fact that a second party of Japanese had outflanked Baldwin's platoon, which remained under cover during the day, and at nightfall made for Boyland's post at Hatu-Lia. After gruelling experiences, in steep, jungle-tangled country, they and Laidlaw's platoon had all reached Hatu-Lia by 7th March, and the company was together for the first time since it had landed on the island.

This meant a great deal. Under test, it had stood up to the tough, flexible sort of warfare for which the unit, but few others in the Allied forces, had been trained. Its losses had been slight. Though Portuguese reports were that 4,000 Japanese had landed, and 200 had been killed in the action at the airfield, the company had emerged from the first shock of assault a compact, alert fighting body, undaunted by the disappearance of the Dutch force from the scene of action, or by the Japanese numbers and tactics. Its members scorned messages from the Japanese urging them to surrender, though rumours were current that they would be treated as spies if captured.

---

[3] Pte R. Knight, WX13454; 2/2 Indep Coy. Fettler; of Kalgoorlie, WA; b. Smethwick, Staffs, England, 28 Jan 1911. Killed in action 2 Mar 1942. (Knight's correct name was W. P. Cotter.)

[4] Pte H. E. Mitchell, WX9344; 2/2 Indep Coy. Farmer; of Kuringup, WA; b. Katanning, WA, 14 Jan 1907. Killed in action 2 Mar 1942.

[5] One of them, Pte A. R. Hollow (of Cue, WA), had portion of his face blown away. Such was Dunkley's skill that he kept him alive, and Hollow subsequently underwent plastic surgery in Australia.

There was, however, anxious speculation about the fate of Australia, for the message about the raid on Darwin was the last home news the company had received. And what had happened to the main body of Sparrow Force in Dutch Timor?

Brigadier Veale had completed the reconnaissance he undertook on arrival on Timor, when on 19th February the news of the Darwin raid reached him. He was in a difficult position. The units which were to have built up the Australian force to the strength of a small brigade group had not arrived; his own staff was incomplete. In these circumstances he wisely instructed Colonel Leggatt to put his (Leggatt's) plan for the defence of the airfield into operation, to keep the airfield open as long as possible, and then to withdraw on Su, some 30 miles east of Champlong. Leggatt ordered his force to stand ready for action. During the evening a watching point at Semau Island, flanking Koepang Bay to the south-east, reported that thirteen unidentified warships and transports were approaching from the north-west. Rear headquarters were moved to Tarus, north-east of Usapa-Besar on the road leading to the north coast and Portuguese Timor. Veale also moved his headquarters to Tarus, intending to go next day to Champlong where he could organise some form of defence in that area and at the same time give Leggatt the freedom of action a battalion commander might expect. A report was received during the night from the Independent Company that Dili was being shelled from the sea. Then silence fell on events in that area.

Early on 20th February a report arrived that the Japanese had begun to land at the mouth of the River Paha, which reached the south coast at a point almost due south of Usapa-Besar. Tracks led from the mouth to roads into Koepang, but owing to the smallness of the forces on the island the spot was undefended. (It was to meet such a contingency as this that one company had been organised as a mobile reserve.) The Japanese landing was a serious threat to the rear of the force at Koepang. Sparrow Force engineers were ordered to blow their prepared demolitions on the Penfui airfield as authorised by Veale; and the reserve company (Captain Trevena) was sent to positions based on Upura, astride the road to Koepang from the south coast, along which the Japanese might advance. The company was machine-gunned from aircraft while the move was being made. Veale, who meanwhile had moved from Tarus to Babau farther east, suggested to Leggatt that Sparrow Force move to Champlong; but as demolitions were incomplete, Leggatt decided against this. Veale and his headquarters troops themselves moved to Champlong, as arranged.

Veale's plan was to give Leggatt what assistance he could from Champlong, where the limited reserve supplies were concentrated, and if the Independent Company arrived from Portuguese Timor, to use it as a reserve wherever required. His Signals Officer, Captain Parker,[6] tried with-

---

[6] Lt-Col G. E. Parker, OBE, NX34821. HQ Sparrow Force; CSO 7 Div Sigs 1943-45. Lighting engineer; of Earlwood, NSW; b. Adelaide, 23 May 1914.

out success to reach Australia by wireless from the 2/40th Battalion's station at Champlong, and from a point several miles farther along the Su road. Soon, most unfortunately, Veale was also out of wireless communication with the 2/40th Battalion. Veale decided that Champlong could not be held long, whereas Su could be held for some time by a battalion group—and as mentioned Leggatt had been instructed to withdraw his force there when he could no longer hold the airfield. Consequently Veale decided to maintain a small defensive position astride the road west of Champlong, move all stores to Su, and then his headquarters. He arrived at Su on the 21st February.

The Japanese were acting swiftly meanwhile. Their bombers attacked the fort at Klapalima on the 20th, mortally wounding the commander, Major Wilson.[7] The air force report centre, transferred from Penfui to Champlong, received at 9.30 a.m. that day a report that hundreds of Japanese paratroops were landing five miles north-east of Babau.[8] The whole force was jeopardised by the landing of these paratroops astride the only road into the centre of the island, particularly as it cut the battalion off from its main ammunition dumps and supplies at Champlong. The only men in the Babau area were the cooks and "B" Echelon personnel, and the men of headquarters company, together with a few patients and medical orderlies in a small dressing station. Captain Trevena's company was summoned back to Babau, and the men in the threatened areas were ordered to defend them meanwhile. Klapalima was again bombed, and both guns there, having become ineffective as a result of the destruction of their communications, were put out of action by their crews.

After the destruction of the guns Leggatt redeployed his force. Captain Roff's company, which had been ordered to evacuate its position on the beach and move to a prepared position for defence of the fort, was ordered to the airfield. Captain Johnston's company was ordered from its beach position to a prepared position in defence of the Usapa-Besar road junction. Lieutenant Sharman's[9] platoon was to send out a fighting patrol to Liliba to contact the enemy. The N.E.I. force was ordered to move its headquarters to Tarus (to join Sparrow Force rear headquarters) and to take up a position from Liliba to Upura astride the Baun road.

An advanced party of the paratroops entered Babau at 10.50 a.m., and met stiff resistance from two improvised platoons of Australians, armed only with rifles, plus artillerymen fighting as infantry. After suffering severe losses the Australians were forced out of the village early in the afternoon, and withdrew to Tarus.

---

[7] Maj A. J. McL. Wilson, SX11358; OC 2/1 Hvy Bty 1941-42. Solicitor; of South Yarra, Vic; b. Geelong, Vic, 28 Dec 1902. Died of wounds 20 Feb 1942.

[8] The OC AASC detachment, Captain J. F. Read, subsequently related that on the morning of 10th February he observed from Champlong a large carrying plane, manoeuvring in an area between Champlong and Penfui. The day was wet and cloudy and visibility was limited, but with the aid of binoculars he detected what appeared to be a billowing camouflaged parachute blowing along the ground and towards the sea. He noted the bearing and advised headquarters, but searches were unsuccessful. On that and subsequent nights telephone communications between Champlong and headquarters at Penfui were interrupted, and a voice mocked the caller. Read and other officers believed that the voice was of a Japanese paratrooper.

[9] Lt T. M. Sharman, TX2880; 2/40 Bn. School teacher; of Cygnet, Tas; b. Devonport, Tas, 28 Apr 1918.

When Trevena's company became available it advanced on Babau. It attacked from a start-line about 500 yards west of Babau at 4.30 p.m. The left platoon, advancing through maize fields, forced its way into the eastern end of the village. The other platoons, under mortar and machine-gun fire, advanced to the market place, Lieutenant Corney[1] being killed in an attack on a machine-gun post. A considerable number of paratroops were killed in the village and a useful number of automatic weapons captured, but enemy machine-guns firing from the concealment of the maize made the Australians' position untenable. When it was almost dark, and there seemed to be hundreds of Japanese moving into the village, Trevena withdrew his men to Ubelo, a good defensive position.

The situation after the day's fighting was reviewed at a headquarters conference at Penfui at 8 o'clock on the night of 20th February. The Japanese were astride the line of communication between Penfui and the supply base, with a force too large for Trevena's company to overcome. Leggatt therefore decided to withdraw from the airfield. He intended to use his force to recapture Babau and Champlong (presumed to have been occupied by the enemy) obtain the supplies it needed, and then wage guerilla warfare on the Japanese.

He ordered the force to concentrate at Tarus, and movement thither began at 10 p.m. Johnston's company remained in position until all other troops had withdrawn past the Usapa-Besar junction, and then it withdrew across the Manikin River. Sappers of the 2/11th Field Company demolished the bridge.

At Tarus about midnight Leggatt gave instructions for a second attack on Babau at 5.30 a.m. on the 21st. All company commanders and Colonel Detiger, the Dutch commander, were present. Leggatt explained that his headquarters would be at a point 500 yards west of Ubelo. Roff's and Trevena's companies, each with a section of carriers, an armoured car, and a mortar detachment under command, would lead the attack from a start-line at Ubelo.

Trevena's company began to advance at 5.30 but was halted for a time by a Japanese paratrooper in the maize at the left of the road. This man was disposed of, but the advance continued only slowly; there were no troop-carrying vehicles and the men were very tired, having had little rest for the three previous nights. At 8.30 a.m. it was reported that about 300 more paratroops had been landed in the same area as on the previous day. From 7 a.m. Japanese aircraft were over the Australian column strafing and dive-bombing. The gunners of the 79th Light Anti-Aircraft Battery—a veteran unit which had served in the Battle of Britain—shot down several aircraft and damaged others.[2]

---

[1] Lt D. N. Corney, TX2154; 2/40 Bn. Farmer; of Richmond, Tas; b. Perth, WA, 1 Feb 1916. Killed in action 20 Feb 1942.

[2] In the four days of fighting the battery reported the shooting down of 14 aircraft.

Leggatt and his adjutant, Captain Maddern,[3] joined the forward companies at 10.30 a.m. They were then about 800 yards from the outskirts of Babau. After a rest the advance was continued at midday, with Trevena's company astride the road and Roff's on its left. Soon after the advance was resumed the companies came under very heavy fire. Trevena ordered his two right-hand platoons to withdraw 200 yards preparatory to a wide flanking movement, but the platoons, still under heavy fire and losing men, moved back almost to Ubelo. Leggatt and Maddern came forward again at 2 p.m. and Leggatt ordered Trevena to prevent the enemy from moving towards Ubelo; but they could not find Roff, although they found one of his platoons almost in Babau, protecting a light anti-aircraft gun of the British battery.

Leggatt thereupon returned to Ubelo and ordered Burr's company forward from Tarus to reinforce Roff's. At the same time he ordered that all vehicles should move to Ubelo within a perimeter to be formed by Johnston's company and Trevena's and men from the fixed defences. The anti-aircraft battery too was moved into the perimeter.

Meanwhile Roff's company (with two platoons of its own and the remaining platoon of Trevena's company) had won a brilliant success. They had moved round the left flank, cleared the paratroops from the maize fields there and then taken Babau. In a building that seemed to be the enemy's headquarters Roff (who was wounded but carried on) and two men had killed 10 paratroops, including their commander. Corporal Armstrong[4] advanced under heavy fire with a Lewis gun, established himself in a building from which he could enfilade an enemy group, and drove it off, killing five. Lieutenant Williams[5] led his platoon with great dash. Maps and equipment were captured. Only isolated Japanese remained in Babau when the Australians moved out.

Leggatt then decided to move the whole force into Babau that night. Johnston's company entered unopposed at 8 p.m. and by 5.30 a.m. on 22nd February the force was concentrated there, with Roff's company forward on the right, Johnston's on its left, Burr's on the left rear, Trevena's on its right and the transport within the perimeter. The Dutch force did not take part in this movement.[6]

At Babau the savagery of the Japanese again revealed itself. It was found that several Australians, including a medical orderly, had been tied to trees, and their throats cut. One man, forced by the paratroops to carry a wireless set, had been bayoneted when he collapsed of exhaustion. He was still alive when his comrades found him, but died later. Some

---

[3] Lt-Col N. P. Maddern, MBE, NX34734; 2/40 Bn. Regular soldier; of Wayville, SA; b. Adelaide, 29 May 1919.

[4] Cpl J. H. Armstrong, TX3283; 2/40 Bn. Labourer; of Launceston, Tas; b. Beaconsfield, Tas, 19 Feb 1919. Died while prisoner about 16 Jun 1943.

[5] Lt R. G. Williams, TX2146; 2/40 Bn. Draper; of Derby, Tas; b. Derby, 7 Aug 1920.

[6] The Dutch account states that "as there were not enough vehicles the Netherlands troops came too late to join the Australians in their battle against these paratroopers". A fuller description of the movements of the Dutch force appears later in this chapter.

men of the fixed defences who had been sent on their way to hospital at Champlong on the 20th had been intercepted, tied together, and shot.

At this stage it seemed likely that from 300 to 500 paratroops were between Leggatt's force and Champlong, and that the enemy was in Koepang. Leggatt decided to move the whole force on to Champlong, beginning at 8 a.m. with Roff's company, followed by Johnston's and Trevena's. Burr's was to protect the rear. The carriers and mortars were allotted to the forward companies and the anti-tank and anti-aircraft guns were distributed along the column. At 7 a.m. Japanese paratroops surrounded an anti-aircraft gun that had moved outside the perimeter to join the convoy then forming up. The gunners held them off until one of Johnston's platoons attacked and drove them away.

All rations and ammunition in Babau having been issued, the head of the column passed the start-line punctually at 8 o'clock. About a mile from Babau a road-block was seen at the bridge over the Amaabi River and many Japanese, with a mountain gun, were seen digging in on the Usau ridge over which the road passed. Roff decided to move round the left—the more covered approach—cross the river and attack the ridge.

Only the left platoon (Warrant-Officer Billett[7]), however, managed to cross the river, and it suffered a number of casualties in doing so. The others, under heavy fire, waited until support could be given by the mortars. They then

> moved well round the left flank and finally attacked, but were driven out by superior numbers. . . . Hundreds of the enemy appeared to be occupying the village [Usau], most of them being concentrated on the reverse slope of the ridge, and both front and flanks of the village were protected by an organised defence.[8]

Two more mortar detachments were sent forward to Roff and throughout the morning these fired on the ridge. At 10 a.m. Johnston's company attacked on the right but could not continue because the approach was across 400 yards of open ground well covered by the enemy's fire. A second attack at midday also failed. At 1.30 Leggatt and Maddern went forward to Johnston, and there Leggatt decided that an attack on that flank could not succeed. He therefore ordered the company back to the main road preparatory to a three-company attack. Leggatt then reconnoitred the left, and after his return summoned the company commanders to report at 4.30 p.m. for orders. These were that, after a mortar and small arms bombardment and after the engineers had removed the roadblock, the battalion would attack Usau ridge, with Johnston's and Burr's companies forward supported by the fire of Roff's company, the medium machine-guns and mortars. The start-line would be the river left of the road. Roff's company was to advance as soon as Johnston's gained its first objective. At 4.35 p.m., 25 minutes before the attack was due to begin, heavy firing was heard from the rear of the column still near

---

[7] Lt B. H. Billett, TX3756; 2/40 Bn. Plumber; of Burnie, Tas; b. Burnie, 27 Mar 1919. (In the subsequent attack Billett continued to lead his platoon though twice wounded.)

[8] Sparrow Force (Timor), Report of Action by Lt-Col W. W. Leggatt.

Babau, and word soon arrived that an enemy column about 400 strong had approached moving along the road in fours. Trevena's company, guarding the convoy, with 30 men of the fixed defences, went into action and soon dispersed the enemy, but this fight continued throughout the evening.

The fire support for the attack on Usau ridge was intense, and the ridge became obscured by dust and smoke. Lieutenant Stronach,[9] Sergeant Couch,[1] and five others of the engineers removed the road-block without anyone being hit, and at 5.25 the attack went in. Roff's company on the right met fierce fire and soon he and his second-in-command, Lieutenant Gatenby,[2] had been killed and a platoon commander and several N.C.O's wounded.[3] Johnston's company soon gained their first objective—a knoll on the left of the road at the entrance to the village. At this stage the enemy still occupied the ridge to the right, the troops on the right were pinned down, Johnston's company was clearing the enemy from the village and the reverse slope, and Burr's, having made a wide sweep on the left, was approaching the village at right angles to the road, having lost heavily during its advance. The ridge was strewn with Japanese dead.

Leggatt and Maddern moved forward to the knoll as soon as Johnston captured it. They brought a Japanese machine-gun on the knoll into action against the Japanese pinning down Roff's company, but quickly ran out of ammunition. Leggatt then moved forward to control the forward companies, leaving Maddern to deal with the mopping-up of the Japanese who were holding up Roff.

Maddern ordered "R" Company to rush the ridge. This company consisted of reinforcements who had enlisted in December 1941, arrived in Timor on 16th January with little training, and were now attached to Johnston's company; the men killed all the surviving Japanese but one, whom they captured. This prisoner later jumped into a trench and opened fire with a machine-gun, necessitating another charge by "R" Company. Maddern then ordered the survivors of Roff's company under the only remaining officer, Lieutenant McLeod,[4] to occupy a position on the forward slope of the ridge to protect the convoy as it and Trevena's company moved through. From 6.5 p.m. the vehicles moved through Usau. Trevena's company, fighting from a series of rearguard positions, had protected them against the strong enemy force in the rear; some vehicles, including two anti-tank vehicles, had been knocked out and two anti-tank guns

---

[9] Lt G. F. Stronach, NX35043; 2/11 Fd Coy. Works superintendent; of Mackay, Qld; b. Newcastle, NSW, 12 Jan 1912.

[1] Sgt R. J. Couch, QX17723; 2/11 Fd Coy. Labourer; of Nimbin, NSW; b. Ballina, NSW, 24 Aug 1905.

[2] Lt N. R. Gatenby, TX2123; 2/40 Bn. Pastoralist; of Forest Vale, Cressy, Tas; b. Longford, Tas, 1 Jan 1912. Killed in action 22 Feb 1942.

[3] Leggatt recorded that in the main attack at Usau, Roff "led his company up the ridge over open ground against the enemy entrenched positions. His outstanding gallantry and leadership gave courage and confidence to his troops. . . . His loss was a severe blow to the Force. He would have made a very fine and inspiring battalion commander." Roff, of English birth, had been headmaster of Launceston Grammar School.

[4] Lt T. R. McLeod, TX2152; 2/40 Bn. Pastoralist; of Richmond, Tas; b. Macquarie Plains, Tas, 25 Jun 1919.

destroyed for lack of vehicles to tow them. Captain Groom[5] had been wounded in this fighting, but carried on.

The convoy was halted one mile beyond Usau at 7 p.m.; picquets were posted and patrols sent out. Leggatt then sent his Intelligence officer, Lieutenant McCutcheon,[6] forward in a carrier to find a defensive area and one where the force could be reorganised for an attack on Champlong. The strength of the force had been so reduced that Leggatt decided to move all the survivors forward in the vehicles. At this stage Captain Johnston was killed when moving forward to give orders to the head of the column. Maddern then went forward and issued orders for the move to begin, and the Intelligence officer reported that the area ahead was clear of the enemy. The men were now nearly exhausted. When, at 9 p.m., the convoy was still not moving Maddern went forward again and found the leading driver asleep. He set the column moving and it was at Airkom by 11.30. Some of the trucks had carried 30 men, and the Bofors tractors and guns carried up to 60.

Leggatt considered that the main body of the Japanese was behind him, but that other Japanese were certainly in Champlong. At midnight he ordered the reorganisation of the column; nine vehicles loaded with wounded were placed in the centre. At 4 a.m. Burr's company was to be ready to move forward in trucks protected by carriers to contact the enemy at Champlong. At the conference at which these orders were given Leggatt pointed out that ammunition, rations and water were almost exhausted and the men were almost worn out; consequently it was necessary to take Champlong quickly to replenish supplies and prepare for further action. At this stage four officers had been killed and six wounded; 21 remained in the battalion and 21 in other units.

Soon after 6 a.m. on 23rd February Lieutenant Sharman's platoon of Burr's company moved off in two trucks preceded by a machine-gun carrier. No news had been received from this little force when, at 7.50, an enemy convoy led by light tanks towing field guns moved up to the tail of the column, the leading tank flying a flag thought at first to be white but later seen to be a furled Japanese flag. When this was realised, the tanks were so close to the rear of the Australian convoy that two anti-tank guns that had been manoeuvred into position could not be fired without endangering the Australians.

The commander of the Japanese force now called upon the Australians to surrender. He said that the Japanese, whose force totalled 23,000, were on both flanks and had one brigade in the rear; if there was no surrender by 10 a.m. the convoy would be bombed continuously and fire would be opened. Leggatt called his officers together and ordered them to obtain the feelings of the troops.

---

[5] Capt J. D'O. Groom, TX2131; 2/40 Bn. Life assurance clerk; of Wynyard, Tas; b. Ulverstone, Tas, 29 Sep 1916.

[6] Lt W. McCutcheon, TX2121; 2/40 Bn. Public servant; of Scottsdale, Tas; b. Orange, NSW, 6 Jul 1903.

All companies and units were unanimous in the opinion that further resistance was useless, as the position in which the Force found itself meant annihilation if the battle was continued. All troops also indicated that they would continue to fight if Commander ordered it. The decision to surrender was made at 0900 hours 23 Feb 1942 and the Japanese made immediate arrangements for wounded to be moved back to Babau.

Many troops, including Major Chisholm of the 2/40th, who was in Champlong when the paratroops landed and was unable to rejoin the battalion, immediately dispersed into the hills; and the decision did not affect Lieutenant Sharman's platoon, which, as mentioned, had set out towards Champlong at 6 a.m.[7]

At 10 a.m. a wave of Japanese bombers appeared and bombed both the Australian and the Japanese convoys, killing some in both forces and destroying four enemy tanks. They made a similar attack at 10.10, but when a third wave of bombers appeared the Japanese had placed many flags around and the aircraft did not attack.

From the beginning the 2/40th and its attached units, tied down to a defensive role, had little chance of doing more than delaying its eventual defeat by mobile forces possessing the initiative and having complete command of the sea and air. The battalion moved or fought for four days with little rest while its strength dwindled and its food and ammunition steadily became exhausted. On the last day it carried out a successful attack with three companies against a well-entrenched Japanese force on its front while at the same time defending its rear against a yet stronger Japanese force. At the time of the surrender the Australian battalion had practically no food or water, only 70,000 rounds of ammunition, 84 officers and men had been killed, and near the rear of its column nine trucks containing 132 wounded or seriously ill men were within close range of the enemy's weapons.[8]

A severe handicap to the battalion throughout the fighting was the lack of effective communications.

Communications from battalion HQ to rifle companies was by runner (wrote Leggatt later) or personal contact by the CO or Adjutant. Radios were inadequate and did not work anyway, while line communication usually was possible only between battalion HQ and the 2 i/c and his HQ with the transport. For these reasons small battles were slowed up, and it was difficult indeed to take advantage immediately of success.

In later discussion Japanese stated that there were only seventy-eight survivors of the paratroops; that a Japanese company which had moved overland from the south coast and joined them had been destroyed; and that further toll had been taken by Trevena's company in its rear-

---

[7] The hospital, originally at Penfui, had been moved to Champlong because of Japanese bombing attacks on the Penfui area. Major R. H. Stevens, in charge, Captain L. O. S. Poidevin, and all other medical personnel remained with the patients as the enemy approached.

[8] The heaviest losses suffered by an Australian battalion in Crete in May 1941 had been those of the 2/11th Battalion: 53 killed and 126 wounded.

guard action.[1] The Australians discovered that the paratroops were armed with .258 carbines; a high proportion of .258 light machine-guns; approximately 2-inch mortars; and hand grenades. Each paratrooper carried a portion of cooked rice wrapped in oiled silk, and a tube filter through which water could be sucked direct into his mouth.

Those Japanese forces which, under the command of *XVI Army*, had been given the task of making a three-pronged advance from Mindanao to a line through Bandjermasin, Macassar and Timor, thus cutting off Java from the east, had now completed their work. The western of these forces comprised the *56th Regimental Group* and the *2nd Kure Special Naval Landing Force* (a battalion group of marines, about 1,000 strong). These had taken Tarakan, Balikpapan, and Bandjermasin in east and south Borneo. The central force comprised the *Sasebo Combined Special Landing Force* (a two-battalion regiment about 1,600 strong) and the *1st Yokosuka S.N.L.F.*, which was built round a battalion of 520 paratroops. This force had taken Menado and Kendari, and the *Yokosuka* had gone to Macassar. The eastern force included the headquarters of the *38th Division*, the *228th Regimental Group* (about 4,500 strong), the *1st Kure S.N.L.F.* (820 strong), and the *3rd Yokosuka S.N.L.F.* (a paratroop and infantry unit about 1,000 strong). As has been seen, the *228th* and the *Kure* attacked Ambon, the *228th* and the *Yokosuka* attacked Timor. The *56th Regiment* was destined now to join the main body of the *XVI Army* in the invasion of Java. It will be seen that the two main forces closely resembled in composition the *South Seas Force* which had advanced to Rabaul: a combined army-navy force built round a brigade or regimental group plus one or more battalions of marines.

As mentioned, Brigadier Veale and Colonel Leggatt had been out of touch during the fighting. At Su, Veale had established outposts, and the Dutch commander at Atambua was instructed to report. He said that no Japanese had landed in his area, and he had no reports from Portuguese Timor. Veale instructed him to move his troops to Su.

On the 23rd Veale learnt that Leggatt had surrendered. Veale had no news from Portuguese Timor, and the only force still available to him comprised about 250 Australians, most of whom were in the Ordnance, Army Service, and Army Medical Corps, with only rifles and a few sub-machine-guns; and about 40 Dutch and Timorese troops. Dutch women and children were encamped about 10 miles north of Su; and the Dutch Resident was anxious to avoid fighting near them. In these circumstances Veale decided that the continued occupation of Su would serve no useful purpose, and now told the Dutch commander at Atambua, who had about 100 troops, to remain there instead of coming to Su. Veale further decided to send a party into Portuguese Timor to contact the Independent Company; and to move the rest of his force to Atambua, taking with him a wireless set possessed by the Dutch Resident. With this set he hoped to

---

[1] All three of the original battalions of the 23rd Brigade had now been rendered ineffective. In retrospect, it seems regrettable that they were not re-formed round the officers and men who evaded captivity or were not with their units at the time. Some 400 officers and men of Rabaul force escaped (and, indeed, the 2/22nd was re-formed in a way for a period in 1943 when a 3/22nd Battalion, an amalgamation of the 3rd Battalion and survivors of the 2/22nd, existed). After the loss of Australian battalions on Crete they were re-formed round cadres of survivors not much larger than those possessed by the 2/21st and 2/40th. As it was, the 23rd Brigade Group, which still possessed its headquarters, the 2/14th Field Regiment, most of its field ambulance, and some sub-units, was filled by adding militia battalions; for a period it retained also the 2/4th Pioneer Battalion which had replaced the 2/22nd when it was sent to Rabaul.

speak to both Java and Australia, and ask that reinforcements be landed on the south coast near the Dutch-Portuguese border.

After an enemy convoy had approached the bridge over the Mina River on the 23rd, and had been fired on and withdrawn, the bridge was blown up (by Lieutenant Doig[2]) and the withdrawal to Atambua began. An outpost was left at the Benain River to destroy the bridge there if a large enemy force approached.

Atambua was a small town in level country flanked on the north by the coastal range and on the east by the mountainous area of the Portuguese border. A road led south, through open country to Besikama, and a fair-weather road led to Dili. Veale decided that if the Independent Company arrived from eastern Timor a stand would be made round Atambua as long as possible, the line of withdrawal being to the south coast and thence eastward into Portuguese Timor. He established posts at the crossroads at Halilulik and at Kefannanu.

On 25th February a Japanese force approached the Benain River; the outpost blew up the bridge and withdrew to Kefannanu. On the 27th Colonel van Straaten arrived from Dili, very fatigued, and reported that the Japanese had taken Dili on the 19th February and that his troops were following him; he had last seen the Independent Company about Villa Maria. He said his troops were very tired and he favoured distributing them in small parties among the villages.

Also on the 27th a strong group of Japanese mounted on ponies crossed the Benain River and advanced on Kefannanu. Veale now decided not to oppose van Straaten's proposal to distribute his men; a major reason was the limited amount of food at Atambua. Veale decided also that, when the Japanese occupied Kefannanu, he would move most of the Australian troops to villages in the north coast area west of Atapupu, allow small organised parties to attempt to reach Australia, and himself move with a small reconnaissance party to south-west Portuguese Timor, where, he considered, there was the best chance of maintaining a force.

This plan was put into operation. All vehicles and surplus stores at Atambua were destroyed; the main body moved to the north coast; and three escape parties set out.[3] Brigadier Veale, with Captains Arnold and Neave[4] and ten other ranks set out for Portuguese Timor on 2nd March; and at the same time Captain Parker and some signallers moved east into Portuguese Timor in an effort to contact the Independent Company.

On the night of the 5th March Veale's party met Lieutenant Laffy[5] of the Independent Company, who was making a reconnaissance south of

---

[2] Capt C. D. Doig, WX11054; 2/2 Indep Coy; 2/2 Cdo Sqn. Farm hand; of Wagin, WA; b. Wagin, 3 Mar 1912.

[3] One of these suffered mishaps and eventually rejoined the main party. Another (Lieutenant Sharman and others) was captured. The third, which set out to join a party of R.A.A.F. men left in the Occusi, north of Su, reached Sumba Island and, eventually, Australia.

[4] Capt R. C. Neave, NX70843. AEME; "Z" Special Unit. Company director; of Killara, NSW; b. Northwood, NSW, 1 Nov 1907.

[5] Capt J. P. Laffy, NX77257. 2/2 Indep Coy and training appointments. Regular soldier; of Newcastle, NSW; b. Redfern, NSW, 14 Nov 1915.

Cailaco, and was in touch with Senhor de Sousa Santos, the Portuguese administrator of the Fronteira Province, with headquarters at Bobonaro.[6] Laffy was told to instruct Major Spence to meet Brigadier Veale at Lolotoi, and Spence arrived there on the night of the 8th March.[7]

While Brigadier Veale's party was moving eastward towards them the men of the Independent Company had been consolidating their position. As previously related, company headquarters had been established by the end of February at Villa Maria, and it was not then known that the 2/40th Battalion had surrendered. After Callinan had spent a day or so at the headquarters, he suggested to Spence that they should endeavour to get further instructions from Leggatt, and inform him that they were quite capable at present of carrying out their secondary role of protecting his rear. The only means of communication with Leggatt was by runner and the time required to cover the one hundred and twenty-odd miles would be considerable. It was agreed that Callinan should go, as he could speak with most responsibility to Leggatt. He set out with Lance-Sergeant Tomasetti[8] and Sapper Wilby.[9] At Laharus they learned that the main force had surrendered. A day was spent assisting Catholic missionaries to restore order locally, and sending messages by Timorese to all Australians in the area that the Independent Company was still fighting. One of these messages brought Captain Parker and party to Laharus, and they returned with Callinan to Cailaco.

On his way back to Cailaco, Callinan pondered what they should do now that the movement back along the road to Koepang was not only

---

[6] The first men of the Independent Company to obtain news of what had happened in Dutch Timor had been Fowler and his party. To them, when they followed the Dutch towards the border after the action at the airfield, it seemed that the whole of their company would seek to rejoin Sparrow Force. Because Thomas had been wounded in the foot, they lagged behind the Dutch during the day, but caught up at night. At Atsabe a pony was found for Thomas, but as his companions continued afoot they stumbled along in a daze, delirious at times with malaria. Nuns at Laharus, a small Dutch mission town across the border, treated, fed, and rested them before they commenced the last stage of their journey. They were overjoyed when a 2/40th Battalion truck appeared and carried them the remaining few miles to Atambua. They were told of the surrender in Dutch Timor and that Brigadier Veale had arrived at Atambua five days before with 225 men. Leaving Thomas in hospital at Atambua, Fowler, Poynton, and Hancock joined Veale's group.

[7] A Dutch official account of what happened to the Dutch force stationed at Koepang when the Japanese invaded the area states: "The Australians had suffered material losses in this action, so that, in the opinion of the Commander of the battalion, continuing the battle against stronger enemy forces that had meanwhile advanced with motorised detachments through Timor was impossible. A truce applied for by him was declined by the Japanese Commandant."

After the surrender of Sparrow Force, "the Territorial Commander decided to retire to the interior of the country with the Netherlands troops still available and some Australian detachments, with the purpose of joining the forces in Portuguese Timor. After a march through heavy mountainous country, the mouth of the Mina River was reached from where the march was continued, at first in a north-easterly and then in a northerly direction. . . .

"On March 4th, 1942, the advance was checked by an enemy company south of Niki-Niki provided with machine-guns and a piece of mountain artillery. Our exhausted men were no longer able to engage successfully this well-equipped enemy force, so that a great number of the forces that originally made up the Dutch garrison of Timor fell into enemy hands."

The account continues that there were about 225 Dutch troops at Atambua at the end of February. When a report reached them that the Japanese were approaching, evacuation began on 1st March. Later, when it was discovered that the Japanese were not at Atambua or thereabouts, the commander of the Atambua detachment decided to rally the Dutch troops there for guerilla action against Su and Koepang.

[8] L-Sgt W. E. Tomasetti, VX28767. 2/2 Indep Coy; 2/27 Bn. Clerk; of Malvern, Vic; b. Brunswick, Vic, 11 Sep 1918.

[9] Pte V. P. Wilby, VX60836. 2/2 Indep Coy; 2/5 Fd Coy; 2/12 Bn. Builders' labourer and seaman; of South Melbourne; b. Bendigo, Vic, 19 Dec 1921.

unnecessary but also undesirable. He formulated a plan based upon earlier discussions with Baldwin about the desirability of having secure bases from which platoons could operate. The base areas for the platoons were selected from the map so that each had a town or village, printed in larger type on the map, within its base area, and they were approximately equally spaced along the southern side of the central range. The size of the type proved to be misleading as an indication of the relative size of the town or village, but the general areas selected were eventually taken up. One selection had, however, been made for them by de Sousa Santos, who had sent a message to Spence saying that troops could and should be quartered at Mape. Baldwin later established his headquarters there.

At Lolotoi on 8th March Brigadier Veale at last obtained a clear picture of the operations of the 2/2nd Independent Company and their present dispositions; and learnt that Callinan and Parker had already been in contact. Veale then set up his headquarters at Maucatar.

The spirit of the Independent Company at this time was evident in their uncompromising response to a demand by the Japanese for their surrender, brought by Ross from Dili. Ross travelled under Japanese escort as far as Liquissa, and thence made his way to Hatu-Lia. He said he had been told by the Japanese commander that all fighting in Dutch Timor had ceased, and that as the Australians in Portuguese Timor were part of Sparrow Force, they also should surrender. If they did not, they would be declared outlaws and if captured would be executed. The reply, swiftly decided upon at a conference of senior officers of the company with Ross on 15th March, was that the company was still a unit, and would fight on.[1]

Again, as at Rabaul and Ambon, the Japanese invasion of Timor had been supported by the Japanese Carrier Fleet. It was this fleet which, at dawn on the 19th February, had launched 81 aircraft at Darwin to neutralise that base in preparation for the coming operations in the Indies. These 81 were joined by 54 land-based aircraft from Kendari; and in the afternoon a second attack was made, by another 54 aircraft. At Darwin or near it the raiders sank the American destroyer *Peary*, four American transports, a British tanker, two large Australian ships and two small ones, killed 238 people and destroyed 10 aircraft.[2]

The plan of attack on Dutch Timor was to land the main part of the force south of the Koepang area with the airfield as a main objective. Part of the *228th Regiment* was given the task of cutting off the defenders' withdrawal to the east. The paratroops were to be dropped about Usau and to cooperate in the attack on the airfields. On the first day the main part of the force reached an east-west line about the centre of the western tip of the island; next day it advanced to Koepang airfield. On this day the right battalion of the regiment became engaged in "desperate" fighting with the Australians withdrawing eastward, whereupon the remainder of the regiment swung east and attacked them, eventually capturing the main body of the Australians near Usau. The Japanese believed that they encountered 1,300 Australians and Dutch troops at Dili. What proportion of the Japanese force landed at Dili could not be ascertained.

---

[1] The later experiences of the Australians on Timor will be described in the next volume of this series.

[2] This raid is described in more detail in the naval and air series in this history and in the next volume of the army series.

A striking demonstration of the flexibility possessed by the army of a Power which commands the sea and air had been given by the *228th Regiment*. It had taken part in the operations against Hong Kong in December; played the main part in the conquest of Ambon in January-February, and now had repeated the achievement in the taking of Timor in February. It will reappear in another theatre in the next volume of this series.

(Australian War Memorial)

Lieut-General V. A. H. Sturdee, Chief of the Australian General Staff, and Major-General H. ter Poorten, who commanded the Allied forces in Java in February-March 1942.

(Australian War Memorial)

Men of the 2/2nd Independent Company in a village in Portuguese Timor.

Sergeants R. C. Hopkins and A. R. Cutter of the 2/2nd Pioneer Battalion, with a Dutch liaison officer, checking positions on a map in the Tjampea area, Java, March 1942.

H.M.T. *Orcades*, carrying members of the A.I.F. from the Middle East, at Batavia, February 1942.

(*Australian War Memorial*)

CHAPTER 22

THE END IN JAVA

THE motley and insubstantial forces which remained in and about Java on the 25th February, after the departure of General Wavell and several of the senior American and Australian commanders, was under the command of Dutch officers; Admiral Helfrich commanded the Allied naval force, General ter Poorten the Allied army, and General van Oyen the combined air forces.

Helfrich's ships included three British cruisers, two Australian, two Dutch, and one American; five British destroyers, four American, and two Dutch; and some Dutch submarines and smaller craft. Commodore Collins[1] remained at Batavia as "Commodore, China Force", in general control, under Helfrich, of the British and Australian ships. The defending air forces included some 18 British fighters and 20 twin-engined aircraft fit for operations; a few American fighters; and ten Dutch squadrons, all much depleted. The Dutch Army totalled some 25,000 troops but, as the Australians had observed early in February, they seemed unlikely to be capable of a very effective resistance. These troops were deployed in four area commands: Batavia area, with two regiments under General Schilling; North Central area, one regiment, under General Pessmann; South Java area, one regiment, under General Cox; and East Java, one regiment, under General Ilgen. The only effective mobile striking units were the two Australian battalions (2/3 Machine Gun and 2/2 Pioneers) under the command of Brigadier Blackburn, a squadron of British tanks of the 3rd Hussars, and a battalion of the 131st American Field Artillery Regiment. The British and Australian contingents, including five British anti-aircraft regiments, two of them without guns, were at length placed under the general control of Major-General Sitwell,[2] who had been Wavell's senior anti-aircraft officer.

Blackburn, a sanguine, gallant and enterprising officer, was a lawyer who had served on Gallipoli in the ranks and won the Victoria Cross as a subaltern at Pozieres in 1916. Between the wars he had risen to the command of a machine-gun battalion, and in 1940 had formed the 2/3rd Machine Gun Battalion. He had led this unit in the Syrian campaign of June and July 1941, in which the 2/2nd Pioneers also fought, as infantry, in a series of costly engagements.

As mentioned earlier, the units which disembarked in Java under Blackburn's command on 19th February were his own battalion and the 2/2nd Pioneers, the 2/6th Field Company of engineers, the 2/2nd Casualty Clear-

---

[1] Vice-Admiral Sir John Collins, KBE, CB; RAN. HMS *Canada* 1917-18; Asst Chief of Naval Staff 1938-39; Comd HMAS *Sydney* 1939-41, British Naval forces in ABDA Area 1942, HMAS *Shropshire* 1943-44, Australian Squadron 1944 and 1945-46. First Naval Member and Chief of Naval Staff 1948-55. B. Deloraine, Tas, 7 Jan 1899.

[2] Maj-Gen H. D. W. Sitwell, CB, MC. GOC Brit Troops Java 1942. Regular soldier; b. 25 Oct 1896.

ing Station, a company headquarters and a platoon of the Australian Guard Battalion (normally employed on guard duties at formation headquarters), and the 105th General Transport Company. On the 20th these troops except the medical unit, which went to Bandung, were given the role of protecting five airfields.

Blackburn decided to organise his force as a brigade. His machine-gun battalion and the other units possessed only rifles and a few Brens and sub-machine-guns at the outset, but in the next few days obtained a less inadequate supply of Brens, some anti-tank rifles, three mortars, 600 grenades, some trucks, a few carriers and "a considerable number of light armoured cars". There was practically no signal equipment. In the first few days some Australian troops from Malaya or destined for Malaya were added: the 2/3rd Reserve Motor Transport Company, 100 reinforcements on their way to Malaya, and one officer and approximately 175 other ranks from Singapore. Out of these resources Blackburn organised a staff[3] and three infantry battalions, which he numbered the 1st, 2nd and 3rd. The 1st (Lieut-Colonel Lyneham[4]) included the 2/3rd Machine Gun Battalion and some engineers and others; the 2nd (Lieut-Colonel Williams) was substantially the 2/2nd Pioneers; the 3rd (Major de Crespigny[5]) included most of the engineers, the detachment of the Guard Battalion, men from Singapore, and some of the reinforcements from Australia.[6] Blackburn organised a supply column from parts of the transport units, and, acting on powers conferred on him by General Lavarack, promoted sufficient officers and N.C.O's to bring his units to full strength in leaders.

Brigadier Blackburn discussed the role of his force with General Schilling on 23rd February, and strongly requested that his force be not dispersed to guard five airfields, but concentrated so that it could be trained for the fighting which seemed inevitable. Two days later General Wavell, on the eve of his departure, saw Blackburn, impressed on him the value to the Allied cause and to Australia in particular of every hour gained by resisting the Japanese invasion; explained that the troops under Blackburn's command were practically the only British troops in Java equipped and trained to fight; and said he was to use them in offensive operations against the Japanese wherever possible.

Blackburn had been instructed the day before that he was under the command of General Sitwell, and on the 25th he sought him out.[7] As a result of discussion Sitwell decided to add to Blackburn's force a signal section from one of the anti-aircraft regiments, the squadron of

---

[3] Maj J. E. M. Calder, OC of 2/6 Fd Coy, a regular officer, became brigade major; and Capt J. J. Edwards became staff captain.

[4] Lt-Col E. D. Lyneham, ED, WX3334; CO 2/3 MG Bn Feb-Apr 1942. Orchardist; of Kalamunda, WA; b. Stawell, Vic, 24 Feb 1905.

[5] Maj J. C. Champion de Crespigny, ED, VX253. I Aust Corps Guard Bn; CO Reserve Bn Blackforce. Advertising manager; of Ballarat, Vic; b. Parkville, Vic, 25 Aug 1908.

[6] Henceforward, however, the battalions will be referred to as 2/3rd Machine Gun, 2/2 Pioneers and the "Reserve Group". The Reserve Group was organised into eight platoons.

[7] An Australian liaison officer, Maj F. A. Woods (of Cambooya, Qld) had been attached to General Sitwell's headquarters.

the 3rd Hussars, and part of the I/131st American Field Artillery Battalion.[8] He decided that the force should be concentrated about Bandung or Buitenzorg;[9] the latter, a hill town on the road and railway from Batavia (the principal administrative centre) to Bandung (the military headquarters), was the site of the principal residence and offices of the Governor-General. Sitwell and Blackburn then called on General ter Poorten and obtained his agreement to these proposals. Ter Poorten decided that the force should concentrate round Buitenzorg, under the command of General Schilling. Sitwell replaced Blackburn's units as airfield guards with the men of two gun-less anti-aircraft regiments, equipped as infantry.[1]

The Japanese had organised two forces to accomplish the final stage of their offensive—the capture of Java. The Eastern Force included the *48th Division* which had been fighting in the Philippines and was now concentrated at Jolo Island in the Sulu Archipelago, and the *56th Regimental Group* which had taken Balikpapan. The 41 transports carrying this force were covered by a naval force of two heavy cruisers and two destroyer flotillas under Rear-Admiral Takagi.

The Western Force was concentrated at Camranh Bay, and included the *2nd Division,* from Japan, and the *230th Regiment* of the *38th Division* from Hong Kong. Its 56 transports were covered by a squadron of four heavy cruisers and by two flotillas of destroyers. To prevent naval intervention by the British fleet in the Indian Ocean, Admiral Kondo's striking force of four battleships and four carriers, having refuelled at Kendari after its attack on Darwin, left there on 25th February and steamed through the Lombok Strait into the Indian Ocean.

On 21st February Admiral Helfrich divided his force into two squadrons, one at each end of the island; a move in which he was influenced by the fact that some of his diminishing stocks of fuel were at Batavia and some at Surabaya. His Eastern Striking Force included the cruisers *De Ruyter, Java* and *Houston* and six destroyers. Most of the ships of the Western Striking Force were engaged on escort work, and for the time being only the cruiser *Hobart* and two destroyers were available for other duties.

On the 25th February Admiral Helfrich, having been informed of the approach of the Japanese Eastern Force, ordered all available ships at the Batavia end to join Admiral Doorman's force at Surabaya and attack. Commodore Collins thereupon sent *Exeter, Perth* and three destroyers eastward, but not *Hobart,* which could not be fuelled in time. Doorman sallied out at dusk on the 25th without waiting for these reinforcements,

---

[8] This battalion had been in the *Pensacola* Convoy, but, whereas the other units in the convoy had disembarked at Brisbane or Darwin, this one had been landed at Surabaya.

[9] Later re-named Bogor; Batavia was later re-named Djakarta.

[1] The British anti-aircraft units with guns were: 77 Heavy AA Regt, 21 Light AA Regt, 48 Light AA Regt. Those without guns were the 6 Heavy AA Regt and 35 Light AA Regt. These units, with other British detachments, contained 3,500 men. There were also some 2,500 Indian drivers, clerks etc in Java.

but failing to find any enemy ships, returned to Surabaya, where the Batavia squadron joined him. Next day there were definite reports of one Japanese convoy approaching from the east and the other from the north. Evidently the invasion was near.

The only ships now remaining at Batavia were the *Hobart*, the old cruisers *Danae* and *Dragon*, and two ancient British destroyers. This force made a sweep northward from 10 p.m. on the 26th to 1 p.m. on the 27th, when it returned to Tanjong Priok, the port of Batavia. It left port again

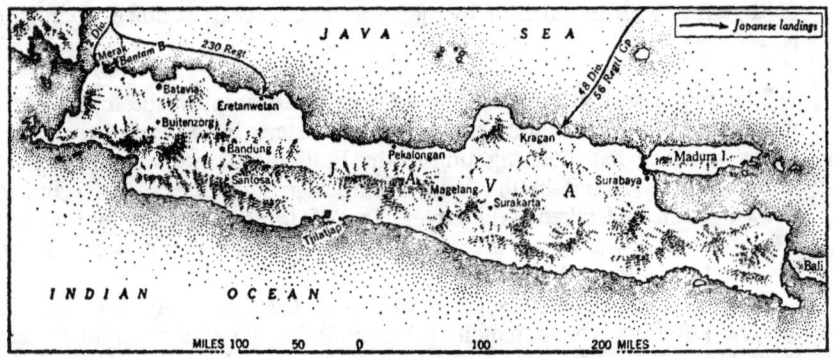

The invasion of Java

just after midnight on the 27th-28th, under orders to sweep northward but if no contact was made by 4.30 a.m., to proceed to Trincomalee through the Sunda Strait. The force made no contact and withdrew as ordered.

Doorman's force of 5 cruisers and 9 destroyers set out from Surabaya at 6.30 p.m. on the 26th under orders to attack the Japanese eastern convoy and then withdraw to Batavia. From 9 a.m. on the 27th the Allied force was shadowed by Japanese aircraft. Doorman returned to Surabaya that afternoon, but, receiving a report of Japanese convoys north and northwest, he immediately set off to intercept. At 4.16 p.m. Doorman's squadron came into action against the Japanese escorting squadron of two heavy cruisers and 14 destroyers. In the five-hour battle that ensued the Dutch cruisers *De Ruyter* and *Java* and two British destroyers and one Dutch destroyer were sunk. Doorman went down with his ship. *Houston* and *Perth* withdrew and reached Batavia at 1.30 p.m. on the 28th.

Thence they departed at 7 p.m. intending to go to Tjilatjap by way of Sunda Strait. In Bantam Bay, just east of the entrance to the strait, they were astonished to find a line of Japanese transports at anchor. They sank four of these and damaged others before the Japanese covering force of three cruisers and nine destroyers arrived. The *Perth* and *Houston* were sunk, firing to the last. Later the Dutch destroyer *Evertsen,* following behind, was damaged and beached. Next morning the cruiser *Exeter* and two destroyers, which had been delayed at Surabaya, were also sunk. Of the Allied ships which had taken part in the long battle only the four

American destroyers survived. They reached Fremantle by way of the Lombok Strait. Admiral Helfrich, on 1st March, resigned command of the Allied naval forces, then almost non-existent, and flew to Colombo on the 3rd. Commodore Collins embarked in the corvette *Burnie* on 2nd March and went to Fremantle. Japanese command of the seas round Java was now undisputed.

The early naval actions had delayed the Japanese landings by 24 hours; but the convoys resumed their courses and landed their troops in eastern and western Java on the night of the 28th February-1st March.

The Eastern Force disembarked at Kragan about 100 miles west of Surabaya, and soon overcame the opposition. The *48th Division* advanced on Surabaya, which it occupied on the 8th. The *56th Regiment* advanced across the island and reached Tjilatjap, which meanwhile had been valuable for the evacuation of men, material and ships, on the 7th.

The Western Force divided into two groups. One (the *230th Regiment*) arrived at Eretanwetan east of Batavia, its objectives being the capture of Kalidjati airfield, and the cutting of the Bandung-Batavia railway at Tjikampek. This force was gallantly attacked by about twelve Hurricanes, but the column aimed at Kalidjati, moving in lorries and tanks, reached the airfield about 10 a.m. The defenders, mostly British anti-aircraft gunners armed as infantry, fought bravely until they had been practically wiped out. The second Japanese column advanced inland and by midday on the 3rd was halted at a destroyed bridge about eight miles short of Tjikampek.

The *2nd Japanese Division* landed in Bantam Bay and at Merak at the western end of Java with the task of advancing on Batavia by the coast road and on Buitenzorg by the southern road through the hills. The main body of the division was to have taken the northern route and one regiment the southern one, but the main body was delayed by destroyed bridges and on the 3rd a second regiment was transferred to the Buitenzorg road.

Both the northern and the southern roads crossed the wide Tjiudjung River about 50 miles west of Batavia and Buitenzorg, and along the eastern bank ran a good road, from Kragilan to Rangkasbitung. There was no other good connecting road but, farther east, tracks able to carry vehicles travelled from about Tangerang on the north road to Djasinga on the south one.

The general Dutch plan was to withdraw, fighting, to the Tjiudjung; demolish the bridges there, and fight a delaying action on that line, and at length fall back to main defensive positions at Tangerang, protecting Batavia, and Leuwiliang, protecting Buitenzorg.

Schilling and Blackburn agreed upon, and ter Poorten and Sitwell approved, a bold plan whereby if the Japanese landed, Blackforce would advance westward along the Buitenzorg road, then north along the connecting tracks to the Batavia road, where it would take the Japanese advancing on Tangerang in the rear. As an alternative Blackforce would attack the Japanese advancing along the southern road. Blackburn emphasised that it would be essential for the Dutch troops to hold Djasinga so as to keep the connecting road open.

Since the 27th February Blackforce had been concentrated near Buitenzorg, ready to carry out one of these plans. Its officers studied the notes on Japanese tactics which, as mentioned earlier, had been compiled by General Allen and Brigadier Berryman during talks with Colonel Stewart of the Argylls.

From Merak, however, the Japanese advanced very swiftly, and by midday on the 1st March were approaching Tangerang and Djasinga. Schilling

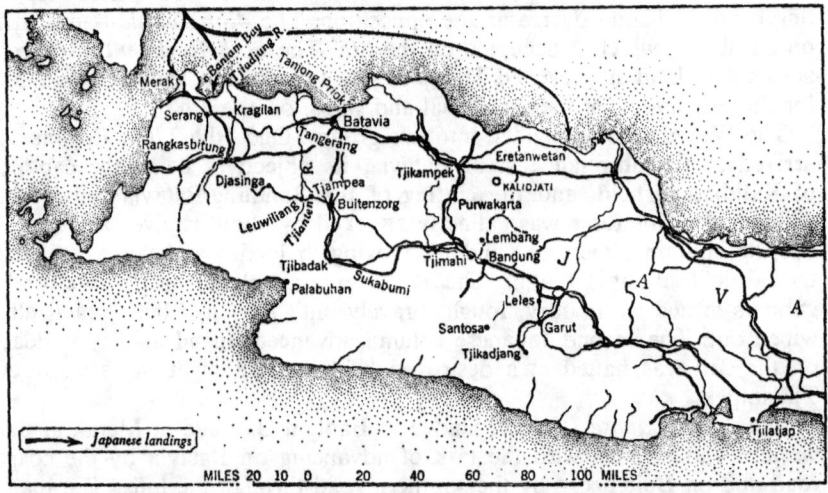

and Blackburn decided that on 2nd March they would first attack the Japanese on the southern road and then advance from the south on Tangerang. Blackforce and an N.E.I. regiment would cross the Tjianten River; Blackforce would hold the centre of the Japanese column and work round its right flank, while the N.E.I. troops attacked its left flank.

Alarmed by the rapidity of the advance of the *230th Regiment* towards Bandung, however, the Dutch commanders decided on the night of the 1st to withdraw all N.E.I. troops about Buitenzorg to Bandung. Schilling informed Blackburn of this and told him that no N.E.I. troops would be left to cover the southern road and that he had no orders for Blackforce. Blackburn thereupon decided to withdraw his force to a position south of Buitenzorg, and obtained permission to do so.

Meanwhile, since the evening of 28th February, Captain Nason's[2] company of the 2/2nd Pioneers had occupied positions overlooking the bridge at Leuwiliang with another company in reserve about 800 yards to the rear. They were there when, at dawn on 1st March, the Dutch engineers blew up the bridge. The Pioneers had just begun to move out in accordance with the new order when, at 4.15 a.m. on the 2nd, Schilling

---

[2] Capt C. H. T. Nason, MBE, MC, VX16136; 2/2 Pnr Bn. Grazier; of Wangaratta, Vic; b. Wangaratta, 18 Oct 1905.

telephoned Blackburn asking him to remain round Buitenzorg and take over all positions being evacuated by the N.E.I. army; two N.E.I. companies would be left with him. Thereupon Blackforce turned about and returned to Leuwiliang, arriving at 6 a.m.

The 2/3rd Machine Gun Battalion now went into position on the left rear of the forward companies of the Pioneers. So far the Australian officers knew practically nothing of the enemy's movements.

> A feature of the Java campaign (wrote the historian of the Pioneers) was the absence of information of any kind about the enemy or the disposition of Dutch troops. It was known that Sumatra was occupied, but thereafter the C.O's repeated enquiries could elicit no news. On one occasion Lieutenant Summons[3] in his capacity as Intelligence officer sought information from Dutch Headquarters concerning enemy movements, and was told that the morning newspaper had not yet been delivered! The next day was to demonstrate just how dangerous this lack of information could be.[4]

In an effort to gain information, one of the reserve companies of the Pioneers sent platoon patrols westward. At 11.50 a.m. on the 3rd a Dutch Intelligence report relayed from Blackburn's headquarters in Buitenzorg stated: "No Japanese landings on Java." Five minutes later five Japanese light tanks arrived at the Leuwiliang bridge from the west. The forward companies opened fire with anti-tank rifles and disabled two of the tanks, and several Japanese who had dismounted were seen to fall. After midday a procession of Japanese trucks arrived, and halted beyond the effective range of small arms. Soon enemy mortars opened fire and a patrol began to ford the river 300 yards south of the bridge. The Pioneers' fire drove this patrol back.

That afternoon the commander of a battery of the 131st American Artillery Regiment came forward and was allotted tasks. His guns soon opened accurate fire at targets on the west side of the river, and the Japanese replied with mortars and infantry guns. In the course of this day the Pioneers lost four killed and five wounded.

Late on the 3rd General Schilling told Brigadier Blackburn that General ter Poorten had decided to counter-attack the Japanese (of the *230th Regiment*) advancing on Bandung from the north-east, and wanted him to hold Leuwiliang with a skeleton force and send the main body of the force to Purwakarta to deliver this attack. Purwakarta was almost 100 miles away in country Blackburn had never seen; and Schilling could not give him the exact position of the enemy or an outline of the proposed attack. Blackburn protested, Sitwell supported him, and the plan was abandoned.

During the night of the 3rd-4th the Japanese did not press on in force, but then and next morning they probed forward in small groups. By 11 a.m. they had infiltrated on the left, where the 2/3rd Machine Gun Bat-

---
[3] Lt W. I. Summons, VX14642; 2/2 Pnr Bn. Student; of Camberwell, Vic; b. Melbourne, 6 Apr 1920.
[4] E. F. Aitken, *The Story of the 2/2nd Australian Pioneer Battalion* (1953), p. 120, on which the following account of the battalion's experiences in Java is chiefly based.

talion was in position, and Captain Guild's[5] company of the Pioneers was sent forward from Tjampea to make a counter-attack to relieve pressure on this flank of the 2/3rd.

In the early hours of the 4th March General Schilling, at Batavia, warned Brigadier Blackburn that the Japanese advance from the east had been so rapid that General ter Poorten had decided to abandon Batavia and Buitenzorg and concentrate round Bandung. At Schilling's headquarters at 9 a.m. that day Schilling asked Blackburn to hold the enemy west of Buitenzorg for a further 24 hours while his forces round Batavia withdrew to Bandung. Blackburn agreed to do so, and decided to withdraw on the night of the 4th-5th to a narrower front some miles nearer Buitenzorg. Consequently he issued a warning order that the force would break contact at 6.30 p.m. and withdraw to Sukabumi, one company of the 2/3rd Machine Gun and the squadron of the 3rd Hussars forming the rearguard. Guild's company of the Pioneers, however, was out of contact. The machine-gunners could not find it, nor could Colonel Williams when he went forward in an armoured car, nor a second officer who went out in an armoured car.

At 6.30 p.m. the forward companies thinned out and stealthily withdrew. Heavy rain helped to conceal the movement, which was completed by 9 p.m. The men then boarded their vehicles, the last of which reached Sukabumi early on the 5th; but the 118 officers and men of the lost company were missing.

At 3 p.m. on the 5th, all N.E.I. forces having withdrawn through Buitenzorg, the rearguard also fell back to Sukabumi. A conference of senior Allied officers was held at Bandung at 6 p.m. on the 5th, when ter Poorten announced that guerilla warfare would be impossible because of the great hostility of the Indonesians towards the Dutch; Bandung could not be defended for long; on the other hand the High Command could operate only from Bandung. He added the surprising statement that he had instructed his troops to disregard any order he might later give to cease fighting. General Sitwell said that the British troops would fight on if any Dutch did so, and was allotted an area about Santosa south of Bandung. He and Air Vice-Marshal Maltby arranged to move into this area early on the 6th, and sent a report of the proceedings to Blackburn.

Meanwhile, on orders from Bandung, Blackforce had withdrawn to east of Bandung. At dawn on the 6th Blackburn received a message from Sitwell giving him permission to take independent action if the N.E.I. forces capitulated.

In the next two days Blackburn reconnoitred the mountain country south of Bandung and had quantities of rations concentrated there. On the night of the 7th-8th Blackforce moved into the area. Some 1,750 armed men of the R.A.F. were also assembling there. At 9 a.m. on the 8th ter Poorten broadcast that resistance had ceased and all were to lay down their arms.

---

[5] Capt D. D. Guild, VX15341; 2/2 Pnr Bn. Architect; of St Kilda, Vic; b. Seymour, Vic, 7 Dec 1916. Missing believed died 1 May 1942.

Learning of this an hour later, Blackburn withdrew his force to an area round Tjikadjang, covering the roads leading to the south coast. On the afternoon of the 8th, judging further resistance useless, Air Vice-Marshal Maltby and General Sitwell issued the Dutch order to all British units. The Australian force remained in its position during the 9th, 10th and 11th. Blackburn tried to send a message to Australia informing the Government of his situation, but later learnt that wireless communications had ceased before it was sent.

> The rainy season had commenced (he wrote later); my troops would be compelled, if I continued resistance, to be entirely without shelter in mountainous country and I had been unable to obtain an adequate supply of drugs and necessary medicines. Lieut-Colonel N. M. Eadie[6] (my A.D.M.S.) and my regimental medical officers all advised me that without drugs and without adequate shelter the health of my troops would suffer very severely if I remained in the mountains; and this advice was strongly supported by Major-General Sitwell's A.D.M.S. I therefore reluctantly decided that in the best interests of my troops and their lives I must capitulate. Despite the fact that my troops all desired to continue resistance until compelled by force of arms or shortages of food and munitions to surrender, I informed Major-General Sitwell that I would join in the surrender.[7]

On the 12th March the senior British, Australian and American officers signed a formal surrender at Japanese headquarters at Bandung. Before it was signed the Japanese commander agreed to add a passage stating that the rights of prisoners under the Geneva Convention would be observed. Later Japanese officers interrogated General Sitwell.

> An interesting point which came out in the cross-examination (wrote General Sitwell in 1945) was that the Japanese evidently thought there was a complete Australian division in Java as they continually pressed me to give them the name of the divisional commander and refused to believe that the Australian troops who had surrendered were the total numbers present. They also stated that they knew it was quite impossible for an English officer, as I alleged myself to be, to be put in command of Australian troops as the Australians would never agree to such a course of action.[8]

Later General Sitwell was again interrogated about the remainder of the I Australian Corps (which he knew to be on the way to Australia). When he refused to answer questions he was told it might cost him his life. Sitwell pointed out that this was contrary to the Geneva Convention, whereupon his interrogator, a major of the staff of the *Guards Division*, said that Japan only obeyed the Convention when it suited her "the same as England". Sitwell denied the charge against England and was handed over to the Secret Police

> from whom I had a very unpleasant time for the next month being, amongst other things, kept with my hands handcuffed behind my back for the next ten days without a break.

---

[6] Col N. M. Eadie, ED, VX14845; CO 2/2 CCS 1941-42. Consultant surgeon; of Melbourne; b. Bendigo, Vic, 12 Oct 1893.

[7] Report by Brig A. S. Blackburn on operations of the AIF in Java.

[8] H. D. W. Sitwell, *Despatch on Operations in Java 24 Feb 1942 to 20 Mar 1942*.

Not until long afterwards did the 2/2nd Pioneers learn what had happened to their missing company, which was out of contact when the withdrawal from Leuwiliang took place.

As this company neared the threatened flank of the 2/3rd Machine Gun on the 4th March, the men heard firing from a village to the northwest and at 3.30 p.m. attacked towards it on a wide front. Sergeant Croft's[1] platoon became engaged with a strong group of Japanese and maintained a fire fight until dark, when it withdrew towards company headquarters. As Lieutenant Allen's[2] platoon neared the village, advancing through rice fields which offered no cover, it came under fire from two mortars and about seven machine-guns. Allen and Sergeant Ling[3] with about 15 men charged forward, reached the edge of the village and, standing knee deep in water, engaged Japanese who were entrenched there. Captain Guild crawled forward, and at 5 p.m. Allen shouted to him that he was going to charge with fixed bayonets. At that stage only one Australian had been hit, despite prolonged fire. Suddenly Private Byrne[4] stood up and fired three magazines from his Bren. The Japanese scattered. But when the 17 men charged five were soon hit and the advance gained only 20 yards. At dark, seeing more Japanese approaching and an encirclement beginning, the Australians withdrew, carrying their wounded on ground sheets.

The third platoon (Lieutenant Lang[5]) had soon run into an ambush in which two men were killed and others, including Lang, seriously wounded. Lang, who was hit in the hip and stomach, ordered the others to leave him, and the survivors withdrew.

By the morning of the 5th the surviving groups of each platoon were out of touch with each other. Croft's men encountered Japanese in a village, and attacked, losing one man killed and four wounded. Guild now ordered a withdrawal on to Sukabumi across country, as it was evident that the Japanese were between him and the village. They set off carrying their wounded on improvised stretchers.

Croft's platoon, still isolated, broke up into small parties with the object of reaching the mountains and the south coast; but by the 8th all these groups had been captured.

The remainder (67 men under Captain Guild) evaded the enemy and on the 10th reached the main road at Tjibadak between Sukabumi and Buitenzorg, where they were informed that the defending army had capitulated. Guild then divided the company into small groups so that they

---

[1] WO1 T. Croft, EM, VX39726; 2/2 Pnr Bn. Driver; of East Preston, Vic; b. Coburg, Vic, 21 Oct 1915.

[2] Lt R. W. Allen, QX2176; 2/2 Pnr Bn. Salesman; of Ayr, Qld; b. Launceston, Tas, 10 Jul 1909.

[3] Sgt L. F. Ling, VX22828; 2/2 Pnr Bn. Truck driver; of Sandringham, Vic; b. London, 20 May 1908. Killed in action 5 Mar 1942.

[4] Pte M. G. Byrne, WX14594; 2/2 Pnr Bn. Labourer; of East Perth, WA; b. York, WA, 9 Oct 1910. Died while prisoner 10 Apr 1942.

[5] Lt C. W. P. Lang, VX19663; 2/2 Pnr Bn. Regular soldier; of Bedford, England; b. Mooltan, India, 2 Jul 1909. Died of wounds 4 Mar 1942. (He had been commissioned a few days previously.)

might make their way to the south coast west of Tjilatjap and perhaps escape by sea.

Helped by friendly Asians and by Dutch civilians, the company reassembled at Palabuhan on the 13th March and there went to the K.P.M. office to enquire about ships! They found in the harbour the s.s. *Sea Bird*, whose captain told Guild that he would sail if he could find a crew and particularly three engineers. The Australians could not provide marine engineers.

At length, still with local help, Guild joined Lieut-Colonel L. van der Post and three other British officers who were collecting refugees at a camp in the mountains. Van der Post explained that he had a wireless transmitter and his task was to either arrange for the evacuation of refugees or, failing that, to organise guerilla warfare.

During the next few days (wrote Lieutenant Allen afterwards) the men rested and regaled themselves on water-buffalo, poultry and native fruits. The party was then divided into small parties of 10 men each under an officer. They were allocated to four posts within one hour's march of each other and then each post was divided into groups of three and allotted dispersal areas into which they could flee in the case of alarm. Rations were still very good—rice, bully beef, biscuits, tinned milk and beans and reserve supplies were buried at each post. The limiting factor on the length of time the party could hold out was the lack of proper medical care as sickness was taking its steady toll. Wet clothes, mental strain and sheer exhaustion lowered the men's power to resist the various tropical diseases. On 3rd April Pte N. R. C. Gibson[6] died of what appeared to be typhus, Pte E. E. Marshall[7] succumbed on the following day, and one week later Cpl L. W. H. Dunstan[8] and Pte Byrne passed away. To be given a chance of survival sick men were collected together and ordered to move out and surrender in the hope of receiving some medical treatment.[9]

In April the Japanese began to round up the guerillas and on the 20th of that month the occupants of "No. 1 Post", including van der Post, Warrant-Officer Phillips[1] of the Pioneers and 18 others were captured. The loss of van der Post's courage, leadership and organising ability was a severe blow. The guerillas then roamed about the mountains in small groups, one led by Captain Guild and others by Lieutenants Allen and Stewart.[2] On 1st May Guild declared that he would try to reach the coast again and escape by sea. He set off with Stewart, Corporal Hynes[3] and Private Murray.[4] They were never seen again. The others were

---

[6] Pte N. R. C. Gibson, VX19476; 2/2 Pnr Bn. Labourer; of St Kilda, Vic; b. St Kilda, 18 Jul 1919. Died 3 Apr 1942.

[7] Pte E. E. Marshall, VX37351; 2/2 Pnr Bn. Cook's assistant; of West Brunswick, Vic; b. Avoca, Vic, 14 Apr 1912. Died 4 Apr 1942.

[8] Cpl L. W. H. Dunstan, VX30577; 2/2 Pnr Bn. Butcher; of Moonee Ponds, Vic; b. Moonee Ponds, 28 Nov 1917. Died 10 Apr 1942.

[9] Quoted in E. F. Aitken, *The Story of the 2/2nd Australian Pioneer Battalion*.

[1] WO2 F. V. Phillips, VX17884; 2/2 Pnr Bn. Baker; of Collingwood, Vic; b. Benalla, Vic, 9 Sep 1914.

[2] Lt A. I. Stewart, VX19507; 2/2 Pnr Bn. Bank clerk; of Canterbury, Vic; b. Victoria, 25 Feb 1921. Missing presumed died 1 May 1942.

[3] Cpl T. E. Hynes, VX14273; 2/2 Pnr Bn. Shunter; of Geelong West, Vic; b. Geelong, 17 Sep 1915. Missing presumed died 1 May 1942.

[4] Pte A. C. Murray, VX59311; 2/2 Pnr Bn. Labourer; of Albury, Vic; b. Albury, 5 Oct 1905. Missing presumed died 1 May 1942.

at length captured. The last group to be taken, comprising Allen, Private McCrae[5] (who had escaped from Post I when it was captured) and Private Baade,[6] were not captured until 2nd August, five months after the Japanese landed in Java. The total Australian casualties in Java up to the time of the formal surrender were estimated at 36 killed and 60 wounded.

In retrospect it can be clearly seen that from the time the Japanese Navy and Air Force gained mastery of the seas round the Indies and of the air above, no reasonable hope remained of successfully defending Java. Even if I Australian Corps had been landed there and had decisively defeated the *XVI Japanese Army* it would have been cut off from supplies by the Japanese Navy and Air Force; and in the event that navy and air force retained substantial command of the Java Sea until 1945. It was fortunate for the Allied cause and for Australia that the Japanese time-table did not allow time for the Australian Corps to reach Java and be lost there.

In view of these circumstances the other handicaps suffered by the land forces, although very real, were not vital to the issue. They included shortages of equipment; difficulties of terrain and communications; and virtually insurmountable problems of organising adequate cooperation between the various parts of so diversified an army in the short time available.

During the invasion of Java the "disastrous debacle" in the Philippines which General MacArthur had predicted early in February had been coming closer. In the second half of February the line across the waist of the Bataan peninsula was still holding, but Filipino patrols, some moving about in native dress and some employing negritos armed with poisoned arrows, were bringing back information that suggested that the Japanese, though effectively halted, were preparing a decisive assault.

> Heard President Roosevelt talk on what our production will be in 1943-44 (wrote an American officer in Bataan on 23rd February).[7] The President meant to cheer us up. Actually, his talk tends to weaken morale. We are not interested in what the production will be in 1943-44 and 45. All we want are two things, but we want them right now. Unless supplies arrive soon we will be finished by the latter part of March.

On 22nd February President Roosevelt instructed General MacArthur to go to Australia and there take command of the newly-defined South-West Pacific Area. MacArthur protested but at length obeyed, and departed from Manila Bay by motor torpedo boat on the 12th March—the day of the final capitulation in Java. General Marshall informed Lieut-

---

[5] Pte V. L. J. McCrae, VX33502; 2/2 Pnr Bn. Roofer and floorer; of Melbourne; b. Carlton, Vic, 13 Aug 1919.

[6] Pte S. A. Baade, VX18656; 2/2 Pnr Bn. Butcher; of Auburn, Vic; b. Gippsland, Vic, 3 Feb 1913.

[7] Bataan Diary of Maj Achille C. Tisdelle (*Military Affairs*, Fall 1947).

General Brett, commanding American forces in Australia, that MacArthur would call on him to send a flight of heavy bombers to Mindanao to transport some passengers. Soon afterwards MacArthur, having reached Mindanao by motor torpedo boat, asked for long-range bomber aircraft with experienced pilots. Four B-17 aircraft were sent, of which only one reached its destination. MacArthur signalled to Brett that the aircraft was unsuitable and defective and the pilot inexperienced, and sent it back carrying sixteen refugees. Thereupon Brett obtained four new bombers from the Navy, and in these MacArthur and a few staff officers, his wife and child, flew to Darwin.

Throughout March the Japanese High Command sent reinforcements to Luzon: replacements for the *16th Division* and *65th Brigade*; the *4th Division* (11,000 strong) from Shanghai; and a brigade of the *21st Division*, which had been General Terauchi's main reserve.[8] Thus strengthened, Homma launched an offensive on 3rd April and, four days later, had defeated the defenders. On 9th April General King surrendered the force on Bataan.

There remained the fortress of Corregidor, where Wainwright had taken MacArthur's place in command of all forces in the archipelago, and the scattered forces in the southern islands. After heavy air and artillery bombardment, the Japanese landed on Corregidor on the night of 5th May and Wainwright surrendered on the 6th.

Eight days later, after an arduous retreat, General Alexander withdrew his headquarters out of Burma and into India. The defeat of British and American power in East Asia was complete.

In five months the Japanese had conquered the Far Eastern colonies of Britain the United States and Holland, making themselves the new overlords of more than 100,000,000 people. They had severely damaged the American main fleet at a point 5,000 miles distant from Japan and had sunk nearly every sizeable British, American and Dutch ship that had ventured meanwhile into the East Indian seas or the western Pacific. They themselves had lost no naval vessel larger than a destroyer. They had taken the surrender of about 250,000 troops, mostly Asians, but including an Australian division, a British division, and the equivalent of a division of Americans. Only remnants of the defending air forces survived and made their way to Australia and India.

This had been achieved with comparatively modest land forces and at relatively small cost—about 15,000 killed and wounded.[9] The defending army in the Philippines alone numbered as many divisions on paper as the Japanese employed in the whole offensive from Wake Island to Burma.

[8] Thus the *Southern Army*, which initially included ten divisions, now possessed eleven. The four Japanese armies at this stage included the following divisions and independent brigades:
XIV (Philippines): 16 Div, 4 Div, 65 Bde, 62 Regt (of 21 Div).
XV (Burma): 33 Div, 55 Div.
XVI (Java): 2 Div, 38 Div, 48 Div, 56 Bde.
XXV (Malaya): Guards Div, 5 Div, 18 Div.
The main body of the *21 Div* was in Indo-China.

[9] Estimate arrived at by Historical Section of the United Kingdom Cabinet Office.

The Japanese *Southern Army*, however, had been supported by a navy which, after the first day of the war, was by far the strongest in the Pacific or Indian Oceans, and by army and navy air forces of adequate size and considerable efficiency. The navy and air forces had enabled the army formations to land where they pleased and when they pleased, and to be maintained in action.

The Japanese commanders had proved themselves able to conceive and carry out a plan of unparalleled magnitude. At sea, on land, and in the air the Japanese had shown themselves to possess great courage and, generally, had applied their tactical skill with more initiative and vigour than their opponents. The victorious Japanese forces now stood around a vast perimeter which stretched through the central Pacific to New Guinea, and embraced the East Indies, Malaya, Thailand and Burma. In the west they were on the border of India. To the south, within easy range of their aircraft, lay Australia.

PART III
PRISONERS OF THE JAPANESE
by
A. J. SWEETING

CHAPTER 23

CHANGI, BICYCLE CAMP, AND OTHER MAIN CENTRES

THE wave of Japanese victories ending with the capture of Java in March 1942 left in its wake a mass of Allied prisoners, including many Australians. The largest number of Australians (14,972[1]) had been captured at Singapore; other principal Australian groups were in Java (2,736); Timor (1,137); Ambon (1,075) and New Britain (1,049).

After the capitulation at Singapore on 15th February there were more than 50,000 British troops on Singapore Island, including the Australians. At the outset the Japanese were quite friendly, refrained from looting, gave cigarettes to their prisoners, and appeared to be under perfect control. Only picquets entered Singapore on 16th February. Next day the real entry began. A constant stream of trucks, lorries, limbers, cars, motorcycles and bicycles flowed along Bukit Timah road towards the town. Every vehicle flew small Japanese flags, and every driver who had a horn kept on blowing it. "The noise was fierce but cheerful," wrote an observer; "in fact there was a holiday spirit about the whole affair."

On the 16th orders had been issued to the A.I.F., except a small group appointed to act as local police, to pile arms in Tanglin square. At this stage and in the succeeding few weeks the discipline of the prisoners was at a low ebb. In the general acrimony that followed defeat the men blamed their officers for the disaster, junior officers blamed senior officers, and junior formations blamed senior formations.[2] The men were despondent and listless, uncertain of their position in the scheme of things, and obeyed orders grudgingly. Would officers be permitted to exercise any control over them or were they shorn of all power? The bitterness of defeat, and

---

[1] This figure, drawn from Lieut-Colonel Galleghan's "Interim Report—PW Camps, Singapore", is evidently based on the ration strength at Changi. The total number of Australians taken prisoner at this time was estimated by the Central Army Records Office, Melbourne, as 15,384. Either figure represents by far the largest number of Australians ever taken prisoner in a single operation. Previously the largest group of Australian prisoners had been in Crete where 3,109 were taken. The total number of Australian soldiers taken prisoner in 1914-1918 was 4,044.

[2] This attitude is illustrated by the following verse written in Changi and circulated among the prisoners in 1942:

It's the fashion now to laugh
When one talks about the Staff
In a cynical and deprecating way.
But now that they're not manning
The defences at Fort Canning,
I think it's time we let them have their say.

"What really made us sore,"
Says Command, "Is that Third Corps
Simply never would see eye to eye with us"
And "Q" believes that "G"
Were as stupid as can be
And as for "I" they always missed the bus.

Third Corps do not confess,
That they got us in the mess,
But blames the whole disaster on Command;
While the men that did the fighting
Are now all busy writing,
And "sack the bloody lot" is their demand.

the prospect of indefinite captivity by an enemy of whose tradition, customs, outlook and language most of the Australians knew little or nothing made the future seem black indeed.

On 17th February the prisoners were moved by route march to Changi, which was to be Prisoner-of-War Headquarters on Singapore Island for the rest of the war. Changi, situated on the north-eastern tip of the island, was formerly occupied by the British peacetime garrison, and included a collection of large and airy barrack buildings, three storeys high, each storey built to house a company of the regiment in occupation; together with a large number of bungalows and offices for married soldiers and the administrative staffs. Parade grounds and surroundings were well laid out, and lawns and trees gave a pleasant suburban atmosphere to the area.

The A.I.F. area of Changi until June 1944 was the Selarang Barracks, though for a time in 1943 only portion of the barracks square was occupied by the A.I.F. Quarters generally were good, but for long periods they were gravely overcrowded. Many buildings had been bombed and had to be repaired before use. The climate alone saved troops from the worst results of overcrowding, as many slept in the open, either from choice or of necessity. With the ability possessed by Australian troops to make themselves comfortable in the worst of circumstances, many built wood and wire stretchers to lift themselves from the concrete floors.

Soon after the prisoners' arrival in Changi the Japanese administrator issued orders that Allied officers would be responsible for discipline and cases of insubordination would be harshly dealt with if referred to him. There would be no segregation of officers and the administration of the prisoners would rest in their own hands.[3] Despite the initial weakening of discipline, the whole force continued to function as an organised military formation, commanded as before by Lieut-General Percival. His four principal subordinates were Lieut-General Heath, commanding III Indian Corps; Major-General Beckwith-Smith, of the 18th British Division; Major-General Key, of the 11th Indian Division; and Major-General Callaghan, appointed by Percival to replace General Bennett in command of the Australian Imperial Force and the 8th Division. From the outset the Australian divisional staff set about its problems energetically. On the second morning after arrival in Changi officers were called together and warned of the necessity to preserve discipline and obey within reason the orders of their captors. Strictness with hygiene and sanitation were underlined as being essential to survival. All ranks were warned of their liability to military discipline as prisoners of war, and strict supervision of the issue of food and clothing was instituted.

The Japanese ration scale which soon came into effect allowed each prisoner a daily ration of 1.1023 pounds of rice, .11032 pounds of meat, .11032 pounds of flour, .22 pounds of vegetables, .033 pounds of milk,

---

[3] As from 4th March officers were not permitted to wear badges of rank, but were allowed to distinguish themselves by a star on their left breast.

.044 pounds of sugar, .011 pounds each of salt, tea and cooking oil.[4] The first truckloads of rice were greeted by some with enthusiasm. Here at last was something to assuage the pangs of hunger.

> As the unloading parties staggered under the weighty sacks (wrote a young soldier) the onlookers conjured up pictures of gargantuan feasts. Memories of fine white rice cooked by expert Chinese and served at delicious curry tiffins flashed through many minds. And a nice piece of fish; nothing better than a nice piece of fish!
> The dismay, the bitterness of disappointment which followed the first efforts of army cooks to cope with rice defy description. It appeared on the plate as a tight ball of greyish, gelatinous substance, nauseous in its lack of flavour and utterly repulsive. The fish, when it came, which was not often, proclaimed its arrival by an overpowering stench and massed squadrons of flies. To gaze on a sack of rotting shrimps moving slowly under the impulse of a million maggots was a poor prelude to the meals which followed, meals which were nothing but a series of gastronomical disasters.[5]

Prisoners of the Japanese, both at Changi and elsewhere tended rapidly to become food conscious and "such will of the wisp as vitamins, proteins and carbohydrates . . . became household words". The immediate need at Changi, however, was to devise a means by which the rice could be presented to the men in an edible form. To this end mud stoves were built, rice grinders improvised, and, although the rations provided by the Japanese remained atrociously inadequate by Australian standards, the cooking steadily improved, until a remarkable standard of imaginative preparation had been attained.

Changi was dependent on the Johore water supply, and as the pipeline and the causeway carrying the pipes had been damaged, it was apparent that the prisoners would have no direct connection to a water supply for some months. The force had been permitted to bring three or four water carts into Changi, but as the nearest water-point was some miles distant, a limit of half a gallon of drinking water a day for each prisoner was imposed. On 3rd March this amount was slightly increased.

Deep anti-malarial drains which ran through the area were a potential source of water for washing, but these were choked with litter and wreckage. When they were cleaned water was drawn from them for washing and bathing, and in a short time showers, worked by hand, were functioning in the Australian area.

At the end of February 1942 the Japanese administrator had warned the prisoners that they must be self-supporting except for rice by the end of April. On 5th March an A.I.F. gardening scheme was instituted under the direction of Major A. M. Maxwell, formerly a planter in Malaya. All available labour was drafted to the project and by 1st April some 50 acres of land were under cultivation. Besides this communal garden, units were instructed to cultivate every available piece of ground. Steps

---

[4] In October the rice and vegetable rations were increased to 1.1475 lbs and .5975 lbs respectively.
[5] David Griffin, in *Stand-To*, Feb 1952, p. 8. (Griffin was a sergeant in the 2/3rd Motor Ambulance Convoy.)

were taken to conserve the fruit on all coconut and paw paw trees in the area.

On 12th March orders were received that each division must wire in its area. Until then the whole of the Changi area had been accessible to all. Troops had been able to roam from the waterfront on Johore Strait to the sea beach on the east, and thence for several miles to the vicinity of the Changi gaol, where the civilians were interned in March. There a barbed wire fence had been erected to prevent straying and to mark the limit of the prison camp. By 17th March each division had surrounded its area with a double apron of barbed wire and mounted guards at the entrances.[6] Thereafter movement outside divisional areas was restricted to persons or parties carrying flags or special armbands (of which few were available).

Renegade Sikhs were posted by the Japanese to check all traffic between units. Orders were issued that these guards were to be saluted, and the enforcement of the salute by the Japanese as well as the Sikhs themselves was a source of considerable resentment. Later a section of Japanese soldiers was stationed at the northern extremity of the prison camp, but these proved unobtrusive. Despite the barbed wire, however, a fairly free means of intercommunication between areas became possible as time passed. Each division allotted a flag to a "ferry service" which operated hourly, and it became possible by linking up with the service to move throughout the whole area.

A forestry company was organised in March 1942 to cut firewood for the kitchen fires—a task which only the fittest among the ill-nourished prisoners could undertake. Subsequently the A.I.F. forestry team combined with teams from other formations, but up to December 1942 about 2,150 tons had been cut for the A.I.F. alone. Delivery from the cutting area was partly by truck and partly by trailers pulled by teams of prisoners.[7] As the cutting areas became more remote the strain on labour for trailer parties greatly increased.

Replacement and repair of clothing soon became a problem.[8] After supplies from the Base Kit Store, to which the Japanese provided access, were exhausted, diminishing scales of clothing were laid down, and anything which a prisoner possessed above that scale was taken from him and issued to men in need. Mending of clothing and footwear was made difficult by the lack of needles and materials. Sewing machine needles were manufactured in the camp and a machine for making sewing cotton from canvas and other fabrics was devised.

---

[6] There were six principal areas at this stage: the A.I.F.; 18th Division; 11th Division; Southern Area, Temple Hill, and the Hospital area.

[7] These trailers, consisting of motor vehicle chassis, stripped of engine and bodywork, on which a flat platform was built, were a feature of prison life. For the most part they were heavy and cumbersome and were manhandled by teams of prisoners pulling on traces. They were used for the transport of food, fuel and the sick, and in the absence of other means of transport filled a great need.

[8] One battalion commander wrote that on his first battalion parade in Changi "there were two men in Scotch kilts, one in a top hat, another in a lady's white satin cocktail hat, a few in white tennis trousers, and many in tam-o'-shanters".

In the conditions then prevailing flies—fed by corpses, offal, rotting garbage and unprotected latrines—bred in thousands, and outbreaks of diarrhoea and dysentery had begun within a fortnight of the arrival at Changi. The urgency of preventive measures was obvious, and soon hundreds of men were working in shifts digging latrines to a depth of 14 feet and boreholes to 12 feet. The Japanese provided timber to build fly-proof structures over the latrines, and thereafter admissions to hospital declined monthly. By August only 63 were in hospital suffering from these complaints; but in those five months between March and August, 18 had died of dysentery and a further 10 of its after effects.[9]

In May 1942 an A.I.F. Poultry Farm managed by Captain McGregor[1] was established by the headquarters of the 27th Brigade (but later transferred to the control of the A.I.F. as a whole) and the eggs were distributed under medical direction. Between 1942 and June 1945 it produced about 40,000 eggs. Other poultry were privately owned.

The main preoccupations of the prisoners were food and health, but these were not the only ones. Throughout the imprisonment at Changi, and particularly in the early stages, elaborate efforts were made to maintain and improve military efficiency, and from the beginning education and entertainment were organised.

Until April 1943 when large forces were moved out of Changi and the numbers of Australians dropped to fewer than 3,000 (and in May to fewer than 2,000) a mixed brigade was organised on paper to operate against the enemy if the opportunity arose. Many lectures on military subjects were given, classes for N.C.O's were held, drill continued.[2] Air raid precautions were organised. The general staff supervised distribution of wireless news, which was received without interruption on concealed sets.

The leaders at Changi were not long in appreciating the importance of entertainment, education and occupation in a prisoner's life.[3]

---

[9] The medical aspects of the period of captivity are dealt with in A. S. Walker, *Middle East and Far East* (1953), in the medical series of this history.

[1] Capt I. A. McGregor, QX6480; 2/26 Bn. Bank officer; of Brogo, NSW; b. Broken Hill, NSW, 13 Aug 1907.

[2] "The Command determined to maintain full military discipline and establishments, regardless of circumstances or psychology. . . . Accordingly two principles seemed to guide every decision. One, to retain full divisional and regimental staffs pottering round achieving nothing useful at all in divisional and regimental offices; two, to preserve the officers-other rank distinction by as many tactless and unnecessary orders as could be devised. . . . These orders were inspired by a sincere conviction at top level that it was absolutely necessary in the cause of an imminent invasion, which in fact never came, to preserve class distinction by privileges not based upon responsibility."—R. Braddon, *Naked Island*, p. 154 (Braddon was a gunner in the 2/15th Field Regiment).

The introduction of lectures and drill was not entirely welcomed, however, even by the officers upon whom it supposedly conferred privileges. "Our peace was shattered," wrote one young British subaltern, "by a foul series of lectures . . . including three-quarters of an hour's drill before breakfast every day for a fortnight! The troops were as amused and incredulous as we were indignant . . . the basic reason for the anger of . . . nearly all the junior officers was due to the fact that . . . our lecturers, in spite of . . . Spitfires and Churchill tanks, still seemed to prefer to meander back to the plains of Salisbury before such nasty modern things were invented."—J. Coast, *Railroad of Death*, pp. 53-4.

Later, drill was cut to a minimum because of the wear on boots and the inability to replace or repair them.

[3] "So much was bizarre, fearful and uncomfortable by necessity that for intellectual escape—the only variety that was available in Changi—the prisoner strove to attain the virtues of everyday living. Each man created for himself a microcosm into which he could crawl: flowers, hobbies, poultry, painting, writing, what you will. And the most contented prisoner was he who could build the most perfect microcosm and disappear most effectively within it."—David Griffin in *Meanjin*, Autumn 1954.

A comprehensive education scheme was drawn up under the guidance of Brigadier Taylor, with Captain Curlewis as assistant and vocational adviser, and by 1st March three departments—Agriculture, Business Training and General Education—of what came to be known as the "Changi University" were functioning. Other departments or faculties, such as Languages, Engineering, Law, Medicine and Science soon followed. Some of the departments were allied with the immediate needs of the prisoners in Changi. For example, the agricultural classes under Major Maxwell naturally worked hand in hand with the A.I.F. gardening scheme, and of the 1,000 men employed daily in the gardens from 600 to 700 were anxious to continue farming after the war, or sought agricultural training. The enrolment of students for business principles totalled 1,900, with 80 to 90 instructors; there were 870 shorthand pupils, with 20 teachers. For "general or primary education" there were about 2,300 enrolments and 120 teachers. This was the largest of the educational departments, providing elementary instruction in English, arithmetic and geography. Language classes also were included in the sphere of general education, and about 30 qualified instructors were found for some 650 students interested in learning French, Malay, German, Dutch, Spanish or Italian.

The engineering department, like the agricultural, was of practical value to the whole of Changi once it was under way. Of less immediate value was the Legal Department, in which 140 students were enrolled and about 15 lecturers and tutors enlisted. Medicine and Science were coupled in one department, but were studied in two classes. Though small in numbers, both classes flourished, and a course in medicine was given for students who had been in the midst of their studies when war broke out.

A diversity of subjects came under the heading of "Miscellaneous". Classes were held in Commercial Art and Art under the tutelage of the Australian war artist Murray Griffin;[4] a play-reading group was formed, debating societies and groups held regular meetings within units, and bi-weekly educational talks and general lectures covered a wide variety of subjects. Perhaps most popular of all groups or classes was the "Department of Social Studies" consisting of sixteen groups of twelve members, each of whom was required to possess either a practical or academic interest in the principles of economics and contemporary history. The first year in Changi was, in fact, an "era of lectures and clubs".

Nightly the various halls and open air assembly points were thronged with expectant audiences, the more earnest equipped with paper and pencil to note an arresting dictum on political economy or on the prevalence of lice in poultry. The Clubs met with the zeal of revolutionaries. At the "Yachtsmans" the wind howled through a totally absent rigging while the members made a post-war tour along the waterways of France and Germany. Elsewhere the "Sussex Yokels" met in a tavern thickening hourly with reminiscence and dialect. . . .

A body was formed under the ambitious title of "The Social Reconstruction Group". At a formal meeting held on the lawn beneath casuarina trees a panel of

---

[4] V. M. Griffin. Artist; of Melbourne; b. Malvern, Vic, 11 Nov 1903.

chairmen was elected and a comprehensive agenda drawn up. While the general tendency of its policy wavered towards the Left, a strong bracing by the Right curbed the theoretical enthusiasm of the more radical reformers. Meetings were called for each Tuesday night on a grassy slope still singed from the blast of bombs. Guest speakers were invited to address the group and launch the meeting into lively debate.[5]

The comprehensive education scheme initiated in February had to be abandoned when the departure of working parties reduced the number of men in Changi, and depleted the teaching staffs. Thereafter education was supervised by an Education Centre controlled by Captain Greener.[6] Lectures and classes on a wide range of subjects were organised and a library was maintained.

The Australian Concert Party, at first directed by Lieutenant Mack[7] and later (from September 1943) by Acting Staff Sergeant Wood,[8] won a reputation for the originality and excellence of its entertainment. A large garage was converted into a concert hall, and the concert party staged increasingly-elaborate plays, variety shows, and concerts, using scenery, costumes, and musical instruments made in Changi. Much of the script and music was written in the camp, and many of the musical and straight plays were entirely original in concept and production. In addition to local performances the concert party staged entertainment in the areas of other formations. Recordings for broadcast were made at the invitation of the Japanese thrice between 18th October 1943 and January 1944. On each of these occasions the programs drawn up by the Australians for broadcast included the names of as many prisoners as possible, and attempts were made to include, in disguised form, information about diet and organisation.

A variety of games also was played until the prisoners became so weak because of deficiencies in diet that outdoor sport was forbidden for their sake and because medical supplies and anaesthetics upon which football injuries particularly made many demands, had to be conserved.

Dietary deficiencies led to the appointment soon after arrival in Changi of Captain Bennett[9] of the Australian Army Service Corps as director of fishing for the A.I.F. A group of experienced fishermen were enlisted, traps were built of improvised materials, and some hooks and lines obtained. At first the yields were good, but constant damage to traps, and poaching by Malays caused catches to dwindle until, in August, the experiment was abandoned. In the six months 1,693 pounds of fish were obtained, all of which was sent to the hospital.

---

[5] David Griffin, in *Meanjin*, Autumn 1954.

[6] Capt H. L. Greener, NX15946; HQ 8 Aust Div. Journalist; of Sydney; b. Capetown, South Africa, 13 Feb 1900.

[7] Capt V. Mack, QX17732; 2/10 Fd Regt; AGB Depot, Singapore. Regular soldier; of Moonee Ponds, Vic; b. Heywood, Vic, 16 Jul 1896.

[8] Cpl J. Wood, NX65819; 8 Div Sigs. Actor; of Neutral Bay, NSW; b. Forbes, NSW, 11 Nov 1909. Wood was receiving a corporal's pay. Although the office of the Military Secretary allowed liberal promotions in excess of unit war establishments up to the time of the capitulation, none of the acting promotions, so far as is known, made after that time were recognised after release.

[9] Capt J. W. Bennett, NX19301; AASC 8 Div. Accountant; of Bexley, NSW; b. Millthorpe, NSW, 4 Sep 1906.

Perhaps no other activity in Changi or elsewhere was subject to so wide a diversity of opinion as the "Black Market". The official view may perhaps best be indicated by quoting the words of the official report of the A.I.F. in Changi:

> Check and detection of operators [on the Black Market] was undertaken by the "G" Staff, particularly in those cases where trading in drugs was involved. Some convictions were obtained on the evidence thus gathered, but the activities had the effect of lessening considerably the black market operations. Right from the start of our PW life, the question of black market was regarded as serious, involving as it did the creation of a market for stolen goods, the disposal of valuable drugs, the raising of prices of foodstuffs for canteen purchase, and the security angle of illegal contacts.

No doubt, taken from a severely official point of view all this was so. Certainly where such trading encouraged the theft of blankets and clothing which could ill be spared it was a bad thing; and the theft of precious drugs was criminal. Although the operators of the black market sometimes charged prices for goods that bordered on extortion, the prisoners who accepted the goods obtained them without risk while the operator went at first in fear of his life. When the Changi area was wired the Japanese announced that any prisoner found outside the wire would be shot. However, when it was found that the threatened shootings did not take place the number of traders increased, and from their activities, particularly before the canteens were established, flowed a regular supply of food. A minority of such men both at Changi and elsewhere used their accumulated funds for liquor or gross feeding at canteens, or lent money to the desperately ill at extortionate rates of repayment. But the majority with money obtained in this way gave generously to the sick and not a few risked their lives to provide food which saved many.

As in most communities there were men who sought to make profit out of the circumstances in which they and their fellows were placed, and lent money at such high rates of interest, or set so low a rate for Japanese dollars in exchange for the pound sterling that it amounted to usury.[1]

> It is known (said a camp order of 24th July 1943) that persons are lending money in the Japanese dollar currency upon the security of promissory notes, cheques and other negotiable instruments expressed in sterling currency, and that the rate of exchange is often as low as $2.00 to the £1 sterling or its equivalent.

Prices of canteen commodities had jumped to an extraordinary degree and cigarette tobacco at this stage cost 150 to 160 dollars a pound. Thus on the rate of exchange quoted above one pound of tobacco would cost in terms of sterling currency £75.

> There can be no moral justification for charging such a harsh and unconscionable rate (continued the camp order) and those doing so are exploiting for their own profit the needs of their fellow-prisoners due to sickness or misfortune.

---

[1] The Australian headquarters had attempted in 1942 to stamp out the black market by gaining control of all moneys; a camp-wide canvass was made to have all moneys deposited and credited to paybooks. It was intended to use the money thus pooled for collective buying, and issue on a common basis. The canvass was only partially successful and, in fact, lacked the support of some senior Australian officers.

No attempt was made by the camp administration to suppress lending of money at reasonable rates; indeed it would have been undesirable if not impossible to do so. Nevertheless a rate of exchange was fixed and money-lenders were forbidden to accept any negotiable security, promissory note or cheque at a rate of exchange less than 8 dollars local Japanese currency to £1 sterling.

Within a week of their arrival in Changi the Japanese had begun to appreciate the value of the enormous labour potential that had fallen into their hands, and work parties were being formed for tasks in damaged Singapore, on the wharves and godowns of Keppel Harbour, and elsewhere on Singapore Island and the mainland. The first work party, 750 strong, left Changi on 22nd February. By 4th April 5,000 were employed outside Changi; by 16th April, 6,000; and by 5th May, 8,200. The working parties were popular because they freed the prisoners from some of the restrictions imposed in Changi and because men received 4 ounces of meat a day in addition to their ordinary rations. They were also able to buy extras from their canteens when in June working pay became available. Also there were opportunities outside Changi of supplementing the day-to-day rations by looting dumps and raiding godowns (practices in which the Australians rapidly became expert); and the generosity of the Chinese traders and merchants often contributed to their fare.

A variety of tasks were performed. Some parties levelled bomb shelters and filled shell craters; others worked on the wharves, unloading ships or stacking and storing food and merchandise; 2,800 were employed helping to erect a monument to the "Fallen Warriors" at Bukit Timah. Others collected scrap iron and furniture for shipment to Japan. In April a party of 46 went to Mersing to find and demolish mines laid in the area by the A.I.F. as part of the Mersing Defence Scheme. Some of the camps which sprang up at this time—River Valley Road and Sime Road, for example —became permanent areas for the accommodation of prisoners, although the personnel frequently changed; others—Blakang Mati[2] for example— became permanent in both respects. On 14th May the Australian strength at Changi was greatly decreased by the departure of the first large overseas party: "A" Force, 3,000 strong, commanded by Brigadier Varley. This was followed by the departure on 8th July of "B" Force, 1,496 strong, commanded by Colonel Walsh.[3] At this stage the strength of the local Australian work parties amounted to 8,100, and only 2,300 remained in Changi. The next overseas parties left Changi on 16th August, when a group consisting of all senior officers above the rank of lieut-colonel,

---

[2] Blakang Mati, where some 1,000 prisoners (including 600 Australians) served throughout the war, was used as a supply base for the Japanese air force, and the amount of work required of the prisoners was reflected by the activities of that force. There were several notable features about Blakang Mati: accommodation was good, rations were usually sufficient, and there were no deductions of rations for men sick or off duty. During the three and a half years of captivity only 4 men died of the 1,000 there, two of these by drowning and two after they had been evacuated to Changi.

[3] Col A. W. Walsh, OBE, VX40155; CO 2/10 Fd Regt. Regular soldier; of North Balwyn, Vic; b. Tallangatta, Vic, 6 Aug 1897.

brought up to a total of about 400 by the addition of engineers and technicians, and a working party of 1,000 were embarked at Keppel Harbour.

The Japanese sought to persuade prisoners to divulge information of military value, and on 19th February a special order of the day issued by General Yamashita was read to a party of senior officers by Colonel Sugita, who had come to Singapore from Tokyo with a group of Intelligence officers to interrogate the British prisoners. The order said in part:

> When officers or other ranks of the Imperial Japanese Army are investigating any matter, those under investigation must answer all questions put to them according to the best of their knowledge and without evasion. It must be clearly understood that there is no alternative—opposition to this demand will not be tolerated. The attitude of the Imperial Japanese Army towards British prisoners of war will depend upon the strict compliance with the above declaration.

When this order was read General Percival asked Colonel Sugita whether the Japanese subscribed to the Hague Convention on the interrogation of prisoners of war, pointing out that the British had a code of honour which he presumed would be observed by the Japanese. However, no orders were issued either by Percival or Malaya Command prohibiting prisoners from answering questions.

The interrogations of the Australians began in March. A particularly full account of the interrogation of Colonel Thyer exists. He was taken with Colonel Kent Hughes and Lieut-Colonel Stahle to a room in Changi Gaol. They were then taken individually to Sugita.

> He had before him (wrote Thyer) an Australian Army Staff List which was fortunately out of date. It did not show me as having been in Darwin as "G" to H. C. H. Robertson. If it had I should have been very much worried because they were looking for people who knew something of Darwin.

The questions were of a conventional nature. Sugita asked where the five divisions shown in the Staff List were disposed. Thyer said that the secrecy with which the Australian Army acted was as great as in the Japanese Army. Sugita asked what Thyer thought of their campaign in Malaya. Thyer said he thought it a "masterpiece". "Sugita consulted his dictionary and our association moved immediately to a higher plane," wrote Thyer. Afterwards rules were laid down for officers to observe when being interrogated. Since the Japanese had captured all British Army text books, it would be in order to tell them anything that had appeared in a text book, but the answer was to be garbled. So far as Australian defence preparations and the movement overseas of the A.I.F. were concerned, officers should plead ignorance, using the plea of secrecy. The senior officers agreed that adherence to the traditional attitude of restricting information to personal details might spell disaster. At this time a stream of officers was moving to and from Changi Gaol where they were set to writing essays on military subjects. At length Sugita sent for Thyer again and ordered him to explain how the army was disposed for the defence of Australia. Thyer said he could not possibly answer the question, whereupon Sugita altered the question to "How would you use the five divisions to defend Australia?" He was then taken to a warder's cottage where he met Kent Hughes and Stahle. There he learnt that Kent Hughes had been ordered to write a paper on "Administration in a Division"; and Stahle on "Ordnance Administration in a Division". Although the questions asked of Kent Hughes and Stahle were of an innocuous nature, all took the view that to answer would be traitorous. A message setting out the stand they were taking and asking for a direction was sent by Thyer to Percival, but when, two days later, no reply had been received, the Australians drafted letters to Sugita, telling him their reasons for non-compliance. On 21st March Sugita arrived to interview the three Australians. The atmosphere was tense. A copy of Yamashita's order was produced and a somewhat involved discussion, through the interpreter,[4] followed on the ethics of giving orders to prisoners and of prisoners obeying them in certain circumstances. At length a compromise was reached and again through the interpreter Sugita was given the Australian answer: "As Colonel Sugita has given an order we cannot and do not expect him as a soldier to withdraw it. We will obey that order as soldiers and would ask of him that he will not issue any orders, obedience to which would make us traitors to our country. Under such conditions we should have to refuse to obey his orders which we do not wish to do."

On the following day a paper was drafted jointly by the Australians.

We had great fun concocting it (wrote Kent Hughes afterwards). I wrote the first two pages which were an illuminating discourse on the climate and topography of Australia, and how droughts and heavy rains at any old time made it impossible to station troops anywhere with any certainty that they would stay there.

After the paper had been completed the Australians were allowed to leave.

Not all the interviews that took place during this period were concerned with matters of principle or conducted in so tense an atmosphere. One interview which took place in July 1942 between the A.I.F. education officer, Captain Greener, and Lieutenant Yamaguchi was in distinctly lighter vein. After a series of routine questions about Greener's enlistment and his reasons for fighting in Malaya the conversation ranged farther afield.

Yamaguchi: Is it wise, do you think, to appoint a man with only one eye [Wavell] to watch over all India?
Greener: India can be fixed firmly with the glass eye. With the other he will watch the Japanese. (*Japanese laughter.*)
Yamaguchi: Are the Australians not worried that there are so many Americans in Australia, making advances to their women while they are away at the war?
Greener: They do not seem to worry. You see, we have great confidence in our women. (*Laughter.*)

---
[4] Sugita spoke English perfectly, but preferred to conduct the interrogation through an interpreter.

Y. It is said that they are marrying many of your girls. There will be perhaps none left when you get back. Is that not bad?
G. Oh no. Those Americans will stay in Australia and we wish to increase our population.
Y. And who will your young men marry?
G. We shall send for some girls from America. It is only fair. (*Laughter*.)
Y. We are told the Americans in India have better conditions than the British, and they are stuck up.
G. People are often stuck up when they have more money.
Y. But will not such jealousy impair your war effort?
G. In the last war there was much jealousy. American and British troops used to fight in the estaminets in France. Yet we won the war together.
Y. I cannot believe there is affinity of spirit between the Allied Nations sufficient to win the war.
G. Do you believe that there is much affinity of spirit between the Germans and the Italians? (*Loud and prolonged mirth*.)[5]

The skilful parry and thrust of the conversation quite obviously appealed to the Japanese, and the interview concluded harmoniously. Greener was handed a copy of an issue of *Contemporary Japan*, a Japanese journal in English, and given the opportunity of writing a series of articles for publication abroad on life in a Japanese prison camp. Greener, a novelist and journalist, was convinced that he could let the truth be known without offending the Japanese, but A.I.F. headquarters withheld consent to his attempting the task.

Before the departure of the higher ranking officers General Percival appointed Lieut-Colonel Holmes[6] of the Manchester Regiment to command "British and Australian Troops" in Changi, and General Callaghan appointed Lieut-Colonel Galleghan to command the A.I.F. Percival appointed Galleghan also deputy commander of the combined force.[7]

From the day of surrender to the end of August 1942 the prisoners at Changi had been regarded as "captives"—not prisoners of war—by the Japanese.[8] As a result, the prisoners in Changi had seldom seen the Japanese during the first six months of imprisonment, and only those employed outside the camp on working parties came into close contact with them. During this period Colonel Sugita and his Intelligence officers controlled the inhabitants of Changi and the civilian internees in the Changi Gaol, the link between Sugita and the prisoners being Lieutenant Okazaki, the Camp Commandant. In August the camp was placed on a new footing, when Major-General Fukuye, with a large P.O.W. administration staff and numerous interpreters, arrived at Changi.

---

[5] The interview took place on 13th July 1942 and the incidents therein recorded were set down on paper by Greener immediately afterwards.

[6] Col E. B. Holmes, MC. Comd British and Australian Troops, Malaya 1942-45. Regular soldier; b. 3 Jan 1892.

[7] The staff of Headquarters AIF during all or part of the period from August 1942 to mid-1944 comprised: *AA&QMG*, Lt-Col W. W. Leggatt; *DAAG and Legal Officer*, Maj P. L. Head; *DAQMG*, Maj A. N. Thompson; *GSO2*, Maj J. W. C. Wyett and later Maj G. P. Hunt; *GSO3*, Capt F. S. B. Peach; *LO*, Capt N. G. Macaulay; *Supply and Transport*, Capt G. J. Boreham; *CRE*, Maj R. J. Bridgland; *ADMS*, Lt-Col J. Glyn White; *Staff Captains*, Captains N. P. Maddern and J. W. Bennett.

[8] It seems possible that the Japanese were unprepared for the large numbers of prisoners—their own doctrines forbade surrender—and were somewhat embarrassed by them.

The breathing space afforded by Japanese unpreparedness to cope with their prisoner-of-war problem was over, but good use of it had been made by the prisoners. Discipline had been restored, efficient sanitation established; some barracks had electric light, and tap water was becoming available in the camps. The sick were looked after in hospitals, and dental centres functioned, though with much improvisation.

The arrival of Fukuye coincided with a tightening of security, and on 30th August 1942 the Japanese announced that all prisoners should sign the following statement:

I, the undersigned, hereby solemnly swear on my honour that I will not, under any circumstances, attempt escape.

All refused to sign. On 2nd September the Japanese executed four men who had tried to escape and insisted on the senior commanders witnessing the execution. The four men executed included two Australians—Corporal Breavington[9] and Private Gale[1]—who had escaped from a camp at Bukit Timah on 12th May, obtained a small boat and rowed it about 200 miles to the island of Colomba. There in a semi-starved condition they had been rearrested, and at length returned to Singapore where Breavington was admitted to hospital suffering from malaria. At the execution ground Breavington, the older man, made an appeal to the Japanese to spare Gale. He said that he had ordered Gale to escape and that Gale had merely obeyed orders; this appeal was refused. As the Sikh firing party knelt before the doomed men, the British officers present saluted and the men returned the salute. Breavington walked to the others and shook hands with them. A Japanese lieutenant then came forward with a handkerchief and offered it to Breavington who waved it aside with a smile, and the offer was refused by all men. Breavington then called to one of the padres present and asked for a New Testament, whence he read a short passage. Thereupon the order was given by the Japanese to fire.

That day the British and Australian troops, 15,400 in all, including 1,900 Australians, had been concentrated on the Selarang Barrack Square, an area of a little more than eight acres. There were only two water taps and rations were cut to one-third. The commanders negotiated for either an amendment of the declaration or an order, not a request, that it must be signed. Finally the Japanese issued such an order and the British and Australian commanders ordered their troops to sign, explaining what had happened and pointing out that men would die of disease if resistance continued. On 5th September the Japanese allowed the prisoners to move back to their former areas. "The most notable feature of this incident was the cohesion and unity of British and Australian troops, and the fine morale and spirit shown," wrote Lieut-Colonel Galleghan.[2]

---

[9] Cpl R. E. Breavington, VX63100; AAOC. Police constable; of Fairfield, Vic; b. Southend, Essex, Eng, 14 Apr 1904. Executed by Japanese 2 Sep 1942.

[1] Pte V. L. Gale, VX62289; 2/10 Ord Workshops. Fitter and turner; of Balwyn, Vic; b. Toronto, NSW, 13 Feb 1919. Executed by Japanese 2 Sep 1942.

[2] PW Camps, Singapore; interim report by Lt-Col F. G. Galleghan.
Evidently relations between British and Australians in Changi had fallen short of cordiality. "It was not long after taking up life as a prisoner of war at Changi that I became aware of an

In October 1942 the A.I.F. gardening plan commenced under Major Maxwell gave way to a central camp garden scheme outside the perimeter of the A.I.F. area. This was supervised by the Japanese, but in fact was controlled by a prisoner-of-war group known as the "Garden Control Group" as from November, and included Australian representatives. The area of the gardens exceeded 120 acres and at times over 85 acres were under cultivation.[3] By October 1943 410,000 pounds of leaf and root vegetables had been produced and distributed as rations by the Japanese;[4] in addition within the Australian camp area, unit and group gardens continued to be maintained.

In November 1942 the smouldering resentment of the prisoners towards their Sikh guards (whom they regarded as traitors and whose demands became more and more absurd as time passed) culminated in the issue of an instruction by the Japanese to the commander of the Indian garrison at Changi on recognition of salutations made by prisoners of war. This demanded the recognition of all forms of salutations, and forbade entry of Indians into the prisoner-of-war area except on duty, and any form of retaliation by striking for failure of prisoners to salute. These orders, genuinely aimed at removing causes of trouble though they may have been, left loopholes that English-hating Sikhs were not slow to find. Hitherto drafts passing sentries had to salute with Guards-like precision otherwise the offender, escorting officer or whole draft might be beaten up. Now alleged offenders would be drilled in broken English by the Indian guard, or stood to attention for long periods. On some occasions escorting officers were made, at the bayonet point, to strike prisoners.[5]

The number of prisoners in Changi had fluctuated considerably after the departure of the senior officers' party, particularly during October and November 1942, when considerable numbers of British and Dutch prisoners were sent direct from Changi to Thailand. The destination of these "up-country parties" was kept secret. Equally large groups of prisoners, including Australians, from the Netherlands East Indies began to pass through Singapore on their way north. At the end of November a third force ("C"), 2,200 strong (including 563 Australians), was embarked from Singapore for Japan.

---

antagonism directed at everything Australian by a considerable proportion of the Englishmen with whom I came in contact," wrote an Englishman who had lived for many years in Australia and was serving in the Indian Army. This antagonism had its origins partly in faulty propaganda, but partly in the tendency of upper middle class Englishmen to place themselves on pedestals from "which they looked down with amusement on those who did not come up to their standards". G. Round, "Road from Singapore" (in manuscript at the Australian War Memorial).

[3] In October 1,000 men worked in the gardens each day. This number was increased to 1,200 in November and 1,500 in December. This strength was maintained until April, the Australians providing about 800 men a day. After April the numbers dwindled to about 170 a day, of which the AIF provided about 70.

[4] The principal crop was sweet potato, specially fertilised to give a large quantity of leaf, but tapioca, various types of spinach, beans, chillies, egg plant and taro were also grown, despite a lack of suitable manures. Harvesting commenced in March 1943, and by the middle of May ten truckloads of greens a week were being delivered, and sweet potato tubers were cropping 2½ tons an acre.

[5] A description of a clash between the prisoners and the Sikh guards at Changi, including an illuminating conversation between a British officer and the Indian guard commander is given in J. H. H. Coombes, *Bampong Express*, pp. 72-3.

During 1942 the strength of Australians at Changi had seldom exceeded the numbers employed in Singapore and elsewhere on working parties, but in December the Japanese began gradually to concentrate local working parties until by February a peak had been reached when the number of Australians in Changi itself exceeded 10,000. In January a number of senior Allied officers including General ter Poorten, Air Vice-Marshal Maltby and Brigadier Blackburn passed through Changi on the way to Formosa. The purpose of the Japanese in thus concentrating the prisoners was evidently to pool their resources of fit men, for on 5th March Lieut-Colonel Galleghan received a warning order from Malaya Command that a party of 5,000 (to be known as "D" Force), including a maximum of 50 officers, would be required to go north about 15th March. The A.I.F. quota was to be half, but was later reduced to 22 officers and 2,220 other ranks. The Japanese warned that all men would need to be fit for "heavy manual labour in malarial area" and that men who had suffered from malaria or dysentery should be excluded. This order was later amended so that any men fit to work could be included. Lieut-Colonel McEachern was selected to command the Australian part of the force which left in four flights, each of 555 officers and men, between the period 14th and 18th March.

This large force was followed before the end of March by "E" Force, 1,000 strong (including 500 Australians), destined for Borneo, and several others in swift succession. The largest of these and next to depart was "F" Force, 7,000 strong (including 3,600 Australians) which left for Thailand between 18th and 26th April; it was followed by "G" Force, 1,500 strong (including 200 Australians), which sailed for Japan on 26th April; by "H" Force, 3,000 strong (including 600 Australians) which left for Thailand in May; by "J" Force, 900 strong (including 300 Australians, mainly convalescent), which sailed for Japan on 16th May; and by two smaller parties, "K" and "L", mainly medical, which left in June and August for Thailand.

After the departure of the main parties the strength of the Australians in Changi fell to less than 2,500, and the whole camp, including the hospital, was moved to Selarang where, by May, electric light reached all buildings. Few fit men then remained in Changi, which became in fact a backwater of prisoner-of-war activity until December, when remnants of "F" and "H" Forces began to reach Singapore.

It was not until March 1943 that the Australians in Changi received their first letters from home. Six subsequent bulk deliveries were made before the end of the war. The dates of delivery and the numbers of letters received were:

1943		1944	
6 March	40,200	16 January	8,987
4 August	4,942	21 April	18,218
28 August	21,255	12 May	52,382
9 October	663		

Only a proportion of the 146,647 letters thus received at Changi was for the A.I.F. in Singapore. The remainder was sorted under the headings "casualties" and "oversea parties", readdressed, and returned to the Japanese for disposal.

The men were starved for news of home. Consequently on those rare occasions when batches of mail were received at A.I.F. headquarters, "Mail News Summaries" collating the information contained in the letters were produced and circulated. For example, in May 1944 a five-page summary was published which contained over 160 items. These items provided an interesting guide to Australian conditions: from them the prisoners learned, for example, that men's suits were being produced without trouser cuffs; that vests had only two buttons; that beer was 3/- a bottle in Queensland, but only 1/7 in Victoria; that cigarettes were 10d. a packet of 10 (both these last items were declared "hard to get at any price"); that tea, sugar, butter, clothing and petrol were rationed on a coupon system; and that it was hard to get a seat in a railway train. The scarcity of mail from home was paralleled by the limited number and size of letters a prisoner was permitted to send. Postcards were written by all prisoners on 22nd February 1943 and again on 8th December, each limited to 25 words and confined to personal messages. In November 1942 the Australian prisoners had been given the opportunity of writing short messages for broadcast by the Japanese, but this offer was refused. When in March 1943 it was repeated the Australians accepted the offer, having learnt meanwhile that no official prisoner-of-war rolls had reached Australia.[6]

It is difficult to comprehend the attitude of the Japanese towards the prisoners' mail. At the end of the war large quantities of undelivered letters were recovered in almost every area occupied by the prisoners. There is evidence, however, that the dilatoriness in delivery was not caused by a collapse in the channels of communication; for example, a message advising a soldier of his mother's death sent from Australia to Geneva, and relayed to A.I.F. headquarters, Changi, by way of the Japanese Red Cross in Tokyo, reached Changi only fifteen days after the mother had died.

The lot of the administrative staffs at Changi and elsewhere was complicated by a general shortage of paper. Hence one who delves through the records, four feet and a half high, of the headquarters of the 8th Division in captivity, is impressed by the strange assortment of salvaged paper on which the history of this period was written, and the tenacity with which it was preserved. The paper is of all shapes and sizes, ranging from scraps to large 10 by 8-inch sheets, and of all qualities from the best linen to Japanese toilet paper. Some reports were written on Japanese notepaper, others on the prison record sheets of the Changi Gaol; the A.I.F. Concert Party's first annual report was typed on the reverse side of musical score sheets.

---

[6] The problems confronted by the Australian Central Army Records Office, Melbourne, as a result of the Japanese policies towards their prisoners are set out in Appendix 6 to this volume.

The Changi area, looking south-east. Batu Puteh is in the centre foreground.

(Brig F. G. Galleghan)

The move of Australian prisoners at Changi to Selarang Barracks Square. A photograph preserved during captivity of the incident of September 1942.

(*Australian War Memorial*)

Rice distribution from the cookhouse outside Changi Gaol. Photograph taken after liberation.

(*Australian War Memorial*)

A hut of the 50-metre type, used by the Japanese at Changi to accommodate about 250 prisoners.

One of the offshoots of Changi was the Broom Factory. Before the end of 1942 the brooms and brushes at Selarang had worn out, and in November the "R.A.A. Broom Factory" began production with the object of supplying the needs of several large barracks buildings occupied by the three Australian artillery regiments—2/10th and 2/15th Field, and 2/4th Anti-Tank Regiments.

Broom heads were made from the doors of barracks buildings in the Selarang area, which rapidly became doorless; bass brooms, suitable for outdoor work, were made of split bamboo; the centre rib of the coconut palm leaf was used in brooms of the millet type. As the supply of mature bamboo became exhausted, palm leaf ribs were used for all hard brooms, and the tips of the ribs were made into scrubbing brushes. Soft brooms were made of beaten-out coconut fibre; squeegees from old truck tubes.

The program increased month by month as other units called on the factory to supply their needs; materials became harder to get. "Authority," remarks the diarist of the broom makers, "though very pleased to get brooms was not very keen on providing the necessary men and materials," so barter was resorted to. The Detention Barracks, never short of labour to strip the palm fronds, offered to supply large quantities if the factory would keep them in brooms, and this scheme worked admirably.

Various side-lines to the broom factory were developed: chalk was made by precipitation of white clay; glue was manufactured from fish scales; rustless darning needles from hard copper wire. In fact no limit seemed to be placed on the ingenuity of the factory. Toothbrushes were reconditioned; fashionable bosoms made from coconut shells were provided for the female impersonators in the A.I.F. Concert Party; a species of ornamental aloe provided a fibre suitable for soft shaving brushes. After the move to the Changi Gaol the British Brush Factory and the R.A.A. Broom Factory were merged, and became known as the Changi Broom Factory.[7] In the period between October 1942 and November 1944 the Australians produced 1,859 brooms, 202 squeegees, and 706 scrubbing brushes, and thus in no small way contributed to the standard of hygiene in Changi.

There were no major changes in the ration scales at Changi during 1943, but in February a reduction of rice to 15 ounces was ordered, and separate scales for outside workers and camp administrative personnel were introduced by the Japanese. There were, however, several alterations in the type of ration. In September dried fish replaced fresh fish, and later in the year dizu and soya beans, and maize, were at times substituted for part of the rice ration. Rice polishings were issued for a short period in May. Although the official scale remained substantially unaltered short weights were delivered and the prisoners could not remedy the deficiencies. Avitaminosis, of which eye lesions were a principal symptom, was being suffered by 1,000 in February 1943, but ceased to increase in August

---

[7] The Australians permanently employed in the factory were Bdr F. C. Roche, Gnrs A. Baldwin and D. Reisir (2/10 Fd Regt); Gnr A. T. Groves (2/4 A-Tk Regt); and Gnrs J. Woodford and J. Cracknell (2/15 Fd Regt).

when some "Marmite" was received for the worst cases.[8] Malaria became prevalent in March, and when prisoners returned from Thailand the number of cases became so great that a special hospital was formed for them.

The employment of prisoners of war in Changi took a new turn in September when work was begun on the Changi aerodrome. To find the 800 men required daily by the Japanese demanded the employment of many unfit men and others needed for essential camp work. These were organised into parties 100 strong commanded by British and Australian officers. The hours of work in the tropical heat were long—men left camp at 8.30 a.m. and returned at 6 p.m.—and boots and clothing wore out rapidly. This work was continued by groups of varying sizes until the end of May 1945.

In November 1943 Colonel Holmes, who had long been concerned about the severity of punishment inflicted by the Japanese as a penalty for attempted escape and also about the conditions prevailing at Outram Road gaol, where prisoners were undergoing sentence, wrote a courteous and conciliatory letter of protest to the Japanese commander at Changi. He asked that his submission be brought before the notice of General Arimura, who had taken over from General Fukuye, and sought permission for a visit to the gaol of an International Red Cross representative. Holmes and Galleghan presented this to Captain Tazumi, who said that he realised that treatment was not good, but doubted whether even Arimura had the power to intercede officially. At length Holmes was ordered to report alone to the Conference House, where he was addressed by Captain Tazumi in the presence of General Arimura's adjutant. Tazumi declared that, although Japan was a signatory to the 1907 convention, it was also provided therein that prisoners must obey their captors, and that as prisoners they had no rights to protest on any matter. He read extracts from Japanese law to the effect that any Japanese soldiers taken prisoner would be shot on return to Japan. Holmes was instructed that he was no longer to sign letters as Commander, British and Australian troops, but as "Senior Officer, No. 1 PW Camp Changi", and, as punishment, to go each day for a fortnight to the ground levelling party.[9]

In the opinion of the 8th Division's diarist, news bulletins, illicit and prepared and circulated at great risk, ranked in importance second only to food in the prisoners' lives. At the outset the Japanese had issued occasional copies of the *Nippon Times* and made a regular distribution

---

[8] On 11th July 1943 at Changi a circular to all units warned that the Yeast Centre would no longer be able to produce sufficient concentrated extract to make a prophylactic issue, and advised the preparation of a grass soup to help prevent eye trouble. After detailing the method to be used in its preparation, the circular added: "Any type of grass is satisfactory except lalang, and even the latter is suitable if young. Blue couch grass is one of the best." The ingredients were four pounds of grass, cut finely, washed, boiled for ten minutes, allowed to stand for four hours, and flavoured with extract of lemon, if available.

[9] The conditions at Outram Road gaol persisted despite Holmes' protests, and in October 1944 seven Australians were returned to Changi hospital in a condition showing signs of such gross neglect that Galleghan felt compelled again to protest. Of the seven men, two died, all were seriously ill, some dangerously. Two had lost the power of speech, another's sight was failing, yet another was so emaciated that he weighed only 90 pounds. All were incapable of walking, and most were incapable of standing even when supported by two assistants.

of limited numbers of the *Syonan Simbun* (Singapore Times). Both papers were printed in English; both were frankly propagandist in outlook. When this distribution ceased the camp was dependent on news supplied by individuals operating wireless sets, but this, circulated by word of mouth, was in the long run hardly more dependable than the Japanese newspapers mentioned above. In July 1942 Major Bosley,[10] seized by the troops' need of a reliable news service, undertook the production of a daily bulletin which later came to be recognised as the official news bulletin of the A.I.F.[1]

In 1942 the bulletins had seldom exceeded a page and a half of longhand, but in 1943 their length began to increase until each bulletin exceeded seven sheets and two shorthand typists were employed in their production. In April the bulletin was taken over by the Camp Administration and became the official news publication for the whole of Changi. In December the issue of the printed bulletin ceased and the news was issued verbally to representatives of the A.I.F. and other groups in Changi separately. This procedure continued until April 1944, when "a change in policy" caused the cessation of the news bulletin which, in the words of its progenitor, Major Bosley, "had been published and promulgated every day" since its official commencement in 1942.[2]

The change of policy referred to resulted from the concentration of the prisoners on Singapore Island within the Changi Gaol area. Nevertheless, despite the increasing difficulties, a small band of prisoners, including Signalman Sim,[3] Private Wall[4] and Private Taprell[5] of the A.I.F. and Private Thompson of the Volunteers, continued to maintain and operate a receiving set even within the confines of the gaol, and did so until April 1945 when, on the orders of Colonel Galleghan, the receiver

---

[10] Maj W. A. Bosley, MBE, ED, NX71075; Aust Gen Base Depot 8 Div. Commercial buyer; of Pymble, NSW; b. Marrickville, NSW, 10 Mar 1910.

[1] Maintenance of radio sets presented a distinct problem. All radio equipment, including spare parts, in the AIF area, was collected and placed in charge of L-Sgt G. F. Noakes (of Maxwelton, Qld, and Haberfield, NSW) and Sig N. J. Arthur (Fairfield, NSW). As time passed, however, the difficulties of finding serviceable replacements among the stocks in hand increased substantially. An added drain on replacements was caused by a decision to provide up-country and overseas working parties with the means of keeping in touch with the outside world. As a result of this decision "D", "E", "F" and "H" Forces were all issued with complete receiving equipments, or the means of making them. In addition a 15-watt transmitter was built and held against the contingency of it being required by Colonel Galleghan; a 100-watt transmitter was constructed and taken by "F" Force. In the later months of 1942 one transmitter was operated from the central gun emplacement of the Johore heavy battery by Cpl S. K. Elliman (of Claremont, WA) and messages reporting Japanese shipping movements were acknowledged by a station in India.

[2] In March 1944 preparations were made for the periodic transfer of the operating receiver for security reasons. On the night 1st-2nd April the Japanese carried out an abortive search of premises whence the operating receiver had just been removed. The possibility of leakage of information from within the ranks caused Galleghan to order a complete change of all places of concealment. Receivers in use were dismantled and repacked and less serviceable items disposed of. A complete equipment which had been built against the needs of working parties was transferred to the officers' area and operated from 15th November 1944 by Lt R. F. Wright (of Hawthorn, Vic), who supplied news directly to Colonel Galleghan and the officers' area organisation at Changi Gaol.

[3] Sig S. Sim, BEM, NX71306; 8 Div Sigs. Radio mechanic; of Canterbury, NSW; b. Redfern, NSW, 24 May 1920.

[4] Pte D. Wall, NX36620; 2/20 Bn. Commission agent; of Narrandera, NSW; b. Bombala, NSW, 17 Jan 1920.

[5] Pte R. M. J. Taprell, NX10970; 2/20 Bn. Labourer; of Neutral Bay, NSW; b. Darlington Point, NSW, 19 Nov 1917.

was handed to the camp quartermaster.[6] A second receiver was then constructed and thereafter the news was passed verbally to Australian prisoners in the gaol. In the final stages of captivity "flashes" and Australian news items generally were passed to the officers' area organisation for inclusion in their news bulletin.

The move to the Changi Gaol area followed the replacement in March 1944 of Arimura by General Saito as commander of the prisoners in Malaya and Sumatra. The prisoners in the Selarang area (including "F" Force which had by then returned to Changi) were ordered next month to Changi Gaol to make way for Japanese air force units then arriving at the Changi airfield.[7] The move to the gaol—a major feat in the circumstances—was accomplished in May. Only three lorries were allowed as transport, all other haulage being trailers of the type mentioned earlier. The camp was laid out into four main accommodation areas: the gaol building, a hospital, an officers' area, and an other ranks' area comprising 100-metre atap huts outside the gaol wall. The overcrowding was appalling. Into the gaol building itself, designed to accommodate some 600 Asian and 50 European prisoners, were placed some 5,000 prisoners of war. Cells built to house one Asian criminal contained three, frequently four, prisoners, while four senior officers and two batmen lived in an Asian prison warder's family quarters. When the men from Sime Road camp—where most of "H" Force was accommodated after its return from Thailand—and from other smaller camps had returned to Changi there were in the gaol area 11,700 prisoners. This figure included about 5,400 British and 5,000 Australian prisoners of war. The remainder were made up of twelve other nationalities including 1,100 Dutchmen, 50 Americans, and 19 Italian officers and men from Italian submarines. The gaol hospital and the main Selarang hospital installations with about 1,000 patients were moved to Kranji, which then became the principal hospital area for prisoners on the island.

Colonel Holmes had fallen into disfavour with the Japanese since the episode culminating in his relegation to the ground levelling party (as it was euphemistically termed) and in July 1944, without consulting Holmes, the Japanese appointed a new representative officer for the other ranks' camp. Holmes and his deputy, Galleghan (hitherto representative officer) were to take no further part in the camp organisation and administration. This action coincided with large reductions in the numbers of officers permitted by the Japanese to be employed with the troops, and by September the assumption of command of troops by warrant officers; only a few technical officers were allowed to remain for essential light, water and garden services.

---

[6] The set was built in the main from one stolen from a Japanese house in the vicinity of the gaol by Sig Sim in June 1944, and completed from four other sets and parts removed from a Japanese wireless store at Selarang and brought back to camp at considerable personal risk by Sim, Spr P. J. Matthews (of Melbourne) and Gnr W. S. Beadman (of Blackheath, NSW) of the 2/15th Field Regiment.

[7] The civilian internees hitherto occupying the gaol were transferred to the Sime Road camp.
Two noteworthy changes which took place at this time were the introduction in April of Japanese words of command, and the restitution of badges of rank to officers.

A new and difficult era now dawned in the administration of the A.I.F. in Changi. The extent of Lieut-Colonel Galleghan's control over his officers and men was greatly restricted, despite his protests. In addition the Japanese imposed severe restrictions on camp entertainment and lectures. Audiences at lectures were not permitted to exceed 25 in number; and all theatrettes outside the gaol were closed. The gaol theatre equipped with an orchestral pit and wings, curtains and other appliances, was limited to two performances a week, the Japanese declaring that the prisoners were getting far more entertainment than their captors.

On 5th November 1944 about 40 American aircraft raided Singapore; this was followed by a similar raid on 1st January. Thereafter the appearance of Allied aircraft became more frequent until, by July 1945, it had become a daily occurrence.

A most unhappy period in the administration of Changi ended in July 1945 when Lieut-Colonel Dillon[8] was appointed Representative Officer. The A.I.F. then reverted to regular administration of punishments by their own officers; one district court martial was held despite Japanese orders to the contrary.

Meanwhile in March the A.I.F. Concert Party had been disbanded. The Japanese claimed that an item in a current show had offended them, and in consequence General Saito had ordered that the play cease and the theatre be demolished. It was a peculiar ending to a long and valuable history of entertainment; all scripts of entertainments had been submitted to the Camp Office and to Japanese representatives before presentation. It was a blow to the men who had worked together for three years in the party to find themselves being returned to units that they no longer considered their homes.

In March 1945 also the Japanese, who were issuing half rations for the sick, three-quarter rations for semi-sick, and full rations for the fit, cut the rations by roughly 25 per cent, and forbade any pooling of rations. The cut was extremely severe. Thenceforward the prisoners were receiving a daily ration of less than 8 ounces of rice, 4 to 6 ounces of vegetables, and practically nothing else; because of inflation the prisoners' pay was almost valueless.[9] "In common with everyone else, am terribly hungry," commented one prisoner; "am unable to go to sleep at night, for my stomach is empty and feels that it is touching my backbone."[1] That month a Red Cross ship arrived with 1,200 tons of stores, and in April the Japanese began small twice-weekly issues which although not substantial were "wonderfully welcome".[2] The dollar had now lost its purchasing power to the extent that even a relatively well-paid officer—an Australian major for example—was not a great deal better off than a private soldier. At this stage, out of his monthly pay of 170 dollars the Japanese deducted

---

[8] Brig F. J. Dillon, OBE, MC; RIASC. Regular soldier; b. 19 Oct 1898.
[9] Maize flour 8 dollars a pound; sugar 12 dollars.
[1] In April the ration was assessed at from 200 to 700 calories below the basic metabolic standard.
[2] The rations continued to be supplemented in this way for about eleven weeks. The work of the Red Cross in this period is described in A. S. Walker, *Middle East and Far East*, in the medical series of this history.

60 dollars for board and lodging and held 60 in credit, leaving a balance of 50 dollars. The disbursement of this balance was: Camp Maintenance Fund (used to supplement the rations of other ranks), 20 dollars; officers' mess contribution, 9 dollars; unit hospital fund (perhaps), 2 dollars; balance 19 dollars, or enough in fact to buy about a pound of sugar and perhaps a pound of peanuts (if available) at the then ruling rates.[3]

The supply of firewood, always a large problem to the undernourished prisoners, was accentuated in 1944 and in the last twelve months the supply of even the barest minimum was difficult. In August 1945 the Japanese commenced the issue of an oil fuel which obviated an immense amount of labour. So intricate, however, was the prison camp economy that the cessation of the wood supply set up a train of deficiencies: the manufacture of milk of magnesia, dependent on the supply of wood ash, had to be suspended, and the production of tooth powder similarly fell away.

Despite the deterioration in health of the prisoners, the Japanese early in 1945 demanded work parties totalling nearly 6,000 for work around Singapore Island and Johore Bahru. These parties were employed in digging tunnels and defence works. Although they were usually well accommodated and on better rations, the long hours they were compelled to work, the distance of camps from work, and the type of labour all taxed the strength of undernourished men severely. In May work on the aerodrome ceased and fit men from there became available for the working parties. Many were injured by falls of earth during tunnelling, and one death occurred. Towards the end a number of prisoners were wounded during the increasingly severe Allied air raids.

The second largest concentration and transit area for Australian prisoners in 1942 and 1943 was Java where about 3,000 Australians remained after the capitulation of 9th March 1942. Some men remained at large for many months seeking to escape, but many, probably the majority of those who followed the ordinary pattern of surrender, were concentrated in an area to the south-east of Bandung, round the villages of Garut and Leles, and other centres near places of capture. Most of them for a time were allowed much freedom by Japanese pre-occupied with the task of taking over Java. They were free to visit shops and coffee houses in near-by villages, and generally enjoyed what one of them described as an "idyllic existence" in "pleasant surroundings". No rations were provided by the Japanese, but this created no special hardship. A small amount of transport was retained. The prisoners were invited to write letters home without limit as to length. None of these seems to have reached its destination, and the invitation was probably intended by the Japanese merely to provide them with information. An Allied General Hospital in Bandung, formed by members of the 2/2nd Australian C.C.S., and an R.A.F. hospital

---

[3] At that stage almost every delivery of foodstuffs to the canteens was so meagre that it was necessary to hold a ballot and then sell on a roster basis. In June the price of a duck egg was 8 dollars; of a laying fowl 95 dollars.

unit, continued to function until 18th April. The sick were carried there daily by ambulances, which brought back convalescents to camp. Then, at a few hours' notice, the hospital was disbanded, and the staff and most of the patients were marched to an overcrowded native gaol, where "medical arrangements were negligible, rations deplorable, and no recognition was given to medical prisoners".

Late in March advanced parties from Leles (where many of the Australians were concentrated) were sent to Batavia to prepare a camp for the remainder of the prisoners. Instead of being put to the task they were placed in a congested Chinese school, with British and American troops, and did not rejoin their comrades until May. Between 30th March and 14th April most of the Australians in the Leles area were taken by rail to Koenigplein, a suburb of Batavia, where they were billeted in a Dutch barracks—the Bicycle Camp as it was commonly known—which was to be their home for the next six months.

There were at that time at the Bicycle Camp survivors of the *Houston,* about 250 of the battalion of the 15th Punjab Regiment which had fought in Borneo, some British and Dutch troops, and 300 survivors of H.M.A.S. *Perth.* The latter had begun prisoner-of-war life "quite naked". Many had been rescued by a Japanese destroyer after immersion in oil-covered water for between 7 and 15 hours and their clothing had been immediately jettisoned. They had been lodged for some six weeks at Serang in a native theatre or at the local gaol, where lack of food and adequate sanitation had brought a wave of dysentery. At first the Japanese enforced strict discipline, with rifle butts or sticks, and warned the prisoners that any attempt to escape would result in death to all; later they had relaxed and, becoming more friendly, organised daily bathing parties to a near-by canal. "Recreation" at Serang took the form of compulsory physical training—a hardship for men whose physical condition at that time was far below normal. Before their departure for the Bicycle Camp on 13th April they were issued with shorts and shirts, but remained bare-footed. They were commanded by Lieut-Commander Lowe.[4]

After the transfer of the larger group of Australians to the Bicycle Camp, there remained some 600 Australians, mainly of the 2/3rd Machine Gun Battalion, in the Garut area who continued an easy-going existence until June, when they were transferred to Bandung. There they were billeted in the former barracks of a Dutch regiment, which became known as No. 12 PW Camp, Bandung, and joined members of the 2/2nd C.C.S. commanded by Lieut-Colonel Dunlop,[5] and a number of Australians who had remained at large after the general surrender.

Most of the latter had been taken to Sukabumi after capture, and placed in a concentration camp with Indonesians and others. Their hair was close cropped (this became general in Java) and drill orders and

---

[4] Capt R. F. M. Lowe, DSC; RAN. HMAS *Perth* 1941-1942. Of Castlemaine, Vic; b. Clifton Hill, Vic, 30 Aug 1907.

[5] Col E. E. Dunlop, OBE, VX259. Med Liaison Offr, Brit Tps Greece and Crete 1941; 2/2 CCS; CO No. 1 Allied Gen Hosp Java 1942. Surgeon; of Melbourne; b. Benalla, Vic, 12 Jul 1907.

numbering were given in Japanese. The rations at Sukabumi consisted of half-cooked rice and "shadow" soup. Discipline was extremely harsh, there were many pinpricking regulations, and the prisoners were required to fill in questionnaires. Sports competitions had been held by the Japanese between the British prisoners and the native internees and prisoners of war, of whom there were many. In June and July parties were moved from Sukabumi to Tjimahi, about 6 miles west of Bandung, where for a time they were billeted in a Dutch army barracks. The camp was administered by the Dutch under Japanese supervision; sanitary arrangements were good, food was ample, and there was a canteen where tea, sugar and bread could be purchased. In mid-June the transfer of all British troops to Bandung began.

With the arrival of the prisoners from Garut the camp at Bandung was reorganised. Lieut-Colonel Lyneham of the 2/3rd Machine Gun Battalion took over command of the Australians. The camp at this stage possessed poor conveniences: there was a shortage of water, sanitary arrangements were crude, and the camp generally was in a filthy condition. The food ration, of rice and dried potatoes with some green vegetables and a small quantity of meat, was deficient in protein, fats and vitamins.

At the Bicycle Camp conditions were "not bad" from the point of view of the prisoners from Leles; in the eyes of the prisoners from Serang they were "excellent". Accommodation consisted of large brick barrack huts, each holding about 300 men. Water and electricity were laid on; kitchens were well equipped; sanitation was adequate; a good canteen was set up; and secret wirelesses brought news of the outside world. On 14th May all British and Dutch troops were moved elsewhere, and their places taken by Australians from Glodok gaol and the Chinese school (including the advanced party from Leles) and Americans of the 131st Field Artillery Regiment. The numbers held at the Bicycle Camp remained constant thereafter until 4th August, when 20 officers and 20 N.C.O's under command of Lieut-Colonel Leggatt arrived from Timor. In this period the senior officer was Brigadier Blackburn, with a camp staff which included as second-in-command Colonel Searle (U.S. Army), and Wing Commander Davis[6] (R.A.A.F.) as camp administrative officer. The Australians occupied huts on one side of a central camp road; the Americans the huts on the other side. One corner of the camp was fenced off with barbed wire, and contained Major-General Sitwell, Air Vice-Marshal Maltby, and many other senior officers of the British and Dutch Services, including the Governor-General of the Netherlands. In this period rations were poor; only rice, and a small quantity of green vegetables in a thin stew "barely flavoured with pork".

At the Bicycle Camp as elsewhere working parties were sent out and all manner of tasks performed by the prisoners, from filling ditches or rolling steel drums from A to B, to sorting out spare parts for motors. These working parties seem to have been welcomed by the prisoners at

---

[6] Gp Capt R. H. Davis, OBE. Comd No. 1 Sqn RAAF 1941-42. Regular airman; of Archerfield, Qld; b. Sydney, 8 Apr 1912.

the outset for the opportunities they afforded both of escape from the monotony of camp routine, and for bringing articles of value and food into the camp. Lectures and classes were organised on a wide variety of subjects, each one conducted by an expert in his own particular field. A large building was used as a theatre.

In May and June a number of officers were taken away from the camp for questioning by the Japanese. Some were brutally treated and tortured when they refused to divulge information on matters of military importance. One officer who was interrogated at this time recalled that for a month he spent his nights at the gaol and daylight hours at the headquarters of the *Kempei Tai* undergoing questioning. No food was given to him for five days. At the end of that time it was placed before him on a table; he was informed that if he answered the questions put to him the food would be his. At other times

> I was tied to a chair and they kicked it . . . and pushed it round the room. Sometimes I was on the top and sometimes on the side. The ropes tightened when I was being pulled all over the place. They also made me drink water. Their idea was to fill up my lungs, but fortunately I did not get the whole of that. They also tied me to the chair and twisted my legs around. They burnt my feet with cigarette butts. At the end they took me outside, blindfolded me and told me that if I did not answer the questions they would shoot me. . . . They also promised me a house in Batavia and a servant if I would answer their questions, but they got nothing from me.[7]

Others were subjected to treatment even more brutal.

In July the prisoners were ordered to sign an undertaking to obey all orders of the Japanese and not to attempt to escape. When they refused the canteen was closed, and lectures, church services and concerts were forbidden. Communication between officers and men was prohibited and movement between huts restricted. On 4th July (ironically enough, American Independence Day, as an Australian noted) Brigadier Blackburn, the camp staff and hut commanders were placed in the Japanese guardhouse and not allowed to speak to each other. All other officers were marched out of camp. Believing that further resistance might provoke unduly harsh reprisals, Brigadier Blackburn sent a message authorising the Australians to sign the undertaking. The Americans were already doing so.

Prison life soon returned to normal except for certain lectures and classes which continued to be forbidden. Discipline, however, was noticeably tightened, and rigid orders on the payment of compliments were instigated.

> Everybody had to salute every Japanese, irrespective of rank, and the whole compound had to spring to attention, bow or salute (recalled a prisoner). We were not allowed to straighten our backs until the person taking the salute allowed us to stand at ease. . . . If a cook came through the camp we had to salute him. The whole compound bowed or stood up to him. Brigadier Blackburn and Major-General Sitwell were compelled to salute privates and Korean guards.[8]

In September news was received that a large-scale evacuation of prisoners from Java "to a better land where food would be available" and

---

[7] Lt-Col J. M. Williams, CO of the 2/2nd Pioneer Battalion.
[8] Lt-Col J. M. Williams.

prisoners "could earn money to buy extras" was planned. No clue to their destination was given.

On 1st October a small advanced party of Australians, led by Lieutenant Mitchell,[9] left Batavia; on the 7th the personal belongings of all men remaining at the Bicycle Camp were searched, and at 2 a.m. on the 8th more than half the inmates (about 1,200) led by Colonel Williams filed through the gates of the camp and were taken by rail to Tanjong Priok for embarkation on the *Kinkon Maru*. A second group of prisoners (commanded by Colonel Tharp of the 131st Field Artillery Regiment) left the Bicycle Camp on 11th October, and embarked that day on the *Nichi Maru*. The second group contained 362 Australians led by Major Robertson[1] of the 2/6th Field Company. The destination of both groups was unknown. After their departure the camp was for a time empty except for the group of senior officers.

Substantial numbers of Australians remained in Java even after October. At Bandung where there were about 700 Australians, educational classes were started, and a daily news sheet based on a Japanese paper and including camp news was produced. In July the men were paraded according to their States, and Queenslanders and Western Australians were questioned by the Japanese. A few, including Major Wearne,[2] were taken away for further interrogation. At this stage the Australians were in bad odour with the Japanese who complained about their "lack of courtesy". The Japanese "have a dead set on A.I.F.", wrote a diarist. In August meals were getting smaller, and it was all a prisoner could do to save sufficient in three days for one night supper in his room. In September there occurred an epidemic of bashing, mainly caused by prisoners who disobeyed Japanese orders forbidding smoking out of doors. Work parties went out daily, but these, involving carting wood, shifting bomb dumps, or carrying rice, were not particularly strenuous. Meals were served thrice daily, at 8 a.m.—thin rice porridge; 1 p.m.—vegetable soup (no rice); 6 p.m.—rice and soup. There was an issue of meat every second day.

In September a new camp commandant arrived, and as a result of protests bashings diminished. However, the guards seemed to be on the lookout for the least excuse, and tension in the camp was somewhat acute. Working parties went out in large numbers, and an Australian employed handling firewood complained that he "worked solidly till 4 p.m. without food or rest" and that "heavy guards gave no consideration". The civilians were not permitted to wave or smile at the prisoners and the prisoners were not allowed to look at them. "These guards (rawest of raw recruits)," noted the same Australian, "are individually and collectively scared."[3]

---

[9] Lt C. J. Mitchell, VX30705; 2/2 Pnr Bn. Accountant; of East Malvern, Vic; b. Richmond, Vic, 14 Oct 1912.

[1] Maj L. J. Robertson, NX12406. 2/4, 2/6 Fd Coys. Lighting engineer; of Melbourne; b. Melbourne, 19 Jan 1904.

[2] Col W. W. Wearne, OBE, QX6043. 2/9 Bn; BM 24 Bde. Regular soldier; of Brisbane; b. Bundaberg, Qld, 26 Aug 1912.

[3] Sgt A. E. Field, DCM, MM, 2/6 Fd Coy. Field was one of a number of old soldiers who entered captivity. These included the only Australian Victoria Cross winners of the 1914-18 War then serving overseas in the AIF: Sgt Walter Brown, 2/15th Field Regiment; S-Sgt

That month pay was made available to working parties and regimental funds were considerably swelled by officers' pay. A camp café was opened where it was possible to buy eggs and toast, coffee and various trimmings for rice. In October half an ounce of tobacco was being issued weekly. For small offences the Japanese were then inflicting such punishments as standing men motionless in difficult positions for periods varying from two to fifteen minutes, and making Australian N.C.O's slap the faces of their own men. Lack of adequate food was making itself felt and many were suffering from vitamin deficiencies, of which the more common manifestations were aching and burning feet, headaches and ulcerated mouths. That month the camp news sheet reported the shelling of Sydney by submarines in May 1942. "Kempetai greatly impressed by news of cremation of Japs killed in Sydney raid," noted a diarist. "A.I.F. are today very much in the boom."

In November a majority of the Australians (about 1,000) were moved to Makasura, a staging camp of bamboo huts about 4 miles from Batavia, where most of them remained until January. The camp was restricted in size and there was only a small area set aside for recreation. Dunlop, who now commanded the camp, pursued a policy of fostering healthy minds and defeating boredom. Classes begun at Bandung were revived; cricket matches were played; contributions from officers who were now regularly paid were instituted, and from the fund thus created aid was given to all in Makasura regardless of nationality. Little work was done at the camp, although the Japanese created tasks such as sweeping leaves around their headquarters, and carting pebbles from a stream a few miles away. The food situation was not bad, and fruit and sugar were cheap. An occupant of the camp wrote subsequently that one of its outstanding features was "the devotion of most men to things spiritual". Camp services were held, and were attended by large numbers.

> One happy personality was an Australian Catholic Priest who virtually lived with men of all creeds. The fact that he held his morning mass under the palm trees, surrounded by enemies of Christianity . . . as well as cynics within our midst did not detract from the dignity of devotion to God. Every morning that captives prepared the altar they ran the risk of having it kicked over and the faces of worshippers slapped.[4]

The guards were described as "fairly decent", the camp routine not specially tiresome; and in December about 100 radio messages from home were received. The men were allowed to send radio messages home four times a year—in December, February, April and August. These comprised three coded messages out of a selection of 14, and also 20 words freely written, once a year. The radio messages received were in response to some sent earlier.

Walter Peeler, 2/2nd Pioneer Battalion; and Brigadier Blackburn. Brown and Peeler had both understated their ages in order to enlist. Peeler, born in 1887, understated his by 14 years; Brown, born 1885, by 15 years. Peeler survived, but Brown is believed to have been killed while attempting to escape.

[4] F. Foster, *Comrades in Bondage*, p. 64.

On 4th January Dunlop Force (about 900 strong) marched out for Batavia for embarkation. There was at this stage a good deal of movement into or out of the camp. The Australians who remained at Makasura— a few over 100—sometimes fed "like fighting cocks" because rations would arrive after a draft had departed, and perhaps 1,500 rations would have to be eaten by 600. The number of the Australians fluctuated: on the 28th, 350 Australians (mainly 2/40th Battalion from Timor) arrived from Tanjong Priok, and another 100 of mixed units from the Bicycle Camp.[5] Most of the camp posts were then held by Australians. "For once we have got in on the ground floor for paid jobs," commented one of them. In March they were transferred to Tanjong Priok where they shared a camp with American and British prisoners and worked the docks. There were daily swimming parades and weekly concerts. Evidently the condition of officer prisoners was not much below normal. In April a prisoner records witnessing a "sparkling exhibition of Rugby Union football between Aussie officers and the Rest". That month the Australians were moved to the Bicycle Camp, where food was good and well cooked by the Dutch although the rations were rather scanty. The camp routine was: reveille 7.30; check parade 7.40; breakfast 8.30; 9 a.m. working parties sent out; 9.30 general parade. (Those in camp had to remain out of huts and "be doing something".) 10.15 to 10.45 smoko; 12.30 dinner; free till 3 p.m.; smoko 3.45 to 4.15. In May letters were received from Australia; these were dated about June 1942 and were the first letters that some had received for 15 months. That month the prisoners at the Bicycle Camp were divided between Glodok gaol and Makasura, whither 60 Australian officers and 10 sergeants were sent on 19th May.

At Glodok the A.I.F. (mostly 2/40th Battalion) were employed spinning yarn. Food was ample; men were contented, but quarters were very cramped. At Makasura the principal occupation of the prisoners was gardening. In June the Japanese took propaganda photographs at all camps: from the Bicycle Camp a party of "Golfers and Swimmers" was sent to Sukabumi for three days fully equipped with sports gear; a party of 65 left for Bandung for a month's convalescence; and a group of 100 Australians were sent to a theatre in Batavia to provide "applause, laughter, etc." for a prisoner-of-war play that was being filmed by the Japanese. Movement to and from the Bicycle Camp continued. The Japanese were now sending large numbers of prisoners both north and east. Those moving to other areas to the east left from Surabaya; those moving north from Tanjong Priok. At the end of August only about 80 Dutch prisoners and a small number of Australians remained at the Bicycle Camp, but within a few days the number had jumped to over 4,000 and the camp accommodation was badly overtaxed. At that time fish replaced meat on alternate days. On the 26th September a mixed Dutch-British force of 2,500, including Wing Commander Davis and

---

[5] Most of the Timor prisoners had arrived at Surabaya on 25th September, after a two days' voyage from Koepang. Thence they had been sent to Tanjong Priok. A number of them embarked with Dunlop Force.

Lieut-Colonel Lyneham and seven other Australian officers embarked from Tanjong Priok.

Early in 1944 most of the prisoners of war in Java were concentrated in the Batavia area. Some 400 Australians were distributed between Glodok, the Bicycle Camp and Makasura. A few were employed at Adjick on wood cutting, and about 70 were sent to Serang. Some of the Australians were employed in a tobacco factory in Batavia, others in vegetable gardens in the Makasura area. Some medical stores from the British Red Cross were received in June, but most of these were confiscated by the Japanese. That month the meat ration was reduced to offal only, and supplemented by an almost negligible quantity of vegetables and paw paws. In July the island was in a permanent state of brown-out, and the men, learning from the Japanese of heavy sinkings of transports leaving Java and seeing for themselves the pitiful state of the working parties returned from Ambon and elsewhere, did their best to avoid being drafted to oversea parties. In October most of the officers were concentrated at Bandung in what seemed to be a belated attempt by the Japanese to produce a good effect. At Makasura the prisoners in December were passing through what one of them described as "one of the more miserable periods of PW existence . . . much rain, much mud, no news, no sign of action, very little food (now only rice and green leaves with a vestige of offal)". In January 1945 most of the work parties were cut down or cancelled. That month many of the Australians remaining in Java were transferred to Singapore, where some occupied the River Valley camp (recently vacated by parties sent to Japan) and other improvised camps, gradually taking over tasks in the vicinity of the docks from local prisoners of war.

By April most of the remaining British prisoners in Java had been concentrated in a native gaol at Bandung. There, in conditions closely resembling those already described at Changi, some 6,000 were crowded into the gaol under Japanese guards whose attitude towards the prisoners was uncompromisingly harsh almost to the end.

Some of the Australian officers and men who left Singapore before the capitulation and were captured in islands farther to the south were taken to Palembang in Sumatra, where many of them remained until as late as May 1945 before being transferred to Singapore. The principal prisoner-of-war camps at Palembang were the Mulo and Changwa schools and at the airfield, although not all of these were occupied all the time. In September 1942 the men at these camps, some 1,600 in all, included about 60 Australians of the three Services. At Palembang that month, as elsewhere, the prisoners, once sufficient evidence of compulsion had been established, signed forms promising that they would not attempt to escape.

Food supplied by the Japanese consisted of rice, vegetables and proteins in the form of fresh fish, salted fish or dried fish, and occasionally dried meat. The rice ration fluctuated between 190 and 500 grammes, with about 250 grammes of vegetables. The amount of fish or meat supplied averaged about half a cubic inch a day throughout the period of captivity. In 1944 food became steadily less in quantity and inferior in quality; the rice was often full of grit or other impurities, and the vegetables were decayed. When available "snails, rats, cats, dogs, snakes, iguanas, were all eaten". Snails were regarded as "quite a treat from the viewpoint of nourishment".

In May 1945 about 1,400 prisoners were shipped from Palembang to Singapore—a journey lasting five days in conditions so crowded that many of the prisoners had to stand for much of the distance, and a number died.

Among the many hundreds of prisoners of war and internees, including about 220 Australians who remained in Sumatra after this large-scale movement, was a group of Australian nurses, survivors of the sinking of the *Vyner Brooke* and the massacre of nurses on Banka Island in February 1942. After about two weeks at Muntok they had been transferred by ship to Palembang, where the Japanese officers at first endeavoured to persuade them to staff a brothel for their use. The nurses (32 strong) resisted these demands and, after defying threats of starvation, were transferred to bungalows in another quarter of the town where up to 30 prisoners were crowded into one three-roomed house. There they joined Dutch women and children, slept on cement floors and used rice bags and curtains as coverings. Sanitation was inadequate, fuel scarce, and mosquitoes abounded.

Their diet was at first low-grade rice and vegetables, sometimes flavoured by minute portions of duck; later it became more meagre. The nurses did not possess the means to make purchases at the canteen, where beans, sugar and fruit were available, and several developed beri beri. In September 1943 they were transferred, with the women and children, to a desolate camp of bamboo and atap, where leaking huts, mud floors, trench latrines, and the need to draw water from wells, made life still more miserable.

In October 1944 they were returned to Muntok by a small river boat on which 200 women were herded together with barely sufficient space to sit down. Rations became worse than at Palembang; there were few medicines, mcst of the prisoners developed malaria and the hospital, staffed by the Australian nurses, became filled with sick and dying women and children. In February and March 1945 four of the nurses died.

In April they were returned to Sumatra and, after an appalling sea journey during which women and children were packed into the holds of a small ship and for long periods were unable to move from a cramped knee-to-chin position, entered a camp at Lubuklinggau. There they were housed in old and verminous atap dwellings, which leaked during the wet season, and where overcrowding was extreme. The women were expected to work hard at camp maintenance and their health steadily declined. Between April and August four more nurses died. They were buried by their colleagues.

CHAPTER 24

THE BURMA-THAILAND RAILWAY

IT has been seen that large numbers of prisoners were moved from Singapore and Java in 1942 and 1943, and that some of the survivors of these forces were returned to Singapore in late 1943 and early 1944. The destination of these forces at the time of their departure was not known, and while they were absent little information was obtained from the Japanese about how they were employed.

The first main Australian force to leave Singapore was "A" Force, 3,000 strong, commanded by Brigadier Varley. Drawn principally from the 22nd Australian Brigade, it was organised on a three-battalion basis, with an engineer group and a medical group (the latter commanded by Lieut-Colonel Hamilton[1] and drawn mostly from the 2/4th Casualty Clearing Station).[2]

Although at first commanded by an Australian, and entirely Australian in content, it was soon diluted as other parties were merged with it. The force sailed from Singapore on 15th May 1942 in two "small very dirty steamers"—*Celebes Maru* and *Tohohasi Maru*. Only limited space was available, drinking water was scarce; the rations, consisting of rice and stew, seldom reached the consistency of thick soup. On the 17th a small sloop and two other ships carrying Dutch and British prisoners and some Japanese troops joined the convoy off Medan on the east coast of Sumatra. On the 20th the ships reached Victoria Point, Burma, where Green's[3] battalion and a medical and engineer detachment (1,017 strong in all) were disembarked. At Mergui, on the 23rd, Ramsay's battalion (1,000 strong) and 500 British troops from Sumatra were also disembarked.[4] Two days later the rest of the convoy reached the peninsula on the Burma coast near Tavoy.

So ended a 12-day journey (wrote Brigadier Varley in his diary) which will always remain vivid in the minds of all. The congestion of the men in holds; diarrhoea, dysentery, bad latrines etc. I camped on top deck under a tent which leaked like a sieve. As we had rain daily and nightly we had to sit up in our capes to keep bodies dry. Little sleep obtained, all things getting wet. A very small hospital was on this deck which contained Japanese syphilis patients when it was raining. The (sea) captain of this ship was . . . of the N.Y.K. line. . . . He seemed a very decent chap, was apologetic about room on his ship, was under orders therefore [beyond] his control.

For the next few months each battalion was employed at its separate destination on airfield construction. Conditions were not severe. At Mergui the force of 1,500 men was at first crowded into a school capable of

---
[1] Lt-Col T. Hamilton, NX70505, ED. (1st AIF: Pte 30 Bn.) CO 2/4 CCS 1940-42. Surgeon; of Newcastle, NSW; b. Coatbridge, Scotland, 30 Mar 1899.
[2] The battalion commanders were Lt-Col G. E. Ramsay, and Majors D. R. Kerr and C. Green. Lt-Col C. G. W. Anderson was second-in-command to Varley; later Anderson took command of a battalion.
[3] Lt-Col C. E. Green, MBE, WX3435; 2/4 MG Bn. Warehouse manager; of West Perth, WA; b. Perth, WA, 30 Jul 1902.
[4] An Australian surgeon, Lieut-Colonel Coates, accompanied the British troops.

accommodating about half that number, but this gave way to a barracks, which though built largely of bamboo and atap was by far the best they were to encounter as prisoners. A canteen was established, and when work was begun on the aerodrome the poor diet was supplemented by the purchase of eggs, bananas and bread. After some initial misunderstandings the prisoners were treated fairly by Japanese standards. At Victoria Point the Japanese were considered reasonable in their demands for working parties, and, as at Mergui, after a period payments were made to the men and a canteen was established. Accommodation, at first inadequate — the Japanese said they had but recently arrived themselves and had had no time to prepare for the prisoners — later improved, and by June a generous rice ration permitted a considerable amount being used for the production of flour. At this stage the men were receiving better meals than at any time since they had become prisoners. The attitude of the Japanese at this time is indicated by their leniency towards some prisoners who admitted to having gone outside the wire to trade with natives; these were fined three days' pay (Japanese) and the proceeds of the fines were handed back to their unit to purchase extra rations.[5]

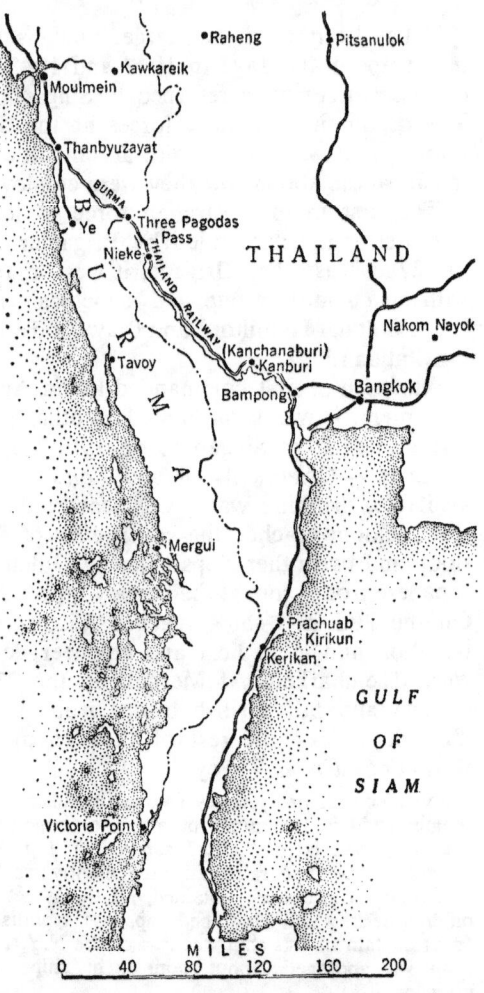

At Tavoy progress on the airfield was delayed partly by the primitiveness of the equipment (although this was a feature of all Japanese undertakings to which prisoners were allotted[6]), partly by the rains and sabotage,

---

[5] Later the Japanese, evidently having forwarded the report of this episode to higher authority, warned Green that any men caught outside the wire would be shot.

[6] At Victoria Point, for example, prisoners were required to straighten nails with stones; at Tavoy, when a party of surveyors was called for, the Japanese were surprised when the prisoners failed to bring with them the necessary surveying equipment.

but also because the Japanese at Tavoy as elsewhere seemed totally unprepared for the arrival of large numbers of prisoners. A fortnight passed before proper guards were posted, and a longer period before the Australians were set to work with picks, shovels, chunkels (large hoe-like instruments) and bags and poles for carrying earth. They were at first billeted in a large hangar "covered with broken rock", evidently prepared for concreting. Rice and some pork and vegetables were provided, but no cooking utensils and little water except from a well which was out of bounds, and in any case lacked a bucket or rope with which to draw the water. A second hangar was occupied by about 1,400 Dutch prisoners. In June conditions improved somewhat when the force was moved to huts. At the end of the month regular fortnightly payments were made to workers and thereafter the rations were supplemented by local purchases from the Burmese. Payment was at the rate of 25 cents a day for working warrant-officers, 15 cents for N.C.O's and 10 cents (about 2d in Australian currency) for privates.[7]

The payment of the men made it possible to buy small quantities of canteen supplies in Tavoy, and Varley observed an immediate drop in sick parades; he concluded that this was "partly psychological" and a result of the pay and better food. "With reason and common sense," wrote Varley, "it is apparent . . . that the tropics to live in are not the horror which we have been led to believe. The men are working daily and getting wet almost daily and yet in spite of bad food for months are quickly getting into good health with reasonable food."

Some optimistic estimates of the duration of the war seem to have been held at this time, and there is a record of a wager of £1 between Brigadier Varley and Colonel Anderson that the war with Germany would end by the beginning of November 1942. The strange circumstances in which members of the force found themselves seem to have resulted in some slackening of standards, particularly among the officers. Varley recorded:

> They have no life—no command, and show signs of slack training. This has been particularly noticeable among AIF this war. All junior officers, or rather a big majority, also NCO's seem to desire to curry favour with the men and are frightened to take full command. Result is that the men soon sum them up as weaklings and discipline generally is undermined. . . . No Army has ever achieved success without strict discipline. The AIF of 1914-18 had it, despite the exaggerated claims of some to the contrary.[8]

The laxness of the Japanese and the friendliness of the Burmese during the early period encouraged some men to attempt to escape, and in June

---

[7] Theoretically officers were paid the Japanese equivalent of their army pay, but a large sum was banked on their behalf by the Japanese, and board and lodgings were deducted. As a result officers received perhaps less than a quarter of their entitlement. However, this was still far in excess of what any man could earn, and it did not fluctuate in proportion to the number of days worked. In February other ranks' pay was increased by 15 cents a day to bring the daily rates for warrant-officers to 40 cents, for NCO's to 30, and for privates to 25.

[8] Varley had served as an infantryman in the old AIF and tended to draw analogies between it and the AIF of 1939-45, sometimes to the latter's disfavour.

a group of eight led by Warrant-Officer Quittendon[9] of the 2/4th Anti-Tank were recaptured after making such an attempt. Despite the protests of the Australian leaders, the eight men were executed without trial.[1] This was a stern reminder both of the difficulties of escape, and of the penalty likely to be incurred. Nevertheless attempts to reach freedom persisted.

By the end of July the airfield had been sufficiently repaired to allow aircraft to land, but the rain, which had begun with a few showers, now increased to a deluge and halted the work.

> We watched fascinated (wrote one soldier) as great clouds brought a solid wall of water sweeping across the drome with the dull roar that heralded its approach for five minutes before the huge drops splashed down upon our sweating bodies. Immediately figures and forms fifty yards away became blurred and indistinct and anything beyond fifty yards was obliterated by the torrent.[2]

In August and September the battalions at Mergui and Victoria Point were gradually concentrated at Tavoy, where work on the airfield continued. Varley endeavoured to maintain the maximum numbers at work, thereby reaping benefits for the men in pay, improved rations, and exercise.[3] The physical condition of the Tavoy group was then very good and comparable with what it had been before they became prisoners. On the other hand Varley found it noticeable that men from Mergui or Victoria Point were not as fit.

By 16th September all work on the airfield had finished, and later that month the movement of "A" Force by ship to Moulmein and thence by rail and road to Thanbyuzayat began. That month a working party of 200 were sent to Ye under Captain Hellyer[4] where they were employed on bridge construction and road repair work. This party was exceptionally well treated. On 3rd October Brigadier Varley reached Thanbyuzayat where he met Colonel Nagatomo, chief of the No. 3 Branch (or Group) of the Thai Prisoner of War Administration and learnt from him the proposed organisation of his force. Varley's headquarters would include a General Affairs Department of 10; a Foodstuffs Department of 17; a Property Department of 17; a Medical Department of 12. The rest of the force would be divided into groups (*kumis*) of 48 to 49 led by a lieutenant (*kumicho*); two such groups would make a *han* under a section commander

---

[9] WO2 M. W. Quittendon, VX45344; 2/4 A-Tk Regt. Fireman; of Windsor, Vic; b. 5 Jun 1905. Executed by Japanese 6 Jun 1942.

[1] The others were Sgt C. Danaher (of Ascot Vale, Vic), Bdrs T. Cumming (Northcote, Vic) and A. W. Glover (Ouyen, Vic), L-Bdr A. A. Emmett (Ouyen, Vic), Gnrs J. A. T. Wilson (Yarram, Vic), A. Reeve (Colac, Vic) and A. H. Jones (Fish Creek, Vic). All were members of the anti-tank regiment. Varley who was compelled to attend the execution noted in his diary: "The spirit of these eight Australians was wonderful. They all spoke cheerio and good luck messages to one another and never showed any sign of fear. A truly courageous end."

[2] R. H. Whitecross, *Slaves of the Son of Heaven* (1951), p. 40.

[3] Workers, in addition to being paid, also received a better ration than non-workers. Later when medical troops were not employed on their routine duties, Varley sent them also out to work in order to get the benefit of increased rations and pay, a step with which Colonel Hamilton, the senior medical officer, agreed.

[4] Maj L. H. Hellyer, NX12561; 2/15 Fd Regt. Public servant; of Artarmon, NSW; b. Leichhardt, NSW, 18 Nov 1908.

(captains and above) known as a *hancho*.[5] The battalion organisations already in existence at this stage persisted. When the concentration of "A" Force was completed Varley, for the first time since his arrival in Burma, would be able to exercise limited authority not only over the "A" Force detachments, but also over the whole of Group 3 (soon to aggregate some 9,000 troops).

The purpose of the Japanese in sending prisoners to Burma and (as will be seen later) to Thailand was to make a railway linking those countries so as to improve the communications of their large army in Burma. In June 1942 these depended on the long and exposed sea route to Rangoon by way of Singapore and the Strait of Malacca and a road from Raheng to southern Burma through Kawkareik to Moulmein, which was unfit for prolonged heavy traffic. The building of the railway which began at Thanbyuzayat in the north and joined the Thailand system at Bampong, 421 kilometres (263 miles) distant, was completed in November 1943, when the various working parties working north from Bampong and south from Thanbyuzayat met about Nieke.

The Japanese plan was that the labour force would be composed of prisoners of war and coolies, under the direction of a railways headquarters at Kanburi. Japanese units engaged in construction would be known as the *Southern Army Railway Corps*. Two railway regiments—the *5th* based on Thanbyuzayat and the *9th* on Kanburi—would work from opposite ends of the line towards the centre at Konkoita. The total number of Japanese employed would be about 12,000. Most of the materials and equipment could be obtained locally, deficiencies being supplemented by bridging material, steel rails and rolling stock from Japan. The Japanese estimated that the work could be completed in 14 months, and at the latest by December 1943.[6]

The railway workers were organised by the Japanese into Groups or Branches; some branches had as few as 2,000 workers, others as many as 12,000. Two prisoner of war groups—Nos. 3 and 5—functioned on the Thanbyuzayat side of the railway; four—1, 2, 4 and 6, plus about 10,000 workers who came under Malayan Prisoner of War administration (as distinct from the Thai one)—worked forward from Bampong in Thailand.

In the northern or Burma sector the work consisted chiefly of clearing dense undergrowth, felling great trees and making embankments and cuttings. In the hilly country the track followed natural gradients and for this reason high embankments would be rare. The track in this sector did not follow a river and there was no good road. Consequently supply difficulties would be accentuated during the wet season. The area to be

---

[5] Finally the Australian staff included: Brigadier Varley, head of bureau; Captain R. S. Griffin, Staff Captain; Lieutenant J. A. Varley, General Affairs; WO2 P. R. Levy, French Interpreter (Nagatomo preferred to conduct interviews in French); two typists and four batmen. There was a similar staff representing the Dutch.
[6] This information has been drawn from SEATIC Bulletin No. 246, "Burma-Siam Railway", dated 8 Oct 1946.

traversed followed an old British survey line abandoned before the war because of the difficulties involved, including the fact that several diseases were endemic throughout the area.

Two days before Varley arrived at Thanbyuzayat work on the railway had begun when "A" Force led by Green's battalion arrived at Kendau, 4.8 kilometres from the base headquarters. On the 5th Anderson's battalion, based at the outset on Thanbyuzayat also began work—consisting at that stage of building an embankment by means of moving earth from the sides of a 50-foot wide strip of cleared jungle and undergrowth.[7] These first arrivals were rapidly followed by other groups—Dutch, British, Australian and American—and between the 29th and 30th October two new Australian groups, Williams and Black Forces, commanded by Colonels Williams and Black,[8] which had arrived at Moulmein on the 25th from Java by way of Singapore, also began work on the line. Williams Force was based at Tanyin at the Kilo-35 camp and Black Force (593 Australians and 190 Americans) at Beke Taung, a camp at Kilo 40. Living conditions at Tanyin are described as

> the best experienced . . . on the Burma section of the railway. The important factor in the treatment received by the prisoners was the character of the Japanese Camp Commandant. . . . Lieutenant Yamada ranked as one of the best commanders that the force came under. . . . In appearance rather grim and forbidding . . . he nevertheless exercised intelligence and tolerance in his camp administration. He rather stretched the rules of the Imperial Japanese Army in regard to prisoners to ensure that Lieut-Colonel Williams received treatment in accordance with his rank. When once he did complain that he himself was not being saluted as he moved about the camp, it was as if to say: "Look here fellows, after all I am the boss here; the least you can do is pay me a little respect occasionally."[9]

At this stage a daily work quota was fixed by the Japanese, each prisoner being required to move .6 cubic metres of earth. Under this system the Australians found that by working hard they were able to complete their daily quota before the fierce midday heat. A ten-minute rest period every hour was permitted but the weekly day of rest, begun at Tavoy, ceased.[1] When the Japanese discovered that the Australians were able to complete their quota early, they increased the amount of earth to be moved. In October the prisoners were ordered to sign undertakings not to attempt to escape. After Varley and Green had been imprisoned and told that they would not be released until they had signed the parole forms, Varley advised his men to do so, as he considered that sufficient evidence of compulsion existed to make the declaration invalid.[2]

The declaration read:

---

[7] In mid-October Anderson's Force moved to Alepauk (Kilo-18 camp).
[8] Lt-Col C. M. Black, ED, NX70821. CO 2/3 Res MT Coy. Business manager; of Bondi Junction, NSW; b. Sydney, 10 May 1898.
[9] E. F. Aitken, *The Story of the 2/2 Australian Pioneer Battalion*, p. 157.
[1] Eventually the Japanese agreed to every tenth day being observed as a day of rest.
[2] At a meeting with Nagatomo Varley was told that "Japan believes in and acts according to her signature of Hague Convention and International Law so far as is necessary. It is very necessary all soldiers sign parole. I cannot do my best for prisoners who have the intention to escape. All my orders must be obeyed. I will insist on this. I have the power to imprison or shoot for disobedience."

I the undersigned hereby swear on my honour that I will not under any circumstances attempt to escape.

In November Group 3 was distributed between camps at Thanbyuzayat and Kilo 40, the main forces being Green's battalion at Kendau (4.8 kilos); a Dutch group at Wagale (8 kilos); Anderson at Alepauk (18 kilos); Williams at Tanyin (35 kilos) and Black at Beke Taung (40 kilos). Hitherto the chaplains of "A" Force had been kept together and afforded no special facilities; but at Thanbyuzayat, once work on the line had begun, Brigadier Varley pressed Colonel Nagatomo to distribute the chaplains among the various camps, and at length this was agreed to.

In November some 200 Korean troops, described by a medical officer as "purely amoral coolie vermin . . . brutal by nature as well as by orders", arrived at Thanbyuzayat to take over guard duty at all camps in Burma. "We are not looking forward to this," noted Varley in his diary, "as our guards here are the best we have had."[3] Varley continued to press for better rations and accommodation, and more medical supplies, but not always successfully:

It is so difficult and heart-breaking to fight for the lives of our men . . . and meet a brick wall on all occasions (he wrote). . . . I have asked that representations be made for a Red Cross ship. Medical reports . . . show deficiencies in drugs. I have asked for beds to keep the sick off the bare boards, where they lie, many without a blanket, losing condition quickly. . . . I have been informed no beds are available. I have asked for rice bags, canvas or any material to make beds. A form of bamboo matting used as walls in native huts is available, but no timber to make the frames. This sort of nightmare goes on.
Cholera broke out in Moulmein and Rangoon a couple of weeks ago and there has now been one death in the village a few hundred yards from our camp. I still cannot get drums (44 gallon) to boil water for men to drink. Water has to be boiled in the kwalis given to cook rice. This is not sufficient and water is a great source of danger.

That month Varley ordered the sale of personal effects of the dead, such as watches, fountain pens, propelling pencils, and the payment of the proceeds into a Red Cross Fund to buy food for the sick. Only wallets and photographs were to be retained for transmission to next of kin. This was a radical departure from normal procedure, but these were exceptional times; it would in any case have been impossible to carry any accumulation of such articles with the force, or adequately to safeguard them.[4]

The summary execution of the Australians in June did not discourage prisoners altogether from leaving the compound and at Thanbyuzayat in November, a Dutch[5] prisoner who went outside the wire dressed in a sarong to trade with the natives was arrested by the Japanese. He pleaded that he had gone outside the wire to buy bananas, but having no money,

---

[3] The Koreans were regarded by the Japanese as an inferior race, and in many instances received treatment little better than that accorded the prisoners. Being themselves treated as inferiors they attempted to treat prisoners as inferiors, and their failure to establish a moral superiority led to frequent incidents.

[4] Soon after this order was issued Nagatomo requested that personal effects be handed to him. "He said he would send them to Tokyo for dispatch to Australia after the war," wrote Varley.

[5] About 50 per cent of the "Dutch" prisoners were Asians.

had traded his shirt. Lieutenant Hosoda,[6] the Japanese commandant at that time, not only forgave him—an Australian at Mergui had been executed for a similar offence—but evidently feeling sorry for the prisoner, gave him money to buy bananas.

Unlike most of the other forces, "A" Force contained a large proportion of over-age Australians—principally members of the 2/3rd Reserve Motor Transport Company to which special conditions of enlistment had applied —and these presented a particular problem in the conditions prevailing on the Burma-Thailand railway. In November 1942 Varley proposed to Nagatomo that the older men, men unfit for heavy work, and the chronic sufferers, be employed on vegetable growing, and on other specialised work such as the repair of boots and clothes, then in a "deplorable condition". However, nothing more seems to have been heard of this proposal, which would have had the effect of earning working pay and rations for partially fit prisoners, and of keeping the force better supplied with clothing and boots.[7]

In December Varley organised a scheme of voluntary contributions from officers' pay towards a Red Cross Fund to be set up to buy extra food for the sick. All camps were prepared to contribute all pay in excess of 20 rupees a month—the officers of Group 3 were paid at higher rates than those of other groups—and such sums were at length paid to a Public Receiver, who accepted the money and issued receipts. The money was then handed to the Red Cross Representative, Mr Murchison, who spent it on hospital patients, patients in R.A.P's, and on improved rations and comforts for those with chronic disabilities who were unable to earn pay.[8]

In December 1942 four more prisoners—three Dutch and one Australian—were executed for attempted escape. The Australian was considered mentally ill by the Australian doctors—as indeed he was—and a plea for mercy on these grounds was made to the Japanese by Varley. At first they seemed willing to spare him; then, without warning, he was taken away and executed. When Varley reproached the Japanese commandant, Lieutenant Naito, he replied that the Japanese medical officer considered the prisoner "mentally sound", and that, as the Dutch officers had been executed for attempted escape, "he had to be fair".

---

[6] Hosoda, noted Varley, was "very humane, bought food for sick at his own expense; helped us in any way he could. Limited by higher command."

[7] At this stage many of the prisoners were in rags; some went to work in underpants or swimming trunks, others with a piece of cloth around their middles like natives.

[8] The rates of pay laid down in Singapore for officers were:

Lt-Col	220.00	Dollars, ticals, rupees or
Major	170.00	yen per month, according
Capt	122.50	to the prisoner's locality.
Lieut	85.00	

These took effect from 16th August 1942. Deductions were made by the Japanese for food, clothing, light and lodging, and these varied from time to time. In Thailand from August 1942 these deductions amounted to 60 ticals a month for all officers; from August 1943 to March 1944 to 20 ticals a month; from April 1944 the deduction was 30 ticals for field officers and 27 for captains and below. In practice the most an officer in Thailand could receive was 30 ticals a month, the rest being placed in a savings account. In Burma, however, officers were allowed to draw up to 70 rupees a month. In the case of junior officers the amount drawn was much less after lodging had been deducted.

In January a second group of prisoners—Group 5—joined the prisoners labouring on the Burma side of the railway. These had come principally from Java and were a mixture of Australians, Dutch and Americans; they operated independently of Group 3. Soon after their arrival Varley wrote to Colonel Nagatomo pointing out the desirability of segregating nationalities into separate camps. He also asked whether the Australians and Americans in Group 5 could be exchanged with an equal number of Dutchmen in Group 3, where in addition to being with their own countrymen they would be with comrades from units to which they had previously belonged. Nagatomo agreed to consider these proposals, but said that a draft of Dutchmen must go to Kun Knit Kway (the Kilo-26 camp) where the Australians of Group 5 were already established. "This is most undesirable," commented Varley, "as they (the Dutch) are a potential reservoir of dysentery . . . also these men will not be able to do much work as they have all been very ill."

Meanwhile Anderson Force at Alepauk had been reinforced by 200 British troops. The number of the sick began to increase. At the beginning of November one man in every three had been classified as too sick to work; in December 300 of the 600 in camp were sick, most of them suffering from leg ulcers or stomach ailments. Varley, who visited all camps for the first time that month, considered Green's camp at Kendau the best, and the Alepauk camp the worst. Many huts had been damaged by time and weather. Portions of roofs had collapsed and been removed.

Between 12th and 25th December Ramsay Force also had begun its labours on the railway, based at Kun Knit Kway. It was then they began to realise, wrote a chronicler of the period, that

so far we had been on a picnic. . . . Conditions were much worse than any we had so far experienced; the huts were only partly weather-proof, food was as bad as at Mergui, work was severe, being set on a piece-work basis. To make matters worse we came, for the first time, under the Korean guards, of whom the less said the better.[9]

On 3rd January Anderson Force moved to the Kilo-35 camp at Tanyin, where they joined Williams Force.[1] Although the staple ration continued to be rice, the cooks had now acquired some dexterity in its preparation. The men experimented with cake-making and prepared "coffee" from carefully roasted rice grains. Each day small parties scoured the surrounding jungle for logs of wood, and at night roaring fires were built, round which "groups of men talked together with the fire-glow lighting their faces against the dark of the surrounding jungle".[2]

By mid-January the deaths in Group 3 totalled 73 (including 24 Australians), a remarkably small number considering the circumstances in which the force was placed. That month Thanbyuzayat was organised as a base hospital for the sick, then numbering 600. In February an out-

---

[9] *Men May Smoke*, p. 63.
[1] Despite the conditions at Alepauk only one man died of sickness in the period spent there by Anderson Force.
[2] R. H. Whitecross, p. 66.

break of pellagra—a vitamin deficiency disease, which ulcerates tongues, gums and lips—affected 80 per cent of the troops at Tanyin and Anarkwan, but by the end of the month it had cleared up. That month a group of three men from Thetkaw camp made a carefully planned and determined attempt to reach India. They were Major Mull,[3] Sapper Bell[4] and Gunner Dickinson.[5] The group reached a few miles north of Moulmein when Dickinson fell out exhausted. As had been agreed, the others went on. Dickinson was recaptured by the Japanese, taken to Thanbyuzayat, and executed without trial. Mull and Bell went on and had reached 100 miles farther north when they encountered a pro-Japanese native patrol. (The Japanese offered substantial rewards to native peoples for the capture of prisoners, and this contributed to the difficulty of escape.) Mull was killed in the encounter, and Bell badly wounded. He was returned to Thanbyuzayat and shot.[6]

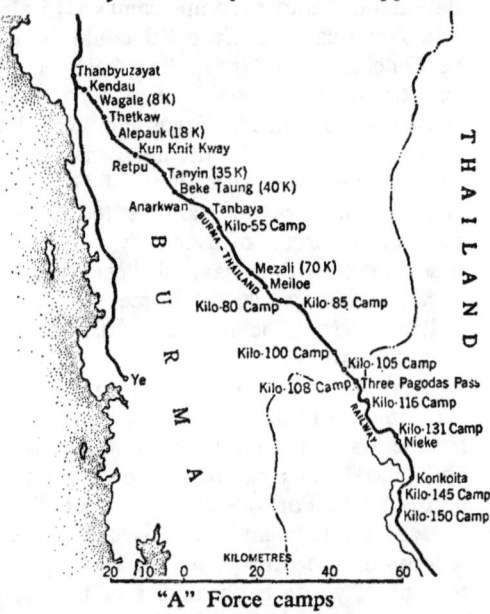

"A" Force camps

From February-March onwards the work became steadily harder, each railway detachment stepping up the amount of earth to be moved by each man until finally the quantity was over two cubic metres a day, whether a man was healthy or sick, big or small.

In March the Japanese announced that all "no duty" (sick) prisoners would be sent to the Retpu (Kilo-30 camp) which had been organised as a hospital area;[7] that the group headquarters would move forward from

---

[3] Maj A. Mull, NX12243; AASC 8 Div. Traveller; of Strathfield, NSW; b. Lahore, India, 8 Apr 1896. Killed 10 Mar 1943. Mull had served as a captain in the British and Indian forces during the 1914-18 War.

[4] Spr A. J. Bell, VX73827; 2/6 Fd Pk Coy. Metallurgist; of Malaya, and Ballarat, Vic; b. Ballarat, 14 May 1913. Executed by Japanese 16 Mar 1943.

[5] Gnr K. J. Dickinson, VX57167; 2/15 Fd Regt. Surveyor; of Bendigo, Vic; b. Collie, WA, 24 Dec 1903. Executed by Japanese 2 Mar 1943.

[6] Like most of the escapers, Bell's behaviour at the execution ground was exemplary. He thanked Lieutenant Naito, who was in charge of the firing squad, for his courtesy and for the privileges extended to him. He shook hands, refused to kneel or sit in a tied position as was the Japanese custom, stating that he would die on his feet, and asked Lieutenant Naito to pass this on to Brigadier Varley. Afterwards Hamilton and Varley were taken to the place of execution. Naito drew up the Japanese guards, and they presented arms to the dead man. "The whole of Bell's behaviour since returning to this camp has been most gallant," commented Varley.

[7] The hospital was organised by Colonels Coates and N. M. Eadie, and Major S. Krantz of the A.A.M.C. "The route home," declared Colonel Coates to the patients of the Kilo-30 camp, "is inscribed in the bottom of every man's dixie. Every time it is filled with rice, eat it. If you vomit it up again, eat some more; even if it comes up again some good will remain. If you get a bad egg, eat it no matter how bad it may appear. An egg is only bad when the stomach will not hold it."

Thanbyuzayat to Meiloe (Kilo-75 camp); and that Anderson and Williams Forces, then at Tanyin, would be combined. They would be known as the "No. 1 Mobile Force", which would lay rails, beginning at Kun Knit Kway. At this stage there were some 9,534 prisoners under the command of Brigadier Varley, including 4,465 Australians, 481 British, 194 Americans, and 4,394 Dutch, but not including about 1,850 in Group 5. The bulk of the Australians—Green, Ramsay and Black Forces—were based at Meiloe. A British-American force was laying rails towards the Kun Knit Kway and the Dutch were concentrated round camps at the 45 and 70 kilo marks. The Kilo-75 camp at Meiloe where Green, Ramsay and Black Forces were based at this time, was set mainly in a valley surrounded by thick jungle. A river ran beside the camp, huts were good, but mosquitoes and sandflies were a torment.

In April the line was heavily reinforced with coolie labour; an article in a Rangoon paper which was delivered to the camp at Thanbyuzayat by the Japanese stated that the youth of Burma were being enlisted into either the Blood Army or the Sweat Army—to defend or work for their country. "These," commented Varley as he witnessed some 2,000 coolies marching past his camp early in April, "must be . . . part of the Sweat Army."

That month Colonel Coates at Retpu complained that a Japanese medical officer had ordered many convalescent patients back to their camps. "Same old trouble," wrote Varley, "Japanese engineers at camps sending men to hospital who cannot do a full day's work and Japanese administrative staff under Colonel Nagatomo sending them back to camp." Nevertheless, it seems evident that the relations between Varley and the Japanese on the Burma side of the line were better than existed elsewhere in Burma or Thailand. This was partly due to Varley's perspicacity in keeping the maximum number of men at work, and his continued efforts to improve conditions,[8] but also because Nagatomo (hamstrung though he may have been in some respects by higher authority) and most of his officers, were reasonable to a degree that would have astonished senior officers charged with liaison between their troops and the Japanese at other times and places. It was largely because of this reasonableness that Varley was able to arrange for truckloads of canteen goods to be delivered in turn to camps in the dry season and the movement forward of "yaks" with Australian drovers which helped to minimise the inevitable losses on the way forward. Some evidence of the amiable relations that existed between the Japanese and their prisoners at Thanbyuzayat at this time is provided by the enthusiasm with which regular sports meetings were attended by both captors and prisoners alike.[9] In May the Retpu hospital was closed and all patients were transferred to Thanbyuzayat. Thenceforward the

---
[8] The best results seem to have been achieved by officers who deferred to Japanese authority on minor matters, and concentrated on taking a definite stand on vital matters affecting the men's lives and health.

[9] At a sports meeting held in April some of the Australians dressed up as "young ladies" to add colour to the scene, and these, amid scenes of great hilarity, pursued an interested Japanese guard some 200 yards to the guardhouse, from which he—evidently having lost "face"—refused to emerge.

Japanese planned to hold hospital patients at each camp. At a conference with Nagatomo that month Varley pressed for assurances that transport would be available to take canteen goods to camps during the wet season, as it would be useless continuing to place orders with merchants without such assurances, and he complained about the length of working hours in outside camps, which he considered was contributing to the increased sick rate. Nagatomo assured Varley that transport would continue to be provided; but said that, while he agreed with Varley, the fixing of working hours rested on the railway commander. Nagatomo said he would ask him whether the hours could be reduced. "Unfortunately he has done this before," commented Varley, "and the Railway commander has not agreed. I have no direct access to him."

In fact, as Varley was now learning, the Japanese Army worked in water-tight compartments; each unit was usually hostile to other units and all were contemptuous of the Korean guards, who never questioned or remonstrated against any order or requirement of the Japanese engineers.[1]

Varley had continued to press Nagatomo to issue orders forbidding the striking of prisoners, and in May this was done. Nagatomo asked Varley to instruct "all P.W. not to treat Japanese guards with disdain" as their looks and actions sometimes irritated the guards. Nagatomo added that the language problem was the greatest barrier to happy relations.[2]

Most camps had one, sometimes more, Allied officers who possessed a smattering of Japanese, and as some camps lacked official interpreters, it was often upon this flimsy thread of understanding that relations between Japanese and prisoner were largely balanced.

Despite Nagatomo's orders, striking of prisoners persisted. The Japanese Army dispensed with charge sheets, trials, and the necessity of finding the accused guilty for minor offences, and permitted two or three-star privates to beat up one-star privates, and one-star privates to beat up Korean guards. Thus it was inevitable that prisoners should be struck, because they were considered of least account of all.[3] The commonest form of immediate punishment consisted of a series of full-arm blows on either

---

[1] The railway engineers usually took no part in the administration of the prisoners' camps. These were normally commanded by subalterns, warrant-officers, NCO's or private soldiers of the Japanese Army. The officer commandants were often lazy and inefficient, but warrant-officers and NCO's were mostly active energetic men, with considerable powers of decision. They carried great responsibilities, for camps of 2,000 were frequently under their command.

[2] The language problem is illustrated by the following incidents recorded in Varley's diary at Thanbyuzayat:
"Lt Naito (who spoke English) asked an Australian driver what was wrong with a truck which would not start. 'The battery is flat,' replied the driver. 'What shape is it usually?' asked Naito. On another occasion when told that there was 'a short' in a vehicle's electrical system, Naito is reputed to have said: 'Make all shorts longer.' "

[3] Any Japanese soldier of whatever rank, if alone, "had no hesitation . . . in giving orders to a battalion [of prisoners]; but in response to orders from a rank one step higher than his own he was an automaton. The Emperor was God, but to O.Rs. any officer was a demigod. Similar prestige attached to seniority among officers; the Japanese commander of Ps.O.W. in Burma was known to bash his second-in-command till he lost his feet and then kick him down the stairs, injuring his back severely: he was then sent out in disgrace to a working camp where he stayed in hospital for six weeks under the care of a P.O.W. medical officer. Nevertheless there were some curious features. A guard commander during his tour of duty, though holding no rank, was supreme in his own domain and even the camp commander could not or would not interfere with one of his guard during a period when he was regarded as the direct representative of the Emperor. Consequently redress for offences by a guard commander or his guard could not be obtained."—Major W. E. Fisher, "Medical Experiences with Ps.O.W. in Malaya, Burma and Siam, 15 Feb 42 to 16 Aug 45".

side of the face—"face-slapping" as it was known—but so small was the self-control exercised by the average Japanese that any convenient weapon, be it bamboo stick, shovel, or even crowbar might be used. Beatings were followed by a period of standing to attention, usually for a number of hours, but sometimes extended to days. Other punishments consisted of holding aloft a heavy weight, or holding at arm's length a pail of water, the prisoner being beaten whenever his arms relaxed.[4]

Meanwhile the No. 1 Mobile Force had begun rail-laying from Kun Knit Kway. The move to that camp was but the first of a series of such moves, involving long hours of work, under the supervision of brutal Korean guards, poor rations and few medical supplies. On 26th April the force moved to the Kilo-45 camp; in May to the Kilo-60 camp. At this stage it entered a period of abject misery. The Kilo-60 camp had been occupied by about 700 coolie labourers, and cholera, smallpox and dysentery stalked the area. Coolies lay dying or had been buried in shallow graves.[5] The wet season commenced and from dawn to dusk under leaden skies the jungle dripped its moisture until already miserable shelters became a reeking bog of mud in places a foot deep. For most prisoners it was their second "wet". Cholera broke out, and the medical officer, Captain Richards,[6] and his two assistants fought selflessly without drugs or outside help for a time to stave it off. At length the Japanese, alarmed lest cholera wipe out the entire mobile force, issued anti-cholera serum. When the epidemic died down only 34 of the camp of 600 had died. At Beke Taung (Kilo-40) a malaria-infested area where men of the mobile force worked for a time on ballasting the line, no quinine was issued by the Japanese sergeant in charge for four weeks, and the health of the men deteriorated rapidly. Sixteen died at the camp and 80 of the remaining 122 subsequently died.

At the Meiloe camp where Black, Green and Ramsay Forces had settled, conditions were little better. The force seems to have been systematically under-supplied with rations, and in May workmen were leaving camp at 9 a.m. and not returning until 4 a.m. That month the force was moved to Kilo-105, and for six days before the move the prisoners—fit and unfit alike—were required to work at an inhuman pace. Light duty men worked from 9 a.m. to 10 p.m.; no-duty prisoners joined them from 2 p.m. to 2 a.m. On the day of the move, men who had completed work that morning were required that evening to begin a 30-kilometres march with all gear to Kilo-105. When the Dutch Kilo-70 camp closed and they were moved to the Kilo-108 camp 800 sick were left behind.

Reports of conditions prevailing at these up-country working camps continued to reach and worry Brigadier Varley, who decided that various

---

[4] A particularly horrifying feature of Japanese punishment was their tendency to strike prisoners in vital places, or to kick, punch or hit with stick, rifle or fist, half-healed ulcers, swollen faces, or broken limbs.

[5] In view of their Greater East Asia doctrine, it was remarkable that the Japanese should exhibit so little concern about the treatment of the native peoples under their dominion. Those employed on the line as coolies, admittedly with only elementary conceptions of hygiene, sanitation and health, suffered a far greater degree of hardship and loss of life than the European prisoners.

[6] Capt C. R. B. Richards, NX70273; RMO 2/15 Fd Regt. Medical practitioner; of Summer Hill, NSW; b. Sydney, 8 Jun 1916.

sections of the line had to be completed to a prescribed schedule and that the "Japanese will carry out schedule and do not mind if the line is dotted with crosses".[7]

In June, except for the Mobile Force, the principal camps were forward of the 75-Kilo mark at 105 and 108, where there were about 1,900 Australians and 2,500 Dutch respectively. At each camp most of the men were employed on road building, as the railway had not been commenced in that area. At the Kilo-105 camp half the troops were without boots and many without shirts or shorts. No holidays were being granted by the Japanese at this stage.

Meanwhile, the Thanbyuzayat headquarters and hospital sited close to a railway marshalling yard and workshops had been thrice visited by Allied bombers, and substantial casualties had been inflicted on the prisoners. Earlier in the year, when the Japanese had issued orders that all prisoners must go to their huts during air raids and remain there under threat of being shot, Varley had pointed out that the huts would not provide protection, and had asked permission to dig slit trenches and lay out a Red Cross of red gravel and white sand.[8] The Japanese approved these requests, but refused to allow the prisoners to construct a symbol —a white triangle on a blue base—to indicate the presence of a prisoner-of-war camp. When on 1st March the area was visited by three Allied bombers, the Japanese guards, according to one diarist

> became very excited, rushed about in all directions, shouting, fixing bayonets, loading rifles; nobody was allowed outside the huts on penalty of being shot, and we were not allowed to use slit trenches. . . . The Japanese remained in their slit trenches for about half an hour after the planes had gone.

In June two heavier raids resulted in the transfer of the group headquarters elsewhere. The first of these was on the 12th, when two bombs, evidently aimed at the railway line and workshops, dropped within the compound. Nine were killed (including five Australians) and 8 wounded (including 2 Australians).[9]

On the 15th a second and heavier raid, apparently directed at the camp, took place. Eight bombs fell in the camp area and a number outside among native coolie lines. Seventeen were killed (including 13 Australians) and many wounded (including an estimated 27 Australians).[1] Next day the Japanese ordered the evacuation of Thanbyuzayat to camps

---

[7] At this stage (24 May) 90 Australians had died or been killed in Burma, and 26 British.

[8] The Japanese could not supply any materials for the work.

[9] As an aftermath officers from the Japanese Department of Propaganda interviewed Varley and asked him what he thought of the bombing. Varley said that the bombs were aimed at the railway line near the camp, and some casualties among the prisoners were men who were working on the outskirts of the camp near the line. He (Varley) was sure that if the Red Cross was maintained the camp would not be deliberately bombed unless, as happened on the 12th, Japanese soldiers fired at the planes from within the camp. However, there was always the likelihood while the camp was sited beside a legitimate target—the railway yards—that it would be hit.

[1] Varley and Black were both wounded. Varley although only lightly wounded had miraculously escaped greater injury. He was temporarily relieved as commander of No. 3 Group by Lt-Col Hamilton of the CCS. Varley's adjutant, Captain Griffin, who at all times "had conducted himself in accordance with the standards of the highest tradition of an Australian officer", was among the dead.

which had fallen into disuse at the 4, 8 and 18 Kilo marks, but refused to provide trucks or railway accommodation to move either the patients or their equipment. Many of the men had not walked more than a few hundred yards for months. Many had scarcely left their beds. Now they were asked not only to make the journey on foot, but to carry all their bedding kit and mess gear into the jungle, to camps where they would be hopelessly overcrowded.[2] Soon after the establishment of his headquarters at Kilo-4, Nagatomo informed Varley that difficulty was being encountered in getting forward rations to the Kilo-105 and Kilo-108 camps —a difficulty that Varley had long foreseen and feared—and that, as it was "useless taking rations there for men unable to work", he proposed bringing back the sick to the Kilo-55 camp. Varley asked that the sick under Colonel Coates at the Kilo-75 camp also be brought back to the Kilo-55 camp, and Nagatomo agreed. Subsequently Varley and Nagatomo went forward to these camps to arrange the movement of the sick, of whom there were about 1,500. At the Kilo-105 camp Varley found a Japanese N.C.O. blitzing the sick parade to get more men:

> He stated (wrote Varley) that Lieut-Colonel Nagatomo had ordered that more men be sent to work. I disbelieved this . . . ordered a sick parade and sent the interpreter to Lieut-Colonel Nagatomo asking him to make an inspection. . . . The sick included hundreds with tropical ulcers varying in size up to a small saucer. Nagatomo was astonished. He ordered that numbers going to work be left to doctors, and he asked what medicines and drugs . . . were required.[3]

In September the Mobile Force had reached the 108-Kilo mark, having in the meantime occupied camps at the 70, 80 and 95-Kilo marks. At this stage it was learnt from Nagatomo that rails would have to be laid by prisoners of Group 3 as far as the 150-Kilo mark, where they would meet parties from Thailand. The men were riddled with tropical ulcers, plagued by dysentery and beri beri, and were working shifts of 24 hours on and 24 off as the Japanese sought to complete the line to schedule. Railway trucks followed the force carrying supplies of rails and sleepers. Locomotives shunted trucks so that the leading bogies carrying the sleepers and rails reached to the very end of the line. Sleepers were then unloaded and dropped in position along the embankment. Next the lengths of rail were run off the bogies in pairs, one from either side:

> Eighteen or twenty sweating men would grasp the rail and holding it up the leading end, quickly run it clear of the bogie and jump clear as it fell on to the sleepers with a resounding Clang! It was pulled into position against the last rail and connected with fish plates and bolts. Spikes were then driven into the sleepers to hold the rail at each end and in the middle. When this had been completed on both sides, the train moved forward to the end of the newly-laid line, where the process was repeated. As each pair of bogies was cleared, they were manhandled off the tracks to make way for the next pair carrying another sixteen rails and sleepers.

> Following the laying gangs at a slower pace came the back spiking gang. Their job was to spike the rails to each sleeper, one spike on each side of the rail on the

---
[2] At the Kilo-8 camp, for example, there was hardly a roof of any kind for a camp of 1,600 men.
[3] On a later visit to the Kilo-55 hospital camp, Nagatomo, having witnessed a leg amputation under primitive conditions, expressed concern and offered to arrange for future cases (of which there were then about 30) to be taken to the Japanese hospital at Moulmein.

straight and two spikes to each sleeper on the curves. Spiking teams were made up of four men: one auger-man who drilled holes in the sleeper with a heavy auger; and one bar-man armed with a steel bar weighing about 25 lb, whose job it was to lever the sleeper tightly against the rail as the remaining two members of the team drove the spike home with lusty blows of 12-lb hammers.

It was all hard work, performed at high pressure. By the time the sun began to drop towards the west the auger-man was certain that his arms would drop off as he drilled his next hole; and the bar now weighed much more than 25-lb, and as fatigue began to tell, the blows of the hammer men were not always accurate and the spike was sometimes bent. If the Jap engineer saw the work stop for a minute for a bent spike to be straightened or pulled out, he bounded along muttering or screaming abuse, and laid about him with his heavy metre stick.[4]

On 17th September the force moved to the Kilo-116 camp, "the worst yet occupied by any P.W.", close to the Burma-Thailand border, a shockingly filthy area where one hut, hastily-cleared of its cholera-stricken occupants to make way for the new arrivals, housed the entire force. Another four or five huts were used to house native labour. The hut could accommodate only half the force at one time, but this presented no special difficulty as 24-hour shifts were being worked and thus only half the force was in camp at the one time. On 30th September the force moved on to an incomplete camp at 131 Kilos, which had formerly been occupied by coolies. Line-laying ceased in this period, because shale cuttings had collapsed farther along the line, and the force was occupied putting ballast beneath sleepers, and restacking sleepers already stacked (a whimsical Japanese method of keeping worn-out men working). The Dutch at the Kilo-108 camp were moved forward to Nieke to hasten the completion of work in the cuttings. On 13th October the Mobile Force (reinforced by 300 Dutch prisoners) recommenced line-laying at a frightful pace. At one stage the men laboured for 33 hours without a rest. By 16th October the two lines had linked about the 145-Kilo mark, and prisoners from Burma were now regularly encountering other forces working north from Thailand.

On 20th November Memorial Services were held by order of the Japanese for the men who had lost their lives at all camps in Burma and Thailand occupied by prisoners of Groups 3 and 5. Large inscribed crosses were erected at the cemeteries, and a letter of condolence was read by Colonel Nagatomo to the assembled prisoners at the Kilo-55 camp and by his representatives at other camps. Two days' rest was granted. That month the Japanese informed the prisoners that fit men would remain in the jungle to maintain the line;[5] "light sick" would go to Bampong in Thailand, and "heavy sick" to a hospital near Bangkok. The food in most camps was now so poor that, although the major work was completed, the death rate began again to rise, particularly in the Kilo-55 hospital camp; and Varley, growing perhaps tired of the repeated failures of Colonel Nagatomo

---

[4] R. H. Whitecross, p. 99.

[5] The quota of fit men set for Groups 3 and 5, both of which were now under command of Varley, was 4,000—far more of course than could be mustered. There were in fact no fit men, only men who were fit compared with others who were sick. Of 884 men in the Mobile Force at this stage, only 24 were graded as fit, including Colonel Williams.

to improve matters, asked for the right to correspond with a representative of a neutral power appointed by the belligerents for the purpose.

Much of the boxed meat received during this period was green and flyblown, and the small cattle (weighing between 100 and 150 pounds) that found their way into the camp were often diseased and would normally have been condemned. The green portion of the boxed meat would be cut away, the maggots washed off, and the remainder of the meat would be eaten. The wisdom of Solomon and the patience of Job were sometimes required to decide whether or not diseased cattle should be used in the cookhouse. One battalion commander who lacked the qualifications needed to decide whether or not an animal should be eaten, developed the practice of asking each of his butchers in turn what he would do if it were thrown out. If the majority said they would eat it themselves, the animal was added to the camp rations.[6]

In December 1943 a godsend in the form of a consignment of Red Cross supplies was received by Varley from Thailand addressed to "British POW Burma" and consigned from the Swiss Consulate at Bangkok. It was left to Varley and the Senior British officer, a captain, to distribute. The British officer said that as the goods were addressed to "British P.O.W." he would not agree to the goods being distributed to other than English prisoners.[7]

> I was staggered by this un-British sentiment (wrote Varley) especially when our Red Cross scheme has been helping English troops the same as all others in the past 14 months. English officers of course have contributed, but owing to their shortage of numbers, and being mostly of junior rank, their contributions have not been in proportion to others. Further . . . the Australian Red Cross officers have borrowed R.6,000 from the Dutch and in this they have likewise benefited, and the Dutch have shown their spirit of cooperation by making the loan.

In the event Varley ordered that the Red Cross supplies be distributed to the most dangerously ill of all nationalities, and this was done.

That month and in January the prisoners began to move eastward in batches to Thailand, where they were reunited with other forces and met comrades they had not seen since Changi. The fit remained in the jungle until the end of March, where they were employed principally in cutting fuel for locomotives, before they too were moved by rail to Thailand.[8]

Group 5 (1,800 strong) which had belatedly been placed under Varley's command, had come from Java, as mentioned earlier. It was a principally Dutch force, but also contained 450 Americans and 385 Australians.

---

[6] At the Kilo-105 camp several boxes of meat arrived in so bad a state that the Japanese commandant complained of the smell. The meat must be eaten forthwith, he declared. The Australian commander replied that it was too bad to eat. The Japanese then ordered the meat to be buried since "I cannot put up with the smell". "His house was 300 yards from where we were," commented the Australian commander . . . "and we had the meat!" Eventually much of the consignment was eaten.

[7] The goods comprised 5 cases of peaches, 5 of jam, 5 of sauce, 13 of sardines, 7 of green peas, 54 of biscuits, 5 of butter, 275,000 cigarettes and 55 cases of soap.

[8] Throughout the period a radio set had been operated at great risk by Lieutenant Watchorn and Sapper T. Stephenson of the 2/12th Field Coy (of Drummoyne, NSW), which kept the men abreast of world events and their optimism at a high level.

The senior officer was Lieut-Colonel Tharp of the 131st U.S. Artillery Regiment; the senior Australian officer was Major Robertson of the 2/6th Field Company. Like Black and Williams Forces, it had left Java in October 1942 for Singapore, but unlike those forces had spent rather longer at Changi, and had not embarked for Burma until 9th January. On its way north the convoy (two transports and a small naval escort) was attacked by Allied aircraft. One ship was sunk with the loss of about 400 Japanese and about 40 Dutch prisoners, and the *Moji Maru,* carrying the Australian and American prisoners, was damaged.

> Moji Maru twice near missed by bombs (says the report of the force). Last stick holing starboard side severely, killing 7 PW's, wounding many others. Many Nips killed and wounded. After-gun blew up killing its crew; forward gun, trained aft, narrowly missed blowing the navigating bridge to fragments. . . . Behaviour of PW's excellent. As ship circled round picking up survivors from the other vessel, sick bay organised on after-deck by Captain Lumpkin, USA and Commander Epstein USN together with Australian, American and Dutch orderlies. Captain Kennedy[9] is to be especially commended for his work in organising cookhouse to get tea and hot water ready and generally in controlling the troops. RAN personnel . . . also Cpl Imlach,[1] Ptes French[2] and Coe[3] were generally outstanding in work of organisation and rescue of Dutch PW's.[4]

On the 17th the troops reached Moulmein, where all prisoners were lodged at the gaol. There they were organised into national groups, each group being broken up into working platoons or *kumis,* as with "A" Force. Between 24th and 28th January the prisoners, now known as "Thai POW Branch 5" were moved from Moulmein to Kilo 18 (Alepauk) on the Burma-Thailand railway. The group commanders were taken to Thanbyuzayat where they met Brigadier Varley and spent a few days before rejoining their forces learning something of the general procedure and requirements of the working parties. On the 26th, accompanied by Japanese guards, all *kumis* began work on railway tasks, with officers acting as foremen. At the outset the task of moving earth to the embankment was set at 1.5 cubic metres a day; holidays were granted every tenth day, and impromptu concerts were organised. Some picnic soccer was also played, the Korean guards joining in and "behaving like a lot of happy gutter kids". The daily task was increased as time passed and the hard work and poor food ("sufficient to keep people just alive who are not engaged in toil") combined to take toll of the men. By 17th March 96 Australians were on sick parade, but a light duty *kumi* helped the Australians to maintain their working quota. Water sufficient only for cookhouse requirements could be drawn from the camp well, but men were permitted to bathe at streams as they returned to camp from working

---

[9] Capt J. Kennedy, TX2084; 2/3 MG Bn. Manager; of Hobart; b. Hobart, 18 May 1912.

[1] Cpl W. Imlach, TX3354; 2/40 Bn. Timber worker, concrete worker, hard rock miner, bullock driver, navvy; of Myrtle Bank, Tas; b. Launceston, Tas, 16 Apr 1906.

[2] Pte J. St G. French, NX36988; 2/2 Pnr Bn. Labourer; of Tamworth, NSW; b. Armidale, NSW, 2 Jul 1919.

[3] Pte J. C. G. Coe, VX39468; 2/2 Pnr Bn. Chauffeur; of Moonee Ponds, Vic; b. Kingston, London, 6 Jan 1916.

[4] Diary of Maj L. J. Robertson, RAE, Commanding Australian Personnel of Thai POW Branch 5, Burma 1943-44.

parties. Each national group maintained its own cookhouse. Cattle were sometimes delivered on the hoof. The rice ration generally measured up to the promised scale, but the bulk of the vegetable issue comprised melons—wryly described by one Australian "as water standing up". However, a canteen was established, and the rations were supplemented by items bought locally, such as duck eggs, vermicilli, tomatoes, *gula* (sugar) and cigarettes. The working men were paid every ten days at fixed rates, and, with the introduction of regular pay, all ranks began to contribute two days' pay in every ten for the purchase of extra food through the canteen for general messing.[5]

In mid-March Group 5 moved to a new camp, sited in rugged, heavily-timbered hills, about Kilo 85. This was in an area partly cleared of jungle; the accommodation consisted of huts newly built of saplings, with bamboo and atap roofs. The Australians were employed in "clearing, cutting and filling tasks". The administrative staffs were whittled down as the Japanese endeavoured to increase the strength of working parties. Early in April the force moved on foot through thick dust to a new location at Kilo 80. There in a bamboo-encrusted hollow, set in thick jungle which prevented any breeze through the camp the numbers of sick increased and it became increasingly difficult to produce work-party quotas. The Japanese threatened that if their demands were not met officers would make up the numbers; and they conducted strict inspections of the sick. Rations improved but working hours lengthened as the Japanese kept the prisoners at work until dark or later to complete the Kilo-80 section of the railway. The longer working hours took toll of the weaker men, and by 6th May, of a total of 322 Australians in camp, it was difficult to muster 220 for outside work. That month *kumis* were returning to camp regularly after midnight, having begun work in the early morning. By 29th May, all work on the Kilo-80 section having finished the force was marched to a camp at Kilo 100, carrying full packs and bedding, the last half of the march being through ankle-deep mud.

At the Kilo-100 camp the total Australians numbered 344; 170 of these were on railway tasks, 75 were sick and the rest were employed as camp staff and on improvements. In June the Australians were finding difficulty in producing the requisite number for working parties and these were made up by levies of the halt and the lame.[6]

At this stage the Japanese stated that the delivery of rations was temporarily impracticable, because of a bridge break near Kilo 75. They reduced the rations of outside workers to two and half normal meals a day, and of inside workers to one and a half. The amount of work required was correspondingly reduced. The low death rate among the Australians convinced the Japanese that they were healthier than other nationalities,

---

[5] The daily rates of pay were: warrant-officers 40 cents; NCO's 30 cents; privates 25 cents.

[6] "The prevailing wet," wrote Major Robertson, . . . "seems to be having a bad effect on the spirits of the weaker-hearted. . . . Refusals to go on camp duties for improvements in camp accommodation and hygiene have recently become more frequent. These men are actually thought little of by the majority of their comrades, the term 'bludger' being applied. It is regretted that a *few* of the officers are sometimes showing a *tendency* to act like disgruntled ORs."

and proportionately larger demands were made on them. Blitzes continued to be carried out on sick parades, and light duty men formed a percentage of the working parties. The commander, Major Robertson, was frequently slapped for failure to produce the requisite numbers. On 22nd July one Australian[7] and two Americans died of suspected cholera.

Sections of the camp were isolated, and working parties reduced. On 2nd August Captain S. Hugh Lumpkin, the medical officer to the force, died after a short illness "undoubtedly aggravated by the mentally torturing task of caring for our sick at all times" especially during the blitz period. The outbreak of cholera was halted, but deaths from other causes continued. In the 72 days to 20th August 62 died at the Kilo-100 camp, including 4 Australians. Some of the deaths were attributable to the depression caused by the damp, dank surroundings and the unsuitable food. The resultant loss of appetite prevented recovery. At this time the strengths of the national groups were: Australian 301, American 363, Dutch 834. The truth of the Coates' dictum that the route to survival lay in the bottom of the troops' dixies seemed to be confirmed by a check made of the eating habits of the troops at this time. This revealed that the Australians ate "all their rice and could eat more"; that the Americans ate less than their issue; and the Dutch, though perhaps more accustomed to a rice diet, ate still less.

By 23rd September the dead numbered 168, including 14 Australians. At this stage because of "decreased cost of living", the amount deducted from officers' pay for board and lodging was reduced to 20 rupees a month. The scale of payment to officers when this took effect was:

	Gross	Board and Lodging	Bank	Nett
Major	170	20	120	30
Captain	122.50	20	72.50	30
Lieutenant	85.0	20	35	30

The general result, adds the report of this force, was "no change in actual pay". In September, although men had continued to die at Kilo 100 at the rate of nearly four a day, and by the end of the month the total dead amounted to 183, only 14 of these were Australians.[8] The troops were then being employed on napping and carrying ballast to the track between Kilo 100 and Kilo 105 for Burmese to lay. On 12th October the first steam train passed the Kilo-100 mark; three Dutchmen died that day bringing the total deaths to 208. That month the Japanese issued instructions that the use of certain words, long since popularised by British and Australian soldiers, must cease. The Japanese soldiers were becoming contaminated!

There was a general improvement in camp conditions at this time. The rain began to ease, rest days became more frequent, rations began to

---

[7] The second Australian to die in Robertson's force since the work began.

[8] At this stage some 30 Australians had died at Kilo 80, which had been established as a hospital area for Group 5, and at other camps along the line.

improve and snakes, "said to taste between fish and rabbit", were abundant. By the middle of October the diarist of the Australian force was able to note that "two days have passed without a funeral". On 12th November the camp received its first mail—six letter cards dated January 1943, all addressed to Java. On 20th November, memorial services, ordered by the Japanese at the cemeteries at Kilo 80 (hospital area for Kilo 100) and Kilo 100 took place, and a "day of feasting" was declared. The work party call up at this stage amounted to 50 per cent of camp strength, working on railway maintenance on a day-on day-off basis. Early in December 1943 "Thai POW Branch 5, Burma" was abolished and the Java Party came under the administration of Group 3. On the 27th began the evacuation of light duty and hospital cases to base camps in Thailand. The departure of Colonel Tharp on the 29th left Major Robertson the senior officer in camp. In January most of the remaining Australians (127 in all) and the remaining Dutch and American prisoners moved to Kilo 105. The gradual reduction of the force by transfer to base camps in Thailand continued until 23rd March when the force was considered wound up. Australian deaths in Burma and Thailand totalled 67. In the period during which Group 5 worked independently of Varley's command, 54 (of 385) Australians, 98 (of 456) Americans, and 322 (of 1,160) Dutch died. The lowest death rate (14 per cent) was suffered by the Australians; the highest (27.7 per cent) by the "Dutch"—largely Asians. The total strengths and deaths in Groups 3 and 5 in the period 15th September 1942 to 20th July 1944 by nationalities showed, however, different proportions:

	Total strength	Deaths	Per cent
Australians	4,851	771	15.8
British	482	133	27.5
Americans	650	128	19.6
Dutch	5,554	697	12.5
	11,537	1,729	

In addition 33 Australian, 17 British and 237 Dutch prisoners died in Burma before work began on the railway. Up to January 1944 the death rate in "A" Force was 13.06 per cent; in Group 3 13.43 per cent—far lower rates as will be seen, than those suffered by any of the forces in which Australians were employed in Thailand.

"During the whole of this tragic period of misery and suffering, Brig Varley's strong personality, his vigorous and fearless championship of the troops, careless of rebuffs and determined to leave no stone unturned for the better treatment of the men, won for him the grudging respect of the Japanese," wrote Lieut-Colonel Anderson, "and I have no hesitation in saying was probably instrumental in preventing a far greater tragedy than that which took place."

While Groups 3 and 5 had been thrusting the railway southwards from Thanbyuzayat towards Nieke, other groups of prisoners had been working northwards from Thailand, as has been mentioned, to meet them. The first Australians to reach the southern end of the railway belonged to Dunlop Force (900 strong) from Java, which arrived at Konyu on the Menam Kwa Noi River on 24th January 1943. There they joined Dutch and British prisoners who were part of the major transfer of prisoners from Singapore which had begun in June of the previous year, gained momentum in October and November, and was soon to be further accelerated.

In Thailand the work forces normally were organised into battalions of about 600 including about 30 officers. From Bampong some of these battalions were taken forward to work camps by truck; others whose members were weak when they set out from Singapore and further debilitated by the heat, crowding and poor rations during a four to five days' train journey, were marched northwards, as a rule at the rate of about 12 miles a day, but sometimes in longer stages, and always by night. The staging camps were inadequate and sometimes filthy, and many marchers spent their nights in the open—a great hardship during the monsoonal season. The prisoners were escorted by Korean guards commanded by Japanese N.C.O's. For administrative purposes the labour battalions were organised, as in Burma, into groups. Irrespective of seniority the Allied commander of a camp occupied by the Japanese group headquarters was regarded by the Japanese as the Allied Group Commander for all matters concerning records and pay. However, his command over other camps in the group was almost non-existent, and the poverty of inter-camp communication together with the typical water-tight compartments in which each camp worked, usually made local commanders the final arbiters of all matters in dispute. In each camp the senior battalion commander acted as Allied camp commander, but where increases or changes in camp strength produced a more senior officer, the seniority of the latter was seldom recognised by the Japanese.

The work-party organisation in Thailand varied between camps, and also from one period to another. At the end of 1942 it had been common for one officer to be sent out with 25 to 30 men; later one officer to 100 men was equally common; and later still, when officers were themselves employed on the line the practice of sending out an officer with other-rank working parties fell into disuse.[9]

In speeches and in private conversations the Japanese officers and men, as in Burma, soon made their attitude towards the prisoners clear.

> During 1942-1943 (states an Australian report) the Japanese claimed to know nothing either of the Hague or the Geneva Conventions. Those who admitted some knowledge of International Law and these conventions expressed what can be taken as the Japanese Army attitude that a signature to the Hague Convention by Japan was binding only on the Government and not on the Army.
> They took the view that it was dishonourable to be taken as prisoners and that, therefore, prisoners of war had no rights or status and were slaves of the Emperor

---

[9] It is doubtful in any case whether the presence of an officer was of any value; they were consistently ignored by the Japanese, and not infrequently made the object of special spite.

for life. We must be punished for fighting against Japan and made to correct our anti-Japanese ideas. . . .

The Japanese did not consider human life of any value when viewed in the light that the railway must be pushed on regardless of the cost. . . . Discipline was enforced by brutality; for example, when standing to attention in front of a Japanese soldier should a prisoner's heels be one inch apart he would be severely beaten. Bashings and other forms of punishment for minor offences were common.[1]

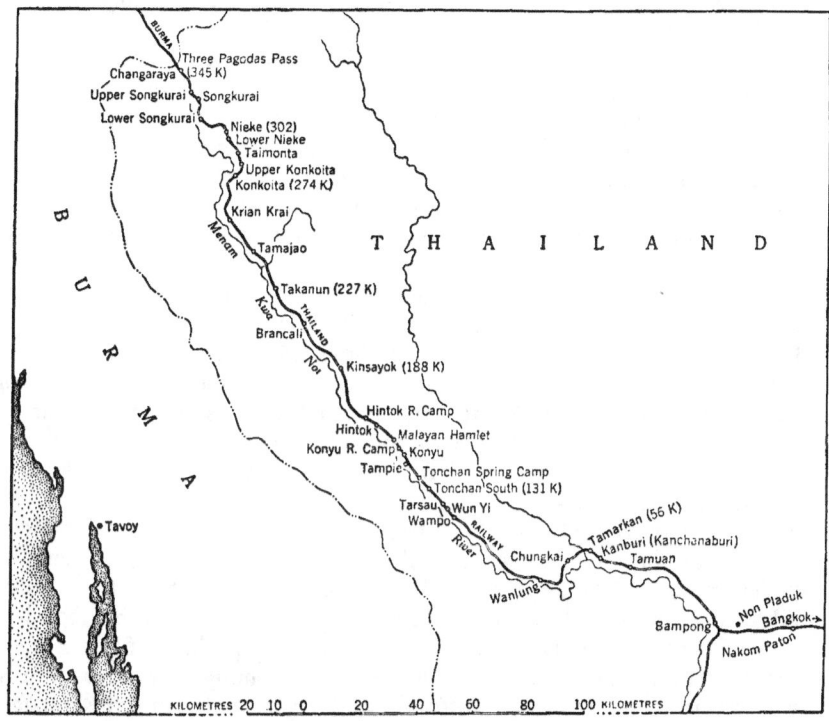

"D", "F" and "H" Force camps

In the Bampong to Nieke sector in which Dunlop and succeeding forces were to be employed, the country was at first flat and open with sparse low bush, but once Wanlung was reached the jungle became thicker and great clumps of prickly bamboo, some as high as 60 feet with bases as thick as a man's thigh, awkward and dangerous to clear, menaced the wayfarer. Farther on the country became hilly, and at Wampo, where a rocky hillside fell steeply into the Kwai Noi River, a great triple-tier viaduct 200 metres long was built. Beyond Tarsau the country rose sharply and became wild, hilly and rugged and covered with dense jungle. This high ground continued beyond Kinsayok and at length began to fall towards Takanun. Between Takanun and Tamajao three or four great cuttings were made. In this area the gradients were often steep and a great

---

[1] Report on Conditions, Life and Work of P.O.W. in Burma and Siam 1942-1945, Brig C. A. McEachern.

many ravines had to be bridged. Near Konkoita the Kwai Noi diverged westward from the track which crossed a tributary and then continued to Nieke.

The Kwai Noi, navigable as far as Takanun in the dry season and as far as Konkoita in the wet, was of great importance during the construction of the railway, both as a means of transport and for its water supply. Also it was rich in fish, although the prisoners seldom were able to take advantage of this.

The jungle was full of exotic orchids, beautiful butterflies and lizards, and "of every kind of biting insect both by day and night". The scenery was often wildly majestic. The rainy season began in May, was at its wettest in July and August, and ended in October. For the next three months the climate was cold. The night temperature sank as low as 45 degrees Fahrenheit and men shivered and prayed for the sun. In February, March and April the weather became hotter and hotter and the camps and roads were deep in dust.

Dunlop Force was organised into two battalions each about 450 strong commanded by Majors Greiner[2] and Woods[3] designated "O" and "P" Battalions respectively. Two other battalions "A" (337 strong commanded by Captain Hands[4]) and "R" (a purely Dutch battalion, 623 strong commanded by Captain Smits) also came under Dunlop's command. The first task of the force was to clear a camp area of bamboo so that huts could be built, but after two weeks of fruitless labour the camp site was abandoned, and on 12th March "O" Battalion (followed a week later by "P") moved to Hintok. "Q" and "R" Battalions also moved from the Konyu area at this time. During the period spent at Konyu the troops had slept in the open, but at the primitive Hintok Road camp, about two or three miles from the river, there were a few dilapidated huts and bamboo lean-tos which had previously housed Indonesian troops in so filthy a condition that they were eventually burnt. The incoming troops at once set to work to build bamboo platforms and erect tents, but the Japanese allowed the prisoners no time to make the area habitable and immediately began to draw upon them for maximum numbers for working parties. From the first camp staff was kept to a minimum.[5]

The difficulties imposed by the smallness of the camp maintenance staff were enhanced by the distance of the camp from the nearest barge-point, and stores had to be manhandled over rough hills a distance of 7 kilo-

---

[2] Maj H. G. Greiner, ED, VX45534; 2/3 MG Bn. Grazier; of Tongala, Vic; b. Echuca, Vic, 19 Feb 1908.

[3] Maj F. A. Woods, MBE, QX6100; S/Capt 21 Bde 1940-41; 9 Div 1941; LO between HQ British tps and HQ AIF Java 1942. Stock dealer; of Ramsay, via Cambooya, Qld; b. Sydney, 5 Aug 1910.

[4] Capt J. L. Hands, WX3335; 2/3 MG Bn. Bank officer; of Perth, WA; b. Bunbury, WA, 4 Mar 1916.

[5] Only 70 were allowed for all administrative and maintenance work for a camp of about 1,000. This allowed 29 cooks, 15 medical personnel (including two doctors, Majors A. A. Moon and E. L. Corlette), 11 clerks, 6 men for anti-malarial work and hygiene, 5 for water duties, 1 bugler and three batmen for the Japanese. Dunlop continued for the time being to be employed as an administrative officer. Cookhouse staffs were usually kept by the Japanese to a minimum of between 1 and 4 per cent of the camp strength. As they were often required to cut their own bamboo for firewood and carry all rations from railhead or riverside their casualties, contrary to popular belief, were often high. At Konyu in 1942-43, for example, the casualties were as high as 50 per cent.

metres. Although Japanese transport frequently used the road, the Japanese engineer officer refused to allow his lorries to be used for this purpose, and as a result the carriage of stores fell heavily on the camp duty section, including officers and volunteer railway workers who made the trip at the end of the day's work.

An almost insuperable obstacle to the work of camp construction, however, was the lack of tools and materials, and it was only with the greatest difficulty at Hintok that deep trench latrines were dug and ultimately provided with timbered roofs and flyproof covers. The timber for the work had to be obtained by felling jungle timber and laboriously splitting it with wooden wedges. While wire was sometimes available for nail-making, at most times wooden pegs had to be manufactured.

It was not surprising that camps should suffer, when similar deficiencies extended even to the railway works. There, for example, a singular lack of good spades existed, although these might have been considered fundamental to any earth-moving project.[6] A lack of means of earth transport made it necessary to devote a large proportion of the labour force to remedy this deficiency by the most primitive means—in bags, on stretchers, or in baskets. In deep cuttings it was common to see a chain of 20 men passing baskets behind two men with digging tools.

The ingenuity of prisoners knew no limits, particularly where the majority stood to benefit. At Hintok, for example, a complete water system, manufactured from bamboo, piped water from a dam several hundred yards to a system of showers and dixie washing points, and was also used to cool condensers in a water distillery plant.[7]

Shelter at Hintok consisted of bamboo and atap huts for both the workers and sick, but in many cases the accommodation for the sick was infinitely the worse of the two.[8] Hospitals were built at a pace which usually lagged behind the number of sick. The Japanese largely disregarded deterioration of huts and tents, gross overcrowding became the rule, and these habitations became infested by rats and other vermin. Bedding was the roughest of bamboo, sometimes even without blankets, let alone mattress or pillows, and, as a rule, the sick lay massed together on continuous bamboo platforms with their feet directed to the only passage through the hut.

For the workers the Hintok section of the line presented special difficulties. It was extremely rocky, with large embankments and deep cuttings, and some of the working camps were so sited that workers had to march over rough hills in all six to seven miles daily.[9] They usually left camp in darkness between 7 and 8 a.m. (Japanese time) and the march and the day's work frequently kept them out for as long as 16 hours a

---

[6] This lack was accentuated after the arrival of large numbers of native workers on the line, when tools of poor quality (for example shovels manufactured from oil drums) were supplied to the workers.

[7] Bamboo served for making huts, beds, brooms, brushes, baskets, water containers and other things.

[8] Workers lived 20 to a leaky hut 16 x 14 feet.

[9] Others had to walk up to 10 miles.

day. By 7th April 85 had been evacuated unfit for work to Tarsau where a hospital had been established and 121 were sick in camp out of a total strength of 873 men. Dunlop attributed this deterioration in the men's health to inadequate rations, inadequate camp staff, lack of footwear and primitive accommodation and medical arrangements.

The primitiveness of the accommodation at Hintok Road camp in comparison with that at other camps was soon remedied, and by May it was recognised as one of the best camps in the area.

> It was a purely Australian camp (wrote a British officer who passed through Hintok with "H" Force on 9th May) and was surrounded by a bamboo palisade. . . . We spent the night under an atap roof on a very wet floor and the Australians were as friendly as they could be—there was little enough they could do to help us for their rations had been skeleton stuff for months. They had however a fair M.I. room that patched us up generously. Several things were unusual about Hintok. The latrines were made of wood, were clean and sixteen feet deep; they had made a complete water system out of hollow bamboo pipes and had rigged up showers in a bath place entirely carpentered from bamboo; and they had a silver bugle blown by a first-rate bugler, who made the calls sound more beautiful with the mountain echoes than I'd ever believed a bugle could sound.[1]

The rations referred to above usually consisted of inferior rice, varying in quantity between 7 and 13 ounces a day depending on the type of work done, and a little dried vegetable and fish, often in a decayed state. In one 10-day period the Hintok camp of 886 men received 33 pounds of pie melon. They were "grossly deficient in proteins, fat and vitamins", in the opinion of Colonel Dunlop, and this combined with their inadequate calorific value rapidly resulted in malnutrition disorders and lowered health.[2] The men were paid when employed on heavy work at rates that prevailed elsewhere. One-third of all such pay was contributed to a messing fund to purchase extra rations through canteen sources and to provide for the sick.[3] When men were evacuated from Hintok it was arranged to send down to base hospitals 10 cents a man a day to assist them. As the number of sick increased, however, this arrangement became a heavy strain on the meagre wages of officers, who were not permitted to use their bank balances for this purpose.

At the end of March the first of "D" Force had begun to arrive in the area and a portion of "S" Battalion of that force brought the strength of the Hintok camp to about 1,000. The commander of the force, Lieut-Colonel McEachern, having arrived, Dunlop was able to persuade the Japanese to relieve him of his duties as an administrative officer, and in April McEachern took command at Hintok.

"D" Force represented a substantial reinforcement of 2,780 British and 2,220 Australian prisoners. The Australians had been drawn mainly

---
[1] J. Coast, *Railroad of Death*, p. 104.
[2] Also the rations, having been plundered before delivery by the Japanese, often bore little relation to the amount which the prisoners were compelled under threat of punishment to sign for.
[3] In particular, eggs supplied by this means saved many lives.

from the artillery units of the 8th Division, and were organised into three battalions.[4] The senior medical officer was Captain Hazelton,[5] there were seven other medical officers and 30 medical other ranks. The Australian portion of the force had left Singapore in four drafts between 14th and 18th March. Like preceding drafts they were taken to Bampong in enclosed steel rice trucks 18 feet by 8 feet into which 36 men were crowded during a journey that took between four and five days. There were no washing facilities or sanitary arrangements, and prisoners were issued with only one pint of water a day, and beaten for attempting to obtain more. At Bampong they were searched, before being taken over the newly-constructed line in open flat rail cars to an open and unguarded area at Kanburi. There for a time they were left to fend for themselves; the many Japanese in the area appeared uninterested in the newcomers, and for a week no parades were held nor instructions received by the force. The men traded personal possessions with local merchants and stall holders, and "everywhere groups of men boiled billies and brewed coffee, fried eggs and bananas and sweated over hot frying pans. Life became one long feast."

At the end of a week this agreeable interlude was shattered by the arrival of a number of aggressive, shouting guards, from whom the prisoners learnt that the week's freedom had been the result of a mistake. It took the guards two days to round up prisoners from the surrounding countryside.

The railway at this stage had progressed no farther than Kanburi and "D" Force was to be employed on embankments and cuttings and difficult tasks along the line where progress had fallen behind schedule. As has been noted, part of McEachern's battalion had gone to Hintok. A second battalion ("T"), of which a record has been preserved, was moved up to Tarsau by trucks and based at Wampo beside a detachment of 200 Japanese engineers who were reasonable in their demands. At the end of two weeks, when a small embankment on which they were initiated to railway work was completed, the men were marched downstream to an old-established camp, whose occupants were the diseased and dejected survivors of an English prisoner-of-war group, and a detachment of brutal guards. There a huge embankment under construction near the camp was well behind schedule and had to be completed in two weeks. The workers were split into two shifts—one to labour at night and one by day. Groups of six Australians were set the task of digging earth and carrying it in stretchers to the top of a high embankment. On arrival the Japanese engineers marked out a plot of ground 6 feet by 3 feet to be dug to a depth of six feet, and indicated that when it was finished the prisoners

---

[4] "S", "T" and "U", commanded by McEachern, Major E. J. Quick and Captain Newton respectively.

[5] Capt A. R. Hazelton, NX35134; AAMC. Medical practitioner; of Artarmon, NSW; b. Sydney, 23 Nov 1915.

would return to camp.[6] Despite various subterfuges the men soon began to feel the strain. At night

> Great fires burnt everywhere and the groups of sweating bodies stood out as they slaved in their pits. A Jap had one man standing on a rock holding a crowbar over his head. Another Jap had two men chasing each other round a tree for hours on end. Yet another . . . had set an unfortunate Englishman the task of rolling a massive boulder up the embankment. Like Sisyphus, the Englishman laboured with his stone only to find it rolled back two feet for every foot gained. Men who had collapsed, lay where they fell until the end of the shift.[7]

After a fortnight's constant work about 100 Australians had fallen out; the rest, now near the point of exhaustion, were ordered to continue until the task was finished. In a nightmare effort, they worked for thirty hours straight. "At its end" (wrote Bombardier Clarke[8]), "we carried dozens of unconscious comrades back to our tents and fell into one of the greatest slumbers of all times."

Thence the Australians were marched north to Konyu, where the main camp was situated on a bamboo-covered plateau about three miles above the river. A second camp on the river (Konyu 2) was the loading point for stores delivered by barge. The Australians were marched to a new area and set to work to construct Konyu 3. Within the day, before the camp was near completion, half the strength of the battalion of 380 men was ordered to commence work on a cutting—"Hell Fire Pass" as it became known. This was in two sections, one about 500 yards long by about 25 feet high, and the other about 80 yards long by 80 feet high. At first the daily task was set at 1½ metres a shift, but within two days it was increased to 2 metres; by the end of the week it had been set at 3 metres, and the layer of earth having been removed, the prisoners were encountering solid rock. Shovels were issued to some men; 8-lb hammers and steel drills to others; and, as the metallic chink of hammers echoed round the hills, ant-like groups of men moved boulders and baskets of rocks out of the now shallow cutting.

By June, rail-laying parties had reached the cutting and the pressure was intensified to speed up its completion. The equipment at the cutting was reinforced by an air compressor, and a dozen Cambodian jack-hammer operators were introduced. Elephants also arrived, and more prisoners, including the fittest of "O" and "P" battalions, Newton's battalion of "D" Force, a battalion of the newly-arrived "H" Force, and some British prisoners. The hours of work lengthened until they reached 18 a day, and this continued for about six weeks until the cutting was completed.[9]

---

[6] Much of the railway work was complicated by a lack of experienced Japanese engineers. The best were employed on the more difficult tasks such as bridgework; the least experienced on embankments. Some of these found it difficult even to calculate a task, and if, for example, a task required the moving of 15 cubic metres of soil, that amount had to be taken from a rectangular hole 3 x 5 metres, and 1 metre deep, and no other shape was allowed.

[7] Hugh V. Clarke, a bombardier in the 2/10 Field Regiment, in an unpublished MS.

[8] Bdr H. V. Clarke, QX17307; 2/10 Fd Regt. Cadet-surveyor; of Brisbane; b. Brisbane, 27 Nov 1919. Clarke has published numerous short stories and sketches of prisoner-of-war life.

[9] Captain Newton estimated that 68 men were beaten to death while working in the cutting.

At night the cutting was lit by about a dozen carbide lamps; by huge lamps constructed of 18-inch long bamboo containers, 4 inches in width, filled with dieseline, with rice sacking for wicks; and by bamboo bonfires.

A second major engineering project in this area was the "Pack of Cards Bridge", Hintok, so named because the bridge, 400 yards long by 80 feet high, fell down three times during construction. It was built of green timber, fastened with wooden wedges, spikes, bamboo ties, rattan or cane rope, and wooden dowls.

> Three weeks ago there was nothing there at all (wrote a prisoner); now there is not only this vast bridge but steam engines bumping slowly over it. . . . Two thousand pre-dynastic slaves . . . had built the entire thing in 17 days! . . . It was characteristically Japanese, not only because it was a crazy wooden bridge that nevertheless functioned, but because no other nation in the world in 1943 would have bashed and bullied, and sweated and slaved prisoners to such fantastic lengths for such an object.[1]

Thirty-one men were killed in falls from the bridge to rocks below, and 29 were beaten to death there.

The wet season had begun on 22nd May, with a 72 hours' non-stop downpour, and camps became "seas of mud walled in by bleak ramparts of jungle or bamboo". Canvas tents began to rot, and footwear, clothing and bedding rapidly deteriorated. Cholera broke out among the native labourers, and despite rigid precautions spread to the prisoners of war. At Konyu the first case occurred on 16th June; at Hintok three days later. Within two months there had been 150 cases at the Hintok camp of which 66 were ultimately fatal. The Japanese greatly feared cholera and patients were relegated to the most deplorable tents in a low-lying area, somewhat downstream of the camp, and frequently covered with several inches of water. Men who caught the disease on railway work were left to lie where they fell until word was sent to the hospital staff.

As the wear and tear on working battalions increased it became increasingly difficult to maintain the numbers required by the Japanese, and pressure upon the sick was increased to the point of "frenzied sadistic brutality".

> Work parades (wrote Dunlop) ultimately became a deplorable spectacle with men tottering with the support of sticks and carried piggyback on to a parade ground, unable to work, in order that fixed figures could be met. Lying cases were frequently carried to the engineers' lines and ordered to work with hammer, axe etc., in a sitting position. The sick were frequently treated with special savagery in order to discourage illness.

As was usual in Japanese working camps, the administration of the prisoners was divided between the local Japanese camp commandant and his staff, with many Korean guards, and the Japanese engineers, who took charge of the workmen and directed their daily activities. Generally speaking the camp commandant and staff were responsible for the hopelessly inadequate camps and medical arrangements for the prisoners; but most of the brutality and actual violence came from the engineers.

---

[1] J. Coast, *Railroad of Death*, p. 96.

The engineer company in charge of the Konyu-Hintok area was commanded by Lieutenant Hirota ("Konyu Kid"[2]), a particularly cruel and sadistic Japanese, whose appearance on the line was invariably associated with waves of brutality. Blows and kicks were a routine measure of punishment and exhausted men who fell out of working parties were beaten and otherwise maltreated. To the sick Hirota displayed a special kind of savagery. On occasions prisoners suffering from diarrhoea and dysentery were not allowed to leave the line. In his treatment of the sick he was abetted by the medical N.C.O., Corporal Okada. Once towards the end of April, when the camp was about to be inspected by a visiting Japanese general, Okada undertook to reduce the hospital numbers by marching about 50 men to a hiding place in the jungle.[3] Although the men were obviously ill, with large tropical ulcers, protein oedema and other disabilities, they were handed over to the engineers to roll 40-gallon oil drums over a rough hillside track and down a steep gradient for several miles to the site of a compressor. If they allowed the drums to get out of control they were beaten.

The relentless demands for fixed numbers of workmen made the lot of medical officers most difficult, because the Japanese were prone to make reprisal raids on the hospital, from which sick were turned out indiscriminately if the required numbers were not produced. Endless daily parades with "heart-breaking comparison" were required to keep the most severely ill in hospital. Frequently men with inflamed and festering feet or ulcers of the legs were made to work on rocks or in rough jungle, and men with diarrhoea and dysentery were not permitted to cease work except during recognised rest periods. Men falling with cholera were left to lie for hours in soaking rain rather than allow workmen to carry them back to hospital. Sometimes men unable to carry on died as a result of beatings. Hostility and pin-pricking tactics towards the sick were everlasting. At times all sick men were required to do some task, and dangerously-ill patients were ordered to kill a stated number of flies with swats. Medical personnel who attempted to protect their patients from Japanese brutality were frequently beaten or stood to attention for long periods.

The Japanese tended to regard sickness as shameful, and to maltreat the sick in the mistaken belief that this would discourage them from falling ill. Camp commanders were repeatedly ordered to allot all rations to the workers and told that it did not matter if the sick died.

In this period the evacuation of the increasing numbers of sick from up-river camps was haphazard and unmethodical. The usual method was by hitch-hiking on empty barges or lorries, but frequently this resulted in sick awaiting transit for days often without attention and with little food. At Tarsau and other places on the Kwa Noi River barge-loads of

---

[2] The prisoners frequently bestowed nicknames upon their captors. Some of these names—"Snake Hips", "Frankenstein", "Leather Lips", for example—seem to have been derived from physical characteristics; others—"the Boy Bastard", "the Turd", "the Maggot"—to express the loathing with which some of the more brutal were regarded by the prisoners.

[3] Visits of high officials were invariably associated with intense pressure upon the sick to secure favourable working figures.

emaciated men frequently arrived, and many died during transportation. Extreme over-crowding occurred at so-called base hospitals, where no warning of the sick who came flooding in could be given.

Yet primitive though such hospitals undoubtedly were, to the human derelicts arriving from working camps on the railway they were "like entering the gates of paradise". At Tarsau, for example, huts were waterproof, the camp was clean, and the food more plentiful than the prisoners had known for weeks. At this period in its history Tarsau was divided into two camps—the hospital area on the river bank, and a smaller camp near by in which fit men were housed. The fit worked on roads in the area, but for the sick work was a thing of the past. The fit camp was divided also for eating purposes into three nationalities, British, Dutch and Australian. The vegetable peelers, who were allowed to keep their peelings, were mainly Australian.

During these grim days the mortality among troops in the Konyu-Hintok area varied from between 12 per cent in the battalions of Dunlop Force to as high as 50 per cent in others. In the period of unrelenting pressure men of various races and differing physiques suffered approximately the same mortality, because, no matter what reserve of physical strength and fortitude an individual possessed, in the long run he was driven to the same level of complete exhaustion and breakdown.[5]

Between 20th August and 2nd September the Japanese began sending large numbers of sick by barge to base hospitals and concentration areas in southern Thailand, reducing the strength of the work forces by as much as 50 per cent. In mid-September, the Hintok sector having been completed, the force was moved to the Kinsayok area. There they remained on railway work until January, when they were returned to Tarsau and thence to Tamuan. Although "D" Force never reassembled as an entity, its total mortality was reckoned at 18 per cent, rather less, as will be seen, than the rate experienced by other forces containing Australians which were employed in Thailand.

"F" Force, the sixth main party containing Australians to depart from Changi, was one of the largest—about 7,000 men including 3,662 Australians and a similar number of British prisoners—and unlike preceding groups it retained its identity throughout the eight months it was away. When it was being formed in April 1943 the Japanese said that the reason for its move was to transfer a large body of prisoners to an area where food was more plentiful and the climate healthier than on Singapore

---

[5] The drain on working battalions in the Hintok area is illustrated by the following figures for 12th August 1943:

Bn	Total Strength	Hospital River Camp Hintok	Hospital Hintok	Elsewhere in Hospital, Konyu and Tarsau	Total in Hospital
O	407	102	87	68	257
P	401	94	67	84	245
S	468	110	41	217	368
T	451	47	86	373	420

Island.[6] The force commander was Lieut-Colonel S. W. Harris of the 18th British Division.

Lieut-Colonel Kappe commanded the A.I.F. contingent, which consisted basically of the 27th Brigade supplemented from other units. This brigade had been kept intact since capitulation. The senior medical officer, who commanded nine other medical officers, one dental officer and 221 other ranks of the medical corps, was Major Stevens.[7]

There were then not 7,000 fit men at Changi, but the Japanese insisted that the size of the force must not be reduced and that 30 per cent of unfit men might be included. The Australians accepted this order with reservations, and finally perhaps not more than 125 unfit Australians were included. In the British force the number of unfit men was estimated at nearly 1,000 with consequences which will be described later.

The force began to leave Singapore on 16th April in a succession of thirteen trains (the first six for the A.I.F.) made up of enclosed steel trucks into each of which 27 or 28 men were crowded. After five days of extreme discomfort, hunger and thirst, each trainload arrived at Bampong, where the men camped under filthy conditions. There they learnt that a march lay ahead, although its extent was not revealed. All heavy kit and stores, including medical stores and tools, were dumped by order of the Japanese in an open space at the side of the road in Bampong, and no guard was allowed. The Japanese had available some six-wheeled lorries and one ambulance. These carried Japanese stores on their first trip north; but few completed a second run, and none a third, as monsoonal rains destroyed long stretches of road. The result was that most of the heavy stores and three-quarters of the medical supplies of "F" Force remained at Bampong. Before the march began most of the men either jettisoned their surplus clothing or sold it to Thai traders.

From Bampong the prisoners marched 180 miles northward, along jungle tracks to the Nieke area, marching by night and resting by day over a period of seventeen days. Control on the march was virtually impossible, as torches had been confiscated during a search at Bampong. Long stretches of road were corduroyed, and snags and holes made marching in the dark difficult and dangerous. Many men wore out their boots and marched on blistered feet. Although some seriously ill men were permitted to remain at Bampong, the guards forced most of them to go on, and before the march was over virtually every fit man was carrying a sick man's gear as well as his own.

Treatment of the sick varied from camp to camp. At some camps medical officers were allowed to leave behind such men as they considered unfit to march. At others they were subjected to much interference and

---

[6] There were other blandishments that suggested the Japanese were either concealing the facts or were ignorant of conditions in Thailand. Bands were permitted to accompany each 1,000 men and gramophones were promised after arrival; canteens were to be established within three weeks; no restrictions were placed on the amount of equipment that could be taken, and transport was promised for the carriage of heavy personal equipment, camp and medical stores and men unfit to march. There were to be no long marches.

[7] Maj R. H. Stevens, NX39043; 2/12 Fd Amb. Medical practitioner; of Kew, Vic; b. Armadale, Vic, 3 Mar 1899.

sometimes were beaten. For example, at Tarsau a Japanese medical officer and Major Bruce Hunt[8] agreed that 37 prisoners were unfit to travel; the corporal of the guard would consent to only ten remaining. The production of a letter from the Japanese medical officer had no effect on the obdurate guard. When the time came for the prisoners to move off, Hunt fell in the 37 men apart from the main parade, and stood with Major C. H. D. Wild, the interpreter, in front of them. The corporal approached with a large bamboo in his hand, and spoke menacingly to Major Wild, who replied in placatory tones.

> The corporal's only reply (reported Hunt) was to hit Major Wild in the face. Another guard followed suit and as Major Wild staggered back the corporal thrust at the major's genitals with his bamboo. I was left standing in front of the patients and was immediately set upon by the corporal and two other guards—one tripped me while two others pushed me to the ground. The three then set about me with bamboos, causing extensive bruising of skull, back, hands and arms, and a fractured left 5th metacarpal bone. This episode took place in front of the whole parade of the troops. After I was disposed of the corporal then made the majority of the sick men march with the rest of the troops.[9]

Repeated check parades at comfortless and sometimes shadeless staging camps interfered with rest periods; Thai bandits attacked and robbed stragglers. Towards the end the night marches "had become grim endurance tests, and even the fittest were suffering severely".[1] No Australians died during the march, but all were very weak and many were seriously ill, particularly with dysentery.

Colonel Harris, who was taken ahead in motor transport to Lower Nieke with the Japanese commander, Colonel Banno, found that virtually no preparations had been made to house and feed the force. Thus when Colonel Pond's battalion (700 men) arrived at Konkoita "no meal was provided until cooks drawn from the ranks of tired men had prepared the usual watery onion stew and rice.[2] No cover was available and men were compelled to lie out in the open in a scorching tropical sun until 1100 hours."[3] When the men moved to a camp area they found that few huts were roofed and those were occupied by coolies; the whole area was filthy and dying natives were lying unattended on the ground.

Pond's battalion was employed on bridge and road construction while the succeeding parties marched through, but on 15th May the Japanese medical men said that cholera had broken out among coolies in the area

---

[8] Maj B. A. Hunt, MBE, WX11177. (1st AIF: 30 Bty AFA.) 2/13 AGH. Medical practitioner; of Perth, WA; b. Sydney, 23 Feb 1899.

[9] In an appendix to "History of 'F' Force", by Lt-Col S. W. Harris.

[1] Report of Activities of AIF, "F" Force. At Changi in May 1944 Colonel Kappe and Captain Curlewis completed this report, a document of about 50,000 words, on which the present summary is mainly based.

[2] The Australian battalion commanders were: 2/26 Bn, Maj C. P. Tracey; 2/29 Bn, Lt-Col S. A. F. Pond; 2/30 Bn Maj N. McG. Johnston. A fourth battalion formed of other than infantry was commanded by Maj J. H. Parry of the AASC.

[3] The prisoners in "F" Force seem to have suffered undue hardship because the Japanese administration of the force was based in Singapore, and there was jealousy between the administrations there and in Thailand. After the monsoonal rains began in May the road from Bampong was useless except to six-wheeler vehicles. Although the river rose and was navigable by mid-June as far north as Nieke, and in fact was used that far by the Japanese engineers and Thai tradesmen, it seems never to have been used for the carriage of sick and stores for "F" Force.

and the battalion was hurriedly marched on to Upper Konkoita. Between that day and the 17th, 1,800 Australians including Major Tracey's battalion from the headquarters area at Lower Nieke reached Lower Songkurai. There on the 16th several cases of cholera were diagnosed among the Australians and others.

Lower Songkurai camp consisted of bamboo huts all of which were roofless except that there were eight tents to cover the officers' quarters. There were no kitchens, and so little water that washing was impossible. There was no hospital accommodation. The prisoner-of-war officers pressed for atap for roofing and urged that enough men should be spared from roadwork—to which all fit men had immediately been allotted—to improve the camp. Gradually an isolation centre and a hospital were built. Cholera vaccine was obtained, and by 25th May all troops had been inoculated; but not before five men had died of the disease. The arrival of more tents, and atap, enabled the huts to be roofed. A secondary wave of cholera began at this time, and before it was got under control a total of 110 had died.

> It was at this stage that Major Bruce Hunt [the senior fit medical officer] made an impassioned and dramatic appeal to the men which finally dispelled the lethargy that had been so apparent, and imbued the men with a new spirit of determination to fight the crisis out. It was one of many such addresses that Major Hunt gave at this and other camps, all of which had an enormous effect on the morale of the force.[4]

On 30th May Majors Johnston[5] and Hunt and the two "battalion" commanders at Lower Songkurai wrote a strongly-worded protest to the senior Japanese officer demanding that work on the railway cease, that medical and other supplies be delivered and that the area be evacuated as soon as the men's health would allow. The letter had the effect of obtaining a four-day suspension of work.

At the end of May "F" Force was distributed among five main camps: No. 1 Camp at Lower Songkurai, about 1,800 Australians; No. 2 Camp at Songkurai, about 1,600 British; No. 3 Camp, Upper Songkurai, 393 Australians; No. 4 Camp, Konkoita, 700 Australians; No. 5 Camp, Changaraya, 700 British. There were a headquarters and hospital at Lower Nieke (soon to be moved to Nieke) of about 200 of each nationality. About 550 Australians and 800 British prisoners had still to reach the regions allotted to "F" Force.

The camps suffered as a whole from a grievous shortage of cooking utensils and food containers, and practically no tools were available either to the prisoners or to the Japanese. Each party had left Bampong carrying some containers and medical stores, but, as the sick gathered at the various staging camps, the containers were left with them and the medical stores were used up in their treatment. Some cooking utensils and containers which had arrived by lorry before the rains began were sent

---

[4] Report of Activities of AIF, "F" Force.
[5] Lt-Col N. McG. Johnston, ED, NX70427; 2/30 Bn. Public servant; of Neutral Bay, NSW; b. West Maitland, NSW, 10 Jan 1906.

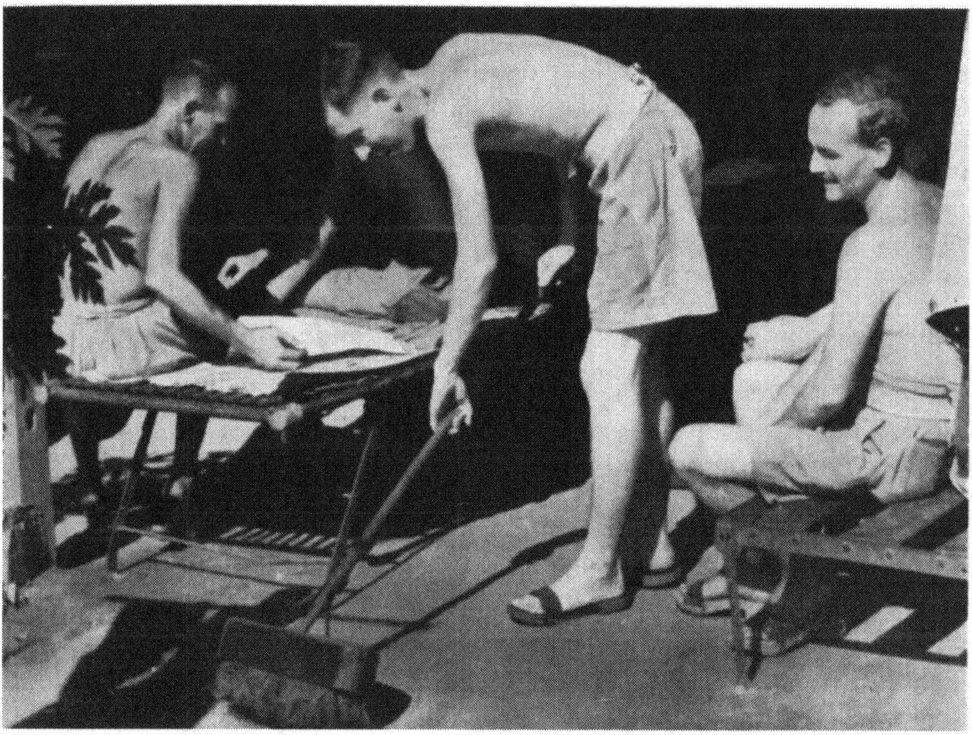

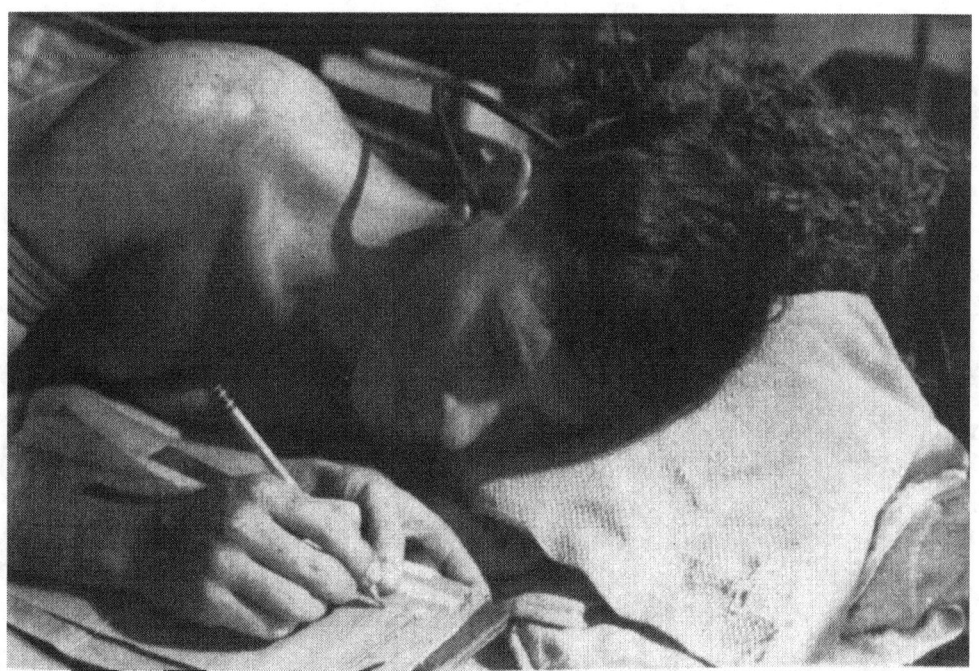

(*Australian War Memorial*)

(*Australian War Memorial*)

News bulletins, illicit, and prepared and circulated at great risk, ranked in importance second only to food in the prisoners' lives. *Top*: The broom wielded by Lieutenant R. F. Wright had a wireless set built into its head. *Bottom*: Wright demonstrating the way news was received.

(Ex-Servicemen's P.O.W. Subsistence Claims Committee)
Steel rice trucks were used by the Japanese to move prisoners from Singapore to Thailand. These trucks, 16 feet long by 8 feet wide, normally carried 30 prisoners of war and their belongings.

(Ex-Servicemen's P.O.W. Subsistence Claims Committee)
A river barge transporting stores and sick prisoners of war on the Menam Kwa Noi River, Thailand.

(*Australian War Memorial*) (*Ex-Servicemen's P.O.W. Subsistence Claims Committee*)

The Burma-Thailand railway and the main road.

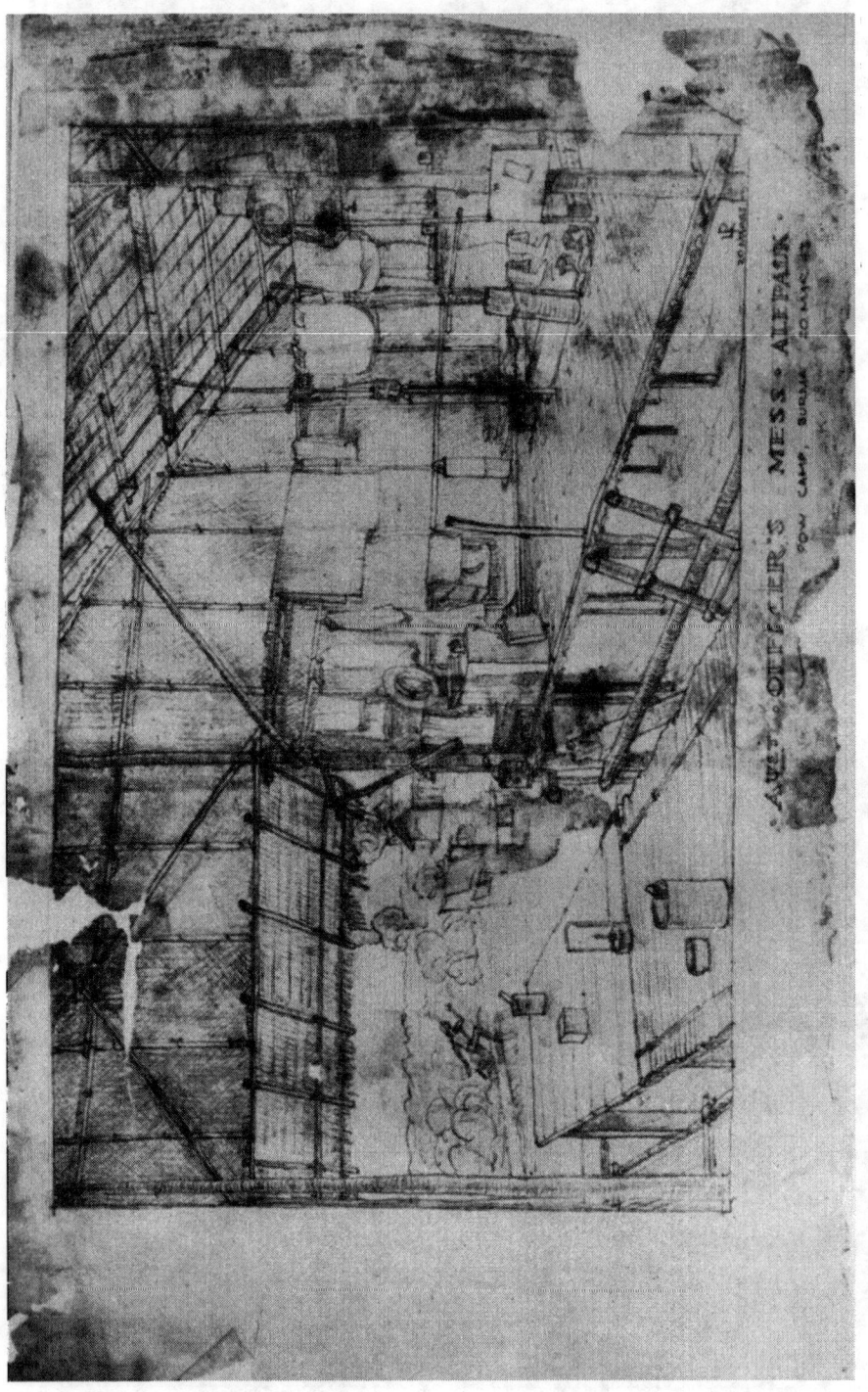

Reproduction of a sketch by Major L. J. Robertson, preserved during captivity, of the Australian officers' mess at Alepauk camp (kilo-18) on the Burma-Thailand railway.

to Lower Songkurai, in expectation of further deliveries. Even so this camp was still poorly provided. Other camps were formed with practically no containers and almost no medical stores.[6]

At Upper Songkurai, a small compact camp close to a water-supply, with a cookhouse near the sleeping quarters, this lack was a serious inconvenience. At the Songkurai and Changaraya camps it was a disaster. The cookhouse at Songkurai, for example, was a quarter of a mile from the camp, and as the numbers of sick increased there was no efficient way of distributing food to the main hospital half a mile away, or to the still more distant isolation hospital. The result was that officers and convalescents spent the entire day trudging through never-ending rain carrying meals to hospital patients in the few buckets and containers that could be spared.

In June, though the fight against cholera at Lower Songkurai had been won, malaria was beginning to make itself felt. The men, now becoming weaker and weaker, many with no boots and all with their clothes in tatters, were being cruelly over-worked. Soon 1,300 out of the 1,890 men at Lower Songkurai were sick; by the end of June 120 had died since arrival; in that month 46 per cent had contracted malaria, 38 per cent dysentery and 9 per cent cholera.

As the Japanese engineers increased their demands for more workers, relations between the Australians and the Japanese commandant became worse, and many stormy interviews took place.

> Men were being driven to work like cattle and not returning to camp until as late as 2330 hours . . . soaked through with rain, tired, footsore and dispirited. After their meal they were often too weary to stand around fires to dry their clothing . . . now rapidly falling to pieces . . . boots . . . were becoming unserviceable and a great number of men were forced to go to work bootless.

At this stage working parties were marching six kilometres and a half to working sites where they were required to manhandle logs 14 feet long by 8 inches in diameter over muddy and waterlogged ground to corduroy the surface of the road. When men collapsed under heavy loads they were compelled by the engineers to carry on, at times being struck with tools and sticks.

Conditions were filthy at Upper Songkurai camp. At first the medical care of the camp was in charge of a sergeant, except when Major Hunt was able to pay a visit from Lower Songkurai, and for a few days rations were issued to coolies who cooked both for themselves and for the Australians. By 8th June 216 men were sick; 7 had died of cholera. Captain Swartz, who took over the camp on 8th June, reorganised it and obtained a big improvement in hygiene and food and "by the end of June this camp was the best in the group, relations with the [Japanese] were reasonable, working conditions and rations fair, and the men generally con-

---

[6] The Japanese administration provided little for cooking purposes except rice boilers (kwalis) which are heavy fixtures and useless for food or water distribution to hospital or outside working parties.

tented".[7] At the Songkurai and Changaraya camps (all British) cholera losses were more severe than elsewhere. In Songkurai 227 of 1,600 died; at Changaraya 159 of 700, almost 25 per cent.

Between Songkurai and Konkoita were the Nieke and Lower Nieke staging camps. Colonel Harris and Colonel Banno (the senior Japanese officer) established their headquarters first at Lower Nieke and then at Nieke proper. The site was a quagmire, but there was less sickness than at other camps and the rations were better, probably partly because Banno was there and partly because of the "untiring leadership" of Lieut-Colonel Dillon, the camp commandant, but also because the camp was a concentration point on the railway and therefore better served with supplies. The number of men frequently changed, the maximum being 1,075, including 450 Australians.

At the end of June only about 700 of the 5,000 men north of Nieke were at work daily, and of those at least half were unfit for heavy work. The remainder, except for Red Cross and administrative troops (including officers), were lying ill in camp hospitals. This state of affairs had been caused at the outset by the general exhaustion of the prisoners and by the demands of the Japanese engineers for maximum numbers, including all fit and convalescent men, to be employed on work parties. These were for such heavy work, seven days a week, as clearing jungle, building bridges, digging cuttings and building embankments, and for roadmaking. Too few men were left for camp maintenance and care of the sick.[8]

At this stage the road from the south was impassable, and to the north difficult. The scale of rations fell below the level required to keep fit men in health, and far below the level required to help sick men back to health. The rations of men in hospital—250 to 300 grammes of rice and a small quantity of beans a day—were fixed at far too low a scale, evidently in the mistaken belief that lack of pay and rations would drive men out of hospital. But this would happen only where men were practising deception, and there could be no deception where the sick were dying in large numbers daily.

In late June the Japanese decided to establish a base hospital at Tanbaya in Burma for the increasing numbers of sick. The hospital was to accommodate 1,700 patients considered incapable of work for at least two months, and Major Bruce Hunt was to command it. The sick far exceeded 1,700 even at that stage, and the selection of patients was extremely difficult. On the one hand it was useless sending men who were unlikely to survive the journey; on the other many were certain to die if retained at the working camps. An advanced party, including Hunt, left for Tanbaya on 1st August, followed by the first batch of sick on the 25th. The journey was unduly prolonged and arduous, and 43 out of 1,700 died on

---

[7] Report of Activities of AIF, "F" Force.

[8] Paradoxically, although the engineers appeared to have complete control of working conditions and seemed insensible of requests for their amelioration, when the condition of the sick was demonstrated to them "they would rush out of the sick huts rather than endure the sight of the results of their inhuman treatment". (Report of "F" Force, Lt-Col S. W. Harris.)

the way. The conditions at staging camps were chaotic, and the sick lay by the side of the road for hours awaiting transport. There was no bedding or straw on the metal floors of lorries or railway trucks, and "guards jabbed ulcerated buttocks to make the sick 'speedo' in their climb into trucks, and stoned them to 'speedo' the unfortunates out again".

The Tanbaya camp fell below even the most dismal expectations. It consisted of a hutted camp without light or water. The amount of medical stores supplied was negligible and rations were at all times poor. They were particularly deficient in vitamin B, vital to patients, practically all of whom were suffering from beri beri.[9] Although men at Tanbaya were required to work only on camp maintenance, in the period 1st August to 24th November 750 patients died, or about 45 per cent of the total patients.

Compared with others, Pond's battalion was unfortunate in two special respects: it was frequently moved from one camp to another and its camps were commanded by Lieutenant Murayama, a particularly cruel and dishonest Japanese. Cholera broke out when it was at Upper Konkoita, roadwork ceased and the rations, always low, dropped to 7½ ounces of rice a day. Dysentery and malaria increased. By 6th June 368 out of the 694 men in the unit were too ill for even light work. On 10th June fit and light duty men (316 all ranks) were moved north to a filthy site near Nieke where groups of 30 or more men had to use 12-men tents. At this stage every man was "suffering severely from hunger pains, weakness and giddiness" although the rice ration had been increased to 12½ ounces a day. By the 17th most of Pond's battalion had been concentrated at the new site. Next morning the battalion began a 40 miles march south to Takanun, the weary sick men "hopelessly weighed down with equipment".

A shuttle system had to be employed whereby fit and nearly fit (who by now were very few) marched to the next camp, erected tents, dug latrines, prepared cookhouses etc. and then returned to the last camp to carry stretcher cases and sick men and their gear forward. To add the last straw to these trials the men repeatedly were ordered back to dig from the mud and then push up the hills the many ox-carts laden with Japanese stores which had become bogged. Over and over again these efforts kept the men on the road until 3 and 4 in the morning, only to start again at 0800 hours.

When it was over more than half the men had no boots, most had no clothing but a loin cloth, and many had developed ulcers.[10] The battalion remained at Takanun for two months, working or marching from

---

[9] A shortage of medical supplies existed throughout "F" Force. At this stage it was estimated that 70 per cent of the men were infected with amoebic dysentery, yet the only issue of a specific drug was 100 1/3rd grain emetine ampoules (sufficient for three patients by normal British standards) to the Tanbaya hospital where there were hundreds in need of it. Anticholera vaccine and quinine were, however, supplied more liberally, although there was seldom enough of the latter for suppression purposes. Many hundreds of cases of beri beri would have been avoided by the supply of rice polishings, used by the Japanese at Kanburi in 1944 to feed their cavalry horses.

[10] The average kit of a prisoner on the Burma-Thailand railway in this period might be made up of an old hat, a pair of boots with leaking soles, no socks, a "Jap-happy" (loin cloth) in which he worked, perhaps a patched pair of reserve shorts; a water bottle, with or without cork, a mess tin and spoon, a leaky foul-smelling groundsheet, two sacks or perhaps a thin blanket, a pack to carry the equipment in, and possibly a share in a mosquito net. These were the total possessions of the average soldier, but many had far less.

8 a.m. until 10.15 p.m. The men rose at 7 a.m. in pitch dark, and usually in pouring rain. Those detailed as mess orderlies staggered up slimy slopes carrying heavy mess dixies of rice. Others, having queued up to sterilise their mess tins in boiling water, received their rice and squatted or stood miserably in the rain while eating it. Immediately afterwards, still in the half light, they lined up again to wash their mess tins and receive their luncheon issue of rice. At dawn the medical officer began sick parade; at 8 a.m. the working parties fell in, and efforts were begun to obtain extra men to replace those whom the medical officer found unfit for work.

At 0815 hours the party moved off across a high level bridge, 80 yards long, the track being constructed of slippery logs 6" wide. Men whose nerves were not equal to the task of negotiating this bridge were compelled to cross a low level bridge two or three feet under water. At 0830 hours a second parade of the work party was held by the Japanese, a check of numbers made and tools issued, and at the conclusion of this the men were herded off to the job about two miles away through deep mud or across sharp flint-like stones or gravel. As half the camp at this stage was without boots the journey always was a trial, stragglers being smacked on the face on arrival for lateness.

Having arrived at the job the men were divided into teams of three or four, one man to pick the cutting face of the rock, one to shovel and two men to carry away the spoil in bamboo stretcher-like baskets. This last duty usually meant a carry of shale, rock or soaking clay for a distance of 50 to 75 yards through yellow oozing clay on a bed of gravel. Again men's feet suffered badly. Almost without exception the periods of work were 50 minutes with a ten minutes break for smoking. When the men were on contract labour, which frequently was the case, the rest period was often used by dysentery and diarrhoea cases to obey nature's call. The break for lunch was taken from 1330 hours to 1500 hours, being reduced to one hour for the last month's work on the railway. . . . Last light at this time of the year was in the vicinity of 2115 hours and usually this was the time for cessation of work. Then followed the collection and counting of tools and baskets, checking of men and the order to return to camp. To many men this return journey was one of the greatest trials of the day. Exhausted from work, feet cut and sore, clothes wet and cold, they set out to pick or feel their way in the dark through the two miles of mud, including a balancing task across three bridges.

Arriving at camp at about 2215 hours, again they would line up to sterilize their mess gear and then draw their evening meal of rice and jungle-leaf flavoured water. The more fortunate would cluster round a fire, and then grope their way down to the river to wash off the day's mud and sweat. Another sick parade, and dressings completed, the men were able, usually by 2300 hours, to don a camp shirt . . . roll themselves in a blanket, probably damp, and lie down under a rotted, dripping tent.[1]

At the outset in "F" Force officers were required to accompany work parties, but at Takanun officers were ordered out to work in special parties on a more favourable contract basis. As time went on sickness reduced their numbers and they became used solely for supervising the men or acting as tally clerks for the number of baskets carried by the men. Suspicions, not perhaps unjustified, that officers were falsifying the figures (at one stage the Korean guards themselves were frequently doing so in order to return to camp the earlier) at length led to their suspension from this

---

[1] Report of Activities of AIF, "F" Force.

task; and as the number of men collapsing at work increased some officers began voluntarily to fill their places with the permission of the guards.

During July conditions at the Songkurai camps became worse. The road became a ribbon of mud, almost impassable except by six-wheeled vehicles. Bridges to the north were repeatedly washed away, and supplies from Burma were irregular. No clothing or boots had been issued and blankets available had been too few even to cover the feverishly ill. Working conditions worsened, and at Lower Songkurai men finishing road work at 9 p.m. faced a return march of two hours through mud and rain in pitch darkness. At the end of the month, of 1,854 men at Lower Songkurai, 1,265 were in hospital, 214 on camp and hospital duties and 375 working. At Upper Songkurai, where conditions were consistently better than at other camps either to the north or south, 229 out of the 430 were hospital patients.

In August 866 Australians of Major Tracey's battalion were concentrated at Songkurai No. 2, where 1,000 British troops were already collected. Conditions there were probably worse than in any other camp, and 600 British troops had died before the Australians arrived. Men had been beaten with wire whips and bamboo sticks to make them work harder, and men too sick to stand had been forced to haul logs and beams from a sitting position. When the Australians arrived hygiene had fallen into neglect. The newcomers built new cookhouses, dug new latrines and cut and stacked wood. At this stage the principal task was the building of a wooden bridge, about 100 feet long over a near-by river, and the prisoners were required to carry logs up to 20 feet long and over 1 foot diameter for distances of 800 feet through mud up to their knees, while being constantly beaten. Lieutenant Abe, the Japanese engineer commander at Songkurai, demanded numbers far in excess of the fit men in camp, and when Tracey protested brought armed guards through the hospital, who turned out by force the first 200 men encountered. Some of the men working on the bridge were knocked into the river 30 feet below it.

By August two-thirds of the men in all camps were hospital patients. A movement began, evidently with the object of concentrating all British prisoners at Songkurai and all Australians (except Pond's battalion at Takanun) at Upper Songkurai. This led to a series of exhausting marches with the men carrying not only their own gear but their blankets and camp equipment, including iron rice boilers, over roads deep in mud. Requests for some motor transport were refused despite the fact that lorries returning empty were moving along the road. On 8th August there were 1,020 Australians, including 403 sick, and 670 British, including 492 sick, in Upper Songkurai. The latrines were flooded by incessant rain; one had broken its confines and a filthy stream oozed through the camp area and passed under the floors of the huts occupied by the hospital, bay after bay of which collapsed under the weight of the sick men who had crowded into them. Cholera broke out, and before it was subdued nearly 50 men had died.

In mid-August Lieutenant Wakabyashi—"the only Japanese officer with whom 'F' Force had to deal who showed the slightest glimmerings of humanity or understanding of his responsibility towards Ps.O.W. under his charge"—told Colonel Harris that the engineers had ordered that, unless the working figure was doubled, all prisoners, sick as well as fit, would be turned out into the jungle to fend for themselves, thus making room for coolies to be brought in who could work. An opportunity for Harris to interview the engineer colonel was created and he was persuaded to allow the prisoners to retain two-thirds of their accommodation, leaving one-third available for fresh labour. The prospect of the prisoners being ejected was a real one, and would otherwise have been carried out despite the monsoon then at its height. "It is a grim recollection," wrote Harris, "that we were able to make available a third of our accommodation only by taking into consideration the number of deaths which would inevitably occur in the next few weeks."[2]

The Japanese seemed determined to break the British troops and to discriminate between them and the Australians. No Englishman was permitted to be employed in the cookhouse or on any other camp duty, so that all were available for working parties despite their age or physical condition. This meant that it became necessary to protect the weaker men by keeping them in hospital until they had recovered sufficiently to take on heavy work. For some days the Japanese reduced the rations of the British troops by one-third, but, by adjustment, the British heavy workers continued to receive the same rations as the Australian. At the end of August 63½ per cent of the men were sick and 100 per cent were suffering from beri beri in some degree. Working hours were increased and the workers were not arriving back in camp until 2 a.m.

> The strain now, both physical and mental, was terrific. Men were too exhausted even to speak and acted more as automatons than human beings. It was only the thought that the end was in sight that sustained them in these days of sheer torture.

"The end" meant the end of the work on the railway. On 18th September it was announced that the main work had been finished and a holiday was granted—the first since the work began in May.

October was relatively peaceful at Songkurai, but at Taimonta, where Pond's unfortunate battalion had now concentrated, "a new form of torture was instituted"—the carriage of railway gear from Nieke to Taimonta or from Taimonta to Konkoita, each return trip a distance of about 15 miles.

> The route was along the line and meant walking on the irregularly placed sleepers or the hard gravel at the sides; the lightest load would be a bundle of five picks, the heaviest an anvil . . . and empty train after empty train would pass without any effort . . . to relieve them. . . . Staggering under their heavy loads, riddled with malaria, with ulcers and cut feet, men collapsed over and over again. . . . On one occasion a warrant-officer, a particularly strong (man) . . . had to drag himself the last three kilometres back to camp on hands and knees.

---

[2] History of "F" Force, p. 22.

The beginning of November brought the final test—a move north to Nieke carrying the sick, including twenty-six stretcher cases. When this was completed most of the Australians of "F" Force were distributed between Nieke and the Songkurai camps. In mid-November the transfer of "F" Force to Kanburi in Thailand and eventually to Singapore began; soon only small rear parties and men too sick to be moved remained.

Of the 3,662 Australians in "F" Force 1,060 had died up to May 1944, including some who died after the return to Changi. Of a similar number of British troops 2,036 died. The average monthly death rate between May and December was over 360. Dysentery and diarrhoea had combined to kill 832 men, while 637 had died of cholera alone. One reason for the large number of British deaths was that a larger proportion of unfit men had to be included in the British force to complete its strength. Colonel Kappe attributed the lower Australian death rate also to "a more determined will to live, a higher sense of discipline, a particularly high appreciation of the importance of good sanitation, and a more natural adaptability to harsh conditions", and to "the splendid and unselfish services rendered by the medical personnel in the Force".

Under the terrible conditions suffered by the force as a whole the bonds of discipline and morale were "stretched to breaking point", wrote Colonel Harris, "but they never quite broke. If they had, probably not one man would have returned alive." Harris decided that the lower death rate among the Australians was due to the fact that they "were all members of one volunteer force with a common emblem and outlook", whereas the other troops were "a heterogenous collection of men of all races and units, many of whom found themselves together for the first time". He considered that the average physical standard of the Australians was "incomparably higher than that of the mixed force of regular soldiers, territorials, militiamen, conscripts and local volunteers" who formed the British half of the force, and they possessed a higher proportion of men accustomed to looking after themselves under "jungle" or "bush" conditions. Also the Australian contingent was undoubtedly fortunate in being able to complete its march and occupy its working camps before the monsoon broke.

While "F" Force had been undergoing privations and hardships in the upper Thailand regions of the line, a new force, "H", had been brought in by the Japanese to reinforce the middle reaches where progress had fallen behind schedule. Like "F" Force it too was to be under the disadvantage of administration by the distant Malayan headquarters. The force had been raised at Singapore in April 1943, in response to a request by the Japanese for a further 3,270 men for employment on the railway. Of these, 600 were to be provided by the A.I.F.[3] The force commander was Lieut-Colonel H. R. Humphries, of the Royal Artillery, and his second-in-command Lieut-Colonel Oakes, who also commanded the

---
[3] "H" Force contained a number of Australians captured in Timor.

Australian part of the force. Twenty-four of the Australian quota were officers, including two medical officers, a dental officer, and a padre.

The movement from Singapore by rail began on 5th May, the Australians leaving three days later. Like preceding forces the men travelled in enclosed steel trucks to Bampong, where the 600 Australians were confined to two atap huts 120 feet long by 20 feet wide. Water was drawn from one well; the latrines, close to the cookhouses, consisted of two slit trenches, with bamboo footrests, "the sight of which was enough to turn the strongest stomach".

> Fly larvae to the number of millions were in the trenches and here, as well as over the whole area of the establishment, flies and numerous other insect pests abounded.[4]

On the 13th, just before midnight, the men set out along a bitumen road on the first stage of the march to Tarsau, about 90 miles northwest of Bampong.

> We had not cleared the town limits (wrote one officer) before men were being sick and requiring assistance. . . . Men fainted and had fits—many threw most of their possessions away—all gasped for breath in the hot night air. . . . Many were grievously sick and very weak, but there were also weak-livered bludgers who couldn't or hadn't the guts to make an extra effort. . . . I would scold, growl, entreat, sympathise, encourage and beg of them to rise, but I might have spoken to the Sphinx—they just lay like dead men, but immediately a Jap guard grunted at them they were up like a shot. These men were just the scum of the A.I.F. . . . The large majority were true blue and helped and encouraged their weaker and sick mates tremendously. . . . We did not arrive at our destination until 10.30 a.m.[5]

The march to Kanchanaburi—an advanced railhead of a kind—was completed in two stages each of about 16 to 18 miles on the morning of the 15th. There a halt was granted, men were inoculated, vaccinated and "glass rodded"[6] before setting out on the final stage to Tarsau. After Kanchanaburi the road degenerated into a dirt track, and when the last leg of the march to Tarsau was reached "every man was limping badly . . . the men were in the last stages of exhaustion, limping, staggering and swaying like drunken men". Some of the groups that followed the Australians were more fortunate in that transport was made available, but at Tarsau, virtually the entrance to the jungle proper, which was reached by Oakes' force on the 19th, there was an almost total absence of tentage or drinking water, and totally inadequate sanitary arrangements.

Thereafter the groups proceeded by stages along jungle paths until they reached their respective camps. At length "H" Force headquarters was set up at Tampie and battalions were along a 20-kilo stretch of railway between Tonchan and Hintok. The Australians were second farthest north at Konyu 2 (afterwards known as Malayan Hamlet) which they reached

---

[4] Report of Lieut-Colonel Oakes.

[5] Major A. E. Saggers' diary. (Saggers was second-in-command to Oakes.) An other-rank member of "H" Force later commented that the prisoners who lay like dead men but were up like a shot when a Jap hove in view were, to his mind, acting quite normally. "A man almost beyond exhaustion point," he wrote, "can often find new energy with a bayonet prodding his rear."

[6] A humiliating test for dysentery performed by the Japanese.

"absolutely worn out" on 21st May. Most of the men had stood up to the march "like heroes", but some were found wanting and imposed unfair burdens on their comrades. The medical officer, Major Fagan,[7] with his medical orderlies, "tended the sick faithfully and lovingly", and "must have walked twice the distance in missions up and down the line", as also did Father Marsden,[8] the padre to the force.[9]

No preparations had been made at Konyu for the incoming troops, but soon a small area was cleared, tents were erected and a cookhouse was prepared. By 25th May the camp strength had grown to over 600. At that time the first working party of 200 men was ordered for work by day with another 200 for work by night. The men, still worn out, were difficult even to the point of insubordination to get working. Here as elsewhere railway work fell into three categories: railway construction, the carriage of rations over long distances during the wet season because of the breakdown in transport; and camp duties. A satisfactory feature of the camp at Malayan Hamlet was that the Japanese permitted Oakes to retain an adequate maintenance staff, and within a short time the camp was enlarged, tents were floored with bamboo, and hospital accommodation improved until, according to Colonel Humphries, it became "easily the best of any in the force".

The principal task allotted to Oakes' force on the railway was the cutting where "D" Force was already employed. Each night masses of rock were blasted away; each morning the broken rock had to be removed —sometimes in small skips but more often in baskets. This work was exceedingly arduous because of the long hours—as many as 15 hours in one stretch—the hurry-up methods of the Japanese, the consequent nervous strain, and the ill-health of men never fully recovered from the effects of the march up to the working sites.

The rations, consisting of rice, and a small amount of dried fish and spinach, were poor at first, but after a few weeks began slightly to improve. Small quantities of yak meat arrived and canteen supplies such as eggs, gula melaka (coconut sugar), tinned fish, biscuits and peanuts became available. Money was limited, however, and the amount of canteen supplies received by individuals extremely small. For example, the cost of providing each man with 1½ eggs or one ounce of sugar or two ounces of peanuts amounted to 100 dollars.

In June the strength of the working parties dropped from 200 to 150 by day and night. The camp strength steadied round 550, but many were ill and unfit for work, and Oakes and his fellow officers fought unceasingly the demands of the Japanese to increase the working party strengths.

---

[7] Maj K. J. Fagan, NX70643; 2/10 AGH. Medical practitioner; of Bookham, NSW; b. Launceston, Tas, 5 Feb 1909.

[8] Rev Fr L. T. Marsden, NX76355. Catholic priest; of Sydney; b. Bundarra, NSW, 12 Jul 1911.

[9] "Above all there was the extraordinary courage and gentleness and the incredible endurance of the medical officer, Major Kevin Fagan. Not only did he treat any man needing treatment to the best of his ability; he also carried men who fell; he carried the kit of men in danger of falling, and he marched up and down the whole length of the column throughout its entire progress. . . . And when at the end of our night's trip we collapsed and slept he was there to clean blisters, set broken bones and render first aid." Russell Braddon, in *Naked Island*, p. 178.

For the officers, the task of providing working parties of the required strength became a nightmare.

> Our guards were concerned only with supplying the workmen demanded by the railway gangers (wrote Oakes). The latter were concerned only with getting the railway built by a certain date. There was nothing personal about the matter at all. It was simply a demand for certain numbers. These men worked 12-hour shifts and were supposed to rest for the other twelve, but there were always ration carrying fatigues, camp fatigues for the Japanese, pulling lorries out of the mud and a hundred and one other distractions.

Towards the end the parades of the sick called to increase the working parties became "ghastly" affairs.

> Men wrapped in blankets, shaking with malaria; men naked except for a loin cloth for fear that they would foul their clothes through the weakness of dysentery; men crying through weakness and nervous strain; men pleading to be allowed to stay back, but the guards adamant.

On the 16th June, Major Fagan reported the first case of cholera, and soon afterwards the man died. That day all men were inoculated. At this crisis in the affairs of Oakes' force, the strength in the area was augmented by the arrival of 266 British troops, who also came under Oakes' command.

Throughout June and July rain continued to fall and deaths from cholera to increase. Over a period of nine days between 26th June and 4th July, 72 men died of cholera alone. The cholera isolation area was "a frightening sight", with dead and dying lying about and the medical orderlies working like heroes. Nevertheless so exhausting at this stage had the work on the railway cutting become that many of the prisoners declared that they would be "glad to be placed in the cholera suspect tents" to rest and be freed from the mental and nervous strain of work "in this hell of a railway cutting". The prisoners were fast becoming demoralised. "Many have dropped their bundle," wrote an officer, "and it is no wonder."[1]

> Time ceased to have any significance (wrote one soldier). No man knew what day of the week nor what week of the month nor even what month of the year it was. . . . If one were to survive it was essential not to acknowledge the horror that lay all around, still more not to perceive the effect it had upon oneself. It was not wise ever to look in a mirror. Life accordingly evolved into a blur of continuous work, people dying, guards bellowing, heavy loads to be carried, fever which came in tides of heat and cold on alternate days, dysentery and hunger. All those became the normal. Upon them, occasionally an event superimposed itself with sufficient violence to be remembered.[2]

Bodies were cremated, sometimes as many as ten at one burning, but the labour involved in gathering fuel was heavy. At length the Japanese prohibited cremations and the dead were buried in mass graves. On 29th

---

[1] It was noticeable that in the early stages of the outbreak many more Australian than British prisoners died of the disease, but within a week the pendulum had swung, and thereafter deaths among the British outnumbered the Australian by almost two to one.

[2] R. Braddon, *Naked Island*, p. 189.

June 454 were in hospital; by 4th July 91 had died, 110 had cholera and there were 118 suspects in a camp about 750 strong.

> The hospital is under fairly good control and organisation (wrote Major Saggers) but the cholera tent lines! God, what a sight—it is just a charnel house . . . the victims just dehydrate—some last up to 11 days, others are dead within 8 hours. They die absolute skeletons. The medical orderlies are heroes—not a whisper of complaint have I heard and they are working like slaves.

Only 120 of Oakes' force were able to work, and these worked in 8 hour shifts, 80 by day and 40 by night. "The 8 hour shifts are helping the men," noted one observer; "they are getting more rest and picking up very slightly but they badly want food." By the 18th, 134 men had died, 118 from cholera, 4 from dysentery, 4 from beri beri and one from diphtheria. One man in every six had died within five weeks.

In August rations began to arrive by rail and deaths to decrease. The men were lice-ridden and the camp was plagued by rats. On the 22nd a large wooden cross, erected by Colonel Oakes, was unveiled by Colonel Humphries at the cemetery, to commemorate the death of 217 prisoners (including 106 Australians). On the 25th 100 "fit" men (83 Australian and 17 British) moved north to Konkoita for other railway work. Early in September the Japanese began returning the remnants of "H" Force to base camps and hospitals at Kanburi. Here although the fit men were reasonably well off, and were issued with footwear, clothing and good food, and canteen supplies and rest did much to restore them, the hospital accommodation was hopelessly inadequate. An Australian has calculated that into an area 150 paces wide by 370 long 2,300 men were crowded. On 20th November the first troops left Kanburi by rail for Singapore and the Sime Road camp, under conditions similar to those encountered earlier, but in cooler weather. They were followed by other batches at intervals until 10th December, when only a few dangerously ill men remained.

One group of "H" Force deserving mention because of the special circumstances of its employment was that known as the "H.6 Officers Party", 320 strong, including 68 Australian officers, and other ranks numbering 60, including one Australian. This group, formed at Changi in May 1943, had been told before its departure that it would be employed in Thailand for camp administration and supervision of labour parties. Like other groups it had been misinformed about conditions in Thailand, and as a result the group included 30 per cent of physically unfit. Also, being one of the last up-country parties to leave Changi, it necessarily included a fairly large proportion of men who on account of their age had been excluded from earlier forces.

When the group arrived at Tonchan South and learned that it was required for labouring tasks on the railway, the officers protested, pointing out to the Japanese that the group was composed largely of unfit, and that it had been sent up solely for administrative duties. These protests were unavailing.

The work performed was of a very heavy nature, such as clearing jungle, felling trees, excavating for cuttings on the railway, cartage of earth, rocks and logs for building up embankments etc. In addition it was often necessary to call on officers who had been out all day to do further work on their return, such as making paths, fetching water for the cookhouse, collecting firewood, unloading lorries and other "chores" necessary to make the camp hospitable.[3]

The work was hard, the hours were long, and the difficulty of liaison with the Japanese resulted in more than the usual number of incidents because of misunderstandings. Officers were struck with pick handles or iron bars almost daily. The food of weak vegetable stew and tea thrice daily was not sustaining, clothing and footwear deteriorated, accommodation for the increasing numbers of sick was insufficient, and all sick other than those actually in bed were forced to make up the working parties. Conditions continued to worsen until June. Camps housing coolie labour sprang up round the H.6 camp and soon it was completely surrounded by areas in which even the most elementary hygiene was neglected. By the end of June almost 50 per cent of the A.I.F. group were sick, mainly with ulcers. On the 28th, when orders were received to send a party north to Hintok River camp, almost every fit officer was required to go. Of the 110 officers who left that day on foot for the 30-kilometres march to Hintok River camp, 28 were A.I.F.[4] Thenceforward the officers' group at Tonchan South began to disperse among other work forces. On 28th August the site was abandoned, and the remaining officers were amalgamated with a group at Tonchan Spring camp.

One small section of "H" Force which remained after the general evacuation to Kanburi included 20 Australian officers commanded by Major Ball who were sent north on foot to Konkoita in late August. A camp site was cleared, tents were erected, and for several weeks the officers were employed on railway construction, working long hours in mixed gangs with Tamils and Chinese coolies, hauling, among other things, heavy baulks of timber by rope up steep river banks. Increasing numbers became too ill to work, and the worst cases were evacuated from time to time to Kanburi. In mid-November the remainder were returned to Kanburi "fit camp", and at length to Singapore.

The deaths in "H" Force totalled 885 (27.37 per cent of the whole force), including 179 Australians. The majority of the Australians died at Malayan Hamlet, but some 50 died after evacuation to Kanburi.

From the Australian point of view redeeming features of the ordeal were the efficient control of medical supplies, a messing fund on a force basis, the maintenance of strict discipline, appearance and morale, "the extreme bravery of Colonel Humphries and his constant endeavour to obviate ill-treatment and remedy injustices, and the perfect harmony that existed between the A.I.F. and the other force commanders at all times".[5]

---

[3] Report by Major A. F. Ball.
[4] These were used to reinforce the Hintok cutting.
[5] Report of Lieut-Colonel Oakes.

The discipline of the officers of No. 3 party (wrote Colonel Oakes of his own force) was at all times of an extremely high order and most certainly an inspiration to me in my command. As regards the other ranks some few exhibited discipline of such a high order that they cannot be too highly commended. The majority . . . behaved themselves and carried out their duties in a most satisfactory manner and compared favourably with other troops. The A.I.F., perhaps owing to their natural training, seemed to stand up to rigorous conditions better than English troops. There were a few whose discipline was bad as they made little attempt to help either themselves, their comrades or the administration. . . . Generally speaking, however, I should say that more decorations for valour were earned during this episode than during any period of battle.

Early in 1943 the Japanese had begun recruiting Tamils, Chinese, Malays and other native labourers from Burma, Malaya, and Thailand to work on the railway. The recruitment was normally by contract for a specified period (usually six months), but the contract period was rarely honoured and coolies were kept working on the railroad until they died or were permanently disabled.

Taken into areas where cholera and dysentery were rampant, where even elementary principles of hygiene were neglected, and where no plan for medical treatment existed, it is not remarkable that the Asian workers died in thousands under the harsh treatment of the Japanese. Soon the medical situation had become chaotic.

Accordingly two forces comprising medical officers and orderlies were formed at Changi in June 1943 for employment on the railroad. Of these forces, "K" consisted of 30 medical officers and 200 orderlies, and "L" of 15 and 100. They were informed before their departure from Changi that they would be going to well-equipped hospitals and that it would be unnecessary to take medical equipment. On arrival at Kanchanaburi in Thailand they learned that they would be treating coolies, and that since "Japanese and other native labour had been grossly maltreated by the Americans at Panama and by the British elsewhere", it was the white man's turn to become "a coolie, to be degraded and to die in thousands". Both forces were split up into parties of one medical officer and four other ranks and distributed among the various coolie camps on the railroad. Coolie hospitals were established at Kanchanaburi in the south, at Wun Yi, Kinsayok, Konkoita and as far north as Nieke. These varied in holding capacity between 2,500 at the Kanchanaburi base to about 800 in those along the line.

The treatment, feeding and supply of medical equipment were particularly bad. Hygiene was exceedingly difficult to control. Cholera and dysentery were rife, and the Tamil particularly . . . will soil his neighbour's area with great cheerfulness. Grave digging was always done by medical personnel and owing to the increased death rate and the lack of staff there were at one time 500 coolies buried in the one grave at Nieke. Major Crankshaw,[6] AAMC, was employed in the IJA cookhouse and on other camp duties, whilst Captain Brown and Captain Eastwood, RAMC, were employed as bath coolies for the IJA.

---

[6] Maj T. P. Crankshaw, VX62081; 2/13 AGH. Medical practitioner; of East Malvern, Vic; b. Ararat, Vic, 17 Mar 1907.

The IJA showed complete indifference to the fate of the sick and labourers. This policy was economically so stupid that one can only suppose that it was due to sheer sadism. On one occasion, one of them killed a patient by putting a pick through his skull, apparently . . . to see how effective a weapon it was. The Nipponese orderlies used to enjoy going about the hospital with a bottle of chloroform and a 10 cc syringe, administering the chloroform intravenously to patients chosen at random and watching the subsequent convulsions and death.[7]

In March 1944 a new phase began with the arrival in Thailand of Japanese-trained Malayan dressers. These had undergone a three-months' course in Malaya and had been sent up to replace British medical personnel who were transferred to coolie work. In the circumstances described above it would be difficult to estimate either the numbers of sick treated along the line or the number of dead. For example, at Nieke in a period of twelve months, about 6,000 cases were admitted to the hospital of whom 1,750 died. The civilian death roll was calculated in August 1944 to amount to 150,000. Although, as will be seen, this was an overestimate, some such number was probably rendered permanently unfit for further work.

A gradual transfer to Kanchanaburi of "K" and "L" Forces began in August 1944 and was completed in February 1945. Deaths among these two forces amounted to about 16.

The magnitude of the task and the degree of suffering incurred by the prisoners may best be comprehended by the examination of some railway statistics, derived partly from Japanese partly from Allied documents collected after the war. Japanese engineers stated that the completion of the railway involved the building of 4,000,000 cubic metres of earthwork, shifting 3,000,000 cubic metres of rock, and the construction of 14 kilometres of bridgework in a period of about ten months "after hastening 6 or 7 months"—all by absurdly primitive means. Altogether 330,000 workers including 61,000 prisoners of war were employed on the railway. The Allied War Graves Registration units decided in 1946 that the number of dead among the prisoners of war amounted to 12,399, including 6,318 British, 2,646 Australians,[8] 2,490 Dutch, and 589 unknown prisoners. The bodies of the American dead were repatriated early in 1946. The total of deaths among the 270,000 labourers drawn principally from Burma, Malaya and Thailand was far higher. Some authorities place it at 72,000, but this figure may under-estimate the dead by as much as 20,000.

By March 1944 the bulk of the prisoners, except for those such as "F" and "H" Forces under Malayan prisoner-of-war administration and consequently returned to Singapore, had been concentrated into main camps at Chungkai, Tamarkan, Kanchanaburi, Tamuan, Non Pladuk and Nakom

---

[7] Report of Lt-Col E. E. Dunlop, Medical Liaison officer, Bangkok, 5 Oct 1945.
[8] The final estimate of the Australian dead is 2,815.

Paton in Thailand.[9] Conditions now began to improve, and there is some evidence that the Japanese had begun to feel apprehensive about the heavy casualties of 1943.[1] This was shown in a series of essays Allied officers were required by the Japanese to write in May 1944, dealing with aspects of railway construction and citing "actual examples of most miserable, most detestable and most painful things or matter (experienced) during the work". Senior Japanese officers from Tokyo visited some camps in Thailand in April and photographs for propaganda purposes were taken purporting to show well-dressed prisoners singing as they worked in the gardens and ideal hospital arrangements in Chungkai, Tamuan, Tarsau and Kanburi.

In February 1944 the Japanese had begun preliminary arrangements for sending parties of technical workers to Japan for employment in heavy industry. However, this plan was altered and at length the Japanese expressed their intention of sending 10,000 men, together with sufficient officers to control them.

The men were drawn from the various groups in Thailand between April and June 1944, after being examined by Japanese doctors, who rejected men suffering from skin complaints and malaria relapses.

The "Japan parties" were concentrated at Saigon whence it was hoped to transport them to Japan. As will be seen, transport difficulties and heavy losses incurred through submarine activities hampered the movement: many were lost on the way; others were taken to Singapore for shipment which did not always eventuate; some remained in Saigon awaiting shipment until the end of the war.

From May 1944 onwards parties ranging in strength from 150 to 600 were sent from base camps in Thailand to work on railway maintenance along the new line, to cut fuel for locomotives, and to handle stores at dumps along the line. The fittest of the prisoners had of course already been earmarked for Japan, but between June and August conditions in these working and maintenance camps were not unduly severe. As the numbers of men decreased, because of the toll taken by disease, conditions worsened. The numbers employed on the railway were too small to encourage merchants to visit the line with canteen supplies, and the railway was overworked carrying military supplies.[2] In some camps there were recurrences of the brutalities that had occurred in 1943; hospital patients, totally unfit for any form of exertion, were beaten and driven out to work. In fact, the only redeeming feature for the men working in the railway gangs along the railway during the winter of 1944-45 was the

---

[9] Some remained at Tarsau until the end of April and at Aparon, Burma, until February 1945, and there were other detachments in Thailand.

[1] Large hospitals such as those at Nakom Paton and Tamuan were established. These, though crude in the extreme, did at least give protection from weather; some of the finest surgical and medical work in the period of captivity took place at these centres. The Nakom Paton base hospital was designed to take 10,000 sick, and eventually held as many as 8,000. It was commanded by Lt-Col A. E. Coates.

[2] According to the records of the *9th Railway Regiment* more than 180,000 tons of supplies and equipment were moved from Thailand to Burma in the period January to December 1944. Thereafter the volume of traffic dropped sharply. In December 115 trains carried supplies from Thailand to Burma. In January 1945, possibly as a result of damage to the railway from air attacks, the number dropped to 60.

facility with which sick could be evacuated to the base in the trains returning empty southwards.

In April 1945 a labour force of about 1,000 (including 120 Australians) was employed making a road between Prachuab Kirikun and Mergui. The road was cut through virgin jungle and working hours were long. No atap roofing for huts was available and a bamboo substitute was not weatherproof. Although rice was plentiful, vegetables were very scarce and small issues of meat were made only at rare intervals. By June the death rate in the party had reached 18 per cent and half the men were sick; by August 25 per cent had died.

Another party of 500 sent to Songkurai, 12 miles south of the Three Pagodas Pass in June 1945 to build defence positions, underwent a gruelling time at the hands of the Japanese, who increased their working hours until the men laboured eighteen hours a day. There were no medical officers and few medical supplies; the rations were restricted to rice and dried vegetables. In the first month eighteen died and beatings were common as the Japanese drove the increasing numbers of sick to work.

A British-Dutch battalion of 400 was sent from Tamuan to Wampo in April to build a road leading westwards to Tavoy. Much of the journey took place at night along jungle tracks. Many of the men were without boots. All had been recently discharged from hospital. They were made to carry heavy burdens, and feeding was inadequate and at long intervals. From Wampo the work consisted of clearing a three-metre track and transporting stores in loads ranging from 25 to 40 kilograms (about 55 to 90 lbs), an average of 26 kilometres (15½ miles) a day. Accommodation was restricted to leaking, overcrowded tents; medical attention was inadequate, and the diet remained consistently at starvation level. Thirteen died in the first month and the number of sick rose rapidly.

Towards the end of July 1945 a group of 800 prisoners (including 100 Australians) commanded by a warrant-officer with two medical officers attached was marched from Nakom Nayok to Pitsanulok, a 600-miles journey which lasted six weeks. A third of the party were suffering from relapsing malaria and over 100 were suffering from chronic amoebic dysentery. Medical supplies were negligible, the rations were very poor, and stores, cooking gear and the sick had to be carried much of the way. Fortunately the capitulation occurred before this epic march was completed, and before more than three had died.

Meanwhile, in the Thailand base camps the discipline had noticeably tightened. In October 1944 ditches were dug round the perimeter of the camps, sentry posts were built and so placed as to cover the entire camp boundaries. As an additional precaution a series of fences were constructed of both barbed wire and bamboo, and embankments were built round most camps to block the prisoners' view of the surrounding country. In addition regulations prohibiting contact with the Thais were rigidly en-

(Ex-Servicemen's P.O.W. Subsistence Claims Committee)
The audience at a camp theatre on the Burma-Thailand railway.

(Ex-Servicemen's P.O.W. Subsistence Claims Committee)
Mess parade at a camp on the Burma-Thailand railway.

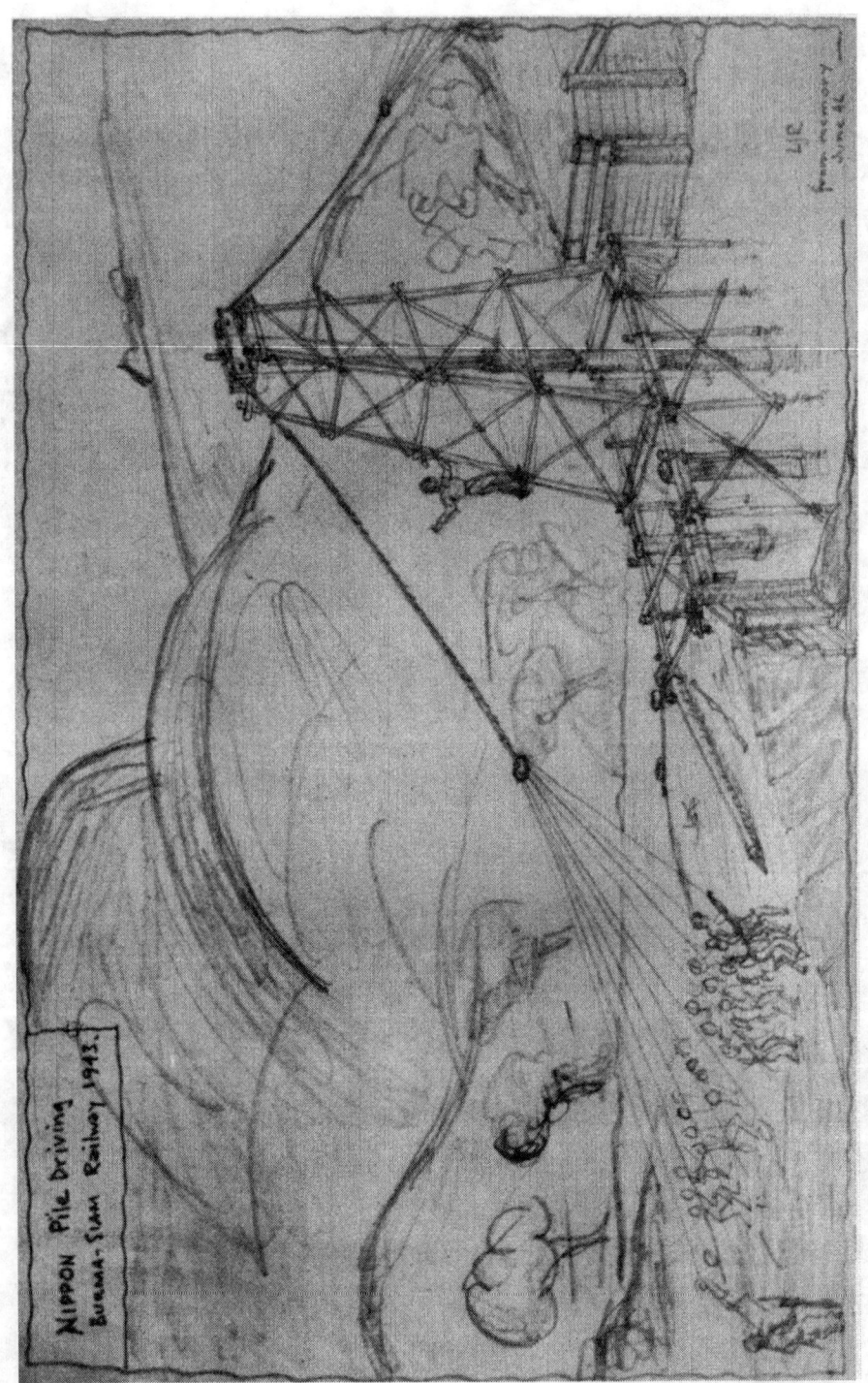

Pile-driving on the Burma-Thailand railway, 1943. Reproduction of a sketch by Maj L. J. Robertson.

forced, the Japanese evidently fearing that the civilians might attempt to enlist prisoners in their resistance movement.

Frequent searches were carried out by the Japanese military police, and officers and other ranks were subjected to third degree by the *Kempei* headquarters at Kanburi. Petty restrictions were imposed. Smoking in the open was forbidden, and permitted in huts only on the condition that a prisoners' both feet were on the ground. Lying down or reading was restricted to certain periods. The half-holiday conceded each week by the Japanese was interrupted by inspections; and men found resting were beaten with bamboo sticks by Japanese guards delegated specially for this duty. Instances of communal punishment were common. A cigarette butt found on the ground might provide an excuse for striking all prisoners in the community and the cancellation of the weekly half-holiday.

The officers, although generally speaking better off in Thailand than the men, never completely won the privileges to which their ranks entitled them. In March 1944 the Japanese had stated that officers would not be required to work other than on light duties in camp for their own benefit —a remarkable concession considering the treatment meted out to the officers' party during the building of the railway. In June, however, when most of the officers had been gathered together at Chungkai to form an officers' battalion, they were ordered to provide 100 officers to work in a vegetable garden outside the camp, the best produce of which was to go to the Japanese. The officers protested, stating that though they could volunteer, they should not be forced to work, and asked that the work be regarded as "voluntary".

The Japanese agreed—evidently the face-saving formula in reverse appealed to them—and 100 "volunteers" were ordered to begin work under their own leaders. The outcome was a notable improvement in health and morale for those employed on outside work.

In November the Japanese demanded that the officers be employed under Japanese control, and issued orders for 70 officers to move a fence round the camp. On 19th November the number of officers so employed was increased to 190, and many officers doing useful voluntary work for the hospital were withdrawn by the Japanese. That month large numbers of officers were sent from Chungkai to Tamarkan, and the delicate matter of officer working parties, overshadowed by deaths from bombing raids and other events, was never quite resolved.

In January 1945 all officer prisoners—about 3,000 all told of British, Dutch, American and Australian nationalities, plus 300 other ranks—were concentrated at Kanburi. There they were expected to build a camp and improve it. Apart from these duties and the construction of defences round the camp as ordered by the Japanese the work was not heavy and, in the words of one officer "when the camp was completed we had very little to do".

Contrary to expectations the removal of officers, except some medical officers and padres, from their men in Thailand and Burma brought no great hardships. As a rule warrant-officers and N.C.O's who had been working with administrative officers took over their tasks, and did magnificent work. In their daily dealings with the Japanese they brought to bear "a mixture of tact, low cunning and firmness"—always necessary if concessions were to be won from their captors—and incidents between Korean guards and the prisoners diminished to a notable degree. This may have been partly because the presence of unemployed officers was a constant source of irritation to the Japanese, as one report suggests, or because of a tendency among certain of the guards to aggravate wherever possible the difficulties of the officers. It may also have been a result of the changed war situation. Whatever the cause the outcome was a triumph for those warrant and non-commissioned officers who bore the burden of liaison with the Japanese in the final stages of captivity.

CHAPTER 25

CAMPS IN BORNEO, JAPAN AND ELSEWHERE

TWO of the larger forces containing Australians which left Changi in 1942 and 1943 went eastwards to Borneo; others, both from Java and Singapore, were taken to Japan. The Australians captured in Timor remained there for six to eight months before being transferred to Java or Singapore, where many of them joined working parties bound for Thailand. In June and July 1942 an attempt was made to transfer to Japan in two drafts the Australians captured on New Britain. One draft containing about 60 officers and 19 Australian women (including 6 Army nurses) arrived safely; the other draft of 1,050 composed principally of troops of the 2/22nd Battalion and 1st Independent Company but also containing about 200 civilians travelled in the *Montevideo Maru*, which was sunk off Luzon in the South China Sea on 1st July. There were no survivors among the prisoners. About 20 Japanese were saved.[1]

These transfers from the outer ring of islands seem to have been part of a systematic attempt by the Japanese to remove European prisoners to areas from which it would be harder to escape, and to replace them by labour forces of Indian and other Asian troops captured in Malaya and elsewhere. (This helps to explain the recovery by Australians of Indian troops during the campaigns in New Guinea in 1945.) In fact by September only the group of Australians captured on Ambon had not been moved elsewhere.

The second large force of Australians to leave Changi was "B" Force (1,496 strong, including 145 officers and an adequate medical staff) commanded by Lieut-Colonel Walsh of the 2/10th Field Regiment. It left Singapore in the *Ubi Maru* on 8th July 1942, and after a nine-days' journey in deplorable conditions disembarked at Sandakan, on the northeast coast of British North Borneo on 18th July. The men were crowded between decks, and had insufficient water. To add to the discomfort of sea travel the between-deck space was covered with about six inches of coal dust. From Sandakan the prisoners were marched to a compound about eight miles from the town, where 1,500 men were housed in huts designed for 300 internees.

At the outset the food ration was 17 ounces of rice a day, supplemented for a time by food brought from Changi. Water was pumped to the camp through a power station and was "muddy and full of bacteria". After about five weeks work was begun on an airstrip about two miles from the camp, on a site selected by the R.A.F. before the war, and the building of a road to the site was commenced. Two runways and extensive bays, revetments and other dispersal and protection areas were to be built. Rations now improved; an issue of fish weighing between 150 and 250

---
[1] It seems possible that the destination of the second draft was Hainan.

pounds was made to the camp thrice weekly, and vegetables also were supplied.

Soon after the arrival of "B" Force the foundations of an elaborate Intelligence organisation were laid, when contact was made with Dr J. P. Taylor, an Australian in charge of the Government hospital at Sandakan, and between the prisoners at Sandakan and the civilian internees who were imprisoned on Berhala Island.[2] The latter were guarded by Japanese and by members of the British North Borneo Constabulary (a locally raised force of Sikhs, Malays and Dusuns—one of the peoples of Borneo—formerly led by British officers) most of whom preferred the old administration to the new. With the aid of the constabulary and of some of the natives of the area, messages, sometimes in cipher, were soon being passed between the two groups of prisoners and Taylor.

In this period some of the officers, particularly Captain Matthews and Lieutenant Wells[3] employed on gardening and fuel parties respectively, were allowed to move outside the compound, and this brought them in touch with friendly Asian inhabitants, including Chinese. These supplied them with a revolver, survey maps of British North Borneo and other local information, and a crystal detector and headphones.

In November a radio receiver was completed by Lieutenant Weynton[4] of the 8th Divisional Signals, helped by Corporals Small[5] and Mills.[6] At first the reception and distribution of news was left to Lieutenant Weynton and Corporal Rickards,[7] but at length the production and distribution within the camp was taken over in its entirety by Lieutenant Weynton, while Matthews and Wells continued the outside contacts. In May 1943 Lieutenant Wells began the building of a radio transmitter from parts built in Sandakan to the prisoners' design.

A devoted corporal of the constabulary was used as a go-between to carry messages from Dr Taylor to the Australian prisoners, and also to supply them between September 1942 and July 1943 with "almost weekly" supplies of medicines, including such items as atebrin, quinine and various sulpha drugs, as well as radio batteries and Intelligence information. On behalf of the Governor, who was interned on Berhala Island, Dr Taylor also organised the collection of money from trusted civilians to form a fund to provide assistance for the prisoners. Gradually an increasingly elaborate Intelligence organisation was built up. Native inhabitants supplied the prisoners with stolen maps of the Sandakan area, showing Japanese dispositions, machine-gun posts and communications, and a message was sent

---

[2] Taylor and other medical staff had been instructed by the Governor to carry on their duties until relieved by the Japanese. When the Japanese occupied Sandakan Taylor had reserves of medical stores sufficient to last "the whole of British North Borneo for at least two years".

[3] Maj R. G. Wells, VX14024; 8 Div Sigs. School teacher; of Tatura, Vic; b. Tatura, 1 Jan 1920.

[4] Lt A. G. Weynton, VX28397; 8 Div Sigs. Secretary and accountant; of Castlemaine, Vic; b. Sydney, 25 Feb 1905.

[5] Cpl A. L. Small, NX26960; 8 Div AASC. Fruit agent; of Coogee, NSW; b. Ballina, NSW, 27 May 1903. Died while prisoner 19 Nov 1944.

[6] Cpl C. C. Mills, TX4197; 2/3 MAC. Motor mechanic; of Bothwell, Tas; b. Hobart, 13 Nov 1906.

[7] Cpl J. Rickards, NX68389; 2/3 MAC. Motor trade employee; of Sydney; b. Torquay, England, 25 Feb 1900.

as far afield as Jesselton, where a force of British prisoners was known to be stationed.[8] As additional information was received, Matthews and Wells collated and tabulated it, each taking responsibility for half the documents thus prepared. Matthews buried his within the camp; Wells arranged to bury his portion outside the local police post.

Meanwhile in September 1942 the Sandakan compound, which was under the control of Captain Susumi Hoshijima from July 1942 to April 1945, was visited by Major (later Lieut-Colonel) Suga, officer-in-charge of all Borneo prison camps,[9] and thereafter control of the prisoners became more rigid. The prisoners were made to count in Japanese on parade, and mistakes in counting resulted in prisoners being slapped, struck with rifle butts, or kicked in the shins. During this period beatings were administered by the Japanese guards, but these "were old soldiers and not so bad". On 12th September a no-escape document was signed by the prisoners after Colonel Walsh had refused to sign and been threatened by a firing squad. Here as elsewhere the prisoners considered that a promise was not morally

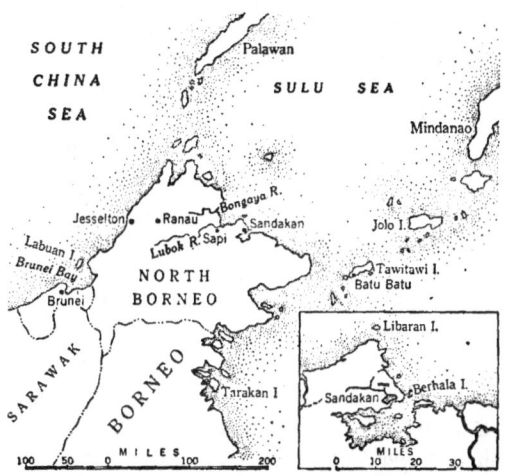

binding once duress had been established. Soon afterwards Colonel Walsh and other senior officers were removed to Kuching, and Major Fleming[1] became commander. In October a Filipino-Chinese guerilla, Mu Sing (one of many such men who had evaded the Japanese and established themselves on Batu Batu, Jolo and other islands unoccupied by the Japanese between North-East Borneo and the Philippines) who had formerly traded in sandalwood round Borneo and owned two power boats, contacted the prisoners, again through the native police, and reported the presence of "B" Force to his commander on Batu Batu. A few weeks later the Australians received a message from Batu Batu stating that Allied submarines would be visiting the island and asking for a report on "B" Force to pass on to them. This was supplied, and at the end of December a second message was received stating that the report had gone on. At the same time (somewhat trustingly perhaps in the circumstances) a map of Batu Batu and details of the organisation of the guerilla force were delivered.

---

[8] These were eventually brought to Sandakan in April-May 1943.
[9] There were evidently four main prisoner-of-war camps in Borneo: at Sandakan, Kuching, Labuan and Jesselton.
[1] Maj F. A. Fleming, VX39089; 2/4 A-Tk Regt. School teacher; of Hawthorn, Vic; b. Kyogle, NSW, 15 Mar 1907.

In January 1943 the civilian internees were transferred from Berhala Island to Kuching, and unofficial control of the constabulary, hitherto vested in a British officer, Major Rice-Oxley, passed to Captain Matthews. In May the guerilla organisation asked Matthews whether he and his party wished to join them, but Major Fleming said that he would prefer them to remain and they did so. Messages from the guerillas were now being regularly passed to the prisoners through the native police by Felix Aziona, a Filipino whose father owned a radio shop in Sandakan; and also to a second group of prisoners now established on Berhala Island.

These newcomers to the area were 500 Australians of "E" Force, which had set out from Singapore in the steamer *de Klerk* on 29th March 1943. Originally 1,000 strong (including 500 British prisoners) "E" Force had suffered the usual discomforts associated with sea travel as guests of the Imperial Japanese Army. The Australians (commanded by Major Fairley) had the choice of sharing the aft hold which housed a leaking cargo of petrol, two small holds adjoining the engine room which were very hot, or a small section of cattle stalls, with double tiers. Indeed the accommodation was so limited that the Japanese guards had used bayonets and rifle butts to force the troops into the space allotted. After disembarkation at Kuching on 1st April, Fairley and Major Carter were removed from command of the Australians by the Japanese, who said that no officer higher than the rank of captain could accompany the force. Thus when the Australian section of the force re-embarked on 9th April it was commanded by Captain R. J. Richardson of the 2/20th Battalion. (The 500 British prisoners remained at Kuching.) On the 14th April the Australians had arrived at Berhala Island by way of Labuan. There, until early June, the time was spent clearing scrub and cutting wood. Although accommodation was limited (500 men in three huts capable of sheltering about 150) the troops were permitted to fish and bathe when off duty, they enjoyed rations good both as to quantity and quality, and a canteen was established. In May a message was sent to "B" Force through the constabulary asking whether Matthews' organisation would help a party of "E" Force, led by Captain Steele, to escape; this was agreed to.

Within a few weeks of the arrival of "B" Force at Sandakan a number of enterprising soldiers had tried to achieve freedom. Four of six A.A.S.C. men who made the earliest recorded attempt were at large only a few days before they were recaptured; two reached a point on the coast about 40 miles south of Sandakan when they too were caught. These six were tried at Kuching and sentenced to four years' imprisonment in Outram Road Gaol, Singapore.

Five men of the 2/29th Battalion who formed a second escape party contacted a wealthy Chinese, Siew Cheow, and with his aid and that of the fund established by the Governor and Dr Taylor lived for some five months in the jungle before being recaptured by the Japanese when attempting to leave Borneo by boat. The average penalty imposed by the Japanese was five years' imprisonment.

On 8th May 1943 Sergeant Wallace[2] and Signalmen Harvey[3] and McKenzie[4] also attempted escape. Some days later Harvey and McKenzie were shot and captured by Japanese guards as they were gathering coconuts near the aerodrome; and Wallace, now alone in the jungle, sought the aid of Captain Matthews and the underground organisation. Because of strict roll calls it was impossible to return Wallace to the compound, and Matthews decided that he should join Steele's party of "E" Force—arrangements for their escape were then well advanced—rather than remain at large.

Meanwhile in April Sergeant Blain,[5] Member of Parliament for the Northern Territory who was imprisoned at Sandakan, approached Lieutenant Wells with a proposal to escape and asked for assistance. At this stage, because of difficulties within the organisation, both Wells and Matthews were reluctant to help, and Blain sent his parliamentary gold pass to Dr Taylor, seeking his assistance. Taylor too was unwilling to help, as were some Chinese from whom Blain also sought aid. At length a message from Blain addressed to Mr Forde, the Australian Minister for the Army, appealing for help, was delivered to Sergeant Wallace.

On 4th June "E" Force was warned to prepare to move to Sandakan, and next night Steele, Lieutenants Wagner, Blow[6] and Gillon,[7] and Privates Butler,[8] McLaren[9] and Kennedy[1] made an uneventful exit from the camp; they were joined by Sergeant Wallace, brought across to Berhala by canoe. It was the beginning of one of the very few successful escapes recorded by prisoners of the Japanese. Three left that night in a small native boat stolen by Wagner and Blow; the others remained on the island for twenty-two days, for the most part within 400 yards of the prison camp. At the end of a tense period of waiting they were taken to Tawitawi, where they rejoined their comrades, and joined the guerilla movement. Wagner and Butler were killed serving with the guerillas; the others survived and subsequently reached Australia.[2]

---

[2] WO2 W. Wallace, NX58809. 2/15 Fd Regt; guerilla forces in Philippines 1943-44. Gaol warder; of Parramatta, NSW; b. Sydney, 1 Mar 1907.

[3] Sig H. F. Harvey, NX49419; 8 Div Sigs. Labourer; of Ingham, Qld; b. Cairns, Qld, 12 Oct 1921. Executed by Japanese 11 May 1943.

[4] Sig D. S. McKenzie (true name T. R. B. Mackay), QX15656; 8 Div Sigs. Pastoral employee; of Roseville,. NSW; b. Rockhampton, Qld, 24 May 1910. Executed by Japanese 18 May 1943.

[5] Sgt A. M. Blain, NX56669. (1st AIF: Cpl 32 Bn.) MHR for NT 1939-49. 2/1 Survey Regt 1940-42. Surveyor; of Nanango, Qld; b. Inverell, NSW, 21 Nov 1894.

[6] Maj R. Blow, DSO, QX4648. 2/10 Fd Regt; guerilla forces in Philippines 1943-44; "Z" Special Unit 1945. Bank clerk; of Hamilton, Qld; b. Grafton, NSW, 13 Nov 1917.

[7] Maj L. M. Gillon, DSO, VX34838. 2/10 Fd Regt; guerilla forces in Philippines 1943-45. Accountant's clerk; of South Yarra, Vic; b. Aspendale, Vic, 17 May 1916.

[8] Sgt R. W. Butler, SX2600. 8 Div Amn Sub Park; guerilla forces in Philippines 1943. Grazier; of Kongorong, SA; b. Mount Gambier, SA, 13 Feb 1913. Killed in action Tawitawi 18 Aug 1943.

[9] Capt R. K. McLaren, MC, QX21058. 2/10 Fd Workshops 1940-42; guerilla forces in Philippines 1943-45. Veterinary surgeon; of Bundaberg, Qld; b. Kirhoaldy, Scotland, 27 Apr 1902. Killed in car accident 3 Mar 1956.

[1] Sgt R. J. Kennedy, VX60861. 2/10 Ord Workshops; guerilla forces in Philippines 1943-44. Rigger; of Moe, Vic; b. Maffra, Vic, 22 Dec 1907.

[2] An account of the subsequent experiences of the party may be found in *Men May Smoke* (a chronicle of the 2/18th Battalion), pp. 82-3, and in H. Richardson, *One Man War* (1957).

Meanwhile in June "E" Force had joined "B" Force at Sandakan which had been reinforced in April by the arrival of about 750 British prisoners from Jesselton. That month the Japanese guards had been relieved by about 100 Formosan guards. During the first twelve months spent at Sandakan only about 24 men had died; except for short periods when mass punishment in the way of reduced rations had been inflicted on the camp the food was adequate. With the advent of the Formosans the treatment worsened. Prisoners on work parties were beaten with pick handles and sword sticks, and stones were thrown at them by the guards. Mass beatings occurred regularly and for no apparent reason:

> My gang would be working all right and then would be suddenly told to stop (said an Australian afterwards). The men would then be stood with their arms outstretched horizontally, shoulder high, facing the sun without hats. The guards would be formed into two sections, one standing back with rifles and the others doing the actual beating. They would walk along the back of us and . . . smack us underneath the arms, across the ribs and on the back. They would give each man a couple of bashes . . . if they whimpered or flinched they would get a bit more.[3]

There seems to have been a fairly severe line drawn between camp technical and administrative staffs and the work parties, and prisoners allotted to camp tasks were not permitted also to work on the airfield. The adequate medical staff of 136 other ranks which had accompanied "B" Force was reduced to 74, and these were given the task of looking after the hospital carrying, in June 1943, some 300 patients. Some of the camp staff who took part in the work parties secretly to make up the numbers and avoid sick men being sent out were punished, when discovered, by confinement to the "cage", among them being Padre Wardale-Greenwood, who was deprived also of his ecclesiastical books. The "cage" at this time was a wooden structure, measuring 4 feet 6 inches by 5 feet 6 inches, barred on all sides, and high enough only to sit in. To enter it a prisoner crawled through a small aperture. Generally confinement in the cage meant sitting to attention throughout the day clad only in shorts or sarong, without mosquito nets, blankets or bed clothing of any kind. Beatings were administered outside the cage twice daily, at the changing of the guard. Sentences varied from a few days to as long as a month, usually for offences trivial by any standards; as much as a week sometimes passed before prisoners were permitted food, and then only on a reduced scale.

Meanwhile the "underground" had continued to function. Preparations for the organisation of the prisoners into a force capable of action in the event of an Allied landing in north-east Borneo were under way when, in July 1943, four Chinese members of the organisation were betrayed to the Japanese. Under torture the Chinese at length admitted having supplied radio parts to Wallace (who had already gone) and unfortunately Matthews' name was mentioned. Thereupon the Japanese instituted a series of *Kempei*-controlled searches of the prison camp, whose object

---
[3] WO1 W. H. Sticpewich.

was obviously the secret radio. Before long not one, but two radios had been discovered and many officers and men (including Matthews, Wells and Weynton) had been arrested. The plot to cooperate with the native inhabitants in the event of Allied landings was also uncovered; Taylor and other civilians concerned in the movement were also arrested. The prisoners were taken to the Military Police headquarters on the outskirts of Sandakan, where all of them were subjected to privations of various kinds, and some were beaten and cruelly tortured. On 25th October 22 Australians, 5 Europeans and about 50 natives—in fact all who had been arrested with the exception of a few natives acquitted of minor charges—were transferred to Kuching, where on 2nd November they entered Kuching gaol. Interrogations began in mid-November and continued at spasmodic intervals until March 1944, when all trials had been completed. Of the 22 Australians one died before trial, one was acquitted, one received six months' imprisonment and the remainder received sentences ranging from 1½ years' imprisonment to 12 years' penal servitude. In March Matthews, the leader of the Australians, was sentenced to death, as were two members of the native constabulary and six natives.[4] Dr Taylor, who had served the Australians so well, was sentenced to fifteen years' imprisonment.

Meanwhile at Sandakan the widespread nature of the underground movement which the investigations had uncovered had evidently convinced the Japanese that a wise course would be to separate the officers from the men. In October surprise marching orders caught the officers unprepared and, within a few hours, having had no time to farewell their men, most were on board a river steamer bound for Kuching, where they remained until the end of the war.[5] A few officers, including Captain Cook[6] (the senior combatant officer), two medical officers, Captains Picone[7] and Jeffrey,[8] and Chaplains Wardale-Greenwood and Thompson[9] remained at Sandakan.

After the departure of the officers the Australians were merged in No. 1 Compound, the British remained in No. 2, and the No. 3 Compound was used as a hospital area. Thenceforward the treatment of the men became increasingly severe. The sickening spectacle of beatings—in which men lost eyes, had teeth knocked out and jaws broken, or were kicked on ulcers or private parts—became almost daily occurrences; prolonged torture of individuals was not uncommon. As the numbers of sick increased the Japanese daily demanded more troops for work than were fit. In the absence of officers the control of the camp and work fell heavily on

---
[4] That month Blain's appeal for help was delivered to Mr Forde in Canberra.
[5] The Australians at Kuching then amounted to 149 officers and 20 other ranks.
[6] Capt G. R. Cook, NX76184; Aust Gen Base Depot, Singapore. School teacher; of Mittagong, NSW; b. Failford, NSW, 27 Oct 1906. Died while prisoner 12 Aug 1945.
[7] Capt D. G. Picone, QX6380; RMO 2/10 Fd Regt. Medical practitioner; of Cooroy, Qld; b. Perth, WA, 14 Mar 1909. Died while prisoner 6 Aug 1945.
[8] Capt R. L. Jeffrey, NX34761; 2/10 AGH. Medical practitioner; of Little Bay, NSW; b. Sydney, 24 Jul 1909. Died while prisoner 24 Jul 1945.
[9] Rev A. H. Thompson, TX6093. Church of England clergyman; of Smithton, Tas; b. London, 27 Mar 1903. Died while prisoner 19 Jun 1945.

N.C.O's. Some of these interposed themselves between the Japanese and their men, and fought to preserve the few rights still remaining.[1]

In August 1944 the Japanese authorised the construction of a prisoner-of-war sign with the letters "P.O.W." in white on a black background. The airport was raided on 23rd September 1944 and two aircraft strafed the camp, killing three prisoners. After that raids ceased—the P.O.W. sign evidently having had the desired effect—until April 1945, when the sign was removed on Japanese orders and destroyed. Soon afterwards the camp was again raided, and about 30 prisoners were killed.

In September 1944 the Japanese had reduced the meals to two a day —at 11.30 a.m. and 5.30 p.m. Up to that time about 120 Australians and 90 British had died at Sandakan. In December the rice ration was reduced to between 5 and 7 ounces daily, although there seems to have been ample rice available even within the camp; in January it ceased altogether. On the 10th work on the airfield also ceased (it had begun to slacken off in September) and work was confined to wood parties, camp duties and the vegetable gardens. At this stage the health of the prisoners was very poor. Rations consisted of about 3 ounces of rice a day issued from a reserve of about 2,000 pounds built up by the prisoners over the previous twenty months, and tapioca and sweet potatoes. Few greens were available— invariably the best produce of the gardens had gone to the Japanese guards —and the canteen had ceased to function in September. The Japanese selected men for work irrespective of their physical condition, and when men complained they were kicked and beaten.

That month eight starving men were arrested for stealing rations from the Japanese quartermaster's store. They were badly beaten and confined for 28 days to the "cage"—an enlarged version of the one already described with slightly more head room—denied blankets or clothes and placed on reduced rations. Each day they were taken out, beaten with sticks and kicked. Two died soon after release; the remainder within a short time. The wonder is not that they died but that they survived so long. Two men caught outside the wire while attempting to reach the tapioca patch suffered similar ordeals and died; another was shot.

Late in January 1945 the Japanese, evidently fearing invasion, began moving the prisoners from Sandakan to Ranau, a small village about 160 miles west of Sandakan. The first group of prisoners totalling 470 (including 350 Australians) began leaving Sandakan in batches of about 50 prisoners a day from 29th January onwards. None of the men were fit on departure; all were suffering from beri beri and malnutrition; 60 per cent were bootless. The Australians were led by Warrant-Officer Watson[2] of the A.I.F. and about 30 guards accompanied them. Captain Jeffrey and the two chaplains, Greenwood and Thompson, also went with the prisoners.

---

[1] An outstanding leader in this regard was Warrant-Officer N. G. Cummings (of East Malvern, Vic) of the 8th Divisional Signals.

[2] WO2 C. Y. Watson, QX17783; 8 Div AASC. Regular soldier; of Ingham, Qld; b. Townsville, Qld, 29 Jan 1900. Died while prisoner 6 Mar 1945.

In March the ghastly policy of withholding medical supplies, of which the Japanese held adequate quantities, and of systematic starvation, resulted in 317 deaths, including 221 Australians. The men were now "walking skeletons"; most weighed between 5 and 6 stone. On the other hand, the Japanese guards were still eating large quantities of rice, and had fish or meat daily as well as soya beans and potatoes. All "looked healthy and well fed".

In May the British prisoners in No. 2 Compound joined the Australians in No. 1. On the 29th the Japanese blew ammunition dumps, and having ordered the prisoners to clear the compound, set fire to the camp, destroying all the force's records. (The 26th Australian Brigade Group had landed on 1st May on Tarakan Island off the north-east coast of Borneo, and by the 28th organised opposition had been overcome.) At that stage about 400 of the 700 prisoners remaining were hospital cases. That evening Captain Cook was told that all prisoners able to walk would be required to move within an hour on a "very short journey"; 500 of the marchers would be supplied by the A.I.F. and 100 by the English. Finally the prisoners were split up into ten parties of 50 and one of 66; the tenth party was composed partly of Australians, partly of British troops, and the last group of 66 were all British. A company of Japanese soldiers acted as escort for the march. These were stationed four to the head and four to the flanks of each group of prisoners, with the remainder of the company at the rear of the column.

As the prisoners assembled for departure the prison buildings and the Japanese barracks were burnt down. For the remaining 290 prisoners, too ill to be moved, no accommodation remained.

Each party was issued with two 100-pound bags of rice, enough for 4 pounds a man, and told that it represented 10 days' rations. Later some salt and sugar were issued. Long before the first halt men were falling by the wayside; at this stage those who lagged behind were driven along with blows from rifle butts. Rice was cooked at the end of each day's march; from that meal sufficient had to be saved for a second meal next morning. Each man's daily ration was reckoned at 100 grammes of rice, but this was reduced after the Japanese had plundered some of the original issue. At the end of the first day's march, when the end of a tarred road was reached, the track became deplorable. The mud was knee deep most of the way for the first part of the journey and the track led over hills so steep that the men had to crawl up and slide down. When stragglers fell out they were not seen again. At each overnight halt the many who could not continue were grouped together and shot after those able to march had been moved on.[3]

On 26th June 142 Australians and 61 Englishmen mustered at Ranau, all that remained of the men who had set out from Sandakan four weeks before. There they joined five Australian prisoners and one Englishman, the only survivors so far as is known of the 470 prisoners who had set

---
[3] Statement by Masao Fukushima of the *Suga Butai*.

out from Sandakan on the first march. From them they learnt that the first group had completed the march in a shorter period, and that only 20 had died before reaching Ranau. They were fitter than the second group when they set out, having been less long on starvation rations. Since then, however, most of the others had died of malnutrition and exhaustion.

At Ranau no provision had been made for the accommodation of the prisoners. The Japanese occupied three huts; the prisoners camped in a valley above the Japanese quarters in an area about 50 yards square devoid of buildings or tents and without provision for cooking. The only shelter was beneath surrounding shrubs, and rain fell constantly. No medical supplies were available to the weary men or treatment of any kind; water had to be carried by hand from a creek half a mile away; the daily food ration amounted to between 70 and 75 grammes of rice, the equivalent of a small cup of rice water with about an inch of rice in the bottom. Within three days 19 men had died. The Japanese ordered out working parties of desperately tired and sick men to cut bamboo for the building of huts (including one for the prisoners), and to carry wood and vegetables. The vegetable-carrying parties had to struggle a distance of 18 to 20 miles a day with loads of between 40 and 50 pounds. The only vegetables the prisoners had were those they stole. At the end of the third day the prisoners were allowed to spread out and build shelters, provided they were well camouflaged. The vegetable-carrying and bamboo-cutting parties continued; and rice-carrying parties, involving the carriage of about 50 pounds of rice over distances of 12 to 13 miles a day, were instituted. Between 30th June and 13th July about 40 Australians and a larger percentage of Englishmen died. The men were now so weak that it was impossible for them to lift the dead to the site of shallow graves; and four men, constantly harried and beaten by the Japanese were taking from three hours and a half to four hours to dig graves two feet deep.

On 18th July a hut 30 feet long by 18 feet wide with a raised floor was completed by the prisoners. Only 72 then survived; 38 occupied the raised floor of the hut; the remainder were so weak and helpless from dysentery that an attempt was made to segregate them by allotting them the area below the floor into which they were able to crawl. As the problem of burying the dead increased the Japanese opened a new cemetery about 20 yards from the prisoners' hut.

The strongest of the starving prisoners were now employed on kitchen duties for the Japanese, or killing, cleaning and carrying cattle for distribution to various Japanese detachments in the area. Eighteen men died on the task of carrying water to the Japanese officers' kitchen alone. This involved carrying daily about 130 buckets of water for 400 yards up an incline so steep that the prisoners could scarcely stand. As the prisoners grew weaker the Japanese openly plundered their gear, beating those who protested, sometimes until unconscious.

On 27th July Warrant-Officer Sticpewich,[4] one of the fittest of the survivors, was warned by a friendly Japanese guard that the time to escape into the jungle had come. If he stayed, the Japanese said, in a very short time he would be killed. Sticpewich, who had received earlier warnings of the impending massacre, warned his comrades and invited them to join him in an attempt to escape. There were then 32 men still alive; six were unconscious; of the others only Private Reither[5] was able to make the attempt.

On the night of 28 July (said Sticpewich) I cooked the meal . . . served it as usual and about half past nine Reither and I sneaked out of camp. The guards on the camp had been doubled from the time we moved . . . to the new hut. . . . The guard house was just above us and there were no sides to our huts so that they had a good view of us. We . . . laid low next day. We were still in the camp area and could see the general confusion in the camp at our escape. . . . We saw the search party go out looking for us and return. . . . At dusk that evening we made our way out along the road towards Ranau. . . . On 2 August, after a lot of adventures I . . . contacted a Kampong chief and prevailed upon him to help us. . . . He did feed and help us and at my instigation sent a coolie with vegetables into the Jap camp to find out how many were still there. The coolie came back and reported that there were still 20 to 21 alive.

If the evidence of the Japanese themselves is to be believed the prisoners remaining at the Ranau camp were already dead. On 1st August all who were able to walk were taken away and shot. The remainder—15 or 17 in so pitiful a condition that it was "impossible for them to attempt to escape"[6]—were hunted out of the hut by Japanese guards.

They were able to just struggle out (said a guard). These people were then taken up the rise at the back of the camp. . . . I then heard the sound of firing and when I went up to look the prisoners were all dead.[7]

Meanwhile a guerilla party operating in the area north of Sandakan had already rescued one Australian. He was Gunner Campbell,[8] who was evacuated on 26th July by flying-boat from the mouth of the Bongaya River to Tawitawi Island, and thence to Morotai. Between 8th and 24th August, a second guerilla party led by Flight Lieutenant Ripley[1] picked up four more survivors. These were Warrant-Officer Sticpewich, whose comrade, Private Reither, overcome by starvation, dysentery and malaria, had died the day Sticpewich was rescued, and Lance-Bombardier Moxham,[2] Privates Botterill[3] and Short.[4] A disused Japanese airstrip on the

---

[4] Capt W. H. Sticpewich, MBE, QX9538; 8 Div AASC. Meat inspector; of Wickham, NSW; b. Carrington, NSW, 4 Jun 1908.

[5] Pte H. Reither, VX48478; 2/4 Res MT Coy. Farm labourer; of Ballarat, Vic; b. Gre Gre via St Arnaud, Vic, 9 Oct 1906. Died 8 Aug 1945.

[6] Statement of Tatsuhiko Yoshikawa.

[7] Statement of Nobunaza Matsuda.

[8] Gnr O. C. Campbell, QX14380; 2/10 Fd Regt. Labourer; of Brisbane; b. Brisbane, 27 Mar 1916.

[1] F-Lt G. C. Ripley, MBE. 1 and 3 Wireless Units RAAF 1943-44; Allied Intelligence Bureau 1944-45. Colonial police officer; of Palestine and Malaya; b. Leeds, England, 30 Apr 1909.

[2] L-Bdr W. D. Moxham, NX19750; 2/15 Fd Regt. Station overseer; of Toongabbie, NSW; b. Sydney, 15 Mar 1912.

[3] Pte K. Botterill, NX42191; 2/19 Bn. Silk and textile printer; of Katoomba, NSW; b. Nyngan, NSW, 1 Mar 1922. The remarkable tenacity and endurance of Pte Botterill are exemplified by the fact that he had spent two periods in "the cage"—one of 12 days, the other of 40 days.

[4] Pte N. A. E. Short, NX58617; 2/18 Bn. Cook; of Woollahra, NSW; b. Enfield, NSW, 30 Aug 1917.

Ranau plain was repaired and at length, on 20th September, the men were flown by Auster aircraft to Labuan.

A sixth survivor had already reached safety. He was Bombardier Braithwaite,[5] who had escaped on 8th June, during the second march to Ranau, soon after crossing the Lubok River. He followed the river northwards towards its mouth, and after a series of remarkable adventures and hardships reached Sapi village, where the native people befriended him and at length took him by boat to Liberan Island. There he was picked up by P.T. boats manned by Americans, and on 15th June reached Tawitawi. He then weighed only 70 lbs.

These six men—Sticpewich, Campbell, Moxham, Botterill, Short and Braithwaite—were the only survivors of some 2,500 British and Australian prisoners who had remained at Sandakan after the transfer of the officers to Kuching. What little is known of the sick who remained at Sandakan after the second march to Ranau is based on the statements of Japanese guards. According to these accounts there were then 292 prisoners in the area. By 10th June 30 had died "from natural causes"; that day 75 were taken under escort to the 8-Mile Post and were not seen again. There were then 185 alive.[6] On 13th July only 53 were still living; that day 23 of the fittest were taken to the airfield and shot; the remainder were now so desperately ill that the Japanese considered they could not last more than a few days "so they were left to die". All were dead by 15th August.

Some 800 miles westward of Borneo lies Ambon where, in February 1942, 791 Australians comprising "Gull Force" entered captivity under naval jurisdiction. The Australians were concentrated at the Tantui Camp, and the Dutch prisoners in a near-by compound. As at Singapore, the Japanese informed the Australian and Dutch commanders that they would be held responsible for the administration and discipline of their men. The commander of the Australians, Lieut-Colonel Scott, thereupon established a headquarters and organised the men into companies and platoons.

Although the Japanese disclaimed any responsibility for the prisoners and insisted that Japan had her own rules for the treatment of prisoners of war, the treatment accorded them was "reasonable". The Australians were allowed access to their clothing and kit bags, which permitted of an equal distribution of clothing among the officers and men. Scott instructed that the prisoners should not cooperate on work likely to assist the Japanese in carrying on the war, and nominal rolls showing false occupations and ages were compiled. In March an escape party was organised which was considered to have reasonable chances of success. The adventures of the escape party which included Lieutenants Jinkins, Jack and Rudder have already been described. By various subterfuges the escape was concealed

---

[5] Bdr J. R. Braithwaite, NX45378; 2/15 Fd Regt. Process engraver; of Coorparoo, Qld; b. Brisbane, 15 Jun 1917. (A detailed account of Braithwaite's experiences was published in *Stand To*, Nov-Dec 1956.)

[6] The figures do not tally precisely

from the Japanese until enough time had elapsed for it to be made good. Afterwards Japanese precautions were tightened, the area of the camp was restricted, and a double barbed wire fence 12 feet high erected round it, with raised machine-gun posts installed at all angles. The Japanese issued orders that the penalty for escape or concealing escape would be death. If escapers were not recovered an equal number of prisoners of equivalent rank would be executed.

Thereafter conditions at Tantui worsened. Discipline slackened, pilfering occurred, men refused fatigue duties, officers and N.C.O's were jeered at, and the whole organisation of the camp began to suffer. At length Scott paraded the camp and warned the men that if they refused to carry out orders he would have to hand them to the Japanese for punishment; N.C.O's would be "peremptorily reverted" for not doing their jobs. In June the camp at Tantui came under the harsh administration of Captain Ando of the Japanese Navy. Recreation of any form, conversation with Ambonese, instructional classes, keeping of diaries, were all forbidden, and nightly inspections took place. Men were beaten with canes or struck with swords, and surprise searches were instigated. In July the Japanese intercepted letters passed between the Dutch prisoners and their wives in an internment camp beyond Ambon. Thirty-four Dutch prisoners including nine officers, two doctors and the padre, their hands tied, were assembled on a rise overlooking the camp in full view of the prisoners. There with pickets, lengths of piping and pickhandles they were flogged by a platoon of young marines.

> These marines fell upon the Dutch like wild beasts and desisted only when every man was unconscious. Ando then rose, struck each unconscious man a blow on the head with a pick handle, entered his car and drove off. The sight on the hill was a ghastly one . . . and at the conclusion the whole rise was slippery with blood. Everyone was filled with horror and fear as it was our first experience of the Japanese way of enforcing discipline.[7]

Soon afterwards the Japanese marines took over as camp guards and a reign of terror began, during which men were beaten and bashed without provocation. At this stage rations, consisting mainly of salvaged Australian stocks and weevily rice, were short, and the prisoners were already showing signs of severe loss of weight. The sick were having difficulty in recovering; drugs were lacking, and malaria cases went untreated; tinea was rife.

In October Scott learnt that a force of 500 (including 263 Australians) would soon leave for what was euphemistically described as a "convalescent camp". Scott and Major Macrae were to accompany the force. Otherwise only sick men were to be included. The stores and equipment of "Gull Force" were divided between the men who were to remain and the group selected for departure. No food was to be taken. Towards the end of the month the force embarked.

---

[7] Lieut-Colonel W. J. R. Scott, "Report of Ambon and Hainan", on which this summary is mainly based.

After the departure of Scott's force 528 Australians remained on Ambon. These were commanded by Major Westley, the senior surviving Australian officer, who also assumed responsibility for a small group of 14 Americans and 7 Dutchmen. The Americans had been captured in New Guinea, whither they had escaped from the Philippines.

Conditions on Ambon continued to be relatively good. The original barracks buildings at Tantui near Galala village continued to be used by the force. These were clean and hygienic. The water supply, drawn from a reservoir, was fresh and clean, and required no treatment, although it was boiled as a precautionary measure. Reasonable opportunities for recreation and entertainment were permitted; weekly concerts were held, and for a time basket-ball was played.

In February the camp was bombed by an American Liberator, and a stick of six bombs blew up a dump of about 200,000 pounds of high explosive aerial bombs placed within the boundaries of the camp by the Japanese. The explosion blew flat most of the camp and more than half was destroyed by fire. Nine Australians were killed, including 5 officers, and about 75 wounded. Westley was then ordered to put a large Red Cross on the roof of one of the few remaining buildings. After some Japanese aircraft had flown over the camp, the Red Cross was taken down. Thereafter requests to the Japanese that the hospital be marked with a Red Cross brought threats of execution. Westley deduced that the area had been photographed for propaganda purposes.

After the bombing the attitude of the Japanese towards the prisoners appreciably hardened. They would not regard the Australian casualties as serious and refused to help. The only Australian medical officer, Captain Davidson,[8] had been killed in the air raid, and the care of the sick and wounded was left to a Dutch medical officer, Captain J. H. W. Ehehart and the Australian dental officer, Captain Marshall.[9]

In March the Japanese prohibited educational classes; and, as conditions became harder and harder, lectures and debates ceased. As 1943 passed the appearance of aircraft over Ambon became more frequent, and the prisoners were set to digging air raid shelters for themselves and the Japanese. In May, 1,200 English prisoners from Java arrived and were sent to Paso. These evidently fared worse than the Australians. A diarist records meeting in December "many Pommies who are army prisoners. They are in very poor health as compared with us. Collected tobacco and gave to them."

Continuously throughout the period of captivity the prisoners were forced to work on military tasks. These included loading and unloading ships, building roads and stores, air raid shelters, tank traps, and gun positions. Protests were disregarded, and if men refused to work they were beaten. At first the demands for working parties were well organised,

---

[8] Capt P. M. Davidson, QX6476; 2/12 Fd Amb. Medical practitioner; of Murgon, Qld; b. Lisbane, Ireland, 1 Oct 1901. Killed in air raid 15 Feb 1943.

[9] Capt G. C. Marshall, VX39263; OC No. 23 Dental Unit. Dentist; of Kew, Vic; b. Melbourne, 28 Sep 1913.

and officers or N.C.O's accompanied them; later officers were prohibited from leaving the camp area, and N.C.O's commanded the parties. At Ambon, as elsewhere, work parties were welcomed because of opportunities they provided for supplementing slender rations, particularly when the prisoners were employed unloading ships, or were brought into contact with the Ambonese who, generally speaking, remained well disposed to the Allies. Towards the end of 1943 mail was received at Ambon and letters were delivered in twos and threes to the men over a period of months. Many were withheld altogether, and not handed over until the end of the war. No outward mail was allowed although permission was repeatedly sought; no parcels were delivered at any time.

For about two months in 1944 the excellent supply of water for bathing purposes was discontinued, and all washing and bathing had to be done in sea water. This was a severe blow to the Australians who place cleanliness high among the virtues.

In March individual gardens which the prisoners assiduously cultivated were prohibited. "We expect that our fowls will be taken from us next," wrote Sergeant Swanton.[1] "The Japanese say there must be no individualism. Suppers are going to be very light in future. We can only cook porridge, as all green things are to be handed into the kitchen."

It is a very poor diet indeed and is having a very marked effect on the health of us all (noted Swanton). Coconuts are now very scarce and it is an island order that none be brought home from [work] parties. No trees are to be climbed and in fact it is almost impossible to get any. The last nut I had was six weeks ago. Any little pieces since then have cost me quite a few cigarettes. Incidentally cigarettes are now the camp currency and are used nearly exclusively for trading, food, etc. It is a great blessing that I am no smoker. . . . Every day one sees heavy smokers sacrificing their much needed meals for smokes. In fact men are now dying every few days from malnutrition.

In August 1944 the town of Ambon was severely damaged by bombing; twelve Liberators dropped bombs across the camp, destroying portion of it, and killing three men.[2] Building materials were then so scarce that damaged huts could not be wholly repaired. The building containing the library was damaged and many of the books were destroyed.

Until August the rice ration was 17 ounces, and some issues of fish and vegetables had been made. This was insufficient for men employed on arduous work, but as has been mentioned prisoners were able at times to supplement the meagre fare by looting and from their own camp gardens. In the period following the August air attack the Japanese

deliberately set out to kill off the prisoners by extra hard labour and short rations. Never at any time were medical supplies adequately available to treat the sick, and often the administration of our hospital was interfered with.

With some exceptions the average Jap guard was not willingly a party to this policy. The blame lies with the Jap Commandant, their officers and particularly

---
[1] Sgt S. M. Swanton, VX25850; 2/21 Bn. Buyer; of East Hawthorn, Vic; b. Elsternwick, Vic, 23 Dec 1913. Died while prisoner 14 Aug 1945.
Swanton wrote his diary in shorthand, which was translated after the war.
[2] The camp was strafed on two other occasions by low-flying aircraft.

Ikeuchi, the Camp Administrator. . . . All protests regarding any matter whatsoever were ignored and in many cases brought reprisal upon the camp. They had to be made through the Camp Administrator, and never got any further. In many cases he even refused to accept them or listen. This applied to both verbal and written requests.[3]

The short rations referred to above amounted in September-October 1944 to 1½ ounces of rice and 7½ ounces of tapioca flour; in January-March 1945 the daily ration was 8½ ounces of rice, supplemented on occasions by sweet potatoes, sometimes bad. Between April and May the ration was only 6 ounces of rice; in June this was reduced to 4 ounces. As part of their wearing down tactics the Japanese deliberately crowded the men in the remaining huts. The Japanese policy appeared to be directed towards breaking the morale of the remaining troops, but this they never succeeded in doing. At times, particularly towards the end when food was desperately scant and the death rate appalling—405 of the 528 Australians who remained on Ambon died in captivity—the men naturally became dispirited, but this was never for more than a few days at a time, and generally speaking morale remained high despite the efforts of the Japanese.

Scott's force disembarked on 5th November 1942 at Hainan, a barren, windswept island east of Indo-China. Though suffering fewer casualties than the group which remained on Ambon, it shared the rather special brutalities which seem to have been reserved by the Japanese for isolated groups which came within their power. The prison compound, four miles from the town of Haicho, covered an area of about ten acres, surrounded by a low barbed wire fence. The living quarters were coolie barracks of a primitive type made of scrap timber and iron. Men slept on the floor on grass mats. No separate accommodation existed for the sick, and officers and men shared huts infested by bugs, cockroaches, rats, lice and fleas. Relations with the Japanese were made increasingly difficult because of the lack of a camp interpreter.[4] Soon after their arrival the prisoners began work on the roads. The Japanese informed them that all must work —it was good for their health—and exhorted them to live "a simple life like the Japanese and to be earnest and diligent". Scott was anxious that officers should accompany the work parties to act as buffers between the men and the Japanese, and he proposed that officers should supervise each work party. At length this was agreed to. An officers' garden was established outside the camp and short walks for officers were permitted. Sergeants were allowed to work in the garden by the Japanese but not compelled to accompany the work parties. On 19th November the Japanese, finding that threats to shoot Scott and his adjutant, Captain Turner,[5] were insufficient to induce the Australian commander to sign

---
[3] Report of Major G. Westley.
[4] Eventually a Dutch chemist, Captain Sticklenberg, performed the remarkable feat of learning to read Japanese without the aid of a dictionary.
[5] Capt J. M. Turner, MBE, EM, VX45196; 2/21 Bn. Bank officer; of North Balwyn, Vic; b. St Kilda, Vic, 26 Aug 1910.

a paper promising the cooperation of the prisoners in the "building of a New East Asia", succeeded by threatening that reprisals would be taken against the whole camp. Scott's health was now failing, in part probably as a result of his bitter and unavailing fight against the Japanese. By January the lack of news and the poor food had reduced the prisoners to a mental state "bordering on despair". Scott called a parade of all ranks and reiterated his policy. He forbade sales of clothing (the prisoners' only asset) and threatened, in cases of stealing, refusal to obey orders, and insolence, to take offenders to the Japanese for punishment.

In February 1943 six Dutch prisoners attempted to escape and punishment was given to the whole camp. A six weeks' period of work without time off began and the poor food and intense heat resulted in a decline in the men's health from which they never really recovered. That month the Japanese endeavoured to persuade Scott to sign a paper promising not to escape, and when Scott refused to comply and to order his men to do so, the Japanese threatened to shoot him. Cases of beri beri now began to occur in increasing numbers. In May and June no vitamin B was issued and only small amounts in July and August. At that stage

a scandalous state of affairs existed and the situation was very alarming (wrote the medical officer to the force, Captain Aitken). Five men had died and many more were dying. The hospital was full of men with atoxia, paralysis and oedema—some able to stagger about and others could not. Every bed held a man with complete oedema of the whole body and gasping for breath. Others in the same condition were being nursed on the floor, propped up against the wall and boxes with kit bags etc; everywhere one looked in the camp one saw men with oedema of the legs and almost every man in the force had the disease to some extent. The Japanese were insisting on 120 men going to work and the work party consisted partly of atoxic and oedematous men scarcely able to stagger to work at which they were flogged and kicked. . . . Various Japanese officers visited the camp during these months and men described above were subjected to roars of laughter.[6]

In August about 150 men were too sick to work. Next month a change of commandants brought an improvement in rations, and a fund established for the purchase of drugs and clothing considerably alleviated conditions. In November a change of command again occurred, the next commandant proving "one of the best commandants". Unfortunately he remained only a short time before being replaced by Warrant-Officer Hukunaga. Thenceforward the camp was commanded by N.C.O's or private soldiers, and the effect was as bad as it could be. Private soldiers had "almost unlimited power . . . over war prisoners"; and they would not pass on complaints or protests to their seniors. At Hainan as elsewhere Japanese photographers arrived during January 1944 to take propaganda pictures of the prisoners' living conditions.[7]

Brutal beatings, sometimes of individuals and at other times of entire working parties, became more frequent as the year progressed. In April

---

[6] Report on Ambon and Hainan, Appendix 22.
[7] For example the remnants of the band were ordered to play and laugh; tomatoes grown and collected for the sick were distributed to a group of men who were told to eat them, and they were photographed while doing so.

an Australian work party accompanied by armed guards was ambushed by Chinese guerillas on its way to a working site. Nine Australians were killed and ten taken prisoner by the Chinese.[8]

In May monthly payments to officers, which had begun in November 1943, were suspended, the officers being informed that the money would be paid into a bank account, but that no prisoner would be allowed to operate on the account; the prisoners must be encouraged to save money in the same way as the Japanese. In October an Australian soldier threatened and abused one of his officers and was sent for punishment to the Japanese. Although the fear of receiving punishment from the Japanese had acted as a considerable deterrent to wrong-doers, hitherto such punishments had not been harsh. On this occasion the offender was tied up and flogged. Thereafter the practice of referring Australians to the Japanese for punishment ceased.

In January 1945 the Japanese began steadily to reduce the prisoners' diet. Next month some Dutch prisoners escaped, and Scott, having learnt from friendly Formosans that the Japanese planned to execute the prisoners in the event of invasion, ordered that an escape team be organised to assist any invading forces and try to bring help to the camp before it was too late.

In March some of the work parties were subjected to "frightful beatings and unbelievable cruelty". On the 17th the sending out of work parties ceased; the electric fence round the compound was strengthened, and the rice ration was again reduced. All surplus rations were confiscated by the Japanese. At this stage starvation loomed as a real threat. Meals were reduced to two a day (at 10 a.m. and 6 p.m.) and there was no way of supplementing the official ration. The prisoners began eating rats and snails and there was a wave of stealing. The Australian commander lacked effective disciplinary powers and appeals to the men by the padre brought no result. At length the men themselves took a hand. They organised a vigilance committee and, after trial, administered corporal punishment to offenders. As a result, pilfering practically ceased. In April the rice ration was reduced to 200 grammes per man per day; drinking water was restricted because of a shortage of fuel to boil it; and the prisoners generally were in so weak a state that they were unable even to water their small gardens. "Most of the men," wrote Captain Aitken, "presented a ghastly picture walking around like skeletons with pot bellies and oedematous legs and faces and with various sores and boils etc. dressed with any old scrap of rag." Since January most of the men had lost about 16 pounds and the average weight of the prisoners was about 8 stone. In April Major Macrae and the special escape party broke out of camp and took to the hills. In May, despite continued protests from Scott, the rice was cut to 168 grammes. In June there was some slight improvement in rations, but men were dying of starvation. The doctor signing the death certificates was told that unless this diagnosis were altered the prisoners would soon learn "what starvation really meant". In July 21 died (includ-

---

[8] Despite an extensive search after the war, none of these Australians was recovered.

ing 5 Australians). Allied aircraft were now appearing almost daily over Hainan, and at the end of the month the Japanese set the prisoners to work digging air raid shelters.

Early in August the rice ration was stopped altogether and the prisoners were placed on a diet of dried sweet potatoes. One prisoner records having tried "rat stew" for the first time on the 14th of that month. The appetite of the men may perhaps best be gauged by the prisoner's appreciation. It was "beautiful", he wrote, "resembling a mixture of chicken and rabbit". Towards the middle of the month the Japanese began to take some interest in the sick and in camp conditions generally. "It was regrettable that the food was difficult, but the men must be very cheerful and pray for release," they said. After the release of the prisoners 250 tons of rice were found in a near-by store.

The movement of Australian prisoners to Japan, Formosa and Korea began in 1942, continued during 1943, and was intensified in 1944, when large numbers began to arrive from Thailand and French Indo-China.

The hardships of overcrowding, primitive accommodation and scant rations normally associated with the sea transport of prisoners were intensified over the longer distances involved in transfers to Japan. The prisoners were usually taken in small cargo ships of 4,000 to 6,000 tons, in numbers aggregating between 500 and 1,500 prisoners. Sometimes the ships were smaller and the numbers of prisoners less. More often than not the prisoners occupied holds already loaded with supplies; some lived throughout the journey on top of coal bunkers. Sometimes holds were sub-divided horizontally at levels which prevented men from standing erect; usually the space allotted to a man and his kit prevented him from stretching out at full length. Holds were often ill-lit; nearly all were poorly ventilated, usually depending on air from open hatchways, or sometimes a wind sock rigged by the prisoners. During storms (and sometimes during submarine attacks) hatches were battened down to protect cargoes, and the prisoners were dependent on forced air systems, which functioned intermittently if at all. At times the atmosphere below decks was stifling, and the heat, particularly in ships of all steel construction, was almost unbearable. Latrines, built of deal and usually overhanging the sides of ships were never available on an adequate scale: on a transport taking prisoners to Korea in 1942 they were on a scale of 3 to 200 men, where normal conditions would demand 1 to 10 men; on a transport in 1943 latrines were on a scale of three to 700 men. The scenes during the inevitable periodic outbreaks of diarrhoea and dysentery were revolting in the extreme.

Rations at sea were usually on the scale prevailing ashore, with rice predominating. Sometimes they were better at sea, although an unexpected delay at a port of call might result in reduced rations for the remainder of the voyage. Such reductions seem to have been the result of poor organisation rather than any considered plan to cause discomfort to the prisoners. Drinking water was rationed; fresh water was seldom available for washing. The length of voyages seems to have varied according to different stages of the war. Thus, in 1942, when ships were sailing direct to Japan, voyages of ten days were not uncommon; in 1943 voyages were taking between 20 and 30 days. In 1944, when the practice had developed of hugging coastlines and travelling by devious and roundabout routes to avoid submarines, voyages took up to 70 days.

At no stage do the Japanese seem to have adopted the practice of marking ships carrying prisoners of war, and this inevitably resulted in much loss of life, particularly during 1944 when the activity of American submarines was becoming more widespread.

A group of 60 officers and 19 women (including 6 army nursing sisters) under Colonel Scanlan was shipped from Rabaul on 6th July 1942 and reached Yokohama on the 15th. The only concession to privacy made by the Japanese was to separate male from female quarters in the hold by a rope. Treatment on board otherwise was reasonable, and after the second day out prisoners were allowed on deck almost without restriction.

Conditions rather more typical of Japanese transports at this time were endured by the Senior Officers' Party, and accompanying groups which embarked at Singapore on 16th August. The Senior Officers' Party, 47 strong, which included Generals Percival and Callaghan and all officers of the full rank of colonel and above then in Changi and fit to travel, was built up to a strength of about 400 by engineers and technicians, including some Australians. Thirteen of the senior officers were Australian. A second group, designated the working party, 1,000 strong, included 6 Australian officers and 90 men. Both groups were at first loaded on to a small tramp steamer, the *Fukai Maru,* but 400, including the senior officers, were embarked on another ship after General Percival had protested. Conditions on both ships remained cramped and uncomfortable even after this rearrangement, particularly so during the delay that occurred before sailing. The Australians on the *Fukai Maru,* for example, were placed in a hold 20 yards long by 15 yards wide with 108 other prisoners. A double tier of bunks, each bunk covered with thin straw matting, was built round the hatchway, allowing each man and his gear a space of 6 feet by 2 feet. Those on the bottom bunks were able only to sit up; those on the top were slightly better off but still unable to stand. The occupants of each hold were allowed on deck for 6 hours a day. Food was fair as to bulk, consisting of two cups of rice and barley, mixed in the proportion of two to one, a cup of watery stew flavoured with either a type of cabbage or onion; and meat and vegetable (36 tins to 1,000 men) five times a day. The ships reached Takao (Formosa), by way of Cape St Jacques, on 29th August, and there the senior officers and accompanying engineers and technicians were disembarked. The working party spent about a fortnight at Takao unloading a cargo of bauxite or working ashore with coolies. It reached Fusan, Korea, on 22nd September, and on the 25th entered a prison camp at Seoul. The engineers and technicians remained on Formosa until November, when 200 of them (including 80 officers) were shipped to Moji together with 300 American prisoners who had arrived from Java. These reached Yokohama on 29th November.

As this group was arriving at Yokohama a force of more than 2,200 prisoners, including 563 Australians of "C" Force (commanded by Lieut-Colonel Robertson), 500 Americans, 950 Dutch, and 200 British airmen, was leaving Singapore on the *Kamakura Maru*. This fast 15,000-ton motor vessel reached Nagasaki on 8th December after a nine days' journey by way of Formosa (where General Heath and Brigadier Maxwell were disembarked). Conditions on board were good by Japanese standards, and all troops were accommodated below decks. This force was distributed to several destinations throughout Honshu. Some of the Australians went to Naoetsu, and the others to Kobe.

Only two substantial groups containing Australians seem to have reached Japan from Singapore in 1943. The first such group was "G" Force, 1,500 strong (commanded by Major Glasgow[9]). The force, formed at Changi, and including 1,000 Dutch, 300 British and 200 Australian prisoners sailed from Singapore in a convoy of five vessels on 26th April. The *Kyokko Maru* in which the prisoners travelled appeared to be the only transport in the convoy carrying prisoners. Conditions aboard this transport were typical of the wretched conditions already described: 700 prisoners (including the Australians) were placed in the forward holds; the aft holds were occupied by Dutch prisoners; ventilation forward was through the hatches; a wind sock was rigged for the aft holds. Men were crowded round the sides of the ship and down the centre of the holds. The individual space allotted worked out at about 5 feet by 2 feet with 4 feet of headroom. Latrines were on the usual inadequate scale. What rescue equipment existed was old and rotted. The rations, however, were comparatively good.

No medical officers or orderlies accompanied "G" Force officially from Changi, but unofficially the Australians took some small medical panniers, the British included four medical orderlies, and the Dutch included one. Dysentery broke out on the second day at sea and by the end of the voyage considerable sickness had developed. The Japanese allowed sick bays to be erected on deck, and the segregation of dysentery cases helped to avert what might easily have become a catastrophe. Two Dutch prisoners died on arrival at Moji on 21st May, and one Australian soon afterwards.

The treatment of Australian and British prisoners in this group was generally good; the Dutch were treated less well. In the early part of the voyage prisoners were permitted on deck for two hours in the morning and two in the afternoon. These periods were later reduced to one hour in the mornings and afternoons. At Moji "G" Force was broken up and contact was lost with the Dutch and British prisoners; the Australians were taken to Taisho sub-camp.

---

[9] Maj R. V. Glasgow, ED, QX6204; 8 Div AASC. Baker and pastrycook; of Red Hill, Qld; b. Brisbane, 23 Mar 1906.

"G" Force was followed soon afterwards by "J" Force, commanded by Lieut-Colonel Byrne, comprising 600 British, 300 Australians (mainly convalescents) and a few American merchant seamen. It sailed from Singapore on 16th May in the *Weills Maru,* an old and slow cargo ship of about 6,000 tons in convoy with three other ships. The prisoners were equally divided between three of the four ship's holds, the fourth being occupied by Japanese troops. The voyage to Japan took 23 days, with halts of four days at Saigon and Takao. On 5th June a torpedo attack affected the ship's engines, resulted in loss of speed and the separation of *Weills Maru* from the remainder of the convoy. On 7th June Moji was reached. There "J" Force was divided into three parties: one party, 150 strong, of sick and unfit prisoners (including 50 Australians) went to a rest camp near Moji; a second, of 250 Australians, went to Kobe; a third, of 550 British, accompanied the Australians as far as Kobe and continued northwards to Hokkaido Island.

As has been mentioned, groups of the fittest prisoners who survived the ordeals of the Burma-Thailand railway were assembled in 1944 in Thailand and Indo-China preparatory to a large-scale movement of prisoners to Japan. Some of these were at first concentrated at Saigon, where they enjoyed good food and conditions. Then the Japanese, having discovered the difficulties and dangers of shipping troops to Japan, began between April and July to transfer large numbers to Singapore. Some remained in Saigon until the end of the war; others reached Singapore, where they were usually accommodated at the River Valley Camp awaiting shipment to Japan. These prisoners and some sent from Java by way of Singapore constituted the bulk of drafts to reach the Japanese islands in 1944 and 1945.

Among the first and largest of such parties to reach Japan in 1944 was a group of 2,250 (including about 1,000 Australians) commanded by Captain Newton. This group left Singapore in two ships on 1st July and arrived at Moji by way of Borneo, the Philippines and Formosa, on 8th September, a voyage of 70 days. The convoy which grew in size at each port of call was at times harassed by submarines and some ships were sunk, but the prisoners arrived without loss.

A force of 2,300 prisoners, under the command of Brigadier Varley, shipped in similar circumstances from Singapore on 6th September was less fortunate. About 1,000 British prisoners of this group were embarked on the *Kachidoki Maru*; 599 British and 649 Australians, with three senior officers including Brigadier Varley, were embarked on the *Rokyo Maru*. They left Singapore in a convoy reinforced by other ships off the Philippines until it totalled seven transports, two oil tankers, and six escorting vessels. The prisoners in the *Rokyu Maru* were crowded into one forward hold, capable of accommodating 187 steerage passengers at normal times, but horizontally subdivided to create two decks, neither of which had a ceiling of more than four feet.

Early on the 12th off Hainan the convoy was attacked by American submarines; an escort vessel was sunk and at 5.30 a.m. the two tankers blew up within a few minutes of each other.

> The night which was pitch black was immediately turned into day. Our transport [the *Rokyu Maru*] which was on the tail end of the convoy was silhouetted beautifully against the two burning tankers. Screams from the Japanese on the bridge heralded the approach of a "tin fish" from the starboard side. It struck a little abaft of amidships and shook the ship from stem to stern. A minute or two later another explosion rocked the ship as yet another "fish" found its mark. Water from the explosion poured over the ship and down the hold in which the prisoners were standing. . . . An orderly evacuation of the hold was made, and although some men were naturally jittery . . . there was no sign of panic. Before the last prisoner was on deck the Japanese had left the ship.[1]

The *Rokyu Maru* remained afloat for twelve hours, allowing the prisoners, none of whom suffered severe injury from the explosions, ample time to escape. The Japanese crew were eventually picked up by Japanese destroyers, whereupon the prisoners took over the abandoned life-boats and went among the rafts and wreckage that littered the sea, picking up their comrades. There were then eleven life-boats, including one which the prisoners had lowered themselves after the Japanese abandoned ship. These separated, one group of four sailing in a westerly direction, the other, of seven, sailing towards the east. On the 14th September the four life-boats were intercepted by Japanese destroyers, one of which picked up 80 Australian and 56 British survivors. The other group was not seen again but the survivors believed the life-boats carrying them had been sunk by naval gun fire which was heard to the east shortly before they themselves were picked up. Among the missing was Brigadier Varley. One hundred and forty-one survivors of the *Rokyu Maru* (including 80 Australians) who had clung to rafts and wreckage, were picked up by American submarines between the 13th and 17th September, taken to Saipan, and thence to Australia. They provided the first authentic news of conditions in Burma and Thailand to reach Australia and the rest of the world.

On the 15th the prisoners rescued from the four life-boats joined survivors of the *Kachidoki Maru* on a tanker in Hainan-To harbour. She had been torpedoed on the night of the 12th-13th September and had sunk within twenty minutes. Japanese naval craft had picked up 520 of the survivors, all of whom had been in the water for at least 24 hours and most for over 40 hours. The water had been coated in oil which burned their skins. Most were naked and were suffering from sunburn; some were moaning with the pain of fractured limbs. Their plight was, in the opinion of an Australian medical officer who had arrived with survivors of the *Rokyu Maru,* equalled only by the sufferings in the "death huts" on the Burma-Thailand railway. On the 16th all were transferred to a whaling mother-ship which sailed for Japan next day, and reached Moji on 28th September. Eight men died during the voyage.

---
[1] A. Bancroft and R. G. Roberts, *The Mikado's Guests,* pp. 163-4. Bancroft and Roberts were Australian naval ratings who had survived the sinking of the cruiser *Perth.*

The first and perhaps the last party to reach Japan from Singapore in 1945 was one, including 600 Australians, which had been assembled at Tamarkan in February of the previous year. After about two months in Saigon, they were taken like others to the River Valley camp in Singapore. During a prolonged stay there they were employed on relatively light duties, but rations were both poor and meagre. On 16th December they were embarked on a passenger ship, the *Awa Maru,* whose modernness led some to expect better conditions than were usual in Japanese transports. In the event, however, 600 men were crowded into a small triple-tiered hold, with about four feet of headroom between tiers. Each tier was capable of accommodating about 200 prisoners. The *Awa Maru* lay in Singapore harbour for ten days of acute discomfort while a convoy of four oil tankers and two merchant ships was assembled. A number of Japanese civilians—men, women and children—also travelled in the ship under similar conditions to the prisoners, except that they were less crowded. The better-class accommodation available on the ship was unoccupied. The prisoners were allowed freedom of the deck during daylight, but at night were herded into the hold. The convoy sailed on 26th December, hugging the coast by day, and often sheltering in small harbours by night. On 15th January it reached Moji, one of the few convoys to reach Japan unscathed in this period—a fact possibly attributable to American pre-occupation in the Philippines. At Moji the men were broken into groups, each of about 200, and, as with earlier drafts, were sent to separate destinations.

Not all the parties of Australians to reach Japan, nor all the convoys, have been mentioned above. Some travelled in small groups in which prisoners of other nationalities predominated and they were often unaccompanied by officers. Just as it would be difficult if not impossible to record the arrival in Japan of all these parties, so too it is impracticable to provide more than representative accounts of the experiences of the larger groups, most of which were broken up and dispersed to different destinations, after their arrival.

Among the first Australians to reach Japan in 1942 was a naval medical officer, Surgeon-Lieutenant Stening,[2] of HMAS *Perth,* who had spent about four weeks at Serang in Java before being suddenly transferred with about a dozen other officers to an interrogation camp near Yokohama. At this camp mass and individual beatings took place, and conditions were more brutal than elsewhere in Japan. The diet was estimated at about 1,200 calories. The men were told that they were not prisoners, but still the enemy, and that they would not be regarded as prisoners until they entered a recognised prisoner-of-war camp. They were treated accordingly. In October, after about five months of these conditions, Stening was transferred to a prisoner-of-war camp. There, after about two months' rest and recuperation, a party of medical officers (including Stening) and

---

[2] Surgeon Lt-Cdr S. E. L. Stening, DSC, RANR. HMAS *Canberra* 1940, *Waterhen* 1940-41, *Perth* 1941-42. Paediatrician; of Sydney; b. Sydney, 14 May 1910.

orderlies was hurriedly organised and sent to the west to the relief of a group of prisoners brought to Japan in a "hell ship". This ship had left Singapore with over 1,000 prisoners on board, and 80 had died of dysentery and starvation between Formosa and Japan; 200 more died after the ship reached its destination.

Better treatment was afforded the 60 officers who also arrived at Yokohama from New Britain in July of that year. These were for the first six weeks billeted at the Yokohama Yacht Club. They were then moved to Zentsuji, on the island of Shikoku, one of the first prisoner-of-war camps to be set up in Japan. In the first year of the war conditions at Zentsuji appear to have justified its description as a propaganda camp; thereafter conditions worsened. As elsewhere the principal discomfort was

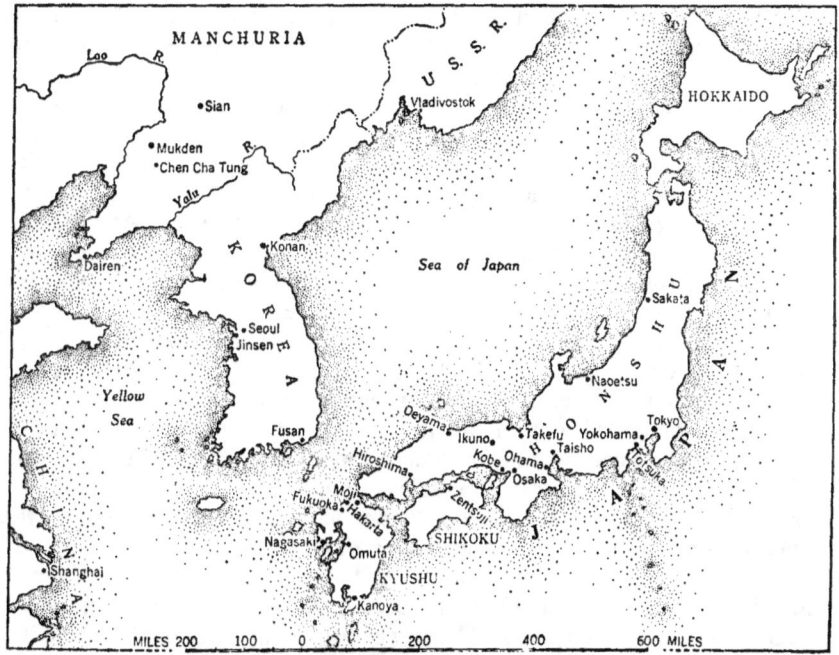

lack of food. Big men suffered most, some losing as much as five stone, but loss of weight was general. Officers (including eventually about 90 Australians) were required to work, but such work was usually only a token—and consistent with the Japanese doctrine that all must work to eat. At Zentsuji the officers gardened for only about two hours a day, and probably benefited from the exercise.

Until mid-1944 at Zentsuji two Japanese newspapers printed in English —*Nippon Times* and *Mainichi*—were regularly received, and the dispatch and receipt of mail seems to have been less of a problem there than elsewhere. An officer has recorded that he received letters each month of 1943, that prisoners were permitted to write home once a month, and that "a fair number" of these reached Australia. Some pay was made available; face-slappings were not severe (the humiliation being worse than the hurt involved); and only two officers died in a period of two years, including one Australian.[3]

In June 1944 the group in Zentsuji camp was broken up into small parties, and 45 officers (including Colonel Scanlan) were taken to a camp at Nisi Asi-Betu on Hokkaido Island. There American and British prisoners were employed in a near-by coal mine. At the Nisi Asi-Betu camp, although living conditions were not good, the officers were better fed than ever before as prisoners. The older officers were employed as gardeners; the younger at the mine head off-loading gravel and timber from the railway trucks; contact between the officers and the men working in the coal mine was forbidden.

The nineteen Australian women who reached Japan from New Britain with Scanlan's party in July 1942 were at length transferred to a camp at Totsuka, about 20 miles from Yokohama, where they remained until the end of the war. Despite the severity of Japanese winters no special issue of blankets was made, and no concessions in the way of additional heating appear to have been granted. Over the three years of captivity each nurse received as clothing a 4-yard length of warm material, tennis socks, a pair of briefs and a singlet. No shoes were issued. At times they were employed digging air raid shelters, carrying bundles of cut wood, or cutting down trees. They were allowed to cultivate their own vegetable gardens, but as happened elsewhere produce ready for eating was usually commandeered by the Japanese. They were also able to earn some pay by knitting small silk bags or manufacturing envelopes, but the rates of pay (for example, 1 sen for 1,000 envelopes) were paltry.

Rations were deficient in quality and quantity, particularly after the first two years. There was an issue each day of one (sometimes two) slices of "mouldy furred bread". Vegetables—the outside leaves of cauliflowers or cabbages, carrot tops, seaweed, lettuce leaves, rhubarb, potatoes, sweet potatoes or radishes—were issued on a diminishing scale.

During the three years spent in Japan the nurses received about 12 individual issues of Red Cross parcels, and one bulk issue. No letters were received and no news. There were no bath tubs in the camp and for the first twelve months only cold showers were available. Thereafter the nurses were able on occasions to obtain hot water from the guards' bath. Generally speaking their guards treated them well, with the exception of one or two who struck them, and Japanese civilians were well disposed. Despite the rigorous conditions and the inadequate rations and medical treatment, the nurses were able to remain moderately healthy and none died in Japan.[4]

The 200 prisoners who accompanied the Senior Officers' Party to Formosa, and were transferred to Japan in November 1942, went to Yoko-

---

[3] The senior officer in this period was Captain Gordon of the cruiser *Exeter*, followed in seniority by Colonel Scanlan of the Australian Army.

[4] Two had died on New Britain before the transfer took place.

hama, where they were billeted in two draughty godowns (bulk storehouses) near the Yokohama market on the sea-front. One godown was used for sleeping, the other for cooking, washing, and stores. The camp was known as Tokyo Branch Camp No. 2; on an average about 500 prisoners were camped there throughout the war. These included British, Australians, Dutch and (mostly) Americans.

The godowns lay in a poorly-drained area about three miles from the dockyard site, where the men were employed on building and repairs to shipping, including such work as welding, riveting and painting. Officers accompanied the daily work parties—principally to watch the interests of the men—for the first few days, but afterwards were not required by the Japanese. The Japanese enforced discipline by reducing rations, by beatings and by mass punishment. Men considered by the medical officers too sick to go to work were beaten and ordered to do so. Men returned to camp from the dockyard as unfit were often beaten personally by the brutal camp commander, Lieutenant Michizawa; in May 1943 when some prisoners were observed smoking in a prohibited area, about sixty men were beaten because the culprits refused to confess.[5] In July 1943 about 50 of the officers who accompanied this group were transferred to Zentsuji, where they remained until that camp was broken up.

About 300 of the Australians, commanded by Lieut-Colonel Robertson, who reached Japan with "C" Force were sent to Naoetsu on the west coast of the island of Honshu; the others, under Captain Paterson,[6] were sent to Kobe, the principal port on the south coast of that island. Robertson's men reached Naoetsu on 10th December 1942, after a 52-hour train journey. The sudden transition from a tropical climate to a northern latitude in midwinter imposed a great strain on the Australians, but the treatment both during the journey and on arrival was good, although food was not plentiful. Naoetsu, a town with a normal population of about 40,000, maintained three factories, and in the summer the port was used for unloading colliers. No. 4 Branch, Tokyo Camp, as it was called, was classified as a permanent camp by the Japanese and was thus included in the periodic distribution of Red Cross supplies. During the first two months the Japanese commander, Lieutenant Shikata, impressed the prisoners as being lenient and capable, and he exercised careful control of his staff. In February, however, he was replaced by a new commandant. Thereafter the prisoners became exposed to the brutality of the camp staff: beatings and bashings of the kind experienced on the Burma-Thailand railway were common; rations were at a starvation level; the steel mill at which the men worked was a mile from the camp; the men were forced to run to and from work, and if they fell down they were beaten. Some men worked 12 and 18 hour shifts for as long as 110 days without a break, either in factories or on the wharves. The lack of

---

[5] The men were paraded by the Japanese and six guards were detailed to beat them up. Each prisoner was struck at least twelve times with full swings to the jaw, and pulled up each time as he fell.

[6] Capt J. Paterson, VX29817; 8 Div Sigs. Accountant; of Balwyn, Vic; b. Kensington, Vic, 22 Mar 1904.

adequate interpreters was a source of continual misunderstanding throughout the whole period of imprisonment. Red Cross stores were pilfered or not issued; men went to work barefooted although adequate supplies of Red Cross boots were available in camp.

The brutal treatment, inadequate rations, and severe winters caused the death of 60 of the 300 Australians, including Lieut-Colonel Robertson, within the first thirteen months. Robertson, weakened by starvation and sickness, died of meningitis in March 1943, having been forced to run four miles every morning for the two months preceding his death. The wearing of overcoats was forbidden within barracks buildings although the temperature even within walls fell below zero during the winter months and snow drifts were as deep as 16 feet. The two-storeyed barracks buildings became infested with lice, fleas and bugs. Mail was withheld in the camp office because the censor refused to release it for as long as two or three months after it was received. None died in this force after about March 1944. Early in 1945 the camp was reinforced by some 400 British, American and Dutch prisoners. As the camp was designed to accommodate only 300 prisoners, conditions thereafter became shockingly overcrowded. Sleeping and messing accommodation was continuously in use, for of necessity one half of the prisoners slept during daylight and the other half during the night.

The Australians of "C" Force who were sent to Kobe under Captain Paterson entered the Kawasaki camp, an area originally used as a children's playground. The camp was new and reasonably well-equipped, and the new arrivals were each supplied with five blankets and eating utensils.

After a period of settling in and elementary tuition in Japanese drill, the troops were divided into working parties, and work at the shipyards became routine. Each day the men rose at 5 a.m., left camp at 6.30, and by route march and train were taken to the shipyards at Kobe. A weekly holiday either on Saturday or Sunday—but sometimes eliminated altogether according to the whim of their captors—was permitted.

In 1943 a concert party was formed. The only news seems to have been that derived from Korean guards at the shipping yards. In June troops were permitted to write home. In July 200 British troops arrived from Korea, bringing the strength at Kawasaki camp to about 600, including 250 Australians and 150 Dutchmen. At the end of the month, however, the officers, with the exception of a few including Captain Paterson were transferred to Zentsuji. By October the barracks rooms were infested with fleas, lice and bugs; and it became common to see fatigued prisoners sitting up at night delousing themselves. Red Cross parcels at the rate of one a man were issued in December. In April 1944 some 2,000 letters —the first from home—were received, and distributed to most men in the camp. At that time, as a result of an attempt by two British prisoners to escape, a number of restrictions were imposed, boundary fences were raised by six feet and sentry boxes were set up about the camp. The prisoners were subjected to roll calls throughout the night and other needless irritations. However, these precautionary measures were gradually relaxed until sentry boxes became empty, and some of the guards, evidently tiring of taking roll calls, allowed prisoners to take them themselves.

Towards the end of 1944 air raid alerts were becoming more common, blackouts were imposed, and the troops' spirits rose at this evidence of increasing Allied power. By January reconnaissance planes were over the camp practically every day, and eventually all prisoners in camp were locked indoors and forbidden to look skywards. Those working at the shipyards were also removed to areas where they could be the more easily controlled. In February Captain Paterson and the other Australian officers were transferred to Ikuno, where they joined Australian officers from Kobe and surrounding camps, and spent the remainder of their captivity with American and British officers at a mining camp in the hills. On 17th March the first raid occurred in which Kawasaki camp was hit. The kitchen, bathroom and huts received direct hits from incendiaries, but no prisoners were injured. In June, as a result of further raids, the Japanese transferred the remaining troops to different camps in the Kobe and Hiroshima areas. Some prisoners were transferred to a mining village in southern Honshu, and were engaged in digging coal. Early in August the Japanese announced the new American "burning" bomb, and all prisoners were ordered to carry a blanket when air raid alarms were sounded.

Taisho sub-camp, to which the 200 Australians of "G" Force who left Singapore in April and arrived in Japan in May 1943 were allotted, was one of a group of camps round Osaka and Kobe.[7] It was a small partially-completed camp containing a barracks, kitchens, wash benches, latrines and hospital, and was about one mile and a half from the Osaka ironworks, whither the men were marched daily, escorted by an armed guard and about eighty factory guards carrying sticks. The men left camp at 7 a.m., and returned about 5.30 p.m.

No medical officer had accompanied the Australians to Taisho, and until October all medical treatment was carried out by a young ordnance private, James Carr,[8] who in the course of his duties had many arguments with the Japanese and received some severe beatings. Then Major Akeroyd, formerly at the Itchioka Stadium hospital, who had reached Japan from New Britain, arrived at Taisho to become the camp medical officer.[9] Thenceforward a qualified medical officer was usually available.

The rations at Taisho, though at the usual modest level, were supplemented in December by some small Red Cross supplies—principally sugar, and tins of bully beef and meat and vegetable—and again in January 1944, when sufficient American Red Cross parcels arrived to issue one to each officer and man. In December 640 American Red Cross parcels

---

[7] The headquarters camp was at Itchioka in Osaka.
[8] Pte J. G. Carr, NX44072; AAOC. Storeman-clerk; of Croydon, NSW; b. Glebe, NSW, 16 Jun 1921.
[9] Akeroyd was replaced in March 1944 by Lt Louis Indorf of the Dutch army, and subsequently by Surgeon Lt Stening of HMAS *Perth*.

were received at the camp, and out of this issue a half parcel was issued to each man at Christmas. The Japanese held the remainder of the parcels and thereafter "it was found advisable to give the Jap Q.M. a small present of cheese, cigarettes, jam or sugar, otherwise issues would have been so small as to be of no value to the men's health".[1]

The treatment of prisoners at Taisho appears to have varied with individual guards. Discipline was at all times strict; sometimes it was unjust. The weaker prisoners, the sick, and the medical officers seem particularly to have suffered from the attentions of the Japanese medical staff and the Japanese camp commandant. The officers (only two had accompanied the force) were informed that under the Geneva Convention they were not compelled to work, but that there would be no food for them unless they did.

In March 1945 widespread fires caused by heavy incendiary raids on Osaka affected the Taisho camp, but there were no casualties. At the end of March Major Glasgow and Lieutenant Evans[2] were transferred to Oeyama, where they found themselves the only Australians in a camp of some 600 British, Canadian and American prisoners. The men were employed at a nickel mine and smelting works. The officers cultivated vegetable gardens and were employed twice daily hauling to the camp, by hand cart and on their backs, firewood from mountains about two miles distant. At other times they unloaded coal and rice trucks, or performed menial tasks about the camp. Glasgow and Evans, who arrived at this camp on 31st March with a group of other officers, were struck by the low morale and dull mentality of the prisoners, most of whom appeared to have had their spirits crushed by the inhuman treatment of the camp staff. Conditions improved somewhat after their arrival, but the food supplies, which are described as being "worse than at any other camp", continued to be bad and gradually became worse.

Soon after the departure of Glasgow the Taisho sub-camp was broken up; the medical officer, Stening, and 160 prisoners were moved to Takefu, and the remainder of "G" Force (between 20 and 30 prisoners) to Akanobe. At Takefu, a camp in a valley north of Osaka, the prisoners were employed as labourers in an ironworks. Food was reasonably good at first, with fair supplies of fish, but later it deteriorated. Stening fought hard both as camp commander and medical officer in the interests of the men, until 3rd September when he was joined by Glasgow and Evans from Oeyama. The group of prisoners who went to Akanobe were employed during the last few months in a copper mine; the poor food and long working hours caused all to lose weight and health deteriorated.

Most of the Australians who reached Japan in 1943 seem to have gone to the Kobe-Osaka area, as did the 300 Australians who arrived with "J" Force. The latter went to the Kobe House camp, situated within the Kobe city area, close to the harbour edge and a jumble of wharves and

---
[1] Maj R. V. Glasgow, Report on Taisho Sub-Camp, Osaka.
[2] Lt L. A. R. Evans, SX12186; 8 Div Amn Sub Park. Chartered accountant; of Adelaide; b. Adelaide, 15 Jun 1907.

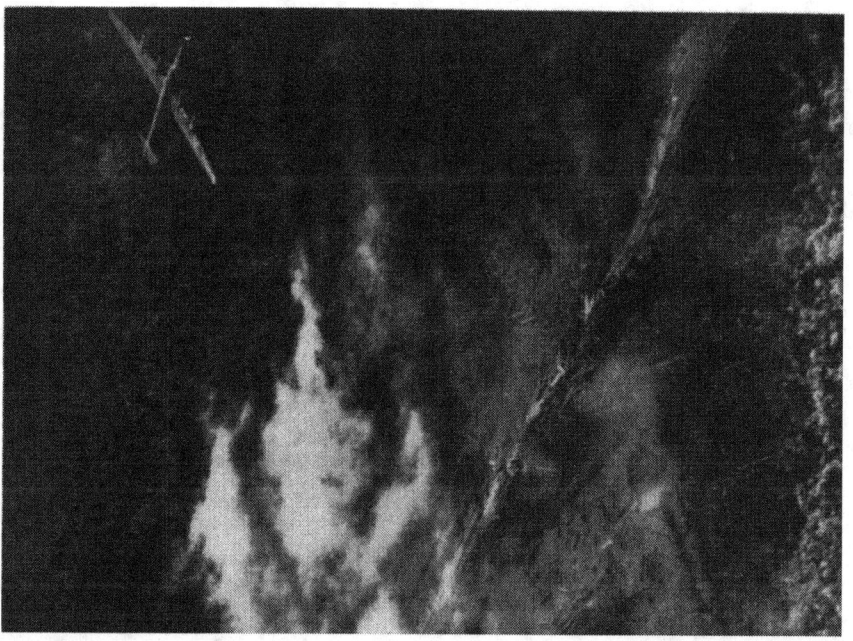

(R.A.A.F.)

A 200-foot bridge, built by prisoners of war about ten miles south of Thanbyuzayat, after low-level attacks by R.A.F. Liberators, 22nd March 1945.

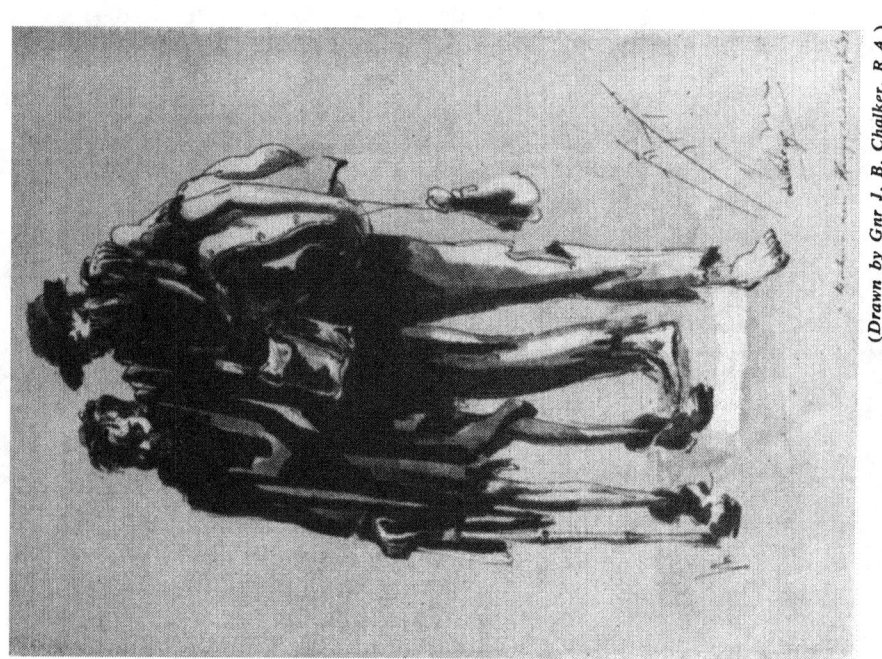

(Drawn by Gnr J. B. Chalker, R.A.)

"Working men" on the Burma-Thailand railway, Kenyu area, January 1943.

(Ex-Servicemen's P.O.W. Subsistence Claims Committee)
A better type of jungle camp on the Burma-Thailand railway.

(Drawn by Gnr J. B. Chalker, R.A.)
Cholera hospital, Hintok.

godowns. The camp itself consisted of two warehouses bounded by three streets and connected at the rear by a narrow, partly-covered alleyway, lined with wash benches and taps. It was poorly lit, ill-ventilated, dirty, verminous and crowded, with no exercise yard and very little entrance for sunlight.

The camp was already occupied, when the Australians arrived, by some 400 prisoners, mainly British from Hong Kong, but included a mixed lot of merchant seamen employed, as the Australians were soon to be, as wharf labourers and factory hands. Until the arrival of the Australians there had been no doctor at the Kobe House camp, and from the time of its inception in October 1942 about 120 prisoners had died.

The staple diet at Kobe was unpolished rice supplemented by beans, vegetables in season, and by fresh meat and dried and fresh fish. Kobe House was one of fourteen prisoner-of-war camps in the area, and although there as elsewhere a ration scale had been laid down, whether or not it was adhered to depended largely on the whims of the Japanese camp commandant.

Outdoor workers received extra food from companies for which they worked, and the prisoners supplemented their rations by stealing as opportunity offered. Non-workers—the sick and indoor staff and the officers—were allowed only half rations by the Japanese, but by common consent rations were pooled and evenly distributed. At first a Japanese doctor visited the sick at fortnightly intervals, and if a patient required surgical treatment or pathological investigation it was usually possible to persuade him to dispatch the patient to the Kobe prisoner-of-war hospital. Before the opening of this "show" place, such patients were sent to the Itchioka Stadium hospital, Osaka, "a cold place of cruelty, starvation and death".

The Australians in this force were fortunate in that, being convalescents, they arrived in Japan fairly well equipped—too well equipped in fact, for they were at first denied current Japanese issues of clothing, except for blankets. Later they received work and rest suits for summer and winter wear, and appropriate shirts and underclothes. In summer blankets were issued on the scale of three a man; in winter the issue was increased to five. At the end of the first winter troops received a set of warm American Red Cross underwear.

Hot baths were provided during the winter on rest days—twice a month —when fuel was available, and wash benches and taps were numerous, but the latrines became a breeding ground for flies, and in summer "maggots abounded on the walls and floors". Cigarettes were at first distributed regularly, soft drinks and cordials occasionally, and camp life gradually improved as a better understanding developed between prisoners and captors. This led to a relaxation of the harsh Japanese discipline, and the provision in August 1944 of musical instruments, the organisation of concerts, and the granting of permission on rest days for reading and card games.

Life (wrote one Australian) was at first extremely unpleasant, but as time went on and our hosts discovered . . . that we had initiative, and that some sign of leniency or kindness produced more and better work, conditions of life improved. From our point of view it was realised too that some of the restrictions and impositions were actually for our benefit, and that all Nipponese were not brute beasts, and that by humouring them and by playing with them as with children many benefits could be obtained.

In the close confinement of the Kobe House camp, however, differences in outlook and temperament as between British and Australian prisoners became accentuated. The Australian group contained a large proportion of over-age men and all were considered to be convalescents on departure from Changi. As a result sick parades were at first immense, consisting mostly of Australians largely with trivial ailments. Captain Boyce[3] concluded that the Australians were "pampered" so far as medical treatment was concerned. On the other hand, while the comparison between British and Australian sick rates was unflattering to the Australians, the British were acclimatised, and the Australians considered that they had all the best jobs and held on to them.

At the outset some Australians committed breaches of Japanese military discipline, leading to severe punishments, displayed a lack of gratitude for things done for them, and did little to help their comrades who were ill. (Later this attitude changed and in February 1944 the Australians were contributing a quarter of their supply of Red Cross milk for distribution among the sick.) On the credit side was the fact that they "would not and could not pretend to toady for favours to the Nips". As time went on and the health of the Australians began to improve they stood up to the cold better than the British, although they tended to succumb the more quickly to changes in temperature. By April 1944 sick parades had dwindled and the Australians, many of whom had never been employed on a working party before their arrival in Japan—and at first resented it—had "learned to loot and scrounge" and "could out-trade the British who played havoc with them earlier".

In March 1945 the incendiary bombing already mentioned played havoc with Kobe, and the end of that month saw the gradual transference of prisoners elsewhere. On the 31st all officers, except the medical officers, were transferred to an officers' camp in the mountains. Air raids continued, and in May three batches of Australians left the Kobe House camp. At that stage most of the working camps in Kobe had been evacuated to safer places, but Kobe House was evidently retained because of its proximity to the wharves and the need to continue the handling of cargoes. When the batches of Australians had gone only 76 of the original "J" Force remained, a minority group in a mixed camp without officers.

On 5th June all buildings in the camp were destroyed by fire in an incendiary raid lasting two and a half hours. Casualties were surprisingly light; the Australians escaped with a few burns of primary or secondary

---

[3] Capt C. R. Boyce, QX23158. 2/13 AGH; 2 Convalescent Depot. Medical practitioner; of Goodna, Qld; b. Toowoomba, Qld, 21 Apr 1899. (Boyce, from whose report much of the information in this account is derived, was the medical officer to "J" Force.)

degree and some cuts and abrasions; British prisoners had a worse time, and three suffered burns of third degree, but all recovered. Three Japanese guards, occupying an air raid shelter built by the prisoners, received fatal burns. That night the whole camp began a long march with stretcher cases and salvaged kit through still-burning Kobe to Kawasaki camp, already evacuated as unsafe by other prisoners.[5] The new camp was considered better from the prisoners' point of view because it gave greater access to fresh air and sunshine; but worse from the Japanese because its distance from the wharves, docks and factories led to loss of working time. This caused the Japanese to look for a suitable site nearer the town—a difficult task because all but a few buildings in the city area had been gutted by fire or bombing—and on 21st June the move of the prisoners to Wakinohama camp took place. At that stage only about 50 of the original "J" Force remained. The new camp was a partially burnt-out brick building, formerly used as a school. There was ample accommodation, and for the first time in Japan the prisoners had some of the advantages of sewerage. They were plagued, however, by mosquitoes, flies and fleas, and their food was mainly salvaged and dirty rice, but vegetables were becoming available. The Japanese declared that because of the food shortage in Japan all rations must be reduced to a minimum, but it so happened that from the end of July the prisoners received food in large quantities. However, rice did vanish from the rations and its place was taken by barley and sorghum.

Frequent air raids in the concluding stages of the war kept the men on the alert; kits and blankets were always packed and visits to shelters were many. Adequate rest was impossible and nerves and tempers were on edge.

The 1,000-odd Australians who reached Japan in September 1944 with Captain Newton, after a voyage lasting seventy days, were distributed to several destinations.[6] One group of about 200, of which a record survives, went to Nagasaki, and thence by ferry to a vast dockyard built on an island in Nagasaki Bay. The island housed some 70,000 workers and was equipped with five docks. The camp, which already housed 1,000 American, British and Dutch prisoners, and was surrounded by barbed wire, was reasonably well built in a series of long low wings, each wing containing a row of cubicles and bunks in double tiers. The men slept side by side on mats with their personal equipment piled at their heads. After some cursory training the men were allotted tasks at the dockyards, connected with shipbuilding, usually as welders, riveters, drillers, riggers, or platers.

They rose each day at 4 a.m., marched about a mile to the dockyard, and worked until 6 p.m. with a break of half an hour for lunch. Summary slappings and punchings were accepted as a normal part of the day's

---

[5] Thither the Kobe POW Hospital, situated before the raid in the foothills behind Kobe House, was also evacuated.

[6] Captain Newton went to Hiroshima PW Camp 9B Ohama.

routine. Beatings about the buttocks with baseball bats (2 to 4 strokes) were administered by Japanese marines for the more serious offences. Their blows, struck with full force, were feared by the prisoners because of the damage an ill-judged or malicious stroke might cause to the spine.

Here as elsewhere in Japan the prisoners were plagued by a series of regulations which tended to make their lives within barracks a misery. Caps had to be worn outside the room—even to visit the latrine or clean teeth; yet to wear them within the barracks room was a punishable offence. Tags were issued in several colours, denoting that a prisoner was sick, on light duties, or insane; other tags hung at the end of a prisoner's bunk indicated his whereabouts. Thus a tag had to be hung on each occasion a prisoner visited the latrine, which on a rice diet was as often as nine times a night. Community baths of hot salt water were available every third night. A rest day was granted every tenth day.

The Australians were at first unable to eat all the food given to them, and for a time British, Dutch and American prisoners were able to gather surplus food from the tables. Gradually, however, the Australians became as hungry as the rest. Winter converted the island into a snow-bound quagmire and many died of pneumonia. Early in 1945 air raids began to occur with increasing severity and confined the prisoners to air raid shelters for long hours. Ships were sunk in the bay and the dockyards strafed. In May some of the Australians were transferred to Nakarma and came under command of Dutch officers. (Their own officers had been transferred elsewhere soon after arrival in Japan.) There they relieved "several hundred emaciated Dutchmen" who had been toiling in the coal mines for two years. From Nakarma the prisoners could see and hear Moji—40 miles away—being regularly bombed. Work in the coal mines ceased after a time and some of the Australians answered a call for experienced oil drillers.[7] These were taken to Fukuoka, a well-made town on the west coast of Kyushu, as a preliminary to being moved to Manchuria. About half the prisoners at Fukuoka were Americans; the other half Dutch and Indonesians. The camp was situated in a thin forest of pine trees on the shores of the bay, and the huts, atap-roofed with earthen floors, looked as though they might have been transplanted bodily from Thailand. About 50 British sailors and soldiers were there, and also a small band of Australians from Nagasaki, who had answered a call for skilled carpenters and had been taken to Fukuoka to load trains! There the food was so bad and there was so little of it that hunger was seldom appeased. The Japanese, however, seemed little better off themselves. Each day and night B-29's raided the area, destroying supplies, dislocating transport and sinking shipping both at Fukuoka and near-by Hakarta.

---

[7] One Australian has asserted that he was able to pass muster as an oil driller merely by describing what he had once seen of the drilling of an artesian bore in central Queensland. "Most primitive; most primitive," hissed the Japanese examining officer. "We will give you most modern equipment."—See "The Specialists" by Hugh V. Clarke in *Stand To*, Jan-Feb 1955.

The 600-odd survivors of the ill-fated expedition which included Brigadier Varley were also divided between several destinations after their arrival at Moji in late September. One group of 300 British prisoners went to Yokohama; 50 Australians went to Tokyo; 290, including 29 Australians, were taken to Sakata, on the west coast of the island of Honshu about the 39th Parallel. Ten seriously ill men remained at Moji.

There is no record available of the Australians who went to Tokyo but Captain Richards of the A.A.M.C. who accompanied the prisoners to Sakata considered that their physical state was one of extreme exhaustion aggravated by starvation and disease. Upon arrival they were billeted in a rice store, poorly ventilated and lit, and slept on wooden floors covered by grass mats. Work of a type usually done by coolies was begun three days after arrival, and about three days' holiday a month was granted thereafter. The working hours—$9\frac{1}{2}$ hours a day—were not long by coolie standards, but the ration scale—60 grammes of rice, barley and beans, plus horse or pig offal on rare occasions—was grossly deficient in protein, fats and vitamins. Apart from small quantities of seaweed, the only vegetable supplied was a particularly obnoxious form of dried spinach with small food value. Because of the long working hours no regular recreation or amusements were provided, and on holidays the men were too tired to play games. On Christmas Day 1944, however, the Japanese staff made genuine efforts to arrange an impromptu concert, which was thoroughly enjoyed.

In 1945 eight men died of pneumonia during what was described as the severest winter experienced in Japan for 70 years, and a further ten died of other causes before the war ended.

The final force of Australians to reach Japan with which this account is concerned were the 600 who reached Moji in January 1945. Like preceding forces it was broken into groups which were sent to separate destinations.

One group of 90 Australians went to Fukuoka Camp No. 22, where they were accommodated in a good building divided into rooms each holding ten men. Blankets and mattresses were provided and facilities for bathing were adequate. For the first three weeks the new arrivals were officially resting; in fact they were employed digging air raid shelters. Food during this period was on an extremely low scale. At the end of that time most of the prisoners were employed in a coal mine about a mile from the camp, and rations improved slightly. The men worked on a quota system—which meant that when the quota was finished they returned to camp—but the quota was remorselessly increased until they were working about 15 hours a day and getting little sleep off duty because of the constant air raids. In February 1945 Red Cross parcels were received and issued to the prisoners; afterwards much of the supplies were plundered by the Japanese and only minute quantities were issued to the prisoners of war.

As elsewhere, individual beatings were common, and sometimes Sergeant Irio, regarded as a particularly cruel Japanese, indulged in mass punishments, in which all of the prisoners were compelled to kneel for hours in the snow, sometimes with bamboo sticks under their knees. By 15th August there was not a fit man in the camp (for months there had been no meat or fish issue) and Sergeant Irio's savagery had reduced the prisoners to a state of nervous breakdown.

A second group of about 200 went by rail to Omuta, at that time one of the largest prisoner-of-war camps in Kyushu, containing about 1,700 British, American, Dutch and Australian prisoners, where they also were employed in a coal mine. The Americans, having arrived first in 1943, held all the best jobs in the camp, such as in the hospital and kitchen. The camp was sited between the town of Omuta and the sea on ground reclaimed by tippings from mine workings; the organisation of the camp was complex (regulations similar to those at Nagasaki were rigidly policed), but on the whole was considered fairly efficient. There was, for example, a reasonably equipped hospital run by four medical officers (including Captain Duncan[8] of the A.A.M.C.); a communal bath; a barber's shop, and a canteen of sorts. The camp, surrounded by a 12-foot high wooden fence electrified at its top by three strands of wire, provided the best accommodation the Australians had seen since Changi, though it was midwinter when they arrived and snow was falling.

Work was divided according to nationalities: the British prisoners worked in a zinc foundry; the Dutch (100 all told) in coal stalls near the camp and on coaling of ships; the Americans and Australians jointly worked the coal mine.

The work either at the pithead in the bitter winter, coaling the trucks below ground, or at the coal face itself, was arduous and at times dangerous. Water coursed through the mine from an underground stream, and none knew when a fall would take place. Although at the outset there were occasional Red Cross parcels—as a prize for the section having the highest attendance figures in a month!—the men were continually hungry and most of them found the starvation rations during the Japanese winter harder to bear than ever before. Some considered the work in the coal mines more arduous than on the railway because in the jungle they had rested for ten minutes every hour, whereas in Japan there were no rest periods. Much petty stealing took place, and an Australian commented that unlike other camps—River Valley Road, for example—it was rash even to hang out clothes for drying without mounting guard on them. An involved system brought by the Americans from the Philippines of trading in food had developed, and men craving tobacco were able to trade their meagre rations for cigarettes. "Rice now, for rice and soup tomorrow" meant that a prisoner was consuming only his soup at the present meal, and trading his rice with someone who would promise to

---

[8] Capt I. L. Duncan, NX35135; RMO RAE 8 Div. Medical practitioner; of Wollongong, NSW; b. Glen Innes, NSW, 29 May 1915.

pay it back on the morrow plus soup as interest—in other words his entire meal.

In June the Japanese foremen in the coal mine were exhorted to produce more coal. Thenceforward the prisoners were relentlessly driven, and beatings and punchings became even more common. From the more brutal guards there was torture. The men were now at the limits of their physical resources, and rather than endure the tyrannical conditions imposed in the coal mines some chose to injure themselves in order to obtain release. That month, although the camp escaped damage, Omuta and the surrounding area were being regularly bombed. In July and August Allied aircraft were over Japan in force every day. Much of the off-shift time was spent in air raid shelters where proper rest was impossible; in July an incendiary raid destroyed many of the camp huts. On 9th August 730 multi-engined planes were counted in the skies above Omuta. That day the entire western sky seen from the prison camp "from sea level to zenith was a mass of billowing smoke". About 40 miles to the west lay Nagasaki, laid waste in one awesome moment by an atomic bomb.

Meanwhile the Senior Officers' Party had also come to Japan, though only in passing. The larger part of their time had been spent on Formosa. After arrival there in August 1942 they had gone to a camp of crude coolie huts at Heito where they were compelled to sign declarations promising not to escape. About a fortnight later they were transferred to Karenko, on the east coast, where American senior officers from the Philippines had already arrived. (They were joined later by senior British and Dutch officers from the Netherlands East Indies, and by the Governor of Hong Kong, Sir Mark Young.) At this stage there were about 400 prisoners housed in a barracks designed to accommodate about 120. At Karenko the Japanese introduced a policy seemingly "calculated to degrade all officers and subject them to mental torture and physical starvation", and the most senior officers were sometimes slapped or knocked down by Japanese privates without reason, or for trivial ones.

The food ration sank to a very low level; all lost weight—one officer whose normal weight was 13 stone 6 pounds dropped to 8 stone 8 pounds in the period spent at Karenko—and most of the prisoners suffered from dysentery and malaria. A work program was introduced; senior officers worked as farm labourers, clearing ground and planting gardens with sweet potatoes, tomatoes and beans. Although the work was not hard the prisoners were soon so debilitated that, in the words of one elderly officer, "we could hardly lift the hoes we were made to use on the farm".

The Japanese introduced a pay system but the greater part of the pay went into a "Post Office Savings Account" which officers were unable to broach. However, the Japanese allowed the prisoners a small credit which they could use at the canteen to purchase fountain pens, notebooks and other such articles of which evidently there were plenty. No food was available at the canteen, although large supplies existed on the island.

Conditions improved early in 1943, and face-slapping practically ceased. In April about 80 officers of the rank of brigadier and above were transferred for a short period to Tamasata, about 60 miles to the south, where they remained until after the visit to Formosa of an International Red Cross inspecting officer had been completed. In June a small party of governors and generals was moved to a camp built for the purpose at Mosak near Taihoku, the capital of Formosa, where they enjoyed improved treatment and food. That month the remaining prisoners were transferred by boat and rail to Shirakawa, a dark and dismal camp in a marshy area encircled by hills. There farmwork was reintroduced and continued intermittently until June 1944. That month as a result of the refusal of officers to "volunteer" for work the Japanese began systematically to persecute them—night roll calls were instituted, music (except at weekends) and the playing of cards were forbidden, and prisoners were not allowed to go to bed before lights out (9.30 p.m.) or to lie on a bed during the day.

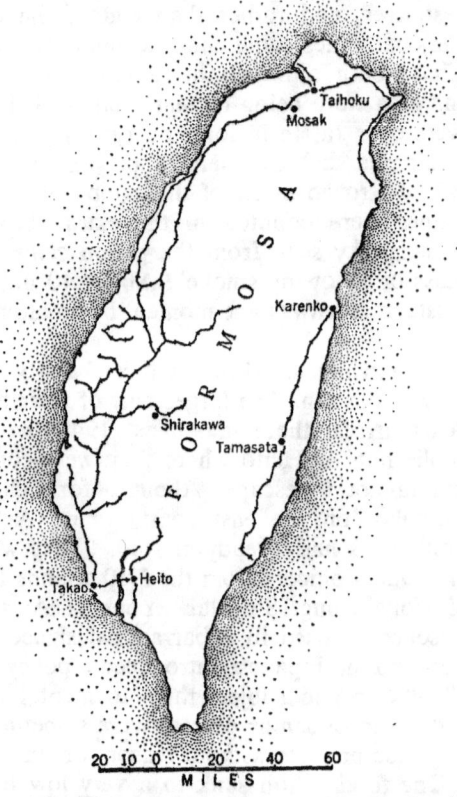

These tactics continued until October when the Japanese, evidently fearing an invasion of Formosa, transferred the senior officers by air or by sea to Japan, and thence by sea and rail to Manchuria by way of Korea. The treatment in Japan during this move was easily the best they received as prisoners. At length most of the Australian officers, with British and American colleagues, were concentrated at Chen Cha Tung (Liayuanchow) in northern Manchuria where they occupied an old stone, two-storeyed barracks built by the Russians as a prison. The senior officers and governors had arrived a month earlier. The treatment at this camp was on the whole better than in Formosa and the rations—soya beans, bread and vegetables—more filling and sustaining than the normal rice diet. Also there were sufficient Red Cross supplies to enable parcels to be issued for a time on a scale of about one every three weeks. Except for digging slit trenches, no work was done in Manchuria by the senior officers, and generally speaking other ranks who accompanied them had to perform only such camp duties as were essential to survival. Some clothing was provided by the Japanese, and although temperatures sometimes fell as low as minus 50 degrees Fahrenheit, and cases are reported of some officers remaining in bed practically all day in order to keep warm, the senior Australian officers seem not to have suffered unduly because of the cold.[9]

In May most of the prisoners in Manchuria were concentrated near Mukden, where before long some 2,000 Allied prisoners were gathered. Rations were twice reduced, and the buying of food outside camp was forbidden. Time dragged, but a secret wireless provided a daily news service that encouraged flagging spirits.

Two of the remoter northern camps where small numbers of Australians were imprisoned were at Seoul and Konan on the Asian mainland. Some ninety Australians had arrived at Seoul on 25th September 1942 with the working party of 1,000 which had left Singapore with the Senior Officers' Party the previous month. Seoul was the headquarters camp for all prisoners of war in Korea. There they were required to sign undertakings not to attempt to escape and were addressed by Colonel Noguchi in the following terms:

I am Colonel Noguchi (he said through an interpreter). We are fighting for the emancipation of the nations of East Asia, firm and unshakeable in our resolve that our enemy Britain and U.S.A. should be crushed. Australia is on the verge of capture, India of rebellion. We have already sunk 2,801 vessels and destroyed 4,500 aircraft. The Nippon Army is under the Imperial Command of the Emperor who is the personification of God, so that the Imperial troops are to be called the troops of God. Now you have become prisoners of war through struggling against God's army are you not feared to the marrow? Hostile feelings in your hearts against us cannot go permitted. We will punish you if you against our regulations or attempt to escape. According to your malice feelings so shall we limit your freedom or treat you with severity or lenity.

Sign parole as proof of your non-hostility or be placed under restraint. Grumbling against food, clothing, or housing is strictly prohibited.

You have come to Japan not as honoured guests—you must endure.

At Seoul all drill and commands had to be given in Japanese; blankets were issued on a scale of five per man. The first working parties were not sent out to local factories until 27th October—a month after the prisoners' arrival. Snow fell for the first time on 8th November, but stoves were not lit until 5th December. A Red Cross representative had visited the camp in November, and in February Red Cross rations arrived in camp and were issued—after a Japanese guard had been detected eating them! In March prisoners were allowed to write their first letters and an officers' garden was started. In August the first mail for the prisoners arrived at the camp, but there was none for the Australians. The flow of Red Cross parcels, which had been issued on a scale of 6½ a man, ceased at this

---

[9] In December 1944 some senior officers, including Callaghan and Blackburn, were transferred to Sian.

time. In September a number of prisoners (including one Australian officer and 50 men) were transferred to Konan; Red Cross supplies were replenished in January, but by March food was scarce and eggs were not available. In May, as a result of complaints, the bread issue was increased to 10 ounces and the amount of rice for outside working parties also increased; rice for inside workers, however, was correspondingly reduced.

Conditions at Konan seem to have been similar to those which prisoners had been exhorted to endure at Seoul. The prisoners were accommodated in rooms 50 by 25 feet in which 40 men lived, slept and ate on Japanese bed platforms. Four to six blankets were issued, depending on the seasons. The rations—24 ounces of rice a man daily, plus plentiful supplies of vegetables in autumn and winter, and ample fish in winter and spring—were generally satisfactory as regards quantity. From November 1944 American Red Cross parcels on the scale of a half parcel per month were issued. Heating in the barracks was reasonable, with a concrete stove constantly burning in each room from 21st November to 21st March. The men were employed in factories, breaking stone, shifting limestone, and stoking furnaces. Discipline was greatly relaxed by Japanese standards, because this was a working camp with men out at all hours. Nevertheless the usual face slappings and unfair punishments persisted, although these were promptly taken up by British officers in the camp.

At Konan as at other places the Japanese seemed to reserve a special brand of ill-treatment for the sick. The hospital was ill-equipped, no extra food was provided for patients and the attitude of a visiting Japanese doctor was callous and arbitrary. Frequently men unable to perform their duties by reason of high temperatures, bad feet, or legs were ordered out to work. Only minute quantities of medical supplies were made available.

What steps had been taken by the Allies by August 1945 to organise for the impending liberation of the prisoners of the Japanese?

As early as 1942 the War Office in London had begun to consider problems involved in the repatriation of prisoners and was seeking Dominion agreement in principle to plans which had been drawn up by the Imperial Prisoners of War Committee covering prisoners in both Europe and Asia. In brief these plans envisaged British control of repatriation of Commonwealth prisoners in Europe, but the division of the Far East into convenient areas of Dominion responsibility, with some measure of United States control in Japan proper and the Philippines.

Towards the end of 1944 a draft directive was submitted to the Combined Chiefs of Staff, and detailed planning began. Commanders-in-Chief in the Pacific were made responsible for the protection, maintenance and evacuation of all United Nations prisoners of war within their respective operation zones, but were to coordinate their plans. These were to ensure provision for prisoners of war in any armistice agreement made with the enemy, to take control of prisoner-of-war camps, to see that liberated prisoners were properly cared for, to send back nominal rolls, to preserve enemy records concerning prisoners, and to apprehend enemy personnel charged with their maltreatment. The directive required countries concerned to inform the British War Office and the American War Department of the numbers and locations of their nationals held by the Japanese (although this was a task beyond the capacity of most) as well as any special requirements for their handling after recovery. Members of national forces to which prisoners belonged were to be used in reception depots at the earliest possible stage of evacuation (a point which had been stressed by Australian planners from the outset). Priority in evacuation was to be given to sick and wounded, but no other distinction was to be made among recovered servicemen in respect either of rank or arm of the Service.

The surrender terms imposed obligations on the Japanese to ensure the safety and well-being of all prisoners and internees and to supply adequate food, shelter, clothing and medical care until Allied forces took over. Until this occurred prisoner-of-war camps were to be handed over to the command of the prisoners' leaders.

The task of recovery faced by the organisation created for this purpose, known as R.A.P.W. & I.—Repatriation of Allied Prisoners of War and Internees—was hardly less complex in August-September 1945 than that faced by the chronicler who endeavours to follow in detail a decade later the group and individual experiences of the prisoners. As an illustration of the widespread distribution of prisoners throughout East Asia,[1] the largest numbers of Australians were congregated on Singapore Island and Johore (5,549); 4,830 were distributed in several camps and on a number of working parties in Thailand and remote areas of Burma; 265 were in French Indo-China; about 750 were distributed throughout the islands of the Netherlands East Indies, with the largest group (385) in Java, and in Sumatra (243); about 100 were on Ambon; two were at Macassar, seven on Bali; another 150 were at Kuching in British North Borneo. About 2,700 were distributed between Japan, Korea and Manchuria. About 200 remained on Hainan.[2]

The Australian Army, however, was well organised for the imminent recovery operations, particularly in South-East Asia, for in June General Blamey had been warned by Admiral Mountbatten that impending operations in Malaya might result in the release of large numbers of prisoners of war (including Australians). Although these operations did not eventuate, the Australian contribution to a reception scheme based on India—advanced parties of the 2nd Australian P.W. Reception Group[3] (Brigadier Lloyd[4]) and contact teams—had begun to arrive in Ceylon

---

[1] Estimated by the Japanese at 192,895, including 93,762 prisoners of war. The bulk of the internees were Dutch.

[2] This distribution of prisoners of war was not known to the Australian Government at the time. The best estimates placed 8,000 Australians in Japan, 5,000 in South-East Asia, 500 in Java, 2,000 in Borneo, and 2,000 in other locations. Some 3,000 were unaccounted for.

[3] The 1st Australian P.W. Reception Group was based in the United Kingdom.

[4] Brig J. E. Lloyd, CBE, DSO, MC, ED. (1st AIF: Lt 23 and 24 Bns; Indian Army.) CO 2/28 Bn 1940-42; comd 16 Bde 1942-43, 2 Aust PW Reception Gp 1945. Of Perth; b. Melbourne, 13 Apr 1894.

and India before the war ended. Then, when it became apparent that the Australian Reception Group would be receiving prisoners direct from the recovery areas, it was expanded to make it more self-contained until it included 1,250 officers and men, a 600-bed hospital, and some 10,000 tons of stores and equipment. Two ships (including the *Duntroon*) used for taking the group direct to Singapore would be used to evacuate prisoners to Australia. The hospital ship *Manunda* was to be used to evacuate unfit prisoners from Singapore to an Australian hospital at Labuan, thus speeding up its turn around. No plans could be made for the concentration or transfer of other Australians in South-East Asia until reliable estimates were received of their numbers. Eventually, however, the bulk of the prisoners from Saigon, Thailand, Java and Sumatra were transferred to Singapore for onwards passage. Prisoners recovered in western Borneo were accommodated by the 9th Australian Division at Labuan; others recovered in northern Borneo and in islands of the Netherlands East Indies (including Ambon) were to be taken to Morotai, where the 1st Australian P.W. and Internee Reception Unit had been established since June.

Whereas the 2nd Australian Reception Group in Singapore would work with British, Indian and Dutch recovery organisations and be principally concerned with the recovery of Australian prisoners and internees, the 3rd Reception Group (Brigadier Wrigley[5]), which established its headquarters near Manila in the Philippines on 19th August, would be required to work closely with American recovery organisations, with the larger task of being the principal receiving depot for all Commonwealth—except Canadian—prisoners and internees recovered in Formosa, Japan and Korea. Some 26 Australian contact teams were attached to American formations and reached Japan, but the bulk of the work there was done by Americans and in strict accordance with methods of procedure established by the American Army. The Australian and other contact teams were attached only to assist in dealing with specific problems applicable to their own nationals, and, in the case of the Australian contact teams, to British nationals also. The Australian Reception Group at Manila was augmented by the attachment of a British section (representing the three Services) about 250 strong, and a small Indian Army detachment of 32—a rather inadequate contribution so far as the British were concerned to the task of repatriating some 16,000 prisoners, the larger portion of whom would necessarily be British.

Meanwhile, on 15th August Mountbatten's South-East Asia Command had been extended to include part of the adjacent South-West Pacific Area, including Java, Borneo, Dutch New Guinea, and part of French Indo-China, but not Timor, and embraced the areas where most of the Australians were to be found. Mountbatten, his command poised for the capture of Malaya, had orders already in train for the occupation of that

---

[5] Brig H. Wrigley, CBE, MC, VX171. (1st AIF: S-Sgt 3 Inf Bde, Capt 60 Bn; Indian Army.) CO 2/6 Bn 1941-42; comd 20 Bde Sep-Oct 1942, 3rd PW Reception Gp 1945. Oil company representative; of Sale, Vic; b. Scarsdale, Vic, 1 Dec 1891.

and other areas (ships were actually at sea) when General MacArthur, who had been created Supreme Commander for the Allied Powers to make arrangements for the surrender of the Japanese, issued orders that the actual documents of surrender in theatres other than his own might only be signed after his own had been signed; and that no landing or reoccupation by military forces might be made until after the formal signature of the surrender document in Tokyo. The formal surrender had been fixed for 31st August; but because of a typhoon striking the coast of Japan the ceremony was postponed until 2nd September. Thus the liberation of the prisoners was delayed for more than a fortnight.

On 27th August Japanese delegates, who had arrived in Rangoon in response to a request by Mountbatten, signed a preliminary agreement which enabled instructions to be sent out through Field-Marshal Terauchi to senior Japanese commanders concerned, ordering them to assist and obey the British commanders of the reoccupation forces, who would be acting with Mountbatten's authority and in his name. Operations for the recovery of the prisoners began next day when aircraft began dropping pamphlets over all known camps in the South-East Asia area, with the object of spreading the news of the Japanese capitulation to the guards and the prisoners themselves. Immediately afterwards the delivery of stores and relief troops began, and before the military landing in Malaya on 5th September took place some 120 relief personnel had been flown into known prison camps in the command, and 950 tons of supplies delivered. Between 3rd and 8th September the headquarters and a brigade of an Indian division were flown into Bangkok and about 190 tons of stores delivered by air. On 13th September the *Duntroon* and a cargo vessel arrived at Singapore from Sydney carrying the 2nd Australian P.W. Reception Group and its accompanying hospital.

Meanwhile news of the end of the war had reached the prisoners in most areas without delay, through unofficial sources such as secret wirelesses or from friendly civilians; the Japanese announcement usually followed some days later.

In Changi Gaol a secret wireless permitted the prisoners to follow the negotiations for surrender from the time of President Truman's broadcast from Washington on the Potsdam decisions, through the exchange of notes and broadcasts on 10th and 11th August, up to the joint announcement by Mr Attlee and President Truman on 15th August that Japan had accepted the Allied demand for unconditional surrender. One young soldier imprisoned in Changi Gaol who wrote his recollections of the events closely preceding that day recalled that on 10th August

shortly after midnight, the official and pirate radio operators had their greatest moment. Crouched in the darkness beside their faintly glowing machines they heard from London the breath-taking news. . . . The penalty for wireless operating was death. The only safeguard was secrecy. Yet who could rest all night with this stupendous fact bursting within him?

Out of the cells they came, dark shadows slipping along the corridors. "Wake up." Sleepers felt themselves shaken as the words were hissed in their ears.

"What's up?" Another party to unload rice perhaps, or another move.

"The news—it's all over son, Japan is out. Down at home they are going mad and God-knows-everything."

"Who says so?" a voice is heard drawling sarcastically. Everyone had been caught by rumours.

"It's right, I tell you, I heard it myself. The Nips are going for the Parker.[6] You are free, Digger. Think of it; free."

In their excitement and desire to convince the doubters, the newsbringers were half choking.[7]

In the less settled camps round Singapore Island and in Johore the first indications of impending peace were rumours among native people and the cancellation of work parties. An Australian from Java employed on the Singapore waterfront recalled that there had been persistent rumours of peace or an armistice since 10th August, and that the date 24th August had been freely mentioned as having great significance. On the 17th the Japanese officially confirmed the news at Changi; at other camps some work parties were not sent out; others returned from work early. A warrant-officer in charge of a working party of 200 Australians at Jurong road was urgently summoned before a Japanese administrative officer about 5 p.m. and informed that, as it was raining and the ground slippery, there was a likelihood of "Australian soldiers slipping and hurting themselves", and that all men were to rest on the 18th and "have plenty of food". This perhaps unprecedented solicitude was almost as convincing as the official confirmation. The reactions of the prisoners varied according to individual temperament and circumstances. Some at first elated later felt depressed, or were worried about what might have occurred during prolonged absences from homes; an Australian in Thailand decided that there was "very little display of emotion; just a more cheerful atmosphere". The official announcement "fell absolutely flat". Some prayed; others visited comrades in hospital; one found the news "too big, too stunning for instant assimilation"; most complained of an inability to sleep. One Australian soldier employed on a work party in Singapore broke out of camp (as others must have done), sat down at a street stall and ate a gargantuan meal of rice, fish and sambal (generic name for condiments served with oriental dishes), at a cost of 25 dollars.

As I ate (he wrote soon afterwards) various onlookers added perhaps another piece of fish or sambal, or a cup of excellent coffee . . . one stall-holder from a competitor stall brought me another meal of rice, while the stall-holder where I was eating added more fish and sambal. . . . He then left to return with an excellent cigarette whilst I sipped away at my lovely coffee and, lolling back with cigarette and coffee, passed a remark that it was equal to Raffles, which brought down the house.[8]

On the day of the official Japanese announcement working parties began to return to Changi from Singapore and Johore. By 21st August Changi

---

[6] Such was the power of American advertising that this was a way of saying the Japanese were reaching for a pen to sign a surrender document.

[7] David Griffin, in *Stand-To*, February 1952.

[8] Sgt A. E. Field. Field records having increased in weight by 21 pounds between 18th and 31st August.

camp held some 12,000 prisoners; 3,800 British, Dutch and Australian prisoners were distributed among three other camps on the island. About 14,000 Indian prisoners were also to be repatriated. On the 28th Allied aircraft dropped leaflets in English, Japanese and Korean, ordering the Japanese to lay down their arms but to continue to care for the prisoners of war and civilian population and giving advice to the prisoners on the organisation created for their recovery. On the 30th two combatant officers, two doctors and two medical orderlies as well as a small supply of stores were dropped by parachute; next day many stores were dropped by parachute on Changi airfield. On 5th September the 5th Indian Division and a number of recovery teams were landed, and within a week prisoners were leaving by air for the south.

Even to isolated working parties in Burma news of the liberation was not long delayed. At one camp on the Mergui road, where for the previous month the prisoners had been witnessing a pilgrimage of broken Japanese soldiery returning from Burma, only ten fit men remained out of about 300 British, Australian and American prisoners. About mid-August the attitude of the Japanese suddenly changed and liberal supplies of quinine and blankets were made available. Work ceased; then early on the 19th the Japanese announced excitedly that the war was over.[9] A few days later parachute troops were dropped, and then with what seemed amazing celerity the men were transferred to a hastily erected seaside camp at Kerikan. They were next taken by Dakota aircraft to Rangoon, and eventually conveyed to Australia and other destinations.

Similarly elsewhere in Burma and Thailand the news was not long delayed. An account which survives of one large working camp in Thailand reports that members of a working party first learnt of the impending liberation on 12th August from a Thai who had heard it on his wireless. The 15th August was a holiday, the first for many weeks. Next day working parties which had been marched out to working sites were returned to camp and dismissed. Work parties assembled after breakfast on the 17th were also dismissed. Half-way through the morning word was circulated that there would be a parade, to be announced by bugle call, at which all men in camp must be present.

At 11 a.m. the bugle sounded (wrote a chronicler of the 2/2nd Pioneer Battalion). It was not the lugubrious Japanese call which for so long had been the summons to parade. It was the old familiar "Fall in A, Fall in B, Fall in every Company!" There was a tremendous din of chatter as 2,500 British, Australians and Americans took their places on the parade ground.

The senior prisoner in the camp, a British warrant-officer, climbed on to a box in front of the parade. The noise subsided, and the silence was complete as he spoke.

"Gentlemen!" he said, "this is the happiest moment of my life. The Japanese commandant has asked me to inform you that the war has ended!"

For perhaps ten seconds there was not a sound. The unbelievable had happened, and it first had to be believed. Then the air was rent with sound as 2,500 men yelled and shouted as they had never done before.[1]

---

[9] An Australian prisoner recorded that the Japanese themselves were so much out of touch with the progress of the war that they were unable to say who were the victors.
[1] *The Story of the 2/2nd Australian Pioneer Battalion*, p. 176.

By the end of September the majority of Australian prisoners recovered in Singapore, Java and Sumatra had been evacuated to Australia, either by ship or by air from Singapore; in addition half the prisoners from the Bangkok area had been similarly evacuated or were staging through Singapore.[2] Some 350 Australians were flown from Bangkok to Rangoon before the plan to repatriate them through Singapore was able to take effect. So rapid in fact had been the evacuation of the prisoners from these areas that some were arriving inadequately equipped for leave at Australian ports; and these arrivals were a source of complaints that eventually reached Mr Forde, the Minister for the Army. "Please have full report for me on my arrival Melbourne," he telegraphed General Blamey on 9th October . . . "and advise me who is responsible for neglect to supply clothing to these men and who has consequently brought disrepute upon army for its treatment of returning prisoners of war." The facts were that the speed of evacuation from Singapore was outstripping the time needed for adequate stocks of clothing to reach the reception group by sea. Rather than delay the departure of the prisoners arrangements were made for clothing to be dispatched by air to Darwin and other ports of call, but the difficulty of estimating the proportions of the different sizes required made it probable that whatever happened some prisoners would be lacking a few items.

Generally speaking, the more remote the area the longer the news of the surrender took to reach it. Thus at Hainan the prisoners were not informed until the evening of 25th August that the war had ended, although there as elsewhere the period after 15th August was made notable by improved rations after a long period of semi-starvation. On the 17th—the prisoners had then been confined to the compound for five months—they received their first meal of rice for over a fortnight; on the 21st much to the surprise of everyone two pigs arrived with the rations; on the 23rd the Japanese caused another surprise by providing some medical supplies. On the 25th the Japanese painted "P.W." in large letters on the roof of the camp, and that evening the men—no longer prisoners—were informed that the war was over and that soon "an American captain would be arriving by parachute to take charge of the Island of Hainan". The Japanese swamped the camp with medical supplies on the 26th, and next day an American bomber appeared and dropped 30 parachutes with other supplies. Colonel Scott conferred with an American recovery team which arrived that day, and learnt that his men would be moved to Samah, where Americans from Kunming had set up a headquarters, and be evacuated thence to the Philippines. This move took place on 5th September. Messages were dropped to Major Macrae and his party of escapers, telling them also to go to Samah. There was evidently some duplication of the arrangements for recovery of prisoners from Hainan—perhaps inevitable in the circumstances—for on 12th September the British

---

[2] The work of the reception group was facilitated both at Singapore and Bangkok by the excellence of the records maintained by the prisoners of war, and by the fact that nominal rolls, prepared by the prisoners themselves, were awaiting the Reception Group's arrival.

UNIT	ORIGINAL UNIT	1/3 Aus Mt. bay.	RANK	NAME
	UNIT TRANSF. TO	2/3 M. AC	Lieut	Hamilton G.T.

BATTLE TAKEN PART IN	DATE	8/2/42 to 15/2/42	PLACE	Shadana harbor to Singapore

COMERADE(S) KILLED IN ACTION DIED OF WOUND OR SICKNESS	NAME	UNIT	DATE	PLACE
	None Killed			

A. Experiences on the battlefield (Battle conditions and situations under which one fought, battle conditions immediately prior to capitulation, things admired about the Japanese force, etc)

Was not on the battlefield

B. Confessions from the battlefield (Tragidies, from the standpoint of both the individual and the unit, things that were sad, dreadful, frightful, suffering, happy, etc.)

None for "A"

C. Your opinion, or impression, about the Japanese force (Before the battle, on the battlefield, since capitulation, etc.)

Did not come in contact with them
Being a P.O.W. I have not had the opportunity to study the Japanese

D. Is it profitable, or advisable, for Great Britain to fight against Japan? Reasons.

E. Your opinion concerning the establishment of the Greater East Asia

Have been a P.O.W. for 2 years, I have not come in contact with the population upon the establishment

F. How long do you think this war will last? When do you think you can return to your home country?

Until secret

A Japanese questionnaire circulated to prisoners of war in Korea in 1944.

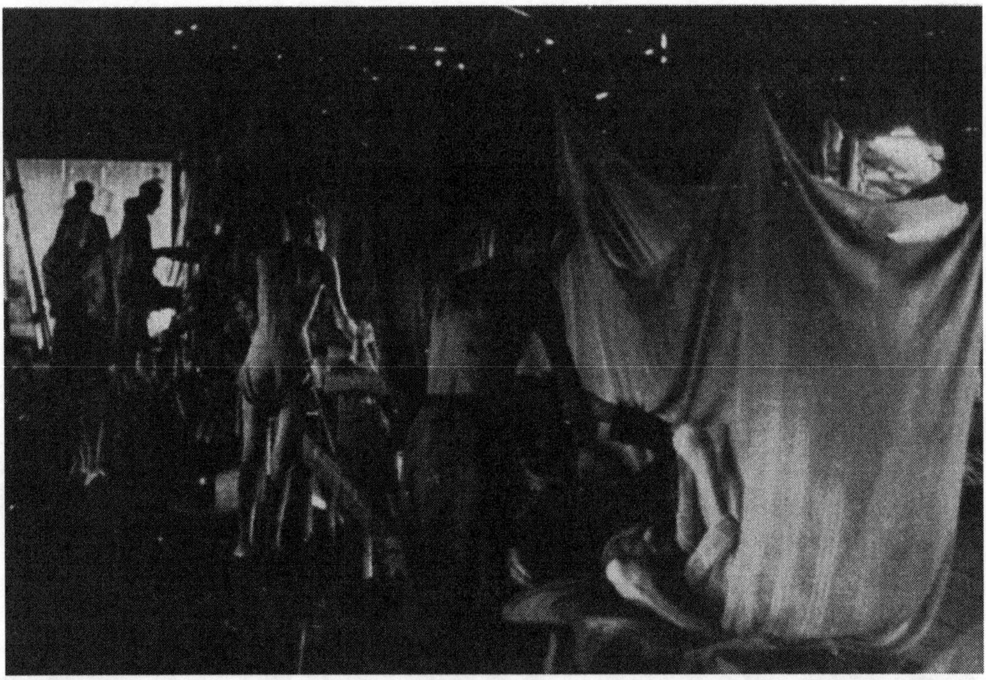

(Australian War Memorial)
Prisoner-of-war camp hospital, Bakli Bay, Hainan Island, with the Dutch ward to the right.

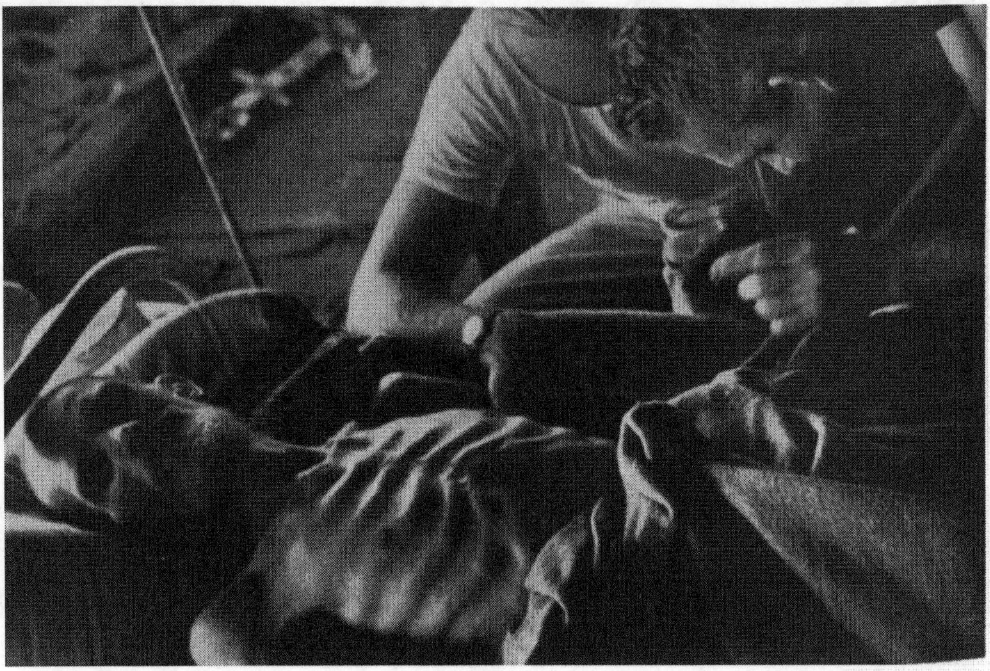

(Australian War Memorial)
Members of an American recovery team giving plasma to a Dutch prisoner of war in the camp hospital at Bakli Bay.

TO ALL ALLIED PRISONERS OF WAR

THE JAPANESE FORCES HAVE SURRENDERED UNCONDITIONALLY AND THE WAR IS OVER

WE will get supplies to you as soon as is humanly possible and will make arrangements to get you out but, owing to the distances involved, it may be some time before we can achieve this.

YOU will help us and yourselves if you act as follows:—

(1) Stay in your camp until you get further orders from us.

(2) Start preparing nominal rolls of personnel, giving fullest particulars.

(3) List your most urgent necessities.

(4) If you have been starved or underfed for long periods DO NOT eat large quantities of solid food, fruit or vegetables at first. It is dangerous for you to do so. Small quantities at frequent intervals are much safer and will strengthen you far more quickly. For those who are really ill or very weak, fluids such as broth and soup, making use of the water in which rice and other foods have been boiled, are much the best. Gifts of food from the local population should be cooked. We want to get you back home quickly, safe and sound, and we do not want to risk your chances from diarrhoea, dysentery and cholera at this last stage.

(5) Local authorities and/or Allied officers will take charge of your affairs in a very short time. Be guided by their advice.

Dropped over Changi P.W. camp on 28 Aug '45

Copies of this leaflet were dropped over Changi on 28th August 1945. The reverse side contained instructions to the Japanese about the treatment of prisoners. The annotation on the left of the leaflet has been made by the diarist of the 8th Australian Division.

Released prisoners of war congregate round the entrance to Changi Gaol.

(*Australian War Memorial*)

(R.A.A.F.)
Released prisoners of war about to embark on a hospital ship.

(Australian War Memorial)
Survivors from Ambon on board a corvette bound for Morotai. The rapid improvement in the physical appearance of the prisoners after a few weeks' rest and good treatment is illustrated by the contrast between the Ambon survivors, picked up directly from a Japanese prison camp, and those in the top photograph, after a short time in the hands of an Australian Reception Group.

destroyer *Queenborough* arrived at Samah (its captain knew nothing of the American organisation) and embarked Colonel Scott and 90 others (including 30 Australians) for Hong Kong, leaving Macrae in charge. "It was on the evening of this day," recorded Scott, "that we had our first taste of bread for more than three years." On the 18th the British aircraft carrier *Vindex,* having embarked the remainder of the Australian prisoners at Samah, also arrived at Hong Kong, collected Scott and his party and sailed that day direct for Australia.[3] On 3rd October the men disembarked at Sydney.

On Ambon Island confirmation of the peace was not received until September, although on 21st August the Australian commander, Major Westley, was informed that a state of armistice existed. The Japanese, however, emphasised that it was not peace, but that terms were being discussed and the war might continue. Nevertheless, when Westley demanded improved rations and medical supplies, and the cessation of work parties, the Japanese agreed. For a fortnight, however, they refused to allow Westley to communicate with the nearest Allied commander. Then on 7th September, in response to renewed demands, a message addressed to Army Headquarters, Melbourne, written and signed by Westley was dispatched. The message which echoed the Australian's perplexity was picked up by signals control, 93rd United States Division on Morotai, and relayed to Australian advanced headquarters there. It read in part:

As senior officer of 123 Australian, 8 American, 7 Dutch troops and 1 American civilian prisoners of war in Amboina I request clarification of the situation and definition of our status.

On the 8th a reply was received from Morotai. A naval detachment was being sent and would reach Ambon on 10th September. Four corvettes arrived as promised and that afternoon the men embarked. On the 12th they reached Morotai, where 63 of the 123 survivors were admitted to hospital. Two died at Morotai.

In Manchuria rumours of the impending liberation reached the Mukden camps as early as 10th August. On 14th August the number of workers employed at factories was reduced; on the 16th work at the factories ceased altogether. That day five Americans flown in from General Wedemeyer's headquarters in China arrived before the Japanese had received the news, and were at first roughly handled. On the 17th the Japanese themselves confirmed the news, and next day the prisoners took over the administration of the camps. On the 20th a Russian commission arrived, disarmed the Japanese guards in front of the prisoners and placed them in the guard room, over which a guard formed by the prisoners was mounted. On the 24th began the evacuation of the sick and senior officers by air. On the 30th an American recovery team arrived; the prisoners began to receive American clothing, chocolates and tinned fruit in increasing quantities. On 11th September many were taken by rail to Dairen,

---

[3] The deaths in the period spent at Hainan were estimated at 114, including 68 Australians.

near Port Arthur, whence they sailed in a hospital ship for Okinawa. The Australians were evacuated by air or sea to Manila to the reception camps very efficiently run by Brigadier Wrigley's group. The way home thence was by ship or air; some who had left documents buried in Changi were flown to Morotai and thence to Singapore where they were allotted transport to Australia.

News of the impending liberation reached some camps in Japan almost as quickly as it reached the Japanese people. At other camps official confirmation was delayed for one or two days. Throughout the morning of 15th August radios had been warning the Japanese people to stand by for a special announcement, and at noon long blasts on the air raid sirens summoned them to their radios.

At Wakinohama, in response to the air raid sirens, all Japanese staff were assembled at the camp office and the prisoners were herded to a distant end of the camp. The Japanese told the prisoners nothing of the Emperor's broadcast which followed, but at its end "all looked stunned and forlorn". Work parties returning to camp that evening brought back news that the war was over. Each told more or less the same story, wrote Captain Boyce: "Nips to the radio at noon . . . crying Nip women and dejected men; hanchos lining the men up for the return home, shaking hands with them and saying, 'Sayonara . . . aster shigoto ni', or 'Goodbye . . . no work tomorrow'; and in one case an indiscreet Nip said that Nippon had lost the war." Thenceforward work ceased. The Japanese commandant appealed to the prisoners to carry on as usual and to maintain law and order, and provided western food on demand and large quantities of medicines and surgical equipment which had been withheld for months. Discipline declined for a time, and a group of six officers (including one Australian) was sent to Wakinohama to endeavour to restore order. On the 26th Allied aircraft began dropping food and clothing, and next day a Red Cross representative visited the camp for the first time since the troops had arrived in Japan. Australians, mostly thin and gaunt, who had been transferred in May to other camps began to visit Wakinohama, and were given food and medicines.

On 6th September an American recovery team arrived at the camp to "process" the prisoners. "Processing" meant the preparation of nominal rolls, containing such supplementary information as the prisoner's next of kin, nationality and date of birth, and the examination by both a surgeon and a physician to determine each prisoner's state of health and, in consequence, his mode of travel—by air, hospital ship or other form of sea transport—from Japan. Before the end of the day men were leaving by train for Yokohama, and thence by air and sea for Okinawa and Manila.

The pattern of events was similar at most of the camps. Working parties were cancelled at Fukuoka on the 15th; on the 17th the prisoners were paraded and informed that the Emperor had decided to end hostilities. Prisoners were asked to be patient and remain in camp. In the following days clothing, food, medical supplies and other comforts were dropped to them. Some went visiting near-by towns—such as Fukuoka and Hakarta—in the interval pending the arrival of recovery teams; others travelled farther afield to Tokyo. Fukuoka had been heavily pounded by bombers and offered few attractions; the city of Hakarta was a scene of desolation and chaos. The civilians were not hostile, and many of the Japanese soldiers saluted as they passed the prisoners. At Nakarma positions had been reversed to the extent that the former mine-*hanchos* had taken over positions as batmen to Australian prisoners, and on the occasion of one Australian's visit were industriously polishing their boots. On the whole the released prisoners both in Nakarma and Fukuoka acted without malice towards their former captors; and any incidents which occurred were provoked rather by high spirits than by revenge. The Japanese, in the opinion of one ex-prisoner, could hardly have been more hospitable, and "most of them changed overnight from sons of heaven to ordinary human beings". On 10th September an American aircraft landed at Fukuoka and that day thirty Australian prisoners left on the first leg of their journeys back to their homeland.

It was much the same at Omuta. Work stopped after the Emperor's broadcast of the 15th. That night Red Cross food was issued for the first time for months. Next morning the prisoners received jackets, long trousers and rubber boots. On the 17th they learnt that the war had ended, and huge yellow letters "PW" were laid about the camp on black backgrounds. On the 19th American aircraft dropped supplies by parachute.

> One of the inexplicable things about the war was our sudden change of attitude towards the Japanese once peace was declared (wrote one Australian). Up to the very last day the fierce discussions which had taken place during the whole of our captivity as to what would happen to the Japs . . . when we were released were continued. . . . But when the day of release finally came there were very few . . . who remembered their threats, and not many Japs were beaten up. Our minds were wholly taken up with the wonderful realisation of being free men again. In our new-found happiness we wanted to forget the past.[4]

Recovery teams did not reach Omuta until 13th September. When they arrived they found that of the camp strength of 1,700, 506 (including 126 Australians), had, in the parlance of the day, "shot through" to Kanoya from where, an American war correspondent had told them, they could get away by plane. This proved "too much of a temptation," wrote an Australian contact officer, and a large number tried to make their own way. Those who patiently awaited rescue teams at Omuta began their journey homeward within 48 hours of their arrival.

The first British Commonwealth repatriates from Japan reached Australian reception camps at Manila on 4th September, and included the Australian nurses who had gone to Japan from Rabaul. From 9th September the liberated prisoners began to reach Manila by sea and air in increasing numbers. By 17th October, when the bulk of the recovery had

---

[4] R. H. Whitecross, *Slaves of the Son of Heaven*, p. 241.

been completed, 14,692 prisoners of war or internees had either passed through or were held by the Australian Reception Group. Of these 11,500 were British, 2,680 Australians, 27 New Zealanders, 160 Indians, 123 Burmese, 131 Malays, 48 Chinese, 8 Portuguese. Although the evacuation of British prisoners presented no great difficulty—most were shipped to the United Kingdom by way of the United States, and only negligible numbers by air—no shipping was made available for the transport of Australians until early October, and the number of R.A.A.F. Liberator aircraft was woefully inadequate. At the end of September fewer than 400 Australians had been evacuated from Manila. By 4th October some of the Australians had been in camp 24 days. That day some 1,500 were embarked on the aircraft carriers *Formidable* and *Speaker*, made available for the voyage to Australia by the Commander of the British Pacific Fleet, Admiral Fraser, after General Berryman, who was General Blamey's Chief of Staff, had placed before him the predicament of the Australian Reception Group. A steady outgoing by air continued until 16th October, when only 816 repatriates remained for evacuation of whom five only were Australian. Soon these too had gone. On the 24th the Australian Reception Group, its work at Manila completed, embarked for Australia.

The foregoing account of the experiences of Australian prisoners during three years and a half of adversity has been drawn from the writings and recollections of men of all ranks. Any comment is theirs. The present chronicler considers that any opinions he might offer would serve only to blur the record.[5]

More than one-third of the Australian soldiers who were prisoners of the Japanese died in captivity; 13,872 were recovered and 7,777 died—nearly three times the number killed in battle in, for example, the 9th Australian Division during its four campaigns. Among the 7,777 who died 123 were officers. Of those who did not return from Japanese prison camps, 2,336 died in Thailand, 1,783 in Borneo, 718 in Ambon, 479 in Burma, 284 in Malaya, 200 in New Britain, 190 in Japan. The number lost at sea was 1,515; 27 were executed for attempted escape, 193 were known to have been executed for other reasons, and 375 others were believed to have been executed. By comparison, of 7,116 Australian soldiers who were prisoners of Germany and Italy only 242 died in captivity. Australian soldiers who escaped from imprisonment in German or Italian camps numbered 582. Only about eight of the Australian soldiers captured in Malaya succeeded in escaping, evidence partly of the ruthless treatment of recaptured men by the Japanese, and partly of the difficulties in the way of successful escape by Europeans in Asian countries where they were conspicuous and whence, to reach Allies, they had to make long journeys through jungle and perhaps across the sea.

---

[5] The impact of the period is reflected in the large number of books about prisoner-of-war life published both in Australia and abroad. A list of books by Australian prisoners of the Japanese is given in Appendix 7 to this volume.

APPENDIX 1

AUSTRALIANS IN MISSION 204

IN 1941 the British Army began preparations to give technical aid and training to the Chinese guerillas who were operating against the Japanese. A Military Mission named "204 Mission" was established in Chungking to direct this work and the Chinese agreed to raise six guerilla battalions to each of which a demolition squad of British officers and other ranks would be attached.

Meanwhile at Maymyo in Burma a Bush Warfare School had been established for training the British squads in guerilla tactics. To it were sent a number of Britons with knowledge of the interior of China and volunteers from British units in Hong Kong, Burma and Malaya; from commando units in the Middle East; and from the 8th Australian Division. This school trained a force about 250 strong organised initially into six contingents.

The Australian contingent was about 40 strong and was drawn from seven units of the 8th Division. The men who volunteered for this special service were discharged from their units in the 8th Division on 27th July 1941 and shipped to Rangoon, whence they travelled to Maymyo.[1] There and elsewhere in northern Burma they engaged in strenuous training for the following six months.[2]

Mission 204 did not set out for China until 25th January 1942. At the air force station at Lashio the men were loaded into vehicles containing six months' rations and large quantities of explosives, and in these they made the hazardous journey over the Burma Road to Kunming where they were reloaded into Chinese Army trucks. In these the journey continued over frozen and sometimes snow-covered roads. Near Hochi on 15th February the Australians loaded their stores and some trucks into a train, and on 17th February they reached quarters at Kiyang, having travelled 2,100 miles in 25 days.

At this stage the men began to get restless. Their departure from Burma had been delayed for six weeks after Japan attacked; this, according to one Australian diarist, was due to "awful staff work". It was originally intended that the force should operate about Canton and Shanghai; now the plan was to operate in the Changsha-Hankow-Nanchang area in northern Kiangsi, but at the end of March no move had been made. On 16th March news arrived that Major-General Dennys, head of Mission 204, had been killed in an air crash at Kunming. He was succeeded by

---

[1] The chief instructor and, later, commandant of this school was Major (later Brigadier) J. M. Calvert of the Royal Engineers who, as mentioned, had been one of the instructors of the Australian and New Zealand Independent Companies.

[2] A lively account of the Australians' experiences in Burma and later is given in *The Surprising Battalion* (1945) by W. Noonan, a member of the force.

Brigadier Bruce,[3] an Indian Army officer and noted Himalayan mountaineer.

The men of the Mission were now very fit, having done long route marches in the mountains carrying packs weighing about 30 lbs, but

combined training with the Chinese battalions has been anything but successful (wrote one officer). Their standard of training is not very high; operations would be difficult and hazardous. Nevertheless I like the officers of our [Chinese] battalion and I think that if the first few shows hold an amount of luck, future operations may be fair.

On 20th April, after weeks of training interspersed with parties and other diversions, an operation order arrived from headquarters in Chungking: the force was to operate in Burma. The plan was to walk from the

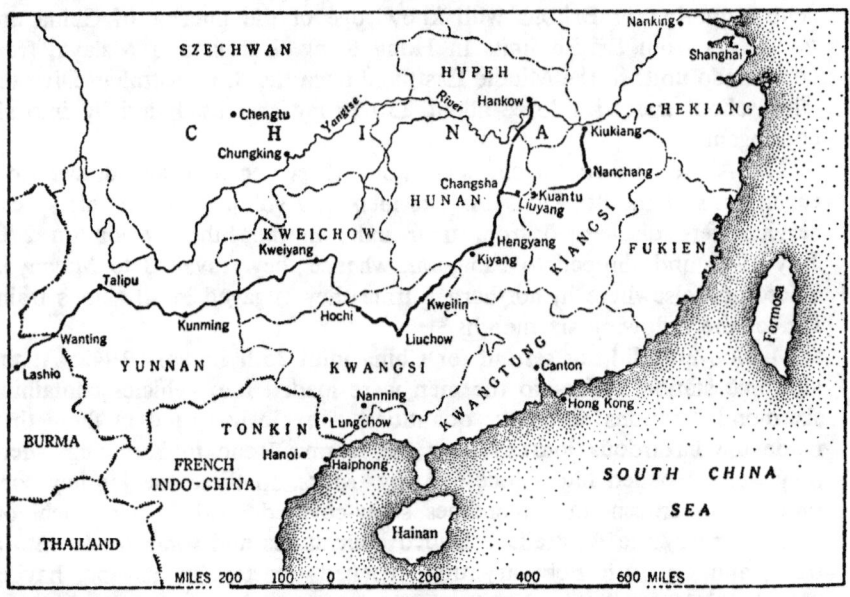

railhead 275 miles to Kweiyang, and travel thence by truck to Lashio. The force set out by rail on 2nd May and then was brought back again. On 5th May "everyone is hoping and wishing that we shall be flown to India and this Mission abandoned". On 31st May General Bruce, with the Australian Minister at Chungking, Sir Frederic Eggleston, arrived at the camp; they brought news that the force would operate in northern Kiangsi as originally planned. The force—now three contingents, including one of Australians commanded by Major Braund[4]—went by rail to Hengyang, then by river sampans to Changsha, which was reached on 8th June. On 18th June the sampans reached Liuyang; by 27th June they had reached

---

[3] Maj-Gen J. G. Bruce, CB, DSO, MC. Deputy Director Military Operations, India, 1941-42; Maj-Gen i/c British Military Mission, China, 1942; DCGS Indian Army 1944-46. Regular soldier; b. 4 Dec 1896.

[4] Maj F. N. B. Braund, NX12551. 2/19 Bn; Mission 204; 2/4 Bn. Solicitor; of Turramurra, NSW; b. Neutral Bay, NSW, 8 Jan 1914.

Kuantu and stores were off-loaded. Thence the force set off, with coolies as carriers, towards their area of operations. They travelled over the mountains often in heavy rain and came to disease-ridden country near the Kiangsi border where a Chinese colonel informed them they would not last a month.

The impression was growing among the Australians that the Chinese did not want foreign troops but only foreign equipment; and that Mission 204 was an embarrassment to the Chinese. They were becoming aware of the jealousies and mistrust that existed between one Chinese commander and another, and that treachery was not infrequent. The men's quarters were filthy and the men began to fall sick in increasing numbers. In the second week of July two men died, presumably of typhus. Others now had malaria and dysentery. At one stage the troops had received no mail for six months. In August there was more exhausting marching in the area west of the Nanchang-Kiukiang railway and illnesses increased, but there was still no indication that the force would be allowed near the Japanese.

In October and November the contingents moved back to Kunming where General Bruce met them and spoke to them sympathetically. Thence on 29th October the Australians were flown to Assam and taken by train to Calcutta. From India the Australian contingent sailed for home.

APPENDIX 2

"ABDACOM" DIRECTIVE TO SUPREME COMMANDER, DATED 3RD JANUARY 1942

Following for General Wavell from Chiefs of Staff

Begins. By agreement among the Governments of Australia, Netherlands, United Kingdom and United States, hereinafter referred to as the ABDA Governments.

1. *Area.*—A strategic area has been constituted to comprise initially all land and sea areas including general regions of Burma, Malaya, Netherlands East Indies and Philippine Islands more precisely defined in Annexure 1. This area will be known as ABDA area.

2. *Forces.*—You have been designated as Supreme Commander of ABDA area and of all armed forces afloat ashore and in air of ABDA Governments which are or will be (*a*) stationed in area (*b*) located in Australian territory when such forces have been allotted by respective Governments for service in or in support of the ABDA area. You are not authorised to transfer from territories of any ABDA Government land forces of the Government without consent of local commander or his Government.

3. The Deputy Supreme Commander and if required a Commander of the Combined Naval Forces and the Commander of Combined Air Forces will be jointly designated by the ABDA Governments.

4. No Government will materially reduce its armed forces assigned to your area nor any commitment made by it for reinforcing its forces in your area except after giving to other Governments and to you timely information pertaining thereto.

5. *Strategic concept and policy.*—The basic strategic concept of the ABDA Governments for conduct of war in your area is not only in immediate future to maintain as many key positions as possible but to take offensive at the earliest opportunity and ultimately to conduct an all-out offensive against Japan. The first essential is to gain general air superiority at the earliest moment through employment of concentrated air power. The piece-meal employment of air forces should be minimised. Your operations should be so conducted as to further preparations for the offensive.

6. General strategic policy will be therefore:—

   (*a*) to hold Malaya barrier defined as line Malay Peninsula, Sumatra, Java, North Australia as basic defensive position of ABDA area and to operate sea, land and air forces in as great depth as possible forward of barrier in order to oppose Japanese southward advance;

   (*b*) to hold Burma and Australia as essential support positions for the area and Burma as essential to support of China and to defence of India;

(c) to re-establish communications through Dutch East Indies with Luzon and to support Philippines garrison;
(d) to maintain essential communications within the area.

7. *Duties, responsibilities and authorities of Supreme Commander.*—You will coordinate in ABDA area strategical operations of all armed forces of ABDA Governments where desirable to arrange formation of task forces whether national or inter-national for executing specific operations and appointing any officers irrespective of seniority or nationality to command such task forces.

8. While you will have no responsibilities in respect of the internal administration of the respective forces under your command you are authorised to direct and coordinate the creation and development of administrative facilities and the broad allocation of war materials.

9. You will dispose of reinforcements which from time to time may be despatched to the area by ABDA Governments.

10. You are authorised to require from commanders of the armed forces under your command such reports as you deem necessary in discharging your responsibilities as supreme commander.

11. You are authorised to control the issue of all communiques concerning the forces under your command.

12. Through channels specified in paragraph 18 you may submit recommendations to the ABDA Governments on any matters pertaining to the furthering of your mission.

13. *Limitations.*—Your authority and control with respect to the various portions of ABDA area and to forces assigned thereto will normally be exercised through commanders duly appointed by their respective Governments. Interference is to be avoided in administrative processes of armed forces of any of the ABDA Governments including free communication between them and their respective Governments. No alterations or revision is to be made in basic tactical organizations of such forces and each national component of a task force will normally operate under its own commander and will not be sub-divided into small units for attachment to other national components of task forces except in cases of urgent necessity. In general your instructions and orders will be limited to those necessary for effective coordination of forces in execution of your mission.

14. *Relations with ABDA Governments.*—The ABDA Governments will jointly and severally support you in the execution of duties and responsibilities as herein defined and in the exercising of authority herein delegated and limited. Commanders of all sea, land and air forces within your area will be immediately informed by their respective Governments that from a date to be notified all orders and instructions issued by you in conformity with the provision of this directive will be considered by such commanders as emanating from their respective governments.

15. In the unlikely event that any of your immediate subordinates after making due representation to you still considers obedience to your orders would jeopardise national interests of his country to an extent

unjustified by the general situation in ABDA area he has the right subject to your being immediately notified of such intention to appeal direct to his own Government before carrying out orders. Such appeals will be made by most expeditious methods and copies of appeals will be communicated simultaneously to you.

16. *Staff and assumption of command.*—Your staff will include officers of each of ABDA Powers.

You are empowered to communicate immediately with national commanders in area with view to obtaining staff officers essential your earliest possible assumption of command. Your additional staff requirements will be communicated as soon as possible to ABDA Governments through channels of communication described in paragraph 18.

17. You will report when you are in position effectively carry essential functions of supreme command so your assumption of command may be promulgated to all concerned.

18. *Superior Authority.*—As supreme commander of ABDA area you will always be responsible to ABDA Governments through agency defined in Annexure II.

ANNEXURE I.—BOUNDARIES OF ABDA AREA

The ABDA area is bounded as follows:—

North.—By boundary between India and Burma, thence eastward along Chinese frontier and coastline to latitude 030 degrees north, thence along parallel 030 degrees north to meridian 140 degrees east. (Note.—Indo-China and Thailand are NOT included in this area.)

East.—By meridian 140 degrees east from 030 degrees to the Equator, thence east to longitude 141 degrees east, thence south to the boundary of Dutch New Guinea (and to) coast on south coast, thence east along southern New Guinea coast to meridian 143 degrees east, then south down this meridian to the coast of Australia.

South.—By the northern coast of Australia from meridian 143 degrees east westward to meridian 114 degrees east, thence north-westward to latitude 015 degrees south, longitude 092 degrees east.

West.—By meridian 092 degrees east.

2. Forces assigned to ABDA and adjacent areas are authorised to extend their operations into other areas as may be required.

ANNEXURE II

1. On all important military matters not within the jurisdiction of supreme commander of ABDA area, U.S. Chiefs of Staff and representatives in Washington of British Chiefs of Staff will constitute agency for developing and submitting recommendations for decisions by President of U.S. and by British Prime Minister and Minister of Defence. Among chief matters on which decision will be required are:—

(*a*) Provision of reinforcements.
(*b*) Major changes in policy.
(*c*) Departures from supreme commander's directive.

2. This agency will function as follows:—
   (*a*) Any proposals coming either from Supreme Commander or from any of the ABDA Governments will be submitted to Chiefs of Staff Committee both in Washington and in London.
   (*b*) The Chiefs of Staff Committee in London will immediately telegraph to their representatives in Washington to say whether or not they will be telegraphing any opinion.
   (*c*) On receipt of these opinions the U.S.A. C's of S. and representatives in Washington of British C's of S. will develop and submit their recommendations to President and by telegraphing to Prime Minister and Minister of Defence. Prime Minister will then inform the President whether he is in agreement with these recommendations.

3. Since London has machinery for consulting Dominion Governments and since Dutch Government is in London the British Government will be responsible for obtaining their views and agreement for including these in the final telegrams to Washington.

4. Agreement having been reached between President and Prime Minister and Minister of Defence the orders to Supreme Commander will be despatched from Washington in the name of both of them.

APPENDIX 3

GENERAL BENNETT'S ESCAPE

ON 17th November 1945 Mr Justice Ligertwood was appointed by the Prime Minister of Australia to be a Commissioner to inquire into and report on the circumstances of and connected with the action of General Bennett in relinquishing his command and leaving Singapore; whether at the time Bennett had the permission of any competent authority for such action; whether Bennett was, and if so when, a prisoner of war; whether it was Bennett's duty to remain with the forces under his command; whether in all the circumstances Bennett was justified in relinquishing his command and leaving Singapore.

The Commission opened its sittings in public on 26th November and sat continuously until 13th December 1945. The transcript of the evidence covered 480 pages of foolscap.

In Part I of his subsequent report, Mr Justice Ligertwood set out what he considered to be the material circumstances relating to General Bennett's action. He found that:

"In relinquishing his command and leaving Singapore General Bennett did not have the permission of any competent authority. There was, in fact, no competent authority who could give him such permission. General Percival could not do so because he had signed the capitulation under which he had agreed that General Bennett as one of the troops under his command would be surrendered. Even the Australian Government could not have given him such permission because it was within the competence of General Percival to agree that General Bennett as one of such troops would be surrendered, and the capitulation bound the Australian Government as much as it did General Percival.

"At the time General Bennett left Singapore he was not a prisoner of war in the sense of being a soldier who was under a duty to escape. He was in the position of a soldier whose commanding officer had agreed to surrender him and to submit him to directions which would make him a prisoner of war.

"Having regard to the terms of the capitulation I think that it was General Bennett's duty to have remained in command of the A.I.F. until the surrender was complete.

"Having regard to the terms of the capitulation I find that General Bennett was not justified in relinquishing his command and leaving Singapore."

Part II of the report dealt with the reasons and motives which actuated General Bennett in deciding to escape. In this the Commissioner found:

"(*a*) General Bennett was the first Australian General to meet the Japanese in battle in jungle conditions.

"(b) He acquired valuable information and experience in Malaya relating to Japanese strategy and tactics and evolved successful counter measures.

"(c) He genuinely believed that Australia was in peril and that it was of vital importance to the safety of the country that he should return to take a leading part in its defence.

"(d) He genuinely, but in my opinion mistakenly, believed that immediately upon the cessation of hostilities the whole of the British Forces on Singapore Island had been surrendered to the Japanese and that he was a prisoner of war under a duty to escape if he could.

"(e) He genuinely, but in my opinion mistakenly, believed that the terms of the Cease Fire order requiring the troops to remain in their positions was a Japanese order directed to prisoners of war and one which he was in duty bound to disregard if he saw the opportunity of escaping.

"(f) He genuinely believed that he had done all he could for his men and that if he remained he would be immediately segregated from them and could not give them any further assistance.

"(g) The escape was a hazardous enterprise and involved no reflection on General Bennett's personal courage.

"(h) He did in fact bring back valuable information to Australia which was used in the training of the A.I.F. in jungle warfare.

"(i) His decision to escape was inspired by patriotism and by the belief that he was acting in the best interests of his country."

In 1948 an eminent military lawyer, Lieut-Colonel Fry,[1] published in the University of Queensland Law Journal (and later in pamphlet form) a lengthy examination of the "Legal aspects of the departure of Major-General Gordon Bennett from Singapore". Fry's summary of his conclusions was:

The Royal Commissioner decided that the Bukit Timah memorandum was a capitulation, but did not state clearly whether it made provision for an unconditional or conditional surrender. Nevertheless, whether it was or was not a "capitulation", conditional or unconditional, would seem to be immaterial in applying the rules of international law to General Bennett's departure from Singapore.

The material point seems to be whether surrender (conditional or unconditional) took place at 2030 hours on 15th February. If so, General Percival and his forces at that hour became prisoners of war, and as such were each individually entitled to attempt to escape; and any stipulation to the contrary would be inconsistent with the Prisoners of War Convention and customary laws of war, and, therefore, invalid. The Royal Commissioner was of opinion that the surrender did not take place at 2030 hours on 15th February. He seems to have based his decision upon the view that the Bukit Timah memorandum should be interpreted to mean the surrender was not to occur unless and until General Percival's forces were "behind the wires" of prisoner of war camps. The Bukit Timah memorandum does not expressly say this, and his opinion does not seem to be supported by international practice, convention or text-writers.

---

[1] Lt-Col T. P. Fry, ED, QX6266. DJAG HQ I Aust Corps 1940-41; LSO HQ III Corps 1942-44; AD of Research, LHQ 1944-45. Barrister; of Ascot, Qld; b. Brisbane, 19 Jun 1904. Died 24 Sep 1952.

The rules of international law and facts of this particular case provide reasonable grounds for holding an opinion, contrary to the Royal Commissioner's findings, that unconditional surrender took place at 2030 hours on 15th February, and that at that moment the personnel of General Percival's forces acquired the status of prisoners of war.

If, however, the Royal Commissioner was correct as to the time of surrender, and if, therefore, General Bennett was not a prisoner of war at 2200 hours on 15th February, what at that moment were his status, rights and duties? The Royal Commissioner seems to have held that, at that moment he was neither a prisoner of war nor a combatant, but a soldier who must obey Japanese orders, including an implied Japanese command not to escape. That is, he had the status, rights or duties of neither a prisoner of war nor combatant. This idea that, by means of a "capitulation" the victor can, by a simple device of postponing the moment of surrender, deprive enemy soldiers of their status of combatants without substituting for it that of prisoners of war would seem to be without validity as a principle of international law, and capable of opening the flood-gates to wholesale evasion of international safeguards.

The Royal Commissioner based his report on an interpretation of international law, and did not discuss General Bennett's action from the standpoint of Australian military law, which placed him under no inflexible obligation to remain on Singapore Island.

Whatever may be thought of the validity of the Royal Commissioner's findings and views in General Bennett's case, the dramatic nature of the General's escape and public interest excited by the inquiry have made it essential for the future guidance of Australian soldiers to remove their present doubts. It is suggested this can only now be done by the issue of clear, unequivocal instructions as to the precise time at which, in each possible set of governing circumstances, they are as soldiers obliged by the law of their country to attempt to escape. These instructions should make clear the circumstances in which international law and the customs of nations will afford them protection.

APPENDIX 4

ORDEAL ON NEW BRITAIN

AFTER the Japanese had driven Colonel Scanlan's force from its positions near Rabaul on 23rd January 1942, two main lines of retreat developed. One led westward to the Keravat River, and thence to the north coast; the other south-east to the south coast. In both directions the country was mountainous, rugged, covered with dense growth, and intersected by deep ravines along which ran fast-flowing streams. The little food available in the jungle was largely of a kind which the men had not been trained to recognise.

No plans had been made for the situation which then arose. Orders such as "go bush", "break up into small parties" and "every man for himself" which soon began to circulate implied a cessation of military organisation and control. As the troops withdrew they left their communication and supply routes, and along the tracks they were to traverse few stores of food, ammunition or medical supplies had been organised or established. For the moment the only course open to the men was to escape in mechanical transport down the roads to the south so far as the roads ran. Soon trucks and carriers were transporting troops to the rear and being subjected to bombing and machine-gunning from the air.

Lieutenant Selby, the anti-aircraft artillery officer of the force, later recalled one such journey.

> We walked at a brisk pace, only taking cover when diving planes roared down on us. Eventually a truck dashed by, then pulled up in answer to our hail and we climbed aboard. At frequent intervals planes would dive on us, their machine-guns blazing, and we would leap off the track and take cover by the roadside. . . .
> At Toma . . . we came to Rear Operational headquarters. I told the sergeant-major there that I wished to report to the Colonel. He went into the tent and returned, saying: "The Colonel's orders are that each man is to fend for himself." Less than a mile farther on the road petered out and the jungle began. A large portion of my battery was waiting for me by the roadside but a number had gone on with various groups of infantry. Along the road was a long string of abandoned vehicles, filled with rations, munitions and stores of all descriptions. The sight of the rations made me feel hungry and glancing at my watch I was surprised to see that it was just after midday. I could not leave that string of trucks to be picked up by the enemy intact and [we] set to work demolishing the trucks . . . but left the food in case more troops should be coming through.

Meanwhile Captain Appel, in accordance with his final instructions from battalion headquarters to cover the withdrawal, remained in the Vunakanau area until mid-afternoon of 23rd January. Then, following the direction taken by Captain McInnes and others, he too moved off towards the Keravat, crossed the river and two miles farther on reached a bivouac area already selected by his second-in-command, Captain Cameron.[1] There

---
[1] Lt-Col A. G. Cameron, DSO, VX44906. 2/22 Bn 1940-42; CO 3 Bn 1942-43, 2/2 Bn 1943-45. Bank clerk; of Elwood, Vic; b. Brunswick, Vic, 16 May 1909.

he found about 160 men, mostly from his own and McInnes' companies but including some headquarters and anti-tank people.

The Vulcan beach defenders under Captain Field, who had been ordered by Major Owen soon after 7 a.m. to withdraw to Four Ways, made slow progress through thick bush and by dusk had reached a position only half a mile from Four Ways. Next morning a native reported to Field that Four Ways and Vunakanau had been occupied, cutting off the road to Tobera. Skirting Four Ways, the party moved on through the jungle, avoiding the roads and eventually reaching the Keravat four days later.

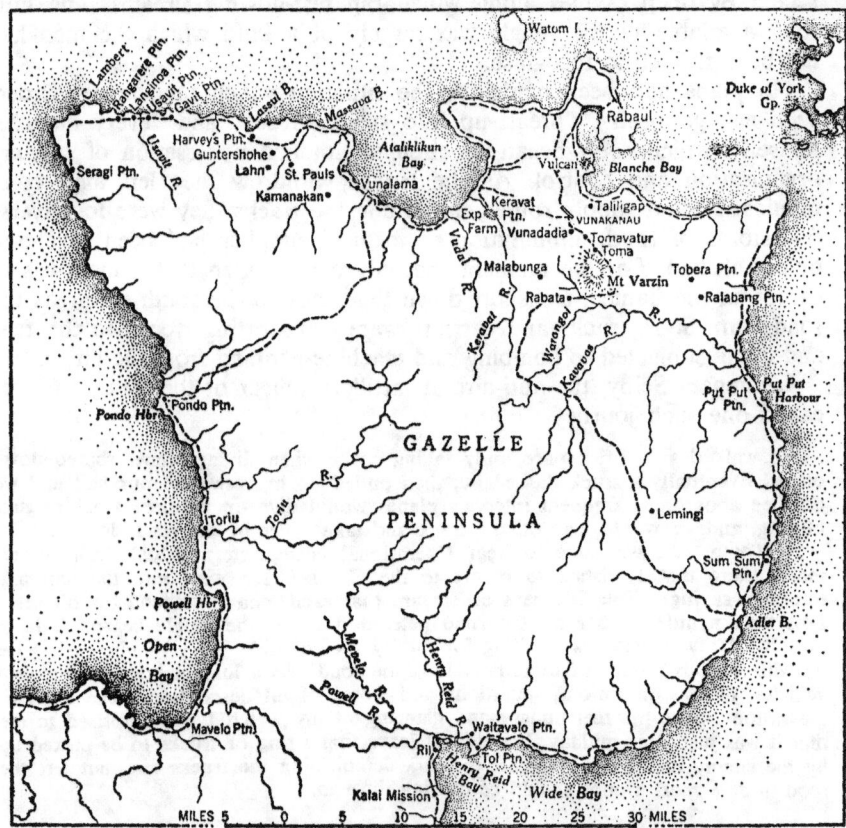

On the way other stragglers joined the party which on arrival numbered fifty-nine. After crossing the river the men moved on towards Keravat Farm, which they found to be occupied by Japanese. A civilian told Field that Japanese were moving in large numbers towards the Vudal River, south-west of Keravat. His move would necessarily continue in that direction. The men were very tired, some were sick, and all had been practically without food for four days.

Field called them together. He told them that he himself had no intention of surrendering; that those who wished to continue with him could do so; the alternative was surrender. He gave them half an hour to make their decisions. Six elected to go on, the remainder to return to Keravat and surrender. They would remain in their present position until the afternoon, they said, to allow Field and his men to get clear. It was then 27th January. All told, the rations for the seven men amounted to one tin of bully beef, a cucumber and two and a half biscuits.

Meanwhile, on the 24th, Travers, who had bivouacked his company near Toma the previous night, was confronted with a situation similar to that which Field was to face when he reached the Keravat River. He knew nothing of the movements of the rest of the force, or of the order to withdraw, and decided that the injured and those who considered themselves unfit to attempt the formidable task of reaching either the north or south coasts on foot should surrender. With Lieutenant Donaldson he set off at 8 o'clock to reach an agreement with the Japanese. The two officers walked to Vunadadia, thence to Malabunga Junction, and after a two hours' journey returned to Toma, having seen no sign of the enemy. Travers then advised those who were resolved to escape to split up into parties as they saw fit, allowing the direction they took to be influenced by their knowledge of the country they were to traverse. The majority of the men made their way to the south coast; but parties under Donaldson and Tolmer, amounting to about twenty men in all, eventually linked with other escapers on the north coast, the main group of whom had set out westwards from Keravat on the 24th.

Appel had organised the men into groups consisting of carrying parties with advance and rear-guards, and by 5 p.m. on the 26th had reached the Kamanakan Mission. There, realising the condition of his men and sensing a lowering of spirits, he held a muster parade totalling 285 all ranks and appealed to the men not to allow themselves to be captured. He said that he would establish camps in the hills where he would re-train them and make them fit to fight again. The men responded well to his appeal.

He sent forward Lieutenant Smith[2] and Corporal Hamilton[3] on horseback to Lassul Bay, Sergeant Jane[4] and Corporal Headlam[5] to Massava, and appointed Captain Cameron his liaison officer. The force, divided into a headquarters and four groups commanded by Captains McInnes and McCallum,[6] Lieutenant Bateman[7] and Appel himself, was established at St Paul's, Guntershohe, Lahn and Kamanakan. On 27th January Kamanakan was shelled by Japanese naval craft; next day two large Japanese forces were landed at Massava and Lassul Bay. McInnes, who reached

---

[2] Capt D. O. Smith, VX23843. 2/22 Bn; 2/2 Pnr Bn. Apprentice plumber; of St Kilda, Vic; b. Carlton, Vic, 9 Oct 1918.

[3] Capt J. McK. Hamilton, MBE, VX44959. 2/22 Bn; "Z" and "M" Special Units. Wool valuer; of Geelong, Vic; b. Bairnsdale, Vic, 26 Feb 1915.

[4] Sgt H. A. Jane, VX28644. 2/22 Bn; 112 Lt AA Bty. Salesman; of Malvern, Vic; b. Benalla, Vic, 7 Apr 1918.

[5] WO2 J. M. Headlam, VX20614. 2/22 Bn; 112 Lt AA Bty; Flying Officer in RAAF 1945. Farmer; of Hobart; b. Launceston, Tas, 2 Jan 1913.

[6] Capt J. T. McCallum, VX45853; 2/22 Bn. Grazier; of Colac, Vic; b. Winchelsea, Vic, 12 Dec 1911.

[7] Lt P. J. Bateman, VX44398; 2/22 Bn. Law clerk; of Caulfield, Vic; b. Maryborough, Vic, 9 Oct 1914.

Lassul on the 29th, saw landing craft loaded with Japanese coming ashore. He withdrew his men and soon afterwards met Captain Appel, who had arrived with a second group of escapers. McInnes, who believed that the Japanese were likely to advance on Lahn, advised his men to split up into small parties, to facilitate escape. The alternative was surrender. Appel, however, took his company, now numbering about 120, four miles beyond Lahn into the mountains where, in pouring rain, the men spent the night. Next morning he moved them to a village westwards of Lahn, where they sheltered in small huts.

There he was approached by an officer and some of the N.C.O's who declared they should give up because of the poor physical condition of the men, the lack of food and the adverse weather. Eventually, after a further conference in which McInnes participated, Appel (still unconvinced of the hopelessness of the situation) set off with a small party, including McInnes and three N.C.O's, for Lassul Bay. Before he left Appel ordered his men to follow in an hour's time. He felt that it was imperative that the men should have comfortable conditions that night, but hoped that the Japanese had left Lassul Bay because he had seen transports and destroyers moving out to sea.

About two miles from Lassul the party took a wrong track which led through Guntershohe and took the party five miles out of its way. Appel was afraid lest the delay result in the rear party arriving first at Harvey's Plantation:

> I forced two kanakas to carry two packs and set off [said Appel later]. Captain McInnes . . . said he would accompany me from Guntershohe. The distance was seven miles. We ran every part of the way which was flat or downhill. Captain McInnes knocked up and I reached Harvey's approximately 12 minutes after the troops. We stopped at Harvey's house, which is 2 miles from the beach, and kanakas said the Japanese had left during the afternoon. . . .

Greatly relieved by this discovery, Appel now set about organising food supplies, establishing reconnaissance and standing patrols (finding in the process that some men had abandoned their arms). Within the next few days most of the men from McInnes' dispersed group, who found themselves unable to penetrate the jungle, had been found and brought back to the Lassul Bay area. A headquarters was formed at Harvey's, and the troops, then totalling 413, were dispersed along the 30 miles of coastline between Ataliklikun Bay and Cape Lambert in groups ranging from the smallest of four at Vunalama under Lieutenant Tolmer to the largest of 194 under Captain Appel at Lassul Bay.

Meanwhile McInnes and a party of seven men had moved to Langinoa Plantation, about three miles east of Cape Lambert. There they remained until 16th February, when they set off in a boat navigated by Mr J. McLean of the near-by Rangarere Plantation, who had taken the place of one of McInnes' men, and to whom the pinnace belonged. Their course took them to the southern end of New Ireland, where they met Mr Kyle,[8]

---
[8] Lt A. F. Kyle, DSC; RANVR. Missing presumed died 1 Sep 1942.

formerly the assistant district officer at Namatanai, who was also a coastwatcher. A message was sent to Port Moresby requesting that a flying-boat be sent to pick them up, but none could be spared. There the party remained until 30th April, although the Japanese twice visited the area, when they shipped in a larger vessel and in May reached Port Moresby.

Captain Appel, a pharmacist by profession and on that account able to give considerable assistance to the many sick, remained in the Lassul Bay area where he continued to be an inspiring and energetic leader.

On 14th and 15th February Japanese forces landed again at Lassul and at Gavit, capturing about 160 men without resistance. At Lassul Appel was able to approach within 60 yards of the Japanese who were sharing a meal with their prisoners, whom they appeared to treat well.

> My troops were smoking what must have been Japanese cigarettes [said Appel afterwards] . . . were guarded by Japanese with fixed bayonets. Our troops were unarmed but their hands were not tied. At 1815 the Japs marched the men down to the beach, lit numerous small fires and slept on the beach all night.
> I sent two of my men down to the beach and they observed that our troops were given breakfast in the morning. After breakfast the hands of our captive troops were tied behind their backs and they were put in a pinnace and taken out to a transport.

Afterwards the Japanese distributed messages[9] in writing urging the Australians to surrender, and Appel, afraid lest his exhausted and ill-fed men be persuaded, covered over 100 miles in the next five days, riding, walking and swimming, visiting his scattered parties and urging them to hold out.

At midnight on 21st February Corporal Headlam rode into Appel's camp with heartening news for the fugitives. An evacuation scheme had been prepared by the Assistant District Officer at Talasea, Mr McCarthy,[1] and he was on his way to meet the party.

In January McCarthy had been pursuing the normal duties of a district officer at Talasea. On the 23rd he had been at Cape Gloucester cratering the airfield, and that day had seen numbers of Japanese aircraft heading for Rabaul. He hurried back to Talasea, and by the 30th had established his radio in the Kalingi area, some 90 miles to the west, at the western end of the island overlooking the Dampier Straits. On his way he had gathered up a number of civilians and established a base camp at Karai-ai. On the 28th he received a message from Commander Feldt,[2] naval Intelligence officer at Moresby, ordering him to take his wireless to Toma, in the vicinity of Rabaul, and send news of Colonel Scanlan's force, of which nothing had been heard since the invasion. A further message ordered

---

[9] One such message read:
"To all sick Australian soldiers and all other Australian soldiers who are at Mr Harvey's bungalow tonight or early tomorrow are herewith commanded to be on the beach at Lassul at about 12 noon tomorrow. Put out a white flag and signal the ship to come in and pick you up. If no signal ship will pass and leave you back to walk to Vunakambi. Your life will be guaranteed.
Commander Ogama."

[1] Lt-Col J. K. McCarthy, MBE, NGX258. "Z" and "M" Special Units; Angau and BBCAU. District officer; of Talasea, New Britain; b. St Kilda, Vic, 20 Jan 1905. (McCarthy was commissioned as a lieutenant and temporary captain in Angau on 14 Feb.)

[2] Cdr E. A. Feldt, OBE. (1914-18 War; Lt RAN.) Officer i/c Coastwatchers. District Officer and Warden; of Wau, NG; b. Ingham, Qld, 3 Jan 1899.

him to take possession of the *Lakatoi* (179 tons), believed then to be at Kapepa Island, east of the Willaumez Peninsula, and use it to evacuate the civilians.

McCarthy had at this time under his command two small pinnaces, the *Lolobau* and the *Aussi*, each about 5 tons. He loaded the civilians aboard them and set off for Kapepa, arriving there early in the morning of 1st February, but the *Lakatoi* had gone. Leaving the civilians to go to Salamaua in the *Lolobau*, McCarthy and Marsland,[3] a local planter who had volunteered to accompany him, set out in the *Aussi* with a native crew

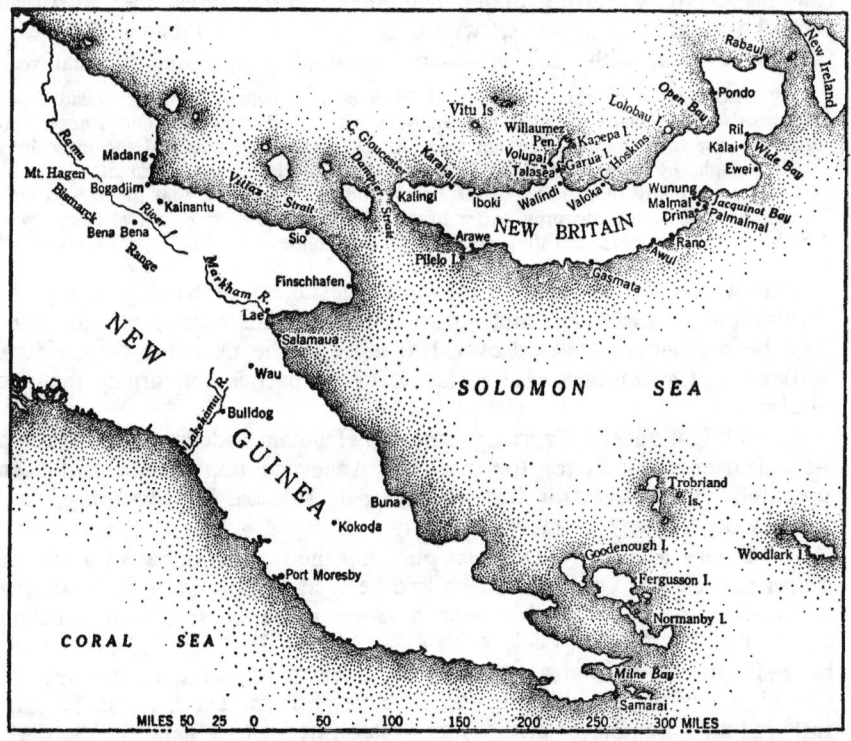

and sixteen police boys intending to take his wireless to Toma. He was followed in an open boat by Douglas,[4] another planter who had volunteered for the journey and was determined to assist, and a Chinese, Leong Chu.

At Open Bay natives informed them that the Japanese had occupied Pondo Plantation to the north, and that two destroyers had been seen in Powell Harbour. McCarthy thereupon crossed the bar at the mouth of the Toriu River and established a camp some seven miles upstream. Thence Marsland made a trip to Pondo and discovered that the Japanese had left the area, after machine-gunning it and blowing up the ships and small

---

[3] F-Lt G. H. R. Marsland, MBE, RAAF. Planter; of Talasea, New Britain; b. Melbourne, 1 Dec 1912.

[4] Lt K. C. Douglas, RANVR. Planter; of Talasea, New Britain; b. Hobart, 13 Nov 1903.

boats in the harbour. On the 9th he met Captain Cameron, liaison officer to the force on the north coast. Cameron had with him a group of nine soldiers, armed and in good spirits, a teleradio, and a small pinnace. On the 11th, accompanied by Marsland and Lance-Corporal Tuddin[5], Cameron met McCarthy near Toriu. By the 14th McCarthy's teleradio was able to transmit, and about midday a message drafted and signed by Cameron was sent to Port Moresby outlining the engagement at Rabaul and telling of subsequent events so far as they were known. It was the first news from the area received by the outside world since the message dispatched by Figgis on the morning of 23rd January.

On 15th February Cameron received a wireless message from headquarters at Port Moresby granting him permission, if guerilla warfare seemed impossible, to proceed with his party to Salamaua. Cameron replied that he would do so.

Then occurred an unfortunate dispute between Cameron and McCarthy, both exceptionally determined men, which cannot fairly be disregarded since McCarthy later claimed that Cameron's actions jeopardised his entire evacuation scheme. Briefly, McCarthy wished Cameron to cooperate with his pinnace in the evacuation scheme he had devised and which had been approved by Port Moresby. Cameron, who had already received instructions to proceed to Salamaua, agreed to cooperate provided approval was gained from Port Moresby and drafted a message seeking permission, which he handed to McCarthy for transmission. Later when an attempt was made to take over Cameron's pinnace and teleradio, Cameron, pending a reply to his message to Port Moresby, refused to agree. What Cameron did not know was that although McCarthy had accepted his message he did not send it, and at no stage did he intend to do so. He felt, he declared later, that Cameron was overriding his authority even by questioning it.

On the 20th Cameron, having given McCarthy a pistol for Frank Holland,[6] a local timber-getter who was going through to the south coast to look for Colonel Scanlan and rescue other survivors, set out for Salamaua and arrived there on 3rd March with his eleven men after a voyage lasting eleven days.

Meanwhile McCarthy, having despatched Holland on 20th February to the south coast, moved north from Pondo to Seragi where he met Sergeant Jane and Corporal Headlam, the two energetic and competent N.C.O's who had been reconnoitring the coast ahead of Appel's main force. They were suffering from malaria, but took McCarthy to Langinoa where about thirty troops were found on the verge of starvation. They had eaten all available poultry and European food on the plantation but "had failed to recognise 50 hectares of bearing tapioca growing within 20 yards of them", McCarthy recalled later.

---

[5] Cpl J. A. Tuddin, VX24244. 2/22, 2/4, 2/2 Bns. Road worker; of South Yarra, Vic; b. St Arnaud, Vic, 1 Dec 1905.
[6] Capt F. Holland, MBE, VX102689; "Z" Special Unit. Tractor driver and timber getter; of New Britain; b. Enfield, England, 15 Oct 1907.

At Langinoa Headlam offered to ride on ahead and warn Appel of the impending arrival of McCarthy. It will be recalled that he arrived at Lassul Bay and met Appel at midnight on the 21st. That night Appel, who had earlier received warnings that the Japanese would be returning to Lassul Bay on the following day to accept the surrender of the remainder of his men, moved them about four miles inland to Lahn. On the 22nd he met McCarthy on the Usavit River and after hearing his plan agreed to have at least 145 men at Pondo within seven days. A minority of the men did not wish to take part, and McCarthy issued orders through Appel that surrender would later mean court martial for "desertion to the enemy". Eight sick and wounded men, not well enough to make the move, were left at a hospital established at St Paul's under Major Akeroyd,[7] who had volunteered to remain, and during the next five days groups of men began to arrive at Pondo, assisted by native carriers over the final stages of the march through the mountains.

It now became apparent that the one ship available to ferry the men, numbering nearly 200, gathered near Pondo, would be inadequate. McCarthy placed Lincoln Bell[8] (another timber-getter) in charge of the *Aussi* and set Marsland and Tolmer, two sergeants (Beaumont[9] and Hunt[10]), and a civilian, D'Arcy Hallam, to repair the small schooner *Malahuka*, which had been partially destroyed by the Japanese. After five days and nights of intensive work she was launched and the ferrying of the troops down the coast began.

After one trip to Lolobau Island the *Malahuka* broke down, but sometimes on foot, at other times in canoes, and occasionally by pinnace, the red-headed and energetic McCarthy (aided in particular by Appel and Tolmer) continued the movement westwards. At Walindi on 8th March he met Patrol Officer Harris[1] who had arrived with a flotilla of schooners from Madang, and thereafter the movement continued apace. On 9th March Holland, who had been anxiously awaited by McCarthy, arrived at Open Bay from the south coast with a party of twenty-three, including Colonel Carr, after a two days' journey from Ril across the mountainous Mukolkol country. By the 15th most of the troops had reached Walindi, more than fifty arriving from Valoka in twenty canoes which McCarthy had organised. By this time five wireless posts were operating and direct communication between all points in the evacuation scheme was constant.

From Walindi the fit men walked to Garua Mission and thence across the Willaumez Peninsula to Volupai Plantation. The sick were transported round the peninsula in the *Gnair* and thence to Iboki, about 60

---

[7] Maj J. F. Akeroyd, MBE, ED, VX18194. RMO 2/22 Bn. Medical practitioner; of Frankston, Vic; b. Brunswick, Vic, 17 Dec 1909.

[8] Lt L. J. Bell, RANVR. Planter, trader and timber-cutter; of Powell Harbour, New Britain, and Sandy Bay, Tas; b. Wandeela, Qld, 1906. Killed in action 1 Apr 1943.

[9] Sgt J. R. Beaumont, VX22662. 2/22 Bn and 1 Water Tptn Group. Motor mechanic; of Prahran, Vic; b. Glenferrie, Vic, 29 Dec 1908. Died of injuries 24 Mar 1943.

[10] Sgt H. C. Hunt, VX101857. Coast Defence Bty, Rabaul; Darwin Fixed Defences; BCOF. Regular soldier; of Hampton, Vic; b. North Brighton, Vic, 2 Dec 1910.

[1] Capt G. C. Harris, PX98; Angau. Patrol officer; of Lae, NG; b. 4 Jun 1911. Executed by Japanese 25 Mar 1944.

miles to the west. Other ships of the flotilla then assisted in bringing the remainder of the men from Volupai to Iboki, where food was plentiful and a hospital had been established under a tireless and devoted woman, Mrs Gladys H. Baker, a plantation owner of Vitu Islands who had refused to be evacuated with other women and children in December.[2] At Iboki McCarthy learnt that the *Lakatoi* was at Vitu, and on 19th March sent a party of men under Marsland to arrest her. On the 20th, the *Lakatoi's* master and mate having agreed to cooperate, the main body of the troops moved to Vitu. Next day, loaded with stores, water and fuel and carrying a total of 214,[3] the *Lakatoi* set sail for Australia. The empty ships *Totole* and *Umboi* were returned to Madang and the *Gnair*, with W. Money[4] as master, followed the *Lakatoi* in its passage down the Vitiaz Straits. On the 22nd the *Lakatoi* met the *Laurabada* at the eastern end of Papua, and, after receiving food and medical supplies, continued her voyage southwards. On the 28th the survivors were disembarked at Cairns.

> Of all on board [recorded Feldt], six only were fit men . . . the rest were sick, debilitated by poor and insufficient food . . . weakened by malaria and exposure. Most had sores, the beginnings of tropical ulcers, covered by dirty bandages. Their faces were the dirty grey . . . which betokens malaria; their clothes were in rags and stank of stale sweat. They were wrecks, but they were safe, and some would fight again.[5]

The main routes of withdrawal to the south coast were from the Malabunga and Toma roadheads across the Warangoi and Kavavas Rivers either to Lemingi at the foot of the Bainings, or to Put Put Harbour on the east coast of the Gazelle Peninsula. A number of tracks radiated from Lemingi to the south coast, but the principal ones led to Adler and Wide Bays. Both were ill-defined, rough and hard going. The route from Put Put followed the coast to Adler Bay.

The commander of the force, Colonel Scanlan, after issuing to Carr his orders for the withdrawal, had remained at Tomavatur for about an hour deliberating whether to attempt to reach the south coast or to surrender. Eventually, accompanied by five others, he set out for Malabunga and joined other assorted groups trudging along the track to Lemingi.

Some of the men who arrived at Malabunga during the afternoon of the 23rd January were advised to take three days' rations from abandoned

---

[2] An advanced party of eighteen had passed through Iboki and by 10 Feb reached Kalingi. Thence they were evacuated to the mainland in the *Thetis* and on 14 Mar reached Bogadjim. Eventually, after many days of painful progress, they reached Mount Hagen. On 13 May they were taken by plane to Thursday Island and from there by sea to Townsville, arriving on 23 May.

[3] The total comprised:

AIF, NGVR	162
NGAU	6
European Police	6
Civilians	16
European Crew	4
Native Crew	18
Other natives	2

[4] Capt W. A. Money, MC, MM, NG2360. Angau and "M" Special unit. Plantation owner; of Talasea, New Britain; b. London, 9 Aug 1895.

[5] *The Coastwatchers*, p. 65.

trucks there and push on about five miles to a police barracks. By 5 p.m. about 200 who obeyed these instructions had gathered there. It was nearing dusk and about half the party decided to stop at the barracks until morning; the others to attempt to reach Lemingi Mission. One soldier[6] who elected to go on described the trip:

> We walked along in line in pitch dark. Each had his hand on the man in front. If a man in front came to a log he'd say "log" and the word would go back along the line. I was the twentieth in the line at the beginning and by midnight I was last and dropped off. I pulled a groundsheet over me and slept in the rain. Next morning I followed the track and came up with the others in a village about 1700.

By the 25th advanced parties of the force had begun to arrive at Father Maierhofer's mission at Lemingi, and the following day it was estimated that 300 officers and men were there. The missionary provided tea, rice and native foods, and the men slept at the station and in the neighbouring village.

Early on the 26th an advanced party under Captain Nicholls[7] left Lemingi to push on over the mountains to the coast. That day and the next other parties followed. Soon after leaving Lemingi the track dropped away steeply for about 2,000 feet. It was muddy and slippery, and the men slid most of the way to the fast 30-yard-wide river below; after wading it, they followed all day a track which climbed steeply. There were few villages. The men, wet, muddy and weary, were strung out along the track and had to rest every hundred yards or so.

Soon they broke up into groups of about twelve men. As they entered the villages the natives disappeared, but the men found taro roots, and cooked them for food. Otherwise rations were meagre. Each day found them growing weaker through lack of food and the effort needed to climb ragged mountains and cross swift rivers.

> Our hands, never dry, were cut and torn [recalled one soldier]. It was painful even to close them to grip the rough vines, and our bodies were bruised and stiff from innumerable falls.

The advanced party arrived at Adler Bay at 4 p.m. on the 27th. As they neared the coast they heard sounds of gun fire, and Lieutenant Best[8] and Private Ross[9] went ahead to reconnoitre. They returned with the news that civilians and Chinese, who were camped at Adler Bay, were flying a white flag and desired to surrender. At the bay Nicholls' party met Colonel Field[1] of the N.G.V.R., who told them it was no use going on and advised surrender. Nicholls' men pulled down the white flag. During the 28th and 29th groups of men from Lemingi continued to arrive. A dress-

---

[6] Sgt A. L. Frazer, NX58247; 8 Div AASC and Mil Hist Section. Press photographer; of Manly, NSW; b. Annandale, NSW, 26 Apr 1915.

[7] Maj H. W. Nicholls, V83714. (1st AIF: Lt 4 Div Arty.) S/Capt NG Area; LHQ 1942-45. Horticulturist; of Red Cliffs, Vic; b. Ballarat, Vic, 5 Jul 1898.

[8] Lt E. W. Best, VX44505; 2/22 Bn. Advertising agent; of Melbourne; b. Melbourne, 11 Sep 1917.

[9] Dvr J. C. Ross, NX58814; AASC 8 Div. Motor driver; of Arncliffe, NSW; b. Sydney, 13 Mar 1913.

[1] Lt-Col C. R. Field. (1st AIF: 2 MG Bn.) CO NGVR. Director of Public Works, Rabaul; b. 11 Sep 1895. Lost in sinking of *Montevideo Maru* 1 Jul 1942.

ing station was set up by members of the 2/10th Field Ambulance,[2] where the men were able to obtain sticking plaster, mercurochrome and small quantities of quinine. Food was abundant and the men slept in huts in a large village.

Meanwhile other soldiers were advancing by the route through Put Put. One party was led by Major Owen, the resolute commander of the company on Vulcan Beach. He had withdrawn soon after 7.30 a.m. on the 23rd with Captain Silverman and the R.A.P., and eventually overtook some Japanese near Taliligap. In skirting them Owen became separated from the rest of his party and spent the night close to Vunakanau, which he found also to be occupied. On the 24th, near a church at the foot of Mount Varzin, he met Lomas' platoon, which had been joined by Lieutenant Dawson, and was told that all resistance had ceased and the troops had been instructed to fend for themselves. Owen thereupon assumed leadership of the group, now amounting to thirty-six, and announced his intention of reaching the south coast.

On the 25th they met the acting Administrator (Major Page[3]) and three other administrative officials. Page warned them that he had already sent a note to the Japanese informing them of his location and asking to be picked up. He added that the soldiers would be foolish to stay in the area. Acting on this advice Owen pushed on to the Ralabang Plantation house, reaching it soon after dusk.

> There we found three civilians [said Dawson later] who said they could not give us any food. I lifted a plate of scones off the table and said: "This will do for the time being." Eventually they gave us enough food for one day, but said they could not give us more as they had more than 300 natives to feed and did not know how long it would be before they could get rice from the Japanese. The unreality of their outlook shocked us.

Thence on the 26th the party reached the Warangoi River, followed its course on foot and by rafts, and on the 28th reached Put Put. On the 31st they too reached Adler Bay where they found a considerable number of troops waiting to surrender.

Colonel Carr had set out on the 23rd with a small headquarters party for Malabunga where, about midday, he met a naval officer, Lieutenant MacKenzie,[4] and some ratings. Native carriers detailed to carry MacKenzie's wireless set onward from Malabunga had not arrived there and lest it fall into Japanese hands MacKenzie had ordered that it be destroyed. Its destruction removed any possibility of continued resistance under one command until a new wireless could be obtained, said Carr later.

That afternoon and next day the headquarters group, now amalgamated with MacKenzie's naval party and numbering twenty-one in all, toiled along a rough jungle track until they reached a village 15 miles south of

---

[2] The nurses had been left by Major Palmer at Vunapope on the morning of the 23rd under the care of Chaplain J. L. May (of Hobart) and the Mission sisters.
[3] Maj H. H. Page, DSO, MC. (1st AIF: Maj 25 Bn.) Govt Sec NG 1923-42, A/Adm Sep 1941-42. B. Grafton, NSW, 8 Aug 1888. Lost in sinking of *Montevideo Maru* 1 Jul 1942.
[4] Lt-Cdr H. A. MacKenzie, DSC, RAN. Naval Intelligence Office, Rabaul 1941-42. Of Claremont, WA; b. Claremont, 25 Oct 1907. Died 4 Jul 1949.

Malabunga. They remained there for a week, sending back patrols to report the movements of the Japanese. From these Carr learnt that the enemy had not penetrated beyond the Warangoi River to the east, Malabunga Junction in the centre, and the Keravat River to the west, and that the Australians were pushing on in small parties on the main routes already described. On the 24th pamphlets[5] had been dropped ordering them to surrender. On the 26th Major McLeod and Lieutenant Figgis joined the headquarters group, and some days later the move continued. On 1st February, at Lemingi, Father Maierhofer proved as helpful to Carr's party as he had been to earlier arrivals. He estimated that nearly 400 men had passed through in the preceding week, among them, Carr learnt, being Colonel Scanlan.

The battalion headquarters party was now at the rear of a long and weary procession of men. On the morning of the 28th the withdrawal westwards from Adler Bay had begun. The coastal route lay along coral rocks, or through mangrove swamps; the men camped in deserted villages at night and mosquitoes made life a torment; little food was to be found. By midday on the 31st the advanced party reached Wide Bay, where they met four air force men who had rowed round the coast in a dinghy.[6] Tol Plantation house, the men discovered, had already been visited by the Japanese. They had shot the cattle and taken the pigs and sheep, but had left untouched the furnished house, complete with bed linen. The weary men caught and killed a stray pig, made linen lap laps, bathed and shaved, and afterwards revelled in the luxury of a roast pork dinner.

By 1st February the escapers at Tol had grown, according to some estimates, to 200, and small fires tended by groups of men were burning throughout the area.

We told them to put out the fires, but they were too tired to worry [recalled one soldier]. They just didn't care any more.

That morning a float-plane came over and some of the leaders, convinced that the signs of occupation would bring the Japanese, warned the men to leave the area. Many pushed on that day, among them Sergeant Smith's[7] party, which had been joined by seven members of "A" Company, and now totalled twenty in all. Best and Nicholls, after conferring with Private O'Neill,[8] who had demonstrated outstanding qualities as a leader during the journey down the coast, left the following morning, accom-

---

[5] They read:
> To the Officers and Soldiers of this Island
> SURRENDER AT ONCE!
> and we will guarantee your life, Treating you as war prisoners. Those who RESIST US WILL BE KILLED ONE AND ALL. Consider seriously, you can find neither food nor way of escape in this island and you will only die of hunger unless you surrender.
> January 23rd 1942
> Japanese Commander in Chief.

[6] Other groups arrived during the day. One party of thirteen men led by Sergeant F. S. Smith of the 2/22nd Battalion had travelled direct from Lemingi to Wide Bay, over scarcely known tracks, and arrived that morning after being lost for a day and a half in the Baining Mountains.

[7] Sgt F. S. Smith, VX30515. 2/22, 2/4 Bns. Barman; of Brighton, Vic; b. Carlton, Vic, 1 May 1909.

[8] Pte F. E. G. O'Neill, VX23947; 2/22 Bn. Packing machinist; of East Preston, Vic; b. Carlton, Vic, 4 Jul 1917.

panied by twelve others. They met a party of five engineers under Captain Botham[9] at the mouth of the Henry Reid River, crossed the three rivers which run into Henry Reid Bay and bivouacked for the night of 2nd February near Kalai Mission.

That day Major Owen, accompanied by Sergeant Morgan[1] and Private Glynn,[2] had set out from Adler Bay on a fast trip to Tol. Owen feared that food was being wasted and was determined to get ahead of the troops in order to organise the available supplies.[3] During the day he passed about 150 troops going to Tol, and on his arrival that afternoon found about 100 already there. After learning that food was scarce at Tol but said to be plentiful at Kalai Mission, Owen decided to push on. He set out early next morning, having been joined by Majors Mollard and Palmer and Captain Goodman[4] and a small body of troops. They were crossing the second river at 7 a.m. when five enemy landing craft, heavily laden with troops, appeared heading for Tol Plantation. As they neared the beach the Japanese began to shell and machine-gun the area. Other groups who had recently left Tol either heard or saw the arrival of the Japanese and hastened away.

On the 3rd there remained at Tol and at Waitavalo, about a mile north, some seventy men. Twenty-two elected to surrender and, carrying white flags to the Japanese on the beach, were taken prisoner. Others attempted to escape through the plantation areas into the bush but many were captured. The Japanese systematically combed the areas adjacent to Henry Reid Bay, and parties of prisoners unable to cross the rivers at their mouths[5] except by boat were brought to the concentration point at the Tol native labour quarters. The troops were fed at midday and at night. The Japanese contributed some rice towards their evening meal and permitted the use of a fire to cook it. When night fell the men were imprisoned in a large hut. Fires were lit round it and tended by the Japanese throughout the night.

Early next morning the prisoners were assembled outside the hut and marched to Tol Plantation house. There two Australian officers who had headed the surrender party the previous morning were separated. A piece of cloth on which Japanese characters had been written was attached to the belt of each officer, and an attempt made to separate from the others the men who had comprised the surrender party. Of about forty

---

[9] Maj W. G. Botham, DCM, VX114261. (1914-18: Lt Bedfordshire Regt; Pilot Officer 80 Sqn RAF.) OC Fortress Engrs, Rabaul 1941-42, Brisbane Fixed Defences 1942-43. Engineer; of Box Hill, Vic; b. London, 3 May 1897.

[1] L-Sgt J. A. Morgan, VX21651. 2/22, 2/4 Bns. Farmer; of Hedley, Vic; b. Yarram, Vic, 13 Mar 1912.

[2] Pte V. P. Glynn, VX24088. 2/22, 2/4 Bns. Stevedore; of Geelong, Vic; b. Geelong, 20 Jul 1911.

[3] In addition a group of armed natives from the NG Constabulary had got ahead of the troops, and interpreting too literally an order to "live off the country" had plundered the villages, stirred up the natives and were responsible for much of the desolation encountered by the Australians on their journey down the coast.

[4] Capt C. E. Goodman, VX44904; 2/22 Bn. Stock and station agent; of Bairnsdale, Vic; b. Bairnsdale, 23 Sep 1909.

[5] The Henry Reid River, too deep to ford at its mouth, was easily fordable 200 yards upstream.

men who claimed this distinction twenty were separated and marched away.

When they had gone the remainder were lined up in fours, and their names, ranks and army numbers entered in a book. Paybooks, photographs, letters and personal items were collected and heaped together; the hands of the prisoners were tied behind their backs with cord and they were linked together in groups of nine or ten. The men rested for a while. Some of them were given water to drink and allowed to share Japanese cigarettes. Then, led by three Japanese and with each group separated from the other by soldiers carrying spades and fixed bayonets, the men moved off through the plantation. The parties soon divided, going in different directions into the long undergrowth.

I decided that this was a shooting party [said one survivor later] and that if one were to be shot one might as well be shot trying to escape as be "done in" in cold blood. I was fortunate in that the line I was in happened to be not roped together and that I was No. 2 in the line. . . . In the beginning the procession made its own track through the cover crop and secondary growth which was springing up, but after a time emerged for a short distance upon the track proper through the plantation. It was here that an "S" bend in the path with secondary growth overgrown with cover crop presented an opportunity for me to escape and I availed myself of it. Turning the first bend of the "S", I nipped out of the line and ducked down behind a bush on the other bend of the "S". The chap next to me called "Lower, Sport", and I accordingly crouched further into the scrub.[6]

A survivor from another party, Private Collins,[7] was in a group of men linked together by cord. When his party halted in the plantation an officer drew his sword, cut the rope joining the first man to the others, and motioned him into the bush. A Japanese soldier followed with a fixed bayonet. Collins, last in the line, heard a man cry out, and saw the Japanese return wiping his bayonet. Others were cut away from the group and led into the bush. One man broke loose and tried to escape, but the officer hit him with his sword and then shot him. Clissold[8] of the 2/10th Field Ambulance, who was wearing a Red Cross brassard, had it torn from his arm. When he asked if he could be shot, the officer, in Collins' presence, complied.

Finally, only Collins and the officer remained. The latter took up a rifle and motioned Collins to walk. After a few paces he fired, hitting Collins in the shoulder and knocking him to the ground. Another shot hit him in the wrists and back. The Japanese departed. Collins lay still on the ground for a time, then finding that the last shot had severed the cord round his wrists and that his hands were free, got up and walked

---

[6] Lt (then Pte) A. L. Robinson, DCM, NGX263; NGVR and Angau. Clerk; of Rabaul, and Dalley, Qld; b. Townsville, Qld, 7 Dec 1903. Killed by natives, New Britain, 12 Dec 1948. (Robinson wandered for three days in the bush, his hands still tied and in a shocking condition, before meeting a party of civilians who released him from his bonds and treated his hands; eventually he joined Holland's party from the north coast.)

[7] Dvr W. D. Collins, NX57343; 2/10 Fd Amb. Truck driver; of Sans Souci, NSW; b. Miranda, NSW, 7 Jun 1918.

[8] Pte T. B. Clissold, NX57642; 2/10 Fd Amb. Labourer; of Emu Plains, NSW; b. Emu Plains, 1 Jul 1912. Executed by Japanese 4 Mar 1942.

away, passing the bodies of about six of his comrades lying still on the ground.[9]

Another survivor, Lance-Corporal Marshall,[1] endured a similar ordeal. When the group he was with entered the undergrowth, each was unlinked from the line and taken into the bush with a Japanese soldier. When Marshall's turn came he was stabbed from behind with a bayonet, receiving three wounds—in the back, the arm and side, and lower down on his side. He fell, and lay still, feigning death. Soon afterwards he heard cries, followed by rifle shots. He concluded that any man who moved was fired upon. After lying for a time on the ground, bleeding freely, he managed to release one of his hands. When dusk fell he arose, and saw three or four men lying on the ground. After a few days' wandering in the bush he was picked up by a party of Australians, including Lieutenants Lomas and Dawson, who had themselves narrowly escaped capture.

> Marshall . . . attempted to run away (wrote Dawson afterwards). He was delirious, walking along with an empty tin in one hand, the other tucked in his shirt front, which was full of blood. He had used the tin for drinking river water. We caught him, and learned the story of the massacre of Tol.

Other survivors spoke of subsequent killings on that grim day. Gunner Hazelgrove[2] was one of a party of six who had entered Tol Plantation, unaware of the presence of the Japanese, soon after the first massacre, and had been surprised and captured. They were taken to a house near the beach where the party met an interpreter with the Japanese, dressed in shirt and shorts, who appeared to be English. As they arrived the interpreter said "All right boys, you can put your hands down now." He spoke like an Australian, said Hazelgrove, later. At the Tol Plantation house Hazelgrove saw a large pile of equipment. Identity discs and personal belongings were taken from his party. Their hands also were tied behind their backs, and they were roped together. After marching them through kunai grass for about a quarter of a mile the Japanese, without warning, fired. Hazelgrove was hit in the back, fell, and lay very still. The Japanese threw palms over them and left. After struggling for two hours Hazelgrove freed his wrists from the bonds, and got up. Around him his five comrades lay dead. Somehow he struggled to the beach, where in a confused state he remained for two days before a party of artillerymen under Lieutenant Selby picked him up and cared for him.

Private Cook,[3] of the 2/10th Field Ambulance, survived another such execution. About 9.30 on the 4th he and a group of seven others had been walking along the track towards Tol when they met an N.C.O. of

---

[9] Collins wandered for three days in the bush and then found his way back to the plantation. The Japanese had gone. He found two men with bayonet wounds, who were seriously ill, took them to a house and there left them. Eventually he met Major Palmer, who took him under his care.

[1] L-Cpl C. Marshall, VX25254; 2/22 Bn. Truck driver; of Prahran, Vic; b. Melbourne, 10 Jan 1911.

[2] Gnr M. Hazelgrove, N109824; Rabaul AA Bty. Carpenter; of Bega, NSW; b. Bega, 27 Oct 1922.

[3] Pte W. Cook, NX56978; 2/10 Fd Amb. Oiler; of Campsie, NSW; b. Alexandra, NSW, 28 May 1908.

the 2/22nd Battalion, who told them that he believed the Japanese had left Tol, but to remain where they were until he made certain.

We waited just off the track, four of us, having a game of cards and the other four cooking some food (said Cook later). Our first intimation that the Japs were there was when the four who were cooking ran past us, muttering "The Japs are on us." We were at the edge of the jungle. I myself ran into the jungle and hid. I saw my seven mates walk out with their hands up so I went back with them. It was roughly about 1030 hours. We were taken to the main track under a party of Japanese, in charge of whom was a sergeant.

Soon other small parties of Japanese arrived with more prisoners, until the group totalled twenty-five. At Tol the Japanese separated a civilian police officer from them, they were tied together, and made to sit down in the plantation. The ambulance men protested that they belonged to the Red Cross, but the brassards they were wearing were torn from their sleeves. The Australians were then taken away in twos and threes. Cook was in the second last group of three. In sign language they were asked whether they would prefer to be bayoneted or shot. They asked to be shot. As they reached the bottom of the track, three other Japanese with fixed bayonets intercepted and fell in behind them:

They then stabbed us in the back with their bayonets (Cook related). The first blow knocked the three of us to the ground. Our thumbs were tied behind our backs and native lap laps were used to connect us together through our arms. They stood above us and stabbed us several more times. I received five stabs. I pretended death and held my breath.

The Japanese then walked away. The soldier who was lying next to me groaned. One Japanese came back and stabbed him again. I could not hold my breath any longer, and when I breathed he heard it and stabbed me another six times. The last thrust went through my ear, face and into my mouth, severing an artery which caused the blood to gush out of my mouth. He then placed coconut fronds and vines over the three of us. I lay there and heard the last two men being shot.

After an hour Cook was able to rise. He untied the cloth which connected him to his mates, and staggered towards the sea, about 50 yards away. After a few steps he again collapsed. Eventually he regained consciousness, reached the beach and, the instinct for self preservation strong even in that weakened state, walked along it in the water to avoid leaving traces of blood. At dusk he saw the smoke of a near-by camp fire and stumbled towards it. Next morning he found a small party of soldiers under Colonel Scanlan camped close to where he had spent the night. Scanlan dressed his wounds while Cook told his story.[4]

Another survivor, Private Webster,[5] was among eleven men who reached Tol on 3rd February. Next morning they were surprised and captured by a Japanese patrol. They were marched to Waitavalo House, tied, lined up in the bush and fired upon. Hit in the arm and side Webster fainted.

---

[4] Cook later lost his voice as a result of the wound in his throat, but partially recovered it. In 1951, at work on the maintenance of railway rolling stock, he was knocked down and run over by a train. He survived, but lost both legs.

[5] Pte H. J. Webster, VX23821; 2/22 Bn. Truck driver; of North Melbourne; b. Melbourne, 1 Jun 1920.

When he recovered the Japanese had gone. Only one of his comrades, Private Walkley,[6] remained alive. After hiding near the plantation for three days, the two men set off for help. Webster, who was ahead, missed Walkley and searched for him without success. Eventually Webster too met Colonel Scanlan's party.

In a summary of these events and after interrogating all the available survivors and independent witnesses who had passed through the area, a Court of Inquiry reported in May 1942 its conclusion that

> there were at least four separate massacres of prisoners on the morning of 4th February, the first of about 100, the second of 6, the third of 24 and the fourth of about 11. These figures are only approximate.[7] Witnesses were pressed by the Court as to whether they could suggest any explanation as to the cause of the Japanese action, but none of them can advance any explanation of the Japanese onslaught upon them, and none saw anything which might have provoked it. All the men had surrendered or been captured and held in captivity for some time before being slaughtered.
>
> The Court accepts as absolutely reliable the evidence of the above men. Each of them appeared truthful and had a clear recollection of the events he was describing. This conclusion is supported by the fact that each of the five wounded men bore wounds consistent with his account, and Robinson's hands were tied when he was picked up.
>
> The Court considers that their evidence is further supported by the fact that each of the six was subsequently picked up, quite independently, by other parties and gave an account of his experiences agreeing with his present testimony. It is in the highest degree improbable that such an account could, in the circumstances, have been concocted.

After the massacre the movement westwards continued. Two small parties got ahead of the main group. One comprising seven men under Corporal Hamill,[8] which passed through Tol on 2nd February, had by the 15th reached Awul, 50 miles east of Gasmata. There from a missionary, Father Culhane, they learned that Gasmata was in Japanese hands, and went into the mountains, emerging five miles west of it. Using native canoes they reached Pilelo, an island off the New Britain coast near Arawe, and on 2nd March left in a missionary's pinnace for Finschhafen.

The party under Nicholls and Botham reached Wunung on 10th February. Thence Lieutenant Best set out in a pinnace with eight men, but his party was captured at Gasmata. By the 13th Nicholls and Botham reached Father Culhane's mission at Awul and, having secured a pinnace, sent back a message to Rano (where some of the men had remained) asking for a volunteer to steer it. One man who had been a seaman said

---

[6] Pte N. W. Walkley, VX23167; 2/22 Bn. Spinner; of Preston, Vic; b. Glenelg, SA, 15 Nov 1919. Died of wounds 1 Mar 1942. Walkley, grievously wounded, was found later by Lieutenant Figgis, who reached Tol on 14th February.

[7] In 1945 officers of the War Graves Commission uncovered the remains of 158 victims of the massacres. How many of these were soldiers and how many civilians will never precisely be known.
The difficulty of sheeting home such crimes was demonstrated after the war. Investigating officers, having traced the massacre to Japanese combatant troops, eventually obtained the names of two of the principals concerned—a lieut-colonel and a doctor—but both committed suicide. As a result no War Crimes Trial has taken place in connection with this atrocity.

[8] Cpl R. J. S. Hamill, VX24129; 2/22, 2/4 Bns. Pulp cutter; of Forrest, Vic; b. Colac, Vic, 24 Sep 1917.

he would not risk the journey, but Private Frazer, who had sailed on Sydney Harbour, offered his services.

They said only one man (Frazer related) but O'Neill said he was going too. We got tins of meat and goldfish[9] and a canoe. Three miles out in the bay two Zeros shot us up. We put into shore and left the canoe. O'Neill was now delirious from the sun. I dragged him to a village and got two natives to carry him. At Father Culhane's we found some "A" Company boys sick, and the rest half a mile farther on. Father Culhane said the Japanese had captured Gasmata and we would not get past.

He (Father Culhane) had a 20-foot pinnace, old, with a diesel engine capable of 4 knots and mast on which we rigged a sail. We got a compass off a schooner which had been wrecked on the reef. Father Culhane put O'Neill to bed with a temperature of 105. We took a 44-gallon drum of water, two 44-gallon drums of dieseline and two kerosene tins of cooked rice. I was to steer and sail the boat and Sergeant Elton[1] was to look after the engines. The idea was to make for the Trobriands due south at dusk. We'd painted the boat black with pitch and set off at dusk twenty-five days after the landing.

200 yards out someone trod on the feed pipe and it broke. It took an hour to change and we had to row to keep off the reef. Two men wanted to go back, but O'Neill stood up, swaying with fever, and said he'd shoot anyone who wanted to do so. Three miles out a hot cap on the motor burst. It took an hour to put on a spare. These were the only spares we had.

Five miles out we ran into weather in the dark. To steer south meant being side on and we were shipping waves. So we steered south-east for one hour and south-west for an hour. In four days we hit the Trobriands. At one stage it rained for half a day. We saw no aircraft or boats. Most were seasick; only Elton and I were not. They lay helpless, unable to eat rice. We'd given up hope on the fourth day when a boy said he saw land. It took only two hours to reach it. We passed the first island, and sailed on looking for a mission. We passed another two islands and turned right through more islands and came to a channel marked by a post. We'd come along the only possible channel all the way from Rabaul with a map from an atlas as our only guide.

On the 20th February, Nicholls' party of eleven were joined in the Trobriands by a group of civilian escapers. On the 24th they reached Samarai; three days later they were flown to Port Moresby where they gave details of the retreat down the south coast of New Britain and asked that help be sent.

Among the troops who passed through Tol after the massacre was Colonel Scanlan, who as related had met some of the survivors, including Privates Cook and Webster, soon after the event. Two messages[2] had been left at Waitavalo, one addressed to Colonel Scanlan, urging him to surrender and "beg mercy" for his troops.

---

[9] Slang for tinned herrings and tomato sauce.

[1] Lt J. R. Elton, VX101862. Rabaul Fortress Coy Engrs; AEME. Regular soldier; of Middle Park, Vic; b. Melbourne, 12 Aug 1917.

[2] The messages read:
"To Commander Scanlan: Now that this Island is took and tightly surrounded by our Air Forces and Navy you have no means of escape. If your religion does not allow you to commit suicide it is up to you to surrender yourself and to beg mercy for your troops. You will be responsible for the death of your men."
"To Officers and Australian troops: Surrender yourselves. You will die of hunger or be killed by wild savages as there is no means of escape. You will be treated as prisoners of war and when the war is over you will be returned to your Motherland. Today we caught many prisoners but killed only those that attacked us.
                        Japanese Commander-in-Chief of landing at Wide Bay."

On the evening of the 8th Scanlan reached Kalai Mission, where a number of troops were gathered under Major Owen. A Mission priest told Scanlan that he knew of no scheme for rescuing the men and if they proceeded farther westward they would run short of food. In his opinion there was no alternative but to return to Rabaul and surrender.

The disorderly withdrawal of his force from Rabaul, the events at Tol, and the implications of the sentence "surrender yourself and beg mercy for your troops" must have weighed heavily upon Scanlan. Unaware how events were shaping elsewhere or of any attempt or plan to rescue the survivors, and in the light of the Japanese message, Scanlan decided his duty was to surrender. He told Major Mollard his reasons and asked him to address the men. That night Mollard gathered the troops together, told them that he had decided to return with Colonel Scanlan, and gave them his reasons.[3] His speech "through its sheer hard logic depressed me more than anything which had happened on the track", wrote Lieutenant Selby later.

After the departure of Scanlan and Mollard on the 10th, Owen, as senior officer on the south coast, took command. That day he began the movement westwards from Kalai, travelling with a party of twenty-three including the medical officer (Major Palmer) and three of the survivors from Tol—Hazelgrove, Marshall and Webster. The party reached Draak on the 17th, and were joined there by a further survivor of the massacre—Private Cook. By the 23rd the men were at the Malmal Mission at Jacquinot Bay, where they were generously helped by Father Harris. (It was his pinnace that Best and his party had taken on their voyage to Gasmata.) When Owen learned that the Japanese had occupied Gasmata, he decided that it was useless to continue the move westward. Camps were established at Wunung and Drina plantations for about 50 and 100 troops respectively. Several of the men had died on the march from Tol, and others were extremely ill.

As it seemed likely that the wait on the south coast would be long, and to keep the men occupied, Owen set them to work planting vegetables. Before long, however, sickness had depleted the workers until they seldom exceeded 10 per cent of the camp strength. In a medical report on the condition of the troops at this time, Major Palmer wrote that

---

[3] Similar reasoning probably influenced others to surrender. Mollard's conclusions were:
The announcement that he was a prisoner of war would relieve the anxiety of his wife and relatives.
Malaria had already attacked the party and as quinine supplies ran out would eventually prove fatal.
Clothes were beginning to fall to pieces and there would be no means of replacing them.
The natives were already showing signs of indifference and when they saw the great white master fleeing from the enemy and dying of malaria and exhaustion they would lose all their respect and might even become actively hostile.
Food supplies were so precarious that there was a very real danger of death from starvation.
The Japanese would probably want something tangible to show for their conquest and would probably work all the plantations on the coast for copra. In so doing they would round up any Australian troops in the locality and it would become impossible to live on any plantation.
It was impossible for white men to live a native life indefinitely in that climate and there was no guarantee that even should they survive till the end of the war they would be repatriated. There was always the possibility of the war dragging on for many years and then ending in a compromise whereby the Japanese might well be allowed to retain their conquests in the Bismarck Archipelago.
They had not seen a single friendly reconnaissance plane to date and there was a grave doubt as to whether the authorities in Australia would or could make any effort to rescue them.

100 per cent of the men have been inflicted with malaria and have had at least one recurrence; 90 per cent have had two or more recurrences, 10 per cent have daily rigours or sweating at night, 33 per cent only are able to do any sort of work. At least 15 per cent of the men are suffering from such a degree of secondary anaemia and debility following attacks of malaria, diarrhoea and the privations of the journey and lack of food that it will not be possible to keep them alive more than a few weeks.

On 5th April, however, a party sent out by Owen returned from Awul with a supply of stores and trade goods; that day Owen received welcome orders to concentrate his men at Wunung for evacuation.

How had this come about? On 7th February, leaving Figgis and MacKenzie to go by the direct route to Wide Bay, Carr and the bulk of his party had left Lemingi for the south coast. On the 14th, they met Scanlan and Mollard returning to surrender. On the 26th they overtook Figgis and MacKenzie at Ewei, where they were repairing a 12-foot dinghy. At Ril on 4th March Carr learnt from warrant-officers of the New Guinea constabulary of the evacuation scheme being organised on the north coast. A few days later, led by Frank Holland, Carr's party, now accompanied by Collins and Robinson, two survivors of the Tol massacre, set off for McCarthy's rendezvous. They took with them a message drafted by MacKenzie to be sent on McCarthy's teleradio to the Naval Office, Port Moresby, stating that he and Figgis would endeavour to concentrate the remaining men on the south coast at Palmalmal, and there each Wednesday and Saturday afternoon would keep watch for aircraft and for any instructions that might be dropped to the force.

It was in response to this message that Lieutenant Timperly[4] of Angau, taking a teleradio with him, had slipped across from the Trobriands to Palmalmal in a fast launch, arriving on 5th April. At midday Major Owen received a message from Captain Goodman to concentrate his men at Wunung. "They must be here today, as tonight is the night," the message warned.

Then began a harrowing forced march for the men at Drina. Some were able to make only slow progress, supported at each side by their comrades; others were so weak they had to be carried on improvised stretchers. It was after midnight when the weary, over-wrought men arrived at Palmalmal, to discover that so far only Timperly's pinnace had arrived. By the 9th over 150 soldiers and civilians had gathered at the evacuation point. That morning the *Laurabada* arrived, captained by Lieutenant Ivan Champion.[5] She lay concealed during the daylight and at dusk the troops filed aboard. On the 12th the *Laurabada* reached Port Moresby, whence the survivors were shipped in the *Macdhui* to Townsville.[6]

---

[4] Capt A. T. Timperly, MBE, PX176; Angau. Civil servant; of Ipswich, Qld; b. Ipswich, 30 Dec 1915.

[5] Lt I. F. Champion, OBE; RANVR. Assistant resident magistrate; of Bwagaoia, Misima, Papua; b. Port Moresby, 9 Mar 1904.

[6] The *Laurabada* brought out 131 soldiers, 4 RAN and 21 civilians. One man had died during the voyage.

One small party which could not reach the evacuation point in time to catch the *Laurabada* was brought out under the leadership of the former radio superintendent at Rabaul, Mr Laws,[7] in a salvaged launch more than a month later. The party landed at Sio, whence the men walked by way of Bogadjim to Bena Bena, and were flown to Moresby.

Another group of nine led by Lieutenant Dawson, having learnt from Lieutenant Figgis of McCarthy's scheme on the north coast, followed the route taken by Colonel Carr, but arrived too late to be evacuated in the *Lakatoi*. They were led by friendly natives to Mavelo Plantation, and thence by canoe reached Valoka Mission at Cape Hoskins. At the end of March Dawson at Garua, following the route of earlier escapers, met Lincoln Bell, who had remained in New Britain after McCarthy's departure, and through him sent a message to Port Moresby, giving the names of his men. On 14th May, after periods spent at Iboki and in the Vitu Group, the party was picked up at Bali Harbour by Lieutenant Harris in the schooner *Umboi*. On the 16th they reached Bogadjim and met Lieutenant Boyan[8] of Angau. He led them to Kainantu in the Upper Ramu. There they were joined by several other Australians and learnt that they must go to Bena Bena for evacuation. At Bena Bena the weary Australians were told that only Americans (survivors of a Mitchell bomber which had made a forced landing in the area) were to be flown out; they must walk by way of Wau to the south coast, where they would be picked up by small ships.[9] They reached Wau on foot on 15th July and were ordered to walk thence over the Ekuti Range to Bulldog and down the Lakekamu River to the south coast of New Guinea. Dawson protested and eventually all except Dawson himself were evacuated from Wau by air. Dawson's odyssey had not ended. He remained with the 2/5th Independent Company until the end of September, when, suffering from dysentery, he walked over the Ekuti Range along a track which climbed to about 8,500 feet through moss forest until at length he reached the mouth of the Lakekamu; there he was picked up by a small vessel and taken to Port Moresby. (In 1945 he was back on New Britain as a battalion commander.)

The strength of Colonel Scanlan's force at Rabaul on 23rd January was 1,396. Of these this narrative has recorded the escape of over 400, either by their own enterprise or with the guidance and help of those members of a force soon to become known as A.N.G.A.U. In addition some 60 civilians and four members of the R.A.N. were embarked either on the *Lakatoi* or the *Laurabada,* and about 120 members of the air force were taken off in flying-boats on 23rd and 24th January—an indication of what might have been done had an organised withdrawal and evacua-

---

[7] Lt D. A. Laws, P479. Angau and "M" Special Unit. Radio engineer; of Rabaul; b. Brisbane, 26 Jul 1909. Killed in action 5 May 1943.

[8] Capt R. H. Boyan, PX150; Angau. Patrol officer; of Aitape, NG; b. Sydney, 30 Jun 1913.

[9] Evidently a higher estimate was held of the value of these relatively fit American aircrew than of the weary survivors from New Britain. Four aircraft—two Boston A-24's, a DH-86, and a Spartan Moth—were lost attempting to rescue the Americans from Bena Bena.

tion scheme been planned before the invasion. About 800 became prisoners.[10]

Also remaining on New Britain and New Ireland were some 300 civilians. Most of the women and children had been evacuated between mid-December and early January. What opportunities had there been to evacuate the remaining civilians? On 16th January, the Acting Administrator at Rabaul, having learnt that a Japanese invasion was believed imminent, sent an urgent radiogram to the Commonwealth Government asking for action to evacuate the civil population. On the 21st the Prime Minister's Department in Canberra replied asking the Administration at Lae to supply the numbers and the whereabouts of unessential civilians so that the question could be considered. It was then too late. Attempts by the Administration at Lae to gain wireless touch with Rabaul on the 22nd failed; Rabaul had been attacked that morning, and the *Herstein* in which Page hoped all civilians might be embarked lay burning in the harbour.

It is doubtful whether, even if granted opportunity to escape at this last moment, all the civilians would have chosen to go. Many of them had spent their lives hewing out plantations from the jungle and were reluctant to abandon their life's work; others no doubt were swayed by responsibilities to their native labourers; a percentage under-estimated the consequences of remaining or over-estimated the dangers of travelling in small craft (some of which had left Rabaul as late as the day before the invasion) over long distances exposed to air attack; some were elderly and could not have faced the hardships entailed in escaping; some of the administrative officials considered it their duty to remain at their posts.

After the invasion most of the civilians were gathered in the vicinity of Rabaul where a camp was established by the Japanese for civil and military prisoners at Malaguna road.[1] On 22nd June, 849 military prisoners, and about 200 civilians were embarked at Rabaul on the *Montevideo Maru*. On 1st July the *Montevideo Maru* was torpedoed and sunk by an American submarine off Luzon in the South China Sea. All the prisoners were lost, including a large number of the men responsible for the development of the territory in the two previous decades. In the first week of July the officers and nurses of Scanlan's force were also shipped from Rabaul "in a dirty old freighter packed in a hold", related one nurse. "We were all mixed together and spent nine days sweating and starving before we reached Japan."[2]

---

[10] Soon after the Australians entered captivity the Japanese permitted them to write letters home. Several mail bags containing these letters were dropped during an early air raid on Port Moresby. On the outside of one of the bags was a message in English to Maj-Gen Morris stating that "no doubt the addressees would be glad to receive the contents of 'this bomb'." The letters enabled Morris' headquarters to compile a fairly complete roll of that part of the Rabaul garrison taken prisoner.

[1] See *Pacific Islands Year Book* (1950), pp. 30-32, for an account by Gordon Thomas of Rabaul under Japanese occupation.

[2] A brief account of the experiences of this group in Japan is given in Chapter 25.

APPENDIX 5

FUTURE EMPLOYMENT OF A.I.F.: GENERAL STURDEE'S PAPER OF 15TH FEBRUARY 1942

IN view of the present situation in the S.W. Pacific Area and of information which has just come to my knowledge, I consider that the future employment of the A.I.F. requires immediate reconsideration by War Cabinet.

2. At the present moment we are in the process of transferring 64,000 troops of Aust. Corps from the M.E. to the ABDA Area. The first flight of 17,800 is now in Bombay being restowed into smaller ships for disembarkation in N.E.I. If any change is to be made, action must be taken immediately.

3. So far in this war against Japan we have violated the principle of concentration of forces in our efforts to hold numerous small localities with totally inadequate forces which are progressively overwhelmed by vastly superior numbers. These small garrisons alone without adequate reinforcement or support never appeared to have any prospect of withstanding even a moderate scale of attack. In my opinion, the present policy of trying to hold isolated islands with inadequate resources needs review.

4. Our object at the present time should be to ensure the holding of some continental area from which we can eventually launch an offensive in the Pacific when American aid can be fully developed. This postulates the necessity for keeping open the sea and if possible the air reinforcing routes from U.S.A. This area to be held must be large enough so that, if we are pressed seriously by the Japanese, we will have room to manoeuvre our defending forces and not get them locked up in a series of small localities, e.g. islands, where the garrisons are overwhelmed piecemeal and are consequently lost as fighting resources for the duration of the war. Sacrifices of this nature can only be justified if the delay occasioned to the enemy's advance is such that the time gained enables effective measures to be organised for taking the offensive.

5. Present indications are that in the near future the only portion of N.E.I. that is likely to remain in Allied hands is Java. The Dutch Military Forces there amount to some 55,000 organised into two divs (according to information dated Nov 1941), concentrated in two groups around Batavia and Surabaya. The centre of the island is devoid of troops except a few small posts. These forces consist of a small proportion of Dutch whites, the remainder being native. They are entirely immobile in the sense that they cannot fight out of the area in which they are at present located, as they rely very largely on civil resources for their supply, transport, repair, signals, provost and other services. In fact, they should be regarded more as well equipped Home Guards than an Army capable of undertaking

active operations in the field according to the developments of the strategic situation.

6. The Dutch themselves will probably fight well, but are inexperienced and probably not highly trained. The rank and file are natives whose fighting qualities are doubtful under conditions of modern warfare. It is unlikely that they are as good as British Indians, who so far have not been very successful against the Japanese.

7. General Wavell's present plan is to distribute the A.I.F. and the accompanying British Armoured Bde as follows:—

South Sumatra: 7 Div and some Corps Troops.

Central Java: 6 Div and balance of Corps Troops. British Armoured Bde.

South Central Java: Depots and Base Units.

The prospects of 7 Div being able to reach South Sumatra in time seem doubtful even at the best estimate. If they are unable to go to Sumatra, it seems probable the whole Corps would be located in Central Java. Assuming that the move of the A.I.F. can be completed in time, the defence of the whole of Java would then depend on Aust Corps of two divisions, one British Armoured Bde and two inadequately organised and immobile Dutch divs tied by lack of maintenance services to Batavia and Surabaya respectively.

8. Java is some 600 miles long with an average width of about 100 miles. It is highly developed with internal communications (roads and railways) and possesses few of the topographical obstacles encountered in Malaya. Its natural resources are well distributed and very favourable to the Japanese forces living on the country. With the present command of the sea enjoyed by the Japanese and the local air superiority they can concentrate, landings can be effected in any portion or portions of the island they choose.

9. It is known that Japan has several divisions in reserve in addition to those that could be spared from Malaya and the Philippines. Her limitations therefore appear to be shipping, her losses of which to date are comparatively small.

The prospects of the successful defence of Java are therefore far from encouraging.

10. Even assuming the successful defence of Java, this island does not provide us with a continental base from which we could build up Allied strength to take the offensive. It would be continually subject to air bombing from adjacent N.E.I. islands in Japanese hands, and the sea approaches would be open to continuous attack from Japanese naval and air forces from near-by bases.

Valuable as the holding of Java would be to impede the Japanese advance southwards, it cannot provide a strategic base upon which Allied strength can be built up owing to its comparatively small size, the long sea route from U.S.A. and the uncertainty of keeping such route open for the enormous quantity of shipping needed to develop U.S.A. resources in manpower and fighting equipment.

An equally important factor is that, if Timor is lost, we are unable to ferry fighter and medium bomber aircraft by air to Java from their assembly bases in Australia.

11. The most suitable location for such a strategical base is Australia. It has the shortest sea route with U.S.A. of any considerable area of continuous land. Its extent is such that it cannot be completely overrun by the Japanese if we concentrate our available resources for its immediate protection whilst American strength is arriving. It has an indigenous white population which provides considerable fighting forces. It has sufficient industrial development to form a good basis for rapid expansion with American aid. Its northern shores are sufficiently close to Japanese occupied territory to make a good "jumping off" area for offensive operations, whilst its southern areas are sufficiently far from Japanese bases to ensure a reasonable degree of immunity from continuous sea and air bombardment bearing in mind the growing strength of U.S.A. Naval and Air forces.

It can therefore be accepted that Australia meets the requirements of a strategic base from which to develop our ultimate and decisive offensive.

12. The only other alternatives seem to be India and its neighbour Burma. The latter is already in the front line, more difficult of access even than Java, and possesses insufficient development to be capable of rapid expansion. It is, however, most important to keep the Burma Road open to retain China in the war. India is a long sea route from U.S.A. and approaches via the Bay of Bengal will probably be difficult of access. It is a "black" country, and the attitude of its population is likely to be uncertain if the whole of the N.E.I. falls into Japanese hands in addition to Malaya and Singapore.

Therefore, Australia provides the logical answer.

13. Our immediate problem is how best to assure the security of this country pending the arrival of sufficient American forces not only to safeguard this strategic base, but also to develop the offensive against Japan.

The A.M.F. is progressively being built up to some 300,000 but it lacks much of its essential fighting equipment and is inadequately trained at present. Having regard to the size of the continent, it is inadequate against a maximum scale of attack by Japan. The cream of its trained and experienced officers have gone abroad with the A.I.F. and large numbers of its other ranks are in the elementary stages of training. Even when fully trained, a matter of many months, its numbers are inadequate to defend the vital areas within the 12,000 miles of coastline.

14. It is therefore very evident that considerable risks are at present being taken with the security of this country, which appears to be the only practicable base from which the offensive can ultimately be launched. The return of the available A.I.F. from abroad, some 100,000 trained

and war experienced troops, complete with war equipment and trained staffs, would in my opinion more than double the present security of this country.

15. To hold Java (if this is practicable) and to lose Australia would be little solace to Australia, the British Empire or the Allied cause.

Alternatively, if Australia is held and Java lost together with over three-fifths of the Australian Corps, the Australian potential for providing its quota of military forces for the eventual offensive would be very greatly reduced.

16. In view of the foregoing, I have no alternative but strongly to recommend that the Govt give immediate consideration to:—

  (*a*) The diversion to Australia of:—
    (i) that portion of the A.I.F. now at Bombay and en route to Java;
    (ii) the British Armoured Bde in the same convoy.
  (*b*) The diversion of the remaining two flights to Australia.
  (*c*) The recall of 9 Aust Div and remaining A.I.F. in M.E. at an early date.

17. Since the above was written, a cable has been received from General Lavarack (copy attached) which endorses the basis of the views I have expressed. He refers therein to an appreciation by General Wavell. This is not so far available to me.

(Sgd) V. A. H. STURDEE
Lieutenant-General
15 Feb. 42.   Chief of the General Staff.

Addendum by Chief of the General Staff:

General Wavell's appreciation just received, which only confirms the views submitted. (Intl'd) V.A.H.S.

APPENDIX 6

CENTRAL ARMY RECORDS OFFICE AND THE PRISONERS OF THE JAPANESE

DURING the war it was not advisable for the relatives of prisoners of the Japanese to be told all about the efforts of the Central Army Records Office to collect information about the prisoners. The following extracts from a History of Central Army Records Office during the War of 1939-45 written by Captain L. I. Parker set out the problems which confronted that office as a result of Japanese policies concerning prisoners, and its efforts to solve them.

The Japanese Government steadfastly refused to comply with the terms of the International Convention. Therefore, nothing was known as to the fate or whereabouts of members of the A.I.F. until letters from our men were received in Australia. By arrangement with the Chief Censor, all these letters, of which there were some thousands, were examined for evidence of the whereabouts of the writer and other casualty information. The casualty category of the writer was changed from "Missing" to "Prisoner of War", and that of any personnel mentioned in the letters who could be identified from "Missing" to "Missing believed Prisoner of War" or "Missing believed Deceased" according to the evidence recorded.

The actual place of internment of any individual soldier was still uncertain, and reports reached A.H.Q. that there was evidence the Japanese were moving prisoners of war, but the extent of these movements and who had been moved was not known.

Numerous requests were received by the Echelon organisation for information relating to personnel who were in Malaya, on the island of Ambon, in Rabaul and other occupied Japanese territory, and there were many very bitter complaints of the inability of the Army to supply information relating to such personnel. The plain fact was that the Army had no authentic information regarding thousands of personnel missing in operations or believed to be taken prisoners in operations against the Japanese, and all efforts to obtain information through the appropriate channel of communication proved resultless.

Later on the Japanese did report the removal of some officers from Rabaul to Japan, and reported from time to time the death of personnel, but the general position remained obscure until the recovery of prisoners of war at the cessation of hostilities.

Early in March 1943, the Japanese apparently considered that the anxiety of the Australian Government for news of prisoners of war had potential propaganda possibilities and commenced a series of cunningly conceived radio broadcasts. The names of several prisoners of war would be given in these broadcasts with messages for next of kin, relatives or friends, which included statements extolling the virtues of the Japanese.

Copies of all such broadcasts, which were recorded by the Broadcasting Receiving Stations, Short Wave Division of the Department of Information, were forwarded to 2nd Echelon A.H.Q.

Serious consideration of these broadcasts was given by the Prime Minister, the Minister for Information, and Officers of the Department of Information and Publicity Censorship, regarding the policy to be adopted, and it was suggested to the Minister for the Army that in conveying the information to next of kin it should be pointed out that, as the messages came from enemy sources, they should be accepted with the reservation that part or parts of them may not be authentic. This policy was adopted by 2nd Echelon A.H.Q. [the base records organisation] when despatching copies of messages to next of kin.

A number of letters broadcast by the Japanese in November 1943 contained internal evidence that they were written about a year before the date of their broadcast. It was difficult to understand why these messages should have been held so long. The delay was a pungent commentary on the repeated claim of the Japanese-controlled broadcasting station at Batavia that it was conducting its message service by radio in order to overcome the inevitable delay in sending letters through regular Red Cross channels.

During the period of the broadcasts the Batavia Radio maintained a continual emphasis on the fighting qualities of the Japanese forces, and nearly every letter broadcast from a prisoner of war contained a tribute to the fighting spirit of the Japanese. The Batavia Radio also broadcast an offer to cooperate in a two-way exchange of radio greetings.

To assist Records Offices in answering the very considerable number of enquiries from next of kin, etc., concerning the well-being of Australian prisoners of war, a situation which necessarily called for the exercise of considerable tact and courtesy, they were provided with Intelligence information such as the following, the source of the information, of course, not being made known to the enquirer:—

"Two of the chief objectives which Japanese propagandists hope to achieve through their prisoner of war propaganda are—(a) to aggravate war weariness in Allied countries and so pave the way for a negotiated peace; and (b) to deter the Allies from bombing Tokyo and other cities in Japan.

"To obtain the first of these objectives the Japanese use broadcasts by Allied Prisoners of War (and/or their impersonators) over enemy stations to paint the Japanese as chivalrous and peace loving people who hate war as much as you and are kind and generous to prisoners of war; describe the Japanese and their national aims as misunderstood, and stress the desire of prisoners of war to be home with their loved ones and the mental anguish which their imprisonment entails not only for themselves but for their wives, children and mothers at home as well.

"Wireless programmes introducing these broadcasts frequently contain dramatic scenes in which Allied soldiers are portrayed on the verge of madness in the jungle, the death of the P.W. through illness and wounds despite the efforts of the Japanese to save them, sob stories of the horrors of war and appropriate incidental music."

As it was apparent that the Japanese Government had no intention of establishing satisfactory channels of communication with prisoners of war, in August 1944 authority was given for the institution of a two-way short wave message service in respect of prisoners of war in the Far East.

The scheme was administered by the Australian Prisoners of War Relatives' Association in conjunction with the Australian Broadcasting Commission. All messages were lodged with the P.W. Relatives' Association. The messages were then forwarded to the Prisoners of War Information Bureau, which in turn passed them to 2nd Echelon A.H.Q. for the checking of next of kin, who were the only persons eligible to send a message. After the check the P.W.I.B. prepared the message for the censorship authorities and the short wave division of the A.B.C.

Individual messages consisted of 25 words excluding address and were broadcast daily for one hour, messages being restricted to one from each next of kin.

Replies to outward messages were broadcast from Japanese controlled radio stations at Singapore and Batavia, but there was no evidence that other Japanese broadcasting stations were monitoring outward messages or whether messages reached Australian prisoners of war other than those held in Singapore and Java.

This service was discontinued on 28th August 1945.

A telegraph message service between prisoners of war and civilian internees in Japanese hands and their relatives in Australia was inaugurated on 15th January 1945. This service was introduced by the Australian Red Cross Society, and under arrangements made by the Department of External Affairs and the Postmaster General's Department each next of kin or authorised sender could send one telegram per year. Each telegram was restricted to a maximum of ten words, excluding address and signature, and the charges for the service, both as regards outward messages to Japan and replies, were borne by the Australian Red Cross Society. . . .

For the purpose of assisting recovery teams in their search, lexicographical rolls of A.M.F. prisoners of war and missing in campaigns against the Japanese were made up to the 30th June 1944 as follows:—

(i) By theatre of operations in which personnel were serving—100 copies.
(ii) By units—200 copies.
(iii) Prisoner of war locations as recorded at date of compilation of roll—200 copies.

Copies of these rolls were distributed among the members of the reception groups and 2nd Echelon components in Australia, Directorates of Prisoners of War and Internees, Prisoner of War Information Bureau and the Australian Red Cross Society.

Interrogation Statement forms (AAF A.119) were printed and copies forwarded to the interrogation officers and, in addition, copies of photographs of missing and prisoners of war.

In making the preparations as detailed above it was fully realised that the tracing of missing and prisoners of war personnel in all theatres of war in which operations were conducted against the Japanese presented special problems, in view of the numbers and various forces involved, and the fact that little and in some cases no information had been received from the Japanese regarding Allied personnel in those theatres.

It was planned, in fairness to anxious next of kin of those who would not be recovered, that the interrogation of recovered prisoners of war should be made in the prisoner of war recovery camps prior to embarkation for Australia, and that the first information sought would be regarding deaths and the whereabouts of unrecovered personnel.

While an immense amount of information was obtained in the recovery camps and transmitted to Australia, so rapid was the recovery and movement to Australia of recovered prisoners of war by transport vessels and aircraft that a good deal of interrogation had to be completed after the arrival of personnel in Australia, in particular of those who had been flown out of campaign areas by aircraft.

To facilitate the speedy and efficient control of all casualty information obtained, Army forms B.199(a) and B.103 of all prisoners of war and missing were concentrated at 2nd Echelon A.H.Q. and a casualty index sheet opened for each recovered person, on which all particulars of recovery and events subsequent to recovery were recorded.

During the period early September to middle November 1945, 2nd Echelon A.H.Q. received, verified, collated and transmitted to next of kin or to the appropriate authority information concerning the recovery or death of over 20,000 Australians and 30,000 Allied personnel.

To cope with this immense amount of work, the staff of the casualty section was augmented by officers and staff from other sections of 2nd Echelon. This work was carried on 24 hours daily by 3 shifts each of 8 hours' duration until the end of November, by which time all next of kin and appropriate Allied authorities had been notified, and the information recorded.

APPENDIX 7*

BOOKS BY AUSTRALIAN PRISONERS OF THE JAPANESE

Aitken, E. F. *The Story of the 2/2nd Australian Pioneer Battalion.* Melbourne, 2/2nd Pioneer Battalion Association, 1953.
Bancroft, A., & Roberts, R. G. *The Mikado's Guests.* Melbourne, Paterson Printing Press, N.D.
Braddon, R. *The Piddingtons.* London, Werner Laurie, 1950.
Braddon, R. *The Naked Island.* London, Werner Laurie, 1952.
Bulcock, R. *Of Death But Once.* Melbourne, F. W. Cheshire, 1947.
Forbes, G. K., Clayton, H. S., Johnston, D. S., & Britz, J. H. *Borneo Burlesque.* Sydney, produced by H. S. Clayton, 1947. Limited edition.
Foster, F. *Comrades in Bondage.* London, Skeffington & Son, N.D.
Greener, L. *No Time to Look Back.* London, Victor Gollancz, 1951.
Jacobs, J. W., & Bridgland, R. J. (editors). *Through: The Story of the Signals 8 Australian Division and Signals A.I.F. Malaya.* Sydney, 8 Division Signals Association, 1950.
Jeffrey, Betty. *White Coolies.* Sydney, Angus & Robertson, 1954.
Kent Hughes, W. S. *Slaves of the Samurai.* Melbourne, Oxford University Press, 1946.
McCabe, G. *Pacific Sunset.* Hobart; Oldham, Beddome & Meredith, N.D.
Penfold, A. W., Bayliss, W. C., & Crispin, K. E. *Galleghan's Greyhounds: The Story of the 2/30th Australian Infantry Battalion.* Sydney, 2/30th Battalion Association, 1949.
Rivett, R. *Behind Bamboo.* Sydney, Angus & Robertson, 1946.
Simons, Jessie Elizabeth. *While History Passed.* Melbourne, William Heinemann, 1954.
Summons, W. I. *Twice Their Prisoner.* Melbourne, Oxford University Press, 1946.
Whitecross, R. H. *Slaves of the Son of Heaven.* Sydney, Dymock's Book Arcade, 1951.
Ziegler, O. L. (editor). *Men May Smoke.* Sydney, 2/18th Battalion Association, 1948.

* Only books describing the life of prisoners of war are included.

APPENDIX 8

ABBREVIATIONS

A—*Assistant*
AA—*Anti-aircraft*
AA&QMG—*Assistant Adjutant and Quartermaster-General*
AAMC—*Australian Army Medical Corps*
AASC—*Australian Army Service Corps*
ABDA—*American, British, Dutch, Australian*
ACH—*Area Combined Headquarters*
Adm—*Admiral*
Admin—*Administrative*
ADMS—*Assistant Director Medical Services*
Adv—*Advanced*
AEME—*Australian Electrical Mechanical Engineers*
AFA—*Australian Field Artillery*
AFC—*Australian Flying Corps, Air Force Cross*
AG—*Adjutant-General*
AGH—*Australian General Hospital*
AHQ—*Army Headquarters*
AIF—*Australian Imperial Force*
Amb—*Ambulance*
AMF—*Australian Military Forces*
AMLO—*Australian Military Liaison Officer*
AN&MEF—*Australian Naval and Military Expeditionary Force*
Angau—*Australian New Guinea Administrative Unit*
AOC—*Air Officer Commanding*
Armd—*Armoured*
Arty—*Artillery*
ATIS—*Allied Translator and Interpreter Section*
A-Tk—*Anti-tank*

Bde—*Brigade*
BEF—*British Expeditionary Force*
BGGS—*Brigadier-General, General Staff*
BGS—*Brigadier, General Staff*
BHQ—*Battalion headquarters*
BM—*Brigade Major*
Bn—*Battalion*
Brig—*Brigadier*
Bty—*Battery*

Capt—*Captain*
CASC—*Commander Army Service Corps*
Cav—*Cavalry*
CCS—*Casualty Clearing Station*

CDH—*Combined Defence Headquarters*
Cdo—*Commando*
CE—*Chief Engineer*
CGS—*Chief of the General Staff*
CIGS—*Chief of the Imperial General Staff*
C-in-C—*Commander-in-Chief*
CO—*Commanding Officer*
Col—*Colonel*
Comd—*Command, Commander, Commanded*
Comdt—*Commandant*
Coy—*Company*
Cpl—*Corporal*
CRA—*Commander, Royal Artillery (of a Division)*
CRE—*Commander, Royal Engineers (of a Division)*

D—*Deputy, Director, Directorate*
DAAG—*Deputy Assistant Adjutant-General*
DADOS—*Deputy Assistant Director Ordnance Services*
DAPM—*Deputy Assistant Provost Marshal*
Div—*Division*
DJAG—*Deputy Judge Advocate-General*
DMI—*Director of Military Intelligence*
F—*Fighter (of aircraft)*
FB—*Flying-boat*
Fd—*Field*
FELO—*Far Eastern Liaison Office*
FMSVF—*Federated Malay States Volunteer Forces*

Gen—*General*
GHQ—*General Headquarters*
GOC—*General Officer Commanding*
GR—*General Reconnaissance (of aircraft)*
GSO1—*General Staff Officer, Grade 1*

HQ—*Headquarters*
Hvy—*Heavy*
Hyg—*Hygiene*

IJA—*Imperial Japanese Army*
Ind—*Indian*
Indep—*Independent*
Inf—*Infantry*
Int—*Intelligence*

LAD—*Light Aid Detachment*
LH—*Light Horse*
LHQ—*Land Headquarters*
LO—*Liaison Officer*
L of C—*Lines of Communication*
Lt—*Lieutenant*

MAC—*Motor Ambulance Convoy*
Maj—*Major*
MD—*Military District*
ME—*Middle East*
MG—*Machine-Gun*
MT—*Motor Transport*
Mtd—*Mounted*

NCO—*Non-Commissioned Officer*
NEI—*Netherlands East Indies*
NF—*Night fighter (of aircraft)*
NGAU—*New Guinea Administrative Unit*
NGF—*New Guinea Force*
NGVR—*New Guinea Volunteer Rifles*
NT—*Northern Territory*

OC—*Officer Commanding*
OR—*Other Rank*
Ord—*Ordnance*

Pk—*Park*
Pnr—*Pioneer*
POW, PW—*Prisoner of War*
Pte—*Private*

R—*Royal, Reserve*
RAAF—*Royal Australian Air Force*
RAE—*Royal Australian Engineers*
RAF—*Royal Air Force*
RAP—*Regimental Aid Post*
RAN—*Royal Australian Navy*
Regt—*Regiment*
Res—*Reserve*
RFA—*Royal Field Artillery*
RMO—*Regimental Medical Officer*
RN—*Royal Navy*

SAA—*Small Arms Ammunition*
SD—*Staff Duties*
SEATIC—*South-East Asia Translator and Interpreter Centre*
Sgt—*Sergeant*
Sig—*Signals, Signalman*
Spr—*Sapper*
Sqn—*Squadron*

TB—*Torpedo-bomber (of aircraft)*
Tpt—*Transport*

INDEX

AA News Bulletin, 397n
ABBOTTS, Sgt F., 219
ABBREVIATIONS, 684-5
ABDA COMMAND (Sketch p. 200), 201, 266, 279, 305, 341, 452, 455, 457, 462, 675; creation of, 183-4, 200-1; Supreme Commander appointed, 201-2, his directive, 646-9; organisation of, 205-6; Australian representation on, 255-6, 260; Darwin included in, 259; reinforcement of, 272, 451n; Allied strength, 442; dissolution, 456, 458, 461
ABE, Lt, 579
ABERDEEN ISLAND (Map p. 171), 173
ABYSSINIA, 19, 33, 79, 255
ADAM PARK (Sketch p. 374), 369
ADAM ROAD (Sketch p. 360), 360-1
ADB-1 PLAN, 81
ADEN, 463
ADJICK, 539
ADLER BAY (Sketch p. 654), 661-2, 663-5
ADMIRALTY ISLANDS (Map p. 393), 396
AFGHANISTAN, 31, 103
AILEU (Sketch p. 478), 479
AIRCRAFT: Allied, number required for defence of Malaya, 18, 41; role in Malaya, 20, 47, 100; British production and distribution, 21, 43, 103; Far East requirements, 44-6, 51, 146, 286; strength in Malaya, 49-50, 77, 90, 121n, 163, losses, 141, reinforce Malaya, 169, 182, 203; strength in Philippines, 89, losses, 129; strength in Burma, 108; losses at Pearl Harbour, 127; strength and reinforcement of America, 445, 458, 473-4, 677. Japanese, Intelligence estimates of, 58, 83, 137; strength available, 82, 115; strength in Pearl Harbour attack, 132; strength in Malaya, 134, 141; in Darwin raid, 493. *Types: Albacore*, 244n, 266; *Auster*, 604; *Beaufort*, 45; *Blenheim*, 15, 49, 50, 108, 121n, 180, 442; *Boston*, 673n; *Brewster Buffalo*, 58, 83, 108, 121n, 141n, 143, 144, 168, 244n, 289, 423; *Catalina*, 121n, 123, 125, 135, 399, 426; *Dakota*, 637; *DH-86*, 673n; *Flying Fortress*, 89, 128, 177, 444, 507; *Glenn Martin*, 141n, 223; *Hudson*, 15, 44n, 49, 50, 121n, 122, 123, 124, 125, 137, 138, 169, 266, 398, 399, 418, 419, 422, 423, 426, 427, 468, 473; *Hurricane*, 169, 184, 221, 257, 289, 317, 365, 442, 499; *Liberator*, 606, 642; *Mitchell*, 673; *Spartan Moth*, 673n; *Super Fortress*, 626; *Tomahawk*, 108, 423; *Vildebeeste*, 49, 108, 121n, 122, 123, 125, 266; *Walrus*, 107; *Wirraway*, 15, 44n, 49, 398, 399, 423; *Zero*, 129, 137, 399, 670
AIRFIELDS, 108, 163, 168, 291, 299, 396, 446, 447, 496-7; Allied development of, 45, 48; effect army dispositions in Malaya, 107, 149, 193, 257, 342; constructed by prisoners of war in Burma and Borneo, 541-4, 593
AIRKOM (Sketch p. 468), 488
AIR RAID PRECAUTIONS, 126, 152, 287
AIR RAIDS: Allied, on Singapore Island, 531, 532; on Thanbyuzayat, 554; on Sandakan, 600; on Ambon, 606-7; on Japan, 621-2, 624-5, 626, 629; Japanese, on Singapore, 126, 152, 287, 370-1, 372; on Penang Is, 156; on Manila, 177; on Rabaul, 398-400; on Kavieng, 412; on Ambon, 426-7; on Rangoon, 463; on Darwin, 475, 493; efficacy against ground forces, 263n
AITKEN, Maj E. F., 501n, 505n, 546n, 683
AITKEN, Capt W., 434, 609-10
AKANOBE, 622
AKEROYD, Ma J. F., 621 660 f.n.
"ALBATROSS"; *see* PIESSE, Maj E. L
ALBATROSS CHANNEL (Sketch p. 413), 412, 415
ALBURY, 31
ALEPAUK (Sketch p. 550), 546-7, 549, 555, 558
ALEXANDER, Field Marshal Rt Hon Earl, 461, 464, 507
ALEXANDRA BARRACKS (Sketch p. 374), 369; massacre at, 374
ALEXANDRA ROAD (Sketch p. 360), 370, 373
ALEXANDRA SWITCHLINE, 370
ALEXANDRIA, 24, 253, 371
ALFORD, Pte F. J., 480

ALICE SPRINGS, 59, 69
ALLEN, Maj-Gen A. S., 35, 443n 444n, 457, 500
ALLEN, Lt R. W., 504, 505-6
ALLIED GEOGRAPHICAL SECTION, 471n
ALOR STAR (Maps pp. 139, 158), 133, 149-50, 157
ALOR STAR AIRFIELD, 121n, 125, 140, 142-3, 365
AMAABI RIVER (Sketch p. 468), 486
AMAHAI (Sketch p. 439), 439
AMAHUSU (Sketch p. 421), 425, 429n, 430, 431-2, 434, 435
AMA KENG (Map p. 286; Sketch p. 310), 291, 299, 309, 313-15, 316, 317n, 318-20, 322
AMBON (Ske.ch p. 421), 420, 422, 425, 428-9 430, 437
AMBON, BAY OF (Sketch p. 421), 420, 429, 435; mining of, 422, 430, 436
AMBONESE, THE 428-9, 430-1, 607
AMBON ISLAND (Map p. 393; Sketch p. 421), 184, 206, 256n, 260, 271, 284, 392, 441, 442, 451n, 466, 473, 490, 493, 494, 539; Australian reinforcement of, 59, 69, 76, 83, 130, 418, 419-20 422-4; Japanese plans, 111, 179, 418; Allied reasons for defence of, 272; criticism of employment of Gull Force on, 419n, air raids on, 423, 426; invasion of, 427-38; escapes from 433, 438-40; prisoners of war in, 511, 593 604-8, 633, 679, deaths, 608, 642, release and repatriation, 634, 639
AMBUSHES, at Gemencheh, 212-16; at Nithsdale, 266-9; in Timor, 478-9, 480
AMENITIES, in Malaya 72
America; see Wakefield
AMERICA, UNITED STATES OF, 5, 14, 16, 40-1, 58, 59, 73, 74, 79, 111 122, 127, 163, 169, 176, 184, 190, 191n, 253, 287, 371, 442, 449, 507, 631, 632-3, 642, 675 676-7; nava¹ strength fixed at Washington Conference 1: acquires Hawaii and Philippines, 4; and Japan, 10-12, 17-18, 26, 38, 50, 93, 108-9, 132, imposes economic sanctions, 22, freezes Japanese assets, 87, 90, declares war, 130-1; collaboration with Great Britain, 12, 13, 25, 37, 39, 52-3, 54, 55, 76, 80, 91, 202, 383; accelerates defence program, 22-3, 38; leases bases in British West Indies, 39; passes Lend-Lease Act, 55; cracks Japanese diplomatic code. 56, 90-1, 95, 109; Japanese plan surprise attack, 75, 110, 131; strategy in Far East, 80-1; diverts aid to Russia, 91; and defence of Philippines, 89, 94, 391; effect of Pearl Harbour attack, 135-6; Curtin's appeal, 182-3; signs Atlantic Charter, 200n; and creation of ABDA Command, 201, 646-9; plans development of Australia as base, 441, 445, 450, 451n
AMERICAN AIR FORCES, 205, 272, 422, 426 440 458n, 474. 531 677; strength in Philippines, 89n, 177, losses, 129; losses at Pearl Harbour, 127; strength in Java, 458, 495
—AMERICAN VOLUNTEER GROUP, in Burma, 108
AMERICAN ARMY, 53 55, 90n, 206, 507; MacArthur appointed commander in Far East 88; in Philippines, 89, 205, 389-91; reinforces Australia, 256n, 446n; strength in Java, 458
—DIVISIONS: *41 Inf*, 446n, 451; *93 Inf*, 639; *Philippine*, 177
—ARTILLERY: *131 Fd Regt*, 495, 497, 501, 534, 536, 538; *49 Arty Bn*, 474
—CAVALRY: *26 Regt*, 89n
—INFANTRY: *31 Regt*, 89n
AMERICAN GOVERNMENT, 54, 93, 256, 451
—CHIEFS OF STAFF, 76, 81, 89, 183-4, 202, 648-9
—CONGRESS, 22, 91, 131, 136
—HOUSE COMMITTEE ON FOREIGN AFFAIRS, 55
—JOINT PLANNING COMMITTEE, 54
—NATIONAL DEFENCE RESEARCH COUNCIL, 23n
—NAVY DEPARTMENT, 55, 90n
—STANDING LIAISON COMMITTEE, 38-9
—STATE DEPARTMENT, 18, 90n
—WAR DEPARTMENT, 55, 446n, 633
AMERICAN NAVY, 24, 25, 27, 44, 75, 90n, 114, 396 423n, 440, 446, 507, 677; strength fixed at Washington Conference, 1; role in event of war, 12, 53-4, 80; and Singapore base, 17-18, 38-9, 54, 122; expansion of, 22-3; Japanese surprise attack, 55, 108; Japanese estimate of, 80; strength at Manila,

AMERICAN NAVY—*continued*
  90, 177; strength in Pacific after Pearl Harbour, 127, 145, 253; allotted to Anzac Area, 201; strength in ABDA Area, 205, 495; at Balikpapan, 416-17; off Bali, 456
  —FLEETS: *Asiatic*, 53, 80-1, 90, 122, 177; *Atlantic*, 80; *Carrier*, 440-1; *Pacific*, 80-1. 126-7, 131-2, 440
  —MARINE CORPS, 23n, 128, 441; *4th Regt*, 89n; *6th Defence Bn*, 128
  —SUBMARINES, 442, 615
AMERICANS, THE, 341-2, 521-2, 587; united by Pearl Harbour attack, 136n
AMMUNITION: *anti-aircraft*, at Rabaul, 402; *anti-tank*, at Rabaul, 402n; *field*, 244, 326, 341; expenditure at Muar, 229n, 245; expenditure at Nithsdale, 268n; British expenditure on Singapore Island, 327, restrictions and shortages, 299, 300, 306, 327, 375 377; Japanese expenditure and shortages, Singapore Island, 306, 373-4, 380; *machine-gun*, 311
ANAMBAS ISLANDS (Map p. 88), 142, 207, 305
ANARKWAN (Sketch p. 550), 550, 553
ANDERSON, Lt-Col C. G. W., VC (Plate p. 270), 68, 70, 226, 228-9 231 234-5, 237-40, 242-4, 246, 248, 256, 272, 296, 298, 304, 305n, 368-9, 543, 546-7, 549, 551, 561; commands 2/19 Bn. 86; takes command at Bakri, 233, orders withdrawal, 236; orders withdrawal from Parit Sulong, 245; awarded VC, 246; General Bennett's appraisal of, 249
ANDERSON, Maj R., 233, 242
ANDERSON, Maj R. H., 213, 218-19, 262-3, 318
ANDERSON, Lt S. F., 431-2, 434
ANDERSON, Maj-Gen W. M., 76n
ANDERSSEN, Capt L. N., 354-5, 357
ANDO, Capt, 605
ANGLO-JAPANESE ALLIANCE, 13
ANG MO KIO (Map p. 344), 364, 368
ANKETELL, Lt-Col M. J., 258n, 363
ANTI-COMINTERN PACT, 4
ANZAC AREA (Sketch p. 200), creation of, 200-1; naval reinforcement of, 451n
ANZAC CLUB, 72
APARON. 589n
APARRI (Map p. 178), 177
APPEL, Lt-Col E. S., 398n, 400-1, 406-7, 409, 653-4, 655-7, 659-60
Aquitania, British transport, 60, 258n
ARAWE (Sketch, p. 658), 669
ARCHER, Lt J. C., 404
ARIMURA, Maj-Gen, 528, 530
ARITA, Hachiro, 15-16, 17
ARMSTRONG, Cpl J. H., 485
Army Quarterly, 7n, 8n
ARNEIL, Sgt S. F. 218n, 219n
ARNOLD, Lt-Col G. J., 474, 491
ARTHUR, Sig N. J., 529
ARTILLERY, 86; shortages in Indian Army, 19; strength and deficiencies in Malaya, 41. 44, 49, 77 82, 95, 102-3, Australian equipment in Malaya, 101; in Philippines, 89-90; at Hong Kong, 107, 170-2; in Burma 108; on Singapore Island, 291-2, 295-6, 297n, 299, 300, 306, 310-11. 327, 331, 375, 379n; on Ambon, 419n, 426. *Anti-aircraft*, at Singapore. 106 291, 398; in Java. 442; in Ceylon, 459. *Japanese*, 270n, 299, 303, 308; organisation and equipment of regiments, 115; strength available for attack on Singapore Island, 306, 327
ARU ISLANDS (Sketch p. 439), 439-40
ASHKANASY, Lt-Co M., 86n, 305n
ASIA, 13, 71, 94n, 451n; spread of communism in, 4; repatriation of prisoners from, 632-42
ASIANS, THE, 209, 342, 382, 507, 547n, 593, 594; in Malaya, 49 66, 157, 160, 165, 190, 287 294. 368: relations with Australians, 62, 72; behaviour under air attack, 152, 288, 372; aid escapers. 505; on Burma-Thailand railway. 587-8
Asosan Maru. Japanese transport, 125n
ASSAM. 645
ASSHETON. Lt-Col C. F., 298, 309, 312, 319, 321-2; commands 2/20 Bn, 99n
ASUN (Map p. 139), 147
ATALIKLIKUN BAY (Sketch p. 654), 656
ATAMBUA (Sketch p. 467), 467, 475, 479, 490-1, 492n
ATAPUPU (Sketch p. 467), 467, 491
ATLANTIC CHARTER, 91-2, 199-200

ATLANTIC OCEAN, 18, 19, 26, 52, 80, 92, 127, 253, 423n; convoy protection in, 53; American strategy in, 53n, 54; proposed American naval reinforcement of, 81
ATLANTIC WALL. 326n
ATOMISTICS, study initiated, 23
ATROCITIES; *see* EXECUTIONS; MASSACRES
ATSABE (Sketch p. 478), 492n
ATTLEE, Rt Hon Earl, 635
AUCHINLECK, Field Marshal Sir Claude, 46n, 103, 145, 163, 184, 255n
Aussi, pinnace, 658, 660
AUSTIN, Lt R. W. L., 244
AUSTRALIA, 3n, 7, 40n, 53, 55n, 69, 71, 73-4, 81-2, 98, 101, 102, 114n, 146n, 169, 170n, 190, 191n, 199, 214, 252, 259n, 271, 294, 357, 365, 371, 377, 380, 384, 389, 395n, 396, 410, 432, 435, 440, 457-8, 465, 473-4, 481n, 482-3, 491, 496, 503. 506-7, 521-2, 523n, 526, 547, 597, 615, 618, 631, 634, 638, 642, 661; granted mandate over New Guinea, 1; trade relations with Japan, 5-6; defence of, 8, 11, 24-5, 39, 456-7; response to European War, 13, 14; aid to Malaya, 15, 19, 20, 21, 44, 51-2, 60, 83; likelihood of Japanese invasion, 24-5, 41, 43, 56; represented at Singapore Conferences, 41, 76, 80, 163; aircraft production, 45; informed of Beat-Hitler-first policy, 53n; reduction of Japanese staffs in, 57; army strength in, 59, 258n; divided responsibilities of, 61; appoints Government Representative in Singapore, 91-2; declares war on Japan, 130; represented on Far Eastern War Council, 145; development as U.S. Pacific base, 177, 182, 183, 256n. 286. 441, 446. 449, 450, 451-2, 460, 675, 677; representation in higher direction of war, 184, 205-6, 255-6. 260; signs Atlantic Charter, 200n; and ABDA Command, 201-2, 646; agrees to reinforce Ambon and Timor, 418, 419, 466; provides weapons for N.E.I. Army, 442; return of AIF to, 444, 445-6, 447, 449, 450, 452, 459, 460, 677-8
AUSTRALIA HOUSE, 459
AUSTRALIAN AIR FORCE, 13, 43, 45, 58, 265-6, 419n, 642; reinforces Malaya, 44n, 49; plans striking force based on Darwin, 76; in Malayan campaign, 123, 223, 244n, withdrawn to N.E.I., 341; strength in ABDA area, 260, 451n, 458; at Rabaul, 397, 398, 399-400, 673; on Ambon, 423n, 426, 435, 439; in Timor, 472-3, 474, 491n
  —SQUADRONS: *No. 1*, 44n, aircraft of, 121n; at Kota Bharu, 122-3, 125. 137-8; *No. 2*, in Timor, 419, 468-9, 474; *No. 8*, 44n, 121n, 124; *No. 13*, in Ambon, 418-19, 422, 427; *No. 21*, 44n, 121n; *No. 453*, 121n, 144, 168-9
AUSTRALIAN ARMY, 76, 130n, 419. 423n, 520; challenges Singapore base theory, 7-8; studies Japanese language, 8-10; represented on ABDA Command, 256n; strength in ABDA Area, 259-60; lessons of Malaya circulated to, 381n, 443n; strength of, 445, 677; organises repatriation of prisoners of war, 633-4. *See also* AUSTRALIAN IMPERIAL FORCE
  —ARMY HEADQUARTERS, 9, 32, 57, 65, 67, 70, 85, 116, 154. 256n, 374-5, 376n, 385n, 415, 419, 472, 639, 679; administration of Gull Force, 419n, 420, 422-4, 432; *Second Echelon*, 680-2
  —ARTILLERY: *Rabaul AA Bty*, 394, 398-9, 401-2, 402-3, 653; *Praed Point Bty* (CD), 394-5, 400
  —AUSTRALIAN NEW GUINEA ADMINISTRATIVE UNIT, 661n, 672, 673
  —CAVALRY: *1st Bde*, 35
  —CENTRAL ARMY RECORDS OFFICE, 511n, 526, 679-82
  —COMMANDS AND MILITARY DISTRICTS: *Eastern Comd*, 34; *Southern Comd*, 424; *2 MD*, 9; *7 MD*, 259n, 418, 423n, 474
  —DIRECTORATE OF PRISONERS OF WAR AND INTERNEES, 681
  —DIVISIONS: *2nd*, 29, 33
  —HOME FORCES HQ, General Bennett suggested as commander, 97
  —INFANTRY: *4th Bde*, 31; *5th Bde*, 29; *8th Bde*, 28, 85; *9th Bde*, 33; *3 Bn*, 490n: *3/22 Bn*, 490n; *18 Bn*, 29; *30 Bn*, 29; *35 Bn*, 30; *56 Bn*, 29, 30; *64 Bn*, 32; *Melbourne University Regt*, 31; *New Guinea Volunteer Rifles*, 394, 402, 404, 661n, 662; *Sydney University Regt*, 29; *No. 7 Inf Trg Centre*, 84
  —MILITARY BOARD, 34, 69, 101-2, 384-5
  —NEW GUINEA AREA HQ, 397-9, 408

INDEX

AUSTRALIAN ARMY—continued
—RABAUL FORTRESS SIGNALS, 406
—VOLUNTEER DEFENCE CORPS, 34
—WAR GRAVES DIRECTORATE, 669n
AUSTRALIAN BROADCASTING COMMISSION, 681
AUSTRALIAN COMFORTS FUND, 72
AUSTRALIAN FOOD RELIEF MISSION, 28
AUSTRALIAN GOVERNMENT, 8, 39, 163, 182, 259n, 288, 303, 353, 375, 376, 385n, 633n, 646, 650, 674, 678, 679; restricts trade with Japan, 5-6; bans export of iron ore, 18n; offers brigade group for Malaya, 51-2; and Beat-Hitler-First policy, 53n, 81, 164; sends representative to Portuguese Timor, 57-8; holds forces in readiness to reinforce Timor and Ambon, 76; agrees to develop air bases for American bombers, 89; presses for reinforcement of Singapore and Far East, 92, 252-3, 286, 352; seeks representation in higher direction of war, 183-4; agrees to dispatch of I Aust Corps to Far East, 190; employment of I Aust Corps, 443, 445, 447, 449-52; defence of Portuguese Timor, 446, 469, 471; opposes diversion of AIF to Burma, 459. See also AUSTRALIA
—ADVISORY WAR COUNCIL, 57, 255, 256, 271, 272, 286, 447-9, 448-9, 464n
—ARMY, DEPT OF, 55n, 69, 101-2, 154, 167, 419n, 680
—CHIEFS OF STAFF, 20, 23, 24-5, 45, 58-9, 76, 256n, 272, 392, 396-7, 474
—CIVIL AVIATION, DEPT OF, 57
—DEFENCE COMMITTEE, 40
—EXTERNAL AFFAIRS, DEPT OF, 23, 164, 204, 288, 376, 681
—INFORMATION, DEPT OF, 73, 680
—NAVY, DEPT OF, 9
—PRIME MINISTER'S DEPT, 9, 674, 680
—POSTMASTER-GENERAL'S DEPT, 681
—WAR CABINET, 14-15, 20-1, 23, 25, 26-7, 34, 40, 45, 58, 59, 76, 81-2, 83, 93n, 101, 102n, 122, 130, 256, 286-7, 365, 385, 392, 396-7, 419, 447, 449, 474, 675
AUSTRALIAN IMPERIAL FORCE: First, 1 Div, 33; 2 Bde, 32; 3 Bde, 33; 15 Bde, 35; 5 Bn, 31; 6 Bn, 32, 33; 44 Bn, 258n. Second, 51n, 76; raising of, 13-14; employment and distribution, 20, 44-5, 59, 71, General Sturdee's paper, 675-8; strength in Australia, 83; training of, 95, 381n, 443n; attempt to concentrate in Middle East, 102; proposed reinforcement of Malaya with Middle East AIF, 154, 164, 183; recalled to Australia, 444-52, 459-60; strength in Java, 458
—CORPS: Anzac, 85; I, 28, 34, 59, 65, 85, 184, 256n, 503; concentration and employment, 25, 27; proposed reinforcement of Malaya, 163, 190, 202-3; planned employment in Java and Sumatra, 260, 272, 371n, 442-3, 506; recalled to Australia, 444-52, 459-60; in Sumatra, 454-5, in Java, 457; necessity for diversion to Burma examined, 460-5; III, training of, 381n
—DIVISIONS: Armoured, 1st. 164, 418; Infantry, distribution, 95; 6th, 13, 14, 20, 33-4, 35, 85, 258n, 459n; move to Far East approved, 190; planned employment in Java, 443n, 444, 676; return to Australia recommended, 447; destination undecided, 450, 451n; offered to augment garrison of Ceylon, 460; 7th, 13, 28, 33, 34-5, 85-6, 258n; raising of, 14; proposed dispatch to Malaya, 20, 25; sent t: Middle East, 26-7; move to Far East approved, 190; planned employment in NEI, 371, 443n, 444-5, 676; proposed employment in Burma, 447-8, 449, 450-2, 464-5; evacuates Java, 457; proposed diversion to Ceylon, 459; 8th, 35, 36, 41n, 61, 74, 83-4, 86, 93, 96n, 97, 153-4, 286, 418, 507, 567, 643; formation of, 14, 28-36; staff of, 34-5, 85-6, in Changi, 522n; training of, 31, 65-9, 70-1, 95-6, 167-8; retained in East Asia, 59; advanced party dispatched to Malaya, 60; arrives Singapore, 62; GOC's directive, 65; relations with British, 68, 72n, 73, 96-7, 165n, 336n, 523; dispersion of, 69-70, 101; role in Malaya, 72-3, 79, 97-8, 106, 198-9, 203, 241; strength in Malaya, 77, 86, 101, 102; forms administrative headquarters, 101; dispatch of detachments to Ambon and Timor approved, 130; reinforcements, 96, 184, 189, 258n, 296, 371n; functions as Westforce, 206, 209, 210-21, 222, 225-6, 228-9, 230, 233, 235, 238n,

AUSTRALIAN IMPERIAL FORCE—continued
242, 244, 249-50, 254, 257-61; splitting of in Johore, 207; first contact with Japanese in Johore, 225n; withdraws to Singapore Island, 262, 270, 273, 277, 279, 281, 282-3, 290n; reinforcement of, 258, 290; role on Singapore Island assigned, 254, strength on Singapore Island, 289, 341-2; assigned command of Western Area, 292-3, 295, frontage allotted, 296-7; functions as Western Area headquarters, 300, 301-2, 304-5, 308, 322, 326-7, 329-31, 335-6, 337-9, 346, 348, 351-2, 358, 362, Area reinforced, 317, 323, 325; allotted front in final perimeter, 336-7; issues orders for counter-attack to regain Kranji-Jurong line, 345; AIF perimeter planned, 361; stragglers in Singapore, 366; in final perimeter, 369-70, 374-5, 379; official evacuation organised, 373, 383, 387; ordered to remain at posts, 378; surrenders, 380-1, 382-3; numbers taken prisoner, 511; 9th, 35, 85, 258n, 459n, 634, 642; recall of, 445, 447, 450, 451n, 460, 678
—FORCES: Blackforce, 454, 511; formed in Java, 457, attempted extrication, 459; in Java, 495-6; operations of, 499-503, 504-6; Eastforce; see 22 Aust Bde; Gull Force, 260, 419, 473; operations of, 420-40; in captivity, 604-8, 608-11, 638-9; Robin Force, 473; Roseforce, 185-6; Sparrow Force, 260, 419, 423n, 470-1, 475, 511; strength and composition, 467-8, dispositions, 472-3; reinforcement, 474; operations of, 482-93; Westforce; see 8 Aust Div
—ARTILLERY: HQ RAA 8 Div, 62, 297n, 310-11, 364-5, 375; 2/4 A-Tk Regt, 60n; armament, 86; at Gemas, 210, 217, 220; at Bakri, 225, 227; at Batu Anam, 230; on Singapore Island, 297, 304, 337, 346; at Rabaul, 394-5, 402; on Ambon, 421n; in Timor, 468n, 486, 487-8; in captivity, 527, 544; 2/10 Fd Regt, 60n; armament, 86, 101; at Mersing, 251, 252; at Nithsdale, 267, 268n; on Singapore Island, 297-8, 300-1, 326-7, 331-2, 339, 359, 362, 364-5; in captivity, 527, 568, 593; 2/14 Fd Regt, 419, 490n; 2/15 Fd Regt, armament, 84, 86, 101; at Gemas, 210, 219; at Segamat, 211; at Muar, 222-3, 224; at Bakri, 226-7, 228-9, 233-4, 242-3, 245, losses, 249; at Ayer Hitam, 264; at Namazie Estate, 271; at Ayer Bemban, 277-8; on Singapore Island, 297, 300-1, 315, 322, 326-7, 343, 351, 359, 362; in captivity, 515n, 527, 530n, 536n; 2/1 Hvy Bty, in Timor, 468n, 483
—CAVALRY REGIMENTS: 8th, 86; 9th, 86
—CHAPLAINS DEPT, in captivity, 547, 583, 591, 598-9, 600
—ENGINEERS: RAE 8 Div, 303, 324n; 2/6 Fd Coy, 457, 495, 496n, 536, 558; 2/10 Fd Coy, 60n, 251, 297, 314, 315, 320-1, 324, 325; 2/11 Fd Coy, 421n, 427, 468n, 482, 484, 487; 2/12 Fd Coy, 84, 213, 261, 297, 332-3, 557n; 2/6 Fd Pk Coy, 84; 2/1 Fortress Engrs, 468n; 8 Div Forestry Team, 514
—INDEPENDENT COMPANIES: formation of, 83-4, 418, 643n; 1st, in New Ireland, 396, 398, 412-16; in captivity, 593; 2/2nd; in Timor, 467-8, 469-72, 475-82, 490, 491-3; 2/3rd, 397; 2/5th, 673
—INFANTRY: Brigades: 16th, 85, in Ceylon 443n, 460n; 17th, 443n, 460n; 18th, 448; 21st, 448, 463; 22nd, 101, 106n, 266, 272; formation, 28, 29-31; employment decided, 52; sails to Malaya, 60-1; arrives Singapore, 62, 77; in Malaya, 67n; training of, 68-71; in Mersing-Endau area, 98-9, 99-100, 121, 198-9, 203, 221, 222-3, 225-6, 241, 250, 251-2, designated Eastforce, 207, 241, 251, 254, 260, withdrawal to Singapore Island, 261, 269, 270, 279, 281; crosses Causeway, 283; on Singapore Island, 297, 298-9, 306, 308-17, 318-27, 328-9, 330-1, 336-7, 343, 345, 350, 358-9, 360, 361-2, 362-3, 365, 377, casualties, 345n; in captivity, 541; 23rd, 69, 83, 84, 394, 418, 467; formation of, 28-9, 31-2; removed from command 8 Div, 101; strength in NT, 419; failure to reform battalions, 490n; 24th, formation of, 28-9, 31; sent to Egypt, 35; 25th, 448; 26th, 601; 27th, 69, 85, 97, 121, 356, 364; formation of, 35-6; employment decided, 83; arrives Singapore, 84, 86; role in Johore, 98-9, 100, 154, 167, 198; training of, 101; units of, 106n; at Segamat, 210-11, 214, 221, 231; withdraws to Yong Peng, 235-6, 240, condition of, 250; at Ayer Hitam, 257, 260, 262-4; in withdrawal to Singapore Island, 270-1, 277-9, 281-2; in Causeway sector, 296-7, 298, 301, 318, 325-6, 328-33; placed under

INDEX

AUSTRALIAN IMPERIAL FORCE—*continued*
command 11 Indian Div, 338-9, 340, 342-3; ordered to recapture Bt Panjang, 354-5; sector allotted in final perimeter, 337; withdraws from Northern Area, 362; in final perimeter, 370; in captivity, 515, 572. *Battalions*, 305n; 2/1st, 85; 2/5th, 85; 2/9th, 85; 2/11th, 489n; 2/18th, 60n, 62, 106n, 185n, 347, 597n; raising of, 29-30; in Mersing-Endau area, 99, 250, 251-2; at Nithsdale, 262, 266-9; on Singapore Island, 296, 297-8, 300, 302, 306, 308n, 309, 312, 313-15, 319, 320-2, 323-4, 335-6; on Reformatory road, 337, 345, 350, 358-9, 363; 2/19th, 60n, 62-3, 68, 86, 106n, 185n, 268, 272; raising of, 29-30; in Mersing-Endau area, 99, 225n, 250; reinforces Muar sector, 226; at Bakri, 228, 229, 231-5; withdrawal from Bakri, 236-40, 241-49; on Singapore Island, 296-7, 298-9, 302, 304-5, 308-9, 315-16, 319, 321, 324, 335, 347, 369; 2/20th, 60n, 106n, 185n, 304, 347, 358, 360, 596; in Mersing-Endau area, 99, 250, 251-2, withdraws to Jemaluang, 262, 266; on Singapore Island, 297-8, 302, 305-6, 309, 311-13, 319-20, 321-2, 323-4, 335, 358; 2/21st, 467; history of, 418-19; on Ambon, 420-38; escapers, 438-40; not re-formed, 490n; in captivity, 511, 604-11, 638-9; 2/22nd, raising of 31-2; arrives Rabaul, 394; at Rabaul, 397-410; not re-formed, 490n; in captivity, 511, 593; withdraws from Rabaul, 653-74; 2/26th, 106n, 185n, 269, 354, 364; raising of, 35-6; arrives Singapore, 84; in Johore, 99, 100, 210, 264; at Namazie Estate, 270-1, 275-7; at Ayer Bemban, 277-9; withdraws to Singapore Island, 281-2; in Causeway sector, 297-8, 304, 329-30, 331-3, 339, 343, withdraws, 333, 338, 355, 356-7; at Tyersall Park, 362; in captivity, 573n; 2/27th, 85; 2/29th, 106n, 185n, 318, 328, 352, 356; raising of, 35-6; arrives Singapore, 84; role in Mersing area, 99; in Segamat area, 100, 211; reinforces Muar area, 225; at Bakri, 226, 227-9, 230, 233-5, withdraws, 236-49; on Singapore Island, 296-7, 298; reinforces 22nd Bde, 309, 317, 319; at Tengah airfield, 322-4; withdraws to Bulim line, 326; in Kranji-Jurong line, 335-7, 339, 340; role allotted for recapture of Kranji-Jurong line, 343; at Bt Panjang, 345-6; at Bt Timah, 351; on Reformatory road line, 358; in Tanglin area, 362; factor of tiredness in reinforcements, 371n; in captivity, 573n; 2/30th, 86n, 100, 106n, 185n, 249, 357, 381n; raising of, 36; arrives Singapore, 84; role in Johore, 99, 154; at Gemas, 210, 212-21, 225; withdraws to Fort Rose Estate, 230; at Yong Peng, 257-8; at Ayer Hitam, 261, 262-4; at Namazie Estate, 275-7; withdraws to Singapore Island, 279-80, 282; in Causeway sector, 297-8, 301, 318, 329-30, 331-3, 338, 342-3; at Mandai road, 354-6; under command 53rd Bde, 362; withdraws to final perimeter, 364, 368; in captivity, 573n; 2/40th, 418, 423; raising of, 32; employment decided, 419; arrives Koepang, 467-8; in Timor, 472-3, 475, 482-9, 492-3; not re-formed, 490n; in captivity, 538; "Merrett Force", formed, 324; on Reformatory road, 337, 345; in Sleepy Valley Estate, 347-8; Snake Gully Rifles, 360, 364; Special Reserve Bn, formed, 302, 304; on Singapore Island, 317, 319 322-3, 324, 325-6, 328, 335-6, 337, 340, 345, 347, 348-9, 349-50; "X" Bn, formed, 304, 337; loss of, 345, 347-8; "Y" Bn, on Reformatory road, 358, 363
—MACHINE-GUN BATTALIONS: 2/3rd, arrives Oosthaven, 454; in Java, 454, 457, 495-6, 501-2, 504; in captivity, 533, 534; 2/4th, 83, 304; employment decided, 101, 184, 189; arrives Singapore, 258; on Singapore Island, 272, 297, 298, 302-3, 311, 313-14, 317, 319, 321, 323, 335, 345, 358-9, 362, 363-4
—MEDICAL, 389, 490; *Casualty Clearing Stations*: 2/2nd, 457, 495-6, 532, 533; 2/4th, 60n, 541, 554n; 2/2nd Con Depot, 168, 370; *Dental Units*, 17th, 60n; 22nd, 468n; 23rd, 421n; *Field Ambulances*, 2/9th, 60n, 251, 297; 2/10th, 84, 297, 370, 395, 401, 663, 666, 667; 2/12th, 370, 421n, 436, 468n, 489n; *Fd Hyg Sec*, 2/5th, 60n; *General Hospitals*, 2/10th, 60n, 62, 167, 362, 370, 387; 2/13th, 362, 368, 370, 374, 386, 387; 2 Mobile Bacteriological Lab, 60n; Nursing Service, 362; massacre at Banka Island, 386-7; in captivity, 406n, 540, 612, 618, 641, 663n

AUSTRALIAN IMPERIAL FORCE—*continued*
—MISCELLANEOUS 8 DIV UNITS: *Cash Office*, 60n; *Concert Party*, 517, 526, 527, 531; *Gen Base Depot*, 99n, 101, 279n, 357, 364, 366
—ORDNANCE: *8 Div*, 302, 490; *8 Div Base Kit Store*, 514; *2/4 Fd Wksp*, 60n; *73 LAD*, 359; *75 LAD*, 468n; *104 LAD*, 421n, 425; *2/2 Ord Store*, 60n
—PIONEER BATTALIONS: 2/2nd, arrives Oosthaven, 454; in Java, 457, 495-6, 500-2, 504-6, 535, 536n; in captivity, 637; 2/3rd, 419n; 2/4th, 83, 419, 474, 490n
—POSTAL UNIT, *8 Div*, 60n
—PRISONERS OF WAR RECEPTION GROUPS: *1st*, 633n; *2nd*, 633-4, 635, 638; *3rd*, 634, 640, 641-2; *1st PW & Internee Reception Unit*, 634
—PROVOST COY: *8 Div*, 60n
—SECURITY SERVICE, 60n
—SERVICE CORPS: AASC 8 Div, 62, 302, 421n, 468n, 483n, 490, 573n, 596; 105 Gen Tpt Coy, 457, 496; *Motor Amb Convoy*, 59; 2/2nd, 60n; 2/3rd, 513n; *Res MT Coys*, 59; 2/3rd, 146, 156, 165, 283, 383, 457, 496, 548; 4 Sup Pers Sec, 60n
—SIGNALS 8 AUST DIV, 60n, 213, 242, 245, 308, 317, 329, 350, 356, 360, 364, 373, 383n, 421n, 468n, 594
AUSTRALIAN LABOUR PARTY, 5, 8
AUSTRALIAN MANDATED TERRITORIES, 398n
AUSTRALIAN NAVY, 9, 13, 122, 417, 419n, 533, 558, 672n, 673; role in event of Pacific war, 41, 43-4, 45; strength in ABDA Area, 451n, 495
—NAVY OFFICE, 398n
—AUSTRALIA STATION, 57
—NAVAL COLLEGE, 398n
—COASTWATCHERS, 398n, 656-7
AUSTRALIAN PRISONERS OF WAR INFORMATION BUREAU, 681
AUSTRALIAN PRISONERS OF WAR RELATIVES ASSOCIATION, 681
AUSTRALIAN RED CROSS SOCIETY, 680-1
AUSTRALIANS, THE, 61, 62-3, 71-2, 388, 389n, 523, 557, 566, 580, 586, 624
AVITAMINOSIS, 527-8, 537
Awagisan Maru, Japanese transport, 125n, 135, 137n
Awa Maru, Japanese transport, 616
AWUL (Sketch p. 658), 669, 672
AXIS POWERS, 17, 23, 37, 41, 52, 94, 136, 183, 199, 283
Ayato Maru, Japanese transport, 125n, 137n
AYER BEMBAN (Map p. 262; Sketch p. 278), 277-9
AYER HITAM (Map p. 262; Sketches pp. 237, 263), 64, 198, 225, 231, 241, 250, 257-8, 259-61; action at, 262-4
AYER KUNING (Sketch p. 211), 212n
AYER MOLEK (Sketch p. 384), 388
AYER RAJA ROAD (Map p. 344), 337, 358
AZIONA, Felix, 596

BAADE, Pte S. A., 506
BABAU (Sketch p. 468), 482, 487, 489; action at, 483-4, 485-6
BABINGTON, Air Marshal Sir John, 40, 77
BABO, 419n
BADANG (Sketch p. 124), 125
BAGUALA BAY (Sketch p. 421), 425
BAHAU (Sketch p. 208), 209
BAHREIN, 371
BAIKAL, LAKE (Map p. 30), 16
BAINING MOUNTAINS, 661, 664
BAKER, Mrs Gladys H., 661
BAKRI (Sketches pp. 211, 228), 222-4, 259, 272; action at, 225-30, 231-5; withdrawal from, 236-49
BALDWIN, Gnr A., 527n
BALDWIN, Maj R. R., 471, 481, 493
BALI (Map p. 393), 392, 416, 453, 475, 633; invasion of, 456
BALI HARBOUR, 673
BALIKPAPAN (Maps pp. 112, 393), 122, 259, 284, 418, 497; Japanese plans, 392; invasion of, 416-17, 490
BALING (Map p. 158), 156, 160, 162
BALL, Maj A. F., 210, 219, 586n
BALL, R. A., 9n
Ballarat, Australian corvette, 456
BALLENTINE, Brig G. C., 258, 299, 315, 323, 325-6, 340, 359, 363; commands 44 Indian Bde, 297
BAMBOO ROAD (Sketch p. 401), 407
BAMPONG (Sketches pp. 542, 563), 545, 556, 562-3, 567, 572, 574, 582

INDEX

BANCROFT, A., 615n, 683
BANDJERMASIN (Sketch p. 179), 284, 490
BANDUNG (Sketches pp. 498, 500), 206, 419, 440, 495, 497, 499, 500-503, 532-3, 539; prisoners of war at, 536
BANGALORE, 444n
BANGKOK (Map p. 30; Sketch p. 542), 64, 92, 134, 141n, 556-7, 635, 638
BANHAM, Maj C. F. W., 265
BANKA ISLAND (Sketch p. 384), 383, 385; massacre on, 386-7; prisoners of war on, 540
BANKA STRAIT (Sketch p. 384), 385
BANNO, Colonel, 573, 576
BAN SADAO (Map p. 139), 140
BANTAM BAY (Sketches pp. 498, 500), 498-9
Barham, British battleship, 253
BARNES, Pte J. H., 318
BARNES, Lt W. G., 350
BARSTOW, Maj-Gen A. E., 106n, 142, 192, 210, 223, 270, 273; commands 9 Indian Div, 77; killed, 274
BARTON, Col N. D., 420
BARTON, Sgt S. J., 242
BATA, SUNGEI (Sketch p. 148), 150
BATAAN PENINSULA (Sketches pp. 88, 390), 205, 341-2; withdrawal to, 177-9; operations on, 389-91; surrender of, 506-7
BATANG BERJUNTAI (Sketch p. 188), 193
BATAN ISLAND (Map p. 178), 177
BATAVIA (Map p. 112; Sketch p. 498), 204-5, 383, 442, 444n, 446-8, 457, 480, 495, 497-9, 502, 533, 536, 538-9, 675, 681
BATCHELOR FIELD, 177
BATEMAN, Lt P. J., 655
BATHURST, 83
BATTERY ROAD (Sketch p. 401), 395
BATU ANAM (Map p. 54; Sketches pp. 208, 211), 198-9, 206, 210-11, 223, 230
BATUANJUT (Sketch p. 421), 431
BATUANJUT, CAPE (Sketch p. 421), 425
BATU BATU (Sketch p. 595), 595
BATUGONG (Sketch p. 421), 428
BATUMERAH (Sketch p. 421), 431
BATU PAHAT (Map p. 262; Sketches pp. 99, 211), 100, 168, 198, 203, 207, 222, 224-5, 230-1, 236, 238, 241, 249-50, 254, 256-7, 258-9, 260, 264-5, 271
BATU PEKAKA (Map p. 158), 161
BATU TIGA (Sketch p. 208), 207
BAUN ROAD (Sketch p. 468), 483
BAYLISS, W. C.; see PENFOLD, A. W., BAYLISS, W. C. and CRISPIN, K. E.
BAYNES, Lt V., 381n
BAYONETS, use of, 70n, 215, 232, 239, 262, 267, 276, 278, 314, 332, 348, 349n, 350, 363-4, 477, 504
BAZAR-TETE (Sketch p. 478), 471, 479, 480-1
BAZLEY, A. W., 33n
BEACHLIGHTS, employment on Singapore Island, 301, 309, 310-11, 318, 331-2
BEADMAN, Gnr W. S. R., 530n
BEALE, Maj R. F. S., 323, 325, 335, 350, 374, 377
BEAN, C. E. W., 35
BEATTIE, Pte R. G., 218
BEAUMONT, Sgt J. R., 660
BECKWITH-SMITH, Maj-Gen M. B., 294, 512
BEIRNE, Capt B. R., 298, 356-7
BEKE TAUNG (Sketch p. 550), 546-7, 553
BELL, Spr A. J., 550
BELL, Lt L. J., 660, 673
BENA BENA (Sketch p. 658), 673
BENAIN RIVER (Sketch p. 467), 491
BENGAL, BAY OF (Sketch p. 448), 47, 371, 677; Japanese strength in, 451n, 464
BENGKALIS ISLAND (Sketch p. 384), 388
BENNETT, Lt-Gen H. Gordon (Plate p. 47), 8n, 82n, 93, 99, 106n, 145, 153, 197, 221, 228, 233-4, 241-2, 243, 245n, 246, 249, 254, 256-7, 271-2, 274, 279, 281-2, 283, 297, 298-9, 300, 304, 305n, 308-9, 323, 329, 335, 338, 346, 348, 352-3, 354n, 357-8, 359, 361, 363, 370-1, 372-3, 374, 376, 379n, 512; commands 8 Aust Div, 32-5; sets age limits for officers, 36; flies to Malaya, 60; his directive, 65, application of, 72-3, 97, 207; problems of, 65-7; endeavours to concentrate division, 69, 70, 98, 101; relations with Brigadier Taylor, 70; promotion of senior officers, 85-6; relations with General Percival, 96-8; granted right to communicate with Minister for the Army, 101-2; urges transfer of AIF division in Middle East to Malaya, 154, 182;

BENNETT, Lt-Gen H. Gordon—*continued*
on Japanese tactics, 155, 164, 168; attends Dec 1941 Singapore Conference, 163n; orders reconnaissance of Gemas-Muar line, 167, 198; reports to Sturdee, 23 Dec, 181-2; plans defence of Johore, 199; commands Westforce, 203, 206; directs defence of Muar-Segamat line, 210, 212, 214, 222, 223, 225, 226; orders withdrawal behind Sungei Segamat, 230-1; orders recapture of Bukit Pelandok, 236; resumes command of troops on Muar road, 240; issues orders for withdrawal to Singapore Island, 261-2, 270; plans escape, 273, 377, 380-1; commands Western Area, 293; propounds policy of aggressive defence, 301, 303; orders formation of Special Reserve Battalion, 302; orders reserves to 22nd Brigade sector, 317; orders counter-attack to recapture Ama Keng, 322; ordered to stabilise on Kranji-Jurong line, 325; withdraws headquarters to Holland road, 326; allotted role in defence of Singapore, 336-7; ordered to recapture Kranji-Jurong line, 339-40, 343, 345; issues orders for recapture of Bukit Timah, 350-1; plans final AIF perimeter, 361, 369; appoints Varley to command 22nd Brigade, 362; restricts Australian artillery fire, 375; issues orders for units to remain at posts, 378; compiles training manuals, 381n; escapes, 383-4; attends War Cabinet meeting, 385; Ligertwood inquiry, 650-2
BENNETT, Capt J. W., 517, 522n
BENOIT, Sig M. A. W., 245
BENTENG (Sketch p. 421), 422, 425, 434
BENTENG BATTERY, 430, 435
BENTONG (Sketch p. 208), 209
BENUT (Map p. 262), 260-1, 264-5, 273
BENUT, SUNGEI (Map p. 262), 261, 264
BERESFORD, Pte E. S., 359
BERHALA ISLAND (Sketch p. 595), 594, 596-7
BERI BERI, 540, 555, 585, 609
BERIH, SUNGEI (Map p. 286; Sketch p. 310), 297, 299, 302, 309, 315-16, 321, 326
BERLIN, 37, 38, 75, 79, 80, 90
BERNAM, SUNGEI (Sketch p. 188), 189
BERRYMAN, Lt-Gen Sir Frank, 442-3, 457, 500, 642
BESIKAMA (Sketch p. 467), 491
BEST, Lt E. W., 662, 664, 669, 671
BETONG (Maps pp. 139, 158), 146, 156
BEVERLEY, Capt F. G., 231-2, 236-7, 238, 242, 245
BHAMO (Sketch p. 461), 16
BIAS BAY (Map p. 30), 11
BICYCLE CAMP, 533, 534-6, 538-9
BIDOR (Map p. 188), 187, 189
BIG DIPPER ROAD (Sketch p. 401), 395, 402, 405
BILIN RIVER (Sketch p. 461), 461-2
BILLETT, Lt B. H., 486
BILLINGS, Cpl, 384n
BINGHAM, Cpl G. J. W., 245, 350
BINNEN BAY (Sketch p. 421), 420-1, 429, 437
BISMARCK ARCHIPELAGO (Sketch p. 413), 392
BLACK, Lt-Col C. M., 146n, 546-7, 551, 553, 554n, 558
BLACKBURN, Brig A. S., VC, 495, 499, 500-1, 502, 525, 534-5, 536n, 631n; arrives Oosthaven, 454-5; commands AIF in Java, 457, role, 496-7; surrenders, 503
BLACK SEA, 141
BLADIN, Air Vice-Marshal F. M., 80n
BLAIN, Sgt A. M., 597, 599n
BLAKANG MATI, PULAU (Map p. 286), 231, 519
BLAKE, Maj-Gen D. V. J., 206, 418
BLAMEY, Field Marshal Sir Thomas, 33, 35, 85, 95, 97, 101, 256n, 633, 638, 642; visits Malaya, 102; career compared to Wavell's, 255
BLANCHE BAY (Sketches pp. 394, 401), 392, 395, 401
BLAND, Pte J. R., 216n
BLANJA (Map p. 158), 166, 181
BLOW, Maj R., 597
BOBONARO (Sketch p. 478), 492
BOGADJIM (Sketch p. 658), 661, 673
BOGOR; see BUITENZORG
BOMBAY (Sketch p. 448), 160, 182, 190, 444-5, 448, 463, 675, 678
BOND, Lt-Gen Sir Lionel, 14, 40, 78, 107
BONEGILLA, 31, 36, 418
BONGAYA RIVER (Sketch p. 595), 603
BONIN ISLANDS (Map p. 112), 410
BONNEY, Lt L. G., 245
BOOTH, Capt E. H., 355

BOOTH, Lt L. H., 218-19, 220
BOREHAM, Capt G. J., 522n
BORNEO (Map p. 42; Sketches pp. 179, 595), 7, 48n, 51, 78, 111, 122, 454, 490, 533, 614, 634; invasion of, 110, 179-81; prisoners of war sent to, 525; deaths among, 642
BORNEO, BRITISH NORTH (Sketches pp. 88, 179, 595), 41, 47, 205, 593; British strength in, 106, 121; invasion of, 111, 134, 169, 179-81; prisoners of war in, 593-604, 633; B.N.B. Constabulary, 594, 596
BORNEO, DUTCH (Map p. 393; Sketch p. 179), 205-6, 259, 392; invasion of, 179-81
BOSLEY, Maj W. A., 529
BOSS, Capt J. A., 219
BOSTOCK, Air Vice-Marshal W. D., 41n
BOTHAM, Maj W. G., 665, 669
BOTTERILL, Pte K., 603, 604
BOUCHER, Rear-Admiral M. W. S., 53n
BOUGAINVILLE (Maps pp. 30, 393), 1n, 396
BOUMAN, Capt E. P., 429, 430-1, 435
BOWDEN, V. G., 163, 366; appointed Australian Government Representative in Singapore, 91-2; respresents Australia on Far Eastern War Council, 145; cables and reports to Australia, 164-5, 182, 288-9, 353, 365; assesses leaders in Malaya, 204-5; leaves Singapore, 376-7; death of, 385-6
BOWRING, Capt W. B., 296, 339, 345, 351-2
BOYAN, Capt R. H., 673
BOYCE, Capt C. R., 624, 640
BOYES, Lt-Col A. H., 210, 276-7, 298, 330, 337, 345, 347; commands 2/26 Bn, 35; commands "X" Bn, 304
BOYLAND, Capt G., 472, 480
BRACHER, Capt W. P., 238
BRADDELL ROAD (Sketch p. 374), 361, 369
BRADDON, Gnr Russell, 515n, 583n, 584n, 683
BRADLEY, Maj B. H. J., 347, 348
BRADLEY'S HEAD, 60
BRAITHWAITE, Bdr J. R., 604
BRAND, Capt V., 243
BRAUND, Maj F. N. B., 644
BREAVINGTON, Cpl R. E., 523
BREN CARRIERS, at Gemas, 220
BRENNAN, Dr E. T., 397n
BRENNAN, Sgt R. N., 332
BRERETON, Maj-Gen Lewis H., 129, 458n; commands Allied Air forces ABDA Command, 205
BRETT, Lt-Gen George H., 256n, 458n, 507; appointed Deputy C-in-C ABDA Command, 205
BRIDGEFORD, Lt-Gen Sir William, 443, 457
BRIDGES, in Malaya, demolition of, 212n, 213-14
BRIDGES, Maj W. F. N., 72
BRIDGES, Maj-Gen Sir W. T., 72
BRIDGLAND, Maj R. J., 522n, 683
BRINK, Col Francis G., 381n
BRISBANE, 441, 497n; diversion of *Pensacola* convoy to, 127
BRISBY, Cpl H. H., 362
BRISTOW, Capt V. G., 413, 415
BRITAIN, BATTLE OF, 136, 144, 287, 484
BRITAIN, GREAT, 4, 32, 35, 40n, 43, 45-6, 57, 63, 74-5, 85, 94-5, 111, 121, 136, 145, 146n, 147, 163, 279, 352-3, 371, 423n, 461, 503, 507, 631, 642; naval strength, 1, 12; decides to build Singapore Base, 3; trade relations with Australia, 5-6; and Japan, 6-7, 10-12, 16, 17, 26, 39, 51-2, 109, freezes Japanese assets, 87, 90; plans and policies in Far East, 7, 8-9, 13, 17-18, 80-3, 189-90; American aid to, 17, 37-8, 53, 55; proposes dispatch of AIF to Singapore, 19, 25, 83; suspends transit of war materials to China, 21-2, reopens Burma Road, 38; withdraws troops from Shanghai and Tientsin, 23; collaboration with America, 39, 55, 76, 91, 109, 449; and Burma, 50; Far East reinforcement policy, 53-4, 76, 82-3, 103, 164, 183-4, 252-3; strength compared to Japan, 59; Japan plans to attack, 110, 132; relations with Thailand, 141n; interests in Borneo, 179; machinery for handling Pacific problems, 191n; signs Atlantic Charter, 200n; and ABDA command, 201, 646-8; represented on Combined Chiefs of Staff, 202; Dominion representation in higher direction of war, 255-6; effect of fall of Singapore on, 383. See also BRITISH GOVERNMENT
BRITISH, THE, 80, 384n, 522, 524, 587; use of term, 15n; relations with Australians, 72, 420, 523, 557, 566, 580, 586, 624

BRITISH AIR FORCE, 47, 48, 52, 74, 126, 129, 141n, 205, 278n, 287, 499, 502, 532-3, 593; strength in Malaya and Far East, 13, 49-50, 58, 82-3, 163, 207, 271; estimated requirements in Malaya, 41, 164, 166n; role in Malaya, 43, 100, 107, 221, distribution, 121n; strength compared to Japan's, 59; strength in Burma, 108, reinforcement, 190; in Malayan campaign, 123, 125, 143-4, 151, 169, 180, 265-6, losses, 141-2, 266, reinforcement, 146, 169, 182-4, 190, 221, 257; strength in Java, 272, 442, 458, 495; on Singapore Island, 294, 303, 317, 352, 365, 379, withdrawn from, 281, 289, 325-6, 341, 373; in Sumatra, 365, 453, 454-5
—AIR COMMAND, FAR EAST, 121, 124-5, 137-8, 143-4, 154, 180, 265, 341
—NORGROUP, 168
—SQUADRONS: No. 21, 169; No. 27, 121n; No. 34, 121n; No. 36, 121n; No. 60, 121n; No. 62, 121n; No. 100, 121n; No. 205, 121n; No. 243, 121n
BRITISH ARMY, 32n, 52, 63, 110, 205, 255, 306, 342, 353, 453, 455, 458, 520; strength in Malaya, 13, 49, 77, 102-3, 207, 221, requirements, 41, 164, 166n, reinforcement of, 81, 190; withdrawn from Shanghai and Tientsin, 23; relations with air force in Malaya, 48, lacks air support, 352; weaknesses in Far East, 58; training of, 68, 95-6, 186, 381n; relations with AIF, 68, 72n, 73, 96-7, 165n, 336n, 420, 523; tactics in Malaya, 107; strength in Hong Kong, 107, 170, casualties, 176; strength on Singapore Island, 271, 289-90, 341, 342, evacuation of, 372-3, surrender of, 379, losses, 382, 511; strength in Java, 458, 495, 497n; strength in Burma, 462-3
—GENERAL HEADQUARTERS, FAR EAST, 47
—GENERAL HEADQUARTERS, MIDDLE EAST, 85
—BRITISH EXPEDITIONARY FORCE, 78, 166
—COMMANDS: *Aldershot Command*, 78; *British Tps in China*, 170; *Malaya Command*. 61, 69, 96, 106, 137, 154, 180, 185, 191, 193, 204, 221, 294, 307, 322n, 326, 352, 375n, 382, 520, 525; and training 63, 67, 70; employment of AIF, 65, 72-3; General Percival appointed commander, 78; lacks Indian and Australian representation, 97; endeavours to raise labour force, 107; and Operation Matador, 138-9; imposes artillery ammunition restrictions on Singapore Island, 299-300, lifts restrictions, 327; fears seaborne attack, 305; plans perimeter defence of Singapore, 337; allots vacancies for official evacuation party, 373; *Northern Command*, 458; *Southern Command*, 461
—AREA COMMANDS: *Northern Area*, 293, 295-6, 304, 327, 339, 362, 368; *Southern Area*, 293, 295-6, 353, 514n
—FORTRESS TROOPS: *Hong Kong*, 170, 174, 176; *Penang*, 156n; *Singapore*, 106, 168, 206-7, 254, 293
—DIVISIONS: *Armoured*, distribution among major theatres, 95; *Infantry*, distribution, 95; compared with Japanese divisions, 115: *6th*, 86, 459n; *18th*, 95n, 184, 202, 257, 450n, 451n, 507, 512, 514n, 572; diverted to Far East, 145; reinforces Singapore, 182, 189-90, 221, 287, 289-90, 304, role assigned, 254, 293; on Singapore Island, 294-5, 304-5, 336, 339, 341-2, 357-8, 361, 364; *44th*, 78; *70th*, 447, 459
—BRIGADES: *Armoured*, 7th, diverted to Burma, 445, 460, 462-3, 464; diversion to Australia proposed, 446, 678; proposed employment in Java, 676; *Infantry*, East Bde, at Hong Kong, 173, 175; West Bde, at Hong Kong, 173-4, 175; *53rd*, 184, 203, 221, 225-6, 231; in Malayan campaign, 257-8, 260, 273, 289, at Bt Pelandok, 235-6, 240-1, 241-2, 244, 256, at Benut, 261, 264; on Singapore Island, 357, 362, 364, 368-9, 373; *54th*, 290, 339, 353, 369; *55th*, 290, 339, 353, 369
—FORCES: *Dalforce*, 293-4, 298, 312, 377; *Eastforce*: see 22 Aust Bde; *Massy Force*, 353, 358-9, 360, 369; *Roseforce*, 163; *Tomforce*, 339, 343, 350-1, 352-3, 354n, 358-9, 369; *Westforce*; see 8 Aust Div
—ARMOUR: *3rd Hussars*, 454-5, 495, 497, 502; *7th Hussars*, 463; *100th Light Tank Sqn*, 353; *2nd Royal Tank Regt*, 463
—ARTILLERY: strength and employment on Singapore Island, 291-2, 300, 327. *Anti-aircraft*, in Java, 442, 495, 499; in Sumatra, 454-5; *6th Heavy AA Regt*, 221, 497n; *21st Light AA Regt*, 497n; *35th Light AA Regt*, 221, 497n; *48th Light AA Regt*, 497n; *77th Heavy AA Regt*, 497n; *79th Light AA Bty*, in Timor, 468n, 474, 484-5, 486. *Anti-tank*, 231; *80th A-Tk Regt*, 147; *85th A-Tk Regt*, 221,

INDEX 693

BRITISH ARMY—continued
339; 2nd A-Tk Bty, 187; 273 A-Tk Bty, 187. Coast, 293; 11th Coast Regt, 156n; Hong Kong and Singapore Fortress Arty, 156n. Field, 5th Regt, 191, 297n, 326-7, 343, 359, 362; 88th Regt, 159, 187; 135th Regt, 221; 137th Regt, 147, 194-5; 155th Regt, 146, 195; 73rd Bty, 125
—ENGINEERS, 375; *36th Fortress Coy*, 156n; *287th Field Coy*, 221
—INDEPENDENT COMPANIES, formation of, 83; *1st*, 106, 162
—INFANTRY BATTALIONS, distribution in Indian Army, 104; 2/Argyll and Sutherland Highlanders, 106n, 153, 185, 272, 359, 381n, 388n, 443n, 500; training of, 67; in Malayan campaign, 156, 161-2, 165-6, 189, 194-5, 283; on Singapore Island, 293, 324-5, 336, 339, 343, 346; 5/Bedfordshire and Hertfordshire, 358, 364, 369n, 370, 379; British Bn, formed, 188; in Malayan campaign, 189, 208, 231, 259, 265; on Singapore Island, 296, 340, 345, 348-9, 350, 359; 1/Cambridgeshire, 353; 2/Cambridgeshire, 221, 265n; in Malayan campaign, 225, 230-1, 259-60, 264; Cameronians, 463; 2/East Surrey, 49, 106n; in Malayan campaign, 147, 150, 157, 159; 2/Gordon Highlanders, 104, 106n, 261, 269, 272, 359, 361, 388; in Malayan campaign, 264, 271, 275, 277, 279; cross Causeway, 283; on Singapore Island, 352, 358, 363-4, 369-70; King's African Rifles, 79; King's Own Scottish Borderers, 388; 1/Leicester, 106n; at Jitra, 147-8, 149, 150-1; 2/Loyals, 104, 106n, 206, 211, 225, 231, 258, 261, 262-4; at Bt Pelandok, 235-6, 240-1, 244, 257; on Singapore Island, 369n, 370, 379; 1/Manchester, 104, 106n, 258n; 1/Middlesex, 172-3, 174-5; 4/Norfolk, 339, 351; 5/Norfolk, 221, 231, 259, 265n; relieve 2/19 Bn, 226; at Batu Pahat, 260-1; 6/Norfolk, 221, 238, 261, 265n; at Bt Pelandok, 225, 228, 230-1, 235-6; 18th Reconnaissance Bn, 339, 350, 351-2; 2/Royal Scots, 172-3, 175; 1/Seaforth Highlanders, 49; 1/5 Sherwood Foresters, 339, 351, 362; 4/Suffolk, 353; West African Frontier Force, 78
—MISSION 204, 51, 643-5
—ROYAL ARMY MEDICAL CORPS, 388, 389
—SEARCHLIGHT REGIMENT: *5th*, 301, 309, 310-11, 331
BRITISH EMPIRE, 5, 7, 14, 48n, 51, 54, 82, 93, 136, 201n, 253, 286, 341-2, 678
BRITISH GOVERNMENT, 14, 15, 18, 40, 45-6, 54, 58, 76, 81-2, 93, 109, 130, 182, 191n, 255, 469, 471, 475n; reaffirms policy of stationing main fleet in European waters, 6; proposes dispatch of AIF Div to Malaya, 19-20, 23, 25; requests preparation of Indian divisions for overseas service, 44; emphasises need for protection of Singapore Naval Base, 53n; proposes dispatch of I Aust Corps to Far East, 190; Far East reinforcement policy, 252-3; destination of I Aust Corps, 449, 451n, 459
—ADMIRALTY, 92, 122n, 130, 144, 452
—AIR MINISTRY, 169
—CHIEFS OF STAFF, 24, 46, 79, 141, 153n, 163-4, 166, 184, 285-6, 447, 457-8, 460, 462-3, 465, 648-9; estimate length of time Singapore required to hold out, 14; place reliance for defence of Malaya on air power, 18, 40-1, estimate requirements, 51; Far East reviews and appreciations, 19-20, 23-4, 82-3, 145-6, 169, 189-90; review situation in Middle East, 21; collaborate with American Chiefs of Staff, 52-3, 76-7; and Operation Matador, 93, 122;
—CHIEFS OF STAFF COMMITTEE, 7, 284
—COLONIAL OFFICE, 13, 48, 191n, 375
—DEFENCE COMMITTEE, 81, 451n, 169
—DOMINIONS OFFICE, 53n, 191n, 256, 450, 457
—ECONOMIC WARFARE, MINISTRY OF, 191n
—FOREIGN OFFICE, 13, 191n
—FUTURE OPERATIONAL PLANNING SECTION, 81
—HOME DEFENCE, MINISTRY OF, 13
—HOUSE OF COMMONS, 26, 75, 451n
—INDIA OFFICE, 191n
—INFORMATION, MINISTRY OF, 74, 191n
—OVERSEAS DEFENCE COMMITTEE, 13
—TREASURY, 13, 107
—WAR CABINET, 91, 136, 184, 256, 341, 447
—WAR OFFICE, 93, 96, 122, 255n, 457, 462; offers instructors for Australian Independent Coys, 83; hampers raising of labour force in Malaya, 107; warns Brooke-Popham of impending collapse of

BRITISH GOVERNMENT—continued
Washington negotiations, 121; asks for Australian reserve motor transport coys, 146n; destination of I Aust Corps, 444, 450; plans repatriation of prisoners of war, 632-3
BRITISH ISLES, 136n; probable loss envisaged by United States, 54
BRITISH NAVY, 10, 22, 25, 39, 45, 90, 114, 145, 283, 287, 371, 396, 417, 446, 497, 507, 642; strength fixed at Washington Conference, 1; stationing of fleet in Far East, 6, 15, 24, 76, 81, 82; commitments, 7; role in event of war in Far East, 8, 12, 24; and Singapore Base, 15, 18, 19-20, 24, 27, 44, 78, naval reinforcement of, 92, 103; in Mediterranean, 23-4, 51-2, 56, 83; Japanese estimate of, 80; at Hong Kong, 108, 172, 174; in Malayan campaign, 141-2, 144, 205, 294, 379, 388, 389, transfers to Java, 204, 372; reinforced in Indian Ocean, 253; strength in Java area, 271-2, 442, 495
—CHINA STATION, 74, 80, 93, 145n; merged with Eastern Fleet, 122n
—EASTERN FLEET, 122, 145n, 146
—CHINA FORCE, 495
—"Z" FORCE, 142, 143-5
—MARINES, 293, 325
—STAFF COLLEGE, 78
BRITISH OVERSEAS AIRWAYS CORPORATION, 444n
BRITZ, J. H., 683
BROADBENT, Brig J. R., 9-10, 70, 86n, 361, 373, 377, 383, 389; appointed AA and QMG 8 Div, 28
BROADCASTS, in captivity, 526, 537, 679-81
BROOKE-POPHAM, Air Chief Marshal Sir Robert (Plate p. 47), 48-9, 59, 74, 82n, 83-4, 100, 107, 108n, 121, 145-6 164, 168, 392; appointed C-in-C Far East, 46; extent of command, 46-7, 50-1; visits Australia, 58; urges reinforcement of Hong Kong, 77; optimistic of ability of Singapore to operate as fleet base, 81; and Operation Matador, 92-3, 109, 122-5; urges aircraft reinforcement of Malaya, 141; approves withdrawal from Kelantan, 153; seeks Indian Army reinforcements, 160-1; replaced, 166; assessment of, 204
BROWN, Capt, 587
BROWN, Cecil, 74n
BROWN, Lt G. V., 264
BROWN, Sgt W. E., VC, 536n
BRUCE, Rt Hon Viscount, 169, 449-50
BRUCE, Capt A. L., 130n
BRUCE, Maj-Gen J. G., 644-5
BRUNEI, STATE OF (Sketch p. 179), 48n, 179
BRUNEI BAY (Sketch p. 179), 179
BUCHANAN, Pte A. D., 434
BUCKMAN, Sgt G. I., 223
BUITENZORG (Sketch p. 498), 497, 499, 500-2, 504
BUJANG MELAKA (Map p. 188), 187
BUKA PASSAGE (Map p. 393), 396
BUKIT BANANG (Map p. 262), 259
BUKIT BELAH (Sketch p. 237), 225, 235
BUKIT BROWN (Sketch p. 360), 357
BUKIT LANGKAP (Sketches pp. 99, 251), 99, 153, 251
BUKIT MANDAI (Maps pp. 286, 344), 291, 330, 338, 343
BUKIT PANJANG (Maps pp. 286, 344), 291, 306, 315, 322, 328-9, 333, 338-9, 345-6, 351, 357; recapture ordered, 354-5; plan abandoned, 355-6
BUKIT PAYONG (Map p. 262; Sketch p. 237), 228, 244
BUKIT PELANDOK (Map p. 262; Sketch p. 237) 225, 230, 231, 256-7, 264; 53rd Bde at, 235-6, 240-2, 249
BUKIT TIMAH (Maps pp. 286, 344), 186, 291, 519
BUKIT TIMAH RIFLE RANGE, 351, 367
BUKIT TIMAH ROAD (Map p. 344; Sketch p. 360), 337, 346, 350-1, 352-3, 359-61, 362, 369, 379, 511
BUKIT TIMAH VILLAGE (Maps pp. 286, 344; Sketch p. 360), 291, 309, 325, 336-7, 339, 340-1, 345-6, 347-8, 349, 350-2, 354, 356, 359n, 362, 364, 366-7, 379-80, 523, 651
BUKIT TINGGI, 358
BUKUM, PULAU, 366
BULCOCK, F-Lt R. P., 683
BULIM (Map p. 286; Sketches pp. 310, 324), 303, 315, 318, 320, 322-6
BULIM LINE (Sketch p. 324), 323-4, 325-7, 335, 339
BULLDOG (Sketch p. 658), 673
BULLITT, William C., 38
BULLWINKEL, Sister Vivian, 386-7
BULOH, SUNGEI (Map p. 286), 306
BULOH KASAP (Sketch p. 211), 211, 235
BUNDY, McGeorge, 391n

INDEX

BUONA VISTA (Sketch p. 374), 361, 369
BUONA VISTA ROAD (Sketch p. 374), 361, 363, 369, 370
BURMA (Map p. 30; Sketches pp. 461, 542), 10, 16, 21, 41, 45, 47, 84, 102, 107, 134, 141*n*, 160, 169, 205, 210*n*, 259, 281, 284, 443, 450*n*, 457, 459, 562, 576, 579, 588, 589*n*, 591, 615, 643, 644; defence plans, 43-4, 50, 58, 206; reinforcement of, 79, 190, 191*n*, 285-6, 445, 460; British strength in, 108, 461; transferred to India Command, 108*n*, 146, 456, 461, included in ABDA Command, 201, 202, 646, 648; Japanese plans, 111; proposed employment of AIF in, 444, 446-7, 448-9, 450-2, 456, 460-5; and Great Britain, 449; invasion of, 461-4; British withdrawal from, 507; prisoners of war in, 541-57, 633, deaths among, 561, 642, release and repatriation, 637; *see also* BURMA-THAILAND RAILWAY
BURMA DEFENCE FORCE, 50, 79, 108
—1ST BURMA DIVISION, 461, 462, 464
—2ND BURMA BRIGADE, 461
—BURMA RIFLES, 462
BURMA ROAD, 16, 39, 50, 201, 285, 447, 449-50, 460, 643, 677; closed, 21-2; reopened, 38
BURMA-THAILAND RAILWAY (Sketches pp. 542, 550, 563), 519, 525, 589-90, 614, 619; "A" Force on, 546-57; Group 5 on, 557-61; Dunlop Force, 562-6; "D" Force, 566-71; "F" Force, 571-8; "H" Force, 581-7; employment of coolie labour, 573, 575, 580, 586, 587-8; casualties incurred, 549, 553, 554*n*, 560-1, 566-71, 581, 585-6, 588, 591, 642; news of conditions reaches Australia, 615
BURMESE, THE, 543, 550-1, 560; demand removal of British control, 50
BURNETT, Air Chief Marshal Sir Charles, 424*n*
BURNETT, Capt J., 41*n*
Burnie, Australian corvette, 455, 499
BURNS, Lt J. L., 414
BURR, Capt D. F., 472, 485-6, 487-8
BURT, Capt S. F., 236, 305*n*
BURU ISLAND (Sketch p. 439), 419*n*, 422
BUSH, Dr Vannevar, 23*n*
BUTLER, Mt (Map p. 171), 174
BUTLER, Sgt R. W., 597
BYRNE, Lt-Col L. J. A., 29, 86*n*, 614
BYRNE, Pte M. G., 504-5

CAHILL, Capt R. L., 243
CAILACO (Sketch p. 478), 492
CAIRNS, 661
CAIRO, 47, 57, 205
CALCUTTA (Sketch p. 448), 444*n*, 449-50, 464-5
CALDECOTE, Lord, 19, 20
CALDER, Maj J. E. M., 496*n*
CALIFORNIA, 170*n*, 441
CALLAGHAN, Maj-Gen C. A. (Plate p. 15), 69, 86*n*, 153, 241, 297*n*, 300, 304, 362, 382, 522, 612, 631*n*; appointed CRA 8 Div, 28; commands 8 Div, 381, 512
CALLINAN, Lt-Col B. J., 83*n*, 475-6, 477, 478-9, 492-3
CALVERT, Pte C. L., 318
CALVERT, Brig J. M., 84, 643*n*
CAMBERLEY, 78, 85
CAMBODIA, CAPE (Sketch p. 88), 123, 135
CAMERON, Lt-Col A. G., 653, 655, 659
CAMIGUIN ISLAND (Map p. 178), 177
CAMOUFLAGE, Japanese use of, 349
CAMPBELL, Capt A., 479
CAMPBELL, Maj H. A., 388
CAMPBELL, Gnr O. C., 603, 604
CAMRANH BAY (Sketch p. 88), 87, 122, 180, 453, 497
CANADA, 11, 39, 53, 183; reinforces Hong Kong, 95; signs Atlantic Charter, 200*n*
CANADIAN ARMY, reinforces Hong Kong, 107, strength at, 170
—ROYAL RIFLES OF CANADA, 95, 172-3, 175
—WINNIPEG GRENADIERS, 95, 172-4
CANBERRA, 9*n*, 32, 39, 599*n*, 674
Canberra, Australian cruiser, 61
Canopus, steam yacht, 469
CANTEENS, in captivity, Singapore, 518-19; in Sumatra, 540; in Burma, 543; on Burma-Thailand railway, 551-2, 559, 585; in Borneo, 600; on Formosa, 629
CANTON (Map p. 30; Sketch p. 644), 11, 114, 269, 643
CAPE, Col T. F., 474
CAPES, Maj G. H., 9, 10
CAROLINE ISLANDS (Map p. 30), 1
CARPENDALE, Brig W. St J, 106*n*, 146, 149, 159
CARPENTARIA, GULF OF (Sketch p. 439), 201, 439

CARR, Lt-Col H. H., 394, 397, 399, 405-6, 407-8, 660, 663-4, 672-3; commands 2/22 Bn, 31-2
CARR, Pte J. G., 621
CARR, Lt W. P., 239
CARTER, Maj W. A., 99, 312, 596
CARTY, Capt L. A., 384*n*
CASEY, Rt Hon R. G., 17-18, 25, 39-40, 182, 183*n*, 450-1, 459
CASUALTIES: in air raids, Malaya, 126, 156, 287; at Darwin, 493; *American*, at Pearl Harbour, 127; *Australian*, 489*n*; in Malaya, 220, 249, 264, 268, 278, 345*n*, totals, 382; at Rabaul, 410; at Kavieng, 416*n*; on Ambon, 436; in Timor, 488, 489; in Java, 506; in captivity, 554, 642; *British*, in *Prince of Wales* and *Repulse*, 144; at Hong Kong, 176; in Malaya, 382; *Indian*, in Malaya, 151, 155, 193; *Japanese*, 70*n*, 151, 176, 220, 249, 382, 412, 481, 489, 507
CAUCASUS, 145
CAUSEWAY (Maps pp. 286, 344; Sketch p. 328), 272-3, 279, 290-1, 293, 296, 300-1, 315, 325-6, 327-8, 335, 340, 342-3, 364; withdrawal across, 281-2; demolition of, 283; dispositions, 297-8; Japanese bombardment, 308; patrol activity, 318; withdrawal from, 329-33, 338
CAVITE (Map p. 178), 177
CELEBES (Maps pp. 30, 393), 111, 205-6, 259, 392, 420; Japanese plan invasion, 179
Celebes Maru, Japanese transport, 541
CERAM (Sketch p. 439), 420, 439, 440
CEYLON (Sketch p. 448), 47, 371, 387, 443*n*, 444*n*, 463, 633; planned British reinforcement of, 447; diversion of AIF to, 459-60
CHALLEN, Brig B. S., 231, 259, 261, 264-5, 296; commands 6/15 Indian Bde, 207
CHAMPION, Lt I. F., 672
CHAMPION DE CRESPIGNY, Maj J. C.; *see* DE CRESPIGNY, Maj J. C. CHAMPION
CHAMPLONG (Sketch p. 468), 468, 472, 475, 482-4, 486, 488-9
CHANGARAYA (Sketch p. 563), 574-6
CHANGI (Map p. 286), 96, 248*n*, 293, 352, 380, 539, 557-8, 571-2, 581, 585, 587, 593, 612-13, 624, 640; withdrawal from, 361, 364; move of prisoners to, 382-3; prisoners of war at, 511-32
CHANGI AIRFIELD, 528, 530, 532, 637
CHANGI BLACK MARKET, 518
CHANGI BROOM FACTORY, 527
CHANGI DETENTION BARRACKS, 527
CHANGI EDUCATION CENTRE, 517
CHANGI GAOL, 514, 520, 522, 526-7; concentration of prisoners in, 529-32; liberation of prisoners, 635-7
CHANGI UNIVERSITY, 516-17
CHANGI YEAST CENTRE, 528*n*
CHANGKAT JONG (Sketch p. 188), 189
CHANGLUN (Map p. 139), 140, 147
CHANGSHA (Sketch p. 644), 643-4
CHANGWA SCHOOL, 539
CHAPLAINS, Australian, in captivity, 523, 537, 547, 583, 591, 598-9, 600
CHAPLIN, Lt W. J., 425, 431
CHAPMAN, Col James A., 57; estimates Japanese intentions, 114*n*
CHAPMAN, Capt W. A. M., 431, 433, 439-40
CHEMOR (Sketch p. 188), 184
CHEN CHA TUNG (Sketch p. 617), 630
CHENDEROH LAKE (Map p. 158), 165, 166
CHIANG KAI-SHEK, Generalissimo, 21-2, 39, 94*n*, 464
CHIFLEY, Rt Hon J. B., 650
Childs, American seaplane tender, 417
CHINA, 6, 10, 14, 16, 19, 24, 26-7, 33, 50, 91, 93, 108-9, 111, 113, 115-16, 117, 132, 141, 204, 256, 283, 334, 342, 446-7, 450, 451*n*, 462, 639, 677; and Japan, 1, 2, 3, 10, 17, 18, 58, 87, Japanese strength in, 114; spread of Communism in, 4; trade with Australia, 5; supply routes to, 16, closing of, 21-2; relations with United States, 17, 38-9, 94*n*, 201*n*, 449; first Australian Minister appointed, 92; effect of fall of Hong Kong, 176; signs Atlantic Charter, 200*n*; and ABDA Directive, 202, 646, 648; Mission, 204, 643-5
CHINESE, The, 50, 165, 172, 204, 209, 248, 279*n*, 281, 285, 303, 324*n*, 341, 395, 450, 519, 594-5, 596-7, 598, 610, 658, 662; population in Malaya, 64, at Hong Kong, 170, in Timor, 466; behaviour under air attack, 288*n*, 372; in Dalforce, 293; employed on Burma-Thailand railway, 586, 587-8

CHINESE ARMY, 3, 201n; Mission 204 to, 643-5
—V Chinese Army, in Burma, 462
CHINESE HIGH SCHOOL (Sketch p. 360), 359
CHINESE MOBILISATION COUNCIL, 204
CHISHOLM, Maj J., 472, 489
CHISHOLM, Capt J. W. S., 308n, 315, 320, 358, 363
CHISMON, Sgt, 384n
CHISWELL, L-Sgt G. A., 480
CHOA CHU KANG (Map p. 286; Sketch p. 310), 315, 319, 321-2
CHOA CHU KANG ROAD (Map p. 286; Sketch p. 310), 291, 297, 299, 303, 315, 319, 321, 324-5, 327-8, 330, 335-6, 339, 356
CHOLERA, in Burma-Thailand, 547, 553, 556, 560, 569-70, 573-4, 575-6, 577, 579, 581, 584-5, 587
CHONDONG (Sketch p. 124), 142
CHRISTMAS ISLAND (Map p. 42), 106
CHRISTOFF, Sgt G. J., 249
CHUNGKAI (Sketch p. 563), 588-9, 591
CHUNGKING (Map p. 30; Sketch p. 644), 16, 51, 643-4
CHURCHILL, Rt Hon Sir Winston, 14, 46, 57, 75, 190, 191, 199, 252, 254, 256n, 292, 295, 306, 354, 371, 372n, 376, 383, 446, 648, 649; on Burma road closure, 21, 38; Far East reinforcement policy, 23-4, 26-7, 51-2, 56, 76, 81, 83, 91, 142n, 164, 253; and defence of Hong Kong, 50, 77, 107; Menzies' assessment of, 82; visits USA, 91, 136, 169; naval reinforcement of Indian Ocean, 92; learns of sinking of *Prince of Wales* and *Repulse*, 145; requests consideration of movement of I Aust Corps to Singapore, 163; on British reinforcement of Malaya, 182-3, 209-10; assigns ABDA Command to Wavell, 183-4, 201, 205; on defence of Singapore, 284-5, 341-2, reinforcement of, 286-7; destination of I Aust Corps, 447, 449-52, 460, 462, 465; proposes Wavell as C-in-C India, 458
CIANO, Count, 37
CLANCY, Sister Veronica, 387n
CLARK, Lt A., 402
CLARK, Maj J. R. P., 394
CLARKE, Brig D. W., 83n
CLARKE, Lt G. R., 218
CLARKE, Bdr H. V., 568, 626n
CLARK FIELD (Map p. 178), 129
CLARK KERR, Sir Archibald, 93
CLAYTON, H. S., 683
CLEMENS, Lt P. W., 219
CLINTON, Pte F. R., 410
CLISSOLD, Pte T. B., 666
CLOTHING, in captivity, 514, 548n, 554, 575, 577n, 604, 618, 623, 638
CLUNY ESTATE (Sketch p. 188), 194-5
COAST, Lt J., 515n, 566n
COASTWATCHERS, 398n, 656-7
COATES, Lt-Col Sir Albert, 389, 550n, 551, 555, 560, 589n
COATES, Col J. B., 325, 335, 340, 345, 348-9, 384, 388; commands 6/15 Indian Bde, 296
COCHRANE, Pte J. R., 216n
COCKLE CREEK (Sketch p. 413), 414
CODES, Japanese, broken by America, 56, 90-91, 95, 108-9, 130-1
COE, Pte J. C. G., 558
COHEN, Maj R. H., 312
COLLETT, Pte F. G., 216n
COLLINS, Vice-Admiral Sir John, 163n, 495, 497, 499
COLLINS, Dvr W. D., 666-7, 672
COLOMBA ISLAND, 523
COLOMBO (Sketch p. 448), 50, 122, 388, 447-8, 450n, 452, 457, 463, 499
COLVIN, Admiral Sir Ragnar, 15, 80n
COMBINED CHIEFS OF STAFF, 260, 457, 465; lack of Australian representation on, 184; creation of, 203; and destination of I Aust Corps, 444; recommend diversion of 7 Aust Div to Burma, 447; defence of Java, 456, 458-9; plan repatriation of prisoners of war, 632-3; issue directive to Supreme Commander ABDA Area, 646-9
COMBINED DEFENCE HEADQUARTERS, at Halong, 423; at Koepang, 472
COMMUNICATIONS, in Malaya, 64, 231n, 245
COMMUNISM, in Japan and China, 4; in Malaya, 204
COMORO RIVER (Sketch p. 478), 471
CONVOYS, Allied, 53, 60-1, 221; *Pensacola*, 127, 474, 497; air protection of, 143, 163, 168, 191, 304n; naval protection of, 204, 205; from Middle East, 443n, 444-5, 446-7, 447-8, diverted to Burma,

CONVOYS, ALLIED—*continued*
450-2, 462-3, not tactically loaded, 464; to Timor, 474. Japanese, 154, 169, 305; Malaya invasion, 122-3, 123-4, 134-5, 265-6; Borneo invasion, 180, 416-17; New Britain invasion, 400; Ambon invasion, 427; Sumatra invasion, 453-4; Bali invasion, 456; Java invasion, 497
COOK, Capt G. R., 599, 601
COOK, Pte W., 667-8, 670-1
COOMBES, J. H. H., 524n
COOPER, Lt J. H., 262, 276
COOTAMUNDRA, 30
COOTES, Lt R. J. G., 239
CORLETTE, Lt-Col E. L., 564n
CORNEY, Lt D. N., 484
CORNFORTH, Lt R. G. W., 319
CORREGIDOR (Sketch p. 390), 177, 285, 287, 390; surrenders, 507
COTTER, W. P., see KNIGHT, Pte P.
COUCH, Capt N. W., 360, 364
COUCH, Sgt R. J., 487
COUSENS, Maj C. H., 315-16, 319, 321
COX, Maj-Gen, 495
CRACKNELL, Gnr J. G., 527n
CRAIG, Lt C., 251n
CRAIGIE, Sir Robert, 4n, 17n
CRANKSHAW, Maj T. P., 587
CRAWFORD, Lt B. D. G., 232, 246
CREDNER ISLAND (Sketch p. 394), 406
CRETE, 154, 205, 257, 281, 345n, 418, 459n, 489n, 490n
CRISPIN, K. E.; see PENFOLD, A. W., BAYLISS, W. C. and CRISPIN, K. E.
CROFT, Sgt R. F. T., 247, 248
CROFT, WOI T. M., 504
CROSBY, Sir Josiah, 93, 141n
CULHANE, Rev Father, 669-70
CUMMING, Brig A. E., VC, 192, 348n
CUMMING, Bdr T. S., 544n
CUMMINGS, WO N. G., 600n
CURLEWIS, Capt A. H., 353-4, 377, 381n, 516, 573n
CURNOW, Pte M. W. V., 248n
CURRAN, Lt K. S., 477, 479
CURTIN, Rt Hon John, 57, 169, 287, 443-4, 462; challenges Singapore Base theory, 8; suggests test mobilisation of Australian forces, 57; approves dispatch of AIF to Ambon and Timor, 130; urges reinforcement of Singapore, 182, 209, 286; his "Australia looks to America" message, 183; requests Australian representation on United Command of forces resisting Japan, 184; criticises British Far East reinforcement policy, 252-3; expresses confidence in General Bennett, 385; proposes Australia as main base and return of AIF to, 446, 449, 450, judgment vindicated, 465; informed of diversion of 7 Aust Div to Rangoon, 451-2; seeks withdrawal of *Orcades* troops from Java, 456-7, 459; offers two Australian brigades to augment Ceylon garrison, 460
CUTTER, Sgt A. R. (Plate p. 495)
CYPRUS, 104n

DAIREN (Sketch p. 617), 639
DALLEY, Lt-Col J. D., 293, 377
DAMPIER STRAIT (Sketch p. 658), 657
Danae, British cruiser, 498
DANAHER, Sgt C. E., 544n
DARWIN (Map p. 30; Sketch p. 439), 41, 44, 57, 69, 101, 122, 130, 169, 184, 201, 206, 258n, 260, 371, 418-19, 423-4, 426-7, 438, 443, 466-7, 468, 474, 497, 507, 520, 638; reinforcement of, 15, 43, 59, 76, 83; development of, 45, 89; included in ABDA Command, 259; bombing of, 450, 475, 482, casualties, 493, Carrier Fleet's role in attack, 111
DAVAO (Map p. 178), 132, 177, 437
DAVAO GULF (Map p. 178), 129
DAVIDSON, Capt P. M., 606
DAVIES, Sgt J. L., 229, 242, 245
DAVIS, Gp Capt R. H., 534, 538-9
DAWKINS, Maj C. B., 85, 86n, 167, 292-3, 297n, 309, 343; appointed BM 22 Bde, 29; killed, 351
DAWSON, Lt-Col B. G., 405-6, 411, 663, 667, 673
DE ABREU FERRIERA DE CARVALHO, Manuel, 466n, 469-70, 471
DEAKIN, Brig C. C., 97n, 187, 193
DE CRESPIGNY, Maj J. C. Champion, 496
de Klerk, Japanese transport, 596
DELBRIDGE, Cpl A., 476

DELHI, 202, 205, 461, 463
DEL MONTE FIELD (Map p. 178), 177
DEMOLITIONS: in Malaya, 142-3, 147, 160, 168, 212*n*, 213, 251, 261, 281, 283, 318, 326, 332-3, 341; in Borneo, 179-80, 417; at Rabaul, 400; in Ambon, 427; in Sumatra, 455; in Timor, 477, 482
DEMPSEY, Maj J., 474*n*
DENNIS, Lt D. J. A., 415
DENNYS, Maj-Gen L. E., 50-1, 643
DEN PASAR AIRFIELD, 475
DEPRESSION, TRADE, 4, 5
DERHAM, Col A. P., 69, 86*n*; appointed ADMS 8 Div, 29
De Ruyter, Dutch cruiser, 454, 456, 497; sunk, 498
DESERTERS, from Singapore, 376, 383, 387, 388-9
DE SOUSA SANTOS, Antonio, 492-3
DETIGER, Lt-Col, 467, 469-70, 484
DEVER, Pte L. C., 218
DEVIL'S PEAK PENINSULA (Map p. 171), 173
DIARRHOEA, 515, 570, 581
DICKINSON, Gnr K. J., 550
DIGNEY, Cpl H., 440
DILI (Sketches pp. 467, 478), 57, 466-7, 469, 470-2, 475, 476-7, 478-9, 480, 482, 491, 493
DILI AIRFIELD (Sketch p. 478), 466, 481; Australians occupy, 470, 471; action at, 475-8
DILL, Field Marshal Sir John, 451*n*
DILLON, Brig F. J., 531, 576
DIPANG (Sketch p. 188), 185, 187
DIPHTHERIA, 585
DISCIPLINE: *Australian*, in Malaya, 96, 366, 377; in 2/21 Bn, 418; in captivity, 511-12, 515, 522, 531, 534, 543, 587, 605, 609, 610. *British*, 341. *Indian*, 113, 338, 535, 536-7
DIXON, Lt G. W. P., 414-15
DJAMBI (Sketch p. 384), 384*n*, 388
DJAMBI RIVER, 384*n*
DJASINGA (Sketch p. 500), 499, 500
DJAUL ISLAND (Sketch p. 413), 415
DOBBIE, Lt F. A., 321
DOBBIE, Lt-Gen Sir William, 292
DOBO (Sketch p. 439), 439, 440
DOIG, Capt C. D., 491
DOLAMORE, Capt W. H., 320-1
DOMINICAN REPUBLIC, 200*n*
DOMINIONS, THE, 82, 109, 632; limitations placed on naval strength, 1; machinery for consultation, 649
DONALDSON, Capt J. G., 406, 409-10, 655
DONOHUE, Capt K. G. C., 218
DOOLAN, Sgt A. A., 215, 216
DOORMAN, Rear-Admiral K. W. F. M., 453-4, 456, 497-8
DORMAN-SMITH, Sir Reginald, 108, 463
DOUGLAS, Lt K. C., 658
DOYLE, Mr, 414
DOYLE, L-Cpl C. E., 476-7, 478-9
DRAAK, 671
Dragon, British cruiser, 498
Dragonfly, British gunboat, 264-5
DRINA (Sketch p. 658), 671-2
DRUMMOND, Matron Irene M., 386-7
DUFF COOPER, Rt Hon Sir Alfred (later Lord Norwich), 93, 164, 288*n*, 303; appointed Minister of State in Far East, 91, 145; civil defence in Malaya, 191; on Malayan civil administration, 283; position as Resident Minister lapses, 204
DUFFY, Lt-Col D. J., 213-14, 215-16, 217*n*, 264, 275-6, 331-2
DUKE, Brig C. L. B., 235-6, 240-1, 244, 261, 264-5, 362, 368
Duke of York, British battleship, 92
DUKE OF YORK ISLANDS (Sketch p. 394), 399
DUMAS, Sgt H. S., 312
DUNCAN, Capt D. I. McI., 238
DUNCAN, Brig H. C., 226, 228-9, 231, 233, 238-9; commands 45 Indian Bde, 210
DUNCAN, Capt I. L., 628
DUNKIRK, 144, 283
DUNKLEY, Maj C. R., 471, 481*n*
DUNLOP, Col E. E., 533, 537, 562-3, 564, 566, 569, 571
DUNSTAN, Cpl L. W. H., 505
Duntroon, Australian transport, 634, 635
DURBAN, 169, 371
Durban, British cruiser, 61
DUSUNS, THE, 594

DUTCH, THE, 24-5, 38, 80, 109, 396, 420, 424*n*, 450, 457-8, 466, 472; relations with Japanese, 55, 110; Australian cooperation with, 59, 69, 76, 418; interests in Borneo, 179; aid escapers, 388, 389*n*, 439, 505; relations with British, 447, with Portuguese, 471, with Indonesians, 502
DUTCH AIR FORCE, strength in Far East compared to Japanese, 59; in Malaya, 121*n*, 123, 141*n*, 223; in Borneo, 180; sinks *Nana Maru*, 417; in Ambon, 422, 423*n*, 426; strength in ABDA area, 442, in Java, 495
DUTCH ARMY, 206, 439, 440; in Borneo, 181, 416-17; in Ambon, 421-2, 423*n*, 424, 425-6, 427-9, 430-1, 432, 434-5, 437; in Sumatra, 444, 453-4, 455; in Java, 441-3, 445, 495, 499, 500-1, 502-3, 675-6; in Timor, 467, 468*n*, 469-70, 471-3, 475-6, 478-9, 480-1, 483, 485, 490-1, 492*n*
DUTCH GOVERNMENT, 93, 469, 475*n*, 646, 649
DUTCH NAVY, 205, 416-17, 422, 423*n*, 507; submarine operations, 125, 180, 417, 442; strength in Java area, 495
DYSENTERY, 426, 469, 515, 553, 555, 570, 577, 581, 585, 587, 590, 602, 613, 617

EADIE, Col N. M., 503, 550*n*
EAST AFRICA, 68, 255, 475*n*
EAST ASIA, 3*n*, 22-3, 26, 28, 37, 41, 55, 127, 132*n*, 145, 507, 631; Japanese ambitions in, 14, 16, 37, 56, 132; British weaknesses, 17; British-American cooperation in, 38; defence plans, 40; retention of 8 Aust Div in, 59; trend towards war in, 74-5; unified Allied Command established, 201; *see also* FAR EAST
EASTERN GROUP CONFERENCE, 40
EASTERN GROUP SUPPLY COUNCIL, 40*n*
EASTWOOD, Capt, 587
EATHER, Maj-Gen K. W., 85
EATON, Lt R. W., 220, 330
ECHO, Mt (Sketch p. 374), 370
EDEN, Rt Hon Sir Anthony, 141*n*
EDGLEY, Capt J. L., 266-7, 268
EDUCATION, in captivity, 516-17, 535-6, 537
EDWARDS, Maj J. J., 496*n*
EGGLESTON, Sir Frederic, 92, 644
EGYPT, 14, 19, 21, 23-4, 27, 35, 103, 205, 448
EHEHART, Capt J. H. W., 606
EISENHOWER, Gen of Army, Dwight D., 88, 89*n*; urges development of Australia as American base, 177, 441
EKUTI RANGE, 673
ELLIMAN, Cpl S. K., 529*n*
ELLIOTT, Brig C. M. L., 85
ELRINGTON, Lt-Col M., 241, 262-3
ELTON, Lt J. R., 670
EMMAHAVEN (Sketch p. 384), 388
EMMETT, L-Bdr A. A., 544*n*
Empress of Asia, British transport, 304
Encounter, British destroyer, 455
ENDAU (Map p. 54; Sketch p. 99), 64-5, 98-9, 123, 153, 199, 207, 225, 250, 267; 22 Aust Bde takes over defences, 98; withdrawal from, 251; Japanese invasion, 265-6
ENDAU, SUNGEI (Sketch p. 251), 98, 153, 251*n*, 266
ENGGOR (Map p. 158), 166
ENGLAND; *see* BRITAIN, GREAT
ENOGGERA, 31
Enterprise, American aircraft carrier, 440-1
ENTERTAINMENT, in captivity, 515, 516-17, 531, 606, 620, 623, 627
EPSTEIN, Cdr, 558
EQUIPMENT: *Aust*, 20; *British*, in Malaya, 44, 151; *Japanese*, 116-17, 543, 565, 574-5; *Philippine Army*, 90
ERETANWETAN (Sketch p. 498), 499
ERI (Sketch p. 421), 429-30, 432, 434; dispositions at, 425; withdrawal to, 433
ERMERA (Sketch p. 478), 471, 480
ESCAPES, from Singapore, 348*n*, 376-7, 378, 642, 650-2; from Ambon, 433, 436, 438-40, 604-5; from Timor, 491; from Borneo, 596-7, 602-3, from Hainan, 610; Japanese attitude to, 528, 535, 539, 543-4, 546-7, 595
EUROPE, 6, 7, 10, 11, 13-15, 17-18, 23, 26, 37, 48*n*, 52, 54, 61, 71, 75, 78, 191*n*, 632
EUROPEANS, THE, in Malaya, 49, 64, 157, 190-1, 287, behaviour under air attack, 372; in NEI, 442
EVANS, Lt L. A. R., 622

INDEX 697

EVATT, Rt Hon Dr H. V., 204
Evertsen, Dutch destroyer, 498
EWART, Maj A. C. M., 312, 319
EWEI (Sketch p. 658), 672
EXECUTIONS, at Alexandra Barracks, 374; on Banka Island, 385-7; in Timor, 480; in captivity, 523, 543-4, 548, 550, 642; *see also* MASSACRES
Exeter, British cruiser, 454, 497-8, 618*n*

FABER, MT (Sketch p. 374), 370
FAGAN, Maj K. J., 583, 584
FAIRBAIRN, Hon J. V., 32
FAIRLEY, Maj J. G., 361, 377, 396
FAR EAST, 2*n*, 9-10, 11, 18, 24, 50, 89, 94, 166*n*, 205, 287, 353, 365; discussion of term, 3*n*; trade relations in, 5, 7; stationing of British fleet in, 6-7, naval reinforcement of, 144, 146; British plans and policies, 7-8, 13, 17, 19-20, 51, 82-3; role of American fleet in, 12, 54; Japanese ambitions, 17, 56, strength, 82, strategy, 371, German-Japanese collaboration, 75; British reinforcement policy, 46, 51-2, 54, 58, 76, 79, 80, 82, 92, 95, 145-6, 169, 189-90, demands subordinated by Beat-Hitler-First policy, 53, 103, policy criticised, 253; comparison of forces in, 59; publicity arrangements, 73-4; Allied coordination of command in, 81, 93, 183, 199-202, 256; British Resident Minister of State appointed, 91, 145; role of Hong Kong in, 170, 176; transfer of AIF to, 190, 444; British machinery for control of problems in, 191*n*; Japanese conquest of, 507-8; repatriation of prisoners, 632-44; *see also* EAST ASIA
FAR EAST COMBINED INTELLIGENCE BUREAU, 82*n*, 137*n*, 376*n*
FAR EAST COMMAND, 81, 137, 201; C-in-C appointed, 46, 166; extent of, 50, Burma transferred to India Command, 146; AOC appointed, 77; lapses, 205
FAR EASTERN COUNCIL, LONDON, 256
FAR EASTERN WAR COUNCIL, 43, 157, 164, 191; created, 145; becomes War Council, Singapore, 204
FARREL, Pte A. B., 232
FARRER ROAD (Sketch p. 360), 360-2, 369
FEIS, H., 108*n*
FELDT, Cdr E. A., 398*n*, 657, 661
FERGUSON, Capt G. B., 298*n*
FIELD, Sgt A. E., 536*n*, 636*n*
FIELD, Lt-Col Hon C. R., 662
FIELD, Maj D. F., 404, 654-5
FIFTH COLUMN, 168, 173
FIGGIS, Maj P. E., 406, 659, 664, 669*n*, 672-3
FIJI (Map p. 30), 19*n*, 441
FILIPINOS, THE, 391, 595-6
FINSCHHAFEN (Sketch p. 658), 669
FISHER, Gnr H. M. M., 223*n*
FISHER, Maj W. E., 552*n*
FISK, Lt-Col E. K., 373
FLEMING, Maj F. A., 595-6
FOGDEN, H. W. T., 72
FOLEY, Paymaster Capt J. B., 80
FOOCHOW (Map p. 112), 114
FOOD SUPPLIES, Singapore, 354, 377; Bataan, 390-1
FORBES, Lt G. K., 683
FORDE, Rt Hon F. M., 597, 599*n*, 638
Formidable, British aircraft carrier, 642
FORMOSA (Map p. 30; Sketch p. 630), 4*n*, 111, 113, 129, 132, 525, 614, 617-18; prisoners of war in, 611, 612-13, 629-30, 634
FORMOSAN GUARDS, 598
FORT CANNING (Map p. 286; Sketch p. 374), 294, 352, 354, 357, 371, 377, 380
FORT ROSE ESTATE (Sketch p. 211), 230
FORT STANLEY; *see* STANLEY, FORT
FOSTER, Victoria, 84, 418
FOSTER, F., 537*n*. 683
FOUR WAYS (Sketch p. 401), 396-7, 401, 404-5, 406-7, 408, 654
FOWLER, Cpl J. F., 479, 492*n*
FRANCE, 12, 18-19, 26, 32, 38, 51, 71, 77-8, 89, 136*n*, 166, 255*n*, 258*n*, 397, 418, 424; naval strength fixed at Washington Conference, 1; fall of, 14, 15; reaches agreement with Japan about bases in Indo-China, 87. *See also* FRENCH GOVERNMENT
FRASER, Admiral of the Fleet Lord, 642
FRASER, Capt A., 414-15
FRASER, Col W. E., 269*n*, 303-4, 325, 346, 351
FRASER'S HILL (Map p. 54), 64, 193
FRAZER, Sgt A. L., 662, 670

FREMANTLE, 60, 61, 258*n*, 389, 457, 499
FRENCH, Pte J. St G., 558
FRENCH GOVERNMENT, 55; agrees to prohibit certain supplies through Indo-China, 16; yields to Japanese demands in Indo-China, 26, 87
FRENCH NAVY, limitations placed on strength, 1; affects British strategy in Far East, 26
FRONTIERA PROVINCE (Sketch p. 478), 492
FRY, Lt-Col T. P., 651-2
FUEHRER CONFERENCES ON NAVAL AFFAIRS, 198*n*, 371*n*
FUEL, in captivity, 514, 532
Fukai Maru, Japanese transport, 612
FUKUOKA (Sketch p. 617), prisoners of war at, 626, 627-8, 640-1
FUKUSHIMA, Masao, 601*n*
FUKUYE, Maj-Gen, 522-3, 528
FUSAN (Sketch p. 617), 612
FUSES, 244*n*

GAHAN, Capt N. J., 229
GALALA, 606
GALE, Pte V. L., 523
GALLEGHAN, Brig F. G., 210, 213-14, 220, 262-3, 275-6, 277*n*, 298, 301, 329, 511, 523, 525, 528-9, 530-1; commands 2/30 Bn, 35-36; disposes 2/30 at Gemas, 212-13, orders counter-attack, 217; commands AIF Changi, 522
GALLIPOLI, 30, 32-3, 424, 495
GANNON, Sig B. I., 478
GAP, THE (Sketch p. 360), 361, 369-70
GARDENING, in captivity, 513-14, 516, 524, 607-8
GARNER, Sgt D. F., 213, 215-16
GARRARD, Lt H. G., 409
GARRETT, Brig K. A., 106*n*, 146-7, 149-50, 159
GARUA (Sketch p. 658), 660, 673
GARUT (Sketch p. 500), 532-3, 534
GAS, 276, 278*n*
GASKIN'S HOUSE, 406, 409
GASMATA (Sketch p. 658), 399, 669-70, 671
GATENBY, Lt N. R., 487
GAVEN, Capt F., 358
GAZELLE, CAPE (Sketch p. 394), 399
GAZELLE PENINSULA (Sketch p. 654), 392, 396, 661
GEIKIE, Lt N. B. C., 213, 215-16
GELDARD, Capt H. S., 382
GEMAS (Sketches pp. 211, 212), 64, 182, 210, 212, 222-3, 225, 227, 230, 235, 249; recces of, 167, 198; road-block at, 217-21
GEMAS, SUNGEI (Sketch p. 211), 217
GEMENCHEH, SUNGEI (Sketch p. 212), 217, 261; ambush at, 212-16
GENEVA, 526
GENEVA CONVENTION, 220, 503, 562-3, 622
GEORGE VI, King, 136
GEORGETOWN (Map p. 158), 156
GERMAN ARMY, 100, 205, 255, 270*n*; at Tsingtao, 113, 117
GERMAN NAVY, 19, 371, 394
GERMANS, THE, 395, 522
GERMANY, 7, 11, 14, 16, 54, 83, 135, 198, 210, 341, 442, 446, 543, 642; Pacific colonies annexed, 1, 52; relations with Japan, 3-4, 13, 17, 75, 80, 110, 136; invades Norway, 15; assembles invasion fleet, 26; signs Tripartite Pact, 37; and Russia, 46*n*, 79, 87, 91, 145; and Greece, 51; Allied decision to concentrate against, 53, 189; Japanese military mission to, 133, 270*n*; effect of Japanese successes on, 371
GESER ISLAND (Sketch p. 439), 439
GIBRALTAR, 24
GIBRALTAR HILL (Sketch p. 267), 100, 266
GIBSON, Capt J. E. M., 313
GIBSON, Pte N. R. C., 505
GIBSON, WO W., 388*n*
GILBERT ISLANDS (Map p. 30), 111
GILINGIL PLANTATION (Sketch p. 413), 416
GILL, G. Hermon, 125*n*
GILLON, Maj L. M., 597
GIN DRINKER'S BAY (Map p. 171), 129*n*
GIN DRINKER'S LINE (Map p. 171), 129 170, 172
GLADE ROAD (Sketch p. 401), 407-8, 410
GLADSTONE, Prime Minister, 92*n*
GLASGOW, Maj R. V., 613, 622*n*
GLASGOW, Maj-Gen Hon Sir William, 34
GLASSFORD, Vice-Admiral W. A., 416-17
GLASSON, Lt D. J. R., 229
GLODOK GAOL, 534, 538-9
GLOUCESTER, CAPE (Sketch p. 658), 657

GLOVER, Bdr A. W., 544*n*
GLYNN, Pte V. P., 665
Gnair, 660-1
GOBLE, Air Vice-Marshal S. J., 53*n*
GONG KEDAH AIRFIELD (Sketch p. 124), 121*n*, 125, 142
GOODE, Capt A. E., 413-14
GOOD HOPE, CAPE OF, 182
GOODMAN, Capt C. E., 665, 672
GOPENG (Sketch p. 188), 185, 187
GORDON, Capt O. L., 618*n*
GORDON, WO2 V. M. I., 213, 215
GORT, Field Marshal Viscount, VC, 46*n*, 166
GOULBURN, 31
GOVERNMENT HOUSE, Singapore (Map p. 286; Sketch p. 374), 304, 361, 373
GRANT, Lt W. G., 402-3, 404-5, 407
GREATER EAST ASIA CO-PROSPERITY SCHEME, 56
GREECE, 51-2, 54, 85, 200*n*, 255, 257, 345*n*, 418, 446, 451*n*, 452
GREEN, Lt-Col C. E., 541-2, 546-7, 549, 551, 553
GREENER, Capt H. L., 517, 521-2, 683
GREINER, Maj H. G., 564
GRENFELL, Capt Russell, 8*n*
GREW, Joseph C., 17, 55
GRIFFIN, Sgt D., 513*n*, 515*n*, 636*n*
GRIFFIN, Capt R. S., 322, 359, 545*n*, 554*n*
GRIFFIN, V. Murray, 516
GRIK (Map p. 158), 64, 156, 159, 160-2, 165-6
GRISEK (Sketch p. 211), 222
GROOM, Capt J. D'O., 488
GROVELLY, 31, 36
GROVES, Gnr A. T., 527*n*
GROWNS, Cpl F. W., 479
GRUNERT, Maj-Gen George, 89
GUADALCANAL (Map p. 30), 396
GUAM (Map p. 30), 1*n*, 127, 177, 411; Japanese plan, 111, attack on, 128, 132, 176
GUERILLA WARFARE, 84, 186, 426-7, 438; in Timor, 480-2, 492*n*; in Java, 502, 505-6; on Batu Batu, 595, 596; on Tawitawi, 597; in Borneo, 603; in China, 643-5; failure to wage in New Britain, 659
GUILD, Capt D. D., 502, 504-5
GULLETT, Hon Sir Henry, 32
GUNONG PULAI (Map p. 262), 273
GUNTERSHOHE (Sketch p. 654), 655-6
GURUN (Map p. 158), 149, 150-1, 157, withdrawal from, 159

HAAD YAI (Map p. 54), 64
HACKNEY, Lt B. C., 227, 233*n*, 239-40, 245-6, 247-8
HAGEN, Mt (Sketch p. 658), 661*n*
HAGUE CONVENTION, 520; Japanese interpretation of, 528, 546*n*, 562
HAICHO, 608
HAIG, Field Marshal Earl, 32
HAINAN ISLAND (Map p. 30; Sketch p. 88), 11, 19, 114, 134, 593*n*, 615; prisoners of war on, 608-11, 633, liberation and repatriation, 638-9
HAINAN-TO HARBOUR, 615
HAIPHONG (Map p. 30), 16
HAITI, 200*n*
HAKARTA (Sketch p. 617), 626, 641
HALE, Sgt K. G., 403*n*
HALIFAX, 183*n*
HALIFAX, Rt Hon Earl, 53*n*
HALILULIK (Sketch p. 467), 491
HALLAM, D'Arcy, 660
HALMAHERA ISLAND (Map p. 30), 420
HALONG (Sketch p. 421), 420, 422, 423*n*, 426, 428; Area Combined HQ at, 423-4
HAMAGUCHI, Eizo, 2
HAMILL, Cpl R. J. S., 669
HAMILTON, General Sir Ian, 3
HAMILTON, Capt J. McK., 655
HAMILTON, Lt-Col T., 541, 544*n*, 550*n*, 554*n*
HANCOCK, Sig P., 479, 492*n*
HANDS, Capt J. L., 564
HANKOW (Sketch p. 644), 643
HANN, L-Cpl I. G., 216
HANOI (Map p. 30), 16
HARIKAWA, Maj, 434-5
HARRIS, Rev Father, 671
HARRIS, Capt F. L., 232, 248
HARRIS, Capt G. C., 660, 673
HARRIS, Lt-Col S. W., 572-3, 576, 580-1
HART, Admiral T. C., 122; appointed Chief of Naval Staff ABDACOM, 205

HARTLEY, General Sir Alan, 458
HARVEY, WO2 C. R., 415
HARVEY, Sig H. F., 597
HARVEY'S PLANTATION (Sketch p. 654), 656
HASSON, Pte J., 475
HATA, General Shunroka, 16-17
HATU-LIA (Sketch p. 478), 480-1, 493
HAWAII (Maps pp. 30, 112), 1, 18, 53, 75, 80, 111, 126, 132*n*, 253, 451*n*; American acquisition of, 4*n*; air link with Philippines established, 89; Japanese plan surprise attack on, 110
HAWKER, C. A. S., 6*n*
HAWKINS, Pte G. A., 436
HAYDON, Professor J. F. M., 9*n*
HAYES, Lt-Cdr J. O. C., 283
HAYES, Pte K. M., 480
HAYMAN, Pte V. J., 357
HAZELGROVE, Gnr M., 667, 671
HAZELTON, Capt A. R., 567
HEAD, Lt H., 213, 216
HEAD, Maj P. L., 86*n*, 279*n*, 522*n*
HEADLAM, Air Commodore F., 469
HEADLAM, WO2 J. M., 655, 657, 659-60
HEATH, Lt-Gen Sir Lewis, 96, 100, 106, 124, 142, 149, 150-1, 156, 160-1, 162, 181, 191-2, 193, 197-8, 199, 214, 231, 244*n*, 251, 254, 257, 259, 260-1, 262, 268, 271, 279, 282, 303, 325, 338-9, 352, 354, 358-9, 360-1, 512, 613; arrives Malaya, 78; career, 79; recommends withdrawal from Kelantan, 153; orders evacuation of Penang, 160; orders withdrawal from Kuantan, 192; placed in command Muar front, 230; issues program for withdrawal to Singapore Is, 269-70; allots command of bridgeheads, 272; Comds Northern Area, 293, 336-7; abandons Naval Base area, 357
HEATHCOTE, Lt C. T., 321
Heather, launch, 384*n*
HECKENDORF, Sgt E. E., 216
HEINL, Col Robert D., 127*n*
HEITO (Sketch p. 630), 629
HELFRICH, Vice-Adm C. E. L., 497; commands Allied Navy in Java, 495; resigns command, 499
"HELL FIRE PASS", 568-9
HELLYER, Maj L. H., 544
HELY, Air Vice-Marshal W. L., 41*n*
HENDY, Lt L. F. G., 218, 355
HENGYANG (Sketch p. 644), 644
HENMAN, Lt O. R. T., 251*n*
HENNESSY, Col P., 175*n*
HENRY, Lt L. D., 402
HENRY REID RIVER (Sketch p. 654), 665
Herald (Melbourne), 287*n*
Herstein, Norwegian merchantman, 399, 674
HILLVIEW ESTATE (Sketch p. 347), 297
HILTON, Pte E. P., 218
HINTOK (Sketch p. 563), 564-5, 567, 569, 570-1, 582, 586
HINTOK ROAD CAMP (Sketch p. 563), 564, 566
HIROHITO, Emperor; *see* JAPAN, EMPEROR OF
HIROSHIMA (Sketch p. 617), 621
HIROSHIMA PRISONER-OF-WAR CAMP 9B, 625*n*
HIROTA, Lt, 570
Hiryu, Japanese aircraft carrier, 427
HISTORICAL SECTION, U.K. CABINET OFFICE, xii, 507*n*
HITLER, Adolf, 53, 54, 81, 198-9, 200*n*, 326*n*, 371; on collaboration with Japan, 75; conceals decision to attack Russia from Japan, 80; on Pearl Harbour, 136
HITU-LAMA (Sketch p. 421), 421, 425, 427-8, 435, 437
HITU PENINSULA (Sketch p. 421), 420, 428
Hobart, Australian cruiser, 60-1, 454, 497-8
HOCHI (Sketch p. 644), 643
HODGSON, Lt-Col W. R., 204, 288
HOKKAIDO ISLAND (Map p. 30; Sketch p. 617), 614, 618
Holbrook, American transport, 474
HOLLAND, 14, 16, 18, 77, 256, 442, 447, 507; represented at December 1941 Singapore Conference, 163; signs United Nations Declaration, 200*n*
HOLLAND, Capt F., 659, 660, 666*n*, 672
HOLLAND ROAD (Map p. 344; Sketch p. 360), 326, 338, 346, 350-1, 358, 363-4, 369
HOLLOW, Pte A. R., 481*n*
HOLLY, Pte C. J., 478-9
HOLMES, Col E. B., 528, 530; commands British and Australian troops in Changi, 522
HOLMES, Maj-Gen W., 392

INDEX 699

HOLMES, Pte W., 409
HOMER, Lt R., 305
HOMMA, Lt-Gen Masaharu, 390-1, 507
HONG KONG (Maps pp. 30, 171), 6, 11, 16, 41, 47, 82n, 127, 132, 179, 284, 373, 437, 453, 494, 497, 623, 639, 643; passage of war materials to China prohibited, 21; value of, 50; reinforcement of, 58, 77, 95; British strength on, 107-8; Japanese plans, 111; attack on, 128-9; fall of, 170-76
HONG KONG VOLUNTEER DEFENCE CORPS, 107, 173, 175
HONSHU ISLAND (Map p. 30; Sketch p. 617), 613, 619, 621
HOOK, L-Cpl R. L., 350
HOOPER, Pte N. S. W., 478
HOPKINS, Harry L., 450-1
HOPKINS, Sgt R. C. (Plate p. 495)
HORE, Maj F., 336, 339
HORII, Maj-Gen Tomitaro, 411, 412; Comds *South Seas Force*, 410
Hornet, American aircraft carrier, 440
HOSADA, Lt, 548
HOSHIJIMA, Capt Susumi, 595
HOSKINS, CAPE (Sketch p. 658), 673
Houston, American cruiser, 90, 474, 497, 533; sinks, 498
HOWELLS, Capt E. R., 219, 356
HUDSON, Pte W. D., 477
HUGHES, Colonel, 174
HUGHES, Maj L., 236, 245
HUGHES, Rt Hon W. M., 7; states problem of Japan in Pacific, 1-2; argues against reliance on British Navy, 8
"HUGHESLIERS", 174
HUKUNAGA, WO, 609
HULL, Cordell, 17, 18, 22n, 25, 39, 52n, 53, 56, 91n, 132n; supports Lend-Lease, 55; negotiates with Admiral Nomura, 87, 94-5, 108, 130-31
HUMPHRIES, Lt-Col H. R., 581, 583, 585-6
HUNAN PROVINCE (Sketch p. 644), 16
HUNT, Maj B. A., 573-4, 575-6
HUNT, Maj G. P., 522n
HUNT, Sgt H. C., 660
HUNT, Capt W. G., 245
HUNTLEY, Cpl N. L. S., 216
HUTTON, Lt K. W., 350
HUTTON, Lt-Gen Sir Thomas, 108n, 206, 461-3
HUTUMORI (Sketch p. 421), 428, 437
HYNES, Cpl T. E., 505

IBA FIELD (Sketch p. 88), 129
IBBOTT, Lt A. G. C., 237
IBOKI (Sketch p. 658), 660-1, 673
IBRAHIM, H. E., Sir, Sultan of Johore, 48n, 98, 102, 242, 273, 357, 366, 389
IKEUCHI, Lt, 608
IKUNO (Sketch p. 617), 621
ILGEN, Maj-Gen, 495
IMLACH, Cpl W., 558
IMPERIAL CONFERENCE OF 1937, 6
IMPERIAL DEFENCE COLLEGE, 32, 78, 166
IMPERIAL PRISONERS-OF-WAR COMMITTEE, 632
INDERAGIRI RIVER (Sketch p. 384), 385, 388
INDIA, 7, 9, 25-6, 28, 32, 40-1, 43-4, 51, 57, 63, 73, 95, 108, 111, 146, 201, 210n, 285, 290n, 348n, 371, 384n, 387, 389, 445, 449, 451n, 458, 462-3, 464-5, 507, 521-2, 529n, 550, 631, 634, 644-5, 677; drawn upon for reinforcements, 19, 49, 79, 160-1; proposal to train AIF in, 20; defence of, 58; relations with Britain, 103-4; signs Atlantic Charter, 200n; and ABDA directive, 202, 646, 648
INDIAN ARMY, 45, 202, 272, 514, 523n, 524, 644, 676; strength in Malaya, 13, 49, 77, 102; reinforcement of, 184, 189, 258; expansion and distribution, 19, 44, 79, 95, 104n; recruits officers from 1st AIF, 31; training of, 68; reinforces Burma, 79, strength in Burma, 103; compared with Japanese Army, 82n; lacks representation on Malaya Command, 97; estimate of, 103-4; strength in Hong Kong, 107, 170; effect of Japanese tanks on, 147; strength on Singapore Island, 289-90; discipline, 338; casualties in Malaya, 382; strength in Java, 497n
—INDIA COMMAND: Burma included in, 108n, 146, 456, 461; removed from, 201; Wavell proposed as C-in-C, 458
—CORPS: *III*, 93, 146n, 153, 158, 167-8, 169, 215, 233, 304, 512; arrives Malaya, 78; composition and

INDIAN ARMY—*continued*
distribution, 79, 106n; role, 97, 106, quality of, 103; in Malaya, 98, 124, 140, 142, 198, 199, 202-3, 206-7, 212, 214, 225, 236, 279, 282; reinforcement of, 160-1, 164; condition assessed, 250; role on Singapore Island allotted, 254, 293; on Singapore Island, 272, 294, 296, 301, 329, 336
—DIVISIONS, distribution of, 95; 4th, 19, 104n; 5th, 19, 79, 104n, 637; 6th, 19, 104n; 7th, 19; 8th, 19, 104n; 9th, 104n, 142, 155, 187, 207, 241; formed, 19; arrives Singapore, 77; deployment, 79, composition, 106n; reinforcement of, 161, 184; at Kuantan, 163, 168, 191-2; in Johore, 203, 206, 209-11, 231, 235, 260, 262, 270, 274, 277, 281-2; on Singapore Island, 293, 296; 10th, 10, 104n; 11th, 104n, 140, 146, 162-3, 165, 198, 207, 241, 254, 340, 364, 512, 514n; arrives Malaya, 49, deployment, 79, composition, 106n, reinforcement, 161, 184; in Malaya, 72, 106, 138, 150-1, 157, 159-60, 166, 192, 194, 196-7; reorganisation of, 163, 203; in Johore, 207, 208-9, 225, 257, 259, 260-1, 270, 273, 279, 281, 282-3; on Singapore Island, 293-4, 330, 336, 343, 354, 361, 369, 373; 14th, 19n; 17th, 19n, 160, 210n, 461-2, 464; 19th, 19n; 20th, 19n; 34th, 19n, 459
—BRIGADES, allocation of British regular battalions to, 104; 6th, 104; arrives Malaya, 49; composition, 106n; at Jitra, 146-7, 149, 150-1; at Gurun, 159, 160; amalgamated with 15th Bde, 163; 6th/15th, 166, 193, 207, 241, 384, 388; formed, 163; at Kampar, 181, 185, 187, covers withdrawal, 189, 193; at Slim River, 194; at Batu Pahat, 231, 259, 260, withdraws, 261, 264-5; dispersed, 271; on Singapore Island, 296, 325, 328, 335-6, 340, 343, 345-7, 348-9, 350; 8th, 207, 192; arrives Malaya, 49; composition, 106n; at Kota Bharu, 106, 125, 137-8, 142; withdraws from Kelantan, 153, 155; in Johore, 211, 235, 240, 257, 260, 262, 270, 273-5, 277, 282; on Singapore Island, 293, 296, 342, 357, 364; 12th, 67, 70, 79, 97n, 98, 104, 106, 156, 162, 166, 333, 384; composition, 106n; in Malaya, 153, 160, 162-3, 166, 181, 184, 187, 189, 193, 194-6; withdrawn to Singapore, 207; reorganised, 225n; on Singapore Island, 293, 317, 323-4, 327, 335-6, 339, 343, 345-6, 350, 357; 13th, arrives Burma, 79; 15th, 104, 160; composition, 106n; at Jitra, 146-7, 149, 151; at Gurun, 159; amalgamated with 6th Bde, 163; 16th, in Burma, 79, 461; 22nd, 125, 231; composition, 106n; at Kuantan, 31, 191; in Johore, 211, 240, 257, 260, 262, 270, 273, 274-5, 277, 279, 281n; loss of, 277n, 281n, 282, 293, 300; 28th, 106, 140, 241; arrives Singapore, 93, 95; composition, 106n; at Jitra, 146-7, 149, 151; withdraws to Kampar, 159, 160, 166, 181, 185, 188; at Slim River, 189, 193-5, 196; in Johore, 260, 273, 279, 281; on Singapore Island, 298, 329-30, 333, 357, 364; 44th, 336-7, 343, 365, 377; reinforces Malaya, 189; arrives Singapore, 258; history, 290; on Singapore Island, 293, 296-7, 299, 304, 308, 315-16, 323, 325-6, 328, 335, 340, 358, 361, 363-4, 369, 370; 45th, 231, 258, 290n, 299; diverted to Malaya, 160-1, 184; arrives Singapore, 189; role in Johore, 203, 206; in Muar battle, 210, 222, 225-6, 228-30, 233, 235-6, losses, 249; 46th, 461; 63rd, 464
—COLUMNS: *Krohcol*, 140, 146, 150, 156, 160; *Laycol*, 140, 146
—ARTILLERY, lack of, 19; *10 Mountain Bty*, 146, 160; *21 Mountain Bty*, 125; *22 Mountain Regt*, 146-7
—CAVALRY: *3rd Cav Regt*, 156n, 261, 353
—INDEPENDENT COMPANIES: *1st*, 162, 165, 186-7, 189, 193
—INFANTRY BATTALIONS: *2/10 Baluch*, 106n, 125, 211, 274, 296, 343, 354-5, 359, 364; *2/17 Dogra*, 106n, 207, 251; *3/17 Dogra*, 106n, 125, 137, 211; *2/12 Frontier Force Regt*, 106n, 125, 138, 155, 192-3, 211; *1/13th Frontier Force Rifles*, 106n, 125, 138, 211, 230, 296; *2/18 Garhwal*, 106n, 192, 211, 257, 260, reformed as Garhwal Battalion, 296; *5/18 Garhwal*, 222, 224, 226-7, 229, 236, 262, reformed as Garhwal Battalion, 296; *Garhwal Battalion*, 296; *2/1 Gurkha*, 106n, 147-8, 151, 189, 194, 195-6; *2/2 Gurkha*, 106n, 149, 150-1, 188, 194, 279, 333; *2/9 Gurkha*, 106n, 149, 150-1, 157, 166, 194-5; *4/19 Hyderabad*, 106n, 142, 166, 194, 294, 325, 336, 339, 343-4, 345; *2/9 Jat*, 106n, 147, 149, 150, 251, reformed as Jat Battalion, 296; *4/9 Jat*,

INDIAN ARMY—continued
222, 224, 226, 228-9, 231, 233-4, 236, 239, reformed as Jat Battalion, 296; *Jat Battalion,* 296, 340, 345, 348; *6/1 Punjab,* 297, 299, 340; *5/2 Punjab,* 97n, 106n, 161, 165-6, 187, 193, 194; *1/8 Punjab,* 106n, 140, 147, 159, 251; *7/8 Punjab,* 297, 299, 340; *1/14 Punjab,* 106n, 147, 149; *2/14 Punjab,* 172-3; *5/14 Punjab,* 106n, 146, 149, 156, 160, 189, 194-5; *6/14 Punjab,* 297, 299, 340; *2/15 Punjab,* 106n, 121, 179-80, 181, 533; *2/16 Punjab,* 106n, 140, 147, 159; *3/16 Punjab,* 106n, 140, 146, 149, 156, 160, 166, 231, 235, 241, 261, 296, 340; *5/7 Rajput,* 172-3, 174-5; *7/6 Rajputana Rifles,* 222, 223-4, 226, 229, 236; *5/11 Sikh,* 106n, 211, 235, 260, 262, 270, 277n, 353
—LABOUR COMPANIES, 107
—MEDICAL: Alexandra Mil Hospital, 374; Tyersall Base Hospital, 359
—STATE FORCES, 106n; *Bahawalpur Infantry,* 296; *1st Hyderabad,* 125; *Jind Infantry,* 299, 319, 322-3; *1st Mysore State Infantry,* 125
INDIAN CONGRESS PARTY, 103-4
INDIAN OCEAN (Sketch P. 448), 23, 41, 47, 106, 182, 201, 290, 371, 459, 463, 497; British strength in, 43-4; reinforcement of, 45, 82, 92, 145, 189, 253; Japanese supremacy in, 508
INDIANS, THE, in Burma, 50; in Malaya, 64n, 65, 209
INDO-CHINA (Maps pp. 30, 112), 11, 16, 18-19, 21, 39, 41, 56n, 59, 75-6, 94, 102, 108n, 111, 121, 123, 126, 134, 141n, 154, 162, 180, 284, 290, 444n, 446, 507n, 608, 611, 614, 648; Japanese gain air bases in, 24-5, 26, 87, 111; signs Peace Treaty with Thailand, 55-6; Japanese strength in, 114, 292; prisoners of war in, 633, 634
Indomitable, British aircraft carrier, 92
INDONESIA, REPUBLIC OF; *see* NETHERLANDS EAST INDIES
INDONESIANS, THE, 387, 424, 433-4, 442, 533; relations with Dutch, 502
INDORF, Lt Louis, 621n
Induna Star, 412, 413, 415-16
INGLEBURN, 31
INISHI, Rear-Admiral, 56n
INTELLIGENCE, 57, 162, 501, 594; Allied, 8-10, 57, 67, 114n, 131, 196, 443-4, of Japanese Army, 20, 82n, 172; of Japanese Air Force, 58, 82, 137; Japanese, 74, 115-16, 306-7, 411n
IPOH (Map p. 158; Sketch p. 188), 140, 146n, 151, 153, 163, 181, 184, 185, 207
IPOH AIRFIELD (Map p. 105), 168, 221
IRAN; *see* PERSIA
IRAQ, 77, 103, 104n, 145, 205; Indian Army reinforcement of, 79, 95
IRIO, Sgt, 628
IRON ORE, 18n, 38
IRRAWADDY RIVER (Sketch p. 461), 16, 464
IRVING, Brig R. G. H., 85
ISKANDOR (Map p. 158), 166
ISLAND GOLF CLUB (Maps pp. 286, 344), 357, 364
ISMAY, Gen Rt Hon Lord, 27, 163-4, 452n
ITALIAN AIR FORCE, 82
ITALIAN ARMY, 19, 27, 79, 255
ITALIAN NAVY, 1, 19, 39, 51
ITALY, 1, 23, 33, 51, 54, 135, 210, 522, 642; signs 10-year pact with Germany and Japan, 37; Japanese military mission to, 133
ITCHIOKA STADIUM HOSPITAL, 621, 623
ITO, Maj-Gen Takeo, 434, 436-7

JACK, Lt-Col A. G., 440, 604
JACOBS, J. W., 683
JACQUINOT BAY (Sketch p. 658), 671
JAKARTA: *see* BATAVIA
JALUIT (Map p. 30), 441
JAMAICA, 92
JAMES, Capt D. H., 371n
JANE, Sgt H. A., 655, 659
JAPAN (Map p. 30; Sketch p. 617), 19-20, 33, 43-4, 45-6, 51-2, 61, 66, 69n, 73-4, 76-7, 89, 91, 123, 126, 129, 133, 135, 141, 166, 176-7, 179, 182-4, 191n, 200, 201n, 202, 205, 252-3, 256n, 259, 286, 391-2, 410, 418, 434n, 442, 446, 449, 451n, 452, 456, 460, 466, 469, 472, 474, 497, 503, 519, 545-6, 563, 630, 643, 646, 675-7; granted mandate over German colonies in Western Pacific, 1; problems of, 1-2; attacks China in Manchuria, 3, 10-11; relations with Germany, 3-4, 14, 38, 75, 80, 87, 136, 270n, 371;

JAPAN—continued
trade developments, 5-6, 7, 39; language studied in Australia, 9-10; remains aloof from European war, 13; and Netherlands Indies, 15-16; attempts to seal supply routes to China, 17, 21-2; relations with America, 17-18, 22, assets frozen, 87, 90, relations ruptured, 108-9, 130-1; Australian Minister appointed, 23; gains bases in Indo-China, 24-6, 39, 56, 87, 140; threat posed by, 27, 93-4; Australian Food Relief Mission to, 28; conjectural role in event of war, 41, 58-9, 114n; and Thailand, 50, 55-6, British plans to forestall in, 92, 122; Allied strategy, 53, 80-3; reduces staffs in Australia, 57; relations with Russia, 55, 78-80, 93; diplomatic communications intercepted, 56, 90n, 108-9; plans offensive, 109-113, 121; scope of offensive, 127, 131-2, 507-8; movement of prisoners to, 524-5, 539, 589, 593, 611-16, 674, 679; prisoners of war in, 616-29, release and repatriation, 632-3, 634-5, 640-2
JAPAN, EMPEROR OF, 56n, 109, 113, 631, 640, 641
JAPANESE, THE, 1-3, 65-6, 74, 285, 341, 373, 380, 466, 512, 514, 518, 522, 528, 533, 535, 536-7, 539, 543-4, 556, 562-3, 568, 591, 595, 596-7, 598-9, 600, 605, 609-10, 618-19, 625-6, 628-29, 630; Intelligence estimate of, 67; relations with British, 80; code of behaviour, 113; massacre prisoners, 246-8, 374, 386-7, 410, 436, 603, 604, 665-9; ill-treat sick, 565, 569, 570, 572-3, 576-7, 579, 584, 588-9, 609, 623, 632; treatment of subject peoples, 553n, 587-8
JAPANESE AIR FORCES, 111, 121, 128, 129-30, 138, 205, 251, 278n, 282, 363, 416, 453, 519n, 530; estimates of, 58, 82, 131, 137, 172; strength, 59, 115, performance, 144; attack Pearl Harbour, 126-7; attack Philippines, 132, 177; in Malayan campaign, 134, 137, 141, 142-3, 156, 168, 181, 187, 207, 217, 221, 223, 230, 233, 242, 243, 270, 304; attack *Prince of Wales* and *Repulse,* 143, 144; in Borneo, 180; efficacy of attacks on ground troops, 263n; in attack on Singapore Island, 287, 289, 299, 317, 320, 352, 362, 367, 381-2, role, 306, 308, losses, 365; in Bismarcks campaign, 398-400, 412; in attack on Ambon, 423, 426-7, 437; attack Rangoon, 463; in Timor campaign, 473-4, 483-4, 489; attack Darwin, 475, 493; in Java campaign, 506; achievements, 508
—AIR CORPS: *3rd,* 381; *12th,* 381; *57th,* 381
—AIR FLEETS: *Eleventh,* 56n
—AIR FLOTILLAS: *21st,* 144; *22nd,* 144; *24th,* 111, 411
—AIR GROUPS: *3rd,* 134
JAPANESE ARMY, 22, 55n, 79-80, 117, 125, 129, 133, 138, 146-7, 149-50, 151-2, 153-4, 156-7, 159, 161, 165, 170, 186, 205, 207, 209, 212, 217n, 220-1, 224-5, 229, 246-8, 249, 250, 267, 284, 304, 305-7, 333, 353, 366-7, 374, 376, 378-9, 382-3, 385, 390-1, 410-12, 427, 435, 464, 480-1, 485-6, 493, 520, 545-6, 552-3, 560, 596, 631; political influence, 2; blockades British Concession area in Tientsin, 10; estimates of, 20, 82n, 100, 172, 278n; quality and characteristics, 113-14; strength and dispositions, 135, 162, 290, 341, 437n, 488; establishes technical missions in Berlin and Rome, 38; invades Indo-China, 87; staff and intelligence organisation, 115-16; tactics, 116, 155, 166-7, 172, 176, 196, 472-3; employment of water transport, 333-4; achievements in Malaya, 382; attitude to Hague and Geneva Conventions, 503, 562-3; casualties, 507
—AREA ARMIES: organisation of, 115; *Kwantung Army,* 3; *Southern Army,* 115; composition, 110-11, 114; achievements, 507-8
—ARMIES: organisation of, 115; XIV, 110, 111, 390, 507n; XV, 110, 111, 134, 186-7, 507n; XVI, 133n, 490, 506; composition, 110-11, 507n; XXIII, 173; XXV, 116, 333, 374n; composition, 110-11, 507n; experience, 114; plans attack on Malaya, 133-4; move to, 134-5
—DIVISIONS: number and distribution of, 114; organisation, 115; Guards, 111; history of, 114; composition, 113n; in Thailand, 134; in Malaya, 186-7, 207-8, 224, 228, 230, 246, 258-9, 265, 269; in attack on Singapore Island, 306-7, 331, 333-4, 352, 354, 366-7, 373, 503, 507n; 2nd, 111; in Java, 497, 499, 507n; 4th, in Philippines, 507; 5th, 111; history, 114; composition, 133n; in Malaya, 133-5, 150n, 151, 186, 189, 193, 196, 207, 220, 249, 262-4, 269, 507n; in attack on Singapore

INDEX

JAPANESE ARMY—continued
  Island, 306, 316-17, 333-4, 350, 352, 366-7, 373, 379; **16th**, 111, 177, 507; **18th**, 111, 133, 180, 269, 380; history, 114; composition, 133*n*; in Malaya, 134, 207, 507*n*; in attack on Singapore Island, 306, 316-17, 334, 347, 350, 352, 359, 363, 366-7, 369; **21st**, 111, 507; **33rd**, 111; in Burma, 461, 507*n*; **38th**, 111, 497; at Hong Kong, 173; in Ambon, 434, 436-7; in Sumatra, 453; in Timor, 490; in Java, 507*n*; **48th**, 111; in Philippines, 177, 390; in Java, 497, 499, 507*n*; **55th**, 111, 134, drawn upon for *South Seas Force*, 410; in Burma, 461, 507*n*; **56th**, 111, 133, 134
  —BRIGADES, 114; *9th Infantry*, 133, 149, 220; *21st Infantry*, 111, 133, 220; *23rd Infantry*, 133*n*; *35th Infantry*, 133*n*, 180; *56th Infantry*, 507*n*; *65th Infantry*, 111, 390, 507
  —FORCES: *Mukaide*, 220; *South Seas*, 410-12, 490
  —REGIMENTS: infantry organisation, 115; *3rd Konoye*, 133*n*; *4th Konoye*, 133*n*, 189, 193, 207, 208, 224, 249, 259, 261, 331; *5th Konoye*, 133*n*, 207, 224, 230, 265; **11th**, 133, 149, 189, 193, 220; **21st**, 133*n*, 207, 220; **41st**, 133, 149, 150*n*, 189; **42nd**, 133, 149, 151, 162, 193, 196, 220; **55th**, 133*n*, 269; **56th**, 111, 133-4, 191, 359, 416, 490, 497, 499; **62nd**, 507*n*; **114th**, 133, 359; **124th**, 133*n*, 134, 180; **143rd**, 134; **144th**, 111, 410, 411-12; **228th**, 173-4, 437, 490, 493-4; **229th**, 173-4, 175, 453; **230th**, 173-4, 497, 499, 500-1
  —ARMOURED UNITS: 488; regimental organisation, 115; *3rd Tank Group*, 133*n*; *1st Medium Tank Regt*, 133*n*, 220, 306; *2nd Medium*, 133*n*; *5th Reconnaissance Regt*, 150*n*; *6th Medium Tank Regt*, 133*n*; *14th Light Tank Regt*, 133*n*, 306
  —ARTILLERY: 270*n*; regimental organisation, 115; employed against Singapore Island, 303, 305-6, 308, 367, strength available, 327; ammunition shortage, 373-4, expenditure, 380; *3rd Independent Mountain Regt*, 133*n*; *3rd Heavy Field Arty Regt*, 133*n*; *18th Heavy Field Arty Regt*, 133*n*; *17th Field Air Defence Unit*, 133*n*; *21st Heavy Field Arty Bn*, 133*n*; *3rd Trench Mortar Bn*, 133*n*; *5th Trench Mortar Bn*, 133*n*; *14th Indep Mortar Bn*, 133*n*
  —ENGINEERS, 116; *4th Indep Engr Regt*, 133*n*; *15th Indep Engr Regt*, 133*n*, 410; *23 Indep Engr Regt*, 133*n*; *5th Indep Heavy Bridging Coy*, 133*n*; *21st Bridging Material Coy*, 133*n*; *22nd Bridging Material Coy*, 133*n*; *27th Bridging Material Coy*, 133*n*; *10th River Crossing Material Coy*, 133*n*; *15th River Crossing Material Coy*, 133*n*; *21st River Crossing Coy*, 133*n*
  —INFANTRY BATTALIONS: strength assembled for attack on 22 Bde front, Singapore Island, 306, 316
  —MISCELLANEOUS UNITS: *96th Airfield Bn*, 266; *1st Balloon Coy*, 133*n*
  —PARATROOPS, 453, 483-5, 486, 489-90, 493
  —POLICE: *Kempei*, 117, 503, 535, 537, 591, 598-9; *2nd Field Military Police Unit*, 133*n*
  —RAILWAY UNITS: *Southern Army Railway Corps*, 545; *2nd Railway Unit*, 133*n*; *5th Railway Regiment*, 545; *9th Railway Regiment*, 545, 589*n*
  —SIGNALS UNITS: equipment of, 116; *25 Army Signal Unit*, 133
JAPANESE GOVERNMENT, 22, 365, 391, 562; influence of armed forces, 2; treatment of prisoners of war, 679-81
  —JAPANESE PLANNING BOARD, 109
JAPANESE MANDATED ISLANDS (Map p. 30), 1, 59, 80, 397
JAPANESE NAVY, 23-4, 38, 56*n*, 80, 134, 177, 371, 373, 399, 410, 414, 433, 605; strength fixed at Washington Conference, 1; China proposes sneak attack on, 39; battleship strength, 92; plans attack on Pearl Harbour, 110; strength and organisation, 114-15, 145; attacks Midway, 128; in Pearl Harbour attack, 132; off Endau, 265-6; in Bali Island action, 456; in Java campaign, 497, 506; achievements of, 507-8
  —FLEETS: *Combined Fleet*, 110, 132, 437*n*; *First*, 111; *Second*, 111; *Third*, 111, 179; *Fourth*, 111, 398, 410, 411; *Carrier Fleet*, 111, 132, 427, 441, 493, 497
  —FORCES: *Southern*, 115, 134
  —MIDWAY NEUTRALISATION UNIT, 132
  —SPECIAL NAVAL LANDING FORCES, 410, 427; organisation of, 114; *Kashima*, 414*n*; *1st Kure*, 437, 490; *2nd Kure*, 416, 490; *6th Kure*, 114;

JAPANESE NAVY—continued
  Maizuru, 414*n*; *Sasebo*, 417, 490; *1st Yokosuka*, 490; *2nd Yokosuka*, 180; *3rd Yokosuka*, 490
  —SUBMARINES, 126, 132, 143-4, 371
JAPANESE RED CROSS, 526
JARDINE'S LOOKOUT (Map p. 171), 174
JASIN (Sketch p. 99), 100
JAVA (Map p. 30; Sketches pp. 498, 500), 76, 181, 202, 205-6, 260, 266, 271, 281, 371-2, 381*n*, 383-4, 385, 387, 388-9, 421, 447-8, 451*n*, 452-3, 454, 460, 463, 466, 469, 474-5, 490-1, 546, 549, 557-8, 561-2, 593, 606, 614, 616, 646, 678; Japanese plan attack, 110-11, 390, 497; Allied strength in, 442, 445, 456, 458, 495-6; planned employment of I Aust Corps in, 443, 444-5, 446-7, 451*n*, 457, 459, 463, 675-7; evacuation of, 458; organisation and role of Blackforce, 496-7; invasion, 497-505; guerilla warfare in, 505-6; Japanese strength in, 507*n*; prisoners of war in, 511, 532-9, 541, 633, 681, repatriation, 634, 638
Java, Dutch cruiser, 454, 456, 497-8
JAVA SEA (Map p. 498), battle of, 497-9; Japanese supremacy established, 506
JEATER, Lt-Col W. D., 60, 99*n*, 357; commands 2/20 Bn, 29-30
JEFFREY, Sister Betty, 683
JEFFREY, Capt R. L., 599, 600
JEHOL PROVINCE (Map p. 30), 3
JEMALUANG (Map p. 105; Sketch p. 251), 98-9, 100, 153-4, 168, 198, 226, 231, 241, 250-1, 252, 257, 261-2, 266, 268-9
JEMENTAH (Sketch p. 211), 211
JEPHSON, Lt-Col E. W. F., 297*n*, 327
JERANTUT (Map p. 105; Sketch p. 192), 155, 168, 192-3
JESSELTON (Sketch p. 595), 595, 598
JESSUP, Capt H. E., 377, 381*n*
JINKINS, Maj W. T., 425, 427, 429, 432, 434-5, 440, 604
JITRA (Maps pp. 54, 139; Sketch p. 148), 153, 157, 196, 198; defence line established, 140; dispositions, 146-7; action at, 147-52
Johan van Oldenbarneveldt, Dutch transport, 84
JOHNSON, Sgt C. H., 320
JOHNSON, WO1 D., 440
JOHNSON, Nelson T., 39
JOHNSTON, D. S., 683
JOHNSTON, Capt N. H., 472, 483, 485-6, 487-8
JOHNSTON, Lt-Col N. McG., 573*n*, 574
JOHNSTONE, Maj F. T., 213, 267-8, 315, 320
JOHORE, STATE OF (Map p. 54), 47-8, 58, 65, 78-9, 100-1, 153-4, 182, 197, 253-4, 285, 291*n*, 292, 303*n*, 633, 636; defence plans and requirements, 93, 98, 106, 162-3, 164, 167-8, 198-9, 202-3, 206-7; appointment of Director-General of Civil Defence in, 191; withdrawal to, 207, 209; dispositions in, 210-14; operations in, 214-21, 222-49, 250-52, 260-71, 272-83; first contact between AIF and Japanese in, 225*n*
JOHORE, SULTAN OF; *see* IBRAHIM, H. E. Sir
JOHORE, SUNGEI (Map p. 280), 254
JOHORE BAHRU (Maps pp. 54, 286), 48, 64, 98, 101, 254, 259, 268, 273, 279, 281 308, 366, 380, 529*n*, 531; restrictions placed on artillery targets in, 299, 300-1, lifted, 304
JOHORE STATE FORCES, 106, 251, 321, 324
JOHORE STRAIT (Map p. 286), 47, 272, 281, 283, 288, 290-1, 293, 297, 300, 305, 318, 333, 341, 373, 514; patrolling of, 301, 305; Japanese cross, 316, 327, 331, 333-4, 366-7
JOINT BOARD OF DEFENCE, 39
JOLO ISLAND (Sketches pp 178, 595), 497, 595
JONES, Gnr A. H., 544*n*
JONES, Maj F. A., 213, 215-16, 217, 275-6
JONES, Cpl J. N., 403
JOO LYE ESTATE (Sketch p. 267), 262
JORAK (Sketch p. 211), 222
Jukka Maru, Japanese transport, 417
JULIUS, Maj W. W., 222, 226-7, 233
JURONG (Map p. 286; Sketch p. 324), 303, 326
JURONG I (Map p. 344; Sketch p. 347), 345; action at, 347-8
JURONG, SUNGEI (Map p. 286; Sketch p. 324), 291-2, 293, 297, 301, 303, 306, 323-4, 325-6, 327, 335, 340
JURONG ROAD (Map p. 286; Sketch p. 324), 291, 297, 303, 306, 321, 323-4, 326-7, 335, 340, 346-8, 367, 636

K.12, Dutch submarine, 125*n*
Kachidoki Maru, Japanese transport, 614-15
KAHANG (Sketch p. 99), 99, 241, 251
KAHANG AIRFIELD (Sketch p. 99), 99, 257, 262, 266
KAJANG (Map p. 54; Sketch p. 208), 62, 207-8
KAI ISLAND (Sketch p. 439), 439
KAINANTU (Sketch p. 658), 673
KAI TAK AIRFIELD (Map p. 171), 129
KALAI MISSION (Sketch p. 654), 665, 671
KALIDJATI AIRFIELD (Sketch p. 500), 499
KALILI HARBOUR (Sketch p. 413), 415
KALINGI (Sketch p. 658), 657, 661*n*
KALLANG AIRPORT (Map p. 286; Sketch p. 374), 121*n*, 291, 294, 325, 361-2, 364-5, 369, 379
Kamakura Maru, Japanese transport, 613
KAMANAKAN (Sketch p. 654), 655
KAMPAR (Sketch p. 188), 181, 185; defence of, 187-8, 189
KAMPAR, SUNGEI (Map p. 188), 187
KAMPONG BAHRU, 62
KAMPONG JAWA (Map p. 344), 335
KAMPONG SLIM (Sketch p. 188), 194-5
KANBURI (Sketches pp. 542, 563), 545, 567, 581-2, 585-6, 587-9, 591
KANCHANABURI; *see* KANBURI
KANGAR (Map p. 139), 146
KANGKAR, SUNGEI (Map p. 286), 291
KANJONG IMAM (Sketch p. 148), 147
KANOYA (Sketch p. 617), 641
KAPEPA ISLAND (Sketch p. 658), 658
KAPINGAMARANGI ISLAND (Map p. 30), 1*n*
KAPITZ, Lt-Col J. R. L., 421, 424, 426-7, 428-9, 431, 434-5
KAPPE, Brig C. H., 41*n*, 60, 85, 86*n*, 373, 387, 572, 573*n*, 581; appointed CSO 8 Div, 85; forms "Snake Gully Rifles", 360
KARACHI, 444*n*
KARAI-AI (Sketch p. 658), 657
KARENKO (Sketch p. 630), 629
KARUMBA (Sketch p. 439), 439
KATHERINE, 467*n*
KATO, Masuo, 4*n*
KATONG (Map p. 286), 370
KAUT (Sketch P. 413), 413-14, 415
KAUT HARBOUR (Sketch p. 413), 413, 415
KAVAVAS RIVER (Sketch p. 654), 661
KAVIENG (Map p. 393; Sketch p. 413), 396, 398, 411; Japanese plan capture, 392; air attack on, 399, 412; Japanese invasion, 414-16
KAVIENG AIRFIELD (Sketch p. 413), 413, 414
KAWAMURA, Major-General, 149
KAWASAKI CAMP, 620-21, 625
KAWKAREIK (Sketch p. 542), 545
KAY, Sgt B. G., 432
KEARNEY, Capt P. D., 215
KEAT HONG (Sketch p. 310), 315, 317, 323, 335, 339
KEDAH, STATE OF (Maps pp. 54, 139), 64, 140, 150, 164, 209; defence requirements, 93
KEDAH, SUNGEI (Map p. 158), 150, 157
KEDAH PEAK (Map p. 158), 157, 159
KEEGAN, Maj R. W., 231-2, 233, 236-7, 242, 248, 302, 315-16, 321, 347-8
KEFANNANU (Sketch p. 467), 491
KEITEL, Field Marshal W., 80*n*
KELANTAN, STATE OF (Map p. 54), 64-5, 138, 149, 162, 166, 191; defence requirements, 93; withdrawal from, 142, 153, 155
KELANTAN, SULTAN OF, 142
Kelena, 251*n*
KENDARI (Map p. 393), 206, 259, 392, 416-18, 427, 474, 490, 493, 497
KENDAU (Sketch p. 550), 546-7, 549
KENNEDY, Capt J., 558
KENNEDY, Pte N., 406
KENNEDY, Sgt R. J., 597
KENT-HUGHES, Colonel Sir Wilfrid, 8*n*, 69, 72*n*, 86*n*, 101, 279, 361, 366, 382, 520-1, 683; appointed DAQMG 8 Div, 28; appointed AA&QMG 8 Div, 373
KEPPEL GOLF LINKS (Sketch p. 374), 379
KEPPEL HARBOUR (Map p. 286), 291-2, 294, 519, 520
KERAVAT EXPERIMENTAL FARM (Sketch p. 654), 654-5
KERAVAT RIVER (Sketches pp. 394, 654), 396, 407-8, 653-5, 664
KERAVIA BAY (Sketch p. 401), 403, 412
KERIKAN (Sketch p. 542), 637
KERR, T. -Col D. R., 541

KEY, Maj-Gen B. W., 138, 142, 225, 231, 241, 257, 259, 261, 264, 273, 282, 338, 340, 342-3, 354*n*, 512; commands 8 Indian Bde, 106*n*; orders withdrawal from Kota Bharu, 142; appointed GOC 11 Div, 207; orders 53 Bde to clear road to Parit Sulong, 236; endeavours to expedite attack, 240
KHLAUNG NGAE (Maps pp. 54, 139), 140
KIANGSI (Sketch p. 644), 16, 643-4, 645
KIDO, Marquis Koichi, 56*n*
KILGOUR, Major, 389
KILO-4 CAMP, 555
KILO-55 CAMP (Sketch p. 550), 555, 556
KILO-60 CAMP, 553
KILO-80 CAMP (Sketch p. 550), 555, 559, 560*n*, 561
KILO-85 CAMP, 559
KILO-95 CAMP, 555
KILO-100 CAMP, 559-60, 561
KILO-105 CAMP (Sketch p. 550), 553-4, 557*n*, 560-1
KILO-108 CAMP (Sketch p. 550), 553-4, 555
KILO-116 CAMP (Sketch p. 550), 556
KILO-130 CAMP (Sketch p. 550), 556
KILO-150 CAMP (Sketch p. 550), 555
KIMMEL, Admiral H. E., 108
KING, Fleet Admiral Ernest J., becomes Chief of US Naval Operations, 440-1
KING, Maj-Gen Edward P., 507
KING, Capt J. C., 130*n*
KING, Maj-Gen R., 85
Kinkon Maru, Japanese transport, 536
KINSAYOK (Sketch p. 563), 563, 571, 587
Kinta, British merchantman, 383
KIRKLAND, Sgt A. J., 403
KIUKIANG (Sketch p. 644), 645
KIYANG (Sketch p. 644), 641
KLANG (Sketch p. 208), 207
KLANG, SUNGEI (Sketch p. 208), 207-8
KLAPALIMA (Sketch p. 468), 468, 472; Japanese attack on, 483
KLUANG (Map p. 54; Sketch p. 99), 64, 70, 98-9, 153, 203, 207, 241, 250, 254, 257, 260, 262, 269, 279*n*, 306
KLUANG AIRFIELD (Sketch p. 99), 99, 257, 262, 266; British air attacks on, 365
KNIGHT, Pte P., 481
KNOX, Franklin, 53, 55
KOBE (Sketch p. 617), 613-14, 619; prisoners of war at, 620-21, 622-5
KOBE HOUSE CAMP, 622-5
KODIANG (Maps pp. 54, 139), 146-7, 148
KOENIGPLEIN, 533
KOEPANG (Sketches pp. 467, 468), 69*n*, 130, 271-2, 417, 419, 466-7, 468-9, 470-2, 474-5, 482, 486, 492-3, 538*n*
KOEPANG BAY (Sketch p. 468), 466, 468, 472, 482
KOH RONG (Sketch p. 88), 123
KOKOPO (Sketch p. 394), 395, 401-2, 404-5, 406*n*, 409, 411
KOKOPO RIDGE ROAD (Sketch p. 401), 396, 401-2, 405-6; action on, 407, 408-10
KOLBANO (Sketch p. 467), 475
Komet, German raider, 52
KONAN (Sketch p. 617), prisoners of war at, 631-2
KONDO, Admiral N., 497
KONKOITA (Sketches pp. 550, 563), 545, 564, 573-4, 576, 580, 585-7; *see also* UPPER KONKOITA
KONOYE, Prince Fumimaro, 2*n*, 37; becomes Premier, 22; resigns, 94
KONYU (Sketch p. 563), 562, 564, 568-71, 583
KONYU 2; *see* MALAYAN HAMLET
Koolama, Australian transport, 473
KOREA, 2, 113, 620, 630; annexed by Japan, 1; Japanese strength in, 114; prisoners of war in, 611-12, 631-2, 633
KOREAN GUARDS, 546-7, 549, 552-3, 558, 562, 569, 578, 592, 620
Kortenaer, Dutch destroyer, 456
KOTA BHARU (Map p. 54; Sketch p. 124), 64, 87, 106-7, 124, 130, 132*n*, 133-4, 153; air force based on, 121*n*; air operations from, 122; Japanese invasion of, 125-6, 135, 137-8, 142
KOTA BHARU AIRFIELD (Sketch p. 124), 125, 137, evacuation of, 138
KOTA TAMPAN (Map p. 158), 165
KOTA TINGGI (Map p. 54; Sketch p. 99), 98, 251, 262, 266
KOWLOON (Map p. 171), 170, 173, 176
KOWLOON BAY (Map p. 171), 173

KRAGAN (Sketch p. 498), 499
KRAGILAN (Sketch p. 500), 499
KRA ISTHMUS (Map p. 42), 92, 107, 109; British proposal to occupy, 50, 109, 122-3
KRANJI (Map p. 286; Sketch p. 328), 321, 330, 332; ammunition magazine at, 326, 341
KRANJI, SUNGEI (Map p. 286; Sketch p. 310), 291-2, 296-7, 298, 301, 303, 306, 323-4, 325-6, 327-8, 329, 330-1, 335, 340
KRANJI HOSPITAL, 530
KRANJI-JURONG LINE (Map p. 286), 291-2, 306, 323, 337, 366; reconnaissance of, 301-2, 303; preparations on, 324; General Percival attempts to stabilise on, 325; dispositions on, 326, 327-8, 335-6; withdrawal from, 339-40; attempted recapture of, 343, 346
KRANJI ROAD (Sketch p. 328), 298, 329-30, 333
KRANTZ, Maj S., 550
KRIAN, SUNGEI (Map p. 158), 160, 162-3, 166
KROH (Maps pp. 54, 158), 64, 133, 140, 146, 149, 151, 156, 160-1, 162
KUALA DUNGUN (Map p. 280), 65
KUALA KANGSAR (Map p. 158), 64, 156, 160, 163, 165-6
KUALA KRAI (Map p. 54), 138, 142, 153, 155
KUALA KUBU (Map p. 54; Sketches pp. 188, 208), 64, 168, 187, 191, 209
KUALA LIPIS (Map p. 105), 142, 155, 168, 191
KUALA LUMPUR (Map p. 54; Sketch p. 208), 48, 62, 72, 79, 96, 168-9, 193, 198, 203, 220, 248n, 279n, 306; British withdrawal from, 208-9
KUALA LUMPUR AIRFIELD (Map p. 105), 168, 193
KUALA SELANGOR (Sketch p. 188), 185, 193
KUANTAN (Map p. 54; Sketch p. 192), 64, 106-7, 133-4, 143, 153, 168, 250, 269; defence of, 163; withdrawal from, 191-3
KUANTAN, SUNGEI (Sketch p. 192), 191
KUANTAN AIRFIELD (Map p. 105; Sketch p. 192), 121n, 125, 142, 163, 191; defence of, 192-3; British air attack on, 221
KUANTU (Sketch p. 644), 645
KUCHING (Map p. 30; Sketch p. 179), 121, 180, 595n, 596; capture of, 180-1; prisoners of war at, 595-6, 599, 633
KUDAMATI (Sketch p. 421), 425; defence of, 429-32; surrender of, 434
KULAI (Map p. 262), 258, 277-8, 279, 281-2
KUN KNIT KWAY (Sketch p. 550), 549, 551, 553
KUNMING (Map p. 42; Sketch p. 644), 16, 638, 643, 645
KUPANG (Map p. 158), 46
KURE, 114
Kuretake Maru, Japanese transport, 417
KURILE ISLANDS (Map p. 112), 111
KURUSU, Saburo, 94-5, 127, 130-31, 132n
KUSUNOSE, Colonel, 410
KUWADA, Lt-Col, 411
KWAJALEIN ATOLL (Map p. 112), 132; American strikes on, 441
KWANGSI PROVINCE (Sketch p. 644), 16, 114
KWANTUNG PROVINCE (Sketch p. 644), 3n
KWEICHOW PROVINCE (Sketch p. 644), 16
KWEIYANG (Sketch p. 644), 644
KYLE, Lt A. F., 656-7
Kyokko Maru, Japanese transport, 613
KYUSHU ISLAND (Sketch p. 617), 626, 628

LABIS (Sketch p. 211), 211, 230-1, 235-6, 240
LABUAN ISLAND (Map p. 30; Sketches pp. 179, 595), 51, 595-6, 634
LAE (Sketch p. 658), 279, 396, 399, 674
LAFFY, Capt J. P., 491
LAHA (Sketch p. 421), 424, 432, 434, 436, 438
LAHA AIRFIELD (Sketch p. 421), 419-20, 422-3, 425, 426-7; fight for, 435-7
LAHANE (Sketch p. 478), 479
LAHARUS (Sketch p. 467), 492
LAHN (Sketch p. 654), 655-6, 660
LAIDLAW, Maj G. G., 471, 479, 480-1
LAITIMOR PENINSULA (Sketch p. 421), 420-2, 425-6, 427-8, 429, 435, 437
Lakatoi, motor schooner, 658, 661, 673
LAKEKAMU RIVER (Sketch p. 658), 673
LAKUNAI AIRFIELD (Sketches pp. 394, 401), 395, 397-9, 401, 405, 411
LALANG, SUNGEI (Map p. 158), 159
LAMACOTT MISSION, 413
LAMACRAFT, Capt A. M., 213, 217, 219-20

LAMBERT, CAPE (Sketch p. 654), 656
LAMMA ISLAND (Map p. 171), 173
LAMON BAY (Map p. 178), 177
LANCHOW (Map p. 30), 16
LANDING CRAFT, Japanese, 116, 333-4
LANE, Lt-Col C. M., 180-1
LANG, Lt C. W. P., 504
LANGINOA PLANTATION (Sketch p. 654), 656, 659-60
LARKIN, Pte J. W., 30
LASHIO (Sketch p. 644), 16, 464, 643-4
LASSUL BAY (Sketch p. 654), 655-6, 660
LATERI BATTERY (Sketch p. 421), 429, 435
LATHAM, Rt Hon Sir John, 10, 23
LATOURETTE, K. S., 4n
LATUHALAT (Sketch p. 421), 421, 425, 433, 439
LAU-LORA (Sketch p. 478), 479
LAUNCESTON GRAMMAR SCHOOL, 487n
Laurabada, Australian yacht, 661, 672-3
LAVARACK, Lt-Gen Sir John, 8n, 33, 256n, 445, 448, 450, 463, 464n, 496, 678; arrives Java, 442; objects to division of Corps, 443; prepares appreciation on defence of NEI, 444; opposes employment of AIF in Java, 446-7; issues instructions to Blackburn, 454; flies to Australia, 456-7, 459
LAVERTON AIRFIELD, 459
LAWRENCE, Maj K. P. H., 314, 320
LAWS, Lt D. A., 673
LAWSON, Brig J. K., 172-3, 174-5
LAY, Brig W. O., 106n, 140, 146, 149, 159, 273-4; commands 8 Indian Bde, 207
LAYANG LAYANG (Map p. 262), 262, 270, 273-4
LAYTON, Admiral Sir Geoffrey, 93, 122-3, 125n, 141n, 144n, 145; Commander-in-Chief China Station, 40; commands Eastern Fleet, 145n; reinforcement of, 146; transfers to Batavia, 204
LEACH, Capt J. C., 144
LEAGUE OF NATIONS, 22, 392; allots Pacific mandates, 1n; Japan resigns from, 3
LEAVE, 258n; in Malaya, 72, 96
LEDGE, THE (Map p. 139), 140, 146, 149
LEE, Sgt G. F., 332
LEGASPI (Map p. 178), 177
LEGGATT, Lt-Col Sir William, 423, 467-70, 472-3, 475, 482-7, 488-9, 490, 492, 522n, 534
LEIGHTON HILL (Map p. 171), 175
LELES (Sketch p. 500), 532-3, 534
LELET PLATEAU (Sketch p. 413), 415
LEMBANG (Sketch p. 500), 206
LEMINGI (Sketch p. 654), 661-2, 664, 672
LEND-LEASE, 55
LENGA (Sketch p. 211), 210
LENGGONG (Map p. 158), 165
LENNON, Lt J. J., 319
LEONG CHU, Mr, 658
LEREW, Gp Capt J. M., 397, 399
LEUWILIANG RIVER (Sketch p. 500), 499; action at, 500-1, 504-5
LEVY, WO2 P. R., 545n
LEWIS, Pte J. B., 434
Lexington, American aircraft carrier, 128, 440
LIAISON, between Western Area HQ and brigades, 322n; with Indian Corps at Causeway, 333; with Dutch, 418-19, 423n, 424, 429n, 501; between AHQ and Gull Force, 423n
LIANG (Sketch p. 421), 420-1, 427
LIAOTUNG PENINSULA (Map p. 30), 3n
LIAYUANCHOW; *see* CHEN CHA TUNG
LIBARAN ISLAND (Sketch p. 595), 604
LIBYA, 52, 85, 145, 169, 184, 190, 255
LIGERTWOOD, Hon Sir George, 375n, 385n, 650-2
LILIBA (Sketch p. 468), 483
LIM CHU KANG ROAD (Map p. 286; Sketch p. 310), 291, 311-12, 314-15, 319
LIND, Brig E. F., 420, 473; commands 23 Bde, 31; criticises employment of Gull and Sparrow Forces, 418-19
LING, Sgt L. F., 504
LINGAYEN GULF (Map p. 178), 177
LINGGA ARCHIPELAGO (Sketch p. 384), 389
LIQUISSA (Sketch p. 478), 480, 493
LIUYANG (Sketch p. 644), 644
LIVERPOOL, 31
LLOYD, Maj-Gen C. E. M., 206n, 443
LLOYD, Maj D. T., 185, 323
LLOYD, Lt-Col E. E., Longfield, 9-10
LLOYD, Brig J. E., 633
LLOYD, Pte S. K., 357

INDEX

Lolobau, pinnace, 658
LOLOBAU ISLAND (Sketch p. 658), 660
LOLOTOI (Sketch p. 478), 492-3
LOMAS, Maj F. J., 406, 409, 663, 667
LOMBOK STRAIT (Sketch p. 393), 456, 497, 499
LONDON, 13, 14, 18, 26, 40-1, 48, 50-1, 52, 56, 74, 76-7, 78-9, 82-3, 91n, 92-3, 132n, 144-5, 169, 255n, 256, 284-5, 447, 449, 452, 457, 459, 462, 465, 632, 635, 649
LONELY CROSS SPUR, 481
LOOTING, 519
LORENCO MARQUES, 475n
LORENGAU, 396
LOTHIAN, Lord, 17-18, 25, 39
LOVE, Maj F. S., 84n
LOWE, Capt R. F. M., 533
LOWER NIEKE (Sketch p. 563), 573-4, 576
LOWER SONGKURAI (Sketch p. 563), 574-5, 579
LUBOK RIVER (Sketch p. 595), 604
LUBUKLINGGAU (Sketch p. 384), 540
LUMPKIN, Capt S. Hugh, 558, 560
LUNGCHOW (Map p. 30), 16
LUTONG (Sketch p. 179), 179
LUZON (Map p. 178), 202, 342, 593, 647, 674; defence plans, 89-90; Japanese air attacks on, 129; invasion of, 177, 390-1; Japanese reinforcement of, 507
LYE MUN GAP (Map p. 171), 174
LYE MUN PASSAGE (Map p. 171), 173
LYNEHAM, Lt-Col E. D., 496, 534, 539
LYON, Brig C. A., 157
LYON, Lt-Col I., 388
LYTTELTON, Rt Hon O., 91n

McALISTER, Sgt A. J., 262
MACARTHUR, Gen of Army Douglas, 129, 132, 177, 179, 183, 205-6, 390-1, 445n; commands United States Army Forces in Far East, 87-8; career, 89; organises defence of Philippines, 90; considers Japan over-extended, 93-4; warned of possibility of surprise attack, 108; withdraws Luzon forces to Bataan Peninsula, 177; estimate of, 183n; ordered to Australia, 506-8; appointed Supreme Commander Allied Powers, 635
MACASSAR (Maps pp. 112, 393), 284, 474, 490, 633
MACAULAY, Capt N. G., 522n
McBRIDE, Maj I. H., 436, 438-9, 440
McCABE, G., 683
McCALLUM, Capt J. T., 655
MACCALLUM, Brig W. P., 454-5
McCARTHY, Lt-Col J. K., 657-61, 672-3
McCAULEY, Air Marshal Sir John, 163n, 442, 453
McCRAE, Pte V. L. J., 506
McCURE, Lt R. M., 227n
McCUTCHEON, Lt W., 488
Macdhui, Australian transport, 672
MACDONALD, Capt H. C. H., 238
MACDONALD, J. Ramsay, 3
McDONALD, W Cdr J. R. G., 419n
McEACHERN, Brig C. A., 304, 362, 525, 563n, 566-7
McEWEN, Hon J., 23
McEWIN, Capt O. S., 303
McFARLANE, S Ldr A. B., 427n
McGREGOR, Capt I. A., 515
MACHANG (Sketch p. 124), 142, 153; airfield at, 125
MACHINE-GUNS, 86, 305n, 402n, 419n; Japanese, 115
McINNES, Maj C. L., 401-2, 406-7, 408, 653-4, 655-6
MACK, Capt V., 517
MACKAY, Lt-Gen Sir Iven, 33, 35, 97, 350n
MACKAY, Lt I. J., 350, 358, 363
MACKAY, T. R. B., *see* McKENZIE, Sig D. S.
MACKENZIE, Compton, 82n
McKENZIE, Maj C. F. G., 471, 475, 476-8, 479, 481
McKENZIE, Sig D. S., 597
MACKENZIE, Lt Cdr H. A., 663, 672
MACKENZIE, S. S., 392n
McLAREN, Capt R. K., 597
McLAUGHLIN, Paymaster Cdr W. E., 9n
McLEAN, J., 656
McLEOD, Lt-Gen Sir (D.) Kenneth, 108n
McLEOD, Lt-Col N. R., 400, 664
McLEOD, Lt R., 224
McLEOD, Lt T. R., 487
McMILLAN, Capt George J., 128
McNICOLL, Brig-Gen Sir Walter, 396
MACRAE, Maj I. F., 424, 426, 433, 438-40, 605, 610, 638-9

MACRITCHIE RESERVOIR (Map p. 286; Sketch p. 360), 291, 325, 352-3, 358, 361
MADANG (Sketch p. 658), 660, 661
MADDERN, Lt-Col N. P., 485-6, 487-9, 522n
"MAGIC", code name for intercepted Japanese messages, 56
MAGWE (Sketch p. 461), 464
MAHER, Capt M. B., 234, 242, 244
MAIERHOFER, Rev Father, 662, 664
MAIL, 61; in captivity, 525-6, 537-8, 561, 607, 617-18, 620, 631, 645, 674n; examined by CARO for prisoner-of-war information, 679
MAJOR, Capt J. F., 433
MAJURO, 132
MAKASURA CAMP, 537-9
MALABUNGA (Sketch p. 394), 398, 408, 661, 663-4
MALABUNGA JUNCTION (Sketch p. 401), 407-8, 655, 664
MALACCA (Map p. 54; Sketch p. 208), 62, 211, 223-4, 303n
MALACCA, COLONY OF (Map p. 54; Sketch p. 208), 101, 167, 198-9, 203, 222; administration of, 48; defence plans, 98; role of AIF in, 106
MALACCA, STRAIT OF (Sketch p. 384), 545
MALAGUNA (Sketches pp. 394, 401), 395, 399, 404
MALAGUNA ROAD, 395, 674
Malahuka, motor schooner, 660
MALARIA, 67n, 426, 469, 471, 528, 553, 575, 577, 590, 605, 671n, 672
MALAYA (Maps pp. 30, 54), 41, 45-6, 54, 57, 63, 67-9, 71-2, 85-7, 92-3, 96, 104, 108, 114-15, 121, 123, 126-7, 129, 131, 177, 179, 180, 198, 204n, 206, 254, 284, 288, 290, 293n, 296, 345, 353, 381n, 383, 388n, 389, 419, 443, 451n, 452-3, 463, 472, 496, 507, 513, 520-1, 530, 581, 588, 593, 633, 643, 646, 676-7, 679; reinforcement of, 13-14, 49-50, 76, 81-2, 95, 103, 163-5, 182-4, 189-90, 209-10, 221-2, 258n, British policy, 52-3, 252-3; garrison needed for defence of, 18, 51, 93, strength and deficiencies, 43, 44, 77-8, 102-3, dispositions, 106; Australian reinforcement of, 19, 44n, 45, 52, 59, 60-1, 62, 83, 84, 101, proposed dispatch of 7 Aust Div to, 20, 25, 26; defence plans, 20, 24, 27, 40-1, 58, 78-9, 90, 98, 100, 107, 202-3; civil administration of, 47, 48-9, 145, 190-1, 203-4, 252, 285; British air strength in, 49-50, 77, 163, requirements, 58, distribution, 121n, losses, 141, reinforcement, 257; population, climate, etc., 64-6; publicity policy, 73-4, 84, 141; regarded as backwater by British officers, 97; lacks adequate labour force, 107; Chinese mission to, 109; Japanese plans, 110-11, 116, 125, 133-5; mobilisation ordered, 122; campaign in, 137-40, 142, 146-63, 165-9, 181, 184-91, 191-7, 199, 205, 207, 210-21, 222-49, 250-52, 256-59, 259-69, 269-71, 272-83; air reinforcement route to, 169; included in ABDA Command, 201; leadership in, 204-5; British occupation planned, 634-5; prisoner-of-war deaths in, 642
MALAYA, FEDERATED STATES OF, 48, 62, 72, 168, 198
MALAYAN COMMUNIST PARTY, 204
MALAYAN FARMS (Sketch p. 310), 322, 327
MALAYAN GOVERNMENT, 14, 107
—DEPARTMENT OF INFORMATION, 74
MALAYAN HAMLET (Sketch p. 563), 582-3, 586
MALAYAN KUOMINTANG, 204
MALAYAN POLICE FORCE, 265, 293
MALAY PENINSULA, 27, 62-3, 91, 133, 162, 202, 253, 341, 392, 646
MALAYS, THE, 66, 209, 281, 517, 594; relations with AIF, 62; population in Malaya, 64; attitude to escapers, 248n, 387n; behaviour under air attack, 372; on Burma-Thailand railway, 587-8
MALAYU, SUNGEI (Map p. 286; Sketch p. 310), 306, 327
MALAY VOLUNTEER FORCES
—Federated Malay States Volunteer Force, 104, 281n; establishment of, 14; mobilisation ordered, 122
—Straits Settlements Volunteer Force, 106n, 160-1, 289, 293; calibre, 290
—Brigades: *1st Malaya*, 79, 106n, 290, 293, 340, 358, 361, 369, 370, 373-5; *2nd Malaya*, 79, 106n, 293, 361, 369
—Battalions: *1 Malay*, 106n, 300, 369, 370, 379; *2 Malay*, 335, 340; *1 Perak*, 185n; *3 Bn SSVF*, 156n
MALMAL MISSION (Sketch p. 658), 671

INDEX

MALTBY, Maj-Gen C. M., 174-5, 176; commands British Tps in China and Hong Kong, 170
MALTBY, Air Vice-Marshal Sir Paul, 365, 442, 502-3, 525, 534; commands British and Australian air units of ABDA Command, 341
MALUM ISLAND (Map p. 30), 1n
MANCHUKUO, 3, 22
MANCHURIA (Map p. 30; Sketch p. 617), 6, 14, 22, 55, 113, 626; Japan gains control of, 3; Japanese strength in, 114; prisoners of war in, 630-1, 633, 639-40
MANDAH (Sketch p. 453), 455
MANDAI (Map p. 344), 366
MANDAI, SUNGEI (Sketch p. 328), 331-2
MANDAI KECHIL, SUNGEI (Sketch p. 328), 331-2, 333
MANDAI ROAD (Sketch p. 328), 331, 338, 343, 354, 355-6
MANDAI ROAD VILLAGE (Sketch p. 328), 298, 354
MANDALAY (Sketch p. 461), 462
Manhattan, American transport, 183n
MANIKIN RIVER (Sketch p. 468), 484
MANILA (Map p. 178; Sketch p. 88), 81, 93, 116, 122-3, 127, 129, 177, 390, 634, 640-1; Japanese enter, 179; Australian reception group at, 641-2
MANILA BAY (Sketch p. 88), 89-90, 177, 179, 506
MANOR HOUSE (Sketch p. 374), 362
MANT, Gilbert, 63n
Manunda, Australian hospital ship, 634
MANUS ISLAND (Map p. 393), 396
MAPE (Sketch p. 478), 481, 493
Marblehead, American cruiser, 90
MARCO POLO BRIDGE, 10
Marella, Australian transport, 258n
MARIANA ISLANDS (Map p. 30), 128, 132; placed under Japanese mandate, 1
Marnix van St Aldegonde, Dutch transport, 84
MARRIOTT, Pte H. W., 480
MARSDEN, Chaplain Rev. L. T., 583
MARSHALL, L-Cpl C. E., 667, 671
MARSHALL, Pte E. E., 505
MARSHALL, Gen of Army George C., 53, 94, 108, 177, 441, 506; on proposed visit of US naval squadron to Singapore, 39; rejects ADB1 plan, 81; proposes Wavell as ABDA Command, 184, 201; and reinforcement of Australia, 450
MARSHALL, Captain G. C., 606
MARSHALL, Brig N., 35-6, 85
MARSHALL ISLANDS (Maps pp. 30, 112), 111, 132; placed under Japanese mandate, 1; bombarded by American carriers, 441
MARSLAND, F-Lt G. H. R., 658-9, 660-1
MARTABAN (Sketch p. 461), 451n; loss of, 461
MARTIN, Brig J. E. G., 85
MARTIN, Sgt L. E., 431
Mary Rose, motor launch, 377, 385
MASSACRES, at Parit Sulong, 246-8; at Alexandra hospital, 374; on Banka Island, 386-7; at Tol, 410, 665-9; at Laha, 436; in Borneo, 603-4
MASSAVA (Sketch p. 654), 655
MASSY-BERESFORD, Brig T. H., 352
MASSY-GREENE, Hon Sir Walter, 40
MATADOR OPERATION, 92-3, 109, 121-3, 124-5, 138, 151
MATHESON, Maj G., 394
MATLOFF, M. & SNELL, E. M., 202n
MATSUDA, Nobunaza, 603n
MATSUI, Lt-Gen Takuro, 133n
MATSUOKA, Yosuke, 55-6, 87; becomes Foreign Minister, 22; states Japanese attitude to 10-year Pact, 37-8; on Lend-lease, and American policy, 55; offers Japan's services as mediator, 75; obtains pact of neutrality with USSR, 79; meets Ribbentrop in Berlin, 80; replaced as Foreign Minister, 87
MATTHEWS, Capt L. C., 356, 594, 595-7, 598-9
MATTHEWS, Spr P. J., 530n
MATUPI HARBOUR (Sketch p. 394), 395, 403
MATUPI ISLAND (Sketch p. 401), 396, 401, 404
MAUCATAR (Sketch p. 478), 493
Mauretania, British transport, 60
MAVELO PLANTATION (Sketch p. 654), 673
MAWHOOD, Lt-Col J. C., 83
MAXWELL, Maj A. M., 30, 212n, 228, 513, 515, 524
MAXWELL, Brig D. S. (Plate p. 15), 31, 68, 101, 106n, 210, 212n, 263, 275, 277, 296-8, 300, 304, 325, 327-8 356, 370, 382, 613; commands 2/19 Bn, 29; estimate of, 30; commands 27 Bde, 86; reconnoitres Gemas position, 167; seeks permission for limited

MAXWELL, Brig. D. S.—*continued*
withdrawal from Causeway, 329, delegates responsibility for coordination, 330; problems of, 333; opens headquarters in Holland road, 338; placed under command General Key, 338-9; reports to General Key, 343; ordered to recapture Bt Panjang, 354
MAY, Chaplain Rev J. L., 663n
MAYE, Sister D. M., 413
MAYMYO (Sketch p. 461), 643
MEAL, Sgt F. C., 232-3, 238
Meanjin, 515n
MEDAN (Sketch p. 448), 541
MEDICAL SUPPLIES, in captivity, 517, 518, 577n, 594, 601, 605, 609
MEDITERRANEAN SEA, 26, 51-2, 53-4, 76, 253; British naval commitments in, 19, 23-4, 56, 83
MEIKLEJOHN, Lt J. T., 314
MEILOE (Sketch p. 550), 551, 553-4, 555
MEKONG RIVER, 16
MELBOURNE, 31, 40, 64, 69, 84, 101, 154, 191n, 256, 374, 376n, 384, 385n, 415, 419-20, 423-4, 459, 638-9
MELVILLE, Lt-Col W. S., 213, 217-18, 220
MENADO (Map p. 393), 205, 417, 424, 426; loss of, 392, 490
MENAM KWA NOI RIVER (Sketch p. 563), 562-3, 564, 570
MENGGALA (Sketch p. 453), 455
MENTIPLAY, Lt D. V., 349n
MENZIES, Rt Hon R. G., 14, 72, 82-3, 191n; explains Australian policy in Pacific, 11; proposes conference with British Prime Minister and Dominion representatives, 21; instructs Australian delegation to Eastern Group Conference, 40; visits United Kingdom, 57; cables views on British naval reinforcement of Far East, 76; returns to Australia, 81
MERAK (Sketches pp. 498, 500), 499-500
MERAUKE (Sketch p. 439), 439-40
MERGUI (Map p. 112; Sketch p. 542), 102, 108, 541-2, 544, 548-9, 590, 637
MERRETT, Maj R. O., 312, 319, 322-3, 335, 345, 348; commands Merrett Force, 324
MERSING (Map p. 54; Sketch p. 251), 67n, 70, 107, 123, 133-4, 163, 180, 198, 199n, 203, 241, 254, 260, 262, 266-7; defence plans, 98-9, 100; 22nd Bde at, 121; dispositions, 153-4; operations at, 250, 251-2, 269; evacuation of, 279n; prisoners of war at, 519
MERSING, SUNGEI (Sketch p. 251), 251
MFZALI (Sketch p. 550), 553, 555
MICHIZAWA, Lt, 619
MIDDLE EAST, 13, 14, 19, 20, 23-5, 44-7, 57, 59, 60, 63, 65, 71-2, 76, 85-6, 96, 101, 104n, 145, 153-4, 163-4, 182, 205, 253, 256n, 258n, 381, 418, 447, 451n, 457-8, 460, 643; concentration of AIF in, 26-7, 59; British plans and policies, 21, 52, 81, 83; Indian Army reinforcement of, 79; Minister of State appointed, 91n; Allied strength in, 95; drawn upon to reinforce Far East, 184, 190, 371n, 443-4, 675
MIDWAY ISLAND (Maps pp. 30, 112), 127-8, 132, 176
MILITIA, 59; General Bennett's criticisms, 33-4; strength in Australia, 258n; first militia unit to go into action in Australian territory, 398n
MILLER, Lt H. D., 472
MILLER, Capt W. A., 86n
MILLS, Cpl C. C., 594
MILNE, Lt G. A. C., 402, 404
MINAMI, General Jiro, 2
MINA RIVER (Sketch p. 467), 473, 491, 492n
MINDANAO ISLAND (Map p. 178), 129, 132, 490, 507; Japanese landings, 177
MINES, 194, 251-2, 422, 436
MIRI (Sketch p. 179), 179-80
MISSION—204, 50-1, 643-5
MISSIONARIES, 395; in New Britain, 405, 662, 664, 669, 670-1; in Timor, 492
MITCHELL, Lt C. J., 536
MITCHELL, Pte H. E., 481
Mito Maru, Japanese transport, 411
MOIR, Brig R. G., 193
MOJI (Sketch p. 617), 613-14, 615-16, 626-7
Moji Maru, Japanese transport, 558
MOLLARD, Maj J. C., 398n, 407-8, 665, 671-2
MOLUCCA SEA (Map p. 393), 271, 392, 421
MONEY, Capt W. A., 661
MONEY-LENDING, at Changi, 518-19
MONGOLIA (Map p. 30), 16, 55

Montevideo Maru, Japanese transport, 406*n*, 593, 674
MOON, Maj A. A., 564*n*
MOORE, Lt C. H., 356
MOORHEAD, Brig H. D., 140, 149, 193-4, 235; commands 6/15 Indian Bde, 166; replaced, 207
MORALE, in Malaya, 152, 220, 290, 294, of III Indian Corps, 154, 199; of 2/21 Bn, 418; of US Navy, 440-1; in captivity, 511-12, 559*n*, 574, 581, 586, 608, 622
MORGAN, L-Sgt J. A., 665
MORGAN, Lt-Col M. C., 234, 248*n*
MORISON, S. E., 127*n*, 441*n*
MORO (Sketch p. 384), 388
MOROTAI (Maps pp. 30, 112), 603, 639-40
MORRIS, Maj-Gen B. M., 674*n*
MORRIS, Sgt O., 406, 409
MORRISON, Brig C. E., 189, 265
MORRISON, Dr G. E., 209*n*
MORRISON, Ian, 209*n*
MORRISON, Capt R. H. K., 218
MORSHEAD, Lt-Gen Sir Leslie, 206*n*
MORTARS, at Gemas, 219-20; at Rabaul, 403
MORTON, L., 116*n*, 177*n*, 390
MOSAK (Sketch p. 630), 630
MOSCOW, 61, 79
MOSES, Lt-Col C. J. A., 86*n*, 274, 325, 377, 381, 383
MOTEN, Brig M. J., 85
MOTHER, THE (Sketches pp. 394, 401), 395, 399
MOULMEIN (Sketch p. 542), 544-5, 546-7, 550, 555*n*, 558
MOUNTBATTEN, Admiral of the Fleet Rt Hon Earl, 633-4, 635
Mount Vernon, American transport, 183, 450*n*
MOXHAM, L-Bdr W. D., 603-4
MOYNIHAN, Cpl W. J., 275
MUAR (Map p. 54; Sketches pp. 211, 237), 182, 198-9, 206, 222, 257-8, 290*n*, 296, 299, 305*n*; reconnaissance of, 198; defence plan, 210; battle of, 222-49
MUAR, SUNGEI (Map p. 54; Sketch p. 211), 203, 210-11, 222, 223*n*, 230, 235; Japanese cross, 223-4, 224-5
MUDA, SUNGEI (Map p. 158), 159-61
MUDIE, Lt J. V., 312*n*
MUKDEN (Sketch p. 617), 3, 631, 639
MULL, Maj A., 550
MULLIGAN, L-Cpl C. F., 216*n*
MULO SCHOOL, 539
MUNICH, 30
MUNTOK (Sketch p. 384), 385-6, 540
MURAI, SUNGEI (Map p. 286), 298-9, 302, 306, 313-14, 315-16
MURAYAMA, Lt, 577
MURCHISON, Mr, 548
MURDOCH, Professor James, 9
MURRAY, Pte A. C., 505
MURRAY, WO1 E. A. A., 408
MURRAY-LYON, Maj-Gen D. M., 72, 106*n*, 147, 149, 151, 159; commands 11 Indian Div, 49; requests permission to withdraw from Jitra, 149-50; withdraws to Gurun, 157; replaced, 166
MURRAY RIVER, 31
MU SING, Mr, 595
MUSI RIVER (Sketch p. 453), 454
MUTAGUCHI, Lt-Gen Renya, 133*n*, 317*n*

Nagara, Japanese cruiser, 456
NAGASAKI (Sketch p. 617), 613, 628-9; prisoners of war at, 625-6
NAGASAKI BAY, 625
NAGATOMO, Colonel, 544, 545*n*, 546*n*, 547-9, 551-2, 555-6
NAGLE, L-Sgt A. G., 215
NAGUMO, Vice-Admiral C., commands Japanese Carrier Fleet, 111
NAITO, Lt, 548, 550*n*, 552
Naka, Japanese cruiser, 416
NAKARMA, 626, 641
NAKOM NAYOK (Sketch p. 542), 590
NAKOM PATON (Sketch p. 563), 588-9
NAMANULA RIDGE, 395, 401
NAMANULA ROAD (Sketch p. 401), 395
NAMATANAI (Sketch p. 413), 396, 416, 657
NAMAZIE ESTATE (Sketch p. 275), 271; action at, 275-7
NAMLEA (Sketch p. 439), 422, 427*n*; airfield at, 419*n*
Nana Maru, Japanese transport, 416-17
NANCHANG (Sketch p. 644), 643, 645

NANNING (Map p. 112), 16, 114
NAOETSU (Sketch p. 617), 613; prisoners of war at, 619-20
NASON, Capt C. H. T., 500
NAURU ISLAND (Map p. 30), 52, 130, 132, 394
NAVAL DISARMAMENT, 1-3, 12
NAVE, Paymaster Cdr T. E., 9*n*
NEAVE, Capt R. C., 491
NEE SOON (Map p. 344), 326, 330, 338, 354, 356-7, 364, 366
NEGRI SEMBILAN, State of (Map p. 54), 198
NEGRITOS, THE, in Philippines, 506
NETHERLANDS; see HOLLAND
NETHERLANDS EAST INDIES, 11, 24, 27, 57, 70, 82, 94*n*, 101-2, 111, 115, 121, 141*n*, 179, 182, 202, 294, 366, 396, 420, 424*n*, 444, 450*n*, 451*n*, 452-3, 466, 469, 493, 506-7, 524, 629, 676-7; and Japan, 15-16, 25, 39, 55, 93, 109, freezes Japanese assets, 87, Japanese plan attack, 110, 132; British reinforcement policy, 18, 24, 169, 190, 286; conjectural role in Pacific War, 41; defence plans and requirements, 43, 45; Australian cooperation and reinforcement of, 59, 69, 76, 122, 130, 418, 419; mobilises forces, 152; included in ABDA Command, 201-2, 646; British Air Force withdraws to, 341; planned employment of I Aust Corps in, 371, 443-5, 446-7, 675; Japanese invasion, 392, 453; prisoners of war in, 633-4
NETHERLANDS EAST INDIES ARMY; see DUTCH ARMY
NEW BRITAIN (Map p. 393; Sketch p. 658), 101, 396, 406, 410-11, 415; Japanese task force allotted, 111; evacuation of civilians, 392, 397, 673-4; prisoners of war in, 511, 593, 617-18, 621, Australian deaths, 642; evacuation of, 653-74
NEWBURY, Maj M. W. H., 426, 436
NEW CALEDONIA, 15, 397, 473
NEWCASTLE, NSW, 30, 31
NEW DELHI, conference at, 23, 40
NEW GUINEA (Map p. 30; Sketch p. 658), 10, 76, 111, 132, 176, 259, 279, 392, 396, 416, 419*n*, 420, 439, 465, 507, 606, 634, 648, 673; placed under Australian mandate, 1; extension of air force stations in, 45; administration of, 397*n*, 674; coastwatching service in, 398*n*; role of I Aust Corps in, 460; Indian prisoners of war in, 593
NEW GUINEA CONSTABULARY, 665*n*, 672
NEW HEBRIDES (Map p. 30), 15, 396-7; extension of air force stations in, 45
NEW IRELAND (Map p. 393; Sketch p. 413), 396, 398-9, 411, 415-16, 656; Japanese naval force allotted for capture of, 111
NEWNHAM, Capt C. F., 425, 431-3, 434*n*
NEWS, at Rabaul, 397; in Changi, 515. 526, 528-30; in Java, 534, 536; on Burma-Thailand railway, 557*n*; at Sandakan, 594; in Manchuria, 631; of liberation, 635-41
NEW SOUTH WALES, 29, 64, 146*n*
NEWTON, Maj R. W. J., 232-4, 237-8, 567*n*, 568, 614, 625
NEW ZEALAND, 7, 21, 39. 40*n*, 44-5, 52-3, 56, 61, 76, 82, 201, 256, 371, 441, 446-7, 460; in conjunction with Australia occupies German islands south of equator, 1*n*; presses for British fleet in Far East, 6; sends brigade to Fiji, 19*n*; probability of Japanese invasion of, 24-5, 41, 43; defence links with America and Australia, 39; aircraft deficiencies and requirements, 44; represented at Singapore conferences, 80, 164; declares war on Japan, 130; signs Atlantic Charter, 200*n*
NEW ZEALAND AIR FORCE, dependent on aircraft from Britain, 43;
—No 488 Sqn, 121*n*
NEW ZEALAND ARMY, 14
—Independent Companies, 83-4, 643*n*
NEW ZEALAND NAVY, 43-4, 45
NIBONG TEBAL (Map p. 158), 160
Nichi Maru, Japanese transport, 536
NICHOLLS, Maj H. W., 662, 664, 669-70
NIEBOUER, Mr, 469
NIEKE (Sketches pp. 542, 563), 545, 556, 561, 563-4, 572, 574, 576-7, 580-1, 587-8; see also LOWER NIEKE
Nieuw Amsterdam, Dutch transport, 60
NIKI-NIKI (Sketch p. 467), 492*n*
NIMITZ, Fleet Admiral Chester W., appointed Commander-in-Chief, US Pacific Fleet, 440-1
NINE-POWER TREATY, 10
Nippon Times, 437*n*, 528

NISBET, Brig T. G., 480
NISHIMURA, Lt-Gen Takumo, 224, 230, 249, 259, 261, 333; commands *Guards Division*, 133n
NISI ASI-BETU, 618
NITHSDALE ESTATE (Sketches pp. 251, 267), 100, 252; ambush in, 262, 266-9
NIYOR (Map p. 262), 260, 262
NOAH'S MISSION (Sketch p. 401), 405, 407-8
NOAKES, L-Sgt G. F., 529
NOBLE, Gp Capt C. H., 138
NOBLE, Pte J. A., 216
NOGUCHI, Colonel. 631
NOMURA, Admiral Kichisaburo, 56, 127, 132n; appointed Japanese Ambassador to Washington, 55; negotiates with Cordell Hull, 87, 94-5, 108, 130-31; seeks to be relieved of Ambassadorship, 109n
NON-AGGRESSION PACT OF 1939 (GERMANY-U.S.S.R.), 87
NONA, MT (Sketch p. 421), 425, 427, 429-31, 434
NONA PLATEAU, dispositions at, 425; defence of, 431-2
NON PLADUK (Sketch p. 563), 588
NOONAN, Cpl A. P., 414
NOONAN, W., 62n, 643n
NORDUP (Sketches pp. 394, 401), 395, 411
NORTH AFRICA, 19, 54, 104n, 258n, 418
NORTHCOTE, Stafford, 92n
NORTHCOTT, Lt-Gen Sir John, 41n, 53n; visits Malaya, 69, 76n, 164
NORTH DAUGHTER (Sketches pp. 394, 401), 395, 398
NORTH POINT (Map p. 171), 174
NORTHERN TERRITORY, 69, 101, 177, 418-19, 597
NORTH-WESTERN APPROACHES, 52
NORTH-WEST FRONTIER, 19
"NORTH-WEST ROAD", 16, 21
NORWAY, 15, 200n
NORWICH, Viscount; *see* DUFF COOPER, Rt Hon Sir Alfred
NOTTAGE, Capt S. G., 402n
NOUMEA, 397
NURSES, evacuated from Singapore, 362, 372-3; massacred at Banka Island, 386-7; at Rabaul, 397n, 406n, 612, 663n; in Sumatra, 540; in Japan, 618, 641
NUSA ISLAND (Sketch p. 413), 412
NUSALAUT ISLAND (Sketch p. 439), 439

O.16, Dutch submarine, 125n
OAHU ISLAND, 128; Japanese attack on, 110, 126-7
OAKES, Lt-Col R. F. (Plate p. 15), 226, 302n, 308n, 331, 333, 338, 354-5, 356-7, 581-2, 583-4, 585, 586n, 587; appointed CO 2/26 Bn, 304; takes command 2/26 Bn, 329-30; ordered to coordinate withdrawal from Causeway, 330
O'BRIEN, Maj C. B., 266-7, 268, 314, 315, 347, 348, 363
OCEAN ISLAND (Map p. 30), 127, 129, 130n, 132
OCUSSI (Sketch p. 467), 466, 491n
O'DONNELL, Lt-Col I. J., 85, 86n
OEYAMA (Sketch p. 617), 622
OFFICERS: Aust, 73; selected for 22 Bde, 29-30, for 27 Bde, 35-6; training for higher command, 33-4; promotion in 8 Div, 85-6; training school at Changi, 96; in captivity, 511, 512, 515n, 518n, 530, 543, 548, 559n, 562, 578-9, 584, 585-6, 587, 591-2, 599, 608, 617, 619, 620-1, 622, 629-31, 632, rates of pay, 531-2, 543n, 548n, 560, 610, deaths, 642. British, in Malaya, 96-7, 103. Indian, 104, 290n. Japanese, 113
OGAMA, Cdr, 657n
OHAMA (Sketch p. 617), 625n
OIL, Japanese needs, 11, 179, 371
OKADA, Cpl, 570
OKADA, Rokuo, 9n
OKAZAKI, Lt, 522
OKEY, Maj D. T., 267, 313-15, 320, 363
OKINAWA (Map p. 30), 640
OLDHAM, Capt G. C., 41n
OLDHAM HALL (Sketch p. 374), 362
OLD SILK ROAD, 16
OLLIFF, Maj S. F., 229, 234
OLNEY, Pte J. N., 404
OMUTA (Sketch p. 617), prisoners of war at, 628-9, 641
O'NEILL, Pte F. E. G., 664, 670
ONSLOW (Sketch p. 200), 201
OOSTHAVEN (Sketch p. 453), 453-4; evacuation of, 455-6
OPEN BAY (Sketch p. 658), 658, 660

OPHIR, MT (Map p. 54), 203
Orcades, British transport (Plate p. 495), 446, 448, 454-5, 457, 463
ORCHARD ROAD (Sketch p. 374), 370
ORD, Maj James B., 88
Orion, German raider, 52
OSAKA (Sketch p. 617), 621n, 622-3
OSBORN, CSM J. R., VC, 174
OSHIMA, General, 75, 90
Osprey, launch, 376-7
OTT, General, 87
OTTLEY, Lt D., 305
OUTRAM ROAD GAOL, 528, 596
OWEN, Lt-Col W. T., 401-4, 405-7, 411, 654, 663, 665, 671-2

P.1 AIRFIELD (Sketch p. 453), 453-4
P.2 AIRFIELD (Sketch p. 453), 442, 453-5
PACIFIC OCEAN (Map p. 30), 18, 23, 26, 41, 46, 50, 52, 57, 60, 79, 82, 91, 94n, 108n, 109, 128, 285-6, 395, 440, 451n, 507, 632; allotment of mandates, 1-2; Australia's trade interests, 5; British strategy, 7, 19, machinery for handling problems in, 93, 191n, naval strength, 145; threat of war in, 11, 14-15; role of America in, 13, 27, 39, 40, 53, 54, 55, 80; Japanese ambitions and plans, 17, 55, 56, 110, naval strength, 114; British-American cooperation in, 38; China's proposal for solution of problems, 39; effect of Pearl Harbour, 126-7; German raiders in, 130n; unified command of forces established, 182, 183-4, Australian representation on, 256; naval reinforcement of, 253; American naval offensive begins, 441; Japanese supremacy established, 508; role of Australia, 675, 677
PACIFIC WAR COUNCIL, 256, 452; on destination of I Aust Corps, 447, 449; recommends retention of troops in Java, 459
"PACK OF CARDS BRIDGE", 569
PACT OF STEEL, 37
PADANG (Sketch p. 384), 384-5, 388-9
PADANG BESAR (Map p. 139), 140
PAGE, Sub-Lt C. L., 398
PAGE, Rt Hon Sir Earle, 286, 451n; sent to London, 92; visits Singapore, 93; visits Manila and Washington, 93-4; represents Australia on UK War Cabinet, 169, 447, 449-50, 452; recommends diversion of 7 Aust Div to Ceylon, 459-60
PAGE, Maj H. H., 397n, 663, 674
PAHANG, STATE OF (Map p. 54), 93
PAHA RIVER (Sketch p. 468), 482
PAINTER, Brig G. W. A., 106n, 192, 270, 273, 275
PALABUHAN (Sketch p. 500), 505
PALAU ISLANDS (Map p. 112), 132
PALEMBANG (Sketch p. 453), 180, 305, 385, 442, 539; Japanese attack on, 453; withdrawal from, 454-5; prisoners of war at, 539-40
PALESTINE, 79, 85, 163, 255n
PALLISER, Admiral Sir Arthur, 123, 205, 457
PALMALMAL (Sketch p. 658), 672
PALMER, Lt-Col E. C., 395, 401, 663n, 665, 667n, 671-2
PALOH (Map p. 262), 257, 260
PANAMA, 200n, 587
PANAPAI (Sketch p. 413), 412, 414
Panay, American gunboat, 10
PANCHOR (Sketch p. 211), 222, 224
PANDAN, SUNGEI (Map p. 344), 340
PAPUA, 661; coastwatching service in, 398n
PARATROOPS, Japanese, 453-4, 483-4, 485, 489-90
PARIS, Brig A. C. M., 156, 160-1, 165, 185, 188-9, 195, 293, 317, 323-5, 326, 335, 339-40, 345-6, 384, 388-9; commands 12 Indian Bde, 106; commands 11 Indian Div, 166; reverts to command 12 Indian Bde, 207, 225n
PARIT JAWA (Sketch p. 211), 222, 224, 226-8, 231, 233
PARIT SULONG (Sketches pp. 211, 237), 65, 232-3, 234-5, 242, 245, 256, 272, 296; withdrawal to, 236-40; attempted relief of, 244; massacre at, 246-8; withdrawal from, 248-9
PARKER, MT (Map p. 171), 174
PARKER, Lt-Col G. E., 482-3, 491-2, 493
PARKER, Capt L., 679
PARKER, Col P. W., 240
PARKIN, Lt-Col J. H. D., 260, 262, 277n
PARRY, Maj J. H., 573n
PARRY, Lt K. W., 218

708 INDEX

PASCHKE, Matron Olive D., 387
PASIR LABA BATTERY, 293, 400n; arcs of fire, 300; bombardment of, 316
PASIR MAS (Map p. 139; Sketch p. 124), 64
PASIR PANJANG (Map p. 286; Sketch p. 360), 291, 325, 337, 340, 358, 369
PASIR PANJANG III, 369
PASIR PANJANG RIDGE, 291, 361, 369
PASO (Sketch p. 421), 422, 424-5, 427, 431, 435, 437; defence of, 428-9
PASO ISTHMUS (Sketch p. 421), 420, 422
PATANI (Maps pp. 54, 139), 64, 133-4, 140, 151, 162; Japanese shipping losses, 125n; capture of, 135, 139
PATERSON, Capt J., 619, 620-1
PAY, in captivity, 519, 531, 537, 542-3, 544n, 559n, 560, 610
PAYA LANG ESTATE (Sketch p. 211), 210, 212
PAYA LEBAR (Sketch p. 374), 361, 367, 369
PEACH, Lt-Col F. S. B., 264, 522n
PEARCE, Dvr T. F., 220
PEARL HARBOUR (Maps pp. 30, 112), 39, 90n, 110, 115, 128-9, 145, 176-7, 200, 383, 419, 427, 440-1; Japanese plan surprise attack, 55, 56n; warnings of, 108; task force allotted, 111; attack on, 126-7, 131-2; effect in United States, 135-6
Peary, American destroyer, 474, 493
PEELER, S-Sgt W., VC, 536n
PEGU (Sketch p. 461), 462, 464-5
PEIRCE RESERVOIR (Maps pp. 286, 344), 291, 325, 356, 361, 364
PEIRSE, Air Chief Marshal Sir Richard, 205, 279
PEKING (Map p. 30), 10
PELLAGRA, 550
PENANG ISLAND (Maps pp. 54, 158), 64, 106, 134, 151, 190, 204 290, 294, 372, 451n; administration of, 48; British naval strength at, 103; garrison of, 156; evacuation of, 157, 159, 160; British air attacks on, 365
PENFOLD, A. W., BAYLISS. W. C. and CRISPIN, K. E., 215n, 683
PENFUI (Sketch p. 468), 419n, 468, 472, 475, 483-4, 489
PENFUI AIRFIELD (Sketch p. 468), 466, 468, 473; evacuated by air force, 474-5; demolished, 482; withdrawal from, 484
PENG SIANG, SUNGEI (Map p. 286; Sketch p. 310), 291, 326, 328-30, 339
Pensacola, American heavy cruiser, 127
Pensacola CONVOY, 127, 441, 474, 497n
PERAK, STATE OF (Maps pp. 54, 158), 164, 189, 209
PERAK, SUNGEI (Map p. 158), 64, 133, 159, 160, 162-3, 165-6, 181, 185-6, 189, 196
PERAK FLOTILLA, 185-6
PERCIVAL, Lt-Gen A. E. (Plate p. 47), 82n, 96, 103, 106, 108n, 122, 142. 145, 157, 159, 163-4, 168, 181, 186n, 193, 198, 207, 210, 212, 246, 250, 253, 258-9, 265, 272, 279, 281, 285, 287-8, 298, 303-5, 326, 338-9, 342-3, 346, 348, 354n, 358-9, 362, 369n, 373, 375-6, 381n, 382, 512, 520, 522, 612, 650-1, 652; appointed GOC Malaya, 78-9; requests minimum of 48 battalions for defence of Malaya, 93; relations with AIF, 96-7, 98, 154; endeavours to increase labour force, 107; visits Sarawak, 121; and Operation Matador, 124; orders that battle be fought out at Jitra, 149-50; approves withdrawal from Kelantan, 153; on Japanese tactics, 155, 166-7; authorises withdrawal to Perak, 162-3; orders formation of Roseforce, 185; plans defence of Johore, 198-9, 206, 221; assessment of, 204; reinforces Muar, 225-6; places Heath in command of Muar front, 230; reinforces Bukit Pelandok, 231; orders withdrawal to Yong Peng, 236; orders Bennett to resume command of troops on Muar road, 240; reorganises, 241; organises withdrawal to Singapore Island, 254, 257, 260-1, 271; assumes operational control of Singapore Island, 289-90; plans defence, 292-4; selects AIF lor most dangerous sector, 295; reinforces Western Area, 317, 339; organises perimeter defence of Singapore, 325, 335, 336-7, 343, 360-1, 369; orders counter-attack to regain Kranji-Jurong line, 340-1; on lack of air support, 352; ignores request for surrender, 354; seeks wider discretionary powers, 371-2; negotiates cessation of hostilities, 377, 378-80
PERLIS, STATE OF (Map p. 139), 140, 146; defence requirements, 93; withdrawal from, 147

PERRING, Lt M., 185
PERRY, Capt D. G., 425, 435
PERSIA, 31, 79, 95, 104n, 145
PERSIAN GULF, 371
Perth, Australian cruiser, 533, 615n, 616, 621n; in battle of Java Sea, 497-8
PESSMAN, Maj-Gen, 495
PHILIPPINE AIR FORCE, strength of, 89
PHILIPPINE ARMY, 205, 389-91, 506; expansion and organisation of, 88-90, 177
—DIVISIONS: *11 Filipino*, 90; *21 Filipino*, 90; *31 Filipino*, 90; *71 Filipino*, 90; *Philippine Div*, 90
—REGIMENTS: *Philippine Scouts*, 89
PHILIPPINE CONSTABULARY, 89
PHILIPPINE GOVERNMENT, 89
PHILIPPINE ISLANDS (Map p. 42: Sketch p. 88), 23n, 38, 50, 53, 59, 75, 87, 115, 121, 127-8, 176, 182, 202, 206, 342, 437, 441, 446n, 474, 497, 595, 606, 614, 616, 628-9, 632, 634, 638, 676; United States acquisition of, 4n; defence plans, 80, 89-90; reinforcement of. 94; Japanese plans, 110-11, 116; air attacks on, 129, 132; invasion of, 177-9; included in ABDA command, 201, 646-7; campaign in, 205, 389-91; surrender of, 506-7. *See also* FILIPINOS, THE
PHILIPPINE NAVY, 89
PHILLIPS, WO2 F. V., 505
PHILLIPS, Admiral Sir Tom, 123-4, 145n; appointed C-in-C Eastern Fleet, 122; decides to attack Japanese invasion force, 141-3; death of, 144
PHOSPHATES, 52
PHUQUOK ISLAND (Sketch p. 88), 134
PICKFORD, Capt C., 361
PICKUP, Capt A. C., 228, 242
PICONE, Capt D. G., 599
PIESSE, Maj E. L., 8n, 9-10
Piet Hein, Dutch destroyer, 456
PILELO ISLAND (Sketch p. 658), 669
PIPE-LINE (Maps pp. 286, 344; Sketch p. 328), 291, 293, 330, 343, 345, 351, 355-7
PITSANULOK (Sketch p. 542), 590
PLACE NAMES, INDONESIAN, xiii, 419n
PLACENTIA BAY, 91
PLAYFAIR, G., 191n, 288n
PLAYFAIR, Maj-Gen I. S. O., 256n
PLEASANT, MT (Sketch p. 374), 373
PLENAPS, 81
POIDEVIN, Capt L. O. S., 489n
POINT 85 (Sketch p. 347), 345
POLAND, 200n
POMPONG, PULAU, 389
POND, Col S. A. F., 309, 318, 319, 322-3, 326, 336, 340, 345, 351-2, 362, 573, 577-8, 579, 580-1; appointed BM 27 Bde, 36; commands 2/29 Bn, 296; on factor of tiredness in unseasoned troops, 371n
PONDAI (Sketch p. 211), 212
PONDO (Sketch p. 654), 658-9, 660
PONTIAN, SUNGEI, 250
PONTIAN KECHIL (Map p. 262), 258-9, 260-1, 265, 273
POONA, 290n
POPLE, Maj F. H., 373
PORT ARTHUR, 640
PORT DICKSON (Map p. 54; Sketch p. 208), 62, 63n, 70, 106, 303n
PORT MORESBY (Map p. 112; Sketch p. 658), 44, 57, 258n, 286, 406, 415-16, 657, 659, 670, 672-3, 674n; reinforcement of, 15, 59; expansion of naval station, 45; planned development, 89
PORT SWETTENHAM (Map p. 105; Sketch p. 208), 68n, 185, 193, 208, 303n; airfield at, 193
PORTUGAL, 469, 470; protests at landing of troops in Portuguese Timor, 471, 475n
PORTUGUESE, THE, 420, 466, 481; relations with Dutch, 471
PORTUGUESE ARMY, 467, 475
PORT WELD (Sketch p. 188), 189
POTSDAM DECLARATION, 635
POWELL HARBOUR (Sketch p. 654), 658
POWNALL, Lt-Gen Sir Henry, 256n; appointed C-in-C Far East, 166; assessment of, 204; becomes Wavell's Chief of Staff, 205
POYAN, SUNGEI (Sketch p. 310), 315, 321
POYNTON, L-Sgt J. W., 477, 479, 492n
PRABUMULIH (Sketch p. 453), 454
PRACHUAB KIRIKUN (Sketch p. 542), 590

PRAED POINT (Sketches pp. 394, 401), 395, 397, 400-1, 411
PRESS, THE, 71-4
PRIGGI RAJAH (Sketch p. 384), 388
Prince of Wales, British battleship, 91-2, 122, 142; arrives Singapore, 103; sinks, 143-4
PRISONERS OF WAR: Japanese attitude to, 113, 546n, 562-3; number taken at Singapore, 382, 511; duties of, 385n; interrogation of, 520-2, 535; escape prevention, 523, 528, 535, 543-4, 546-7, 550, 595, 597; pay of, 531-2, 536, 543, 548, 559n, 560, 566; forms of Japanese punishments, 528, 536-7, 552-3, 560, 563, 568-9, 591, 595, 596-7, 598-9, 600, 605, 609, 610, 618, 619, 625-6, 628-9, 630; sea transportation of, 540-1, 558, 593, 596, 611-16, 617, 642, 674; Malay Prisoner-of-War Administration, 545; rail transportation of, 562, 567, 572, 582; Japanese treatment of sick, 565-6, 569-70, 572-3, 576-7, 579, 584, 589, 609, 623, 632; selection of Japan parties, 589; release and repatriation, 632-42; General Bennett's status, 650, 651-2. **American**, in Changi, 530, in Java, 533-4, 538; in Burma-Thailand, 546, 549, 551, 557-8, 560-1, 588, 591, 637; on Ambon, 606, 639; in Japan, 613-14, 618-19, 620-22, 625-6 ,628; in Formosa, 629; in Manchuria, 630: repatriation, 634. **Australian**, 246-8; numbers captured by areas, 511; acting promotion in captivity, 517n; treatment subsequent on Japanese midget submarine raid on Sydney, 537; handling of personal effects, 547; deaths in Burma-Thailand, 554, 561, 588; and Central Army Records Office, 679-82; deaths by areas and causes, 642. **British**, 503; number taken at Singapore, 382, 511; in Changi, 515n, 523-4, 530, 637; in Java, 533-4, 538; in Burma-Thailand, 541, 546, 549, 551, 557, 562, 568, 571-2, 574, 576, 579, 580, 587, 590-1, deaths, 554n, 561, 581, 584, 588; in Borneo. 595-6, 598, 600-1; in Ambon, 606; in Japan, 613, 614-15, 618-19, 620-2, 623-4, 625-6, 628; in Formosa, 629; in Manchuria, 630; liberation and repatriation, 634, 637, 642. **Burmese**, 642. **Canadian**, 622, 634. **Chinese**, 642. **Dutch**, 524; in Changi, 530, 637; in Java, 533-4, 538; in Sumatra, 540-1; in Burma-Thailand, 543, 545n, 546-9, 551, 553-4, 556-7, 558, 560, 562, 564, 571, 590-1, deaths, 561, 588; in Ambon, 604-5, 606; in Hainan, 608, 610; in Japan, 613, 619, 620, 625-6, 628, 633n; in Formosa, 629; repatriation of, 634, 639. **Indian**, 247, 593; repatriation of, 634, 637. **Indonesian**, 626. **Malay**, 642. **New Zealand**, 642. **Portuguese**, 642.
—FORCES: "A" Force, 558; formed, 519; in Burma-Thailand, 541-57; deaths in, 561. "B" Force, formed, 519; in Borneo, 593-4. "C" Force, 613; formed, 524; in Japan, 619-21. "D" Force, 529n, 583; formed, 525; in Burma-Thailand, 566-71, mortality rate, 571. "Dunlop Force", 538, 562-3, 564-6, 571. "E" Force, 529n, formed, 525; in Borneo, 596-604. "F" Force, 529n, 530, 588; formed, 525; in Burma-Thailand, 571-81, deaths, 581. "G" Force, 613-14; formed, 525; in Japan, 621-22. "H" Force, 529n, 530, 568, 588; formed, 525; in Burma-Thailand, 581-7, deaths, 585-6. "J" Force, 614; formed, 525; in Japan, 622-5. "K" Force, formed, 525; in Burma-Thailand, 587-8. "L" Force, formed, 525; in Burma-Thailand, 587-8. **Senior Officers' Party**, 519-20, 522, 524, 612-13, 618; in Formosa and Manchuria, 629-31
—GROUPS: 1 (Thailand), 545; 2 (Thailand), 545; 3 (Burma), 547-9, 551, 555, 561; 4 (Thailand), 545; 5 (Burma), 545, 549, 551. 556, 557-61
—UNITS: *Anderson Force*, 546-7, 549, 551, 553-4, 555-6; *Black Force*, 546-7, 551, 553, 558; *Green Force*, 546-7, 549, 551, 553; *Ramsay Force*, 547, 549, 551, 553; *Williams Force*, 546-7, 549, 551, 553-4, 555-6, 558; *No. 1 Mobile Force*, 551, 553-4, 555-6. "O" *Battalion*, 564, 568, 571n; "P" *Battalion*, 564, 568, 571n; "Q" *Battalion*, 564; "R" *Battalion*, 564; "S" *Battalion*, 566. 567n, 571n; "T" *Battalion*, 567, 571n; "U" *Battalion*, 567n
PROPAGANDA, 62, 72n; British, 74, 141, 190-1; Japanese, 157, 294, 397, 538, 589, 606, 609, 679
PUBLICITY, in Malaya, 73-4, 84, 141, 190-1, 294
PUDU GAOL, 248n
PULFORD, Air Vice-Marshal C. W. H., 145, 168, 281, 373; becomes AOC Far East Command, 77; assessment of, 204; death, 383

PURWAKARTA (Sketch p. 500), 501
PUT PUT (Sketches pp. 413, 654), 395, 661, 663

QANTAS EMPIRE AIRWAYS 444n, 473
QUARRY ROAD (Sketch p. 212), 213-15
Queenborough, British destroyer, 639
Queen Elizabeth, British battleship, 253
Queen Mary, British transport (Plate p. 14), 60-1, 63
QUEENSLAND, 29, 146n
QUETTA, 28, 85
QUEZON, Manuel, 88, 89n; proposes agreement with Japan, 391
QUICK, Maj E. J., 567n
QUIGLEY, Pte J. B., 245
QUINLAN, Lt J. E., 233
QUINN, J. P., 365, 376
QUITTENDON, WO2 M. W., 544

RABALANAKAIA (Sketch p. 401), 395
RABAUL (Map p. 112; Sketches pp. 394, 401), 86, 259, 286, 396, 413, 415n, 416, 418, 427, 441, 451n, 490n, 493, 641, 670-1, 673; decision to base force at, 59, 392; planned development of, 89, 396-7; Japanese plans, 111; garrison of, 394-5, dispositions, 397, 400-3; air raids, 398-400; fight for, 403-10; Japanese account, 411-12; movement of prisoners from, 612, 674, 679; withdrawal from, 653-74
RACECOURSE (Map p. 344), 325, 343, 352, 355, 356-7, 358, 360, 367
RACECOURSE VILLAGE (Sketch p. 360), 352, 359, 360, 363
RADAR, 126, 128, 131
RAFDER, Grand-Admiral Erich, 371
RAFFLES, Sir Stamford, 65
RAFFLES COLLEGE (Sketch p. 374), 382
RAFFLES SQUARE, 126
RAHENG (Sketch p. 542), 545
RAIDERS, GERMAN, in Pacific Ocean, 52, 130n, 394
RAILACO (Sketch p. 478), 471-2, 475, 478-9, 481
RALABANG PLANTATION (Sketch p. 654), 663
RALUANA (Sketch p. 401), 396, 399, 401, 402-3, 404-6, 411
RALUANA MISSION (Sketch p. 401) 402, 404
RALUANA POINT (Sketch p. 394), 395
RAMSAY, Col G. E., 330, 331-2, 338, 342-3, 354-5. 364. 541, 549, 551, 553; commands 2/30 Bn, 329; abandons attack on Bt Panjang, 355-6
RAMSBOTHAM, Capt F., 251
RAMSHAW, F-Lt J. C., 137
RAMU VALLEY (Sketch p. 658), 673
RANAU (Sketch p. 595), death marches to, 600-1; prisoners of war at, 601-2
RANGARERE PLANTATION (Sketch p. 654), 656
RANGKASBITUNG (Sketch p. 500), 499
RANGOON (Map p. 30; Sketches pp. 448, 461), 16, 169, 284, 371, 459, 545, 547, 551, 635, 637-8, 643; reinforcement of. 285; proposed employment of AIF at, 447. 449, 450-2, necessity examined, 460-5; evacuation of, 463-4
RANO (Sketch p. 658), 669
RATIONS, at Changi, 512-13, 515, 517, 523-4, 527-8, 531-2, supplemented by Black Market, 518, on working parties, 519; in Java, 532, 534, 535-6, 538-9; in Sumatra, 539-40; at sea, 541, 611-12, 613; in Burma-Thailand, 542, 544n, 556-7. 559, 566, 576-7, 580, 583; in Borneo, 593-4, 596, 600-1, 602; on Ambon, 605, 607-8; on Hainan, 610, 611; in Japan, 616-17, 618-19, 620-1, 623, 625, 627; on Formosa, 629; in Manchuria, 630-1; in Korea, 632
RAWENG (Sketch p. 188), 193
READ, Capt J. F., 483n
RECONNAISSANCE, AIR: British, 122, 123-4, 138, 143, 151, 169, 230n, 305. Japanese, 144, 411n, 426
RECONNAISSANCE, GROUND: of Muar-Gemas line, 198; of Ambon and Timor, 418-19
RECRUITING, 98; effect of fall of France on, 14; of Res MT Coys, 146n
RED CROSS, in Changi, 528, 531; in Java, 539; on Burma-Thailand railway, 547-8, 557; in Japan, 618, 619, 620, 621-2, 623-4, 627-8, 630; in Manchuria, 630-1; in Korea, 631-2
REED, Cpl G. B., 412
REEVE, Gnr A., 544n
REFORMATORY ROAD (Map p. 344), 337, 345. 347-8, 351, 367; withdrawal to, 340, 349; Japanese attack, 350; defence of, 358-9, 362-5

REID, Pte K. S., 219
REINFORCEMENTS, *Aust*, 96, 258, 296, 473, 487; tiredness factor in battle, 371*n*. *Indian*, 258
REISIR, Gnr D., 527*n*
REITHER, Pte H., 603
RENGAM (Map p. 262), 257, 260, 262, 270
RENGAT (Sketch p. 384), 388-9
RENGIT (Map p. 262), 224, 261, 265
REPATRIATION OF ALLIED PRISONERS OF WAR AND INTERNEES, work of, 633-42
Repulse, British battle cruiser, 92, 122-3, 142; arrives Singapore, 103; sinking of, 144-5
REPULSE BAY (Map p. 171), 175
REPULSE BAY HOTEL, 175
RETPU (Sketch p. 550), 550-1
Reveille, 33*n*
REYNOLDS, Lt P. R., 232, 242, 248
REYNOLDS, Capt W. R., 389
RHIO ARCHIPELAGO (Sketch p. 384), 388
RIBBENTROP, Joachim von, 75, 80, 87
RICE, 49
RICE-OXLEY, Major, 596
RICHARDS, Capt C. R. B., 553, 627
RICHARDS, Cpl R. C., 479
RICHARDSON, Lt G. D., 313
RICHARDSON, Hal, 597*n*
RICHARDSON, Capt R. J. D., 311-12, 319, 347, 596
RICHARDSON, Lt W. J., 348
RICKARDS, Cpl J., 594
RIL (Sketch p. 658), 660, 672
RIPLEY, F-Lt G. C., 603
RITCHIE, Lt J. M., 232
RIVERINA, 30
RIVER VALLEY CAMP (Map p. 286), 519, 539, 614, 616, 628
RIVETT, Rohan, 683
RIX, A. R., 9*n*
ROACH, Lt-Col L. N., 426, 473; commands 2/21 Bn, 31; reconnoitres Ambon, 418; appeals for reinforcements, 420, 422-4
ROBERTS, R. G., 615*n*, 683
ROBERTS, Capt S. S., 357
ROBERTSON, Lt-Col A. E., 250, 315-16, 321, 358, 363, 613, 619; ordered to form Special Reserve Bn, 302; commands 2/19 Bn, 304, 308; death of, 620
ROBERTSON, Lt-Gen Sir Horace, 8*n*, 520
ROBERTSON, Lt-Col J. C., 211, 225, 226-7, 228-9; commands 2/29 Bn, 35-6
ROBERTSON, Maj L. J., 536, 558-9, 560-1
ROBINSON, Lt A. L., 666*n*, 669, 672
ROBINSON, Cpl S. A., 477*n*
ROCHE, Bdr F. C., 527*n*
ROFF, Capt N. H., 472, 483-5, 486-7
ROGERS, Sgt J., 332
"ROKEBY", 31
Rokyu Maru, Japanese transport, 614-15
ROMANUS, C. F. and SUTHERLAND, R., 39*n*
ROME, 38, 79
ROMMEL, Field Marshal Erwin, 253
ROOSEVELT, Franklin D., 18, 22, 38, 55-6, 108, 130, 136*n*, 163, 169, 182, 199, 201*n*, 383, 441, 449, 451, 458, 460, 465, 648, 649; signs Selective Service Bill, 23; issues directive on American policy in Pacific, 52-3; appoints MacArthur Commander US Army Forces in Far East, 87-8; meets Churchill on *Prince of Wales*, 91; appeals to Japanese Emperor, 109; and defence of Philippines, 177, 391; proposes Wavell as ABDA Command, 183-4; appeals to Curtin to divert 7 Aust Div to Burma, 450; orders MacArthur to Australia, 506
ROSE, Lt-Col A. J. C., 67*n*, 185
ROSE, Col H. B., 175
ROSE, Capt J. A., 470
ROSEBERY RACECOURSE, 29, 35
Rosenbaum, Dutch merchantman, 455
ROSS, Gp Capt D., 57-8, 469, 470, 493
ROSS, Dvr J. C., 662
ROSS, Capt J. F., 234, 243
ROUND, G., 523*n*
ROURKE, Brig H. G., 70, 80*n*; appointed GSO 1 8 Div, 28; becomes CRA 7 Div, 85
ROWELL, Lt-Gen Sir Sydney, 86*n*, 95, 98, 101, 422-3
ROYAL MILITARY COLLEGE, DUNTROON, 9, 10, 28
RUBBER, Malayan output, 14, 48
RUDDER, Capt R. O. D., 440, 604

RUSES, *American*, at Midway, 127*n*; *Japanese*, 116-17, 121*n*, 134, 161, 165, 264*n*, 267, 276, 306-7, 346, 432, 437
RUSSELL, Sgt E. S., 263
RUSSELL, Lt G. T., 429
RUSSIA, 1, 16, 21, 94*n*, 136, 183, 341-2; and Japan, 4, 54-5, 79-80, 87, 90, 93; German attack on, 46*n*, 145; transfers divisions from east to west, 80*n*; Allied aid to, 91, 103, 141*n*; signs Atlantic Charter, 200*n*
RUSSIAN ARMY, 79-80, 113, 117, 201*n*, 639
RUSSIAN MARITIME PROVINCES, 87, 93*n*, 131
RUSSO-JAPANESE WAR, 113, 117
RYAN, Pte M. P., 476-7
RYLAND, S Ldr J. P., 419*n*
Ryujo, Japanese aircraft carrier, 454

SABAK (Sketch p. 124), 125
SABANG ISLAND (Sketch p. 112), 169, 206
SABIN, Lt-Col H. L., 278*n*
SAGGERS, Maj A. E., 317, 319, 322-3, 325-6, 340, 345, 347-9, 350, 585; commands Special Reserve Battalion, 304
Sagiri, Japanese destroyer, 180
SAHUM (Map p. 188), 187
SAIGON (Map p. 30; Sketch p. 88), 113, 121, 134 144, 589, 614; 616, 634
SAINT PATRICK'S COLLEGE (Map p. 286), 362
SAINT PAUL'S (Sketch p. 654), 655, 660
ST JACQUES, CAPE (Sketch p. 88), 612
SAIPAN (Map p. 30), 132, 615
SAITO, General, 530-1
SAKAI, THE, 66
SAKAI, Lt-Gen T., 173
SAKATA (Sketch p. 617), 627
Sakewa Maru, Japanese transport, 137*n*
Sakina Maru, Japanese transport, 125*n*
SALAMAUA (Sketch p. 658), 411, 658-9
SALIGARI, Pte E. P., 404
SALWEEN RIVER (Sketch p. 461), 16, 460-1
SAMAH (Sketch p. 88), 134, 638-9
SAMARAI (Sketch p. 658), 670
SAMARINDA (Sketch p. 179), 206
SAMOA (Map p. 30), 441
SAMS, Pte E. W., 216*n*
SANDAKAN (Sketch p. 595), prisoners of war at, 593-604
SANDAKAN AIRFIELD, 597, 600, 604
SANDERSON, Lt R. E., 185
SAN DIEGO, 441
SANDY, Maj D. A., 425-6
SANITATION, at Changi, 515, 523
SANTOSA (Sketch p. 500), 502
SANTUBONG RIVER, 181
SAPARUA ISLAND (Sketch p. 439), 439
SAPI (Sketch p. 595), 604
Saratoga, American aircraft carrier, 440
SARAWAK (Map p. 179), 47, 179; British strength in, 121; invasion of, 180
SARAWAK STATE FORCES, 180-1
SARIMBUN, PULAU (Sketch p. 310), 312
SARIMBUN, SUNGEI (Map p. 30; Sketch p. 310), 298, 312
SAUK (Map p. 158), 165
SAWAHLUNTO (Sketch p. 384), 388
SAYRE, Francis B., 391
SCANLAN, Col J. J., 398, 402, 405-8, 612, 618, 653, 657, 659, 661, 664, 668-9, 670-1, 672-4; arrives Rabaul, 397; orders redeployment, 399, 400-1
SCHILLING, Maj-Gen 495-6, 497, 499, 500-1, 502
SCHOFIELD, WO2 P. A., 220
SCHOOLS, in Malaya, 95
Scorpion, British gunboat, 265
SCOTT, W Cdr E. D., 424*n*, 427*n*, 439
SCOTT, Sir Robert, 74*n*
SCOTT, Col W. J. R., 84*n*, 423, 429-33, 438, 440, 604-6, 608-10, 638-9; represents Gull Force at AHQ, 420; appointed commander of Gull Force, 424; arrives Ambon, 426, problems, 426-7; negotiates surrender, 434-5
SCRIVEN, Lt-Col E. G. B., 85; appointed CRE 8 Div, 28-9; death, 69*n*
Sea Bird, steamship, 505
SEARLE, Colonel, 534
SEDENAK (Map p. 262), 262, 270, 273, 277
SEDILI BESAR, SUNGEI (Sketch p. 99), 99

INDEX   711

SEGAMAT (Map p. 54; Sketches pp. 99, 211), 56, 100, 203, 209-11, 212n, 221, 225-6, 246; withdrawal from, 230-1, 235, 240
SEGAMAT, SUNGEI (Sketch p. 211), 210, 230, 235
SELAMA (Map p. 158), 160, 162, 166
SELANGOR, STATE OF (Map p. 54; Sketch p. 188), 189, 198, 203
SELANGOR, SUNGEI (Sketch p. 188), 193, 207
SELAPUI ISLAND (Sketch p. 413), 414
SELARANG BARRACKS, 512, 525, 527, 530; incident, 523
SELBY, Maj D. M., 394-5, 397-8, 401, 402-3, 653, 667, 671
SELBY, Brig W. R., 194-5, 298; commands 28 Indian Brigade, 166
SELETAR AIRFIELD (Map p. 286), 121, 126, 291
SELETAR RESERVOIR (Map p. 286), 291, 338
SELETAR RIFLE RANGE (Map p. 344), 356, 364
SEMAU ISLAND (Sketch p. 468), 482
SEMAU STRAIT (Sketch p. 468), 466, 472
SEMBAWANG AIRFIELD (Map p. 286), 121n, 144, 223, 244n, 291, 357
SEMBRONG, SUNGEI (Sketch p. 263), 263-4
SENGARRANG (Map p. 262), 259, 261, 264-5
SENTUL, 62, 96n
SEOUL (Sketch p. 617), 612, 631-2
SERAGI (Sketch p. 654), 659
SERANG (Sketch p. 500), 533-4, 539, 616
SEREMBAN (Map p. 54; Sketch p. 208), 62, 63n, 70, 72
SERGIOPOL, 16
SERIA (Sketch p. 179), 179
SERI BAY (Sketch p. 421), 439
SERVICES PRESS BUREAU, 73-4
SEYMOUR, 31
SHANGHAI (Map p. 30), 49, 82n, 507, 643; Japanese landings at, 3; British garrison withdrawn, 13, 21, 23
SHARMAN, Lt T. M., 483, 488-9, 491n
SHAW, Lt, 321
SHAW, Maj J. A. L., 303
SHEARER, Lt J. N., 223n
SHEEHAN, Maj-Gen E. L., 31
SHEPHERD, J., 6n
SHERWOOD, R. E., 23n, 136n
SHIER, Capt F. E., 399, 401-4, 406
SHIKATA, Lt, 619
SHIKOKU (Sketch p. 617), 617
SHING MUN REDOUBT (Map p. 171), 172
Shinonome, Japanese destroyer, 180
SHINTOISM, 2
SHIPPING: *Allied*, 182, 677; German raiders attacks on, 52, 130n, protection of, 53; tonnages handled at Singapore and Sydney compared, 65; losses at Pearl Harbour, 127; movement of AIF from Middle East, 190, 450n; moved from Singapore, 372; losses in Darwin raid, 493; for repatriation purposes, 642. *Japanese*, amount employed for offensive, 110-11; losses at Kota Bharu, 125, 135, 137, at Balikpapan, 417; employed for transport of prisoners, 541, 558, 611-16, 617
SHIRAKAWA (Sketch p. 630), 630
Shokaku, Japanese aircraft carrier, 427
SHORT, Pte N. A. E., 603-4
Shun an, British river boat, 251n
SIAM; *see* THAILAND
SIAM, GULF OF (Sketch p. 88), 122-3, 134
SIAN (Sketch p. 617), 631n
Sibajak, Dutch transport, 84
SIBERIA, 16
SIEW CHEOW, Mr, 596
SIGNALS, Aust, in Malaya, 214, 217n; on Singapore Island, 308, 309-10, 317, 327, 329, 364; at Rabaul, 406; in Java, 496
SIKHS, THE, at Changi, 514, 523-4; in Borneo, 594
SILVERMAN, Capt H. N., 405, 663
SIM, Sig S., 529, 530n
SIME ROAD (Sketch p. 374), 294, 352, 357, 373, 519, 530, 585
SIMMONS, Maj-Gen F. Keith, 106, 168, 254, 272, 281, 292, 297n, 303, 359, 361; commands Singapore Fortress troops, 79; commands Southern Area, 293; allotted role in defence of Singapore, 336-7
SIMONS, Sister Jessie E., 683
SIMONSTOWN, 371
SIMPANG JERAM (Sketch p. 211), 222, 224, 226
SIMPANG KIRI, SUNGEI (Sketch p. 237), 228, 242
SIMPANG RENGAM (Map p. 262), 224, 264
SIMPSON HARBOUR (Sketch p. 394), 395, 399, 403

SIMSON, S-Sgt A. B., 410
SIMSON, Brig I., 375, 376-7; appointed Director-General of Civil Defence in Singapore, 191, 288
SINGAPORE (Map p. 286; Sketch p. 374), 1, 41, 46-7, 53, 57, 60, 64, 69, 72, 74-5, 81, 85, 87, 96, 100, 102, 107, 116, 122-3, 134, 138, 141n, 142, 144, 149, 150-1, 166, 170, 172, 197-9, 201-2, 204-7, 222, 225n, 254, 256, 265-6, 272, 279, 283, 295, 315, 325, 329, 331, 348n, 350, 352-3, 356, 359n, 365, 367, 391, 400n, 442, 444, 446, 450n, 451n, 452, 463, 496, 520, 523-4, 539, 540, 545-6, 548n, 558, 562, 567, 572, 581-2, 586, 588-9, 593, 596, 604, 613, 614, 616, 617, 640, 677; strength of garrison, 13, 63, 103, estimated requirements, 18, 44, 93; reinforcement policy, 13-14, 52, 76-7, 81; Australia's contribution, 15, 19, 45, 51-2, 59, 61-2, 84, its importance to Australia, 24-5, Australian Government representative appointed, 91-2; proposed use by American fleet, 17-18, 38-9, 54, 80; defence plans and problems, 20, 27, 78-9, 93, 98-9, 106, 284-5, 286, 287-8, 292-4, 295-6; Japanese gain bases for attack on, 26, 56; administration of, 48; air reinforcement, 58, 169; population, 65; Japanese plans, 80, 133, 306; naval reinforcement of, 92-3, 103; army reinforcement of, 95, 160-1, 182-3, 184, 189-91, 210, 258, 287, 289-90; Dutch submarines based on, 125n; air attacks on, 126, 152, 287, 370-1, 372, 381, 531; British Resident Minister appointed, 145; proposed dispatch of I Aust Corps to, 163; proposed appointment of Military Governor, 204n, 303; perimeter defence of, 336-7, 340, 343, 361, 368-79; surrender of, 353-4, 378-81, 382-3, 387, 389, 650-2; stragglers in, 366, 376-7; escapes from, 380-1, 383-9, 650-2; prisoners of war at, 511, 519, 525, 541, 585, liberation and repatriation, 634, 635-8; broadcasts from, 681
SINGAPORE CONFERENCES: *Oct 1940*, 40-6, 51, 58, 76-7, 79; *Feb 1941*, 76-7, 392; *Apr 1941*, 94; *Sep 1941*, 93; *Dec 1941*, 163-4; resolutions adopted by America, 108
SINGAPORE CRICKET CLUB, 373
SINGAPORE DAIRY FARM (Maps pp. 286, 344), 298, 346, 356-7
SINGAPORE GOLF CLUB (Map p. 344), 352, 357
SINGAPORE HARBOUR, 372, 385
SINGAPORE ISLAND (Maps pp. 54, 286), 48, 58, 98, 104, 114n, 154, 180, 186, 203, 205, 207, 223, 231, 248n, 251, 261, 264-5, 282, 380, 383, 529, 571-2; compared to Tasmania, 64; army strength and deployment, 79, 106n, 341-2; British air force strength on, 121n, withdraws to, 163, withdraws from, 289, 341; Japanese air attacks, 126, 221, 289; defence plans and preparations, 168, 253-4, 283, 299-302; Director-General of Civil Defence appointed, 191; withdrawal to, 254, 257, 260, 269-70, 271-2, bridgeheads allocated, 272-3; civil administration in, 288, 303, population, 290, morale of, 294-5; artillery defences and employment, 291-2, 295-6, 327; Japanese bombardment of, 299, 303-4, 305, 308-9; Japanese plans, 305-7; operations on, 308-34, 335-67; escapes from, 348n, 376-7, 378; organised evacuation parties, 372-3, 383; casualties, 382; prisoners of war in, 511-12, 519, 531, 633, liberation and repatriation, 636-7; Allied air raids on, 532. *See also* SINGAPORE, SINGAPORE NAVAL BASE
SINGAPORE NAVAL BASE (Map p. 286), 14, 131, 143, 145, 170, 293n, 294, 306-7, 333; construction authorised, 3; role in Pacific War, 6-7; theory examined, 7-8; basing of British fleet on, 15, 18-20, 23-4, 48, 446; effect of fall of France on, 26, opening of, 47; protection of, 153; planned demolition, 288; abandoned, 301, 357; Japanese enter, 373
Singapore Times, 222
SINGAPORE WAR COUNCIL, 288-9; assessment of personalities on, 204; Australian representation on, 365; ceases to function, 376
SINGKAWANG II AIRFIELD (Sketch p. 179), 180-1
SINGKEP ISLAND (Sketch p. 384), 384n
SINGORA (Maps pp. 54, 139), 64, 124, 133-4, 140, 143, 147, 207, 221, 269; plan to forestall Japanese seizure of, 92; Japanese capture, 135, 138; British air attacks, 365
SINGORA AIRFIELD, 138
SINKIANG PROVINCE (Map p. 30), 16
SIO (Sketch p. 658), 673

SIPUTEH (Map p. 158), 166
SITTANG RIVER (Sketch p. 461), 462-3
SITWELL, Maj-Gen H. D. W., 495, 496-7, 499, 501-2, 503, 534-5
SKUDAI (Map p. 262), 258-9, 260, 273, 279, 281-2, 283
SKUDAI, SUNGEI (Map p. 286; Sketch p. 310), 306, 327, 331
SLEEMAN, Lt F. N., 415
SLEEPY VALLEY ESTATE (Sketch p. 347), 345, 347-8
SLIM RIVER (Sketch p. 188), 188, 198, 209; withdrawal to, 189; battle of, 193-7, 202
SLOAN, Cpl J. K., 410
SMALL, Cpl A. L., 594
SMALLPOX, 553
SMITH, Capt D. O., 655
SMITH, Lt D. W., 430
SMITH, Pte F. C., 476-7
SMITH, Sgt F. S., 664
SMITH, L-Sgt H. L., 431
SMITH, Maj I. L., 399, 407-8
SMITH, Pte L. W., 406
SMITS, Capt, 564
SMOKERS, in captivity, 607, 628-9
SMUTS, Field Marshal Rt Hon J. C., 2*n*
SMYTH, Lt F. M., 318
SMYTH, Maj-Gen Sir John, 461, 464
SNELL, Lt, 439
SNELL, E. M.; *see* MATLOFF, M. and SNELL, E. M.
SNELLING, Capt R. R. L., 231, 234, 236, 239, 243*n*
Soerabaja, Dutch cruiser, 469, 470
SOLOMON ISLANDS (Map p. 30), 52; extension of air force facilities in, 45; coastwatching services in, 398*n*
SONGKURAI (Sketch p. 563), 574-6, 579-81, 590; *see also* LOWER SONGKURAI, UPPER SONGKURAI
SONGS, use in battle, 237
SOOK RIVER (Sketch p. 413), 413-14, 415
Soryu, Japanese aircraft carrier, 427
SOUTH AFRICA, 2*n*, 40*n*; signs Atlantic Charter, 200*n*
SOUTH AFRICAN WAR, 71
SOUTH AMERICA, 53
SOUTH AUSTRALIA, 29, 258*n*
SOUTH CHINA SEA (Map p. 30; Sketch p. 595), 121, 129, 284, 593, 674
SOUTH DAUGHTER (Sketches pp. 394, 401), 395
SOUTH-EAST ASIA COMMAND, 634-5
SOUTH-WEST PACIFIC AREA, 634, 675; General MacArthur appointed to command, 506
SPACKMAN, Cpl C. J., 314
Speaker, British aircraft carrier, 642
SPENCE, Lt-Col A., 469-70, 475, 492-3
SPENCER CHAPMAN, Lt-Col F., 83*n*, 84, 186
SPENDER, Hon Sir Percy, 101-2
SPOONER, Vice-Admiral E. J., 281, 288, 372; commands Naval Staff at Singapore, 204; death of, 383
SPORT, at Changi, 517; in Java, 533, 538; on Burma-Thailand railway, 551; on Ambon, 606
STACEY, Col C. P., 174*n*
STAFF CORPS, 33-4, 85
STAHLE, Lt-Col L. R. D., 86*n*, 520-1; appointed DADOS 8 Div, 29
Stand-To, 218*n*, 219*n*, 513*n*, 604*n*, 626*n*, 636*n*
STANLEY, FORT (Map p. 171), 175-6
STANLEY PENINSULA (Map p. 171), 175
STANWELL, Cpl O. M., 363
STARK, Admiral H. R., 39, 53, 81, 108
STAY-BEHIND PARTIES, in Malaya, 186
STEELE, Maj-Gen Sir Clive, 443, 454-5
STEELE, Maj R. E., 223, 596-7
STENING, Surgeon Lt-Cdr S. E. L., 616-17, 621*n*, 622
STEPHENSON, Spr T., 557
STEVENS, Hon Sir Bertram, 40*n*
STEVENS, Brig F. H., 455
STEVENS, Maj R. H., 489*n*, 572
STEWART, Athole, 383*n*
STEWART, Lt A. I., 505
STEWART, Brig I. MacA., 161, 165, 187, 194-5, 272, 283, 336, 339, 346, 381*n*, 443*n*, 500; commands 12 Indian Brigade, 166
STICKLENBERG, Capt. 608*n*
STICPEWICH, Capt W. H., 598*n*, 603-4
STIMSON, Henry L., 22-3, 53, 55, 108, 391*n*
Straits Times, 74*n*, 152, 190, 204*n*, 252, 288*n*
STRATEGY: *Allied*, in Far East, 54, 80-3, 444-5, 675, 677-8; Beat-Hitler-First policy, 53, 81; effect on Malayan campaign, 198-9, 352; in ABDA Area, 202, 206, 646-9; *British*, 52, 189-90, 253; in Far

STRATEGY—*continued*
East, 7, 19-20, 46; in Malaya, 100, 107; in Middle East, 21. *Japanese*, 371, 651
STREET, Brig Hon G. A., 32
STRONACH, Lt G. F., 487
STURDEE, Lt-Gen Sir Vernon (Plate p. 494), 33, 69, 86*n*, 101-2, 164, 181, 199, 271, 419, 424, 446, 459; appointed GOC 8 Div, 28; becomes CGS, 32; recommends General Bennett as GOC 8 Div, 34; visits Malaya, 52; agrees to dispatch of battalion group to Rabaul, 59; suggests Bennett as GOC-in-C Home Forces, 97; interviews Bennett after escape, 384-5; urges return of AIF to Australia, 444-6, 449, 450, 452, 675-8, judgment vindicated, 465; on disembarkation of *Orcades* troops in Java, 447
SU (Sketch p. 467), 482-3, 490, 491*n*, 492*n*
SUEZ CANAL, 23-4, 76, 447, 460
SUGA, Colonel, 595
SUGITA, Colonel, 520-1, 522
SUKABUMI (Sketch p. 500), 502, 504, 533-4, 538
SULU ARCHIPELAGO (Sketch p. 178), 497
Sumanoura Maru, Japanese transport, 417
SUMATRA (Map p. 112; Sketches pp. 384, 453), 106, 110, 151, 169, 180, 202, 206, 221, 238*n*, 266, 272, 281, 284, 305, 348*n*, 365, 371, 383-5, 387-9, 452, 466, 501, 530, 541; Japanese plans, 110-11, 134; bomb stocks withdrawn to, 154; Malayan air force withdrawn to, 289, 326, air force strength in, 442; planned employment of AIF in, 371, 443-5, 448, 451*n*, 676; evacuation of, 449, 454-6; invasion of, 453-4; prisoners of war in, 539-40, 633-4, 638; and ABDA directive, 646
SUMBA ISLAND (Map p. 30), 491*n*
SUMMONS, Lt W. I., 501, 683
SUMNER, Capt A. B., 227, 229
SUMPITAN (Map p. 158), 162, 165
SUM SUM (Sketch p. 413), 400*n*
SUNDA STRAIT (Sketch p. 453), 258*n*, 453-4, 456, 498
Sunday Sun, 33, 34
SUNGEI MURAI ROAD, 315
SUNGEI PATANI (Map p. 105), 149; airfield at, 121*n*, 125, 142, British air attack on, 221
SUNGEI SAYONG HALT (Map p. 262), 261-2
SUNGEI SIPUT (Map p. 158), 166
SUNGKAI (Sketch p. 188), 189, 193
SURABAYA (Sketch p. 498), 272, 416, 456, 474, 497-9 538, 675
SUSUKI, General, 135
SUTHERLAND, R.; *see* ROMANUS, C. F. and SUTHERLAND, R.
SUVA, 44
SUZUKI, Lt-Gen, 380
Swan, Australian sloop, 473-4
SWANTON, Sgt S. M., 607
SWARTZ, Maj R. W. C., 278, 298, 575
SWINDAIL, Cpl D. T., 276
SWISS RIFLE CLUB (Map p. 344), 357
SYDNEY, 28-9, 61, 64, 84, 258*n*, 635, 639, 670; departure of 22 Bde from, 60; shipping handled at, 65; Japanese raid on, 537
Sydney Morning Herald, 47*n*
SYRIA, 85-6, 205, 258*n*, 418, 459*n*, 495
SZECHWAN PROVINCE (Sketch p. 644), 16

TABAR ISLAND (Sketch p. 413), 398
TACO-LULIC (Sketch p. 478), 478
TACTICS, 390; Australian Army fails to develop bush warfare doctrines, 10; in Malaya, 66-7, 100, 161, 168, 186, 210, 222, 232; on Singapore Island, 292-3, 298, 309, 326; on Ambon, 427. *Japanese*, 49, 116, 117, 155, 162, 166-7, 176, 187, 195-6, 235, 314, 317*n*, 326*n*, 472-3; knowledge passed to Australian Army, 377, 380-1, 443*n*, 500, 651
TAIHOKU (Sketch p. 630), 630
TAIMONTA (Sketch p. 563), 580
TAIPING (Map p. 158), 187
Taisan Maru, Japanese naval tanker, 125*n*
TAISHO (Sketch p. 617), 613, 621-2
TAKAGI, Rear-Admiral T., 497
TAKANUN (Sketch p. 563), 563-4, 577-8, 579
TAKAO (Sketch p. 630), 129, 612, 614
TAKEFU (Sketch p. 617), 622
TAKUMI, Maj-Gen, 135
TALASEA (Sketch p. 658), 657
TALILI BAY (Sketches pp. 394, 401), 397, 401-2

INDEX 713

TALILIGAP (Sketches pp. 394, 401), 396, 400, 402, 404-6, 409, 663
TAMAJAO (Sketch p. 563), 563
TAMARKAN (Sketch p. 563), 588, 591, 616
TAMASATA (Sketch p. 630), 630
TAMBILAHAN (Sketch p. 384), 388-9
TAMILS, 586, 587-8
TAMPIE (Sketch p. 563), 582
TAMPIN (Sketch p. 99), 101, 198, 223
TAMPOI HILL (Sketch p. 99), 101, 279n
TAMUAN (Sketch p. 563), 571, 588-90
TAMWORTH, 31, 36
TANBAYA (Sketch p. 550), 576-7
TANGERANG (Sketch p. 500), 499, 500
TANGLIN BARRACKS (Sketch p. 360), 351, 358, 361-2, 364, 368-9, 373-4, 511
TANGLIN HALT (Sketch p. 360), 361, 369
TANJONG MALIM (Sketch p. 188), 163, 193-5
TANJONG PRIOK (Sketch p. 500), 498, 536, 538-9
TAN KAH-KEE, Mr, 204
TANKS, *British*, lack of in Malaya, 77, 93; arrive Singapore, 353; numbers dispatched to Russia, 103; in Burma, 463. *Japanese*, regimental organisation, 115; strength and armament in Malaya, 133n; employed in Thailand, 140, in Malaya, 146, 147-8, 151, 159, 187, 194-5, 217, 219-20, 227, 230, 242, 245, 249, 342, 345-6, 373; in Timor, 488; in Java, 501
TANTUI (Sketch p. 421), 422, 426, 604-7
TANYIN (Sketch p. 550), 546-7, 549, 550-1
TAPRELL, Pte R. M. J., 529
TARAKAN ISLAND (Map p. 393), 205, 416, 426, 601; loss of, 392, 490
TARSAU (Sketch p. 563), 563, 566-7, 570-1, 573, 582, 589
TARUS (Sketch p. 468), 468, 482-3, 484-5
TASMANIA, 29, 64
TATE, Sgt B., 243
Tatsukami Maru, Japanese transport, 417
TAVILO ROAD (Sketch p. 401), 402, 407
TAVOY (Sketch p. 542), 108, 590; prisoners of war at, 541-4
TAWITAWI (Sketch p. 595), 597, 603-4
TAWLIUA MISSION, 405, 411
TAYLOR, Brig H. B. (Plate p. 15), 106n, 269, 272, 283, 297, 308, 311n, 314, 315, 318-19, 321-3, 325, 335, 345, 350, 368-9, 382; commands 22nd Bde, 29; flies to Malaya, 60n; and training, 68-9; relations with General Bennett, 70; assesses Japanese, 100; commands Eastforce, 207; orders withdrawal of Endau force, 251; withdraws headquarters from Mersing, 252; issues orders for Nithsdale ambush, 262; orders withdrawal to Jemaluang, 268; problems on Singapore Island, 298-9; asks for artillery regiment to be placed under command, 300-1; lays down tactics for 22nd Bde, 309; orders occupation of Bulim line, 323-4; reconnoitres Kranji-Jurong line, 326; on Reformatory road, 337, 358-9; relieved of command, 361-2; in Changi, 516
TAYLOR, Capt J. L., 220
TAYLOR, Dr J. P., 594, 596-7, 599
TAZUMI, Capt, 528
TEBBUTT, Maj W. A., 376n
TEBRAU (Map p. 262), 279, 306
TEBRAU, SUNGEI (Map p. 286), 300, 307
TEHORU (Sketch p. 439), 439
TELOK ANSON (Map p. 54; Sketch p. 188), 187-8, 189
TEMELONG (Map p. 158), 165
TEMPLE HILL, 514n
TENANG (Sketch p. 211), 235
TENASSERIM COAST, 108
TENAU (Sketch p. 468), 466-7, 472-3
Tenedos, British destroyer, 122, 143
TENGAH, SUNGEI (Map p. 286), 291
TENGAH AIRFIELD (Map p. 286; Sketch p. 310), 125-6, 291, 299, 306, 309, 315, 317-21, 326-7, 366; air force based on, 121n; air attacks on, 221; abandoned by air force, 303; defence of, 322-3, 325
TERAUCHI, Field Marshal Count Hisaichi, 113, 507, 635; commands *Southern Army*, 110
Tern, motor launch, 384
TER POORTEN, Lt-Gen H. (Plate p. 494), 152, 457, 497, 499, 501, 525; commands Allied army in Java, 206, 495; surrenders, 502
THAILAND (Sketches pp. 88, 563), 18-20, 41, 58, 64, 75-6, 78, 98, 102, 106, 108, 121, 124-5, 127, 187, 207, 365, 446, 507, 524, 528, 551, 556, 593, 611,

THAILAND—*continued*
614-15, 626, 648; Japanese encroachment, 24, 56, 59; British plans, 50, 109; signs peace treaty with Indo-China, 55-6; neutrality violated by Australian officers, 73; seeks Allied assurances against Japanese attacks, 87; and operation *Matador*, 92-3, 122, 123; Japanese plans, 111, 133-4; invasion of, 135, 138-9, 140-1, 146; prisoners of war in, 525, 545, 548n, 557, 561-92, 633, liberation and repatriation, 634, 636-8; Australian deaths in, 642; *see also* BURMA-THAILAND RAILWAY
THAI POLICE, 135, 140
THAIS, THE, 572, 573, 590, 637
THANBYUZAYAT (Sketches pp. 542, 550), 544-7, 549 550-1, 558, 561; air raids on, 554-5
Thanet, British destroyer, 266
THARP, Lt-Col, 536, 558, 561
Thetis, 661n
THETKAW (Sketch p. 550), 550
THOMAS, G., 674n
THOMAS, Pte H. E., 477, 479, 492n
THOMAS, Brig L. C., 339, 350, 351n, 352
THOMAS, Maj R. E., 315-16, 321
THOMAS, Sir Shenton, 48, 73, 93, 145, 191, 204, 252, 281, 288, 361, 373, 375-6, 378; an assessment of, 204
THOMPSON, Pte, 529
THOMPSON, Lt, 359n
THOMPSON, Chaplain Rev A. H., 599, 600
THOMPSON, Maj A. N., 522n
THOMPSON'S RIDGE, 188
THOMSON (Sketch p. 374), 352
THOMSON ROAD (Sketch p. 360), 356-7, 364, 368-9
THORNTON, L-Sgt C. W., 227
Thracian, British destroyer, 174
THREE PAGODAS PASS (Sketch p. 542), 590
"THREE SPURS" (Sketch p. 478), 472, 478-9, 480
THREE WAYS (Sketch p. 401), 396, 400-1, 402, 405-7, 408-9
THURSDAY ISLAND (Sketch p. 439), 44-5, 59, 440, 661
THYER, Col J. H., 82n, 86n, 228, 243-4, 269n, 282-3, 323, 354, 382; appointed CSO 8 Div Sigs, 29; appointed GSO I 8 Div, 85; recommends redisposal of AIF in eastern Johore, 153; visits 45 Bde headquarters, 228; visits 53 Bde, 240-1; on quality of Australian reinforcements, 296; orders reconnaissance of Kranji-Jurong line, 302; interrogated by Japanese, 520-1
TIBAR (Sketch p. 478), 478-9, 480
TIBBITTS, Lt A. H., 246-7
TIDE COVE (Map p. 171), 129n
TIELAND, Maj H. H. L., 428-9
TIENTSIN (Map p. 30), Japanese blockade of, 10; British troops withdrawn, 13, 23
TILL, Lt J. J., 349n
TIME, in Malaya, 122n, 130; in Hawaii, 126n; in Hong Kong, 173
Times, The, 3n
TIMOR (Map p. 393; Sketch p. 467), 41, 43, 111, 184, 206, 256n, 260, 420, 423, 427, 438, 443, 445, 450, 451n, 456, 534, 538, 634, 677; Australian reinforcement of, 59, 69, 76, 83, 130, 418-19, 451n, 474, employment criticised, 419n; Japanese plans, 111, 179, 392; strategical value, 466; garrison of, 467-9; Dutch-Portuguese relations, 471; operations on, 474-94; prisoners of war in, 511, 538n, 593
TIMOR, DUTCH (Sketch p. 468), 471, 492n, 493; population, 466; garrison, 467-8, reinforcement of, 469, 473, 475, dispositions, 472-3, 474-5; operations in, 482-9, 490-2; Japanese account, 493-4
TIMOR, PORTUGUESE (Sketch p. 478), 490; Australian representative appointed, 57; population, 466; garrison, 467; proposed employment of Dutch troops, 469-71, planned replacement with Portuguese troops, 475; operations in, 475-82, 491-3
TIMORESE, THE, 466, 480
TIMOR SEA, 474
TIMPERLY, Capt A. T., 672
TIN, Malayan output, 14, 48
TIPPETT, Lt M. D., 472
Tirpitz, German battleship, 92
TISDELLE, Maj Achille C., 506n
TITI KARANGAN (Map p. 158), 165; rearguard at, 160-2
TJAMPEA (Sketch p. 500), 502
TJIANTEN RIVER (Sketch p. 500), 500
TJIBADAK (Sketch p. 500), 504
TJIKADJANG (Sketch p. 500), 503

714 INDEX

TJIKAMPEK (Sketch p. 500), 499
TJILATJAP (Sketches pp. 498, 500), 389, 456, 498-9, 505
TJIMAHI (Sketch p. 500), 534
TJIUDJUNG RIVER (Sketch p. 500), 499
TOBERA (Sketches pp. 394, 654), 405, 654
TOBRUK, 85, 206n, 459n
TOGO, Shigenori, 108-9, 132n
Tohohasi Maru, Japanese transport, 541
TOJO, General Hideki, 22, 109n; becomes Prime Minister, 94-5
TOKYO (Map p. 30; Sketch p. 617), 9, 17, 28, 55-6, 87, 94n, 108-9, 113, 129, 131, 132n, 390, 397, 437n, 520, 526, 547n, 589, 619, 627, 635, 641, 680
TOL (Sketch p. 654), 664, 670-2; massacre at, 410, 665-9
TOLMER, Maj A. R., 402, 404, 406, 409, 655-6, 660
TOMA (Sketches pp. 394, 654), 400, 406, 408, 410 653, 655, 657-8, 661
TOMASETTI, L-Sgt W. E., 492
TOMAVATUR (Sketch p. 401), 406, 408, 661
TOMPSON, Capt R. C., 220
TONCHAN (Sketch p. 563), 582
TONCHAN SOUTH (Sketch p. 563), 585-6
TONCHAN SPRING (Sketch p. 563), 586
TONKIN (Map p. 30), 16, 26
TOOSE, Capt A. V. C., 269
TORIU (Sketch p. 654), 659
TORIU RIVER (Sketch p. 394), 396, 658
Toro Maru, Japanese transport, 125n
TORPEDOES, AERIAL, Japanese, 144
Tosan Maru, Japanese transport, 125n
Totole, 661
TOTSUKA (Sketch p. 617), 618
TOWNSVILLE, 89, 661, 672
TOYODA, Admiral Teijoro, 87, 90
TRACEY, Maj C. P., 278, 298, 356-7, 537n, 574, 579
TRADE, in Far East, 1-2, 5-6, 7, 15
TRAINING, *Australian*, 31, 36, 59, 96, 246, 258n, 296, 443n, 469, 487, 515, 677; in Malaya, 65-9, 70-1, 100-1, 167, after the campaign, 381n, 500, 651; of Indep Coys, 84, 467n. *British*, 58, 95-6, 103, 226n, 643-4. *Canadian*, 95. *Dutch*, 141n. *Filipino*, 88, 90. *Japanese*, 113-14
TRANSPORT: *motor*, of an infantry battalion, 305n; *water*, use by Japanese in Malaya, 116, 160, 333-4
TRANS-SIBERIAN RAILWAY, 87
TRAVERS, Maj R. E., 401, 404, 406-10, 655
TREMAYNE, Air Marshal Sir John, 40, 77
TRENGGANU, STATE OF (Map p. 54), 65, 191; defence requirements, 93
TREVENA, Maj A. G., 472, 475, 482-4, 485-7, 489
TREVOR, Pte T. C., 216n
TRINCOMALEE (Sketch p. 448), 498
TRIPARTITE PACT, 37-8, 39, 55, 75, 200n
TROBRIAND ISLANDS (Sketch p. 658), 670, 672
TROLAK (Sketch p. 188), 193-4, 195
Tromp, Dutch cruiser, 454, 456
TRONG (Map p. 158), 185
TRONG RIVER, 185
TROPICAL ULCERS, 549, 555
TROTT, Brig W. A., 155, 274, 296
TRUK (Map p. 393), 411
TRUMAN, Harry S., 635
TSINGTAO (Map p. 30), 113, 117
TSUKAMOTO, Lt-Col, 411
Tsuruga Maru, Japanese transport, 417
TUAL (Sketch p. 439), 439-40
TUDDIN, Cpl J. A., 659
TUJU ISLANDS (Sketch p. 384), 383
TULAGI, 396
TUMPAT (Map p. 54), 64
TUNNEL HILL ROAD (Sketch p. 401), 395
TURNER, Capt J. M., 430, 434, 608
TYERSALL PALACE (Sketch p. 360), 346
TYERSALL PARK, 357-8, 359, 362

UBELO (Sketch p. 468), 484-5
Ubi Maru, Japanese transport, 593
UBIN ISLAND (Map p. 286), 305, 307, 331
UGAKI, General K., 2
ULU PANDAN (Map p. 286), 306
ULU PANDAN IV (Sketch p. 360), 358, 363
ULU PANDAN ROAD (Sketch p. 344), 337, 340, 358-9, 362-3
Umboi, motor launch, 661, 673
UNITED KINGDOM; *see* BRITAIN, GREAT

UNITED NATIONS, 632; birth of, 199; declaration, 200n
UNITED SOVIET SOCIALIST REPUBLICS; *see* RUSSIA
UPPER KONKOITA (Sketch p. 563), 574, 577
UPPER SONGKURAI (Sketch p. 563), 574-5, 579
UPURA (Sketch p. 468), 482-3
URANIUM, 23
USAPA-BESAR (Sketch p. 468), 472, 482-3
USAU (Sketch p. 468), 419n, 493; action at, 486-8
USAU RIDGE, 486-7
USAVIT RIVER (Sketch p. 654), 660

Valiant, British battleship, 253
VALOKA (Sketch p. 658), 660, 673
Vampire, Australian destroyer, 103n, 122, 142, 266
Van Dam, Dutch merchantman, 389
VAN DER POST, Lt-Col L., 505
VAN OYEN, Lt-Gen L. H., 495
VAN STARKENBORGH STACHOUWER, T., 469
VAN STRAATEN, Col N. L. W., 469, 470, 475-9, 491
VARLEY, Brig A. L., 262, 266, 268-9, 298, 304, 308n, 312, 314, 315, 319, 320-2, 337, 350, 363, 382, 543-5, 546-9, 550n, 551-2, 553-4, 555, 556-7, 558, 561, 614, 627; commands 2/18 Bn, 29-30; commands 22 Bde, 361-2; commands "A" Force, 519, 541; death, 615
VARLEY, Lt J. A., 228, 236, 238, 240, 250, 545n
VARZIN, MT (Sketch p. 654), 663
VEALE, Brig W. C. D., 483, 490, 491, 492n, 493; commands Sparrow Force, 474; orders withdrawal of 2/2 Indep Coy from Portuguese Timor, 475; problems of, 482
Vendetta, Australian destroyer, 103n
VERNON, Capt J. M., 308n, 313
VERSAILLES CONFERENCE, 1n, 52
VERY LIGHTS, 331n
VICTORIA, 29, 170, 175, 418
VICTORIA CROSS, awarded to J. R. Osborn, 174n; to A. E. Cummings, 192; to C. G. W. Anderson, 246; Australian VC winners taken prisoner, 536n
VICTORIA PEAK (Map p. 171), 170
VICTORIA POINT (Sketch p. 542), 108, 134; Japanese occupation of, 169; prisoners of war at, 541-2, 544
VIGAN (Map p. 178), 177
VIGORS, F-Lt T. A., 144
VILA, 396
VILLA MARIA (Sketch p. 478), 480, 491-2
VINCENT, Maj T. G., 228, 239, 245, 248, 302, 315-16, 321
Vindex, British aircraft carrier, 639
VIOLET HILL (Map p. 171), 175
VIRGINIA CAPES, 53
VISAYAN ARCHIPELAGO (Sketch p. 88), 89
VITIAZ STRAIT (Sketch p. 658), 661
VITU ISLANDS (Sketch p. 658), 660-1, 673
VLADIVOSTOK (Map p. 30), 87
VOLUPAI (Sketch p. 658), 660-1
VUDAL RIVER (Sketch p. 654), 654
VULCAN CRATER (Sketches pp. 394, 401), 395, 401-2, 407, 409; action at, 403-6, 411; withdrawal from, 654, 663
VULCAN ROAD (Sketch p. 401), 395-6, 402, 404
VUNADADIA (Sketch p. 654), 655
VUNAKANAU AIRFIELD (Sketches pp. 394, 401), 395-7, 399, 401, 403, 405-9, 653, 663; Japanese air attacks on, 398; demolished, 400; loss of, 411-12
VUNALAMA (Sketch p. 654), 656
VUNAPOPE MISSION (Sketch p. 394), 401, 663n
Vyner Brooke, British steamship, 386-7, 540

WAGALE (Sketch p. 550), 547, 555
WAGGA WAGGA, 31
WAGNER, Lt C. A., 268, 322, 597
WAINWRIGHT, Lt-Gen Jonathan M., 90, 507
WAI SOON GARDENS (Sketch p. 360), 101
WAITAVALO PLANTATION (Sketch p. 654), 665, 668-9, 670
WAKABYASHI, Lt, 580
WAKATSUKI, Baron, 2
Wakefield, American transport, 183n
WAKE ISLAND (Maps pp. 30, 112), 111, 127-8, 132, 427, 441, 507; invasion of, 176-7
WAKELING, Pte S. W., 434
WAKINOHAMA, 625, 640
WALINDI (Sketch p. 658), 660
WALKER, Col A. S., 68n, 515n, 531n
WALKER, Maj G. H., 351, 377, 381, 383
WALKER, S-Sgt J. W. E., 479

INDEX

WALKER, Capt R. R., 298
WALKLEY, Pte N. W., 669
WALL, Pte D., 529
WALLACE, WO2 W., 597-8
WALLGROVE, 31
WALLIS, Brig C., 172-3, 176
WALLS, Lt R. K., 407-8
WALSH, Col A. W., 519, 593, 595
WALSTAB, Col J., 394
"WALTZING MATILDA", 237
WAMPO (Sketch p. 563), 563, 567, 590
WANKEY, Lt M. E., 311, 319
WANLUNG (Sketch p. 563), 563
WARANGOI RIVER (Sketch p. 394), 395-6, 408, 661, 663-4
WAR CRIMES TRIALS, 669n
Ward, American destroyer, 126
WARDALE-GREENWOOD, Chaplain Rev H., 245, 321, 598-600
WARDELL, Brig A. W., 459
WARDEN, Lt W. G., 267
WARDS, Lt-Col O., 82n
WARHURST, Lt V. I., 349
Warrego, Australian sloop, 474
Warspite, British battleship, 253
WASHINGTON, 17, 25, 39, 53, 55, 90n, 93n, 94, 169, 177, 182, 184, 201n, 255n, 284, 440, 447, 457, 459, 465, 635, 648-9; Staff talks at, 53, 76; Japanese-United States negotiations at, 87, 94-5, 108-9, 121, 123, 130-1, 132n
Washington, American transport, 183n
WASHINGTON AGREEMENT OF 1922, 1, 3, 10n, 170
WATCHORN, Capt A. B., 332-3, 557n
WATCHORN, Capt N. E., 425, 436
WATER-SUPPLY, of Hong Kong, 170, 176; in Johore, 273; of Singapore Island, 291, 354, 366, 370, 372-3, 375, 377, 389; in captivity, 513, 523, 547, 558, 564-5, 582, 593, 606-7, 612
WATKINS, Pte J., 232
WATSON, WO2 C. Y., 600
WATSON, Mark S., 39n, 53n, 93n
WAU (Sketch p. 658), 673
WAVELL, Field Marshal Rt Hon Earl (Plate p. 47), 46n, 47, 91n, 190, 204, 209, 256n, 260, 341, 354, 375, 381n, 384, 424, 442-3, 446, 450, 452-3, 457, 459, 495-6, 521, 676, 678; as C-in-C India, 145-6; proposed as commander ABDA area, 183-4, appointed 201-2, staff of, 205-6, his directive, 646-9; command extended to include Darwin, 259; visits Malaya, 202-3, 206, 222-3, 254, 279, 281, 338-42; orders Percival to fight out battle in Johore, 253; career compared to General Blamey's, 255; authorises withdrawal to Singapore Island, 271-2; on defence of Singapore Island, 284-5, 295; orders withdrawal of air force from Singapore, 289, 341; exhorts Singapore Island troops to fight on, 341-2, 372, 375-6, gives permission for resistance to cease, 378; plans defence of NEI, 371, 443; suggests diversion of AIF either to Burma or Australia, 444; diverts 7 British Armd Bde to Burma, 445; recommends employment of AIF in Burma, 446-7, 449-50, 451n, 463; orders evacuation of Sumatra, 454-5; recommends dissolution of ABDA Command, 456; retains *Orcades* troops in Java, 457; dissolves ABDA Command, 458, 461; estimate of, 458-9; visits Burma front, 460; appointed C-in-C India, 461, 463; halts evacuation of Rangoon, 464; attempts reinforcement of Timor, 474
WEARNE, Col W. W., 536
WEBSTER, Pte H. J., 668-9, 670
WEBSTER, Lt-Col I. G., 455
WEDEMEYER, Maj-Gen Albert C., 639
WEGNER, Pte A. C., 436
Weills Maru, Japanese transport, 614
WEILY, Capt J. G., 232
WELLS, Lt-Gen Sir Henry, 85
WELLS, Maj R. G., 594-5, 597, 599
WENTWORTH, W. C., 8n
WESTBROOK, Capt K. L., 236, 239, 242
WEST BUKIT TIMAH (Map p. 286; Sketch p. 324), 303, 325, 335-6, 340
WESTERN AUSTRALIA, 18n, 29, 258n, 381n
WESTERN DESERT, 91, 102, 459n
WEST INDIES, 39, 59
WESTLEY, Maj G. de V., 425, 429, 430, 433, 606, 608n, 639
WEST POINT, 88

West Point, American transport, 183n
Westralia, Australian transport, 399, 468
WEST RIVER (Map p. 30), 13
WEYNTON, Lt A. G., 594, 599
WHITE, General Sir Brudenell, 15, 32, 34
WHITE, Maj H., 236
WHITE, Lt-Col J. Glyn, 522n
WHITE, Capt S. B. McK., 436
WHITECROSS, Sgt R. H., 544n. 549n, 556n, 641n, 683
WHITFIELD, Col N. H., 28, 61
WIDE BAY (Sketch p. 654), 661, 664, 670n, 672
WIGHT, ISLE OF, 287
WILBY, Pte V. P., 492
WILD, Maj C. H. D., 573
WILDEY, Brig A. W. G., 106
WILKIE, D., 287
WILLAUMEZ PENINSULA (Sketch p. 658), 658, 660
WILLIAMS, Pte D. H., 218
WILLIAMS, Brig G. G. R., 340
WILLIAMS, Lt-Col J. M., 454, 496, 502, 535-6, 546-7, 549, 551, 556n, 558
WILLIAMS, Lt-Col J. W., 234
WILLIAMS, Lt R. G., 485
WILLIAMSON, Pte R. McK., 479
WILLS, Brig K. A., 443-4
WILSON, Maj A. J. McL., 483
WILSON, Gnr J. A. T., 544n
WILSON, Maj J. Edmonds, 396, 412-13, 414-16
WILSON'S PROMONTORY, 84, 467n
WILSTENCROFT, Sgt R., 333
WIRELESS TELEGRAPHY, 214, 217n, 489
WITHYCOMBE, Lt P. S., 223
WONG NEI CHONG GAP (Map p. 171), 174-5
WOOD, Cpl J., 517
WOODFORD, Gnr J. H. G., 527n
WOODLANDS ROAD (Map p. 286; Sketch p. 328) 298, 329, 330-1, 343
WOODLARK ISLANDS (Sketch p. 658), 416
WOODLEIGH (Sketch p. 374), 361, 369
WOODLEIGH PUMPING STATION, 353, 361, 373, 376
WOODS, Capt, 236
WOODS, Maj F. A., 496n, 564
WOOTTON, A. N., 365, 376
WOTJE ATOLL (Map p. 30), 441
WOUNDED, TREATMENT OF, 243n, 244, 246-8, 431
WRIGHT, Lt-Col J. W., 322
WRIGHT, Lt R. F., 529n
WRIGLEY, Brig H., 634, 640
WUNUNG (Sketch p. 658), 671-2
WUN YI (Sketch p. 563), 587
WYETT, Maj J. W. C., 277, 303, 324-5, 522n
WYNTER, Lt-Gen H. D., 7-8

YAMADA, Lt, 546
YAMAGUCHI, Lt, 521-2
YAMAMOTO, Genichi, 437
YAMAMOTO, Fleet Admiral Isoroku, 56n, 110-11, 132, 437n
YAMASHITA, General Tomoyuki, 133n, 134-5, 198, 235, 250, 270n, 366, 382, 520-1; heads military mission to Berlin, 38; commands XXV Army, 133; issues orders for capture of Singapore, 306, requests its surrender, 353-4; accepts surrender, 379-80
YAMPI SOUND, 18n
YANGTSE KIANG (Map p. 30), 10, 13, 283
YE (Sketch p. 542), 544
YELLOW SEA (Map p. 30), 27
YEOWART, F-Lt R. A., 398
YEW TEE (Map p. 286), 298
YOKOHAMA (Sketch p. 617), 613, 616-17, 618-19, 627, 640
YONAI, Admiral Mitsumasa, 22
YONG PENG (Map p. 262; Sketch p. 237), 222, 224-5, 228, 230-1, 233-4, 236, 238, 240-2, 244, 248-9, 256-7, 258, 271
YORK, CAPE, 396
Yorktown, American aircraft carrier, 440-1
YOSHIKAWA, Tatsuhiko, 603n
YOUL, Lt-Col G. D., 418, 423n, 467; appointed CO 2/40 Bn, 32
YOUNG, Sir Mark, 173, 175-6, 629
YUGOSLAVIA, 200n

Zealandia, Australian transport, 468
ZENTSUJI (Sketch p. 617), 617-18, 619, 620
ZIEGLER, O. L., 683
Zuikaka, Japanese aircraft carrier, 427

www.ingramcontent.com/pod-product-compliance
Lightning Source LLC
Chambersburg PA
CBHW070752300426
44111CB00014B/2380